S0-AGC-917

PUBLIC PAPERS OF THE PRESIDENTS

OF THE UNITED STATES

PUBLIC PAPERS OF THE PRESIDENTS

OF THE UNITED STATES

Dwight D. Eisenhower

1954

Containing the Public Messages, Speeches, and
Statements of the President

JANUARY I TO DECEMBER 3I, 1954

PUBLISHED BY THE
OFFICE OF THE FEDERAL REGISTER
NATIONAL ARCHIVES AND RECORDS SERVICE
GENERAL SERVICES ADMINISTRATION

U.S. GOVERNMENT PRINTING OFFICE: 1960

For sale by the Superintendent of Documents, U.S. Government Printing Office
Washington 25, D.C. - Price $7.25

53.035
36p
154

FOREWORD

THERE HAS BEEN a long-felt need for an orderly series of the Public Papers of the Presidents. A reference work of this type can be most helpful to scholars and officials of government, to reporters of current affairs and the events of history.

The general availability of the official text of Presidential documents and messages will serve a broader purpose. As part of the expression of democracy, this series can be a vital factor in the maintenance of our individual freedoms and our institutions of self-government.

I wish success to the editors of this project, and I am sure their work through the years will add strength to the ever-growing traditions of the Republic.

Dwight D. Eisenhower

PREFACE

IN THIS VOLUME are gathered most of the public messages and statements of the President of the United States that were released by the White House during the year 1954. A similar volume, covering the year 1957, was published early in 1958 as the first of a series. The President's foreword is reprinted from that volume.

Immediate plans for this series call for the publication of annual volumes soon after the close of each new calendar year, and at the same time undertaking the periodic compilation of volumes covering previous years. Volumes covering the years 1954 through 1959 are now available.

This series was begun in response to a recommendation of the National Historical Publications Commission (44 U.S.C. 393). The Commission's recommendation was incorporated in regulations of the Administrative Committee of the Federal Register issued under section 6 of the Federal Register Act (44 U.S.C. 306). The Committee's regulations, establishing the series, are reprinted at page 1139 as "Appendix D."

The first extensive compilation of the messages and papers of the Presidents was assembled by James D. Richardson and published under Congressional authority between 1896 and 1899. It included Presidential materials from 1789 to 1897. Since then, there have been various private compilations, but no uniform, systematic publication comparable to the *Congressional Record* or the *United States Supreme Court Reports.*

For many years Presidential Proclamations have been published in the *United States Statutes at Large.* The Federal Register Act in 1935 required that Proclamations, Executive Orders, and some other official Executive documents be published in the daily *Federal Register;* but the greater part of Presidential writings and utterances still lacked an official medium for either current publication or periodic compilation. Some of them were interspersed through the issues of the *Congressional Record* while others were reported only in the press or were generally available only in mimeographed White House releases. Under these circumstances it was difficult to remember, after a lapse of time, where and in what form even a major pronouncement had been made.

CONTENT AND ARRANGEMENT

The text of this book is based on Presidential materials issued during the calendar year 1954 as White House releases and on transcripts of news conferences. Where available, original source materials have been used to protect against substantive errors in transcription. A list of the White House releases from which final selections were made is published at page 1119 as "Appendix A."

The full text of the President's news conferences is here published for the first time. In 1954 direct quotation of the President's replies to queries usually was not authorized by the White House.

Proclamations, Executive Orders, and similar documents, required by law to be published in the *Federal Register* and *Code of Federal Regulations* are not repeated. Instead, they are listed by number and subject under the heading "Appendix B" at page 1132.

The President is required by statute to transmit numerous reports to Congress. Those transmitted during 1954 are listed at page 1138 as "Appendix C."

The items published in this volume are presented in chronological order, rather than being grouped in classes. Most needs for a classified arrangement are met by the subject index. For example, a reader interested in veto messages sent to Congress during 1954 will find them listed in the index under "veto messages."

The dates shown at the end of item headings are White House release dates. In instances where the date of the document differs from the release date that fact is shown in brackets immediately following the heading. Other editorial devices, such as text notes, footnotes, and cross references, have been held to a minimum.

Remarks or addresses were delivered in Washington, D.C., unless otherwise indicated. Similarly, statements, messages, and letters were issued from the White House in Washington unless otherwise indicated.

The planning and editorial work for this volume were under the direction of David C. Eberhart of the Office of the Federal Register, assisted by Warren R. Reid and Mildred B. Berry. The index was prepared by Dorothy M. Jacobson. Frank H. Mortimer of the Government Printing Office developed the typography and design.

WAYNE C. GROVER
Archivist of the United States

FRANKLIN FLOETE
Administrator of General Services

June 22, 1960

CONTENTS

CONTENTS

LIST OF ITEMS

XIII

List of Items

XIV

List of Items

List of Items

List of Items

List of Items

XXI

List of Items

List of Items

List of Items

List of Items

List of Items

List of Items

List of Items

Page

List of Items

List of Items

xxxv

List of Items

xxxvi

List of Items

List of Items

List of Items

List of Items

XL

List of Items

Dwight D. Eisenhower

1954

1 ¶ Memorandum on the Red Cross Campaign.
January 4, 1954

To the Heads of Executive Departments and Agencies:

The Red Cross has long since become an important and valued feature of American life. As a great fellowship, it welcomes all as members. Its activities are so far flung and so vital to our Nation that it seems advisable, occasionally, to remind ourselves of their scope and character. In war it renders so many services, so well, to men fighting for freedom, that among the armed forces no morale factor is more important than the Red Cross. In peace the American spirit of people helping people is demonstrated through Red Cross services. In disasters it mitigates sufferings caused by fire, famine, pestilence, tornado and flood. Through its civilian and military blood donor program it means life to thousands of men, women and children each year. Through its activities the Red Cross is on duty everywhere, in the United States and abroad, in the humblest homes, in great disasters. It serves all creeds, all races, all countries.

The personnel of the Federal Government has set a consistently high standard of generous giving to the Red Cross. I hope this fine record will continue this year under the leadership of the Honorable Arthur E. Summerfield, the Postmaster General, whom I have designated as Chairman of the Government Unit in the 1954 Metropolitan Area Red Cross Fund Campaign. His own wealth of experience in community welfare challenges the hearty and active cooperation of each department head. To give him your support most effectively, you will undoubtedly want to create within your department a Red Cross organization adequate to give everyone an opportunity to contribute and attain the goal desired from your department. Likewise I hope that you will request all personnel in your departmental field offices to help the Red Cross by generous cooperation with their local Red Cross Chapters.

The Red Cross through its purposes, its work and the people who belong to it, helps us to realize man is made of nobler qualities than those of selfishness, greed and personal advantage. The Red Cross gives practical application in a vast human field to those great and noble virtues of man that are the richest heritage from the Almighty.

DWIGHT D. EISENHOWER

2 ¶ Radio and Television Address to the American People on the Administration's Purposes and Accomplishments. *January* 4, 1954

[Delivered from the Broadcast Room at the White House at 9:30 p.m.]

My fellow Americans:

Tonight, I would like to talk to you as individuals and as American families—deeply concerned with the realities of living. We have had a year of progress and can look ahead with confidence.

Our problems are many. We wonder about our Nation's security—the great standing question of peace in the world—and what this may mean in the lives and careers of our sons and daughters. All of us are concerned with the cost of food and clothing and shelter, with taxes and income and savings and jobs, with the schooling, the health and the future of our children and grandchildren, with all the problems and purposes and great hopes that fill our lives.

Believe me—these realities of living, every one of them, are the deep concern, too, of this administration.

From time to time, as we tackle Government's part in the solution of these problems, members of the administration—myself and others—will report to you about our aims, our actions, our progress, and what is being accomplished. This kind of reporting, it seems to me, is one of the great responsibilities of a government which, like ours, rests on the consent of the people. We know that an informed and alert people is the backbone of the free system in which this Republic was conceived and under which it has so greatly prospered.

One such report—and a most important one—I shall deliver to the Congress on Thursday of this week: the State of the Union Message. It will present an outline of this administration's legislative program. Many major phases of the national economy and activities of your Government will be discussed in this report.

I believe you will find it, and the projected program it includes, of great personal interest to you. It will affect your lives—we believe for the better—certainly it represents the philosophy of government by and for the people.

In the preparation of the program to be presented in the State of the

Union Message I am consulting with many senior members of the Congress and have considered the views of a great many other thoughtful persons.

And I hope that this program, because of its purpose of promoting the welfare of all our people, will enlist the support of all of you, regardless of party. It is my earnest hope that the Congress will take quick and effective steps to enact the measures I will recommend.

This evening, I shall not preview the message to be delivered to the Congress on Thursday. However, it is entirely proper that I should review, briefly, the aims and purposes of this administration—in what direction we are headed and how we propose to get there. And, also briefly, some accomplishments of the past 12 months.

This administration believes that Government—from top to bottom—must be manned by men and women of brains, conscience, heart, and integrity. We believe that these men and women must have an intellectual grasp of the problems before them that is matched by their devotion to what is just and humane. Such people are true public servants; not bureaucrats.

Given such men and women, your Government will be unimpeachable in honesty and decency and dignity. It will be an example in solvency and efficiency for all America to follow; and a shining proof to all the world that freedom and strength and a widely shared prosperity go hand-in-hand.

We believe that with such public servants, and backed by your approval, we can take the forward road to a stronger and better America.

This administration believes that no American—no one group of Americans—can truly prosper unless all Americans prosper. We are one family made up of millions of Americans with the same hopes for a full and happy life. We must not become a nation divided into factions, or special groups and hostile cliques.

We believe that the slum, the out-dated highway, the poor school system, deficiencies in health protection, the loss of a job, and the fear of poverty in old age—in fact, any real injustice in the business of living—penalizes us all. And this administration is committed to help you prevent them.

"Help" is the key word of this administration and of the program it presents to the Congress this Thursday. What do we mean by help?

We do not mean monuments to costly and intolerant bureaucracy. We do not mean a timid unwillingness to act. We mean service—service that is effective, service that is prompt, service that is single-mindedly devoted to solving the problem.

You make up the communities of this country, where the everlasting job of building a stronger and better America must have its roots. We will seek to give national effect to your aims and aspirations. To do so, we rely on the good sense and local knowledge of the community and will therefore decentralize administration as much as possible so that the services of Government may be closer to you and thus serve you better.

For we know that you are far more knowledgeable than Washington as to the nature of your local needs. We know also that, as the local partners in any enterprise, you will be incessantly concerned with efficiency and economy—something which we are promoting in all Federal enterprises.

I know that you have unbounded confidence in the future of America. You need only the assurance that Government will neither handcuff your enterprise nor withdraw into a smug bureaucratic indifference to the welfare of American citizens, particularly those who, through no fault of their own, are in a period of adversity.

For this administration, I give you that pledge.

So much for our beliefs and the aims and purposes of this administration. What has been accomplished in the year just past? Let me list a few of these in the briefest possible fashion:

1. The fighting and the casualties in Korea mercifully have come to an end. We can therefore take more satisfaction in other blessings of our daily life.

2. Our own defenses and those of the free world have been strengthened against Communist aggression.

3. The highest security standards are being insisted upon for those employed in Government service.

4. Requests for new appropriations have been reduced by 13 billion dollars.

5. Tax reductions which go into effect this month have been made financially feasible by substantial reductions in expenditures.

6. Strangling controls on our economy have been promptly removed.

7. The fantastic paradox of farm prices, on a toboggan slide while living costs soared skyward, has ceased.

8. The cheapening by inflation of every dollar you earn, every savings account and insurance policy you own, and every pension payment you receive has been halted.

9. The proper working relationship between the executive and legislative branches of the Federal Government has been made effective.

10. Emergency immigration legislation has been enacted.

11. A strong and consistent policy has been developed toward gaining and retaining the initiative in foreign affairs.

12. A plan to harness atomic energy to the peaceful service of mankind, and to help end the climate of suspicion and fear that excites nations to war, has been proposed to the world.

And there is still another accomplishment. Perhaps this one should more properly be called groundwork for an accomplishment.

It is groundwork that has been laid by this administration in the strong belief that the Federal Government should be prepared at all times—ready, at a moment's notice—to use every proper means to sustain the basic prosperity of our people.

I therefore give you this assurance:

Every legitimate means available to the Federal Government that can be used to sustain that prosperity is being used and will continue to be used as necessary.

This administration believes that we must not and need not tolerate a boom-and-bust America. We believe that America's prosperity does not and need not depend upon war or the preparation for war. We know that this great country can make the adjustments necessary to meet changing circumstances without encouraging disaster and without bringing about the economic chaos for which the Communists hope. Our system is the greatest wealth producer in the world—in terms of the life and the well-being of every citizen.

Sound planning and aggressive enterprise must, of course, be accompanied by the indispensable ingredient—a persistent and reasoned faith in the growth and progress of America, a faith which cannot be shaken by self-appointed peddlers of gloom and doom.

Such are a few of the accomplishments of the past year. They promise a new year even more fruitful to the security of the Nation and the welfare of its people.

5

Now, as all of you know, when you set out to build a house, you first must plan and solidly construct a foundation on which to put it—if you hope to live in that house in comfort and security. Since January 20th of last year we have planned and built the foundation for our forthcoming legislative program, constructed under the aims and purposes I have been discussing with you tonight.

It is my legal duty to present this program, in the State of the Union Message, to your elected representatives, the members of the House of Representatives and of the Senate.

It is their duty, in turn, to give it careful study, before taking action on its various recommendations.

It is your right to give it the same thoughtful consideration.

It is a program that does not deal in pie-in-the-sky promises to all, nor in bribes to a few, nor in threats to any. It is a program inspired by zeal for the common good, dedicated to the welfare of every American family—whatever its means of livelihood may be, or its social position, or its ancestral strain, or its religious affiliation.

I am confident that it will meet with your approval.

When the State of the Union Message is delivered to the Congress on Thursday, I hope you will agree with me that it presents an opportunity which will enable us, as a people—united and strong—to push ever forward and to demonstrate to the world the great and good power of free men and women.

We will build a stronger and better America—of greater security and increasing prosperity for all.

3 ¶ Annual Message to the Congress on the State of the Union. *January* 7, 1954

[Delivered in person before a joint session]

Mr. President, Mr. Speaker, Members of the Eighty-third Congress:

It is a high honor again to present to the Congress my views on the state of the Union and to recommend measures to advance the security, prosperity, and well-being of the American people.

All branches of this Government—and I venture to say both of our great parties—can support the general objective of the recommendations

I make today, for that objective is the building of a stronger America. A nation whose every citizen has good reason for bold hope; where effort is rewarded and prosperity is shared; where freedom expands and peace is secure—that is what I mean by a stronger America.

Toward this objective a real momentum has been developed during this Administration's first year in office. We mean to continue that momentum and to increase it. We mean to build a better future for this nation.

Much for which we may be thankful has happened during the past year.

First of all we are deeply grateful that our sons no longer die on the distant mountains of Korea. Although they are still called from our homes to military service, they are no longer called to the field of battle.

The nation has just completed the most prosperous year in its history. The damaging effect of inflation on the wages, pensions, salaries and savings of us all has been brought under control. Taxes have begun to go down. The cost of our government has been reduced and its work proceeds with some 183,000 fewer employees; thus the discouraging trend of modern governments toward their own limitless expansion has in our case been reversed. The cost of armaments becomes less oppressive as we near our defense goals; yet we are militarily stronger every day. During the year, creation of the new Cabinet Department of Health, Education, and Welfare symbolized the government's permanent concern with the human problems of our citizens.

Segregation in the armed forces and other Federal activities is on the way out. We have also made progress toward its elimination in the District of Columbia. These are steps in the continuing effort to eliminate inter-racial difficulty.

Some developments beyond our shores have been equally encouraging. Communist aggression, halted in Korea, continues to meet in Indo-china the vigorous resistance of France and the Associated States, assisted by timely aid from our country. In West Germany, in Iran, and in other areas of the world, heartening political victories have been won by the forces of stability and freedom. Slowly but surely, the free world gathers strength. Meanwhile, from behind the iron curtain, there are signs that tyranny is in trouble and reminders that its structure is as brittle as its surface is hard.

There has been in fact a great strategic change in the world during

7

the past year. That precious intangible, the initiative, is becoming ours. Our policy, not limited to mere reaction against crises provoked by others, is free to develop along lines of our choice not only abroad, but also at home. As a major theme for American policy during the coming year, let our joint determination be to hold this new initiative and to use it.

We shall use this initiative to promote three broad purposes: First, to protect the freedom of our people; second, to maintain a strong, growing economy; third, to concern ourselves with the human problems of the individual citizen.

Only by active concern for each of these purposes can we be sure that we are on the forward road to a better and a stronger America. All my recommendations today are in furtherance of these three purposes.

I. FOREIGN AFFAIRS

American freedom is threatened so long as the world Communist conspiracy exists in its present scope, power and hostility. More closely than ever before, American freedom is interlocked with the freedom of other people. In the unity of the free world lies our best chance to reduce the Communist threat without war. In the task of maintaining this unity and strengthening all its parts, the greatest responsibility falls naturally on those who, like ourselves, retain the most freedom and strength.

We shall, therefore, continue to advance the cause of freedom on foreign fronts.

In the Far East, we retain our vital interest in Korea. We have negotiated with the Republic of Korea a mutual security pact, which develops our security system for the Pacific and which I shall promptly submit to the Senate for its consent to ratification. We are prepared to meet any renewal of armed aggression in Korea. We shall maintain indefinitely our bases in Okinawa. I shall ask the Congress to authorize continued material assistance to hasten the successful conclusion of the struggle in Indo-china. This assistance will also bring closer the day when the Associated States may enjoy the independence already assured by France. We shall also continue military and economic aid to the Nationalist Government of China.

In South Asia, profound changes are taking place in free nations which are demonstrating their ability to progress through democratic methods. They provide an inspiring contrast to the dictatorial methods and backward course of events in Communist China. In these continuing efforts, the free peoples of South Asia can be assured of the support of the United States.

In the Middle East, where tensions and serious problems exist, we will show sympathetic and impartial friendship.

In Western Europe our policy rests firmly on the North Atlantic Treaty. It will remain so based as far ahead as we can see. Within its organization, the building of a united European community, including France and Germany, is vital to a free and self-reliant Europe. This will be promoted by the European Defense Community which offers assurance of European security. With the coming of unity to Western Europe, the assistance this Nation can render for the security of Europe and the free world will be multiplied in effectiveness.

In the Western Hemisphere we shall continue to develop harmonious and mutually beneficial cooperation with our neighbors. Indeed, solid friendship with all our American neighbors is a cornerstone of our entire policy.

In the world as a whole, the United Nations, admittedly still in a state of evolution, means much to the United States. It has given uniquely valuable services in many places where violence threatened. It is the only real world forum where we have the opportunity for international presentation and rebuttal. It is a place where the nations of the world can, if they have the will, take collective action for peace and justice. It is a place where the guilt can be squarely assigned to those who fail to take all necessary steps to keep the peace. The United Nations deserves our continued firm support.

FOREIGN ASSISTANCE AND TRADE

In the practical application of our foreign policy, we enter the field of foreign assistance and trade.

Military assistance must be continued. Technical assistance must be maintained. Economic assistance can be reduced. However, our economic programs in Korea and in a few other critical places of the world are especially important, and I shall ask Congress to continue them in the next fiscal year.

The forthcoming Budget Message will propose maintenance of the Presidential power of transferability of all assistance funds and will ask authority to merge these funds with the regular defense funds. It will also propose that the Secretary of Defense have primary responsibility for the administration of foreign military assistance in accordance with the policy guidance of the Secretary of State.

The fact that we can now reduce our foreign economic assistance in many areas is gratifying evidence that its objectives are being achieved. By continuing to surpass her prewar levels of economic activity, Western Europe gains self-reliance. Thus our relationship enters a new phase which can bring results beneficial to our taxpayers and our allies alike, if still another step is taken.

This step is the creation of a healthier and freer system of trade and payments within the free world—a system in which our allies can earn their own way and our own economy can continue to flourish. The free world can no longer afford the kinds of arbitrary restraints on trade that have continued ever since the war. On this problem I shall submit to the Congress detailed recommendations, after our Joint Commission on Foreign Economic Policy has made its report.

ATOMIC ENERGY PROPOSAL

As we maintain our military strength during the coming year and draw closer the bonds with our allies, we shall be in an improved position to discuss outstanding issues with the Soviet Union. Indeed we shall be glad to do so whenever there is a reasonable prospect of constructive results. In this spirit the atomic energy proposals of the United States were recently presented to the United Nations General Assembly. A truly constructive Soviet reaction will make possible a new start toward an era of peace, and away from the fatal road toward atomic war.

DEFENSE

Since our hope is peace, we owe ourselves and the world a candid explanation of the military measures we are taking to make that peace secure.

As we enter this new year, our military power continues to grow. This power is for our own defense and to deter aggression. We shall not be aggressors, but we and our allies have and will maintain a massive capability to strike back.

Here are some of the considerations in our defense planning:

First, while determined to use atomic power to serve the usages of peace, we take into full account our great and growing number of nuclear weapons and the most effective means of using them against an aggressor if they are needed to preserve our freedom. Our defense will be stronger if, under appropriate security safeguards, we share with our allies certain knowledge of the tactical use of our nuclear weapons. I urge the Congress to provide the needed authority.

Second, the usefulness of these new weapons creates new relationships between men and materials. These new relationships permit economies in the use of men as we build forces suited to our situation in the world today. As will be seen from the Budget Message on January 21, the airpower of our Navy and Air Force is receiving heavy emphasis.

Third, our armed forces must regain maximum mobility of action. Our strategic reserves must be centrally placed and readily deployable to meet sudden aggression against ourselves and our allies.

Fourth, our defense must rest on trained manpower and its most economical and mobile use. A professional corps is the heart of any security organization. It is necessarily the teacher and leader of those who serve temporarily in the discharge of the obligation to help defend the Republic. Pay alone will not retain in the career service of our armed forces the necessary numbers of long-term personnel. I strongly urge, therefore, a more generous use of other benefits important to service morale. Among these are more adequate living quarters and family housing units and medical care for dependents.

Studies of military manpower have just been completed by the National Security Training Commission and a Committee appointed by the Director of the Office of Defense Mobilization. Evident weaknesses exist in the state of readiness and organization of our reserve forces. Measures to correct these weaknesses will be later submitted to the Congress.

Fifth, the ability to convert swiftly from partial to all-out mobilization is imperative to our security. For the first time, mobilization officials know what the requirements are for 1,000 major items needed for military uses. These data, now being related to civilian requirements and our supply potential, will show us the gaps in our mobilization base. Thus we shall have more realistic plant-expansion and stockpiling goals. We shall speed their attainment. This Nation is at last to have an up-to-date mobilization base—the foundation of a sound defense program.

Another part of this foundation is, of course, our continental transport system. Some of our vital heavy materials come increasingly from

Canada. Indeed our relations with Canada, happily always close, involve more and more the unbreakable ties of strategic interdependence. Both nations now need the St. Lawrence Seaway for security as well as for economic reasons. I urge the Congress promptly to approve our participation in its construction.

Sixth, military and non-military measures for continental defense must be and are being strengthened. In the current fiscal year we are allocating to these purposes an increasing portion of our effort, and in the next fiscal year we shall spend nearly a billion dollars more for them than in 1953.

An indispensable part of our continental security is our civil defense effort. This will succeed only as we have the complete cooperation of State Governors, Mayors, and voluntary citizen groups. With their help we can advance a cooperative program which, if an attack should come, would save many lives and lessen destruction.

The defense program recommended in the 1955 Budget is consistent with all of the considerations which I have just discussed. It is based on a new military program unanimously recommended by the Joint Chiefs of Staff and approved by me following consideration by the National Security Council. This new program will make and keep America strong in an age of peril. Nothing should bar its attainment.

The international and defense policies which I have outlined will enable us to negotiate from a position of strength as we hold our resolute course toward a peaceful world. We now turn to matters which are normally characterized as domestic, well realizing that what we do abroad affects every problem at home—from the amount of taxes to our very state of mind.

INTERNAL SECURITY

Under the standards established for the new employee security program, more than 2,200 employees have been separated from the Federal government. Our national security demands that the investigation of new employees and the evaluation of derogatory information respecting present employees be expedited and concluded at the earliest possible date. I shall recommend that the Congress provide additional funds where necessary to speed these important procedures.

From the special employment standards of the Federal government I turn now to a matter relating to American citizenship. The subversive character of the Communist Party in the United States has been clearly demonstrated in many ways, including court proceedings. We should recognize by law a fact that is plain to all thoughtful citizens— that we are dealing here with actions akin to treason—that when a citizen knowingly participates in the Communist conspiracy he no longer holds allegiance to the United States.

I recommend that Congress enact legislation to provide that a citizen of the United States who is convicted in the courts of hereafter conspiring to advocate the overthrow of this government by force or violence be treated as having, by such act, renounced his allegiance to the United States and forfeited his United States citizenship.

In addition, the Attorney General will soon appear before your Committees to present his recommendations for needed additional legal weapons with which to combat subversion in our country and to deal with the question of claimed immunity.

II. STRONG ECONOMY

I turn now to the second great purpose of our government: Along with the protection of freedom, the maintenance of a strong and growing economy.

The American economy is one of the wonders of the world. It undergirds our international position, our military security, and the standard of living of every citizen. This Administration is determined to keep our economy strong and to keep it growing.

At this moment we are in transition from a wartime to a peacetime economy. I am confident that we can complete this transition without serious interruption in our economic growth. But we shall not leave this vital matter to chance. Economic preparedness is fully as important to the nation as military preparedness.

Subsequent special messages and the economic report on January 28 will set forth plans of the Administration and its recommendations for Congressional action. These will include flexible credit and debt management policies; tax measures to stimulate consumer and business spending; suitable lending, guaranteeing, insuring, and grant-in-aid activities; strengthened old-age and unemployment insurance measures; improved agricultural programs; public-works plans laid well in advance; enlarged opportunities for international trade and investment. This mere enumeration of these subjects implies the vast amount of study, coordination, and planning, to say nothing of authorizing legislation, that altogether make our economic preparedness complete.

If new conditions arise that require additional administrative or legislative action, the Administration will still be ready. A government always ready, as this is, to take well-timed and vigorous action, and a business community willing, as ours is, to plan boldly and with confidence, can between them develop a climate assuring steady economic growth.

THE BUDGET

I shall submit to the Congress on January 21 the first budget prepared by this Administration, for the period July 1, 1954, through June 1955.

This budget is adequate to the current needs of the government. It recognizes that a Federal budget should be a stabilizing factor in the economy. Its tax and expenditure programs will foster individual initiative and economic growth.

Pending the transmittal of my Budget Message, I shall mention here only a few points about our budgetary situation.

First, one of our initial acts was to revise, with the cooperation of the Congress, the Budget prepared before this Administration took office. Requests for new appropriations were greatly reduced. In addition, the spending level provided in that Budget for the current fiscal year has been reduced by about $7,000,000,000. In the next fiscal year we estimate a further reduction in expenditures of more than $5,000,000,000. This will reduce the spending level over the two fiscal years by more than $12,000,000,000. We are also reducing further our requests for new appropriations.

Second, despite the substantial loss of revenue in the coming fiscal year, resulting from tax reductions now in effect and tax adjustments which I shall propose, our reduced spending will move the new budget closer to a balance.

Third, by keeping new appropriation requests below estimated revenues, we continue to reduce the tremendous accumulation of unfinanced obligations incurred by the Government under past appropriations.

Fourth, until those claims on our Government's revenues are further reduced, the growth in the public debt cannot be entirely stopped. Because of this—because the government's bills have to be paid every month, while the tax money to pay them comes in with great unevenness within the fiscal year—and because of the need for flexibility to manage this enormous debt, I find it necessary to renew my request for an increase in the statutory debt limit.

TAXES

The new budget provides for a lower level of taxation than has prevailed in preceding years. Six days ago individual income taxes were reduced and the excess profits tax expired. These tax reductions are justified only because of the substantial reductions we already have made and are making in governmental expenditures. As additional reductions in expenditures are brought gradually but surely into sight, further reductions in taxes can and will be made. When budget savings and sound governmental financing are assured, tax burdens should be reduced so that taxpayers may spend their own money in their own way.

While we are moving toward lower levels of taxation we must thoroughly revise our whole tax system. The groundwork for this revision has already been laid by the Committee on Ways and Means of the House of Representatives, in close consultation with the Department of the Treasury. We should now remove the more glaring tax inequities, particularly on small taxpayers; reduce restraints on the growth of small business; and make other changes that will encourage initiative, enterprise and production. Twenty-five recommendations toward these ends will be contained in my budget message.

Without attempting to summarize these manifold reforms, I can here illustrate their tendency. For example, we propose more liberal tax treatment for dependent children who work, for widows or widowers with dependent children, and for medical expenses. For the business that wants to expand or modernize its plant, we propose liberalized tax treatment of depreciation, research and development expenses, and retained earnings.

Because of the present need for revenue the corporation income tax should be kept at the current rate of 52% for another year, and the excise taxes scheduled to be reduced on April first, including those on liquor, tobacco, gasoline and automobiles, should be continued at present rates.

Immediate extension of the Renegotiation Act of 1951 is also needed to eliminate excessive profits and to prevent waste of public funds in the purchase of defense materials.

AGRICULTURE

The well being of our 160 million people demands a stable and prosperous agriculture. Conversely, every farmer knows he cannot prosper unless all America prospers. As we seek to promote increases in our standard of living, we must be sure that the farmer fairly shares in that increase. Therefore, a farm program promoting stability and prosperity in all elements of our agriculture is urgently needed.

Agricultural laws now in effect successfully accomplished their wartime purpose of encouraging maximum production of many crops. Today, production of these crops at such levels far exceeds present demand. Yet the laws encouraging such production are still in effect. The storage facilities of the Commodity Credit Corporation bulge with surplus stocks of dairy products, wheat, cotton, corn, and certain vegetable oils; and the Corporation's presently authorized borrowing authority—$6,750,000,000—is nearly exhausted. Some products, priced out of domestic markets, and others, priced out of world markets, have piled up in government hands. In a world in which millions of people are hungry, destruction of food would, of course, be unconscionable. Yet surplus stocks continue to threaten the market and in spite of the acreage controls authorized by present law, surpluses will continue to accumulate.

We confront two alternatives. The first is to impose still greater acreage reductions for some crops and apply rigid Federal controls over the use of the diverted acres. This will regiment the production of every basic agricultural crop. It will place every producer of those crops under the domination and control of the Federal government in Washington. This alternative is contrary to the fundamental interests, not only of the farmer, but of the Nation as a whole. Nor is it a real solution to the problem facing us.

The second alternative is to permit the market price for these agricultural products gradually to have a greater influence on the planning of production by farmers, while continuing the assistance of the government. This is the sound approach. To make it effective, surpluses existing when the new program begins must be insulated from the normal channels of trade for special uses. These uses would include school lunch programs, disaster relief, emergency assistance to foreign friends, and of particular importance the stockpiling of reserves for a national emergency.

Building on the agricultural laws of 1948 and 1949, we should establish a price support program with enough flexibility to attract the production of needed supplies of essential commodities and to stimulate the consumption of those commodities that are flooding American markets. Transition to modernized parity must be accomplished gradually. In no case should there be an abrupt downward change in the dollar level or in the percentage level of price supports.

Next Monday I shall transmit to the Congress my detailed recommendations embodying this approach. They have been developed through the cooperation of innumerable individuals vitally interested in agriculture. My special message on Monday will briefly describe the consultative and advisory processes to which this whole program has been subjected during the past ten months.

I have chosen this farm program because it will build markets, protect the consumers' food supply, and move food into consumption instead of into storage. It is a program that will remove the threat to the farmer of these overhanging surpluses, a program, also, that will stimulate production when a commodity is scarce and encourage consumption when nature is bountiful. Moreover, it will promote the individual freedom, responsibility, and initiative which distinguish American agriculture. And, by helping our agriculture achieve full parity in the market, it promises our farmers a higher and steadier financial return over the years than any alternative plan.

CONSERVATION

Part of our Nation's precious heritage is its natural resources. It is the common responsibility of Federal, state, and local governments to improve and develop them, always working in the closest harmony and partnership.

All Federal conservation and resource development projects are being reappraised. Sound projects now under way will be continued. New projects in which the Federal Government has a part must be economically sound, with local sharing of cost wherever appropriate and feasible. In the next fiscal year work will be started on twenty-three projects that meet these standards. The Federal Government will continue to construct and operate economically sound flood control, power, irrigation and water supply projects wherever these projects are beyond the capacity of local initiative, public or private, and consistent with the needs of the whole Nation.

Our conservation program will also take into account the important role played by farmers in protecting our soil resources. I recommend enactment of legislation to strengthen agricultural conservation and up-stream flood prevention work, and to achieve a better balance with major flood control structures in the down-stream areas.

Recommendations will be made from time to time for the adoption of:

A uniform and consistent water resources policy;

A revised public lands policy; and

A sound program for safeguarding the domestic production of critical and strategic metals and minerals.

In addition we shall continue to protect and improve our national forests, parks, monuments and other natural and historic sites, as well as our fishery and wildlife resources. I hope that pending legislation to improve the conservation and management of publicly-owned grazing lands in national forests will soon be approved by the Congress.

NATIONAL HIGHWAYS

To protect the vital interest of every citizen in a safe and adequate highway system, the Federal Government is continuing its central role in the Federal Aid Highway Program. So that maximum progress can be made to overcome present inadequacies in the Interstate Highway System, we must continue the Federal gasoline tax at two cents per gallon. This will require cancellation of the $\frac{1}{2}$¢ decrease which otherwise will become effective April 1st, and will maintain revenues so that an expanded highway program can be undertaken.

When the Commission on Intergovernmental Relations completes its study of the present system of financing highway construction, I shall promptly submit it for consideration by the Congress and the governors of the states.

POST OFFICE

It is apparent that the substantial savings already made, and to be made, by the Post Office Department cannot eliminate the postal deficit. I recommend, therefore, that the Congress approve the bill now pending in the House of Representatives providing for the adjustment of certain postal rates. To handle the long term aspects of this, I also recommend that the Congress create a permanent commission to establish fair and reasonable postal rates from time to time in the future.

III. HUMAN PROBLEMS

Along with the protection of freedom and maintenance of a strong and growing economy, this Administration recognizes a third great purpose of government: concern for the human problems of our citizens. In a modern industrial society, banishment of destitution and cushioning the shock of personal disaster on the individual are proper concerns of all levels of government, including the federal government. This is especially true where remedy and prevention alike are beyond the individual's capacity.

LABOR AND WELFARE

Of the many problems in this area, those I shall first discuss are of particular concern to the members of our great labor force, who with their heads, hearts and hands produce so much of the wealth of our country.

Protection against the hazards of temporary unemployment should be extended to some 6½ millions of workers, including civilian Federal workers, who now lack this safeguard. Moreover, the Secretary of Labor is making available to the states studies and recommendations in the fields of weekly benefits, periods of protection and extension of coverage. The Economic Report will consider the related matter of minimum wages and their coverage.

The Labor Management Relations Act of 1947 is basically a sound law. However, six years of experience have revealed that in some respects it can be improved. On January 11, I shall forward to the Congress suggestions for changes designed to reinforce the basic objectives of the Act.

Our basic social security program, the Old-Age and Survivors Insurance system, to which individuals contribute during their productive years and receive benefits based on previous earnings, is designed to shield them from destitution. Last year I recommended extension of the social insurance system to include more than 10,000,000 additional persons. I ask that this extension soon be accomplished. This and other major improvements in the insurance system will bring substantial benefit increases and broaden the membership of the insurance system, thus diminishing the need for Federal grants-in-aid for such purposes. A new formula will therefore be proposed, permitting progressive reduction in such grants as the need for them declines.

Federal grant-in-aid welfare programs, now based on widely varying formulas, should be simplified. Concrete proposals on fourteen of them will be suggested to the appropriate Committees.

The program for rehabilitation of the disabled especially needs strengthening. Through special vocational training, this program presently returns each year some 60,000 handicapped individuals to productive work. Far more disabled people can be saved each year from idleness and dependence if this program is gradually increased. My more detailed recommendations on this and the other social insurance problems I have mentioned will be sent to the Congress on January 14th.

HEALTH

I am flatly opposed to the socialization of medicine. The great need for hospital and medical services can best be met by the initiative of private plans. But it is unfortunately a fact that medical costs are rising and already impose severe hardships on many families. The Federal Government can do many helpful things and still carefully avoid the socialization of medicine.

The Federal Government should encourage medical research in its battle with such mortal diseases as cancer and heart ailments, and should continue to help the states in their health and rehabilitation programs. The present Hospital Survey and Construction Act should be broadened in order to assist in the development of adequate facilities for the chronically ill, and to encourage the construction of diagnostic centers, rehabilitation facilities, and nursing homes. The war on disease also needs a better working relationship between Government and private initiative. Private and non-profit hospital and medical insurance plans are already in the field, soundly based on the experience and initiative of the people in their various communities.

A limited Government reinsurance service would permit the private and non-profit insurance companies to offer broader protection to more of the many families which want and should have it. On January 18 I shall forward to the Congress a special message presenting this Administration's health program in its detail.

EDUCATION

Youth—our greatest resource—is being seriously neglected in a vital respect. The nation as a whole is not preparing teachers or building schools fast enough to keep up with the increase in our population.

The preparation of teachers as, indeed, the control and direction of public education policy, is a state and local responsibility. However, the Federal Government should stand ready to assist states which demonstrably cannot provide sufficient school buildings. In order to appraise the needs, I hope that this year a conference on education will be held in each state, culminating in a national conference. From these conferences on education, every level of government—from the Federal Government to each local school board—should gain the information with which to attack this serious problem.

HOUSING

The details of a program to enlarge and improve the opportunities for our people to acquire good homes will be presented to the Congress by special message on January 25.

This program will include:

Modernization of the home mortgage insurance program of the Federal Government;

Redirection of the present system of loans and grants-in-aid to cities for slum clearance and redevelopment;

Extension of the advantages of insured lending to private credit engaged in this task of rehabilitating obsolete neighborhoods;

Insurance of long-term, mortgage loans, with small down payment for low-income families; and, until alternative programs prove more effective,

Continuation of the public housing program adopted in the Housing Act of 1949.

If the individual, the community, the State and federal governments will alike apply themselves, every American family can have a decent home.

VETERANS ADMINISTRATION

The internal reorganization of the Veterans Administration is proceeding with my full approval. When completed, it will afford a single agency whose services, including medical facilities, will be better adapted to the needs of those 20,000,000 veterans to whom this Nation owes so much.

SUFFRAGE

My few remaining recommendations all relate to a basic right of our citizens—that of being represented in the decisions of the government.

I hope that the States will cooperate with the Congress in adopting uniform standards in their voting laws that will make it possible for our citizens in the armed forces overseas to vote.

In the District of Columbia the time is long overdue for granting national suffrage to its citizens and also applying the principle of local self-government to the Nation's Capital. I urge the Congress to move promptly in this direction and also to revise District revenue measures to provide needed public works improvements.

The people of Hawaii are ready for statehood. I renew my request for this legislation in order that Hawaii may elect its State officials and its representatives in Washington along with the rest of the country this fall.

For years our citizens between the ages of 18 and 21 have, in time of peril, been summoned to fight for America. They should participate in the political process that produces this fateful summons. I urge Congress to propose to the States a constitutional amendment permitting citizens to vote when they reach the age of 18.

CONCLUSION

I want to add one final word about the general purport of these many recommendations.

Our government's powers are wisely limited by the Constitution; but quite apart from those limitations, there are things which no government can do or should try to do.

A government can strive, as ours is striving, to maintain an economic system whose doors are open to enterprise and ambition—those personal qualities on which economic growth largely depends. But enterprise and ambition are qualities which no government can supply. Fortunately no American government need concern itself on this score; our people have these qualities in good measure.

A government can sincerely strive for peace, as ours is striving, and ask its people to make sacrifices for the sake of peace. But no government can place peace in the hearts of foreign rulers. It is our duty then to ourselves and to freedom itself to remain strong in all those ways—spiritual, economic, military—that will give us maximum safety against the possibility of aggressive action by others.

No government can inoculate its people against the fatal materialism that plagues our age. Happily, our people, though blessed with more material goods than any people in history, have always reserved their first allegiance to the kingdom of the spirit, which is the true source of that freedom we value above all material things.

But a government can try, as ours tries, to sense the deepest aspirations of the people, and to express them in political action at home and abroad. So long as action and aspiration humbly and earnestly seek favor in the sight of the Almighty, there is no end to America's forward road; there is no obstacle on it she will not surmount in her march toward a lasting peace in a free and prosperous world.

DWIGHT D. EISENHOWER

NOTE: This is the text of the document which the President signed and transmitted to the Senate and the House of Representatives (H. Doc. 251, 83d Cong., 2d sess.).

The Address as reported from the floor appears in the Congressional Record (vol. 100, p. 62).

4 ¶ Special Message to the Congress on Agriculture. *January* 11, 1954

To the Congress of the United States:

I submit herewith for the consideration of the Congress a number of recommendations affecting the Nation's agriculture.

PART I

The agricultural problem today is as serious and complex as any with which the Congress will deal in this session. Immediate action is needed to arrest the growing threat to our present agricultural program and to prevent the subsequent economic distress that could follow in our farming areas.

I have given assurances to the American farmer that support of existing agricultural laws, including continuance through 1954 of price supports on basic commodities at 90 percent of parity, was a moral and legal commitment that must be upheld. Along with the fulfillment of this commitment, an unending effort has proceeded in the past twelve months to provide the American farmer his full share of the income produced by a stable, prosperous country. This effort requires for success a new farm program adjusted to existing conditions in the Nation's agriculture.

23

This message presents to the Congress that new program. It is designed to achieve the stability and growth in income over the years to which our farmers are entitled and which the Nation must assure in the interest of all 160,000,000 of our people.

STUDIES OF THE PROBLEM

In constructing its program, this Administration resolved to get the benefit of the best thinking of the Nation's farmers, as well as that of its farm experts. Over sixty different survey groups, and more than 500 of the most eminent farm leaders in the country, have participated in these studies. Agricultural colleges and research institutions contributed their work and thought. Scores of producer, processor and trade groups, as well as national farm organizations, gave their findings and proposals. Mail from thousands of individual farmers, and opinion polls among farmers, have been analyzed and weighed. The bipartisan, broadly-representative National Agricultural Advisory Commission has steadily worked and consulted on the problem for the past twelve months. Numerous commodity organizations have been consulted. Many members of the Congress have shared their own rich experience in this effort. Accordingly, as promised a year ago, the most thorough and comprehensive study ever made of the farm problem and of governmental farm programs has been completed.

RECOMMENDATIONS BY COMMODITY

The recommendations which have been reaped from all this inquiry are in the best traditions of bipartisan approach to the Nation's agricultural legislation. They recognize that each farm crop has its own problems and that those problems require specific treatment. Accordingly Part II of this message presents detailed proposals for the treatment of sixteen commodities or commodity groups. I here confine myself to those aspects of the farm program in which all farmers and all citizens are equally concerned.

SOME FUNDAMENTAL CONSIDERATIONS

In its approach to this problem, the Administration has held to the following fundamentals:

1. A stable, prosperous and free agriculture is essential to the welfare of the United States.

2. A farm program must fairly represent the interests of both producers and consumers.

3. However large surpluses may be, food once produced must not be destroyed. Excessive stocks can be removed from commercial channels for constructive purposes that will benefit the people of the United States and our friends abroad.

4. For many reasons farm products are subject to wider price fluctuations than are most other commodities. Moreover, the individual farmer or rancher has less control over the prices he receives than do producers in most other industries. Government price supports must, therefore, be provided in order to bring needed stability to farm income and farm production.

5. A farm program first of all should assist agriculture to earn its proportionate share of the national income. It must likewise aim at stability in farm income. There should therefore be no wide year-to-year fluctuation in the level of price support.

6. No single program can apply uniformly to the whole farm industry. Some farm products are perishable, some are not; some farms consume the products of other farms; some foods and fibres we export, some we import. A comprehensive farm program must be adaptable to these and other differences, and yet not penalize one group of farmers in order to benefit another.

7. A workable farm program must give the Administration sufficient leeway to make timely changes in policies and methods, including price support levels, within limits established by law. This will enable the Administration to foresee and forestall new difficulties in our agriculture, rather than to attempt their legislative cure after they have arisen.

8. Adjustment to a new farm program must be accomplished gradually in the interest of the Nation's farming population and in the interest of the economy of the Nation as a whole.

9. Research and education, basic functions of the Department of Agriculture since its beginning, are still indispensable if our farmers are to improve their productivity and enlarge their markets.

10. The soil, water, range and forest resources of the United States are the natural foundation of our national economy. From them come our food, most of our clothing, much of our shelter. How well we protect and improve these resources will have a direct bearing on the future standard of living of the whole nation.

THE PRESENT AGRICULTURAL SITUATION

Present laws discourage increased consumption of wheat, corn, cotton and vegetable oils and encourage their excessive production. The huge and growing surpluses held by the government act as a constant threat to normal markets for these products. Thus, present law produces results which in turn are hurtful to those whom the laws are intended to help. Partly because of these excessive stocks, farm income has fallen steadily over the past three years.

The urgency in this situation may be illustrated by a few basic facts. During the past year, the investment of the Commodity Credit Corporation in farm commodities more than doubled, increasing by about $2,500,000,000. As a result the financial obligations of the Corporation are pressing hard against the $6,750,000,000 limitation on its borrowing authority. In order to assure that present price support commitments on 1953 and 1954 crops will be covered, I shall request the Congress to take early action to restore the Corporation's capital losses as of June 30, 1953, and to increase its borrowing authority to $8,500,000,000 effective July 1, 1954.

The Government's commodity holdings are enormous. It has investments in more than $2,000,000,000 worth of wheat alone. This includes 440,000,000 bushels owned outright. About 400,000,000 additional bushels are under loan, the greater share of which the government can expect to acquire. This is more than the domestic wheat requirements of the entire nation for a full year.

The cotton carry-over will amount to about 9,600,000 bales. Here again the carry-over is approximately equal to the domestic needs of the entire nation for a full year.

The carry-over of vegetable oils may be about 1,500,000,000 pounds, roughly double the carry-over that should normally be maintained.

Because such tremendous supplies are already in hand, acreage allotments and marketing quotas have had to be applied to wheat and cotton. An appeal by the government for sharp acreage reductions for corn appears unavoidable. These allotments are expected to reduce the acreage planted to these crops in 1954 by the following amounts: wheat, 16.5 million acres; corn, between 5 and 6 million acres; cotton, 3.5 million acres. Without the most careful handling, a diversion within a single year of 25 million acres of productive crop land—

about 8% of the total—from their accustomed use could have the most unfortunate impact on the total economy.

Even these reductions probably will not appreciably lower the surpluses of wheat and cotton because of the likelihood of increased yields that will be sought from the reduced acreage, and because markets will continue to shrink as a consequence of rigid price supports. As for corn, it is estimated that enough diverted land will be used for oats, barley, and sorghums to hold total supplies of feed grains at present levels, thus largely offsetting the purpose of the corn acreage reduction. It is also expected that some 3,000,000 diverted acres may be planted to soybeans, thus aggravating the tremendous oversupply of vegetable oils. The likely production from other diverted acres threatens producers of potatoes, sugar beets, rice, alfalfa, flaxseed, vegetables and many other crops. Therefore, we must move without further delay to treat the fundamental causes of our present excess supplies of farm commodities.

The Nation's agricultural problem is not one of general overproduction: Consumer demand continues at or near record high levels; the average prices of farm products that lack direct price supports have been as high in recent years as those of price-supported products. The problem is rather one of unbalanced farm production, resulting in specific surpluses which are unavoidable under the present rigid price supports. The problem is complicated by the continuing loss of some of those foreign markets on which American agriculture has depended for a large part of its prosperity.

MAJOR FEATURES OF FARM PROGRAM

The new farm program here proposed is consistent with all the foregoing conditions and fundamental considerations. It has five major features:

1. The new program should first be given an opportunity to start operating without the handicap of such large accumulated surpluses. This is to be done by setting aside certain quantities of our surplus commodities, eliminating them from price support computations.

2. The 1948 and 1949 Agricultural Acts were soundly conceived and received bipartisan support. The principles on which they were based are particularly applicable to the agricultural industry today. Although

27

based generally upon those principles, the proposed agricultural legislation of 1954 contains certain new features, improvements and modifications.

3. The amendment to the 1949 Agricultural Act providing for mandatory rigid supports, attuned to war needs and demonstrably unworkable in peacetime, will be permitted to expire. After the 1954 crops the level of price supports for the basic commodities will be gradually related to supply, promising farmers greater stability of income.

4. Modernized parity is to become effective for all commodities on January 1, 1956, as scheduled by law. Provision should be made for moving from the old to modernized parity in steps of five percentage points of the old parity per year until the change from old to modernized parity has been accomplished.

5. The key element of the new program is a gradual adjustment to new circumstances and conditions. Application of modernized parity and the relation of basic crops to supply levels require a transition period to assure a stable farm economy. This transition should be accomplished in a prudent and careful manner to avoid sharp adjustments which would threaten the dislocation of the program.

6. In keeping with the policy of gradual transition, the Secretary of Agriculture will use his authority under the Agricultural Act of 1949 to insure that year-to-year variations in price support levels will be limited.

7. The authority of the Secretary of Agriculture to apply price supports at more than 90 percent of parity when the national welfare or national security requires should be continued.

PARITY AND PRICE SUPPORTS

Under the provisions of the Agricultural Acts of 1948 and 1949 the government will:

1. Support the prices of basic crops of those farmers who cooperate with acreage allotments and marketing quotas when such are in effect;

2. Announce the price support level for various crops before those crops are planted, insofar as practicable;

3. Support price levels at up to 90 percent of parity. For some products a schedule of price floors will also be provided as authorized by the 1949 Act, ranging from 75% to 90% of parity, according to the relationship of total to normal supply; and

4. Vary the price support level one percentage point for every two percentage points of variation in the total supply. If the supply is short, higher support levels will encourage production. If the supply is over-abundant, a lowered price will stimulate consumption. Thus, not only will a floor be placed under all basic crop prices, but variations in price and supply will tend to offset each other, and thus stabilize the income of the farmer.

MODERNIZED PARITY

Parity calculations for most commodities under the old formula are based upon price relationships and buying habits of 40 years ago. Because methods of farm production have changed markedly, the Congress has wisely brought the parity concept up to date. Modernized parity takes account of price relationships during the most recent 10 years. It permits changes in farm technology and in consumer demand to express themselves in the level of price support and restores proper relationships among commodities.

For the basic commodities, the law provides that until January 1, 1956, the old or modernized parity, whichever is higher, shall be used. For all commodities except wheat, corn, cotton and peanuts, modernized parity is already in use.

Equitable treatment of the various commodities requires that we should use modernized parity for all farm products as now provided by law, beginning January 1, 1956.

INSULATION OF SURPLUSES FROM MARKETS

Removal of the threat of huge surpluses of farm commodities from current markets is an essential part of the program here presented. Destruction of surplus commodities cannot be countenanced under any circumstances. They can be insulated from the commercial markets and used in constructive ways. Such uses will include school lunch programs, disaster relief, aid to the people of other countries, and stock-piled reserves at home for use in war or national emergency.

I recommend that authority be provided to set aside reserves up to the value of $2,500,000,000 from the stocks presently held by the Commodity Credit Corporation. Broad discretionary authority should be provided to manage these "frozen" reserves. This authority should be coupled with legislative safeguards to prevent the return of these stocks to domestic or foreign markets so as to cause disturbance in normal trade. Perishable stocks should of course be rotated. Stocks of wheat, cotton, vegetable oils and possibly some dairy products should be set aside after this program takes effect.

The special circumstances relating to the crop and the date of initiating the proposed new program should govern the time for establishing each such commodity reserve. This reserve program will be effective only if it is carefully integrated with the new program as a whole. The insulation of our excess reserves of food and fiber is an essential first step in launching this new program.

EXPANSION OF FARM MARKETS ABROAD

One of our largest potential outlets for present surpluses is in friendly countries. Much impetus can be given to the use of a substantial volume of these commodities by substituting to the maximum extent food and fiber surpluses in foreign economic assistance and disaster relief. I shall request a continuation of the authority to use agricultural surpluses for this purpose.

It is not enough, however, to rely solely on these measures to move surpluses into consumption. No farm program should overlook continued economic growth and expansion. By revolutionary increases in farm productivity during and since World War II, American farmers have prepared our nation to supply an ever greater proportion of the food needs of the world. Developing commercial markets for this expanded production is part of the larger problem of organizing a freer system of trade and payments throughout the free world. Because our farmers depend to a considerable degree on foreign markets their interests will be particularly served by strengthening of the work of the Department of Agriculture in developing market outlets both at home and abroad. In my Budget Message I shall recommend that sufficient funds be appropriated for this purpose.

Meanwhile, a series of trade missions, working in cooperation with our representation overseas, will be sent from the United States, one to Europe, one to Asia, one to South America, to explore the immediate possibilities of expanding international trade in food and fiber. Moreover, the Secretary of Agriculture, in cooperation with the Secretary of State, is organizing discussions for the exchange of views with foreign ministers of agriculture on subjects affecting the use of agricultural surpluses and stockpiles.

USE OF DIVERTED ACRES

In addition to the removal of surpluses and the expansion of markets, special measures must be taken to deal with the use of acreages diverted from crops under allotment. To avoid these difficulties, the number of diverted acres must be reduced to a minimum. The proposed program accomplishes this by increasing the utilization of commodities, thereby reducing the need for acreage restrictions.

When land must be diverted from production, it is essential that its use be related to the basic objectives of soil conservation—to protect and to improve that land. Wherever acreage adjustments are especially difficult, Agricultural Conservation Program funds will be used to help farmers make these adjustments in a manner that will advance soil conservation and long-term efficiency.

SMALL FARMS

The chief beneficiaries of our price support policies have been the 2,000,000 larger, highly mechanized farming units which produce about 85% of our agricultural output. The individual production of the remaining farms, numbering about 3,500,000, is so small that the farmer derives little benefit from price supports. During 1954 the Secretary of Agriculture, in cooperation with the National Agricultural Advisory Commission, will give further special attention to the problems peculiar to small farmers.

CONCLUSION

The agricultural program proposed in this section, and in Part II which follows, will open new market outlets both at home and abroad, not only for current supplies but for future production. It will provide a firm floor on which our farmers can rely while making long-term plans for efficient production and marketing. Year in and year out, it will provide the best prospects for the stability and growth of farm income.

It will help the farmer attain full parity in the market. It will avoid creating burdensome surpluses. It will curtail the regimentation of production planning, lessen the problem of diverted acreage, and yield farm-

It will bring farm production into closer balance with consumer needs. ers greater freedom of choice and action.

31

It will promote agricultural interests, along with the public interest generally. It will avoid any sharp year to year change in prices and incomes.

The program will again stimulate and encourage good farm management. It will prevent arbitrary government control and afford the greatest freedom to the individual farmer. It will provide added incentive to make wise use of all our agricultural resources, and promises the Nation's agriculture a more stable and reliable financial return than any alternative plan.

I urge its early approval by the Congress.

PART II

In this part of the Special Message the principles developed in Part I are applied to specific commodities and commodity groups.

WHEAT

Wheat is a prime example of the results that ensue from a support program which fails to adjust to the level of demand. As of December 16, more than $2,000,000,000 of Commodity Credit Corporation funds were invested in wheat.

The export market, historically vital to our wheat farmers, was itself partly responsible for the expanded production of American wheat during the war and postwar years. To meet the food needs of devastated countries, our farmers continued their high level of production after the war and thus rendered a great service to humanity and to the cause of freedom throughout the world. These expanded outlets have since greatly diminished. Yet the support price has remained at the level associated with wartime needs. The result is that production has continued at wartime levels and, annually, more and more of this production has become surplus.

In foreign markets, the high rigid support program of the United States has become an umbrella for competitors. This has created an artificial competitive situation which has cost the American farmer a substantial part of his world wheat market. During the past two years our exports of wheat outside the International Wheat Agreement have fallen from 220 million bushels to 64 million, while Canada's free market sales have risen from 105 to 161 million bushels. Thus our price policy shrinks the very market that could otherwise help absorb our excess stocks of wheat.

Continuance of present price support levels for wheat would confront us with two undesirable alternatives:

(1) Curtail production to the amount needed for domestic use and very limited exports. This would require a reduction in wheat acreage of about 40 percent—from the 79 million acres planted in 1953 to between 45 and 50 million acres.

(2) Subsidize the consumption of wheat by increasingly severe burdens upon the taxpayer.

The foregoing alternatives make it increasingly clear that the Nation must depart from the high rigid support level for wheat.

It is, therefore, recommended that:

(1) A substantial part of the present excessive wheat carry-over be set aside as an emergency reserve and removed from the market.

(2) After the 1954 crop, the level of price support for wheat be related to supply. Because of the substantial set-aside, computations of the support level under the Agricultural Act of 1949 would insure that changes in support levels would be gradual. The Secretary of Agriculture will use his authority under the Agricultural Act of 1949 to insure that year-to-year variations in price support levels will be limited.

(3) Beginning January 1, 1956, a change be made at the rate of five percent a year from old to modernized parity;

(4) Acreage allotments and marketing quotas be continued, with the anticipation, however, that adjusted support levels will increase the incentive to employ some of the present wheat land for other purposes.

RICE

Price supports for rice at 90 percent of parity have had no recent application. Market prices have been at or above support levels; restraints on production have not been needed; stocks have not accumulated. Nevertheless, present price supports for rice can inhibit an adjustment, if one should be needed, in the same manner that they prevented the adjustment for wheat, when it was needed.

It is therefore recommended that mandatory price supports at 90 percent of parity for rice be allowed to expire after the 1954 crop.

CORN

Corn is a dominant factor in the feed-grain—livestock economy. This economy is based on an interdependent process involving the production

33

of feed, its conversion into livestock products, and its movement into consumption as meat, dairy products and eggs. To hold this economy in balance, prices are a critical factor, encouraging and discouraging livestock production by turns, rationing feed when it is scarce and moving it into use when it is plentiful. For the efficient use of corn, some price freedom is indispensable.

A program of high rigid price supports for feed grains involves the danger of curtailing our livestock industries and limiting the quantity of their products to consumers. We have made great strides in improving the efficiency of corn production and in passing some of those gains on to consumers in the form of reasonably priced livestock products. Our corn support program should be designed to encourage those trends.

Corn is used in the same manner as pasture and hay on farms where grown. Seldom does more than 25 percent of our corn crop move through commercial channels, and the bulk of this is eventually used as feed by other farmers. Farmers, therefore, are the principal users of corn. It follows that a high support price for farmers who produce corn for sale aggravates the cost-price squeeze on other farmers who normally buy corn and competing feeds to produce livestock products.

To guide the corn price support program, the adjustable price and income-balancing features of the Agricultural Act of 1949 on the whole are well suited. The level of support specified is designed to move corn into use. Livestock producers are assured of a steady supply of feed at reasonable prices.

The old parity formula holds the support price for corn too high in relation to livestock prices. Use of modernized parity, scheduled by law to become effective on January 1, 1956, will help to balance these vital price relationships.

It is, therefore, recommended that:

(1) Modernized parity for corn become effective on January 1, 1956, with modification limiting the rate of the transition to 5 percent in any single year;

(2) Except as provided in (3) and (4) the provisions of the Agricultural Act of 1949 become effective for the corn crop of 1955 and subsequent crops;

(3) The Act of 1949 be amended to provide a change, within the range of 75 to 90 percent of parity, of one percentage point in the support price for corn for each one percentage point of change in supply, thereby

giving greater flexibility to corn support prices and tending to prevent the building up of excessive holdings by government;

(4) Legislation be enacted to raise the normal carryover allowance for corn from 10 percent to 15 percent of domestic use plus exports, to become effective for 1955 and subsequent crops. This would help to assure more stable feed supplies and reduce the impact of current carry-over stocks on future production controls and support levels;

(5) Upon adoption of the foregoing recommendation, the system of marketing quotas be abolished.

FEED GRAINS OTHER THAN CORN

The Agricultural Act of 1949 authorizes price support for such non-basic crops as oats, barley, and grain sorghums at not to exceed 90 per-cent of the parity price. The amounts, terms and conditions of price support operations and the extent to which these operations are carried out are determined or approved by the Secretary of Agriculture upon consideration of various factors specified in the law.

Inasmuch as this program has worked satisfactorily, it is recommended that these provisions be continued.

MEAT ANIMALS

The fact that mandatory price supports are ill adapted to meat animals has been recognized by Secretaries of Agriculture for years. The present law provides tools well adapted to deal with the problems peculiar to the livestock industry.

It is recommended, therefore, that the existing conditions with respect to meat animals be continued.

DAIRY PRODUCTS

The Agricultural Act of 1949 requires price support for dairy products at such levels between 75 and 90 percent of parity as are necessary to assure an adequate supply. Sufficient discretionary authority is provided to operate a satisfactory program.

It is recommended that these provisions of law be continued.

POULTRY AND EGGS

Price supports have not been generally desired by the poultry industry. Temporarily, and in special circumstances, price supports can, however, be helpful.

It is recommended, therefore, that:

(1) Provisions of the 1949 Act be continued for poultry and eggs, with discretionary authority for the Secretary of Agriculture to support prices at not to exceed 90 percent of parity;

(2) Discretionary authority be continued to purchase poultry products for use in the school lunch program, in non-profit institutions, and for certain other purposes.

COTTON

Cotton, like wheat, is an export crop whose price is currently supported above the world level. Carryover stocks in the United States have been accumulating rapidly in the past two years. These stocks, probably close to 9,600,000 bales by next August, will approximate a full year's domestic requirements.

Our high rigid price support program stimulates competition of foreign producers and reduces exports. During the twenties and early thirties our net exports of cotton generally exceeded domestic consumption. Current exports amount to hardly a third of our larger domestic requirements.

Our problem is to develop a program which will help growers adjust gradually to changing circumstances, including foreign and domestic competition of rising intensity.

The Agricultural Act of 1949 provides price supports for cotton at a level between 75 and 90 percent of parity, dependent on the supply. Thus changes in supply and price would tend to offset one another, giving a relatively stable income. This plan will allow limited price variation, thus affording growers reasonable market stability and yet offering added inducement for heavier use of cotton in years of abundant supplies.

Separate legislation has made the adjustable pricing provisions of the 1949 Act ineffective for cotton. The Secretary of Agriculture is now required by law to set such marketing quotas and allotments that the required price support level can seldom if ever fall below 90 percent of parity. Instead of relying in part on the schedule of price floors intended in the Act of 1949, the law requires reliance almost entirely on production controls.

It is recommended, therefore, that:

1. A substantial part of the present large carryover of cotton now in prospect be set aside as an emergency reserve and removed from the market.

2. After the 1954 crop, the level of price support for cotton be related to supply. Because of the substantial set-aside, computations of the support levels, under the Agricultural Act of 1949, would insure that changes in support levels would be gradual. The Secretary of Agriculture will use his authority under the Agricultural Act of 1949 to insure that year-to-year variations in price support levels will be limited.

3. Modernized parity becomes effective for cotton as scheduled on January 1, 1956.

4. The Congress repeal the present provisions whereby the maximum use of production restrictions before there can be any reduction of the price support level is required.

TOBACCO

Tobacco farmers have demonstrated their ability to hold production in line with demand at the supported price without loss to the government. The relatively small acreage of tobacco and the limited areas to which it is adapted have made production control easier than for other crops.

The level of support to cooperators is 90 percent of the parity price in any year in which marketing quotas are in effect.

It is recommended that the tobacco program be continued in its present form.

PEANUTS

The law requires that mandatory 90 percent supports for peanuts continue through 1954 and that old parity remain in effect until the end of 1955.

This program, which has experienced some difficulties in adjusting supplies to demand at the supported price, can operate successfully with certain changes.

It is recommended that:

(1) The Agricultural Act of 1949 become effective for peanuts on January 1, 1955.

(2) The shift to modernized parity for peanuts begins as now provided by law on January 1, 1956.

(3) A transitional provision be provided to limit the change from the old to modernized parity to not more than 5 percent per year.

TUNG NUTS AND HONEY

Tung nuts and honey should be in the same category with other products for which price supports are permissive rather than required. It is recommended, therefore, that the mandatory price supports for these commodities be discontinued.

OIL SEEDS

Price support is authorized for soybeans, cottonseed and flax at not to exceed 90 percent of the parity price. It is recommended that the provisions of the Agricultural Act of 1949 be continued for these commodities.

FRUITS AND VEGETABLES

Existing law authorizes the use of 30 percent of general tariff revenues to encourage the exportation and domestic consumption of agriculture commodities. In the event of market distress these funds may be used for limited purchases of market surpluses of such perishable commodities as fruits and vegetables. No purchases may be undertaken unless outlets are available.

It is recommended that:

(1) Present provisions for the use of funds from tariff revenues be continued.

(2) Authorization for the use of marketing agreements be continued and liberalized to

(a) provide for inclusion of additional commodities to which marketing agreements are adapted;

(b) enlarge and clarify the authorization for agencies established under marketing orders to engage in or finance, within reasonable limits, research work from funds collected pursuant to the marketing order;

(c) provide for the continuous operation of marketing agreements, despite short-term price variations, where necessary to assure orderly distribution throughout the marketing season; and

(d) enlarge and clarify the authorization for the use of marketing orders to promote marketing efficiency, including the regulation of containers and types of pack for fresh fruits and vegetables.

POTATOES

It is recommended that legislation be enacted to allow assistance to potato growers in the same manner as is available for producers of other vegetables and of fruits.

38

SUGAR

The Sugar Program, extended in 1951, is operating in a generally satisfactory manner. It is recommended that this program be continued in its present form.

WOOL

Price support for wool above the market level has resulted in heavy accumulations of wool—now nearly 100 million pounds—by the Commodity Credit Corporation and the substitution of imported for domestic wool in our home consumption. Two-thirds of the wool used in the United States is imported; yet our own wool piles up in storage.

A program is needed which will assure equitable returns to growers and encourage efficient production and marketing. It should require a minimum of governmental interference with both producers and processors, entail a minimum of cost to taxpayers and consumers; and align itself compatibly with over-all farm and international trade policies.

It is recommended that:

(1) Prices of domestically produced wool be permitted to seek their level in the market, competing with other fibers and with imported wool, thus resulting in only one price for wool—the market price;

(2) Direct payments be made to domestic producers sufficient, when added to the average market price for the season, to raise the average return per pound to 90 percent of parity;

(3) Each producer receive the same support payment per pound of wool, rather than a variable rate depending upon the market price he had obtained. If each grower is allowed his rewards from the market, efficient production and marketing will be encouraged. This has the further advantage of avoiding the need for governmental loans, purchases, storage, or other regulation or interference with the market. Further, it imposes no need for periodic action to control imports in order to protect the domestic price support program.

(4) Funds to meet wool payments be taken from general revenues within the amount of unobligated tariff receipts from wool.

(5) Similar methods of support be adopted for pulled wool and for mohair, with proper regard for the relationships of their prices to those of similar commodities.

DWIGHT D. EISENHOWER

5 ¶ Special Message to the Congress on Labor-Management Relations. *January* 11, 1954

To the Congress of the United States:

I submit herewith for the consideration of the Congress a number of legislative recommendations affecting labor-management relations. These recommendations are in the interests both of working men and women, and our business and industrial community. In a broader sense, they are in the interests of all our people, whose prosperity is in so great a degree dependent on the existence of genuine mutual respect and good feeling between employers and employees.

This field of legislation has had a long, contentious history. It has taken time for objective principles to emerge which can command mutual acceptance of the fundamentals which govern the complex labor-management relationship. Although the process is not and perhaps never will be complete, we have now achieved a measure of practical experience and emotional maturity in this field which, I do not doubt, is responsible for the relatively peaceful character of recent industrial relations. No drastic legislative innovations in this field are therefore desirable or required at this time.

Federal labor-management legislation at best can provide only the framework in which free collective bargaining may be conducted. It should impose neither arbitrary restrictions nor heavy-handedness upon a relationship in which good will and sympathetic understanding should be the predominant characteristics.

The National Labor Relations Act—known as the Wagner Act and adopted in 1935 by bipartisan majorities—came into being because American working men and women needed the protection of law in order to guarantee them the free exercise of their right to organize into unions and to bargain collectively through representatives of their own choosing. As unions became strong, a need arose to protect the legitimate rights of employees and employers and to protect the general public from the consequences of unresolved labor disputes that created emergencies endangering the health or safety of the nation. To meet this need the Labor-Management Relations Act, 1947, commonly known as the Taft-Hartley Act, was adopted by bipartisan majorities.

In enacting labor-management legislation, the Congress has always built upon the legislation which preceded it. We have never turned backward. The Labor-Management Relations Act, 1947, was no exception. It built upon the National Labor Relations Act, and not only reaffirmed, but reinforced the right of working men and women to organize into unions and to bargain collectively with their employer. The protection of this right is firmly fixed in our law and should remain a permanent policy of our Government.

The Labor-Management Relations Act, 1947, is sound legislation. Experience gained in the operation of the Act, however, indicates that changes can be made to reinforce its basic objectives.

In the area of employer-employee relations the injunction has always been a controversial process. It is apparent, however, that where irreparable damage threatens, the restraining effect of an injunction is required in the interest of simple justice. Nevertheless, where a collective bargaining relationship exists, the issuance of an injunction often has the effect of making settlement of the dispute which led to the injunction more difficult.

Therefore, I recommend that whenever an injunction is issued under the National Labor Relations Act where a collective bargaining relationship exists between the parties, the Federal Mediation and Conciliation Service shall empanel a special local board to meet with the parties in an effort to seek a settlement of their dispute. I further recommend that in secondary boycott cases, the application for an injunction be discretionary.

The prohibitions in the Act against secondary boycotts are designed to protect innocent third parties from being injured in labor disputes that are not their concern. The true secondary boycott is indefensible and must not be permitted. The Act must not, however, prohibit legitimate concerted activities against other than innocent parties. I recommend that the Act be clarified by making it explicit that concerted action against (1) an employer who is performing "farmed-out" work for the account of another employer whose employees are on strike or (2) an employer on a construction project who, together with other employers, is engaged in work on the site of the project, will not be treated as a secondary boycott.

As the Act is now written, employees who are engaged in an economic strike are prohibited from voting in representation elections. In order to make it impossible for an employer to use this provision to destroy a union of his employees, I recommend that, in the event of an economic strike, the National Labor Relations Board be prohibited from considering a petition on the part of the employer which challenges the representation rights of the striking union. I further recommend that for a period of four months after the commencement of the strike, the Board be prohibited from considering a petition on the part of any other union which claims to represent the employees. The prohibition against considering a petition by the employer should continue as long as the strike continues, provided, however, that a reasonable limit of time, which I suggest be one year, be stipulated.

The Act has been interpreted to mean that even though a collective bargaining contract is in force, either party may insist that the contract be reopened for the purpose of bargaining about matters that were not the subject of negotiations when the contract was made. Thus stabilization of the relationship between the parties for the period of the contract can be completely frustrated. I recommend that the law be amended so as to protect both parties to a valid collective bargaining agreement from being required to negotiate during its term unless the contract so authorizes or both parties mutually consent.

The National Emergency provisions of the Act are essential to the protection of the National health and safety. As the Act is now written, the board of inquiry established to inquire into the facts of the dispute causing the emergency must report the facts to the President without recommendations. In order that the President may have the authority to require the board's recommendations, I recommend that after he has received and made available to the public the last report of the board of inquiry (if the dispute has not then been settled), he be empowered to reconvene the board and direct it to make recommendations to him for settlement of the dispute. Although the recommendations of the board would not be binding upon the parties, yet there is real value in obtaining the recommendations of informed and impartial men for the settlement of a dispute which imperils the national health and safety.

Employees engaged in the construction, amusement and maritime industries have unique problems because their employment is usually casual, temporary or intermittent. I recommend that in these industries the employer be permitted to enter into a pre-hire contract with a union under which the union will be treated initially as the employees' representative for collective bargaining. I also recommend that in these industries the employer and the union be permitted to make a union-shop contract under which an employee, within seven days after the beginning of his employment, shall become a member of the union.

Under the Act as presently written, both unions and employers are made responsible for the actions of their agents. In order to make it clear that a union cannot be held responsible for an act of an individual member solely because of his membership in the union, I recommend that the Act be amended to make the traditional common law rules of agency applicable.

The Act presently provides that the facilities of the National Labor Relations Board are available only to those unions whose officials execute affidavits disclaiming membership in Communist organizations. The Communist disclaimer provisions are not presently applicable to employers. I recommend that they be made applicable. Specific proposals for legislation dealing with Communist infiltration generally are now under study. If such legislation is enacted, making the Communist disclaimer provisions of the Act unnecessary, I then will recommend that they be entirely eliminated.

The right of free speech is fundamental. Congress should make clear that the right of free speech, as now defined in the Act, applies equally to labor and management in every aspect of their relationship.

The Act presently prohibits an employer from making payment to a union to assist in the financing of union welfare funds unless the fund meets certain standards. These standards are not adequate to protect and conserve these funds that are held in trust for the welfare of individual union members. It is my recommendation that Congress initiate a thorough study of welfare and pension funds covered by collective bargaining agreements, with a view of enacting such legislation as will protect and conserve these funds for the millions of working men and women who are the beneficiaries.

The Act should make clear that the several states and territories, when confronted with emergencies endangering the health or safety of their citizens, are not, through any conflict with the Federal law, actual or implied, deprived of the right to deal with such emergencies. The need

43

for clarification of jurisdiction between the Federal and the State and Territorial governments in the labor-management field has lately been emphasized by the broad implications of the most recent decision of the Supreme Court dealing with this subject. The Department and agency heads concerned are, at my request, presently examining the various areas in which conflicts of jurisdiction occur. When such examination is completed, I shall make my recommendations to the Congress for corrective legislation.

In the employer-employee relationship there is nothing which so vitally affects the individual employee as the loss of his pay when he is called on strike. In such an important decision he should have an opportunity to express his free choice by secret ballot held under Government auspices.

There are two other changes in the law that I recommend. The authorization which an individual employee gives to his employer for the check-off of the employee's union dues should be made valid until the termination of the collective bargaining contract which provides for such check-off, unless the employee sooner revokes such authorization. The provisions of the Act which require reports from unions concerning their organization and finances should be simplified so as to eliminate duplication in the information required by such reports.

I hope that the foregoing changes will be enacted by Congress promptly, for they will more firmly establish the basic principles of the law. The appropriate Committees of the Congress will, I am certain, wish to keep the law under continuous study and in the light of experience under it propose further amendments to implement its objectives and constantly improve its administration.

Government should continue to search diligently for sound measures to improve the lot of the working man and woman, mindful that conditions and standards of employment change as the products, habits and needs of men and women change. It will be continually a challenge to Government to sense the aspirations of the working people of our country, that all may have the opportunity to fairly share in the results of the productive genius of our time, from which comes the material blessings of the present and a greater promise for the future.

DWIGHT D. EISENHOWER

6 ¶ Special Message to the Senate Transmitting the Mutual Defense Treaty Between the United States and the Republic of Korea.
January 11, 1954

To the United States Senate:

With a view to receiving the advice and consent of the Senate to ratification, I transmit herewith the Mutual Defense Treaty between the United States of America and the Republic of Korea signed at Washington on October 1, 1953.

I transmit also for the information of the Senate a document containing the joint statement by President Syngman Rhee of the Republic of Korea and by the Secretary of State on August 8, 1953, on the occasion of the initialing of the Mutual Defense Treaty in Seoul, and the text of an address by the Secretary of State on the occasion of the signing of the Mutual Defense Treaty on October 1, 1953.

There is further transmitted for the information of the Senate the report made to me by the Secretary of State regarding the aforesaid treaty.

The Mutual Defense Treaty signed by the United States and the Republic of Korea is designed to deter aggression by giving evidence of our common determination to meet the common danger. It thus reaffirms our belief that the security of an individual nation in the free world depends upon the security of its partners, and constitutes another link in the collective security of the free nations of the Pacific.

I recommend that the Senate give early favorable consideration to the treaty submitted herewith, and advise and consent to its ratification.

DWIGHT D. EISENHOWER

NOTE: The treaty and related papers are published in Senate Executive A, 83d Congress. The treaty was approved by the Senate on January 26 and after ratification entered into force November 17, 1954 (5 UST 2368).

7 ¶ Letter to Julius Ochs Adler, Chairman, National Security Training Commission, Concerning the Reserve Establishment. *January* 12, 1954

Dear General Adler:

It meant a great deal to me to have the opportunity to discuss with you plans for arriving at decisions relative to the size and composition of our reserve forces. It will be of immeasurable assistance to the Office of Defense Mobilization, in its preparation of plans for presentation to the National Security Council for developing and maintaining an adequate reserve establishment, to have the benefit of the continued counsel of the National Security Training Commission.

Because of the wealth of information and experience with this problem which your Commission has gained in its long studies and investigations I suggest that you arrange to work closely with the Director of Defense Mobilization, Arthur S. Flemming.

The expression of deep appreciation I feel for the long hours of effort that you and your associates have contributed in the preparation of the excellent report submitted to me has been too long delayed. Your report will be of great value to all who are concerned with meeting this great national military need.

May I as well convey my personal regards to you and to each member of your Commission.

Sincerely,

DWIGHT D. EISENHOWER

NOTE: The report of the National Security Training Commission is entitled "20th Century Minutemen, a Report to the President on a Reserve Forces Training Program" (159 pp., Government Printing Office, 1954).

8 ¶ Citations Accompanying Medals of Honor Presented to William R. Charette, Edward R. Schowalter, Jr., and Ernest E. West.
January 12, 1954

THE PRESIDENT of the United States in the name of The Congress takes pleasure in presenting the Medal of Honor to

WILLIAM R. CHARETTE

HOSPITAL CORPSMAN THIRD CLASS

UNITED STATES NAVY

for service as set forth in the following

CITATION:

For conspicuous gallantry and intrepidity at the risk of his life above and beyond the call of duty as a Medical corpsman, serving with a Marine Rifle Company, in action against enemy aggressor forces in Korea during the early morning hours of 27 March 1953. Participating in a fierce encounter with a cleverly concealed and well-entrenched enemy force occupying positions on a vital and bitterly contested outpost far in advance of the main line of resistance, CHARETTE repeatedly and unhesitatingly moved about through a murderous barrage of hostile small-arms and mortar fire to render assistance to his wounded comrades. When an enemy grenade landed within a few feet of a Marine he was attending, he immediately threw himself upon the stricken man and absorbed the entire concussion of the deadly missile with his own body. Although sustaining painful facial wounds, and undergoing shock from the intensity of the blast which ripped the helmet and medical aid kit from his person, CHARETTE resourcefully improvised emergency bandages by tearing off part of his clothing, and gallantly continued to administer medical aid to the wounded in his own unit and to those in adjacent platoon areas as well. Observing a seriously wounded comrade whose armored vest had been torn from his body by the blast from an exploding shell, he selflessly removed his own battle vest and placed it upon the helpless man although fully aware of the added jeopardy to himself. Moving to the side of another casualty who was suffering excruciating pain from a serious leg wound, CHARETTE stood upright in the trench line and exposed himself to a deadly hail of enemy fire in order to lend more effective aid to the victim and to alleviate his anguish while being removed to a position of safety. By his indomitable courage and inspiring efforts in behalf of his wounded comrades, CHARETTE was directly responsible for saving many lives. His great personal valor reflects the highest credit upon himself and enhances the finest traditions of the United States Naval Service.

DWIGHT D. EISENHOWER

THE PRESIDENT of the United States of America, authorized by Act of Congress March 3, 1863 has awarded in the name of The Congress the Medal of Honor to

FIRST LIEUTENANT EDWARD R. SCHOWALTER, JR.,

UNITED STATES ARMY

for conspicuous gallantry and intrepidity at the risk of his life above and beyond the call of duty in action with the enemy:

First Lieutenant Edward R. Schowalter, Jr., 064 446, Infantry, United States Army, Commanding, Company A, 31st Infantry Regiment, 7th Infantry Division, distinguished himself by conspicuous gallantry and indomitable courage above and beyond the call of duty in action against the enemy near Kumhwa, Korea, on 14 October 1952. Committed to attack and occupy a key approach to the primary objective, the First Platoon of his company came under heavy vicious small arms, grenade and mortar fire within fifty yards of the enemy-held strongpoint, halting the advance and inflicting several casualties. The Second Platoon moved up in support at this juncture, and although wounded, Lieutenant Schowalter continued to spearhead the assault. Nearing the objective he was severely wounded by a grenade fragment but, refusing medical aid, he led his men into the trenches and began routing the enemy from the bunkers with grenades. Suddenly from a burst of fire from a hidden cave off the trench he was again wounded. Although suffering from his wounds, he refused to relinquish command and continued issuing orders and encouraging his men until the commanding ground was secured and then he was evacuated. Lieutenant Schowalter's unflinching courage,

48

extraordinary heroism and inspirational leadership reflect the highest credit upon himself and are in keeping with the highest traditions of the military service.

DWIGHT D. EISENHOWER

THE PRESIDENT of the United States of America, authorized by Act of Congress March 3, 1863 has awarded in the name of The Congress the Medal of Honor to

PRIVATE FIRST CLASS ERNEST E. WEST,
UNITED STATES ARMY

for conspicuous gallantry and intrepidity at the risk of his life above and beyond the call of duty in action with the enemy:

Private First Class Ernest E. West, US 52 151 286, Infantry, United States Army, a member of Company L, 14th Infantry Regiment, 25th Infantry Division, distinguished himself by conspicuous gallantry above and beyond the call of duty in action against the enemy near Sataeri, Korea, on 12 October 1952. He voluntarily accompanied a contingent to locate and destroy a reported enemy outpost. Nearing the objective, the patrol was ambushed and suffered numerous casualties. Observing his wounded leader lying in an exposed position, he ordered the troops to withdraw, then braved intense fire to reach and assist him. While attempting evacuation, he was attacked by three hostile soldiers employing grenades and small arms fire. Quickly shifting his body to shelter the officer, he killed the assailants with his rifle, then carried the helpless man to safety. He was critically wounded and lost an eye in this action, but courageously returned through withering fire and bursting shells to assist the wounded and, while evacuating two comrades, closed with and killed three more of the foe. Private West's indomitable spirit, consummate valor and intrepid actions inspired all who observed him, reflecting highest credit upon himself and upholding the honored traditions of the military service.

DWIGHT D. EISENHOWER

NOTE: The medals were presented by the President at the White House. The text of the citations was read by Comdr. Edward L. Beach, Naval Aide to the President.

9 ¶ The President's News Conference of January 13, 1954.

THE PRESIDENT. Ladies and gentlemen, all this picture-taking session reminds me that this is our first meeting of the year, and so it gives me a chance to say to those that I have not seen before, "Happy New Year." I hope that each of you gets that salary raise that has been so long overdue.

Q. Merriman Smith, United Press: May we quote that, sir?

THE PRESIDENT. If anyone thinks that will have any influence with your publisher, you are at liberty to quote it.

I think, ladies and gentlemen, I have no particular statement of my own. It seems to me I have been making a lot of them lately, and so with your permission we will make this easier by going to questions.

Q. Mr. Smith: Mr. President, after your labor message to Congress, there was some confusion as to precisely what you meant in your recommendation about Government auspices controlling strike votes. Did you mean, sir, that a secret strike ballot should be taken prior to a strike or during a strike?

THE PRESIDENT. Actually, of course, what I was trying to establish was a principle. Nearly all of the suggestions I made for the amendment of the Taft-Hartley were in that tenor, that here is something that should be done. I carefully have avoided the exact details of how these things should be done, because we well know that is a province of the Congress and of its committees in their investigations.

My function, as I see it, is to lay down for their consideration the things that I believe to be principle, and that is exactly what I tried to do there.

So I would accept anything that looks the most practicable and feasible in the circumstances.

Q. John Herling, Editors Syndicate: Mr. President, in view of the sharp disagreement as to the meaning and intention of your recommendation among Republican leadership, not to mention labor leadership as well, would you insist, sir, on having this proposal a part of "must" labor legislation?

THE PRESIDENT. Ladies and gentlemen, within reason, I think we know and can identify those features of bills or of a legislative program that could be classed as "must." They are the things that have to be done. Now, there are certain things which I believe are for the good of the country. I have arrived at those conclusions after long study with all my associates, with people over the country, and I am going to fight for them where I think they are important.

I naturally cannot tell you in advance which I am going to consider the most important and the least important. I don't know how they will come up in Congress and how they will be handled. So I am not going to identify particular details as "must" and "not must" except as they apply to supply bills, legislative bills, security bills in their main outline, such things as that, or where laws expire and something has to be done. Those things must be handled, and they must be handled in a way that will allow the country to go ahead and function properly.

I am not going, though, to try to take each feature of the things I have said and am going to say—I am going to send down lots more messages to Congress—and in each feature of them say that is "must" or that is "not must." I don't think that is my function at least at this moment.

Q. David P. Sentner, Hearst Newspapers: Mr. President, could you say what percentage of your recommended proposals to Congress you would expect to be passed at this session?

THE PRESIDENT. I can't guess. Look: I want to make this very clear. I am not making recommendations to Congress just to pass the time away or to look good or for anything else. Everything I send to Congress I believe to be, and the mass of my associates believe to be, for the good of this country; therefore, I am going to work for their enactment. Make no mistake about that. That is exactly what I am here for and what I intend to do.

But for me to try to say what percentage of these things is absolutely necessary to the existence of this country for another year or until the next session, that is going too far for me.

Q. Nat S. Finney, Buffalo Evening News: Mr. President, I would like to ask a question about your current position on the Bricker amendment, and try to ask it so that it will not be confusing. Will you accept or agree to an amendment which would make it impossible to use the treaty-making power to impose conditions on the individual States which cannot be imposed by regular legislation?

THE PRESIDENT. I must say, you opened up a subject that really requires the space of a lecture to get at exactly what we mean. But I must call this to your attention. When you are talking about the rights of the individual States—and I suppose if you were going to class me as anything else, you would class me as a States' Righter—I would like each of you to ask yourself this question: why was the Constitution formed, and to replace the old Articles of Confederation?

If you will look up the history of the time, you will find that each one of the States under the Articles of Confederation had a right to repudiate a treaty. Because of this fact, the Founding Fathers, who I still think were probably the wisest group of men that were ever brought together in this country, indeed possibly in the world, or such in this governmental field—that is what I am talking about—provided that a treaty properly ratified should take precedence over any State law, including that State's constitution.

That is so that the people, the individual, the representative of the United States—and that means your President and your Secretary of State, or both acting together—meeting a like representative from other nations, can represent one government, and can speak with that much authority. They are not trying the impossible task of representing 48 governments.

Now, there has been a very great deal of concern developing for fear that the treaty-making power may be used to contravene our Constitution. I think some of you, at least, may recall that last July, when Senator Knowland introduced a substitute amendment for the Bricker amendment, I issued a statement. In that statement I said there were certain things to which I would gladly agree, a statement which said that any treaty or any other executive or any kind of international agreement that contravened any article of our Constitution should be null and void, and I would agree to that.

Secondly, I would agree that the votes on these treaties, where they are passed by two-thirds vote in the Senate, should be by yeas and nays to record the purpose of that on the part of its advocates, and to record who was there and how many Senators actually approved.

Also, I stated that the Senate could, whenever it chose, include in its approval that anything in that treaty affecting the internal affairs of the United States could become effective only by an act of Congress.

And, ladies and gentlemen, let me point out one thing else. The power of Congress, by subsequent action, to nullify any article of a treaty has never been questioned. This fear, though, that our Constitution might be damaged has led me to agree to all those amendments. But when you come down to this, that we have to go right back to the general system that prevailed before our Constitution was adopted, then I certainly shall never agree.

Now, as all of you know, it takes a long time to get an amendment passed. This thing, with me, is completely objective. It is completely my concern and my belief of what is good for the future of the United States, not the present. It cannot affect these next 3 years, I am quite sure.

Q. Milton Friedman, Jewish Telegraphic Agency: Mr. President, can you tell us whether you still favor revision of the McCarran-Walter Immigration Act, and whether there was anything significant in your omission of this item from your State of the Union Message?

THE PRESIDENT. No, there was no significance in its omission. As a matter of fact, there were many, many things omitted, and I think I stated that some of these things that were omitted would be the subject of later comment. It happens that this year, up until this time, the details of any studies made on the McCarran Act by the responsible departments have not been submitted to me. And therefore whether we are going to recommend immediate revision, I can't say for certain.

Q. Daniel Schorr, CBS–Radio: Mr. President, is there anything new on the question of channeling defense contracts to chronic unemployment areas?

THE PRESIDENT. Well, there is nothing new on it. There has been, I think, a certain misapprehension about it. You know, the proportion of holdback is normally small in any contract; and then the Secretary of Defense, or the Office of Defense Mobilization, I believe, can channel these contracts to other places only in the event that the lowest bid achieved under normal processes is equaled in that area. It is an attempt to help out in cases of unemployment with useful work rather than with work that wouldn't be so useful to the United States. But I believe that there has been an exaggerated idea that an entire contract would be shoved somewhere just because they had unemployment. There is no such intent.

Q. Mr. Schorr: Will there be any change in that policy as a result of some recent criticism?

THE PRESIDENT. I am not one of those that uses the word "never" very often. I thought when I approved the policy, it was a sound one. I have been proved wrong before in my life, so I am not going to say I can't be proved wrong. But I certainly think that the objective of that policy was good; it was reasonable and certainly was applied only in a limited way. But I am certainly always going to look at it if I see a legitimate case.

Q. John H. Kelso, Boston Post: In line with that same question, a group of New England Congressmen said yesterday that New England is now in a depression, not a recession, and they said that they still had hope, particularly a person from Lawrence, because you told them you would help them during the campaign. Have you any specific plans to help that area?

THE PRESIDENT. You mean, to help Lawrence?

Q. Mr. Kelso: And New England, yes.

THE PRESIDENT. I must say this: I would repeat what I have said often before. There are special problems; there can be no special privileges, as I see it, applying to areas or to class or to anything else. Now, whatever is feasible and possible in the way of credit or work for them or helping small business, which is the big thing that we have talked about there, anything that is feasible within the power of this Government will be done to help all the United States, not merely to help any special section. But if one special section needs these things more than another, then it naturally gets more help, like in the drought problem.

We go into the drought problem not merely because some farmers are suffering and cattle are dying, but because it is good for all the United States to get that thing straightened out and do the best we can with it. And that same approach will be made to any other section of the country.

Q. John L. Cutter, United Press: Mr. President, in discussing the Bricker amendment application, and so forth, you talked about looking to the future, and specified that it cannot affect anything within the next 3 years, I am sure. Does that indicate that you do not intend to remain in office after 3 years?

THE PRESIDENT. There is one thing that I am always advised by my political friends: that is one thing that I never should talk about; if I inadvertently mentioned it here because I was thinking in a specific term, I apologize. Maybe you had better delete the "3 years."

Q. Anthony H. Leviero, New York Times: Mr. President, your proposal to deprive conspirators against the Government of citizenship has aroused considerable interest. Is it your aim to redefine the line between disloyalty and good citizenship? Could you tell us that?

THE PRESIDENT. No, it wasn't that. Here is the point. As of now, there is a law that deprives a man of citizenship if he is convicted of an actual attempt to destroy this Government by force. I believe that if a man is convicted in the courts of deliberately conspiring to do that, he is just as guilty as the attempt. And therefore I am putting him in the same class as the man that attempts.

The Department of Justice has worked up a little list of things, what it means to a man when he loses his citizenship; and I am merely putting a conspirator in the same class as a man who actually attempts it.

Q. Raymond P. Brandt, St. Louis Post-Dispatch: Mr. President, will not that require additional legislation?

THE PRESIDENT. Yes, I think it will.

Q. Mr. Brandt: It will?

THE PRESIDENT. Now, don't let me—I think it will.

Q. Mr. Brandt: Can we get the list from the Department of Justice?

THE PRESIDENT. I think so.

Q. Paul R. Leach, Chicago Daily News: Mr. President, adding conspiracy to the law of 1907, amended in 1940, I believe, is that all that is required?

THE PRESIDENT. I would think so. Now, you are asking me a question you had better ask General Brownell. I think I am correct—we talked this over at length; but after all, you know, that kind of point wouldn't make the exact impression on me that it probably should if I were a lawyer. So I think you had better ask him, but that is my belief.

Q. Sarah McClendon, El Paso Times: Sir, on the Air Academy, the whole question of locating the Air Academy has been reopened, and all applicants have been asked to resubmit bids, after a Commission worked for years with the help of paid Government professional experts to find seven sites. Will you say what you think about reopening this?

THE PRESIDENT. I will say this: this is the first time I have heard of this. But I will say this also: here is a question in which, I think, I have exhibited admirable restraint. [*Laughter*]

You will recall when I came back from Europe in 1945, I believed in one thing: the Air Force ought to be organized separately. I believe, after we proved that West Point and Annapolis could not be sufficiently large enough, I believe the Air Forces ought to have an academy. I believed that. I was on a board to help decide that, after I had made up my own mind long before. I personally think I know exactly where it ought to be; I have kept my mouth shut, and I would never admit to anyone where I think it should be. So I say I will look into this; I had not heard of this reopening.

Q. Richard L. Strout, Christian Science Monitor: Mr. President, could you assist us in getting a press conference with Mr. Brownell? You just suggested that we should have one. Some of us have been trying to get one for some months now. [*Laughter*]

THE PRESIDENT. Well, I will tell you, everybody has his own method of operating. I don't know over in the Department of Justice whether it is proper and to the best interests of everybody to have periodic press conferences.

I would say that when there is a legitimate request made for information, the information would be forthcoming. How he should put it out is something else. That is for his decision, and if I can't trust Cabinet officers for that, I would have a pretty hard time.

Q. Marvin L. Arrowsmith, Associated Press: Mr. President, on the basis of Secretary Dulles' preliminary talks with Ambassador Zaroubin, are there any indications that Russia is acting in good faith interest in your atomic pool proposal?

THE PRESIDENT. I don't believe, Mr. Arrowsmith, that you could make a conclusion that would be that far-reaching. I would say this: it is encouraging that Mr. Dulles and the Ambassador have had talks in a friendly atmosphere, and that there is some attempt being made in that kind of atmosphere to find out exactly what each other means so as to pursue the subject. I don't believe you could say that there is any kind of proof of anything.

Q. Lloyd M. Schwartz, Fairchild Publications: Mr. President, I wonder if you could give us some of the reasoning behind your recommendation in your agriculture message for a direct payment system for the wool growers?

THE PRESIDENT. Well, it is a long and involved story.

We produce quite a small proportion of our wool, and there is a provision in the law now that sets up a target of 360 million pounds a year as what we would like to produce domestically. You see, wool has always in the past, at least, been a very critical material in time of war, and you would like to have a reserve produced here.

Now, when we are making that small proportion though of our own requirements, meaning that small proportion from domestic sources of our own requirements, it seemed bad to put up a tariff which would be another bar, another obstruction, in international trade, and where we would have the whole United States paying this much money in order to reach this 360 million pounds target or anything under it.

So the idea was to take from the general revenues, because there is produced by this tariff some six times as much as would be involved in the payments made to the domestic producers. It seemed a good idea to do it that way in this one article.

Now, it was a long and inner struggle with me to come to this decision, but I did because I thought it was the best under the circumstances.

Q. Robert G. Spivack, New York Post: Mr. President, in the State of the Union Message, I believe the figure of 2200 security risks was used, and I wondered if there is any breakdown available now on that since the 1456 figure?

THE PRESIDENT. No detailed report has yet been made to me, and it is perfectly understandable. The Civil Service Commission has a very hard job, and there have been more than one hundred and eighty some thousand people dropped, whose positions have not been filled; so this 2200 is not a great number.

The only thing that I can tell you about them is—and some of them, by the way, probably resigned without knowing of these derogatory remarks, or at least had not been notified by us of these derogatory remarks on their record. There were 2200 people against whom the Government intended to move because they believed them to be security risks, remarks already on their records showing that there was some doubt. Those 2200 have gone in one form or another.

Q. Hazel Markel, Mutual Broadcasting System: Mr. President, your predecessor has said within the last few days that it, in his opinion, was highly probable or possible, at least, that a woman might be President. I wonder, after a year in your office, which is conceded to be the hardest job in the world, if you think it is possible that a woman might handle those arduous duties?

THE PRESIDENT. You know, it makes a subject that we could have, I

think, a very interesting conversation on; but it is possible that out of my
deep respect for women's intelligence as well as my admiration for their
many other qualities—[*laughter*]—that I might reach the conclusion that
they had too much sense—[*laughter*]—to want the job.

I would know of no reason why a woman's brain and heart couldn't
be used there as well as a man's; but I don't think she would like it.

Q. Chalmers M. Roberts, Washington Post: Mr. President, Secretary
Dulles said in his speech last night that the National Security Council
and yourself had made a decision, a basic decision he called it, that in
the future we would confront any possible aggression by what he called,
and I quote, "a great capacity to retaliate instantly by means and at places
of our own choosing." Could you elucidate on that somewhat for us, sir?

THE PRESIDENT. No, I think no amplification of the statement is either
necessary or wise. Let us put it this way: the more destructive that becomes, a bomb or any other article or missile that you can carry, the more
value you place on the element of surprise in war. In other words, Pearl
Harbor threw a defeat on us because of surprise. But if you could imagine
multiplying the effect of Pearl Harbor, then you will see something of
what the element of surprise has come to be. About your only defense
is the knowledge that there is a strong retaliatory power.

He was merely stating what, to my mind, is a fundamental truth and
really doesn't take much decision; it is just a fundamental truth.

Q. Anthony H. Leviero, New York Times: Have these new weapons
caused any change in our concept of balanced forces?

THE PRESIDENT. You know, it is an odd thing: every time I read about
balanced forces in the papers, there seems to be a connotation that this
means 33 percent for one, 33 percent for the next, and so on, and this
applies both to men and to money. Now, to the professional, balanced
forces means something entirely different. It means forces that are adjusted to the needs of the time or the needs of the battle.

When we went into Normandy, and there are some of you here that
went in with me, you will remember on the first few days we had a terrific
preponderance of naval and air strength because it was difficult to get
ground strength. But as time went on, the ground strength grew as compared to these other two; but at all times we felt we were balanced with
respect to the job we had.

Now, when I say, therefore, "balanced," I think we are achieving every day a better balance. But it is not balance in the sense of one-third, one-third, one-third.

Q. Oscar E. Naumann, New York Journal of Commerce: Mr. President, yesterday the Assistant Secretary of Agriculture said the Department is considering a proposal to sell a large quantity of surplus butter and cottonseed oil to Russia. Are you in favor of selling our farm surpluses to Russia, if she wants to buy them?

THE PRESIDENT. Well, you made a long jump from the statement that I had heard. I called up, just before I came over here, and they said there was no such statement ever made in the Department of Agriculture. So you are posing a question on something that I am sure there is some misunderstanding somewhere about.

This whole question of trading—East and West—in nonstrategic supplies is constantly under study, and it will be continued to be studied. I will give you my conclusions on it when I see the results of everybody's opinions and analysis.

Q. Clark R. Mollenhoff, Des Moines Register and Tribune: Mr. President, could you tell us what you had in mind in the way of control and protection of welfare funds for the unions, and what caused you to put that in the Message?

THE PRESIDENT. Here we have organisms, as I see it, that function under the auspices of the Federal Government.

Now, any kind of funds that achieve a public basis, to my mind they ought to be out on the table, spread for all to see, that is all. As a matter of fact, I was thinking of the welfare of the people who are supposed to be protected by those funds, that is all.

Q. Mr. Mollenhoff: Were you thinking in terms of State or Federal control on that?

THE PRESIDENT. Well, I always prefer State if it can be done that way.

Q. Alice F. Johnson, Seattle Times: Mr. President, a year ago in your State of the Union Message you recommended statehood eventually for Alaska, under certain circumstances. This year you didn't even mention Alaska. Does that mean that you are less favorably disposed toward granting statehood to Alaska?

THE PRESIDENT. It merely means that the circumstances that I would lay down as the complete justification for Alaskan statehood have not yet arrived.

Q. A. Robert Smith, Portland Oregonian: Mr. President, in your State of the Union address, you spoke of the need for the Federal Government continuing to build resource development projects, and you said in the next fiscal year work will be started on 23 projects. Could you be any more specific about location or type of projects, sir?

THE PRESIDENT. No, not at this moment.

We went over this whole map of the United States, but I can't tell you exactly what they are. There are some—there are one or two—in which everybody is very keen on; and I remember one that affects the Northwest. But there are international as well as other kinds of problems that have to be solved before you can go any further with them.

Q. Robert E. Clark, International News Service: Mr. President, do you have any reports of a Communist buildup of men or material in Korea, in violation of the truce terms?

THE PRESIDENT. No.

Now, the first thing that comes to my mind is—some of the details of that truce agreement now, of course, slip my mind; but, of course, in general the evidence is they have reduced their ground forces, taking out some of them. They have done a very great deal of digging and producing strong defensive lines. They have done a very large amount, a surprisingly large amount, in economic rebuilding in North Korea, apparently treating the North Korean area almost like it was an economic adjunct or part of the land across the Yalu. But as far as actual buildup, I would say, aside from building of certain things that might have a military usefulness, there is no evidence of that kind.

Q. Kenneth M. Scheibel, Gannett Newspapers: Mr. President, if the Congress turns down the flexible farm price plan and extends the 90 percent of parity for another year or 2 years beginning in 1955, would you go along with that or would you veto a measure like that?

THE PRESIDENT. I never can veto anything in advance. I have to wait and take a look, because, let me point this out, there is no item veto possible in the Federal Government. Most States have what they call the item veto. The Federal Government, the President, does not have that right. Consequently, sometimes things are so designed that it is impossible to veto a bill merely because there is some provision of it that you believe to be in error.

Q. Lucian C. Warren, Buffalo Courier-Express: Mr. President, did you have a chance before you sent your labor message to consult with the legislative leaders in Congress, particularly the committee chairmen and subcommittee chairmen about your specific recommendations on labor?

THE PRESIDENT. I can't recall what was the latest conference we had with all these people since last January 20th. These people, every time this subject has come up, have recurrently been brought back in; both Mr. McConnell and Senator Smith, and so on, come back in.

We have talked about these things with numerous people on the Hill. But I can't say and I do not recall that the exact recommendations I sent down were finally put in front of them and read to them.

Q. Marvin L. Arrowsmith, Associated Press: Mr. President, some members of your own party in Congress are saying that your farm program is not politically feasible in this election year. Would you comment on that?

THE PRESIDENT. Well, I don't think I am too smart politically, but I don't believe that anyone can study that problem as long as this administration has studied it, I don't believe you can call in people from every section of this country, go out to them and meet them, talk to them, what are their problems, and believe that this particular system we now have is workable, practicable, and will help farmers. I tell you, I am trying to help agriculture in the utter conviction that a prosperous stable agriculture is essential to this Nation.

Now, if it is not politically feasible, why, we will find out. I believe it is right.

Q. Clark R. Mollenhoff, Des Moines Register and Tribune: Mr. President, was the House Agricultural Committee talked to with respect to the specific agricultural program that you proposed?

THE PRESIDENT. During the course of the year?

Q. Mr. Mollenhoff: No, the specific program as forwarded this week.

THE PRESIDENT [*to Mr. Hagerty*]. We had it last week when Mr. Hope was up?

Mr. Hagerty: Yes.

THE PRESIDENT. I don't know the exact details, but at the meetings of leaders, the general provisions of these bills were placed in front of them. That does not mean to commit them to any complete prior and detailed agreement, but they were all certainly shown to them.

Merriman Smith, United Press: Thank you, Mr. President.

NOTE: President Eisenhower's twenty-fourth news conference was held in the Executive Office Building from 10:33 to 11:07 o'clock on Wednesday morning, January 13, 1954. In attendance: 178.

10   ¶ Special Message to the Congress on Old Age and Survivors Insurance and on Federal Grants-in-Aid for Public Assistance Programs. *January* 14, 1954

To the Congress of the United States:

I submit herewith for the consideration of the Congress a number of recommendations relating to the Old Age and Survivors Insurance System and the Federal grant-in-aid programs for public assistance.

The human problems of individual citizens are a proper and important concern of our government.   One such problem that faces every individual is the provision of economic security for his old age and economic security for his family in the event of his death.   To help individuals provide for that security—to reduce both the fear and the incidence of destitution to the minimum—to promote the confidence of every individual in the future—these are proper aims of all levels of government, including the Federal Government.

Private and group savings, insurance, and pension plans, fostered by a healthy, fully functioning economy, are a primary means of protection against the economic hazards of old age and death.   These private savings and plans must be encouraged, and their value preserved, by sound tax and fiscal policies of the Government.

But in addition, a basic, nation-wide protection against these hazards can be provided through a government social insurance system.   Building on this base, each individual has a better chance to achieve for himself the assurance of continued income after his earning days are over and for his family after his death.   In response to the need for protection arising from the complexities of our modern society, the Old Age and Survivors Insurance system was developed.   Under it nearly 70 million persons and their families are now covered, and some 6 million are already its beneficiaries.   Despite shortcomings which can be corrected, this system is basically sound. It should remain, as it has been, the cornerstone of the government's programs to promote the economic security of the individual.

Under Old Age and Survivors Insurance (OASI), the worker during his productive years and his employer both contribute to the system in proportion to the worker's earnings. A self-employed person also contributes a percentage of his earnings. In return, when these breadwinners retire after reaching the age of 65, or if they die, they or their families become entitled to income related in amount to their previous earnings. The system is not intended as a substitute for private savings, pension plans and insurance protection. It is, rather, intended as the foundation upon which these other forms of protection can be soundly built. Thus the individual's own work, his planning, and his thrift will bring him a higher standard of living upon his retirement, or his family a higher standard of living in the event of his death, than would otherwise be the case. Hence the system both encourages thrift and self-reliance, and helps to prevent destitution in our national life.

In offering, as I here do, certain measures for the expansion and improvement of this system, I am determined to preserve its basic principles. The two most important are: (1) it is a contributory system, with both the worker and his employer making payments during the years of active work; (2) the benefits received are related in part to the individual's earnings. To these sound principles our system owes much of its wide national acceptance.

During the past year we have subjected the Federal social security system to an intensive study which has revealed certain limitations and inequities in the law as it now stands. These should be corrected.

1. *OASI Coverage Should Be Broadened.*

My message to the Congress on August 1, 1953, recommended legislation to bring more persons under the protection of the OASI system. The new groups that I recommended be covered—about ten million additional people—include self-employed farmers; many more farm workers and domestic workers; doctors, dentists, lawyers, architects, accountants, and other self-employed professional people; members of State and local retirement systems on a voluntary group basis; clergymen on a voluntary group basis; and several smaller groups. I urge the Congress to approve this extension of coverage.

Further broadening of the coverage is being considered by the Committee on Retirement Policy for Federal Personnel, created by the Congress. This Committee will soon report on a plan for expanding OASI to Federal employees not now protected, without impairing the independence of present Federal retirement plans. After the Committee has made its report, I shall make appropriate recommendations on that subject to the Congress.

Extension of coverage will be a highly important advance in our OASI system, but other improvements are also needed. People over 65 years of age who can work should be encouraged to do so and should be permitted to take occasional or part-time jobs without losing their benefits. The level of benefits should be increased. Certain defects in and injustices under the present law should be eliminated. I submit the following recommendations to further these purposes.

2. *The Present "Retirement Test" Should Be Liberalized and Its Discrimination Against the Wage Earner Should Be Removed.*

By depriving an OASI beneficiary of his benefit payment for any month in which he earns wages of more than $75, present law imposes an undue restraint on enterprise and initiative. Retired persons should be encouraged to continue their contributions to the productive needs of the nation. I am convinced that the great majority of our able-bodied older citizens are happier and better off when they continue in some productive work after reaching retirement age. Moreover, the nation's economy will derive large benefits from the wisdom and experience of older citizens who remain employed in jobs commensurate with their strength.

I recommend, therefore, that the first $1000 of a beneficiary's annual earnings be exempted under the retirement test, and that for amounts earned above $1000 only one month's benefit be deducted for each additional $80 earned.

To illustrate the effect of these changes: a beneficiary could take a $200 a month job for five months without losing any benefits, whereas under present law he would lose five months' benefits. He could work throughout the year at $90 a month and lose only one month's benefit, whereas under present law he would lose all twelve.

Approval of this recommendation will also remove the discriminatory treatment of wage earners under the retirement test. Self-employed persons already have the advantage of an exemption on an annual basis, with the right to average their earnings over the full year. The amendment I have proposed would afford this advantage, without discrimination, to all beneficiaries.

3. *OASI Benefits Should Be Increased.*

Today thousands of OASI beneficiaries receive the minimum benefit of twenty-five dollars a month. The average individual benefit for retired workers approximates fifty dollars a month. The maximum benefit for an individual is $85 a month. For OASI to fulfill its purpose of helping to combat destitution, these benefits are too low.

I recommend, therefore, that benefits now being received by retired workers be increased on the basis of a new formula to be submitted to the appropriate Committees by the Secretary of Health, Education, and Welfare. This formula should also provide increases for workers retiring in the future, raising both the minimum and the maximum benefits. These increases will further the objectives of the program and will strengthen the foundation on which its participants may build their own security.

4. *Additional Benefit Credits Should Be Provided.*

The maintenance of a relationship between the individual's earnings and the benefits he receives is a cornerstone of the OASI system. However, only a part of many workers' annual earnings are taken into account for contribution and benefit purposes. Although in 1938 only the first $3000 of a worker's annual earnings were considered for contribution and benefit purposes, statistical studies reveal that in that year 94% of full-time male workers protected by OASI had all of their earnings covered by the program. By 1950 less than half of such workers—44%— had their full earnings covered by the program, so the Congress increased the earnings base to $3600.

Today, the earnings base of $3600 covers the full earnings of only 40% of our regular male workers. It is clear, therefore, that another revision of this base is needed to maintain a reasonable relationship between a worker's benefits and his earnings.

I recommend, therefore, that the earnings base for the calculation of OASI benefits and payroll taxes be raised to $4200, thus enabling 15,000,000 people to have more of their earnings taken into account by the program.

5. *Benefits Should Be Computed on a Fairer Basis.*

The level of OASI benefits is related to the average of a worker's past earnings. Under present law periods of abnormally low earnings, or no earnings at all, are averaged in with periods of normal earnings, thereby reducing the benefits received by the retired worker. In many instances, a worker may earn little or nothing for several months or several years because of illness or other personal adversity beyond his power of prevention or remedy. Thus the level of benefits is reduced below its true relation to the earning capabilities of the employee. Moreover, if the additional millions of persons recommended for inclusion under OASI are brought into the program in 1955 without modification of present law, their average earnings will be sharply lowered by including as a period of no earnings the period from 1951 to 1955 when they were not in the program. I recommend, therefore, that in the computation of a worker's average monthly wage, the four lowest years of earnings be eliminated.

6. *The Benefit Rights of the Disabled Should Be Protected.*

One of the injustices in the present law is its failure to make secure the benefit rights of the worker who has a substantial work record in covered employment and who becomes totally disabled. If his disability lasts four years or less, my preceding recommendation will alleviate this hardship. But if a worker's earnings and contributions cease for a longer period, his retirement rights, and the survivor rights of his widow and children may be reduced or even lost altogether. Equity dictates that this defect be remedied. I recommend, therefore, that the benefits of a worker who has a substantial work record in covered employment and who becomes totally disabled for an extended period be maintained at the amount he would have received had be become 65 and retired on the date his disability began.

The injustice to the disabled should be corrected not simply by preserving these benefit rights but also by helping them to return to employment wherever possible. Many of them can be restored to lives of usefulness, independence and self-respect if, when they apply for the preservation of their benefit rights, they are promptly referred to the Vocational Rehabilitation agencies of the States. In the interest of these disabled persons, a close liaison between the OASI system and these agencies will be promptly established upon approval of these recommendations by the Congress. Moreover, in my message of January 18 to the Congress, I shall propose an expanded and improved program of Vocational Rehabilitation.

COSTS

I am informed by the Secretary of Health, Education and Welfare that the net additional cost of the recommendations herein presented would be, on a long-term basis, about one-half of one percent of the annual payrolls subject to OASI taxes. The benefit costs will be met for at least the next fifteen to twenty-five years under the step-rate increases in OASI taxes already provided in the law.

PUBLIC ASSISTANCE

An important by-product of the extension of the protection of the OASI system and the increase in its benefit scale is the impact on public assistance programs. Under these programs States and localities provide assistance to the needy aged, dependent children, blind persons and the permanently and totally disabled, with the Federal Government sharing in the cost.

As broadened OASI coverage goes into effect, the proportion of our aged population eligible for benefits will increase from forty-five percent to seventy-five percent in the next five or six years. Although the need for some measure of public assistance will continue, the OASI program will progressively reduce, year by year, the extent of the need for public assistance payments by the substitution of OASI benefits. I recommend that the formula for Federal sharing in the public assistance programs for these purposes reflect this changing relationship without prejudicing in any manner the receipt of public assistance payments by those whose need for these payments will continue.

Under the present public assistance formula some States receive a higher percentage share of Federal funds than others. In the program of old-age assistance, for example, States making low assistance payments receive up to eighty percent Federal funds in defraying the costs of their programs. States making high assistance payments receive about sixty-five percent of Federal funds in that portion of the old-age assistance payments which is within the $55 maximum for Federal participation.

This variation in Federal participation is the result of a Congressional determination that the Federal sharing should be higher for States which, because of low resources, generally make low assistance payments. In order better to achieve this purpose, I recommend that a new formula be enacted. It should take into account the financial capacity of the several States to support their public assistance programs by adopting, as a measure of that capacity, their per capita income. Such a new formula will also facilitate the inclusion, in the old-age assistance program, of a factor reflecting the expansion of OASI.

The present formula for Federal sharing in public assistance programs requires adjustment from another standpoint. Under present law, the Federal Government does not share in any part of a monthly old-age assistance payment exceeding $55. Yet many of these payments must exceed this amount in order to meet the needs of the individual recipient, particularly where the individual requires medical care. I consider it altogether appropriate for the Federal Government to share in such payments and recommend, therefore, that the present $55 maximum be placed on an average rather than on an individual basis. Corresponding changes in the other public assistance programs would be made. This change in the formula would enable States to balance high payments in cases of acute need against low payments where the need is relatively minor. In addition, great administrative simplification would be achieved.

A new public assistance formula should not become effective until the States have had an opportunity to plan for it. Until such time, the 1952 public assistance amendments should be extended.

The recommendations I have here submitted constitute a coordinated approach to several major aspects of the broad problem of achieving economic security for Americans. Many other phases of this national problem exist and will be reflected in legislative proposals from time to time to the Congress. The effort to prevent destitution among our people preserves a greater measure of their freedom and strengthens their initiative. These proposals are constructive and positive steps in that direction, and I urge their early and favorable consideration by the Congress.

DWIGHT D. EISENHOWER

11 ¶ Special Message to the Congress on the Health Needs of the American People. *January* 18, 1954

To the Congress of the United States:

I submit herewith for the consideration of the Congress recommendations to improve the health of the American people.

Among the concerns of our government for the human problems of our citizens, the subject of health ranks high. For only as our citizens enjoy good physical and mental health can they win for themselves the satisfactions of a fully productive, useful life.

THE HEALTH PROBLEM

The progress of our people toward better health has been rapid. Fifty years ago their average life span was 49 years; today it is 68 years. In 1900 there were 676 deaths from infectious diseases for every 100,000 of our people; now there are 66. Between 1916 and 1950, maternal deaths per 100,000 live births dropped from 622 to 83. In 1916, ten percent of the babies born in this country died before their first birthday; today, less than 3 percent die in their first year.

This rapid progress toward better health has been the result of many particular efforts, and of one general effort. The general effort is the partnership and teamwork of private physicians and dentists and of those engaged in public health, with research scientists, sanitary engineers, the nursing profession and the many auxiliary professions related to health protection and care in illness. To all these dedicated people, America owes most of its recent progress toward better health.

Yet, much remains to be done. Approximately 224,000 of our people died of cancer last year. This means that cancer will claim the lives of 25,000,000 of our 160,000,000 people unless the present cancer mortality rate is lowered. Diseases of the heart and blood vessels alone now take over 817,000 lives annually. Over seven million Americans are estimated to suffer from arthritis and rheumatic diseases. Twenty-two thousand lose their sight each year. Diabetes annually adds 100,000 to its roll of sufferers. Two million of our fellow citizens now handicapped by physical disabilities could be, but are not, rehabilitated to lead full and productive lives. Ten million among our people will at some time in their lives be hospitalized with mental illness.

There exist in our Nation the knowledge and skill to reduce these figures, to give us all still greater health protection and still longer life. But this knowledge and skill are not always available to all our people where and when they are needed. Two of the key problems in the field of health today are the *distribution* of medical facilities and the *costs* of medical care.

Not all Americans can enjoy the best in medical care—because not always are the requisite facilities and professional personnel so distributed as to be available to them, particularly in our poorer communities and rural sections. There are, for example, 159 practicing physicians for every 100,000 of the civilian population in the Northeast United States. This is to be contrasted with 126 physicians in the West, 116 in the North central area, and 92 in the South. There are, for another example, only 4 or 5 hospital beds for each 1,000 people in some States, as compared with 10 or 11 in others.

Even where the best in medical care is available, its costs are often a serious burden. Major, long-term illness can become a financial catastrophe for a normal American family. Ten percent of American families are spending today more than $500 a year for medical care. Of our people reporting incomes under $3000, about 6 percent spend almost a fifth of their gross income for medical and dental care. The total private medical bill of the nation now exceeds nine billion dollars a year—an average of nearly $200 a family—and it is rising. This illustrates the seriousness of the problem of medical costs.

We must, therefore, take further action on the problems of distribution of medical facilities and the costs of medical care, but we must be careful and farsighted in the action that we take. Freedom, consent, and individual responsibility are fundamental to our system. In the field of medical care, this means that the traditional relationship of the physician and his patient, and the right of the individual to elect freely the manner of his care in illness, must be preserved.

In adhering to this principle, and rejecting the socialization of medicine, we can still confidently commit ourselves to certain national health goals.

One such goal is that the means for achieving good health should be accessible to all. A person's location, occupation, age, race, creed, or financial status should not bar him from enjoying this access.

Second, the results of our vast scientific research, which is constantly advancing our knowledge of better health protection and better care in illness, should be broadly applied for the benefit of every citizen. There must be the fullest cooperation among the individual citizen, his personal physician, the research scientists, the schools of professional education, and our private and public institutions and services—local, State, and Federal.

The specific recommendations which follow are designed to bring us closer to these goals.

CONTINUATION OF PRESENT FEDERAL PROGRAMS

In my Budget Message appropriations will be requested to carry on during the coming fiscal year the health and related programs of the newly-established Department of Health, Education, and Welfare.

These programs should be continued because of their past success and their present and future usefulness. The Public Health Service, for example, has had a conspicuous share in the prevention of disease through its efforts to control health hazards on the farm, in industry and in the home. Thirty years ago, the Public Health Service first recommended a standard milk sanitation ordinance; by last year this ordinance had been voluntarily adopted by 1558 municipalities with a total population of 70 million people. Almost twenty years ago the Public Health Service first recommended restaurant sanitation ordinances; today 685 municipalities and 347 counties, with a total population of 90 million people, have such ordinances. The purification of drinking water and the pasteurization of milk have prevented countless epidemics and saved thousands of lives. These and similar field projects of the Public Health Service, such as technical assistance to the States, and industrial hygiene work, have great public value and should be maintained.

In addition, the Public Health Service should be strengthened in its research activities. Through its National Institutes of Health, it maintains a steady attack against cancer, mental illness, heart diseases, dental problems, arthritis and metabolic diseases, blindness, and problems in microbiology and neurology. The new sanitary engineering laboratory at Cincinnati, to be dedicated in April, will make possible a vigorous attack on health problems associated with the rapid technological advances in industry and agriculture. In such direct research programs and in Public

Health Service research grants to State and local governments and to private research institutions lies the hope of solving many of today's perplexing health problems.

The activities of the Children's Bureau and its assistance to the States for maternal and child health services are also of vital importance. The programs for children with such crippling diseases as epilepsy, cerebral palsy, congenital heart disease, and rheumatic fever should receive continued support.

MEETING THE COST OF MEDICAL CARE

The best way for most of our people to provide themselves the resources to obtain good medical care is to participate in voluntary health insurance plans. During the past decade, private and non-profit health insurance organizations have made striking progress in offering such plans. The most widely purchased type of health insurance, which is hospitalization insurance, already meets approximately 40 percent of all private expenditures for hospital care. This progress indicates that these voluntary organizations can reach many more people and provide better and broader benefits. They should be encouraged and helped to do so.

Better health insurance protection for more people can be provided.

The Government need not and should not go into the insurance business to furnish the protection which private and non-profit organizations do not now provide. But the Government can and should work with them to study and devise better insurance protection to meet the public need.

I recommend the establishment of a limited Federal reinsurance service to encourage private and non-profit health insurance organizations to offer broader health protection to more families. This service would reinsure the special additional risks involved in such broader protection. It can be launched with a capital fund of twenty-five million dollars provided by the Government, to be retired from reinsurance fees.

NEW GRANT-IN-AID APPROACH

My message on the State of the Union and my special message of January fourteenth pointed out that Federal grants-in-aid have hitherto observed no uniform pattern. Response has been made first to one and then to another broad national need. In each of the grant-in-aid programs, including those dealing with health, child welfare and rehabilitation of the disabled, a wide variety of complicated matching formulas have been used. Categorical grants have restricted funds to specified purposes so that States often have too much money for some programs and not enough for others.

This patchwork of complex formulas and categorical grants should be simplified and improved. I propose a simplified formula for all of these basic grant-in-aid programs which applies a new concept of Federal participation in State programs. This formula permits the States to use greater initiative and take more responsibility in the administration of the programs. It makes Federal assistance more responsive to the needs of the States and their citizens. Under it, Federal support of these grant-in-aid programs is based on three general criteria:

First, the States are aided in inverse proportion to their financial capacity. By relating Federal financial support to the degree of need, we are applying the proven and sound formula adopted by the Congress in the Hospital Survey and Construction Act.

Second, the States are also helped, in proportion to their population, to extend and improve the health and welfare services provided by the grant-in-aid programs.

Third, a portion of the Federal assistance is set aside for the support of unique projects of regional or national significance which give promise of new and better ways of serving the human needs of our citizens.

Two of these grant-in-aid programs warrant the following further recommendations.

REHABILITATION OF THE DISABLED

Working with only a small portion of the disabled among our people, Federal and State governments and voluntary organizations and institutions have proved the advantage to our nation of restoring handicapped persons to full and productive lives.

When our State-Federal program of vocational rehabilitation began in 1920, the services rendered were limited largely to vocational counseling, training and job placement. Since then advancing techniques in the medical and social aspects of rehabilitation have been incorporated into that program.

There are now 2,000,000 disabled persons who could be rehabilitated and thus returned to productive work. Under the present rehabilitation program only 60,000 of these disabled individuals are returned each year to full and productive lives. Meanwhile, 250,000 of our people are annually disabled. Therefore, we are losing ground at a distressing rate. The number of disabled who enter productive employment each year can be increased if the facilities, personnel and financial support for their rehabilitation are made adequate to the need.

Considerations of both humanity and national self-interest demand that steps be taken now to improve this situation. Today, for example, we are spending three times as much in public assistance to care for non-productive disabled people as it would cost to make them self-sufficient and taxpaying members of their communities. Rehabilitated persons as a group pay back in Federal income taxes many times the cost of their rehabilitation.

There are no statistics to portray the full depth and meaning in human terms of the rehabilitation program, but clearly it is a program that builds a stronger America.

We should provide for a progressive expansion of our rehabilitation resources, and we should act now so that a sound foundation may be established in 1955. My forthcoming Budget Message will reflect this objective. Our goal in 1955 is to restore 70,000 disabled persons to productive lives. This is an increase of 10,000 over the number rehabilitated in 1953. Our goal for 1956 should be 100,000 rehabilitated persons, or 40,000 persons more than those restored in 1953. In 1956, also, the States should begin to contribute from their own funds to the cost of rehabilitating these additional persons. By 1959, with gradually increasing State participation to the point of equal sharing with the Federal government, we should reach the goal of 200,000 rehabilitated persons each year.

In order to achieve this goal we must extend greater assistance to the States. We should do so, however, in a way which will equitably and gradually transfer increasing responsibility to the States. A program of grants should be undertaken to provide, under State auspices, specialized training for the professional personnel necessary to carry out the expanded program and to foster that research which will advance our knowledge of the ways of overcoming handicapping conditions. We should also provide, under State auspices, clinical facilities for rehabilitative services in hospitals and other appropriate treatment centers. In addition, we should encourage State and local initiative in the development of community rehabilitation centers and special workshops for the disabled.

With such a program the Nation could during the next five years return a total of 660,000 of our disabled people to places of full responsibility as actively working citizens.

CONSTRUCTION OF MEDICAL CARE FACILITIES

The modern hospital—in caring for the sick, in research, and in professional educational programs—is indispensable to good medical care. New hospital construction continues to lag behind the need. The total number of acceptable beds in this nation in all categories of non-Federal hospital services is now about 1,060,000. Based on studies conducted by State hospital authorities, the need for additional hospital beds of all types—chronic disease, mental, tuberculosis, as well as general—is conservatively estimated at more than 500,000.

A program of matching State and local tax funds and private funds in the construction of both public and voluntary non-profit hospitals where these are most needed is therefore essential.

Since 1946, nearly $600 million in Federal funds have been allocated to almost 2,200 hospital projects in the States and Territories. This sum has been matched by over one and a quarter billion dollars of State and local funds. Projects already completed or under construction on December 31, 1953, will add to our national resources 106,000 hospital beds and 464 public health centers. The largest proportion of Federal funds has been and is being spent in low-income and rural areas where the need for hospital beds is greatest and where the local means for providing them are smallest. This Federally stimulated accomplishment has by no means retarded the building of hospitals without Federal aid. Construction costing in excess of one billion dollars has been completed in the last six years without such aid.

Hospital construction, however, meets only part of the urgent need for medical facilities.

Not all illness need be treated in elaborate general hospital facilities, costly to construct and costly to operate. Certain non-acute illness conditions, including those of our hospitalized aged people, requiring institutional bed care can be handled in facilities more economical to build and operate than a general hospital, with its diagnostic, surgical and treatment equipment and its full staff of professional personnel. Today beds in our hospitals for the chronically ill take care of only one out of every six persons suffering from such long-term illnesses as cancer, arthritis, and heart disease. The inadequacy of facilities and services to cope with such illnesses is disturbing. Moreover, if there were more nursing and convalescent home facilities, beds in general hospitals would be released for the care of the acutely ill. This would also help to relieve some of the serious problems created by the present short supply of trained nurses.

Physical rehabilitation services for our disabled people can best be given in hospitals or other facilities especially equipped for the purpose. Many thousands of people remain disabled today because of the lack of such facilities and services.

Many illnesses, to be sure, can be cared for outside of any institution. For such illnesses a far less costly approach to good medical care than hospitalization would be to provide diagnostic and treatment facilities for the ambulatory patient. The provision of such facilities, particularly in rural areas and small isolated communities, will attract physicians to the sparsely settled sections where they are urgently needed.

I recommend, therefore, that the Hospital Survey and Construction Act be amended as necessary to authorize the several types of urgently needed medical care facilities which I have described. They will be less costly to build than general hospitals and will lessen the burden on them.

I present four proposals to expand or extend the present program:

(1) Added assistance in the construction of non-profit hospitals for the care of the chronically ill. These would be of a type more economical to build and operate than general hospitals.

(2) Assistance in the construction of non-profit medically supervised nursing and convalescent homes.

(3) Assistance in the construction of non-profit rehabilitation facilities for the disabled.

(4) Assistance in the construction of non-profit diagnostic or treatment centers for ambulatory patients.

Finally, I recommend that in order to provide a sound basis for Federal assistance in such an expanded program, special funds be made available to the States to help pay for surveys of their needs. This is the procedure that the Congress wisely required in connection with Federal assistance in the construction of hospitals under the original Act. We should also continue to observe the principle of State and local determination of their needs without Federal interference.

These recommendations are needed forward steps in the development of a sound program for improving the health of our people. No nation and no administration can ever afford to be complacent about the health of its citizens. While continuing to reject government regimentation of medicine, we shall with vigor and imagination continuously search out by appropriate means, recommend, and put into effect new methods of achieving better health for all of our people. We shall not relax in the struggle against disease. The health of our people is the very essence of our vitality, our strength and our progress as a nation.

I urge that the Congress give early and favorable consideration to the recommendations I have herein submitted.

DWIGHT D. EISENHOWER

12 ¶ Letter to President Hoover Regarding the Commission on Organization of the Executive Branch. *January* 18, 1954

[Released January 18, 1954. Dated January 16, 1954]

Dear Mr. President:

I appreciate very much your thoughtfulness in writing me relative to the progress that has been made by the Commission on Organization of the Executive Branch of the Government.

The nation is faced with basic issues that must be resolved in every one of the areas that you have selected for study. You have enlisted the services of some of our most outstanding leaders for membership on the task forces that you have established to carry forward these studies. Please convey to them my personal appreciation of their willingness to serve in this manner.

As you know I have a very real interest in the outcome of the work of the Commission. We are determined to do everything we can to put into effect sound principles of management in the conduct of the affairs of government. I look forward to having the benefit of your recommendations.

The time, thought, and energy that you are putting into this program as Chairman of the Commission is a source of real inspiration to all of us. The country is to be congratulated that you have once again been willing to undertake leadership in this work.

Sincerely,

Dwight D. Eisenhower

NOTE: President Hoover's letter follows:

My dear Mr. President:

We have made progress in the major setup of the Commission on Organization of the Executive Branch of the Government. The Commission was created by Public Law No. 108 of July 10, 1953. The membership of the Commission was completed in the latter part of August and the Commission held its first meeting on September 29, 1953.

The Presidential appointees to the Commission are: The Honorable Herbert Hoover, Attorney General Herbert Brownell, Jr., The Honorable James A. Farley, Director of Defense Mobilization Arthur S. Flemming.

The Vice President's appointees are: Senator Homer Ferguson, Senator John L. McClellan, Dean Solomon C. Hollister of the School of Engineering at Cornell University, Dean Robert G. Storey of the School of Law at Southern Methodist University.

The Speaker's appointees are: Congressman Clarence J. Brown, Congressman Chet Holifield, The Honorable Joseph P. Kennedy, Mr Sidney A. Mitchell.

The Honorable John B. Hollister is the Executive Director. Five of these members served on the Reorganization Commission of 1947–50.

As of the present we have created the following nine major Task Forces to undertake investigations and to make recommendations. They are:

The Business Organization of the Department of Defense, Chairman Charles R. Hook and more than 10 members. The various Task Forces already on work on fractions of these problems will be represented on this Committee and another such Task Force will be created on Procurement;

Water Resources Development and Power, Chairman Admiral Ben Moreell and 25 members;

Medical Services, Chairman Chauncey McCormick and 15 members;

Personnel and Civil Service, Chairman President Harold W. Dodds and 9 members;

Legal Services and Procedure of the Executive Branch of the Government, Chairman Judge James M. Douglas and 15 members;

Use and Disposal of Surplus Property, Chairman General Robert E. Wood and 7 members;

Subsistence Management, Chairman Joseph P. Binns and 8 members;

Budgeting and Accounting, Chairman J. Harold Stewart and 6 members;

Lending Agencies, Chairman Paul Grady and 10 members.

In addition we are conducting staff investigations of certain other agencies as directed by the law. In all our work we have sought to avoid duplication with the work in progress for efficiency and economy by other Commissions, Committees of Congress and the Departments.

The members of the Task Forces are chosen solely because of their experience in different fields. I have considered it in the public interest not to include representatives of any particular group interest. The representatives of such groups will be given full hearings.

The problems to be solved require a determination of fact and the deduction of recommendations therefrom. For the purpose of amassing the facts, each Task Force has been given adequate research staff. The recommendations of the Task Forces and of our staff will be reviewed by the Commission.

Due to the large proportion of voluntary service, the cash expenditures and outstanding obligations from September

29 to December 31, 1953 are $152,035. Our paid staff comprises three persons, an Assistant to each Commissioner, together with research employees of the Task Forces. Such clerical help as we require is mostly secured on a reimbursable basis from the Executive Departments so as not to create a permanent staff.

Thus far, over 115 leading professional and administrative citizens have been enlisted upon our Task Forces. I will forward to you a list of them and of the other men and women associated in the work.

Yours faithfully,

HERBERT HOOVER

13   ¶ Statement by the President on the Approval by the Netherlands Parliament of the European Defense Community Treaty.   *January* 20, 1954

I HAVE just learned that the Netherlands, through action today by the First Chamber, has completed legislative action on the treaty to create the European Defense Community.

The Netherlands thus becomes the first country to complete the necessary legislative processes. I am gratified at the steady progress toward the achievement of conditions in Europe which will insure permanent peace and prosperity.

14   ¶ Annual Budget Message to the Congress: Fiscal Year 1955.   *January* 21, 1954

To the Congress of the United States:

I am transmitting herewith the Budget of the United States for the fiscal year ending June 30, 1955.

The budget message is divided into two parts. The first part is a general statement summarizing the budget and a number of its most important aspects. The second part includes pertinent details of my tax and legislative programs, and of the budget. Together the two parts comprise my budget message.

When this administration took office on January 20 of last year one of its first concerns was the budget for the 1954 fiscal year, which had been sent to the Congress on January 9, 1953, by the previous administration.   With the cooperation of the Congress that budget promptly was revised and reduced.   This new budget is the first prepared entirely by this administration.

It provides adequately, in my judgment, for the national defense and the international responsibilities of the Nation—responsibilities which we must undertake as a leader of the free world.   On the success of this leadership depends our national security and prosperity.   The budget also provides adequately for the current needs of the Government and for constructive forward steps in our domestic responsibilities and programs.

The recommended budget continues the strengthening of our military posture; our progress in the development and production of atomic weapons; the expansion of our system of continental defense; assistance in the development of the military strength of friendly nations; and programs for rapid mobilization if an emergency should arise.

Authority is recommended for new and advanced work on the peace-time uses of atomic energy in the earnest hope that present international relations can be improved and the wonders of nuclear power can be turned gradually to the development of a more abundant life for ourselves and all mankind.

The budget contains provisions for legislative recommendations for expanding the coverage and increasing the benefits of our social security system; for promoting better housing conditions and more widespread home ownership in the Nation; for improving our system of education; for conserving our natural resources; for helping prevent the ravages of floods and soil erosion; for encouraging the expansion of adequate health and hospital care for our people; and for other constructive domestic purposes designed to strengthen the foundations of a stable and prosperous economy.

This budget continues the progress that has been made during the past year in reducing both requests for new appropriations and Government expenditures.   The reductions in expenditures already accomplished, together with those now proposed, justify the tax reductions which took effect January 1 and the further tax revisions I am recommending. These lower taxes will encourage continued high capital investment and consumer purchases.   Despite the substantial loss of revenue caused by these tax reductions, we have moved closer to a balanced budget.

One of the first problems of this administration was to bring the budget under better control. That was substantially accomplished in the revision of the original budget document for the fiscal year 1954. Now an amount approximately equal to the savings made in this new budget is being returned to the public in tax reductions and tax revisions. This amount substantially exceeds the estimated budget deficit.

In preparing this budget the administration has directed its attention to essential activities and programs rather than to those which some might consider desirable and appropriate, at this time, for the Federal Government to undertake. It assumes fairly stable conditions, internally and externally, during the period it covers. It allows for the continuing heavy demands of the national security programs on the budget. But as we continue to reduce and eliminate the less desirable or the unnecessary Government expenditures, it will become possible to turn to other purposes which are the most desirable in terms of their benefits to all of the people.

This budget marks the beginning of a movement to shift to State and local governments and to private enterprise Federal activities which can be more appropriately and more efficiently carried on in that way. The lending activities of the Reconstruction Finance Corporation; the services provided by the Inland Waterways Corporation; certain agricultural activities; and some aspects of our health, education, and welfare programs are examples of this type of action. In those cases where Federal participation is necessary, the effort of this administration is to develop partnerships rather than an exclusive and often paternalistic position for the Federal Government.

This budget also benefits from material savings from the decreased costs of Federal operations resulting from our constant effort to improve the management of Government activities and to find better and less expensive ways of doing the things which must be done by the Federal Government.

The total effect of the recommendations for the 1955 budget, under existing and proposed legislation, is shown with comparable figures for earlier years in the following table. The table also reflects certain technical adjustments for 1955 and prior years which do not affect the budget surplus or deficit and are described in part II of this message. Both receipts and expenditures include, insofar as can be determined, the estimated budgetary results of my recommendations for new legislation.

BUDGET TOTALS

[Fiscal years. In billions]

	1950 actual	1951 actual	1952 actual	1953 actual	1954 estimated [1]		1955 esti- mated
					Budget docu- ment	Cur- rent	
New authority to incur obliga- tions.....................	$49.3	$82.9	$91.4	$80.2	$71.8	$60.7	$56.3
Receipts:							
Under existing legislation...	36.5	47.5	61.4	64.6	68.0	67.4	61.5
Under proposed legislation..	.....	.....	.....	.....	.....	.2	1.2
Total receipts...........	36.5	47.5	61.4	64.6	68.0	67.6	62.7
Expenditures:							
Under existing legislation...	39.6	44.0	65.4	74.0	75.6	70.9	64.5
Under proposed legislation..	.....	.....	.....	.....	2.3	([2])	1.1
Total expenditures.......	39.6	44.0	65.4	74.0	77.9	70.9	65.6
Surplus (+) or deficit (−)...	−3.1	+3.5	−4.0	−9.4	−9.9	−3.3	−2.9
Cumulative unspent balances of appropriations at end of year....................	[3]14.1	[3]50.3	68.8	78.7	67.4	66.5	54.1

[1] References to 1954 are to the 1954 budget document of January 9, 1953, as presented to the Congress, and to currently revised budget estimates.

[2] Less than 50 million dollars.

[3] Estimated. Detailed accounting data are not available.

General budget policy.—This administration is dedicated to greater efficiency and economy in meeting the Nation's security requirements and the necessary and valid functions of the Government.

The current estimates of the 1954 budget show that the requests for new appropriations were reduced about 12.5 billion dollars, new obligational authority was reduced more than 11 billion dollars, and expenditures were reduced 7 billion dollars below the totals estimated in the 1954 budget document of the previous administration.

Similar reductions continue in the budget recommended for the fiscal year 1955. Recommended new obligational authority is 4.4 billion dollars less than the current estimate for the fiscal year 1954, 15.5 billion dollars less than recommended for that year in the 1954 budget document, and 23.9 billion dollars less than in 1953. Estimated expenditures for the fiscal year 1955 are 5.3 billion dollars less than the current estimate for the fiscal year 1954, 12.3 billion dollars less than recommended in the 1954 budget document, and 8.4 billion dollars less than in 1953.

Thus, new obligational authority has been reduced 15.5 billion dollars and estimated expenditures have been reduced 12.3 billion dollars since this administration took office.

These reductions justified lower taxes. Without tax reductions, a budget surplus was in sight for the fiscal year 1955.

So that most of the new savings could be passed along to the taxpayers of the Nation as a whole, with beneficial effects on our entire economy, I believed it best to adopt a course leading toward the twin goals of a balanced budget and tax reductions.

The reductions in 1954 expenditures were devoted to reducing the large deficit forecast in the 1954 budget document. The anticipated savings in 1955 budget expenditures already have been reflected in the tax reductions of January 1 of this year and are also reflected in the tax revisions I am recommending in this message.

Together these tax reductions will total nearly 5 billion dollars.

We will still have a budgetary deficit of slightly less than 3 billion dollars for the fiscal year 1955, as now estimated. But we will continue determined efforts for economy to reduce that deficit during the 1955 fiscal year.

Furthermore, despite the loss of cash revenue from the tax reductions and revisions, the total cash transactions of the Government with the public are now estimated to show a small cash surplus for the fiscal year 1955.

Budget totals, fiscal year 1954.—The actual budget deficit for the fiscal year 1953 was 9.4 billion dollars. The budget deficit for the fiscal year 1954, indicated in the 1954 budget document, was 9.9 billion dollars. The current estimates of the budget for that year show a budgetary deficit of 3.3 billion dollars.

Total Government cash transactions with the public include the receipts and payments of the social security and other trust funds which are not considered part of the budget. In 1953 the excess of cash payments to the public over receipts from the public was 5.3 billion dollars. The 1954 budget document estimated an excess of cash payments of 6.6 billion dollars. Present estimates indicate an excess of cash payments over receipts in 1954 of more than 200 million dollars, a reduction of 6.4 billion dollars in the cash deficit originally estimated.

Budget totals, fiscal year 1955.—The budget for the fiscal year 1955 is estimated to show a deficit of 2.9 billion dollars.

Fiscal year:	Deficits (in billions)
1952	$4.0
1953	9.4
1954:	
As estimated, January 9, 1953	9.9
Revised estimate	3.3
1955 estimate	2.9

The presently estimated deficit for the 1955 fiscal year is in sharp contrast to a deficit forecast made by the Bureau of the Budget prior to transmission to the Congress of the 1954 budget document. This projection of the programs in existence and contemplated in the 1954 budget document, under the tax laws as they then existed, indicated a deficit for the 1955 fiscal year about five times greater than the deficit now estimated.

Budget receipts and expenditures for the fiscal year 1955 are estimated as follows:

	Receipts	Expenditures (in billions)
Under existing legislation	$61.5	$64.5
Under proposed legislation	1.2	1.1
Total	62.7	65.6

Budget receipts allow for an estimated loss of revenue, totaling nearly 5 billion dollars, from the tax reduction which took effect January 1 and from the cost of recommended tax revisions, insofar as these will apply to the 1955 fiscal year. On a full-year basis the revenue loss will approach 6 billion dollars.

The total cash transactions of the Government with the public show an estimated excess of receipts from the public over payments to the public of more than 100 million dollars in the fiscal year 1955.

This record of progress toward a balanced budget is the result of a determined and continuous effort to bring the financial affairs of the Government under control.

New obligational authority.—My recommendations for new appropriations and other new obligational authority for the fiscal year 1955 amount to 56.3 billion dollars, a further reduction from the amounts enacted during the last several years.

Fiscal year:	New obligational authority (in billions)
1952	$91.4
1953	80.2
1954:	
As estimated, January 9, 1953	71.8
Revised estimate	60.7
1955, as recommended	56.3

New obligational authority includes new appropriations, additions to borrowing authority, and certain adjustments to the authority of agencies to incur obligations. The above figures are on a comparable basis, reflecting certain adjustments in composition and definition made in this budget, partly to conform to congressional practices. Details are shown in the second part of this message.

The accumulated unexpended balances of prior appropriations as of June 30, 1953, of 78.7 billion dollars, will be reduced to 66.5 billion dollars by June 30, 1954, and to 54.1 billion dollars by June 30, 1955, as now projected.

The lower levels of new obligational authority and of accumulated unexpended balances for 1954 and 1955 lead to less expenditures in these and in future years. In the revision of the 1954 budget and in the 1955 budget the trend clearly is toward a balanced budget.

Budget expenditures.—Total budget expenditures in the fiscal year 1955 are estimated at 65.6 billion dollars.

Fiscal year:	Expenditures (in billions)
1952	$65.4
1953	74.0
1954:	
As estimated, January 9, 1953	77.9
Revised estimate	70.9
1955 estimate	65.6

Proposed expenditure programs for 1955 fall in three broad categories: national security, major programs relatively uncontrollable under existing and proposed legislation, and all other Government programs.

Expenditures for major national security programs—for the military functions of the Department of Defense, the mutual military program, atomic energy, and stockpiling of strategic materials—dominate the budget and are estimated at 44.9 billion dollars in the fiscal year 1955. This compares with a presently estimated 48.7 billion dollars in 1954 and 50.3 billion dollars in 1953. These amounts are about the same percentage of total budget expenditures in each of the 3 years.

Closely related to these major security programs are other activities for national security included elsewhere in the budget. Our foreign economic assistance and information programs are particularly essential to deter aggression and strengthen the world forces for peace.

Proposed reductions in major national security expenditures in 1955 represent the largest single element of reduction from the current year's level of expenditures. I emphasize, however, that these savings result from revisions in programs, from shifts in emphasis, from better balanced procurement, and from improved management and operations. Our security is being strengthened—not weakened. Further, while expenditures for some programs in this category will be reduced, others will be increased.

Of the four major national security programs, proposed 1955 expenditures for the Atomic Energy Commission and for the mutual military program will be at the highest levels since the initiation of the two programs.

Within the Department of Defense the fiscal year 1955 expenditures on behalf of our airpower will be the largest since World War II. Allocations of expenditures for our continental defense program will be greater than in any previous year.

Expenditures for stockpiling—the fourth of the principal programs in the major national security category—will be less than in the fiscal year 1954, as a result of approaching fulfillment of stockpile requirements in certain categories and of lower world market prices for materials still required for the stockpile.

Budget expenditures for certain Government activities are, by law, relatively nondiscretionary, and depend largely on factors outside the annual budgetary process. While relatively few in number these represent a large amount of dollars and the budget each year has to provide funds for them. For example, once the laws are placed on the statute books, grants to States for many purposes depend upon the extent to which States take advantage of Federal grant-in-aid programs; veterans' pensions depend upon the number of qualified veteran applicants; farm price supports depend upon the size of crops and the demand for supported commodities; and interest payments on the national debt depend upon the amount of the debt and the rate of interest.

In the fiscal year 1955 it is estimated that budget expenditures of 14.1 billion dollars will be required to support these programs. This amount is about the same as presently estimated for 1954 and almost 800 million dollars less than similar expenditures in the fiscal year 1953.

Budget expenditures for other Government activities, which contain more elements controllable through the budget process, are reduced an estimated 2.2 billion dollars below the fiscal year 1953 and 1.5 billion dollars below the present estimate for 1954. This is a reduction, over the two fiscal years, of about 25 percent in the cost of these numerous day-to-day operations of the Government. These activities cover, in number, a large majority of the items in the budget, although the amount involved is about one-tenth of total budget expenditures.

Some substantial reductions in this category will result from a lessened postal deficit and management and program savings in many other departments. On the other hand, estimated expenditures for the Tennessee Valley Authority, urban development and redevelopment, college housing loans, the National Science Foundation, fish and wildlife resources, the school lunch program, and several other programs of domestic importance will be the largest in our history.

Budget receipts and taxes.—Budget receipts under existing and proposed legislation are estimated to be 62.7 billion dollars in the fiscal year 1955. This is 4.9 billion dollars less than presently estimated 1954 receipts; 1.9 billion dollars less than 1953, and 1.3 billion dollars more than 1952.

Total Government expenditures and taxes are now so high that we must choose our path carefully between inadequate revenues on the one hand and repressive taxation on the other. I am anxious to have taxes reduced as fast as that can be done without building up inflationary deficits. It is the determined purpose of this administration to make further reductions in taxes as rapidly as justified by prospective revenues and reductions in expenditures. The objective will be to return to the people, to spend for themselves and in their own way, the largest possible share of the money that the Government has been spending for them.

The start toward tax reductions is justified only because of success in reducing expenditures and improving the budgetary outlook. That outlook permits me to make some proposals for tax reform and reductions for millions of taxpayers at this time which represent much-needed improvements in our tax system. These proposals are directed toward removing the most serious tax hardships and tax complications, and reducing the tax barriers to continued economic growth. The proposals will encourage the initiative and investment which stimulate production and productivity and create bigger payrolls and more and better jobs. The details of these proposals are many and represent much cooperative work by the House Ways and Means Committee and its staff and the Treasury Department. In part II of my budget message, I list and describe 25 important tax revisions.

I do not believe that the budgetary situation will permit further reductions of taxes at this time. Hence, I repeat my recommendations of last May that the reductions in the general corporate income tax be deferred for 1 year; that the excise tax rates, scheduled to be reduced on April 1, including those on liquor, tobacco, automobiles, and gasoline, be continued at present rates; and that any adjustments in the other excise taxes be such as to maintain the total yield which we are now receiving from this source.

Debt management.—A sound dollar is the cornerstone of financing policy under this administration. The problem of debt management is not only one of offering securities for cash or refunding which the market will take, but of appraising the economic situation and adapting financing plans to it, so that as far as possible debt management does not contribute to either inflation or deflation.

This means close cooperation with the Federal Reserve System, whose duty it is under the law to administer the money supply, with these same objectives in view.

Nearly three-quarters of the debt we inherited a year ago matures within less than 5 years or is redeemable at the holder's option. Too large a proportion is in the hands of banks. This is the result of financing over a period of years too largely by short term issues at artificially low interest rates maintained by Federal Reserve support. These policies contributed to cheapening the dollar.

A start has been made in lengthening the maturities of the debt, as well as obtaining a wider distribution among individuals and other nonbank investors. In our 1953 debt operations, maturities were lengthened in 5 out of 9 times.

There is every reason to look forward with confidence to this country's ability to put its financial house in better order without serious disruption of credits or markets. The stream of the Nation's savings is huge, larger than ever before; the financial system is sound. With a reasonable assurance of sound money of stable buying power there is no better investment than securities of the United States Government.

The national debt is now close to the legal limit of 275 billion dollars. In view of the wide swings in receipts and expenditures and their unpredictability, it is not prudent to operate the huge business of the United States Government in such a straitjacket as the present debt limit.

These difficulties will become worse as we move forward in the year. We shall be close to the debt limit and our cash balances will be dangerously low on several occasions in the first half of the calendar year.

In the second half of the calendar year, when tax receipts are seasonally low, there will be no way of operating within the present debt limit.

For these reasons, I renew my request to the Congress to raise the debt limit.

Proposed legislation.—Legislative proposals are reflected in separate messages or are included in the appropriate sections of part II of this message.

A summary of the budgetary impact of the legislative program also is given in part II.

In summary, I emphasize that this budget carries out the policy of this administration to move toward reduced taxes and reduced Government spending as rapidly as our national security and well-being will permit.

By using necessity—rather than mere desirability—as the test for our expenditures, we will reduce the share of the national income which is spent by the Government. We are convinced that more progress and sounder progress will be made over the years as the largest possible share of our national income is left with individual citizens to make their own countless decisions as to what they will spend, what they will buy, and what they will save and invest. Government must play a vital role in maintaining economic growth and stability. But I believe that our development, since the early days of the Republic, has been based on the fact that we left a great share of our national income to be used by a provident people with a will to venture. Their actions have stimulated the American genius for creative initiative and thus multiplied our productivity.

This budget proposes that such progressive economic growth will be fostered by continuing emphasis on efficiency and economy in Government, reduced Government expenditures, reduced taxes, and a reduced deficit. The reduced request for new obligational authority promises further that, barring unforeseen circumstances, the budgets I shall recommend in the future will be directed toward the same objectives.

DWIGHT D. EISENHOWER

PART II

To the Congress of the United States:

This, the second part of my budget message, discusses in considerable detail my recommended program for the Government for the fiscal year 1955.

I now present and describe my legislative proposals for taxes, and summarize my other legislative proposals, indicating their budgetary impact. This is followed by a presentation and discussion of the pertinent details of the budget.

TAX PROPOSALS

Our whole system of taxation needs revision and overhauling. It has grown haphazardly over many years. The tax system should be completely revised.

Revision of the tax system is needed to make tax burdens fairer for millions of individual taxpayers. It is needed to restore normal incentives for sustained production and economic growth. The country's economy has continued to grow during recent years with artificial support from recurring inflation. This is not a solid foundation for prosperity. We must restore conditions which will permit traditional American initiative and production genius to push on to ever higher standards of living and employment. Among these conditions, a fair tax system with minimum restraints on small and growing businesses is especially important.

I believe that this proposed tax revision is the next important step we should take in easing our tax burdens. After it is completed, further reductions in expenditures can be applied to our two objectives of balancing the budget and reducing tax rates.

A year ago I asked the Secretary of the Treasury to undertake a complete review of the tax system and make recommendations for changes. The Committee on Ways and Means of the House of Representatives had already started constructive examination of the tax laws with the same objectives.   Extensive hearings were held by the committee during the late spring and summer.

The proposed revisions are the result of a year's intensive work.   The collaboration between congressional and Treasury staffs in the development of a tax revision bill has been very close.   It may, I hope, provide a precedent for similar collaboration in other fields of legislation.

I shall not list here all the detailed points developed for the revision of the tax laws.   The following recommendations cover the major points.

They will substantially reduce the more glaring inequities, thereby helping vast numbers of our people in their individual tax burdens.   They will reduce the more serious restraints on production and economic growth. They will promote investment, which provides new and better methods of production and creates additional payrolls and more jobs.

The revisions will also make the law simpler and surer, with benefits to both taxpayers and the Government.   They will in many ways prevent abuses by which some taxpayers now avoid their rightful share of tax burdens by taking unfair advantage of technicalities.

1. *Children earning over 600 dollars.*—At present, parents cannot claim as a dependent any child who earns over 600 dollars a year.   This discourages children in school or college from earning as much as they can to help in their support.   I recommend that a parent should be permitted to continue to claim a child as a dependent regardless of the child's earnings if he is under 18 or away from home at school, as long as he is in fact still supported by the parent.   Such dependents should, of course, continue to pay their own income tax on earnings above 600 dollars.

2. *Heads of families.*—At present, a widow or widower with dependent children is denied the full benefit of income-splitting available to married couples.   It seems unfair to tax the income of a surviving parent with dependent children at higher rates than were applied to the family income before the death of one of the partners in a marriage.   I recommend that widows and widowers with dependent children be allowed to split their income as is now done by married couples.

This same tax treatment should be authorized for single people supporting dependent parents.   Furthermore, the present requirement that dependent parents must live with their children for the children to qualify for this tax treatment should be removed.   It is often best for elderly people to be able to live in their own homes, and the tax laws should not put a penalty on family arrangements of this sort.

3. *Foster children as dependents.*—At present, foster children and children in process of adoption may not be claimed as dependents. I recommend that such children be allowed as dependents.

4. *Expenses of child care.*—Some tax allowance can properly be given for actual costs of providing care for the small children of widows or widowers who have to work outside the home. The same tax privilege should be given to working mothers who, because their husbands are incapacitated, provide the principal support of their families.

5. *Medical expenses.*—The present tax allowances for unusual medical expenses are too limited to cover the many tragic emergencies which occur in too many families. I recommend that a tax allowance be given for medical expenses in excess of 3 percent of income instead of 5 percent as at present. I recommend further that the present ceiling of 1,250 dollars for a single person with a maximum ceiling of 5,000 dollars for a family should be doubled so that the maximum for a family will be 10,000 dollars. However, to avoid abuses in medical deductions, I recommend that the definition of medical expenses be tightened to exclude both ordinary household supplies and certain indirect travel expenses.

6. *Medical insurance and sick benefits for employees.*—Insurance and other plans adopted by employers to protect their employees against the risks of sickness should be encouraged by removing the present uncertainties in the tax law. It should be made clear that the employer's share of the costs of providing such protection on a group basis will not be treated as income on which the employee is liable for tax. This principle should be applied to medical and hospital insurance as well as to a full or partial continuation of earnings during a sickness.

There should be no tax discrimination between plans insured with an outside insurance company and those financed directly by the employer. At present, payments received by a person while sick are entirely nontaxable if made under an insured plan. This makes it possible for a person subject to high tax rates to have a much larger net income while on sick leave than while at work. To prevent abuses, I recommend that a limit of 100 dollars a week be placed on tax-free benefits, but this exemption should be extended only to plans meeting certain general standards.

7. *Pension and profit-sharing plans for employees.*—The conditions for qualification for special tax treatment of employers' pension plans

are too involved. Such plans are desirable. I recommend that the rules be simplified and that greater discretion be given in establishing plans for different groups of employees, so long as there is no discrimination in favor of key executives or stockholders.

Under present law, the value of a future pension to a surviving widow or child of an employee is included in the husband's taxable estate, even though the survivors may not live to receive the full benefits and there may be no cash available to pay the tax. I recommend that such value should not be included in an estate but that the survivors continue to pay tax on the pension in the same manner that it was taxed to the person first receiving it.

At the same time, to avoid unfair competition with ordinary taxpaying businesses, I recommend that pension trusts be restricted in the same manner as tax-exempt foundations. They should also be subject to rules in regard to percentage distribution of their assets comparable to those applying to regulated investment companies.

8. *Taxation of annuities.*—Under the present tax law, a person buying an annuity is taxed on a relatively large part of each payment until his cost is fully recovered, at which time the full amount becomes taxable. The tax rule is so strict that often a person is not likely to get his capital back tax free unless he lives beyond his life expectancy. I recommend that the tax treatment of annuities be determined on the basis of the life expectancy of the person receiving it. This will permit the hundreds of thousands of people who buy annuities to recover their capital free of tax over their life expectancies and will avoid any change in the tax status of an annuity during a person's lifetime.

9. *Double taxation of dividends.*—At present, business income is taxed to both the corporation as it is earned and to the millions of stockholders as it is paid out in dividends. This double taxation is bad from two standpoints. It is unfair and it discourages investment. I recommend that a start be made in the removal of this double taxation by allowing stockholders a credit against their own income taxes as a partial offset for the corporate tax previously paid. This will promote investment which in turn means business expansion and more production and jobs.

Specifically, I recommend that the credit be allowed on an increasing scale over the next 3 years. For this year, I recommend that a credit of 5 percent be allowed; for 1955, a credit of 10 percent; and, in 1956 and later years, 15 percent. To avoid shifts in the payment dates of corporation dividends, these credits should apply to dividends received after July 31 of each year. To give the full benefit immediately to small stockholders, I recommend that the first 50 dollars of dividends be completely exempted from tax in 1954 and that the first 100 dollars be exempted in 1955 and later years.

10. *Estimated returns.*—The burden on those required to file estimated tax returns should be reduced by increasing the number of optional ways in which an individual can estimate his tax without being subject to penalty for an underestimate. I recommend also that the penalties resulting from underestimates be simplified by being stated as a 6-percent interest charge on deficiencies.

11. *Filing date.*—To reduce the burdens of preparing and filing returns in the early months of the year, I recommend that the March 15 filing date for individuals be changed to April 15.

In the taxation of business the same objectives of fairness, simplicity, and reduction of tax barriers to production and normal economic growth are important. The present tax law should be revised on the basis of these standards.

Particular attention should be given in the revision of the law to the problems of small and growing business concerns. I cannot emphasize too strongly the social and economic importance of an environment which will encourage the formation, growth, and continued independent existence of new companies.

12. *Depreciation.*—A liberalization of the tax treatment of depreciation would have far-reaching effects on all business and be especially helpful in the expansion of small business whether conducted as individual proprietorships, partnerships, or corporations. At present, buildings, equipment, and machinery are usually written off uniformly over their estimated useful lives. The deductions allowed, especially in the early years, are often below the actual depreciation. This discourages long-range investment on which the risks cannot be clearly foreseen. It discourages the early replacement of old equipment with new and improved equipment. And it makes it more difficult to secure financing for capital investment, particularly for small business organizations.

I recommend that the tax treatment of depreciation be substantially changed to reduce these restrictions on new investment, which provides a basis for economic growth, increased production, and improved standards of living. It will help the manufacturer in buying new machinery and the storekeeper in expanding and modernizing his establishment. It will help the farmer get new equipment. All of this means many more jobs.

Specifically, I recommend that business be allowed more freedom in using straight-line depreciation and in selecting other methods of depreciation. Larger depreciation charges should be allowed in the early years of life of property by the use of the declining-balance method of depreciation at rates double those permitted under the straight-line method. Other methods which give larger depreciation in early years should be accepted, so long as they do not produce deductions which exceed those available under the declining-balance method.

The new methods of depreciation should be allowed for all investments in buildings, equipment, and machinery made after January 1, 1954. This would include farm buildings and equipment and new construction of commercial and industrial buildings and rental housing.

Faster depreciation, it should be noted, will merely shift the tax deductions from later to earlier years. It will not increase total deductions. The change should, in fact, increase Government revenues over the years because of the stimulation which it will give to enterprise and expansion.

In addition to the tax treatment of depreciation, which is important for all business, there are other features of the tax law which are of special importance to small business.

13. *Research and development expenses.*—At present, companies are often not permitted to deduct currently for research or development expenses. This rule is especially burdensome to small concerns because large companies with established research laboratories can usually get immediate deductions. I recommend that all companies be given an option to capitalize or to write off currently their expenses arising from research and development work. Our tradition of initiative and rapid technical improvements must not be hampered by adverse tax rules.

14. *Accumulation of earnings.*—At present, the penalty tax on excessive accumulations of corporate earnings operates to discourage the growth of small companies which are peculiarly dependent on retained earnings for expansion. The tax in some form is necessary to prevent avoidance of individual taxes by stockholders, but I recommend that the law be changed

to make the Government assume the burden of proof that a retention of earnings is unreasonable.

15. *Taxation of partnerships.*—The tax law applicable to partnerships is complex and uncertain. I recommend that it be simplified and made definite. It should be possible to form partnerships and make changes in them without undue tax complications.

16. *Optional tax treatment for certain corporations and partnerships.*—Small businesses should be able to operate under whatever form of organization is desirable for their particular circumstances, without incurring unnecessary tax penalties. To secure this result, I recommend that corporations with a small number of active stockholders be given the option to be taxed as partnerships and that certain partnerships be given the option to be taxed as corporations.

17. *Corporate reorganizations.*—The tax law applicable to reorganizations and recapitalizations of corporations is also complex and uncertain. This part of the law should be simplified and made sufficiently definite to permit people to know in advance the tax consequences of their actions.

The owners of small corporations frequently find it necessary to rearrange their interests in a corporation in anticipation of estate taxes, to secure new capital, or to make stock available for a new management group. I recommend that the tax law permit tax-free rearrangements of stockholders' interests in corporations, so long as no corporate earnings are withdrawn. Such changes will remove some of the tax pressures which force the sale of independent companies to larger corporations. At the same time, the law should be tightened to prevent abuses by which corporate earnings are withdrawn through the issuance and redemption of corporate securities. It should also be amended to avoid abuses through the purchase of corporations to acquire their rights to loss carryovers.

18. *Loss carryback.*—At present, losses may be carried back and offset against prior earnings for 1 year and carried forward to be offset against future earnings for 5 years. I recommend that the carryback be extended to 2 years. This will benefit established companies which become distressed. The 5-year carryforward should be continued to permit new businesses to offset their early losses against later profits.

19. *Soil conservation expenses.*—At present, only limited and uncertain tax deductions are allowed for soil conservation expenses on farms. I recommend that such deductions be allowed up to 25 percent of the farmer's gross income.

20. *Accounting definitions.*—Tax accounting should be brought more nearly in line with accepted business accounting by allowing prepaid income to be taxed as it is earned rather than as it is received, and by allowing reserves to be established for known future expenses.

21. *Multiple surtax exemptions, consolidated returns, and intercorporate dividends.*—I recommend that the law be tightened to remove abuses from the use of multiple corporations in a single enterprise. I also recommend that the penalty tax on consolidated returns and intercorporate dividends be removed over a 3-year period.

22. *Business income from foreign sources.*—I recommend that the taxation of income from foreign business investments be modified in several respects. The investment climate and business environment abroad are much more important than our own tax laws in influencing the international flow of capital and business. Nonetheless, our capital and management know-how can be helpful in furthering economic development in other countries, and is desired by many of them. Our tax laws should contain no penalties against United States investment abroad, and within reasonable limits should encourage private investment which should supplant Government economic aid.

Specifically, I recommend the following new provisions in our taxation of business income from foreign sources:

(*a*) Business income from foreign subsidiaries or from segregated foreign branches which operate and elect to be taxed as subsidiaries should be taxed at a rate 14 percentage points lower than the regular corporate rate. This lower rate of tax should apply only to earnings after January 1, 1954.

(*b*) The present definition of foreign taxes which may be credited against the United States income tax should be broadened to include any tax other than an income tax which is the principal form of taxation on business in a country, except turnover, general sales or excise taxes, and social security taxes. This country, by its tax laws, should not bring indirect pressure on other countries to adapt their tax systems and rates to ours.

(*c*) The overall limitation on foreign tax credits should be removed. This limitation discourages companies operating profitably in one foreign country from starting business in another foreign country where operations at a loss may be expected in the first few years.

97

(*d*) Regulated investment companies concentrating on foreign investments should be permitted to pass on to their stockholders the credit for foreign taxes which would be available on direct individual investments.

23. *Payment dates of corporation income tax.*—Over the past several years, corporation income tax payments have been gradually shifted forward into the first two of the regular quarterly dates. By 1955, the entire tax will be due in two equal installments in March and June.

The irregularity of tax receipts increases the problems in managing the public debt and is an unsettling influence in the money markets. The irregularity of tax payments also may make it harder for corporations to manage their own financing.

I recommend that, beginning in the fall of 1955, a start be made in smoothing out corporation income tax payments by requiring advance payments in September and December before the end of the taxable year. Each of these payments should be made at 5 percent of the amount due for the entire year in 1955, rising to 25 percent each in 1959 and later years.

These advance payments will require estimates of income for the year somewhat comparable to those now required of individuals. Though estimates of profits are difficult to make accurately, no payments will be required before the middle of the ninth month of a business year.

24. *Administrative provisions.*—The administrative features of the tax laws are unnecessarily complex. Different provisions have been adopted over the years to deal with particular problems, with little regard to consistency. Specifically, I recommend that the parts of the law covering assessments, collections, interest and penalties, the statute of limitations, and other administrative provisions be simplified and brought together in one place. This will result in savings to both taxpayers and the Government.

An effective and fair administration of the tax laws is vital to every individual in the country. The Internal Revenue Service has been revitalized during the past year and is being organized and managed on a basis that will assure fair and equal treatment to all taxpayers, maximum realization of taxes from revenue laws, and the contribution by each taxpayer of the share of the cost of Government that Congress intends that he should make.

The regulations and administration of the tax laws are being tightened to prevent abuses by which a small minority of taxpayers avoid their fair share of taxes by misuse of expense accounts and other improper practices.

25. *General simplification of tax laws and other revisions.*—The revision of the tax laws should be comprehensive. Many unnecessary complications have developed over the years. The entire Internal Revenue Code needs rewriting and reorganization.

Jointly, the Treasury Department and the staff of the congressional committees have developed many recommendations for changes other than those which I have described here. Some of these relate to the estate and gift tax, and the administrative provisions of the excise taxes.

The review of the present tax system in the Treasury Department has not yet led to final conclusions in many other situations that require further study before any recommendations for change can be properly made. These subjects include the tax treatment of capital gains and losses, the special problems of the oil and mining industries, the tax treatment of cooperatives and organizations which are wholly or partially tax exempt, as well as the provision of retirement income for people not covered by pension plans.

The tax reforms and revisions covered by the foregoing 25 recommendations make the income tax system fairer to individuals and less burdensome on production and continued economic growth. After their adoption, further reductions in Government expenditures will make possible additional reductions in the deficit and tax rates.

I do not believe that the budgetary situation justifies any tax reductions beyond those involved in the proposed tax revision and in the tax changes which occurred on January 1. Accordingly, I repeat my recommendation of last May that the reduction in the general corporate income tax rate be deferred for another year.

Excise taxes provide a relatively small proportion of our total tax revenues. In the fiscal year 1955, they are estimated to produce 10 billion dollars at existing rates as compared with 20 billion dollars from corporation income taxation and 30 billion dollars from individual income taxes. Of this 10 billion dollars, more than half comes from the excise taxes on liquor, tobacco, and gasoline.

Because of the present need for revenue, I recommend that the excise taxes scheduled to be reduced on April 1, including those on liquor, tobacco, automobiles, and gasoline, be continued at present rates; and that any adjustments in the other excise taxes be such as to maintain the total yield which we are now receiving from this source.

SUMMARY OF OTHER LEGISLATIVE PROPOSALS

The administration has developed a dynamic, progressive, and at the same time wholly practical legislative program. Its major outlines are set forth in the State of the Union Message, which I delivered to the Congress on January 7. Since that date, I have forwarded to the Congress the details of my recommendations with respect to the steps which I believe should be taken: (1) To modernize and make effective our agricultural laws (January 11); (2) to bring up to date and to improve the Labor-Management Relations Act of 1947 (January 11); (3) to extend and make more equitable the old-age and survivors insurance system (January 14); (4) to chart a new course in Federal cooperation and support for putting up-to-date medical and hospital care at the disposal of our citizens (January 18). On January 25 I shall present a program which will, for the first time, bring together into a coordinated and forward-looking set of policies the housing and community development programs of the Federal Government. Within a few days thereafter, I expect to make certain recommendations with respect to amendments to the Atomic Energy Act. These are discussed in more detail in subsequent sections of this message.

These measures, together with the legislative proposals which will be presented in the course of the next several months with respect to foreign assistance and trade, are the foundation stones for the legislative program of this administration. All of them call for extensions of existing legislation or the enactment of new legislation. All of them are necessary. They will help us to protect the freedom of our people, to maintain a strong and growing economy, and to concern ourselves with the human problems of the individual citizen.

Keyed to these foundation stones are the other individual measures which I have already recommended or which I shall recommend as soon as the necessary information upon which to base recommendations can be prepared. To some extent these other measures are basically improvements in program and are less precisely definable in terms of new costs attributed to them.

SUMMARY OF OTHER LEGISLATIVE PROPOSALS

1955 BUDGET

[Fiscal years. In millions]

Function and program	1954–1955	
	Recommended new obligational authority	Estimated expenditures
EXTENSION OF PRESENT MAJOR PROGRAMS		
National security:		
Military public works, Department of Defense...........	$1,108.0	$100.0
Mutual military program............................	2,500.0	700.0
International affairs and finance:		
Mutual economic and technical cooperation...........	875.0	300.0
Surplus agricultural commodities disposal..............	300.0	....
Contributions to voluntary international programs.......	135.0	70.0
Agriculture and agricultural resources: Increase in borrowing authority of the Commodity Credit Corporation....	1,750.0	....
Transportation and communication:		
Federal-aid highway program........................	575.0	....
Forest highways...................................	22.5	....
Subtotal, extension of present major programs.........	7,265.5	1,170.0
NEW LEGISLATIVE PROGRAM		
Social security, welfare, and health:		
Grants to States for public assistance..................	108.0	108.0
Expansion of grants for hospital construction...........	62.6	5.6
Program to stimulate wider coverage and greater benefits from private health insurance......................	26.2	1.1
Expansion of vocational rehabilitation services for the disabled..	8.8	7.8
Creation of a National Commission for Health Improvement..	0.3	0.3
Housing and community development: Advance planning of local public works..............................	[1] 10.0	3.0
Education and general research:		
Program to strengthen the Office of Education..........	0.3	0.3
National Conference on Education....................	[1] 2.0	[2] 1.8
Agriculture and agricultural resources: Cooperation with State and local agencies on watershed protection........	3.0	2.4
Natural resources:		
Aid for non-Federal development of water resources.....	10.0	10.0
Federal projects...................................	0.5	0.4
Transportation and communication:		
St. Lawrence Seaway...............................	105.0	5.8
Proposed postal rate increases (increased revenue).......	−240.0	−240.0
Labor and manpower: Expansion of unemployment compensation coverage: Administrative costs.................	22.1	22.0

[1] Recommended for the fiscal year 1954.

[2] Includes 1.5 million dollars in the fiscal year 1954.

Summary of Other Legislative Proposals—Continued

1955 budget—Continued

[Fiscal years. In millions]

	1954–1955	
	Recommended new obligational authority	Estimated expenditures
Function and program		
NEW LEGISLATIVE PROGRAM—continued		
General government:		
Unemployment compensation for Federal civilian employees....................................	$25.0	$25.0
Increase in Federal payment to the District of Columbia..	10.0	10.0
District of Columbia public works program.............	7.0	5.0
Subtotal, new legislative program:		
1954...	12.0	1.5
1955...	148.8	−33.0
Total legislative proposals:		
Fiscal year 1954................................	12.0	1.5
Fiscal year 1955................................	7,414.3	1,137.0

Proposed Legislation Affecting Trust Funds

1955 budget

[In millions]

Function and program

	1955 estimated
Social security, welfare, and health:	
Expansion and improvement of old-age and survivors insurance:	
Additional receipts..	$100.0
Additional disbursements......................................	408.0
Net accumulation in reserve..................................	−308.0
Labor and manpower:	
Extension of coverage of unemployment insurance:	
Additional deposits by States................................	145.0
Additional withdrawals by States..............................	60.0
Net accumulation in reserve..................................	85.0

To the extent that it has been possible to assess with reasonable accuracy the cost of major measures in the legislative program, estimates have been included in this budget. These estimates are summarized above. One recommendation, the proposed increase in postal rates, would add to Federal revenues. Other minor measures, in themselves too small to be identified in summary tables, are discussed and recommended in respective summary sections and chapters of this budget. Their total cost is small and has been adequately provided for in the reserve for contingencies.

DISCUSSION OF THE BUDGET

I now present and describe pertinent details of the budget. The figures shown in the budget are careful estimates based on present and foreseeable conditions. Changes in the budget can result from congressional action. Still others can result from economic factors which change the price of goods purchased by the Government or the incomes received and taxes paid by the citizens of the Nation. Changes in international and domestic conditions could alter this budget before the end of the fiscal year 1955.

The presentation of the figures in the budget for the fiscal year 1955 reflects two significant clarifications.

First, the appropriation to the railroad retirement trust fund equal to the taxes under the Railroad Retirement Tax Act has been excluded from the totals of budget expenditures and deducted from the total of budget receipts. This does not affect the budget surplus or deficit, and has been applied to the figures for all the years shown in this budget so that they are on a comparable basis.

This change properly presents an item which has previously overstated both budget receipts and expenditures in an equal amount. The collection of employment taxes on the railroad industry is in effect collections for a trust fund and not for Government operations. Their transfer to the trust fund should be made directly as a deduction from receipts and not shown as a budget expenditure.

The second significant clarifying change in presentation relates to the fact that the budget expenditure totals in the past have understated the scope of the Government's activities in that they included only the net basis of the spending by a number of enterprises which are engaged in business-type operations with the public. In the course of carrying out their functions, each of these public enterprises receives money from its customers or clients—interest and collections on loans or payments for goods delivered or services rendered. By law, most public enterprises may use their receipts and collections to carry on the operations for which they were created. These receipts and collections from the public in the fiscal year 1955 total 11 billion dollars.

The public enterprise activities are carried on through "revolving funds." Some of the enterprises are organized as Government corporations; others, such as the Post Office, are unincorporated.

In the summary tables of previous budgets, the receipts of such funds were subtracted from expenditures and only the difference was reported as a budget expenditure. In those cases where receipts exceeded expenditures for the year a negative figure was included in the summary expenditure tables. While the use of either the gross figures or the net figures produces an identical effect on the budget surplus or deficit, the former method of presenting only net figures in the summary tables did not reveal the full scope of the Government's financial transactions.

When Government agencies engaged in lending activities use their collections on old loans to make new loans, the net expenditure figure fails to disclose the volume of new lending and the new risks involved.

In this budget, the summary tables present the expenditures of the public enterprise funds on both a gross and net basis. The difference reveals the magnitude of receipts from the public in the "revolving funds."

BUDGET RECEIPTS

The estimates of budget receipts for the fiscal year 1955 in the following table are in accordance with my recommendations for taxes, and are based upon the continuation of business conditions, personal income, and corporation profits at substantially the present high levels.

BUDGET RECEIPTS

[Fiscal years. In millions]

Source	1953 actual	1954 estimated	1955 estimated
Individual income taxes:			
Existing legislation	[1] $32,478	$33,433	$30,908
Proposed legislation	....	....	−585
Corporation income taxes:			
Existing legislation	21,595	22,809	19,694
Proposed legislation	....	....	570
Excise taxes:			
Existing legislation	9,943	10,038	9,221
Proposed legislation	....	189	1,018
Employment taxes:			
Federal Insurance Contributions Act:			
Existing legislation	[1] 4,086	4,600	5,369
Proposed legislation	....	....	100

[1] Estimated.

BUDGET RECEIPTS—Continued

[Fiscal years.   In millions]

Source	1953 actual	1954 estimated	1955 estimated
Employment taxes—Continued			
Federal Unemployment Tax Act:			
Existing legislation..........................	$276	$290	$292
Proposed legislation..........................	....	....	16
Railroad Retirement Tax Act...................	626	640	640
Railroad Unemployment Insurance Act..........	10	....	....
Estate and gift taxes...........................	891	955	955
Customs......................................	613	590	590
Internal revenue not otherwise classified..........	49	....	....
Miscellaneous receipts..........................	1,827	2,313	2,454
Total receipts...............................	72,394	75,857	71,242
Deduct:			
Appropriation to Federal old-age and survivors insurance trust fund:			
Existing legislation..........................	4,086	4,600	5,369
Proposed legislation..........................	....	....	100
Appropriation to railroad retirement trust fund...	625	640	640
Refunds of receipts:			
Existing legislation..........................	3,120	2,988	2,644
Proposed legislation..........................	....	....	−153
Adjustment to daily Treasury statement basis.......	+30	....	....
Budget receipts..............................	64,593	67,629	62,642

Budget receipts exclude refunds of overpayments made to taxpayers and also exclude the employment taxes which are appropriated and transferred to the old-age and survivors insurance trust fund and to the railroad retirement trust fund.   Since these items are also excluded from budget expenditures, the surplus or deficit is not affected.

APPROPRIATIONS AND OTHER BUDGET AUTHORIZATIONS

New obligational authority represents the total of all new authorizations enacted by the Congress permitting Government agencies to incur financial obligations.   In addition to new appropriations, it includes mainly authorizations to enter into contracts prior to the enactment of appropriations, and authorizations to make expenditures from borrowed money.

NEW OBLIGATIONAL AUTHORITY BY MAJOR PROGRAM

[Fiscal years. In billions]

Major program	1953 actual	1954 estimated Budget document [1]	1954 estimated Current estimate	1955 recommended
National security...................	$57.2	$49.1	$39.3	$34.9
Veterans' services and benefits..........	4.1	4.6	4.2	4.0
International affairs and finance........	2.2	1.9	1.2	1.5
Social security, welfare, and health......	1.9	1.9	1.9	1.8
Housing and community development...	1.5	.7	.6	.2
Education and general research........	.3	.2	.2	.2
Agriculture and agricultural resources...	1.3	1.5	2.3	2.8
Natural resources...................	1.4	1.4	1.0	1.0
Transportation and communication.....	1.9	2.1	1.8	1.5
Finance, commerce, and industry	.1	.1	.1	([2])
Labor and manpower.................	.3	.3	.3	.3
General government..................	1.4	1.5	1.1	1.0
Interest............................	6.6	6.4	6.6	6.9
Reserve for contingencies.............	....	.1	.1	.2
Total..........................	80.2	71.8	60.7	56.3

[1] Adjusted for purposes of comparability.

[2] Less than 50 million dollars.

In prior years, new obligational authority has included all reappropriations. In conformity with congressional procedures, this budget does not include as new obligational authority reappropriations for two large programs, the mutual security program, and the construction program of the Atomic Energy Commission. These are authorized annually but are in effect continuing programs. The resulting reduction in reported new obligational authority is offset by a corresponding increase in the unspent balances of appropriations brought forward from one fiscal year to the next. New obligational authority in this budget also excludes the appropriation equivalent to taxes for the railroad retirement account, which has been discussed elsewhere. These changes are set forth in the following table:

NEW OBLIGATIONAL AUTHORITY—RECONCILIATION

[Fiscal years. In millions]

Description	1953 actual	1954 estimated Budget document	1954 estimated Current	1955 estimated
New obligational authority, midyear review basis	$81,373	$72,883	$63,981	....
Deduct reappropriations for:				
Mutual security program	447	....	1,944	....
Atomic Energy Commission—construction	65	404	679	....
Appropriations for railroad retirement taxes	625	660	640	....
New obligational authority, present basis	80,236	71,819	60,718	$56,283
Deduct authorizations other than current appropriations	7,879	7,504	8,889	9,260
Current appropriations	72,357	64,315	[1] 51,829	47,023

[1] Includes supplemental appropriations estimated in this budget at about 0.5 billion dollars; hence appropriations actually enacted are 51.3 billion dollars.

The Congress enacted increasing amounts of new obligational authority after the beginning of hostilities in Korea in June 1950. This new obligational authority was much greater than the amount of budget expenditures for each year and also greater than budget receipts in each year. Thus it represented commitments for future spending in excess of the revenues then being provided by the tax system.

The estimate of total appropriations and other authorizations for the fiscal year 1954 and, likewise, the total of my recommendations for new obligational authority for the fiscal year 1955 are less than estimated budget expenditures and also less than estimated budget receipts for the corresponding years. This is in direct contrast to the substantial excess of appropriations over revenues in recent prior years. It means we now are reducing the large amount of outstanding unfinanced commitments incurred under past appropriations and are making possible lower future levels of expenditures.

The major national security programs still require the largest part of our new budgetary authorizations. Of the total new obligational authority recommended for the fiscal year 1955, 34.9 billion dollars, or about 62 percent, is for the military functions of the Department of Defense, the atomic energy program, the mutual military program with our allied nations of the free world, and the stockpiling of strategic and critical materials.

In the detailed review which the appropriations committees and the Congress make of the operations of each agency and its budget proposals before enacting new obligational authority it is necessary to have the budget proposals set forth separately for each agency. Part II of the 1955 budget document is organized on such a basis. It presents summary and detailed information on my recommended appropriations for each agency. The individual appropriations are supported by schedules which reconcile the amount of the appropriation recommended with the obligations which are expected to be incurred. The obligation figures are reconciled with the estimated expenditures. The activities carried on within the appropriations and the workloads involved are also described for individual appropriations.

This grouping of the budget proposals by agencies, as contrasted with grouping by program or function principally employed in the budget summaries, is not only required for congressional action but is also the essential presentation for those of our citizens who are interested in following the progress of the budget proposals in the Congress.

The following table is derived from part II of the 1955 budget document. It shows that the new obligational authority I am recommending for the fiscal year 1955 is 56.3 billion dollars. This is 35.1 billion dollars less than the highest post-Korean amount of 91.4 billion dollars enacted for the fiscal year 1952. It is 15.5 billion dollars less than the amount recommended to Congress for the fiscal year 1954, in the budget document dated January 9, 1953, and 4.4 billion dollars less than the currently revised estimate for the fiscal year 1954.

UNEXPENDED BALANCES

In some cases, a considerable time period elapses between the enactment of an appropriation and the expenditure of all the Federal funds appropriated. For example, several years may elapse between the time a contract is negotiated pursuant to an appropriation for aircraft or other heavy military equipment and the time all the equipment ordered has been delivered and paid for by the Government. Thus many of the expenditures being made by the Government in the fiscal years 1954 and 1955 result from obligational authority enacted and from contracts negotiated in prior years.

NEW OBLIGATIONAL AUTHORITY BY AGENCY

[Fiscal years. In millions]

Agency	1953 *actual*	1954 *estimated* Budget document [1]	Current estimate	1955 *recommended*
Legislative branch....................	$76	$85	$83	$67
The Judiciary........................	28	29	29	30
Executive Office of the President.......	9	8	9	9
Funds appropriated to the President....	1,908	1,532	932	1,185
Independent offices:				
Atomic Energy Commission..........	4,079	1,593	1,042	1,366
Veterans Administration.............	4,191	4,554	4,273	3,893
Other.............................	1,050	1,134	665	592
General Services Administration........	317	395	163	155
Housing and Home Finance Agency....	1,357	506	454	85
Department of Agriculture.............	1,510	1,659	2,499	2,935
Department of Commerce.............	911	1,078	982	973
Department of Defense:				
Military functions...................	48,776	41,319	34,495	30,993
Mutual military program...........	4,236	6,119	3,800	2,500
Civil functions.....................	598	688	505	580
Department of Health, Education, and Welfare...........................	1,934	1,773	1,863	1,806
Department of the Interior.............	590	664	499	488
Department of Justice.................	173	187	179	178
Department of Labor.................	295	332	299	388
Post Office Department (general fund)..	660	669	439	89
Department of State..................	241	332	142	269
Treasury Department.................	7,279	7,101	7,250	7,471
District of Columbia (general fund).....	18	12	16	31
Reserve for contingencies.............	....	50	100	200
Total...........................	80,236	71,819	60,718	56,283

[1] Adjusted for purposes of comparability except for reorganization transfers.

During the fiscal year 1955, it is estimated that 45 percent of total budget expenditures will be from obligations incurred under appropriations and other authorizations enacted in years before 1955, and 55 percent will be from the new obligational authority I am recommending for 1955.

The reductions in appropriations that were made last year and the further reductions I am recommending for the fiscal year 1955 decrease the accumulated backlog of outstanding commitments which lead to later budget expenditures. Balances of appropriations unexpended at the end of the year and still available for expenditure during the next year are shown in the following table for each fiscal year since 1950. The amounts shown have been modified to reflect related technical changes in handling reappropriation items (see pp. 106–107) and to restrict unexpended balances to items of appropriations, excluding, for example, public debt authorizations. For the most part, these appropriation balances have been obligated or committed, but the expenditures take place one or more fiscal years after the enactment of the appropriation.

UNEXPENDED BALANCES OF APPROPRIATIONS

[In billions]

Fiscal year	Amount brought forward into the year	Amount carried over to next year
1950	[1] $11. 5	[1] $14. 1
1951	[1] 14. 1	[1] 50. 3
1952	[1] 50. 3	68. 8
1953	68. 8	78. 7
1954 estimated	78. 7	66. 5
1955 estimated	66. 5	54. 1

[1] Estimated. Detailed accounting data not available.

BUDGET EXPENDITURES

Budget expenditures in the fiscal year 1955 are estimated at 65.6 billion dollars, a reduction of 5.3 billion dollars from the revised estimate of the fiscal year 1954 expenditures, a reduction of 12.3 billion dollars from the expenditures estimated in the 1954 budget document, and a reduction of 8.4 billion dollars from actual expenditures in the fiscal year 1953.

As mentioned earlier, the summary tables in the budget have been made more revealing by the presentation of expenditures of public enterprises on both a gross and a net basis. The difference between the gross and net figures reveals the magnitude of the receipts and collections of the "revolving funds" which are used for making new loans and other expenditures.

In the summary tables of this budget, these receipts are labeled "applicable receipts of public enterprise funds." The table on the following page shows both gross and net figures for the fiscal year 1955, compared with net figures (on the old basis) for 1954 and 1953.

BUDGET EXPENDITURES BY MAJOR PROGRAM

[Fiscal years. In millions]

Major program	1955 estimated			1954 estimated Budget expenditures (net)		1953 actual
	Gross expenditures	Applicable receipts of public enterprise funds	Budget expenditures (net)	Budget document	Current estimate	Budget expenditures (net)
National security.......	$44,860	(1)	$44,860	$54,700	$48,720	$50,274
Veterans' services and benefits..............	4,223	$31	4,192	4,564	4,160	4,298
International affairs and finance..............	1,885	635	1,250	2,161	1,779	2,216
Social security, welfare, and health..........	1,807	(1)	1,807	1,919	1,947	1,910
Housing and community development........	1,903	2,180	−277	509	57	549
Education and general research.............	223	....	223	288	278	277
Agriculture and agricultural resources........	6,752	4,386	2,366	1,827	2,654	2,936
Natural resources.......	1,337	234	1,103	1,381	1,172	1,358
Transportation and communication..........	4,277	2,859	1,418	2,111	1,856	2,077
Finance, commerce, and industry.............	917	755	162	150	164	76
Labor and manpower...	282	1	281	303	265	281
General government....	1,164	4	1,160	1,554	1,175	1,439
Interest...............	6,875	....	6,875	6,420	6,600	6,583
Reserve for contingencies.................	150	....	150	40	75	....
Adjustment to daily Treasury statement basis................	....	....	....	....	....	−292
Total..............	76,655	11,085	65,570	77,927	70,902	73,982

1 Less than 500,000 dollars.

The fuller presentation in the summary tables does not have any effect on the budget surplus or deficit, or upon the changes in the public debt. Nor does it indicate any new method of financing these Government-owned enterprises. However, it does give a more complete disclosure of the Government's financial transactions with the general public.

As indicated in the preceding table, the term "budget expenditures" refers to the net expenditure figures. The term "gross expenditures" will be used wherever the activities of public enterprises are discussed on a gross basis. The table which follows shows the gross figures for all 3 years, reduced to the older net basis by a single deduction for each year at the bottom of the table.

GROSS EXPENDITURES BY MAJOR PROGRAM

[Fiscal years. In millions]

		1954 *estimated*		
Major program	1953 *actual*	*Budget document*	*Current estimate*	1955 *estimated*
National security.....................	$50, 274	$54, 700	$48, 721	$44, 860
Veterans' services and benefits..........	4, 327	4, 590	4, 190	4, 223
International affairs and finance........	2, 656	2, 604	2, 249	1, 885
Social security, welfare, and health......	1, 910	1, 921	1, 947	1, 807
Housing and community development...	2, 118	1, 696	2, 357	1, 903
Education and general research........	277	288	278	223
Agriculture and agricultural resources...	6, 448	6, 362	8, 087	6, 752
Natural resources.....................	1, 499	1, 568	1, 349	1, 337
Transportation and communication.....	4, 474	4, 570	4, 446	4, 277
Finance, commerce, and industry.......	1, 205	897	1, 151	917
Labor and manpower.................	284	306	267	282
General government..................	1, 444	1, 558	1, 178	1, 164
Interest.............................	6, 583	6, 420	6, 600	6, 875
Reserve for contingencies..............	....	40	75	150
Adjustment to daily Treasury statement basis...............................	−292	....	....	....
Subtotal.......................	83, 207	87, 520	82, 895	76, 655
Deduct applicable receipts of public enterprise funds........................	9, 225	9, 593	11, 993	11, 085
Budget expenditures (net)..........	73, 982	77, 927	70, 902	65, 570

The figures for gross expenditures in this and related tables are derived from the detailed accounts of each Government agency contained in part II of the 1955 budget document. On this basis, both the gross expenditures and the applicable receipts include some transactions relating to private bank loans guaranteed by the Commodity Credit Corporation and by the Export-Import Bank which involve no use of governmental funds. These amounts are:

GROSS EXPENDITURES AND APPLICABLE RECEIPTS, GUARANTEED LOANS

[Fiscal years. In millions]

Program and agency	1953 actual	1954 estimated Budget document	1954 estimated Current estimate	1955 estimated
International affairs and finance: Export-Import Bank.....................	$4	$5	$82	$188
Agriculture and agricultural resources: Commodity Credit Corporation.......	340	383	1,564	274

In the sections of this message discussing international affairs and agriculture, these figures are excluded from the totals to make them comparable to the basis used in other public enterprise accounts. This has no effect on net budget expenditures.

My recommendations for each of the major programs of Government listed in the above tables are discussed in detail later in this message. Budget expenditures by agency are described in detail in part II of the 1955 budget document, and are summarized in the table on the following page.

The analysis on page 115 shows that budget expenditures for the national security program and for those items which are relatively fixed under provisions of existing and proposed legislation amount to an estimated 59 billion dollars in the fiscal year 1955, 90 percent of all budget expenditures.

The remaining "all other," 6.6 billion dollars, or 10 percent of the total, include some items related to the first two categories. For example, those related to our national security effort are the international programs for economic development, the Selective Service System, and civil defense. Examples of programs which are partly controllable through the budgetary process are the mortgage purchases of the Federal National Mortgage Association and a few relatively small grant-in-aid programs. The bulk of this category is made up of expenditures for the day-to-day operations of the Government, such as law enforcement and administration, tax collection, the various regulatory agencies, the administration of other services rendered to the public, and the cost of direct civil public works.

BUDGET EXPENDITURES BY AGENCY

[Fiscal years. In millions]

Agency	1955 *estimated* Gross expenditures	Applicable receipts of public enterprise funds	Budget expenditures (net)	1954 *estimated* Budget expenditures (net) Budget document[1]	Current estimate	1953 *actual* Budget expenditures (net)
Legislative branch............	$66	......	$66	$70	$63	$61
The Judiciary................	30	......	30	28	29	27
Executive Office of the President...................	9	......	9	8	10	9
Funds appropriated to the President...................	1,622	$242	1,380	1,956	1,702	1,828
Independent Offices:						
Atomic Energy Commission..	2,425	(2)	2,425	2,700	2,200	1,791
Veterans Administration.....	4,235	70	4,165	4,494	4,190	4,334
Other....................	3,795	3,317	478	979	520	830
General Services Administration......................	753	2	751	1,126	936	1,107
Housing and Home Finance Agency....................	1,712	2,097	−385	380	−103	385
Department of Agriculture.....	4,760	2,263	2,497	2,031	2,945	3,217
Department of Commerce.....	1,028	49	979	1,031	1,080	1,063
Department of Defense:						
Military functions...........	37,575	(2)	37,575	45,500	41,550	43,610
Mutual military program....	4,275	......	4,275	5,700	4,200	3,954
Civil functions.............	654	114	540	640	617	813
Department of Health, Education, and Welfare..........	1,789	2	1,787	1,904	1,949	1,920
Department of the Interior....	562	34	528	659	549	587
Department of Justice........	176	......	176	184	184	171
Department of Labor........	362	1	361	321	299	300
Post Office Department (general fund)....................	2,775	2,686	89	669	440	659
Department of State..........	214	......	214	317	159	271
Treasury Department.........	7,653	208	7,445	7,178	7,292	7,325
District of Columbia (Federal contribution)...............	35	......	35	12	16	12
Reserve for contingencies......	150	......	150	40	75	......
Adjustment to daily Treasury statement basis.............	......	......	......	......	......	−292
Total...................	76,655	11,085	65,570	77,927	70,902	73,982

[1] Adjusted for purposes of comparability except for reorganization transfers.
[2] Less than 500,000 dollars.

The record of budget expenditures since the outbreak of aggression in Korea in June 1950 shows considerable variation in the relative changes from year to year in the three major categories shown. While expenditures for national security have risen markedly and those for uncontrollable major programs have fluctuated within rather narrow limits, Government spending in all other categories has been steadily declining.

ANALYSIS INDICATING CONTROLLABILITY OF NET BUDGET EXPENDITURES

[Fiscal years. In millions]

		1954 *estimated*		
Description	1953 *actual*	*Budget document*	*Current estimate*	1955 *estimated*
National security program.............	$50,274	$54,700	$48,720	$44,860
Relatively uncontrollable major programs under existing and proposed legislation:				
Legislative and the Judiciary.........	88	98	92	96
Interest on public debt and refunds...	6,583	6,420	6,600	6,875
Claims and judgments...............	129	65	148	135
Veterans' compensation, pension, and benefit programs..................	3,383	3,524	3,232	3,244
Payments to employees' retirement funds...........................	324	430	34	32
Payments to Railroad Retirement Fund for military service credits..........	33	35	35	....
Grants to States for public assistance...	1,330	1,340	1,389	1,293
Grants to States for unemployment compensation and employment service administration.....................	202	208	190	205
Veterans' unemployment compensation.............................	26	47	40	61
Unemployment compensation for Federal employees.....................	....	....	....	25
Federal-aid highway grants..........	509	540	541	555
Conservation of agricultural land resources........................	273	254	225	196
Removal of surplus agricultural commodities........................	82	75	205	233
Agriculture price support............	1,943	729	1,404	1,165
Total..........................	14,905	13,765	14,135	14,115
All other...........................	8,803	9,462	8,047	6,595
Net budget expenditures...........	73,982	77,927	70,902	65,570

NET BUDGET EXPENDITURES

[Fiscal years. In billions]

Description	1950 actual	1951 actual	1952 actual	1953 actual	1954 estimated	1955 estimated
National security program.....	$13.0	$22.3	$43.8	$50.3	$48.7	$44.9
Relatively uncontrollable major programs.................	15.6	12.1	12.3	14.9	14.1	14.1
All other...................	11.0	9.6	9.3	8.8	8.1	6.6
Total..................	39.6	44.0	65.4	74.0	70.9	65.6

RECEIPTS FROM AND PAYMENTS TO THE PUBLIC

Budget receipts, expenditures, and the budget surplus or deficit reflect transactions of funds which belong to the Federal Government. There are many other financial transactions of the Federal Government which involve funds the Government holds in trust for others, such as the social security trust funds. The transactions of these trust funds are shown separately in part III of the 1955 budget document. They are not included in the budget totals of receipts and expenditures. As a rule, the trust funds are now building up accumulations; that is, as they build reserves for future liabilities, they are currently taking in more money than they pay out.

By consolidating the trust funds with the budget transactions, and by eliminating intragovernmental and certain noncash transactions, it is possible to obtain a measure of the flow of money between the Federal Government as a whole and the public.

RECEIPTS FROM AND PAYMENTS TO THE PUBLIC, EXCLUDING BORROWING

[Fiscal years. In millions]

	1953 actual	1954 estimated Budget document	1954 estimated Current esimate	1955 estimated
Cash receipts from the public..........	$71,282	$75,150	$74,932	$70,842
Cash payments to the public..........	76,554	81,797	75,166	70,727
Excess of cash receipts.............	....	....	....	115
Excess of cash payments............	5,272	6,647	234	....

The trust funds of our social security system reflect the increase in rate provided under existing law and the expected increase in payments resulting from proposed legislation increasing the coverage and benefits.

If the automatic increase in rate had taken place with no recommendation for increased coverage and benefits, the excess of cash receipts
over payments estimated for the fiscal year 1955 would have been a
greater amount.

NATIONAL SECURITY

This budget is based on a new concept for planning and financing our
national security program, which was partially applied in the budget revision recommended last spring for the fiscal year 1954. Our military
planning in previous years had been based on several successive assumed
fixed dates of maximum danger, which were extended from time to time
with procurement and personnel plans focused to achieve maximum readiness by each such date. This budget is aimed instead at providing a
strong military position which can be maintained over the extended period
of uneasy peace.

It points toward the creation, maintenance, and full exploitation of
modern airpower. Our military planners and those of the other nations
of the free world agree as to the importance of airpower. But air forces
must be complemented with land forces, amphibious forces, antisubmarine
warfare forces, and fighting ships. The added emphasis on airpower
complements our plans for improving continental defense against possible
enemy attack. We expect to continue to improve the combat effectiveness
of our forces by the application of new weapons and new techniques, and
ultimately achieve far greater flexibility than heretofore attainable. The
reassembly of our strategic reserve forces will be as dictated by world
conditions and the forces kept in a high state of readiness to cope with any
possible acts of aggression. This budget aims toward building to a maximum effectiveness all of this complex of military strength. It provides
greater expenditures for airpower in the fiscal year 1955 than in any year
since the close of World War II. The reorientation of our defense strategy
makes this possible within a lower level of total expenditures for national
security.

With the shift in emphasis to the full exploitation of airpower and
modern weapons, we are in a position to support strong national security
programs over an indefinite period with less of a drain on our manpower,
material, and financial resources.

Today there is a truce in Korea. After 3 years of hostilities, we are
now in the first year of an armed peace. But we are a long way from

achieving the kind of peace that is our goal. As long as the Communist threat to the free world exists, we must plan to maintain effective military strength in close cooperation with the other nations of the free world.

Our basic security objective is to prevent another outbreak of aggression. We must create the necessary deterrent to any possible aggressor by maintaining a strong military position at home and abroad. To do this takes determination, human and material resources, and careful planning.

The national security section of the budget includes not only the military functions of the Department of Defense, but also the mutual military program, the development of atomic energy, and the stockpiling of strategic and critical materials. These four major programs are related and designed for the basic purpose of our security. They complement each other and must be assessed in conjunction with the long-range planning which underlies the fiscal and legislative programs of this administration.

The previous history of our military budgets has been one of feast or famine, depending upon the state of world affairs. In peacetime, appropriations have customarily been much reduced. In wartime, financial considerations have been largely ignored. Our present budgetary plans represent a departure from these practices. They provide for the continued maintenance of a strong military force which is within the financial capability of a sound economy. We cannot afford to build military strength by sacrificing economic strength. We must keep strong in all respects.

It will be noted from the table on pages 120–121 that expenditures for the Department of Defense and the stockpiling program have been reduced in the fiscal year 1954 and I am recommending a further reduction for the fiscal year 1955. The reduction in the total Department of Defense expenditures will be effected despite the fact that expenditures for aircraft, shipbuilding, electronics, guided missiles, construction, research and development, and many other defense programs will continue at close to record peacetime levels. I am also recommending some increased expenditures in the fiscal year 1955 for the mutual military program and for atomic energy which will bring expenditures for these two programs to record levels. Nevertheless total spending for national security is estimated to decline about 1.6 billion dollars from the fiscal year 1953 to 1954, and an additional 3.9 billion dollars from 1954 to 1955.

This decline in national security expenditures reflects the dynamic long-range plan recommended by the Joint Chiefs of Staff for our military forces, the savings resulting from the economies effected by this administration, the cessation of hostilities in Korea, and the decrease in procurement—particularly with respect to vehicles, ammunition, and soft goods—made possible by the improved supplies and materiel position.

The defense team, both military and civilian, is working hard toward improvement of the organization, procedures, and methods of the entire Defense Establishment. Already much progress has been made. The Office of the Secretary of Defense has been reorganized, and the administrative structures of the three military departments are under review, with the purpose of making Secretaries of these departments truly responsible administrators and establishing clearer lines of responsibility within this concept. This will help in achieving the maximum economies that can be realized through improved management and administration.

Considerable progress has been made in standardizing military procurement, and it is planned to reduce sharply the present approximately 4 million different procurement items. This alone will ultimately save hundreds of millions of dollars in procurement, warehousing, and distribution costs. The adoption of commercial maintenance practices for aircraft, vehicles, and other equipment is currently saving millions of dollars.

Better transportation methods are being worked out which will produce additional economies. Savings are also being effected in personnel, procurement, and supply activities. Through these and similar economy programs, more defense for the taxpayers' dollar will be realized.

Consistent with these plans for a sustained military capability at the lowest possible cost is an integrated plan of continental and civil defense. Such planning is necessary in order to hold our civilian losses from possible enemy attack to a minimum.

Last summer I told the American people that "the Soviets now have the capability of atomic attack upon us, and such capability will increase with the passage of time." I made this statement shortly after it was established that the Soviet Union had successfully detonated a thermonuclear device which, if successfully converted into an offensive weapon and if exploded over our American cities, would be capable of effecting unprecedented destruction.

The administration has taken a number of actions to deal with this serious prospect. Funds are included in the Department of Defense budget to expand the system of continental defense which coordinates the actions of our radar outposts and our air, naval, and land forces. It will provide improved early warning of enemy attack and the men and equipment to resist any such attack. Expenditures for continental defense in the fiscal year 1955 are expected to be greater than ever before in our history.

This budget reflects a new concept of civil defense which takes account of the destructive threat of modern weapons and which emphasizes improved warning of impending attack and planning for the dispersal of populations of potential target cities in advance of enemy attack.

NATIONAL SECURITY

[Fiscal years. In millions]

	Expenditures					
Item	1950 *actual*	1951 *actual*	1952 *actual*	1953 *actual*	1954 *estimated*	1955 *estimated*
Gross expenditures:						
Direction and coordination of defense.................	$10	$12	$13	$15	$12	$13
Other central defense activities......................	199	353	379	394	438	562
Army defense..............	3,983	7,469	15,635	16,242	14,200	10,198
Navy defense...............	4,100	5,582	10,162	11,874	11,300	10,493
Air Force defense...........	3,600	6,349	12,709	15,085	15,600	16,209
Proposed legislation.........	......	......	......	......	......	100
Subtotal—Department of Defense..............	11,892	19,765	38,898	43,610	41,550	37,575
Mutual military program:						
Present programs.........	130	991	2,442	3,954	4,200	3,575
Proposed legislation.......	......	......	......	......	......	700
Development and control of atomic energy............	550	897	1,670	1,791	2,200	2,425
Stockpiling of strategic and critical materials..........	438	654	837	919	770	585
Total..................	13,010	22,307	43,847	50,274	48,720	44,860
Deduct applicable receipts.....	(¹)	(¹)	(¹)	(¹)	(¹)	(¹)
Net budget expenditures.......	13,010	22,307	43,847	50,274	48,720	44,860

¹ Less than 500,000 dollars.

NATIONAL SECURITY—Continued

[Fiscal years.   In millions]

New obligational authority

Item	1950 actual	1951 actual	1952 actual	1953 actual	1954 estimated	1955 recommended
Direction and coordination of defense....................	$11	$12	$14	$15	$13	$13
Other central defense activities..	180	432	419	400	762	548
Army defense................	4,392	19,588	21,354	15,221	12,777	8,236
Navy defense................	4,359	12,484	16,220	12,689	9,526	9,882
Air Force defense.............	5,428	15,203	22,375	20,451	11,417	11,206
Proposed legislation...........	......	......	......	......	......	1,108
Subtotal—Department of Defense................	14,370	47,719	60,382	48,776	34,495	30,993
Mutual military program:						
Present programs............	1,359	5,222	5,291	4,236	3,800	......
Proposed legislation.........	......	......	......	......	......	2,500
Development and control of atomic energy..............	794	1,919	1,266	4,079	1,043	1,366
Stockpiling of strategic and critical materials...............	425	2,910	579	134	......	......
Total new obligational authority................	16,948	57,770	67,518	57,225	39,338	34,859

Much planning, organization, and training remains to be done, however, to make this strategy of civil defense fully effective at all levels of government. It will be the Federal responsibility, as reflected in this budget, to provide warning of impending attacks, and to stockpile medical supplies. The Federal Government will not assume the responsibilities which belong to local governments and volunteer forces, but will supplement State and local resources, provide necessary information on weapons effects, and advise and assist States and localities.

Many activities throughout the budget are related, directly and indirectly, to the national security. They are not all classified as national security for many reasons. Civil defense is one of these activities. The major part of continental defense is in the military budget, but, because of the community aspect of the civil defense program, funds for it are included as heretofore in the section on housing and community development.

Department of Defense.—The total of the first six items listed in the preceding table indicates the portion of our national security expenditures which is used for the direct support of our military forces. For these items the budget recommends 31.0 billion dollars of new obligational authority and estimates expenditures of 37.6 billion dollars in the fiscal year 1955. These expenditures are 4.0 billion dollars less than the amount now estimated for 1954. The revised estimate for 1954 is 2.1 billion dollars less than the actual spending in 1953—in marked contrast with the expectation in the budget document of January 9, 1953, that such expenditures in the fiscal year 1954 would exceed those in 1953.

The changing military situation following the sudden attack on Korea brought unbalanced programs and uncoordinated financing during the fiscal years 1951 to 1953. Steps have been, and will continue to be, taken by this administration to bring these factors into balance. One result has been the elimination of the previously forecast increase in expenditures in 1954. Because of the long lead-time needed to procure military equipment, the expenditures have not come down to the level of the new obligational authority. In 1954, with new obligational authority of 34.5 billion dollars, the expenditures are estimated to be 41.6 billion dollars. Likewise, in 1955, though I am recommending 31 billion dollars in new obligational authority, the expenditures are estimated at 37.6 billion dollars.

At the outbreak of hostilities in Korea we had about 1.5 million men under arms. The Korean fighting and general defense buildup brought this figure up to an average of 2.4 million in the fiscal year 1951; to an average of 3.5 million in fiscal year 1952 and a peak strength of 3.7 million in the last quarter of that fiscal year; and to an average of 3.6 million in fiscal year 1953.

Recently, I announced our plan to withdraw two Army divisions from Korea and return them to the United States as an initial step in the progressive reduction of United States ground forces in Korea. This withdrawal is made possible by the cessation of hostilities, the increased mobility and striking power of our air and other combat forces, and by the increasing capabilities of the Republic of Korea forces. This action does not impair our readiness and capacity to oppose any possible renewal of Communist aggression with even greater effect than heretofore if this should be necessary. United States military forces in the Far East will be maintained at appropriate levels, with emphasis on highly mobile naval, air, and amphibious units. Funds are provided to the Department of Defense in this budget for the continued support of Republic of Korea forces at a high level of effectiveness.

As the striking power of our combat forces is progressively increased by the application of technological advances and the growth of airpower, the number of military personnel is being reduced. Total military personnel is scheduled to be reduced from the present level of more than 3.4 million to approximately 3.3 million by June 30, 1954, and a little over 3 million by June 30, 1955. On this basis, this budget provides for an average of 3.2 million military personnel during the fiscal year 1955, compared with an average of 3.4 million during the fiscal year 1954.

The efficiency of our combat forces is contingent upon having experienced, well-trained career personnel. In the State of the Union Message I indicated that pay alone will not retain in the Armed Forces, in competition with industry, the necessary proportion of long-term personnel. We must provide a more generous use of other benefits important to service morale.

Under the long-range plan recommended by the Joint Chiefs of Staff, the number of Army divisions may be less than those currently organized, but increased mobility and the availability of modern weapons will provide each division with increasingly greater striking power. As part of the program to improve continental defense, the number of guided-missile antiaircraft battalions will be increased substantially.

At the present time, the Air Force, Navy, and Marine air forces have a total active inventory of approximately 33,000 aircraft, of which approximately one-third are jet aircraft. The emphasis on airpower is reflected in the objective of increasing the active aircraft inventory to more than 40,000 during the next 3 years, with more than half of these aircraft to be jets. At that time the Air Force will have 137 wings—of which 126 will be combat wings—augmented by appropriate combat support units. Naval airpower will include 16 carrier air groups and 15 antisubmarine warfare squadrons, while the Marines will maintain 3 Marine air wings. In each case, these units will be supplemented by appropriate combat support units.

The Navy, in addition to increasing its effective air strength, will continue to modernize the fleet, with emphasis on the combatant elements. The Marine Corps will maintain three combat-ready divisions.

The military plan for forces to be maintained in the fiscal year 1955 permits a reduction of approximately 600 million dollars in the expenditures required for military pay, allowances, and other direct military personnel costs. Operation and maintenance—sometimes called housekeeping—is being held to a minimum, and expenditures in this area will be reduced.

Major procurement expenditures as a whole will decline by about 15 percent from 1954 levels, but the 14.5 billion dollars expected to be spent for this purpose will still be almost four times as great as the amount spent during the fiscal year 1951—the first year of buildup following the attack in Korea. Because the capital investment will already have been made for much new equipment and for a considerable portion of the desired mobilization reserve of materiel and supplies, expenditures for vehicles, ammunition, production equipment, and some other major equipment items will be lower in 1955. The accumulation of mobilization reserves is being scheduled over an extended period of time, with a view toward keeping production facilities of key military items in continued production. Provision of capital equipment and modernization of aircraft will continue at a rapid pace in 1955, and expenditures for aircraft procurement for the Air Force and naval aviation will be at the same general level as in 1954. Aircraft procurement expenditures will account for 22 percent of total Department of Defense expenditures in 1955, compared with 20 percent in 1954, 17 percent in 1953, and 13 percent in 1952. Shipbuilding expenditures will continue at approximately the same level as in 1954, but the new obligational authority I am recommending will provide for a slightly higher level of shipbuilding in the years immediately ahead in order to meet the problem of "block obsolescence" of the fleet, a major portion of which was built during World War II.

Expenditures for military public works in the fiscal year 1955 will be maintained at the 1954 level, as work progresses on air bases, antiaircraft and radar sites, and other necessary installations. Expenditures for reserve components are expected to increase by about 20 percent as the buildup of a vigorous reserve program continues. Research and development will continue at a high level.

The following table shows, by major cost category, the elements making up the Department of Defense budget.

DEPARTMENT OF DEFENSE

[Fiscal years. In millions]

Cost category	1950 [1] actual	Budget expenditures 1951 actual	1952 actual	1953 actual	1954 estimated	1955 estimated	New obligational authority 1955 estimated
Military personnel............	....	$7,148	$11,152	$11,556	$10,910	$10,335	$10,673
Operation and maintenance..	....	6,444	11,855	10,335	8,979	8,769	9,107
Major procurement and production..	....	(3,976)	(11,478)	(17,123)	(17,273)	(14,546)	(7,303)
Aircraft......	....	2,412	4,888	7,416	8,425	8,310	4,399
Ships........	....	381	624	1,191	1,005	990	1,150
Other........	....	1,183	5,966	8,516	7,843	5,246	1,754
Military public works........	....	439	1,819	1,913	1,687	1,650	1,109
Reserve components......	....	537	476	521	560	675	710
Research and development..	....	758	1,163	1,412	1,425	1,350	1,352
Establishment-wide activities.	....	621	656	666	735	740	739
Working capital (revolving) funds........	....	−158	299	84	−19	−490	....
Total.......	$11,892	19,765	38,898	43,610	41,550	37,575	30,993

[1] Detail not available.

Mutual military program.—Because our own national security is vitally dependent on the continued strength of our allies throughout the free world, we have undertaken over the past several years to assist them in building the military forces necessary to deter Communist aggression from without or subversion from within. Since the beginning of the mutual defense assistance program in fiscal year 1950, when the armed strength of the free world was at low ebb, 18 billion dollars have been made available to furnish military equipment and training to friendly nations. More than half of this amount will have been spent by the end of the fiscal year 1954. This assistance, combined with their own resources, enables our allies and friends to equip and train an equivalent of 175 army divisions, about 220 air force squadrons, nearly 1,500 naval aircraft, over 440 naval vessels, and related combat and logistic units to back up these forces.

These friendly forces located in key strategic areas for the defense of the free world are largely supported by the countries themselves. In addition, substantial forces are exclusively supported by our allies. Without all of these forces the United States would be faced with a potential defense burden so costly that it could well sap the economic vitality of our Nation. These forces constitute an integral part of the military strength of the free world.

Since the mutual military program is so closely integrated with our own military plans and program, it is shown this year in the defense chapter of part II of the budget, and is discussed here as part of our national security program. Because the mutual military program is also an integral part of our foreign policy, the Secretary of Defense will continue to carry out his responsibilities for the mutual military program under the foreign policy guidance of the Secretary of State and within the terms of the mutual security legislation passed by the Congress.

In this budget, mutual military program funds are shown under the new obligational authority of the Department of Defense. However, this arrangement is being reviewed and my recommendations will be set forth in connection with the authorizing legislation I shall recommend to the Congress. This authorizing legislation should permit adjustments in the composition of our aid programs to meet changing needs due to new international developments. It is therefore essential that the Congress maintain the present Presidential powers of transferability of all foreign assistance funds, whether for military, technical, or economic assistance.

The recent Paris meeting of the North Atlantic Treaty Organization set realistic force goals for the 14 member nations, which will provide for a substantial increase in the defensive strength of NATO. The mutual military program provides the bulk of the initial equipment and certain mobilization reserves needed to meet these new goals. Meanwhile, our allies are themselves carrying heavy burdens. Their military budgets during the period of this program exceed by many times the value of the equipment we have so far delivered. They have expressed their determination to continue their efforts at high levels.

Despite the progress which NATO has made, we are nevertheless faced with a serious need to achieve the unity in Europe which is necessary for strength and security in the North Atlantic area. As is well known, the treaty constituting the European Defense Community is not as yet in effect. It is not necessary for me to dwell on the reasons why the EDC is urgently needed. However, I am convinced that the Europeans who must decide on this essential next step toward building a European community are fully aware of what is at stake and will in the near future reach their decisions.

NATO is engaged in a reappraisal of strategy and tactics to reflect the prospective availability of atomic and other new weapons. These studies, to be meaningful, require the dissemination of certain information regarding atomic weapons to NATO commanders. This will have a significant impact on NATO planning and provide a greater measure of security for all. I shall recommend that the Congress amend the Atomic Energy Act to permit us to disseminate classified information to our allies with regard to the tactical use of atomic weapons. This, of course, would be accomplished under stringent security regulations. It is essential that action on this matter be taken by the Congress during the current session.

In Indochina, where the French Union and Associated States forces are holding back Communist efforts to expand into the free areas of Asia, the United States is making a major contribution by providing military equipment and other military support. The amount as well as the timeliness of this military assistance will be an important factor in improving the situation. Additional native forces must be trained and equipped to preserve the defensive strength of Indochina. This assistance is required to enable these gallant forces to sustain an offensive that will provide the opportunity for victory.

We have helped the Chinese Nationalist forces to strengthen the defense of the Island of Formosa. This assistance will be continued as will assistance to other countries of the free world such as the Philippines, Thailand, and some of the American Republics.

The mutual military program, like our domestic military program, is now designed to build strength for the long pull rather than meet a given target date. Accordingly, we will concentrate on helping equip forces which our allies can themselves support over a long period of time, with minimum dependence upon aid from the United States. We have succeeded in substantially reducing the need for additional funds in fiscal year 1955 compared to previous years.

Our mutual security program continues in two related parts—the economic and technical program is much smaller in amount than the mutual military program and is discussed in a later section under international affairs. In that section is a comparative summary of the combined program.

Development and control of atomic energy.—In my speech before the United Nations on December 8, 1953, I made proposals looking toward a resolution of the atomic danger which threatens the world. My budgetary recommendations for the program of the Atomic Energy Commission for the fiscal year 1955 contemplate both new efforts to advance peacetime applications of atomic energy and also additional production of fissionable materials. All men of good will hope that these fissionable materials, which can be used both for peace and for military defense, will ultimately be used solely for peace and the benefit of all mankind.

Under the recommendations in this budget, expenditures of the Atomic Energy Commission will rise in the fiscal year 1955 to the highest point in our history. Operating costs will rise significantly as newly completed plants are brought into production. Capital expenditures will continue at a high level as construction goes forward on major new plants authorized in recent years. New obligational authority recommended in 1955 is above that provided in 1954, because of the expansion in operations. Initiation of new construction projects will be at a lower level than in recent years, and they will be limited essentially to facilities directly related to the production program and to several urgently needed research and development facilities. In all areas of activity the Commission is making strenuous efforts to effect economies; results are being accomplished in the reduction of unit costs.

The increase in expenditures for operations from 912 million dollars in the fiscal year 1954 to 1,182 million dollars in 1955 is due primarily to expanded operations at the Commission's facilities at Oak Ridge, Paducah, Portsmouth, Hanford, and Savannah River, as plants are completed and placed in operation. To meet the greater requirements for raw materials for this enlarged productive capacity, increased amounts of uranium ores and concentrates will be purchased. Due to vigorous efforts in recent years to expand our sources of supply in this country and abroad, increased amounts are now being made available to match the increase in requirements.

Atomic reactor development will be focused particularly upon the development of industrial atomic power for peacetime uses. The Commission will move forward on the construction of a large atomic power reactor to be initiated in the fiscal year 1954, marking a significant advance in the technology of peacetime atomic power. Research and development, including construction of experimental facilities, will continue also on several other types of reactors which show promise of ultimately producing power at economic rates.

The launching—this month—of the first atomic submarine, the U. S. S. *Nautilus*, will be followed in the fiscal year 1955 by the launching of the U. S. S. *Seawolf*, a second atomic submarine of different design. Research on the more difficult problems of aircraft propulsion by atomic energy will continue.

With the advent of various technical developments relating to atomic power and with the greater availability of raw materials and fissionable materials, the time has arrived for modification of the existing atomic energy legislation to encourage wider participation by private industry and by other public and private groups in this country in the development of this new and uniquely attractive energy source for peaceful purposes. Such widespread participation will be a stimulating and leavening force in this important field and will be consistent with the best traditions of American industrial development. The congressional Joint Committee on Atomic Energy last summer held public hearings which have served a most useful purpose of identifying and developing both the problems and the opportunities which emerge as preparations are made to depart from the Federal Government's existing monopoly in this field. Legislation is being recommended to the Congress which would encourage such participation and yet retain in the Federal Government the necessary controls over this awesome force.

Further amendment of the Atomic Energy Act is needed also to enable us to realize the full value of our atomic energy development for the defense of the free world. I shall recommend amendments which would permit, with adequate safeguards, a greater degree of exchange of classified information with our allies, in order to strengthen their military defenses—as already mentioned—and to enable them to participate more fully in the development of atomic power for peacetime purposes. I shall recommend also an amendment which would permit the transfer of fissionable material to friendly nations to assist them in peacetime atomic power development, particularly those nations which are supplying us with uranium raw materials. This proposed amendment, as well as the previously mentioned amendment, will provide adequate safeguards for the security of the United States. These legislative recommendations are independent of my recent proposal for the establishment of an international agency to advance the peacetime benefits of atomic energy, for which additional legislation would be needed.

It is now feasible to plan to terminate Federal ownership and operation of the towns of Oak Ridge, Tennessee, and Richland, Washington. To enable the citizens of these communities to manage their own affairs in a more normal fashion, legislation will be recommended which would permit them to purchase their own homes and to establish self-government in these communities.

Stockpiling of strategic and critical materials.—Considerable progress has been made in the fulfillment of the national stockpile goals, and further substantial progress is expected during the fiscal year 1955. By the end of 1955 about 50 of the 73 materials objectives will be virtually completed. Consequently, expenditures will decline sharply from 919 million dollars in 1953 to 770 million dollars in 1954 and 585 million dollars in 1955. The total value of all stockpile objectives is estimated at 7.2 billion dollars, of which about 5.5 billion will be on hand by June 30, 1955, to meet industrial and mobilization requirements in times of emergency. In addition to these direct expenditures from stockpile appropriations, the borrowing authority provided under the Defense Production Act, discussed in the finance, commerce, and industry section of this message, is used primarily for expanding the supply of critical materials. Net expenditures under this authority are estimated at 381 million dollars in the fiscal year 1954 and 308 million dollars in 1955. Therefore, a total of nearly 900 million dollars will be spent in the fiscal year 1955 to assure an adequate supply of critical materials in the event of an emergency.

VETERANS' SERVICES AND BENEFITS

Since 1940 the number of veterans has risen nearly fivefold and it is still increasing rapidly as men are discharged from the Armed Forces. There are now more than 20 million veterans, who, with their families, constitute 40 percent of our people. Over 300 laws provide a variety of special benefits and services to this large segment of our population.

It is our firm obligation to help our veterans overcome the handicaps which they incurred in the service of the Nation so they can return to their normal civilian pursuits. We must first of all do what we can to ease the burdens of veterans disabled in service and the families of those who have died from service causes. This is our primary responsibility, and generous benefits to them are the core of our veterans' programs.

Secondly, we must make available readjustment aids through well-conceived and properly administered programs for those veterans discharged after service during national emergencies.

Finally, we must remember that the best way to help our millions of veterans is by making it possible for them to share fully in the economic

VETERANS' SERVICES AND BENEFITS

[Fiscal years. In millions]

Program or agency	Expenditures 1953 actual	Expenditures 1954 estimated	Expenditures 1955 estimated	Recommended new obligational authority for 1955
Gross expenditures:				
Readjustment benefits:				
Education and training..................	$659	$473	$554	$350
Loan guaranty and other benefits (Veterans Administration).....................	112	89	37	37
Unemployment compensation (Labor Department)...........................	26	40	61	56
Compensation and pensions................	2,420	2,485	2,535	2,535
Insurance and servicemen's indemnities......	102	105	75	72
Hospitals and medical care:				
Current expenses........................	657	693	694	689
Hospital construction....................	100	84	60	44
Other services and administration (Veterans Administration and other)..............	251	221	207	176
Total............................	4,327	4,190	4,223	[1] 3,959
Deduct applicable receipts:				
Insurance programs (Veterans Administration).....................................	1	2	3	....
Other services and administration (Veterans Administration, primarily canteen services)...................................	28	28	28	....
Net budget expenditures...................	4,298	4,160	4,192	....

[1] Compares with new obligational authority of 4,132 million dollars in 1953 and 4,229 million dollars in 1954.

and social gains of our country. This means assuring them adequate job opportunities. It also means assuring them, both during and after military service, of the same protection under the broad social-security programs that is provided for nonveterans. Progress in achieving these objectives will lessen the need for pensions and other special benefits for the vast majority of veterans who, fortunately, did not incur disabilities during their service.

The appropriations recommended in this budget will enable the Government to discharge fully our obligations to veterans in the coming fiscal year. Funds are included to provide for all essential benefits and services, in some cases exceeding the amounts spent in any previous year. At the same time allowance has been made for anticipated savings from improvements in efficiency, resulting in part from a general reorganization of the Veterans Administration.

Readjustment benefits.—Education and training and loan guaranty benefits are provided for veterans of World War II and the current emergency. In addition, special vocational rehabilitation assistance is provided for service-disabled veterans of both periods, and unemployment compensation is available to veterans of the Korean conflict.

Expenditures of 652 million dollars for all readjustment benefits in the fiscal year 1955 are estimated to be about 8 percent higher than in the current year. While expenditures for benefits to veterans of the Korean conflict are increasing, outlays for education and training, rehabilitation, and loan guaranty benefits to World War II veterans are declining. Thus, the proportion of total outlays for all readjustment benefits going to veterans of the Korean conflict is expected to rise from about one-half to about four-fifths in the one year.

During the fiscal year 1955 an average enrollment of 537,000 veterans—more than 30,000 above the previous year—is expected in school, job, and farm training courses. Of this number, an estimated 412,000 are veterans of the Korean conflict.

A decline in expenditures for loan guaranty and other benefits from 1953 to 1955 reflects the discontinuance of payment by the Government of a gratuity up to 160 dollars on each guaranteed loan issued after September 1, 1953.

Unemployment compensation payments to veterans will increase. This is the result of the growth in the number of eligible veterans.

While existing legislation was intended to provide benefits during the transition period after discharge, it does not include a limit on the time during which veterans may apply for unemployment compensation. I recommend that the law be changed to provide for a time limit for filing claims after discharge. This should provide reasonable time for veterans to make their readjustment to civilian life and to establish benefit rights under the general unemployment compensation program. Limits are now provided in the Servicemen's Readjustment Assistance Act for other benefits.

Compensation and pensions.—The estimated expenditures of 2.5 billion dollars will provide for compensation and pension benefits to an average of 3.3 million individuals and families. This total includes nearly 1.8 billion dollars in compensation payments to service-disabled veterans and families of those veterans who have died from service-connected causes, and 700 million dollars for non-service-connected pensions. It also includes 45 million dollars for subsistence payments to an average of 20,000 disabled veterans in the vocational rehabilitation program and for 115,000 burial awards.

Expenditures for compensation and pensions have increased sharply in the last decade, and the long-run outlook on the basis of present laws and veteran population is that these expenditures will rise to double their present annual amount within several decades. At the same time, a large proportion of the present or potential recipients of these benefits will also qualify for payments under the Government's old-age and survivors insurance program.

While the conditions under which veterans are entitled to compensation and pension benefits are largely specified by law, the Administrator of Veterans' Affairs necessarily has important responsibilities for their administration, and the budget estimates for the fiscal year 1955 assume additional efforts to prevent unsound practices and abuses.

Insurance and servicemen's indemnities.—The Government reimburses the veterans' insurance trust funds for payments made for deaths traceable to war hazards in the case of policyholders under the national service life insurance contracts issued mostly to World War II veterans and under the United States Government life insurance policies issued to veterans of earlier periods. The Government also pays certain other insurance benefits directly to policyholders. Insurance payments are expected to decline from 84 million dollars in the fiscal year 1954 to 45 million dollars in 1955.

Since the enactment of the Servicemen's Indemnity Act of 1951 as a substitute for a Government life insurance program, the families of servicemen who die on duty or within 120 days after separation are paid benefits at the rate of $92.90 a month for 10 years. These payments are expected to increase 41 percent from the 1954 level to 30 million dollars in 1955.

Hospital and medical care.—The estimates for current expenses of the veterans' hospital and medical programs will provide for an average of 110,200 patients in Veterans Administration and contract hospitals and 25,700 members in Veterans Administration and State domiciliary facilities during the fiscal year 1955. The cost of caring for the increase of about 2 percent in the hospital load compared to the level now estimated for 1954 is offset, however, by lower amounts for the medical and dental outpatient care programs. The lower estimates for the dental outpatient care program are based primarily upon the recommendation that the Congress extend for 1955 the language enacted for the fiscal year 1954 in Public Law 149, 83d Congress, limiting dental treatment for noncompensable disabilities to those cases for which application for treatment is made within one year of discharge.

The budget includes recommended new obligational authority of 44 million dollars for new construction and improvements, including 30 million dollars to complete new hospitals at San Francisco and Topeka, toward which the Congress made an initial appropriation for the fiscal year 1954.

I am recommending increased appropriations to provide for an average employment in the Veterans Administration medical and hospital programs of 136,000 during the fiscal year 1955, an increase of 10,500 from average employment in 1953 and 3,000 more than in the current year. This increase provides for operation of the new hospital facilities which have been constructed.

Other services and administration.—General administrative expenses of the Veterans Administration are estimated to decline further in the coming year as the result of declining workloads for readjustment of World War II veterans as well as improved performance resulting from better organization and greater efficiency. Average employment of 35,600 in Veterans Administration nonmedical programs is estimated for 1955, 11 percent below employment in the current year and 17 percent less than in 1953.

Trust funds.——Under the United States Government life insurance and national service life insurance trust funds, nearly 7 million policies continue in force, carrying 44 billion dollars of life insurance issued before enactment of the Servicemen's Indemnity Act of 1951. The receipts of these funds now roughly balance their disbursements. The transactions of these, as of other, trust funds are not included in the budget totals.

VETERANS' LIFE INSURANCE FUNDS

(Trust funds)

[Fiscal years. In millions]

Item	1953 *actual*	1954 *estimated*	1955 *estimated*
Receipts:			
Transfers from general and special accounts......	$84	$75	$36
Interest on investments........................	200	208	208
Premiums and other..........................	427	522	485
Total....................................	711	805	729
Expenditures:			
Dividends to policyholders.....................	190	297	217
Benefits and other...........................	470	533	524
Total....................................	660	830	741
Net accumulation (+) or withdrawal (−).......	+51	−25	−12
Balance in funds at close of year..............	6,613	6,588	6,576

INTERNATIONAL AFFAIRS AND FINANCE

My budget recommendations for the international programs of the Government will enable us to hold our newly won initiative in world affairs and move toward a lasting peace. The budget for international affairs and finance includes funds required for the conduct of our foreign affairs, for the programs for economic and technical development abroad, and for our foreign information and exchange program.

The mutual military program, which was formerly included in the budget along with these programs under the heading "International security and foreign relations" has been discussed in this budget message as part of the national security program. At the same time, military assistance is intimately related to and must be administered in the furtherance of our foreign policy.

The extent of our assistance under both the mutual military program and mutual economic and technical program is shown in a summary table below. This table covers all components of the present mutual security program. This entire program is directed toward the establishment of conditions overseas which, in one way or another, contribute to our own security and well-being.

MUTUAL SECURITY PROGRAMS, MILITARY AND ECONOMIC

[Fiscal years. In millions]

	1953 *actual*	1954 *estimated*	1955 *recommended or estimated*
Expenditures:			
Mutual military program.....................	$3, 954	$4, 200	$4, 275
Mutual economic and technical program.........	1, 702	1, 300	1, 125
Total....................................	5, 656	5, 500	5, 400
New obligational authority:			
Mutual military program [1].....................	4, 236	3, 800	2, 500
Mutual economic and technical program [2]........	1, 907	926	1, 010
Total....................................	6, 143	4, 726	3, 510

[1] Does not include reappropriations of $321 million for 1953 and $1,763 million for 1954.
[2] Does not include reappropriations of $128 million for 1953 and $179 million for 1954.

Our national security and international programs are designed to deter would-be aggressors against the United States and other nations of the free world, and to strengthen our efforts for peace by all appropriate means including diplomatic negotiations with the Soviets. With a position of strength, an effective conduct of our foreign relations by the Department of State is the keystone of our efforts to win our way to peace. There has never been a time when the future security and welfare of our country were more dependent upon the exercise of wise leadership in the realm of world affairs. My recommendation for funds for the Department of State will enable it to meet this challenge.

Some countries are still facing such economic conditions that they are not able solely by their own efforts to support the desired military effort or to provide for the economic growth and progress essential to our mutual objectives. It is thus still necessary that supplementary goods, services, and technical skills be provided by the United States. It is for these purposes that funds for economic and technical development are requested for fiscal year 1955.

Through our information and exchange program we are attempting to achieve a clear understanding by others of our aims, objectives, and way of life and a better understanding by us of the aspirations and cultures of other countries. Such mutual understanding increases our ability to exercise strong, sympathetic, and cooperative leadership in the mutual efforts of free peoples to achieve their common goals.

INTERNATIONAL AFFAIRS AND FINANCE

[Fiscal years. In millions]

Program	Gross expenditures			Net expenditures			Recommended new obligational authority for 1955
	1953 actual	1954 estimated	1955 estimated	1953 actual	1954 estimated	1955 estimated	
Conduct of foreign affairs...	$150	$129	$125	$150	$129	$125	$116
Economic and technical development:							
Present program [1]	2,396	1,943	1,105	1,960	1,555	658	15
Proposed legislation	....	....	370	....	....	370	1,010
Surplus agricultural commodities disposal (proposed legislation)	....	....	....	....	....	....	300
Foreign information and exchange activities	106	95	97	106	95	97	105
Total	2,652	2,167	1,697	2,216	1,779	1,250	1,546

[1] Gross expenditures exclude private bank loans guaranteed by the Export-Import Bank and net repayments thereof in the amounts of 4 million dollars in 1953, 82 million dollars in 1954, and 188 million dollars in 1955.

During the past year progress has been made toward the accomplishment of the objectives of our international programs. Not only have our allies and friends grown in military strength, but also a continued high level of production and increased gold and dollar reserves have permitted European countries to become more nearly self-supporting. This improvement makes it possible for estimates of expenditures for economic and technical programs included in this budget to be significantly lower than the already reduced level of the fiscal year 1954. Significant contributory factors in this progress have been our assistance in past years and the positive and constructive fiscal and other economic measures which have been taken by the other countries themselves. As a result the fiscal year 1955 represents, in a sense, a period of transition from heavy dependence by a large number of countries upon massive bilateral economic assistance from the United States to the use of such assistance in more limited circumstances. Progress in such a transition will generally depend upon the extent to which our own policies, and those of our friends, contribute to increased private investment, increased exports to the United States, internal financial and economic reforms in some countries, and multilateral cooperation for the achievement of strong and self-supporting economies.

Conduct of foreign affairs.—The burden of the vastly enlarged responsibility involved in our international affairs falls heavily upon the Department of State since the Secretary of State is the officer responsible, under the President, for the development and control of all foreign policy and for the conduct of our relations with foreign governments and international agencies. Successful discharge of this broad responsibility calls for wise and informed diplomatic support to our national leaders in negotiations carried on at the highest levels as at Bermuda and Berlin. It requires the day-to-day representation of our national interest through some 273 diplomatic missions and consular offices abroad. We also must continue to give our firm support to the United Nations and other international organizations, and bear a part of the costs of these organizations and their programs. A successful administration of our foreign policy requires the State Department to report and appraise political, economic, and social conditions and trends abroad; to provide foreign policy guidance to all agencies carrying on programs overseas; and to coordinate in the field all foreign policy aspects of overseas programs. Finally, advice must be furnished as to the foreign policy implications of domestic programs.

Net budget expenditures for the conduct of foreign affairs in the fiscal year 1955 are estimated at 125 million dollars. This expenditure represents a decrease of 4 million dollars from 1954, resulting from reduction of personnel and other costs of the Department of State including the curtailment of civilian occupation activities in Germany.

Economic and technical development.—Net budget expenditures for economic and technical development in the fiscal year 1955 are estimated at 1,028 million dollars, compared with 1,555 million dollars in the fiscal year 1954 and 1,960 million dollars in 1953.

This budget, as did the fiscal year 1954 budget, reflects proportionately greater emphasis on programs in Asia, Africa, and Latin America. It contemplates new appropriations for aid to very few European countries.

In the Far East there is a need for contributions to provide for relief in Korea and, now that hostilities have been terminated, for an expanded reconstruction program for that war-devastated country. Funds are also recommended to maintain the strength and security of Formosa and to support further the effort of our friends combating Communist aggression in Indochina. This budget also provides for technical assistance and economic development in India, Pakistan, the Philippines, and other nations of Asia to encourage continued progress in their efforts to improve the living conditions of their people.

With respect to the Near East the budget provides for helping relieve the plight of Arab refugees through contributions to the United Nations refugee agency, and for technical assistance and supplementary economic development in the Arab States, Israel, and Iran.

Provision is also made in the budget for continuing the technical assistance program for Latin America. This program, which has existed for a number of years, contributes to a reduction of social and economic problems upon which communism feeds and which hampers the development of stable and growing economies.

Surplus agricultural commodities.—I plan to request authority soon to use a part of our accumulated surpluses of agricultural products to assist in strengthening the economies of friendly countries, and otherwise to contribute to the accomplishment of our foreign policy objectives. Authority will be requested to use for this purpose over a 3-year period up to 1 billion dollars worth of commodities held by the Commodity Credit Corporation. This budget anticipates a request for a supplemental appropriation of 300 million dollars for the fiscal year 1955 to reimburse that Corporation for commodities used.

This program for use of agricultural surpluses is designed to complement our general program of economic and technical development and must be closely coordinated with it. The program for use of surplus agricultural commodities involves the use of stocks held by the Commodity Credit Corporation. No additional budget expenditures will be required for these commodities.

139

It should be emphasized in connection with this program that it is purely temporary, predicated upon adoption of our domestic agricultural program which should not involve the continued accumulation of large surpluses. Special safeguards will be provided which will require that commodities furnished must be in addition to amounts which otherwise would have been imported and must not displace the usual marketings of the United States and friendly countries.

Foreign information and exchange activities.—This budget includes expenditures of 97 million dollars for foreign information and exchange activities, including those functions conducted by the new United States Information Agency. This is an increase of 2 million dollars over the expenditures for foreign information and exchange programs in the fiscal year 1954.

In October, on the advice of the National Security Council, I directed the United States Information Agency to develop programs which would show the peoples of other nations that the objectives and policies of the United States will advance their legitimate aspirations for freedom, progress, and peace. I believe that if the peoples of the world know our objectives and policies, they will join with us in the common effort to resist the threat of Communist imperialism and to achieve our mutual goals. It is essential that the United States Information Agency have the tools to carry out this mission.

The United States Information Agency will reach 77 free countries through radio, press, motion pictures, or information centers and will reach 10 Iron Curtain countries through radio broadcasts.

My budget recommendations for information and exchange activities include 15 million dollars of new obligational authority for educational exchange programs. These programs are designed to promote a receptive climate of public opinion overseas through the exchange between the United States and over 70 foreign countries of students and persons who are leaders important to the present or future of their nations.

SOCIAL SECURITY, WELFARE, AND HEALTH

I believe that, along with the essentials of protecting the freedom of our people and maintaining a strong and growing economy, we must make greater and more successful efforts than we have made in the past to strengthen social security and improve the health of our citizens. In so doing, we build for the future, and we prove to the watching world that a free Nation can and will find the means, despite the tensions of these times, to progress toward a better society.

The keystone of our social security program today is the system of old-age and survivors insurance, under which nearly 70 million people are insured and 6 million people are presently receiving benefits. The economic protection afforded by this social insurance is now accepted as basic in our society. Yet there are serious defects in the system. In my recent social security message, I submitted specific recommendations to remedy these defects.

The legislation to improve old-age and survivors insurance will not directly affect the budget totals, since this program is financed through

SOCIAL SECURITY, WELFARE, AND HEALTH

[Fiscal years. In millions]

Program or agency	Expenditures			Recommended new obligational authority for 1955
	1953 actual	1954 estimated	1955 estimated	
Gross expenditures:				
Public assistance:				
Present program	$1,332	$1,391	$1,187	$1,202
Proposed legislation	......	......	108	108
Promotion of public health:				
Present program	316	289	281	234
Proposed legislation	......	......	7	89
Aid to special groups:				
Vocational rehabilitation:				
Present program	25	25	21	21
Proposed legislation	......	......	8	9
School lunch	83	83	68	68
Indian welfare and other	48	51	54	54
Accident compensation	43	42	43	43
Prisons and probation	29	27	28	29
Retirement and dependents insurance (Railroad Retirement Board)	33	35	......	....
Defense community facilities and services	1	4	2	....
Total	1,910	1,947	1,807	[2] 1,857
Deduct applicable receipts	([1])	([1])	([1])	....
Net budget expenditures	1,910	1,947	1,807	....

[1] Less than 500,000 dollars.

[2] Compares with new obligational authority of 1,886 million dollars in 1953 and 1,919 million dollars in 1954.

payroll taxes which go into a trust fund, and the expenditures are made from the fund rather than from the general budget accounts. However, the legislation should lessen the need for expenditures from the general budget accounts to help the States pay public assistance to the needy aged and to dependent children, as old-age and survivors insurance takes over a larger and larger role in providing them with basic protection.

To reflect this development, legislation is being prepared to reduce Federal grants to States for old-age assistance as old-age and survivors insurance continues to take over an increasing share of the load. My social security message has set forth these recommendations in more detail.

This administration flatly opposes the socialization of medicine. Under the traditional American approach, private and nonprofit medical and hospital insurance programs have grown steadily and now cover a large segment of the population. Yet there is still a long way to go. Many families are not protected; many health costs are not insured. Positive action to promote the health of all our people has been recommended in my recent message.

The budget estimates for the fiscal year 1955 provide for the costs of the proposed legislation to improve the health of the people and also for the improvements and expansion of vocational rehabilitation services for the disabled. Experience has proved that these efforts pay for themselves many times over.

Including the proposed legislation, net budget expenditures for social security, welfare, and health in the fiscal year 1955 are estimated at 1,807 million dollars. This is 140 million dollars less than estimated expenditures in 1954. The decline results mainly from an expected reduction in public assistance grants to the States.

Public assistance.—Under present law the Federal Government contributes, according to a statutory formula, to State expenditures for assistance payments to four groups of people in need—dependent children, the aged, the blind, and the totally disabled. With the expansion of the social security program, it is now feasible to recommend a new formula for public assistance grants which will more adequately recognize the varying financial needs of the several States and the appropriate role of the Federal Government in meeting these needs. The legislation which I am recommending would provide for a permanent formula to replace the present temporary increase in the Federal share which expires next

September 30. This new formula includes specific provision for a related reduction in Federal grants to States for old-age assistance as the improved old-age and survivors insurance program takes over an increasing share of the load. A transition period for adjusting both Federal and State procedures will be necessary.

The decrease of nearly 100 million dollars in estimated expenditures for public assistance is made possible primarily by the proposed improvement in old-age and survivors insurance, which will reduce the need for supplementation by public assistance.

Promotion of public health.—The budget provides for initiating our new program to help assure adequate medical and hospital services. The main elements of this program are:

1. Establishment of a limited reinsurance service to encourage private and nonprofit health insurance organizations to offer broader health protection to more families on a basis which would reinsure the special additional risks through premiums modeled on sound insurance principles. The capital for this program will be provided initially by the Federal Government and repaid from fees.

2. A broadening of the present Federal grant-in-aid program for hospital construction to stimulate provision of diagnostic and treatment centers, rehabilitation facilities, nursing homes, and additional chronic disease hospitals, and to help finance State surveys of their needs for such facilities.

The new program is estimated to require new obligational authority of 89 million dollars for the fiscal year 1955, of which 7 million dollars would be spent in that year.

Budget expenditures for all public health programs under existing legislation, excluding medical care for military personnel and veterans, are estimated at 281 million dollars in the fiscal year 1955. About one-half of this amount will be for grants to universities and medical schools for medical research and training, for clinical and laboratory research conducted by the Federal Government, and for operation of the Public Health Service hospitals. The Public Health Service hospitals primarily furnish hospital and medical care to American merchant seamen. The budget provides funds to continue these special services while the Department of Health, Education, and Welfare has this program under review.

Other expenditures will be for grants-in-aid to State governments and local communities for hospital construction, general health services, maternal and child health, and the control of specific diseases, such as tuberculosis, cancer, mental illness, and heart ailments. With the major communicable diseases, including tuberculosis and venereal diseases, diminishing in importance as public health problems, greater emphasis is being given to the chronic diseases which are becoming more prevalent.

Vocational rehabilitation program.—The estimate for the present program of vocational rehabilitation reflects congressional action, taken in the 1954 appropriation act, to require that a larger portion of the program be financed by the States. To revitalize the vocational rehabilitation program, I have recommended that we redefine our objectives so as to make possible a substantial increase in the number of persons rehabilitated.

School lunch program.—Budget expenditures shown for the school lunch program for fiscal years prior to 1955 include funds for the purchase of commodities for distribution to the States, as well as for cash payments to the States. The amount recommended for 1955 will maintain cash payments to the States at the same level as in 1954. In addition, it is expected that larger Federal contributions of surplus agricultural commodities will be made to the program. These contributions are financed from a permanent appropriation to the Department of Agriculture. As a result, total Federal aid for the school lunch program, including cash payments and surplus foods distributed under the program for the children are estimated at 218 million dollars in the fiscal year 1955 compared with 206 million dollars in 1954.

Railroad retirement.—As described earlier, the railroad retirement program is reported in this Budget in the same manner as the old-age and survivors insurance program and appears in the tables on that basis. The change does not affect the budget deficit.

Trust funds.—The old-age and survivors insurance system is operated through a trust fund, which receives the payroll contributions and pays the benefits and administrative expenses. The tax rate rose to 2 percent each on employers and employees, effective January 1, 1954. My proposals for expanding and improving the program will raise receipts by an estimated 100 million dollars, benefit disbursements by 400 million dollars, and administrative expense by 8 million dollars in the fiscal year 1955.

SOCIAL SECURITY, WELFARE, AND HEALTH

(Trust funds)

[Fiscal years. In millions]

Fund and item	1953 actual	1954 estimated	1955 estimated
Federal old-age and survivors insurance trust fund:			
Receipts:			
Present program:			
Appropriation from general receipts..........	$4,086	$4,600	$5,369
Deposits by States.........................	44	100	135
Interest and other.........................	387	442	477
Proposed legislation.........................	....	....	100
Payments of benefits, construction, and administrative expenses, and tax refunds:			
Present program............................	−2,748	−3,368	−3,809
Proposed legislation.........................	....	....	−408
Net accumulation.........................	1,769	1,774	1,864
Balance in fund at close of year................	18,364	20,138	22,002
Railroad retirement fund:			
Receipts:			
Appropriation from general receipts...........	658	675	640
Interest on investments.....................	89	98	105
Payments of benefits, salaries, and expenses.......	−465	−490	−513
Net accumulation..........................	282	283	232
Balance in fund at close of year................	3,183	3,466	3,698
Federal employees' retirement funds:			
Receipts:			
Employee contributions.....................	425	427	427
Transfer from budget accounts and other.......	321	31	30
Interest....................................	215	227	236
Payments of annuities and refunds, and expenses..	−363	−421	−448
Net accumulation..........................	598	264	245
Balance in funds at close of year..............	5,652	5,916	6,161

The Government also operates separate retirement programs for railroad workers, mentioned above, and for Federal civilian employees.

HOUSING AND COMMUNITY DEVELOPMENT

Good housing and the development of adequate community facilities are essential to the welfare of our people and to the stability and growth of our economy. Over the years the Federal Government has undertaken a wide variety of programs to assist our citizens in obtaining better housing. These programs, however, have been designed in the main to meet short-run emergencies or they have been developed piecemeal without a clear underlying policy. As a result, housing laws have become a patchwork which only experts can understand. Excessive reliance has been placed on direct participation by the Federal Government in areas where, properly encouraged, local governments or private enterprise could have carried a larger share of the total responsibility. Different Federal programs have too often worked at cross-purposes, resulting in heavy expense without commensurate gains. In some instances, they have aggravated inflationary price increases instead of working toward lower housing cost for the ultimate consumer. Finally, the weaknesses in the organization of Federal housing activities have prevented us from realizing the full potentialities of present programs.

At my request, the Advisory Committee on Housing Policies and Programs, under the chairmanship of the Housing Administrator, has intensively examined all Federal housing activities. After consideration of its report and the Administrator's recommendations, I am proposing a series of changes which have three important objectives: First, they would reorient existing programs to emphasize the initiative of private enterprise and the role of local governments. Second, they would fill important gaps in the present housing program and at the same time eliminate numerous unnecessary and obsolete activities. Third, they would strengthen the administration of these programs to assure the most economical and effective use of Federal funds in improving the housing conditions of the Nation.

To carry out these proposals I shall recommend major changes in legislative authority. I shall also submit a reorganization plan which will permit a more logical grouping of operating programs and give the Housing Administrator appropriate authority to supervise these programs and to determine major policies. Pending final decision on important details, estimates for these proposals are not specifically set forth in this budget. However, they will not have a significant effect on the Federal budget in the fiscal year 1955.

Most housing and community development programs involve both expenditures and receipts. In the fiscal year 1955 gross expenditures will total an estimated 1,903 million dollars, but receipts will exceed these expenditures by 277 million dollars. These net receipts compare with

HOUSING AND COMMUNITY DEVELOPMENT

[Fiscal years. In millions]

Program or agency	Gross expenditures			Net expenditures			Recommended new obligational authority for 1955
	1953 actual	1954 estimated	1955 estimated	1953 actual	1954 estimated	1955 estimated	
Urban development and redevelopment............	$25	$68	$97	$21	$38	$48	....
Aids to private housing:							
Housing and Home Finance Agency:							
Federal Housing Administration.............	124	118	94	−43	−30	−69	....
Federal National Mortgage Association......	645	590	488	379	62	−166	....
Other..............	15	16	4	−25	−38	−28	$4
Veterans' housing loans (Veterans Administration)...............	92	109	84	70	78	44	....
Treasury (Reconstruction Finance Corporation)...	.....	.....	.....	−6	−50	−11	....
Farm housing (Department of Agriculture).........	19	17	.....	19	17	.....	....
Public Housing programs...	1,027	1,222	956	1	−220	−234	77
General housing aids:							
Housing and Home Finance Agency:							
College housing loans...	14	37	62	14	36	58	....
Other..............	5	3	3	5	3	3	3
Provision of community facilities:							
Present programs........	31	53	34	23	43	3	6
Proposed advances for public works planning...	.....	.....	3	.....	.....	3	....
Defense housing..........	28	31	1	28	31	1	....
Civil defense.............	78	76	70	51	74	68	86
Disaster loans and relief....	15	17	7	12	13	3	....
Total...............	2,118	2,357	1,903	549	57	−277	¹176

¹ Compares with new obligational authority of 1,526 million dollars in 1953 and 628 million dollars in 1954.

net expenditures of 549 million dollars in 1953 and the revised estimate of net expenditures of 57 million dollars in 1954. The great improvement in the fiscal outlook over the 2 years reflects mainly the fact that purchases of mortgages by the Federal National Mortgage Association are declining and sales are rising. Increased private financing for the public housing program is also reducing the need for Federal outlays.

Urban development and redevelopment.—Too many families in our cities today are living in substandard housing in deteriorating and slum neighborhoods. Since 1949 the Federal Government has been providing loans and grants to local governments for clearance and redevelopment of slum areas. Most local projects approved for Federal assistance are still in the planning stage, but by the end of the fiscal year 1955, clearance and redevelopment operations will be completed or underway for 180 projects, compared to 43 projects begun by June 30, 1953. Net expenditures in 1955 are estimated to rise to 48 million dollars, of which 39 million dollars represents grants to local communities to cover two-thirds of the net cost of projects which they have completed, or on which they have made substantial progress.

This acceleration is encouraging, but clearing slums provides only a partial answer. Effective progress in redeveloping our cities will require (1) enlistment of greater local and private participation, (2) slum prevention as well as elimination, and (3) rehabilitation of rundown houses and neighborhoods. To help attain these objectives, I shall recommend legislation broadening the present program to authorize loans and grants for the conservation, rehabilitation, and renewal of neighborhood areas. Important changes should also be made in mortgage insurance authority of the Federal Housing Administration and in the low-rent public housing program, so that these programs can contribute more effectively to sound redevelopment. All of these aids should be fully coordinated and should be provided only in areas where the local community has adopted and is carrying out its part of an effective program to arrest urban decay.

Federal Housing Administration.—As one of the major Federal aids to private housing, the Government insures mortgage loans made to finance housing construction or purchase. In the fiscal year 1955 under existing programs the construction of an estimated 190,000 new homes and the purchase of 126,000 existing homes will be financed with the aid of mortgages insured by the Federal Housing Administration. Receipts from premium income and other sources will exceed expenditures by an estimated 69 million dollars.

To encourage the substitution of private financing for Federal outlays in the areas of greatest housing need, I shall urge the Congress to authorize two new mortgage insurance programs, as well as to liberalize certain existing programs. Specifically, the Federal Housing Administration should now be authorized to insure private credit used for the rehabilitation of obsolete neighborhoods. It should also be given authority, on an experimental basis, to insure mortgages with small down payments and with the balance payable over a long period, to finance inexpensive homes for lower income families, particularly families displaced by rehabilitation and slum-clearance programs. Additional authority should be provided to adjust down payments and maturities for insured mortgages to the extent consistent with overall economic policy. I shall also recommend simplification of the basic housing laws by the elimination of numerous inactive or unnecessary programs and by simplification of the structure and operations of the existing mortgage insurance funds. At the same time, measures will be recommended to strengthen the insurance funds.

Federal National Mortgage Association.—The Federal National Mortgage Association buys and sells mortgages insured by the Federal Housing Administration or guaranteed by the Veterans Administration. Gross expenditures are estimated at 488 million dollars in the fiscal year 1955, mainly for purchase of mortgages to finance military and defense housing under commitments made in earlier years. By 1955 the supply of private funds is expected to be adequate in most areas to provide financing for most other types of mortgages without Federal support.

The policy of this administration is to sell the mortgages now held by the Association as rapidly as the mortgage market permits. Assuming satisfactory market conditions, receipts from these sales and from other sources in 1955 will exceed expenditures by an estimated 166 million dollars. This contrasts with net expenditures of 379 million dollars in 1953, and 62 million dollars estimated for 1954.

The legislation which I shall propose would provide authority to establish, from time to time, maximum interest rates and other terms on insured and guaranteed mortgages with the objective of encouraging an adequate, but not excessive, supply of private mortgage funds for all parts of the country. This proposal would make unnecessary in the future large Government purchases of mortgages such as were required in the past, whenever interest rates made such mortgages unattractive to private lenders. I shall also recommend the initiation of a new program, financed in large part from private funds, to furnish many of the secondary market facilities now provided by the Federal National Mortgage Association.

Other aids to private housing.—Net expenditures for direct housing loans to veterans are estimated at 44 million dollars in the fiscal year 1955, compared with 78 million dollars in 1954. Sales of loans to private investors are expected to rise as a result of the recent increase in the rate of interest on these loans. Under existing law, disbursements will be made during 1955 only on loans for which commitments are made prior to the expiration of lending authority on June 30, 1954.

Authority for farm housing loans under title V of the Housing Act should be permitted to expire on June 30, 1954. Most of the essential needs can be met under other authorities and funds available to the Farmers' Home Administration.

The loans of three other programs will be substantially liquidated in the fiscal year 1954. These include mortgages held by the Reconstruction Finance Corporation, loans made by the Housing Administrator to the Alaska Housing Authority, and loans to various prefabricated housing manufacturers.

Public housing.—As already indicated, I shall propose a new mortgage insurance program and other measures to encourage provision of private housing for low-income families. If these proposals prove effective, the need for future construction of low-rent public housing will be reduced. As an interim measure, however, the present public housing program should be continued at the level considered necessary to meet the needs of low-income families, particularly those displaced by slum-clearance and urban rehabilitation activities. Accordingly, my recommendations for the fiscal year 1955 in this budget would authorize construction of approximately 35,000 low-rent public housing units by local housing authorities, with the assistance of Federal loans and annual contributions adequate to assure the low-rent character of these units.

An estimated 956 million dollars in temporary Federal loans and other expenditures will be necessary to finance the operations of the low-rent and other public housing programs during the fiscal year 1955. Receipts from private refinancing of local housing authority obligations and other sources are estimated to exceed these expenditures by 234 million dollars. All except 8 million dollars of the 77 million dollars in new obligational authority requested is for payment of annual contributions under contracts made in prior years.

College housing.—Under the Housing Act of 1950 the Housing Administrator makes direct loans repayable over 40 years to finance student and faculty housing at colleges and universities. Net expenditures for such loans in 1955 will rise to 58 million dollars, largely under commitments made in prior years. By June 30, 1955, over 200 loans will have been approved. These will finance construction of housing accommodations for about 50,000 students and faculty members. Wherever possible, private financing of these loans will be encouraged.

Provision of community facilities.—The sharp reduction in net expenditures for provision of community facilities reflects mainly liquidation by the Treasury of loans to public agencies which were originally made by the Reconstruction Finance Corporation. No appropriations are being requested at this time for new loans to public agencies.

To encourage State and local governments to prepare for possible future expansion in public works construction, I am recommending legislation to authorize Federal advances to them for planning future construction. If the authority is granted, I shall request a supplemental appropriation for the fiscal year 1954 of 10 million dollars, with estimated expenditures of 3 million dollars in 1955.

Civil defense.—Expenditures for civil defense are included in housing and community development because of their community aspects, but the program is discussed in this message under national security. Federal expenditures for civil defense are estimated at 68 million dollars in the fiscal year 1955.

EDUCATION AND GENERAL RESEARCH

The citizen in a democracy has the opportunity and the obligation to participate constructively in the affairs of his community and his Nation. To the extent that the educational system provides our citizens with the opportunity for study and learning, the wiser will their decisions be, and the more they can contribute to our way of life.

I do not underestimate the difficulties facing the States and communities in attempting to solve the problems created by the great increase in the number of children of school age, the shortage of qualified teachers, and the overcrowding of classrooms. The effort to overcome these difficulties strains the taxable resources of many communities. At the same time, I do not accept the simple remedy of Federal intervention.

It is my intention to call a national conference on education, composed of educators and interested citizens, to be held after preparatory conferences in the States. This conference will study the facts about the Nation's educational problems and recommend sensible solutions. We can then proceed with confidence on a constructive and effective long-range program. Pending the outcome of these conferences and the development of our educational program, the Federal Government is providing assistance to those communities where school needs have been greatly increased by the activities of the Federal Government.

Budget expenditures for education and general research activities in the fiscal year 1955 are estimated at 223 million dollars. This figure does

EDUCATION AND GENERAL RESEARCH

[Fiscal years. In millions]

Program or agency	Budget expenditures (net)			Recommended new obligational authority for 1955
	1953 actual	1954 estimated	1955 estimated	
Promotion of education:				
Office of Education:				
Assistance for school construction and operation in federally affected areas...........	$201	$199	$139	$99
Vocational education....................	25	26	25	25
Grants for colleges of agriculture and the mechanic arts........................	5	5	5	5
Educational conference and other proposed legislation............................	......	1	1	(¹)
Other................................	3	3	3	3
Educational aid to special groups.............	7	7	7	9
Library and museum services................	11	12	12	12
General-purpose research:				
National Science Foundation..............	4	7	12	14
Bureau of the Census....................	13	9	10	10
National Bureau of Standards..............	8	9	9	8
Total.................................	277	278	223	² 185

¹ Less than 500,000 dollars.

² Compares with new obligational authority of 328 million dollars in 1953 and 217 million dollars in 1954.

not include amounts spent for education and research in connection with the military, veterans', atomic energy, and certain other programs— which are classified in other sections of the budget.

Sixty-two percent of the expenditures for education and general research in the fiscal year 1955 will be for grants to those local school districts that have been burdened by Federal activities. Another 13 percent will be for grants to States to help support their vocational education programs and their land-grant colleges. The Federal Government also assists Howard University and educational institutions for the deaf and blind, and it maintains major library and museum services at the National Capital. Expenditures shown for general-purpose research are for programs of the Census Bureau, the National Bureau of Standards, and the National Science Foundation.

Promotion of education.—Responsibility for education in the United States belongs to the State and local governments. The Federal Government has for many years provided financial assistance for land-grant colleges and some other educational activities. The Office of Education also disseminates information on educational trends and good practices. In recent years, the problems of education have been increasing in severity while this service has been reduced. My budget recommendations provide for an expansion of this basic activity.

The proposed national conference and preparatory State conferences will be most important steps toward obtaining effective nationwide recognition of these problems and toward recommending the best solutions and remedies. I recommend immediate enactment of the authorizing legislation and appropriations so that preparations for the individual State conferences as well as the national conference can begin at once.

Within the appropriation recommended for the Office of Education in this budget is provision to expand the studies and consultations through which it promotes better practices in education. One problem to which particular attention will be given is the meager education received by children of migrant agricultural workers. Because these children move with their parents from State to State, the problem of providing for their education can be solved only through special effort on a cooperative interstate basis.

In addition, I recommend that legislation be enacted which will enable the Office of Education to join its resources with those of State and local agencies, universities, and other educational organizations for the conduct of cooperative research, surveys, and demonstration projects. Legislation is necessary to make this cooperative effort effective.

An advisory committee on education in the Office of the Secretary of Health, Education, and Welfare should be established by law. This recommendation carries forward an objective of the reorganization plan under which the Department was created last year. This committee, composed of lay citizens, would identify educational problems of national concern to be studied by the Office of Education or by experts outside the Government, and would advise on action needed in the light of these studies.

For these new activities directed toward the improvement and strengthening of our basic educational services, I am including 300,000 dollars in the 1955 budget and recommending a 1954 supplemental appropriation of 2 million dollars.

The last session of the Congress enacted legislation to extend temporarily the laws under which assistance has been provided to local school districts burdened by Federal activities, and to improve the original laws so that they will provide the aid economically and to the areas most acutely affected. As a result of these improvements, the recommended appropriation of 59 million dollars for school-operating assistance in the fiscal year 1955 is 14 million dollars below the amount for 1954. This assistance is provided to more than 2,000 school districts, with enrollments of almost 5 million children, of whom almost 1 million qualify for assistance because their presence is related to Federal activities.

The appropriation of 40 million dollars for school construction recommended for 1955, together with the 1954 appropriation of 70 million dollars, will provide for the most urgent classroom needs of the school districts eligible for this aid under the extended program. These funds are being used to help build almost 5,000 classrooms to serve 140,000 children.

Aid to special groups.—A construction program now underway at Howard University will provide facilities for double the enrollment in the schools of medicine, dentistry, pharmacy, and related health fields. This budget includes funds for the construction of the preclinical medical building, the last unit necessary to make this expanded enrollment possible. Although the university is not limited to any group, it serves as an important center of higher education for Negroes. The expanded enrollment, therefore, will help to alleviate the shortage of doctors, particularly Negro doctors.

Enrollment at the Columbia Institution for the Deaf has been increasing in recent years. Steps now being taken to enable the college to reach an accredited status in the near future include the provision of additional teachers and funds for the construction of a library-classroom building. One-third the cost of this building is being provided by contributions, primarily from former students.

General research.—The National Science Foundation was created by the Congress in recognition of the need to formulate an adequate scientific research policy for the Nation. It is now engaged in intensive studies to that end, and is giving particular attention to the size and composition of the research activities of the Federal Government.

The Congress, at its last session, amended the basic act of the Foundation, removing the ceiling on appropriations to this agency in order to permit steps toward increasing the responsibility of the Foundation for the general-purpose basic research of the Federal Government. Approximately one-half of the 6-million-dollar increase I am recommending in the appropriation for the Foundation for the fiscal year 1955 is in reality a transfer of the responsibility and the financing for certain basic research programs from the Department of Defense to the National Science Foundation. The remainder of the increase is needed to expand basic research.

Within the appropriation for the National Bureau of Standards, there is also provision for an increase in basic research.

Additional basic research is needed to build up the fund of knowledge on which will be based the development of new crops for agriculture, new methods of safeguarding health, new tools for industry, and new weapons. A further important result is the training which basic research projects provide for graduate students in our universities. The number of trained scientists graduating each year falls short of the needs of our growing economy and is still declining. Enlargement of the research program and the related fellowship program will help counteract this trend.

Funds are requested for the fiscal year 1955 to permit the Census Bureau to conduct a sample census of agriculture. This census will provide essential data for current needs.

AGRICULTURE AND AGRICULTURAL RESOURCES

My recommendations for Federal agricultural programs are designed to help in the solution of pressing immediate problems such as the hardships arising from severe drought in major farm areas, the squeeze on livestock producers resulting from lower cattle prices, and the disposal of excess stocks of wheat, cotton, vegetable oils, and dairy products which have been accumulated under provisions of price-support laws presently in force. They also take into account our long-run goals—promotion of a more stable and healthy farm economy, conservation and improvement of our basic agricultural resources, and provision of an adequate supply of food and fiber to match the needs of our increasing population.

AGRICULTURE AND AGRICULTURAL RESOURCES

[Fiscal years. In millions]

Program or agency	Gross expenditures			Net expenditures			Recommended new obligational authority for 1955
	1953 actual	1954 estimated	1955 estimated	1953 actual	1954 estimated	1955 estimated	
Stabilization of farm prices and farm income:							
Price support, supply, and purchase programs (CCC):							
Existing programs [1]	$2,874	$2,832	$2,951	$1,831	$1,152	$1,105	....
Proposed legislation...........	......	......	......	......	......	......	$1,750
International Wheat Agreement.......	131	84	89	131	84	89	....
Removal of surplus agricultural commodities........	82	205	233	82	205	233	180
Sugar Act.........	63	65	65	63	65	65	60
Federal crop insurance...........	27	37	33	5	9	3	6
Agricultural adjustment programs...	13	44	43	13	44	43	42

[1] Gross expenditures exclude private bank loans guaranteed by the Commodity Credit Corporation and net repayments thereof in the amount of 340 million dollars in 1953, 1,564 million dollars in 1954, and 274 million dollars in 1955.

AGRICULTURE AND AGRICULTURAL RESOURCES—Continued

[Fiscal years. In millions]

Program or agency	Gross expenditures			Net expenditures			Recommended new obligational authority for 1955
	1953 actual	1954 estimated	1955 estimated	1953 actual	1954 estimated	1955 estimated	
Financing farm ownership and operation:							
Farm Credit Administration......	$1,936	$2,012	$2,164	—$83	—$1	$42	$25
Farmers' Home Administration......	177	193	168	177	193	168	168
Disaster loans and emergency feed...	47	315	66	16	181	—17	......
Financing rural electrification and rural telephones.........	239	250	232	239	250	232	137
Agricultural land and water resources:							
Agricultural conservation program...	308	256	196	251	242	165	195
Soil Conservation Service, flood prevention and other:							
Existing programs.	66	73	69	66	73	69	66
Proposed legislation..........	......	......	2	......	......	2	3
Research and other agricultural services.	145	157	167	145	157	167	159
Total...........	6,108	6,523	6,478	2,936	2,654	2,366	[2] 2,791

[2] Compares with new obligational authority of 1,333 million dollars in 1953 and 2,302 million dollars in 1954.

The Secretary of Agriculture has recently reorganized the Department to increase administrative efficiency and to make more effective the various services the Department renders. Activities have been grouped into major units consisting of closely related programs, and provision has been made for greater emphasis on research and extension work directed to the improvement of farm products, reduction of production and marketing costs, and broadening of both the foreign and the domestic markets for farm products.

Gross expenditures for agricultural programs in the fiscal year 1955 are estimated at 6.5 billion dollars. Repayments of loans and the sale of commodities constitute most of the receipts of the public enterprises carrying on certain of these programs. These receipts are estimated at 4.1 billion dollars. Hence, net budget expenditures in the fiscal year 1955 are estimated at 2.4 billion dollars. This is 288 million dollars less than estimated net expenditures in 1954 and 570 million dollars less than in 1953.

Stabilization of farm prices and farm income.—Price support activities of the Commodity Credit Corporation, which account for nearly one-half of the estimated 1955 net budget expenditures for agriculture and agricultural resources, have dominated the trend of these expenditures in recent years. There is no better evidence of the tremendous budgetary significance of these activities than the increase of about 2.5 billion dollars during the past calendar year in commodities held by the Corporation and in price support loans. Furthermore, present prospects indicate that, under present law, large additional budgetary outlays will be required for these activities in the fiscal year 1955. It is clear, therefore, that a thorough reconsideration by the Congress of the provisions of existing price support laws is needed not only in the interest of farmers, but also in the national interest.

In my recent special message, I recommended improvements in the price support legislation both to deal with the immediate problems arising from our large surpluses of agricultural commodities and to chart a course for the future that will more effectively achieve the goals of farm price supports. In most instances the reduction in budget expenditures which can be expected from improved and more flexible price support provisions will begin to be effective in the fiscal year 1956.

It is impossible, because of many variable factors, to estimate with any certainty the expenditures under these programs. Based upon the best information now available, it appears that the gross price support expenditures of the Commodity Credit Corporation, which reflect mainly the loans made and commodities acquired during the year, will be 3 billion dollars in the fiscal year 1955. Anticipated receipts of 1.9 billion dollars from loan repayments and commodity sales will result in net expenditures in the fiscal year 1955 of 1.1 billion dollars. These net expenditures for price supports are expected to be 47 million dollars lower than in 1954, and 726 million dollars below the high level reached in 1953.

The reduction in expenditures from the 1953 level is due primarily to the application of marketing quotas on wheat and cotton and acreage allotments on corn which are intended to reduce production from the 1954 crops. The estimates for the fiscal years 1954 and 1955 also reflect greater emphasis given to private financing of price support operations. This, coupled with the customary timing for loan maturities, will result in a substantial proportion of the price supports on the 1953 and 1954 crops not becoming a Government expenditure until the loans held by private institutions mature, which will occur in 1955 and subsequent fiscal years.

All obligations of the Commodity Credit Corporation, whether in the form of borrowing from the Treasury or commodity loans held by banks and guaranteed by the Corporation, constitute a use of the statutory borrowing authority of 6.75 billion dollars. With the large volume of commodity loans and inventories now held and the increases expected in 1954 and 1955, it is estimated that the obligations of the Corporation may exceed its present borrowing limit during the annual peak, probably February 1954, and rise to a still higher level in the fiscal year 1955. I shall recommend to the Congress early in this session a supplemental 1954 estimate of 775 million dollars to restore borrowing authority to the Corporation, through cancellation of notes owed the Treasury, in an amount equal to the sum of the Corporation's capital impairment as of June 30, 1953, the advances during 1953 for control of foot-and-mouth disease, and the cost of operations under the International Wheat Agreement. This note cancellation will require immediate action by the Congress to insure that the Corporation can fulfill its statutory responsibilities under the present price support program.

I shall also recommend legislation to increase the borrowing authority of the Corporation by 1.75 billion dollars, effective July 1, 1954. This recommended increase in borrowing authority takes into account the increased commitments by the Government which would result from the proposed increase in the minimum 1954 cotton acreage allotment. While these commitments will be made in the fiscal year 1955, the cash expenditures by the Commodity Credit Corporation will not occur until 1956.

The recommended new obligational authority for the Corporation will meet the minimum foreseeable needs, provided steps are taken through new legislation to place our farm price support program on a sound basis for the future. A further request for additional borrowing authority may be necessary at a later date if conditions result in this amount being insufficient to provide for the commitments and expenditures required during the period the presently applicable price support provisions remain in effect.

Under the revised International Wheat Agreement, which became effective in the fiscal year 1954, our export quota for wheat has been reduced because of the withdrawal of Great Britain from the Agreement. Moreover, the maximum export price has been raised from $1.80 to $2.05 per bushel. As a result, expenditures under this program are expected to be only about two-thirds as much as in 1953 when our guaranteed export quota was larger and the spread between the domestic price and the export price of wheat was wider. While expenditures under the Wheat Agreement will be less in 1955 than in earlier years, the loss of wheat exports may increase wheat surpluses and thus cause larger outlays by the Commodity Credit Corporation under the price support program than would otherwise occur.

The permanent appropriation for the removal of surplus agricultural commodities, enacted in 1935, is equivalent to 30 percent of the customs receipts for the preceding calendar year. In the fiscal year 1955 there will be available from this authority a carryover of 241 million dollars from prior years plus 180 million dollars of new authorization. This total of 421 million dollars compares with estimated expenditures in 1955 of 233 million dollars. Of this amount 150 million dollars of surplus commodities purchased under this program is estimated to be distributed to the national school lunch program in 1955, as compared with 123 million dollars in 1954 and 52 million dollars in 1953. This permanent appropriation will be used also to strengthen the work being done by the Foreign Agricultural Service in cooperation with the Department of State in developing new foreign markets for our agricultural products.

Financing farm ownership and operation.—The Farm Credit Act of 1953, enacted by the last session of the Congress, restored the Farm Credit Administration to an independent status under the supervision of the Federal Farm Credit Board created by that legislation. It is the policy of this administration, through the Farm Credit Administration, to strengthen cooperative credit services on the basis of sound business-credit standards, and to increase farmer participation in the ownership and control of the Federal farm credit system to the end that the investment of the United States in the federally sponsored agricultural credit institutions may be retired within a reasonable time.

The cooperative credit institutions supervised by the Farm Credit Administration make both long- and short-term loans to farmers and to farmers' cooperatives. Short-term loans by the production credit associations are financed largely through the federally owned intermediate credit banks. Gross expenditures of these banks, which reflect mainly new loans, are expected to be approximately offset by receipts from loan repayments in the fiscal year 1955.

Direct loans to farmers by the Farmers' Home Administration, primarily for farm ownership, production and subsistence, and water facilities, are intended to supplement the credit services provided by private and cooperative credit agencies. The principal purpose of these loans is to help borrowers improve their financial situation so that they can qualify for private or cooperative credit. In the fiscal year 1955, the regular loan program will be continued at about the same level as that provided in 1954. Collections of principal and interest on old loans, which approximately equal new loans made, go directly into miscellaneous receipts of the Treasury and are not deducted from budget expenditures of this program.

Existing legislation does not provide adequately for the financing of group water facilities and related small water supply projects. Proposals for legislation will be submitted at a later date to broaden the geographical area within which water facilities loans may be made, and to increase the loan limit.

The volume of special disaster loans to farmers increased sharply during the first half of the fiscal year 1954. This increase resulted mainly from loans made to stockmen and other farmers in drought-stricken areas to help them finance feed purchases and thereby avoid drastic liquidation of their livestock holdings. The Federal Government also contributed emergency feed from stocks acquired in price support operations and absorbed a part of the cost of making other feed available to farmers in these areas.

As of December 18, 1953, the Federal Government under this program had committed 52 million dollars to supply 1.4 million tons of feed concentrates and over 5 million dollars to cover the Federal Government's share of the cost of the hay program which is administered by the States. A recommendation will be made to the Congress shortly to assure a continuation of advances to States for assistance in distributing hay to farmers and ranchers in the drought areas. In addition, meat purchases of 86 million dollars by the Government up to December 16, 1953, financed from the permanent appropriation for removal of surplus agricultural commodities, have resulted in the removal of about 780,000 head of cattle from the market. The disaster loan program, along with provision of emergency feed and purchases of meat by the Department of Agriculture, supported livestock prices at a time when the market otherwise would have been more depressed by forced liquidation of livestock. The need for new loans and other emergency assistance is expected to be greatly reduced by the spring of 1954, and collections during the fiscal year 1955 on disaster loans made in prior years should exceed new loans made.

Financing rural electrification and rural telephones.—The need for rural electrification loans has become less as the proportion of our farms that are electrified has increased. About 91 percent of our farms are now electrified. Only about 42 percent of our farms, however, have telephone service. The budget recommendations for these two programs in the fiscal year 1955 provide loan funds sufficient to finance substantial further expansion of electrification and telephone services in rural areas. In order to reduce the need for future Federal aid, this administration also is exploring possible arrangements whereby more private capital can be made available to finance telephone services in rural areas.

Agricultural land and water resources.—The need for greater emphasis on conservation and development of our agricultural land and water resources was set forth in my special message to the Congress on this matter on July 31, 1953. The budget estimates provide for 66 million dollars under existing legislation to continue and improve the technical and advisory services of the Soil Conservation Service and for related activities.

Additional work should be undertaken with a view to strengthening our vital upstream conservation activities. Farmers increasingly realize that it is in their own interest to do more of this work. Because the Nation as well as farmers and local communities receive benefits, this work should be a joint responsibility. Existing law, however, does not provide an adequate basis for cooperative upstream development. The 1955 budget, therefore, includes 3 million dollars under proposed legislation to permit the Department of Agriculture to cooperate with State and local agencies in the planning and installation on small watersheds of the necessary protective facilities, and to provide for better conservation, development, utilization, and disposal of water. This will supplement the 11 million dollars to be spent under existing law for watershed protection and flood prevention projects.

In conformance with the forward authorization for the 1954 crop year enacted in the 1954 appropriation act, the budget provides 195 million dollars for the agricultural conservation payment program in the fiscal year 1955. A proposed revision of this program will be recommended to the Congress. The proposal involves no expenditures in the fiscal year 1955.

Research and other agricultural services.—To achieve a more efficient and stable agriculture and to provide for the future needs of a growing population, increased attention must be given to research and educational work on problems of agricultural production, soil conservation, and marketing. The 1955 budget includes 112 million dollars for research and extension work, an increase of 18 million dollars over the estimate for the fiscal year 1954. This work is done in cooperation with State and private agencies. The budget recommendations will provide for a needed expansion of research on marketing and utilization of farm products and of other scientific research conducted by Federal agencies, and increased payments to States for related cooperative research programs. This budget also will provide greater Federal contributions to the Federal-State extension program.

The recommended increase in Federal appropriations for cooperative research and extension work is accompanied by a recommended decrease in appropriations for certain regulatory activities carried on jointly with the States. The budget contemplates elimination of Federal contributions for tuberculosis and brucellosis indemnity payments and curtailment of Federal quarantine and similar operations in a number of insect and plant disease programs. The shift in responsibility for continuation of these programs is in accordance with the policy of this administration that the Federal Government should withdraw from activities which we believe can be more appropriately carried on by private enterprise or by State and local governments.

A strengthening of agricultural research and the wide dissemination of improved techniques through extension work will contribute to the efficiency of farm production and marketing, benefiting both producers and consumers. This will provide the solid foundation for a more prosperous and stable agriculture and ultimately for less reliance on Government price support and other financial aids.

NATURAL RESOURCES

My recommendations for the natural resources programs of the Government are based on a reappraisal of the responsibility which the Federal Government should exercise in the development of our resources. At the same time, the recommendations have been made with due regard to our overall fiscal position. To keep the Federal financial burden at a minimum while defense expenditures remain high, some improvements and program expansions which might be desirable have not been included in this budget. Emphasis has been given to careful planning to insure sound development of our natural resources. Such development should be timed, whenever possible, to assist in leveling off peaks and valleys in our economic life.

A strong program of resource conservation and development is necessary to support the progressively expanding demands of our increasing population and to contribute to the economic growth and security of the Nation. Achievement of this goal requires a combined effort on the part of States and local communities, citizens, and the Federal Government. To the greatest extent possible, the responsibility for resource development, and its cost, should be borne by those who receive the benefits. In many instances private interests or State and local governments can best carry on the needed programs. In other instances Federal participation or initiative may be necessary to safeguard the public interest and to accomplish broad national objectives.

Estimated net expenditures of 1.1 billion dollars in the fiscal year 1955 will provide for the management and protection of the resources which belong to all the people and which are under the jurisdiction of the Federal Government. About three-fourths of this total will be for flood control, irrigation, power, and multiple-purpose river basin development. The remainder will be spent on the management, development, and protection of our national forests, parks, and other public lands, and for mineral and fish and wildlife resources and basic surveys. Activities to advance the peacetime applications of atomic energy, which will be of increasing significance in 1955, are discussed with other activities of the Atomic Energy Commission in the national security section of this message.

NATURAL RESOURCES

[Fiscal years. In millions]

Program or agency	Gross expenditures			Net expenditures			Recommended new obligational authority for 1955
	1953 actual	1954 estimated	1955 estimated	1953 actual	1954 estimated	1955 estimated	
Land and water resources:							
Corps of Engineers: Flood control and multiple-purpose projects:							
Existing program......	$579	$416	$361	$579	$416	$361	$342
Proposed legislation: Aid for non-Federal development of water resources..............			5	....	....	5	5
Department of the Interior:							
Bureau of Reclamation: Irrigation and multiple-purpose projects:							
Existing program.....	235	182	167	231	180	164	160
Proposed legislation: Federal projects....	....	....	(1)	....	....	(1)	(1)
Proposed legislation: Aid for non-Federal development of water resources..........	....	....	5	....	....	5	5
Power transmission agencies................	65	64	53	65	64	53	39
Indian lands resources..	32	36	35	29	35	34	27
Bureau of Land Management and other......	14	16	15	14	16	15	16
Tennessee Valley Authority.................	315	366	439	184	195	212	142
Department of State.....	15	9	5	15	9	5	2
Federal Power Commission................	4	4	4	4	4	4	4
Forest resources...........	107	116	110	107	116	110	108
Mineral resources........	41	41	39	38	38	36	36
Fish and wildlife resources...	34	37	38	34	37	38	36
Recreational use of resources................	30	34	34	30	34	34	29
General resource surveys and other..............	28	28	27	28	28	27	27
Total.................	1,499	1,349	1,337	1,358	1,172	1,103	2 978

[1] Less than 500,000 dollars.

[2] Compares with new obligational authority of 1,396 million dollars in 1953, and 1,026 million dollars in 1954.

Land and water resources.—Under my recommendations in this budget, the Federal Government will spend an estimated 858 million dollars for the conservation and development of land and water resources in the fiscal year 1955. A major part of this represents investment in assets which will yield benefits long into the future.

This administration is developing a sound and uniform national policy for the conservation, improvement, and use of water and related land resources, designed to assure that future programs are not only responsive to local requirements but are consistent as well with the needs of the Nation as a whole. As a step in this direction, a statement of principles has been issued on the generation, transmission, and disposal of electric power. Standards for the justification of proposed water resources projects are currently being reviewed by the executive branch. Special attention is being given to requirements for the sharing of costs among private beneficiaries, State and local groups, and the Federal Government. Also, the Congress has established commissions to examine resource programs, as well as other Federal activities, and to make recommendations with respect to them. As the various studies are completed, I shall make specific legislative recommendations to the Congress.

This administration has also taken and will continue to take steps to encourage non-Federal interests to formulate plans and undertake development of water resources, including hydroelectric power, which are consonant with the best use of the natural resources of the area. An outstanding example of cooperation between various levels of government— State, Federal, and international—in multiple-purpose development of a resource is the proposal for the development of the St. Lawrence River. It would also be in the public interest for construction to be undertaken, on a non-Federal basis, to realize the power potential of the Niagara Falls site.

Basic resource surveys and advance engineering and design activities will be carried on in 1955 at rates necessary to provide for further development of our resources. Federal activities in projects or plans will not imply any exclusive reservation of such projects to Federal construction or financing or preclude local participation in them. Needed projects to be constructed by the Federal Government may include those which, because of size and complexity, are beyond the means of local, public or private enterprise.

My budget recommendations also provide for the continuation of river basin work now underway. Less urgent features of the projects, not required for operation of going or completed units, will be deferred. Budget expenditures of the Bureau of Reclamation and the Corps of Engineers include an estimated 443 million dollars in the fiscal year 1955 to carry on construction of about 160 river basin development projects. A substantial amount of these expenditures is for multiple-purpose development for irrigation, flood control, navigation, and hydroelectric power. During the fiscal year 1955, 20 projects will be completed or substantially completed, including 9 flood control projects, 5 irrigation projects, and 6 multiple-purpose projects with power facilities.

In furtherance of the policies of this administration, I am recommending the starting of some new projects or new units of existing projects by the Corps of Engineers and the Bureau of Reclamation, as well as the resumption of some previously deferred projects. The budget recommends commencing work on 6 irrigation and water supply projects, 8 local flood prevention projects, and 8 navigation projects, one of which I recommend starting in the fiscal year 1954 with supplemental funds. In addition, it provides for resumption of work on 2 flood control reservoirs and 2 river and harbor improvements. This work is estimated to cost a total of 184 million dollars, with expenditures of 20 million dollars scheduled for the fiscal year 1955. Together with the St. Lawrence Seaway, this totals to 23 new projects and 4 resumptions in the budget. The navigation projects, including the St. Lawrence Seaway, are discussed in this message with the transportation and communication programs. Recommendations for related watershed protection and flood prevention activities of the Department of Agriculture are discussed in the section on agriculture and agricultural resources.

The new local flood prevention works, to be constructed by the Corps of Engineers, are relatively small projects and can be completed within 3 years. The detailed plans preliminary to construction have been completed. Each of the projects has a favorable ratio of benefits to costs and provides for a reasonable degree of financial cooperation by local interests. Resumption of work is proposed on 2 flood control reservoirs, each of which is about one-third completed.

The new projects recommended for the Bureau of Reclamation include 3 projects already authorized and 2 projects under legislation I am proposing. Commencement of work is also recommended on a new pumping unit of an irrigation project now under construction. These are small or intermediate-sized developments. In their selection, consideration has been given to the benefits of supplemental irrigation for established farming areas, to more intensive and beneficial use of existing water supplies, and to the ability of the water users to make a reasonable repayment of the investment. In the case of one of the projects which requires authorization, I have recommended to the Congress that provision be made in the legislation for repayment within 50 years of all reimbursable costs, and that construction of the project be made contingent on the assumption by the State, together with local organizations, of financial responsibility for reimbursable costs beyond the ability of the water users to repay. This principle is in line with the policy of this administration that, to the greatest extent possible, the cost of these developments should be borne by those who receive the benefits.

In accordance with this administration's policy of encouraging State and local undertakings, there is included in the budget an initial appropriation of 10 million dollars under proposed legislation to enable the Corps of Engineers and the Bureau of Reclamation to cooperate with States, local governments, or private groups in the development of their water resources. It is thought that there are projects on which State and local interests could go forward with some Federal assistance. Such assistance should be provided on an equitable financial basis and should be limited to projects from which benefits would accrue to the general public.

The power policy of this administration recognizes the willingness of State and local groups to participate in providing additional power facilities. Where the necessary transmission facilities are not being provided on reasonable terms by other public or private agencies, the Department of the Interior will construct and operate transmission lines that are economically feasible and are necessary for proper interconnection and operation of Federal generation plants, and those that are required to carry power to load centers within economic transmission distances. As a result of this policy and the approaching completion of transmission systems required for carrying out arrangements for marketing power from Federal projects under construction, combined expenditures of the Bonneville, Southeastern, and Southwestern Power Administrations in the fiscal year 1955 will be less than in 1954.

Under the Federal Power Act, licensees of hydroelectric projects which benefit from headwater impoundments of other projects, either public or private, must make annual payments to the upstream developer in accordance with benefits received. The Federal Government is not required to make similar payments when Federal projects derive such benefits. In simple equity, this should be done. I recommend enactment of legislation which would require such Federal payments.

Although no appropriations are included in the 1955 budget for new power generation units by the Tennessee Valley Authority, expenditures will increase for continuation of construction of power plants presently underway, and for operation of power plants after they are completed. Expenses for operation of flood control, navigation, and fertilizer facilities will continue at about the 1954 level. Expenditures for power and fertilizer operations are more than offset by the income from sales. In order to provide, with appropriate operating reserves, for reasonable growth in industrial, municipal, and cooperative power loads in the area through the calendar year 1957, arrangements are being made to reduce, by the fall of 1957, existing commitments of the Tennessee Valley Authority to the Atomic Energy Commission by 500,000 to 600,000 kilowatts. This would release the equivalent amount of Tennessee Valley Authority generating capacity to meet increased load requirements of other consumers in the power system and at the same time eliminate the need for appropriating funds from the Treasury to finance additional generating units. In the event, however, that negotiations for furnishing these load requirements for the Atomic Energy Commission from other sources are not consummated as contemplated or new defense loads develop, the question of starting additional generating units by the Tennessee Valley Authority will be reconsidered.

In order to carry out the power policy of this administration which requires an interest charge on the Federal investment in power facilities to reimburse the Treasury for the cost of providing funds, a proposal is being developed for submission to the Congress to provide that an adequate rate of interest be paid to the Treasury on public funds invested in power facilities of the Tennessee Valley Authority. For this purpose, I have requested that a study be undertaken by the agency in cooperation with other executive agencies.

National forests and other public lands.—The development and use of our public lands should be on a businesslike basis with due regard for proper conservation and for the rights and interests of States and private citizens. Programs of the Forest Service and the Bureau of Land Management provide for the management, development, and increasing use of the valuable timber, forage, and mineral resources of the national forests and public lands, and also for the protection and use of these lands for their strategic watershed and other public values. Receipts from the use of these lands, estimated at 154 million dollars in the fiscal year 1955, are shared with the States and counties in which the lands are located.

The budget contemplates the withdrawal of Federal financial participation in certain phases of State and private forestry cooperation, with greater assumption of responsibility by local interests. At the same time, emphasis will be placed by the Forest Service on cooperative research. Increased funds are recommended to complete construction of access roads needed to salvage the timber in the beetle-infested and windblown forest areas of Washington and Oregon.

Expenditures for the management and protection of our national parks, monuments, and historic sites will be somewhat above the current-year level, so as to provide for improved services to the increasing number of visitors. This increase is largely offset by a reduction in expenditures for construction. Federal aid to States for fish and wildlife restoration, financed by special taxes on fishing and hunting goods, will increase.

As a part of the administration's objective of charging reasonable fees for services or facilities provided by the Government for private individuals or groups, consideration is being given to adjustments which would result in increased receipts to the National Park Service, thus returning to the Treasury a larger amount of the costs of maintaining and operating our national parks.

Expenditures on Indian land resources will provide for soil conservation work and further development of water supplies and timber and range resources necessary for their economic development. In the fiscal year 1955 appropriations will be reduced from their level in 1954 as a result of the slowing down or deferring of some construction projects—which will be accomplished without jeopardizing the overall objectives of the Indian programs.

Mineral resources.—I have recently appointed a Cabinet committee to establish guidelines for the prudent use and development of domestic mineral resources and to assure our growing economy of necessary mineral supplies in time of emergency. The report of this committee, expected within the next few weeks, should be helpful in resolving many of the problems facing the mineral producers of the Nation.

The Bureau of Mines will continue its basic research programs in the fiscal year 1955 for the aid of private development of resources, with emphasis on expanding the utilization of minerals in abundant supply and the development of suitable substitutes for materials in short supply. The Federal Government will also encourage private development by undertaking basic resource surveys, providing incentives for exploration of high priority minerals, and assisting in the development of oil and gas reserves of the Outer Continental Shelf.

TRANSPORTATION AND COMMUNICATION

Efficient transportation and communication services are essential to the national economy and the national security. At my request, an intensive reappraisal of Federal responsibilities is underway both by the regular departments and agencies and by special commissions. The general principles guiding this reappraisal are that the national interest will usually be served best by a privately owned and operated industry, which is supported by a minimum of Federal funds or Federal basic facilities and services operated at the lowest feasible cost and financed, where possible, by charges levied on the users of the services.

In the fiscal year 1955 net budget expenditures for transportation and communication programs will decline to an estimated 1,418 million dollars, compared with 1,856 million dollars in 1954 and 2,077 million dollars actually expended in 1953. The largest decrease is the anticipated reduction of the postal deficit by operating savings and by increased postal rates. Sizable reductions have also been made in other large programs.

New legislative authority is required to move more rapidly toward putting the postal service on a self-supporting basis and to establish a corporation to operate the Washington National Airport. I am also recommending legislation to permit us to participate in the St. Lawrence Seaway, and to continue and strengthen the Federal-aid highway program.

Promotion of aviation.—The rapid development of aviation has been materially assisted by numerous services and by direct financial assistance provided by the Federal Government. These aids have included basic scientific research in aeronautics, establishment and operation of airways, enforcement of safety regulations, assistance in construction of airports,

TRANSPORTATION AND COMMUNICATION

[Fiscal years.   In millions]

Program or agency	Gross expenditures			Net expenditures			Recommended new obligational authority for 1955
	1953 actual	1954 estimated	1955 estimated	1953 actual	1954 estimated	1955 estimated	
Promotion of aviation:							
Civil Aeronautics Administration..............	$161	$146	$121	$161	$146	$121	$104
Civil Aeronautics Board (subsidies to air carriers).	.....	54	80	.....	54	80	73
National Advisory Committee for Aeronautics..	78	91	77	78	91	77	58
Promotion of merchant marine:							
Maritime Administration.	358	262	156	235	196	107	102
Inland Waterways Corporation................	12	1	(1)	.....	—2	—1	....
Provision of navigation aids and facilities:							
Coast Guard...........	230	236	190	230	236	190	181
Corps of Engineers:							
Present programs......	113	102	106	113	102	106	103
Proposed legislation (St. Lawrence Seaway)...	.....	.....	6	.....	.....	6	105
Panama Canal Company..	106	102	99	—10	—2	—1	....
Provision of highways:							
Bureau of Public Roads:							
Present programs......	550	592	582	550	592	582	10
Proposed legislation....	.....	.....	.....	.....	.....	.....	598
Alaska roads and other...	22	20	17	22	20	17	13
Postal service:							
Present program.........	2,775	2,775	2,775	659	440	330	329
Proposed increase in postal rates................	.....	.....	.....	.....	.....	—240	—240
Regulation of transportation.	17	16	16	17	16	16	16
Other services to transportation...................	45	42	45	15	—40	21	22
Regulation of communication...................	7	7	7	7	7	7	8
Total................	4,474	4,446	4,277	2,077	1,856	1,418	2 1,482

1 Less than 500,000 dollars.

2 Compares with new obligational authority of 1,925 million dollars in 1953 and 1,756 million dollars in 1954.

and direct provision of subsidies to airmail carriers. While need for some aid continues, the increasing maturity of this industry requires thorough reevaluation of the promotional responsibilities of the Federal Government. At my request, the Air Coordinating Committee is now undertaking a comprehensive review of our aviation policy.

With growing maturity, the airline and aircraft manufacturing industries should assume increased responsibility for air safety. Improved procedures of traffic control, elimination of older-type facilities, and curtailment of less essential services should permit an expanded volume of air traffic to be handled safely with reduced Federal expenditures for operating programs. Expenditures for construction programs are likewise declining.

As a result of these developments, expenditures of the Civil Aeronautics Administration can be reduced and we can still fulfill the basic Federal responsibilities for providing air-navigation aids, traffic control, and safety services. Budget expenditures in the fiscal year 1955 are estimated to be 25 million dollars less than in 1954, and 40 million dollars less than in 1953.

I am recommending appropriations for new airways facilities amounting to 5 million dollars, which will permit further progress on the modern very high frequency system of navigation aids and certain other improvements. Pending completion of current studies, no provision is made in the budget for additional appropriations for grants to State and local governmental units for airport construction.

In addition, the time has come when consideration should be given to requiring the users of the airways facilities to share the costs of providing this service.

Reorganization Plan No. 10 of 1953, transferring the subsidy portion of airmail payments from the Postmaster General to the Civil Aeronautics Board, makes it possible for the first time for Congress to consider this major aid to aviation as a separate budget item. For both 1954 and 1955, these subsidy payments are estimated at approximately 80 million dollars, based primarily on existing route patterns and mail rates. The subsidy expenditures were included in the Post Office Department through September 1953. The separation of compensatory mail payments, which remain in the Post Office, from subsidy payments is a necessary first step toward a more effective review of expenditures for civil aviation as well as for the postal service.

The scientific research in aeronautics conducted by the National Advisory Committee for Aeronautics will continue in the fiscal year 1955 to be devoted almost entirely to support of the military programs for the development of new and improved aircraft, guided missiles, and propulsion systems. The budget provides for a strong continuing program in aeronautical research and for initial operation of the three new large supersonic wind tunnels now under construction. Nevertheless, expenditures will be 14 million dollars less than in the fiscal year 1954 because of the sharp decrease in construction expenditures as projects are completed. The superior performance of our jet aircraft in Korea and the even better performance of newer types now in production has been possible because of the basic research and wind-tunnel testing done in previous years. Much of the work will also contribute eventually to improving the performance, safety, and comfort of civil aircraft. Future possibilities are hinted by the recent performance of our research airplanes, one of which attained a speed of over 1,600 miles per hour—two and one-half times the speed of sound.

Merchant marine.—Federal aid to the merchant marine consists primarily of operating and construction subsidies to offset the differences between American and foreign costs. This program is designed to promote a healthy merchant marine as a nucleus capable of rapid expansion to meet national-defense needs. The sharp reduction in expenditures will result almost entirely from virtual completion of construction of the 35 Mariner-class vessels authorized in 1951.

Expenditures for operating subsidies have been rising steadily, and in 1955 will account for 85 of the 107 million dollars in net expenditures for maritime programs. These increases reflect not only faster payment of earlier obligations but also higher levels of subsidy resulting from the increased operating costs in recent years. The size and rising trend of expenditures for these subsidies make it essential to consider legislative changes to provide for more effective budgetary control consistent with the basic objectives of the maritime program.

Operating programs of the Maritime Administration show a downward trend. By the end of the fiscal year 1955 the emergency operation of Government-owned cargo vessels will be reduced to about 47, compared to a high of 538 in 1952. Ships withdrawn from operation are being maintained in the national-defense reserve fleet to meet future emergency needs.

The physical assets of the Inland Waterways Corporation were sold as of July 1, 1953, in accordance with this administration's policy of removing the Federal Government from an activity which is appropriately private. The terms of sale fully protect the public interest in the continuance of the common-carrier barge service along the Mississippi and Warrior Rivers.

Navigation aids and facilities.—The expanded search-and-rescue facilities of the Coast Guard established in support of Department of Defense activities are being curtailed. Moreover, the fact that our transoceanic civil aviation no longer has a requirement for ocean weather stations has made it possible to reduce the number of these stations to those required by the Department of Defense, which in the future will finance them. These and other realinements will permit Coast Guard financed expenditures to be reduced from 236 million dollars in fiscal 1954 to 190 million dollars in fiscal 1955.

The Corps of Engineers will carry forward at minimum levels the maintenance work required for continued operation of river and harbor projects. Construction will also continue in 1955 at economic rates on 13 channel, harbor, or lock and dam projects, including one project to be initiated by a proposed 1954 supplemental appropriation. Seven other projects will be initiated and 2 deferred projects resumed in 1955. These projects have been selected on the basis of assuring the expeditious movement of traffic in existing harbors or waterways serving important requirements of commerce or national security. Emphasis has been given to small- or intermediate-sized projects for which detailed engineering plans have been completed. Not only do the benefits of these projects exceed their costs, but also, except for four high-priority projects of national interest, local beneficiaries will make a reasonable financial contribution.

In my State of the Union Message I again strongly recommended enactment of legislation to create a Government corporation to work, along with Canada, on the construction and operation of the proposed St. Lawrence Seaway. This proposal, now before the Congress, represents one part of a broad development of the great potential of the St. Lawrence River for electric power and for navigation. The power features of the International Rapids section are expected to be constructed in part by the Province of Ontario and in part by the State of New York. The seaway legislation would permit the Federal Government, in cooperation with

Canada, to build the remaining navigation facilities needed for ocean-going vessels to reach the Great Lakes. The total amount to be invested by the United States in the seaway is now estimated at 105 million dollars, with first-year expenditures of 6 million dollars. As I have previously indicated, not only would the seaway make a major contribution to national security, but over a period of years the tolls received by the United States from the prospective commercial use should permit the Federal investment to be fully repaid. Joint participation with Canada in this undertaking will assure that all legitimate American interests are taken into account in the construction and operation of this vital transportation link.

Highways.—Expenditures under the Federal-aid highway program of grants to States for highway construction have been rising during the past year, and will continue to rise in the fiscal year 1955 under commitments made pursuant to the Highway Act of 1952. The 1955 expenditures will be the highest in history. Emphasis in the selection of new projects will be given to the national system of interstate highways, which comprises the most important routes for interstate commerce and national defense. Of the 555 million dollars of estimated expenditures under the Federal-aid program in the fiscal year 1955, about 150 million dollars will be spent for projects in the interstate system. Other construction programs of the Bureau of Public Roads will involve expenditures of 27 million dollars, mainly for direct construction of forest highways and defense access roads.

We should give increased attention to eliminating the existing inadequacies of the national system of interstate highways. Pending development and review of detailed proposals for extension of the Federal-aid highway program, I am including under proposed legislation the 575-million-dollar level of the existing authorization. Similarly, I am including the prevailing annual rate of 22.5 million dollars for the forest-highway program. No appreciable expenditures will be made under the proposed authorizations in the fiscal year 1955.

Postal service.—Measured both in dollars and in employees, the postal service is big business. But, in its management, the modern methods which have so greatly increased the efficiency of private business have too often been ignored.

Last February, I announced "a program directed at improving service, while at the same time reducing costs and decreasing deficits." Progress is being made toward achieving these objectives and will continue.

First, we are speeding the delivery of mail by many new steps without significant change in costs of handling. Later window hours, later pick-ups, changes in transportation patterns and schedules, experiments in carrying first-class mail by air, and many other projects have been made effective or are now being tested. The results will become increasingly apparent in the next year.

Second, to obtain a clear-cut measure of the cost of operating the postal service, the payment of airline subsidies has been transferred by reorganization plan to the Civil Aeronautics Board, and legislation enacted to require Government agencies and the Congress to reimburse the Post Office for the cost of handling their mail.

Third, we have initiated many economies and are planning others. Reduced mail-handling costs through efficient modern techniques already have resulted in substantial savings. This program is well underway but will take a long time to complete, since the new methods will require employee training and development of new machines.

Fourth, the deficit has been further reduced by increases in rates which the Postmaster General could change. Increases in parcel-post rates, foreign-mail rates, and others subject to administrative discretion have in the main put these services on a self-supporting basis.

The results of these and other improvements are already visible in the financial operations and outlook. Despite an estimated increase in mail volume of almost 2 billion pieces, gross expenditures of 2,775 million dollars in the fiscal year 1955 will remain unchanged from 1954. With higher operating revenues, the deficit under existing postal rates will continue to decline:

	Million
1953 (actual)	$659
1954 (estimated)	440
1955 (estimated)	330

No business, public or private, can prosper unless its management is free to use the best available methods of operation and to set prices adequate to cover the costs of an efficient operation. Legislation is already before the Congress to authorize the Post Office Department to acquire needed modern postal facilities, through long-term leases with title acquired at the end of the term. Other legislation is required to correct archaic administrative and personnel practices, and to enable expanded use of more modern transportation methods.

Most important, prompt and favorable action by the Congress is needed to increase postal rates. I am recommending increases in rates sufficient to yield as a minimum an additional 240 million dollars in revenues in the fiscal year 1955. These revenues would reduce the 1955 postal deficit to 90 million dollars. Adequate rates, together with further major economies in postal operations, are expected to put the postal business on a self-supporting basis. This will continue to be our policy.

Regulation.—Three regulatory commissions carry out the Government's responsibility to protect the public interest in reasonable rates and adequate, safe transportation and communication: Interstate Commerce Commission, Federal Communications Commission, and Civil Aeronautics Board. Although their duties have substantially increased in recent years, anticipated improvements in management and procedures make it unnecessary to request any significant appropriation increases. For example, the centralization of administrative responsibility and the reorganization of existing activities in the Interstate Commerce Commission should make possible more effective use of available funds. By the end of the fiscal year 1954, the Federal Communications Commission should be substantially current in handling applications for television stations, so that the funds required for its activities, except for a new program of monitoring frequency usage, will be smaller in the fiscal year 1955 than in 1954.

Receipts of public enterprise funds.—Two-thirds of the gross expenditures of 4,277 million dollars for transportation and communication programs in the fiscal year 1955 will be financed from receipts of public enterprise funds. Postal receipts account for the bulk of these revenues. Substantial receipts are also anticipated from tolls and other revenues of the Panama Canal Company, and from vessel operations of the Maritime Administration.

FINANCE, COMMERCE, AND INDUSTRY

Within the limits set by requirements of national defense and the needs of the national economy, we are steadily reducing direct banking and business operations of the Federal Government. For example, the Reconstruction Finance Corporation is being liquidated, and the Government's synthetic rubber plants are being offered for sale. At the same time, the programs of the Department of Commerce to promote trade and industry are being strengthened and the Small Business Administration has

FINANCE, COMMERCE, AND INDUSTRY

[Fiscal years. In millions]

Program or agency	Gross expenditures			Net expenditures			Recommended new obligational authority for 1955
	1953 actual	1954 estimated	1955 estimated	1953 actual	1954 estimated	1955 estimated	
Promotion of defense production:							
Expansion of defense production..............	$390	$562	$546	$89	$381	$308	....
Reconstruction Finance Corporation...........	516	349	270	−98	−233	−65	....
Other.................	121	27	16	84	−5	−4	$4
Business loans and guarantees:							
Reconstruction Finance Corporation (Treasury):							
Loans..............	128	44	10	7	−95	−121	....
Other..............	18	122	5	−29	97	−19	....
Small Business Administration................	.....	13	31	.....	12	25	
Promotion or regulation of trade and industry:							
Department of Commerce.	17	17	22	17	17	22	22
Other.................	9	10	11	9	10	11	11
Promotion or regulation of financial institutions......	6	7	6	−3	−20	5	5
Total................	1,205	1,151	917	76	164	162	[1]42

[1] Compares with new obligational authority of 134 million dollars in 1953 and 97 million dollars in 1954.

been established to meet the special needs of small business. Regulatory agencies are simplifying their procedures and putting greater stress on cooperation rather than compulsion, without reducing protection to the public.

Gross expenditures for finance, commerce, and industry programs are expected to be 917 million dollars in the fiscal year 1955, a reduction of 234 million dollars from 1954. About 60 percent of these expenditures are for financial assistance provided under the Defense Production Act. Another 30 percent are for the production programs administered by the Reconstruction Finance Corporation—primarily rubber and tin. Anticipated receipts of these enterprises as a group will decline about as much as their expenditures. Accordingly net expenditures of 162 million dollars in 1955 will be about the same as in 1954.

Expansion of defense production.—The Defense Production Act authorizes extensive financial assistance to assure expansion of productive capacity and of the materials supply necessary for our defense. With the help of purchase commitments, loans, and advances already made, much of the needed expansion is now under way. As a result, the aluminum productive capacity of the United States has doubled since 1950 and supplies of machine tools, titanium, copper, nickel, and other critical items have also substantially increased.

These programs are financed under the borrowing authority of 2.1 billion dollars provided in the Defense Production Act. Gross expenditures in the fiscal year 1955 are estimated at 546 million dollars. Of this amount 296 million dollars will be spent for purchases of materials and 165 million dollars for loans and advances to producers. Most of these expenditures arise from commitments already outstanding. Since a large part of the materials to be acquired under this authority will be sold to the military stockpile of strategic and critical materials to meet its objectives, this program is intimately related to the stockpiling program discussed in the national security section of this message. Receipts from these sales and from sales to private industry, together with repayments of loans and advances, are estimated at 238 million dollars in 1955, reducing net expenditures to 308 million dollars.

Reconstruction Finance Corporation—production programs.—Expenditures and receipts of the rubber, tin, and abaca fiber programs currently administered by the Reconstruction Finance Corporation will continue to decline sharply in 1955, primarily as a result of reduced operations anticipated in the tin program.

By the end of the present fiscal year, the Government will have completed purchases of tin for the national stockpile. World supplies are already adequate to meet current requirements. As a result, there may no longer be a need for continued operation of the Government tin smelter in 1955. Pending outcome of international negotiations, the budget assumes withdrawal of the Government smelter from operations at the end of the fiscal year 1954.

During the fiscal years 1954 and 1955, annual production of synthetic rubber is estimated at about 600,000 tons— a reduction from the 712,000 tons produced in 1953. Present experience indicates that this level of production will meet all of the anticipated national needs for synthetic rubber. Although the Rubber Facilities Disposal Act authorizes sale of Government plants to private ownership before the end of the fiscal year 1955, plans are not yet far enough advanced to include estimated receipts from such disposal in the 1955 budget.

The production programs will be transferred to another agency before June 30, 1954, as provided in the Reconstruction Finance Corporation Liquidation Act.

Business loans and guarantees.—The regular business loan program of the Reconstruction Finance Corporation is now in liquidation as a result of legislation enacted last year on the recommendation of this administration. The Treasury Department will administer the liquidation after June 30, 1954. We plan to sell a major part of the Corporation's loans to private financial institutions. To meet commitments previously made, some expenditures will continue, but repayments and sales of loans will result in estimated net receipts of 121 million dollars in 1955.

A new program of loans to small businesses has recently been established in the Small Business Administration. The 1955 budget assumes that about 350 loans will be authorized in the fiscal year 1954, and about 700 in 1955. This would almost exhaust the available appropriation of 55 million dollars by the end of 1955. Loans will be made where private credit on reasonable terms is unavailable, and, whenever possible, they will be made jointly with private banks. The Small Business Administration also assists small concerns in obtaining a fair share of Government contracts, and provides them with technical and financial advice.

Department of Commerce.—In accordance with this administration's declared policy, most emergency controls over business have been removed. The business programs of the Department of Commerce have been reorganized to provide a simpler and more effective basis for carrying on both regular business services and continuing responsibilities under the Defense Production Act. The Business and Defense Services Administration provides general services to business, assists in mobilization preparedness, and administers relevant current defense activities. The Bureau of Foreign Commerce assists in promoting international trade, primarily by providing American business with information on opportunities to buy and sell abroad. The Office of Business Economics provides data on the American economy and analyses of economic and business trends for a wide range of business and Government purposes. I am recommending small increases in the appropriations for these programs so that the Department can adequately carry out its responsibilities to foster and promote industry and commerce.

LABOR AND MANPOWER

My budget recommendations for the labor and manpower programs of the Federal Government are designed to help the Nation's productive system function smoothly and efficiently, by providing economic safeguards for workers, by helping bring together jobseekers and jobs, and by helping to recruit the working forces for defense and other industries. Workers will continue to be given protection against substandard wages and working conditions and against income losses due to unemployment. Orderly labor relations will be fostered, and the amicable settlement of disputes will be assisted by mediation.

Including proposed legislation, budget expenditures for labor and manpower programs are estimated at 281 million dollars during the fiscal year 1955, an increase of 16 million dollars from the current fiscal year. Approximately three-fourths of total budget expenditures for these programs is for administering the job placement and unemployment compensation services.

Although many of our workers benefit from the existing Federal-State unemployment compensation system, the present Federal law does not include employees of firms with fewer than eight persons nor does it include Federal civilian employees. I recommend prompt extension of the system to these workers. Seventeen States already provide coverage of most firms with one or more employees, and most other States have legislation which will permit immediate coverage when the Congress acts. Amendments to State laws to achieve full coverage will be needed in only a dozen States. This preparedness on the part of the great majority of States will permit rapid extension of this valuable protection after the Federal law is amended. Additional revenues will more than offset the administrative costs resulting from such extension. An estimate of the benefit costs for Federal employees is included under general government.

Placement and unemployment compensation administration.—Gross expenditures in the fiscal year 1955 for administering the Federal-State placement and unemployment compensation services under present law are estimated at 192 million dollars, 7 million dollars below the current year. A decrease of about 30 million dollars will result from a change in

LABOR AND MANPOWER

[Fiscal years. In millions]

Program or agency	Expenditures			Recommended new obligational authority for 1955
	1953 actual	1954 estimated	1955 estimated	
Gross expenditures:				
Placement and unemployment compensation administration:				
Department of Labor:				
Present program................	$212	$199	$192	$223
Proposed legislation to broaden unemployment insurance:				
Federal civilian personnel.......	....	....	2	2
Other workers.................	....	....	20	20
Labor standards and training:				
Department of Labor.............	13	12	12	12
Mine safety (Department of the Interior and other)................	4	5	5	5
Military manpower selection: Selective Service System and National Security Training Commission..............	33	30	31	32
Labor relations....................	13	14	13	13
Labor information, statistics, and general administration: Department of Labor...........................	7	7	7	7
Defense production activities: Department of Labor.................	2	(1)	....	....
Total..........................	284	267	282	2 314
Deduct applicable receipts: Farm labor supply revolving fund..............	3	2	1	....
Net budget expenditures..............	281	265	281	....

[1] Less than 500,000 dollars.

[2] Compares with new obligational authority of 282 million dollars in 1953 and 267 million dollars in 1954.

financial arrangements, by which advance payments to each State before the opening of each fiscal year will be reduced from an amount covering three months' operations to an amount for one month. Part of this reduction will be offset, however, by a higher estimated rate of expenditures for this program resulting from increases in salaries provided by State laws to employees who administer the services, some rise in the expected number of unemployment compensation claimants, and provision for weekly filing of claims and weekly payment of benefits. The weekly claims system, replacing the biweekly method currently in use in most States, will provide more satisfactory service to the claimants and, by permitting more frequent contact, should reduce the possibilities of fraudulent or erroneous payments. These factors may make necessary a request for a supplemental appropriation for the current fiscal year.

This administration has already recommended enactment of legislation to transfer annually to a special account in the unemployment trust fund, an amount equal to the difference between the receipts of the Federal unemployment tax and the administrative costs of operating our joint Federal-State unemployment security program. The initial transfer, based on receipts and expenditures in the fiscal year 1955, would be made at the beginning of the fiscal year 1956.

My recommendations in this budget provide for continued operation of the system for recruiting qualified workers from Mexico for seasonal employment on farms in the United States. These workers are needed to supplement our domestic farm-labor supply. The 1954 appropriation for this recruitment program was based on legislation which was to have expired on December 31, 1953. This authority has now been extended until December 31, 1955, and funds are included in the budget to pay for operations during the rest of the fiscal year 1954, as well as in the fiscal year 1955.

The railroad unemployment insurance taxes and expenditures which were previously included in budget accounts are now entirely included in trust accounts.

Labor standards and training.—Budget expenditures for the minimum-wage and maximum-hour regulatory programs in the fiscal year 1955 are estimated at about the 1954 level.

The social and economic plight of migratory farmworkers has been studied repeatedly. Up to now, little positive action to better these conditions has been taken by the Federal Government. This budget includes a recommended appropriation of 100 thousand dollars to enable the Department of Labor to provide leadership in establishing a cooperative Federal-State program in the fiscal year 1955.

Military manpower selection.—Although a reduction in military personnel is planned, calls by the Department of Defense in 1955 to replace men drafted in 1953 will require an increase of 676 thousand dollars in estimated expenditures of the Selective Service System. This budget provides also for continuing a small staff for the National Security Training Commission.

Labor relations.—Budget expenditures of 13 million dollars in the fiscal year 1955 are estimated for the independent labor relations agencies—the National Labor Relations Board and the mediation services. Emphasis will be placed on providing improved services to employers and employees of industries and establishments strategically situated in interstate commerce.

Unemployment trust fund.—Under present law, unemployment compensation benefit payments in the fiscal year 1955 are expected to be somewhat higher than in 1954 because of an increase in claims of short duration and liberalization of benefits by States. Receipts in 1955 are estimated somewhat lower than in the current fiscal year. The legislation I am recommending to broaden unemployment compensation coverage will increase both the receipts and the benefit payments. Trust-fund transactions are not included in the totals of budget receipts and expenditures.

UNEMPLOYMENT TRUST FUND

[Fiscal years. In millions]

Item	1953 actual	1954 estimated	1955 estimated
Receipts:			
Deposits by States and railroad unemployment taxes:			
Present programs	$1,391	$1,344	$1,329
Proposed legislation extending coverage	....	....	145
Interest	203	222	216
Payments:			
State and railroad withdrawals for benefits:			
Present programs	−1,004	−1,095	−1,195
Proposed legislation extending coverage	....	....	−60
Net accumulation, including proposed legislation	590	471	435
Balance in fund at close of year	9,244	9,715	10,150

GENERAL GOVERNMENT

Net expenditures for general government functions are estimated at 1,160 million dollars for the fiscal year 1955, compared with 1,175 million dollars in the fiscal year 1954. These expenditures are chiefly for the traditional Government activities not specifically classified elsewhere—making and enforcing the laws, collection of revenues, management of the public debt, and custody and management of public buildings and records.

GENERAL GOVERNMENT

[Fiscal years. In millions]

Program or agency	Expenditures			Recommended new obligational authority for 1955
	1953 actual	1954 estimated	1955 estimated	
Gross expenditures:				
Legislative functions................	$48	$46	$47	$46
Judicial function...................	27	29	30	30
Executive direction................	11	13	11	11
Federal financial management:				
Tax collection....................	269	277	265	266
Customs collection, debt management, and other....................	173	177	166	165
Other central services:				
Central property and records management..........................	179	158	156	155
Civil Service Commission..........	21	16	15	16
Other...........................	14	19	21	23
Unemployment compensation for Federal civilian employees (proposed legislation)......................	....	....	25	25
Retirement for Federal civilian employees...........................	324	34	32	32
Protective services and alien control:				
Federal Bureau of Investigation.....	71	77	78	78
Immigration and Naturalization Service.............................	40	41	39	39
Other...........................	22	29	22	21
Territories, possessions, and District of Columbia:				
District of Columbia:				
Present programs................	12	16	20	14
Proposed legislation.............	....	....	15	17
Territories and possessions..........	48	47	46	42
Other general government:				
Payment of claims and relief acts....	137	149	135	....
Weather Bureau..................	27	26	25	25
Other...........................	21	24	16	14
Total..........................	1,444	1,178	1,164	[1] 1,019
Deduct applicable receipts............	5	3	4	....
Net budget expenditures..............	1,439	1,175	1,160	....

[1] Compares with new obligational authority of 1,337 million dollars in 1953 and 1,033 million dollars in 1954.

Federal financial management.—During the past year the Internal Revenue Service has improved greatly the administration of Federal revenue laws. Further economies will be made by cutting overhead expenses. These savings of several million dollars will be used to strengthen the field audit staff and to obtain more effective collection and enforcement. Auditing of tax returns and settlements are being speeded up. Tax collection has been decentralized so that most decisions in individual cases can now be made in district offices near the taxpayer. The reduced staff in Washington is concerned primarily with developing overall policies and assuring uniformity in administration throughout the country. Nevertheless, serious problems remain. For example, despite the improvement in auditing, the backlog of unaudited returns and uncollected accounts has increased for several years. Strenuous efforts are being made to reverse this trend, both to increase collections and to permit a more prompt determination of taxpayers' liabilities.

Further reduction in expenditures by the Bureau of the Public Debt will be achieved in the fiscal year 1955 by revisions in the savings bond promotion program to place greater emphasis on the sale of larger denomination bonds, elimination of uneconomic sales outlets, and other economies. A large volume of savings bonds is now reaching maturity, but redemptions of these matured bonds are relatively low, since most owners are taking advantage of their right to continue to hold them at 3 percent interest.

Central property and records management.—Substantial reductions have been made in the expenditures of the General Services Administration for management of Government property and records. The fiscal year 1955 estimate of 156 million dollars is 23 million dollars below actual 1953 expenditures and 2 million dollars below the revised 1954 estimate. These savings primarily result from material reductions in building space rented for Government use, made possible in part by reductions in the scope of Government operations and accomplished through an aggressive and critical examination of requirements. In addition, numerous savings are being achieved by the General Services Administration which reduce the budget requirements of other agencies throughout the Government. Real property requirements and holdings are being reexamined and property determined to be surplus is being disposed of as rapidly as possible. Purchases of new materials have decreased as a result of elimination of unnecessary inventories by reduction in the number of separate types of items carried in inventories and by better utilization of property already on hand. Significant progress also is being made in controlling the volume of records, in their economical storage, and, when they are no longer essential, in accelerating their disposal.

Civil Service Commission.—As part of the program for strengthening the merit system of the Federal civil service, the budget provides funds to improve the standards used for the recruitment and transfer of personnel and to further the career development of Government employees. The Civil Service Commission expenditures as a whole, however, will decrease with improved management practices and with a decline in prospective workloads for the examination and placement of applicants and for the investigation of persons employed or seeking employment in the Federal service.

I am recommending legislation to strengthen further the merit system and to provide conditions of employment for Federal personnel more nearly comparable to those in private enterprise. Certain legal restrictions initiated at the beginning of the present national emergency on the appointment and promotion of Federal workers should be removed. The present statutory limits on the number of high-level executive and scientific positions should be raised. Government agencies should be permitted to select employees from among the top five rather than the top three on Federal civil-service registers. Existing inequities in overtime-pay practices should be corrected. Building and maintenance workers should be added to the categories of employees paid at rates prevailing locally in private employment for similar occupations. The incentive-awards program should be consolidated and improved in order to eliminate costly administration and to increase employee interest in greater efficiency and economy. The cost of these changes in the main can be absorbed within the appropriations recommended for the agencies concerned.

Unemployment compensation for Federal workers.—I strongly recommend extension of the unemployment compensation system to give Federal employees the same benefits as are now provided to most workers in private employment. This will require an estimated 25 million dollars in expenditures for benefit payments in the fiscal year 1955. This program could be administered under contractual arrangements made through the Department of Labor with existing State unemployment compensation systems.

Retirement for Federal civilian personnel.—An appropriation of 30 million dollars is recommended to permit the continued payment to retired Federal workers of temporary cost-of-living increases as authorized by the Congress in 1952. The budget also includes 2 million dollars to pay annuities under special laws.

The civil-service retirement system is financed jointly by employee contributions and appropriations by the Government. The Congress, at its last session, however, did not appropriate for the Government's payments to the fund. The resumption of these payments is not included in this budget. Recommendations for financing this system as well as other retirement programs for Federal personnel will be determined after the Committee on Retirement Policy for Federal Personnel completes its study and reports to the Congress on or before June 30, 1954.

Protective services and alien control.—The Federal Bureau of Investigation, as the investigative arm of the Department of Justice, obtains evidence for use in legal actions involving violations of Federal law. The crime rate throughout the country has put an increasing burden on the Bureau. The Bureau also has primary responsibility for coordinating investigations in the executive branch necessary for the Nation's internal security. Such investigations continue at peak levels. It is essential, therefore, that the Bureau staff be adequate to discharge these responsibilities.

District of Columbia.—I strongly recommend enactment of legislation to finance the expanded public works construction urgently needed in the National Capital. This legislation would authorize an increase of 9 million dollars in the annual Federal payment to the general fund of the District of Columbia, and an additional 1 million dollars for full payment for all water and related services. It would authorize 107 million dollars of additional interest-bearing loans to the District over the next decade, of which an estimated 5 million dollars would be spent in the fiscal year 1955. These expenditures by the Federal Government would be accompanied by substantial increases in taxes paid by District taxpayers. This legislation would, for the first time in recent years, place Federal payments to the District government on a level commensurate with the Federal Government's position in and its demands upon the District. It would permit the District to start a long-term program of public works necessary to make the Capital City worthy of our great Nation.

Territories and possessions.—The Federal Government also has special responsibilities for administering the various Territories and possessions, including the Canal Zone and the Trust Territory of the Pacific Islands. Included in this budget are certain necessary increases in expenditures for continuing the civilian administration of the Trust Territory, except those islands in the northern Marianas returned to the jurisdiction of the Navy. I recommend that the Congress enact at an early date legislation establishing the basic form of government for the Trust Territory to replace the present temporary arrangements.

Intergovernmental relations.—A Commission on Intergovernmental Relations is now studying the proper role of the Federal Government in relation to the State and local governments. It is giving particular attention to fiscal relationships, such as Federal grants-in-aid, tax sources, and intergovernmental tax immunities, and will report shortly on certain aspects of its assignment.

Claims and relief acts.—The payment of certified claims makes up the total expenditure figure of 135 million dollars estimated for claims, judgments, and private relief acts in the fiscal year 1955. Most of these payments are for claims resulting from activities of the Department of Defense. The apparent decline of 14 million dollars in expenditures in the fiscal year 1955 is due to the usual omission in the budget year of any specific estimate for other claims, judgments, and relief acts.

Receipts of public enterprise funds.—The operations of the Virgin Islands Corporation account for most of the 4 million dollars in receipts of public enterprise funds.

INTEREST

Primarily as a result of the large increase in the public debt during World War II, interest payments now account for about 10 percent of Federal expenditures. Interest payments are fixed primarily by the size of the public debt and by interest rates on debt already outstanding.

Interest on the public debt.—Interest payments on the public debt in the fiscal year 1955 are estimated at 6,800 million dollars. This is an increase of 275 million dollars over estimated expenditures for the current fiscal year, and 297 million dollars above actual expenditures in 1953.

The increase in 1955 reflects both the higher average interest rates and the larger public debt. The average rate on the interest-bearing public debt rose from 2.33 percent on June 30, 1952, to 2.41 percent on De-

INTEREST

[Fiscal years. In millions]

Item	Budget expenditures (net)			Recommended new obligational authority for 1955
	1953 actual	1954 estimated	1955 estimated	
Interest on public debt...............	$6,503	$6,525	$6,800	$6,800
Interest on refunds of receipts..........	75	70	70	70
Interest on uninvested trust deposits.....	5	5	5	5
Total.........................	6,583	6,600	6,875	[1] 6,875

[1]Compares with new obligational authority of 6,583 million dollars in 1953 and 6,600 million dollars in 1954.

cember 31, 1953, primarily because of the refinancing of maturing obligations at the higher market rates prevailing. As the result of the deficit financing during the same period the public debt has increased from 259 billion dollars to 275 billion dollars (including about one-half billion dollars not subject to the statutory debt limitation).

The budget of the United States is the financial expression of the administration's program for the coming fiscal year. An understanding of its scope and content is a high challenge to every citizen.

When I took office a year ago, I promised the Congress and the people that this administration would seek to chart a fiscal and economic policy which would reduce the planned deficits and bring the budget into balance.

I warned that this would not be easy. There still are heavy national security requirements. Substantial expenditures are by law relatively nondiscretionary. The far-reaching activities of the Federal Government are extremely complex.

Despite these inherent difficulties, we have made great progress. Federal expenditures have been cut substantially, tax reductions have been made justifiable, and the budgetary deficit has been sharply reduced.

We have, furthermore, made appropriate provision for our national security and for our international obligations and we have been able to propose certain increases in Federal expenditures to advance our domestic well-being and to foster economic growth.

I firmly believe, therefore, that this budget represents a plan of government which will not only protect our way of life but will also strengthen our economic base and enhance the welfare of all our people.

Dwight D. Eisenhower

NOTE: As printed, references to special analyses appearing in the budget document have been deleted.

15 ¶ Memorandum Concerning Purchase of Savings Bonds by Government Employees.
January 22, 1954

Memorandum to the Heads of Departments and Agencies:

The nation's economic welfare requires the widest possible distribution of the national debt through the continued sale of United States Savings Bonds to the people. To this end it is important that Government employees continue their leadership in the purchase of Savings Bonds through the Pay Roll Savings Plan.

The Interdepartmental Savings Bond Committee established by Executive Order No. 9953 of April 23, 1948, provides a vehicle for the effective promotion of the Pay Roll Savings Plan. This Committee is composed of the heads of the several executive departments and agencies or their designated alternates.

I therefore request that each of you give the fullest cooperation to the Chairman, Mr. Edward F. Bartelt, Fiscal Assistant Secretary of the Treasury, in the work of the Committee. Any of you who will be unable to work personally with the Committee should immediately designate an alternate from among the senior officials of your department or agency.

Dwight D. Eisenhower

16 ¶ Memorandum Transmitting Report of the Commission on Foreign Economic Policy.
January 23, 1954

WITH THIS MEMORANDUM, I am transmitting a copy of the Report to the President and the Congress by the Commission on Foreign

Economic Policy. The Commission, as you know, was set up, at my request, by the Congress to study and report on the over-all foreign economic policy of this country.

I am anxious that Executive Departments and Agencies with responsibilities in the area of foreign economic policy proceed immediately with an intensive review of this report as a first step in the formulation of a unified Administration program to be submitted to the Congress for its attention during the current session.

I am confident that, on the basis of the Report, it will be possible to develop a program that will advance the best interests both of the United States and of the free world.

DWIGHT D. EISENHOWER

NOTE: A copy of this memorandum was sent to the heads of all departments and agencies having responsibility for foreign economic policy.

The Commission on Foreign Economic Policy, of which Clarence B. Randall served as Chairman, was established pursuant to the act approved August 7, 1953 (67 Stat. 472). The Commission's report (94 pp.), transmitted to the President and the Congress on January 23, 1954, together with a minority report (20 pp.), transmitted January 30, were published by the Government Printing Office (January 1954).

17 ¶ Special Message to the Congress on Housing. *January* 25, 1954

To the Congress of the United States:

I submit herewith measures designed to promote the efforts of our people to acquire good homes, and to assist our communities to develop wholesome neighborhoods in which American families may live and prosper.

The development of conditions under which every American family can obtain good housing is a major objective of national policy. It is important for two reasons. First, good housing in good neighborhoods is necessary for good citizenship and good health among our people. Second, a high level of housing construction and vigorous community development are essential to the economic and social well being of our country. It is, therefore, properly a concern of this government to insure that opportunities are provided every American family to acquire a good home.

In working toward this goal, we must not be complacent. The Federal government must provide aggressive and positive leadership. At the same time actions and programs must be avoided that would make our citizens increasingly dependent upon the Federal government to supply their housing needs. We believe that needed progress can best be made by full and effective utilization of our competitive economy with its vast resources for building and financing homes for our people.

The building of new homes provides only a partial solution to the housing problem. The Nation has tremendous assets in its 37,000,000 existing non-farm homes. The fact that 20,000,000 of these are owner-occupied demonstrates the continuing efforts of our people to have their own homes, where they can raise their families in self-respect and in good surroundings. But 19,000,000 of our existing non-farm homes are more than 30 years old. We must encourage the conservation and improvement of our existing supply of homes for the important contribution this can make to the raising of national housing standards.

Our housing deficiencies continue to be serious. Millions of our people still live in slums. Millions more live in run-down, declining neighborhoods. The national interest demands the elimination of slum conditions and the rehabilitation of declining neighborhoods. Many of our local communities have made good progress in this work and are eager to make further substantial improvements but are hard put to find the needed resources.

The knowledge, the skills, the resources and, most important, the will to do this job already exist in the Nation. We have a private home-building industry and home-financing institutions that are strong and vigorous. We have a highly skilled labor force. Savings are high. While some of our communities are financially hard-pressed, they are increasingly alert to the need both for improving their existing physical plants and for sound growth and development proportionate to their expanding populations. We have the unlimited resources which grow from the independence, pride and determination of the American citizen. I am convinced that every American family can have a decent home if the builders, lenders, and communities and the local, State and Federal governments, as well as individual citizens, will put their abilities and determination energetically to the task.

To help find the best way to meet our national housing needs, I recently appointed an Advisory Committee on Government Housing Policies and

Programs, consisting of leading citizens experienced in the problems of housing, mortgage finance, and community development. Under the Chairmanship of the Housing and Home Finance Administrator, this Committee has made an exhaustive study of existing Federal housing programs. It has also analyzed numerous proposals for the development of a program better adapted to our present housing requirements. The conclusions of this Committee, and the results of our own studies and experience in administering present housing laws, are reflected in the recommendations I am about to propose. Several of these recommendations provide an entirely new approach to the task of meeting our housing needs.

I. NEIGHBORHOOD REHABILITATION AND ELIMINATION AND PREVENTION OF SLUMS

In order to clear our slums and blighted areas and to improve our communities, we must eliminate the causes of slums and blight. This is essentially a problem for our cities. However, Federal assistance is justified for communities which face up to the problem of neighborhood decay and undertake long-range programs directed to its prevention. The main elements of such programs should include:

First. Prevention of the spread of blight into good areas of the community through strict enforcement of housing and neighborhood standards and strict occupancy controls;

Second. Rehabilitation of salvable areas, turning them into sound, healthy neighborhoods by replanning, removing congestion, providing parks and playgrounds, reorganizing streets and traffic, and by facilitating physical rehabilitation of deteriorated structures;

Third. Clearance and redevelopment of nonsalvable slums.

Existing housing programs permit an effective attack on only the third of these essential tasks. A new approach will help our communities to deal effectively with the other two. I, therefore, make the following recommendations:

1. Title I of the Housing Act of 1949 should be broadened. It should make available a program of loans and grants for the renovation of salvable areas and for the outright elimination of nonsalvable slums. Under this program, there would be immediately available from existing authorizations approximately $700,000,000 of loan funds and $250,000,000 in capital grant funds. As our communities are enabled by this broadened

authorization to increase the scope and pace of their efforts, I shall request such additional loan and grant authorizations as can be effectively used.

2. The Federal Housing Administration should be authorized to insure private credit used to rehabilitate homes in declining neighborhoods. This new program should be limited to specific areas where the local community has given adequate assurances that it will carry out a workable plan of neighborhood renewal.

3. A program of matching grants to States and metropolitan areas should be established to enable smaller communities and metropolitan area planning agencies to do the planning job which is necessary to arrest the spread of slum conditions. I recommend that the Congress authorize the appropriation of $5,000,000 for this purpose.

II. CONSERVATION AND IMPROVEMENT OF EXISTING HOUSING

Because of the housing shortages that developed during the depression and war years, recent Federal housing activities have been directed mainly to increasing the production of new homes. But while the high demand for new homes will continue, and while private activity will be encouraged to meet that demand, we must also undertake the long-delayed job of maintaining existing homes in good condition. Millions of our people live in older homes in which they have invested their savings; our people and our economy will greatly benefit if these homes can be kept in good repair and are brought up to modern standards of comfort and convenience.

It is not enough, therefore, to rehabilitate homes in obsolete neighborhoods. To encourage the maintenance and improvement of homes wherever located, I recommend the following additional amendments to the National Housing Act:

1. The maximum permissible terms authorized for the insurance of loans on existing homes should be made comparable to those available for new housing. This amendment will end the present discriminatory policy which favors the purchasing of new as against existing homes. It should have the important additional advantage of facilitating the trading in of older homes on new home purchases.

2. The maximum loan which can be insured under Title I of the National Housing Act to repair and modernize single-family homes should be increased from $2,500 to $3,000 and the maximum term should be

extended from three years to five years. Comparable revisions should be made in loan limitations and terms authorized for the rehabilitation of multiple dwellings. Since the terms of such loans have not changed for fifteen years, these adjustments are obviously needed to help our citizens repair and improve their homes.

III. HOUSING FOR LOW-INCOME FAMILIES

The continued lack of adequate housing, both new and used, for low-income families is evidence of past failures in improving the housing conditions of all of our people. Approval of my preceding recommendations will increase the opportunities of many families with low incomes to buy good older homes. But a more direct and more positive approach to this serious problem must be taken by the government. I recommend, therefore, a new and experimental program under which the Federal Housing Administration would be authorized to insure long-term loans of modest amounts, with low initial payment, on both new and existing dwellings, for low-income families. The application of this new authority should be limited to those families who must seek other homes as a result of slum rehabilitation, conservation, and similar activities in the public interest. I recognize, as did the Advisory Committee, that this program represents a challenge to private builders and lenders. In order to assist them in meeting this challenge, a greater proportion of the risk should be underwritten by the Federal Housing Administration than it regularly insures. The successful development of this program will afford a much greater proportion of our lower income families an opportunity to own or rent a suitable home.

Until these new programs have been fully tested and by actual performance have shown their success, we should continue at a reasonable level the public housing program authorized by the Housing Act of 1949. I recommend, therefore, that the Congress authorize construction, during the next four years, of 140,000 units of new public housing, to be built in annual increments of 35,000 units. Special preference among eligible families should be given to those who must be relocated because of slum clearance, neighborhood rehabilitation, or similar public actions. The continuance of this program will be reviewed before the end of the four-year period, when adequate evidence exists to determine the success of the other measures I have recommended. In addition to this requested extension of the public housing program, the Housing Administrator will recommend amendments to correct various defects which experience has revealed in the present public housing program.

IV. HOUSING PROBLEMS OF MINORITY GROUP FAMILIES

It must be frankly and honestly acknowledged that many members of minority groups, regardless of their income or their economic status, have had the least opportunity of all of our citizens to acquire good homes. Some progress, although far too little, has been made by the Housing Agency in encouraging the production and financing of adequate housing available to members of minority groups. However, the administrative policies governing the operations of the several housing agencies must be, and they will be, materially strengthened and augmented in order to assure equal opportunity for all of our citizens to acquire, within their means, good and well-located homes. We shall take steps to insure that families of minority groups displaced by urban redevelopment operations have a fair opportunity to acquire adequate housing; we shall prevent the dislocation of such families through the misuse of slum clearance programs; and we shall encourage adequate mortgage financing for the construction of new housing for such families on good, well-located sites.

V. MODERNIZATION OF NATIONAL HOUSING ACT

There are certain deficiencies and numerous obsolete and unnecessary provisions in the National Housing Act. The Housing Administrator will present to the appropriate Committees of the Congress a number of proposals to modernize this basic law. These recommendations will include a scale of mortgage ceilings more realistically related to the increased cost of both single-family and multi-family structures and complementary revisions in mortgage ceilings for cooperative projects.

VI. ADJUSTMENT OF PERMISSIBLE TERMS OF GOVERNMENT INSURED OR GUARANTEED MORTGAGES

Because inflationary or deflationary pressures can be accentuated or diminished by mortgage credit terms, government operations in connection with the insurance or guarantee of mortgage loans should be judiciously adjusted to prevailing economic conditions. The Congress has already given the President limited authority to adjust from time to time, in the light of economic conditions, the permissible terms on government guaranteed and insured mortgages. I urge the Congress to broaden this authority to cover all loans insured by the Federal Housing Administration and guaranteed by the Veterans Administration. Such authority would permit adjustments, within appropriate statutory limits, in maximum interest rates and in loan-to-value ratios and maturities. This action by the Congress would materially strengthen our ability to stabilize economic activity and high levels of production and employment. A fuller discussion of the importance of this recommendation will be included in the Economic Report to be submitted to the Congress on January 28.

VII. SECONDARY MORTGAGE MARKET

In recent years the Federal National Mortgage Association has functioned as a primary lender rather than as a secondary source of mortgage credit. As a result the Federal government now finds itself with substantial frozen investments in guaranteed and insured mortgages. Because of the terms on which these mortgages were written and the prices at which they were purchased, they are not readily salable in the private market. The following changes should therefore be made:

1. The Federal National Mortgage Association should be reorganized to require the users of the facility to invest funds on a basis which would eventually permit the full retirement of government funds from secondary mortgage market operations. The Federal government should be enabled to purchase the initial stock of the reorganized association, but private capital funds supplied by the users of the facility should be built up to speed the retirement of the government's initial investment.

2. The reorganized Federal National Mortgage Association should be given three basic responsibilities:

First, it should be authorized to issue its own non-guaranteed debentures on the private market. With the funds so obtained, it can perform a desirable service by buying mortgages at market rates in areas where investment funds are scarce, for resale in areas where there is a surplus of funds. There is need for an organization to carry out this true function of a secondary market.

Second, the new Association should be authorized to manage and liquidate present mortgage holdings which are government-owned assets. It should be made clear that such liquidation is to be accomplished in an orderly manner and in such a way as to protect the interests of the individual borrower. Since Treasury funds were used in the acquisition of these assets, all proceeds of this liquidation should be returned to the Treasury.

Third, the President should be enabled to authorize the Federal National Mortgage Association to borrow directly from the Treasury for the sole purpose of purchasing certain kinds and types of insured and guaranteed loans when the President determines such action to be necessary in the public interest. For this purpose the borrowing authority of the Association should be limited to a reasonable amount to be made available from the present Treasury borrowing authorization of the Association. Although outright primary support for certain types of loans may be desirable in the public interest from time to time, this support should be clearly identified as the direct use of Treasury funds for mortgage purchasing, and the extent of such support should be closely controlled.

Approval of these recommendations will correct the most serious defects of the present mortgage purchasing operations of the Federal government and will authorize an effective secondary market facility, relying primarily on private financing. It will also provide flexible authority under which the Federal government could directly purchase mortgages, should economic conditions and the public interest indicate the need for such action.

VIII. REORGANIZATION OF FEDERAL HOUSING ACTIVITIES

The present organization of Federal housing activities is unsatisfactory. The Housing and Home Finance Agency is a loosely knit federation of separate organizations. Its present structure is cumbersome, inefficient and lacks clearcut recognition of administrative authority. The result is confusing to the public. Neither the Congress nor the Executive Branch can expect it to achieve good and efficient management under its present structure. I shall, therefore, submit to the Congress a reorganization plan to provide a better grouping of housing activities headed by an Administrator with adequate supervisory authority.

I believe that this message offers the means whereby our Nation may provide more and better homes for our families. By applying these recommendations we shall add to the comfort and the health of our people; we shall strengthen the economic and social fibers of our Nation; and we shall reinforce the freedom and self-reliance which have brought greatness to our land. I urge, therefore, that the Congress give to these recommendations its early and favorable consideration.

DWIGHT D. EISENHOWER

18 ¶ The President's News Conference of January 27, 1954.

THE PRESIDENT. Ladies and gentlemen, I have one or two items I think may be of some interest.

As you know, President Bayar and his wife are going to be here this evening as visitors to our Government, and there will be a formal dinner for them this evening. I am delighted to have them, of course. Turkey has emerged a very modern and sturdy nation and great friend of ours, and so I regard it as a great privilege to have the opportunity of paying a compliment to them.

The other item that certainly interests me and, I hope, you, is coffee.

I want to be very careful what I say. I am going to read one or two sentences, they are not particularly for quotation, but I don't want to misquote the Federal Trade Commission. I understand they are going to have a press conference themselves, so I am not trying to steal their story. I just want to tell you, up to date, what I know about it.

On January 13 they started a preliminary investigation to see what was the trouble about coffee prices in this country. They discovered enough that they thought a full-scale investigation was indicated, and is going to take place.

Now, the Chairman said that the Commission will give particular attention to the charge that domestic trading in coffee futures on the Coffee and Sugar Exchange is restricted to certain types of coffee, and that all domestic coffee prices are tied in in some ways to the Exchange price.

What it all means and comes down to is that they are going to try to determine first whether the law has been violated and, secondly, to publish all the facts in an economic report.

Of course, the Commission will maintain liaison with the Department of Justice.

Just exactly what is going on, no one seems to know. Of course, we do know there is a shortage. Back in the thirties there was a great surplus;

there was a reduction in planting, I believe even a cutback in the acreage devoted to coffee, and now demand has caught up. Add to that a few frosts and things like that; it's been bad, and it's bad for all of us in coffee at this time. Anyway, the Trade Commission is making a full investigation of the matter.

In the past week, as you know, the Randall Commission reported to me, and I have sent copies of the Randall Commission Report to each executive agency of Government.

Now, the idea of the Commission was conceived in line with the whole general policy of developing a stronger America. It has to be examined by all interested agencies to make certain that in trying to achieve that effort, we don't damage or harm seriously, at least, any great group in America. To that I would never be a party, because the attempt is to develop the economy of America, make it stronger, not to make it weaker.

Because of the very dedicated work all these people did, I think all of us owe them a debt of thanks. Certainly I feel so. And I feel that Mr. Randall himself has worked so hard on it that he still has a field of usefulness as we analyze and present these conclusions in the form of specific recommendations. So I have retained him as a Special Consultant to the White House, which he has agreed to, to help out in that way for the time being.

Now, let's see if I had anything else here. I think that is all the special items I have. We'll go to questions.

Q. Merriman Smith, United Press: Mr. President, in your recent speech to the Anti-Defamation League of B'nai B'rith, you spoke quite highly of part of the American code of behavior being that the accused had the right to face his accuser. A California Congressman, a Democrat named Condon, yesterday before the House Un-American Activities Committee, asked for the right to face his accusers. He had been mentioned in an AEC report as being a Communist, and he denied that. I wonder if you think your code, as you spelled it out for the Anti-Defamation League, would apply in his case?

THE PRESIDENT. Well, Mr. Smith, you are asking me to take one off-the-record expression of conviction, translate it quickly into a specific case, and make an application in another quick conclusion.

I certainly believe earnestly in the general statement that I made before. This case, I really have had no connection with. As I understand, it was done in the Atomic Energy Commission.

Just what can be done in these cases, I am not certain, but I do think that this man has got to be given every right to clear himself. This is the first time I knew he had been accused of being a security risk, and I don't know any of the circumstances; but I certainly believe that if we are going to have decency and justice for the individual in this country, he has got to be given full opportunity in some way to establish the falsity of charges.

Just how that works out in a specific case, I think I will have to pass that one for a moment. Maybe there will be a report made on it to me, on that subject; I don't know.

Q. Raymond Brandt, St. Louis Post-Dispatch: Mr. President, on this Randall Commission Report, after the agencies have reported, will you send a special message to Congress?

THE PRESIDENT. I haven't any fixed conclusions; I suppose I will, yes, I think I will. That was certainly my original intention.

Q. Mr. Brandt: And it will follow the general line of the majority report, if you can find out the majority? [*Laughter*]

THE PRESIDENT. It is being analyzed now, but there is, generally speaking, a majority opinion runs through it. The recommendations I make will be based upon the Report and upon the analyses made by the several Departments of Government.

Q. Ray Scherer, National Broadcasting Company: I have a question allied to Mr. Smith's, and I would like to ask you to comment, if you will, sir, on a development in Norwalk, Connecticut. It appears this morning on the front page of a paper that is generally deemed to be reliable, and it goes like this: "The names and addresses of residents of this city whose record of activities are deemed to be Communistic by the local Post for the Veterans of Foreign Wars, are being forwarded by it to the Federal Bureau of Investigation."

THE PRESIDENT. Now, what do you want me to comment?

Q. Mr. Scherer: Whether you think this fits in with the expressions in your B'nai B'rith speech: "It was learned today that a special committee formed from men from all walks of life had been created to sift the suspects." Do you think this might be a threat to civil liberties?

THE PRESIDENT. Well, I don't believe you can stop anybody from putting something down and sending forward names; but I believe that there are libel and slander laws in our country, and if a man makes or a group of people make false charges against someone, they have to be responsible for their own statements. So just what this one is, I don't know; I had not heard of it, and I am not sure what opinion I would have on this at all.

Q. Sarah McClendon, El Paso Times: In line with that same thing, we learned at Mr. Brownell's press conference last week, and I believe Mr. Donald Dawson stated this in the paper this morning, that if you are employed by the Federal Government and you suddenly leave or quit, your friends may think you have been fired for security reasons; you have no means of proving to them. I know a man who quit the State Department the other day, and he said, "Please don't put it in the paper; I am just quitting, but somebody will think I have been fired for security reasons." Is there some way we can devolve a system for tagging these people, like the Army does, with honorable discharges and dishonorable discharges?

THE PRESIDENT. Of course, this whole thing is a very confused business, and since there have been so many hundreds of thousands, millions of people employed by the Government, unusual and cloudy cases arise.

As I told you before, our idea is here that we should not charge anyone with disloyalty or subversive activity unless that is proved in a court of law, and I don't believe that we should. We talk and try to devise a scheme whereby those people whose records gave you some evidence that they were not good security risks in the Government should not be there employed.

Now, that is all that we have ever tried to say about this thing. Certainly no one that I know of has ever gone a bit further.

As to differentiating between the person who gets, let's say, a letter of commendation when he goes, and the other, I think it ought to be possible. You bring up a point of this thing, I must tell you, that I had not thought about; but I think something like that ought to be possible. Certainly, I am going to ask about it and see whether it can be done.

Q. Mrs. May Craig, Maine Papers: Mr. President, last night in a speech at a pro-Bricker amendment dinner, it was charged that the Status of Forces legislation of the last year, which subjected American soldiers to foreign courts in NATO countries does, in fact, deprive them of constitutional rights. When I was in France last September, Americans told me that our American soldiers were so being deprived in their opinion. Has that been brought to your attention in relation to any cases of American soldiers?

THE PRESIDENT. Well, in this complicated business of trying to make America stronger in the world, you do run into a variety of situations involving individuals.

Now, I don't know what the people argue. The Status of Forces agreement was one for which I worked very seriously when I was in Europe, for this reason: fundamentally, any foreigner in the United States can be tried by a United States court if he commits a crime of any kind, and we have units of other nations come here occasionally. This same thing happens in a foreign country.

Now, these people, let me point out, are our partners. In no case where we make agreements with other nations are we trying to establish or act like they're satellites. That is a philosophy that seems to me repugnant to the whole concept of freedom, of liberty.

And remember this: the Status of Forces agreement, as I recall the provisions—after all, it is 2 years ago that I studied them—any crime that is committed between individuals of our units, they are tried by us; anything that happens when the man is on official duty, they are tried by us.

The actual time when the man is exposed to some kind of action by a foreign court is when he is on leave, and he is in exactly the same status, as a practical measure, as you were when you went there.

Now, if you had committed an offense in France, or wherever you were, would you have expected to come back to the United States to be tried? You would have been tried, and you would accept that risk when you go over there.

The difference is that a soldier is ordered over, but he does have his post, he does have his unit, and it is still expected then that when he goes off of his own territory and goes off on leave, on his own personal status, that he does become responsible to their courts. Even there, there are certain safeguards in the way he is represented and the information given to our embassies.

Now, this same thing applies to people who are here. All these treaties are reciprocal, and that is the thing to remember. They are arranged so as to do justice to the very greatest possible extent to the individual, and to meet national needs.

Q. Charles von Fremd, CBS Television: Mr. President, yesterday Senator Young said that during the campaign you always promised the farmers nothing less than 90 percent of parity, and he challenged your flexible price supports at 75 to 90 percent of parity. I would like to ask you, do your recent agricultural recommendations represent a change in your thinking on this matter, and if so, why?

THE PRESIDENT. Well, now, let me ask you one question: did you go to the trouble to read my speeches in the campaign?

Q. Mr. von Fremd: Yes, sir; I did.

THE PRESIDENT. All right; then, did you find anything that said I ever promised permanent rigid price supports at 90 percent? Ever? Any place?

Q. Mr. von Fremd: Mr. President, I am just referring to the remarks of Senator Young yesterday.

THE PRESIDENT. I know, but I don't answer individuals; I answer questions directed to principles and ideas. I am not engaged in argument with individuals.

Q. Mr. von Fremd: My question then, sir, is your present plan, which you submitted on agriculture, does that represent in any way a change in your thinking?

THE PRESIDENT. None at all.

Actually, what I promised was this: I said there is on the books a law, an amendment to the acts of '48 and '49, which carries rigid price supports through December of 1954; that law will be rigidly enforced, and there will be no attempt to tamper with it.

In the meantime—and I promised this in every talk I ever made about agriculture—we will get together the most comprehensive, the most broadly based groups of actual farmers and farm students and agricultural intellectuals, and all the rest of them, get them together to devise a program that seems to meet best the needs of our country; that is exactly what I said. That is exactly what we have done, and we have come up with a program in which I believe. I believe it to be as nearly adapted to the needs of this country as we can possibly devise at this moment.

Q. Marvin Arrowsmith, Associated Press: Mr. President, would you comment on Molotov's demands for a Big Five Conference including Red China and world problems?

THE PRESIDENT. Well, of course, my attitude about these things, I think, is known; but in any event we do have a conference now going on in Berlin to which our representative has gone.

I have, as you know, I hope, the utmost confidence in Secretary Dulles and his wisdom, and I know there is going to be no change in policy. He is going to stick to and, so far as he is able in that conference, carry out the beliefs and policies of this Government.

I don't think that it is in order for me to speak in detail of my opinions at the moment. He is now on the front line and is carrying out the job, and I am backing him up.

Q. Robert Spivack, New York Post: The Peiping radio, I understand, has been having a propaganda field day with the case of Corporal Dickenson, and while I am sure that he will be given a fair trial, I wonder if you feel that there is any better way of handling the cases of these men who admit their mistake, and had the courage to break with the Communists.

THE PRESIDENT. I have two remarks on that: I was so disturbed when I saw it in the paper that I got hold of Secretary Wilson, and we discussed it.

By no means do I think that this investigation was started merely because the man had been for a moment saying he believed he'd stay Communist and stay over there.

I think there must be something else to it, although I personally am not very well informed on that. This is the fact: they said they were going to put him, I believe, before a court-martial. Actually, any court-martial in the Army—and here I can speak from a little bit more experience—is preceded by a very long investigative process.

If, say, you put a man in to prefer charges against him, those charges are handed to an impartial and objective group, sometimes individuals, sometimes a group, and a long investigation goes through to determine whether there are real grounds for trying this man.

That investigation will, just as a matter of law, take place; and I know that Secretary Wilson himself is keeping close touch with it to see that no injustice is done.

Certainly, I am sure that I know of no Army man or anybody else who would punish a man for a simple mistake committed under the most trying of circumstances, and who later repented. After all, we can read the tale of the prodigal son profitably occasionally.

Q. Daniel Schorr, CBS Radio: Mr. President, aside from the Dickenson case, as such, do you have any thoughts on the whole vexing problem confronting this country in the form of those who signed germ warfare confessions, and those 21 who remained behind?

THE PRESIDENT. Well, the 21 who remained behind, I don't know of anything you can do, except to take the action the Services did. Secretary Wilson just decided to separate them from our Services under dishonorable conditions.

Now, for these people who come back, I think there has to be a real investigation and study to see what to do with them.

We must not, sitting here in the comparative safety of Washington— there are dangers of another kind, at least—[*laughter*]—let us not be too sure of what we would have done under these same circumstances.

What I would hope that the Services do as they investigate this thing is to have some real sympathy in their hearts as they look into it. And I must say this: my own experience, my long experience with the armed services, was that usually you can find there the full average measure of decency and humanity when you are forced into this business of judging and passing judgment upon the weaknesses or failures of others. I think that there will be no attempt on the part of anybody to be harsh in these cases.

Q. Robert L. Riggs, Louisville Courier-Journal: Mr. President, we took up with Mr. Brownell the matter of breaking down these 2200; that was on your advice, I believe. Mr. Brownell said we ought to go to the Civil Service Commission, and I see by the papers that Mr. Young of the Civil Service Commission has notified a Congressman that it is up to the White House and the National Security Council. We are going around in circles, are we not, sir?

THE PRESIDENT. Well, probably what he said is because he is compelled, under an Executive order that I issued some time back, to make reports to us; I hadn't thought of that when I mentioned it before. You see, the Attorney General drew up this security order, as opposed to the so-called loyalty boards and so forth, and I was thinking of him as a man who was more intimately aware of the circumstances than I was.

Now, it is possible that there is some kind of a time thing on it; but on the other hand, I don't know whether there can ever be any real breakdown into specific categories that you people might like.

I will have to ask Chairman Young myself what this thing is developing into. But as far as I am concerned, I am trying to protect the service of the United States and do no one damage, if I can help it. That is the reason I answered one question awhile ago that I believe there ought to be some way of showing when people are separated with complete honor and for reasons of their own, and when they are just something else.

But a poor security risk—I am not going to say that what we deem to be a poor security risk under statements made on the record reaching clear back into babyhood, I am not going to say that he is a disloyal person; I just won't do it because I don't necessarily believe it.

Q. Mr. Riggs: Sir, a moment ago you said you were not aware of anyone who used any such terms. Governor Dewey has used the words "spies and traitors," and then referred to 1400 security risks.

THE PRESIDENT. When I said anyone, I meant anyone that was within this administration. I am sorry.

Q. Norman Carignan, Associated Press: Mr. President, last Thursday you held a meeting at the White House with your brother, Dr. Milton Eisenhower, and several Cabinet officers and other Government officials dealing with Latin America. And I gather it dealt with the loan policy towards Latin America. I wonder if you could tell us something about the meeting and any conclusions reached?

THE PRESIDENT. I merely can say this: the meeting ended with an agreement that there would be an intensive study by several of the interested agencies as to exactly what some of these specific problems are, and whether there should be any change in policy as of now. I would think it would be a little while before their answers would be available.

Q. Edward Sims, Columbia (S.C.) State and Record: Ever since you made the statement in Augusta about unemployment areas and defense contracts for unemployment areas, there has been, of course, intense interest in my section and other sections; and this morning there is a report out that you have assured or the Government has assured—not you personally—20 percent of the defense contracts to unemployed areas. Is that something new? Would you comment on that at all?

THE PRESIDENT. In no case do I think there is a fixed rule of that kind. For example, suppose you are going to build a ship, how can you take 20 percent of a ship and put it some place else? Certain things just have to be done as units.

As I explained to you before, the great mass of these procurement orders will go out in the normal routine manner, lowest bidder and lowest responsible bidder, and that is that.

The law allows the withholding of a certain percentage—even that can differ—that can be put out then for negotiated bids as long as the bid is as low as the lowest bid you got in the normal line of communication. I believe that 20 percent is merely the maximum, that is what I understand.

Q. Jerry O'Leary, Washington Evening Star: Mr. President, do you see any signs of agreement between the opposing sides on the Bricker amendment? Do you have any information of a possible agreement?

THE PRESIDENT. Well, I can only say that certain of my associates down on the Hill keep hoping for it. So far as I know, there is nothing different from what you see in the papers.

Q. Richard Wilson, Cowles Publications: Some people have characterized your legislative program as an extension of the New Deal. I think former President Truman is one that has done that. Would you care to comment or discuss that?

THE PRESIDENT. I think the best comment on that is to go and take a look at the budget. Take a look at the budget he proposed, and what we did, and the direction in which we are going.

Q. Mr. Wilson: How would you draw a distinction between the two?

THE PRESIDENT. The difference in the direction in which it would go. One was going further and further into debt and at an increasing rate; and the other is trying to reduce the expenditures of Government and go the other way.

Now, let me point out: there were a number of things that started in the late 1920's and early 1930's that were continued on throughout the New Deal. The RFC notably is one.

I don't think anyone attempts to say that everything that was done by some political opponents, or by a political school in which he did not believe, is necessarily evil or bad for the country. I believe our job, I believe the job of this administration or any other that will come after it, is to take the situation as it exists, and what is good for the country.

I believe that we use titles, appellations, what do you call them, meanings of words that seem to get all confused—liberal, progressive, and all the rest of them. Nevertheless, I think it would be safe to say this:

when it comes down to dealing with the relationships between the human in this country and his Government, the people in this administration believe in being what I think we would normally call liberal; and when we deal with the economic affairs of this country, we believe in being conservative.

Now, I quite admit that there can be no distinct line drawn between the economy and the individual, and I am ready to say also that such a little capsule sort of description of an attitude can be pulled to pieces if you want to. But, in general, that is what we are trying to do. The difference here is that the Government's position, the Government's growth, the Government's activity under this new administration is to try to have its functions in conformity with the Constitution of this country; but in doing so, to make certain that the individuals realize that Government is a friend and is not their enemy in any way.

That is, by all odds, certainly an abbreviated answer to such a question, but I do think that all the way along we have showed the difference between this philosophy, the philosophy of this Government, and that of the New Deal.

Q. James Reston, New York Times: I wonder, sir, if you can give us any report about the Atomic Energy discussions you have had with the Soviet Ambassador, or rather that Mr. Dulles has had.

THE PRESIDENT. No, there is no report at this time. I don't know when there will be one, actually.

Q. Robert Clark, International News Service: Mr. President, your social security message would seem to have answered this, but I have been requested to ask you whether the administration has abandoned its original proposal to cut back to 1½ percent social security tax.

THE PRESIDENT. Well, last year, of course, I asked for its freezing for a year. Now my recommendations extend social security to something like ten million more people and increase the benefits, and it seems to us necessary to allow the 2 percent to go into effect.

Merriman Smith, United Press: Thank you, Mr. President.

NOTE: President Eisenhower's twenty-fifth news conference was held in the Executive Office Building from 10:33 to 11:02 o'clock on Wednesday morning, January 27, 1954. In attendance: 185.

19 ¶ Remarks of Welcome to President Bayar of Turkey. *January* 27, 1954

President and Madame Bayar:

It is a great privilege to speak for the American people and the Nation's Government in bidding you welcome here to the Capital.

On the personal side, Mrs. Eisenhower and I are very proud to have you, the Head of the great and friendly State of Turkey, as guests at the White House.

NOTE: The President greeted President Celal Bayar and Mme. Bayar on the North Portico of the White House at 5:00 p.m. A translation of President Bayar's reply follows:

I can hardly express the emotions that I feel at the warm acclaim that I have received ever since I have set foot on American soil.

I was very happy to accept the very kind invitation of that great soldier and statesman, your President Eisenhower, and of Mrs. Eisenhower. I am very proud to convey to them and to the American people the warm affection and the greetings of my Nation.

20 ¶ Toasts of the President and President Bayar at the White House. *January* 27, 1954

Your Excellency, Madame Bayar, distinguished guests of two countries:

Tonight, this company—this Capital—this country—is honored by the presence at this board of the Head of the Turkish Republic. We gladly seize the opportunity afforded us by his presence, to salute a nation which is one of the most gallant and staunchest defenders of freedom in the modern world.

The evolution of Turkey, taking place within the span of a single generation, is one of the marvels of our time. Fifty years ago—and there are a number of us here who can remember that long—the events, the names, and the faces of Turkey were little known to us. Our understanding of the country and its people was very meager indeed.

And then the change. Today we recognize it as a modern, progressive country, one that we are proud to call ally in the great problems that face the free world today. This great change was brought about by a dream of a group of men, a group of men headed by Mustafa Kemal Ataturk. He had a dream that with a band of devoted associates they translated into reality—by service, unselfish and dedicated service, to their country. Forgetting themselves, they gave their lives and their talents to the nation to which they belonged.

And since 1923 we see the transformation that has taken place. Now the great Ataturk is dead, but his work lives on, and our guest of honor this evening is one of the original band that worked with him to bring about this great change, and to make Turkey the nation she is today: great, and growing greater every day.

Our guest of honor, since that day in 1923, has been almost continuously in the Assembly of his country. He has held almost every position in his government, including that of Prime Minister, and now is honored by holding the highest position in the land.

In a feeble effort to show some of the appreciation of this Government and its people, for Turkey as a nation and its people, our Government has awarded to our guest of honor the Legion of Merit in the grade of Chief Commander, the highest honor that this Government can give to anyone in time of peace not a citizen of this country. And with your permission, I shall read the Citation:

"The President of the United States of America, authorized by Act of Congress July 20, 1942, has awarded the Legion of Merit, Degree of Chief Commander, to Celal Bayar, President of the Turkish Republic, for exceptionally meritorious conduct in the performance of outstanding services:

"The Turkish people have shown their confidence in Celal Bayar by entrusting him with high offices throughout his long public career, but especially when he was honored by being placed in the highest and most responsible position in Turkish public life—that of the Presidency of the Republic. In this high office, he has contributed greatly to the enrichment of that goodwill which characterizes the relationship between Turkey and the United States. Under his firm leadership, Turkey has continued to actively support those ideals which are cherished by free peoples everywhere, thus contributing effectively to the hopes for freedom and peace throughout the world." Signed by the President.

Now, my friends, as we lift our glasses to our guest of honor, let us remember that through him we do so, also, to the great nation of Turkey and its people—a people whose future we shall watch with interest, and wish for them everything that is good in a free world.

Ladies and gentlemen, President Bayar of Turkey.

NOTE: The President proposed this toast at a state dinner at the White House at 9:45 p.m. President Bayar responded in Turkish. Thereafter the following translation was read by John F. Simmons, Chief of Protocol:

Mr. President:

I am deeply moved by the warm reception and the manifestations of genuine friendship which I have experienced since I set foot on American soil.

I am particularly happy, as your guest this evening, to enjoy your solicitous hospitality in this legendary residence.

The emotion that I felt on listening to your kind words about my country was not only stirred by the sincere feelings which you so well expressed, but it was also due to the fact that I realized how well this country understood the revolution which has taken place in my country since the day that, under the leadership of one of her sons devoted to the cause of civilization and humanity, she changed her destiny until the day she won her place in the community of free countries and assumed her duties in the service of humanity.

There is no doubt that the words that you, a great general and outstanding statesman, have spoken as the highest authority of the great American nation, will be a source of endless joy to all my countrymen.

I also wish to thank you for your kind and gratifying words about myself. As you have said, I do in fact cherish the moral satisfaction of having worked together, from the first day to the last, with Kemal Ataturk, the saviour of my country, the founder of modern Turkey, and the architect of the Turkish Revolution.

But the group who rallied under Ataturk and who were then called "the na-tional force," are a symbol of the Turkish nation who pinned their destiny on him in the cause of a free and independent Turkish land, and for the ideal of a free and independent world according to the highest human concepts.

Today, these goals of the Turkish nation have been attained. Turkey shares the responsibility of a common fate with those nations of the free world who are making sacrifices for their liberty and independence. The happiest manifestation of that is in the firm ties which bind our two countries to each other.

I am very proud to hear that your government has decided to confer upon me the Legion of Merit, which is the highest award given in time of peace to a foreign citizen, in recognition of his services.

I accept this great honor, fully conscious of its worth, as a valuable token of the friendship of the American people towards my nation, which at the moment I represent on friendly American soil.

Turkey considers it a human and national duty to cooperate with the peoples who are striving for the realization of the ideals of a free world and genuine peace. No matter how strenuous and dark may be the road that leads to that objective, she is determined to walk hand in hand with her allies. For the Turkish nation, liberty is the mainstay of life. And I am convinced that the souls of the Turkish and American nations find communion on that motto above everything else.

When, therefore, our sons shake each other's hand on the road on which our countries are determined to walk arm in arm, they feel the mutual determination and confidence of two great spirits.

I raise my glass to your health, and to the health of Mrs. Eisenhower. I drink to the happiness and prosperity of our great ally, the United States.

21   ¶ Annual Message Transmitting the
Economic Report to the Congress.
January 28, 1954

To the Congress of the United States:

I am herewith presenting my Economic Report, as required by Section
3 (a) of the Employment Act of 1946.

In preparing this Report, I have had the assistance and advice of the
Council of Economic Advisers.   I have also had the advice of the heads of
executive departments and independent agencies.

I present below, largely in the words of the Report itself, what I consider to be its highlights.

OUR OBJECTIVES

A great opportunity lies before the American people.   Our approach to
a position of military preparedness now makes it possible for the United
States to turn more of its attention to a sustained improvement of national
living standards.

Our economic goal is an increasing national income, shared equitably
among those who contribute to its growth, and achieved in dollars of stable
buying power.

Sustained economic growth is necessary to the welfare and, indeed, to
the survival of America and the free world.

Although American living standards on the average are now higher
than ever, there are certain groups whose consumption is much less than
it should be.   We can in our lifetime go far toward eliminating substandard living.

A steadily rising national income is the best assurance of harmonious
social and economic adjustments.   There can be no lasting harmony in a
nation in which competing groups and interests seek to divide a constant
or shrinking national output.

ROLE OF GOVERNMENT

The demands of modern life and the unsettled status of the world require a more important role for Government than it played in earlier and
quieter times.

It is Government's responsibility in a free society to create an environment in which individual enterprise can work constructively to serve the ends of economic progress; to encourage thrift; and to extend and strengthen economic ties with the rest of the world.

To help build a floor over the pit of personal disaster, Government must concern itself with the health, security and welfare of the individual citizen.

Government must remain alert to the social dangers of monopoly and must continue vigorous enforcement of the anti-trust laws.

Government must use its vast power to help maintain employment and purchasing power as well as to maintain reasonably stable prices.

Government must be alert and sensitive to economic developments, including its own myriad activities.   It must be prepared to take preventive as well as remedial action; and it must be ready to cope with new situations that may arise.   This is not a start-and-stop responsibility, but a continuous one.

The arsenal of weapons at the disposal of Government for maintaining economic stability is formidable.   It includes credit controls administered by the Federal Reserve System; the debt management policies of the Treasury; authority of the President to vary the terms of mortgages carrying Federal insurance; flexibility in administration of the budget; agricultural supports; modification of the tax structure; and public works.   We shall not hesitate to use any or all of these weapons as the situation may require.

THE CURRENT SITUATION

The year just closed was very prosperous with record output, widely distributed incomes, very little unemployment, and prices stable on the average.

In the second half of the year there was a slight contraction in business leading to unemployment in some localities.   This was due mainly to a decline in spending by businesses for additions to inventory.   Other categories of spending, notably retail sales, have been well sustained.

Our economic growth is likely to be resumed during the year, especially if the Congress strengthens the economic environment by translating into action the Administration's far-reaching program.

BASIS FOR CONFIDENCE

The removal of wage and price controls, the stopping of price inflation, the development of new products available to consumers, and the improved economic condition of the nations of the free world constitute an unusual combination of favorable factors for the future.

While Federal expenditures were being cut in many directions during the past year, outlays on research and development grew and came to 2½ billion dollars out of a total national expenditure on research of 4 billion dollars.   Research has already given us many new industries and products, including atomic energy, radioactive isotopes, electronics, helicopters, jet engines, titanium and heat resistant materials, plastics, synthetic fibers, soil conditioners, and many others.   Outlays on the building of new knowledge must continue since they are our surest promise of expanding economic opportunities.

Because of billions of dollars of savings in Government spending made in this Administration's first year, major tax cuts went into effect on January 1.   More than 5 billion dollars of tax savings are now being left with the American people to increase their purchasing power this year. More will be released to taxpayers as rapidly as additional savings in Government expenses are in sight.

Also favorable to the maintenance of high consumer expenditures growing out of high personal incomes is our wide diffusion of wealth and incomes and the strong urge of Americans to improve their living standards.

Expenditure plans of American business for plant and equipment constitute a powerful support for economic activity.

Despite the record volume of home building in recent years, there is still a good market for housing in this country.   Vacancies in our cities, with few exceptions, are below the level necessary for a healthy competitive market.

A continued rise in State and local expenditures may be expected. There is still, in most parts of the country, a vast backlog of needed schools, highways, hospitals, and sewer, water and other facilities. Federal expenditures will remain a significant sustaining factor in the economy.

Our financial institutions are fully capable of meeting all reasonable credit demands and are in condition to withstand successfully any strains to which they may be exposed.

MEASURES TO STRENGTHEN THE ECONOMY

To protect and promote economic stability we should take bold steps—by modernizing unemployment insurance; by broadening the base and benefits of old-age insurance; by permitting a longer "carry-back" of losses for tax purposes; by granting broad discretionary authority to the Executive to alter, within limits and appropriate to changing circumstances, the terms of governmentally insured loans and mortgages; by establishing a secondary home mortgage market; and by making improvements in the planning of public works programs.

To stimulate the expansive power of individual enterprise we should take action—by revising the tax laws so as to increase incentives and to remove certain impediments to enterprise, especially of small business; by improving credit facilities for home building, modernization, and urban rehabilitation; by strengthening the highway system; and by facilitating the adjustments of agriculture to current conditions of demand and technology.

CONCLUSION

Employment in January, 1954, is somewhat lower than in January, 1953. There seems to be a connection between this fact and the fact that in January, 1953, we were still fighting in Korea and are not doing so today. We can make the transition to a period of reduced mobilization without serious interruption in our economic growth. We can have in this country and in the free world a prosperity based on peace.

There is much that justifies confidence in the future. The Government will do its full part to help realize the promise of that future in its program to encourage an expanding and dynamic economy.

DWIGHT D. EISENHOWER

NOTE: The message and the complete report (225 pages) are published in "Economic Report of the President, 1954" (Government Printing Office, 1954).

22 ¶ Address Recorded for the Republican Lincoln Day Dinners. *January 28, 1954*

My fellow Americans:

You are gathered in this meeting as active, devoted members of a political party. As such, you give of your time, your thought, and your effort to the most important business I know—the public affairs of your country.

You concern yourselves with the conduct and management of government—from the smallest political unit to the topmost levels of the Federal Administration. You are, therefore, in politics—even though you may hold no appointive or elective office. And you should, it seems to me, wear your political badge with some considerable pride. For politics ought to be the part-time profession of every citizen who would protect the rights and privileges of free people and who would preserve what is good and fruitful in our national heritage.

Politics must be the concern of every citizen who wants to see our national well-being increased and our international leadership strengthened. In that combined sense, politics is the noblest of professions. In the ranks of that kind of politics, every American should be enrolled.

You are so enrolled. You chose to enlist in this political endeavor under the banner of the Republican Party.

It so happens that I made the same choice.

I hope that we reached our separate and individual decisions in this important matter for similar reasons and as a result of sincere conviction. For a political party is an instrument to translate into effective action the aims and aspirations of the people. It is therefore essential that the members of a political party—if the party is to be effective—join together to reach a common goal. Unless there is unified support of broad political policy, there is no true political party.

Only in unity can the strength of each of us be multiplied by the total number of all of us. Only in such multiplication of strength can the impact of our efforts be felt with equal force in the Nation's smallest precinct and in the Nation's Capital, alike.

We must generate such an impact if our party—the Republican Party—is successfully to meet the responsibilities of national leadership with which it has been charged by our people.

We will meet that challenge with success if, as we celebrate this one-hundredth anniversary of our party, we seize the opportunity to review its origins and to consider and apply the political philosophy of its first great leader.

A century ago, our party was born as a result of many meetings of little-known men in many sections of the country. Another little-known man in Springfield, Illinois, becoming the leader of that party, later became a "Man of the Ages."

This month, we celebrate his birth and the birth of the party he led. But in every season and in every year and in every month, the man and the party are inseparably linked, one with the other.

In Abraham Lincoln as in no other man, in the wisdom of his statesmanship and in the vast sympathy of his human concern was concentrated the rich promise of our Republican Party.

Beyond all others of his day or since, he most effectively inspired our party to serve the Nation's good—both of the moment and for the centuries. With the country facing the terrible threat of disunity, he made his and the party's first purpose the preservation of the Nation.

From the very moment he repeated the oath as president until the tragic end, Abraham Lincoln's every act and every word were clearly aimed, shaped, sharpened, and designed to serve that single purpose—the preservation of our country.

In the Emancipation Proclamation, at Gettysburg, in his two great inaugural addresses, in countless other utterances and statements—in private letters to friends and critics, within his Cabinet and to the public—over and over and over again, always he seemed to be saying—

> We are the trustees of the American heritage.
>
> In this time, in this tragic war, we have but one responsibility—the protection of that heritage. Every thought we hold, every action that we take, every sacrifice we make—all these must be dedicated, single-mindedly, to this task. We must leave to the future an America that is whole, intact, strong, united—and still the land of freedom.
>
> We are the trustees of the American heritage.

Tirelessly and stubbornly he repeated it. Every tortuous moment of those last 4 years, he lived it.

Through his success, you and I are today the trustees of that same heritage. We, in our time, must pass on to our children's children this America—strong and still the land of freedom.

"The legitimate object of government," declared Lincoln, "is to do for a community of people whatever they need to have done, but can not do at all, or can not so well do, in their separate and individual capacities."

So, preoccupied though he was with the crisis of impending secession and the onrushing tragedy of civil war, he clearly realized that other and continuing responsibilities of government had to be met if this Nation was to remain whole, intact, strong, united, and still the land of freedom.

The same simple but basic philosophy of government he then expressed is still the best guide for the men and women whose official responsibility it is today to direct the legislative and executive affairs of our Nation. Their measure of success will be determined in the degree that they are able to absorb and apply the teachings of that great leader.

In his first inaugural address, Abraham Lincoln also said, "This country belongs to the people who inhabit it." And, at the same time, he made it clear that when the people grow weary of their existing Government, they have the constitutional privilege of changing its course.

Fifteen months ago, the American people—seemingly weary of the course their Government was taking at the time—exercised their constitutional rights and changed that course. You and other hard-working party members like you, aided by millions of Americans of other or no party allegiance, played a vital part in that process—in your neighborhoods and communities, in your counties and your States.

And with victory came added responsibility. On you today—as politicians in the finest meaning of the term—and on your leaders—rests the responsibility of justifying now and for history the mandate of November, 1952. That mandate requires that always we address ourselves to the preservation of this Nation against threat of any kind from any quarter whatsoever. We must preserve its basic system and the freedoms it guarantees to its citizens. It requires also that we share Lincoln's concern for the proper role of government in helping and protecting all our citizens.

It was in such concern that there was recently placed before the Congress this administration's program for consideration and translation into law. Through our unified action, that program will secure our country against the threats of our time and will be doing for our people those things they cannot well do for themselves.

We will justify the people's decision of 1952 only as we attract—with our program—new and willing workers to our ranks; only, with those workers, as we learn the habit and spirit of teamwork; only, with Lincoln, as we remember and apply the wise counsel he gave us in his Second Annual Message when he said:

"The dogmas of the quiet past are inadequate to the stormy present. The occasion is piled high with difficulty and we must rise with the occasion. As our case is new, so we must think anew and act anew."

For we know that each day the world is new, that the problems each day brings are new. But we know also that, though these tasks are new, the approach to them is still the Lincoln approach.

To be dedicated to a single purpose—the freedom, strength, prosperity, and peace of America—and to strive with all that's in us to advance the welfare of her citizens—that is the forward way we must seek for America. That is the legitimate purpose of Lincoln's party—a century ago, today, and always.

NOTE: The President's Lincoln Day address was recorded on film for use by the Republican National Committee. The film was shown for the first time at the Lincoln Day Dinner of the Republican State Central, County, and Town Committees of Rhode Island, held on January 28 in Providence.

23 ¶ Toasts of the President and President Bayar at the Turkish Embassy. *January* 29, 1954

Your Excellency, Madame Bayar, my friends:

A very wise teacher that I greatly admired once observed to me that life is made up of friendships, friendships of various kinds, it is true, and in each case the qualities appropriate to the relationship that exists between the peoples or the groups.

In the world today, there is a free world—and its opponent is a world that is ruled by dictatorial processes behind the Iron Curtain.

The free world is bound together by friendships. The world behind the Iron Curtain is bound together by force, or the threat of force.

If these friendships are strong, then the free world will have unity. And we well know that in unity is strength, as in disunity is weakness and destruction.

The United States has sought friends, and will continue to seek friends, in this world; and it will measure friendships in those qualities that we call the ennobling virtues of man: his courage, his capacity for self-sacrifice, his readiness to stick by his friend until the end—courage, stamina, gallantry.

It is in these terms and these qualities that we so value our friendship with Turkey. We have found her—we have proved her, on the fields of Korea, for our sons are buried together, where numbers of them fought shoulder to shoulder—we have found them to be a nation of courage, of gallantry, of stamina.

To a friendship of this kind, one that has been forged and maintained in common recognition of these values, there are always two others: confidence and faith.

This evening, as I stand here, I say to you, with no shadow of doubt in my mind, that if the free world can be bound together in its entirety by the kind of friendship that binds America and Turkey, we have no more reason to fear the people behind the Iron Curtain than we have to fear ourselves as we sit here at this gorgeous board. [*Applause*]

And so, President Bayar, I am sure that those of my countrymen that are gathered this evening would want me to express to you something more than the polite courtesy that is due to the Head of a State on a visit to this Nation's Capital. They would want me to try to say that we value you and your visit as symbolic of a friendship that exists between our two countries. We value your visit because you bring to us something deeper than anything else in this world: true friendship.

And so, sir, with your permission, we raise our glasses to you, to Madame Bayar, and to Turkey.

NOTE: This toast was proposed at 10:05 p.m. in response to a toast by President Bayar at a dinner which he gave in honor of President Eisenhower at the Turkish Embassy. Immediately after the President finished speaking, President Bayar added in English "And to my hostess."

The toast proposed by President Bayar was given in Turkish. An English translation was then read as follows:

Mr. President, ladies and gentlemen:

I am happy to greet you and Mrs. Eisenhower to this Embassy. Having for many years occupied the center of world attention in the military and political field, you have since acquired renewed stature by being elected to your present position of supreme responsibility, showing the confidence that your great nation has displayed in you.

The people of Turkey are gratified to know that in the trying times that we must all endure in our quest for peace and safety, a victorious and glorified General and experienced statesman like yourself is at the head of the American democracy, which has undertaken great, historical responsibilities.

We learn with gratitude of your magnanimous proposal, calling for the international use of atomic energy in the service of the prosperity and health of mankind. Whatever may be the outcome of this epoch-making proposal, which constitutes the most incontrovertible evidence of the goodwill of the free world, history will always praise your country and yourself for this sublime endeavor. This worthy and humane initiative has proved once again in the eyes of the world the strength of the moral principles forming the basis of United States foreign policy, which has the safeguarding of peace as its main aim.

However ardent may be the love of peace which pervades our spirits, a glance at international relations is sufficient to show that what the free world has so far achieved in the search for peace is yet a long way from giving us the possibility to relax the efforts which we must make to attain that objective. No solution has as yet been found for any of the difficulties which cause the restlessness of the world.

Under these conditions, we have to keep up conscientiously our defense efforts, while we lend renewed vigor to our genuine endeavors for the attainment of peace. I am confident that we shall win the peace that will provide for mankind a life of liberty free of menace.

It is the duty of nations who can grasp realities to walk toward that goal with determination, solidarity, and without being carried away by delusions.

Ever since the day we proclaimed our Republic, we Turks—who are firmly attached to our motto of "Peace at home, and Peace abroad"—have believed that the most effective measure to prevent war is to set up an international organization capable of convincing any prospective aggressor that aggression will not meet with impunity, and to bring up citizens of the world untainted with the vices of envy, greed, and grudge.

The American people, who in the perilous years have set the whole world an example of idealism and magnanimity, may rest assured that they have found in the Turkish nation a firm companion on whom they can rely in every way. The sons of Turkey have fought shoulder to shoulder with your sons under the banner of the United Nations, as a symbol of the human virtues of right and liberty, who have together performed legendary deeds under an able command, and who have died together for a great ideal.

A signpost which stands on one of the frontiers of Turkey reads: "We Turks are proud of our nation, and are prepared to die for it." That motto sums up the outlook on life of the Turkish people.

Mr. President, I drink to your health, and to the health of Mrs. Eisenhower, and to the happiness and prosperity of the American nation.

24   ¶ Statement by the President Upon Signing Bill Amending the Agricultural Adjustment Act of 1938.   *January* 30, 1954

I HAVE TODAY approved H.R. 6665, "To amend the Agricultural Adjustment Act of 1938, as amended."

The principal purpose of the bill is to alleviate the great hardship on many cotton farms that would result from the severe production adjustments required under existing legislation. This is accomplished by increasing the national acreage allotment and modifying the method of apportioning that allotment to farms.

The bill also would permit the Secretary of Agriculture with respect to the 1954 and 1955 crops of wheat to increase acreage allotments and marketing quotas for any class or subclass of wheat determined to be in short supply. At the present time, there is a shortage only of amber durum wheat, which is used in the milling of semolina. Semolina is a type of wheat flour that is used exclusively in the manufacture of macaroni, noodles, and spaghetti.

Finally, this legislation removes the prohibition against the use of funds provided under Section 32 of the Agricultural Adjustment Act for extending assistance to the potato industry. It must be clearly understood that this action provides no basis for a program which might result in the dumping or destruction of potatoes. This is as it should be.

NOTE: As enacted, H.R. 6665 is Public Law 290, 83d Congress (68 Stat. 4).

25 ¶ The President's News Conference of *February* 3, 1954.

THE PRESIDENT. Good morning.

I think that the only statement I have this morning is my apologies for being 5 minutes late. Time slipped by on me. We will go right to questions.

Q. Merriman Smith, United Press: Mr. President, does this Government know the whereabouts of the Russian Far Eastern Mission member, Mr. Rastovorov?

THE PRESIDENT. I have had no detailed reports on it.

Q. Charles Lucey, Scripps-Howard: Mr. President, will you prefer some kind of congressional check on treaty-making power or would you prefer to see no bill at all passed?

THE PRESIDENT. Well, Mr. Lucey, I have tried to make my position clear on this several times. There is undoubtedly an honest fear throughout the United States that the treaty-making power can be used to contravene or to supersede our Constitution. In order to reassure America's population on this score, I am ready to do anything, even if it requires some kind of language in the Constitution.

When it comes to anything, however—and this is where I stick and will not compromise one word—when it comes to the point of using any amendment to change or alter the traditional and constitutional balances of power among the three departments of Government, a feature of our Constitution that is the very genius of our whole system of government, I won't compromise one single word. That is exactly where I stand.

Q. Robert Donovan, New York Herald Tribune: Sir, on the same subject, this Bricker amendment, it is very complicated, and it has now gotten into a very complicated tangle on the Hill. Do you think, sir, it is wise to try to thrash this out without having a new look at it in committee, in view of the technicalities that have now piled up?

THE PRESIDENT. Of course, I am not going to comment on the processes used in the Senate, but I must say it is a complicated matter.

As you people know, it absorbs the time of great numbers of people, studies and arguments. It is very, very intricate, and I go back again and again that that Constitution has served us very well for 165 years. Maybe individuals at times have abused it or maybe here and there we haven't been too accurate in our interpretations—because we have had reversals in interpretations. But, by and large, those people did a job that I don't want to trifle with too much, and unnecessarily. So I do believe that these things must be soberly studied. They must not become in the slightest degree partisan. They must be examined in what is the long-term good of the United States, what is going to be the effect of this two decades from now, and what is it going to be next year. Let's not be in a hurry about such an important thing.

Q. Laurence Burd, Chicago Tribune: Mr. President, there is a report in the news this morning that we have sent 125 air technicians to Indochina to service our bombers over there, and that France has requested 400 more. Do you know, sir, whether we have military personnel in Indochina, and what our plans are on that?

THE PRESIDENT. In many countries of the world we have not only military attachés and their staffs, we have large military missions.

In Indochina, as in numbers of other countries, we have military missions. We do not put people there as fighting units. They are training and technical missions of all kinds, they vary in size, and that is all there is to say on the subject.

Q. Mr. Burd: Do you know if planes are being serviced over there?

THE PRESIDENT. I couldn't say whether they are or not, but we do have a military mission. One of their jobs is instructing in air as well as the rest of the things.

Q. David Sentner, Hearst Newspapers: Mr. President, do you consider the Indonesian [Indochinese] situation critical at the present time?

THE PRESIDENT. Well, it's been critical for so long that it's difficult to just point out a period when it is more than normally critical.

I think this is a fact: all of us have known, in every situation like you have there, that the heart and soul of the population finally becomes the biggest factor of success or failure. By that I mean if the Vietnamese want to be free, if they believe that through this kind of a war they will be free, then you will have probable success.

Q. Anthony Leviero, New York Times: Mr. President——

THE PRESIDENT [*continuing*]. If it goes the other way, you will probably not have the success. So it is critical in the sense that we have had some evidence that there is a lack of enthusiasm we would like to have there.

I am sorry, I just had a lapse: Indonesia——

Q. David Sentner, Hearst Newspapers: I meant Indochinese.

THE PRESIDENT. You did? Then I answered it! [*Laughter*]

I am glad we were both wrong. Some day I must tell you the story of the confusion with a cross-eyed man. [*Laughter*]

Q. Anthony Leviero, New York Times: I am sorry for the interruption, and that is what I meant to call attention to.

THE PRESIDENT. Thank you.

Q. Charles von Fremd, CBS Television: I wonder, sir, if there is anything you can add at this time to the reported Air Force plan to build a world-wide chain of atom bomb storage bases that was discussed up on the Hill?

THE PRESIDENT. I have not seen that.

Q. Mr. von Fremd: It was discussed up on the Hill yesterday in the Armed Services Committee, I believe.

THE PRESIDENT. I didn't know; it has escaped me; I haven't a word to say on it.

Q. Kenneth Scheibel, Gannett News Service: Mr. President, the Government must decide soon what price it will pay for surplus butter under the program which starts this spring. The dairy people have announced they want it kept where it is, but a lot of consumers think it is too high and it should be reduced. Do you know of any plan to reduce the price of butter?

THE PRESIDENT. I'll put it this way: I don't know that the decision has been reached as to where the price would be fixed for next year. Incidentally, I believe I have an engagement now with the dairy people coming in to see me, and I imagine they will talk about that. I do believe this: We can't keep butter priced out of the market and get it used. I just don't believe that, and something, I think, has to be done.

Q. George Herman, CBS Radio: Mr. President, do you agree with Secretary Wilson that the United States is doing 90 percent of the atomic bomb rattling in the world?

THE PRESIDENT. Well, I don't think I ever make just ordinary generalizations that sound like that. I do deplore any spread of hysterical fear in this world. I think that a mature, intelligent people ought to look at the problems and the threats that face them in the world, do the best they can, and have some confidence in the result.

I do deplore, and I think that must have been what Secretary Wilson was trying to say—deploring, let us call it, just spreading of fear.

Q. Nat Finney, Buffalo News: Mr. President, some of the reports from Berlin in the early phases of the conference there suggested, it seems to me, that there was some real progress being made on the discussion of your proposal for an atomic pool. Is there any light you can throw on that for us today?

THE PRESIDENT. No, not of a particularly detailed kind, at least.

I do have, as you would know, I have my daily reports from Secretary Dulles. As I believe I noted last week, he is on the job, the man that enjoys my full confidence. He is doing the best he can to get those agreements of the kind that we believe to be logical and suited to the world situation today, fair to all.

Experience has not given any great reason for assuming tremendous successes, but by the same token, I believe we must always keep trying; that is what we are doing. So far as the atomic side of it is concerned, it would always be possible, of course, that some little advance might be made there even in the absence of advances in the wider political problems; but, as of now, I can't even suggest that that might come about.

Q. Jack Bell, Associated Press: Mr. President, I would like to get back to the Bricker amendment for just a moment. I wonder if you could tell us whether you have any objections to Senator George's substitute proposal for the Bricker amendment?

THE PRESIDENT. Well, I'll tell you, at this moment I am not going to talk about the details of the thing because, as was suggested a few minutes ago, these things are complicated; they are very complicated, and they need long study.

Every time something new appears upon the scene, my advisers and I get together. I get people from outside of Government, inside, and they begin to study it. But until meanings are clear and convictions can be formed, why, I wouldn't want to talk on details.

Q. Mrs. May Craig, New England Papers: Mr. President, if I may go back to the sabre-rattling, our new look puts our dependence on air power and air power weapons, and it is said that they are deterrents of war. Now, if the enemy gets the idea that we will not use them, will they be a deterrent?

THE PRESIDENT. Well, Mrs. Craig, I will tell you: I spent some little time at war, and I don't think that big and bombastic talk is the thing that makes other people fear. I think that a calm going about of your own business, pursuing a steady course, that is the thing that makes him begin to tremble and wonder what you are going to do.

Let me point this out: we fought a number of campaigns over in Europe, and I don't recall once issuing a precampaign statement that "we are big and strong and mighty and tough, and we are going to beat somebody's brains out." *[Laughter]*

We went ahead with our job, our preparations, and when it was necessary, then the thing started.

Our prayer is now that it will never be necessary to do these things, but we are just going about our business like Americans ought to—I hope.

Q. Robert Spivack, New York Post: Mr. President, have you received any preliminary reports yet on the investigation of the high price of coffee, and if so, what they show?

THE PRESIDENT. No, I haven't, except what I expressed last week: that they believed from their preliminary investigation there was sufficient evidence to indicate the need for a much broader and deeper one.

Q. Paul Leach, Chicago Daily News: Mr. President, there has been considerable criticism in the insurance industry of your reinsurance proposal in the health plan. Is there any indication that that will be modified or changed or dropped?

THE PRESIDENT. Not at this moment; it hasn't been suggested to me. In other words, the Secretary of that Department has not come up with any change in plan.

Q. Elmer Davis, ABC Television: Mr. President, is there any more information about the 2200?

THE PRESIDENT. On this 2200, when I found out some little time ago that you people had a very widespread interest in this thing, I said, "Well, let's take a good look."

Here was something that never occurred to me there was going to be this kind of intense interest. We have had several groups since then studying just exactly what we can do, how far we can break these things down, and what information can be put out. When they report to me, I will use some channel to get it to you. Just exactly what the answer is going to be, I don't know.

Q. John Herling, Editors Syndicate: Mr. President, this is a question that ties in with the economic side and the human relations side of your program. On the economic side you referred in your message to Congress that this was not the time for raising the minimum wage; it was a matter of timing. Does this mean that you don't plan to recommend a raise in minimum wages while we are holding the present level of unemployment?

THE PRESIDENT. Well, I think my Economic Report speaks for itself, and if you take any one of these items out of context and begin to talk about it, you can make it mean anything. I really put in many hours of hard work with my advisers on that Report, and I would respectfully refer you to that Economic Report for what I really believe at this moment about the minimum wage scale.

Q. Mr. Herling: Sir, in listing the things that would have to be done in the summary of your Economic Report, the spread of unemployment insurance, and so on, were listed among other things, but minimum wage was not. That is why the question as to whether or not you plan to do something about it this session.

THE PRESIDENT. The Economic Report, I think, makes clear that there would be a very great question about the wisdom of such a move at this particular moment when you are going through, inescapably, a transition from a semiwar economy, or even war economy, and all its controls into a freer economy not supported by great munitions expenditures of all kinds.

It becomes a question of timing, and I am not so certain that I could describe the exact conditions that would have to be prevailing before you would make this recommendation. But I am certain that everybody studying that report and helping to prepare it does believe that it is through the proper distribution of the profits deriving from our form of industry—the widespread distribution—that the prosperity of this country comes about. They believe in getting that done just as far as it is possible.

Q. Mr. Herling: On the human relations side, the Albert Beeson nomination, which is being held up in Congress today, there seems to be a growing doubt in the Senate Labor Committee about how completely Mr. Beeson has severed his relations with his company and the pension plan connected with it. Senator Smith said late last night the White House wants fast action on the nomination one way or the other. Do you have any further or alternative plans in this connection?

THE PRESIDENT. I have no plans at all of any kind in this connection. I had my people search for an individual, I had both the Department and the Labor Departments in this particular thing. We searched and we found a man; we talked to him; we thought he was a good man. We think he is a good man. We put him before the Senate, and it is up to them.

Q. Ray Scherer, National Broadcasting Company: Mr. President, several top Republicans have suggested that there is something unethical, almost un-American, about using this word "recession" in connection with the present business conditions. What could you say about that?

THE PRESIDENT. I hadn't seen those words, at least stated in that way. I think it is a free country; you can use words as you see fit, and attach to them such meanings almost as you see fit.

I think we are going through a readjustment that we have had to after every time we have been in one of these emergencies of any kind in our country. You have to go as intelligently as you can, always remembering that the prosperity of this country lies in the prosperity of its masses, not just of the few corporations or anything else like that. That is the policy we are trying to apply.

I suppose we have receded from something, because not everything is at its peak today, so you have to use the word as you see fit.

I had not heard that particular exhortation.

Q. Marvin Arrowsmith, Associated Press: Mr. President, to go back to the first question of the conference, you said you hadn't received a detailed report, a report on this case of the Soviet agent who is missing in Tokyo. Can you say whether he is in American custody?

THE PRESIDENT. No, I can't say anything, because it just happens to be one of those things that I have had no report of any kind. I assume that when there is really important information to impart, it will be brought to me. Normally it would, certainly.

Q. Harry Frantz, United Press, South American Service: Mr. President, the question may be premature, and I won't press it if you are not prepared, but I just wondered if you are yet ready to give any general indication of your thought and plans with regard to the Tenth Inter-American Conference at Caracas on March 1st? There has even been some speculation that you thought of attending the opening, for example.

THE PRESIDENT. It has been discussed often between my principal advisers in those departments and myself, but there has been no feeling so far that we saw a practicable way for me to get down there at the moment.

Q. Fletcher Knebel, Cowles Publications: Mr. President, after about a year of these press conferences, what do you think of them? Do you like them or not? [*Laughter*]

THE PRESIDENT. You are getting a little personal around here, aren't you? Well, I'll tell you: I think I told you people the first time we ever had a press conference that over a very considerable period of time in which I have been thrown into more or less intimate contact with the press—and that goes back to '41—I feel that there has been between us existing a very fine relationship, in war and in peace.

I have no particular objection even to the so-called needling questions. I think I recognize most of them. [*Laughter*] And I have got some very good friends. I will tell you frankly that one of the difficulties of the particular job I am on is that lots of good friends I have got among the newspaper people I can't pursue as freely as I could at one time, because it isn't understood you are just meeting a friend; you are meeting a newspaperman, and that becomes something else again.

I don't mean to say that I like to give away the time that sometimes these conferences call for, particularly if they come at a very busy period. But all in all, I think I like them; that would be my answer.

Q. George Herman, CBS Radio: Mr. President, last week at our conference you expressed interest in a plan for honorable discharges for people in Government employ. Could you tell us if you have inaugurated any study on that subject?

THE PRESIDENT. I asked about it, and I meant to ask about it this morning, to see whether we had gotten any place at all, but I just overlooked it.

Q. Mr. Herman: You have asked somebody to look into it?

THE PRESIDENT. Oh, yes; I have asked.

Q. Robert Clark, International News Service: Former President Socarras of Cuba was arrested a few weeks ago and accused of trying to smuggle arms out of the United States. We have a Latin-American client who would like to know if his arrest means the United States would not under any circumstances permit the security of another American Republic to be threatened by illegal activities of political exiles?

Q. (Several voices): We don't understand the question.

THE PRESIDENT. Well, the question is, in general, this: that there was apparently some action taken to prevent suspected export of illegal arms, and the question was, then, did this act mean that the United States would always act in the same pattern in the case of any South American country.

Obviously, here is a question that has so many implications you wouldn't even attempt an off-the-cuff, shooting-from-the-hip answer.

Actually there was no detailed report made to me on the primary incident and, therefore, I could not certainly reason from there to a policy until I knew all of the facts. I couldn't possibly answer the question at the moment.

Q. Edward Milne, Providence Journal-Bulletin: Mr. President, I have my usual poor notes on this, on your answer to the question about the 2200. I have you promising to channel something to us, but I don't understand whether you are going to channel the breakdown to us or whether you are simply going to let us know the decision of your associates.

THE PRESIDENT. Well, it could be both—[*laughter*]—but finally I will tell you what we are going to do about it. Now, you just have to give me a little time.

This is an extremely complicated thing. Remember, I insist on one thing: let us not run this Government so as we can throw extraordinary guilt by association or any other way on people that are innocent. At the same time, I am determined that I will not keep people around and give them the privilege of governmental employment if they are security risks. Now, that is all I am trying to do.

It takes time to break it down, and you will get an answer when I can give it and as fully as I can give it, and I don't know how fully that will be.

Q. Robert Spivack, New York Post: Mr. President, this is a personal question, too, but last week when you were telling us about the coffee situation you said that you were intensely interested, I believe, in it yourself. Can you tell us how you take your coffee, and why? [*Laughter*]

THE PRESIDENT. Well, I'll tell you, you asked one that is a bit too personal for me. I happen to be a rather stubborn individual when I think I am being taken in any way or for any reason. I act in my own life in accordance with my convictions; but one reason I am so intensely interested, I have been one of the great coffee drinkers of the United States all my life—most soldiers are, as you know—so I am very interested in getting this coffee back to a price where I think it is reasonable.

Q. Charles von Fremd, CBS Television: Mr. President, I find myself in a quandary regarding Mr. Knebel's question, and I say this with no intention, sir, of being insulting. I wonder, however, if for the sake of the record it might be included that among your friends and the people you would like to get to know better among the newspapermen, if included among them could also be radio and television? [*Laughter*]

THE PRESIDENT. A strange thing about it, some of my best friends have been those people.

Merriman Smith, United Press: Thank you, Mr. President.

NOTE: President Eisenhower's twenty-sixth news conference was held in the Executive Office Building from 10:35 to 10:59 o'clock on Wednesday morning, February 3, 1954. In attendance: 155.

26 ¶ Letter to Walter Reuther, President, United Automobile Workers, CIO, Concerning Economic Growth and Stability. *February* 3, 1954

[Released February 3, 1954. Dated February 1, 1954]

Dear Mr. Reuther:

I have now had an opportunity to read very carefully your letter of January thirteenth reviewing current economic conditions and renewing your proposal for a national conference on employment.

To protect and promote economic stability, we have taken and will continue to take bold steps. The Administration has now outlined a program which, taken in its entirety, is designed to sustain a high level of production and employment throughout our economy. I am well aware of those areas presently experiencing certain economic hardships during this transitional period. From the point of view of Federal action, I believe that the most important attack on these situations is from the standpoint of fostering the over-all health and vitality of our economy. It is with that principle in mind that the economic program of this Administration has been formulated.

Consultation with respect to the various parts of the Administration's program has, of course, been widespread. Continuing steps have been and are constantly being taken to re-examine the policies of the Federal Government affecting economic growth and stability. Special inquiries have been made and are being made into the problems of agriculture, housing, foreign economic policy, taxation, and the relations between Federal, State and local governments. I am gratified to know that you and other members of your group have discussed various aspects of economic growth and stability with the Council of Economic Advisers and with others in the Executive Branch. I hope that such consultations will continue on the wide range of problems that face us. At the present time, I believe this is the most fruitful method of pooling the ideas and experience of all segments of our population.

While we must recognize and seek to deal with particular instances of economic hardship as they arise, it is essential to the achievement of greater national economic strength to maintain a steady, unshakable attitude of public confidence in the capacity of the American economy for continued growth. All of our citizens in positions of leadership have the responsibility of placing in the proper perspective transitional periods such as we are presently passing through.

It is my deep conviction that we can make the transition, now underway, from a wartime to a peacetime economy without serious interruption in our growth as a nation or in the improvement of the living standards of our people. Government policy is now geared to decreasing the difficulties incident to this transition and to strengthening the weapons necessary for this task.

The Economic Report of the President, which was transmitted to the Congress on January twenty-eighth, sets forth and defines an affirmative and constructive overall approach to the problem of creating conditions favorable to sustained economic growth. We shall continue to pursue this objective with unrelenting determination.

Sincerely,

DWIGHT D. EISENHOWER

27   ¶ Veto of Bill Authorizing Commemorative
Coinage for the Tercentennial Celebration of the
City of Northampton, Massachusetts.
February 3, 1954

To the United States Senate:

I am returning herewith, without my approval, S. 987, "To authorize
the coinage of 50-cent pieces in commemoration of the tercentennial
celebration of the founding of the city of Northampton, Massachusetts."

The proposed legislation would authorize the coinage of one million
silver 50-cent pieces in commemoration of the tercentennial celebration
of the founding of the city of Northampton, Massachusetts.

The principal objection to commemorative coins is that they detract
from the fundamental function of the coinage as a medium of exchange.
Multiplicity of designs on United States coins would tend to create confusion among the public, and to facilitate counterfeiting. The Congress
recognized the necessity for limiting the designs of coins by section 3510
of the Revised Statutes which provides that: ". . . no change in the
design or die of any coin shall be made oftener than once in twenty-five
years from and including the year of the first adoption of the design,
model, die, or hub for the same coin: . . ."

I am further advised by the Treasury Department that in the past in
many instances the public interest in these special coins has been so
short-lived that their sales for the purposes intended have lagged with
the result that large quantities have remained unsold and have been
returned to the mints for melting.

I fully recognize the importance to the country of the event which this
coin would commemorate. I recognize, too, that the authorization of
one or two or three of such issues of coins would not do major harm.
However, experience has demonstrated that the authorization of even a
single commemorative issue brings forth a flood of other authorizations
to commemorate events or anniversaries of local or national importance.
In the administration of President Hoover, these authorizations multiplied to the point where he felt compelled to exercise his veto. The same
pattern recurred in the administrations of Presidents Roosevelt and
Truman. In view of this historical pattern, which by now has become

so clear, I think that it is both wiser and fairer to make known my views on this subject at the outset.   I therefore regretfully withhold my approval of S. 987.

As has been suggested in the past, it seems to me wholly appropriate that anniversaries like this one, which the Congress deems it desirable to commemorate, should be recognized by bills authorizing the Treasury to provide suitable commemorative medals at cost.

DWIGHT D. EISENHOWER

28   ¶ Veto of Bill Authorizing Commemorative Coinage for the Tercentennial Celebration of the City of New York.   *February* 3, 1954

To the United States Senate:

I am returning herewith, without my approval, S. 2474, "To authorize the coinage of 50-cent pieces to commemorate the tercentennial of the foundation of the city of New York."

The proposed legislation would authorize the coinage of not to exceed five million silver 50-cent pieces in commemoration of the tercentennial of the founding of the city of New York.

The principal objection to commemorative coins is that they detract from the fundamental function of the coinage as a medium of exchange. Multiplicity of designs on United States coins would tend to create confusion among the public, and to facilitate counterfeiting.   The Congress recognized the necessity for limiting the designs of coins by section 3510 of the Revised Statutes which provides that: ". . . no change in the design or die of any coin shall be made oftener than once in twenty-five years from and including the year of the first adoption of the design, model, die, or hub for the same coin: . . ."

I am further advised by the Treasury Department that in the past in many instances the public interest in these special coins has been so short-lived that their sales for the purposes intended have lagged with the result that large quantities have remained unsold and have been returned to the mints for melting.

I fully recognize the importance to the country of the event which this coin would commemorate.   I recognize, too, that the authorization of one or two or three of such issues of coins would not do major harm. However, experience has demonstrated that the authorization of even a single commemorative issue brings forth a flood of other authorizations to commemorate events or anniversaries of local or national importance. In the administration of President Hoover, these authorizations multiplied to the point where he felt compelled to exercise his veto. The same pattern recurred in the administrations of Presidents Roosevelt and Truman. In view of this historical pattern, which by now has become so clear, I think that it is both wiser and fairer to make known my views on this subject at the outset. I therefore regretfully withhold my approval of S. 2474.

As has been suggested in the past, it seems to me wholly appropriate that anniversaries like this one, which the Congress deems it desirable to commemorate, should be recognized by bills authorizing the Treasury to provide suitable commemorative medals at cost.

DWIGHT D. EISENHOWER

29 ¶ Veto of Bill Authorizing Commemorative Coinage for the Sesquicentennial of the Louisiana Purchase. *February 3, 1954*

To the House of Representatives:

I am returning herewith, without my approval, H.R. 1917, "To authorize the coinage of 50-cent pieces to commemorate the sesquicentennial of the Louisiana Purchase."

The proposed legislation would authorize the coinage of not to exceed two and one-half million silver 50-cent pieces in commemoration of the one hundred and fiftieth anniversary of the Louisiana Purchase.

The principal objection to commemorative coins is that they detract from the fundamental function of the coinage as a medium of exchange. Multiplicity of designs on United States coins would tend to create confusion among the public, and to facilitate counterfeiting. The Congress recognized the necessity for limiting the designs of coins by section 3510 of the Revised Statutes which provides that: ". . . no change in the design or die of any coin shall be made oftener than once in twenty-five years from and including the year of the first adoption of the design, model, die, or hub for the same coin: . . ."

I am further advised by the Treasury Department that in the past in many instances the public interest in these special coins has been so short-lived that their sales for the purposes intended have lagged with the result that large quantities have remained unsold and have been returned to the mints for melting.

I fully recognize the importance to the country of the event which this coin would commemorate. I recognize, too, that the authorization of one or two or three of such issues of coins would not do major harm. However, experience has demonstrated that the authorization of even a single commemorative issue brings forth a flood of other authorizations to commemorate events or anniversaries of local or national importance. In the administration of President Hoover, these authorizations multiplied to the point where he felt compelled to exercise his veto. The same pattern recurred in the administrations of Presidents Roosevelt and Truman. In view of this historical pattern, which by now has become so clear, I think that it is both wiser and fairer to make known my views on this subject at the outset. I therefore regretfully withhold my approval of H.R. 1917.

As has been suggested in the past, it seems to me wholly appropriate that anniversaries like this one, which the Congress deems it desirable to commemorate, should be recognized by bills authorizing the Treasury to provide suitable commemorative medals at cost.

Dwight D. Eisenhower

30 ¶ Letter to Frederic L. Vorbeck, Executive Chairman, United Catholic Organizations for the Freeing of Cardinal Mindszenty.
February 4, 1954

[Released February 4, 1954. Dated February 1, 1954]

Dear Mr. Vorbeck:

I have your telegram of January twenty-third on behalf of the United Catholic Organizations for the Freeing of Cardinal Mindszenty. We in the free world have not forgotten that this is the fifth anniversary of

Cardinal Mindszenty's trial and imprisonment by the Communist authorities in Hungary.

The unjust nature of the proceedings against Cardinal Mindszenty is, of course, well known to the American people. They regarded the attack upon him as a blow against religious freedom in Hungary and an unprincipled attempt to destroy spiritual and moral influences in that country.

The Communist assault upon religious liberty and leadership in Hungary has failed, however, to turn the Hungarian people from their faith in God. The plight of Cardinal Mindszenty and of other churchmen who have suffered at the hands of the Communists has not been forgotten. Their situation continues deeply to concern the people of Hungary and to evoke the sympathy of the free world. Despite the constraints of person and silence imposed on Cardinal Mindszenty and other church leaders by their persecutors, the spirit of these men has defied confinement by the totalitarian State. It has become, indeed, a symbol of faith and freedom for our times.

Sincerely,

DWIGHT D. EISENHOWER

3 1   ¶ Remarks at the Lincoln Day Box Supper.
February 5, 1954

Mr. Vice President, Members of the Cabinet, and Members of the Senate and of the House of Representatives, guests from all over this country, and their ladies and wives, and my very dear—all of you— Republican friends:

In first attempting to acknowledge my very deep appreciation of the cordiality of your welcome, might I say, first that I have had a great inspiration over the past year in working with the representatives, legislative and executive, that you people have sent here to Washington. It has been a great privilege to work with individuals who are dedicated to the good of America, and place America above all personal or other gain.

It is a great privilege to address each of you, the people who throughout this land believe as we do, who support us with your hearts, with your voices, with everything that you have, to make certain that America is going to consistently grow stronger and better—spiritually, intellectually, economically, militarily.

It was only a bit more than four score and ten years ago that a very great man said, "Four score and seven years ago our fathers brought forth upon this continent a new nation, conceived in liberty, and dedicated to the proposition that all men are created equal."

Now, as he ended that great speech, a classic not only in the English language but in philosophical thought, Abraham Lincoln said that "government by the people and for the people and of the people shall not perish from the earth."

That was his philosophy. He uttered those words in a time of crisis. He dedicated his whole being to that one thought, that government by the people and for and of the people should not perish. He endured every indignity. We think of him today as a great leader. Yet he offered to hold McClellan's horse if McClellan would win a victory. There was nothing, no sacrifice he would not make to say we will preserve this nation as it has existed for four score and seven years.

Now, in his time, the threat was a physical one—physical disunion of this great United States. But, my friends, he was only voicing a thought, he was only crystallizing a threat that has been with every type of free government since free government was first conceived. Always there is the struggle between domination by the few, and government of themselves by the many. And he was determined it should not perish.

And in every age and every time, there have been people so dedicated. And it is for that reason that free government exists today. And we are no different from those who have gone before us. We in our time must make certain that the genius of the Constitution and of our government shall not perish, that it shall belong to the young and to those who come after us in the same general form that it has been received by us.

Now, in doing this, Abraham Lincoln said something else of a very profound character. "The legitimate function of government," he said, "is to do for the individuals what they cannot do for themselves, or cannot so well do for themselves." In this we find the expression of his great heart, his determination that government should be interested in people, in that person's disasters, in their privileges, in their rights. Everything that went to enrich their life or to damage that life was a legitimate con-

241

cern of government, and when necessary, government would directly intervene.

So that here we have, really, the compound, the overall philosophy of Lincoln: in all those things which deal with people, be liberal, be human. In all those things which deal with the people's money or their economy, or their form of government, be conservative—and don't be afraid to use the word.

And so today, Republicans come forward with programs in which there are such words as "balanced budgets," and "cutting expenditures," and all the kind of thing that means this economy must be conservative, it must be solvent.

But they also come forward and say we are concerned with every American's health, with a decent house for him, we are concerned that he will have a chance for health, and his children for education. We are going to see that he has power available to him. We are going to see that everything takes place that will enrich his life and let him as an individual, hard-working American citizen, have full opportunity to do for his children and his family what any decent American should want to do.

And so, my friends—by the way, you know, I wasn't supposed to make a speech, I was supposed to get up and greet you and sit down. [*Applause*] Now I am puzzled, I don't know whether you meant it would be a good idea to sit down or not. [*Laughter*] But let me bring this thought to you. This is really what I want to say:

What a glorious challenge we have, what a privilege to live in this time. We know these threats to our system from abroad. We know those things that we have seen happening from within that have alarmed us.

Let us be courageous. Let us lift our chins, our heads, and square our shoulders, and walk right square into it like Lincoln would have walked into it.

Let us not be afraid to be humble, as he was humble when it was necessary. But let us—when it comes down to the basic purpose of the Republican Party: to preserve this Nation as it has existed, and to make government serve the needs of all our people, no matter in what way that needs to be done—let us be just as courageous as Lincoln was courageous as he met the problems of 4 years of dreadful civil war, with brother against brother, with state against state.

If we meet it in that way, it seems to me we will meet it almost with delight—with happiness that it has been given to us, in our time, to serve our country.

Those men who fought on the battlefields of Gettysburg served their country, whichever side they were on. They believed in something. They did it to the utmost of their ability.

If we would do it in that way, we don't have to listen to the prophets of gloom who say that we are going to go into this or that kind of a stumble or fumble or fall. The United States doesn't need to fall.

The reason I believe in the Republican Party is because I believe it is the best political instrument available in this country to serve the United States in this kind of objective: for making certain that every individual American, whatever his station, will recognize that he has the opportunity of a free citizen, to make for himself what he can, and he will have a sympathetic partner—a big-brother partner, in the Federal Government; and that this Nation will persist in the kind of nation that was designed by our forefathers and in which it is now our great privilege to live.

Now, my friends, you have done me a great honor by asking me here, allowing me to address these few thoughts to you. I wonder whether before we break up this party, you would like me to go over and bring my Mamie to greet you?

NOTE: The President spoke at the Uline Arena in Washington at 10:00 p.m.

32 ¶ Remarks Broadcast as Part of the American Legion "Back to God" Program.
February 7, 1954

AS A FORMER SOLDIER, I am delighted that our veterans are sponsoring a movement to increase our awareness of God in our daily lives.

In battle, they learned a great truth—that there are no atheists in the foxholes. They know that in time of test and trial, we instinctively turn to God for new courage and peace of mind.

All the history of America bears witness to this truth.

Out of faith in God, and through faith in themselves as His children, our forefathers designed and built this Republic.

We remember from school days that, aboard a tiny ship of destiny called the Mayflower, self-government on our continent was first conceived by the Pilgrim Fathers. Their immortal compact began with the words, "In the name of God, Amen."

We remember the picture of the Father of our Country, on his knees at Valley Forge seeking divine guidance in the cold gloom of a bitter winter. Thus Washington gained strength to lead to independence a nation dedicated to the belief that each of us is divinely endowed with indestructible rights.

We remember, too, that three-fourths of a century later, on the battle-torn field of Gettysburg, and in the silence of many a wartime night, Abraham Lincoln recognized that only under God could this Nation win a new birth of freedom.

And we remember that, only a decade ago, aboard the transport Dorchester, four chaplains of four faiths together willingly sacrificed their lives so that four others might live.

In the three centuries that separate the Pilgrims of the Mayflower from the chaplains of the Dorchester, America's freedom, her courage, her strength, and her progress have had their foundation in faith.

Today as then, there is need for positive acts of renewed recognition that faith is our surest strength, our greatest resource.

This "Back to God" movement is such a positive act.

As we take part in it, I hope that we shall prize this thought:

Whatever our individual church, whatever our personal creed, our common faith in God is a common bond among us. In our fundamental faith, we are all one. Together we thank the Power that has made and preserved us a nation. By the millions, we speak prayers, we sing hymns—and no matter what their words may be, their spirit is the same—"In God is our trust."

NOTE: The President's remarks were broadcast from the White House at 2:30 p.m. as part of an American Legion program originating in New York City.

33 ¶ The President's News Conference of *February* 10, 1954.

THE PRESIDENT. Good morning. One or two little items that may be of some interest:

First, I hope you will allow me to welcome here a group of press people, press representatives, from the NATO countries. I assume that among them are people I have met many times before during my travels about Europe; anyway, I am glad you are here.

I saw some rumors that the Government was intending to increase the interest rates on these Rural Electrification Administration loans. That is not true.

I told you last December that there would soon be two divisions returning from Korea, if there were no great change in the situation. We expect that very soon the 45th Division will start back, and a little later on the 40th; two National Guard Divisions—the 45th largely from the Oklahoma area, and some other units in it; and the 40th from California. I think the first one will be here in the middle of April, and the next one about the middle of June.

It gives me an opportunity again to pay tribute to these National Guard units who keep themselves organized, their staffs and commanders trained in time of peace, and ready to operate in an emergency. It is part of our reserve element and, of course, very necessary.

As you know, under the law there would normally come about soon a half-cent reduction in the Federal tax on gasoline. You also know in the statements already made that the administration hopes to keep that half-cent tax in order to push the good roads program throughout the United States. In the past, not all of this money has been put out on road construction in matching funds with the States. We hope to do it with all of it, and if we are successful, it will increase the Federal participation, I think, by some $225 million on a matching basis with the States.

There is a Cougar Dam on the McKenzie River. There is a little statement that has been written about it, a very short one, and you will find it outside when you go out. It was merely a statement because it more or less exemplifies the thing we have been talking about quite a while, participation by local communities, municipalities, States, and so on, with the Federal Government in these great developments when such participation is feasible and possible.

Now, that covers the few little statements I had, so we will start with questions.

Q. Merriman Smith, United Press: Mr. President, the Democrats on Capitol Hill say that bipartisan support of certain portions of your program have been endangered by certain statements which have been made by members of the administration, statements ranging from the fact that the Democrats were soft toward subversives in the Government, to labels of political sadism. The Democrats have asked or suggested that you stop the statements; and we wondered if you could discuss the situation in general terms for us.

THE PRESIDENT. Well, I think, first of all, it is quite apparent that I am not very much of a partisan. The times are too serious, I think, to indulge in partisanship to the extreme, and I quite cheerfully admit that there must be Democratic support for the enactment of certain parts of the program. I believe Senator Knowland has often described himself as a majority leader without a majority in the Senate, so it is obvious that if these things are to become law there will have to be some support from the Democratic side.

This one thing, I believe, I can say without appearing to be pontifical or particularly "stuffed shirt" about it: we have, and I have, tried to desperately draw up a program that seems to me to be good for all Americans, which includes Democrats. I don't expect any Democrat to support any program because he happens to be a friend of mine—and I have many friends among them, as some of you would know. I have tried to put out a program that is good for the United States, and it is on that basis that I appeal for help.

I know of no way in which the Chief Executive could stop this kind of thing except among the members of his own executive family, and I must say again that in this region, I have my own doubts that any great partisanship displayed by members of the executive department is really appropriate in this day and time.

Now, there have been from the beginning of parties intemperate statements. They have been hurled back and forth. We seem to survive them and they seem to roll off the backs of political people, after the first flurry is over. I am often amazed when I read some of the statements that were made about Washington even before there were political parties.

If you will look up and read what was said of him in his second administration, where they called him a tyrant, a betrayer of the people, a seeker after a gilded throne on which he wanted to establish a royal dynasty, and so on, these things have been going on a long time.

I don't believe in bitter partisanship. I never believe that all wisdom is confined to one of the great parties; and I certainly have never, in general terms, criticized the other party, that is, to include its great membership.

I believe there are good Americans in both parties, and I believe that the great mass of both parties is fundamentally and naturally sound.

Q. Anthony Leviero, New York Times: Mr. President, isn't it preaching a kind of class warfare for Republican leaders to suggest that all Democrats, whether they are private citizens or officials, whether they are Senators or office holders, suggest that they are tinged with treason or that they are all security risks, without distinction? That is what has been going on.

THE PRESIDENT. You say that is what's been going on? I have seen no such statement; but if any such statement is made, I would consider it not only completely untrue, but very unwise—I mean even from a political partisan standpoint. Who would be so foolish as to call all of another great group treasonous to the United States of America? After all, they fought for America.

Q. William Flythe, Hearst Newspapers: Mr. President, may I ask you about Indochina, sir, if you would care to say anything?

THE PRESIDENT. As I told you last week—I believe I told you last week, didn't that subject come up? I said we had increased the technical side of the training units you send out there. I forget the technical name for them—the training and administrative units that turn over the equipment, and so on—MAAGs, we call them. We have increased that. Now, recently, some of our equipment shipped to Indochina has involved airplanes, and they just didn't have the people to take care of them. So we increased that particular body by some airplane mechanics, who are to be returned from there no later than June 15th.

Q. Mr. Flythe: Mr. President, I wanted to ask you, if I might, if these people could be considered in any way combatant troops?

THE PRESIDENT. No, they are not only maintenance troops, but I see no opportunity of them even getting touched by combat.

Q. Roscoe Drummond, New York Herald Tribune: Mr. President, would you say it would be accurate for us to construe your answer to Mr. Merriman Smith about partisanship as meaning that you would counsel officials of the executive branch of the Government not to engage in extreme partisanship?

THE PRESIDENT. That is correct.

Q. Alan Emory, Watertown Times: Sir, following up Mr. Leviero's question about specific comments from Republicans about the Democrats, I wondered if you would care to comment on these specific statements: one, by a Republican Senator, "that the label 'Democrat' was stitched with the idiocy of a Truman, rotted by the deceit of an Acheson, corrupted by the red slime of a White"; and second, by another Republican Senator, that "the Republicans, when they took over, had found heaps of evidence of treason in the previous administration, and that the Democrats had tampered with the security of the United States."

THE PRESIDENT. Well, I will not comment on anybody's statement as such. I will not engage in personalities, and I think I have stated my position quite clearly as to what I think. I believe this: I believe that the ordinary American is capable of deciding what is temperate and just in fact, and what is just indulging in language for no good purpose that I can see.

Q. Ethel Payne, Defender Publications: Mr. President, last Friday evening at the Lincoln Day box supper at the Arena, the Howard University choir, which was scheduled to sing, was barred from the hall by District police.

THE PRESIDENT. Who?

Q. Miss Payne: The Howard University choir, even though they had their instructions, and had followed out those instructions. Consequently, they were forced to return to the campus without appearing on the program; but, in the meantime, two other singing groups, the Duke and Emory University Glee Clubs were admitted without incident. I wonder if you had been informed of that, and if you had looked into it.

THE PRESIDENT. I not only had not been informed of it—[*confers with Mr. Hagerty*]—I am just told, for the first time that I have heard about this, I am told by Mr. Hagerty that the bus driver was instructed to go around to the door by which I entered, and he refused to go around to that place. I hope there is no connection between those two facts. [*Laughter*] But anyway, that is just what I have been informed.

I would say this: if that choir was barred by the reason that you seem to fear, of anything about race or of color or anything of that kind, I will be the first to apologize to them. I just don't believe that could have happened.

Q. Pat Munroe, Albuquerque Journal: Mr. President, further on the question of bipartisanship, Senator Anderson, perhaps the best friend of your farm program in Congress, is up for reelection, and his probable opponent will be a rather conservative Republican, Governor Mechem. They are saying there that you will probably stay out of the State entirely in the course of the campaign. I think we need a refresher on your plans for helping individuals—helping the Republican ticket in general, this November.

THE PRESIDENT. I have nothing to say on it except to repeat what I said a long time ago. I believe it was before one of our conferences: I am not going into any State and I am not going to participate in local contests. I think that as President I have really no right to do so.

Q. Robert Richards, The Copley Press: Anent that partisan fight, would you say, one, that it is possible to frighten the country into a depression——

THE PRESIDENT. I don't think I heard you start the question.

Q. Mr. Richards: I say, would you say, one, it is possible to frighten the country into a depression; and, two, that efforts to frighten it were of political motivation?

THE PRESIDENT. I think it would be possible to mislead and, to a certain extent, frighten the country; not into a major depression, I doubt that. But I do believe you could have a recession brought about by such statements. On the other hand, I have in the past few months noticed statements that were attributed to at least people of more than one party in this respect, and I believe I will comment on that no more than I have. I don't want to violate my own ideas of fairness.

Q. William Dickinson, Philadelphia Bulletin: Sir, would you permit direct quotation of your answer to Mr. Smith's question, the first one of the conference?

THE PRESIDENT. I wouldn't without taking a look at it. I don't recall the question and I don't recall my answer. But I just believe that the procedures of these conferences have to be observed rather closely or they will become something other than what they are. I hope you don't want me to come in here and begin to think of my grammar and rhetoric and all the rest of it in answering your question, so I would want to take a look.

Q. Marvin Arrowsmith, Associated Press: Mr. President, to go back for a moment to that question on Indochina, there seems to be some uneasiness in Congress, as voiced by Senator Stennis for one, that sending these technicians to Indochina will lead eventually to our involvement in a hot war there. Would you comment on that?

THE PRESIDENT. I would just say this: no one could be more bitterly opposed to ever getting the United States involved in a hot war in that region than I am; consequently, every move that I authorize is calculated, so far as humans can do it, to make certain that that does not happen.

Q. Hazel Markel, Mutual Broadcasting System: Mr. President, there is a report that there has been rather heavy mail at the White House concerning the appointment of a woman to the White House staff. I would like to ask if the mail has been heavy on that score, and if there is consideration being given to such an appointment.

THE PRESIDENT. Well, if there is, I haven't seen it. Now, I don't want to answer your question with just a flat "no" for this reason: as you know, the mail all comes to a great place and it is sorted and segregated and I get my portion of it. I have seen none of it; but I would say and repeat again: I look for brains and ability where I can find it, and if I can find it among the women, I would certainly like to see one of them around here, in one of those important positions.

Q. Joseph Slevin, New York Journal of Commerce: Mr. President, I would like to get back to your highway program announcement at the beginning of the session. You said you hoped to increase, as I understood it, Federal participation by $225 million.

THE PRESIDENT. Well, only in this way: there had been certain of the funds withheld apparently, maybe because the States didn't match them. I am not quite sure of all the facts, but we do hope to step up this program from around $675 million to about $900 million. [*Addresses Mr. Hagerty*] Isn't that correct?

Mr. Hagerty: That is correct.

THE PRESIDENT. That is correct, about $900 million.

Q. Mr. Slevin: Is that in addition to the amount programed in your budget when it went to the Congress?

THE PRESIDENT. The amounts are not programed, except as I spoke of the tax, the cent and a half excise tax, as opposed to two cents.

Q. Mr. Slevin: Is this $225 million in addition?

THE PRESIDENT. The $225 million would be in addition to the one and a half cent yield. You would get a 2 percent yield, which would altogether run about——

Q. Mr. Slevin: I am afraid I didn't make myself quite clear. I meant would the $225 million of Federal expenditures be in addition to the amount the budget said the Federal Government would spend in the next fiscal year?

THE PRESIDENT. As a matter of fact, I have forgotten the item that the Federal budget itself said. I don't believe we gave a specific figure, exact figure, on that, because I thought it was dependent on the amount collected by the tax. I will look up the point and tell you about that.

Q. Will Muller, Detroit News: Mr. President, Detroit, the day before yesterday, was declared a surplus labor area. Do you plan that your order channeling set-asides into surplus labor areas will apply to Detroit, and there will be some relief there in the automotive industry?

THE PRESIDENT. Well, so far as this system gives any relief at all, it goes to every section of the country without exception, provided that the conditions are met. They are, in my mind, very strict conditions. If they are met, why, they would go to Detroit as well as any place else, I suppose.

Q. Edward Milne, Providence Journal-Bulletin: Mr. President, Chairman Wiley of the Foreign Relations Committee urged quite strongly in the Senate on Monday that the whole question of a treaty powers amendment be referred either to a congressional committee or to a Presidential commission for study. Senator Knowland, however, is trying to push ahead with an amendment to be written, as he said, on the floor at this session. Which course do you favor?

THE PRESIDENT. Well, I have had my say, in general, on this whole business of amending the Constitution. As you know, I have no official role in the amending of our Constitution. When an amendment is approved by two-thirds of each House, it goes to the States, and that is that.

Now, as to the procedures that they follow down there, I will leave it to them. I am not going to participate in that.

Q. Mr. Milne: Could I just pursue the question for a moment? Several weeks ago, when the Bricker amendment, as such, was the pending business before the Senate, you made it extremely plain that you were opposed to the Bricker amendment. The pending business, when the Senate returns to the amendment next week, will be the Knowland-Saltonstall-Millikin, and one other Senator's name was attached, Senator Ferguson. I wonder, sir, whether or not you approve that amendment which has been spoken of, at least informally, as an administration amendment?

THE PRESIDENT. Well, as you know, my position was always that there was a certain—normally kept in section 1—that no agreement, no treaty, can be in opposition, or if it is in opposition to the Constitution, have any effect.

I have always thought that was the amendment that would reassure the American people, and nothing else was really necessary. I have examined many, many versions, and where they don't seem to transcend that purpose, in substance, I have not objected. That is all. I have just objected to those things that I believe would hamper the President and the State Department in carrying on the foreign relations of this country, or where there would be an upsetting of the balance of powers established by the Constitution.

Q. Glenn Thompson, Cincinnati Enquirer: Back to the road money——

THE PRESIDENT. To the what?

Q. Mr. Thompson: To the road money.

Q. Sarah McClendon, El Paso Times: Highway money.

Q. Merriman Smith, United Press: Highway money.

THE PRESIDENT. Oh, yes.

Q. Glenn Thompson, Cincinnati Enquirer: Yesterday Congressman McGregor introduced a bill in the House which would increase the Federal contribution to highway building not by $225 million but by $289 million. He described his bill as introduced for the administration. I wondered if your statement of $225 million is an intentional change from that bill?

THE PRESIDENT. Well, the figure that they gave me this morning was 250, and I was merely trying to be conservative. [*Laughter*] I don't know exactly what the amount is.

Q. Mr. Thompson: Mr. President, may I ask what the administration's position is— 225, 250, or 289?

THE PRESIDENT. Well, as a matter of fact, I came in here to talk to you about a principle based on a ½-cent tax; I don't know exactly what the figure is, and I can't be expected to know. Now, I am going to look it up.

Q. James B. Reston, New York Times: Sir, in one of these meetings I believe you referred to your responsibilities as head of the Republican Party. I wonder if you would discuss with us how far those responsibilities cover the activities of the Republican National Committee?

THE PRESIDENT. Well, by organization they don't control it at all. What the President's responsibility as head of the party requires is that he devise a program that is in general conformity with the platform of his party, and that he do his best to get it enacted into law. I think that would be the simplest way to state his major party responsibility.

Now, all parties are organized for business purposes, as you know, in a very detailed way. They head up into the Chairman of the National Committee, and the Chairman of the National Committee is never appointed, as again you well know, without consulting the President as to whether such and such a man is acceptable to him in that position.

But as far as actually directing the affairs of that body, he has no official position whatsoever.

Q. Mr. Reston: I was thinking, sir, of your statement, for example, this morning, suggesting or counseling tolerance upon members of your administration. Would you expect the Chairman of the Republican National Committee to follow such advice?

THE PRESIDENT. Yes, I would.

Q. Daniel Shorr, CBS Radio: Mr. President, should your remarks on Indochina be construed as meaning that you are determined not to become involved or, perhaps, more deeply involved in the war in Indochina, regardless of how that war may go?

THE PRESIDENT. Well, I am not going to try to predict the drift of world events now and the course of world events over the next months. I say that I cannot conceive of a greater tragedy for America than to get heavily involved now in an all-out war in any of those regions, particularly with large units.

So what we are doing is supporting the Vietnamese and the French in their conduct of that war; because, as we see it, it is a case of independent and free nations operating against the encroachment of communism.

Q. Mrs. May Craig, New England Papers: Mr. President, a member of the Senate Armed Services Committee says he fears we are inching our way into war in Indochina, and that the Senate Armed Services Committee was not informed of the sending of additional technicians. Could you tell me to what extent you feel that you are bound to inform the Senate Armed Services Committee of your movements?

THE PRESIDENT. Well, I have not heard of this statement you made, and I should like very much to see and talk to that individual before I speak further, because I make no charges.

I do know this: we try in every significant event that takes place in our international relationships to inform the proper people in the Senate and House—leadership, chairmen, and so on—before we do it, so that they know what's going on. There is no attempt here to carry on the affairs of America in a darkened room.

One thing we must never forget: in the touchiness of today, everything you do has certain risks. Even when we try to give some food to some starving people there was risk in it—we were warned that there would be the gravest consequences likely to follow from such a thing.

Everything you do has its certain risks. Knowing that, we try to keep people informed; and if someone told you that, well, it doesn't agree with my understanding and, therefore, I would want to talk to that person.

Q. Charles Bartlett, Chattanooga Times: Mr. President, leading Republicans down in Tennessee seem to have the idea that you have decided against reappointing Gordon Clapp as Chairman of TVA. I wonder if you could give us some direct insight into that?

THE PRESIDENT. Well, to start with, the answer to that is simple: with respect to the appointments of personnel, you never make a statement until the appointment is announced. You never make a statement about such things; so I am sorry, I can't comment on it.

Q. Sarah McClendon, El Paso Times: I believe, sir, that you had some conversations with the Mexican Ambassador last week. I wonder if you discussed the Mexican labor question? And did he say that a unilateral agreement whereby the United States brings in Mexico would endanger our good relations with that country?

THE PRESIDENT. He just came to ask that certain friendly talks that were going on between us be resumed, and I agreed instantly.

Q. Robert Spivack, New York Post: Mr. President, following up Mr. Reston's question, last Sunday night Leonard Hall said over a TV program that the Republican National Committee was underwriting Senator McCarthy's tour across the country, and that this constituted an endorsement, and that he considered the Senator an asset. This was after the Senator had described the two previous administrations as "twenty years of treason." Do you approve of underwriting the tour or agree with Mr. Hall?

THE PRESIDENT. I don't think my approval or disapproval here is needed, and I am not going to comment any further on that. Particularly, I have said many, many times that I am not going to talk about anything where personalities are involved; I will not do it.

Q. Clayton Knowles, New York Times: Mr. President, you asked for statehood for Hawaii, and it looks like you are going to get it. There is a bill out in the Senate; but there are also bills reported in both the Senate and House for statehood for Alaska. Do you think the time is ripe for Alaskan statehood, as well?

THE PRESIDENT. These things are now separated on the Hill where they are still under discussion. I think rather than start a debate in this body on the same questions, I will wait until they decide; then, if you want to ask me a question again, I will talk about it.

Q. Ray Scherer, National Broadcasting Company: Mr. President, would you give us any inkling of any travel plans you might have in the near future?

THE PRESIDENT. What?

Q. Mr. Scherer: Travel plans, plans to be out of the city.

THE PRESIDENT. I hope to spend next Saturday out of this town. [*Laughter*] I hope that I will get a chance to go shooting.

As you know I went to Europe; I haven't been shooting for 3 years, and I want to see whether I can hit a quail, if that is possible. If I go, I shall go to Secretary Humphrey's farm down in Georgia. That is still hopefully in my plans.

Q. Edward Milne, Providence Journal-Bulletin: Mr. President, I think there has been some oversight here, and nobody has raised the question about 2200 security risks. [*Laughter*]

THE PRESIDENT. You have raised it, and I will let you discuss it. [*Laughter*]

Merriman Smith, United Press: Thank you, Mr. President.

NOTE: President Eisenhower's twenty-seventh news conference was held in the Executive Office Building from 10:30 to 11:01 o'clock on Wednesday morning, February 10, 1954. In attendance: 204.

34 ¶ Statement by the President on the Participation by Eugene, Oregon, in the Multiple Purpose Development of the McKenzie River.
February 10, 1954

BY JOINING with the Federal government in the multiple purpose development of the McKenzie River, the City of Eugene, Oregon, is pioneering in the new concept of power development in the Pacific Northwest.

I have had an opportunity to study the program which the Eugene Water and Electric Board and the Corps of Engineers have jointly developed. Under the plan, the Federal government will undertake the construction of flood control works on the McKenzie and the City will underwrite the cost of construction of power facilities and transmission lines.

This program, when carried to a successful conclusion gives the local people a responsibility in the important development work. It is true partnership and conforms to the power policy of this Administration.

Legislation has been introduced by Senator Cordon and Congressman Ellsworth to carry this policy into effect.

NOTE: The President referred to S. 2920 and H.R. 7815, introduced on February 9.

35 ¶ Letter to Governor Thornton, Chairman of the Governors' Conference 1954, Proposing a Visit to Korea by a Select Group of Governors.
February 11, 1954

[Released February 11, 1954. Dated February 9, 1954]

Dear Dan:

Our country, as you know, has an important stake in the fortunes and destiny of the Republic of Korea. Since the cessation of hostilities there last July, we have continued to improve its military position and have also assumed the task of helping to rebuild its war-torn economy. The results of these endeavors will profoundly affect our leadership and prestige in the Far East and indeed throughout the free world.

I am persuaded that a short visit to Korea by a select group of State executives who are constantly in direct touch with the American people would be highly beneficial. Their personal evaluation of our progress would provide the public with the essential knowledge and broad understanding to which it is entitled.

Accordingly, I would be deeply appreciative if you, together with other members of the Executive Committee of the Governors' Conference, could go to Korea on or about April 1 and, upon your return, give an appraisal of the situation there based on first-hand observation. Will you canvass your Committee and advise me which Governors wish to make the trip?

With kind regard,

Sincerely,

DWIGHT D. EISENHOWER

NOTE: On July 9, 1954, the White House released the text of a report on Korea by Governor Dan Thornton of Colorado, and by Governors John Fine of Pennsylvania and Allan Shivers of Texas who accompanied him on his visit to Korea.

The Governors reported that a good job was being done in administering the U.S. aid programs. "The American and Korean people can be assured that operating overhead is being kept at a minimum and that a full dollar value is being extracted for every dollar spent. Measurable progress has been made toward repairing the devastation wrought by the Communist aggression. We believe that this progress will quicken in the months ahead through the joint efforts of Koreans and Americans."

After citing many examples of progress under the program, the Governors suggested that additional effort be directed toward (a) achieving still better coordination of the U.S., U.N., and Korean programs, (b) encouraging Korea to stimulate private enterprise and private foreign investment through monetary reforms, (c) considering further utilization of U.S. surplus agricultural commodities, and (d) encouraging Korea to take additional measures toward economic and financial stabilization to permit maximum effectiveness in use of aid funds.

A supplemental report to the President on Japan was attached to the release of the Korean report.

36 ¶ Statement by the President on the Appointment of Admiral Jerauld Wright as Supreme Allied Commander, Atlantic. *February* 17, 1954

I FEEL that Admiral Wright is extremely well qualified to perform the duties of Supreme Allied Commander, Atlantic. Admiral Wright has extensive background and naval command experience in positions of vital importance and he is an officer of outstanding character and ability. Admiral Wright has served as Deputy U.S. Representative to the Standing Group of the North Atlantic Treaty Organization and is thoroughly cognizant of the duties and responsibilities of SACLANT. I feel that Admiral Wright will uphold and carry forward the fine traditions and worthy objectives sought by all the NATO nations. I have every confidence that Admiral Wright can make an outstanding contribution to our common defense effort.

37 ¶ Remarks to the White House Conference on Highway Safety. *February* 17, 1954

Mr. Secretary, ladies and gentlemen:

A privilege accorded me is that of coming to this meeting in order to extend to each of you a cordial welcome on behalf of the Government of the United States.

The purpose of your meeting is one that is essentially local or community in character. But when any particular activity in the United States takes 38,000 American lives in one year, it becomes a national problem of the first importance. Consequently, this meeting was called, and you have accepted the invitation, in an understanding between us that it is not merely a local or community problem. It is a problem for all of us, from the highest echelon of Government to the lowest echelon: a problem for every citizen, no matter what his station or his duty.

I was struck by a statistic that seemed to me shocking. In the last 50 years, the automobile has killed more people in the United States than we have had fatalities in all our wars: on all the battlefields of all the wars of the United States since its founding 177 years ago.

We have great organizations working effectively and supported by the Government, to seek ways and means of promoting peace in the world in order that these great tragedies may be prevented—or at least minimized in the future. But we live every day with this problem that costs us so many lives, and not only lives but grief and suffering in the families from which those victims came—to say nothing of the disablement that so many other citizens must bear all through their lives either through their own or someone else's carelessness.

It is one of those problems which by its nature has no easy solution. No one can come along and say that we must have more policemen or more traffic lights or just more roads. It is a problem that is many-sided, and therefore every citizen can contribute something to it if nothing else but his own sense of responsibility when he is driving his car or crossing the street or taking care of his children. But I must say that in each community I do believe that much would be done if the efforts of all of those to whom we give legal responsibility in this affair would have the organized support of all of us. If there were community groups established that could command the respect and the support of every single citizen of that city or that community, so that the traffic policeman, so that everyone else that has a responsibility in this regard, will know that public opinion is behind him. Because I have now arrived at the only point that I think it worthwhile to try to express to you, because in all the technicalities of this thing you know much more than I do. I do want to refer, though, for one moment to this one factor: public opinion.

In a democracy, public opinion is everything. It is the force that brings about progress; it is the force that brings about enforcement of the laws; it is the force that keeps the United States in being, and it runs in all its parts.

So, if we can mobilize a sufficient public opinion, this problem, like all of those to which free men fall heir can be solved. That public opinion is not a thing of passing moment, not a thing to be won to our side all in one day. It is earnest, long, dedicated leadership on the part of everybody who understands the problem, and then having once been formed, it takes the same kind of leadership to maintain and sustain it, so that this problem will not return to us in exaggerated form. And that fear, I believe, is a very real one.

The same list of statistics that I saw said that in 1975—I don't know why I should be bothered about that year, except I have grandchildren—there are going to be 80 million automobiles on our streets and roads and highways.

Now, the Federal Government is going to do its part in helping to build more highways and many other facilities to take care of those cars. But 80 million cars on our highways! I wonder how people will get to highway conferences to consider the control of highway traffic. It is going to be a job.

But that figure does mean this: we don't want to try to stop that many automobiles coming—I am sure Mr. Curtice doesn't, anyway—we want them. They mean progress for our country. They mean greater convenience for a greater number of people, greater happiness, and greater standards of living. But we have got to learn to control the things that we must use ourselves, and not let them be a threat to our lives and to our loved ones.

And so I say all of this comes back to the mobilization of public opinion. This kind of meeting does something in the mobilizing of that opinion. When you go back to your communities, each of you will have an opportunity that is probably as direct and immediate and personal a one as you could probably have in this whole Government of ours. So while I thank you for being here, for doing your part in this kind of job, in this kind of meeting, I also congratulate you on the opportunity that is opening up to each of you in your own communities.

And now again, thank you for the privilege of coming here and meeting you, and saying that I think you are engaged in something—I know you are engaged in something that is not only to the welfare of every citizen of the United States, but I believe that they realize it.

Thank you very much.

NOTE: The White House Conference on Highway Safety was called by the President through a letter to the State Governors released December 14, 1953. Secretary of Commerce Sinclair Weeks served as General Chairman of the Conference. Harlow H. Curtice, to whom the President referred toward the end of his remarks, was Chairman of the group representing business. Later he became Chairman of the President's Committee for Traffic Safety.

The President spoke at the Departmental Auditorium.

38 ¶ Special Message to the Congress Recommending Amendments to the Atomic Energy Act. *February* 17, 1954

To the Congress of the United States:

For the purpose of strengthening the defense and economy of the United States and of the free world, I recommend that the Congress approve a number of amendments to the Atomic Energy Act of 1946. These amendments would accomplish this purpose, with proper security safeguards, through the following means:

First, widened cooperation with our allies in certain atomic energy matters;

Second, improved procedures for the control and dissemination of atomic energy information; and,

Third, encouragement of broadened participation in the development of peacetime uses of atomic energy in the United States.

NUCLEAR PROGRESS

In 1946, when the Atomic Energy Act was written, the world was on the threshold of the atomic era. A new and elemental source of tremendous energy had been unlocked by the United States the year before. To harness its power in peaceful and productive service was even then our hope and our goal, but its awesome destructiveness overshadowed its potential for good. In the minds of most people this new energy was equated with the atomic bomb, and the bomb spelled the erasure of cities and the mass death of men, women, and children.

Moreover, this Nation's monopoly of atomic weapons was of crucial importance in international relations. The common defense and world peace required that this monopoly be protected and prolonged by the most stringent security safeguards.

In this atmosphere, the Atomic Energy Act was written. Well suited to conditions then existing, the Act in the main is still adequate to the Nation's needs.

Since 1946, however, there has been great progress in nuclear science and technology. Generations of normal scientific development have been compressed into less than a decade. Each successive year has seen technological advances in atomic energy exceeding even progressive estimates. The anticipations of 1946, when government policy was established and the Atomic Energy Act was written, have been far outdistanced.

One popular assumption of 1946—that the United States could maintain its monopoly in atomic weapons for an appreciable time—was quickly proved invalid. That monopoly disappeared in 1949, only three years after the Atomic Energy Act was enacted. But to counterbalance that debit on the atomic ledger there have been mighty increases in our assets.

A wide variety of atomic weapons—considered in 1946 to be mere possibilities of a distant future—have today achieved conventional status in the arsenals of our armed forces. The thermonuclear weapon—non-existent eight years ago—today dwarfs in destructive power all atomic weapons. The practicability of constructing a submarine with atomic propulsion was questionable in 1946; three weeks ago the launching of the U.S.S. Nautilus made it certain that the use of atomic energy for ship propulsion will ultimately become widespread. In 1946, too, economic industrial power from atomic energy sources seemed very remote; today, it is clearly in sight—largely a matter of further research and development, and the establishment of conditions in which the spirit of enterprise can flourish.

Obviously, such developments as these within so short a period should have had a profound influence on the Nation's atomic energy policy. But in a number of respects, our atomic energy law is still designed to fit the conditions of 1946.

Many statutory restrictions, based on such actual facts of 1946 as the American monopoly of atomic weapons and limited application of atomic energy in civilian and military fields, are inconsistent with the nuclear realities of 1954. Furthermore, these restrictions impede the proper exploitation of nuclear energy for the benefit of the American people and of our friends throughout the free world.

An objective assessment of these varied factors leads clearly to these conclusions: In respect to defense considerations, our atomic effectiveness will be increased if certain limited information on the use of atomic weapons can be imparted more readily to nations allied with us in common defense. In respect to peaceful applications of atomic energy, these can be developed more rapidly and their benefits more widely realized through broadened cooperation with friendly nations and through greater participation by American industry. By enhancing our military effectiveness, we strengthen our efforts to deter aggression; by enlarging opportunities for peacetime development, we accelerate our own progress and strengthen the free world.

Section 1 of the Atomic Energy Act of 1946 wisely recognizes the need for future revisions of the law. In its spirit and in consideration of matters of the utmost importance to the Nation's defense and welfare, I recommend that the Congress approve a number of amendments to the Atomic Energy Act.

COOPERATION WITH OTHER NATIONS

In this atomic era, the growth of international cooperation for the defense of the free world is the most heartening development on the world political scene. The United States is allied with many friends in measures to deter aggression and, where necessary, to defeat the aggressor. The agreements binding ourselves and our friends in common defense constitute a warning to any potential aggressor that his punishment will be swift and his defeat inevitable. These powerful influences for peace must be made as strong and convincing as possible.

Most of our friends among the nations have had little opportunity to inform themselves on the employment of atomic weapons. Under present law, we cannot give them tactical information essential to their effective participation with us in combined military operations and planning, and to their own defense against atomic attack.

Our own security will increase as our allies gain information concerning the use of and the defense against atomic weapons. Some of our allies, in fact, are now producing fissionable materials or weapons, supporting effective atomic energy research and developing peacetime uses for atomic power. But all of them should become better informed in the problems of atomic warfare and, therefore, better prepared to meet the contingency of such warfare. In order for the free world to be an effective defense unit, it must be geared to the atomic facts of this era.

I urge, therefore, that authority be provided to exchange with nations participating in defensive arrangements with the United States such tactical information as is essential to the development of defense plans and to the training of personnel for atomic warfare. Amendments to the definition of "restricted data" recommended later in this message will also contribute to needed administrative flexibility in the exchange of information with such nations concerning the use of atomic weapons.

To meet a specific defense need existing in 1951, the Congress approved a carefully limited procedure for the communication of information on the processing of atomic raw materials, reactor development, production of fissionable materials, and related research and development. These limitations should now be modified so that the authority to communicate information, adjusted to present conditions, may be better used to our national advantage.

In the development of peaceful uses for atomic energy, additional amendments are required for effective United States cooperation with friendly nations. Such cooperation requires the exchange of certain "restricted data" on the industrial applications of atomic energy and also the release of fissionable materials in amounts adequate for industrial and research use. I therefore recommend that the Atomic Energy Act be amended to authorize such cooperation. Such amendments should prescribe that before the conclusion of any arrangements for the transfer of fissionable material to a foreign nation, assurances must be provided against its use by the recipient nation for military purposes.

Sharing certain information with other nations involves risks that must be weighed, in each instance, against the net advantages to the United States. In each case, we must be guided by such considerations as: The sensitivity and importance of the data, the specific uses to which the information will be put, the security standards of the cooperating nation, its role in the common defense of the free world, and the contributions it has made and can make to the mutual security effort. Such considerations apply to the exchange or communication of information on general defense planning and the employment of conventional weapons as well as to the information that could be exchanged pursuant to these recommendations.

These recommendations are apart from my proposal to seek a new basis for international cooperation in the field of atomic energy as outlined in my address before the General Assembly of the United Nations last December. Consideration of additional legislation which may be needed to implement that proposal should await the development of areas of agreement as a result of our discussions with other nations.

In a related area, present law prevents United States citizens or corporations from engaging directly or indirectly in the production of fissionable material outside the United States, except upon determination by the President that the proposed activity will not adversely affect the common defense and security. Matters that have arisen under this provision have been ordinary business or commercial activities which nevertheless fall within the broad statutory prohibition because they might contribute in some degree, however minor, to foreign atomic energy programs. The President should be enabled to authorize the Atomic Energy Commission to make future determinations of this nature. This amendment is related also to the above amendment concerning the exchange of information with other countries, as arrangements for authorized exchanges of information with friendly foreign governments may involve participation by American citizens or firms in work in foreign countries. The proposed amendment would permit the Atomic Energy Commission also to authorize such participation.

All of these proposed amendments should make it clear that the authority granted must be exercised only in accordance with conditions prescribed by the President to protect the common defense and security.

PROTECTION OF ATOMIC ENERGY INFORMATION

A special category of "restricted data," so defined as to include virtually all atomic energy data of security significance, is now established by law. "Restricted data" are protected in the law by special espionage provisions, provisions relating to the control, dissemination and declassification of such data, and by requirements for personnel security clearances.

Personnel Security. The provisions of the Act relating to security clearances of personnel need improvement in several respects. The Act does not recognize degrees of sensitivity of "restricted data." The same clearance requirements apply to any type of "restricted data," whether it be access by the unskilled construction laborer to "restricted data" of only marginal security significance, or access by a scientist to the heart of atomic weapons information. The Atomic Energy Commission lacks sufficient latitude under present law to determine the extent of personnel investigation needed for adequate security. Many costly background investigations required by present law are unnecessary. The Atomic Energy Commission should be permitted to relate the scope of investigation required under the Act to the significance of the access to "restricted data" which will be permitted.

This amendment is especially pertinent to the proposed broadening of private participation in the development of atomic power. While such private participants will require access to "restricted data" on reactor technology, full investigations of all their employees who will have such access are not warranted because much of the data involved will not have significant security importance. Moreover, such investigations would impede and discourage the desired participation and would be unnecessarily costly both to government and to industry. Where access to more sensitive "restricted data" is involved, the Commission must, of course, require full investigations.

Another security clearance problem relates to personnel of Department of Defense agencies and to the personnel of contractors with those agencies.   The Atomic Energy Commission may now disclose "restricted data" to such of these personnel as have security clearances from the Department of Defense.   The "restricted data" so disclosed by the Commission are thereafter protected in accordance with Department of Defense security regulations.   And yet, contractors of the Commission are precluded by law from granting the same personnel access to the same "restricted data" until they have had AEC clearances, based on investigations by the Federal Bureau of Investigation or the Civil Service Commission.

As applications of atomic energy become increasingly widespread within the Armed Services, the necessity increases for communication of "restricted data" between AEC contractors and participants in related Department of Defense programs.   The present fact that personnel engaged in military programs who have military clearances must be denied access to "restricted data" by AEC contractor personnel impedes cooperation between the Department of Defense and the Atomic Energy Commission in areas of mutual interest and causes unnecessary expense in time and money.   I therefore recommend that the Atomic Energy Commission be enabled to authorize its contractors and licensees to afford access to "restricted data" to personnel engaged in Department of Defense programs who need such data in their work and who possess the proper military security clearances.

The Definition of Restricted Data.   (1) A large body of "restricted data" under present law relates primarily to military utilization of atomic weapons.   The responsibility for the control of much of this weapons information logically should rest with the Department of Defense rather than with the Commission.   Many administrative difficulties that are produced by a dual system of security would be eliminated by the removal of this weapons information from the "restricted data" category and its subsequent protection by the Department of Defense in the same manner and under the same safeguards as other military secrets.

This method of handling weapons information is not possible under present law.   "Restricted data" can be removed from the statutory "restricted data" category only by declassification, upon a determination by the Atomic Energy Commission that the publication of such data would not adversely affect the common defense and security.   Declassification obviously is not the remedy. The remedy lies in reliance upon the standard security measures of the user, the Department of Defense. I recommend, therefore, that the statutory definition of "restricted data" be amended to exclude information concerning the utilization of atomic weapons, as distinguished from information on their theory, design and manufacture.

(2) In addition to information which falls wholly within the utilization category, there is information which concerns primarily the utilization of weapons but which pertains also to their design and manufacture. In order to avoid difficulties in this marginal zone, I recommend legislation which also would authorize removal of such information from the "restricted data" category. This would be done only when the Commission and the Department of Defense jointly determine that it relates primarily to military utilization of atomic weapons and that it can be adequately safeguarded as classified defense information under the Espionage Act and other applicable law.

(3) Consistent with these changes, I recommend that the Department of Defense join with the Atomic Energy Commission in any declassification of "restricted data" which relate primarily to military utilization of atomic weapons and which can be published without endangering the national security. Thus, the Department of Defense will have an appropriate voice in the protection and declassification of such "restricted data" and the responsibilities of the Commission will be clarified with respect to all other "restricted data".

DOMESTIC DEVELOPMENT OF ATOMIC ENERGY

What was only a hope and a distant goal in 1946—the beneficent use of atomic energy in human service—can soon be a reality. Before our scientists and engineers lie rich possibilities in the harnessing of atomic power. The Federal Government can pioneer in its development. But, in this undertaking, the enterprise, initiative and competitive spirit of individuals and groups within our free economy are needed to assure the greatest efficiency and progress at the least cost to the public.

Industry's interest in this field is already evident. In collaboration with the Atomic Energy Commission, a number of private corporations are now conducting studies, largely at their own expense, of the various reactor types which might be developed to produce economic power. There are indications that they would increase their efforts significantly if the way were open for private investment in such reactors. In amending the law to permit such investment, care must be taken to encourage the development of this new industry in a manner as nearly normal as possible, with careful regulation to protect the national security and the public health and safety. It is essential that this program so proceed that this new industry will develop self-reliance and self-sufficiency.

The creation of opportunities for broadened industrial participation may permit the Government to reduce its own reactor research and development after private industrial activity is well established. For the present, in addition to contributing toward the advancement of power reactor technology, the Government will continue to speed progress in the related technology of military propulsion reactors. The present complementary efforts of industry and Government will therefore continue, and industry should be encouraged by the enactment of appropriate legislation to assume a substantially more significant role. To this end, I recommend amendments to the Atomic Energy Act which would:

1. Relax statutory restrictions against ownership or lease of fissionable material and of facilities capable of producing fissionable material.

2. Permit private manufacture, ownership and operation of atomic reactors and related activities, subject to necessary safeguards and under licensing systems administered by the Atomic Energy Commission.

3. Authorize the Commission to establish minimum safety and security regulations to govern the use and possession of fissionable material.

4. Permit the Commission to supply licensees special materials and services needed in the initial stages of the new industry at prices estimated to compensate the Government adequately for the value of the materials and services and the expense to the Government in making them available.

5. Liberalize the patent provisions of the Atomic Energy Act, principally by expanding the area in which private patents can be obtained to include the production as well as utilization of fissionable material, while continuing for a limited period the authority to require a patent owner to license others to use an invention essential to the peacetime applications of atomic energy.

Until industrial participation in the utilization of atomic energy acquires a broader base, considerations of fairness require some mechanism to assure that the limited number of companies, which as government contractors now have access to the program, cannot build a patent monopoly which would exclude others desiring to enter the field. I hope that participation in the development of atomic power will have broadened sufficiently in the next five years to remove the need for such provisions.

In order to encourage the greatest possible progress in domestic application of atomic energy, flexibility is necessary in licensing and regulatory provisions of the legislation. Until further experience with this new industry has been gained, it would be unwise to try to anticipate by law all of the many problems that are certain to arise. Just as the basic Atomic Energy Act recognized by its own terms that it was experimental in a number of respects, so these amendments will be subject to continuing future change and refinement.

––––––––––

The destiny of all nations during the twentieth century will turn in large measure upon the nature and the pace of atomic energy development here and abroad. The revisions to the Atomic Energy Act herein recommended will help make it possible for American atomic energy development, public and private, to play a full and effective part in leading mankind into a new era of progress and peace.

DWIGHT D. EISENHOWER

39 ¶ The President's News Conference of *February* 17, 1954.

THE PRESIDENT. My apologies for being a little early; I am trying to compress my schedule today. I hope, the Lord willing, in about an hour to be on my way to southern California—an area, by the way, which I have never seen, and none of my family. We are anxious to do it.

As usual, of course, there is a small staff going along, I understand a lot of the newspaper people have already departed, and a lot of bills, reports, to read and sign.

There is one little item that I don't know whether it has been published, so I jotted it down: the Queen Mother is going to make a visit to America in November. She is going to participate, I believe, in an English Speaking Union ceremony in New York. She is going to par-

ticipate in the Columbia Bicentennial because, you know—a little commercial for Columbia—their charter was originally granted by King
George II. Then, she will come down to Washington, will spend from
about November 4th to November 6th at the White House, and then,
I believe, will be here in the city at the Embassy for a while longer.

The coffee investigation is proceeding. One reason I bring up the
subject, I was asked by someone in my office whether I thought this
investigation would have any effect on the relationships between the
United States and our people, with South American countries and
peoples. I see no possibility, myself, that it can affect them. The Bra-
zilians, as you know, are as much upset by this coffee rise as the rest of
us. What the investigation is about is to see whether there are any road
blocks thrown between the source of supply in Brazil and South America
and other countries, and the consumers, by speculation and other processes of that kind that account for part of this great price rise. That is
what the investigation is about, not looking into the internal affairs of
any other country.

There is a report due this afternoon, and I believe it will be available
to all of you, from the Presidential emergency board with respect to the
dispute between the Railway Express Agency and the Brotherhood of
Railway Clerks. That report I haven't seen, but it is to be made available, isn't it?

Mr. Hagerty: Four o'clock.

THE PRESIDENT. Four o'clock.

I think that is about all I have in the way of little announcements of
my own, so we will start the questions.

Q. Kenneth Scheibel, Gannett Newspapers: Mr. President, a number
of the farm State Congressmen in both parties are complaining that the
reduction in dairy prices was too severe and should have been done on
a more gradual basis. They feel that the cutback will cause hardships
in some areas and might stir up some resentment against the flexible
program that you advocate. Is there any—would you tell us if there is
any plan to reconsider that decision or are you going to stick with it?

THE PRESIDENT. As you know, I never use the word "never," but,
as of now, I have no thought that it should be reconsidered.

Each of these problems has to be considered on its own merits; you
see, each year under this support program that has been under butter,

each year there has been a new decision to be taken: "Will you again support at 90 percent or will you reduce?"

Now, last year all the conditions were there that called for reduction in accordance with the law as it exists. I, myself, with the Secretary of Agriculture, decided that in view of the fact this came right along after the election, somewhere about the first of March, as I recall, and that it was a problem that had only started a little while before in November, it was only fair to continue the 90 percent for another year and see what happened. We did warn them if this kind of thing continued, the 90 percent rigid price supports could not be maintained. All year long we have been working with dairy associations, leaders of dairy associations, who believe that they have devised for themselves a program which will eventually make them really independent of governmental support. It will require some governmental, I believe, insurance.

So the whole thing is not as sudden as it looked. This had been talked about for a year, looking ahead to the time when we must get butter back to some kind of price where it will be used.

Today we have butter moving directly from creameries to governmental storage. Well, we are trying to get butter back on the dinner table in some way or other, and we believe that is in the best interests, long-term interests, of the dairy people themselves, as well as other farmers, as well as the public. Now, that is the belief.

Q. Daniel Schorr, CBS Radio: Are you satisfied with the results of and the reaction to your remarks on extreme partisanship?

THE PRESIDENT. Well, I have no particular profound comment to make on that question.

I expressed to you people my views about extremism of any kind in this political world, and I didn't particularly offer advice to anyone. I said what I would do and what I thought was only the right and, let us say, the wisest thing to do in our daily political life in this country.

Q. Alan S. Emory, Watertown Times: Sir, I wonder if I could get back to butter for a second. I would like to ask two questions on the subject: first, did Mr. Benson inform you in advance specifically that he was going to lower the supports all the way to 75 percent of parity; and, second, do you see any conflict between the 15 percent drop on dairy products and your farm program proposal that there should be a gradual, probably 5 percent a year drop when the basic crops were changed to flexibility?

THE PRESIDENT. In the first question you are asking me for a test of perfect memory, and I am not sure. We talked over this problem many, many times during the year, and whether or not we agreed it was going to be from 90 to 15 [75] in one particular day, I am not certain. But I did know what the prospects were; therefore, it had certainly my tacit approval before it was ever even thought of.

With respect to the second, I explained that this particular matter in the agricultural field is not like the storable crops. After all, you freeze butter at zero temperatures, and in 18 months, I understand, it is going rancid and deteriorates.

I have also announced as one of my principles—and I think all of you will recall it—that I do not believe it is justified in this day and time to produce American products by the toil of our hands and the sweat of our brows, and then have them spoil. We have got to do something about it.

Now, if you can't do something with it right now, when you have got 270 million pounds of butter in your hands, you have got to make some move to get it moving into commercial lines and, possibly, to turn some of the dairy products themselves into other types of dairy products. So, since this has been going on for a year—it has been under discussion, and actually it was first proposed that we do this in March 1953—there has been, as I say, at least long notice, even though the actual move itself did go from 90 to the lower extreme.

Q. Nat S. Finney, Buffalo Evening News: You sent over your message on the amendments to the Atomic Energy Act today. I wonder if you had any comment as to how urgent you consider that the Congress act on those at this session?

THE PRESIDENT. Well, when you go to talking about degrees and such things, I think it is difficult to give an exact answer.

I will recall to your minds, I think, something that I have talked about before. I was, after all, Commander in Chief; and I suffered, very seriously suffered, under an inability to talk to allies about weapons and kinds of tactics that would be applicable if ever another war broke out, because of the secrecy imposed by this act. So I have always believed, not just this minute but for years backward, that there should be certain reasonable modifications made. So I would say I would like to see them get at it, put it that way.

Q. L. G. Laycook, Nashville Tennessean: Mr. President, several members of Congress contend that the TVA will be crippled because the administration included no requests for funds for new power generating facilities in the budget. Would you care to comment on that?

THE PRESIDENT. Well, I haven't a great deal to say about it that I haven't said before. You will remember this question was up last year and we went through it. There was a struggle between $90 million and $9 million.

I know of no reason why the city of Memphis, if it wanted to, couldn't do something about this matter itself.

But what does disturb me is this: a whole great region of our country saying that it is completely dependent upon the Federal Government and can't move in improving its lot, except with Federal Government intervention.

Now, much as I believe in the partnership between Federal Government, local government, and State government in developing the resources of our country, making them available to all the people at the lowest possible price, I still think that when we relieve local communities, local populations, of all responsibility, all of the participation in the costs of these things, we are running a very dangerous course.

Now, what we are doing with this one is taking a good long survey and a good long look at it. I don't know what the final answer will be, but we are not going, as I say, we are not going to destroy the TVA; that, you can be sure of.

Q. Mr. Laycook: One more question, sir. Have you appointed a commission to make this study that you just spoke of?

THE PRESIDENT. I have not appointed a Presidential commission, no. There have been surveys going on through the Bureau of the Budget.

Q. Richard Harkness, National Broadcasting Company: There were two economic developments yesterday, Mr. President. The Department of Commerce issued its new style census count of unemployment, which showed the figure was rising sharply from the previous estimate; and then an economist of the Federal Reserve Board, Mr. Winfield Riefler, said that already the economic dip was sharper than you had anticipated in your economic message to Congress. Would you comment on that?

THE PRESIDENT. Well, in the first place, the new figures for the Department of Commerce—and I suppose you studied them to see what the difference is—don't necessarily show a sudden rise. They would show a sudden rise possibly if you had this same figure based on this same basis of sample-taking for the last several months. But this is the first one, and we don't know whether the difference comes about through difference in sampling or whether there is actually a sharper rise in January than we had anticipated. I personally think there is a little of both.

I didn't see this other remark that you speak of with the Federal Reserve Board.

Q. Mr. Harkness: That was the testimony before the Joint Economic Committee.

THE PRESIDENT. I would say this: for the last several weeks all of us have been alert to this day by day, trying to make certain that there is no move neglected on the part of the Government that could be helpful, to make sure that we don't have any real recession. And I will tell you this: so far as using the powers of the Government are concerned, why, we are using them gradually. Now, if this thing would develop so that it looks like we are going into anything major, I wouldn't hesitate one second to use every single thing that this Government can bring to bear to stop any such catastrophe in this country.

I have said that often, and I say it again; but you also don't want to throw the Government wildly out into all sorts of actions, lashing around everywhere, until you know what you are doing. It is a very dangerous move, I should say.

Q. John Herling, Editors Syndicate: Mr. President, there are current reports that you favor a larger grant of power to States in the handling of labor relations, and I wonder whether they are correct reports.

THE PRESIDENT. I have made no commitment, no talk of any kind, except what you have already seen in the amendments I sent, to the Taft-Hartley bill, to Congress.

Q. Mr. Herling: Well, some pro-Eisenhower union men are asking the question whether or not you would favor such an extension of power to States in labor relations, even if it meant the States would enact legislation that would lead to what has been described as union-busting legislation.

THE PRESIDENT. Well, I have never believed in union-busting. You are propounding here a hypothetical question which I have never talked about, and I would be foolish to try any shooting-from-the-hip answer to that one, I will tell you.

Q. Robert L. Riggs, Louisville Courier-Journal: Sir, on your TVA answer, did I get the correct impression that you were advocating the city of Memphis building a steam-generating plant?

THE PRESIDENT. No, I didn't advocate anything; but, I said, what would stop them if they wanted to?

What I did say is this: I am fearful when I see any great section of the United States saying that they cannot do a single thing in industrial expansion or any other kind of expansion unless the Federal Government moves in and does it for them; that is just what frightens me.

Q. Mr. Riggs: Your point was the city could build it if they wished?

THE PRESIDENT. I think so; I don't know any reason why they shouldn't. Someone tells me that there is an element in the contract down there that sort of estops the kind of action which would take place wherever you had free enterprise or greater freedom. I am not quite sure what that item is, but I was told that just in the last few days.

Q. Sarah McClendon, El Paso Times: Mr. President, this unilateral Mexican labor program is being blocked in the House Rules Committee. Is that being done at your request, pending the outcome of the resumption of these negotiations in Mexico City on the bilateral labor program?

THE PRESIDENT. I assure you I didn't know it was blocked in the Rules Committee; I didn't know anything about it.

Q. David P. Sentner, Hearst Newspapers: Mr. President, would you care to comment upon any expected results from the Big Four Conference or any lessons from it?

THE PRESIDENT. Well, I suppose lessons are of all kinds, positive and negative, and so on.

I don't think there is any comment to make. The Secretary of State is coming back soon. He is going to report immediately to bipartisan groups in both Senate and House, and to the appropriate committees in each case. He will report to me early next week, as soon as I come back; and I will possibly then, at whatever press conference follows that, have something to say about his evaluation.

I have had nightly reports from the Secretary, and I think I am fairly well acquainted with his thinking; but it is only fair, I think, both to him and to me, before I comment publicly to wait and have a chat with him.

Q. Joseph R. Slevin, New York Journal of Commerce: Mr. President, do you think the economic downturn has reached a point where consumers should get larger tax concessions than your program called for?

THE PRESIDENT. Well, I can't give you an affirmative answer to that one at this moment.

As you know, the Economic Report states that that is a measure to bring in very quickly when you see this thing spread very definitely.

I should think that March ought to be sort of the key month. March is a month when, I am told, employment begins normally to pick up and you have a definite upturn in the curve. Now, if that isn't true, I should say then we would have a very definite warning that would call for the institution of a number of measures; possibly this tax reduction would be one of the first considered, although I can't say for certain.

Q. Jack L. Bell, Associated Press: Mr. President, Senator Carlson said earlier today that there would be a statement issued on the 2200. He didn't make it clear exactly where the statement would be issued. If there is such a statement, would you care to comment on it now in advance of issuance, and tell us something about it?

THE PRESIDENT. Well, no. [*To Mr. Hagerty*] Didn't you tell me that the Civil Service Commission, I think, is going to have a preliminary statement on this thing sometime—today, is it?

Mr. Hagerty: Yes, 4:00 o'clock.

THE PRESIDENT. Four o'clock. But I think that their final answer that they will put out will take a little bit of time to compile, but they are going to have a statement to make on it sometime this afternoon.

Q. Andrew F. Tully, Scripps-Howard: Mr. President, what has become of your plan for an international atomic energy pool?

THE PRESIDENT. As a matter of fact, it is not dead, and I wouldn't be at all surprised to see some further negotiation in a group jointly set up to do some private talking on it. I don't know yet what is going to happen, but it is still alive.

Q. Mr. Tully: Did Mr. Dulles and Zaroubin get anywhere in their discussions?

THE PRESIDENT. I think I have said enough on that; thank you very much.

Q. Louis Lautier, National Negro Press Association: Is there any way to distinguish between aid to the anti-Communist forces in Indochina and support of colonialism?

THE PRESIDENT. Well, of course. You have asked the very question that is the crux of this whole thing at this moment. There is no colonialism in this battle at all.

France has announced several times, and most emphatically last July, that they are fighting to give the three associated states their freedom, their liberty; and I believe it has been agreed they would live inside the French Union, but as free and independent states.

Now, as I see it, the Vietnamese are fighting for their own independence, and I have no trouble at all making the distinction that you speak of.

We are not trying to help anybody support and maintain colonialism.

Q. Henry Pierre, Le Monde (Paris): Mr. President, there have been some reports that General O'Daniel will be sent back to Indochina with increased responsibilities. Does it imply, in your opinion, some criticism about the way the Vietnamese troops have been trained up to now?

THE PRESIDENT. No. I think, first of all, to get a real answer to your question why there should be a change in the head of that mission out there—Trapnell, I believe, is there now—I believe you better go to the Defense Department; but it merely means there would be a man to relieve Trapnell in Indochina.

Q. Helene C. Monberg, Colorado Newspapers: Mr. President, there is a report on the Hill that you would like your good friend Governor Thornton to run for the Senate; is that true?

THE PRESIDENT. Well, I have refused on several occasions to comment on the specific internal and local affairs of any State, particularly their political affairs.

Now, as to a State where I hope to go and spend a pleasant summer, I know I am not going to say anything about it. *[Laughter]*

Q. Mrs. May Craig, Maine Newspapers: Mr. President, Senator Bridges and Senator Symington are going to Italy to investigate the report that Communists are infiltrating into aircraft plants there, and they will also investigate similar reports. Do you think that it is appropriate to impart atomic information and weapons to allies who may be temporarily in a political turmoil?

THE PRESIDENT. Well, Mrs. Craig, there are as many kinds of atomic energy information as there are different types of people in this room. We are not talking about giving anybody information that will help an enemy.

Now, that is the only thing I can say to that.

(Speaker unidentified): Thank you, Mr. President.

NOTE: President Eisenhower's twenty-eighth news conference was held in the Executive Office Building from 1:58 to 2:20 o'clock on Wednesday afternoon, February 17, 1954. In attendance: 178.

40   ¶ Message to Prime Minister Nehru Commending the Indian Custodial Forces in Korea. *February* 19, 1954

Dear Mr. Prime Minister:

Now that the mission of Indian troops is drawing to a close in Korea, I want to express to you my appreciation and that of my countrymen for the performance of the Indian Custodial Forces.

No military unit in recent years has undertaken a more delicate and demanding peacetime mission than that faced by the Indian forces in Korea. The vast majority of prisoners placed in their charge had from months of imprisonment and uncertainty become highly nervous and volatile. The confidence inspired by the exemplary tact, fairness and firmness shown by the Indian officers and men led by their two able commanders, Lt. General Thimayya and Major General Thorat did much to alleviate the fears and doubts of these prisoners. The performance of these officers and their troops was fully in keeping with the high reputation of the Indian Army. They deserve the highest commendation.

With best wishes,

Sincerely,

DWIGHT D. EISENHOWER

41 ¶ Veto of Bill Relating to Claims of Certain Employees of the Bureau of Prisons.
February 22, 1954

To the House of Representatives:

I return herewith without my approval H.R. 395, "To confer jurisdiction upon the United States Court of Claims with respect to claims against the United States of certain employees of the Bureau of Prisons, Department of Justice."

This measure would confer jurisdiction upon the United States Court of Claims to adjudicate the claims of employees and former employees of the Federal Bureau of Prisons, notwithstanding the lapse of time or any provisions of law to the contrary.

The claimants seek compensation for overtime performed on Saturdays during the period beginning in March 1931, and ending in May 1943. They allege that they were not granted compensatory time off on some other work day as required by the so-called Saturday half-holiday law of March 4, 1931. Even for the most recent of the claims the six-year statute of limitations expired several years ago.

The claims in these cases relate to work performed at different times over a period of more than twenty years. The official time and attendance records which would be required to prove or disprove the issues of fact have been disposed of periodically in the regular manner. Without doubt, necessary witnesses have died or are otherwise beyond reach. This is the very kind of situation which proves the wisdom of a statute of limitation. Without it in such cases it is doubtful whether we can have efficient and orderly administration of the affairs of government.

If I were to approve this enactment, I could not in good conscience refuse to approve other bills setting aside the statute of limitations on old claims for overtime or other compensation for either individuals or groups of Federal personnel who delayed in presenting their claims.

Leaving aside these very important issues of principle and going to the legislative record of this bill, it would appear that the measure has been under consideration in one form or another since the first session of the 80th Congress. Each successive review by the Department of Justice has indicated that within the then existing statutory framework, Bureau of Prisons employees were granted appropriate time off.

In this connection, it must be remembered that the matter of authorizing payment of overtime compensation to Federal employees has been of gradual development. For almost fifty years, between 1893 and 1942, except where there was express authorization to the contrary, the statutes prohibited the payment of additional compensation for extra hours of service, and there was no law of general applicability establishing weekly hours of duty of Federal per annum employees.

The outbreak of World War II brought a close to the haphazard approaches to this problem. Under war-time laws and those enacted since, definite statutory limits were established to govern the work week, overtime compensation, and holiday pay. Without doubt, by present standards, the working conditions of the Bureau of Prisons employees for a great part of the period in question would be considered onerous. But they were no more onerous than those applicable to many other groups of Federal employees. I believe it would be a mistake to single out the group covered by H.R. 395 for the purpose of dealing retroactively with an hours-of-work situation which existed during a long-past period that began almost twenty-three years ago.

Furthermore, I do not see how this bill could work full justice. Turnover in employment in the classes of employees covered by it was very high, and I have the gravest doubts that the intended benefits would reach more than the relatively few who would become aware of the existence of this act if I were to approve it.

I am in favor of providing Federal employees with the fullest opportunity to adjust grievances. I believe, however, that it is fair to confine them generally to the limitations of law and other reasonable conditions. This case, in my opinion, is especially an instance where the law and the principles of orderly administration should be permitted to prevail.

For these reasons I return the bill without my approval.

DWIGHT D. EISENHOWER

42   ¶ Veto of Bill for the Relief of Mrs. Anna Holder.   *February 23, 1954*

To the House of Representatives:

I return herewith H.R. 3733, "For the relief of Mrs. Anna Holder."

This measure, in directing the payment to Mrs. Anna Holder of the sum of $10,000, would provide a special legislative settlement of her claim that she is entitled to that amount from the Government as the beneficiary named in two $5,000 policies of National Service Life Insurance.

These policies matured in May 1945. Mrs. Holder, the sole surviving designated beneficiary, thereupon claimed the proceeds. She established that the deceased serviceman, an orphan, had been reared from early childhood by her parents, and that she occupied a de facto relationship of sister for many years. The Veterans' Administration denied her claim, ruling that she did not come within the permitted classes of beneficiaries prescribed in the National Service Life Insurance Act of 1940, as amended. The correctness of the ruling of the Veterans' Administration under the applicable law is not disputed.

The Congress imposed specific limitations on the classes of beneficiaries permitted to be named under National Service Life Insurance maturing before August 1, 1946. Similarly, the Congress did not vest in the Veterans' Administration authority to grant exceptions from the general rule.

Therefore it seems to me irrelevant and unwise to accept as justification for this bill, the fact that Mrs. Holder could now qualify as a beneficiary under existing law, which was not made retroactive.

On the other hand, I believe that it is relevant to take fully into account several other factors of great importance in connection with the National Service Life Insurance program as it existed up to 1946. The insurance was issued at peace-time rates which it was recognized would provide but a small fraction of the cost of the program if the United States should become involved in a war. Consequently, provision was made that all benefits payable because of deaths due to the extra hazard of military service would, in effect, be paid from appropriated funds. This was done by reimbursing the trust fund for such costs. Under these circumstances, it was considered desirable to restrict those eligible for benefits to the categories of persons to whose support the veteran might be obligated to contribute.

Finally, I cannot overlook considerations of equity to all beneficiaries as contrasted with the individual case in which the deceased veteran named an ineligible person as the beneficiary of his insurance. I have expressed the view, on other occasions, that uniformity and equality of treatment to all who are similarly situated must be the steadfast rule if the Federal programs for veterans and their beneficiaries are to be operated successfully. Otherwise, inequities are compounded, as is fully revealed by statistics reported by the Veterans' Administration. More than 3,200 claims of designated beneficiaries for the proceeds of National Service Life Insurance have been denied because they were not within the prescribed classes of beneficiaries. A great number of them involved relationships which appear to have been just as close and as real as that claimed by Mrs. Holder.

In my judgment, this is not a case in which the circumstances are so unique or exceptional as to justify a waiver of the law. I, therefore, withhold my approval from the bill.

DWIGHT D. EISENHOWER

43 ¶ Statement by the President on Proposed Improvements in the Federal Personnel Program. *February* 24, 1954

I HAVE been long convinced that a program combining the best practices of progressive private employers with the special demands of public service would greatly benefit our Federal career system and its employees, and would improve the efficiency of its administration.

In keeping with this conviction, I recently designated a subcommittee of the Cabinet to carry on studies with other special groups to determine how best to adjust pay inequities and provide other necessary elements of a well-rounded personnel program. Many of the elements of such a program have since been recommended to me and approved by the Cabinet. As approved by me, these elements are:

1. Reclassification, job evaluation and a new pay scale for the Postal Field Service as recommended by the Postmaster General.

2. Readjustment of inequities in the Classification Act pay scale.

3. A program of contributory Group Life Insurance, on a voluntary basis, for all Federal employees.

4. A program of contributory Medical Care and Hospitalization Insurance open to all Federal employees on a voluntary basis.

5. Unemployment insurance, according to recommendations made in my Budget Message.

6. Improvement of governmental pension plans which will be based on recommendations of the Committee on Retirement Policy for Federal Personnel.

7. Continuing study of the wage board pay system and the extension of that system to certain jobs now under the C.P.C. schedule of the Classification Act.

8. Repeal of the "Whitten Amendment" in order to remove certain restrictions on Federal appointments and promotions established during the Korean emergency.

9. Additional improvements in Federal personnel administration, including:

(a) Longevity pay increases in grades above GS–10;

(b) Increase in the number of positions in the three highest grades under the Classification Act;

(c) Revision of overtime pay and premium pay provisions;

(d) Development of a stronger incentive awards program; and

(e) Substitution of a "Rule of Five" for the present "Rule of Three" in selecting eligibles from the Civil Service lists.

Recommendations covering much of this program have already been sent to the Congress and are scheduled for early action. The contributory life insurance and medical care and hospitalization insurance programs will be presently submitted to the Congress for later consideration and analysis.

44   ¶   Letter to Prime Minister Nehru of India Concerning U.S. Military Aid to Pakistan. *February* 25, 1954

[Released February 25, 1954. Dated February 24, 1954]

Dear Mr. Prime Minister:

I send you this personal message because I want you to know about my decision to extend military aid to Pakistan before it is public knowledge and also because I want you to know directly from me that this step does not in any way affect the friendship we feel for India.   Quite the contrary.   We will continually strive to strengthen the warm and enduring friendship between our two countries.

Our two Governments have agreed that our desires for peace are in accord.   It has also been understood that if our interpretation of existing circumstances and our belief in how to achieve our goals differ, it is the right and duty of sovereign nations to make their own decisions.   Having studied long and carefully the problem of opposing possible aggression in the Middle East, I believe that consultation between Pakistan and Turkey about security problems will serve the interests not only of Pakistan and Turkey but also of the whole free world.   Improvement in Pakistan's defensive capability will also serve these interests and it is for this reason that our aid will be given.   This Government's views on this subject are elaborated in a public statement I will release, a copy of which Ambassador Allen will give you.

What we are proposing to do, and what Pakistan is agreeing to, is not directed in any way against India.   And I am confirming publicly that if our aid to any country, including Pakistan, is misused and directed against another in aggression I will undertake immediately, in accordance with my constitutional authority, appropriate action both within and without the UN to thwart such aggression.   I believe that the Pakistan-Turkey collaboration agreement which is being discussed is sound evidence of the defensive purposes which both countries have in mind.

I know that you and your Government are keenly aware of the need for economic progress as a prime requisite for stability and strength. This Government has extended assistance to India in recognition of this fact, and I am recommending to Congress a continuation of economic and technical aid for this reason. We also believe it in the interest of the free world that India have a strong military defense capability and have admired the effective way your Government has administered your military establishment. If your Government should conclude that circumstances require military aid of a type contemplated by our mutual security legislation, please be assured that your request would receive my most sympathetic consideration.

I regret that there has been such widespread and unfounded speculation on this subject. Now that the facts are known, I hope that the real import of our decision will be understood.

With best wishes,

Sincerely,

DWIGHT D. EISENHOWER

45 ¶ Statement by the President on Military Aid to Pakistan. *February* 25, 1954

ON FEBRUARY 19th, Turkey and Pakistan announced their intention to study methods of achieving closer collaboration on various matters including means designed towards strengthening peace and security. This Government welcomed this move and called it a constructive step towards better ensuring the security of the whole area of the Middle East. The Government of Pakistan has now asked the United States to grant military assistance.

I have said repeatedly that regional groupings to ensure security against aggression constitute the most effective means to assure survival and progress. No nation can stand alone today. My report to the Congress on June 30, 1953, stated that we should strengthen efforts towards regional political, military and economic integration. I, therefore, under the authority granted by the Congress, am glad to comply with Pakistan's request, subject to the negotiation of the required MDAP agreement.

This Government has been gravely concerned over the weakness of defensive capabilities in the Middle East. It was for the purpose of helping to increase the defense potential in this area that Congress in its last session appropriated funds to be used to assist those nations in the area which desired such assistance, which would pledge their willingness to promote international peace and security within the framework of the United Nations, and which would take effective collective measures to prevent and remove threats to peace.

Let me make it clear that we shall be guided by the stated purposes and requirements of the mutual security legislation. Those include specifically the provision that equipment, materials or services provided will be used solely to maintain the recipient country's internal security and for its legitimate self defense, or to permit it to participate in the defense of the area of which it is a part. Any recipient country also must undertake that it will not engage in any act of aggression against any other nation. These undertakings afford adequate assurance to all nations, regardless of their political orientation and whatever their international policies may be, that the arms the United States provides for the defense of the free world will in no way threaten their own security. I can say that if our aid to any country, including Pakistan, is misused and directed against another in aggression I will undertake immediately, in accordance with my constitutional authority, appropriate action both within and without the UN to thwart such aggression. I would also consult with the Congress on further steps.

The United States earnestly desires that there be increased stability and strength in the Middle East, as it has desired this same thing in other parts of the free world. It believes that the aspirations of the peoples in this area for maintaining and developing their way of life and for realizing the social advances close to their hearts will be best served by strength to deter aggression and to reduce the fear of aggression. The United States is prepared to help in this endeavor, if its help is wanted.

46 ¶ Statement by the President Marking the Opening of the Red Cross Drive. *February* 28, 1954

My fellow Americans and Red Cross members:

Americans believe in the Red Cross.

I personally believe in it, first, because I know from my own experience the great good it accomplishes in war and peace; second, because I believe in the fundamental principle of Red Cross—the principle of people helping people.

Through the Red Cross, Americans have helped the men and women in our armed forces. In generation after generation, American servicemen have turned to the Red Cross with their personal problems, their family emergencies, and the Red Cross has responded. It has responded quickly and generously.

Through the Red Cross, the people of this Nation have constantly relieved the pain and suffering of fellow citizens trapped by natural disasters. The homeless and the hungry have been sheltered and fed. Victims of disaster, lacking the means to rebuild and refurnish their homes, have found in the Red Cross the assistance they needed.

And because the American people have donated their blood as well as their money, the Red Cross during the last decade has given life itself to the wounded and the sick. The blood donated by the American people has saved not only the wounded on the battlefields of World War II and Korea, but the sick and injured in more than three thousand hospitals here at home.

The Red Cross has provided, and with your help will continue to provide, vast quantities of blood products—products such as gamma globulin, which helps our children avoid the horrible paralysis caused by polio.

So much for the material contributions of the Red Cross. But beyond all this—the Red Cross abundantly provides faith in the innate goodness of people, in their ability to work together for the Nation's good. It exemplifies the enormous power which kindness and generosity can exert to move men closer to the day when the rule of force will be banished from the world, and when the Golden Rule will guide the actions of mankind.

Through your Red Cross you give special meaning to this faith in humanity. I am confident that this year, as in the past, the American people will join the Red Cross in its magnificent efforts to comfort our fellow men.

47   ¶ Message Recorded for the Observance of World Day of Prayer.   *March 2, 1954*

My friends in many lands:

It is profoundly moving to realize that the 1954 World Day of Prayer is to be observed, in appropriate services, by many millions of people around the globe.   These services, beginning in New Zealand and the Tonga Islands, west of the international date line, follow the sun throughout the day, and end 24 hours later, in St. Lawrence Island in Alaska.

Prayer seems to bring closer together in mutual understanding, the people who unite in its practice.

At the very beginning of our own national life, at a time when the Constitutional Convention was plagued by dissension and on the point of breaking up, Benjamin Franklin suggested that all join him in a moment of prayer.   After that silent moment, the delegates suddenly seemed to be united in their purposes, and there was born the great document by which we live.

Throughout the history of this country, all the men and women we most revere as inspired leaders constantly sought Divine Guidance in the discharge of their public responsibilities.

Today the innermost longing of mankind is for peace; peace for all nations, for all men, everywhere.

The hosts of people who take part in this World Day of Prayer are seeking the help of the Almighty to find the way toward the goal of peace, toward the triumph of freedom and the unity of men.

In this noble purpose all men of good will may devoutly join.

NOTE: The President's words were broadcast throughout the world by the Voice of America, as recorded and as translated into some 37 languages.   World Day of Prayer (March 5) was sponsored by the United Church Women of the National Council of Churches of Christ in the United States.

48   ¶ The President's News Conference of *March 3, 1954.*

THE PRESIDENT. Ladies and gentlemen, as you know, the Governor of Puerto Rico made a visit to the capital yesterday, to join with all of us here in an expression of his sentiments of regret at the tragic events on Capitol Hill 2 days ago.

I was, of course, pleased to welcome him for that purpose, because while we all knew what the sentiments of the mass of Puerto Rico were, it was, I thought, a very splendid gesture on his part to come up and state them, you might say, officially.

We start out—I have got one statement that I want to make as my complete and full expression on one incident of recent weeks.

[*Reading*] I want to make a few comments about the Peress case.

The Department of the Army made serious errors in handling the Peress case and the Secretary of the Army so stated publicly, almost a month ago. The Army is correcting its procedures to avoid such mistakes in the future. I am completely confident that Secretary Stevens will be successful in this effort.

Neither in this case, nor in any other, has any person in the executive branch been authorized to suggest that any subordinate, for any reason whatsoever, violate his convictions or principles or submit to any kind of personal humiliation when testifying before congressional committees or elsewhere. [*Discontinues reading*]

For the benefit of those of you who are making statements, Mr. Hagerty has insisted on duplicating this, and you will probably get a copy of it.

[*Resumes reading*] In a more general sense, I have certain observations to make. They are:

1. We must be unceasingly vigilant in every phase of governmental activity to make certain that there is no subversive penetration.

2. In opposing communism, we are defeating ourselves if either by design or through carelessness we use methods that do not conform to the American sense of justice and fair play.

3. The conscience of America will clearly discern when we are exercising proper vigilance without being unfair. That conscience is reflected in the body of the United States Congress. We can be certain that its members will respond to America's convictions and beliefs in this regard.

Here I must repeat something that I have often stated before. The ultimate responsibility for the conduct of all parts of the executive branch of the Government rests with the President of the United States. That responsibility cannot be delegated to another branch of Government. It is, of course, likewise the responsibility of the President and his associates to account for their stewardship of public affairs.   All of us recognize the right of the people to know how we are meeting this responsibility and the congressional right to inquire and investigate into every phase of our public operations.

Manifestly, in a government such as ours, successful service to 160 million people demands a true spirit of cooperation among the several branches of Government, especially between the executive and the legislative branches.   Real cooperation is possible only in an atmosphere of mutual respect.

I spent many years in the Army, during the course of which I sometimes appeared before committees of the Congress.   Sometimes I was a direct witness; more often, in my early years, at least, I was merely a so-called technical assistant to the man testifying.

In all that time, I never saw any individual of the Army fail to render due and complete respect to every member of Congress with whom duty brought him in contact.   In all that time, I never saw any member of the Congress guilty of disrespect toward the public servants who were appearing before him.   In the tradition of such mutual respect I grew up in the governmental service.   It is that tradition that I intend that the executive branch will observe and apply as long as I hold my present office.

Now, I have only a few additional comments.

First, all of us know that our military services and their leaders have always been completely loyal and dedicated public servants, singularly free of suspicion of disloyalty.   Their courage and their devotion have been proved in peace as well as on the battlefields of war.   America is proud of them.   I am certain that no one in any governmental position wants to have his own utterances interpreted as questioning the lasting debt that all of us as Americans owe to the officers and enlisted men and women of the armed services.   In this tribute to the services, I mean to include General Zwicker, who was decorated for gallantry in the field.

Second, except where the interests of the Nation demand otherwise, every governmental employee in the executive branch, whether civilian or in the Armed Forces, is expected to respond cheerfully and completely to the requests of the Congress and its several committees.   In doing so it is, of course, assumed that they will be accorded the same respect and courtesy that I require that they show to the members of the legislative body. Officials in the executive branch of the Government will have my unqualified support in insisting that employees in the executive branch who appear before any type of executive or congressional investigating body be treated fairly.

Third, obviously, it is the responsibility of the Congress to see to it that its procedures are proper and fair. Of course, I expect the Republican membership of the Congress to assume the primary responsibility in this respect, since they are the majority party and, therefore, control the committees. I am glad to state that Senator Knowland has reported to me that effective steps are already being taken by the Republican leadership to set up codes of fair procedure.

Fourth, there are problems facing this Nation of vital importance. They are both foreign and domestic in character. They affect the individual and collective future of all of us. The views of myself and my associates on these matters have been outlined in the proposals for legislation we have submitted to the Congress. They deserve the undivided and incessant attention of the Congress, of the executive branch, of the public information media of our Nation, of our schools, and even of our churches. I regard it as unfortunate when we are diverted from these grave problems—of which one is viligance against any kind of internal subversion—through disregard of the standards of fair play recognized by the American people. These incidents are all the more useless and unfortunate in view of the basic dedication of every loyal American to the preservation and advancement of America's safety, prosperity, and well-being. [*Ends reading*]

And that is my last word on any subject even closely related to that particular matter.

Q. Merriman Smith, United Press: Mr. President, this is not closely related, but Senator McCarthy yesterday questioned the wisdom of Secretary Dulles having removed from Mr. McLeod the authority over personnel problems in the State Department. I wonder if you could tell us your feeling on that.

THE PRESIDENT. Well, the assignment to duty of any administrative officer in any department of Government is the responsibility of the head of that department, and no one else's whatsoever. I hold the head of department responsible to me for proper operation of that department. He is, in turn, responsible for everything that goes on within it.

Q. Donald Shannon, Salt Lake City Deseret News: I think this is quite far removed from anything you were talking about. The term of Interstate Commerce Commissioner James K. Knudson expired in December. Why hasn't the renomination gone up, and will it eventually be sent to the Senate?

THE PRESIDENT. It has not been submitted to me yet. I haven't had anything on that brought to my desk.

Q. Richard Harkness, National Broadcasting Company: Would you comment, sir, on suggestions that special labor camps be formed to contain alleged and suspected subversives in the Armed Forces?

THE PRESIDENT. Well, I don't believe I will comment on this at the moment. Renewed attention has been given to this whole problem within the Armed Forces, they are coming up with a plan, and I will be perfectly ready to comment on their whole plan after it is once submitted. But I don't believe that I want to comment on a suggestion of that kind which I never before heard.

Q. Mr. Harkness: Mr. President, if I may continue, sir.

THE PRESIDENT. Yes.

Q. Mr. Harkness: This is not part of the Army's plan, as I understand it. It is, to the contrary, a suggestion of Senator McCarthy.

THE PRESIDENT. Well, as I say, I don't care to comment on it at the moment because I don't know how it would work out.

Q. Sarah McClendon, El Paso Times: Sir, totally aside from that, but somewhat related to what you said about humiliation before committees and fair play—totally aside from the merits or demerits of Chief Justice Warren or his accuser—don't you think it smacks of totalitarianism for a witness before a congressional committee on a confirmation case to be harassed by the Justice Department and the Metropolitan Police and the Capitol Police when he is there to testify, in a free country?

THE PRESIDENT. Well, you are asking a question based on a premise that I do not know to be true. I know about this only what I have read in the papers, and that said that there was a man who was a fugitive from justice, and the legal authorities of our country were taking care of their own responsibilities.

I should say this: if they did have responsibility and didn't discharge it, we would have cause to worry. I don't know anything about the merits of the case.

Q. Mrs. McClendon: Sir, if I may continue, I believe later they decided that they didn't have enough to arrest the man there—of course, that would be a question of fact—but what I am getting at is arresting a man through efforts of the Department of Justice in the Halls of Congress when he comes before a congressional committee to say, as an American, he wants to testify.

THE PRESIDENT. I believe that that is something that will have to be tested by the good sense of the enforcement officers, and the decisions of courts.

I haven't heard the particular circumstances that you describe. I just knew from the papers that a man, appearing to testify, was wanted somewhere else, and officers were called upon to do something about it.

Q. Alice Dunnigan, Associated Negro Press: Mr. President, the question has been under discussion on Capitol Hill as to whether Labor Secretary Mitchell's letter sent to the chairman of the Senate Committee on Labor and Public Welfare last week endorsing the Ives equal employment opportunity bill, with enforcement powers, expresses the position of the administration on this measure. Would you like to clarify your position on that?

THE PRESIDENT. I have made my position clear many dozens of times. I believe there are certain things that are not best handled by punitive or compulsory Federal law.

Now, not only is Secretary Mitchell allowed in his own person to have views different from me on certain particular details of governmental activity, but any other Cabinet officer is so allowed and so authorized, and I don't consider it any matter of disloyalty to me.

He expressed his own personal views, and I respect his personal views, but I don't want around me a bunch of yes-men.

Q. McClellan Smith, Radio Television Daily: Mr. President, Chairman Reed of the House Ways and Means Committee has said that a 10 percent ceiling should be the maximum on excise taxes. If such a bill goes through, will you veto it?

THE PRESIDENT. I know of no question that is more impossible of answer than what an Executive will do about a future bill with respect to vetoes, because no one knows what is all going to be in that bill; and sometimes, I suppose, you have to swallow a deal of castor oil along with the sweet coating.

Now, as far as that measure is concerned, Secretary Humphrey issued a statement last evening that represents views that he and I had previously discussed; and if you want to know the details of the views, I suggest you take a look at that statement and discuss it down at the Treasury Department.

Q. Edward Folliard, Washington Post: Mr. President, how does the truce in Korea affect the Red Cross, that is, in Red Cross services to the Armed Forces there and elsewhere?

THE PRESIDENT. I don't want to be interpreted here as knowing anything about the law, if there is a law that applies.

So far as I am concerned, every place that I have ever seen troops in the field, we have had the Red Cross; even in this country you have local voluntary groups. I can't see how it would affect it whatsoever.

I had the Red Cross in Germany, after we had an armistice over there, and so I think that the Red Cross goes right ahead performing its many functions, in spite of the fact that shooting has stopped there.

Q. Mr. Folliard: What I had in mind is, is there still the need?

THE PRESIDENT. Oh, indeed. You know, I can't imagine anything more difficult for a very great body of young, impatient, virile Americans than to be cooped up in occupational or other sorts of inactive duties. One of the reasons that the Army has tackled with such enthusiasm and such success the rebuilding of South Korea is because it gives them something constructive to do, and they are doing it.

Now, in that kind of a situation, I think there are many instances where you need the Red Cross far more than you do when the actual fighting is going on, because the fighting and the getting ready for it so absorbs the attention of people.

Q. Anthony Leviero, New York Times: Mr. President, I wonder if you would listen to a question on the Peress case, and if it has been covered I would gladly scotch it. The public has been given two views of that, and one emanating from the Pentagon is that the handling of the case was essentially a redtape and paperwork muddle. I believe you have covered that in your statement.

On the other hand, from the Hill, we get the contention that there was a deliberate covering up and coddling of a Communist. I wonder if you would comment on that point?

THE PRESIDENT. Well, you know, I don't mind. As a matter of fact, I had it in my statement once, because I did want to make some general observations expressing my views in unequivocal terms, and it got so long that I just dropped it out.

Actually, of course, I think that all of the detailed facts that have occurred over these last 10 months are not yet completely known.

I don't for one minute believe that senior officers of the Army or the armed services have been trying to cover up anything of communism.

You do have an unfortunate law—I say "unfortunate"—you do have a law that requires this: if you draft a doctor you are compelled to give him a commission. Well, that puts a great dilemma in front of an administrator in the Army.

Actually there is a case now decided by the appellate courts, I am told, that requires the Army now to pay back pay to a man that they refused to commission; they have to pay back pay as a captain or a major for the past *x* months, I don't know exactly what it is.

So, I would say it was partly confusion—knowing how to handle such cases.

You people might be amused a little bit to know that when I was in Europe a few years back, the French had to come up with this problem; after all, when you have got 25 or 30 percent of your people registered or voting in the Communist Party, and then you have a universal military service law bringing them in, think of their problem.

Well, I used to discuss with them how they handled it. They did, of course, try to keep these people out of sensitive positions. And they had this one remarkable and very encouraging result: that the people who came into the Army as Communists, less than a quarter of them went out as such. They learned some things in the Army, apparently, they hadn't known before.

Q. Mrs. May Craig, New England Papers: Mr. President, last year Senator Margaret Smith of Maine introduced a bill to outlaw the Communist Party or any similar organization under another name. Would you favor that?

THE PRESIDENT. I can't tell you for sure, Mrs. Craig, for this reason: when I came down here, one of the first things I asked was for a study on that, and lawyers have been fighting over it ever since.

There seems to be a constitutional bar in just outlawing a particular political party in this country, and I believe that all convictions that have been secured against these leaders have been not on the word "Communist" but on their being a part of a conspiracy to destroy the American form of government by force. So I don't know whether it can be done, and there certainly I wouldn't want to commit myself on something that was constitutionally so abstruse.

Q. Lloyd Schwartz, Fairchild Publications: Mr. President, I would like to ask whether you have decided to reject a Tariff Commission proposal for special fees on imports of wool, now before you.

THE PRESIDENT. There is going to be an announcement a little later in the week, a public announcement; I could possibly just tie the thing up a little, but I have already approved certain actions, and for certain reasons, and they will be explained in a public statement. It will be out, I think, in 2 or 3 days.

Q. Robert Spivack, New York Post: Mr. President, as you know, before the Army and General Zwicker were involved, witnesses had been abused also on the Hill, and one of the ideas that has been kicking around, which I don't think we have ever asked for your comment on, is the idea of combining these investigations under more responsible leadership. Would you tell us how you feel about that?

THE PRESIDENT. I have constantly stated that I recognize and respect the right of Congress to investigate into anything that it finds it necessary to investigate. Manifestly also, the business of determining their own rules, their own procedures, is a matter for the conscience of the Congress, and I have tried to point out that in the long run, certainly they are going to be responsive to the general will of the United States. I can state nothing more definite on that.

Q. Nat Finney, Buffalo Evening News: Are you satisfied with the outcome of the debate on the Bricker amendment on Capitol Hill?

THE PRESIDENT. The only thing I can say is that I am very pleased that we can devote our efforts to concrete and specific parts of a program that I believe to be absolutely essential for building a stronger and better America; that is all I can say on it.

Q. Robert Richards, Copley Press: How do you think the Republicans are coming along with your advice to be kinder to Democrats? [*Laughter*]

THE PRESIDENT. I got a letter on it within 5 minutes before I came over here. I got a letter on it from a man in Maine who, at least, cheered my words, and maybe I will pass his letter around.

Q. Marietta Dake, Niagara Falls Gazette: Mr. President, I was wondering whether you instructed the Republican leadership to see to it that each committee has at least one Republican and one Democrat in attendance at all times?

THE PRESIDENT. I can't possibly instruct the Senate as to its procedures. They have reported to me as to what they are planning to do, and I will wait until their program comes out, which certainly should be shortly.

Q. Anthony Leviero, New York Times: Mr. President, Chairman Young of the Civil Service Commission reported yesterday to a committee on the subversive cases, the security risk cases. I wonder if you have any comment on that report?

THE PRESIDENT. Only one thing, and that is to emphasize to you ladies and gentlemen once more, I never used the word "subversives" in connection with the program that this administration designed to get rid of undesirables of any kind in this administration. I simply stated we are going to get rid of security risks.

Now, Mr. Young is attempting to give you such information as is available and is proper to give out, and your problems will have to be with him.

My own opinion is that they were bad security risks, and that is all.

Q. Mr. Leviero: Well, Mr. President, following that up, long before this administration came into office, people were claiming they were treated unfairly, both under the loyalty and security programs. Has any thought been given to making characterizations of "unsuitable" instead of "security risks" where it relates to people who are not disloyal?

THE PRESIDENT. You bring up a word I had not thought of, but it might be, it might be that they could find—I think they did it, though, on this basis: if you find these people you call unsuitable by reason of personal habits or anything else, they become risks. I had this problem in the war. I had men when we were planning secret operations, if it was brought to me and proved that they were men that drank and, therefore, were a little bit indiscreet in their social contacts, they were removed and in some cases reduced. The same principle, I think, applies; but you may have an idea that our people can look at.

Merriman Smith, United Press: Thank you, Mr. President.

NOTE: President Eisenhower's twenty-ninth news conference was held in the Executive Office Building from 10:32 to 10:58 o'clock on Wednesday morning, March 3, 1954. In attendance: 256.

49 ¶ Statement by the President on the Administration's Program for the Domestic Wool Industry. *March 4,* 1954

ON JULY 9, 1953, on the advice of the Secretary of Agriculture, I requested the United States Tariff Commission to make an investigation, under Section 22 of the Agricultural Adjustment Act, to determine the effect of imports of certain varieties of sheep's wool on the operation of the domestic price-support program for wool.

I now have the Report of the Tariff Commission, in which a majority of its members recommend the imposition of certain fees on imports of wool in addition to the prevailing duties.

At the same time as the Tariff Commission inquiry was initiated, I requested the Secretary of Agriculture to make a comprehensive study of the domestic factors which have contributed to the decline in sheep numbers and wool production in the United States, with a view toward the development of a sound and prosperous domestic wool industry consistent with an expanding international trade.

On the basis of this study, which was carefully analyzed and discussed by the interested agencies of the Executive Branch, I determined that domestic wool growers required continued price or income assistance in a more effective form than is now provided. I accepted the principal recommendations of the Secretary of Agriculture, which provide for government assistance to growers under an incentive payment plan during periods when wool prices are below the desired support level.

These recommendations have been submitted to the Congress. Hearings have been held before the Senate Committee on Agriculture and Forestry and a bill embodying these recommendations has been approved by that Committee. The enactment of this program by the Congress would eliminate the necessity for an increase in import fees or other limitations on wool imports, a course of action which I do not believe would best serve either the wool growing industry or the national interest. I am confident that this new program will appreciably contribute to the achievement of a sound and prosperous domestic wool industry, an essential component of a healthy overall economy and a strong defense.

In view of the fact that the Administration's new wool program is specifically designed to help remedy those conditions which prompted the Tariff Commission's investigation, I am taking no action on the Commission's Report.

50 ¶ The President's News Conference of *March* 10, 1954.

THE PRESIDENT. I have only one announcement. It is very inconsequential. Sometime during the coming week I shall probably go on the air to discuss the general contents of the tax program. As you know, the administration is committed—the administration of the Republican Party—to a program, the pieces of which have gone down to the Congress in the form of legislative proposals and, all together, make up a plan of action that we believe to be good for the United States.

Of that, taxes is part. The purpose of taxes is, of course, to get the money to pay the bills for the things you have to do, or believe desirable for Government to do, for its people—and to do it in such a way as to cause not only the least damage to the economy but to the great mass of people that make up the United States, and cause the burdens to be distributed in such a way that we will not impede the very progress you are trying to advance.

So it will be discussed. The only point of my making the statement now is that the tax program will be discussed in its relationship to what we are trying to do in a broad program.

That is the only statement I have to make. We will go right to questions.

Q. Merriman Smith, United Press: Mr. President, do you feel that there is a need for any additional Republican reply on a nationwide basis to Adlai Stevenson other than Vice President Nixon's speech Saturday?

THE PRESIDENT. Well, I don't sense any particular need myself. I think all you people know how greatly I admire the Vice President, how much I trust him. I have confidence that he will place the facts as he understands them, and as all of us in a position of responsibility in the Republican Party understand them, before the people; and that will be that.

Q. Robert G. Spivack, New York Post: Mr. President, in connection with the selection of Vice President Nixon to reply, does that mean that

Senator McCarthy will not be speaking for the party in the '54 campaign?

THE PRESIDENT. You pose a question that I don't suppose anyone in the world can answer. I suppose when he speaks, he will say he is representing what he chooses. The Republican Chairman has made it quite clear in this instance who has been selected to speak for the party, and that is that.

Q. Martin Agronsky, American Broadcasting Company: It has been reported, sir, that you personally chose the Vice President to respond to Mr. Stevenson, and communicated your wishes to Mr. Hall; is that correct?

THE PRESIDENT. There was a meeting at which I participated, and I don't remember that I was the one that suggested it. I most certainly concurred heartily. I can't remember, frankly, who made the first suggestion that Mr. Nixon should do it, but I certainly concurred heartily.

Q. Richard L. Wilson, Cowles Publications: Mr. President, last Saturday night the proposition was put forward that the Republican Party is half Eisenhower and half McCarthy. Would you care to comment on that?

THE PRESIDENT. At the risk of appearing egotistical—and you can so interpret it if you choose—I say nonsense.

Q. Edward T. Folliard, Washington Post: Mr. President, this is related to Merriman Smith's question. Do you think that the big networks have been fair in giving time to the Republican National Committee to answer Governor Stevenson rather than to Senator McCarthy? McCarthy feels that the networks have been unfair.

THE PRESIDENT. I am not going to make the decisions that, of course, the Federal Communications Commission makes, and that the networks make on their own responsibility. Personally, I think that the networks have certainly discharged their responsibility for being impartial when they give to the Republican National Committee the right to answer as they see fit.

You know, suppose any one of you would make a speech, whatever party you belong to, and mention 20 names on the other side; now, does the network have to give 20 different people the right to get up and answer, or is it a party thing?

There must be some limit to this sort of thing. I believe as long as they give to responsible, acknowledged heads of the organization part of the party—the Chairman—the right to determine this, why, that is justice.

Q. Mrs. May Craig, Maine Newspapers: Mr. President, do you not regard the Stevenson speech as a part of the Democratic campaign for Congress, and therefore it should be answered by the party—by the Republican Party?

THE PRESIDENT. Yes, indeed I do. Of course I do.

Q. Roscoe Drummond, New York Herald Tribune: Mr. President, will you tell us whether you find yourself in substantial sympathy with it, or what your reaction is to it if that is not correct, to Senator Flanders' talk yesterday in the Senate?

THE PRESIDENT. Well, I was perfectly certain I wasn't going to get through this morning without getting that question. [*Laughter*]

And I thought about it on the way over. [*Laughter*]

Now, certainly, I can agree with this part: the Republican Party is now the party of responsibility, so charged by the people of the United States in the elective process. And when Senator Flanders points up the danger of us engaging in internecine warfare, and magnifying certain items of procedure and right and personal aggrandizement, and all such questions, to the point that we are endangering the program of action that all the leadership is agreed upon and we are trying to put across, then he is doing a service when he calls the great danger to that kind of thing that is happening.

Now, I am not going to be in a position of endorsing every word he said or how he said it. I don't know; all I saw of it was a little bit of thing on television last evening, and so I know you wouldn't ask me just to say I underwrite it. But I do say that calling attention to the grave error in splitting apart when you are in positions of responsibility and going in three or four different directions at once is just serious, that's all.

Q. Anthony H. Leviero, New York Times: Mr. President, I wonder if you would put that much on the record, the answer to that question.

THE PRESIDENT. I will tell you what you can do. I believe they keep a transcript; after the meeting is over, Mr. Hagerty can see how many errors of grammar, of which I was guilty, when I stated it—[*laughter*]— and if he thinks it is worthwhile stating it, or if it is all right, you can put it in.

Q. Richard L. Wilson, Cowles Publications: Can we include that "nonsense" part in that quotation?

THE PRESIDENT. I forget. I said about—half and half, you said? That was the question?

Q. Mr. Wilson: Yes.

THE PRESIDENT. As far as I am concerned, you can use my influence with Mr. Hagerty. [*Laughter*]

Q. Laurence H. Burd, Chicago Tribune: I would like to ask about the Manion resignation. We have never had any statement from the White House on it. Dr. Manion said he was asked to resign by Sherman Adams, presumably because of his stand on the Bricker amendment and the TVA. My question is, can you tell us who was responsible for the Manion resignation and why it was asked for?

THE PRESIDENT. Actually, Dean Manion, a very estimable man, was entitled to his own opinions on those certain items, and they were never questioned. I knew where he stood on certain things when I asked him to do a certain job. But he was busy and couldn't do the job that he was asked for. The job requires a continuous devotion to that kind of work. As a matter of fact, we are hunting for the man now that can give full time to that kind of work.

Q. Mr. Burd: It was a question of time, was it not?

THE PRESIDENT. So far as I was concerned, yes.

Q. M. Stewart Hensley, United Press: Senator Anderson yesterday formally called up his amendment to tack Alaska onto the Hawaiian statehood bill. Do you have any comment on that at all?

THE PRESIDENT. Well, our leadership has promised to do its best to keep them separate, and I personally favor that plan.

You people know where I have stood on this business of statehood for the two Territories. You know that I take a platform seriously. I am trying very much to carry out the basic promises of the Republican platform. I note that some of them are paralleled in the Democratic platform. So I don't see any reason why each of these subjects can't be handled on its own merits.

Q. Robert G. Spivack, New York Post: Mr. President, this is on a less controversial subject. Have you ever had your coffee report?

THE PRESIDENT. Ever had what?

Q. Mr. Spivack: The report on the coffee investigation that you announced.

THE PRESIDENT. No, I haven't. Will you look that up? I don't know whether that is completed, the major one. I gave you the results of the preliminary, which they said, you will remember, justified a full-scale investigation. The reports on that full-scale, I have not had.

Q. Kenneth M. Scheibel, Gannett Newspapers: Mr. President, there seems to be increasing support in Congress and among the farm organizations that we sell part of our surplus butter to Russia for 40 or 50 cents a pound, provided part of that surplus is made available in this country at a reduced price. Could you tell us if you would favor such an arrangement?

THE PRESIDENT. I haven't heard just exactly that one. I, of course, believe that where the United States interests indicate the need for a barter arrangement to get something that we need and can preserve in place of butter which we apparently don't need, because it is in storage, and which is perishable, that would be a good deal, in my estimation.

Q. Mr. Scheibel: Would you extend that to include all the other farm surpluses we have, swapping for materials?

THE PRESIDENT. Certainly, the great surpluses. I really believe we should look for ways to trade them advantageously to the United States. That is what barter is, that is what trade is, that is what made this country, in many ways; and I don't think we should fear now our ability to trade to the best interests of the United States. But, on the other hand, I realize there are a thousand different considerations that apply to this delicate thing of disposing of these surpluses, both at home and abroad.

Q. Paul Shinkman, Radio Stations WASH–FM and WDON: Prime Minister Churchill said last week that he still felt that a four-power conference at the top level would be helpful in the foreseeable future. Do you have any comments on that subject?

THE PRESIDENT. Of course, I have disagreed with Winston—with the Prime Minister in the past. Here, in this one, I will put it this way: I fail to see at this moment what good could come out of it. Of course, there are always the possibilities of great difficulty coming.

Now, I have approved numbers of conferences for our Secretary of State participating with other foreign ministers. Incidentally, I must say, I think he has handled himself like a master. I know of no one who could have done better than Secretary Dulles in representing the best interests of the United States in the most confusing and trying of circumstances. I think we are fortunate to have such a man.

Q. Charles S. von Fremd, CBS Television: Mr. President, the Colonel Schwable case has raised an important argument, the two sides of which you are probably quite familiar with, with your distinguished military background.   On the one side, the military naturally fears from the standpoint of precedence to have its men admit to false confessions, while from the humanitarian standpoint, it is easy to understand and sympathize with a man who makes a false confession under duress or torture. Not referring specifically to the Colonel Schwable case, sir, can you give us your general views on this entire military situation, or problem?

THE PRESIDENT. Well, when you begin to talk about military problems, you must certainly relate that problem to the times in which you live.

If you will go back to our Revolutionary War times, you will find there were codes that existed among professional fighting men that were almost independent of international law.   If you captured a general, he was your guest; you took him in; you were very nice to him.   He might be the guest of the conquering general for 2 or 3 days.

There was a sort of understanding that controlled most of our contacts with the enemy, and out of that were translated really the rules of land warfare to which many nations adhered.

Today, with hatreds and prejudices sharpened, all brought about by very deep, underlying differences in ideologies, the very basis by which we live—we think we are a religious civilization; our opponents in the world believe in a materialistic dialectic and nothing else, that only materialism has anything to do with man's happiness, man's progress, and man's concern—these bring about very, very great changes.

Now, you must remember that all the early part of my life I was studying the campaigns, the conduct of past wars and past heroes of mine— a Lee and a Washington, people like that.

Today you have got to be a rather understanding individual if you presume to criticize severely someone who has given way to the things that these men have had to endure.   Indeed, I read only recently that one psychiatrist said that there is no man on earth that under the continued process of brainwashing can fail to make the confession desired of him.

There is, of course, like all things, a rule of reason that applies.   You can't take back such people and ask young America to follow them enthusiastically. On the other hand, we mustn't condemn them too severely. It is a very, very hard problem. And I must say this: in some 13 years— or something like that, maybe they are not continuous, they seem almost that—that you have to sit in judgment on other humans' failures, legal and other failures, you have to sit in and take final action on them, it is a very trying thing. First of all, you must think of punishment as being instituted for the protection of society, the society that you know. On the other hand, you have justice to the individual. Frequently your opinions and convictions differ. It is a very, very difficult problem, and sometimes that is one of the burdens you wish could be removed from your shoulders. I carried it a long time, and I have no really definite answer for it. Sorry.

Q. Marvin L. Arrowsmith, Associated Press: Mr. President, there has been a great deal of talk among some Republicans lately that the word has gone out from you that you want much more emphasis on the positive aspects of the administration's program. Possibly your answer on the Senator Flanders' speech gives some of the reasons, but I wonder if you could tell us if that is so, if you feel there should be more of that emphasis.

THE PRESIDENT. Mr. Arrowsmith, I thought I had emphasized that right here in one of these meetings. I don't believe that things negative promote the happiness of people. I believe that you must go forward in the spiritual and intellectual, cultural, economic development of this country if we are going to make it a place where 161 million people can live in happiness—and the increasing population can live in happiness.

Now, all the things that distract from that effort, they are sometimes necessary. All of these things, these corrective, and therefore punitive measures, are sometimes necessary; but what I complain about is their overemphasis. The overemphasis of those things to the exclusion of a positive program of human welfare, human advancement, that is what I complain about. I think it is very wrong. And I have certainly appealed to everybody that I can reach with my voice to give their attention—not necessarily to agree with every single item in this program, but for goodness' sake, to take out what is good and to stand behind it, and to give less attention to subjects that are unworthy, really, of occupying our time from morning until night.

Q. Edwin Dayton Moore, United Press: Mr. President, are you going on both television and radio with your tax talk? And do you have any idea what night it will be?

THE PRESIDENT. As a matter of fact, I haven't even asked for time yet.

Actually, what I mean is this. I want most informally and as simply as I can to explain the philosophy underlying a tax program, what it means. I assume, because I believe this is the practice, I assume that it will be on both television and radio because, I assure you, it will be nonpartisan as far as I am concerned.

Q. Paul R. Leach, Chicago Daily News: Will that be next week, Mr. President?

THE PRESIDENT. I think so.

Q. Mr. Leach: Not this week?

THE PRESIDENT. Well, what are we on now? We are on Wednesday. Next week.

Q. Sarah L. McClendon, El Paso Times: Mr. President, we all know how you feel about the Bricker amendment and about keeping the powers of the executive branch independent of the others. But if some examples of flagrant cases, where the international executive agreements negotiated by agencies of the executive branch of the Government were presented to you, where these agreements, made internationally, violate internal law, would you be inclined to reconsider those agreements and to disapprove them?

THE PRESIDENT. Well, it is a very intricate hypothetical question. I haven't seen these agreements, and I don't know exactly what I would do. But I will say this: if I have gotten so rigid in any conviction of theory that I can't take any case that is put in front of me and try to decide it with such enlightenment as God has given me according to what I believe to be the best interests of the country, then certainly they ought to move rapidly to impeach me. I certainly would try to do so.

Q. James J. Patterson, New York News: Mr. President, Senator Stennis said yesterday that we were in danger of becoming involved in World War III in Indochina because of the Air Force technicians there. What will we do if one of those men is captured or killed?

THE PRESIDENT. I will say this: there is going to be no involvement of America in war unless it is a result of the constitutional process that is placed upon Congress to declare it. Now, let us have that clear; and that is the answer.

Q. Anthony H. Leviero, New York Times: Mr. President, Chancellor Adenauer suggested the other day that we ought to return the seized German assets in this country. I wonder if any decision has been reached on that.

THE PRESIDENT. Well, there has been no decision. It has been a subject of study since, I think, almost the first day I came into this office. It is a very difficult one. I personally believe that this matter should be settled, cleared up, once and for all, and we get out of the business. That is what I am trying to do.

Q. John Herling, Editors Syndicate: Mr. President, do you plan to send up a supplementary message on labor relations to Congress?

THE PRESIDENT. I don't know. There is probably never a week goes by that there are not serious talks on some phase of labor relations, someone coming in to make a recommendation. There is no plan at this moment to send a specific message up; however, that doesn't preclude the fact that I could.

Q. A. Robert Smith, Portland Oregonian: Mr. President, about 3 weeks ago, you issued a formal statement at your news conference endorsing a dam in Oregon, Cougar Dam, and you said that this exemplified what you have meant all along as a partnership proposal—that the Federal Government would build the dam and the local utility would install the generators.

At about the same time, a group of Arkansas Senators and Representatives called on Mr. Dodge at the Budget Bureau, in trying to urge him to have the Federal Government proceed to build several additional dams on the White River. They reported that he said that hereafter the partnership policy was the only thing that would be followed in the construction of dams in the West, and in the South, too; that is, only in cases where local utilities would install the generators. Now, can you clarify that?

THE PRESIDENT. Well, it has never been stated in that way. If you will go back over every statement that I have ever made about this question of public power, you will find, on the erection of these multiple-purpose dams, that wherever it is feasible, I want local participation; because I believe you will get greater economy and greater care in the operation and the building and the use to which the dam is put.

Now, it is also acknowledged in every single statement, there can be cases where it is so exclusively to the Federal advantage to do this thing, of course, they will do it then. The rule of looking for the partnership is exactly what I hope to follow, but I don't preclude the possibility that these others come up. Of course, they do.

Q. Garnett D. Horner, Washington Star: Mr. President, do you have any travel plans for this weekend that you can tell us about?

THE PRESIDENT. As a matter of fact, I hope to go up to Camp David, if I can. Now, there is still doubt in the way, but I want to go up and take a look. As a matter of fact, from there, I think I might say, I would hope to roam around at least as far as a little local golf course that some of you may know about.

Q. Mrs. May Craig, Maine Newspapers: Mr. President, could I have a second question? Would you comment on Stevenson's criticism of your "new look" defense program?

THE PRESIDENT. Well, of course, I comment on nothing that other individuals say. I would merely comment, here, this: I have spent a long time in the military services. In all the really important positions I ever had, I dealt with the three services, not with the single one—I mean, in important positions in higher rank.

I am concerned about the security of this country, I hope, as seriously as any single individual alive. If I have too much confidence in my own judgment here, well, that is for someone else to say, and I am therefore subject to criticism. But I will say this: I am doing nothing in the security departments that I don't believe is for the welfare and the security and the continued safety of the United States of America, and I am not going to demagogue about it.

Q. William V. Shannon, New York Post: Mr. President, along that line, there has been criticism that, unlike Presidents Roosevelt and Truman, that this administration has engaged in insufficient prior consultation with the leaders of the opposition party in forming defense and foreign policy. Would you care to comment on that?

THE PRESIDENT. You say they are complaining because we are guilty of insufficient?

Q. Mr. Shannon: Yes.

THE PRESIDENT. You haven't heard the statements made to me that they were never consulted in the last 20 years, according to my reports, except after a decision has been made—the fait accompli, and here it is. That has been the complaint made to me. We have been going to extraordinary lengths, and they look at me sometimes rather askance because of my insistence on it.

I would say the shoe is on the other foot so far as my reports go.

Q. Anthony H. Leviero, New York Times: Apropos of the "new look" question, Mr. President, is there any change in the procedures of the Joint Chiefs of Staff in considering defense policies? Any change since you came?

THE PRESIDENT. None at all. Look. Let us go back to that question again for a minute. We recognize one thing, and one thing has caused the new look, so called. As you know, I despise all slogans; I don't think they are truly descriptive of anything. But we were in an emergency pointing up toward some fancied date. They selected July 1, 1952, '54, or whatever—you pick the date—but we were working toward that.

What I ask all of us to remember is this: the free world is picking up a burden that it may have to carry on indefinitely. We can't look forward to a solution to the problems we have inherited as of next year or even in the next decade, possibly not in our lifetime. We have got to be able to carry this forward and in such a way that it will not wreck the very concepts on which all free government is constituted.

Now, all that we are trying to do is to get these things so put together in view of their extraordinary, almost extravagant, cost and expense, to get all these things put together so that the free world can pick up this burden which is bound to remain a burden, and do it in a way that we don't have to abandon it at a critical point along the road, or we don't have to get hysterical with fear because we are afraid we are not doing too much.

Remember, there are considerations on both sides of such problems or they wouldn't be problems. But we must, I insist, be ready for the long term, and that's a fact.

Merriman Smith, United Press: Thank you, Mr. President.

NOTE: President Eisenhower's thirtieth news conference was held in the Executive Office Building from 10:33 to 11:01 o'clock on Wednesday morning, March 10, 1954. In attendance: 181.

51 ¶ Remarks at Conference of the National Association for the Advancement of Colored People.   *March* 10, 1954

Ladies and gentlemen:

From time to time the President of the United States has the privilege of appearing before a body of Americans assembled here in Washington to extend to them greetings on behalf of the administration and of the Federal Government here located.

And certainly, more often than not, he also has the privilege of extending felicitations and well wishes in the prosecution of their work.

It is the last part of this statement that I want to refer to for a moment. My welcome to you is warm and sincere, but I should like also to take your time to talk about the good wishes that I extend for the prosecution of your work.

I believe most sincerely in the statement of Lincoln that this nation was dedicated to the proposition that all men are created equal.   I believe with the writers of the Declaration of Independence that men are endowed by their Creator with certain rights.   And furthermore, I believe that the vast majority, the great mass of Americans want to make those concepts a living reality in their lives.

I was talking only a few minutes ago with some of your leaders in the anteroom just off this hall.   I had a chance to express my belief that all of us can take inspiration from this one thought: the great faith of the American people taken in the mass.

There are vociferous minorities.   There are people who, for selfish or for fearful reasons, do not fully live up to the concepts held and so eloquently stated by our Founding Fathers—or by Lincoln.   But, by and large, the mass of America wants to be decent, and good, and just.

Our people do not want to make differentiations among people based upon inconsequential matters of nature involving color and race.

Admitting quickly—even if sadly—that the ideals of those people have not been reached, let us still remember this: this same thing is true of everything we do in life.   Ideals are really never reached by imperfect humans.   But the striving for them makes better both the great body we are trying to affect and ourselves.

And so—and I hope, my dear friends, that doesn't sound like a sermon—I am merely trying to state my beliefs as fully and as frankly as I know how to do. But I believe that this struggle, this one that in your case now has gone on for, lo, these many decades, is producing results on the part of the administration.

I stated my own personal views many times before the election. I have tried to state them since. Wherever Federal authority clearly extends, I will do the utmost that lies within my power to bring into living reality this expression of equality among all men.

By no means do I come here to make a political statement or to outline for you what has been done. But I do submit that in the two areas that I spoke about in the campaign, definite progress has been made. It is in the areas of all the armed services and where their territories and functions and activities extend, and right here in the District of Columbia. With respect to these, I expressed certain convictions and determinations. Not in all cases have the full results been achieved. But we are still trying. I know of no other slogan that is so good for all of us as once we have determined upon and visualized a worthy ideal, to keep on trying with all that is in us.

I wish for each of you an enjoyable time in this Capital. I hope that you, aside from the fruitfulness of your work, have the satisfaction of seeing something around this town that you will carry back with really fond memories. I hope that you will find something just outside of the beauty of the buildings and the niceness of nature.

For all of you—good luck and goodbye.

NOTE: The President spoke in the Departmental Auditorium at 12:30 p.m.

52 ❡ Statement by the President on the Approval by the Belgian Parliament of the European Defense Community Treaty. *March* 12, 1954

I HAVE JUST been informed that Belgium, by the vote of its Senate today, has completed all parliamentary action leading to ratification of the treaty establishing the European Defense Community. Belgium has thus become the third nation whose legislature has taken this important step.

One of the most important conditions essential to assuring lasting peace will be met when an integrated and, therefore, stronger European Community has been built.   I am gratified that steady progress is being made toward this goal.

53   ¶ Remarks on Dedicating by Remote Control the First Power Unit at Fort Randall Dam, South Dakota.   *March* 15, 1954

Governor Anderson, and all Americans participating in the ceremony at Fort Randall Dam this morning:

It is both an honor and a privilege to be able to gather with you people by the means of this long distance cable in dedicating the first power unit that Fort Randall Dam will operate.

The occasion is significant not only to the individuals who will benefit directly from the flood control features, the navigation, the power, the irrigation—everything that will come from this dam.   It is a symbol also of what we all over America must do about our most precious natural resource.   By this I mean water.   Water uncontrolled, improperly used, can cause us more damage in this country, possibly, than almost any other single element.   Properly used, properly harnessed, it can be our greatest resource.

It is one of my most earnest ambitions, an ambition shared so far as I know by every political leader of both parties in Washington and elsewhere and by all of my associates in the Cabinet—to make certain that we find the best and most intelligent ways of participating through a combination of Federal, State, and local assets in developing the water resources of our country so as to be of lasting benefit for the whole Nation, now and always.

And now, my friends, with these very few, but very earnest remarks, it is my privilege to press the key that will start in operation this first power element at Fort Randall Dam.

NOTE: The President spoke in the Cabinet Room at 12:30 p.m.

54 ¶ Radio and Television Address to the American People on the Tax Program. *March* 15, 1954

[Broadcast from the White House at 9:00 p.m.]

Good evening, my friends:

I would like to talk with you tonight about something that concerns each of us personally and directly—especially on March 15th. I want to talk about our taxes—and about the new tax program that Congress will debate this week.

Now, I can talk only about a few essential facts in this program because, my friends, this 900-page book is the new tax program, and this 500-page book is the explanation made by the Ways and Means Committee of the House of Representatives to the House regarding this bill. You and I tonight will be discussing only a very few of the high spots.

Now, we recognize, of course, that taxes are necessary. We know that through taxes our Government gets the money to carry on its necessary functions. The most costly is defense.

Only at our peril may we pursue a penny wise, pound foolish policy in regard to the Nation's security. In the past year, we have been able to make real savings in defense costs. But despite these savings, 70 cents out of each dollar spent by your Government still go for defense purposes.

The remaining 30 cents go for many things: to meet our obligations to veterans—to carry on important activities overseas—to pay the interest on the gigantic public debt—and to do within our country what Abraham Lincoln described as "those things which the individual cannot do at all or so well do for himself."

I know how burdensome your taxes have been and continue to be. So we are watching every expenditure of Government—to eliminate waste, duplication, and luxury. But while we are insisting upon good management and thrift in Government, we have, at the same time, asked the Congress to approve a great program to build a stronger America for all our people.

So let me give you some examples of the things we want to do in this program:

We want to improve and expand our social security program.

313

We want a broader and stronger system of unemployment insurance.

We want more and better homes for our people.

We want to do away with slums in our cities.

We want to foster a much improved health program.

We want a better and a lasting farm program, with better reclamation and conservation.

We want an improved Taft-Hartley Act to protect workers and employers.

We want wider markets overseas for our products.

We want—above all—maximum protection of freedom and a strong and growing economy—an economy free from both inflation and depression.

Most of these things cost money. Without adequate revenue, most of them would be abandoned or curtailed. That is why our tax proposal is the cornerstone of the entire effort. It is a tax plan designed to be fair to all. I am sure you join me in the hope that the Congress, before it adjourns, will approve this program for a stronger America.

And along with this great plan for America, we want also to reduce your taxes so you can save or spend more of your own money, as you personally desire.

Now, to reduce taxes, we had to find some way of saving money, for despite many years of heavy taxation, our Government has been running deeper and deeper into debt. A year ago, this administration inherited a budget calling for a spending program that we have since reduced by twelve billion dollars. Of this total saving, seven billion dollars is being made this year.

Now, seven billion dollars is so much money—even in Washington—that it's hard to know what it really means. Let's see if we can get some idea of how much it is.

The money American farmers got last year for all the corn and all the wheat grown in our entire country was seven billion dollars.

The money Americans paid in all of last year for household utilities and for fuel amounted to seven billion dollars.

The money Americans pay each year for doctor, dentist, medical and hospital bills is seven billion dollars.

Now, I think you will agree that we have, indeed, saved a lot of money. Without these savings, there could have been no tax relief for anyone. Because of these savings, your tax cuts were possible.

On January 1st this year your taxes were cut by five billion dollars. The tax revision program now in Congress will cut taxes by over one and a half billion dollars more. The total may be nearly seven billion dollars. Thus the Government is turning back to you about all that we expect to save this year. Meanwhile, we are seeing to it that the Government deficit, instead of growing, may continue to shrink.

Now, in the light of all this, let's look at the tax program now in Congress.

To start with, it is the first time in half a century that our tax laws have been completely overhauled. This long overdue reform of old tax laws brings you benefits which go beyond the tax reductions I have just mentioned. Millions of individual taxpayers—many of you listening—will benefit. Now here are some of the ways in which you will benefit:

You will have larger deductions for your medical expenses.

There will be special deductions for the cost of child care for those among you who are widows who work.

Fairer tax treatment for the widows of policemen and firemen and others who have fraternal or private pension plans.

Fairer tax consideration for those of you who are retired.

Deductions of up to $100 a week for those of you receiving sickness or accident benefits.

There are, in addition, important provisions to encourage the growth and expansion of industry, the creation of jobs, and the starting of new and small businesses.

Now, one of these provisions is of particular interest to those among you who have made or want to make investments to help meet the expenses of a growing family or to meet the requirements of old age. This year, we proposed to reduce by a modest amount or percentage the existing double taxation on dividend income.

This will be important to all of us, whether our savings are large or small. It will encourage Americans to invest in their country's future. And let us remember this most important fact: the average investment needed to buy the tools and facilities to give one of our workmen a job runs about eight to ten thousand dollars. The more we can encourage savings and investments, the more prosperous will be 160 million American citizens.

Just as we need more spending by consumers, so we need buyers for items produced by heavy industry—for lathes and looms and giant gen-

erators.   The making of these things gives jobs to millions of our people.
This carefully balanced tax program will encourage this kind of produc-
tion.   It will make new jobs, larger payrolls, and improved products.
It will give us lower price tags on many of the things we want and need.

And here is another important part of this program.   It concerns the
income tax on corporations.   Under the law, this tax would be reduced
two weeks from today.   Now I have asked the Congress to keep this
tax at 52 percent and not to permit it to go down to 47 percent at this
time.   The extension of this extra tax on corporations will provide
enough money to pay the costs of the benefits this tax revision program
will bring to individuals and business.

So, there you have, in broad outline, the new tax revision program.
I most earnestly hope that the Congress will pass it.

But—this is an election year.   Some think it is good politics to promise
more and more Government spending, and at the same time, more and
more tax cuts for all.   We know, from bitter experience, what such a
policy would finally lead to.   It would make our dollars buy less.   It
would raise the price of rent, of clothing, and of groceries.   It would
pass on still larger debts to our children.

Some have suggested raising personal income tax exemptions from
$600 to $800, and soon to $1,000, even though the Federal budget is
not in balance.   You've seen this kind of deal before.   It looks good on
the surface but it looks a lot different when you dig into it.

The $1,000 exemption would excuse one taxpayer in every three from
all Federal income taxes.   The share of that one-third would have to be
paid by the other two-thirds.

I think this is wrong.   I am for everybody paying his fair share.

When the time comes to cut income taxes still more, let's cut them.
But I do not believe that the way to do it is to excuse millions of
taxpayers from paying any income tax at all.

The good American doesn't ask for favored position or treatment.
Naturally he wants all fellow citizens to pay their fair share of the taxes,
just as he has to do, and he wants every cent collected to be spent wisely
and economically.   But every real American is proud to carry his share
of that national burden.   In war and peace, I have seen countless examples of American pride and of the unassuming but inspiring courage of
young American citizens.   I simply do not believe for one second that

anyone privileged to live in this country wants someone else to pay his own fair and just share of the cost of his Government.

Aside from that, let's just be practical. The loss of revenue involved in this proposal would be a serious blow to your Government.

A $100 increase in the exemption would cost the Government two and a half billion dollars. To increase the personal exemption to one thousand dollars would cost eight billion dollars. This, of course, would be on top of the large tax cuts our savings have already made possible this year.

Now, in your interest I must and will oppose such an unsound tax proposal. I most earnestly hope that it will be rejected by the Congress. Especially, I hope you feel the same way.

Every dollar spent by the Government must be paid for either by taxes or by more borrowing with greater debt. To make large additional savings in the cost of Government at this moment means seriously weakening our national defense. I do not know any friend of the United States who wants that, under present world conditions. Now the only other way to make more tax cuts now is to have bigger and bigger deficits and to borrow more and more money. Either we or our children will have to bear the burden of this debt. This is one kind of chicken that always comes home to roost. An unwise tax cutter, my fellow citizens, is no real friend of the taxpayer.

Now, this evening I mustn't overlook those among us who are professionally faint hearted. They have been arguing lately that we are on the very brink of economic disaster. Viewing with gloom is only to be expected in the spring of an election year. The truth is, we do not have a depression. And what's more, as I have said time and time again, your Government will continue to use its full powers to make sure that we don't have one.

A month ago, I expressed to the Congress my conviction that we would be able to go from wartime to peacetime conditions without serious economic trouble. Nothing has happened since to change my mind.

Some unemployment has developed in different parts of the country, but the Nation as a whole continues to be prosperous. Unemployment has reached about the level it was in the spring of 1950. The broad program I have proposed to the Congress will strengthen our economy. When it is approved by Congress, it will both increase the number of jobs and help make every man secure in the job that he has.

Of course, everyone wants tax reductions of the right kind, at the right time.   That specifically includes this administration.   This has been proved by the large tax cuts we have already made possible this year.   But at this time economic conditions do not call for an emergency program that would justify larger Federal deficits and further inflation through large additional tax reductions.

My friends, a century and a half ago, George Washington gave us some good advice.   He said we should keep a good national defense.   He also said we should not ungenerously impose upon our children the burdens which we ourselves ought to bear.

I know you and I agree with Washington on these points.

We agree, too, on efficiency in Government, and on a forward-looking program for a stronger America—an America whose people know good health and prosperity—who are secure, day and night, from fear at home or abroad.   That is the aim of this tax program.

That goal, my fellow citizens, is a goal worthy of our people.

55   ¶ Letter to the Governors of the States and Territories Requesting Them To Serve as Honorary Chairmen, United Defense Fund.
March 16, 1954

[Released March 16, 1954. Dated March 15, 1954]

Dear Governor ——————:

Some time ago, I accepted the Honorary Chairmanship of the United Defense Fund.   I did this because of my deep conviction that the defense of this country depends upon the voluntary activities of its citizens, as well as upon the authority of government.   I am delighted that General of the Army Omar N. Bradley has accepted, at my request, the active campaign chairmanship.

There is great need this year for an aggressive campaign for financial support for the United Defense Services.   We have moved from a fighting war to an armed peace, but the problem of sustaining the high morale of our defense forces is no less acute than during time of actual combat. If we are to maintain the United Defense Services—particularly those of the USO—on the desired high level, the understanding and support of the American people are vital.

In the task of marshalling this support, we hope to enlist as leaders the official heads of State and Territorial Governments. Accordingly, I am asking each State and Territorial Governor to serve as Honorary Chairman for the United Defense Fund in his State or Territory. I hope that it will be possible for you to accept this important assignment.

Sincerely,

DWIGHT D. EISENHOWER

56 ¶ Statement by the President Upon Signing Bill Providing for Protection of Mexican Migrant Labor. *March* 16, 1954

ON SIGNING this legislation, I wish to dispel any misconceptions which may exist regarding its purpose. The basic purpose is to enable this Government to give Mexican migrant labor the protection of our laws.

Whenever United States employment is at such a level that Mexican workers are needed to supplement the United States labor force, and whenever they can be spared temporarily from Mexico, we of course welcome their valuable assistance to our farming community if they will cross the border legally. The problem of adequate control and protection of Mexican workers in the United States has in recent years been the subject of searching analysis by the Governments of the United States and Mexico, working both independently and together.

The two Governments, after more than four months of careful study and friendly negotiation—conducted in an atmosphere of mutual respect worthy of two sovereign neighbors—announced on March 10 that they had concluded a renewed and improved Migrant Labor Agreement. While neither Government assumes that this Agreement will prove to be the final answer to the whole complex problem, it provides necessary means for moving forward to more complete solutions.

Unforeseeable future developments may some day lead the two Governments to determine that formal agreement on this subject is no longer desirable but that appropriate action by each within its own jurisdiction is still essential. Authority has existed for a number of years for the

Attorney General to admit Mexican farm workers under whatever conditions he alone may establish, but because of the wording of applicable legislation there has not been adequate authority for United States governmental measures for protection and placement of the workers at any time there should not be an agreement with Mexico. The present law is precautionary in that it removes this disability and enables the Secretary of Labor to perform these functions of protecting and placing migrant workers which are so important to both United States and Mexican interests, at any time these services may be required.

NOTE: As enacted the bill (H.J. Res. 355) is Public Law 309, 83d Congress (68 Stat. 28).

57   ¶ The President's News Conference of *March* 17, 1954.

THE PRESIDENT. I trust, ladies and gentlemen, everybody is wearing his proper emblem and done up in green this morning.

Someone asked last week about the coffee investigation. We inquired, and the Chairman says that the investigation is coming along in good form, and they should have a report in the near future.

There is one other little item, an Executive order that will be published, I guess this afternoon, having to do with this research and development.

The only reason I mention it is because of the tremendous impression and impact it makes on me when I look at the sums that the Government spent for research and development only a matter of 12, 13 years ago, and what we are spending now. When you have an item of more than $2 billion in your budget, you have something that takes, of course, not only the finest scientific brains you can find in the United States to supervise and coordinate it, but it is really big business of a very large order; I believe in 1940, in all departments, that ran to $100 million. I think that Mr. Hagerty will have a statement to put out somewhere along about 4:00 o'clock.

I think that is all I have, so we will go to questions.

Q. Merriman Smith, United Press: Mr. President, Representative Sterling Cole, the Chairman of the Joint Congressional Atomic Energy

Commission, said last night that we now have a hydrogen bomb and can deliver it anywhere in the world. I wonder if you could discuss that?

THE PRESIDENT. No, I wouldn't want to discuss that. I hadn't seen the statement, and I don't recall what we have released. My embarrassment at this moment is not that I wouldn't be glad to talk over certain of these things if I could recall how far we have gone in releasing information on the point, but when you say "can deliver anywhere in the world," why, of course, I guess that assumes that you have the right places from which to do it, and the machines, and so on.

I would say that was a question not to be discussed until I was more sure where I am standing.

Q. Mrs. May Craig, Maine Newspapers: Mr. President, he did put in the reservation if we have bases near enough. He did say we do not have nonstop planes that can take it there now.

THE PRESIDENT. I didn't read what he said; and I am sorry, Mrs. Craig, I don't believe I will discuss that this morning because I just don't think it is wise for me to do so until I check up. It is possible that I have said so much in the past that I would be perfectly justified in discussing it in some detail this morning.

I will tell you what I will do; I will look up and see where we stand, and if it comes up at our next conference, why then, I will discuss it if I should do so. But I just don't want to go off the deep end here when I don't know where I'm standing.

Q. Edward T. Folliard, Washington Post: Mr. President, I would like to ask you about a reply you made to a question last week. You had been asked about Indochina, about the possibility of a war growing out of an incident in Indochina, and you made this reply:

"I will say this: there is going to be no involvement of America in war unless it is a result of the constitutional process that is placed upon Congress to declare it. Now, let us have that clear; and that is the answer."

What I wanted to ask, Mr. President, is this: does that mean that if an aggression came, one, say, like the aggression in Korea in 1950, that you would hold up action until Congress debated the matter and then declared war?

THE PRESIDENT. Well, of course, you are trying to foresee every possible condition that can arise.

Last week we were talking about Indochina, and I believe the question was concerning the possibility of one of our men, or one or two, getting killed, and what that would mean. I tried to reply very emphatically, and I still don't back away from the generalization I made in this general sense. But let us take an extreme case: suppose, while we are sitting here, right at this minute, there came a message flashed over the United States that coming up from the south somewhere were a great fleet of airplanes, and we had positive evidence that they were intent upon spreading destruction in the United States.

Now, if there is anyone here or any citizen of the United States who would hold me guiltless if I said, "We will sit here and try to get in touch with Congress," well, then, I don't know who they are.

That is an extreme case, and we must be careful not to make generalizations just in terms of taking care of extremes.

You can go right on down the line until you can have something where you say, "Well, the best interests of the United States are involved in this incident taken with someone else, but there is plenty of time to discuss it with Congress."

But when you come down to the matter of self-preservation, quick reaction to a threat against your life, I believe there is a rule that applies to nations exactly as it does to the individuals: you don't call a policeman if your life is actually in danger; if you have nothing else to do but run, you at least try to do your best.

I think that a rule of reason must apply here. But as far as trying to involve in any kind of circumstances the United States in a complete war—after all, war involves many things. There are all sorts of relationships changed in the world. We are talking now about just defense against that sudden attack.

Then, of course, you have the congressional.

Q. Mr. Folliard: Mr. President, the argument was made in 1950 that speed was very urgent, that it was necessary to move very quickly.

THE PRESIDENT. Well, I don't remember exactly about that. I remember I was up in Canada, as a matter of fact, when it happened, and I came out of Canada.

But if I recall, the first order was that there would be air support given to the South Koreans, the Republic of Korea troops; so there was plenty of time then to discuss what further action you would take, plenty of time to discuss it by Congress, I should think.

I am not trying to judge or to pass judgment on what happened. I am merely saying that there arise occasions in the handling of anything that is as complicated as a great country such as ours in its relationships with other countries, that you can't always predict exactly how you will handle a thing.

We must, once in a while, trust to the judgment of humans and of people; that is why Government is so much dependent upon the people holding it.

I am merely trying to say in my statements, I am against violating the Constitution. Actually, this thing was so well debated, you know, when the Constitution was passed, that it is implicit, I think, in our whole document that the President must act against sudden unexpected aggression. They debated just exactly that point when they passed that provision that the Congress would declare war.

Q. William P. Flythe, Hearst Newspapers: Mr. President, could you say anything about the status of the negotiations with Russia on the joint development of atomic energy for peaceful purposes?

THE PRESIDENT. No, I can't say anything about it because the conversations that are going on are still on very much of a private basis. I can't say anything.

Q. Ethel Payne, Defender Publications: Mr. President, Vice President Nixon said on his return from Asia that every act of racial discrimination or prejudice in the United States hurts America as much as an espionage agent who turns over a weapon to a foreign enemy. He added that every American citizen can contribute towards creating a better understanding of American ideas abroad by practicing and thinking tolerance and respect for human rights every day of the year. We know also that you have taken the firm stand along these same lines.

Do you not feel then, that the continuance on our statute books of the McCarran-Walter Act containing the national origins quota system, which discriminates against Asiatic people from southeastern Europe and from the West Indies, is harming our foreign policy, and will there be any proposal made to Congress on immigration which might alleviate these conditions?

THE PRESIDENT. As you know, you are bringing up a very broad, but it is a very vital question to us.

Now, there has not been brought to me from the State Department this act and its immediate and direct effect upon our relationships with other countries, so there have been no discussions between me and the State Department officials on the point.

I do say that I believe as we come closer and closer to living by the principles enunciated in our founding documents, our own situation abroad is going to be better, and that is the kind of thing for which I strive. I am not going to be a bull in a china shop and destroy things. I am working for things; that is what I am trying to say.

Q. Richard Harkness, National Broadcasting Company: If I may go back, sir, to the question raised by Mr. Folliard. Yesterday, Secretary of State Dulles said that he interpreted our NATO obligations and our obligations under our Latin-American pacts to retaliate in the event of an attack on one of our allies, and that there was no need for you to go to Congress for a declaration of war in such an event. On the other hand, thinking back, I discovered that the Senate Foreign Relations Committee, in approving the NATO pact in June 1949, this committee said that the treaty gave no authority to the Chief Executive that was not there in the absence of a treaty. Would you comment on Mr. Dulles' speech?

THE PRESIDENT. As a matter of fact, I don't think, by any manner of means, Mr. Dulles meant his remarks to say that I would have the authority to declare war. But there is a difference between an act of war and declaring war—I mean an act of violence.

I come back again to the obvious right of self-protection, self-preservation, if you are attacked and you have notice. What would you do if you suddenly were facing a gigantic Pearl Harbor? This thing isn't academic. When you get into that extreme, you are going to act, do whatever you think will save best the people of the United States, and would most quickly diminish the power of the other fellow to repeat it.

Now, this whole thing within hours has to be before the Congress. They have to act on this. After all, you can't carry on a war without Congress. They have to appropriate the money, provide the means, the laws, and everything else. So Congress would have to come in on an emergency basis, if they were absent; or if they were here they would start meeting at night quickly. Things would have to move at the most tremendous speed. But I believe there is a great gulf between what the President would do to protect the United States and an actual declaration of war.

Now, I could be mistaken, and I would not argue it. I would like to discuss it with Foster Dulles but, having talked to him, I am sure that we are absolutely in agreement as to what we mean about it.

Q. Richard L. Wilson, Cowles Publications: Mr. President, on this general subject there is another point involved. Mr. Dulles has outlined the policy of retaliation, and in some quarters that has been interpreted as meaning that if you have a local war or a local situation that the retaliation might be against Moscow or Peiping or some major point. Could you discuss that question of the local warlike situation?

THE PRESIDENT. Mr. Wilson, there is one thing I can tell you about war, and almost one only, and it is this: no war ever shows the characteristics that were expected; it is always different. What we are trying to say now is to express a generalization that would apply in an infinite variety of cases, under an infinite variety of provocations, and I just don't believe it is possible.

I think that what has got to be decided is how deeply is the safety and security of America involved.

We do know that there are weapons now in being that give more than ever to the attacker a tremendous advantage, the man who attacks by surprise. The element of surprise, always important in war, has been multiplied by the possibility of creating such widespread destruction quickly. Therefore, any President should be worse than impeached, he should be hanged, I should say, if he didn't do what all America would demand that he do to protect them in an emergency.

But when it comes to saying that where on the fringe or the periphery of our interests and of wherever we may be, that any kind of an act on the part of the enemy would justify that kind of thing, that I wouldn't hold with for a moment; I don't think anybody else would.

Q. Mr. Wilson: Well, the point has been made, sir, that the policy which Mr. Dulles outlined on January 12th would mean that we wouldn't take part in wars like the Korean War or the Indochinese War, but that if we did do anything to meet the threat of those local wars, it would be a direct attack upon the major aggressor at some point most desirable for us.

THE PRESIDENT. Well now, I will tell you: Foster Dulles, by no stretch of the imagination, ever meant to be so specific and exact in stating what we would do under different circumstances. He was showing the value to America to have a capability of doing certain things, what he believed that would be in the way of deterring an aggressor and preventing this dread possibility of war occurring.

So no man, I don't care how brilliant he is, would undertake to say exactly what we would do under all that variety of circumstances. That is just nonsense.

Q. Marvin L. Arrowsmith, Associated Press: Mr. President, I would like to get clear on one point. You are talking throughout here about the possibility of Presidential action in the case of an attack without going to Congress first?

THE PRESIDENT. I am talking about things you would have to do in 2 minutes, that is all.

Q. Martin S. Hayden, Detroit News: Mr. President, since our last press conference, a Senate committee has released certain documents in which they allege that your Secretary of the Army made threats against the Senate committee, and offered to turn in the Navy and the Air Force if he could get a favor from the committee. I wanted to ask you just this, sir: as the man responsible for the Executive, are you at all disturbed about these reports and these allegations against this man in your administration?

THE PRESIDENT. Well, to say that a thing like that causes no concern to a Chief Executive would, of course, be ridiculous. After all, I have plead and plead for positive action to try to get our minds off these petty quarrels, negative results of calling each other names, and getting ahead with something that is good for the United States. I believe that with all my being, so every time that these things occur and upset people on the Hill and get them separated from the Executive, why, of course, it is serious.

Now, when you ask me whether I believe Secretary Stevens, of course I do. If I didn't believe him, if I didn't have faith and confidence in him, he wouldn't be where he is; of course I believe in him. I don't say he can't be mistaken, I should make that clear. I don't know, there may be something that he has been misinformed on; but so far as his integrity and honesty are concerned I stand by him.

Q. Kenneth M. Scheibel, Gannett News Service: Mr. President, a bill has been introduced in the House to change the St. Lawrence Seaway legislation which has been approved by the committee, substituting Federal funds and putting in private capital to finance that project. Could you give us the administration viewpoint on the use of private capital rather than Federal?

THE PRESIDENT. I don't quite—you say substituting Federal funds?

Q. Mr. Scheibel: Substituting private capital for Federal money.

THE PRESIDENT. I haven't seen the exact language of any amendment proposed, but I would say this: I stand behind the bill as it came out of committee; that is what I should like to see enacted.

Q. Robert G. Spivack, New York Post: Mr. President, there has been considerable speculation as to what the renewed fighting in Indochina means, and I wondered if, on the basis of any reports you have—well, some of the speculation goes along the lines that it is for the psychological effect on the Geneva conference; and others is that it means a renewal of Russian belligerency; and then there are some others. I wondered how you interpreted it.

THE PRESIDENT. No, I have no exact interpretation of those things, as none of us has. Strange and weird things are happening in this war.

There was a movement, a very strong movement, you know, to the south and southwestward. Now, the spearheads of that force moved back to around this town, whose name I can never pronounce, but it is probably at the tip of your tongue, all of you. I assume that this force, having made all of this move down there, has now decided to see if they can accomplish something that they would consider a very great victory, if they could really defeat this French force that is holding this citadel and town.

It wouldn't look like it was planned originally for that, because otherwise why waste all the time going on south. But they have come back. The fighting season, I believe, there will soon be drawing to a close because of the rains; so it looks to me like a battle just to try to overpower the French in that region.

It may be something else; I haven't asked really my G–2 boys to give me their interpretation of the movement.

Q. Sarah McClendon, El Paso Times: Sir, Congressman Rayburn and Congressman Cooper and Senator George undertook to answer you on taxes last night. I wonder if you would like to answer them on this point: they say the dividend features of this tax bill would give only 6 families out of every 1,000 great benefits, and 80 percent of the people would not be benefited by the bill, and that those with incomes less than $5,000 would really suffer.

THE PRESIDENT. U.S. Steel is probably taken as the example of big business, owned by rich families.

There are 300,000 men working for U.S. Steel; there are 300,000 stockholders in U.S. Steel. Fifty-six percent of those stockholders are men who draw less than $5,000 a year in their total incomes. Of that number, I think there is a total of 46 percent below the $4,500 mark, which is the average wage of the steel earners.

There are more stockholders in U.S. Steel that are in the bracket $2,000 to $3,000 income than there are in any other thousand-dollar bracket in the whole list of stockholders.

Now, to say that the bill that we have designed and worked on all these months is designed to help rich people, is an error.

Q. Gould Lincoln, Washington Evening Star: Your speech on taxes has been interpreted in some quarters as meaning that you would veto the tax bill if it should contain the large exemptions proposed by some Congressmen. Would you tell us something about that?

THE PRESIDENT. As I have explained here before, it would be dangerous to say in advance what bills a President should veto and should not. As you know, the President does not have the power of the item veto; and he has to take the bill or reject it. I explained before, sometimes you have to take very unpleasant features along with an otherwise good bill. However, any bill that in my opinion is going to wreck us or put us in an impossible situation, then I have got to sit down with it and decide whether the bad features are more important than the good. That is about all I can say.

But I do say this: I notice some of the people that suddenly want to cut our income way down are the very people who just a very few months ago were saying "We will not increase the debt limit." Now, they must have some answer to that one.

Q. Milton B. Freudenheim, Akron Beacon Journal: Mr. President, yesterday you were visited by your Commission to sell the Government's synthetic rubber plants. I wondered if you have any comment on the progress of that effort?

THE PRESIDENT. Only that they think they are making real progress. I believe there is a date set, before long, when this particular phase of expiration and all that comes to an end, and then start long negotiations. I know they believe that they are making real progress.

Q. Robert J. Donovan, New York Herald Tribune: Sir, I had a question collateral to Mr. Hayden's on these investigations. There have been reports that all these embroilments have impaired morale in the Army and, particularly among officers. Have you had any reports, sir, on that; or, in your judgment, is that likely?

THE PRESIDENT. No, I haven't had any specific reports on it, but I will tell you: I would suspect that inside their hearts a lot of people hurt. The Army, and all the rest of the services, are rightfully very proud of the kind of service they have rendered to the United States.

Now, when they find, sometimes rightly—well, as a matter of fact, it hurts more when it is rightly. When they are rightly criticized for the mistakes or errors or blunders of someone at the top of the services, they feel pretty low. When they are accused unjustly there is, I suppose you would say, a mixture of anger, resentment, and rather a great deal of sadness.

They are people who are not articulate; they are not around making speeches in commercial clubs and all that sort of thing. They are people to whom I think we all owe a lot, and we ought to stand up and very carefully differentiate against anyone we think may have made a mistake and may have made a blunder, and these great armed services.

There is a man for example, I see in the paper, who built a dog house. Well, he ought to live in it. I mean, he did it with Federal funds. [*Laughter*]

Q. Edward T. Folliard, Washington Post: Mr. President, I would like to go back to the matter of Secretary Dulles and the doctrine of "massive retaliation." As you told Mr. Wilson, you can't foresee the things you might do under varying circumstances. Perhaps we are confused, because we have been led to believe that Secretary Dulles had enunciated some new doctrine. Is it a new doctrine, sir?

THE PRESIDENT. Oh, no, not at all.

Q. Mr. Folliard: Then there is nothing new about that?

THE PRESIDENT. After all, let's remember this: the American sailors tried to fight back at Pearl Harbor, didn't they?

Q. Mr. Folliard: Yes.

THE PRESIDENT. Well, that was an act of war; it was an act of violence, at least. We would have been amazed had they not done it.

If you can imagine such things happening on a larger scale, who is the man who has to act quickly? The President of the United States, as the Commander in Chief of the Armed Forces; he has got to do something.

But when it comes down to saying that merely because in some corner of the world our vital interests are hurt, we are going to decide in advance such great and extraordinary action that the Congress really has no way of backing up, that wouldn't be right.

Q. Mr. Folliard: Last week, Mr. President, you said you didn't particularly care for slogans, but we have had this, we have been hearing now about the "new look," the "new look" in defense, "new look" in foreign policy; is it true, sir, would we be wise to assume that nothing new has happened in the matter of military——

THE PRESIDENT. Have you got 3 minutes to listen to a lecture?

Q. Mr. Folliard: Yes, sir. [*Laughter*]

THE PRESIDENT. All right. "New look": now, what do we mean? We mean this: we are not fighting with muzzle-loaders in any of the services. Every single day things change in this world, and any staff or any group of leaders doing his job is re-examining the world situation, the advances of science, the whole situation, geographic and otherwise, of our country and of others, to see what is it that we now need most to insure our security and our peaceful existence.

You cannot possibly say that the kind of a unit and organization that I took to war or took over across the Channel in 1944 would have any usefulness today whatsoever. For example, you will recall we landed on June 6; we got out of that narrow little beachhead on about July 25. All right; behind that we built up two artificial harbors and we were landing over the beaches. What would two atomic bombs have done to the whole thing?

So you just simply can't take, in warfare or in any contemplation of war or preparation for war, take old patterns and say that is by which we live.

All that the "new look" is is an attempt by intelligent people to keep abreast of the times; and if you want to call your today's clothes the "new look" as compared to what Lincoln wore, all right, we are in the "new look." But I just don't like this expression because it doesn't mean much to me.

I mean that we are striving our best to meet the grave responsibilities that are placed upon people whose job is to protect this country. Let me point out this: I hear people say "bigger army." Now, our most valued, our most costly asset is our young men. Let's don't use them any more than we have to.

For 40 years I was in that Army, and I did one thing: study how can you get an infantry platoon out of battle. The most terrible job in warfare is to be a second lieutenant leading a platoon when you are on the battlefield.

If we can do anything to lessen that number—remember this: we are planning right now the greatest peacetime army we have ever held, one million men in time of peace.

What are we talking about? It is, I think, there is too much hysteria. You know, the world is suffering from a multiplicity of fears. We fear the men in the Kremlin, we fear what they will do to our friends around them; we are fearing what unwise investigators will do to us here at home as they try to combat subversion or bribery or deceit within. We fear depression, we fear the loss of jobs. All of these, with their impact on the human mind makes us act almost hysterically, and you find hysterical reactions.

We have got to look at each of those in its proper perspective, to understand what the whole sum total means. And remember this: the reason they are feared and bad is because there is a little element of truth in each, a little element of danger in each. That means that finally there is left a little residue that you can meet only by faith, a faith in the destiny of America; and that is what I believe is the answer.

This "new look"—the "new look" is just our effort to solve in one field, that of the direct military attack, to produce the best results we can for the protection of America. To call it revolutionary or to act like it is something that just suddenly dropped down on us like a cloud out of the heaven, is just not true, just not true.

Q. Roscoe Drummond, New York Herald Tribune: Mr. President, may I ask a quick question, and that is, do you think the time will come when we will have a press conference in which events do not require us to ask a question about unwise investigators? [*Laughter*]

THE PRESIDENT. I will tell you, Mr. Drummond, coming over this morning I said to one of my associates, I said, "You know, if one name comes up I am going to ask permission whether we couldn't have one press conference without this particular subject coming up." [*Laughter*]

Q. Mrs. May Craig, Maine Newspapers: Mr. President, if you are able to talk to us at your next press conference about Mr. Cole and what he said on the hydrogen and atomic bombs, would you consider answering the question as to why we do not have planes which can deliver the hydrogen bomb from continental United States?

THE PRESIDENT. Of course, there are some of these questions that you had maybe get in the best engineers from Lockheed, and Consolidated and Boeing; ask those people, because there are certain limitations on every plane that is flying in the air today.

However, I will look into the thing and see how much has been put in the public domain. I am perfectly ready to try to place in such perspective as I can, out of my experience before this group, such facts as are already in the public domain. But let me make perfectly clear, I am not going to release anything here that hasn't been released before.

Q. Clark R. Mollenhoff, Des Moines Register and Tribune: Mr. President, has the White House given up in its effort to obtain the resignation of Colonel Johnson from the ICC?

THE PRESIDENT. What are you talking about? [*Laughter*] It is a question I know nothing about; I don't know the name; I don't know what you are talking about.

Q. Mr. Mollenhoff: Is it correct, Mr. President, that you don't know that Mr. Adams has had Mr. Johnson at the White House on a couple of occasions to discuss that?

THE PRESIDENT. I suppose there are 500 people a day going in that office that I know nothing about. I don't know what you are talking about, so I don't have any answer whatsoever.

Q. Robert G. Spivack, New York Post: Mr. President, on this question of fears, I think I can detect in all the questions that have been asked you here about the war question, there is one fear that seems to be involved, and that is the possibility of our involvement in the Indochina war if our men who are over there are further attacked. I know this came up last week at the press conference.

THE PRESIDENT. And I gave my answer. You read it and you will find it is exact.

Merriman Smith, United Press: Thank you, Mr. President.

NOTE: President Eisenhower's thirty-first news conference was held in the Executive Office Building from 10:31 to 11:02 o'clock on Wednesday morning, March 17, 1954. In attendance: 167.

58 ¶ Veto of Bill for the Relief of Wilhelm Engelbert. *March* 17, 1954

To the United States Senate:

I return herewith, without my approval, S. 153, a bill "For the relief of Wilhelm Engelbert."

This measure would grant the status of lawful permanent residence in the United States to Mr. Engelbert upon payment of the required visa fee.

Mr. Engelbert is a native and citizen of Germany who was born in Dortmund, Westphalia, on July 27, 1905. He entered the United States illegally on December 31, 1926, as a deserting seaman, with the intention of remaining here permanently.

Between 1926 and the outbreak of World War II in 1939, the alien did nothing to regularize his status in the United States. In fact, according to the record set forth in the Committees' reports upon this bill, his actions indicate clearly that he thought of himself as a German and showed his allegiance time and again as that of a German national.

After the United States entered World War II, Mr. Engelbert was interned as an enemy alien. He remained an internee until July 1, 1948. In due course, a warrant for his deportation to Germany was issued in 1943. This warrant, issued on grounds of illegal entry, was outstanding at the time of his release from alien enemy proceedings. Applications for reconsideration and reopening of the deportation hearings have been denied by the Board of Immigration Appeals.

Although it appears that to a certain extent Mr. Engelbert's motives in becoming a member of the Nazi party, registering for service in the German army, equipping himself with German money to defray the cost of a trip to Germany, and other acts demonstrating allegiance to Germany, may have been dictated by a desire to assist his mother and to obtain legal entry into the United States, the fact remains that he did nothing to regularize his status for some twelve years. Furthermore, from 1939 until the end of World War II there is nothing in the record of this case to indicate that Mr. Engelbert showed real willingness to accept the responsibilities of a permanent resident of the United States. On the contrary, he sought repatriation to Germany during the war, and it was not until after

333

victory had been assured in Europe in 1945 that he withdrew his application and requested adjustment of his immigration status.

Under these circumstances, I see no basis for setting aside the requirements of the immigration law.

DWIGHT D. EISENHOWER

59 ¶ Veto of Bill for the Relief of the Estate of Mrs. Margareth Weigand.   *March* 17, 1954

To the United States Senate:

I return herewith, without my approval, the enrolled bill (S. 502), "For the relief of the estate of Mrs. Margareth Weigand."

Kurt F. Weigand, the son of Margareth Weigand and a German citizen resident in the United States, was interned in 1942 as an enemy alien. Following his release from parole in 1945, he died in Fargo, North Dakota, by accidental drowning. Owing to his coverage under the Social Security Act, his mother, a resident and citizen of Germany, became entitled to a lump sum death benefit award. The amount of the award was vested in the Attorney General by Vesting Order 17973, dated May 31, 1951, which was issued in accordance with the provisions of the Trading With the Enemy Act. This bill would provide for the return of the amount so vested to the estate of Mrs. Margareth Weigand. Mrs. Weigand was alive at the date of issuance of the vesting order.

Section 39 of the Trading With the Enemy Act, as amended, in general prohibits the return of property or interests in property vested from nationals of Germany or Japan unless such nationals are eligible for return under the provisions of section 32 of the Act. Mrs. Weigand did not file a claim under section 32 for return of the amount vested, and the record contains no indication that she would have been eligible for return. Her ineligibility would disqualify her successors in interest. If ineligible, the enactment of the bill would authorize the transfer of the property to the beneficiaries of her estate contrary to existing general law.

Moreover, even if these beneficiaries were eligible for the return of the property, this bill would bestow a preference on them by setting aside the claims procedures prescribed by general law. There is no apparent reason for singling out the beneficiaries for preferential treatment of any nature.

The reasons urged in support of this measure would equally apply to the cases of thousands of other enemy nationals whose property in the United States was vested pursuant to the provisions of the Trading With the Enemy Act.

DWIGHT D. EISENHOWER

60 ¶ Statement by the President Upon Signing Executive Order Strengthening the Scientific Programs of the Federal Government. *March 17, 1954*

SCIENCE has a vital role in our Nation's security and growth. During the past half-century, it has brought about a vast transformation in industry, in agriculture, in medicine, in transportation, and in communications. Military science has been revolutionized by technological development. The impact of science is increasingly felt in every field of public policy including foreign affairs. All this has been brought about through a combination of vision, initiative, business enterprise, a strong educational system, and the dedicated enthusiasm of the scientific community.

The responsibilities of the Federal Government toward science have likewise changed greatly. In 1940, the Federal Government spent about one hundred million dollars in supporting research and development. The budget which I have just transmitted to the Congress calls for expenditures for these purposes in the next fiscal year of over two billion dollars. This is convincing evidence of the important role of science and technology in our national affairs.

This rapid expansion of Federal responsibility requires prudent administration. More than half of all the investment in the Nation today for scientific research and development is being made by the Federal Government. In large measure, these Federal funds are paid to industry and educational institutions for the conduct of research and development projects. Thus our Federal policies and practices regarding research and development are felt immediately and substantially by industry and our educational institutions.

335

More than ninety percent of this Federal support is presently going into applied research and development. This is the practical application of basic knowledge to a variety of products and devices. However, only a small fraction of the Federal funds is being used to stimulate and support the vital basic research which makes possible our practical scientific progress. I believe strongly that this Nation must extend its support of research in basic science.

While the Executive Order which I have signed today calls upon the National Science Foundation to carry out important responsibilities in regard to scientific research, it is also designed to strengthen the conduct and support of vital research and development in the several agencies where science is important in achieving their assigned missions.

This order will, for the first time, set in motion important steps leading to a thorough and continuing review of the status of the Federal Government's activities in science, and thus enable the Government, together with industry, higher education, and the scientific community to move forward with assurance toward the achievement of the Nation's goals.

I expect and believe that this order will clarify the position of the Government toward the support and advancement of science in the Nation, and that it will contribute in a constructive sense to the development of our national policy in this important and critical area.

NOTE: Executive Order 10521, "Administration of Scientific Research by Agencies of the Federal Government," is published in title 3 of the Code of Federal Regulations, 1954 Supplement, p. 49.

61 ¶ Citation Accompanying Medal of Honor Presented to Ola L. Mize. *March* 18, 1954

THE PRESIDENT of the United States of America, authorized by Act of Congress March 3, 1863 has awarded in the name of The Congress the Medal of Honor to

SERGEANT FIRST CLASS (THEN SERGEANT)

OLA L. MIZE, USA

for conspicuous gallantry and intrepidity at the risk of his life above and beyond the call of duty in action with the enemy:

Sergeant Mize, Infantry, United States Army, a member of Company

K, 15th Infantry Regiment, 3d Infantry Division, distinguished himself by conspicuous gallantry and outstanding courage above and beyond the call of duty in action against the enemy near Surang-ni, Korea, on 10–11 June 1953.   Company K was defending "Outpost Harry," a strategically valuable position, when the enemy launched a heavy attack.   Learning that a wounded comrade lay helpless at a friendly listening post, Sergeant Mize with a medical aid man moved through intense enemy fire and rescued him.   On returning to his position Sergeant Mize organized an effective defense and inflicted heavy casualties against the continuously and fiercely attacking enemy.   During this period he was knocked down three times by the concussion of artillery and grenade blasts but each time he dauntlessly arose and resumed the violent combat.   When enemy onslaughts ceased temporarily with the enemy in possession of friendly emplacements in the outpost area, he led his few remaining men from bunker to bunker, firing into the apertures, throwing grenades at the entrenched foe, and effectively neutralizing their positions.   When an enemy soldier suddenly stepped from cover prepared to fire at one of Sergeant Mize's men, Sergeant Mize killed him saving the life of his fellow-soldier.   After rejoining the platoon, he observed that a friendly machine gun had been overrun.   Unhesitatingly, he fought his way to the position, single-handedly killing ten of the enemy and dispersing the remainder.   Fighting his way back to his command post he took a position to protect several wounded soldiers.   Later, securing a radio, he directed friendly artillery fire upon the attacking enemy's routes of approach and at dawn he helped regroup for a counterattack which drove the enemy from the outpost.   Sergeant Mize's valorous conduct and unflinching courage reflect lasting glory upon himself and uphold the noble traditions of the military service.

Dwight D. Eisenhower

NOTE: The President presented the medal to Sergeant Mize at Lowry Air Force Base at 11:30 a.m. on September 7, 1954, in the presence of relatives and friends.

62 ¶ Statement by the President Upon Approving Recommendations for the Development of the Upper Colorado River Basin. *March 20, 1954*

I HAVE TODAY approved recommendations for the development of the Upper Colorado River Basin.

The general plan upon which these recommendations are based has been prepared by the Secretary of the Interior. The Secretary's recommendations have been reviewed by the Bureau of the Budget. Legislation embodying the Administration's recommendations is being prepared for introduction in the Congress.

This is a comprehensive, well-planned development of a river basin. The close Federal-State cooperation upon which the Secretary's plan is based also carries out this Administration's approach to water resource development.

The development will conserve water, enabling the region to increase supplies for municipal uses, industrial development, and irrigation. It will develop much-needed electric power.

The development calls for sound financing. The legislation now being drafted will set up a fund for the entire project so that it will be constructed and paid for as a basin program.

Construction of the Echo Park and Glen Canyon dams, two of the large projects in the basin plan, is recommended. These dams are key units strategically located to provide the necessary storage of water to make the plan work at its maximum efficiency.

The legislation being drafted will authorize a number of projects which will put to use the waters of the Upper Colorado. This authorization will become effective following further consideration by the Secretary of the Interior, with the assistance of the Secretary of Agriculture, of the relation of these projects to the wise use and sound development of the basin.

I am deferring my recommendation on the Shiprock unit of the Navajo project until the Secretary has completed his study.

I hope the Congress will give early consideration to enactment of the Administration's legislative proposal. I firmly believe development of the Upper Colorado River Basin, in accordance with its provisions, is in the national interest.

NOTE: The recommendations approved by the President, together with related papers, are printed in Senate Report 1983 (83d Cong., 2d sess.).

63 ¶ The President's News Conference of *March* 24, 1954.

THE PRESIDENT. I have nothing of my own this morning, and we will go right to questions.

Q. Merriman Smith, United Press: Mr. President, the Republican leadership has said that Senator McCarthy should not participate in an investigation in which he is involved; yet the Senator insists on the right of cross-examination in an investigation of the dispute between his committee and the Army. What are your feelings, sir, in this matter?

THE PRESIDENT. Well, I have no feelings at all about a particular situation or technicality of which I know nothing.

I am perfectly ready to put myself on record flatly, as I have before, that in America, if a man is a party to a dispute, directly or indirectly, he does not sit in judgment on his own case, and I don't believe that any leadership can escape responsibility for carrying on that tradition and that practice.

Q. Richard Harkness, NBC Radio: May we quote you on that?

THE PRESIDENT. No. You have the regular—I don't mind. You can go and see Mr. Hagerty as usual on that particular point; but if every time I say something I am to be quoted, why, I will come over here with written answers.

Q. Merriman Smith, United Press: Mr. President, can we have Mr. Romagna [official reporter] read back the last part of your reply—some of us missed it—without asking for a direct quotation?

THE PRESIDENT. OK.

Q. S. Douglass Cater, Jr., The Reporter Magazine: Mr. President, last year you urged passage of the Refugee Relief Act, but to date only a handful of people have been admitted under that. Do you have any knowledge as to whether the difficulty lies in the legislation, or the administration, or where it does lie?

THE PRESIDENT. Well, I haven't any late and detailed report on it.

What I do have is a statement that they have had great difficulty in trying to streamline procedures in accordance with the prescriptions of the act itself, as passed, and to get the thing rolling.

It has been reported to me they are striving to do so. I would hope that this logjam loosens up very shortly. I will look it up again.

Q. John Herling, Editors Syndicate: I believe in your press conference of February 17th, in reply to a question on the economic situation, you referred to March as being sort of the key month as to action by the Government in regard to rising unemployment, and if unemployment continued to rise at that time then action other than has been pursued would be called for. Now, unemployment has risen, sir, and I wonder whether there is an administration policy that has been projected at this time?

THE PRESIDENT. I don't recall the exact words. I implied and indicated that March would normally be a rather significant month, that is, a month when normally, seasonally, there is an upturn. I don't believe I said that instantly there would be programs set, I said there would be a new examination of the problem and it would cause real concern.

It is difficult to talk about this question without taking a little bit more time than just a "yes" or "no," ladies and gentlemen.

Coming out of a war economy, going back into a peacetime economy, has traditionally caused, in every country, very, very marked fluctuations, sometimes marked by great inflation, lowered productivity, all that sort of thing.

What has been the task that has really been going on for quite a while, but especially since last July, has been trying to make this transition, with a cutback on all kinds of war production, ammunition and everything else being used in Korea, in such a way as to cause the least damage.

There has been, of course, a continuous rise in unemployment since that time. The figures for March are, of course, not all in, and they won't be in until sometime in early April.

A contributing cause here, they tell me, although I am not so sure of the effect of this one, is that Easter being late, the ladies have not been buying as rapidly as they normally do this time of year and all kinds of qualifying conditions enter into this thing.

The only thing that I am sure of, up to this moment—we study this every single day of our lives, there is a conference in my office on this subject every single day—there is nothing that has developed that would call for a slambang emergency program being applied at this moment. That doesn't mean that we are not watching everything.

Many things have been done. There is easier credit, there is cheaper money, there are things of that kind; there are housing and building programs before the Congress which should be helpful.

There is every kind of thing constantly under consideration that we can think of that would be helpful. But we just don't believe this is the time to move on an emergency basis; because if we do, we could easily distort the picture very badly.

Q. Daniel S. Schorr, Columbia Broadcasting System: Mr. President, are you satisfied with the progress of your legislative program through Congress?

THE PRESIDENT. I think there have been several times when we have discussed exactly what this word "satisfied" means.

I truly believe that the rounded program sent to Congress represents a crying need in the United States. I believe it will insure its progress; I believe it will insure an upturn in the economy; I believe it will insure greater prosperity and happiness for all of us; distribution of inescapable burdens and a stronger America, which is, after all, the ultimate goal.

Now, the longer we put that off, to my mind, the more we are failing to take advantage of our opportunities to do what we should.

Q. William P. Flythe, Jr., Hearst Newspapers: Would you care to say anything, sir, about the conference at Geneva with reference to Indochina and Communist China? That is a large order.

THE PRESIDENT. Of course, you are asking a question that we can take the rest of the time on. I would say only a very few things.

One, I don't believe that it is necessary to argue the importance of all this great southeast Asian area and the southwest Pacific, its importance to the United States and to the free world. Indonesia, our friends in Burma and Siam and Malaya, the Philippines, all in that region, it is of the most transcendent importance.

This fighting going on in Indochina, no matter how it started, has very manifestly become again one of the battlegrounds of people that want to live their own lives against this encroachment of Communist aggression; that is what it is.

With respect to Communist China, at this moment, in the forthcoming conference, I haven't much to say. I have expressed certain of the reasons why we took the attitude that we do toward Red China, and until those conditions have changed, there is no change in our attitude or our situation.

Q. Pat Monroe, Salt Lake City Deseret News: Mr. President, on December 8, before the U.N., in your Operation Candid Speech, you said that the free people of the world must be armed with the significant facts, that is, atomic facts, of today's existence, and yet a lot of us have found what has been called the uranium curtain of secrecy at the Atomic Energy Commission closing ever tighter.

My specific question concerns the possible resumption of press conferences there at the Atomic Energy Commission, if and when.

THE PRESIDENT. Well, I will tell you, I wouldn't give you a positive answer that that is a good thing to do.

I do believe this, that entering the atomic age, you people have legitimate questions—and all America and possibly the world—affecting this whole development. You have a right to ask them at places, specifically to me or the White House or other places, when information can be given without definitely jeopardizing the security of the United States.

I shall try, after Admiral Strauss comes back from the Pacific, to review this whole question with him again and determine, if we can, what is the scope or the limits of the things of which I can talk. I promised this last week, not realizing, I guess, at that moment that he was a long ways from my side. I want to put off any further discussion until he comes back.

Q. Mrs. May Craig, Maine Newspapers: Mr. President, in relation to that, my question to you last week was aimed at clarifying your position on the emphasis to be put on bombers based in the United States rather than depend on overseas bases which might or might not be available to us in war.

THE PRESIDENT. Now, Mrs. Craig, you are talking about something that I won't talk about. I am not going to say what I consider, except I do consider myself a military man in that respect, and my lifetime was spent in it. I am not going to try to give an evaluation of the one kind of a base as against another at this moment. I don't think it would be wise at all.

Q. Ethel Payne, Defender Publications: Mr. President, since you have said that you are in favor of using Federal authority, where it is proper to do so, in the program of ending racial discrimination, will you urge the Congress to act favorably on S. 262, the bill to prohibit segregation in interstate travel?

THE PRESIDENT. I will take a look. I haven't heard of the bill; I will take a look, because I am not sure. I would have to consult the Attorney General and see what he says about our authority there.

Q. Joseph C. Harsch, Christian Science Monitor: Mr. President, would you give us a soldier's appreciation of the battle at Dien Bien Phu?

THE PRESIDENT. Well, it is extremely difficult unless you are on the spot.

I have talked to a number of people. Frankly, the odds that are just given in numbers, the comparative odds, the attacker against the defender—if you had a well-chosen defensive position, I would say the odds were all in favor of the defender.

Now, I suppose most of you have looked at the map, and you know this position is in the valley astride a river; that it is not too long. With some 21 battalions, I believe it is, they are trying to defend a position that is completely dominated by the observation that the attackers have on the two ridges, the ridges on the side of the river. So that makes it anything but pleasant.

Some of you here were unquestionably at Anzio—that was after I left Italy, but I have gone back to that battleground—and there all the Allied Forces were in an almost impossible position.

They were lying on the plain, and the enemy had all of the observation positions to place all the artillery where they wanted to, and it is a terrible thing on morale.

So, I think one of the things, one of the intangibles, that you would have to be present to evaluate is what is the effect of this continuing situation where they are getting shot at all the time and don't believe they are shooting back effectually; what is that effect on morale?

Now, there is no need to tell you people that followed battles in the war, morale is everything. So long as a unit thinks it can win, it can win; but, of course, many things go into making it up.

I would say right now, as I see it, there is no reason for good troops to despair of coming out of the thing all right. Now, it is not an easy one.

By the way, I asked one specific question you might be interested in. I find there is a colonel commanding the unit, and he was put there because apparently he is a very brilliant commander. I said, "Well, if

I were the commander in the field, and I had a colonel commanding that thing, he would have been a general the day before yesterday." [*Laughter*] In any event, there is apparently a very brilliant, fine, young soldier commanding the place, and doing a gallant job, and they did promise to put my remark on his record after it came out.

Q. Nat S. Finney, Buffalo Evening News: Mr. President, there has been a good deal of complaint about the statistics of unemployment, complaint about confusion in the two series. Do you have any plans to do anything about that?

THE PRESIDENT. Well, they are doing something about it. They have a group that is checking every single new installment of statistics to try to figure out what these things mean, and are going to adopt the one that is the most accurate—I think that is the broader one. But to get adjustment between the two, it is going on right along.

I think it is unfortunate that the thing happened to be put into effect when we did have a rise, and when we are also rightfully concerned with rising unemployment and, therefore, it puts an element of confusion in the thing that wouldn't normally be there. But they are working as hard as they can to get it straightened out and to produce the honest facts, that I assure you. No one is trying to be clever about this, but to get the straightforward facts.

Q. Frank van der Linden, Nashville Banner: Mr. President, a week ago you had a conference here with Mr. Harry Carbaugh of Chattanooga, and he came out later and said you discussed the possibility of making him the Chairman of TVA. A statement came through Mr. Hagerty's office, said he could not serve the full time; and some of the Democrats in the Senate have said that that indicates maybe he won't get the job, that it is a face-saver, they say. I wonder if you have a comment on that?

THE PRESIDENT. Face-saver?

Q. Mr. van der Linden: Yes. They say that he was just being given a nice welcome treatment here, and that he will be brushed off—that is the Democrat view on it.

THE PRESIDENT. I think that they flatly said that I had no decision to announce because I had reached none, and that is the absolute truth.

Now, the other two items that you heard, so far as I know, are also the absolute truth.

Q. Donald R. Larrabee, New Bedford Standard-Times: Mr. President, there has been criticism in some quarters of the fact that this administration has retained a 1948 Presidential directive which denies loyalty and security data to congressional committees. I would like to ask you if you would care to comment on the charge that this has hampered the work of congressional committees, and should be revoked or revised?

THE PRESIDENT. You start off with a statement of which I am not presently informed.

There are certain types of files that will never be released by the executive departments. The FBI files are inviolate, and are going to remain so as long as I am here.

Now, if there are other kinds of files—they tell me they do forward certain summaries and factual information, as long as it is fact; I don't know exactly how it is done—it is a question you might look up and provide the answer for, Mr. Hagerty. I don't know enough about it to talk about it further.

Q. Paul Scott Rankine, Reuters-Australian Associated Press: Mr. President, there have been some expressions of concern overseas that your policy of instant retaliation against aggression, that it might not involve consultation between the United States and its allies, either in advance of or during the kind of emergency which you discussed with us last week. I wondered if you could clarify the situation?

THE PRESIDENT. Well, I explained to you last week one type of emergency in which a commander in chief would have no recourse, and that was when you were directly under the kind of thing, in a glorified way, that happened at Pearl Harbor. But I believe that the Prime Minister answered one part of your question very accurately, yesterday, when he said we had all the arrangements for instant consultation that could possibly be made and, particularly, with respect to any use of the bases there. With other of our friends in the North Atlantic Alliance, particularly those we work very close with—Canada, for example—we are always in consultation.

Q. Charles J. Greene, Jr., New York Daily News: Returning, sir, to your first question about a man sitting in judgment upon himself, McCarthy is insisting as late as yesterday afternoon, that he no longer wishes to sit in judgment, that he has withdrawn from any voting on the committee, that all he wants and must have is the right to cross-examine the witnesses.　Will you comment on that?

THE PRESIDENT. No.　Many times, I told you, I don't know enough about the specific case to comment, even if I should.　There are certain things that the leadership and the people down there cannot escape responsibility for, and I am not going to try to prejudice the case by commenting on details of which I know nothing.　I state my principle on which I stand.

Q. Marvin Arrowsmith, Associated Press: We have been asked whether you care to comment on the Senate rejection yesterday of the resolution to unseat Senator Chavez.　It was turned down, as you probably saw.

THE PRESIDENT. I have no comment whatsoever.　I would say again you are talking about something that certainly is strictly the Senate's business.

Q. Sarah McClendon, Galveston News-Tribune: Sir, you have been asked, I believe, to keep the Texas City tin smelter open.　That request was made by Senator Johnson and Congressman Thompson; and in view of the situation in Indochina, I wonder if you have made up your mind to reverse the budget and keep it open?

THE PRESIDENT. No, I haven't made up my mind about it.　As a matter of fact, the question has been reopened for study, but I have not made up my mind to keep it open.

Q. George E. Herman, CBS Radio: Mr. Hagerty told us yesterday that you would not be commenting on the atomic energy test, but I wanted to ask you a question on the fringe, if you have no objection. Some anti-American newspapers in Japan and other countries in the Far East, have been seizing upon these cases of radioactive poisoning to make some very strong anti-American propaganda.　I wonder if you would care to give us some statement of policy of the Government of its responsibility towards the rest of the world in these tests?

THE PRESIDENT. It is quite clear that this time something must have happened that we have never experienced before, and must have surprised and astonished the scientists.　Very properly, the United States has to take precautions that never occurred to them before.

Now, in the meantime, I know nothing about the details of this case. It is one of the things that Admiral Strauss is looking up, but it has been reported to me that the reports were far more serious than the actual results justified.

Q. Robert G. Spivack, New York Post: Mr. President, there have been stories in papers around the country by various Republican leaders expressing the hope that you will actively take part in the 1954 congressional campaign, and that you will be visiting their communities or making a speaking tour. Have you any thoughts on that?

THE PRESIDENT. I have expressed my thoughts before this body time and again, and I am sure that there is no one here that is really mistaken about what I mean and what I have said. If there is, you can bring the question up next week.

Q. Alan S. Emory, Watertown Daily Times: Mr. President, this week the House Rules Committee, after beginning action on the St. Lawrence Seaway project, decided to postpone until April first additional hearings and, possibly, a vote. This action was taken with the presence before the committee of both the leading proponents and opponents of the project from the House Public Works Committee, and the postponement has resulted in some charges of stalling even by your own backers who consider this a major part of the administration program. I wonder, sir, if you intend to ask the House leadership to expedite action on the Seaway?

THE PRESIDENT. So far as I know, they have got it scheduled for its place in their program, and I am not going to ask them to upset a whole program of work.

Frankly, I think the House has been doing an awfully good job. No one has asked me about it, but if you would like to ask my opinion about the tax fight the other day, why, I would say I think they did a magnificent job. They did it for the good of the country and, I would say, with a minimum of concern for their own particular welfare or ambitions.

They did it because they thought it was a fine program. Of course, we had some few, thank goodness, Democrats who felt the same way about it; but I think the House has been doing a fine job. I can certainly ask when they expect this to come out, but I have the minimum of criticism for the group.

Q. David Sentner, Hearst Newspapers: Mr. President, in your promise to review the atomic weapons public relations problem, will that include the possibility of having members of the press invited to any future hydrogen bomb test?

THE PRESIDENT. Well, I will ask. I hadn't thought of it. I think rather than comment on it right now, I will take it up, I will say that. So the discussions will include that.

Q. Carroll H. Kenworthy, United Press: Mr. President, when you were talking about the French Colonel at Dien Bien Phu a few minutes ago, did you say you recommended that to the French General who saw you the other day?

THE PRESIDENT. Well, I said I recommended it; I don't know whether I recommended it to——

Q. Mr. Kenworthy: You spoke to the French General?

THE PRESIDENT. I said I thought it would be a good thing to do.

Q. Mr. Kenworthy: And you told it to the Frenchman?

THE PRESIDENT. I told it to a Frenchman who promised it would be put on his record.

Q. Ray L. Scherer, NBC Radio: General MacArthur said the other day you called him down here to get his views on certain subjects. Could you tell us any more about that visit with the General?

THE PRESIDENT. Well, I didn't see General MacArthur's statement afterward, but he and I have been very closely associated since 1930, and I have never found any talk with him profitless. We talked about the general conditions in the Far East, where he spent so many years of his life.

We talked over general situations, implications of various things that we saw in our reports, and it was not intended to reach definitive conclusions or plans or anything else. It was merely an exchange of views from an old friend; that is what it was.

Q. Lloyd Schwartz, Fairchild Publications: Mr. President, a Supreme Court decision recently appears to have knocked out about sixteen of these State right-to-work laws which provide for use of injunction against picketing and boycotts and the like. I wanted to ask, have you definitely abandoned any plan to send up a message on this to Congress to correct this?

THE PRESIDENT. There has been no definite decision on it. As a matter of fact, I didn't know about the Supreme Court decision you are speaking of this morning.

Q. Robert J. Donovan, New York Herald Tribune: Sir, your compliment to the House naturally begs the question on a certain other branch on Capitol Hill. [*Laughter*]

THE PRESIDENT. Then I am glad you brought it up; I would like to make it clear. After all, all of us know that the rules of the Senate differ from those of the House; possibly because the House is such a large body, they have to have firmer disciplinary control.

But in any event, let us remember this also, that all revenue bills have to start in the House. There the extensive hearings are held, which often helps to shortcut the work in the other House.

I was asked a question about the House Rules Committee, I wasn't asked about the Senate. Now, they have to have a little more time, as we all know.

Q. Joseph Chiang, Chinese News Service: Mr. President, Generalissimo Chiang Kai-shek once again was elected by the people, the free people, of China as President of the Republic of China. Do you have any comment to that, sir?

THE PRESIDENT. Well, I don't think I have any comments. As you know, I know the Generalissimo, and I like him.

When I go there, or when I have been out in that region, I like to see him; but I don't know anything at all about what I should say or what comment you would expect from me now. I really don't.

Merriman Smith, United Press: Thank you, Mr. President.

NOTE: President Eisenhower's thirty-second news conference was held in the Executive Office Building from 10:31 to 10:58 o'clock on Wednesday morning, March 24, 1954. In attendance: 212.

64 ¶ Statement by the President Upon Signing Bill To Amend the Natural Gas Act. *March* 27, 1954

I HAVE TODAY approved H.R. 5976, a bill "To amend section 1 of the Natural Gas Act."

This measure preserves the authority of the Federal Power Commission to regulate the rates which may be charged for natural gas moving in interstate commerce up to the time it reaches the State in which it will be wholly consumed. At the same time the bill makes it possible to remove from Federal regulation persons and facilities receiving gas within or at the boundary of a State if all of the natural gas so received is to be used within that State.   The bill contains a Congressional declaration that these matters are primarily of local concern and subject to regulation by the several States.   The removal is operative only if the States exercise and enforce jurisdiction over rates and services.

I have approved this bill because of my conviction that the interests of the individual citizen will be better protected when they remain under State and local control than when they are regulated or controlled by the Federal Government.   I shall support State regulation of functions and matters which are primarily of local concern whenever possible and when not contrary to the national interest.

The State regulation provided in H.R. 5976 presents a new challenge to the State governments and their regulatory commissions.   This measure places the responsibility for protection of consumer interests for intra-state matters squarely where it belongs—in the hands of the people of the States and their duly elected or appointed officials.   I believe effective and competent discharge of that responsibility will result.

If experience should demonstrate that the Act creates a larger area of regulation by the States than they will be able to handle effectively in the public interest, I shall promptly recommend that the Congress take whatever remedial action appears to be necessary.

NOTE: As enacted, H.R. 5976 is Public Law 323, 83d Congress (68 Stat. 36).

65   ¶ Letter Accepting Resignation of Joseph M. Dodge as Director of the Bureau of the Budget. *March 27, 1954*

[Released March 27, 1954. Dated March 2, 1954]

Dear Joe:

I must, of course, respect your wish to leave governmental service after so many years devoted to it.   I cannot in conscience ask you to reconsider in view of the reasons you give for your decision.   But I assure you that it is only with the greatest reluctance that I accept your resignation as Director of the Bureau of the Budget.

Your services during these past fourteen months in office have been invaluable to the country.   Your competence and knowledge in an exceedingly difficult field have immeasurably helped solve the gigantic fiscal and management problems that have faced this Administration. On the more personal side, I shall sorely miss your advice, counsel and your friendly helpfulness. In fact, I have every intention of imposing upon you from time to time to give me your thoughts and opinions on some of the knotty questions that will continue to arise.

In thinking back over the governmental positions you have been called to fill since the beginning of World War II, I am struck by the fact that not only has each been an important one but most of the assignments have been almost on an emergency basis. In each your reputation for efficiency and dedication to the public good has continued to grow. As a consequence, you will leave behind you in the government service a host of admiring friends; I know that each of them would join me now in wishing for you the greatest of happiness and success in the years to come.

With warm personal regard,

As ever,

DWIGHT D. EISENHOWER

NOTE: In his letter of resignation Mr. Dodge referred to his work in revising the original 1954 budget and to his intention, known to the President, of resigning soon after the 1955 budget was presented to the Congress. His letter was released with the President's reply.

66 ¶ Statement by the President on the Ratification by Germany of Treaties Relating to the Proposed European Defense Community. *March* 29, 1954

PRESIDENT HEUSS of the Federal Republic of Germany has signed the treaty establishing the European Defense Community and the Convention on Relations with the Federal Republic, thus completing final ratification of these treaties by the Federal Republic.

I am gratified that one more country has now completed all phases of ratification of these treaties which are designed to assure a stronger European community and thereby contribute to the establishment of lasting peace.

67   ¶ Special Message to the Congress on Foreign Economic Policy.   *March* 30, 1954

To the Congress of the United States:

I submit herewith for the consideration of the Congress recommendations concerning the foreign economic policy of the United States.

Due to the urgency and significance of our problems in this area, I previously recommended, and the Congress approved, the establishment of the Commission on Foreign Economic Policy. Its membership, consisting of seventeen elected officials and private citizens, was drawn from all parts of the country and represented diverse points of view. The Commission's report, prepared in the American tradition of full debate and vigorous dissent, has been carefully reviewed by the various Executive Departments of the Government and forms the basis for the program I submit in this message.

Before the Commission began its deliberations I said to its members, "I commend to you an attitude both realistic and bold. Above all, I urge you to follow one guiding principle: What is best in the national interest."

The national interest in the field of foreign economic policy is clear. It is to obtain, in a manner that is consistent with our national security and profitable and equitable for all, the highest possible level of trade and the most efficient use of capital and resources. That this would also strengthen our military allies adds urgency. Their strength is of critical importance to the security of our country.

Great mutual advantages to buyer and seller, to producer and consumer, to investor and to the community where investment is made, accrue from high levels of trade and investment. They accrue no less in trade from nation to nation than in trade from community to community within a single country. The internal strength of the American economy has evolved from such a system of mutual advantage.

In the press of other problems and in the haste to meet emergencies, this nation—and many other nations of the free world—have all too often lost sight of this central fact. World-wide depression and wars, inflation and resultant economic dislocations, have left a sorry heritage: a patchwork of temporary expedients and a host of restrictions, rigidities, interferences and barriers which seriously inhibit the expansion of international trade. Thus are impeded the very forces which make for increased production, employment and incomes.

The tasks of repairing the physical damage caused by the catastrophe of war have been substantially achieved. The creation of an adequate system of defense for the free world is well advanced. Most of the countries which suffered the ravages of war have made remarkable headway towards financial stability and increased production. Their own efforts have been greatly aided by our assistance, and yet, despite this recovery, we and other free nations are still severely limited by the persistence of uneconomic, man-made barriers to mutual trade and the flow of funds among us.

Together we and our friends abroad must work at the task of lowering the unjustifiable barriers—not all at once but gradually and with full regard for our own interests. In this effort, the United States must take the initiative and, in doing so, make clear to the rest of the world that we expect them to follow our lead.

Many foreign restrictions have been imposed as a consequence of the so-called "dollar gap." This phrase has become the symbol of the failure of the free world to find a lasting solution to the imbalance of international payments. We should no longer fill it by major grants to enable other nations to secure what they need but cannot buy. Our aim must not be to fill the dollar gap, but rather to help close it. Our best interest dictates that the dollar gap be closed by raising the level of trade and investment.

The United States stands ready and able to produce and sell more than the rest of the world can buy from us. The inability of many foreign countries to buy our goods in the volume we would like to sell does not arise from any lack of desire for these goods. Such is far from the case. Instead it arises out of an inability of these nations to pay—in dollars— for the volume we have to sell.

Dollar grants are no lasting solution to this impasse.

The solution is a higher level of two-way trade. Thus we can sell and receive payment for our exports and have an increasing volume of investment abroad to assist economic development overseas and yield returns to us. Greater freedom from restrictions and controls and the increased efficiencies which arise from expanding markets and the freer play of economic forces are essential to the attainment of this higher trade level.

Failure so to move will directly threaten our domestic economy, for it will doom our efforts to find ways by which others, through their own efforts, can buy our goods. The only practicable alternative is to reduce exports. Our farms would have to sell less, since the products of 40 million acres, amounting to 10 to 12 percent of our agriculture, would have to find their market outside our own country. Moreover, if their export markets were curtailed, American factories now selling their products throughout the world would have to reduce employment. It is a very important fact that over 4 million American workers depend on international trade for their employment.

Beyond our economic interest, the solidarity of the free world and the capacity of the free world to deal with those who would destroy it are threatened by continued unbalanced trade relationships—the inability of nations to sell as much as they desire to buy. By moving boldly to correct the present imbalance, we shall support and increase the level of our exports of both manufactured and agricultural products. We shall, at the same time, increase the economic strength of our allies. Thus shall we enhance our own military security by strengthening our friends abroad. Thus shall we assure those sources of imports that supplement our domestic production and are vital to our defense. Thus shall we raise our standard of living and aid in the development of a better world for all of us and our children.

TARIFFS

I am convinced that the gradual and selective revision of our tariffs, through the tested method of negotiation with other nations, is an essential ingredient of the continuing growth of our domestic economy. An expression of our willingness to negotiate further will offer needed leadership towards the reduction of trade and payments barriers that limit markets for our goods throughout the world.

The Commission on Foreign Economic Policy recommended a three-year extension of the Trade Agreements Act with amendments to authorize:

a. Reduction, pursuant to trade agreement negotiation, of existing tariff rates on commodities selected for such negotiations by not more than 5 percent of present rates in each of the three years of the new act;

b. Reduction, by not more than one-half over a three-year period, of tariffs in effect on January 1, 1945, on products which are not being imported or which are being imported only in negligible volume; and

c. Reduction, over a three-year period, pursuant to trade agreement negotiation, to 50 percent ad valorem, or its equivalent, of any rate in excess of 50 percent ad valorem, or its equivalent.

I have approved these recommendations of the Commission and urge their adoption by the Congress. I may also recommend special provisions for negotiation with Japan in view of the economic problems of that country.

The foregoing authority does not contemplate across-the-board tariff reductions. The peril point and escape clause procedures would, of course, be preserved, and the three proposed types of rate reduction would not be cumulative. Tariff reductions would be made selectively on specific commodities, and only after notice and hearings in accordance with past practice. This would represent our part in the gradual and careful approach to the whole problem of improved trade which the world so urgently needs. No sudden, sharp, or widespread adjustments within our economy would be involved.

These escape clause and peril point provisions of our tariff legislation are designed to mitigate injury to our domestic producers from tariff reductions. Whenever recourse is had to these provisions, I shall carefully consider the findings and recommendations of the Tariff Commission. My responsibilities for the welfare of the nation require that I continue to base my decisions at times on broader grounds than the Tariff Commission is empowered to consider. The Commission on Foreign Economic Policy supports this position.

I have approved the Commission's recommendations that the United States withhold reductions in tariffs on products made by workers receiving wages which are substandard in the exporting country. This policy shall be placed in effect. I have also approved the Commission's recommendations concerning raising of labor standards through consultative procedures and cooperation in international conferences such as those sponsored by the International Labor Organization.

These recommendations for renewal and amendment of the Trade Agreements Act are based on the plain truth that if we wish to sell abroad we must buy abroad.

THE GENERAL AGREEMENT ON TARIFFS AND TRADE

Since 1948, virtually all the major trading nations of the world, including the United States, have become parties to a General Agreement on Tariffs and Trade. This Agreement has been the principal arrangement by which we in the United States have sought to carry out the provisions and purposes of the Trade Agreements Act.

The Commission on Foreign Economic Policy has recommended that the United States renegotiate the organizational provisions of the Agreement, so that the contracting parties acting collectively would confine their functions to sponsoring multilateral trade negotiations, recommending broad trade policies for individual consideration by the legislative or other appropriate authorities in the various countries, and providing a forum for consultation regarding trade disputes.

I shall act promptly upon this recommendation. At the same time, I shall suggest to other contracting parties revisions of the substantive provisions of the Agreement to provide a simpler, stronger instrument contributing more effectively to the development of a workable system of world trade. When the organizational provisions of the Agreement have been renegotiated, they will be submitted to the Congress for its approval.

CUSTOMS ADMINISTRATION AND PROCEDURE

The problems of tariff classification, of proper valuation of imported articles and of procedures for administering the customs are complex and perplexing. Over the years these problems have grown to the point where they now constitute an unwarranted and unintended burden on trade.

The United States may be no worse in this regard than many other nations, but good business practice alone is sufficient to require:

a. Simplification of commodity definitions, classifications and rate structure;

b. Improvement in the methods of valuation of imports; and

c. Establishment of more efficient procedures for customs administration.

To this end I shall propose legislation providing for the simplification of the commodity definitions and rate structures in the Tariff Act, after a study by the Tariff Commission, and subject to appropriate standards to be established by the Congress. Such legislation should also provide

356

for a better method of classification of articles not enumerated in the tariff schedules, and for such improvement in the statutes governing the administration of customs procedures as can be made at this time. In this connection I am directing the Department of the Treasury to keep customs procedures under continuous review and to report to the Congress annually on the difficulties and delays in processing goods through Customs, together with recommendations for action to eliminate such obstructions. I further recommend that the anti-dumping law and procedures under it be changed so far as necessary to permit speedier and more efficient disposal of cases and to prevent undue interference with trade during investigation of suspected dumping.

To provide an improved basis for customs valuations I urge adoption of the Treasury's valuation proposals. These are embodied in H.R. 6584 which has already been passed by the House of Representatives.

U.S. INVESTMENT ABROAD

An increased flow of United States investment abroad could contribute significantly to the needed expansion of international trade. It also could help maintain a high level of economic activity and employment in the United States. Further, such investment contributes to the development abroad of primary resources needed to meet our own ever-increasing needs even while it helps to strengthen the economies of foreign countries. In view of the great importance of private investment to our foreign economic policy, I emphasize the necessity for passage of the Administration tax bill already recommended to you and already advanced in your considerations which provides for:

a. Taxation of business income from foreign subsidiaries or from segregated foreign branches which operate and elect to be taxed as subsidiaries at a rate 14 percentage points lower than the regular corporate rate;

b. Broadening the definition of foreign taxes which may be credited against the United States income tax to include any tax, which is the principal form of taxation on business in a country, except turnover, general sales taxes or excise, and social security taxes;

c. Removing of the overall limitation on foreign tax credits; and

d. Permitting regulated investment companies concentrating on foreign investment to pass on to their stockholders the credit for foreign taxes which would be available on direct investment.

Further to encourage the flow of private investment abroad, we shall give full diplomatic support, through our activities here and through our missions and representatives in the field, to the acceptance and understanding by other nations of the prerequisites for the attraction of private foreign investment. We shall continue to use the treaty approach to establish common rules for the fair treatment of foreign investment.

In connection with legislation authorizing the Mutual Security Program I suggest that the Congress consider the desirability of broadening the existing authority to guarantee against losses on new investment abroad, so as to cover losses caused by war, revolution and insurrection.

The Commission has pointed out that uncertainty as to the application of United States antitrust laws to the operations of American firms abroad is a deterrent to foreign investment. It recommended that our antitrust laws be restated in a manner which would clearly acknowledge the right of each country to regulate trade within its own borders. At the same time, the Commission insisted that it should be made clear that foreign laws or established business practices which encourage restrictive price, production or marketing arrangements will limit the willingness of United States businessmen to invest abroad and will reduce the benefits of such investment to the economies of the host countries.

I have requested the Department of Justice to consider this recommendation in connection with its current study of the antitrust laws.

BUY AMERICAN LEGISLATION

At present certain of our laws require that, in specified Federal or Federally-financed procurement, preference be given to domestic firms over foreign bidders. Except where considerations of national security, persistent and substantial unemployment, or encouragement of small business require otherwise, I agree with the Commission that it is improper policy, unbusinesslike procedure and unfair to the taxpayer for the Government to pay a premium on its purchases.

I request, therefore, that legislative authority be provided to exempt from the provisions of this legislation the bidders from nations that treat our bidders on an equal basis with their own nationals. Meanwhile, the Executive Branch is clarifying the application of these preference principles to government procurement. It will limit the price differential favoring domestic producers over foreign bidders to a reasonable percent dependent upon the circumstances over and above whatever tariffs may apply. Discretionary authority, however, must be continued to permit special consideration in government procurement for the requirements of national security, for the problems of small business and of areas where persistent and substantial unemployment exists.

RAW MATERIALS

This country is blessed with abundant mineral resources, but we must make the most of them if we are to satisfy the ever-increasing appetite of an expanding economy and at the same time maintain an adequate defense posture. We must recognize, however, that it is not possible for this nation, or any other nation, to produce enough of every metal and mineral needed by modern industry. These materials are not evenly distributed throughout the world. We have to depend on one another. Our foreign economic policies, therefore, must encourage the relatively easy flow of these materials in international trade.

The Commission has made two sets of recommendations which I believe will materially assist in achieving an orderly expansion of mineral production both here and abroad.

The first is that the United States Government should make a constructive contribution toward greater stability of world prices of raw materials by moderating or relaxing impediments to international trade, by encouraging diversification of foreign economies, by avoiding procurement practices which disturb world prices, by consultation with other nations, and by tempering the fluctuations in our own economy.

The second calls for increased encouragement of investment in overseas production by our citizens and the nationals of other countries.

I heartily endorse these recommendations.

The Commission also recommended that domestic sources for raw materials required for military purposes should be assured by direct means and not by tariffs and import quotas. I believe that normally this is sound.

However, I have appointed a special Cabinet committee which is now surveying the whole field of our minerals policy and have drawn their attention to these recommendations.

AGRICULTURE

Perhaps no sector of our economy has a greater stake in foreign trade than American agriculture. In recent years, for example, one-third of our wheat, forty percent of our cotton and rice, and one-fourth of our tobacco and soybeans have been exported. It is highly important to maintain foreign markets for our agricultural products.

Any program designed to serve the interests of American agriculture must take due account of the necessity for export markets. Put in the words of the Commission, "It is necessary to harmonize our agricultural and foreign economic policies without sacrificing the sound objectives of either." I am convinced such reconciliation is possible. Acceptance of the recommendations in my Agricultural Message of January 11 will, I feel certain, help accomplish this objective.

MERCHANT MARINE

With respect to our ocean shipping, we must have a merchant marine adequate to our defense requirements. I subscribe to the principle that such support of our merchant fleet as is required for that purpose should be provided by direct means to the greatest possible extent. Such a policy, however, requires a careful analysis of the means available for providing direct support, its possible effects on foreign flag vessel carryings, and its total costs before a specific program can be recommended.

The Department of Commerce has already studied this problem at length. Its findings will be further reviewed within the Executive Branch in order to develop specific recommendations to transmit to the next session of the Congress, in addition to the proposals submitted by the Executive Branch that are now before the Congress.

INTERNATIONAL TRAVEL

International travel has cultural and social importance in the free world. It also has economic significance. Foreign travel by Americans is a substantial source of dollars for many countries, enabling them to pay for what we sell them.

While the promotion of tourism is primarily a responsibility of the countries which welcome visitors, and is a function for private enterprise, there are some specific governmental actions which can be helpful. For example, there is H.R. 8352 which increases the duty-free allowance for tourists from $500 to $1000, exercisable every six months. I recommend its passage. From time to time I may have other recommendations for legislative action to stimulate travel.

Meanwhile, in the Executive Branch, I shall instruct the appropriate agencies and departments, at home and abroad, to consider how they can facilitate international travel. They will be asked to take action to simplify governmental procedures relating to customs, visas, passports, exchange or monetary restrictions and other regulations that sometimes harass the traveler.

ECONOMIC AID AND TECHNICAL ASSISTANCE

Assistance extended in the past by the United States to other free nations has played an effective part in strengthening the national security, developing important resources, and opening up significant opportunities, for ourselves and for others. It has also carried with it, in many instances, particularly in technical cooperation and famine relief, a deep humanitarian response by our people. However, economic aid cannot be continued indefinitely. We must distinguish between an emergency and a chronic malady, between a special case and a general rule.

I subscribe, therefore, to the principle that economic aid on a grant basis should be terminated as soon as possible consistent with our national interest. In cases where support is needed to establish and equip military forces of other governments in the interest of our mutual defense, and where this is beyond the economic capacity of another country, our aid should be in the form of grants. As recognized by the Commission, there may be some cases in which modest amounts of grant aid to underdeveloped countries will importantly serve the interest of security. I further agree that in other situations where the interest of the United States requires that dollars not otherwise available to a country should be provided, such support to the maximum extent appropriate should be in the form of loans rather than grants.

In extending such loans, we must be careful not to interfere with the normal lending activities and standards of the Export-Import Bank. The International Bank is the primary institution for the public financing of economic development. The Export-Import Bank will consider on their merits applications for the financing of development projects, which are not being made by the International Bank, and which are in the special interest of the United States, are economically sound, are within the capacity of the prospective borrower to repay and within the prudent loaning capacity of the Bank.

I approve the recommendations of the Commission on Foreign Economic Policy that the United States participation in technical cooperation programs should be pressed forward vigorously. Such programs should concentrate on providing experts and know-how rather than large funds or shipments of goods except for necessary demonstration equipment. They should not provide capital for investment but should be so administered as to fit into the programs of development of the assisted countries and they should be related to any private or public investment likely to be forthcoming.

Review of the requirements for the Mutual Security Program has been conducted with these principles in mind and substantial reductions in grant aid have been made by this Administration. The legislation which I shall later propose for the Mutual Security Program will reflect these principles.

EAST-WEST TRADE

In viewing the problems of other nations of the free world, we are forced to recognize that the economies of some of them have been weakened by the disruption of the broad historic pattern of trade between East and West.

Curtailment of our aid programs will increase the pressures for resumption of such trade. A greater exchange of peaceful goods between East and West—that is, goods not covered by the Battle Act nor otherwise considered strategic—so far as it can be achieved without jeopardizing national security, and subject to our embargo on Communist China and North Korea, should not cause us undue concern. I shall, of course, take appropriate action to ensure that our security is fully safeguarded.

CONVERTIBILITY

The Commission rightly regards positive progress toward currency convertibility as an indispensable condition for a freer and healthier international trade. Steps toward enabling holders of foreign currencies to convert them freely into other currencies deserve our encouragement.

The Commission has correctly observed that the initiative and responsibility for introducing currency convertibility must rest with the countries concerned. I am happy to say that such initiative is being taken. The British and other members of the Commonwealth of Nations have met twice, in London and in Sydney, to consider plans for convertibility of the pound sterling. The United Kingdom and other important nations of Europe have discussed their aims with us. Individually they are taking constructive steps affecting their own currencies. In addition, discussions among them which are now under way in connection with the renewal of the European Payments Union are being largely influenced by their desire to prepare the way for convertibility.

I have approved the Commission's recommendations for cooperation in strengthening the gold and dollar reserves of countries which have prepared themselves for convertibility by sound internal and external policies. These recommendations do not call for new action by the Congress. Authority and procedures for this purpose already exist. The United States will support the use of the resources of the International Monetary Fund as a bulwark to strengthen the currencies of countries which undertake convertibility. In addition, a study is now being made, as suggested by the Commission, of the possibility of standby credits from the Federal Reserve System.

CONCLUSION

What I have outlined to you is a minimum program which should be judged as a whole. Its various parts are interrelated; each requires the other.

Conceived as a whole, this program consists of four major parts:

Aid—which we wish to curtail

Investment—which we wish to encourage

Convertibility—which we wish to facilitate and

Trade—which we wish to expand

I consider it essential that we achieve each of these objectives, which we must clearly understand are closely interlocked: As we curtail our aid, we must help to close the dollar gap by expanding our foreign investment and trade. This expansion will be facilitated by a return to convertibility of foreign currencies. The return by our friends abroad to convertibility will be encouraged if our trade policy leads them to expect expansion of our foreign trade and investment.

Unless we are prepared to adopt the policies I have recommended to expand export and import trade and increase the flow of our capital into foreign investment, our friends abroad may be discouraged in their effort to re-establish a free market for their currencies. If we fail in our trade policy, we may fail in all. Our domestic employment, our standard of living, our security, and the solidarity of the free world—all are involved.

For our own economic growth we must have continuously expanding world markets; for our security we require that our allies become economically strong. Expanding trade is the only adequate solution for these two pressing problems confronting our country.

DWIGHT D. EISENHOWER

NOTE: The report of the Commission on Foreign Economic Policy was published by the Government Printing Office (Jan-   uary 1954). See also note to Item 16, above.

68 ¶ The President's News Conference of *March* 31, 1954.

THE PRESIDENT. As you can suspect, ladies and gentlemen, from the picture-taking this morning, we are trying a little bit of an innovation.

There has been some slight interest shown in the tests recently conducted in the Pacific, and for this reason, I brought along with me this morning the expert in that field. After I take a certain share of the press conference time, I am going to turn the rest of it over to him. Of course, this will also give me a unique privilege of seeing someone else in this particular spot![1]

One of the things that I should like to take a moment to talk about is the excise taxes.

The excise taxes, of course, have reduced revenues a very considerable amount more than I recommended. Nevertheless, from the beginning it was acknowledged that here was a field that was open to discussion. There is one school of thought that believes that cutting of excise taxes can have such a great effect in stimulating of business that the revenues will not be hurt as much as we estimate.

In any event, the bill, continuing certain needed excise taxes on beyond April 1st—that is tomorrow—is going to be signed. I will sign it today. I accept it wholeheartedly, and we are certainly hopeful that any damaging results will not be as great as might be.

I should like to call attention to this one fact: on figures furnished to me by the Treasury, this will be the greatest single tax reduction in dollars ever accomplished by the American Government, $7,400,000,000 reduced

---

[1] The President referred to the Chairman of the Atomic Energy Commission, Lewis L. Strauss. See note at end of this news conference.

in one year in taxes. This includes, of course, the reduction in income taxes of January 1st, the abolition of the excess profits tax, and this excise tax. That will be a huge amount of money in the hands of private citizens to spend themselves; and, certainly, we have every reason to believe that it will be a stimulating factor in our economy.

Another point to discuss just briefly is housing. There has been a lot of different kinds of thinking on public housing. I think most of you are aware of the general provisions of the plan that I submitted to the Congress some couple of months ago, and I am informed that Mr. Wolcott's committee is bringing out that program largely in the same form as presented to him.

Now, in the public housing factor, there has been a very considerable struggle, but I am delighted that yesterday the leadership succeeded in getting the necessary appropriations so that approximately 35,000 public housing units can be constructed this year. And the authorization will certainly be accorded to go for a like amount or something of that order next year, in the authorization committee.

The other item that I wanted to mention was the Randall report, and my message to Congress on foreign trade. I think the report and the message largely speak for themselves, but I do want to make this one observation: in making this kind of an adjustment, in trying to move from an era in which our friends abroad had to depend so markedly on direct aid into an era where expanded trade will be of benefit to all of us, certain difficulties, even certain hardships can occur not only in our country but in others.

The Government is alert to that situation, will constantly be vigilant to see that any damage of that kind does not become one that is unjustified as you think of the welfare of the 160 million people, and will take such steps as are necessary to prevent them from becoming either widespread or severe. But that there will be some adjustments of that kind is, of course, inevitable.

I do believe that in this day and time, the free world must come more and more to realize that in an expanding, healthy, two-way trade lies our best insurance that the doctrines of statism cannot come in and overcome our whole idea of free government. Within our own country we don't feel that danger so intimately; the danger, in other words, is not in position, let us say, of breathing down our necks. But in some of the others it is, and we have got to take all of those things into consideration as we stand firmly for a principle which, in the long run, is for the good of all of us. It is going to take very great firmness because, as I say, there are bound to be some maladjustments and difficulties.

Now, that was my speech for the morning, ladies and gentlemen; and the rest of my time that I have allocated to myself, we will take up with questions.

Q. Merriman Smith, United Press: I wonder if you could explore for us, sir, or amplify on Secretary Dulles' speech the other night in which he spoke of our readiness to take united action in the Far East.

THE PRESIDENT. Well, of course, the speech must stand by itself. I should say that I was over every word of it beforehand; Secretary Dulles and I, as usual, find ourselves in complete agreement.

I have forgotten the exact words that he used in respect to the question you raised, but he did point out that it is in united action of all nations and peoples and countries affected in that region that we can successfully oppose the encroachment of communism, and should be prepared to meet any kind of attack that would come in there. He pointed out the great value of the region to all the free world and what its loss would mean to us.

So, I think, aside from just the assertion that we are seeking that kind of united action among all our friends, that the speech otherwise must stand by itself.

Q. Martin Agronsky, American Broadcasting Company: Mr. President, I wondered if I could ask one more specific question along those lines. The united action has been interpreted generally as indicating, perhaps, intervention, direct intervention or direct use, more accurately, of American troops. Can you comment on that—if necessary?

THE PRESIDENT. Well, I have said time and again that I can conceive of no greater disadvantage to America than to be employing its own ground forces, and any other kind of forces, in great numbers around the world, meeting each little situation as it arises.

What we are trying to do is to make our friends strong enough to take care of local situations by themselves, with the financial, the moral, the political and, certainly, only where our own vital interests demanded any military help.

But each of these cases is one that has its own degree, let us say, of interest for the United States, its own degree of risk and danger; consequently, each one must be met on its merits.

I couldn't possibly give you a general rule of what the United States would do in a situation, because no one could know all of the circumstances surrounding it. I think the best answer I ever heard in diplomacy was that given by France, I believe, to Germany in late August or late July of 1914. When Germany asked her her intentions, she said, "France will do that which her best interests dictate," and that is about the only answer I believe you can give, except in terms of very great generality.

Q. Garnett Horner, Washington Evening Star: Mr. President, reports from Europe indicate that the European Defense Community project is bogging down. That raises again the question of whether we have all our policy eggs in that EDC basket, or whether there is some alternative in mind if EDC fails. Could you comment on that?

THE PRESIDENT. Well, I just say this. I have been threatened with defeat before, and I don't fight my second battle on the supposition that it is going to occur.

I am all out for the approval of EDC and establishing it as a factor that will insure Europe's safety. Until that question is definitely settled—and I still firmly believe in the affirmative—I am not going to comment on what else could happen.

Q. Robert G. Spivack, New York Post: Mr. President, an explosive situation seems to be building up in the Middle East between the Arab States and Israel, which the Soviet Union seems to be exploiting, if not fomenting. I wondered if you favored bringing the Israel-Arab dispute before the U.N. Security Council, the whole dispute?

THE PRESIDENT. I couldn't comment on that at the moment. It would be, I think, speaking a little bit recklessly.

We have had a very definite program of our own that we have supported—when I say "of our own" I don't mean it quite that way—we have thoroughly approved the idea that is implicit in the U.N. plan that through some economic unity there we would achieve a better, let us say, psychological and political union; therefore, we have been very strongly supporting the plan of development, including water development and sharing, that we hoped would be effective.

There is, of course, so much emotionalism in the thing that you can't tell from day to day how it is going to come out. But I do say it is a case where both sides ought to restrain their partisans and their extremists, use a little bit of reason, and depend upon the judgments of outside people.

Q. Francis M. Stephenson, New York Daily News: I wonder, is the Federal Government planning to take any action in the New York waterfront strike?

THE PRESIDENT. The question is about the New York waterfront strike.

I, of course, want to be careful that I don't pretend that I am going to get into a field where it is so technical that I couldn't possibly expect to know the answers; so I will talk a little bit in generalities but, I think, clearly enough to show intention and concern.

Any strike of this kind is of the utmost importance to the whole Nation and, therefore, to your Federal Government.

Whenever we touch this delicate transportation system of the United States and affect it seriously, we affect the economy, we affect the living, the welfare of many thousands; we affect even such things as health and sanitation, that sort of thing. So these things become serious instantly.

The second they occur, every department of Government that has any possible connection instantly keeps abreast of the situation: the Attorney General; the NLRB—largely independent—of course does so, and determines such things as elections and all that sort of thing; at the same time, Federal courts, an independent branch, take action. Finally it becomes necessary to make sure that their orders are obeyed.

There is also, of course, the understanding in America that everything is handled locally as long as it can be, and you don't bring down Federal agencies until it is necessary. There are city authorities, there are State authorities; they are doing their best, and again we have one of those cases where partnerships must be observed.

The Federal Government has certain grave responsibilities imposed by law, but there are also the police powers and that sort of thing in keeping order that reside in the local authorities. So it is a question of partnership. Our Attorney General, the NLRB, the Secretary of Labor, everybody, is keeping up with this as closely as possible, and to keep me informed as to the whole situation, so that if it does become the responsibility of the Federal Government to take more positive action, we are ready to move in accordance with law, the Constitution, and the merits of the case.

Now, there is very little more you can say, I think, on that matter.

Q. Otto Leichter, Arbeiter-Zeitung, Vienna, Austria, and Swiss and West German Newspapers: Mr. President, do you consider or contemplate any new initiative to obtain an Austrian independence treaty or the withdrawal of all occupation forces, or at least to ease the occupation of Austria?

THE PRESIDENT. I am not sure that I understood every single implication of your question; but, generally, it was, do we have any new approach now to secure a general approval of the Austrian treaty.

About the only observation I could make on it is this: for now, I think it is, 6 or 7 years, we have stood firmly for the early completion of the Austrian treaty, believing it to be wholly unjust and unnecessary to continue the occupation of that country, in view particularly of the facts that early in the war it was agreed that Austria had been occupied country and not an instigator of the war. So I know of no reason that we shouldn't continue to stand on that belief; as a matter of fact, I know we do, and we will certainly be alert to every possible way of easing the situation. But when you come down to asking me to predict success or what could be a brand new approach, I could not comment.

Q. George E. Herman, CBS Radio: Mr. President, the last few weeks the Soviet Union has broken a considerable amount of precedent by publishing the details of nuclear and thermonuclear explosions. Could you tell us what your feelings are on their policies and intentions in making public these facts lately?

THE PRESIDENT. No, I don't really know.

We have had many discussions on them—I would say inconclusive; but there are some who believe that it is indicating a slight change in public policy that might indicate a greater readiness to negotiate earnestly and honestly.

We are trying to keep ourselves in position so that, at any sign of negotiating honestly, we can do so with confidence, on the plan that I suggested last December—which would be merely a beginning. All things like that, we would certainly welcome in view of the situation in the world today.

Q. Ray L. Scherer, National Broadcasting Company: Mr. President, the last couple of weeks several members of your team have announced they are returning to private life: C. D. Jackson, Mr. Kyes, and Mr. Dodge. Could you discuss with us the problem of inducing such men to stay in Government?

THE PRESIDENT. Today, I think it is perfectly clear to all of us, with the family responsibilities that men have, with the tax situation that they have, children to educate, and all of that sort of thing, it is only natural that they think this kind of public duty should be shared.

Now, each of the three men you name promised to stay a year. In each case, because of certain changes in the program and the need for having very intelligent expositions before the committees of the House and the Senate, they have agreed to stay a little longer.

They are difficult to replace, but in at least two instances I am sure we have two very able and capable men to take their places.

I believe that any government such as this is not wholly damaged by some rotation of people, bringing fresh people in from the outside as long as they are capable in themselves and dedicated.

The three men that are going, that you just named, I couldn't speak of them in terms of too great praise. I think they have done a remarkable job. I am indebted to them, and I think the people are indebted to them. So it is not easy for any people to fill their shoes, but when you can do it, a certain amount of that rotation is good rather than bad.

Q. Clark R. Mollenhoff, Des Moines Register and Tribune: Mr. President, several weeks ago I had asked if the White House had given up its efforts to obtain the resignation of Chairman Johnson of the ICC, and at that time you stated that you had no knowledge of that, and I wondered if you had an opportunity to acquaint yourself with the ICC problem of personnel.

THE PRESIDENT. As a matter of fact I forgot about that question. Will you make a note, and I will. [*Confers with Mr. Hagerty*]

As a matter of fact, Mr. Hagerty says that I make an answer that is very, very unusual for me, because he says "No comment." I don't know anything about it, but I will try again to look it up. [*Laughter*]

That is my last question, and now Mr. Strauss is going to take over. I didn't realize that time had gone.

NOTE: During the remainder of the news conference the Chairman of the Atomic Energy Commission, Lewis L. Strauss, read from a prepared statement making public those portions of his report to the President of March 30, 1954, as could be released without compromising the national security. The Chairman described his visit to the AEC proving grounds in the Marshall Islands where he witnessed the second part of the thermonuclear weapons tests for which Bikini and Eniwetok served as bases of operations. After

reading from his statement Mr. Strauss answered queries from members of the press.

The statement was released by the White House. Excerpts of the statement were published in the Department of State Bulletin (vol. 30, p. 548).

President Eisenhower's thirty-third news conference was held in the Executive Office Building from 10:30 to 11:09 o'clock on Wednesday morning, March 31, 1954. In attendance: 235.

69 ¶ Letter to Lindsay Warren Regarding His Retirement as Comptroller General of the United States. *March 31, 1954*

Dear Mr. Warren:

It is with a great deal of regret that I agree to the request in your letter to retire on April 30, 1954, as Comptroller General of the United States. It is unfortunate from every viewpoint that you are unable to complete your full term after thirteen and one-half years of outstanding service in that important position. Not only has your service been long, it has also embraced the period of tremendous responsibility in government incident to the conduct of the second World War, the postwar military and foreign aid programs, and the Korean conflict. However, I can certainly understand that it would be inadvisable to continue in this very demanding office against the advice of your doctors.

You have left a lasting mark on government in the great program of the General Accounting Office and can take deep pride in so vast a contribution to better, more efficient governmental operation.

I appreciate the fine cooperation you have given this Administration. Please accept my warm good wishes for a fully satisfying and happy retirement.

Sincerely,

Dwight D. Eisenhower

70 ¶ Statement by the President on the Death of General Hoyt S. Vandenberg. *April 2, 1954*

THE NATION mourns the passing of a devoted and able military leader, General Hoyt S. Vandenberg, and will hold him in grateful remembrance.

Gallant commander, a decade ago, of our tactical air force in Northwest Europe; unswerving advocate of the precepts and cause of the United States Air Force; a forceful fighter for a strong national defense—General Vandenberg was a courageous and tireless leader. He has left a lasting imprint on the Service he loved so well and on the nation he served with all his strength and skill.

News of his untimely death brings sorrow to his host of civilian and military friends, among whom I was privileged to be numbered.

71   ¶ Statement by the President on the Fifth Anniversary of the Signing of the North Atlantic Treaty.   *April* 4, 1954

FIVE YEARS AGO today, the signing of the North Atlantic Treaty launched a unique working partnership among the Atlantic peoples. Their alliance for the preservation of peace and mutual defense against Communistic aggression is now a mighty bulwark of the free world.

NATO symbolizes the unity of free men in an age of peril.   Fourteen nations, diverse in language and economy and custom and political structure, are joined within it because each nation is determined to sustain its own independence.   Dedicated to a common purpose, their strength is multiplied, their inexhaustible energies are pooled.

During my service with NATO there were many uniforms worn, many tongues spoken at my headquarters.   But daily I found new inspiration in the unity of spirit among my comrades.

The inspiration remains with me; a cherished memory, a heartening proof that free men—united—can face any peril unafraid.   NATO is visible evidence that, in cooperation among the free peoples, we can best preserve our common heritage of freedom against any threat.

72   ¶ Radio and Television Address to the American People on the State of the Nation.   *April* 5, 1954

[Delivered from the Broadcast Room of the White House at 8:30 p.m.]

Good evening, my friends:

This evening I want to talk to you about a very big subject.   I want to talk to you about this great country of ours.   I should like to ask you, with me, to make a quick survey of its strength, its problems, its apprehensions, and its future. Particularly I would like to talk to you about what you and I can do about its future.

Now, as we first take a look at the strength of America, you and I know that it is the most productive nation on earth, that we are richer, by any standard of comparison, than is any other nation in the world. We know that we have great military strength—economic—intellectual. But I want to call your particular attention to spiritual strength.

Now, I don't think it is amiss, in this season of the year that has so many religious overtones, that we call attention to this fact: that in conception, our Nation had a spiritual foundation, so announced by the men who wrote the Declaration of Independence. You remember what they said? "We hold that all men are endowed by their Creator with certain rights." That is very definitely a spiritual conception. It is the explanation of our form of government that our Founding Fathers decided upon.

And now, today, that spiritual strength is just as great in its requirements as it has ever been in our whole history. By this I mean it is very important that you and I value the spiritual things that they had in mind when they founded this country.

For example, the things that were stated in the Bill of Rights, the things that announce the rights that every single individual has in this country; his equality before the law, his right to worship as he pleases, and think as he pleases, and talk as he pleases, just so he does not trespass on the rights of others. And the other part of the spiritual strength we need today is the same stamina and courage and gallantry that our forefathers had in defending those rights.

I want to call your attention to this particular part of the American strength, because without all this everything else goes by the board. We must be strong in our dedication and our devotion to America. That is the first element of our entire strength. But all in all, this total strength of America is one of those things we call—and the world calls—unbelievable.

Now why, then, with all this strength, should we be worried at times about what the world is doing to us? Actually we see threats coming from all angles—internal and external, and we wonder what is going to happen to us individually and as a Nation.

Now, perhaps I can illustrate some of the reasons for this concern of today. Thirty-seven years ago tomorrow, our country entered the First

World War. At that time, I was a lieutenant serving with the United States Infantry in Texas. My regiment was armed, as were all other regiments, with the same kind of equipment, at least as to type and general character of power, as were the regiments that fought the Spanish-American War. Now, only a year ago, the hydrogen bomb was exploded in the Pacific. Last month, another series of tests was undertaken.

Now, this transfer of power, this increase of power from a mere musket and a little cannon, all the way to the hydrogen bomb in a single lifetime, is indicative of the things that have happened to us. They rather indicate how far the advances of science have outraced our social consciousness, how much more we have developed scientifically than we are capable of handling emotionally and intellectually. So that is one of the reasons that we have this great concern, of which the hydrogen bomb is merely a dramatic symbol.

None of the questions that bothers us today has an easy answer. And many of them have no answers at all, at least in their complete sense. We may only do our best, and from there on make sure that we are doing all that human beings can do to meet these problems.

This is not greatly different from what the ordinary American family does. It has the problems of meeting the payments on the mortgage, paying for the family car, educating the children, laying aside some money for use in case of unexpected illness. It meets these problems courageously. It doesn't get panicky. It solves these problems with what I would call courage and faith, but above all by cooperation, by discussing the problem among the different members of the family and then saying: this is what we can do, this is what we will do, and reaching a satisfactory answer.

The problems of America are the family problems multiplied a million-fold. That is what we are talking about tonight.

Now I am not going to try to talk about all these problems. We can talk about water conservation, and soil erosion, and handling of the public debt, and all of these things that bother us day by day in our daily lives. But I am going to confine myself this evening to discussion of just four or five of these.

For example, we are concerned about the men in the Kremlin. We are concerned about the Atomic Age. We are concerned about the loss of our international friends in exposed areas of the world—the loss of them to the Communist dictatorship. We are worried about Communist penetration of our own country, and we are worried about the possibility of depression, and the loss of jobs among us here at home.

Now, the greater any of these apprehensions, the greater is the need that we look at them clearly, face to face, without fear, like honest, straightforward Americans, so we do not develop the jitters or any other kind of panic, that we do not fall prey to hysterical thinking.

Sometimes you feel, almost, that we can be excused for getting a little bit hysterical, because these dangers come from so many angles, and they are of such different kinds, and no matter what we do they still seem to exist. But underlying all of these dangers is one thing: the threat that we have from without, the great threat imposed upon us by aggressive communism, the atheistic doctrine that believes in statism as against our conception of the dignity of man, his equality before the law—that is the struggle of the ages.

Now, the H-bomb—the H-bomb and the Atomic Age. They are not in themselves a great threat to us. Of course not. The H-bomb is a threat to us only if a potential aggressor, who also has the secrets of the H-bomb, determines to use it against us. And against that, then, we have to make our provisions, to make certain that sensible men have done every possible thing they can to protect ourselves against that threat.

Communism seeks to divide us, to set class against class, good people against good people, when those good people should be standing together in defense of liberty and against communism. Because of that, we must take counsel among ourselves and stand together and let nothing tear us apart.

So let us first, then, take these purposes one by one, and think of some of the counterbalancing factors against the threat itself. By this I mean, take the Kremlin. When we say that word, we mean the politburo, and we think of what may be its designs against us, what may be the dictator's intentions with respect to war or aggression, his plans to enslave the world. Of all of these, of course, war poses to us the gravest threat, because of its destructive qualities.

Now let us take the first of what I would call the counteracting or counterbalancing factors. The very fact that those men, by their own design, are in the Kremlin, means that they love power. They want to be there. Whenever they start a war, they are taking the great risk of losing that power. They study history pretty well. They remember Mussolini. They remember Hitler. They have even studied Napoleon very seriously. When dictators over-reach themselves and challenge the whole world, they are very likely to end up in any place except a dictatorial position. And those men in the politburo know that.

So we have the first of these counteracting or counterbalancing factors, against the possibility of their declaring war. There are many risks of every kind in war. Among other things, the Russians have a system of satellites—captive satellites. Now they know, again, the risks of indulging in war when you have captive satellites.

Napoleon went into Russia in 1812 with exactly that kind of army. The Grand Army of France had been reinforced by Prussians and others of the regions that Napoleon had conquered, whose soldiers he had impressed into his own army. As quickly as he met his first disaster, they began to desert.

The Russians know all that. That very system of satellites could be, in a war of exhaustion, a very great source of weakness. They have, as compared to us, economic weaknesses, and after all a strong economy is necessary, if you are going to push through to victory in a modern war.

The Russians produced last year something less, probably, than half a billion barrels of oil. We produced two and a quarter by ourselves. We produced something over twice as much steel as they produced. Now these are strong elements in our economy, when you are going to use so much of your production to wage a war, particularly a war of exhaustion.

Now all of these things are deterrents upon the men in the Kremlin. They are factors that make war, let us say, less likely. As long as they know that we are in position to act strongly and to retaliate, war is not a decision to be taken lightly. Yet I admit—and we must all admit—that it remains a possibility they might do this, in a fit of madness, or through miscalculation.

Of course, as I mentioned before, the H-bomb is dangerous because those people have its secrets, possess and have exploded, as they did some months back, such a bomb. But we know, with respect to that bomb, we are not going to start a war. It is not going to be used by our initiative. And I have just talked about this sobering effect of the risks of war upon the men in the Kremlin. Of all those sobering effects, none is greater than the retaliation that will certainly be visited upon them if they would attack any of our nations, or any part of our vital interests, aggressively and in order to conquer us.

In addition to all this, we devote ourselves to civil and continental defense, in order to make certain that we have the best possible chance to live through such a catastrophe, as well as to inflict upon the enemy such losses that he would quit fighting. But since insanity still exists, I again say there is still an element in that threat that we must calculate very coldly and very carefully.

Now the next thing that we fear, or concerning which we are apprehensive, is this idea of Communist infiltration into our own country, into our Government, into our schools, into our unions, into any of our facilities, any of our industries, wherever they may be, and wherever those Communists could damage us. Now, it would be completely false to minimize the dangers of this penetration. It does exist. We know some of them are here. Yet, let me give you now some of the counterbalancing factors.

First of all, this fear has been greatly exaggerated as to numbers. In our country today, there are possibly some 25 thousand doctrinal Communists. The FBI knows pretty well where they are. But the headlines of the newspapers would sometimes have you think that every other person you meet is a Communist. Actually, 25 thousand out of 160 million people means about one out of six thousand. But they are dangerous.

Now our great defense against those people is the FBI. The FBI has been doing, for years, in this line of work, a magnificent job. They are a great bulwark, and any one of you can notify them today about real valid facts which you have, and they will be on the job doing something about it. They are that kind. So great is the story that they have to tell that I am not going to attempt to tell it tonight. Instead, I have asked the Attorney General on next Friday night, to come before you and give you a complete account of what the FBI has been doing about this.

Along with this, this fear of Communist penetration, comes another fear that is related to it, the fear that we will use intemperate investigative methods, particularly through congressional committees, to combat communistic penetration.

As I pointed out before, it is minute. The great mass of governmental people, Government workers, civilian and in uniform, people in our schools, and everywhere else that we can think of, are just as dedicated as you and I. They are just as loyal. But this fringe still has to be hunted out, and as I say, you will get a full report of what the FBI is doing on this.

Now, the congressional committee. One of its functions—when it was set up as the congressional investigative committee it was to be your protection against the unwarranted attacks of an overpowering executive. It was to look after your civil liberties, to make certain that your liberties were not eroded away.

Now, ladies and gentlemen, I admit that there can be very grave offenses committed against an innocent individual, if he is accused, possibly, by someone having the immunity of congressional membership. He can lose his job. He can have scars that will be lasting. But in the long run, you may be certain of this: America believes in, and practices, fair play, and decency and justice. In this country, public opinion is the most powerful of all forces. And it will straighten this matter out wherever and whenever there is real violence done to our great rights.

And now the next fear I want to touch upon is the fear of losing international friends, the fear that comes to us, or the apprehension that comes to us, when we consider that exposed areas of the world, not so strong as we are, not so strong in materials, or in this world's riches, or militarily, may fall prey to the subversion, the deceit, the bribery, and the propaganda that is practiced by the Russians.

Now, some of these areas are very, very important to us, not merely because of the necessary materials we get from them—tin, tungsten, rubber, manganese, and all the things we need to keep our economy going—but because those people, if regimented under the Communist dictators in the Kremlin, could make them stronger and stronger as against us, as the free world was chipped away.

Now, let us take, again, some of the counterbalancing values. Did you ever stop to think there is no nation in the world that has ever freely adopted communism in a vote of the people? On the contrary, every time Communists have taken over a country, even Russia, it has been done by a very small minority practicing violence. Or through some slick method, or political move it has gotten control of the country, establishing a gestapo or other method of police control and has ruled that country.

Moreover, there is a growing understanding in the world, of the decency and justice of the American position in opposing the slavery of any nation. We do not believe that any nation, no matter how great, has a right to take another people and subject them to its rule. We believe that every nation has a right to live its own life. Every bit of aid we give, every cooperative effort we undertake, is all based upon the theory that it is cooperation among equals.

The other night, a newspaper by a curious error, spoke of allies as "appliances" instead of alliances. Now the one mistake we must never make is to think of our friends in the international world as being tools of ours. They are not. They are friends of ours. And as they are friends, they are equals to us.

The United Nations was conceived with one idea: that cooperative effort among great and free, peace-loving nations could establish peace in this world. That the United Nations authorizes coalitions in different areas of the world designed for the same purposes and in the same spirit. We believe in these. In every corner of the world, whether it is to protect the southwest Pacific, or NATO in Europe, or wherever it is, we believe that the interested nations should band together, and in cooperative spirit, maintain the freedom of those countries against any kind of communist aggression. Still, some of these nations are weak; they are indecisive. And we have our disappointments in trying to build them up. So we have again that form of apprehension to take into our calculations, prepare for and prepare against.

Now I want to take up, just very briefly, the fear of depression and loss of jobs. You will hear people talking about the level of 3,700,000 unemployed. And it is very true. And it is a figure that comes about as a result of our efforts to go from a war to a peace economy. That figure happily shows every sign now of leveling off. The last report was only a few thousand greater than the one just earlier.

But these people who look on it so gloomily never say to you that there are more than 60 million people today gainfully employed in the United States, entirely aside from the 3,500,000 that are in the armed services. We have a number of peacetime jobs and an employment that is very near to an all-time high. We have great insurance plans in this country against loss of jobs. We have a farm program to protect the farmer against disaster. We have the great savings of our people near an all-time high. And then we have the great requirements of the 160 million people of good income, and that is the kind of thing that gives employment and insures the productivity of our farms and factories.

But aside from this, my friends, we have also a Government that is ready to act whenever necessary. Now one of the important things in this kind of problem is the attitude of your Government. I have tried to define our Government several times as one that is completely liberal in its relationship to people, but earnestly tries to be conservative when it deals with your money and your economy.

Now already there have been many measures taken to ease and to accommodate this transition from war to peace economy. We have made loans easier and facilitated construction. We have reduced and are reducing to some extent the surpluses that overhang our agricultural market. We are trying to increase our markets abroad, stimulating production, and so on. But there are many, many more plans in reserve, ready to use if necessary. Among these, of course, is public construction, further lowering of taxes, increasing your money to spend in many ways, and that is something to be brought out if necessary. But on the other hand, your Government does not intend to go into any slambang emergency program unless it is necessary.

Now, my friends, I should say that the one great aspiration of America is a free, peaceful, and prosperous world. To have a free, peaceful, and prosperous world, we must be ever stronger; we must be ever stronger not only in the things I have mentioned but particularly in this spiritual sense, in the belief—the faith that we can do certain things. We must have the faith that comes from a study of our own history, from the inspiration of leaders like Washington and Lincoln, and what our pioneering forefathers did.

But as we look at the whole problem, and we sum up these apprehensions of which I have just spoken, we find that each of them has a certain lingering element of truth in it. And so we have plans, and this administration has presented to the Congress a plan—a legislative program. In that program there is ample measure for defense, civil, and continental defense and for the deterrent effects of our atomic development. We have lowered taxes so that six billion dollars or more have been turned back to the public so as to stimulate production. We have farm programs— taxes—trade—mutual security—housing—social security—health programs—all of these things. My friends, if they are done, we will be certain of a stronger America that will be capable of bringing closer to us this peaceful, prosperous, and secure America.

But I say, again, that it is the American belief in decency and justice and progress, and the value of individual liberty, because of the rights conferred upon each of us by our Creator, that will carry us through, as we study and plan these things. There must be something in the heart as well as in the head. So as we do this, as you and I approach our problems in this way, I assure you we don't have to fear. I don't mean to say, and no one can say to you, that there are no dangers. Of course there are risks, if we are not vigilant. But we do not have to be hysterical. We can be vigilant. We can be Americans. We can stand up and hold up our heads and say: America is the greatest force that God has ever allowed to exist on His footstool.

As such it is up to us to lead this world to a peaceful and secure existence. And I assure you we can do it.

Good-night, my friends.

73 ¶ The President's News Conference of
April 7, 1954.

THE PRESIDENT. We will go right to questions this morning, ladies and gentlemen.

Q. Merriman Smith, United Press: Mr. President, concerning the hydrogen bomb, are we going to continue to make bigger and bigger H-bombs and, as the H-bomb program continues or progresses, are we learning anything that is directly applicable to the peacetime uses of atomic energy?

THE PRESIDENT. No, we have no intention of going into a program of seeing how big these can be made. I don't know whether the scientists would place any limit; and, therefore, you hear these remarks about "blow-out," which, I think, is even blowing a hole through the entire atmosphere.

Q. (Questioner unidentified): What was that, sir?

THE PRESIDENT. I say you hear statements, comments like "blow-out" and all of that sort of thing.

We know of no military requirement that could lead us into the production of a bigger bomb than has already been produced.

Now, with respect to the potentiality of this development for peacetime use, our people study, I think in almost every aspect of human affairs, how this whole atomic science, this nuclear science, can be applied to peacetime uses.

It would be rash to say that the hydrogen bomb doesn't add to the possibilities; yet, at the moment, I know of no direct connection or direct application of the hydrogen bomb principle to peacetime power.

I asked that very question of the scientists, and they gave an answer as nearly as I have just stated it as I can recall.

Q. Walter Ridder, St. Paul Pioneer Press and Dispatch: Sir, on that subject, a certain Senator said last night there had been a delay of 18 months in the production of the hydrogen bomb, and suggested it was due to subversion in Government. Do you know anything about that?

THE PRESIDENT. No, I know nothing about it. I never heard of any delay on my part, never heard of it.

Q. Mrs. May Craig, New England Papers: Mr. President, aren't you afraid that Russia will make bigger hydrogen bombs before we do?

THE PRESIDENT. No, I am not afraid of it. I don't know of any reason for building a bigger bomb than you find to represent as great an efficiency as is needed or desirable, so I don't know what bigger ones would do.

Q. Joseph Harsch, Christian Science Monitor and NBC: Mr. President, would you care to say anything to us about the loyalty and patriotism of Edward R. Murrow?

THE PRESIDENT. I am going to say nothing at all about that.

First of all, I don't comment about people, I don't comment about things of which I know nothing.

I will say this: I have known this man for many years; he has been one of the men I consider my friend among your profession. That is what I do know about him.

So far as indulging in philosophical discussion, I can't remember any instance; but I do say that he has been one of those that over the years, in the war, when he was working in London, and so on, I always thought of him as a friend.

Q. Robert Richards, Copley Press: Mr. President, would you mind commenting on the strategic importance of Indochina to the free world? I think there has been, across the country, some lack of understanding on just what it means to us.

THE PRESIDENT. You have, of course, both the specific and the general when you talk about such things.

First of all, you have the specific value of a locality in its production of materials that the world needs.

Then you have the possibility that many human beings pass under a dictatorship that is inimical to the free world.

Finally, you have broader considerations that might follow what you would call the "falling domino" principle. You have a row of dominoes set up, you knock over the first one, and what will happen to the last one is the certainty that it will go over very quickly. So you could have a beginning of a disintegration that would have the most profound influences.

Now, with respect to the first one, two of the items from this particular area that the world uses are tin and tungsten. They are very important. There are others, of course, the rubber plantations and so on.

Then with respect to more people passing under this domination, Asia, after all, has already lost some 450 million of its peoples to the Communist dictatorship, and we simply can't afford greater losses.

But when we come to the possible sequence of events, the loss of Indochina, of Burma, of Thailand, of the Peninsula, and Indonesia following, now you begin to talk about areas that not only multiply the disadvantages that you would suffer through loss of materials, sources of materials, but now you are talking really about millions and millions and millions of people.

Finally, the geographical position achieved thereby does many things. It turns the so-called island defensive chain of Japan, Formosa, of the Philippines and to the southward; it moves in to threaten Australia and New Zealand.

It takes away, in its economic aspects, that region that Japan must have as a trading area or Japan, in turn, will have only one place in the world to go—that is, toward the Communist areas in order to live.

So, the possible consequences of the loss are just incalculable to the free world.

Q. Diosdado M. Yap, Manila Chronicle: Mr. President, next Friday marks the 12th anniversary of the fall of Bataan. Would you care to make any comment on it?

THE PRESIDENT. Well, I have been asked by General Romulo to send a message to a meeting, which I have done. If I haven't already signed it, I have been working on it, I know that.

Q. Raymond Brandt, St. Louis Post-Dispatch: Mr. President, what response has Secretary Dulles and the administration got to the request for united action in Indochina?

THE PRESIDENT. So far as I know, there are no positive reactions as yet, because the time element would almost forbid.

The suggestions we have, have been communicated; and we will have communications on them in due course, I should say.[1]

Q. Robert G. Spivack, New York Post: Mr. President, do you agree with Senator Kennedy that independence must be guaranteed the people of Indochina in order to justify an all-out effort there?

THE PRESIDENT. Well, I don't know, of course, exactly in what way a Senator was talking about this thing.

I will say this: for many years, in talking to different countries, different governments, I have tried to insist on this principle: no outside country can come in and be really helpful unless it is doing something that the local people want.

Now, let me call your attention to this independence theory. Senator Lodge, on my instructions, stood up in the United Nations and offered one country independence if they would just simply pass a resolution saying they wanted it, or at least said, "I would work for it." They didn't accept it. So I can't say that the associated states want independence in the sense that the United States is independent. I do not know what they want.

I do say this: the aspirations of those people must be met, otherwise there is in the long run no final answer to the problem.

Q. Joseph Dear, Capital Times: Do you favor bringing this Indochina situation before the United Nations?

THE PRESIDENT. I really can't say. I wouldn't want to comment at too great a length at this moment, but I do believe this: this is the kind of thing that must not be handled by one nation trying to act alone. We

---

[1] On April 10, 1954, the White House released a statement by the Secretary of State shortly after his talk with the President before leaving for London and Paris. Secretary Dulles stated that he would consult with the British and French governments about the problems involved in creating "the obviously desirable united front to resist communist aggression in Southeast Asia." The Secretary continued: "The communist bloc with its vast resources can win success by overwhelming one by one little bits of freedom. But it is different if we unite. . . . Our purpose is . . . to create the unity of free wills needed to assure a peaceful settlement which will in fact preserve the vital interests of us all."

In a statement released by the White House on April 19, following his return to Washington, Secretary Dulles noted that he had found in both capitals recognition of the need for exploring the possibility of establishing a collective defense.

The full text of both statements by the Secretary of State are published in the Department of State Bulletin (vol. 30, pp. 590, 668).

must have a concert of opinion, and a concert of readiness to react in whatever way is necessary.

Of course, the hope is always that it is peaceful conciliation and accommodation of these problems.

Q. Charles von Fremd, CBS Television: I would like to go back to the A- and H-bomb matter for just a moment, sir. Due to the concern and the arguments in the British House of Commons in the past week, do you think it possible or wise to have a renewal of the passage of atomic energy information or hydrogen information between the two countries?

THE PRESIDENT. Well, exactly how much information you have to pass back and forth, I am not sure.

This whole development has a curious history, and, I believe, the Prime Minister tried to trace some of the several steps the other day in the House of Commons.

Originally, I think it was clearly evident that there was supposed to be a complete exchange of information. Then there was a new agreement made in '48—intervening was the Atomic Energy Act. And now, the Atomic Energy Commission is—I don't know whether it has as yet presented the bill, but it has been working on a bill, at least, you might say to modernize the law under which we operate.

The original bill, let me call your attention, was drawn under the theory we could keep the secret of the manufacture of the atomic bomb. Well, the second that went out and was disproven, then you have a new condition, and there should be now some revision of law.

As to exactly how much information we should exchange, I am not certain; but I do know this: when it comes down to the exchanging of the information that is necessary in order for allies to work together intelligently, both for the prevention of war or in the tragic occurrence of war for operating efficiently, that much, of course, we must do now.

Q. Alice Johnson, Seattle Times: Mr. President, last week the Senate passed a measure enabling both Hawaii and Alaska to achieve statehood. If the House should pass that measure, would you veto the bill?

THE PRESIDENT. I believe I have made a rule here never to predict what I will do. I am sometimes like the man, you know, who in a speech was introduced a little bit overgenerously; and he said, "*I* am even going to be interested in what I am going to say, because there certainly have been great predictions made about it." [*Laughter*]

Here we have a situation for which I have stood for a long time, Hawaiian statehood.

I thought there were certain considerations of national security, and so on, that made the other case a separate one.

If these bills are put together, I will have to take a look at them at the time and study and decide what I believe to be right at that moment. I just can't predict.

Q. Mrs. Johnson: May I ask one more allied question? Governor Heintzleman of Alaska recently suggested that statehood should be given only to the populated area of Alaska. Would you favor such a move as that?

THE PRESIDENT. I don't know whether I would favor it. It certainly is a different problem; and I would look at it with an entirely different viewpoint than I would if we had all those outer reaches, barren outer reaches, that are lying on the Bering Sea and the Arctic Ocean, included. It would be a different problem in my mind.

Q. Ethel Payne, Defender Publications: Mr. President, in your housing message to Congress on January 25th you said the administrative policies governing the operations of the several housing agencies must be, and will be, materially strengthened and augmented in order to assure equal opportunity for all of our citizens to acquire, within their means, good and well-located homes. Then there was a further reference to the misuse of slum clearance laws to dislocate persons. I would like to know what administrative regulations have been issued by the housing agencies to implement this part of the message.

THE PRESIDENT. You have asked a question that I will have to ask Mr. Hagerty to look up for next week. I know this: I know that every administrative part of Government knows my policy and is trying to do it. Now, they may be slow getting around to it, sometimes.

Q. Robert Clark, International News Service: Secretary Dulles has said that the Chinese Communists are awfully close to open aggression in Indochina. Can you tell us what action we are prepared to take if their intervention reaches the point of open aggression?

THE PRESIDENT. No, Mr. Clark, I couldn't answer that one for the simple reason that we have got this whole troublous question now under study by a group of people.

The only thing I can say is that here is a problem that is of the utmost moment to all of us, not only the United States, to the free world. It is the kind of thing to which there is more attention given, I guess, at the given moment of real acute occurrence than almost any other thing.

It is getting study day by day, and I can't tell you what would be the exact reaction.

Q. Sarah McClendon, El Paso Times: Sir, I found many Senators and House members this week who said that while you were allaying their fears, that Secretary Dulles was making them fear more, and I wonder if he is going to clear his statements on Indochina with you?

THE PRESIDENT. So far as I know, Secretary Dulles has never made an important pronouncement without not only conferring and clearing with me, but sitting down and studying practically word by word what he is to say.

Now, I am not aware of any antagonism between the statements he has made and I have made.

I have plead with America to look facts in the face; I have plead with them not to minimize what the possibilities of the situation are, but to realize that we are 160 million of the most productive and the most intelligent people on earth; therefore, why are we going around being too scared?

Now, on the other hand, we would be completely foolish not to see what these facts are and what their potentialities are.

I see those two statements as completely compatible, not as incompatible.

Q. Marvin Arrowsmith, Associated Press: Mr. President, you have touched on this, but I wonder if you could tell us whether there is any truth to these reports in the last couple of days that the United States is asking some of the other free nations to join in a joint declaration warning Communist China against any aggression in Southeast Asia?

THE PRESIDENT. No; in approach, Mr. Arrowsmith, you call attention to the problem and say that this looks like a place where the interests of all of us are involved, and now let us talk this over. You don't propose the answer before you study it, put it that way.

Q. Kenneth Scheibel, Gannett Newspapers: Sir, could you tell us how soon you expect to name a successor to Mr. Warren, the Comptroller General?

THE PRESIDENT. No, I can't tell you.

Q. Henri Pierre, Le Monde (Paris): Mr. President, would you say that the last statement of the Secretary of State of last week about

Indochina has improved the chance of reaching a negotiated solution at Geneva of the Indochinese controversy?

THE PRESIDENT. Your question is really, do I think there is a good chance of reaching a negotiated solution?

Q. Mr. Pierre: That is right.

THE PRESIDENT. Well, I wouldn't class the chances as good, no, not one that the free world would consider adequate to the situation.

I must say, let me make clear again, I am certain the United States, as a whole, its Congress and the executive portions of its Government, are ready to move just as far as prudence will allow in seeking any kind of conciliation or negotiated agreement that will ease any of the problems of this troubled world. But one thing: we are not going to overstep the line of prudence in keeping ourselves secure, knowing that the agreements we made have some means of being enforced. We are not simply going to take words. There must be some way of making these things fact and deed.

Q. Robert Riggs, Louisville Courier-Journal: Does the executive branch want any action by Congress now about Indochina?

THE PRESIDENT. Not at this moment. I should point out, with all the sincerity I have, there is nothing partisan about this problem. There is nothing, so far as I know, in which the executive branch and the Congress are apart. We not only must confer upon the broadest scale with the leaders of Congress as we proceed toward a decision, we go just as far as they would think it would be necessary in such a conference. If some specific authority or anything else were necessary, it would be asked for after the leaders had already agreed on a bipartisan basis this is what we should do.

I know of nobody that is trying to escape his responsibility in this whole business, because we realize that it is America and the free world we are talking about, and nothing else.

Q. Martin Agronsky, American Broadcasting Company: Mr. President, in response to the question about whether you knew anything of Senator McCarthy's charge that the building of the H-bomb had been delayed for 18 months as a result of Communist influence in our Government, you replied you didn't know anything about that. That might leave the implication, sir, that there is some possibility of truth in that charge. It is a very serious charge, of actually high treason in Government.

THE PRESIDENT. I don't know. As a matter of fact, I don't know of any speech, first of all; I get from here the first knowledge that there was a speech. But, secondly, I have been very close to the Chairman of the Atomic Energy Commission. He tries to keep me informed not only of present developments but of history. He has never mentioned such a thing as you speak of, and I gave a perfectly honest answer: I never heard of it.

Q. James Patterson, New York News: Mr. President, as the last resort in Indochina, are we prepared to go it alone?

THE PRESIDENT. Again you are bringing up questions that I have explained in a very definite sense several times this morning.

I am not saying what we are prepared to do because there is a Congress, and there are a number of our friends all over this world that are vitally engaged.

I know what my own convictions on this matter are; but until the thing has been settled and properly worked out with the people who also bear responsibilities, I cannot afford to be airing them everywhere, because it sort of stultifies negotiation which is often necessary.

Q. John W. Vandercook, American Broadcasting Company: Going to a change of subject, sir, the most recent figures of the Bureau of Census have indicated that possibly unemployment is leveling out; that statement has been made. Would you care to say, sir, whether you have reckoned a specific figure or proportion of unemployment which might be regarded as acceptable or permissible as an average in the American life?

THE PRESIDENT. Well, in the economic conferences, we talk about that possibility a very great deal. But let us remember, the economy of America is not a static thing; you cannot say 6 percent equals so-and-so, and that is disaster, and something else is prosperity. It is a fluid thing, and you must keep touch with it.

Now, the last figures I saw, apparently the total of employment rose about 50,000 in March and apparently unemployment rose about 50,000, sort of canceling each other out, but showing a very definite flattening out of the curve of the rise of unemployment.

There are other rather encouraging signs in the economy. The thing is now, I think, to keep in touch with it day by day to be ready to move with everything you have, to give it a boost in the right direction. But again, as in all other things, let's don't be panicky about it, let's be straightforward. This is one field where I have no intention of trying to conceal anything from the American public that we find out. It is just what do we do at any given moment, and it is not always easy, but we are doing our best.

Q. Mr. Vandercook: May I ask a related question, sir?

THE PRESIDENT. Yes.

Q. Mr. Vandercook: Do you have in mind so far any intention of proposing legislation to assist the States to continue unemployment benefits beyond the 6 months' period, as that 6 months, in many instances, is running out?

THE PRESIDENT. I have forgotten for sure whether that was in the bill that went to the Congress or not. I remember the subject was discussed by Mrs. Hobby in front of me, and I would have to ask Mr. Hagerty to give you the exact thing as to whether it was actually in the bill.

Merriman Smith, United Press: Thank you, Mr. President.

NOTE: President Eisenhower's thirty-fourth news conference was held in the Executive Office Building from 10:32 to 10:57 o'clock on Wednesday morning, April 7, 1954. In attendance: 197.

74 ¶ Statement by the President on the Approval by the Luxembourg Parliament of the European Defense Community Treaty.
April 7, 1954

I HAVE JUST learned of the vote of the Luxembourg Parliament, approving ratification of the treaty establishing the European Defense Community. Luxembourg has thus become the fourth of the six European Defense Community nations whose Parliament has taken favorable action.

This represents further significant progress in the establishment of this Community. The integration of the defense forces of France, Germany, the Benelux nations and Italy will do much to assure conditions in Europe which will contribute to the peace and security of that area.

75   ¶ Statement by the President Upon
Approving the Joint Resolution Providing for the
Observance of Bataan Day.   *April 8,* 1954

I HAVE TODAY approved Senate Joint Resolution 143 providing for
the observance of April 9, the twelfth anniversary of the fall of Bataan,
as Bataan Day.

The intervening years since Bataan have little dimmed the bitterness
of defeat, the sorrow at the terrible human loss.   Nevertheless, that day
was a day of glory.   Philippine and American soldiers wrote a heroic
chapter in military history.   As comrades in arms they proved in defeat
that men of righteous purpose and firm resolve can endure suffering and
death and fight with courage and tenacity.

Bataan Day reminds us of the close ties which bound our two countries in adversity and by which we are still joined in happier circumstances.   We are bound no longer in a relationship of dependence, nor
by common peril, but in a far richer bond—that of free and sovereign
nations with like aims and aspirations.

On this twelfth anniversary of the fall of Bataan, let us remember with
a full measure of gratitude those brave and gallant men of our two
countries who stood and fell together in the cause of freedom.

NOTE: As enacted, Senate Joint Resolution 143 is Public Law 328, 83d Congress (68
Stat. 51).

76   ¶ Remarks at Ceremony Marking the
Issuance of the First Stamp Bearing the Motto
"In God We Trust."   *April 8,* 1954

General Summerfield and distinguished guests:

The size and greatness, the influence of America have come to be an
accepted fact in the modern world.

In trying to describe these characteristics and qualities of our country,
we are often tempted to do it in terms of the height of our buildings, the
extent of our roadways, the speed of our automobiles, the wonderful
gadgets that we use in our houses.

But America was great, America was a symbol of hope to many millions of people long before these modern appliances were even discovered by the genius of man.

Throughout its history, America's greatness has been based upon a spiritual quality, which seems to me is best symbolized by the stamp that will be issued today, and in honor of which issuance we are here gathered.

The Flame of Liberty symbolizes the determination of America always to remain free, to remain a haven of the oppressed and a ready acknowledgement that all men in the attainment of human aspirations and worthy aspirations are dependent upon an Almighty.

It seems to me in these two concepts we have a true description of the greatness of America.

The reason that I was particularly honored to come here today, aside from the opportunity of meeting with friends, was to be a part of the ceremony which now gives to every single citizen of the United States, as I see it, the chance to send a message to another. Regardless of any eloquence of the words that may be inside the letter, on the outside he places a message: "Here is the land of liberty and the land that lives in respect for the Almighty's mercy to us." And to him that receives that message, the sender can feel that he has done something definite and constructive for that individual.

I think that each of us, hereafter, fastening such a stamp on a letter, cannot fail to feel something of the inspiration that we do whenever we look at the Statue of Liberty, or read "In God We Trust."

NOTE: The ceremony was held in the office of Postmaster General Arthur E. Summerfield. The stamp was an 8-cent issue. See also Item 77 below.

77 ¶ Remarks at Luncheon Meeting of the National Conference of Republican Women. *April 8, 1954*

Madam Chairman, and ladies:

To illustrate the state of confusion in which I sort of find myself at this moment, I think I should tell you a story about three cross-eyed men who were called before a cross-eyed judge. And in starting the examination, he said to the first, "What's your name?" And the second one said, "John Smith." The Judge said, "I didn't speak to you," and the third one said, "I know it."

For some reason or other, I thought I was to come to a business meeting of this organization and that I was to step in and more or less wave a hand and be on my way. I found that, as you can see, that I was a little wrong.

I have just come from assisting in the dedication of a new stamp. Sounds like a very commonplace and ordinary sort of thing to do. It was thrilling—and I will tell you why it was to me. Not only because of the company there gathered—representatives of all the great religious groups of the United States, and of our Government, and of others. The stamp has on it a picture of the Statue of Liberty, and on it also is stated "In God We Trust."

By putting on the Flame of Liberty, it seems to me it places America before the world, not as the greatest nation because of its tall buildings and its automobiles, but because it represents a concept of human dignity, that here all the world can enjoy this liberty, all of those who come to her shores; and also a Nation whose greatness is based on a firm unshakeable belief that all of us mere mortals are dependent upon the mercy of a Superior Being.

Now the reason this seems so thrilling is not just those thoughts, but the opportunity it gives to every single individual who buys the stamp to send a message—regardless of the content of a letter. You may, by placing that stamp on a letter, send a message of hope to those who are oppressed, or let us say, of inspiration and reawakening to our own friends and those among us who will be reminded thereby that this is the land of the free and in God we trust. So each of those stamps, I think, is a worthy messenger of the American system. And as I can see this, every proper, every dedicated political worker is exactly the same.

The Republican Party is by no means a conspiracy among people who simply thirst for power. The Republican Party is an agency of America, which means an agency for spreading further in the world this concept of the dignity of the human, our dependence upon a Superior Being.

And in those two concepts we find vast room to develop every single good thought, idea, program, for the benefit of our own citizens, and to serve as worthy leaders in the same way for the entire world.

Ladies and gentlemen—are there any gentlemen here?—I cannot tell you how great I believe to be the opportunity that now lies before America, and before the Republican Party of that country.

Now, I understand—I have been told—that 52 percent of the votes cast for the Republicans in the last national election were by women. Consequently, I must say that it would appear the majority of my gratitude to the people for the work they did in advancing the kind of theory of which I have been trying so haltingly to speak, belongs to the women.

I want to tell you now two tiny stories, one occurring this morning in my office. There is a man visiting us from Australia. He is head of the steel union—the iron and steel union of Australia. His name is Short. He is a very thoughtful, very earnest, and very sincere man. And he was talking about defeating communism. He fought for 15 years within his union to defeat communism, and finally did it, and is now chairman of that union, the greatest in Australia. He has, therefore, acquired a very great deal of experience, a lot of which we could possibly use. He does not believe that the defeat of communism lies merely in economic measures, in trying to raise the standard of living. He believes it is in work—work and organization. And he made the report that women are great workers, and if they believe something, if they are dedicated to it, their energy is tireless, their determination unbounded.

Not long ago I had the great pleasure of playing a round of golf—at least I went along—with Ben Hogan. Ben Hogan is, of course, the great golfer of our time—of these modern days. I said to him, "Do you think that such and such a young man will be a champion who can take your place?" And he said, "It depends entirely on how seriously he takes his job and how hard he will work." He said, "He has got everything; that's all he needs to do."

I think that the tribute that I should like to bring to Republican women this morning is this: whenever they have come to my office, and their representatives, they have sought opportunities to work, opportunities better to organize, missions to carry out—something to do. I have yet to have a delegation of women come to my office and insist that so and so be appointed to this or to that, or that we lower taxes even on handbags. They have come as dedicated people, ready to work, appreciating the seriousness of their job.

I could wish that that kind of attitude and that kind of spirit was shared by every single American, no matter what their political faith, no matter what their political convictions. Because in the long run, it is only as America expresses with all its might what it believes, in its heart and its mind, are we going to be safe and secure in a free and prosperous world. If we do that we cannot fail. We must have that kind of dedication to win.

I am very grateful to you for asking me over in front of this distinguished body. I hope you have had a fine time here. I hear that you have been briefed by most of my Cabinet officers. And I get that every week, so I know you are very well informed about everything that is going on.

Thank you.

NOTE: The President's opening words "Madam Chairman" referred to Bertha Adkins, Assistant to the Chairman of the Republican National Committee. Later the President referred to Laurence E. Short, National Secretary of the Federated Iron Workers Association of Australia.

78 ¶ Remarks at the "Help Korea" Trains Ceremony. *April 9, 1954*

FIRST OF ALL, I think I may speak for the people of the United States in thanking you three gentlemen—and you, Mrs. Willkie—for your part in mobilizing the gifts of America to go to a country where they are so badly needed.

I think I can speak, also, for the nation, in thanking the railroads for being so helpful and cooperative in showing such a sympathetic attitude toward this great need.

I want to speak for just a moment about my pride in what the Army has done. The Army had a long and grueling experience out in that country, as did, of course, all our fighting forces. Yet so impressed were our soldiers by the great need out there, and by the gallantry of their ally, that they themselves contributed more than 25 million dollars. This was completely aside from all of the work they did in providing the know-how for reconstruction of schools, hospitals, roads, bridges—all the things that were destroyed in the war.

So as they excite my pride, you people excite my thanks. I am certain that all of us are going to have our sentiments stirred very deeply in this country by your efforts. I am sure the response will be everything that you expect.

Now to each of you—good luck.

NOTE: The President spoke in the Rose Garden at 2:30 p.m. In the opening paragraph he referred to Dr. Howard A. Rusk, President of the American Korean Foundation, Henry C. Alexander, National Chairman of the Help Korea Trains campaign, Philip A. Hollar, Vice President of the Association of American Railroads, and Mrs. Wendell L. Willkie, National Chairman of the Women's Division of the American Korean Foundation.

79 ¶ Citation Accompanying Medal of Honor Presented to Benjamin F. Wilson. *April* 10, 1954

THE PRESIDENT of the United States of America, authorized by Act of Congress March 3, 1863 has awarded in the name of The Congress the Medal of Honor to

FIRST LIEUTENANT (THEN MASTER SERGEANT)

BENJAMIN F. WILSON, UNITED STATES ARMY

for conspicuous gallantry and interpidity at the risk of his life above and beyond the call of duty in action with the enemy:

Lieutenant Wilson, Infantry, United States Army, a member of Company I, 31st Infantry Regiment, 7th Infantry Division, distinguished himself by conspicuous gallantry and indomitable courage above and beyond the call of duty in action against the enemy near Hwach'on-Myon, Korea, on 5 June 1951. Company I was committed to attack and secure commanding terrain stubbornly defended by a numerically superior hostile force emplaced in well-fortified positions. When the spearheading element was pinned down by withering hostile fire, he dashed forward and, firing his rifle and throwing grenades, neutralized the position denying the advance and killed four enemy soldiers manning submachine guns. After the assault platoon moved up, occupied the position and a base of fire was established, he led a bayonet attack which reduced the objective and killed approximately twenty-seven hostile soldiers. While friendly forces were consolidating the newly-won gain, the enemy launched a counterattack and Lieutenant Wilson, realizing the imminent threat of being overrun, made a determined lone-man charge, killing seven and wounding two of the enemy, and routing the remainder in disorder. After the position was organized, he led an assault carrying to approximately fifteen yards of the final objective, when enemy fire halted the advance. He ordered the platoon to withdraw and, although painfully wounded in this action, remained to provide covering fire. During an ensuing counterattack, the commanding officer and first platoon leader became casualties. Unhesitatingly, Lieutenant Wilson charged the enemy ranks and fought valiantly, killing three enemy soldiers with his rifle before it was wrested from his hands, and annihilating four others with his entrenching tool. His courageous delaying action enabled his comrades to reorganize and effect an orderly withdrawal. While directing evacuation of the wounded, he suffered a second wound, but elected to remain on the position until assured that all of the men had reached safety. Lieutenant Wilson's sustained valor and intrepid actions reflect utmost credit upon himself and uphold the honored traditions of the military service.

DWIGHT D. EISENHOWER

NOTE: The President presented the medal to Lieutenant Wilson at Lowry Air Force Base at 11:30 a.m. on September 7, 1954, in the presence of relatives and friends.

80 ¶ Statement by the President on the Death of Senator Griswold of Nebraska. *April* 12, 1954

I WAS SHOCKED to hear the news of the sudden and tragic passing of Dwight P. Griswold. As Governor of Nebraska, Chief of the American Mission for Aid to Greece, and as a member of the United States Senate, Senator Griswold was a devoted public servant and a distinguished legislator. Although he had served in the Senate less than two years, his long experience in government made him a valuable member of the Upper House; one whose advice and counsel were widely sought. The nation can ill afford to lose the services of such a fine American as Dwight P. Griswold.

81 ¶ Memorandum to the Administrator, Housing and Home Finance Agency, Directing Him To Take Custody of the Records of the Federal Housing Administration. *April* 12, 1954

Memorandum for:

   The Administrator

   Housing and Home Finance Administrator

In order to facilitate the investigations which are being conducted by the Executive Branch of the Government and any other actions necessary or proper to insure the fidelity of operations under the National Housing Act, you are hereby authorized and directed to take custody forthwith of all files and records of the Federal Housing Administration, both in Washington and the field, pertaining to Title I and Section 608 of the National Housing Act, and such other files and records as you find proper for such purposes.

DWIGHT D. EISENHOWER

NOTE: On April 16 a White House release stated that the President had directed all appropriate agencies to cooperate fully in the investigation of the Federal Housing Administration being conducted by Albert M. Cole, Administrator of the Housing and Home Finance Agency. The release further stated that the President had similarly directed all agencies to assist in any investigations by committees of the Congress into FHA activities in the field of small property improvement insurance and the financing of privately-owned rental housing projects.

82 ¶ Message to the King of Laos on the 50th Anniversary of His Accession to the Throne. *April* 15, 1954

[Released April 15, 1954. Dated April 14, 1954]

His Majesty Sisavang Vong

King of Laos

Luang Prabang, Laos

It is an honor to send personal greetings to Your Majesty on the fiftieth anniversary of your accession to the throne. I wish at the same time to express my hope that the people of Laos will continue for many years to benefit from your wise and courageous leadership which has been so vital a factor in the inspiring defense of your Kingdom against foreign aggression.

DWIGHT D. EISENHOWER

NOTE: This message was released at Augusta, Ga.

83 ¶ Exchange of Messages Between the President and the President of France and the Chief of State of Viet-Nam Concerning the Defenders of Dien Bien Phu. *April* 16, 1954

IN COMMON with millions of my countrymen, I salute the gallantry and stamina of the Commander and soldiers who are defending Dien Bien Phu. We have the most profound admiration for the brave and resourceful fight being waged there by troops from France, Vietnam, and other parts of the French Union. Those soldiers, true to their own great traditions, are defending the cause of human freedom and are demonstrating in the truest fashion qualities on which the survival of the free world depends. I would be grateful if you would convey to the Commander of the gallant garrison of Dien Bien Phu this expression of my admiration and best wishes.

DWIGHT D. EISENHOWER

NOTE: Identical messages were sent to President Coty of France and to the Chief of State of Viet-Nam, Bao Dai.

President's Coty's reply follows:

I have transmitted without delay, to the fighting men of Dien Bien Phu and to their chiefs the message you sent to me. The Expeditionary Corps and the National Armies of the Associated States are fighting in Indo China not only for the safeguard and the independence of the Associated States but also for the common ideal adopted by the whole free world, as our American friends know so well. Our soldiers will proudly welcome this testimony by the former Commander-in-Chief, who led the allied troops to victory in the fight against oppression.

RENE COTY

The reply from the Chief of State of Viet-Nam follows:

At moment when all who here participate in battle for dignity of man are bound by anxiety and animated by hope your message is a precious comfort.

The moving battle of Dien Bien Phu symbolizes the determination of communism to impose its rule without regard for the suffering of the people.   Also opens all eyes to reality of force and wills which refuse to bow before the Red despotism.

Before this dramatic circumstance, the Vietnamese people unite in determination and recognizing the disinterested aid given them by the great American nation address to it the expression of their gratitude and friendship.

BAO DAI

The messages were released at Augusta, Ga.

84   ¶ Statement by the President Regarding Relationships With the Proposed European Defense Community.   *April* 16, 1954

AS THE TIME APPROACHES for historic decision on the remaining measures required to put into effect the European Defense Community Treaty, it is appropriate for me to state clearly the United States position on the relation between the European Army and the European Community on the one hand, and the North Atlantic Treaty Organization and the broader Atlantic Community on the other hand.   The essential elements of this position, which have been discussed with leaders of both political parties in the Congress, may be simply stated.

The United States is firmly committed to the North Atlantic Treaty. This Treaty is in accordance with the basic security interests of the United States and will steadfastly serve these interests regardless of the fluctuations in the international situation or our relations with any country.   The obligations which the United States has assumed under the Treaty will be honored.

The North Atlantic Treaty has a significance which transcends the mutual obligations assumed.   It has engendered an active practical working relationship among the Atlantic nations.   Through the North Atlantic Treaty Organization, the United States and its allies are working to build the concrete strength needed to deter aggression and, if aggression occurs, to halt it without the devastation or occupation of any NATO country.   These nations are also seeking to make the Atlantic Alliance an enduring association of free peoples, within which all members can concert their efforts toward peace, prosperity, and freedom.

The European Defense Community will form an integral part of the Atlantic Community and, within this framework, will ensure intimate and durable cooperation between the United States forces and the forces of the European Defense Community on the continent of Europe.   I am convinced that the coming into force of the European Defense Community Treaty will provide a realistic basis for consolidating Western defense and will lead to an ever-developing community of nations in Europe.

The United States is confident that, with these principles in mind, the Western European nations concerned will proceed promptly further to develop the European Community through ratification of the European Defense Community Treaty. When that Treaty comes into force the United States, acting in accordance with its rights and obligations under the North Atlantic Treaty, will conform its actions to the following policies and undertakings:

(1) The United States will continue to maintain in Europe, including Germany, such units of its Armed Forces as may be necessary and appropriate to contribute its fair share of the forces needed for the joint defense of the North Atlantic area while a threat to that area exists, and will continue to deploy such forces in accordance with agreed North Atlantic strategy for the defense of this area.

(2) The United States will consult with its fellow signatories to the North Atlantic Treaty and with the European Defense Community, on questions of mutual concern, including the levels of the respective Armed Forces of the European Defense Community, the United States and other North Atlantic Treaty countries to be placed at the disposal of the Supreme Commander in Europe.

(3) The United States will encourage the closest possible integration between the European Defense Community forces on the one hand, and United States and other North Atlantic Treaty forces on the other, in accordance with approved plans with respect to their command, training, tactical support, and logistical organization developed by the military agencies and the Supreme Commanders of the North Atlantic Treaty Organization.

(4) The United States will continue, in conformity with my recommendations to the Congress, to seek means of extending to the Atlantic Community increased security by sharing in greater measure information with respect to the military utilization of new weapons and techniques for the improvement of the collective defense.

(5) In consonance with its policy of full and continuing support for the maintenance of the integrity and unity of the European Defense Community, the United States will regard any action from whatever

quarter which threatens that integrity or unity as a threat to the security of the United States. In such event, the United States will consult in accordance with the provisions of Article 4 of the North Atlantic Treaty.

(6) In accordance with the basic interest of the United States in the North Atlantic Treaty, as expressed at the time of ratification, the Treaty was regarded as of indefinite duration rather than for any definite number of years. The United States calls attention to the fact that for it to cease to be a party to the North Atlantic Treaty would appear quite contrary to our security interests when there is established on the continent of Europe the solid core of unity which the European Defense Community will provide.

NOTE: The President's statement was transmitted through the Department of State to the Prime Ministers of Belgium, France, Germany, Italy, Luxembourg, and the Netherlands.

85 ¶ Telegram Inviting the Governors of States Afflicted by Dust Storms To Attend Conference at the White House. *April* 16, 1954

[Released April 16, 1954. Dated April 15, 1954]

I AM DEEPLY CONCERNED about the consequences of the dust storms which have afflicted your State and others in the southwestern part of the United States, coming as they have upon the heels of serious and extended drought. This concern extends not only to measures to alleviate suffering and protect property, but to measures which will meet the problem on a longer run basis. This involves all levels of government in working out a cooperative program for improved land utilization and soil conservation. You are invited, along with Governors of other seriously affected states, to attend in the Cabinet Room of the White House a conference to discuss this problem at 2:30 p.m. April 26, 1954. I am hopeful that you will find it possible to be present.

DWIGHT D. EISENHOWER

NOTE: This telegram was sent to the following Governors: Allan Shivers of Texas, Johnston Murray of Oklahoma, Edward F. Arn of Kansas, Edward L. Mechem of New Mexico, and Dan Thornton of Colorado.

86   ¶ Remarks to the 63d Continental Congress of the National Society of the Daughters of the American Revolution.   *April* 22, 1954

Madam President, and members and friends of this great typically American Society:

It is a tremendous honor that you accord me by inviting me to appear before you, even though very informally and briefly.   My first message is from Mrs. Eisenhower who, for once in a long lifetime, bowed to my wishes and remained at her little place of rest down in Georgia while I came to bring you greetings from the family.

I want to talk to you for a few moments from the standpoint of the application of the great principles for which this Society stands, which this Society supports, the application of those principles to today's life.

I think we would not have to go to any great length to describe what we mean by those basic principles.   Our Founding Fathers in writing the Declaration of Independence put it in a nutshell when they said, "We hold that all men are endowed by their Creator with certain rights."

In that one phrase was created a political system which demands and requires that all men have equality of right before the law, that they are not treated differently merely because of social distinction, of money, of economic standing, indeed of intelligence of intellectual capacity, or anything else.

It acknowledges that man has a soul, and for that reason is equal to every other man, and that is the system, that is the principle—that is the cornerstone of what we call the American system.

There are, of course, dozens of auxiliary principles that go along with this one, but rip out this one and you have destroyed America, while many others could be at least revised, studied, and considered without necessarily damaging our whole governmental and political structure.

Now, how do we apply such a system in a world where there is present one great power complex that stands for the exact opposite?   Remember, in the phrase I quoted to you, "Men are endowed by their Creator."   Our system demands the Supreme Being.   There is no question about the American system being the translation into the political world of a deeply felt religious faith.

The system that challenges us today is the atheistic. It is self-admitted as an atheistic document. They believe in a materialistic dialectic. In other words, there are no values except material values. It challenges us today in every corner of the globe.

Now, how do we approach Indochina, or debt management, or taxes, or France, or any other problem that looms up as important to us, in a world where no nation may live alone? How do we oppose the idea of the equality of men, which means group action by cooperation among men, as against this dictatorial, atheistic policy that treats men merely as an agent, as a pawn, as an atom, to be used according to the dictates of the ruler? That is the problem of today.

It would be interesting if we could have the counsel of Washington, of Madison, or of Jefferson, or of Franklin today, after all this span of almost two centuries, if they could sit with us and counsel with us on these problems. They cannot do it. We find, like all other generations, we have our problems. I hold they are not insoluble. America can do it.

But remember, among equals, group action is done to the greatest extent possible by cooperation. You are a free individual. The general limits of your freedom are merely these: that you do not trespass upon, the equal rights of others.

In the same way, in a free society of nations, we don't dictate to one of our friends what they must do. And we certainly won't tolerate any attempt of theirs to dictate to us what to do.

We are a society of equals, both nationally and internationally. And that is the problem. How do we marshal the great intellectual, scientific, economic, financial, spiritual resources of such a great aggregation of equals against a single dictatorial, ruthless enemy that threatens, through every possible type of aggression, the peace of the world?

Now, those are the problems. And I want to say several things. First—I think possibly I am talking about the reasons that I venerate and admire the Daughters of the American Revolution, because the very fact that you preserve this Society means that you do venerate the system that was established by our forefathers. Your lives, or at least this part of your lives, your public service, is dedicated to the preservation of those principles. If we are then united in spirit, we develop a power that is unknown to regimentation.

Woodrow Wilson said, in far better words than could I, something of what I am trying to get at. He said, "The highest form of efficiency is the spontaneous cooperation of a free people."

What I am trying to talk about is the great power, the great force, that is developed by people who believe in certain causes, or a certain principle, with their whole heart and soul.

You know, there was an old feeling among people that you could not have great elan, great esprit, in a service and at the same time an iron discipline. People that believe that ought to read the story of Cromwell's Ironsides. They had not only stern discipline but a great elan, because they believed in something. They went into battle singing hymns.

I sometimes wish that as we approach a concentration, a mobilization of ourselves, of the powers of which we are capable, that we would meet in the idea of singing, whether it's America the Beautiful, or something else, but coming together in the idea that here is a spirit, a belief, a determination that can't be whipped by anything in the world. And that's all we need.

If any of you would follow your imagination to travel around the world, you would find that still in the control of that part of the world we call independent, outside the Iron Curtain, there is a great preponderance of the world's material resources, a great preponderance of human beings, a great intellectual capacity, particularly in certain centers, a great culture, great scientific advancement; in the aggregate resources so overwhelming as compared to the Iron Curtain countries that you sometimes wonder why we grow tense, we grow fearful.

And that brings me back again to my one single theme. It is because we instinctively fear a power that is in the hands of a single dictatorial group or person. How do we combat that power? Again I say, by a spiritual unity among ourselves that is indestructible, among ourselves as individuals, among the nations that we are proud to call friends.

Now, that is a rough chart, as I see it, of the way we will win the cold war, and prevent a hot war, because we will bring to bear in this search and quest for peace all the great spiritual, intellectual, and material values which the free world can concentrate to this one purpose.

Underneath it all must lie this common understanding, this common purpose: the love of liberty, the belief in the dignity of man, and in that to brush aside all minor problems as unimportant, the determination to press forward in that quest.

Now, the kind of unity of which I speak, my friends, is not regimentation. By no means do I believe that democracy can live if each person is compelled to think the same thoughts and agree on all the multitudinous details that go to make up the legislative history of a land. But I do say this: we must be bound together in common devotion to great ideals, in common readiness to sacrifice for the attainment of those ideals, and in a common comprehension of our situation in the world, where we are living, how we are living, and what in broad outline we must do to achieve that victory. Then, if our spiritual dedication is up to the task, we cannot fail.

Now, that is something that I believe this Society does for our people. It increases, and keeps alive, and nurtures that dedication to the dignity of man, to the greatness of our country, and the right of every man to walk upright, fearlessly, among his own equals.

I do hope that during this week you have had a grand time in Washington. I hope that it will not be 7 years that shall pass before I see you again.

Thank you, and good day.

NOTE: The President spoke at Constitution Hall at 3:15 p.m. His opening words "Madam President" referred to Mrs. Gertrude S. Carraway, of New Bern, N.C., President General of the Daughters of the American Revolution.

87 ¶ Address at the Dinner of the American Newspaper Publishers Association, New York City. *April* 22, 1954

President Chambers, President Hoover, Mr. Speaker, distinguished members of this great audience:

For the cordiality of your welcome, I am profoundly grateful. Thank you very much. I am most distinctly honored by your invitation to speak to you.

The responsibilities and the constructive influence of the American press make this a significant occasion to me; one that I welcome. From personal experience, in war and in peace, I have come to recognize your dedication to truth and to the welfare of your country. You deserve the applause of free men, everywhere.

You are, of course, cosmopolitan in thought and in character, at least I am quite well aware, after sitting between the St. Louis Post-Dispatch and the Minneapolis Star and Tribune, that you are not members of a one-party press.

Eight years ago—almost to the day—I addressed the Bureau of Advertising. At that moment, the horror of war was a bitter memory of the recent past. A revulsion against war or any reminder of war possessed our people. The atmosphere was charged with emotionalism that could have destroyed our military strength. Fortunately, our newspapers did not then permit us, nor are they now permitting us, to forget the ever-present reality of aggressive threat.

Aggression is still a terrible reality, though on all the continents and the islands of the earth, mankind hungers for peace. This universal hunger must be satisfied.

Either the nations will build a cooperative peace or, one by one, they will be forced to accept an imposed peace, now sought by the Communist powers, as it was by Hitler.

But free men still possess the greater portion of the globe's resources and of the potential power to be produced from those resources. They possess scientific skill, intellectual capacity, and sheer numbers in excess of those available to the Communist world. Consequently, free men can have a cooperative peace, if with hearts and minds cleansed of fear and doubt, together they dedicate themselves to it in unity and in understanding and in strength.

It is urgent that we try to clarify our thinking about the prospect. Let us start with our own present position. This Nation is a marvel of production, rich in total wealth and individual earnings; powerful in a unique combination of scientific, military, economic, and moral strength. For generations our country has been free from the devastation of war in her homeland and is blessed with staunch and friendly neighbors. We covet no nation's possessions. We seek only the friendship of others. We are eager to repay this priceless gift in the same coin.

Surely, the United States—by all the standards of history—should possess a genuine peace and tranquility.

But our Nation today is not truly tranquil. We, her people, face a grave danger which, in essence at least, all of us understand. This danger, this peril calls for two far-reaching policies or purposes behind which all in our country should be solidly united. They are:

First: All our efforts must be bent to the strengthening of America in dedication to liberty; in knowledge and in comprehension; in a dependable prosperity widely shared; and in an adequate military posture.

Second: This strength—all of it—must be devoted to the building of a cooperative peace among men.

Now these are the fixed purposes of the vast majority of our people. But in a world of ideological division, competitive rivalry, turbulent crisis in one place and political upheaval in another, their achievement demands far more than good intentions or glowing words.

If we are to build and maintain the strength required to cope with the problems of this age, we must cooperate one with the other, every section with all others, each group with its neighbors. This means domestic unity, about which I talk incessantly. Unity does not imply rigid conformity to every doctrine or position of a particular political figure. But it does require a common devotion to the cardinal principles of our free system; shared knowledge and understanding of our own capacities and opportunities; and a common determination to cooperate unreservedly in striving toward our truly important goals. This type of unity is the true source of our great energy—our spiritual, intellectual, material, and creative energy.

Furthermore, our people, strong and united, must cooperate with other nations in helping build a cooperative peace. Such cooperation requires the American people to increase their understanding of their fellowmen around the globe. Likewise, the nations beyond our shores must come to understand better the American people—particularly our hopes and our purposes. And, because of the relatively greater stake we have in world stability, because history has decreed that responsibility of leadership shall be placed upon this Nation, we must take the initiative in the development of that genuine international understanding on which a cooperative peace must be built.

In these truths I find my justification for this appearance before you. The increase of understanding and knowledge is a task that cannot be accomplished solely by our schools or our churches or from political platforms. The malignant germs of misunderstanding and misinformation are at work in the minds of men 24 hours of every day. To combat them challenges the study and the effort of every individual who occupies any position of influence on public opinion.

Every newspaper, every magazine, every radio and television station has the mission of bringing home to all our people and to as many other people of the world as we can reach, the facts of existence today. But this is not enough.

Every agency of human communication also must help people everywhere achieve perspective with respect to facts. Suppose the American press should faithfully report the details of every crime committed in our country, but should be invariably silent on the apprehension and punishment of criminals. Would there not soon be created a universal impression of national lawlessness, disorder, and anarchy? Facts must be related one to the other in truthful perspective. Only within such framework shall we reach clear decisions in the waging of the continuous struggle for a stronger America, and a peaceful world.

Domestic unity and strength as well as international understanding depend, therefore, in great part, on the free flow of information, and its balanced presentation.

Now I am not suggesting that the cause of domestic unity would be served by any attempt of yours to slant the news, or to turn your news columns into editorials. The consequent loss of public respect and confidence would soon destroy the influence of the press. But I do believe most earnestly that the press should give emphasis to the things that unite the American people equal to that it gives to the things that divide them.

News of events which divide may be more spectacular than news of developments which unify. But a free press can discharge its responsibility to free people only by giving all the facts in balance. Facts in perspective are vital to valid citizen judgments. Sound judgment is crucial to the preservation of freedom. Hence a free press can sustain itself only by responsibly reporting all the facts and ideas—the spectacular and the unspectacular, the unifying facts and the divisive.

Could not reader-understanding be as powerful a criterion in newspaper offices as reader-interest?

Need these two qualities be incompatible? I think not. Certainly, the great journalists of our day, in critically examining and reporting on a legislative proposal must inevitably deal with such constructive questions as:

Does it or does it not tend to sustain our economy; to provide needed military strength; to increase our understanding of others or others' understanding of us? Does it give us a more secure position internationally? Does it promise to preserve and nurture love of liberty and self-dependence among our people? Does it improve our health and our living standards? Does it insure to our children the kind of nation and government we have known?

If proposed laws and policies are described as mere battle grounds on which individuals or parties seeking political power suffer defeat or achieve victory, then indeed is the American system distorted for us and for the world. If the fortunes of the individual supporting or opposing a measure become, in our public accounts, as important as the principle or purpose of the project and its effect upon the Nation—then indeed are we failing to develop the strength that understanding brings. If the day comes when personal conflicts are more significant than honest debate on great policy, then the flame of freedom will flicker low indeed.

I trust you do not view my remarks as an attempt to tell you how to run your own business. I am, however, willing to take the risk of your misinterpretation. James Madison once wrote: "A popular government without popular information or the means of acquiring it is but a prologue to a farce or a tragedy or perhaps both." So we are talking of a problem that the responsible governmental official cannot ignore, just as none of you can close your eyes to it.

We are not moving toward farce or tragedy. But knowledge of the facts and of their interrelationships is more than ever essential to the solution of human problems.

I know that to present the facts in perspective is a difficult task. The haste of living creates reader impatience. It discourages complete explanation and places a premium upon cliches and slogans. We incline to persuade with an attractive label; or to damn with a contemptuous tag.

But catchwords are not information. And, most certainly, sound popular judgments cannot be based upon them.

On the steady, day-by-day dissemination of complete information depends our people's intelligent participation in their own government. For them that is no light thing. The decisions they must make are crucial in character and worldwide in scope. On them depends all the necessities and comforts of life—from the amount of money in their pocketbooks, the pavement on their highways, the housing in their towns, to the sort of country they will leave behind as a heritage to their children. They need full and accurate information. Your newspapers can give it to them. On every question where they have it, their decisions will be sound.

Now if increased knowledge and understanding are necessary to promote the unity of our people, they are equally necessary to the development of international cooperation. At this juncture in world affairs, ignorance of each other's capacities, hopes, prejudices, beliefs, and intentions can destroy cooperation and breed war.

Nowhere on this planet today is there an impregnable fortress, a continent or island so distant that it can ignore all the outer world. If this is not to be the age of atomic hysteria and horror, we must make it the age of international understanding and cooperative peace. Even the most rabid Marxist, the most ruthless worshipper of force, will in moments of sanity admit that. International understanding, however, like domestic unity, depends—in large part—on the free, full flow of information and its balanced presentation.

But recent reports state that 75 percent of all the people who inhabit the earth live under censorship. Illiteracy affects vast numbers in many areas of the globe. And, of course, there are language and cultural barriers. Understanding cannot, under these circumstances, be easily or quickly achieved. Into the vacuum caused by censorship and illiteracy, pours the positive and poisonous propaganda of the Soviets. For 24 hours each day, it pours in.

The Communist propaganda machine, for instance, tirelessly tells all the world that our free enterprise system inevitably must collapse in mass unemployment, industrial strife, financial bankruptcy. Time and again, communistic propaganda has shifted and reversed its tactics. But this one charge is firmly fixed in the party line from Marx to Malenkov.

Our United States Information Service, cooperating with similar efforts by friendly nations, seeks to combat propaganda with truth. Every dollar we put into it, when wisely used, will repay us dividends in the triumph of truth and the building of understanding. But our official Information Service is properly limited in purpose, as it is in size. The mass of information of us and to us must flow through the established publicity media of the several nations. Of all these we think ours the best and the most efficient.

Yet, a study in which, I am told, many of you cooperated, shows that the average daily newspaper in the United States prints about four columns a day of news stories from abroad. I do not know whether that is too little, too much, or about right. But I do know that in this amount of daily space it is hard to inform the American people about relevant happenings in all other countries.

Two-thirds of this foreign news was found to be about important official ceremonies and events in other countries—about their internal political crises, their foreign relations involvements, their official statements and pronouncements. Very little of the news had to do with the man in the streets, or with his social, educational, cultural, civic, and religious life and history. Yet an understanding of these is indispensable to an understanding of a nation.

The same specialists who studied this question also examined many European newspapers. There, too, news about the average American was scant. Those among you who have spent years abroad have undoubtedly been amazed by the frequency with which misleading or distorted opinions of our individual and national life are expressed by citizens of other countries.

It is always disconcerting to hear foreign friends speaking disparagingly of the American civilization as a collection of shiny gadgets. It is alarming to know that we are considered so immature in world politics as to be ready to provoke a war needlessly and recklessly. It is even worse to learn that we are often judged as power-hungry as the men in the Kremlin.

Because of a tragic failure to understand us and our purposes, the citizen of Western Europe frequently looks upon America and the U.S.S.R. as two great power complexes, each seeking only the most propitious moment in which to crush the other by force. He believes also that, in the meantime, each seeks alliances with nations throughout Europe with the sole purpose of using them as pawns when the moment of crisis arrives. We know that we seek only peace, by cooperation among equals. Success in this great purpose requires that others likewise know this, also.

As individuals we are frequently pictured abroad as rich, indifferent to all values other than money, careless of the rights of others, and ignorant of the contributions others have made to the progress of Western civilization. Undoubtedly these misconceptions are partially the result of Communist propaganda. But they flourish in the lack of comprehensive, truthful two-way information.

Here at home we need fuller and better information of others, if we are wisely to direct our policies toward real security. Many of us incorrectly assume that all other countries would like to live under a system identical or similar to ours. Some believe that all foreigners are lazy or decadent—that few pay taxes, that they hate us for the sole reason that we are prosperous. We hear often that the people of a particular nation are cowardly, or have no love of country, or pride in their citizenship. Too often we think of them as physically weak, intellectually shallow, and spiritually defeated.

Of course, there are individuals everywhere who fit these descriptions—but it is dangerous to us and to peace when we carelessly speak in generalities of this kind, characterizing an entire nation.

We live in a small world, and only by a cooperative effort of the free peoples occupying important areas can we build security and peace. It is not a question of turning the press, radio, television and newsreels into media of sugar-coated propaganda, "selling" America to the Frenchman, France to the German, and Britain to the American.

It is quite different from that. I repeat: for understanding we need the facts and the perspective within which they fit. I am sure that the free press in all free countries has made real progress in this direction. But I think a lot more can, and by all means should, be done. The future of all of us depends upon it.

No group can be more effective in such accomplishment than you of the American Newspaper Publishers Association. Here, indeed, is an endeavor worthy of your talents and skills.

Within the framework of friendly alliances, we are joined with hundreds of millions among the free nations in working agreements, primarily concerned with military security, but inescapably dealing with every hope and every concern of daily life. Together we live in a mighty arena, bounded by the polar regions, practically encircling the globe, peopled by men and women of independent nations. These peoples, with scanty information and understanding of one another, are now allies of convenience under Communist threat; but tomorrow they could be full partners permanently joined in mutual understanding, impelled by common aspirations. Among the nations of that vast arena, at least, war can become unthinkable—quickly. A cooperative peace among them is no mirage of the dreamer.

Within the United Nations, we possess a global forum where we can plead the cause of peace so that even the men of the Kremlin must listen. Their ears may be stopped to the spirit of our words. Their minds, however, cannot forever be shut to the facts of the age within which we—and they—must live, physically separated one from the other by a few hours of flight.

We cannot hope with a few speeches, a few conferences, a few agreements to achieve the most difficult of all human goals—a cooperative peace for all mankind. Here may I say, my friends, that your representatives in the diplomatic world have no other thought or no other purpose than that which I have just stated: the achievement of a cooperative peace among the free nations and eventually to enlarge that by appealing to the commonsense, representing the facts of the world as they are today to all others, so that even the iron wall must crumble and all men can join together.

To lead that kind of effort, we are blessed—and I say we are blessed, and I believe it from the bottom of my heart—with a man whose whole life has been devoted to this one purpose, who from babyhood has studied and thought and contemplated how to achieve this one great goal of human kind, well knowing that within his lifetime perfection cannot be attained, but to do his part in reaching it. I cannot tell you how sincerely I believe that every one of us—every one of 160 million people—owes a great debt of gratitude to Foster Dulles.

Free men do not lose their patience, their courage, their faith, because the obstacles are mountainous, the path uncharted. Given understanding, they invariably rise to the challenge.

Never, then, has there been a more compelling and rewarding time to work for international understanding, to labor for cooperative peace.

I most firmly believe that the American people's decision to strengthen our country—in moral leadership, in intellectual stature, in military posture, in a dependable prosperity widely shared—will be realized. Underlying that decision is a tremendous spiritual energy which I believe to be adequate to every test. I believe that it grows from day to day as our people become more and more aware of the deadly nature of the world's struggle.

I most firmly believe, too, that world leadership in the cause of cooperative peace lies within the capacity of America. This capacity will be realized when everyone here present uses his mind and his will and all his resources, in union with others of like influence, to bring about the understanding, the comprehension, the determination we need. Freedom of expression is not merely a right—in the circumstances of today, its constructive use is a stern duty. Have we, have you as publishers, the courage fully to exercise the right and perform the duty?

Along with patriotism—understanding, comprehension, determination are the qualities we now need. Without them, we cannot win. With them, we cannot fail.

Thank you very much.

NOTE: The President spoke at the Waldorf-Astoria Hotel at 9:00 p.m. His opening words referred to Stuart M. Chambers, President of the Association, President Herbert Hoover, and the Honorable Joseph W. Martin, Jr., Speaker of the House of Representatives.

88 ¶ Remarks at the Birthplace of Abraham Lincoln, Hodgenville, Kentucky. *April* 23, 1954

Senator Cooper, my fellow citizens:

Long have I looked forward to an opportunity to visit this Shrine, which is so truly American. Now, never in my wildest moments did I picture in my mind this kind of occasion. I saw myself driving up in an ordinary jalopy, and stopping with my family to look and visit this great spot.

I am truly honored by the courtesy you show me in being here today, that I may greet you and bring a word of welcome from your far-off Capital, Washington.

I think I could best express my feelings about Lincoln in this way. In my office in the White House I have sketches of four great Americans on the wall: one is—and the oldest—Benjamin Franklin; George Washington, Abraham Lincoln, and Robert E. Lee.

Abraham Lincoln has always seemed to me to represent all that is best in America, in terms of its opportunity and the readiness of Americans always to raise up and exalt those people who live by truth, whose lives are examples of integrity and dedication to our country.

I would like to speak about two or three characteristics of Lincoln that I think most of us could now remind ourselves, possibly with profit. He was a great leader. I would like to remind you of the methods he

415

used in leadership. You can find no instance when he stood up in public and excoriated another American. You can find no instance where he is reported to have slapped or pounded the table, and struck the pose of a pseudo-dictator, or of an arbitrary individual.

Rather, the qualities he showed and exhibited were forbearance in the extreme—patience. Once he called upon General McClellan, and the President went over to the General's house—a process which I assure you has been reversed long since—and General McClellan decided he did not want to see the President, and went to bed.

Lincoln's friends criticised him severely for allowing a mere General to treat him that way. And he said, "All I want out of General McClellan is a victory, and if to hold his horse will bring it, I will gladly hold his horse."

This means one thing: Lincoln's leadership was accomplished through dedication to a single purpose, the preservation of the Union. He understood deeply the great values that unite us all as a people, Georgia with New York, and Massachusetts with Texas—California with Florida. He knew that there were divisive influences at work, but he knew also they were transitory in character—they were flaming with heat, but they were made of stuff that would soon burn itself out.

The true values of America, he understood, are enduring, and they hold us together. And so he was patient. He was forbearing. He was understanding. And he lives today in our hearts as one of the greatest that the English-speaking race has produced, and as a great leader. Yet never did he fall into the false habit of striking a Napoleonic attitude at any time and under any provocation.

We remember his words because they still mean for us, and still explain to us, what this great country is: the greatest power on God's footstool that has been permitted to exist. A power for good, among ourselves, and in all the world. And he—this great Lincoln—was the one who did so much to give us the opportunity to live at a time when that would be so. When America's leadership in the world is necessary to the preservation of freedom and of liberty in that world, just as his presence in the sixties was necessary to the preservation of liberty and freedom and union of this Nation.

Thank you again for the great honor you do me for coming out here. I cannot tell you how happy I am, at last, to have the opportunity of coming to the birthplace of Lincoln, a man who for me—like for all of you—has been an idol since the days of my first memories.

Thank you, and goodbye.

NOTE: The President spoke at noon.

89 ¶ Address at Transylvania College, Lexington, Kentucky.   *April* 23, 1954

President Rose, Senator Cooper, Dr. Thomas, and members and friends of this great College:

It is my unique privilege and honor to bring to this gathering a salute from the national Government on the 175th anniversary of the founding of this institution.   This honor that I feel does not find its source merely in an age which by American standards is truly venerable.   It comes from many things, that this institution is a member of that great body of institutions that has two great dedications: the preservation, the enrichment, and the dissemination of knowledge; and the propagation and increase of that faith in the dignity of man, in the capacity of man that is the cornerstone of our great free system of Government.

If you will pardon me for referring to Dr. Thomas' address, and particularly allow me first to say that I am overwhelmed by the overgenerosity of his concluding remarks with respect to myself, I would want to make this point: it is indeed refreshing to have a distinguished scientist stand in front of a body of educated people and publicly proclaim that the spiritual values of America are its true values, transcending all of the intellectual and scientific and political and material progress we have made.

Now, what exactly do we mean by these spiritual values?   We mean, I think, those characteristics of man that we call ennobling in their effect upon him—courage—imagination—initiative—a sense of decency, of justice, and of right.   The faculty of being ready to admit that the limit placed upon our personal rights is that we do not transgress upon similar rights of others.   All of which, in a very real sense, is a translation into a political system of a deeply-felt religious faith.

Our forefathers acknowledged this when they wrote, in their first great document: "We hold that all men are endowed by their Creator

417

with certain rights." They did not hold that these rights were yours and ours today because we are born here, because of our height, or weight, or any other characteristic physical or geographical in character, but because you were a child of your Creator. They acknowledged that, in attempting to explain our Government to the world, which they stated in the Declaration of Independence, that that is what they were trying to do. They said, Man is endowed by his Creator with certain rights.

Now, Transylvania, it seems to me, shows certain of these spiritual qualities in its very founding. To come out to this country 175 years ago—and I have been doing some mental arithmetic, sitting here at my seat on the platform—I think that adds up to 1779, and if I am wrong I am sure I will be corrected by those present—but that was 2 years before Yorktown, that was 4 years before the treaty of peace with Britain, that was 8 years before the meeting of our Constitutional Convention.

Ladies and gentlemen, it is almost overpowering to think that someone at that time, coming west of these Alleghenies, and before we were even a nation, before the War of Independence had been successfully concluded, was establishing here an institution to disseminate knowledge and to propagate and to promote and to sustain these great spiritual values that are at the heart of our system.

It seems to me that everybody who in the past has graduated from this institution, who today is privileged to serve in it, or to be here a student, has a great heritage of tradition and understanding that cannot fail to enrich his life as long as he shall live.

One of the great figures identified with this school is, of course, Henry Clay, a man of great courage and forthrightness, and who preached reason as opposed to emotionalism, who strove to get people to use the faculties with which they were endowed, to help solve the problems of the day, and not to give way to mere prejudice.

About 125 years ago he said, once, "Government is a trust. The officers of government are its trustees. And both the trust and the trustees were created for the benefit of the people." That statement of his is not only accurate today, but he summed up in one single sentence, it seems to me, all of the great reasons why it is necessary that Americans today stand shoulder to shoulder in defense of the values that brought about the founding of this College, and the establishment of this country, as against an institution, a doctrine which states government exists to direct people, and people are mere pawns of government, although they clothe their purpose in their rather euphemistic slogan, a dictatorship of the proletariat. It is still dictatorship, and the exact antithesis of the definition given to us by Clay.

Now the point I want to make, again I refer to the address of Dr. Thomas, when he talked about the terrifying power of the atom bomb and the hydrogen bomb. But let us remember this: in a democracy, there is only one truly great force, an overwhelming public opinion.

Woodrow Wilson put it this way: "The highest form of efficiency," he said, "is the spontaneous cooperation of a free people." If you will consider the force that can be generated by the vast majority of 160 million people, with the highest level of education in the world, with the greatest material prosperity and productivity, and with the greatest understanding in their hearts of what freedom and the dignity of man means, if you will try to get some conception of what that force can be, my friends, you will realize that they can conquer the atom bomb and hydrogen bomb, or anything else in this world to which they set their minds and their hearts.

Now, great power can be used for good or for evil. As Dr. Thomas explained, the atom bomb and the scientist's laboratory may produce the force that spells destruction for a city. But it can also produce, or they can also produce, things of vast benefit for all human kind, to make life richer and happier.

Now, so can public opinion. If not based upon fact—fact as seen in its proper perspective—then it can go wrong. So again I think it is—we can repeat, the function of such an institution as this is to place the facts before us in proper perspective, then to relate those facts and that perspective to the faith by which we live.   Out of those two things will grow this public opinion that will insure the safety and security of America.

In the kind of understanding, in the kind of power of which I speak, then we would understand that no nation can live alone today. Just as so many others are dependent upon the products of our laboratories, our factories, and our farms, so are we very definitely dependent upon many of the materials that we use.

All of the original atom bombs, for example, were made of material brought almost exclusively from central Africa. But tin and tungsten and rubber and platinum and many other items used in our daily lives, we do not produce.

We cannot live alone. Understanding of these facts, and again our dedication to freedom and liberty, are bound together, and they begin to emerge into policy as this happens. The words "Dien Bien Phu" are no longer just a funny-sounding name, to be dismissed from the breakfast conversation because we don't know where it is, or what it means. We begin to understand that in a far-off corner of the globe is an agony of conflict, where no matter how it started, has become again a testing ground between dictatorship and freedom, a desire on the one side to give a people the right to live as they shall choose, and on the other side to dominate them and make them mere additional pawns in the machinations of a power-hungry group in the Kremlin and in China.

And then we begin to understand why the special conflict is of such importance to us. When we begin to picture the possibility of more hundreds of millions, starting with this neck in the bottle in Indochina, spread over all Southeast Asia and through the great islands of the Pacific, then we begin to get an understanding of what your representatives in international conferences are striving to preserve for you: basically the same freedom that your Founders brought to this spot. That Lincoln came here and talked about. That Jefferson Davis and others imbibed here. Understanding of the facts, coupled with the faith in America—the spiritual faith that all things are possible to us, if we unite behind them, and they are decent and right.

I should like to make clear, before I say goodbye, that when I talk about united, I do not mean united behind special labels or behind the political doctrines of any particular figure. I am not talking about the details of taxes, which none of us likes. I am not talking about anything that must be argued out freely in our public forums, if we are to reach democratic answers. I am talking about the basic ideals of America. In fact, the kind of thing that, when we stop to think, would be the richest heritage we could pass on to our own children—and I am old enough to talk in terms of grand-children: a faith in this country, and in our God, in themselves, that they can proceed down the road of time, doing all and more than all these past great figures that we today revere, respect, and salute, have done for us.

For the very great courtesy you have paid me in the invitation to appear before you, my profound thanks. If, through you, I could extend my thanks, also, to every person who gave me a smile on the streets of this city, and in the sections I have traveled today, I would be grateful indeed.

Thank you.

NOTE: The President spoke at 4:35 p.m. His opening words referred to Dr. Frank A. Rose, President of Transylvania Col- lege, John Sherman Cooper, U.S. Senator from Kentucky, and Dr. Charles Allen Thomas, President of the Monsanto Chemical Company.

90 ¶ Remarks at the 42d Annual Meeting of the United States Chamber of Commerce. *April 26, 1954*

Ladies and gentlemen:

One of the most pleasant duties that falls to the lot of the President is the opportunity, from time to time, to welcome here in the Capital city bodies of Americans, normally organized according to function or activity in the country, or to some basic purpose. They come here to meet and consult together, and in so doing they consult with members of the Government, and bring us counsel, bring us in touch with the areas lying outside of the District of Columbia, and, we think, greatly to our advantage. We hope that sometimes this is a two-way road. So I do bid you welcome, in the name of the Executive Branch of Government. In fact, I am sure I may speak for the entire Capital in saying we are honored to have you here, the members of the United States Chamber of Commerce.

I think each of us senses that when we meet, as you are meeting today, we are doing so in a time of great decisions. I think it is no longer necessary to enter into a long argument or exposition to show the importance to the United States of Indochina and of the struggle going on there. No matter how the struggle may have started, it has long since become one of the testing places between a free form of government and dictatorship. Its outcome is going to have the greatest significance for us, and possibly for a long time into the future.

We have here a sort of cork in the bottle, the bottle being the great area that includes Indonesia, Burma, Thailand, all of the surrounding areas of Asia with its hundreds of millions of people, and its geographical location that controls lines of communication, to say nothing of the great products of the region, some of which we must have.

Moreover, it is a region with which the newly formed and democratic type of government in Japan must trade. If it is denied the opportunity to trade with that area, how can Japan with its 85 million people exist and develop into a civilization that we would consider dependable, in that it also tried to live in the concept of dignity of the human and according to the precepts of free government?

And then we turn our eyes to Geneva, and we see representatives of great—and some antagonistic—powers meeting there, trying to arrive at some situation that at least we could call a "modus vivendi." We do not hope, I think, very soon to have the type of understanding that we believe we can ultimately develop among ourselves as to great issues. But we would hope that the logic of today's situation would appeal to all peoples, regardless of their ruthlessness, so that they would see the futility of depending upon war, or the threat of war, as a means of settling international difficulty.

That conference is meeting in the terms of another great development of our time: the atomic age, which has so greatly increased the destructive power of weapons that we sometimes visualize in a single destructive and surprise attack, almost a decisive act in the event of an outbreak of hostilities.

In all these things we must, of course, prevent ourselves always from overexaggerating danger, just as we refuse to become complacent because of our historical position of geographic isolation. We do look at them seriously. I am sure that every American that I know looks at them seriously. But I am certain also that America does not forget the power that is concentrated in the faith that we have, in the character of our Government, the character of the system under which we live, and our confidence that by putting our shoulders to the wheel, we can pull through any difficulty.

The great problem is to meet the difficulty in time, so that it does not become a major catastrophe, but that we do adhere to the old principle, "A stitch in time saves nine." But as we think about all of these crises in the world, and their effect upon us, it does illustrate emphatically a doctrine by which the Chamber of Commerce has long lived: that no nation can live alone. We are dependent upon others, as they are dependent upon us, a truth that you have well exemplified in all your actions for many years, including your support of the United Nations.

Admittedly an imperfect instrument for the settlement of these great difficulties, and for the elimination of these great threats of danger, it is still a forum where the world can still talk instead of fight. And that, in itself, is a great advance. It has, in my opinion, accomplished so much in the late years that because the things it has prevented have not happened, we sometimes overlook them.

I think our attitude toward the United Nations should be support, and betterment, and improvement.

Now, because we do have the purpose in this world of promoting peace, of better understanding, of starting by promoting this understanding among nations who are disposed to be friendly to us—the nations still independent, there is one truth we must always remember. I can put it in military terms: you can do nothing positive in a campaign unless you have a firm base from which to start.

In the same way, the United States can do nothing positive in the form of leading the world toward cooperative security, unless it is firm and confident at home.

And so the legislative programs that are submitted to the Congress by the executive departments, that are carefully worked out with consultations with people such as yourselves, and with agricultural, financial, and labor organizations throughout the country, and other people, have as their purpose a firm, sound economy at home, and reasonable, enlightened policies abroad.

In this foreign field there is just one item to which I should like to call your attention this morning: the Report of the Randall Committee, and the message placing it before the Congress for suitable action.

The point I want to make is this: it is a moderate program—if you like, a middle-of-the-road program. It attempts to evaluate and understand and recognize the needs of certain types of industries at home, at the same time that it recognizes the great and crying need for sound relationships with our friends abroad. The additional truth, that we cannot forever be an Atlas, and through gifts and grants and loans—it has become, almost, grants—supporting the rest of the world. But there must be a method worked out by which with mutual profit to all of us, trade can go ahead, strengthening their economies and their standards, as ours are strengthened. Recognizing that adjustments and certain sacrifices have to be made to bring this about, it also recognizes that there is no sacrifice here implied or involved that is half as great—a twentieth as great—as the risk of bringing about a falling apart of cooperative security, and increasing the danger of war.

So you do meet at a time when grave issues are being studied and examined by people who are—like you—ordinary Americans longing for peace, striving to see that peace shall be our lot, and shall be our prize. They do it exactly as you do it, by meeting together, by discussing the problems, by trying to find a solution which adheres to commonsense and to logic, that avoids the extremes on both points, by trying to go down that broad middle way where the great and vast majority of Americans— indeed of the world—can go in perfect accord and unity.

I would say only one additional thing. From war I learned one lesson that I recall right this minute. And that is this: a long face never solved any difficult problem. As you approach these problems you must do so in the confidence that America is great and is powerful, and that it can do anything when we are united among ourselves. You must do so in the certainty that you are striving for the positive factors of happiness and enjoyment in this life, and not in the mere negative idea that we are avoiding destruction or disaster this one day. There must be an approach that reflects confidence, courage, and the certainty that you—and your children—are going to have this great America, and live in it, and be as proud of it and its past as we are this day.

Frankly, my friends, I think I possibly owe you an apology. I came over to say "Welcome" to this Capital City. But as I came, I found my mind so engaged with so many of these other things, and I know that you have so often been helpful, I couldn't avoid talking a bit seriously this morning.

Thank you very much.

NOTE: The President spoke at the opening session in Constitution Hall.

Regarding the Randall Report and the message placing it before the Congress, see Items 16 and 67.

91 ¶ Recorded Interview by Mrs. John G. Lee, National President, League of Women Voters. *April* 26, 1954

THE PRESIDENT. Ladies of the League of Women Voters: As you know, circumstances prevented me from accepting your invitation to address you. Because of this, your President, Mrs. Lee, has suggested that she ask me two or three questions of interest to the League, and that I answer them, our conversation to be recorded. This I am delighted to do. She is in my office now. Mrs. Lee.

Mrs. Lee: Mr. President, the League of Women Voters urges all citizens to work in the party of their choice and to be willing to assume the responsibilities of public office. Do you think that women have a useful contribution to make in this regard?

THE PRESIDENT. Well, most certainly I do. After all, I am told that 52 percent of the vote on the Republican side in the national election a year and a half ago was cast by women. I am biased, of course, but I think they then made a very useful contribution.

So far as the responsibilities of public office are concerned, my position is made clear, I think, by the number of women I have appointed to key posts in the Federal Government. There were 34 in the first year. The more women of the same caliber we have in Government the better off we will be.

Mrs. Lee: Mr. President, the League of Women Voters believes the main focus of United States foreign policy should be, first, to strengthen cooperatively the economies of the free nations, and second, to build our defenses into a workable system of collective security within the framework of the United Nations whenever possible. Would you comment on the individual's role in the achievement of these ends?

THE PRESIDENT. Well, American foreign policy must be founded on America's understanding of her relationships to the rest of the world, arrived at through widespread study of relevant fact. The results of this study are expressed in a sound public opinion, which is of course the real power in a free system. Thus America becomes essentially unified in support of applicable foreign policy, and only when based on such unity can any foreign policy be successful. Every individual American within the limits of his ability and influence can add something to the building of a sound public opinion, to the unity of America.

An organization such as the League of Women Voters can multiply the contribution of its individual members by fostering programs and discussion groups that help a community to learn the facts of existence in the world of 1954. In addition to unity at home, we must have mutual understanding among the free peoples. All of us, whether we live in Maine or Kansas or Texas, in Ceylon or Iceland or Turkey, must come to recognize that basically we are all moved by the same human aspirations, the same general purposes, the same determination to live our lives in freedom according to the dictates of conscience, the same desire for a just and lasting peace.

Again, every individual, and particularly an organization such as yours, can help increase international understanding. Every time we refuse to be stampeded by a prejudice, every time we correct a falsehood, we are doing something for understanding of others by ourselves. Every time we help others to learn the truth about America, we move that much closer to international understanding.

Mrs. Lee: Mr. President, in our opinion the United States has an important stake in the expansion of world trade. Could you tell us what you consider to be the primary considerations in this matter with which the citizens should be concerned?

THE PRESIDENT. The first consideration, I think, should be the enlightened self-interest of the United States. When a problem in world trade arises, and a solution is proposed, I think we should apply to it this question: does this solution, regardless of all else, increase the overall strength of our country, or enhance its influence, or strengthen its position of leadership? If there is a net gain to America in the proposed solution, we should reject all counsel that is rooted in prejudice or in the belief that we can get along without the rest of the world.

The second consideration, I think, should be the reduction of the man-made barriers between the free nations. The more closely we are joined with the other free nations of the world, the greater is our own national security in this generation. Very few Americans, in my opinion, would today urge that we abandon all our alliances, and all our friendships, and retreat into continental isolationism. But we can wall ourselves off in isolation by a stubborn refusal to promote the freest possible trade with others that is consonant with the stability of our own economy.

The third consideration concerns our ultimate goal of a cooperative peace in the world. A principal avenue to cooperation between peoples is trade that is mutually advantageous. The Yankee clipper ships of a century ago were outstanding ambassadors of goodwill for our country. Their modern counterparts on the ocean lanes and the airways of the world can be effective builders of a cooperative peace. The hungry, the disease-ridden, the impoverished, are easily moved by threats and promises and propaganda. Through trade we create opportunities for raising standards of living in other countries, and we win friends who are dependable, we make the world more stable. Only a stable world can be a truly peaceful world.

Mrs. Lee: Thank you, Mr. President. We of the League of Women Voters deeply appreciate your courtesy in taking time out during a very busy day to talk with us.

92 ¶ The President's News Conference of *April* 29, 1954.

THE PRESIDENT. Ladies and gentlemen, I have no announcements this morning; we will go right to questions.

Q. Merriman Smith, United Press: Mr. President, I wonder if you could tell us what are the prospects of our getting involved in Indochina, involved in the sense of use of combat strength there?

THE PRESIDENT. I have expressed myself, I think, rather emphatically on this point several times.

I remember in a press conference, say, of a month ago or more, a question was asked; I said we would not get into a war except through the constitutional process which, of course, involves the declaration of war by Congress.

Now, as to what we have been doing in Indochina: as you know, within the terms of the Mutual Assistance Pact, we provided technical assistance, we provided money, we provided equipment. That is as far as that bill authorized the Executive to go, and that is as far as we have gone.

Now, as to speculating on the future, I wouldn't want to do that too much this morning, Mr. Smith, for the simple reason that we now have a conference called for the ostensible purpose of trying to find compositions for all the Asian troubles; and it would be, I think, inappropriate for me to speculate as to what might happen in the distant future.

Q. Joseph Harsch, Christian Science Monitor: Mr. President, in a recent speech you referred to the desirability of a modus vivendi in Indochina. Could you give us anything further on your thoughts, what is in your mind, by a modus vivendi?

THE PRESIDENT. Well, only this: you are steering a course between two extremes, one of which, I would say, would be unattainable, and the other unacceptable.

It wouldn't be acceptable, I should think, to see the whole anticommunistic defense of that area crumble and disappear. On the other hand, you certainly cannot hope at the present state of our relations in the world for a completely satisfactory answer with the Communists. The most you can work out is a practical way of getting along.

Now, whether or not even that is possible, I don't know; but when you come down to it, that is what we have been doing in Europe—the whole situation from Berlin all the way through Germany is really on a practical basis of getting along one with the other, no more.

Now, I think that for the moment, if you could get that, that would be the most you could ask.

Q. Edward Michelson, Boston Herald and Traveler: I have a question about our air defense.

THE PRESIDENT. About what?

Q. Mr. Michelson: Air defense, continental defense. Senator Saltonstall has said on two occasions now that he believes that our defenses are adequate in terms of the present threat. He has said so since talking with Admiral Strauss and Admiral Radford, and I wondered whether his views as to the adequacy of our defenses reflects your point of view on that score.

THE PRESIDENT. I haven't seen Senator Saltonstall's specific statements, but he well knows, as do all of us here, that a defense is not something that is static. Never is a defense completely adequate. There are improvements going on always.

I am only guessing at an interpretation of a statement I did not read, but I would say that he believes that we are on a program that will bring about the kind of results that he believes necessary. To that extent I can say that I can agree that we are on a program that brings about that state that, you know, I think we have referred to as "respectable posture" in this respect.

Q. Anthony Leviero, New York Times: Mr. President, yesterday a rider was introduced into the House, a rider to the appropriations bill, which would restrict the President's authority to send troops to Indochina or anywhere else in the world without the prior approval of the Congress. I wonder how that squared with your view of the President's constitutional powers to act in an emergency?

THE PRESIDENT. Well, I am not going to talk about constitutional interpretations because it scarcely needs to be said I am not a lawyer. But I do believe this: first, an appropriation bill is not the place to legislate—legislation should be studied in committees, and worked out and adopted thoughtfully; secondly, I believe in this day and time, when you put that kind of artificial restriction upon the Executive, you cannot fail to damage his flexibility in trying to sustain the interests of the United States wherever necessary.

Q. Harry Dent, Columbia (S.C.) State and Record: Mr. President, Mr. Benson has suggested that you would veto any farm bill that would extend even for 1 year the present 90 percent support levels. Would you, sir, would you veto any bill passed by Congress to extend——

THE PRESIDENT. I have several times said that I never prophesy in advance what I am going to do about vetoing bills. I would have to take a look at the bill that came up and study it. I would study it with him, and of course his advice would be important advice to me.

Q. Mrs. May Craig, New England Papers: Mr. President, can you say whether it is true that the French have asked us for air intervention and that it was refused on British urging?

THE PRESIDENT. No British advice or counsel has entered whatsoever in any conversations between the British and ourselves as to what we should do in any specific instance, of the kind of help we should give to France. The matters have been discussed with them on the basis of the constitutional rights and authority of the Executive, and they have been discussed with the proper people in Congress constantly; but the British conversations have been on a much broader basis than any such thing as you bring up.

Q. Charles Lucey, Scripps-Howard: Could you tell us something about your visit with Senator Williams of Delaware, sir; specifically, did he go into anything that might lead to further inquiries into corruption?

THE PRESIDENT. I am not trying to duck, I am just trying to recall exactly what that conversation was.

As I recall, he brought up a certain instance. He and I have been talking about these instances ever since back in 1952 when I was a nominee and not President. I have very great respect for the quiet, effective way he digs into things in Government.

He pointed out certain areas that he thought certainly would bear investigation, and I promptly turned them over to the proper departments of Government. In fact, I asked him to go see those departments, which he did, and he reported to me they have had further conversations.

Q. Mr. Lucey: Would you care to name those departments?

THE PRESIDENT. I think I would wait a little while; I don't think it is necessary to say.

Q. Edward T. Folliard, Washington Post and Times Herald: Mr. President, Folliard, Washington Post [pause] and Times Herald. [Laughter] This bears on what Mrs. Craig was asking you: did the French Government ask our Government for air aid, that is to say, airplanes manned by American pilots to help out in Indochina, and did we turn down the request?

THE PRESIDENT. Mr. Folliard, I would have no objection to answering that question at an appropriate time, but right now we have got a conference going on in Geneva, and our Secretary of State is there representing the interests of the United States. We are trying to get a solution, and I think it is a good time not to say too much about it. But if you will bring that question up after the Geneva conference is over, I would suspect that I can give you quite a little resume of the chronological events.

Q. Robert J. Donovan, New York Herald Tribune: Mr. President, May 1st is nearly on us, and the congressional season is getting along. Do you feel, sir, that the preoccupation of the country and, to some extent, of the Congress, with this Senate investigation is putting a serious roadblock in front of your program?

THE PRESIDENT. Well, Mr. Donovan, while I try to cultivate patience, I don't believe that I am primarily a very patient man; so when I think that there is a course of action that looks like it is for the good of the United States, I am never quite satisfied until it is all done.

Now, I am assured by the congressional leaders that they are going to enact the program that I have placed before them; that at the present time the work of the committees and of the Congress is not being delayed. But I must say this: again, I cannot exaggerate or overstate the importance of getting a program that represents, as I see it, the best interests of this great country—get it on the books, and soon, so as to give confidence to ourselves, and to strengthen the stand that we have to take everywhere in the world. And I mean strengthen our own economic position, to know what we are trying to do in the field of foreign affairs, of trade, of our tax bills, our expenditure program, everything. All this is important, so that we stand as a united people; and when I say "united," I don't mean all of us agree as to details, I mean united behind such a broad program to take care of ourselves abroad.

Q. Sarah McClendon, Galveston News-Tribune: Mr. President, I believe you said you had under study the Texas City tin smelter's closing, and Senator Lyndon Johnson asked the Senate this week to adopt a resolution to keep that open for 1 more year in view of the situation in Indochina. He said if Indochina falls, the free world would be cut off from 65 percent of its tin from Indonesia. Have you made up your mind what you are going to do about that?

THE PRESIDENT. That particular resolution of which you speak, or amendment, whatever it was, I haven't seen. Now, a Congressman from Texas visited me yesterday, and he said he thought that the program involving that smelter was "on the rails," I believe was the word he used.

Q. Mrs. McClendon: Did he say that a group of Bolivians were going to try to buy the plant?

THE PRESIDENT. He said something to that effect. But so far as we are concerned, you must remember this: American purchasing is based upon American estimates of its needs and stockpiles. Now, those estimates are subject to review. What was correct 5 years ago is not necessarily correct now, and there may be more purchasing and more need. But the fact is that there is law that governs what we may do in these lines, including running, let us say, of a smelter, merely to get tin to put in the stockpile. So it is not just as easy as saying you will do it; you have to have a basis of need.

Q. Milton Friedman, Jewish Telegraphic Agency: Mr. President, three Republican Senators and six Republican Congressmen have put in a bill to revise the McCarran-Walter Immigration Act, and I wonder if you could tell us, in view of your previously expressed interest in such revision, what is your attitude toward a bill of this nature?

THE PRESIDENT. I haven't read the bill, but, as you know, I have urged that there be a complete review of the original act in order that we may take out of it what appear to be palpable injustices and inequities— certainly to study all of them to see whether there is not something we may do. Secondly, the asking for the emergency legislation of last year was to provide an avenue by which refugees and others of Europe could come into the United States. As you know, the administration of that bill has been slow and difficult, and what I have been putting my attention on lately is trying to get the administration of that bill so straightened out that that can work effectively.

Q. Ernest Mickel, Dodge Newspapers: Mr. President, there has been some confusion recently over the forced resignation of Federal Housing Commissioner Hollyday. Could you give us the exact reasons why he was asked to resign, sir?

THE PRESIDENT. There is an investigation going on, not only at my direction or certainly approval, but in which I have directed every interested department in Government to cooperate. I have also directed that so far as any proper or appropriate committee of Congress is investigating this matter, they cooperate with such committee.

Now, until that answer is clearer than it is now, until these decisions have been reached, I wouldn't like to comment on any individual's part in it.

Q. Louis Lautier, National Negro Press Association: Mr. President, during the 1952 presidential campaign, at Atlantic City, you said in a speech that you would take up with the Governors of the several States the question of fair employment practices. Since the Governors met here this week, I was wondering whether anything had been done along that line?

THE PRESIDENT. I didn't address them this time except most informally; they came to dinner at the White House, and no specific thing came up.

Whether or not this subject was taken up at this session of the Governors, I do not know; but implicit in everything that I have ever said is the hope and the expectations that States will move on this in an enlightened and forward-looking way.

Q. Robert Clark, International News Service: Some Democrats have complained that they have not been adequately consulted on Indochina, and they don't know enough about the administration's policy on this and other matters that are being taken up at Geneva. Do you think there is any justification for such a complaint?

THE PRESIDENT. The question is whether there has been proper pursuance of the policy of bipartisanship in our foreign relations, especially with respect to Indochina.

I don't want to pass judgment on someone else's opinion as to whether or not they have been treated fairly, because in this question of bipartisanship does arise this one question all the time: I don't, nor does any representative of mine, go before, let's say, a full joint session of both parties in both houses of Congress, and explain the situation.

You do get in leaders who are presumably most intimately connected with the subject. Since the first of the year—I have looked up the record only recently—there have been numerous consultations of this kind. During this month alone with respect to Indochina—there are three meetings this month, in April alone. So I would say that so far as it is feasible and possible, we do everything we can to keep both parties informed of developments.

We go on the theory—and I think it is correct—that, after all, no difficulties abroad affect only one party here at home; they affect all the United States, and we are trying to get the composite view and a composite understanding of the problems.

[*Mr. Hagerty conferred with the President*]

Mr. Hagerty is afraid I left the inference, these three meetings in April, that I participated in them; they were by the Secretary of State.

Q. Marvin Arrowsmith, Associated Press: Mr. President, the congressional elections are still some way off, but do you at this time see any one overriding issue in this year's campaign?

THE PRESIDENT. I am a great believer in policy and the execution of policy. I believe the issue is, are we going to have a record of accomplishment during these past 2 years of legislative and other types of programs that are good for the United States, or have we dillydallied by the way? I think if we have a good program, that's that; if we haven't, it will be something else again.

Q. Kenneth Scheibel, Gannett Newspapers: Mr. President, you told us some time ago that you did not feel the Communists-in-Government problem would be an issue this year. Have you had any reason to change your view on that?

THE PRESIDENT. No, for this reason: I explained one evening on the television talk, and then the Attorney General went on the air later, showing exactly what was going on and what we are doing.

I don't mean to minimize, and I haven't in anything I have ever said, the danger that the United States incurs when there are these people in Government or in other sensitive positions like in industrial plants that are of great importance to the United States security. But I do say that the Government and its proper sections are alert to the problem, are doing everything that is humanly possible to find them, unearth them, and get rid of them, if there are any there; I am not saying or intimating that there are individuals of this kind, I am talking straight to the point of the purpose of these investigations and these examinations. We are doing everything that is humanly possible.

Q. Francis Stephenson, New York Daily News: Mr. President, I think you have received a number of invitations this week to speak in some rather important States. I am wondering if you can tell us your plans in that regard?

THE PRESIDENT. I haven't really, definitely, formed a detailed plan, as you know, for the rest of the year. I do like to go and visit; sometimes I pick up commitments that I have made as long as 2 or 3 years ago, and go and fulfill the commitments.

I expect to move around, to talk about the program that has been laid before the Legislature, what has been done about it, and what we must look toward in the future. I expect to talk about this Government, how it is getting along, its needs, its problems, and try to point out what I believe to be logical ways to approach the solution.

Now, I have told you time and again I do not intend to go out and, as a barnstormer, participate in a local election contest; that is not my business.

Q. Nat Finney, Buffalo Evening News: Mr. President, the Oppenheimer case has broken since we last had an opportunity to talk to you. I wonder whether you could throw for us any light on this question: was this matter taken up again, I believe it has been stated, at your direction or with your knowledge, as an application of the new security order routinely, or was there fresh information which, in effect, caused it to be brought up de novo?

THE PRESIDENT. Well, I would say this: here was a case that, because of its character, it seemed to me could be handled only in accordance with the processes that had been approved and laid down by scientists and others involved in this most delicate and most sensitive subject of scientific research in our Government.

For all scientists I have the greatest admiration, and I am certainly keenly aware of the obligations America owes them.

In this case, and because of the great sensitivity of the subject, because of evidence—put it this way: not evidence, allegations; I would like to correct myself very emphatically, allegations—it seemed that the only thing to do was to assemble the kind of investigating board that had been agreed upon in the past, and at its head I secured the services of a man that I consider to be one of the finest Americans I know.

Until, again, they have reached some conclusion, I am not going to comment further on it.

I must say this: I have known Dr. Oppenheimer and, like others, I have certainly admired and respected his very great professional and technical attainments; and this is something that is the kind of thing that must be gone through with what I believe is best not talked about too much until we know whatever answers there may be.

Q. Alice Dunnigan, Associated Negro Press: Mr. President, the Bureau of Engraving and Printing has been charged with defying the recommendations of the Civil Service FEPC Board by refusing to reappoint apprentice plate printers.

The Fair Employment Board was said to have agreed 6 months ago that the apprentice plate printers at the Bureau were victims of racial discrimination. These findings have allegedly been made known to Mr. Philip Young of the Civil Service Commission, but have never been released publicly. Do you plan to take any steps to have the FEPC Board's recommendations and decisions made public and to have the Bureau of Engraving and Printing fulfill its obligations under the Servicemen's Readjustment Act?

THE PRESIDENT. Have you gone to the proper departments of Government to ask that question? I mean, have you gone to the Bureau of Engraving, and have you gone to the Civil Service Commission and asked that question?

Q. Mrs. Dunnigan: I haven't asked that question, but I understood——

THE PRESIDENT. The reason being, I like to come here completely prepared as well as I can to answer the questions that come up; but when

435

you ask me about the details of how some particular thing has been handled, I can't be expected, I think, to know too much about it. Now, I will ask Mr. Hagerty to look up this particular question and give you an answer in time, but I simply am not able to say anything about that.

Q. A. E. Salpeter, Haaretz, Tel Aviv: Mr. President, in view of the decision to grant military assistance to Iraq, has the administration considered similar assistance to Israel?

THE PRESIDENT. I have forgotten for the moment what is the state of our negotiations with Israel. I know that we have rendered them economic assistance.

We are not rendering anyone assistance to start a war or to indulge in conflict with others of our friends. When we give military assistance, that is for the common purpose of opposing communism. So if we do, and when we do, give military assistance to any region or any nation in that region, it is not for the purpose of assisting them in any local war of any kind.

Q. Edward Folliard, Washington Post and Times Herald: I would like to go back, sir, to what you said about modus vivendi. It is a question of interpretation. I may not have caught all you said, but I caught this much: that you want to get along on a practical basis, as we are now getting along in Europe. Since Germany is partitioned, and since you draw that analogy, is there a danger, sir, that people, some people, might think that our Government would be agreeable to a partition in Indochina?

THE PRESIDENT. Well, I didn't mean, Mr. Folliard, to endorse, even by indirection, any specific means of getting along. I pointed out that a completely trustworthy peace, one in which we could have confidence as between ourselves and the Communist world today, seems to be something over the horizon. We work toward it; we have not achieved it, and I think we would be foolish to think we could do this quickly.

On the other hand, we also understand what the loss of this region would mean to us. There is fighting going on, and of course everybody would like to see fighting stopped. But I am merely talking about some solution that would be acceptable to us and would stop the bloodletting, and have a result of trying to improve that region in its economy and standards of living, and so on.

I have no particular method that I am thinking about at the moment.

Q. James Reston, New York Times: I wondered, sir, whether, in view of this situation in Indochina, you are considering any upward revision of your defense budget?

THE PRESIDENT. Not at this moment in any overall way. Now, there have been specific items suggested to me in which we might do something, but not in any overall or marked way.

Q. Frank van der Linden, Charlotte (N.C.) Observer: Mr. President, are you planning to go down to Charlotte on May 18th—you accepted an invitation this week. I wondered, in view of your statement regarding the congressional campaigns whether or not you plan to say a few kind words down there for Congressman Charles Jonas, Republican down there?

THE PRESIDENT. Well, I would say this: I certainly never intend to say anything bad about any friend of mine. [*Laughter*] But I should like to remark this: the invitation brought to me included Senator Hoey, and the Democratic Governor of North Carolina, so I don't believe you can put it entirely on Mr. Jonas.

Q. John Kenton, New York Journal of Commerce: I wonder if you have any comment, sir, on the statement by Representative Noah Mason of Illinois, quoting Mr. Leonard Hall as saying that he had engaged the services of Senator McCarthy to speak for 3 solid months during the campaign this fall in so-called doubtful Republican districts?

THE PRESIDENT. Mr. Mason quoted who? Leonard Hall?

Q. Mr. Kenton: Leonard Hall; yes, sir.

THE PRESIDENT. I would say this: Leonard Hall hasn't said that to me.

Q. Anthony Leviero, New York Times: Mr. President, I wanted to return to the question of Dr. Oppenheimer again to get a bit of clarification. In the investigation of the allegations you mentioned, is it the aim, was it the aim, to keep the investigation within the security system of the executive branch and thus avoid a public hearing in Congress?

THE PRESIDENT. I am not trying to interfere with any proper execution of its duties by Congress; but, on the other hand, as I have said many, many times, the investigation of these things, allegations, any kind of incident of this sort, falls right squarely upon the shoulders of the Executive. And when it was brought to me I directed the action that has been taken.

Q. Mrs. May Craig, New England Papers: Mr. President, might I ask one technical question: you expressed disapproval of legislation on an appropriation bill. My understanding of the proposal is to restrict the expenditure of the funds in the defense appropriation, to provide that you may not send troops to Indochina without Congressional consent?

THE PRESIDENT. I took it that the questioner gave me the scope of the amendment; I have not read it myself, but I suppose that is what it meant.

Q. Mrs. Craig: There are resolutions relating to that, but the particular thing is a restriction on the expenditure of the money.

THE PRESIDENT. That would be, in my opinion, a poor place to make legislation; secondly, I just want to point this out, that I think the whole process is a wrong way to approach the cooperative work that must be done between the legislative branch and the executive branch in representing us properly abroad.

Q. Arthur Sylvester, Newark News: Mr. President, at the McCarthy hearing yesterday, Secretary Stevens was rather chided for letting the Army go so long under pressure by Mr. McCarthy in behalf of Private Schine, and he subsequently testified that his two bosses were Mr. Wilson and the President of the United States, and said he had taken it up with Mr. Wilson. I wondered if Mr. Wilson had taken this problem up with you during the 7 months?

THE PRESIDENT. You mean talking about this private?

Q. Mr. Sylvester: Yes, and pressure being put on for him.

THE PRESIDENT. I never heard of him. I never heard of him.

Q. Richard Wilson, Cowles Publications: Mr. President, as a former commanding general of the United States Army, what do you think of all the excitement at the Capitol over the privileges granted this private?

THE PRESIDENT. I trust that you ladies and gentlemen will excuse me for declining to talk at all about something that—the whole business— that I don't think is something to talk about very much. I just hope it is all concluded very quickly. That's all.

Merriman Smith, United Press: Thank you, Mr. President.

NOTE: President Eisenhower's thirty-fifth news conference was held in the Executive Office Building from 9:01 to 9:35 o'clock on Thursday morning, April 29, 1954. In attendance: 142.

93 ¶ Remarks to the Leaders of the United Defense Fund. *April* 29, 1954

Mr. Chairman and ladies and gentlemen:

Anyone who has spent 40 years in the armed services could not possibly meet such a gathering as this without seeking for words in which to express a very deep and very lasting appreciation for the work you are undertaking.

The soldier abroad does not lead a particularly happy life, particularly in all of those things that have to do with his home, his community, and his country. He gets a sense of isolation.

As I see it, the big thing that the United Defense Fund does, and through a number of channels, is to keep that man understanding that he is part of America, no matter where he comes from, what may be his city, what may be his race, or his religion—he still thinks, through this kind of effort, primarily of America, and of himself as an American.

Napoleon once said that the moral is to the physical in war as three is to one. And every soldier since then has wondered why Napoleon was such a piker in the ratio that he gave. I would say that ten to one would be a far closer approximation of the truth.

Nobody can win anything in the world unless he believes he can win; unless therefore he is ready to dedicate himself, all his efforts and all his talents, to that job. That is esprit. That is morale. You have got to have something in which to believe. You have got to have leaders, organization, friendships, and contacts that help you to believe that, and help you to put out your best.

Now that is the kind of thing that you people are doing for the American armed services, no matter where they are. It is a terribly important function. And so, while I could have found many ways, I suppose, had I taken time to say this in shorter time, in more succinct and emphatic words, I do say again: thank you all very sincerely.

I thank General Bradley, my old comrade in arms, my classmate from West Point, my great associate in World War II, for taking the job of the chairmanship of this great organization for this coming year. I would guarantee his success because I have made that kind of commitment before, and always came through. And I want to thank another of my old comrades, Jimmy Doolittle, for what he did in the year just

439

passed.   Indeed, we have concocted an opportunity for me to do again what I have so often done in the past, and that is to give Jimmy a decoration.   This is in the form of a Citation which with your indulgence I will read.

THIS CITATION IS PRESENTED BY THE

UNITED DEFENSE FUND

TO

J. H. DOOLITTLE

1954 NATIONAL CAMPAIGN CHAIRMAN

For Distinguished Service in mobilizing leadership throughout the country and for stimulating support of the voluntary services designed to strengthen the national defense program.

NOTE: The President spoke in the Rose   "Mr. Chairman" referred to Lt. Gen.
Garden at 9:30 a.m. His opening words   James H. Doolittle.

94   ¶ Special Message to the Congress Transmitting Reorganization Plan 1 of 1954: Foreign Claims Settlement Commission of the United States.   *April 29, 1954*

To the Congress of the United States:

I transmit herewith Reorganization Plan No. 1 of 1954, prepared in accordance with the Reorganization Act of 1949, as amended.

The reorganization plan establishes a new Government agency, the Foreign Claims Settlement Commission of the United States; transfers to that Commission the functions of the War Claims Commission and of the International Claims Commission of the United States; and abolishes the latter two Commissions.

The Foreign Claims Settlement Commission will be composed of three members appointed by the President by and with the advice and consent of the Senate. The President will designate one of the members as Chairman of the Commission. The Chairman will be responsible for the internal management of the affairs of the Commission. The reorganization plan contains provisions designed to assure smooth administration of functions during the period of transition to the new organization.

The War Claims Commission was created as a temporary agency by the War Claims Act of 1948. The Commission was made responsible for settling certain claims of former United States World War II prisoners of war, civilian internees captured or in hiding to avoid capture in the Philippines, Guam, Wake Island, and the Midway Islands, and certain religious organizations in the Philippines which had aided American forces during the war. In 1952, the Commission was assigned, additionally, the administration of claims of Philippine religious organizations which sustained losses of their educational, medical, and welfare facilities in the war, and of benefits to United States prisoners of war for inhumane treatment during internment by the enemy.

From its inception in 1949 to April 1, 1954, approximately 500,000 claims were filed with the War Claims Commission, and approximately $134,000,000 was paid to claimants. Approximately 96,000 remaining claims are in the process of settlement, and the Commission must complete action on them, together with such appeals as may be filed, by March 31, 1955.

The International Claims Commission was established within the Department of State by the International Claims Settlement Act of 1949. Its immediate function was to adjudicate claims covered by a settlement of $17,000,000 which was deposited with the Government of the United States by the Yugoslav Government primarily to compensate our nationals for losses sustained through nationalization of properties. The act also authorized the Commission to settle such claims as might be included later in any similar agreement between the United States and a foreign government. Subsequently, the Commission was assigned the administration of a $400,000 settlement negotiated with the Government of Panama.

From its establishment in 1950 to April 1, 1954, the International Claims Commission has settled 531 claims out of a total of 1,622 filed. Of this total, 1,555 claims were against Yugoslavia and 67 were against Panama. Under the act, settlement of the remaining Yugoslav claims must be completed by December 31, 1954.

The accompanying reorganization plan has substantial potential advantages. The Foreign Claims Settlement Commission will be able to administer any additional claims programs financed by funds derived from foreign governments without the delay which has often characterized the initiation of past programs. Moreover, the use of an existing agency will be more economical than the establishment of a new commission to administer a given type of foreign claims program. Consolidation of the affairs of the two present Commissions will also permit the retention and use of the best experience gained during the last several years in the field of claims settlement. The declining workload of current programs can be meshed with the rising workload of new programs with maximum efficiency and effectiveness.

A proposed new claims program now pending before the Senate would provide benefits similar to those paid to World War II victims under the War Claims Act for losses and internments resulting from hostilities in Korea. The executive branch of the Government has recommended approval of this program by the Congress. I now suggest that this program be assigned by law to the Foreign Claims Settlement Commission.

There should also be assigned to this new Commission the settlement of such of the claims programs as may be authorized from among those recommended by the War Claims Commission in its report made pursuant to section 8 of the War Claims Act. That report, posing many complex policy, legal, and administrative problems, is now being reviewed by executive agencies; and recommendations will soon be sent to the Congress.

By peace treaties and an international agreement, the United States has acquired the right to utilize certain external assets and settlement funds of several countries. A total of about $39,000,000 is available to indemnify claims of United States nationals against the Governments of Roumania, Hungary, Bulgaria and Italy, arising out of war damage or confiscations in those countries. In addition, claims growing out of United States losses from default on obligations and nationalization of properties may be settled by awards from $9,000,000 realized from an agreement made in 1933 with the Soviet Union, known as the Litvinov Assignment. Action by the Congress is necessary before these various funds may be assigned for settlement, and recommendations of the executive branch in this connection will be transmitted at an early date.

In addition to the reorganizations I have described, the reorganization plan transfers to the Foreign Claims Settlement Commission the functions of the Commissioner provided for in the Joint Resolution of August 4, 1939. These functions involve the receipt and administration of claims covered by the Litvinov Assignment. The office of Commissioner, for which funds have never been appropriated and which has never been filled, is abolished.

The reorganization plan does not transfer the War Claims Fund or the Yugoslav Claims Fund from the Department of the Treasury, or divest the Secretary of the Treasury of any functions under the War Claims Act of 1948, as amended, or under the International Claims Settlement Act of 1949, as amended. It does not limit the responsibility of the Secretary of State with respect to the conduct of foreign affairs. The reorganizations contained in the reorganization plan will not prejudice any interest or potential interest of any claimant.

After investigation, I have found and hereby declare that each reorganization included in the accompanying reorganization plan is necessary to accomplish one or more of the purposes set forth in section 2(a) of the Reorganization Act of 1949, as amended. I have also found and hereby declare that it is necessary to include in the accompanying reorganization plan, by reason of reorganizations made thereby, provisions for the appointment and compensation of officers specified in section 1 of the plan. The rate of compensation fixed for each of these officers is that which I have found to prevail in respect of comparable officers in the executive branch of the Government.

The statutory citation for certain functions of the Secretary of State with respect to the International Claims Commission which are abolished by the reorganization plan, is the third and fourth sentences of section 3(c) of the International Claims Settlement Act of 1949, 64 Stat. 13, as amended.

It is at this time impracticable to specify the reductions of expenditures which it is probable will be brought about by the taking effect of the reorganizations contained in the plan.

Reorganization Plan No. 1 of 1954 provides a single agency for the orderly completion of present claims programs. In addition, it provides an effective organization for the settlement of future authorized claims programs by utilizing the experience gained by present claims agencies. It provides unified administrative direction of the functions concerned, and it simplifies the organizational structure of the executive branch. I urge that the Congress allow the reorganization plan to become effective.

DWIGHT D. EISENHOWER

NOTE: Reorganization Plan 1 of 1954 is published in the U.S. Statutes at Large (68 Stat. 1279) and in the 1954 Supplement to title 3 of the Code of Federal Regulations (p. 101). It became effective on July 1, 1954.

95 ¶ Special Message to the Congress Transmitting Reorganization Plan 2 of 1954 Relating to the Reconstruction Finance Corporation.   *April* 29, 1954

To the Congress of the United States:

I transmit herewith Reorganization Plan No. 2 of 1954, prepared in accordance with the Reorganization Act of 1949, as amended. The reorganization plan assigns to appropriate agencies the liquidation of certain affairs of the Reconstruction Finance Corporation.

First, the reorganization plan transfers to the Export-Import Bank of Washington loans made to foreign financial institutions and to foreign governments, including a loan to the Republic of the Philippines; all foreign bonds and securities acquired in the liquidation of Corporation lending programs; and functions with respect to the liquidation of those assets. The Bank is this Government's principal instrument for the administration of similar matters and can readily integrate the liquidation of the transferred assets with its other activities in the field of foreign finance.

Second, the reorganization plan transfers to the Small Business Administration loans made by the Reconstruction Finance Corporation to victims of floods or other catastrophes, together with the function of liquidating those loans. The Small Business Administration is responsible for a similar loan program. Thus, by this transfer, related activities are concentrated in a single agency for effective administration.

Third, the reorganization plan transfers to the Federal National Mortgage Association, in the Housing and Home Finance Agency, real estate mortgages made or acquired under the authority of the RFC Mortgage Company and the Defense Homes Corporation, and the function of liquidating these assets. The Association is responsible under its basic authority for the servicing, liquidation, and sale of the bulk of residential real estate mortgages held by the Government of the United States.

Through its field offices, the Association maintains continuous relationships with lending and investing institutions specializing in home financing. It is, therefore, the Federal agency best situated to liquidate the assets of a similar type transferred to it by the reorganization plan.

Under existing authority, the completion of the liquidation of the assets and the winding up of the affairs of the Reconstruction Finance Corporation will be carried out under the direction of the Secretary of the Treasury after the succession of the Corporation expires on June 30, 1954. The reorganization plan modifies that arrangement by placing responsibility for the completion of each of the activities described above under the jurisdiction of an agency responsible for a similar continuing program. Thus, the reorganization plan facilitates the orderly and expeditious liquidation of the affairs of the Corporation.

It is not, however, practicable at this time to specify the reductions of expenditures which it is probable will be brought about by the taking effect of the reorganizations contained in the plan.

After investigation, I have found and hereby declare that each reorganization included in Reorganization Plan No. 2 of 1954 is necessary to accomplish one or more of the purposes set forth in section 2(a) of the Reorganization Act of 1949, as amended.

I urge that the Congress allow the reorganization plan to become effective.

DWIGHT D. EISENHOWER

NOTE: Reorganization Plan 2 of 1954 is published in the U.S. Statutes at Large (68 Stat. 1280) and in the 1954 Supplement to title 3 of the Code of Federal Regulations (p. 102). It became effective on July 1, 1954.

96 ¶ Remarks to the President's Committee on Employment of the Physically Handicapped. *April* 29, 1954

GENERAL MAAS has extended to me the privilege, ladies and gentlemen, of saying a few words of appreciation for the work that is being done by this grand Committee for the rehabilitation of people that we used to call disabled.

I am not going to stand long before you today. I just want to tell you that I have had a chance to read part of the essay by little Miss Kreidler, and I found a thought that appealed to me mightily. It was this: that the new approach to this problem that we call rehabilitation is not to say what is wrong with someone, but what you can do, or what is it that you can be trained to do, what are your capacities. Never mind the incapacities because, she very carefully points out, we all have them, and I suppose she will admit she has some herself.

The essay goes on to say, if you are not good at figures and can't keep your own checkbook straight, you shouldn't try to be an accountant, so that is your disability. But whatever it is that anyone can do best, the needs of society require that we discover those and develop them to the utmost, in order that that individual can render a service to society of which she or he is capable.

This seems to me to be such a positive and fine kind of approach to the whole problem that it puts it instantly into a realm or into a level where all of us can look at it in our own way, to the very best effect.

And the point is we don't need to work only for others—we, of course, are working for ourselves. We can try to find out what we can do, what our defects are, and avoid that kind of work. I could name a lot of them; that I could do right quickly.

And that, I think, is the lesson I have learned today. Aside from that, I bring to each of you thanks for your great interest in this kind of thing— because of what you are doing for others, for yourselves, and most of all, for our country.

Thank you very much.

NOTE: The President spoke at the annual meeting of the Committee in the Departmental Auditorium. His opening words referred to Gen. Melvin J. Maas, Chair- man of the Committee. Later he referred to Shirley Kreidler of Trenton, N.J., first-place essay winner.

97 ¶ Remarks to the Defense Advisory Committee on Women in the Services. *April 30, 1954*

I WANT TO SPEAK for one second, ladies, about morale. I know something about the work that you people are doing to sustain in America respect for the Armed Forces and to support them in the work that they are doing for all of us.

Morale among the Armed Forces is the indispensable ingredient, and I know something about producing it. It is this: in the field, a man is more affected by his home town, excepting letters from home, than by any other single thing.

He can have good commanders. He can be well-fed. He can be well-clothed. He can be fired and inspired by victories, but he has got to know that the home front not only respects and appreciates the work he is doing, but also is for him from top to bottom.

In doing your part to assure the Armed Forces of today, in times of, let us say, sort of peaceful cold war instead of active campaigning, you are doing more than your part.

And I, as Commander in Chief of those Forces, want to express to each of you a personal word of thanks and of appreciation.

NOTE: The President spoke at the Pentagon Building.

98 ¶ Memorandum Directing the Departments and Agencies to Take Part in a Civil Defense Test Exercise. *April* 30, 1954

To the Heads of all Departments and Agencies:

On June 14 and 15, 1954, a nation-wide Civil Defense test exercise will be held in cooperation with the Dominion of Canada. United States Territories and Possessions will also participate.

The task of civil defense is vital to our national life. It demands preparedness that can do more than limit the damage of a war-time disaster. It means developing a preparedness, a vigilance, so impressive as to deter aggression itself. This awareness must touch every community, every citizen of our land.

Therefore, I hereby direct each department and agency of the Executive Branch of the Government, both at the national and field level, to take part in this civil defense exercise, to cooperate fully with Federal, State and local civil defense authorities, and to the extent feasible under the terms of Executive Order, dated April 22, 1954, to authorize the release of Federal employees who are enrolled in local civil defense organizations to perform such civil defense duties as are assigned during this exercise.

DWIGHT D. EISENHOWER

99 ¶ Statement by the President on the Dust Bowl Emergency. *May 4, 1954*

LAST WEEK, at my invitation, the Governors of Colorado, Kansas, New Mexico, Oklahoma and Texas met the representatives of interested Departments and Agencies of the Federal Government to discuss remedial action in connection with the dust bowl emergency.

The Governors attending that conference expressed their approval of legislation to make additional Federal funds available to supplement state efforts directed at alleviating the wind erosion problem.

In order that prompt action may be initiated in this critical situation, I am today authorizing the allocation of $10,000,000 from the President's Disaster Relief Fund to the Secretary of Agriculture. This will enable the Federal Government to move swiftly in aiding the dust bowl area pending final Congressional action in this matter. The revised version of S.J. Res. 144, now before House and Senate conferees on the Third Supplemental Appropriation Bill, has been worked out in cooperation with the Senators and Governors of the states affected by this serious wind erosion.

I have been gratified by the teamwork evident during these discussions. This kind of cooperation will contribute significantly to a speedy and effective attack on this menacing problem.

100 ¶ Remarks to the President's Conference on Occupational Safety. *May 4, 1954*

Secretary Mitchell, ladies and gentlemen:

First, I have the privilege of bidding you welcome to the Nation's Capital on behalf of the administration—indeed, of the entire Government. Next, I should like to thank each of you, to express to you some measure of the sense of obligation I feel that you have responded to my invitation to give up your own time and to devote your own energies and talents to this problem of providing for safety against the accidents of industry.

It is a subject that is brought to my attention frequently. Like you, I read about it in the papers and am appalled by its frequency. And I have people around me, the Secretary of Labor, and his assistants, who never let me forget it. There are people on the Hill, like Senator Saltonstall, who always tell me I must do something about it.

That something to do about it is what we hope now you are going to help advance and develop.

They showed me a statistic only this morning, that the days lost in 1953 because of industrial accidents would have built one million six-room houses. Well, when I think of all of the effort and mental agony, and argument and difficulty we go through in order to get started a program of house-building for those who are not properly housed in this country, it would seem, if we could put these two problems together and get a common solution, we would have a great deal done quickly.

You read in your papers about all the different types of problems that beset our country, and you read the differing opinions as to the approach that should be made. You read of Indochina and the various ways we ought to try to help solve the difficulties of that troubled section. We read of India and Pakistan, and of differences in Europe, the differences of opinion among other nations, and among ourselves—about taxes, and so forth.

But among us there is certainly no difference about this one thing: we ought to stop accidents among our people. Particularly we ought to stop the kind of accident that apparently is so often brought about by lack of training, or through carelessness.

If you can help reduce this appalling bill—and I know you can—the appalling bill the Nation must pay, not only in terms of the material things we have lost, but in the suffering of people who undergo the accidents, or the loss of life that occurs, the charge upon our hospitals and all the rest of it, then you will indeed be doing something that you can definitely and clearly know is in the interests of the United States. It is one place where you will unquestionably not have to answer the arguments and the criticisms of those that disagree, because there should be none.

So it is with unusual warmth and enthusiasm that I welcome this body here, representatives of business, of labor, of education, and every other kind of activity that represents and makes up this great America.

449

I hope also that while you are here, in addition to the constructive work that you will do and the contributions you will make, you will thoroughly enjoy your visit to the Capital City. I assure you, you have come at a moment when through some propitious circumstance the temperature is more fitting to sightseeing and enjoyment than it normally is at this time of year.

Thank you very much.

NOTE: The President spoke in Constitution Hall. His opening words "Secretary Mitchell" referred to Secretary of Labor James P. Mitchell.

101　¶ The President's News Conference of *May* 5, 1954.

THE PRESIDENT. First, ladies and gentlemen, I should like to record my intense satisfaction that the Governor General of Canada found it possible to return the courtesy visit that I made to that country some months ago.

I was delighted he had a chance to address the assembled Houses of our Congress. It goes without saying that the destinies of our two countries are very closely linked. Because, indeed, of our geographical similarity in certain respects, sometimes our economic interests are competitive and they lead to long discussion, sometimes possibly argument; but I must say that our relationship with Canada stands as almost a model, as I see it, for international relationships everywhere.

I am highly pleased that the Governor General could come down here and voice the same sentiments.

Now, I am going to talk for a few minutes about the Indochina affair. The statement that I read will, before the end of this conference, be outside in mimeographed form, so I assure you you don't have to take notes of what I have to say here, but I do want to make a few things crystal clear.

[*Reading*] With the return of the Secretary of State from Geneva, there will of course be a series of conferences on foreign affairs, both within the executive department and between the Secretary of State and bipartisan groups of the Congress. Because of these forthcoming conferences and the probability that the Secretary of State will himself have something to say, and because also of the delicate nature of the issues now pending before the Geneva conference, I shall limit my comments on the Indochina situation to this written statement.

United States foreign policy has consistently supported the principles on which was founded the United Nations. The basic expression of this policy was the Vandenberg resolution in 1948. The United States believes in assuring the peace and integrity of nations through collective action and, in pursuance of the United Nations principle, has entered into regional security agreements with other nations. Examples are the Inter-American Agreement, the NATO Agreement, and numerous pacts in the Pacific. These arrangements are invariably to assure the peaceful security of the contracting nations and to prevent likelihood of attack; they are not arrangements designed primarily for waging war.

The Geneva conference, now 9 days old, has produced no surprises. The expressed fears of some have proved unfounded.

It has not been a "Five-Power" conference as the Soviet Union tried to make it.

It has not involved establishing express or implied diplomatic recognition by the United States of the Chinese Communist aggressors.

The Korean phase of the conference has been organized. Here the Communists came up with a scheme for Korean unification which was a Chinese copy of the Soviet scheme for the unification of Germany. Under their proposal no election measures could be taken without Communist consent, and there could be no impartial supervision of the election conditions or of the voting.

This scheme was rejected for Germany. Secretary Dulles tells me that it is equally unacceptable to the Republic of Korea and to the United Nations members which took part in the Korean war under the United Nations Command now represented at Geneva.

The Indochina phase of the conference is in process of being organized and the issues have not yet been clarified. In this matter a large measure of initiative rests with the governments of France, Viet-Nam, Laos, and Cambodia, which are the countries most directly concerned.

Meanwhile, plans are proceeding for the realization of a Southeast Asia security arrangement. This was publicly suggested by Secretary Dulles in his address of March 29. Of course, our principal allies were advised in advance. This proposal of the Secretary of State was not a new one; it was merely reaffirmation of the principles that have con-

451

sistently guided our post-war foreign policy and a reminder to interested Asian friends that the United States was prepared to join with others in the application of these principles to the threatened area. Most of the free nations of the area and others directly concerned have shown affirmative interest, and the conversations are actively proceeding.

Obviously, it was never expected that this collective security arrangement would spring into existence overnight. There are too many important problems to be resolved. But there is a general sense of urgency. The fact that such an organization is in the process of formation could have an important bearing upon what happens at Geneva during the Indochina phase of the conference.

The countries of the area are now thinking in constructive terms, which include the indispensable concept of collective security. Progress in this matter has been considerable, and I am convinced that further progress will continue to be made. *[Ends reading]*

Now, until certain of these things have occurred, the conferences and so on, I shall have nothing further to say about the Indochina situation.

With that one comment, why, we will proceed to questions.

Q. Marvin L. Arrowsmith, Associated Press: Mr. President, last week you expressed the hope that there would be an early end to the Army-McCarthy hearings. Yesterday the Army counsel objected to a Republican proposal to cut them short. Do you see any administration conflict there? Do you still favor a quick end to those hearings?

THE PRESIDENT. Well, last week, of course, when we failed to get through a conference without this subject coming up again, I noted in reading most of the accounts that my appearance upon answering seemed to be more important than what I had to say, so I will try to be very careful. *[Laughter]*

I did say that I hoped that these hearings would be quickly concluded; but by the word "concluded," I meant, of course, with effective answers to whatever were considered by the committee to be the main issues involved, and from the principals concerned.

I am going to say just one more thing about it, and then I wouldn't be surprised that I would bar questions of this nature—*[laughter]*—for a few weeks at least.

Our only hope now is that America may derive from this incident advantages that are at least comparable to what we have suffered in loss of international prestige, and I venture to say, judging from my correspondence, national respect, self-respect.

Now, that is just about the way I look at it, and I have nothing further to say.

Q. Edward J. Milne, Providence Evening Bulletin: Mr. President, point of order! [*Laughter*] This may be out of order, but I would like to pursue this and go just one step further, if I may. I would like to ask whether or not Secretary Stevens, who is now in his tenth day on the stand, has your full backing in his course of conduct?

THE PRESIDENT. Secretary Stevens was selected for his present job with great care, upon the recommendation of people that have known him for a long time. His record was carefully examined. I know of nothing that would cause me to lose confidence in Secretary Stevens' administration of the Army, and on that basis I'd back him up to the limit.

Q. Diosdado M. Yap, The Manila Chronicle and Bataan Magazine: Mr. President, it is reported that General Romulo discussed with you the question of the Philippine defense, and the interest of the President of the Philippines in the Anti-Communist Pacific Alliance Pact. Would you care to make any comments on this matter?

THE PRESIDENT. I am not trying to be evasive here, but I must admit I don't recall the exact subjects of General Romulo's call upon me. We are old friends from Philippine days, and we discussed many things, personal and otherwise.

I do not recall that the specific things that you mentioned came up, except that he did point out that President Magsaysay instantly announced his readiness to go along with the United States in an effort of the kind suggested, publicly.

Q. Ethel Payne, Defender Publications: Mr. President, I would like to refer to the question asked you on April 7th, as to whether the several housing agencies had issued any regulations to implement the statement in your housing message to Congress, that everything should be done to assure good and well-located homes for all citizens. You said then that you would have an answer later for this.

So far as we have been able to learn, no such specific regulations have been forthcoming. May I cite to you the situation at Levittown in Pennsylvania as an example where members of minority groups are being barred.   I would like to know if you have any information at this point on this matter.

THE PRESIDENT. Just a minute.   [*Confers with Mr. Snyder*]

Mr. Snyder tells me that there have been some reports come to the White House, but they are of a general character; and the only hope of getting a detailed report, such as you describe, is to go to the FHA people themselves, that department.

Q. Pat Munroe, Salt Lake City Deseret News: I wonder if you have any comments, sir, on the slow progress in Congress of your bill to develop the Colorado River in the Rocky Mountain area near your summer headquarters.

THE PRESIDENT. Well, my summer headquarters is on the eastern slope.   [*Laughter*]   As a matter of fact, it was for 1 year; I never know whether it will ever be again, of course.

This is an involved matter, as you know.   One of the beliefs, one of the convictions, I hold is that water is rapidly coming to be our most valuable national resource—that is, material resource—and that we have to have surveys covering the entire Nation in order to act intelligently in any specific area, whether it is reclamation or flood control, navigation or whatever.

One thing that appealed to me about the Colorado River project was that it seemed to be at least a completely integrated plan going from the headwaters down on and integrating with the Lower Colorado River project which was developed some years ago, and taking care of our commitments to Mexico which, I believe, are on the order of 75 million acre-feet over a period of 10 years.

A vast thing like this takes a lot of study.   They are naturally going to study it in the committees of Congress, just as we continue to study it. I would never expect any particular plan to go through in every detail as it has been originally recommended; but I do say that whatever is approved out of this will be in accordance with a general plan of an integrated use of our water resources of the Nation.

Q. John Herling, Editors Syndicate: Mr. President, can you tell us what your attitude is toward the so-called States rights amendment introduced by Senator Goldwater of Arizona to the Taft-Hartley legislation which would, in effect, surrender to the States certain rights which now belong to the Federal Government under the Taft-Hartley law?

THE PRESIDENT. Well, the exact language of the Goldwater amendment I haven't in front of me; but this question of the rights of the State to act in labor disputes has been, of course, one of great discussion, not only for many months but throughout the history of labor legislation.

My own general feeling is that as long as the rights, privileges, of labor and employer set up by the Taft-Hartley Act are not violated, the traditional responsibilities of the State for health, for keeping the peace, and so on, should not be interfered with. Now, the exact language here is going to have to be worked on and hammered out.

This is what I have to say about it: as a matter of urgency there are certain things in the interests of the great laboring group of the United States and, therefore, the United States as a whole that we believe should be done to the Taft-Hartley Act, and we passed those recommendations to Congress. I would dislike to see them halted by extraneous matters that could be handled, I think, on their own; but I am not prepared to discuss in detail the language of Mr. Goldwater's amendment.

Q. Robert E. Clark, International News Service: Mr. President, Secretary Dulles has drawn his sharpest criticism since taking office because of what some people are contending is a major diplomatic defeat for American foreign policy at Geneva. Do you have any comment on that?

THE PRESIDENT. Well, I would say this: you can't count a battle lost that is still going on. I would say further, United States foreign policy, like the foreign policy of all other nations, is designed in this belief: that it serves the enlightened self-interest of the country that it is drawn up in favor of.

Now we continue to work along that line. If any ally disagrees or if someone with hostile intent is able to put over some idea of his, you continue to work; you never give up working persistently and as intelligently as you know how for the best interests of the United States. So there is no such thing as acknowledging a defeat in the execution of foreign policy, as I can see it.

Q. Roscoe Drummond, New York Herald Tribune: Mr. President, the Democratic National Committee is meeting here in Washington today and tomorrow, and I wondered if, by chance, you would have any message you would like to deliver to the assembled Democrats?

THE PRESIDENT. I haven't been invited, Mr. Drummond. [*Laughter*]

Q. Kenneth M. Scheibel, Gannett News Service: Mr. President, there are reports that you have advised your leaders in Congress you will accept a 1-year extension of the 90 percent farm program; is that true?

THE PRESIDENT. I never have heard of such reports. I believe to say what I would accept and what I would veto falls again under my general approach, you might say principle, of not promising in advance what you will do with any particular bill because you don't know what will be its other features. The exact statement that you make I have never made.

Q. Frank van der Linden, Nashville (Tenn.) Banner: Mr. President, yesterday a group of TVA Congressmen came to see you and asked you again to reappoint Gordon Clapp as Chairman of TVA. They quoted you afterward as saying that there wouldn't be any partisanship in the selection of a TVA Chairman; and I wondered if we should interpret that as meaning that you would reappoint Mr. Clapp?

THE PRESIDENT. Well, that is a curious interpretation.

I say there will be no politics, so far as I can eliminate them—I mean, as far as I know and can feel and sense in the appointment to a post where I believe the highest kind of professional competence is needed.

Q. Laurence H. Burd, Chicago Tribune: Mr. President, are you fully satisfied with Secretary Dulles' handling of the Geneva negotiations, and do you expect him to return there?

THE PRESIDENT. To answer the last part of your question first, the need for his return or not returning will be determined by himself. After all, he is a mature man and an experienced man.

Now, I would say this: I would never answer a question with respect to anyone, did he over a period of weeks act exactly, let's say, according to standards of perfection.

I will repeat this: Foster Dulles, in my opinion, is the greatest Secretary of State in my memory, and he has my unqualified support in what he is doing; so far as I know, I have agreed in advance to every policy he has ever brought forward.

Q. (Questioner unidentified): I would like to ask, do you see anything in the current business and employment situation that justifies the conclusion that an upturn already is under way with no further Government intervention necessary?

THE PRESIDENT. Well, Government is never entirely free in these modern days from exercising some influence on the economy, with Government and quasi-governmental organizations, the Federal Reserve Board,

Treasury, interest rates, everything. So, you say seeing no need, it is inescapable, there is some effect of governmental action upon the economy.

Now, just as I cautioned against too pessimistic an outlook some weeks ago, I would caution against looking at this thing through too rosy glasses now. The economy of our country is a delicate affair, and it takes watching every day. But I would say this: in my late reports there has been a preponderance, I would say, of favorable factors over unfavorable; that is about all I can say.

Q. Sarah McClendon, San Antonio Light: Mr. President, the Soviet Embassy in Mexico City yesterday announced, according to the Associated Press, they would invite trade with Mexico in meat, cotton, and other items. The State Department says this is not outside the realm of your policy so far as East-West trade is concerned if it is not in vital war materials. But some of these products, like meat, we exclude from this country. I wonder if you see any potential danger?

THE PRESIDENT. Well, I haven't discussed this. As a matter of fact, you are reporting something I hadn't heard of, it hadn't come to my desk. I haven't discussed it with anybody, and I would have to have a chance to take a look at it before I make an answer.

Q. Fletcher Knebel, Cowles Publications: Mr. President, could you say whether since the McCarthy-Army hearings have started, that you have called Secretary Stevens?

THE PRESIDENT. I what?

Q. Mr. Knebel: Whether you have called him and talked to him?

THE PRESIDENT. Oh, I have talked to him several times. I don't know whether I have called him; I know that I have talked with him several times. As a matter of fact, the last time was only, I think, Friday noon.

Q. James M. Daniel, Rocky Mountain News: Did I understand you to say, sir, that you might not be coming to the Summer White House in Denver?

THE PRESIDENT. I said I could never be sure of what one can do, and so no matter where my heart lies, I have to follow the dictates sometimes of very hard and obvious facts in life.

Q. Mr. Daniel: Not even a vision of coming out this summer? [*Laughter*]

Q. Raymond P. Brandt, St. Louis Post-Dispatch: Mr. President, do you plan any further measure for the Randall report to get congressional support for it?

THE PRESIDENT. Well, we are constantly studying the ways and means of proceeding with that report which, as you know, I consider a very fine middle-of-the-road approach to our foreign trade, and I sent a long statement.

There are many ramifications. Some of the parts of that study, I think, will take long examination and analysis, and they will unquestionably be matters probably of some long debate. Others are not argumentative, and so it will be a question, I should think, of how rapidly can you get these various things implemented. On that, I am not going to quit by any manner of means.

Q. Mr. Brandt: The Reciprocal Trade Agreement law expires in June——

THE PRESIDENT. Yes, June 12th.

Q. Mr. Brandt: Do you think there is a possibility it will merely be extended, and then these other matters will be taken up?

THE PRESIDENT. Well, really I don't want to guess, Mr. Brandt, for the simple reason that I don't know exactly what Congress is going to do, and I don't want to appear that I am going to be horribly disappointed if they don't do it my way. As long as they see the essentials of the situation and meet them, why, of course, that is what I want. Some of these things have to be done quickly and some slowly.

Q. Mrs. May Craig, New England Papers: Mr. President, the Air Force has decided not to court-martial prisoners who may have broken in captivity. The Army has court-martialed one corporal. The Marine Corps has made an in-between decision. Do they come up to you for a general policy consideration in view of the "brain-washing" technique of the enemy?

THE PRESIDENT. Well, of course, they don't have to. As a matter of fact, the things that have to come to my desk, as I recall, are all of those offenses for which court-martial finds a punishment of death or, I believe, dismissal of an officer.

They don't have to come to me, but you must remember I spent a long time in the Army and so, frequently, they come up to me for conversations that are unofficial.

This is the only thing I feel that I can guarantee: that there will be justice tempered with mercy in all of these cases, because there is a very

458

deep understanding of the tremendous pressures that can be placed upon people. But do not make the error of thinking that all of these cases are identical; they are far from identical. There are wide and vast differences; therefore, you can't merely say, because in one case such-and-such a conclusion was reached, that that is applicable to all. So I don't know what will finally come up to me. It has been impossible to make a statement that would be applicable to all of them.

Q. Mrs. Craig: Sir, I asked you that because there has been a proposal that a commission be set up to study these new techniques of the enemy and how our men can be prepared against them. My thought was that, perhaps, that would come to you.

THE PRESIDENT. Well, that I think would.

Q. Joseph Chiang, Chinese News Service: Mr. President, some news stories that appeared in various newspapers in Far Eastern countries advocate a strong movement to organize among the free people of Asia united action to check the Communist invasion against Asia. It was also pointed out that they welcome interest by Americans in support of their cause. Do you have any comment on that, sir?

THE PRESIDENT. I think, if you will read carefully the statement I made this morning, the written statement, of which you will get a copy outside, you will find as much of an answer as I can make at this moment.

(Speaker unidentified): Thank you, Mr. President.

NOTE: President Eisenhower's thirty-sixth news conference was held in the Executive Office Building from 10:30 to 10:55   o'clock on Wednesday morning, May 5, 1954. In attendance: 157.

102 ¶ Statement by the President Upon Signing the Federal-Aid Highway Act of 1954. *May 6, 1954*

I AM VERY GRATIFIED that this important measure has now become law. I am especially glad that the scope and pace of our efforts to make up our highway deficiencies will be considerably increased.

In recent years the nation has accumulated tremendous highway needs which are becoming increasingly acute. Our highways badly need modernization and expansion to accommodate today's vastly increased motor traffic. Large-scale improvement is needed simply to remedy deficiencies not met in the past.

This legislation is one effective forward step in meeting these accumulated needs. It keeps in the States, as I deeply believe it should, primary responsibility for highway construction. At the same time, it recognizes the responsible relationship of the Federal Government to the development of a sound, naionwide highway system.

The almost two billion dollars authorized by the new law is the largest two-year sum ever provided for Federal highway programs. Nevertheless, the needs are so great that continued efforts to modernize and improve our obsolescent highway system are mandatory.

The public will welcome, I am sure, the fact that funds equivalent to revenue from Federal gasoline taxes will now be used entirely for the improvement of the nation's highways.

I am especially interested in the studies to be made by the Secretary of Commerce under the new law, and in the related studies under way in the Commission on Intergovernmental Relations. Continuances of work on the Inter-American Highway and Rama Road is also important.

NOTE: The Federal-Aid Highway Act of 1954 is Public Law 350, 83d Congress (68 Stat. 70).

103 ¶ Remarks at the 22d Annual Convention of the Military Chaplains Association. *May* 6, 1954

Mr. Chairman, ladies and gentlemen:

I am somewhat embarrassed by the extravagance of the language your presiding officer used to describe certain of my simple convictions and beliefs. I am astonished that this group of public servants—this group of Chaplains—should have found it desirable from their viewpoint to present to me such an award, one that I assure you will be treasured by me and my family.

The last time that I can remember addressing a group of Chaplains was in the Hague. It was the last group that I addressed before I came home from Europe, in the early spring or summer of 1952. I can well remember the subject I took that day, as I had the opportunity, exactly as this one, to go before that body and to bid them welcome to a particular spot for a particular purpose. Then it was all the Chaplains of SHAPE, the great international organization, as you know, designed to preserve the peace in Europe.

Today it is my privilege to extend to you on behalf of the administration a welcome to the Capital City. What I talked about was what I thought was a dereliction of duty on the part of the Chaplains. And I had a—I thought—very definite reason for talking in that way. I thought they were far too modest, far too much like shrinking violets, and were normally hiding their lights behind trees, if not bushels, instead of getting out where they belonged and doing something about things. And we really had quite a nice time before I got away. But I still think that some modicum, at least, of criticism is applicable.

Now, I don't know to what source we trace our faith, its beginnings in our hearts and minds. But it was certainly not difficult for me to build up an intensive religious faith as long as I was as dedicated as I think I am—to a free system of government among people. To me it makes no sense, without a religious foundation. And indeed, our forefathers could not explain the new system they set up in America except by saying our Creator has endowed us with certain basic rights, thereby establishing, as far as this Government was concerned, a divine source for its beginnings.

Now, in its application to the Army, why does an Army fight? Why do people go into the armed services, either voluntarily or in response to the behest of Government? Why do they meet the tests of battle, and do it courageously?

Because there is a certain sense of values that are important to them. They have a cause for which to fight.

Now, if we fail to get that cause in their minds fixed as comprehending the very source of the things for which they are fighting, the whole system that provides them a free home, a free way of life, free education, free expression, all based on a religious foundation—if we don't get that across to them, I say the Army, Navy, Air Force, is not as good as it can be.

Cromwell's men marched into battle singing hymns. They were highly disciplined, and greatly and wildly enthusiastic about the cause for which they fought. Now you may have been a Cavalier instead of a Roundhead in your sympathies, but you do have to admit that that was a most efficient Army, and they sang while they hewed off heads with a sweep of their swords. Now they believed they saw a direct connection between

461

the risking of their lives, and what they were doing and something very deep in their souls.

These things may be basic. You may say, well everybody knows that. Well, everybody doesn't know it. Everybody doesn't stop to think about it. And entirely aside from all of the, let us say, routine—normal duties of the Chaplain, as I see it, our great service is to get over and make sure every individual knows what his country stands for, and therefore what is the basic cause for which he fights.

This need became very real with me in the early days of World War II. I know of no question that I was asked by the private soldier, as I would roam around in the various fronts and along the roadways, through depots—I know of no question that was asked me as often as "Well, General, why are we here?" And particularly if they picked up some paper that showed there was some strike going on in the United States, as there was at that time, as I recall. "Why are we here fighting like this? These people aren't supporting us"—or words to that effect.

To get over to them that they were defending a free way of life, and that that free way of life was imbedded deeply in the religious faith of their fathers—that was the simplest and best answer I could give them.

And I believe it can be done ahead of time, and I don't believe we have to ask our fighting men of any service to go into battle not knowing what he is fighting for.

I conceive that to be a job of the Chaplains, and at least, let us say, you have worked efficiently, but you haven't completed the job—that we know.

Now of course I am honored to appear before such a body. Not only is it a wonderful feeling to come back among the uniforms, I am glad to see your ladies with you. Mostly I don't have that privilege. I seem to address stag dinners mostly—or luncheons. To each of you my felicitations, my best wishes for an enjoyable period here in the Nation's Capital, and a continuation of your work among our armed services to help raise and keep up to the highest possible pitch the morale and the spiritual strength that we so badly need, as we defend freedom against totalitarianism in this world.

Thank you very much.

NOTE: The President spoke at a luncheon meeting at the Sheraton-Park Hotel in Washington. His opening words "Mr. Chairman" referred to Brig. Gen. Henry Darlington, N.Y.N.G. ret., President of the Association. The President was presented with a citation "for emphasizing the spiritual values of our nation."

104 ¶ Exchange of Messages Between the President and the President of France on the Fall of Dien Bien Phu. *May 7, 1954*

My dear President Coty:

The entire free world has been inspired by the heroism and stamina displayed by the gallant garrison at Dien Bien Phu. Their devotion and the quality of their resistance have been so great that that battle will forever stand as a symbol of the free world's determination to resist dictatorial aggression and to sustain its right of self-determination and its dedication to the dignity of the human being. France has in the past suffered temporary defeats, but always she has triumphed in the end to continue as one of the world's leaders in all things that tend to bring greater richness to the lives of men. Those who fought and died and suffered at Dien Bien Phu should know that no sacrifice of theirs has been in vain; that the free world will remain faithful to the causes for which they have so nobly fought.

With expressions of my personal regard,

DWIGHT D. EISENHOWER

NOTE: President Coty's reply (released May 13) follows:

To the President of the United States:

The tribute of the President of the United States to the defenders of Dien Bien Phu goes straight to the heart of the French people. Our profound gratitude, Mr. President!

The soldiers and veterans of France and the French Union will be proud that the Chief who led the Armies of Liberty to victory salutes in this magnificent resistance the symbol of the inflexible resolution of all men who, throughout the world, are and wish to remain free. It is a well-deserved honor for the soldiers of de Castries.

France, who, as you note, Mr. President, has always risen above her reverses, can now once again surmount a trial so painful and so glorious with all her energy and all her courage in close solidarity with the peoples whose destiny is joined with her destiny.

Our heroes' sacrifice will make dearer and more sacred to all the cause for which many have fallen and all have fought beyond human strength.

RENE COTY

105 ¶ Exchange of Messages Between the President and the Chief of State of Viet-Nam on the Fall of Dien Bien Phu. *May 7, 1954*

Your Majesty:

On behalf of the American people I should like to express to you and the people of Viet-Nam our admiration for the gallant men of the Vietnamese forces who, together with their comrades of the French Union, for two months so heroically defended Dien Bien Phu against insuperable odds. It is sad indeed that the fortress and its brave defenders have fallen to the enemy, but we can be heartened in the knowledge that their sacrifice has not been in vain. Not only have they taken a terrible toll of the enemy, but, I think more important, their heroic resistance to the evil forces of Communist aggression has given inspiration to all who support the cause of human freedom. Those brave men made their sacrifice in order that individual freedom and national independence for the people of Viet-Nam should not be lost to Communist enslavement. We of the free world are determined to remain faithful to the causes for which they have so nobly fought.

With expressions of my personal regard,

DWIGHT D. EISENHOWER

NOTE: His Majesty Bao Dai's reply (released May 13) follows:

To the President of the United States:

I have received with deep emotion the noble message of May 8 in which you have wished express, in name people United States and in your name, admiration for valiant soldiers of Vietnamese forces who have defended heroically Dien Bien Phu, with their French Union comrades, for two months.

The Vietnamese people and I are profoundly touched by these expressions. We express to you our heartfelt gratitude and we ask you to convey it to the great American people who have already given us so many proofs of friendship.

The fall of Dien Bien Phu is in effect a painful occurrence which affects us very much and affects the peoples of the French Union and the free world.

In spite of their heroism inscribed henceforth in history, the defenders of the fortress were swamped by the forces of those who, having subjugated to their designs and fanaticized by their untrue propaganda a certain number of my fellow countrymen, aspire to extend Communist dominion over my country as over all the free nations.

I think as you that their sacrifices have not been in vain. For our struggle, which will be able to surmount this reverse, we can draw a great comfort in the determination of the American people and in your personal will of aiding the free forces who resist Communist imperialism.

Please accept, Mr. President, the expression of my personal feeling of sincere affection.

BAO DAI

106 ¶ Remarks at the Capitol at the Dedication of the Rotunda Frieze. *May* 11, 1954

Mr. Chairman, Mr. Vice President, Mr. Speaker, members of this distinguished audience:

No man could find words to describe the color and romance—the dignity and majesty—of this spot.

The frieze above us, the paintings and statuary surrounding us, are symbolically representative of more than 400 years of American history. It is fascinating to contemplate, for only a brief moment, the nature of that 400 years. At its beginning, man moved at the same rate and by the same means that were used by the Pharaohs—the horse, the ox, and the tiny sailing vessel were the best means at hand.

In the last panel of this great frieze above us is represented the invention of the machine that now allows man to travel almost at the speed that the earth turns toward the sun. Soon, undoubtedly, he will do so.

We find here represented the great fusion of foreign bloods that brought about this Nation that became America. The Spaniards in their explorations; the French in their colonization and their assistance to the colonists as they fought the War of Independence; the English; and, finally, in the great artistry of the Italians. These are representative of the bloodstreams that, joining here in this great country of promise and opportunity, have produced the great Nation that is symbolized here in this Rotunda.

But more than being merely a compressed history of America, this spot is in a very real sense the heart of America. In this room, and in the rooms immediately adjoining, our "greats" have trod and spoken— Lincoln, and Webster, and Clay, and Jackson—all those names that thrill us merely by uttering them.

Immediately in front of me, for generations, all Presidents of the United States have taken their oath of office. Here indeed is not only a spot that reminds us of America, of her past, and her achievements, but it is one that in a very real sense is America.

And now this frieze, through the genius of an American artist, has been completed. But the thought does not cross our minds that the history of America is completed. Atop the Capitol dome the great statue still faces the east—the rising sun—ready to meet the challenge of the day.

And so the mind is intrigued with the thought as to what would be depicted in another frieze, if it should be started, or if there should be additional panels provided somewhere.

Of course, we cannot guess at the exact incidents of our history that could be there emplaced, but we do know this: they would not be there to commemorate the shattering effects of an atom bomb or a hydrogen bomb. There would be depicted progress that brings happiness to humans. There would be something that would imply and indicate and record a stronger America—stronger spiritually, intellectually, economically, in every way needed to allow America to serve her role in leading the world to a more secure and peaceful existence.

Certainly, there would be panels commemorating significant events in the long quest that man has made toward peace, and which indeed must soon reach some kind of fruition, or the alternative is bleak indeed.

But we have confidence, as we look at the record of America's past, that she can so lead. She has not failed. She will not.

And so, as I gather here today with this distinguished company, accorded the great honor of dedicating this frieze to all those future Americans who from this day on shall come here and gain renewed inspiration to do their work, I pray with you, and I share your confidence, that that future will be one of increasing strength, increasing security for all America, and all the world.

And so, in that sense, in that spirit, I dedicate this frieze to the future of America.

NOTE: The President's opening words "Mr. Chairman" referred to Thomas A. Jenkins, U.S. Representative from Ohio. Representative Jenkins introduced the bill providing for the completion of the frieze and served as a member of the committee for the execution of the project. The subjects of the new panels by artist Allyn Cox are the Civil War, the Spanish-American War, and the invention of the airplane by the Wright Brothers. The dedication exercises were held at 11:00 a.m.; for full text see Congressional Record (vol. 100, p. 6369).

107 ¶ The President's News Conference of *May* 12, 1954.

THE PRESIDENT. Ladies and gentlemen, my only announcement this morning is a very short one, but there is a 30-year struggle and study that has terminated. Tomorrow morning I sign the Seaway bill at 9:00 o'clock.

That is my single announcement; we will go to questions.

Q. John Cutter, United Press: Mr. President, last week Senator McCarthy testified that an Army security officer gave him classified FBI information which the Attorney General later said was done without authorization. Would you care to comment on the propriety of such actions?

THE PRESIDENT. Well, the question is of two parts. One involved the Senator: I said last week that I was going to take a little vacation in commenting on that particular incident, and so I won't talk about that part of it.

What I assume you are talking about is the propriety of an individual officer or civilian giving away classified information involving the security of our country, giving it away to anybody. That is so reprehensible that when we talk about security in the Federal services, what we are talking about is ways and means of keeping such things secret.

Now, in the Army or in any of the services, an enlisted man, when he takes an oath, includes in that oath to obey the orders of the superior officers set above him and the Army regulations itself.

Are we to assume that an enlisted man has one kind of loyalty to the Government and to the commanders set over him, and an officer a lesser one? It is perfectly ridiculous.

The soul of an Army, the soul of a defensive force, is the certainty that everybody responds to the laws of the land and to the orders of the superiors all the way up to the Commander in Chief. Assume otherwise, and how would you fight a battle?

I give an order to you people as division commanders or something of that nature to carry out your part of the battle, and you decide that isn't the thing to do—well, if ever we get to adopting that theory in the military or in our civilian organization, we had better disband.

On the contrary, fortunately, their sense of loyalty all the way through— and I don't refer merely to the fighting services—their sense of loyalty and dedication to their country and the obligations of their service is high indeed; and I am proud of them. But let us not for one second ever think of condoning insubordination, and particularly wherein, as in this case, there are special laws that apply to the release of confidential information.

Q. Edward Folliard, Washington Post and Times Herald: Mr. President, former President Truman made a speech at the National Press Club the other day, and the essence of it was this: that in these critical days foreign policy should be taken out of the political arena; that this is impossible so long as Republican political assassins are calling Democrats traitors, and that the only one who can put an end to these charges of treason is the President of the United States. Do you have any comments, sir?

THE PRESIDENT. I wouldn't answer anyone who finds it proper to criticize me and my actions, but I will call your attention to what I have said before: that question came up here in a press conference—whether I considered Democrats to be disloyal persons, and that sort of thing. I ridiculed the idea and said not only did I have a great many personal friends among them, but they were just exactly as loyal as all other Americans. I cannot discern in my own mind any difference between the loyalty, dedication, patriotism of people depending upon a particular party to which they belong in this country. I have said that always.

Q. Paul Leach, Chicago Daily News: Mr. President, getting back to the previous question, has any effort been made to discover who gave classified information to Senator McCarthy?

THE PRESIDENT. I don't know; I have had no report on that.

Q. Anthony Leviero, New York Times: Mr. President, again on the first question, if an enlisted man or an officer feels his superiors are derelict in throwing disloyal people out of the services, don't they have some recourse outside of the regular command channels by filing a complaint with the Inspector General?

THE PRESIDENT. That's right; that's right.

As a matter of fact, in every unit I have ever commanded, everybody along the line, if he had something that weighed on his heart heavily, had a right to get to me. I have had enlisted men, when I was commanding an entire theater of operations, come to me to give me ideas; and some of them were awfully good.

Q. Alan Emory, Watertown Times: I have two closely allied questions, sir, and neither has to do with the St. Lawrence Seaway! [*Laughter*]

Sir, I wonder if you were concerned over the increasing Democratic attacks on administration foreign policy, and if so, what proportion of those attacks you ascribe to election year politics, and what proportion to genuine concern over world affairs?

THE PRESIDENT. I never attack another's motives. I don't know what the motivation is; but so far, I think, as is possible and practicable, the foreign affairs of the United States are handled on a bipartisan basis.

I note that yesterday the majority leader in the Senate in a talk gave an exact record, put in the Congressional Record, of how many times the State Department alone had called in or dealt with bipartisan groups in an effort to keep them informed in advance of what is going on.

As a matter of fact, I am astonished in the way that you now have this interest in this question for the simple reason that I believe no one was interested in that statement yesterday.

As I recall, the figure he gave for the State Department alone in 16 months is 91 such meetings. There are, of course, all sorts of meetings through the FOA, through the Defense Department and others. For my own part, I even took all of that part of my State of the Union speech and, before giving it last January, had in a bipartisan group, went over the whole thing with them, and asked for their comments.

Now, this goes along all the time. Manifestly, you cannot go down to the last individual; it is a selected group, but always are the leadership and those principally concerned brought into those things. I don't know any other way in which the bipartisan policy, in which I firmly believe, can be carried out.

Q. Raymond Brandt, St. Louis Post-Dispatch: Mr. President, the minority groups say that they were not consulted in advance about the massive retaliation idea.

THE PRESIDENT. Well, I am not going to take each single idea here and say that these people were consulted in advance. That idea, that phrase, has become used as very descriptive of a particular policy. Actually something of the kind is implicit in everything we have been doing for many, many months, even long before we came in here; so I think that phrase has been overworked myself.

Q. Anthony Leviero, New York Times: Mr. President, the main point of criticism on bipartisanship has been that this administration has not used as many Democrats as the Democrats used Republicans, such as Lovett, and Mr. Dulles and McCloy. I wonder what your comments are on that?

THE PRESIDENT. Well, I don't know; possibly we haven't used as many. I have never added it up, but I do know this: one man that, I think even before I came down to the inauguration, I asked—I am not going to say my memory is exact, but I think it is—I asked to stay on because of my respect for his approach to the entire problem of foreign affairs, that was David Bruce. I worked with him in Europe; I believe implicitly in his wisdom and in his tact, his breadth of approach. He is one man at least that has been kept. And, of course, we have many foreign service officers—it never occurred to me to ask what their politics is—and ambassadors, and so on. But it is possible that we haven't used quite as many; I wouldn't answer that one now.

Q. Roger Stuart, New York World-Telegram and Sun: Mr. President, following your recommendation last January that the voting age be lowered to 18, there has been some action along that line in Congress. Moreover, opinion polls carried on throughout the country seem to reflect a considerable degree of support for the proposal. Would you comment, sir, on your view as to how the public has reacted to your recommendation, and whether you are pleased with the response?

THE PRESIDENT. Well, I could not claim that I am in as close a touch to the public reaction to that suggestion as you people are, possibly.

Also, when I said 18, I picked an age out of the air. As I recall, I based it on this: if a man is old enough to risk his life, it is entirely logical that he have some voice in the decision which sent him there. I have had people say 19 would be a better age on the basis that a man, under our Selective Service System, never really goes to a battlefield until he is 19. I haven't looked up the exact laws, I don't think I would quarrel too much as to the exact months a man has to be; but I think some age like that is correct. The only comments I have had, of course, are favorable, but that could easily be because the others haven't written to me.

Q. Garnett Horner, Washington Star: Mr. President, Secretary of Defense Wilson said yesterday that the Army and the Defense Department, as a whole, was entirely capable of handling any security risk problems, and that he felt that no more congressional investigations of the military in that regard were necessary. Would you tell us your feelings? Do you agree with him?

THE PRESIDENT. Of course, when you ask me such a question you are asking only for a feeling, because I left active connection with the Army quite a while ago.

My own experience in the Army was most heart-warming from the standpoint of its dedication and loyalty. I know that its great mass of people are dedicated, patriotic people.

Now, I don't see why there isn't ample authority in the Defense Department, certainly there is ample will there, to take care of this problem.

As to the occasional and proper investigation into particular things from the outside, I think they are good, just as I believe that an Inspector General's service is necessary to a Secretary of the Army and to the Chief of Staff. I believe that an occasional good look-see into various things is good.

There is an old saw in the services: that which is not inspected deteriorates.

I believe in inspections, but I believe also that the Federal services, the armed services, are perfectly capable in the long run of taking care of this with satisfaction to the United States.

Q. Charles von Fremd, CBS Television: Mr. President, should the proposed Southeast Asian Defense Alliance be created, as Secretary Dulles and others have suggested, do you think that the Associated States of Indochina, Laos, Cambodia, and Viet-Nam should be members of such organization?

THE PRESIDENT. Most certainly I would hope that they would voluntarily express such a conviction and such an intention.

In this connection, some have assumed that there has been a difference of opinion between the Secretary of State and myself as to exactly what we meant. I think I have assured this group several times that I know of no important announcement made by either one of us in this regard that isn't the result of long and serious conferences. If there are any differences ever detectable in our utterances, it must be because of language and not because of any intent.

Now, I understand that Mr. Dulles said we will not give up; no matter what happens down there, we will never give up even if these three should fall. I think—I know he was talking about another step that could be detrimental to the interests of the free world, and what would you do then. Naturally, all of us want to save them because of their importance, but it has to be done on their invitation.

Q. Mr. von Fremd: Mr. President, I asked the question with no reference to a difference between you and Secretary Dulles.

THE PRESIDENT. Yes; I know, yes.

Q. Mr. von Fremd: The reason for it is there have been some reports that the British or the French Government might very well be against the Associated States being a member of such an alliance.

THE PRESIDENT. Well, I must make this point which I have tried to make, again, several times: no nation can be saved to the free world unless it itself wants to be saved. Freedom, by its very definition, cannot be possessed by someone who doesn't want freedom; so unless those states are enthusiastic parties to such an arrangement, then it could have no immediate right interfering with their business, as I see it.

Q. Mrs. May Craig, Maine Papers: Mr. President, General Mark Clark has said that we are so short of manpower we cannot fight another war without drafting women for noncombat service. Have you considered that?

THE PRESIDENT. Well, when you say "war" you are talking about such a variety of situations and conditions that you can't possibly, as I see it, fasten to the word or to its possibility any particular set of conditions here.

I think this is correct: you could not expand the military activities on active service greatly beyond what we were carrying on at the end of the Korean war, without going to some general form of mobilization; though I would doubt, until the thing became far more serious, whether there would be earnestly studied a proposition for drafting women.

Now, of course, General Clark was with me in Britain, as were many of you people, and you saw what women did in the armed services in relieving men to go off to more difficult physical tasks. So I assume he, with that lesson, was trying to point out that we could get into a serious thing, and then women could help immeasurably.

Q. John Herling, Editors Syndicate: Mr. President, last week the Department of Labor and Department of Commerce issued a joint report on the employment situation, and in spite of a slight seasonal rise in employment, it showed a decrease in employment in manufacturing. Now this week the CIO is having a full employment conference here, and next week the A.F. of L. Executive Council is going to take up the matter of what they call rising unemployment now in, especially, manufacturing. Does the administration have any plans to deal with that problem, the problem of unemployment in manufacturing?

THE PRESIDENT. Well, it seems this morning I am going back and reminding you of things I have said so often in the past.

In this problem there is continuous study, there is never any relaxation of the effort to keep abreast of the times and where we will probably be tomorrow. This is done by statistical branches, by the bureaus and the departments concerned, and by the economic advisers who get together, consolidate their thinking. As a matter of fact, you may know, Mr.

Burns appears before the Cabinet at every meeting to give a short résumé of what he believes is going to happen.

So far as human beings can be prepared for the things that judgment shows may happen, of course we try to be prepared.

Q. George Herman, CBS Radio: Mr. President, since we seem to be going into the past, a few weeks ago you told us of your theory of dominoes about Indochina, the neck of the bottle——

THE PRESIDENT. Yes.

Q. Mr. Herman: Since the fall of Dien Bien Phu, there has been a certain amount of talk of doing without Indochina. Would you tell us your administration's position; is it still indispensable to the defense of southeast Asia?

THE PRESIDENT. Again I forget whether it was before this body I talked about the cork and the bottle. Well, it is very important, and the great idea of setting up an organism is so as to defeat the domino result. When, each standing alone, one falls, it has the effect on the next, and finally the whole row is down. You are trying, through a unifying influence, to build that row of dominoes so they can stand the fall of one, if necessary.

Now, so far as I am concerned, I don't think the free world ought to write off Indochina. I think we ought to all look at this thing with some optimism and some determination. I repeat that long faces and defeatism don't win battles.

Q. Robert Riggs, Louisville Courier-Journal: Next Tuesday Mr. Clapp's term expires, as Chairman of TVA. Are you now ready to appoint a new one, sir?

THE PRESIDENT. I believe that in such cases I make an announcement as soon as decisions have been made, but I have none to make this morning.

Q. Sarah McClendon, El Paso Times: Sir, I know that Mr. Philip Young, the Civil Service Commissioner, is opposed to honorable discharges for Federal employees because he said if you gave some dishonorable discharges that would brand people separated from the services, perhaps, subversives or otherwise unsatisfactory persons. But I see you have given him authority to write the merit regulations for the civil service merit system; and I wonder if, before doing that, you discussed with him in any way the possibility of honorable discharges?

THE PRESIDENT. Oh, as a matter of fact, it was discussed not only with him, but in a very broad way with department heads, and so on.

Now, here is one of those things where you have to leave matters with the people that are working them out. If I could see here a clear advantage or disadvantage one way or the other, of course, that would be my responsibility to decide it. But I really believe that such things as this are best handled by department heads and by the Civil Service Commission; that is what they are there for, to study them.

Q. Douglass Cater, The Reporter Magazine: Mr. President, Senator McCarthy has attacked your Executive order maintaining the secrecy of the security files or the files dealing with security matters, as well as the members of the Board. Would you give us your thinking behind that order as to why that information should be kept from members of the Congress?

THE PRESIDENT. There are certain secrets in the United States that should be given only to those who absolutely need to have them in making their decisions. Even within the Government people are very cautious and careful, and I am one of them. I have had leaks in war that caused sleepless nights wondering what was happening.

The point comes in, of course, that it is human judgment that determines when an item of information is this delicate, and because we are a republic, a free country, and because the public is entitled to every bit of information that you can give out, inevitably a conflict occurs.

I have found myself more often than not in specific arguments on the side of giving out more. But because I am on that side, there are certain things that I wouldn't give out to anyone; in fact, there would be nothing that would ever get me to agree to it.

Now, our Government being so big, employing 3½ million in our armed services today and some 2½ million in civil service, quite definitely no one human being can make the decisions—what is to be given out and what is not.

We have, through an order that we worked on many, many weeks and was issued some time last year, tried to define as well as we can a policy for these people to follow; but as long as those individuals decide these matters in their own departments as well as they know how and in accordance with the oath of office that they have taken, we must support them. That means I must, and I think the public must.

Q. Robert Spivack, New York Post: Mr. President, continuing that point, do you feel that members of what we might call this McCarthy spy network are to be regarded as security risks?

THE PRESIDENT. That is a question I don't believe I will answer.

Q. Frank O'Brien, Associated Press: Mr. President, a report was published this week that Commissioner of Internal Revenue T. Coleman Andrews would leave his job before the end of this administration, and that he could not go too quickly to please some persons in the administration. This report added that some people in the administration felt that in his handling of FHA "windfall profits" he had been not entirely loyal to the Republican administration. Would you tell us if there is any dissatisfaction with Mr. Andrews?

THE PRESIDENT. The only thing that has ever been asked of a man in that kind of position is: is he loyal to the Government of the United States, that is, to the Constitution and to his job. I can't conceive that such a man would be asked to be loyal to some kind of party label.

Now, certainly George Humphrey has never expressed to me the slightest word of dissatisfaction with Mr. Andrews. On the other hand, he has expressed often very great satisfaction with his work. My own contacts with Mr. Andrews, which have not been frequent, have certainly been cordial when I met him. So far as I know, he has been doing a grand job, and no one has come up to me to recommend his dismissal, I assure you, or hinted that he was thinking of resigning. This is news to me.

John Cutter, United Press: Thank you, Mr. President.

NOTE: President Eisenhower's thirty-seventh news conference was held in the Executive Office Building from 10:32 to 10:59 o'clock on Wednesday morning, May 12, 1954. In attendance: 157.

108 ¶ Remarks at the Annual Conference of the Society for Personnel Administration. *May* 12, 1954

Mr. Chairman and ladies and gentlemen:

In the few moments that I am allotted on this stand, there are three sub-subjects on which I should like to speak to you.

First is, of course, my privilege of bidding you welcome to this Capital

City on behalf of the administration, and to hope that you will find here not only profitable meetings but real enjoyment during your stay.

The second is to express great admiration for the kind of work you are doing in developing policies and methods that apply to the employment of people in masses.

It is a simple enough thing to establish a good relationship with one individual, but when we go into the great organisms that modern life demands—great organisms of personnel—then, of course, policy must serve as a guide for many, many hundreds of sub-executives.

Unless we are wise in the development of those policies, we will not get from governmental and civilian organisms the kind of service we must have. Public service requires the finest types of humans. Along with being intelligent people, people of integrity and probity, they must be dedicated people; because always, somewhere, if they are capable, is held before them material reward in some other job that would far outstrip what they are given in the public service.

So we must achieve, then, a morale—an esprit—and a sense of dedication, that keep in all of these organisms the finest we can produce. Because, through them, our lives are affected—through these organisms they are affected in many ways. Whole philosophies can develop out of real operations by these bodies.

So I not only am interested in your work, I would hope that every department of the Federal Government that can possibly assist you would show a readiness to cooperate, an anxiety to cooperate, in what you are doing that would be measured only by their recognition of the importance of your work. And I am sure that that will be high.

Now the third related subject I wanted to bring up is not about the methods and the systems and the planning and the ideas that engage your attention. In the specific sense, you unquestionably know more about those than I. But I think I can claim a little experience in dealing with humans as individuals. And so I want to talk for just a moment about the personal relationship that must exist in all personnel systems.

Sometimes, in our studies and in planning of how we will do certain things to promote justice and fairness, opportunities for merit to go up and security for all that are working loyally, we forget that the person who is to be affected by this policy is another individual just like our-

476

selves. He is subject to the same kind of fears, the same kind of hopes, with the same kind of ambitions and aspirations, the same kind of worries and problems that we all have. So we tend to become mechanical.

I believe in the most intense personal application to personnel problems in every organism that you can think of. I believe that there is more to be gained by the boss letting his people know that if necessary— if they have got something that is really on their hearts—they can get all the way up to him. That is far more important than the exact accuracy of some policy intended to promote justice and fairness for all.

I admit you need policies, but without this human element, they are sterile and negative.

The personal quality is something we call leadership. And so I think, in a word, what I am saying is—don't forget that all the policies that you can devise must presume and assume leadership.

Now, strangely enough, everybody thinks he is a leader, that he has splendid qualities, that everybody should like him, and everything is lovely and that is that! Do you know there are languages that do not include the word "leadership"? They do not even comprehend the general meaning that I think most of us have in mind when we use that word.

Now I think, speaking roughly, by leadership we mean the art of getting someone else to do something that you want done because he wants to do it, not because your position of power can compel him to do it, or your position of authority. A commander of a regiment is not necessarily a leader. He has all of the appurtenances of power given by a set of Army regulations by which he can compel unified action. He can say to a body such as this, "Rise," and "Sit down." You do it exactly. But that is not leadership.

Now a leader makes use of the powers inherent in a position, as he establishes the influence of his leadership. But this is only a part. He never rests there. He gets over to the individual with whom he is working that he does hope to understand that individual, that he is sympathetic when a child is sick, or anything else is happening that troubles that individual.

I have worked for a long time with bodies of public servants, both in uniform and without. I am convinced that this item concerning which I presume to take up some of your time is not only of importance, it is of growing importance. And again, I give you the reason: because we must organize hierarchies of command reaching from somebody who is the boss, on down three or four, then on down three or four more until you have millions. It becomes more difficult for personal qualities to reach down to the last individual.

Now, there is the problem. How do you pick your people? How do you impress those that you meet so that they in turn will take their own methods and their own ways? Some leaders are scrawny little people, and some are big and handsome guys, and so on. It makes no difference: if they have got this in their hearts, they can be leaders. That is the job that I think, as you study policies, as you study methods, you must never forget. We must assume it, and presume it, and insist upon it. And no man and no woman who shows a lack of concern about this matter, who dismisses it, should ever be allowed to go too high in the service. Because humans are still humans, they will respond to human consideration, to human kindness, to human courtesy—which are at the same time the cheapest and most valuable items that I know in dealing with another.

I thank you very much indeed for the honor you have done me by inviting me before you.

Good luck to you.

NOTE: The President spoke at the Statler Hotel in Washington. His opening words "Mr. Chairman" referred to Dr. Erwin D. Draheim, President of the Society for Personnel Administration.

109 ¶ Statement by the President on the Death of Senator Hoey of North Carolina.
May 12, 1954

I HAVE JUST LEARNED of the sudden death of the senior Senator from North Carolina, Clyde R. Hoey. A member of the House of Representatives, a former Governor of his State, and a member of the United States Senate since 1945, Senator Hoey has a long and distinguished record of public service to his State and nation. Mrs. Eisenhower joins with me in extending our sympathy to his family and to his many friends.

110 ¶ Remarks Upon Signing the St. Lawrence Seaway Bill. *May* 13, 1954

I AM VERY HAPPY, in the presence of this distinguished company, to sign this bill.

I think it is particularly fortunate that we have with us the Ambassador from Canada, because this bill is intended to set in motion the great project which will operate to the benefit of both our countries.

This marks, of course, the legislative culmination of an effort that has taken 30 years to reach this point. Now work can begin on the great project itself. That work, we all hope, will progress rapidly without interruption to a successful completion, so that the benefits of this great project can come to all our people on both sides of that great river.

NOTE: The President signed the bill in the Conference Room at the White House. Among those present were Canadian Ambassador A. D. P. Heeney, Senator Homer Ferguson of Michigan, Senator Alexander Wiley of Wisconsin, and Representative George A. Dondero of Michigan.

The St. Lawrence Seaway Bill is Public Law 358, 83d Congress (68 Stat. 92).

111 ¶ Remarks at the Armed Forces Day Dinner. *May* 14, 1954

Mr. Toastmaster, and members of this distinguished gathering:

First, I should like to express my appreciation to Secretary Anderson, as I think each of you would, for an address that was not only scholarly but, so far as I was concerned, was inspiring. I am grateful for it.

And now, as I trust you know, the speech-making is over. The rest of the time, I am informed, can be given over to rambling reminiscences. And for my part, I could not possibly of my own complete freedom choose an audience with which I would rather reminisce than this one.

Forty-three years ago this month I was privileged first to take the Soldier's Oath to his flag and to his country. I assure you, when those flags came through tonight, that thrill was just as real as it was 43 years ago.

Now, of course, in any reminiscing among servicemen, why there is usually quite a—you might say—traffic jam, everybody trying to get in

479

his word.   But this evening, I am sort of given the privilege of the chair, and so you will have to let me do this particular part of it.

Some of you here were in the Army in 1911.   Indeed, this morning I was visited by Senator Martin of Pennsylvania, who reminded me of the Spanish American War, and I felt like a recruit.   Then, we had the Benet-Mercier automatic rifle.   Probably most of you never heard of it.   A second lieutenant didn't have a gold bar, he had nothing on his shoulder; he was called a shavetail.   Life was rather simple.   And of course, even then they were saying, "The Army isn't what it used to be."   And someone would then remark, "And it never was."   But we thought we were very wise.

I remember my professor somewhere along about 1912 gave a long and very learned lecture on the possibility of a European war, and proved by the lack of gold and money reserves in Europe that no war in Europe could possibly last more than 30 days.   That was before World War I—since which time the world has been topsy-turvy.   At times I think most of us my age felt we were living in a squirrel cage, and were frequently tempted to say: "Why this is where I came in."

And we can't get out.   All sorts of things bother us: the terrible power of destructive weapons, the uncontrolled ruthlessness of unbridled ambition, the wonder whether democratic forms, with their admitted weaknesses in administrative work, can possibly hold their own against masses of people and productive enterprises all directed by one single head.   Of course, it is well to remember what happened to the dictatorships of the past that even seemed as great and terrible in their time, on down through Rome, and Genghis Khan, Napoleon, and Hitler and Mussolini—all gone.

Through those 40 years, of course, we were just people developing. This country was bringing out automobiles, and at times there were general orders on the post that you should be especially careful if you happened to own one of these things because the mules in the colonel's Dougherty wagon would be frightened.   And the mules are gone.

Well, we thought many things, the same things as we think now.

For example, I remember as a very respectable second lieutenant, I was walking the proper distance behind two lordly captains—and you know, it was sometimes the second lieutenant's job to see that the captain got home in the evening without the major knowing.   In any event, these two captains were talking. They were talking about the possibility of a poker game that evening. It sounded rather intriguing to both. One of them said, "Well, I will tell you. It sounds very good, and I will go home and I will talk to Mary. If she is doing something this evening, I will get hold of you—I will call you up and come to the poker game." And the other one said, "You will talk to Mary? What are you, a man or a mouse?" And he said, "Of course I am a man, my wife is scared of a mouse!"

Ladies and gentlemen, as I look back over these 43 years, I don't think we have changed much.

And so I am going to talk just for one moment of a few of the things that I learned in those 43 years. They are very simple things. They are nothing, I think, that you would call erudite. They are nothing that would be called intellectual attainments. They are simply great faith. I have been in difficult places with Americans—many Americans. From them I have gained an inspiration, an inspiration that free men can do anything when they are united in a common cause, and set their hearts to that cause.

Secretary Anderson has sketched for us this evening something of the dangers we face, something of the nature of the ideological conflict in the world, something of the policy to which we must devote ourselves, and the faith that we must hold if we are to win through.

And I should like to reinforce, or add to what he said, this one thought: never forget the strength of freedom of the free world. We know how much we value our right to worship as we please, to speak as we please, to choose our own occupations, to try to give to our children the kind of training in beliefs and faith that we believe will make them happiest. We know the values we place on those things.

If at times we seem to ignore them, if we are torn by doubts or current fears, or our attention is diverted by unworthy scenes, even in our National Capital, we still know that we are America. The heart of America is sound. It is sound now that we shall pass on to those a little younger than us, those that are coming behind us, we shall pass on to them the same kind of right to hold up their heads, to be proud both of opportunity and of their freedoms, of their liberties that we inherited.

Knowing that, we begin to get sacrifices and costs in their proper perspective. I think, possibly, that for any one of us Patrick Henry may have overstated the case when he said, "For me, give me liberty or give me death."

But for this race, he did not overstate it.   This race will live in liberty. It will not die.   It will live, and live in liberty.

Perhaps, ladies and gentlemen, a man did not have to be in the armed services all these years to gain these truths.   But for me there is where I learned them, because there is where my life was spent.

So I thank every associate I have ever had in the armed services, be he Marine, or Navy, or Air, or Army.   In all these years, I have nothing to look back upon but pride in those men, and the certainty that they represented America—America's strength, not only in armed might, but in spirit and determination, confidence in themselves, their country, and their God.

Thank you.

NOTE: The President spoke at the Statler Hotel in Washington.   His opening words "Mr. Toastmaster" referred to Lewis L. Strauss, Chairman of the Atomic Energy Commission.   He also referred to Robert B. Anderson, Deputy Secretary of Defense.

112   ¶ Letter to General Wladyslaw Anders of the Polish Armed Forces in Exile on Commemoration of the Battle of Monte Cassino. *May* 17, 1954

[Released May 17, 1954. Dated May 7, 1954]

Dear General Anders:

I am happy to write in connection with your recent letter on plans to commemorate the battle of Monte Cassino.

That famous battle has come to represent the heroism and sacrifices of the Polish soldiers in the past war against the forces of totalitarianism in Europe.   It will stand through the years as a symbol of the Polish nation's inextinguishable love of freedom.

Today, the Polish people are again faced with foreign oppression and are meeting the test with the same qualities of heroism.   We in America are convinced that this courage and faith in freedom will not be in vain and that the cause of liberty and justice will prevail, as it did at Monte Cassino ten years ago.

Sincerely,

DWIGHT D. EISENHOWER

Lieutenant General W. Anders, C.B.
18, Queen's Gate Terrace
London, S.W. 7, England

113 ¶ Letter to the Secretary of Defense Directing Him To Withhold Certain Information from the Senate Committee on Government Operations. *May 17, 1954*

Dear Mr. Secretary:

It has long been recognized that to assist the Congress in achieving its legislative purposes every Executive Department or Agency must, upon the request of a Congressional Committee, expeditiously furnish information relating to any matter within the jurisdiction of the Committee, with certain historical exceptions—some of which are pointed out in the attached memorandum from the Attorney General. This Administration has been and will continue to be diligent in following this principle. However, it is essential to the successful working of our system that the persons entrusted with power in any one of the three great branches of Government shall not encroach upon the authority confided to the others. The ultimate responsibility for the conduct of the Executive Branch rests with the President.

Within this Constitutional framework each branch should cooperate fully with each other for the common good. However, throughout our history the President has withheld information whenever he found that what was sought was confidential or its disclosure would be incompatible with the public interest or jeopardize the safety of the Nation.

Because it is essential to efficient and effective administration that employees of the Executive Branch be in a position to be completely candid in advising with each other on official matters, and because it is not in the public interest that any of their conversations or communications, or any documents or reproductions, concerning such advice be disclosed, you will instruct employees of your Department that in all of their appearances before the Subcommittee of the Senate Committee on Government Operations regarding the inquiry now before it they are not to testify to any such conversations or communications or to produce any such documents or reproductions.   This principle must be maintained regardless of who would be benefited by such disclosures.

I direct this action so as to maintain the proper separation of powers between the Executive and Legislative Branches of the Government in accordance with my responsibilities and duties under the Constitution. This separation is vital to preclude the exercise of arbitrary power by any branch of the Government.

By this action I am not in any way restricting the testimony of such witnesses as to what occurred regarding any matters where the communication was directly between any of the principals in the controversy within the Executive Branch on the one hand and a member of the Subcommittee or its staff on the other.

Sincerely,

DWIGHT D. EISENHOWER

NOTE: Attorney General Brownell's memorandum of March 2, 1954, was released with the President's letter. The memorandum traces the development from Washington's day of the principle that the President may, under certain circumstances, withhold information from the Congress.

Taking the doctrine of separation of powers as his text, the Attorney General stated that it is essential to the successful working of the American system that the persons entrusted with power in any one of the three branches should not be permitted to encroach upon the powers confided to the others.

The memorandum continues: "For over 150 years . . . our Presidents have established, by precedent, that they and members of their Cabinet and other heads of executive departments have an undoubted privilege and discretion to keep confidential, in the public interest, papers and information which require secrecy.

American history abounds in countless illustrations of the refusal, on occasion, by the President and heads of departments to furnish papers to Congress, or its committees, for reasons of public policy. The messages of our past Presidents reveal that almost every one of them found it necessary to inform Congress of his constitutional duty to execute the office of President, and, in furtherance of that duty, to withhold information and papers for the public good."

As for the courts, they have "uniformly held that the President and the heads of departments have an uncontrolled discretion to withhold . . . information and papers in the public interest; they will not interfere with the exercise of that discretion, and that Congress has not the power, as one of the three great branches of the Government, to subject the Executive Branch to its will any more than the Executive Branch may impose its unrestrained will upon the Congress."

Among the precedents cited in the Attorney General's memorandum are the following:

President Washington, in 1796, was presented with a House Resolution requesting him to furnish copies of correspondence and other papers relating to the Jay Treaty with Great Britain as a condition to the appropriation of funds to implement the treaty. In refusing, President Washington replied "I trust that no part of my conduct has ever indicated a disposition to withhold any information which the Constitution has enjoined upon the President as a duty to give, or which could be required of him by either House of Congress as a right; and with truth I affirm that it has been, as it will continue to be while I have the honor to preside in the Government, my constant endeavor to harmonize with the other branches thereof so far as the trust delegated to me by the people of the United States and my sense of the obligation it imposes to 'preserve, protect, and defend the Constitution' will permit."

President Theodore Roosevelt, in 1909, when faced with a Senate Resolution directing his Attorney General to furnish documents relating to proceedings against the U.S. Steel Corporation, took possession of the papers. He then informed Senator Clark of the Judiciary Committee that the only way the Senate could get them was through impeachment. The President explained that some of the facts were given to the Government under the seal of secrecy and could not be divulged. He added "and I will see to it that the word of this Government to the individual is kept sacred."

"During the administration of President Franklin D. Roosevelt," the Attorney General's memorandum states, "there were many instances in which the President and his Executive heads refused to make available certain information to Congress the disclosure of which was deemed to be confidential or contrary to the public interest." Five such cases are cited, including one in which "communications between the President and the heads of departments were held to be confidential and privileged and not subject to inquiry by a committee of one of the Houses of Congress."

114 ¶ Address on Freedom Celebration Day, Charlotte, North Carolina. *May* 18, 1954

Governor Umstead, members of this distinguished gathering:

First, may I pay to each of you my personal thanks for the cordiality of your welcome. To each of you who along the street or in this gathering has given me a smile or a wave, I am eternally grateful, and I say this most feelingly and most sincerely.

Any American with a modicum of modesty would at times be overwhelmed by the intensity and the importance of the problems that he would meet, if he were called upon to serve in the chief official position of this country. He would find, as I have found, and as all before me in the same office have found, that his great inspiration, his great source of help is going back and meeting his friends in the street, in gatherings such as this, so that he may know that the heart of America is always sound, and America's judgment—when based on information—is always correct.

If he can carry that conviction into international conference, into domestic discussion with political and business and other leaders, he can be certain that in the long run, if he hews to that line, he will have done his duty, insofar as his God gave him the ability to do it.

And so you may understand something, then, of the true pleasure I feel in being with you here today, to join with you, my own fellow Americans, in saluting, first, our armed services, those men and women of ours who have worn the uniform of our country, proudly, well, and effectively—who have defended our flag at home and abroad for lo all these decades since the founding of our country—in whose accomplishments we have always found tremendous pride and satisfaction.

Today, as in all other decades of our history, we are still confident of our armed services, from their secretaries and high commanders on down to the last private in the ranks.

And it is not difficult to understand this pride, because these people are of us. They are Americans. They come from this crowd. They sit among you people, who have worn that uniform. There are others who will. Some of you in that great throng this day are in the service, and serving your country. Still others have sons and brothers and husbands and sweethearts serving. We know that they are sound, because they are America.

And we have met, in addition, for the traditional purpose of honoring those men of long ago—patriots in their time—who signed the Mecklenburg Convention. Now the historical record of that particular moment in history 179 years ago has been disputed by some, particularly those who claim that they are the descendants of the true authors of all early historical documents of that kind. Now, to me, that is not important. The important thing is that here, this great segment of America wants to be known as the originators of our historical documents of freedom.

Did you take no pride in freedom today, why would you meet to claim such an honor? I will tell you this: in my States of Texas and Kansas, could we today prove that there were at least three settlers in each of those States, today we would prove to you that we not only started the Revolutionary War, wrote all the documents, won the war, but started the Nation. And I thoroughly believe, as long as all Americans are anxious to claim kinship, not necessarily by blood descent, but by spirit, by admiration, by closeness of feeling with those men who did those great deeds, then indeed is America safe.

And so it matters not exactly how many men were gathered in that cabin to sign a document. It matters not that part of the document had to be reconstructed from memories of those who were present, the fact is that it was an immortal step in our development, because today people venerate the occurrence.

As we today worship freedom as they worshipped freedom, we are doing our part, as they did theirs, in sustaining it for all, both of this generation and those to come.

And that, my friends, is the great problem, is the great task, of this generation of America. The world has practically eliminated physical barriers as among nations and among continents. But, the world today, although joined physically by a few hours of flight or by an instant in telecommunications, is further apart in idea, in political belief, in basic philosophy, than it ever was—even before the discovery of the Western World.

There are two camps, one which believes—as did the men of Mecklenburg—that government should be founded and should be sustained to serve people—in other words, that the most important element of a nation is the individual that composes it; another doctrine, discarding and rejecting all thought of spiritual values on which such a concept is based, saying the only values in the world that mean anything are materialistic values, and so, in order that they may survive, they intend to destroy the whole concept that those forefathers of yours handed on down, and in which you meet here today.

Indeed, the gathering of such a group as we have here is in itself a monument to what has happened in America, a monument to the type of civilization and government under which we live.

If such a meeting should occur in the Soviet country, it would be there to hear a doctrine propounded by the dictator. It would come there by the routes laid out by the dictator. It would cheer when told to cheer, and leave when told to leave, and go exactly to where its members were told to go.

Here we do not do that. And so we have the true value of a meeting fully expressed, because people are here—because they want to.

I realize that in the time and life such as ours, all of us are torn by worries as we meet, no matter how uncomplainingly—the problems of living, the problems of paying the taxes, the payments on the car, maybe the mortgage on the house, of educating the children. We are still torn by the worries that come about with the knowledge that science has brought us a great power for self-destruction in this world, even while no one has seemed, yet, to devise a means whereby we can escape the consequences of such discoveries and devote them exclusively to the betterment of mankind.

At this time and place, I cannot outline in detail what your Government is trying to do in this regard. But I do want to leave with you today one pledge: your Government, in all its parts, is devoted to one thing, and one thing only, a fair and just peace for all mankind.

Every move—every move that it makes on the international checker-board, every program that it devises and supports for enactment at home, is to seek that road toward peace, with an America that is strong, in its spirit, in its devotion to freedom, intellectually—in its educational and mental attainments, economically strong, with a wide distribution of all the productivity of this great country; and finally, militarily strong so that we may be secure and safe as we seek out this road and make more certain that we can find it.

In a nutshell, ladies and gentlemen, that is what all of us joined together in Washington are trying to do. Despite the arguments that you see in your headlines, despite all the things that distract us from these important aims and purposes of Government, that basic thought, that basic aim, is there—always.

Ninety-nine percent of all the public officials that you have in city councils, in your State governments, in your Governors chairs, and in Washington, are devoted to that one purpose, because all Americans know that until we have peace, we cannot march forward to attain the dream that was held—and so clearly stated—by the men of Mecklenburg.

And now, permit me again a personal reference, before I go and start my journey back to Washington. From the moment I stepped off my plane to meet your Governor, I have met many old friends. Everywhere I have encountered nothing but warm hospitality. I thank the people who served the lunch, the orchestras, and the choirs that entertained us with their art. I thank five old classmates of mine from West Point who came here today to give me a chance to say Hello to campaigners of 1911. Everybody here—to each of you, my thanks.

Good luck, and I hope I will be seeing you.

NOTE: The President spoke in Freedom Park at 2:40 p.m.

115 ¶ The President's News Conference of *May* 19, 1954.

THE PRESIDENT. Ladies and gentlemen, it is awfully nice once in a while to have a piece of news come to your notice that is very pleasing. If you have noted the action of the Senate Banking and Currency Committee in restoring the housing program of the administration, you can understand that I am highly pleased. I sincerely hope the conferees will find a way of supporting that program very definitely and unequivocally.

Now, with that out of the way, we will take the other questions.

Q. Marvin L. Arrowsmith, Associated Press: Mr. President, both Republicans and Democrats on the Senate permanent investigating subcommittee have expressed the opinion that as a result of your order to Secretary Wilson on Monday, it may be impossible to get at the whole truth in the controversy. They have expressed the hope that you will rescind or at least relax that order. Do you have any such intentions, sir?

THE PRESIDENT. Well, I shall not only answer your question, but I think I shall go a little bit beyond your question and talk about this matter a moment, if you will allow me.

First, I have no intention whatsoever of relaxing or rescinding the order, because it is a very moderate and proper statement of the division of powers between the Executive and the Legislative.

Now, when I saw in the paper allegations to the effect that the issuance of that order could be used as a reason or excuse for calling off hearings, I was astonished. Lest there remain any doubt as to why the meeting of January 21st was called, I will tell you exactly why. There was an investigation going on in which an executive department of Government—Defense Department, and principally the Army—was engaged with a committee of Congress. Finally, there was proposed to them a question which they could not answer by themselves because it involved an Executive order.

It was proposed that they bring up the records—the records of the loyalty boards and the individuals who comprised those loyalty boards.

Under an Executive order of long standing, that was impossible, so they had to have advice. Since, of course, an Executive order is an instrument drawn by the President, they asked an adviser or two of mine to be there, and it was done, I believe, in the Attorney General's office. That was the purpose of that meeting, to decide whether this question could be answered affirmatively or should be answered negatively under the terms of that Executive order.

Now the only reason I issued the order was because I saw an investigation going ahead where it appeared that there was going to be a long sidetrack established, and go into a relationship between the President and his advisers that had no possible connection with this investigation, and which in any event would directly and instantly raise the old question of the proper division of powers between the Executive and the Legislature.

Far from trying to get any investigation off the track, I was merely trying, with the timely statement, to keep it on the rails.

I will say with respect to that investigation, as I have told you before, I hope it is concluded as soon and expeditiously as possible, but conclusively so that the principals tell their stories openly and fully, and so the public can know the facts, but so these extraneous matters and these things that roam all up and down the alleys of Government, of every kind of thought and idea, are kept out of them. Now I hope that disposes of my order.

Q. Robert G. Spivack, New York Post: Mr. President, may I just ask you one question? In commenting on your last sentence in your remark, when you say you hope the principals all testify, do you mean all the principals who have not testified up to now? Is that what you were referring to?

THE PRESIDENT. Well, I don't want to be so completely specific in this thing, because certainly I am not trying to tell any committee how to conduct its investigations; but I do believe that two or three main issues were raised. All the principals to those two or three main issues should be questioned. Some of them have been questioned.

Incidentally, I think in this regard, and in order to assure in the public mind what Mr. Stevens so often said before, I have no doubt that he will have something to say about the disassociation between his administration of the Army and this meeting of last January 21st.

Q. Robert E. Clark, International News Service: Mr. President, in connection with that, the main issue in the hearings at this moment appears to be whether the authority for the Army's actions passed from Stevens to a higher level at the January 21st meeting. Can you tell us whether Stevens——

THE PRESIDENT. I think Mr. Stevens' announcement can take complete care of that, Mr. Clark, but I should say this: that at that meeting there was no attempt made, there was nothing brought up that could intimate such a thing.

Q. Anthony Leviero, New York Times: Mr. President, is there anything in that letter of yours that should be interpreted as meaning that the January 21st conference meant to suppress any of the essential facts that this committee could use in this investigation?

THE PRESIDENT. Oh, no, nothing. As a matter of fact, as you can well know, ladies and gentlemen, I can't stay too close to the details of this argument, and I don't know what is the latest and most intense question that is brought up. So, the letter which I signed, I had directed the beginning of its preparation long before in order to clarify our own minds, get the best legal opinion as to where this thing was. You can see how long it took; did you see all of the—in the attached memorandum how the historical examples were recited merely to show that this is no new doctrine? We are just trying to preserve the essentials of our Government.

Q. Gould Lincoln, Washington Star: Mr. President, would it be correct to say that the White House OK'd the preparation and submission of the Army report on Senator McCarthy and Mr. Cohn?

THE PRESIDENT. It would not.

Q. Harry C. Dent, Columbia (S.C.) State and Record: Mr. President, do you have any advice to give the South as to just how to react to this recent Supreme Court decision banning segregation, sir?

THE PRESIDENT. Not in the slightest. I thought that Governor Byrnes made a very fine statement when he said, "Let's be calm and let's be reasonable and let's look this thing in the face."

The Supreme Court has spoken and I am sworn to uphold the constitutional processes in this country; and I will obey.

Q. Mr. Dent: Mr. President, one more question. Do you think this decision has put Mr. Byrnes and Mr. Byrd and other Southern leaders who supported the Republican ticket in 1952 on the political hotspot, so to speak, since it was brought out under the Republican administration?

THE PRESIDENT. The Supreme Court, as I understand it, is not under any administration.

Q. Sarah McClendon, El Paso Times: A question along that same line, sir, do you expect that this ruling will, however, alienate many of your Southern supporters politically?

THE PRESIDENT. This is all I will say: I have stood, so far as I know, for honest, decent government since I was first mentioned as a political figure. I am still standing for it, and they will have to make their own decisions as to whether they decide that I have got any sense or haven't.

Q. David P. Sentner, Hearst Newspapers: Mr. President, did you say whether you were aware in advance of the calling of the so-called conference on January 21st——

THE PRESIDENT. The what?

Q. Mr. Sentner: Were you aware of a conference being called in advance on January 21st in the Attorney General's office?

THE PRESIDENT. Well, I wouldn't answer it in any event because, after all, we do come to a place here where you can't go into detail; but my memory wouldn't serve me anyway. I couldn't remember such a thing.

Q. Clark R. Mollenhoff, Des Moines Register and Tribune: Is it proper that the loyalty conversations are the only thing barred by your order, things outside of the scope——

THE PRESIDENT. I think the order stands on itself. After all, it has a certain amount of legal terminology which I have had to study and try to comprehend. I think the order should be read and just interpreted for itself.

Q. Mr. Mollenhoff: Mr. President, under the past administration T. Lamar Caudle testified with relation to conversations with Howard McGrath, and several Treasury Department employees were called to testify with relation to conversations with John Snyder. I wonder if there is any distinction between this case and those cases which you would like to make?

THE PRESIDENT. I believe this: I believe situations can arise in this vast executive department where officials, knowing that something is not a matter of a confidential nature and exchange of views, can make their own decisions. You will recall both in that order and anything I have ever said, that the executive department stands ready always in every proper way to cooperate with the Congress.

We at least know this: you can't make our form of government work without cooperation. We are careful in this particular only to keep the proper division between their powers and the Executive powers and authorities and responsibilities, so confusion does not result.

Now I am not going to try to take every case that could possibly arise in this vast executive department and here give an answer as to what should happen.

Q. Mr. Mollenhoff: Mr. President, do you feel that there is a danger of this precedent being used though in the future? In the past there were conversations between Fall and Denby in the Harding administration that would have fallen within the pale of this, as I would interpret it. I wonder if there was some distinction?

THE PRESIDENT. Well, you will have to read the order and decide yourself.

Q. Kenneth M. Scheibel, Gannett Newspapers: Mr. President, could you tell us your reaction to the reported shipment of arms to Guatemala from behind the Iron Curtain?

THE PRESIDENT. Well, it is disturbing. I think that, above all, it highlights the circumstances, the background, that led to the adoption of the resolution at the Caracas conference regarding communism in this country.

To have the Communist dictatorship establish an outpost on this continent to the detriment of all the American nations, of course would be a terrible thing; that was the reason for the Caracas resolution.

Q. Charles L. Bartlett, Chattanooga Times: Mr. President, Gordon Clapp's term as Chairman of the TVA ended yesterday. I wondered if you had any farewell comment on his service in that post?

THE PRESIDENT. All of the reports that have come to me are that he has operated as a very fine administrator and without any fear, favor, or affection.

Q. Chalmers M. Roberts, Washington Post and Times Herald: Mr. President, I wonder if you could tell us anything about the current conversations between this Government and France on Indochina, as to your understanding of their scope and progress?

THE PRESIDENT. Well, as far as the conversations just between representatives going on in Paris, of course there is nothing to say about them.

I can say this: I can remind you again of the background that is still stable, so far as this country is concerned. If any of you may recall, on April 16th, 1953, I made a talk on the world situation, promotion of peace, and in it I most clearly pointed out, went to some trouble to point out, that there should be collective arrangements for assuring the security of southeast Asia.

That, remember, is the basic policy of the United States; that it is only through collective security among several nations that you can establish a political background in which it is possible to defeat Communist aggression.

Now, any talks that are going on anywhere, in which the United States is a part, always go ahead with that background.

Q. Mr. Roberts: Is it your understanding, sir, that we are trying to get that collective security before the close of the Geneva conference?

THE PRESIDENT. Such things cannot be forced. They are long weary conversations, and in one form or another have been going on for a long time, as I say, witness my own public statement of well over a year ago, witness the public statements of the Secretary of State.

I don't know and I can't tell you anything about it; or at least I couldn't report, I say, any detail that would indicate progress or lack of progress. They are just going ahead, is all I can say.

Q. Mrs. May Craig, Maine Newspapers: Mr. President, may I ask one more question about the investigation? The question before the committee as outlined there was whether the direction of the investigation had been shifted on January 21st from the narrow issue of the Department of Defense and the Army to the White House and the Attorney General. Mr. John Adams testified that just before that on January the 19th, he felt the issues had got beyond him, particularly in relation to the loyalty aspect, and that therefore he had taken it up with the Department of Justice, and then the 21st conference took place.

THE PRESIDENT. Just a moment; I told you that that particular question of course was beyond them because it involved an Executive order, and that is the reason he was justified in saying that.

Q. Mrs. Craig: Yes, but the question of the Capitol, as voiced by all these Senators, was whether from that day on the whole course of this controversy was shifted to the White House.

THE PRESIDENT. Well, as I intimated before, I am sure you will be satisfied by the Secretary of the Army's statement on this. If you are not, you may raise it again at the next press conference. I think I have made it clear.

Q. Alan S. Emory, Watertown Daily Times: Mr. President, late last week Governor Dewey suggested that a solution to two of our problems might be if we drank less coffee and more milk. I wonder if you had any comment on that? *[Laughter]*

THE PRESIDENT. Well, I don't know if you have to drink less coffee, because most of us like it. But I am sure of this. I would like to see Americans drink more milk. That will help solve one of my problems.

Q. Kenneth M. Scheibel, Gannett Newspapers: Mr. President, in that connection Secretary Benson wants to put milk-vending machines in all of the Government buildings. Will you support him in that proposal?

THE PRESIDENT. Someone on my staff came along and said that he was 2 years late or a year late. We have had them in our office for a long time. I think it's a pretty good idea.

Q. Mr. Scheibel: Would you recommend them for the other Government buildings?

THE PRESIDENT. I think I would have to let them decide that themselves. I'm in favor of drinking milk.

Q. Dayton Moore, United Press: Mr. President, when do you think you will appoint a new Chairman or reappoint Mr. Clapp to the TVA?

THE PRESIDENT. As soon as I find a man who is completely nonpolitical in his position and status, who is in my opinion a professionally well-qualified man, whose general philosophical approach to such affairs agrees with mine, and whose integrity and probity is above reproach; and that is a hard job.

Q. Joseph R. Slevin, New York Journal of Commerce: Mr. President, in your foreign economic message to Congress at the end of March, you mentioned modifying the "Buy American Act" regulations through administrative action. I wonder if you could tell us what the status of those plans is at this time?

THE PRESIDENT. Modifying the "Buy American Act"?

Q. Mr. Slevin: Modifying the regulation, Executive regulation.

THE PRESIDENT. No, there has been no recent report made to me on this subject. Now, it does come up every time we talk about the plan and our hope of promoting a freer trade with our friends in the world; but I don't know about the details of which you speak, and I will have to have them looked up and given you.

Q. Douglass Cater, The Reporter Magazine: Mr. President, would you give us any estimate of what you think the effect would be if this Senate investigation were called off at this time?

THE PRESIDENT. Well, I don't think the facts have been brought out. This has aroused a great interest in the United States.

Now, make no mistake; I am anxious to see it cease, with all of the principals once telling their story. Ladies and gentlemen, let me say again I just don't think anything today deserves to absorb the attention of the United States as compared to the study it should be making of our foreign situation, our foreign policy, as it is applied to the various areas of the world, where does lie our enlightened self-interest, where do we best support the whole theory of the hanging together, the cooperation amongst the nations of the free world, the program as it is applied to our own country in the terms of taxes and farm programs and everything that is there to keep us strong so we can pursue intelligently and with confidence a peaceful program in the world.

Nothing, nothing can be so important as that kind of a program and its enactment at this time. Consequently, much as I want to see this thing settled conclusively, and so that we do know the facts, let the chips fall where they may. Let's get the facts out and then let's go on about the important business of this Government; and I personally feel, ladies and gentlemen, there is no time to waste.

We should stand in great issues as a more united people looking at the same set of facts; and I don't mean, as I have told you so often, I don't mean agreeing with me or with anybody else in details of procedure and methods. But let's see what it is we are trying to do in the world, and then let's get ahead with it.

I am sorry to make a speech.

Q. Frank van der Linden, Charlotte (N.C.) Observer: Judging from your reception down in Charlotte yesterday on the trip, would you say the Republicans have a good chance of carrying that part of North Carolina this fall?

THE PRESIDENT. Well, I wouldn't make such suggestions, for this reason: we know that the South is traditionally Democratic. But I will say this: I got very great support for the speech I just have now made you, and many, many, many men saying to me, "I hope we can get ahead with it," of all parties.

Q. Nat S. Finney, Buffalo Evening News: Mr. President, there have been some reports that the conversations with Russia as to your atomic pool plan have, in effect, broken down. Can you throw some light on that for us today?

THE PRESIDENT. I would merely say this: with certain of my advisers who are close in this, I am studying as hard I can to see how the United States can go ahead in some enlightened form, some enlightened method along this line without waiting on anybody else.

Q. Laurence H. Burd, Chicago Tribune: Mr. President, can you say what you think the prospects are of Great Britain joining in the Southeast Asia Pact?

THE PRESIDENT. No, I can't, because I don't know.

Q. Mr. Burd: Do you think we could build an effective pact back there without Great Britain's support?

THE PRESIDENT. Well, after all, you must remember that Australia and New Zealand are the countries of the British Commonwealth of Nations that are directly involved. I should say that with the proper Asiatic nations, which of course I lay down as a *sine qua non,* and Australia and New Zealand, we might possibly work out something that would be maybe not as satisfactory or as broad as you would like it, but could be workable.

Q. Roscoe Drummond, New York Herald Tribune: Mr. President, could you say whether you think that the atomic energy law should be revised so as to give more authority to the Chairman of the Commission?

THE PRESIDENT. Well, it is a detail, I must tell you, that I am not quite sure how the law is written. And Mr. Drummond, I will say this— no recommendations have been made to me on the subject, so I could add this—I have the utmost faith in Admiral Strauss, and if you could make certain that there was always going to be a man there of that caliber, why I could stand a lot of authority in his hands.

(Speaker unidentified): Thank you, Mr. President.

NOTE: President Eisenhower's thirty-eighth news conference was held in the Executive Office Building from 10:32 to 10:54 o'clock on Wednesday morning, May 19, 1954. In attendance: 183.

116   ¶ Special Message to the Congress on
Contributory Group Life Insurance for Federal
Employees.   *May* 19, 1954

To the Congress of the United States:

I propose for the consideration of the Congress a plan of contributory group life insurance for Federal civilian employees.

Three months ago I expressed my conviction that a well-rounded personnel program was needed to benefit the Federal career system and its workers and to increase the administrative efficiency of the government. A program was envisaged that would combine the best practices of progressive, private employers with the special requirements of public service.

With this type of personnel program as our objective, thorough studies were made to determine how best to provide its necessary elements, and most of these have been recommended to the Congress. An additional essential element is contributory group life insurance. Such a plan I now recommend to the Congress.

Excepting those excluded by their own request or for administrative reasons, this plan would provide all civilian employees of the legislative, executive and judicial branches with group life insurance approximately equal in amount to one year's salary during active service prior to age 65, and with reduced benefits thereafter. The amount would be doubled if the employee should die by accidental means. Employees retiring on an immediate annuity, after fifteen years of service, would have insurance protection without further cost to them. Others terminating their employment would be able, without medical examination, to convert their insurance to individual policies at rates applicable to their attained age.

By means of this plan government workers could supplement their own insurance programs at minimum expense. The cost of the plan would be shared by the government and participating employees, each agency paying from existing appropriations about half of its employees' costs. Thus employees could take advantage of the low contribution rate of twenty-five cents bi-weekly for each one thousand dollars of life insurance.

In order to have advantages under this plan that are normally available to private employers, it is proposed that the insurance be cooperatively underwritten through the facilities of a large group of life insurance companies having experience in employee group insurance benefits. These companies would establish a single administrative office to assure the utmost economy in the operation of the plan.

The functions normally performed by the employer in a group insurance plan would, under this plan, be performed in the government by the Civil Service Commission. A Council on Group Insurance, consisting of the Secretaries of the Treasury and Labor and Director of the Bureau of the Budget, would be established to review the program and advise the Commission on policy matters.

In summary, two predominant features make this plan especially advantageous to the government and its personnel. First, employees are better enabled by this low-cost life insurance protection to carry out their responsibilities to their families. Second, the plan is another essential element in the development of a comprehensive personnel program that applies to government service the best practices of progressive, private employers.

A draft bill to effectuate this plan has been prepared by the Civil Service Commission and is being submitted to the Congress. I earnestly recommend that the Congress give this plan early favorable consideration.

DWIGHT D. EISENHOWER

117 ¶ Exchange of Messages Between the President and the King of Laos on the Occasion of Constitution Day. *May* 20, 1954

[Released May 20, 1954. Dated May 10, 1954]

His Majesty Sisavang Vong
King of Laos
Luang Prabang, Laos

To Your Majesty and to the people of Laos on the occasion of Constitution Day, I am delighted to send the best wishes of the people of the United States.

It is our fervent hope that your sovereignty and independence will be strengthened and preserved. I am convinced that the forces of freedom, working in unison, will repulse the Communist imperialism that would enslave your Kingdom and your people.

In this crucial struggle of all free men against those who would reduce Laos to the status of a satellite of world Communism, I know that Your Majesty and the people of Laos will continue to provide an heroic and inspiring example for all.

DWIGHT D. EISENHOWER

NOTE: His Majesty Sisavang Vong's message of May 12 follows:

To the President of the United States of America:

Your Excellency was good enough on the occasion of the anniversary of the Laotian Constitution to extend to me and to the people of Laos the best wishes of the United States of America. In the name of the people of Laos and in my own name I thank Your Excellency for that friendly message. The Kingdom of Laos has struggled and continues to defend its territory against the foreign invasion with the same stubbornness. It can continue the struggle only with the substantial assistance of the United States of America and the moral and material support of the free world.

SISAVANG VONG

118 ¶ Remarks to the Committee for Economic Development. *May 20, 1954*

Mr. Kestnbaum, ladies and gentlemen:

It is a special privilege that I have of extending to this group a welcome to the Capital City.

I think that among this group I would find a greater average of old acquaintances and personal friends than almost any other which I could meet, by reason of the fact that when I was President of a University you even allowed me to belong to your organization.

In spite of this, I am not going to make the mistake of talking economics to such a group—maybe it is because you so well know my limitations that I will not talk about it.

But I should like to mention a few things that I think are associated with your work. First, I believe that in such a group as this lies a great part of the major decisions—power for making these major decisions—that are going to determine the character of our future, not only immediately but over a longer period.

Many of those decisions are business decisions. It is a matter of great gratification, not only to me but to every associate I have in the admin-

istration, both on the legislative and executive side, that the decisions—
that we can see the effects of—that you have been making reflect an
optimism and a confidence that we believe is one of the greatest factors
necessary to ensure that America will continue to march forward as it
has been marching.

Your expenditures for capital investment, plant improvement, and
greater productivity are the decisions of very courageous and forward-
looking people—the same kind of people that have brought America to
its position today.

Now, of course, in their sum, all of the things that Government does
affects all of you far more, possibly, than they did in a simpler day.
When I look over the list today and see great public works programs in
buildings and roads, great expenditures for defense equipment, farm
programs, great extensions in the security programs, old-age pensions,
and all of this sort of thing, I am really staggered by the sum total that
is poured into our economy, in a direct way, by the Government.

Nevertheless, that is still not the important part. It is the wisdom, the
forward-looking capacities of our businessmen that are going to make
America, and keep America, the healthy, economic organism that will
bring the happiness and progress to our people.

Along with it I want to suggest only one thing where I believe the
Government, with you, has a mission. That is the constant teaching
that the problem of the economic development of the United States is
more than mere economics; it is of the heart; it is the spirit; it is made
up of such factors as courage, confidence, pride, and patriotism—faith.

We do not keep security establishments merely to defend property or
territory or rights abroad or at sea. We keep the security forces to defend
a way of life.

Now everybody knows that no security force is any good at all unless
it is one of high morale, belief, and conviction. Consequently, the first
thing we must do, it seems to me, is to believe in this system of freedom
with all our hearts, to realize we are defending, first of all, our great
system of freedoms and of rights. Everything we do that seems to im-
pinge upon them, although at times we may think it is necessary in their
modification, we must examine carefully and say how far may we go and
still not ruin this system. Where do we establish the line beyond which
we must not step, unless we are going to go and lose internally what we
so desperately try to defend against externally?

I believe all the way through we must in this manner of faith recognize a relationship between free government and a religious faith. I believe that if there is no religious faith whatsoever, then there is little defense you can make of a free system. If men are only animals, why not try to dominate them?

We reject all these theories that are so earnestly promulgated by the totalitarian dictatorships. They have to believe or teach those things in order to get people to accept their domination.

We don't believe them.

That is the kind of thing that I believe Government can stand for and preach, along with you, as you try in a material way to bring greater opportunity to all men for jobs, for raising their standards of living. We must constantly remember that men do not live by bread alone. And the Government, and every leader of a business or profession must band together to show that the United States is a great organism of free men who put freedom above all other values.

I sometimes think that Patrick Henry may have overstated the case— for any one of us may not quite accept and live by his immortal statement, "Give me liberty or give me death." But I still believe that that statement is true for our race.

We will accept nothing over and above freedom. And as long as we live that—and believe in it—and do our work in that spirit, to my mind, America is not only safe but America is going forward in the expanding and growing economy that will bring greater and greater happiness to our people, security for us, and promote peace in the world.

Thank you very much.

NOTE: The President spoke at the Shoreham Hotel in Washington. His opening words "Mr. Kestnbaum" referred to Meyer Kestnbaum, Chairman of the Board of Trustees of the Committee.

119 ¶ Letter to Charles H. Percy of Chicago
Concerning the President's Foreign Economic
Policy Proposals. *May* 20, 1954

[Released May 20, 1954. Dated May 19, 1954]

Dear Mr. Percy:

It is gratifying to have your letter of May fourteenth expressing strong
support for the foreign economic policy proposals contained in my Message to the Congress of March thirtieth. In that Message I set forth
what I believe to be a minimum essential program for the building of a
stronger America as an integral part of a strong and economically vigorous free world. Because I consider the enactment of that program indispensable to the work that this Administration must do in the national
interest, I have given much thought to the means by which such enactment can best be assured.

As you know, several recommendations in my Message on foreign
economic policy can be carried out without further legislative authority.
Among these are clarification of the application of the Buy American
legislation, assistance through the International Monetary Fund and the
Federal Reserve System to nations which undertake convertibility of
their currencies, renegotiation of the organizational provisions of the
General Agreement on Tariffs and Trade for submission to the Congress,
encouragement to overseas investment through giving full diplomatic support to United States investors abroad and through actions to encourage
more extensive travel.

Accomplishing enactment of the heart of the program—extension of
and amendment of the Trade Agreements Extension Act of 1951, as
amended—would, I believe, best be served by careful and deliberate
action taken on the basis of extensive and unhurried hearings. In this
way the wide public support for the program that I know exists and to
which you attest, will have adequate time and opportunity to express
itself. Moreover, those who are opposed would have full opportunity
to be heard. It is my hope and expectation that the Committee on
Ways and Means, following the pattern of its historic work last year
on the tax bill, will initiate consideration of the trade agreements aspect
of the program in ample time so that full and adequate hearings may

be completed between now and the convening of the Congress next January. Under this procedure the prospect for consideration by the Congress early next year is excellent.

Since the present Act expires on June 12, 1954, a simple one-year extension will, of course, be required for the interim period.

In addition to initiating hearings on the vital subject of extension and amendment of the Trade Agreements Extension Act, there is much else that should be accomplished in this session of the Congress to carry into effect the recommendations of my Message of March thirtieth. The tax incentives for foreign investment provided for in H.R. 8300 will, I am confident, become law shortly. I look forward to enactment in this session of the increase in the tourist allowance from $500 to $1,000 as provided in H.R. 8352, now pending before the House Ways and Means Committee. It is my hope that the Congress will shortly complete action on H.R. 6584, dealing with customs valuation, a bill which has already passed the House and is now pending in the Senate Committee on Finance. Simplification of commodity definitions and rate structures in the Tariff Act based upon a study by the Tariff Commission, and a better method of classifying articles not enumerated in the tariff schedules should be authorized. Improvement in the statutes governing the administration of customs procedures and changes in the anti-dumping law and procedures to speed up its administration should also, I believe, be provided at this session.

Accomplishment of these things now would represent substantial progress in which we all could take satisfaction. With these first steps behind us, the Congress will be in a position early next year to undertake immediate consideration of the vital part of the program—the further amendment and extension of the Trade Agreements Extension Act. This overall program will provide the forward motion in our country essential to progress the world over in raising levels of profitable trade and investment. It is my deep conviction that in this direction lies the greater security for America that comes from a stronger free world.

Sincerely,

DWIGHT D. EISENHOWER

NOTE: Mr. Percy's letter of May 14 was released with the President's reply. The letter referred to a meeting in the President's office on April 29 at which Mr. Percy served as spokesman for a group of businessmen, and to their subsequent finding of much interest, throughout the country, in the President's foreign economic policy proposals.

120 ¶ Remarks at the Annual Convention of the National Rivers and Harbors Congress.
May 25, 1954

Mr. Chairman, ladies and gentlemen:

First, permit me on behalf of the administration, and I am sure all of Washington, to bid you a very warm welcome to this city for your deliberations. We hope that you find your meeting not only profitable but enjoyable.

I have just heard it said that every President in the past 53 years has endorsed the work of this Congress. Here is one case where I certainly intend to set no precedent of a negative sort, and I join in the list of those who have endorsed your work.

Now, if I may impose on a bit of your time before you can make inroads on your luncheon, I should like to tell you of just one or two of the reasons why I feel so strongly in this matter.

I have become convinced that before very long, America will almost unanimously look upon water as its single greatest resource. Everywhere we find evidence of its destructiveness when badly used or when not controlled. We have a very great lack of it in some areas, even down to one project proposed for drinking water—just isn't enough drinking water for three cities in one of our States.

Along with it, of course—when we are conserving and handling water correctly—goes soil conservation. So I won't even take your time to digress into that field, but simply stick to the water end of it.

Now, as an old soldier, I have a horror of piecemeal action. There are among you old soldiers who have attended Fort Leavenworth and have heard of all the lessons they taught us and the criticisms of doing things piecemeal. I learned that, and I believe it. So when a project is proposed that seems to me to be unrelated to all of the necessities of a river valley or of a slope in which it is located, I am very cold and unsympathetic. I believe that we have got to go to the Continental Divide and find from there on to the sea where each drop of water falls and what we are going to do with it until it reaches the sea. I believe that any lesser survey of our water resources, our water uses, and our water control, is completely piecemeal, and we should reject it.

When we begin to talk about dams on streams, or soil conservation way upstream, I believe they are two related subjects and should be dealt with together.

Now I know that a body such as this is doing valuable work every day. My anxiety is to have the Government cooperate with you and to be so organized that it can effectively operate and cooperate with you without the necessity of running to half a dozen departments in the executive branch. I shall do this, and am doing it.

There is being organized, first, a Cabinet committee on water resources that will be announced either this evening or tomorrow. It will have on it the Defense Department, the Interior Department, and the Agriculture Department. The heads of those Departments will be the members, and they will coordinate with bodies such as this, with the Hoover Commission, and with Members of Congress, to devise on behalf of the executive departments a broad water program that will cover this continent from ocean to ocean and from the Canadian border to Mexico.

Under this Cabinet committee will be organized an operating committee so that the policies determined upon by the Legislature—the National Legislature—and the Cabinet committee can be implemented. This operating committee, in turn, will be able to meet with you and your representatives on an operating basis.

In this way, we hope that not only will the Federal Government be coordinated in this great endeavor, but that the actual activities which you people so deeply study will be coordinated as far as the Federal executive department is concerned. We will then be able to plan to use our water for power, for irrigation, for its control so that it doesn't flood out our other resources and wash away soil, for navigation, for the proper use of our harbors. That will be our task.

There are other individuals in Government that will be members of these committees, when necessary. These will be permanent committees established for this purpose. And certainly I do hope that in this one field the great wisdom and experience that can be brought to us by the professionals in the field, the people who study it, such as you do, by the policy-making groups in the Congress, by our own executing agencies in the executive department and branches, all can be brought together. We hope that all can work to the end that we will make certain that we won't wake up some two decades from now and regret that we did not act intelligently back in 1954 with respect to this greatest of all national resources.

Now in this very crude and informal way, I have tried to tell you why I am interested in your work. If I haven't made you understand it now, I don't know what else to say. So with this brief interlude—for which I thank you, and thank you for the compliment of inviting me before you—I will say goodbye. Good luck to each of you.

NOTE: The President spoke at the Mayflower Hotel in Washington. John L. McClellan, U.S. Senator from Arkansas, was President of the Congress, and Overton Brooks, U.S. Representative from Louisiana, was Vice President and chairman of the Convention.

121 ¶ Veto of Bill Providing for the Conveyance of Lands Within Camp Blanding Military Reservation, Florida. *May 25, 1954*

To the House of Representatives:

I return herewith, without my approval, H.R. 7512, a bill to provide for the conveyance of the federally-owned lands which are situated within Camp Blanding Military Reservation, Florida, to the Armory Board, State of Florida, in order to consolidate ownership and perpetuate the availability of Camp Blanding for military training and use.

Generally, the bill provides for the conveyance of federally-owned lands within Camp Blanding Military Reservation, Florida, to the Armory Board, State of Florida, upon conditions designed to permit coordinated management of the natural resources of both the Federal and State lands within the reservation and to insure that all of such lands will continue to be available for military use. I wish to emphasize my agreement with these objectives.

However, I cannot approve Section 2(4) of the bill in its present form. This section would authorize the State of Florida to dispose of "interests or rights in land by lease, license, or easement or by contract of sale of timber or timber products" upon the condition that in the case of Federal lands and within nine months after the enactment of the bill into law, the State of Florida and the Secretary of the Army shall have reached an agreement governing the disposition of the revenues from such operations. Again, there can be no objection to such cooperative action between

Federal and State governments. However, Section 2(4) further provides "that prior to the consummation of the agreement with the State of Florida or board, the Secretary of the Army or his designee shall come into agreement with the Committees on Armed Services of the Senate and of the House of Representatives concerning the terms of such agreement." Because of this provision of the bill, I cannot approve it.

The purpose of this clause is to vest in the Committees on Armed Services of the Senate and House of Representatives power to approve or disapprove any agreement which the Secretary of the Army proposes to make with the State of Florida pursuant to Section 2(4). The practical effect would be to place the power to make such agreement jointly in the Secretary of the Army and the members of the Committees on Armed Services. In so doing, the bill would violate the fundamental constitutional principle of separation of powers prescribed in Articles I and II of the Constitution which place the legislative power in the Congress and the executive power in the Executive branch.

The making of such a contract or agreement on behalf of the United States is a purely executive or administrative function, like the negotiation and execution of government contracts generally. Thus, while Congress may enact legislation governing the making of government contracts, it may not delegate to its members or committees the power to make such contracts, either directly or by giving to them a power to approve or disapprove a contract which an executive officer proposes to make. Moreover such a procedure destroys the clear lines of responsibility for results which the Constitution provides.

I believe it to be my duty to oppose any such departure from constitutional procedures. However, I am confident that the true purpose of the Congress in the enactment of this provision was to facilitate administrative action, while at the same time not neglecting its own responsibilities. I suggest that this could be properly accomplished by requiring specific reports from the Executive as to action taken. These reports could serve as the basis for further Congressional action in case the Congress so desired. Accordingly, I recommend that H.R. 7512 be modified and reenacted.

DWIGHT D. EISENHOWER

NOTE: A modified bill was enacted on July 14, 1954, as Public Law 493, 83d Congress (68 Stat. 474).

122 ¶ Letter to Secretary McKay Establishing a Cabinet Committee on Water Resources Policy. *May 26, 1954*

Dear Mr. Secretary:

The conservation and use which we make of the water resources of our Nation may in large measure determine our future progress and the standards of living of our citizens. If we are to continue to advance agriculturally and industrially we must make the best use of every drop of water which falls on our soil, or which can be extracted from the oceans. It is my desire that this Administration furnish effective and resourceful leadership in establishing national policies and improving the administrative organization needed to conserve and best utilize the full potential of our water resources.

During the more than a century in which the Federal Government has played a vital part in the harnessing and development of water resources, our policies have been modified repeatedly to reflect changing needs and priorities. Unfortunately, we have often relied on piecemeal or stop-gap measures. In other instances the policies covering different Federal Agencies concerned with similar water resources have been inconsistent. Accordingly, it is both fitting and necessary for us to undertake a comprehensive review looking toward modernization of Federal policies and programs in the field of water resources. We must do this with a full realization that the States, communities and private citizens are vitally concerned with the policies and actions of the Federal Government.

To meet the needs to which I have referred above, I am establishing a Cabinet Committee on Water Resources Policy. The committee shall undertake an extensive review of all aspects of water resources policy. Its recommendations for the strengthening, clarification and modernization of water policies, together with a suggested approach to the solution of organizational problems involved, are to be submitted to me not later than December 1, 1954.

I am designating you the Chairman of the Cabinet Committee on Water Resources Policy. The Secretary of Defense and the Secretary of Agriculture will serve with you on the committee as full members, and

I am so notifying them by copies of this letter. The Secretary of Commerce, the Secretary of Health, Education and Welfare and the Director of the Bureau of the Budget will participate on an ad hoc basis. My Advisory Committee on Government Organization will be glad to cooperate wherever possible.

The Commission on Organization of the Executive Branch of the Government, under the Chairmanship of former President Hoover, is undertaking a comprehensive study of water and power policies and organization. The Cabinet Committee should be prepared to assist in the Executive Branch consideration and review of the Hoover Commission recommendations.

Several Departments and Agencies are presently charged with responsibilities directly affecting the conservation and use of water and each such Agency is capable of making an important contribution to the reexamination and revision of water resources policy. By means of another letter, I am also approving the establishment of an Inter-Agency Committee on Water Resources as provided in an Inter-Agency Agreement proposed through the initiative of your Department. The Inter-Agency Committee on Water Resources will provide a facility for improving the coordination of existing policies, programs and activities of the participating Departments and Agencies concerned with water and land resources investigation, planning, construction, operation and maintenance. I shall expect the Inter-Agency Committee to assist the Cabinet Committee in every way possible in order to insure that the Cabinet Committee has the opportunity to utilize fully the skills and experience of the Executive Agencies.

Sincerely,

DWIGHT D. EISENHOWER

NOTE: The release containing the text of this letter to the Secretary of the Interior listed the following agencies as members of the Inter-Agency Committee on Water Resources: Departments of the Interior, Agriculture, Commerce, Health, Education, and Welfare, and Army; and the Federal Power Commission. The release added that the Labor Department would have associate membership. The President's letter approving the establishment of the Inter-Agency Committee was not released.

123 ¶ Statement by the President on Receiving the Air Coordinating Committee Report on U.S. Aviation Policy. *May* 26, 1954

BECAUSE the last comprehensive review of United States aviation policy was completed approximately six years ago, current guidance is critically needed by the aviation industry, by government and by the public.

On September 23, 1953, I requested that the Honorable Robert B. Murray, Jr., as Chairman of the Air Coordinating Committee, direct that committee to review and, for my consideration, make recommendations on United States aviation policy. The report was prepared with the help of appropriate representatives of the aviation industry, local governments and other groups directly concerned with aviation matters. The Committee has accomplished this task in a fashion that could make its report a milestone in the progress of American aviation.

The report has been presented to me, and reflects this Administration's central objective in this field—to strengthen American aviation. In order to carry out this broad policy, the Committee has made certain specific recommendations in such phases of aviation as air transport routes and subsidy, air cargo, airports and airways, aviation safety, mobilization planning, and some aspects of aircraft manufacturing. In each case, the Committee has been guided by the desire to promote the most effective government relationship with the civil aviation industry and to gain the greatest public benefit from every dollar of Government aid expended.

I shall use this report as a guide in the future consideration of questions related to the subject of civil aviation and in making appropriate recommendations to Congress. The review is released for general distribution and information.

NOTE: The report of the Air Coordinating Committee, dated May 1, 1954, was entitled "Civil Air Policy" (71 pp., Government Printing Office, 1954).

124 ¶ Toasts of the President and Emperor Haile Selassie of Ethiopia. *May* 26, 1954

Your Majesty, ladies and gentlemen:

During the past century and a half, there have been entertained within these walls many individuals of distinction—some of our own country, some visiting us from abroad. I think it is safe to say that never has any company here gathered been honored by the presence in their guest of honor of an individual more noted for his fierce defense of freedom and for his courage in defending the independence of his people than the guest of honor this evening.

I read once that no individual can really be known to have greatness until he has been tested in adversity. By this test, our guest of honor has established new standards in the world. In 5 years of adversity, with his country overrun but never conquered, he never lost for one single second his dignity. He never lost his faith in himself, in his people, and in his God.

I deem it a very great privilege, ladies and gentlemen, to ask you to rise and with me to drink a Toast to His Imperial Majesty, the Emperor of Ethiopia.

NOTE: The President proposed this toast at a state dinner at the White House, at 9:45 p.m. The Emperor responded as follows:

I thank you, Mr. President, for the kind sentiments which you have expressed on this occasion, because I take them, not as addressed to me, but to my beloved people.

I have accepted your kind invitation, Mr. President, to come to the United States and visit your nation, because it has offered me the occasion to express the depth of my appreciation and that of my people for your friendship and assistance which encouraged and aided us in resuming our march on the road of progress from which we had been detained by the imperatives of war. That assistance is today, in yet more varied forms, strongly impelling us forward on the path of progressive development.

By your great comprehension of the problems with which Ethiopia is faced, it has been possible for us to achieve, with your help, considerable progress in the solution of the present hour. The smoothness of this collaboration notwithstanding the barriers of distance and language and the breadth and richness of our relations attained during the half-century to which you, Mr. President, have alluded, constitute the supreme manifestation of that extraordinary flexibility of understanding and felicity of spirit with which you, as a nation, have been endowed, and of the trust and confidence which you inspire in the minds of others.

I raise my glass to the men and women of the great and noble American nation, and to its heroic and distinguished chief, President Eisenhower and, last but not least, to his consort and wife who so charmingly represents in her person the women of the United States and the role which they play in giving leadership to American thoughts and ideals throughout the world.

125 ¶ Special Message to the Congress Transmitting Recommendations Adopted by the International Labor Organization. *May* 28, 1954

To the Congress of the United States:

In accordance with the obligations of the United States of America as a member of the International Labor Organization I transmit herewith authentic texts of a Recommendation (No. 91) concerning collective agreements and a Recommendation (No. 92) concerning voluntary conciliation and arbitration, both of which were adopted on June 29, 1951 by the International Labor Conference at its thirty-fourth session, held at Geneva from June 6 to June 29, 1951.

I transmit also the report of the Acting Secretary of State with regard to the two Recommendations, together with a copy of a letter from the Secretary of Labor to the Secretary of State setting forth the coordinated view of the interested departments and agencies of the executive branch of the Government with respect to the Recommendations. I particularly invite the attention of the Congress to the recommendation of those departments and agencies that no legislative action be taken, for the reasons set forth in the above-mentioned letter of the Secretary of Labor.

For action and advice with respect to American Samoa and the Trust Territory of the Pacific Islands (excluding the Northern Mariana Islands with the exception of Rota), and for transmission to the Governments of Alaska, Guam, Hawaii, and the Virgin Islands in order that those Governments may give consideration to the enactment of legislation or other action, I am sending texts of the Recommendations to the Secretary of the Interior. Also, I am transmitting the texts of the Recommendations to the Secretary of the Navy for such action and advice as may be suitable with respect to that portion of the Trust Territory which includes the Northern Mariana Islands except Rota.

Dwight D. Eisenhower

NOTE: The text of Recommendations 91 and 92 and related documents are printed in House Document 406 (83d Cong., 2d sess.).

126 ¶ Special Message to the Congress Transmitting Convention Adopted by the International Labor Organization. *May* 28, 1954

To the Congress of the United States:

In accordance with the obligations of the United States of America as a member of the International Labor Organization I transmit for the consideration of the Congress an authentic text of a Convention (No. 102) concerning minimum standards of social security, adopted on June 28, 1952 by the International Labor Conference at its thirty-fifth session, held at Geneva from June 4 to June 28, 1952.

I transmit also the report of the Acting Secretary of State with regard to the Convention, together with a copy of a letter from the Secretary of Labor to the Secretary of State, setting forth the coordinated view of the interested departments and agencies of the executive branch of the Government with respect to the Convention.

Since, under the constitutional system of the United States, the subject matter of the Convention is appropriate in part for action by the States and in part for action by the Federal Government the Convention is regarded, in accordance with Article 19, paragraph 7(b), of the constitution of the International Labor Organization, as not suitable for ratification but rather for referral to the appropriate Federal and State authorities for their consideration.

I am sending texts of the Convention to the Secretary of the Interior in order that they may be transmitted to the Governments of Alaska, Guam, Hawaii, and the Virgin Islands for such action as may be deemed suitable. I am also transmitting the Convention to the Secretary of the Interior for appropriate action and advice with regard to American Samoa, and to the Secretary of the Interior and the Secretary of the Navy for appropriate action and advice with regard to those areas of the Trust Territory of the Pacific Islands under their respective jurisdictions.

DWIGHT D. EISENHOWER

NOTE: The text of Convention No. 102 and related documents are published in   House Document 407 (83d Cong., 2d sess.).

127 ¶ Remarks to the 44th National Council of the Boy Scouts of America. *May* 29, 1954

Ladies and gentlemen:

It is a very pleasant privilege I have, to come to this meeting to bid you welcome to your Nation's Capital City on behalf of the administration—on behalf of the entire Government, each of whose members I know would like to have me speak for them. We not only hope that you have a very profitable convention, but a very enjoyable time during your visit.

I am privileged to perform this function occasionally. Never have I done so on an occasion where my sentiments were more deeply intertwined than they are on this occasion and with this group. It is one of the honorary positions a President of the United States has, to be an honorary president of your organization. I have been a member of the Executive Council, although I am sorry to say other things have seemed to keep me from working very hard at it for a number of years. And it is one position and one office that I did not resign when I became President of the United States.

I am, of course, not going to take advantage of this particular meeting to talk at great length about the work you are doing. In most instances you know more about it than I do, anyway. But there are two thoughts that occurred to me, as I drove over here, that I thought might be of interest. In your work with the youth of America you have, of course, not only certain official connections or quasi-official connections with the Government of the United States, but you are certainly aware that you have the loyal and earnest, moral support of the entire group in all that you do. In the Four–H Clubs and in the Future Farmers, several departments of Government are themselves engaged in work along lines similar to that you undertake.

With respect to this business of juvenile delinquency, only within the last few days I have recommended for Mrs. Hobby's Department an additional $165,000 to help out in this important work.

Before I leave that term "juvenile delinquency," I want to say this one thing: I hate the term, because I don't think we should ever allow conditions to arise and exist that justify the existence of the term. I think we should find terms that are more positive in their meaning and

515

their connotation, something like "youth training programs," or something so that we may have the words "juvenile delinquency" remembered only in the dictionary, and in the obsolete ones at that.

The other thought that occurred to me was born out of a number of experiences of the morning, how governments and political parties are always seeking for a way to express their purposes. And I suppose because I remembered that I was going to have this opportunity, I thought also of the Scout Oath. I submit that it would be difficult for any political party or any government to state its purposes, at home or abroad, in better terms than mere serious, earnest repetition of the Scout Oath—To do my duty by my God and country.

One of my great heroes of American history is Robert E. Lee, and he said something once, I think, which all of us could remember. He said, "We cannot do more than our duty. We would not wish to do less." So, frankly, when we have said or expressed that first phrase of the Scout Oath, we have said about all that is ennobling in human purpose. But it goes on: To be considerate of others, and to obey the law—to be an integral part of society, that means.

To do my part of the job, to be considerate of others, and to obey the law; and finally, as it goes on, you know—To be physically strong and mentally awake. Was there ever a time when the United States needed to be economically and materially stronger, and when we needed to be more vigilant and mentally awake, and morally straight?

This Government, represented in its Legislature and its Executive departments and its Judiciary, has but one great purpose in its relationships with all other nations: to be morally straight—honest—known as a people and a government of integrity, to be wise enough to determine what methods and procedures will best advance the happiness, the spiritual and intellectual and material welfare of all nations. And, of course, to carry that out, to be physically strong, not to waste our strength where it will do no good, or in chasing visions, but to be strong to carry out these great and noble purposes.

It seems to me, then, that you people in working with Scouts, in the sense of this very noble Scout Oath, are doing a very, very great job of providing an America of just a very few short years from now that will be better and stronger in its position in the world, and among ourselves.

For these reasons, I say again, the heart of this Government is with you in all that you do. Its interests are your interests. Moreover, where it is possible and proper for the Federal Government to intervene in a more direct way, we do it to help out a movement such as the Scouts and we are delighted to do it.

To each of you my thanks for the compliment of asking me before you, and my very, very best wishes for a fine convention.

Thank you.

NOTE: The President spoke at the Statler Hotel in Washington.

128 ¶ Address at the Columbia University National Bicentennial Dinner, New York City. *May* 31, 1954

Mr. Toastmaster, President Kirk, members and friends of Columbia's family, representatives here of Columbia's great sister institutions of learning, fellow citizens and friends:

I have many regrets in memory occasioned by my leaving Columbia University, and I have a new one this evening, that I never had a chance to attend the classes of our Toastmaster.

This occasion has for me particular significance because, for a time, I was intimately associated with those whose life-work is the education of America's youth. I am very proud that, through a brief span in Columbia's two hundred year history, my name was closely joined with that of this great institution. For such expression of personal pride in an association with a home of learning, I have illustrious predecessors.

Thomas Jefferson, for one, at the end of his long life, preferred that posterity should think of him, not as the holder of high office, but for his relationship to the University of Virginia.

He held that the free flow of information was indispensable to the maintenance of liberty. He wrote that if he had to make a choice between a society without newspapers or newspapers without a government, he would prefer the latter. And, of the diffusion of knowledge among the people through schools, he said: "No other sure foundation can be devised for the preservation of freedom and of happiness."

A relentless foe of tyranny in every guise, Jefferson throughout his life was steadfast to a fundamental tenet of Western Society, proclaimed two thousand years ago in the treasury of the Temple at Jerusalem, that the truth will make men free.

The pursuit of truth, its preservation and wide dissemination; the achievement of freedom, its defense and propagation; these purposes are woven into the American concept of education. The American university—neither the property of a favored class, nor an ivory tower where visionaries are sheltered from the test of practice—every American university fundamentally is dedicated to Columbia's Bicentennial theme— "Man's right to knowledge and the free use thereof."

Those who chose the theme of this Bicentennial could not have found a more American one. I say this with apology to scholars of all countries, lest they think that I might be deliberately narrowing a universal principle to a provincial application. But from the very beginning of the Republic, education of the people, freedom for the people—these interdependent purposes have been the core of the American Dream.

Far from being fearful of ideas, the founders of the Republic feared only misguided efforts to suppress ideas.

No less profound was their faith in man's ability to use freedom, for the achievement of his own and his country's good. In the freedom of the individual, they saw an energy that could hurdle mountains, harness rivers, clear the wilderness, transform a continent.

So convinced, they proclaimed to all the world the revolutionary doctrine of the Divine Rights of the Common Man. That doctrine has ever since been the heart of the American faith. Emphatic rejection of this faith is the cardinal characteristic of the materialistic despotisms of our time.

In consequence, the world, once divided by oceans and mountain ranges, is now split by hostile concepts of man's character and nature. Physical barriers and their effects have been largely surmounted. But new barriers seem more insuperable than the old.

Two world camps, whose geographic boundaries in important areas are mutually shared, lie farther apart in motivation and conduct than the poles in space. One is dedicated to the freedom of the individual and to the right of all to live in peace—the other to the atheistic philosophy of materialism, and the effort to establish its sway over all the earth. Watching the two opposing camps are hundreds of millions still undecided in active loyalty.

Today, there is no more important knowledge for each of us to understand than the essential characteristics of this struggle.

One fact stands out stark and clear: of all who inhabit the globe, only relatively small numbers—only a handful even in Russia itself—are fixed in their determination to dominate the world by force and fraud. Except for these groups in the several nations—mankind everywhere—those who still walk upright in freedom; those who hesitate in neutralism; those who must bow to communism—mankind everywhere hungers for freedom; for well-being; for peace. Now, how can a few men thwart the will of hundreds of millions?

Because, answering to no judge in conscience or in public opinion, they are engaged in a relentless and highly organized world campaign of deceit, subversion, and terrorism. And, opposed to them, there is no single, global effort to promote knowledge and cooperation.

They preach a material dogma that is abhorrent to us, a dogma coated with false promises. And they speak it with a single and a tireless voice, while the free world speaks with diverse tongues a message that demands from each responsibility, perseverance, and sacrifice.

Our opponents focus all the weight of government on the single objective they have chosen as the next goal. The free world uses government for the furtherance of human happiness, a front so broad that forward movement is at times almost imperceptible.

To spread their falsehoods, the few who seek world domination possess a global organism ceaselessly engaged in carrying out the orders of their masters. To give the world the truth, the free nations rely largely on the volunteer efforts of individuals—efforts often weak because they are intermittent and uncoordinated.

Possibly in no other way do the Communists so clearly exhibit their fear of the free world achieving real unity as in their persistent efforts to divide and thereby weaken us. They exploit every difference of view among independent nations to make honest discussion falsely appear, not as a valued characteristic of free systems, but as indication of mutual hatreds and antagonisms. This doctrine of divide and conquer they apply not only as between nations, but among groups and individuals of the same nation. They ceaselessly attack our social, industrial, educational, and spiritual institutions, and encourage every type of internecine struggle of whatever kind.

It is very easy to become an unwitting tool or ally of such conniving. For example, there is no other subject or purpose in which Americans are so completely united as in their opposition to communism. Yet, my friends, and I say this sadly, is there any other subject that seems, at this moment, to be the cause of so much division among us as does the matter of defending our freedoms from Communist subversion? To this problem we must apply more knowledge and intellect and less prejudice and passion. Above all, we must not permit anyone to divert our attention from the main battle and to inspire quarrels that eventually find good citizens bitterly opposed to other good citizens, when basically all would like to be joined in effective opposition to communism.

Now, we must, of course, require from the governmental organizations set up for our internal and external security the utmost in vigilance, energy, and loyalty. We must make certain through constant examination that they are so performing their duties. Let us provide any additional laws or machinery necessary to protect America—remembering that protecting America includes also the protection of every American in his American rights. Let us not lose faith in our own institutions, and in the essential soundness of the American citizenry lest we—divided among ourselves—thus serve the interests and advance the purposes of those seeking to destroy us.

The Soviet Communists claim that their cause is timeless, possibly requiring an entire era to achieve desired results. But they know that the truth of freedom possesses an unchanging validity and a cumulative power as more millions learn of it. So the dictators seek to deny to the world the time and opportunity to learn the truth of both communism and freedom. The power-hungry few are therefore persistently aggressive.

In this situation, we, the American people, stand committed to two far-reaching policies—

First and foremost: We are dedicated to the building of a cooperative peace, based upon truth, justice, and fairness.

Second: To pursue this purpose effectively, we seek the strengthening of America—and her friends—in love of liberty, in knowledge and comprehension, in a dependable prosperity widely shared, and in a military posture adequate for security.

In these two policies, there is no iota of aggression, no intent to exploit others or to deny them their rightful place and space in the world. This consideration of others—this dedication to a world filled with peaceful, self-respecting nations—finds its only opposition in militant totalitarianism.

If we are to work intelligently in the cause of freedom, we must study and understand these factors in the world turmoil.

Even when so armed with knowledge, it is not easy for the free world's representatives to negotiate successfully with those who either cannot or will not see the truth or admit the existence of obvious fact.

But surely, even the men in the Kremlin must realize that before all mankind now lies a grand prospect of a far better life for everyone. Its achievement requires only that the scientists of every nation concentrate on the means to a plentiful life rather than on the tools of sudden death; that the millions now under arms be released to fruitful work; that industries of war be converted to the production of useful goods. We have sought and will seek to make this prospect a reality.

Knowledge of the efforts being made by our own Nation to lead the world to this goal is another item of information important to every citizen.

The present administration assumed office 16 months ago, fully aware of the ruthless manner in which the Communists negotiate, conscious of the undependability of their agreements. But we believed that this country's foreign policy must be dedicated to unremitting effort for the preservation of peace, within the enlightened self-interest and fundamental objectives of the United States. Partisan purposes, personal attitudes, all the pressures of lesser interests, we believed, had to be subordinated to this paramount goal.

We knew that every negotiation with the Communists would be fraught with traps and pitfalls but we knew, too, that positive, determined day-to-day toil would pay real dividends among the free nations. We sought a rebirth of trust among all nations—an enduring foundation for a cooperative peace—not a mere breathing space free from imminent crisis.

Every measure we have proposed has been conceived as a step toward this rebirth of trust. These proposals have included an honorable armistice in Korea; a free and united Germany, a liberated Austria; a secure Indochina and southeast Asia; atomic energy harnessed for peaceful purposes under international control.

The first has been achieved. The armistice in Korea, moreover, inaugurated a new principle of freedom—that prisoners of war are entitled to choose the side to which they wish to be released. In its impact on history, that one principle may weigh more than any battle of our time.

Negotiations to unify Germany have been, for the time being, at least, nullified by Soviet demands for a satellite climate in that country. With respect to Austria, the United States, Great Britain, and France agreed to accept State Treaty terms which up to that moment had been acceptable to the Soviet Union. But once this acceptance was announced, the Soviet Union immediately invented new conditions which would enable it, for an indefinite period, to keep military occupation in Austria.

To such a plan we could not agree. Far better, this administration believes, that we end the discussion with the issue still unresolved than to compromise a principle or to accept an agreement whose price might be exacted in blood years hence.

In our effort to find the ways by which the miraculous inventiveness of man should not be dedicated to his death, but consecrated to his life, there have been written exchanges of views between the United States and the Soviet Union. Secretary of State Dulles has personally conferred both at Berlin and at Geneva with the Soviet Foreign Minister, Mr. Molotov. These have not been productive of the results we seek, but we, on our side, are continuing exchanges of views and consultations with the other free nations principally involved.

We intend to proceed with these and other like negotiations, confident in the merits of our cause, realistic in our appraisal of Soviet intention, and assured that our purposes and hopes will survive even the most frustrating series of talks.

To be successful, our peaceful purposes and hopes must of course be clad in obvious truth and constantly proclaimed to the world. Our actions must stand examination by every eye—friendly and hostile and doubtful. We must be forthright and patient in presenting them. Scarcely could we devise, for the cause of peace, a more fitting battle cry than the theme of the Columbia Bicentennial: "Man's right to knowledge and the free use thereof."

Let us not, however, define truth or knowledge of the truth solely in the narrow terms of mere fact or statistic or mathematical equation. Wisdom and human understanding—a sense of proportion—are essential. Knowledge can give us nuclear fission; only wisdom and understanding can assure its application to human betterment rather than to human destruction.

In this light, the Columbia theme is a dynamic idea, a true offspring of the revolutionary doctrine proclaimed by our forefathers. We should preach it—and practice it—fearlessly.

Here, tonight, in this brilliant company and pleasant surroundings, we might easily take for granted, as assured through all time, the preservation and the free use of knowledge. Two hundred years of Columbia history and the existence of thousands of other institutions of learning in our country seem to give validity to such assurance. But can we be sure that possession of these values, even by ourselves, is as indestructible as it is priceless? The bleak history of a dozen nations insistently warns us differently.

Always and everywhere, even though they may never have experienced it—even though they know its values only in their instincts rather than in their minds—men have sought personal liberty; have fought for it; have died for it.

Nevertheless, within the past few decades, the whole philosophy of our Founding Fathers has been rejected by powerful men who control great areas of our planet. The revolutionary doctrines of our free society have not, to America's amazement, swept around the world. Rather, we have too often seen the counterattacks of fascism and of communism substitute for them the police state, with suppression of all liberties and free inquiry. We have too often seen education perverted into an instrument for the use and support of tyranny.

Beyond this, these few decades have seen science confer upon man technical processes whose colossal destructiveness, the virtual obliteration of space as a protective shield, has brought all of us to the frontline of any new war.

Amid such alarms and uncertainties, doubters begin to lose faith in themselves, in their country, in their convictions. They begin to fear other people's ideas—every new idea. They begin to talk about censoring the sources and the communication of ideas. They forget that truth is the bulwark of freedom, as suppression of truth is the weapon of dictatorship. We know that when censorship goes beyond the observance of common decency, or the protection of the Nation's obvious interests, it quickly becomes, for us, a deadly danger. It means conformity by compulsion in educational institutions; it means a controlled instead of a free press; it means the loss of human freedom.

The honest men and women among these would-be censors and regulators may merely forget that the price of their success would be the destruction of that way of life they want to preserve. But the dishonest and the disloyal know exactly what they are attempting to do—perverting and undermining a free society while falsely swearing allegiance to it.

Whenever, and for whatever alleged reason, people attempt to crush ideas, to mask their convictions, to view every neighbor as a possible enemy, to seek some kind of divining rod by which to test for conformity, a free society is in danger. Wherever man's right to knowledge and the use thereof is restricted, man's freedom in the same measure disappears.

Here in America we are descended in blood and in spirit from revolutionaries and rebels—men and women who dared to dissent from accepted doctrine. As their heirs, may we never confuse honest dissent with disloyal subversion.

Without exhaustive debate—even heated debate—of ideas and programs, free government would weaken and wither. But if we allow ourselves to be persuaded that every individual, or party, that takes issue with our own convictions is necessarily wicked or treasonous—then indeed we are approaching the end of freedom's road. We must unitedly and intelligently support the principles of Americanism.

Effective support of principles, like success in battle, requires calm and clear judgment, courage, faith, fortitude. Our dedication to truth and freedom, at home and abroad, does not require—and cannot tolerate—fear, threat, hysteria, and intimidation.

As we preach freedom to others, so we should practice it among ourselves. Then, strong in our own integrity, we will be continuing the revolutionary march of the Founding Fathers.

As they roused in mankind the determination to win political freedom from dynastic tyranny, we can ignite in mankind the will to win intellectual freedom from the false propaganda and enforced ignorance of Communist tyranny. Through knowledge and understanding, we will drive from the temple of freedom all who seek to establish over us thought control—whether they be agents of a foreign state or demagogues thirsty for personal power and public notice.

Truth can make men free! And where men are free to plan their lives, to govern themselves, to know the truth and to understand their fellowmen, we believe that there also is the will to live at peace.

Here, then, in spite of A-bombs, H-bombs, all the cruel destructiveness of modern war; in spite of terror, subversion, propaganda and bribery, we see the key to peace. That key is knowledge and understanding—and their constant use by men—everywhere.

Today, of course, we must have infantry—and planes and ships and artillery. Only so can we be sure of a tomorrow and the opportunity to continue the mobilization of spiritual and intellectual energies. But there is no time to waste if truth is to win the war for the minds of men! Here is the unending mission of the university—indeed of every educational institution of the free world—to find and spread the truth!

We send professors, scholars, and students out to the schools of the free world, to promote understanding of us even as they grow in knowledge and in understanding of others. This practice must be accelerated.

We find room in our own schools for tens of thousands of young men and women from other lands who within the American community learn the truth about us and give understanding of their own people. This effort must be expanded.

The purposes of the free world must not be too limited! Our goal is not merely to react against inroads of Communist lies and attacks. That would be endless and profitless; the tactics of falsehood are limitless. We must join with our friends in a crusade of truth. We must make our aim the building of peace in justice and freedom. That is a worthy objective and a golden reward. Under God, the united energies of free people can attain it.

"The prospect now before us in America," wrote John Adams in 1765, "ought to engage the attention of every man of learning to matters of power and of right, that we may be neither led nor driven blindfolded to irretrievable destruction." And he ended by saying, "Let every sluice of knowledge be opened and set aflowing."

Tonight I think it fitting to repeat John Adams' exhortation, confident that, prompted by reason and armored by faith, we shall speed the advance of knowledge and liberty on their hand-in-hand journey along the avenue of the ages.

My friends, to each of you my thanks for the compliment you pay me in asking me to appear before you, to renew old associations and friendships. Thank you.

NOTE: The President spoke at 9:30 p.m. at the Waldorf-Astoria Hotel in New York City. His opening words "Mr. Toastmaster, President Kirk" referred to Dr. Lyman Bryson, Professor Emeritus of Education, Teachers College, Columbia University, and Dr. Grayson Kirk, President of the University.

129   ¶ The President's News Conference of June 2, 1954.

THE PRESIDENT. Ladies and gentlemen, one word that we seem to find in our daily print more than any other is "Communists"—struggle against communism and Communists in our country and in our Government.

This job of finding them is a day-by-day job 52 weeks a year, has to be conducted without cessation. So, this morning, I called upon the Attorney General to give me a record of statistics to date, what they have done, what has been accomplished in the past months.

They gave me the report under nine items—I should have said this is printed, you will get all of this document; it will be outside, and you will get it—and I think it is an impressive list of accomplishments, and all of it done in absolute accordance with the due processes of law.

A few days ago the Attorney General also, at my direction, prepared a statement with respect to Executive responsibility in maintaining the proper and constitutional division between the authority and responsibilities of the Executive and the Legislature. At my direction, Mr. Hagerty published that.

Now, that constitutes the last word I have got to say on this subject, unless something happens that makes me think I have to say something more—I don't know what it would be—but it is my last word, and I repeat to you my reason: I can't conceive of anything more important to the United States today than the enactment of a legislative program that comprehends the great needs and requirements of all our people today so far as the Federal Government has a hand in them.

As you know, that program is very broad; it touches on such things as workable farm programs, reformation of the tax system, foreign trade; up and down the line there is health, there is housing, and there is social security.

It is a very broadly based program, and positive action in that direction is the thing to which I am going to give my exclusive attention. I am going to talk to everybody I see, to you people every time I see you; I am going to talk to the public, I am going to talk to everybody in Congress that I get a hold of, because I so thoroughly believe that this is a *must* requirement for the United States. When I say that, I don't mean to say every detail or procedure and method and timing; I hope I have sense enough to know that the democratic process requires the meeting of minds and composition of different ideas in order to get things done. I am talking about the spirit and the broad purpose of that program, and that is what I am going to give my attention to. And I will say, ladies and gentlemen, it's very little use asking me questions that don't apply rather directly to that and, of course, to the position of the United States in the world today, that is, in the foreign affairs field.

Now, with that statement of my purpose, why, the meeting is yours.

Q. Richard Wilson, Cowles Publications: Mr. President, last week two Senators have stated publicly their belief that you would submit to Congress a resolution authorizing action in southeast Asia some time before the adjournment. Could you discuss that general possibility?

THE PRESIDENT. Well, Mr. Wilson, I haven't seen those statements, but every possible line of action that could serve the interests of the United States and of the free world is explored daily, all the time, constantly by our staffs—our military staffs, our State Department, and other staffs that have responsibilities in this line; and, of course, such things as that occasionally come up, but I have not, by any manner of means, reached any decision of that kind.

Q. Chalmers Roberts, Washington Post and Times Herald: Mr. President, tomorrow Admiral Carney, on behalf of the Joint Chiefs, is meeting with the British, French, Australian, and New Zealand military officials. Could you tell us what might come out of that, and how it is related to what you just said?

THE PRESIDENT. I can tell you this much: military discussions of this kind are again a continuing process between us and the nations with which we are cooperating in the world.

We have, for example, on the very same subjects that will come up before this meeting, talked with the Philippines and with the military officials of Thailand, and so on.

Now, these particular five—here is getting a group together that, as you know, constitutes the ANZUS organization plus the British and the French. There will be discussed military matters, and military matters only, not matters of political policy. They will discuss what could be done, what should be done, to support the policies that are, of course, originated or at least promulgated through the State Department.

Q. Kenneth Scheibel, Gannett Newspapers: Mr. President, in connection with the legislative program, Congressman Hope the other day, on leaving your office, said that a compromise was inevitable on the farm program. Has there been a new decision by you to accept a compromise?

THE PRESIDENT. I haven't any idea of what he was speaking of in the word "compromise."

I have always insisted that the basic purpose of any reasonable program is to prevent violent fluctuations in the situation of the farmer. I would be the last to claim that there is anything sacrosanct about the program we put forth, but I am prepared to stand up and fight for the principles of that program right down the line, for the simple reason that it was made up by the broadest and most exhaustive kind of examinations and consultations we could make throughout this country, not only in the Capital, but everywhere—representative farmers, farm organizations, legislators, everybody that seemed to have something to do with it. I don't know what he is referring to, but I do say I am not prepared to compromise the principles of that program.

Q. Frederick Kuh, Chicago Sun-Times: Mr. President, you have twice recently referred to our discussions with Russia on atomic energy and on your proposals of last December 8th. Is it your understanding that those discussions have now come to an end or will they go on?

THE PRESIDENT. Well, in the specific item, I don't mean to say they cannot be brought up again and, naturally, will be by our side in any discussion. But the tenor of the Soviet reply to that suggestion and proposal has been such as to, you might say, close the door to immediate accomplishment under the concept that I described in my December 8th speech.

Q. James Reston, New York Times: I wondered, sir, whether you would give us a report as to how those conversations have gone with the Russians on atomic energy—what were the issues?

THE PRESIDENT. Well, I will tell you: while I think I could give you a fairly accurate description of that, here we have a man with my complete confidence, Mr. Dulles, who has conducted most of these hearings directly, and I think it is a question you should put to him because then there will be no error and no mistake.

My reports are, after all, second hand from him; so I think it would be better that he discuss that question with you.

Q. Ruth Montgomery, New York Daily News: Mr. President, you have now completed one-third of your first term. Would you like to say whether it has gone the way you thought it would or make any other observations?

THE PRESIDENT. I think I have told this body before, this group of people, that I didn't enter this kind of a task with any ideas it was going to be a picnic or it was fun.

I have also told you this: there are many frustrations, disappointments and even, you might say, inhibitions that are almost unexpected, even to one who is partially accustomed to living in a goldfish bowl because of my war experiences. But I say this to you also, that you get inspiration from many quarters that you hadn't expected. The number of people who are ready to drop what they are doing to do their very best for the United States of America, for the things in which we all believe, is not only remarkable but it is done sometimes with such a quiet, you might say, ignoring of the sacrifices they are making, that it is highly pleasing and inspiring.

I could tell you a little story—something that happened in my office the other day. A little girl came to see me and took, apparently, very great pleasure in coming to my office. The sense of compliment and flattery I felt, came about in this way: she was stricken 2 years ago when she had a date to come down to see me, stricken with polio, and in her determination to walk again and to fulfill that date, she had broken both legs and had, in that long 2-year struggle, to be laid up with all those injuries to mend. She has had operations on her hands and on her feet and legs, but she finally got there.

When you see courage like that, you don't feel very sorry for yourself any more, is what I say. So that is one of the kind of incidents that comes to your attention that lifts you, possibly—you hope, at least—above yourself.

Q. John Herling, Editors Syndicate: Mr. President, this has to do with an economic question to which you referred earlier. I would like to quote Professor Sumner Slichter of Harvard who spoke to a group here in Washington the other day, and said: "The executive branch of the Government has shown a surprising lack of initiative and enterprise in fighting the recession. I do not know the reason, but I suspect that it is attributable to the influence of the Treasury, which seems to be more interested in keeping the cash budget in balance than in limiting the drop in production and employment." Then he says: "Spokesmen for the administration have said several times that the administration would act if and when action is needed, but the level of unemployment which the administration regards as justifying action seems to be considerably higher than the people of the country will find tolerable."

Would you care to comment on that, sir?

THE PRESIDENT. I think that before this group I have frequently announced my very firm adhering to the democratic process, which means that everybody is not only entitled to his own opinion, but entitled to express it.

I am not going to comment on that gentleman's statement or opinions, but I will ask you this: please go to see the chief of my economic advisers and see what has been done, what have been the measures that have been adopted from time to time, how they have worked, what they are prepared to do, and what we believe about this whole situation; in other words, get his side of the story.

And I might say this, ladies and gentlemen, when I got a man of the caliber of the head of my economic advisers, I gave him just one order: "You are never, by any chance, to develop an opinion and bring it in here to me or to anyone in the Cabinet or in the Legislature that supports someone's political view, including mine. You are to dig out the facts of this economy, and present them as honestly as you and your associates can possibly do it, not only to me but to the public."

I think you will get very honest answers from him.

Q. Charles von Fremd, CBS Television: I wonder, sir, if you have any comments you might be able to give us regarding the decision reached last night in the Oppenheimer case?

THE PRESIDENT. Well, no. I would point this out: this case is going through what is a quasi-judicial process set up by the Atomic Energy Commission. Until they have completely finished that, I think I wouldn't have anything to say. I think at a former time I expressed here my great admiration for what Dr. Oppenheimer has done in the past, and so there is no point in expressing that part of it, which I understand the report brings out again. I think that I will wait until that whole thing is done before I have anything to say.

Q. Roscoe Drummond, New York Herald Tribune: Mr. President, Republicans and Democrats have made different proposals for a code of fair procedure to govern congressional investigations. I would like to ask whether you would think that such an enforceable code, without going into details, would be a logical and desirable part of your legislative program?

THE PRESIDENT. Well, you are asking me one, Mr. Drummond, that I hadn't thought about in those terms before and, therefore, I wouldn't want to answer it too quickly. I wouldn't want to foreclose my right to make recommendations to at least the leaders, maybe of both parties, but I do feel that here we have got something that is a very deep and grave responsibility of the legislators themselves. Before I went any further in it myself, I would want to take a look; I hadn't thought of it in those terms.

Q. Louis R. Lautier, National Negro Press Association: Mr. President, would you care to comment upon the visit of the Emperor of Ethiopia?

THE PRESIDENT. Well, I will say this: not only did I have a very interesting visit with him, but a very enlightening one. Among other things, he brought along what you might call an industrial map of Ethiopia showing the industries of the various sections, and bringing me a few of the products of their country. I was ashamed to say that he could give me some very elementary education that I should have had before.

He was a charming individual, the people with him were interesting and knew their business; and in every way I think it was beneficial.

I am certain of this: in Ethiopia, as in happily many other countries, there is a deep underlying appreciation of America's efforts and an affection for America.

Q. Marvin Arrowsmith, Associated Press: Mr. President, Mr. Shanley said the other day that the Democrats in Congress are trying to ride your coattails to a victory in November. [*Laughter*] And he said at the same time they are trying to block your legislative program. Do you see it that way?

THE PRESIDENT. Well, I will tell you, ladies and gentlemen, this expression "riding your coattails" of course could be a very dangerous one. You don't know, if you are just trying to ride someone else's coattails, where you are going. [*Laughter*]

I would say this: if anyone wants to support a program which I believe has been designed for the welfare of America, if he wants to ride my coattails, he can climb right on; if they'll just support this program, that's all right with me.

Q. Sarah McClendon, El Paso Times: Sir, there seems to have been a lack of organization and purposeful planning on the part of the Republican leadership when they brought up the 18-year-old question, and this has led to charges among many, several, Senators on both sides of the aisle, that the Republican leadership didn't intend for that to pass. I wonder if you discussed this with Mr. Knowland afterwards?

THE PRESIDENT. This is the first time I have heard such an idea.

I felt, as you know, that the young fellows that had to fight wars ought to have some part in the decision as to whether or not we should go to war. I still believe that. To my mind the issue of States rights there was mistakenly brought up because, as I recall, the right of women to vote was brought about by a constitutional amendment; and I merely proposed a constitutional amendment, because I thought the voting age should be lowered. I didn't care if they made it exactly 18, but I thought it should be lowered to take in the vast bulk of these boys who are drafted in time of war.

Q. Laurence Burd, Chicago Tribune: Mr. President, in your opening statement in regard to seeking support for your program, you mentioned that you were going to talk here and there, and you mentioned that you were going to talk to the public. Do you have any particular speaking or traveling plans in mind in that connection?

THE PRESIDENT. No. As a matter of fact, I have made a number of tentative engagements for visits for different reasons at fairs, opening of dams, universities, and so on, where I have no doubt that something of this kind will always be up; but every time I appear, as I say, anywhere from now on, I have just got one idea: get this program enacted.

Q. Robert Spivack, New York Post: Mr. President, counterbalancing what Mr. Shanley said the other day, Senator Symington said during the hearings on the Hill that it was only the Democrats who were backing the administration on the constitutional issues that were raised. Do you think that the Republicans up there are letting you down?

THE PRESIDENT. No, I don't think the Republicans are letting me down. Like every other organization in the world, the Republicans have possibly individuals or splinters that don't go along with the majority beliefs and convictions. I take the platform of the Republican Party very seriously, and I think the rest of them do.

Now, those that stray from there, I don't know what their philosophy, what their attitude is. I believe in it, and am trying to get it done. But I think, on the contrary, that certain of our leaders in most difficult and unusual circumstances have performed very well indeed.

Q. Edward Milne, Providence Journal: Mr. President, do you think Senator McCarthy is hurting your program on the Hill?

THE PRESIDENT. Next question.

Q. George R. Wolff, French News Service (France Presse): Would you tell us something about your talk with the Turkish Prime Minister, Mr. Menderes?

THE PRESIDENT. Well, I just had it just a minute ago. He is a friend of mine that I visited with before. He came to assure the parallel objectives and thinking in Turkey along with that of America and our efforts, to show their appreciation, their good will. We had a very fine conversation.

Q. James T. Rogers, Gannett News Service: A good many people are anxious to know, sir, whether Congressman Sterling Cole will be nominated for Comptroller General. Could you discuss that possibility?

THE PRESIDENT. I believe I have never yet suggested a man's name that was going to be named to a post until he was actually presented to the Senate. I don't think that would be cricket to do that.

John L. Cutter, United Press: Thank you, Mr. President.

NOTE: President Eisenhower's thirty-ninth news conference was held in the Executive Office Building from 10:31 to 10:54 o'clock on Wednesday morning, June 2, 1954. In attendance: 192.

130 ¶ Statement by the President on the Record of the Department of Justice in Dealing With Subversive Activities. *June 2, 1954*

THE DEPARTMENT OF JUSTICE and the Federal Bureau of Investigation are the principal agents of the government in dealing with subversives. The record of legal action speaks for itself. I should like to summarize the latest figures just received from the Department of Justice.

51986—60——37

In the sixteen months this Administration has been in office the Attorney General, working with the Federal Bureau of Investigation and the Immigration and Naturalization Service, has:

1. Arrested 7 Connecticut leaders of the Communist Party last weekend in Connecticut and New York City.

2. Convicted 41 Communist Party leaders—13 in New York City, 7 in Honolulu, 5 in Pittsburgh, 5 in Seattle, 6 in Detroit, and 5 in St. Louis.

3. Indicted 20 additional Communist leaders, including 9 now on trial in Philadelphia and 11 soon to be tried in Cleveland.

4. Ordered the addition of 62 new organizations to the Department of Justice's list of subversive groups, making a total of 255.

5. Secured the conviction of 1 person for treason, and 2 for espionage. 8 others have been convicted for making false statements to the Government—3 have been convicted for perjury.

6. Deported 84 alien subversives.

7. Issued orders for deportation of 268 persons with records of subversive activity or affiliation.

8. Started denaturalization proceedings against 24 naturalized citizens charged with being subversives.

9. Barred entry into this country of 127 subversive aliens, who had arrived at ports of entry.

The constant surveillance of Communists in this country is a 24-hour, 7-days-a-week, 52-weeks-a-year job. It is carried out by the appropriate Federal agencies, in conformance with due process of law. It is being done quietly and relentlessly, and those who best know its effectiveness are the Communists themselves.

NOTE: This statement was brought up to date and reissued on December 7, 1954. As reissued, the enumerated items read as follows:

1. Convicted 50 Communist Party leaders—13 in New York City, 7 in Honolulu, 5 in Pittsburgh, 5 in Seattle, 6 in Detroit, 5 in St. Louis, and 9 in Philadelphia.

2. Indicted 49 Communist leaders.

3. Ordered the addition of 62 new organizations to the Department of Justice's list of subversive groups, making a total of 255.

4. Indicted 1 person for treason, and convicted 2 for espionage. 10 others have been convicted for making false statements to the Government—3 have been convicted for perjury.

5. Deported 129 alien subversives.

6. Issued orders for deportation of 410 persons with records of subversive activity or affiliation.

7. Started denaturalization proceedings against 49 naturalized citizens charged with being subversives.

8. Barred entry into this country of 172 subversive aliens, who had arrived at ports of entry.

131 ¶ Excerpts From Remarks to a Group of Correspondents About To Return to the Scene of the Normandy Invasion. *June* 2, 1954

WELL, I THINK it's just a waste of words for me to tell you how much I would like to go along. I don't know exactly what you are going to do. I was there in 1951, when they had a big ceremony. I hope you will pay my respects to the Mayor of Ste. Mère Église.

I frequently get to questioning myself about—we used to talk a lot about our sacrifices, and so on—about what these sacrifices brought us. Of course, they brought us—and bought us—an immediate safety from the danger then threatening.

What did they bring us in the long run? We know they brought us an opportunity to do something, but what did these sacrifices mean? I have never been able, and probably never will be able, to write down something, myself, to satisfy me.

But I do know this: that out of it all, the people who know war, those that experienced it—you writers, the fighting men—I believe we are the most earnest advocates of peace in the world. I believe these people that talk about peace academically but who never had to dive into a ditch when a Messerschmidt 109 came over, they really don't know what it is.

How long are you going to be gone? A week or 10 days. Probably you won't go through a town there that I haven't been through. You'll see many old friends of mine—some farmers around there, where we used to camp, on down to Granville, the peninsula Cherbourg, and around there. Please give them my warmest greetings. I like them. I really envy you the chance.

NOTE: The President spoke in the Rose Garden. The full text of his remarks was not released.

132   ¶ Memorandum on the Community Chest Campaign in the National Capital Area. *June* 5, 1954

[Released June 5, 1954. Dated June 3, 1954]

To the Heads of Executive Departments and Agencies:

This fall will mark the twenty-seventh successive campaign for the Red Feather agencies of the Community Chests in the National Capital Area. To act as Chairman of the Government Unit in this important appeal, I have been happy to approve the appointment of the Honorable Edmund F. Mansure, Administrator of the General Services Administration.

I ask that you give to Mr. Mansure your fullest measure of support and assistance. I am sure that all persons in authority in the Federal and District Government will be personally interested and will extend their complete cooperation to this important charitable appeal. Such cooperation should logically include the assumption of equitable unit goals, the effective solicitation of all employees, and the setting up of an adequate collection method for the convenience of those who wish to make contributions on an installment basis.

The Community Chest Federation responsible for this annual appeal unites 6 Community Chests and more than 100 Red Feather services in one federated campaign to provide local health, welfare and recreational programs which are so vital if we are to keep our communities healthy and strong.

In the interest of eliminating an additional campaign, the appeal will again include the United Defense Fund which is responsible for the programs of the USO, USO Camp Shows, and United Community Defense Services. These programs continue to be essential to the morale and happiness of our men and women of the Armed Forces both at home and overseas.

It is my hope that all officials and employees will be given the opportunity to contribute and that each will want to do so generously. Each individual's giving should reflect a fair share towards the support of these worthwhile services in effective operation throughout the full year ahead.

DWIGHT D. EISENHOWER

133   ¶ Statement by the President on the 10th
Anniversary of the Landing in Normandy.
June 6, 1954

[Released June 6, 1954. Dated June 5, 1954]

THIS DAY is the tenth anniversary of the landing of the Allied Expeditionary Force in Normandy.   That combined land-sea-air operation was made possible by the joint labors of cooperating nations.   It depended for its success upon the skill, determination and self-sacrifice of men from several lands.   It set in motion a chain of events which affected the history of the entire world.

Despite the losses and suffering involved in that human effort, and in the epic conflict of which it was a part, we today find in those experiences reasons for hope and inspiration.   They remind us particularly of the accomplishments attainable through close cooperation and friendship among free peoples striving toward a common goal.   Some of my most cherished memories of that campaign are those of friendly cooperation with such distinguished military leaders of foreign nations as Field Marshal Montgomery, Admiral Ramsay, Marshal of the Royal Air Force Tedder, Marshal de Lattre de Tassigny, Marshal Juin and Marshal Leclerc.   I recall my pleasant association with the outstanding Soviet soldier, Marshal Zhukov, and the victorious meeting at the Elbe of the Armies of the West and of the East.

These lessons of unity and cooperation have by no means been lost in the trying period of reconstruction since the fighting stopped.   Rather, we see peoples, once bitter enemies, burying their antagonisms and joining together to meet the problems of the postwar world.   If all those nations which were members of the Grand Alliance have not maintained in time of peace the spirit of that wartime union, if some of the peoples who were our comrades-in-arms have been kept apart from us, that is cause for profound regret, but not for despair.   The courage, devotion and faith which brought us through the perils of war will inevitably bring us success in our unremitting search for peace. security and freedom.

134 ¶ Veto of Bill for the Relief of Theodore W. Carlson. *June 7, 1954*

To the House of Representatives:

I am returning herewith without my approval H.R. 3109, 83rd Congress, "An Act For the relief of Theodore W. Carlson."

The bill proposes to grant to Theodore W. Carlson all of the rights, benefits, and privileges which are granted to persons who served on active duty with the United States Army during World War II, and who were honorably discharged from such service after having suffered permanent total loss of vision in one eye as a result of such service.

The evidence discloses that Theodore W. Carlson served in the Army of the United States from February 1941 to October 1941, and from February 1942 to November 1945. In February 1947, he filed a claim for service-connected disability compensation with the Veterans' Administration, alleging an eye condition. In developing that claim, he contended that in February 1945, a foreign body blew into his right eye and had inflamed and infected it; that he was treated at his unit's dispensary, and experienced some relief; that in July or August 1945, the eye condition returned, and he lost the sight in that eye for a short period of time; and that when he again visited the dispensary, he was instructed to apply warm applications, which again resulted in some improvement. In this connection, the medical records of the Army do not confirm the alleged treatment for his eye condition, and when discharged, the veteran claimed no injury to his right eye and the physical examination at that time disclosed no pathology of the eye. Mr. Carlson also claimed that after discharge he suffered recurring periods of blindness, and beginning in August 1947, his sight in that eye was limited to light perception only. He submitted affidavits from his private physicians stating that he was treated on several occasions from December 1945 to August 1947 for moderate inflammation of the eye, and that in November 1947, a diagnosis of retinal detachment and tear involving the macular area of the right eye was established. A third physician stated in 1950 that his examination disclosed an old retinal detachment in the right eye and that it was possible that this could have been produced by injury to the eye while Mr. Carlson was in service.

Since 1947 the veteran's claim for service-connected disability compensation has been very carefully considered on numerous occasions by Veterans' Administration rating boards and at least five times by the Board of Veterans' Appeals. After each consideration it was concluded that the eye disability was not shown to have been incurred in or aggravated by his military service.

The question at issue in this case is basically one of medical judgment, and should not be overruled by private legislation. The possibility raised by the last mentioned physician that Mr. Carlson's eye condition of retinal detachment could have been produced by injury to the eye while he was in service has been considered by the Veterans' Administration. However, based on sound and accepted medical principles, they have held that the evidence does not permit a conclusion that the separated retina initially diagnosed in November 1947 was due either to the inflammatory eye disease first treated approximately two years earlier or causally related to trauma allegedly caused by a foreign body being blown in Mr. Carlson's eye during service.

I consider it unwise to set aside the principles and rules of administration prescribed in the general laws governing veterans' benefit programs. Uniformity and equality of treatment to all who are similarly situated must be the steadfast rule if the Federal programs for veterans and their dependents are to be operated successfully. Moreover, in my opinion the present case does not warrant preferred treatment. Further, I am informed that this would be the first case in which a World War II veteran would, in effect, be placed on the compensation rolls by special legislation. Since there are well over a half million veterans of World War II alone whose claims for disability compensation have been denied in accordance with public laws because the disabilities for which compensation is claimed were not incurred in or aggravated by their military service, approval of this bill would constitute a far-reaching precedent, which I cannot justify.

DWIGHT D. EISENHOWER

135 ¶ Veto of Bill for the Relief of Mrs. Ann Elizabeth Caulk. *June* 7, 1954

To the House of Representatives:

I am returning herewith without my approval H.R. 4532, 83d Congress, "An Act For the relief of Mrs. Ann Elizabeth Caulk."

The bill would authorize and direct the Secretary of the Treasury to pay to Mrs. Ann Elizabeth Caulk the sum of $1,682.80 in full settlement of all her claims against the United States for non-service-connected death pension she would have received if the claim she filed on March 29, 1948, had been considered as having been filed on April 1, 1944.

David H. Caulk, a veteran of honorable service in the Spanish-American War, married the claimant on November 7, 1931, and died of a non-service-connected cause twelve days later. Mrs. Caulk's claim for death pension filed December 31, 1931, was denied for the reason that she had not married the veteran prior to the then applicable marriage delimiting date, September 1, 1922. Effective April 1, 1944, the delimiting date was extended by law to January 1, 1938, rendering Mrs. Caulk potentially eligible for death pension benefits to which she was previously not entitled. However, she did not file a new claim for death pension until March 29, 1948, and under the law pension benefits were paid prospectively from that date.

It appears that favorable action by the Committees which considered H.R. 4532 was based on the theory that the delay in filing claim was due to ignorance of the law on the part of Mrs. Caulk. This reason applied with equal force to many other claimants. Her case certainly arouses one's sympathy, but to prefer it for special treatment to the exclusion of other similar cases would be unwarranted and discriminatory. Further, approval of the bill might serve as a precedent for similar legislation in other cases.

I am opposed to setting aside the principles and rules of administration prescribed in the public laws governing veterans' benefit programs. Uniformity and equality of treatment to all who are similarly situated must be the steadfast rule if the Federal programs for veterans and their dependents are to be operated successfully. Approval of H.R. 4532 would not be in keeping with these principles.

DWIGHT D. EISENHOWER

136   ¶ Remarks at the Washington College Commencement, Chestertown, Maryland.
June 7, 1954

President Gibson, Governor McKeldin, members and friends of the Washington College family:

If you have closely examined your programs for the day, you will see that I am scheduled for no address or talk.   Consequently, any time that I take of yours is indefensible and possibly inexcusable.   But I am so touched by the compliment paid me by this great and venerable institution of learning, that I have the impulse to attempt in a few moments to give you some of the thoughts that crowd my mind today.

I think, first, of those individuals who have been mentioned several times today who founded this college.   I heard it said that there were six young people graduated in 1783.   Unquestionably it must have been a simple curriculum that they pursued, if any curriculum could be called simple that included Latin, Greek, and French.   But, indeed, they were preparing themselves to discharge their responsibilities under a government which, although not yet formed, was already evidencing before the world the principles by which it should live and exist.

One of its great prophets, of course, was Thomas Jefferson.   Again and again he pointed out that liberty could survive only as it was buttressed by knowledge.   No other means could be devised, he thought, other than through real and insistent and persistent and broad education, to prepare people each to carry his burden in the great problem of people governing themselves.

The fortunes of this school, through the intervening 172 years, have had, of course, their ups and downs.   But one thing is certain.   The principle of the need for education of people in a free government has never been lost sight of, and it has upheld those who have been responsible in the President's chair, and in the trustees' positions, in the faculty, and in the student body, indeed, all through these years.   And today we see this magnificent young class come up before their President to receive their degrees in a far more complex age, and they in their turn ready to do their part as citizens.

I hope they will permit me to digress for just a moment, to advert to a statement I heard made here about Washington, D.C. I do want to tell this student body that no matter what they hear about Washington, D.C., I have two United States Senators and one Congressman here today with me to prove that we do need brains. So if you will come down there—so if you will come down there, I am sure that your talents will not be wasted in the service of your country.

And now, ladies and gentlemen, just as this College has come down through the ages, growing larger, inheriting greater responsibilities in this complex age of ours, so has Government done likewise. Starting with a weak form of coalition in a confederacy, we finally evolved a simple form of government which, again in principle, has stood the test of time. It stands today in the same great outlines as it was established in 1787. But, my friends, there all similarity seems to end between the Government of today and that of that far off period.

Sometimes, as I stand outside the White House, I look at it, and I note that the first President that occupied it, John Adams, had his entire office, all his office force, and his living quarters, all within the main part of the building. Succeeding Presidents have built on wings. We have now gone across and taken over one building that used to house three great departments of Government, and we still don't have room for the President's office and the separate offices that are attached to him. This is indicative of what has happened to us in the United States, in the complexities of our economy and industries, and in Government and its complexities. And while this has all happened, that Government and our daily lives have likewise become intertwined.

And so today one of the problems of educated youth and educated adult—every person in the United States who understands—is to determine what is the proper relationship between himself and that Government, and to allow Government to go no further than is necessary, because all governments are greedy. They like to reach out and take everything—indeed, I have found one pamphlet that tells you how to wash the dishes.

Now, ladies and gentlemen, it is perfectly proper, it is perfectly necessary that Government do for us, and with us, many things that at one time in history would have been considered reprehensible and almost a betrayal to our form of government, and these things are done through terms of legislation.

And so we have great social security programs. We have farm programs to prevent the farmer from falling into a disaster concerning which he could have done nothing by himself. We have all sorts of broad tax programs, programs for eliminating slums from the great cities and making certain that every American has a right and an opportunity to get a decent home. All of these things, in health and education, everything we do, are proper spheres for governmental action in working for 160 million people.

But because they are proper spheres, because they come so close to the daily lives of every citizen, it is up to all of us, again 160 million of us, or all of us old enough to understand, to see that all of that service is limited to what must be and what need be—and doesn't overstep and get into something where they are being merely busybodies and taking over those functions of individual life that must be sustained if we are to remain the great country we have become.

These programs are not static things. They are not brought to perfection in any one year, or in any one date. They are constantly evolving things, exactly as your lives, as this country is a gradually evolving thing.

At this moment there is before the Congress a whole series of these things that have been devised to help define this line between the proper function of Government and these fields which it should not enter and should not invade. And it is likewise attempting to establish before all of us that kind of a strength, at home and abroad, that will lead most surely to a life that is secure and peaceful.

And now it would seem improper, I think, my young graduating friends, if I should leave without a word to you directly. During these 172 years your colleagues have heard many commencement orations, none better than you have heard today from your President.

To what he has said, I add just one thought—every one of these 172 commencement addresses, I venture to say, could be summed up in these words: be not afraid to live by those things in which you believe.

My friends, America believes correctly. Has any one of you ever met a man that was willing to say, "I do not love America"? We believe in America. We believe in our system of government. We believe in the American people. We believe in freedom. We believe in liberty. We believe in God.

The only problem is to live up to your own conscience, always having courage to do the thing you believe to be right. The successful American is one that does that.

My friends, again my very great feeling of gratitude for your welcome. To all the faculty, the trustees, the President, the student body of this College, my grateful thanks for the Honorary Doctorate. I am truly complimented.

NOTE: The commencement exercises were held in the afternoon, beginning at 2:00 p.m. The President's opening words referred to Daniel Z. Gibson, President of Washington College, and Theodore R. McKeldin, Governor of Maryland.

137 ¶ Veto of Bill To Amend the Public Health Service Act. *June 8,* 1954

To the House of Representatives:

I return herewith, without my approval, the bill, H.R. 1026, "To amend the Public Health Service Act, with respect to the provisions of certain medical and dental treatment and hospitalization for certain officers and employees of the former Lighthouse Service, and for dependents and widows of officers and employees of such Service."

From 1910 to July 1939, the Lighthouse Service was manned by civilian personnel. On July 1, 1939, under a Reorganization Plan, the Lighthouse Service was absorbed by the Coast Guard. The Coast Guard put into uniform those employees of the former Lighthouse Service who were willing and qualified to accept military appointments. Those employees who wanted to remain civilians were allowed to do so.

This enactment would extend entitlement to medical care and hospitalization at Public Health facilities under certain circumstances to a number of categories of former Lighthouse Service employees, their dependents, and widows. The bill, however, by according such benefits to one group of Federal employees alone, would discriminate against the vast body of Federal workers. In fact, under the enactment, situations would arise in which former Lighthouse Service employees working side by side with other Federal employees and doing exactly the same type of work would enjoy benefits to which their fellow civil servants would not be entitled. H.R. 1026 would also discriminate against uniformed personnel of the Coast Guard, the Coast and Geodetic Survey, and the

Public Health Service. It would establish a statutory entitlement to benefits for the widows of former Lighthouse Service personnel which are not provided generally to the widows of the uniformed personnel enumerated above.

Moreover, the enactment would constitute an unfortunate precedent. Other groups not now entitled to the benefits which would be granted by H.R. 1026 would justifiably consider themselves entitled to benefits comparable to those which would be accorded to the former Lighthouse Service personnel.

I wish to reiterate my strong support for a program of contributory medical care and hospitalization insurance, on a voluntary basis, for Federal employees generally. Such a program would aid Federal employees in meeting their medical and hospital needs and would be fair and equitable to all concerned. Moreover, it would be consistent with my objective of combining the best practices of progressive private employers with the special demands of the public service, thereby improving our Federal career employee system and the efficiency of its administration.

DWIGHT D. EISENHOWER

138 ¶ The President's News Conference of *June* 10, 1954.

THE PRESIDENT. Ladies and gentlemen, the only piece of news I have, and I don't believe it is news any more, is that there is gathered in town a group of people who call themselves "Citizens for Eisenhower Congressional Committee." Their name indicates and implies their support of the program the administration submitted to Congress. So I am going to talk to them tonight under circumstances where, I believe, there will be television and radio; and, of course, I am going to talk about those elements of the program that are now under discussion in Congress and are in different stages of the legislative process.

We will now start the questions.

Q. Merriman Smith, United Press: Mr. President, in 1952 you said during the course of the campaign that you endorsed all Republican candidates for the House and Senate, nominees for the House and Senate. I just wondered if you feel that same way this year?

THE PRESIDENT. Well, you are asking me a question that I dislike just answering in great generality. I did say that I endorsed the candidates nominated by the Republicans of their districts and States, and in accordance with law, because of my earnest belief that the legislative body should be controlled through its committees and organization by the same party that provides the occupant of the White House; that if that were not true, there was always an opportunity to dodge party responsibility. Of course, in that sense, I still believe the same thing, that the Republicans as long as they are in power ought to be in power and be held responsible for every action or lack of action that you can trace to them. But I imagine that you could probably pull out of the hat some specific question that could be most embarrassing; I hope you won't do that. [*Laughter*]

Q. Mr. Smith: Do you have anything on your mind, sir?

THE PRESIDENT. No, I don't.

Q. Ray Scherer, National Broadcasting Company: Mr. President, as a former military commander, would you be in a position to discuss the changing military situation around Hanoi, Indochina, with particular respect to the possible need for outside naval and air help in such a situation?

THE PRESIDENT. Well, now, I don't want to be misunderstood in any way or have my remarks expanded into the field of speculation here as meaning something other than I am talking about, which is now strictly military.

The French Union forces have had a most difficult task, one that would have been made much easier could they have won the true allegiance and loyalty of the Vietnamese with whom they were working. That task is that of holding a great area. You do it on a defensive basis, because you are not trying to destroy anyone—destroy towns, villages, or people—whereas the opponent has had all the initiative that goes with choosing the time and point of attack. Very naturally, they have had a very, very tough time in trying to defend every place, to be strong enough every place, all the time.

In what you might call conventional warfare, the successful commander does not attempt to do any such thing. He collects up his forces, the largest offensive force he can find, goes and defeats the other one, and so secures the victory and the conditions he wants.

But here, it has been sort of an elusive enemy. There were not large concentrations up until the time of Dien Bien Phu; there were not large concentrations you could go and attack. Any attempt to concentrate and move in any one direction merely led to difficulty in another place; so the French have had a very, very difficult time.

Now, within the Delta itself this situation is present, but on a smaller degree because there is not as much territory to defend. I understand that the French are succeeding in concentrating certain mobile detachments that can be used in rapid fashion to relieve and support those areas that now could be attacked; no longer are they isolated by great areas of jungle where really it was out of the question of producing relieving columns, of bringing them in. So the situation in that respect is possibly better than it was.

Now, as far as outside help is concerned, of course they could use it, no question about the improvement of their situation if they had additional military help.

Q. Joseph Harsch, Christian Science Monitor: Sir, about 2 weeks, I think, ago, Admiral Carney said that all dangers this country faced before were trivial as compared to the danger it faces today, but he didn't tell us why that was the case. May I ask you a double question: first, do you concur in that assessment of our present situation; and, if so, can you give us any details about why the danger today is so much greater than anything we ever faced before?

THE PRESIDENT. Well, Mr. Harsch, first of all, I try to avoid calling on history in terms of comparison. I have heard so many people say, "This was the toughest battle ever fought in the history of civilization," and so on; I don't use those terms, because I don't know. I imagine that the people that were living, let's say, in the spring of 1864 in this country could not have believed that there could be any set of conditions that represented more real danger and imminence of destruction to the United States than did those conditions. So I don't think it is necessary to talk in those terms, Mr. Harsch.

I think that what we should talk about is, are we in a truly serious situation? I think you will find that the answer is inescapably "yes," and primarily because the Iron Curtain countries do have the control that is imposed by force.

They have that great unification that allows objectives to be chosen and suddenly attacked. In other words, the whole world in a way is in

547

somewhat the condition I was just describing a little while ago for the French effort to defend all of Indochina.

The free world has to be strong everywhere, you might say, as strong as it can be. But we must not forget that still in the military way the best thing for us to do is to have the central and major forces, the reserves, highly mobile, centrally located, and ready to move when vital interests are threatened in any place.

You know, it is easy, because we say that communism does exist and does achieve this unity and this power by the threat of the knife in the back and force, it is easy to dismiss the appeal that communism has had for very great numbers of people—they have voluntarily adopted it.

What I fear more than anything else in this time, is a failure to look this danger in, you might say, its broad face. We think and concentrate on Indochina, or we think of the possibility of penetrations in the Mideast, or of some other country, one of our friends in Europe, weakening. We have got to remember that the attack is so broad in its character that we cannot be complacent in anything, in the realm of the spirit and the intellectual world, the material world, and the economic.

This is, of course, very general; but let's be very specific: we have just had some of our best educated men in America espouse communism, or at least they have been supporters of communism. Now, why? I don't know. I am puzzled in front of this phenomenon. I just don't know why or see how such a doctrine could appeal to the human spirit, particularly when you see its application in Russia and in the countries where it applies—the use of force, indifference to man and his conditions of living, his intellectual or material or economic. I don't know why it appeals that way, but it does, and we have some of our own, some very intelligent men.

Now, as you go around the world, you find that kind of appeal coupled with bribery, deceit, and corruption and profligate spending of money in some areas, and on top of that, threat—threat of force, the fear of people.

Then I would say, if we would look at this thing in its broad way, we cannot possibly minimize in any way the great problem that America is leading; because whether or not she likes it, whether her leadership has been thrust upon her or whether she has naturally inherited it, she does have the leadership of the free world in forming a like unity on our side, spontaneously or, let's say, cooperatively achieved, so that it can defend against this thing in all three of these fields.

I claim it is not enough just to be militarily strong. I believe there is no defense just in the military; we must be strong in our beliefs, our convictions, in our hearts. We must be strong in our intellectual surety that this is the better system; we must prove it throughout the world, we must prove it to others. Finally, we must be strong militarily so that we gain opportunity and time to do all these things.

I am sorry again for making a speech, but this thing is too complicated, too terribly broad, to define it exactly in any one of these areas; we have to think of it in its whole.

Q. James Reston, New York Times: Mr. President, in your judgment, is the military budget that you have sent to the Congress sufficient to deal with this menace?

THE PRESIDENT. Of course I think it is or I would not approve it; that does not mean that I think it is sufficient to start a war or to do anything of that kind.

What I really believe that the democracies must look in the face is this: you have not only a problem that is broad in scope but it is great in depth.

We don't know, this may last 40 years. Now, what we must devise is such a program of defense in the military field that our country can stand the strain and live under a representative form of government for years and years, taking into consideration the problems that we have, the economic, the intellectual, the spiritual, the military. It seems to me we are on the best road in the defense that we can possibly be on.

Now, that doesn't mean that I am completely satisfied and there are never going to be any changes. I could change at any moment, and I certainly would if there were evidence brought to me that I was mistaken in this regard. This is a changing situation, and you have to live with it and study it and devote everything you have to it. I will tell you this: at any moment I think I am wrong, it will be changed, and I won't be afraid to get up and say I think I was wrong.

Q. Mr. Reston: Sir, what I had in mind was whether the Indochina situation in your judgment had——

THE PRESIDENT. I didn't quite hear you.

Q. Mr. Reston: I say, whether the Indochina—the deterioration of the Indochina situation had, in your judgment, forced you to revise the budget or your thinking about it.

THE PRESIDENT. There has been no change for the moment. I think, if you will go back over the things for the past 15 months that both the Secretary of State and I have been trying to say, we have tried to point out that the United States cannot alone by its military might achieve the policies that we must pursue. There must be—and I go back again to what I have been saying here incessantly—the proper psychological, political bases for these things, for merely to go wage a battle somewhere is perfectly useless, costly and useless.

Now, if we can achieve the proper bases, political and psychological, intellectual, anything else that is necessary, then intervention is achieved in such a way that you are strengthened throughout the world and not merely using up resources to win some local battle.

Q. Ruth Montgomery, New York Daily News: Mr. President, will it be feasible to let Congress adjourn this summer without voting you the power to act in Indochina if it becomes necessary while they are gone?

THE PRESIDENT. Frankly, I have no plan as of this moment to ask for anything that is outside the normal traditional processes in the operation of our Government.

Now, the question you ask can't be answered now. If such a thing would become necessary, it would come up on the crest of some crisis, and you would have to go and lay the problem before Congress and ask them. As of this moment I have no such plan.

Q. William Blair, New York Times: Mr. President, Secretary of State Dulles testified before the Joint Congressional Committee last week on the urgency of an interchange of atomic information with our allies, particularly in relation to NATO. He suggested the situation was such that he would dislike to see the international pool or the interchange idea lost because of the domestic side of the program.

In your mind, sir, are those two programs, domestic and international, inseparably linked or would you prefer one over the other under the existing conditions?

THE PRESIDENT. You have asked, certainly, an extremely complicated problem.

I agree with both statements. There should be a greater interchange with our allies about certain aspects of this whole atomic business.

As you know, our present law which governs our actions in this regard at the moment, was written when we hoped that we could retain a monopoly in the manufacture of this kind of thing. Well, we haven't; so, many of the basic hopes and purposes that underlay the writing of that law are gone, and we should take certainly a new look. I do believe that if we are going to ask allies to work and labor with us cooperatively, we can't sit back and refuse to exchange with them information that could be of the most vital consequences and interest to them in the event of war.

Now, as for the other parts, an atomic pool and progressing with the effort to show all humankind how important these things could be to them, I say we must find ways and means of going ahead with that, regardless. The more people in the world that understand that atomic energy and all of the newly developed sciences can be of benefit to them and do not have to be, and should not be, sequestered off in some dark corner to be used merely for destructive purposes, the greater the moral force will be in favor of general peace, general disarmament, and a better life for all of us.

Q. Douglass Cater, The Reporter Magazine: Mr. President, you have termed it reprehensible for employees of the Government to pass secret information out without authorization. As Commander in Chief of the Armed Forces, do you believe that people should hold Reserve officer commissions in the Armed Forces and in the National Guard who have publicly urged that such secret information be passed out without authorization?

THE PRESIDENT. It is always dangerous, I have found, to answer questions in generalities when you haven't had time to take a look. As far as I am concerned though, when a man has been given the job of helping defend the United States, and has been given a commission or is an enlisted man in that group, I think that his loyalty and his readiness to obey the military laws and the Constitution of the United States should be unquestioned.

Q. Sarah McClendon, El Paso Times: Sir, if the Republican leadership continues to keep the House and Senate from having a chance to vote on extension of reciprocal trade, have you any other tactical moves in mind? What will you do?

THE PRESIDENT. Well, now, to my mind they are not trying to keep them from voting on reciprocal trade. As a matter of fact, I have just been informed that the House committee reported out—you people could tell me whether I am correct—23 to nothing an extension of reciprocal trade.

Q. Mrs. McClendon: They were to meet at 9:30.

THE PRESIDENT. Am I right?

Mr. Hagerty: That is right.

THE PRESIDENT. Twenty-three to nothing, to extend reciprocal trade for 1 year.

Let's be perfectly clear about this: I have heard people say that I have backed away or abandoned the plan that was developed through the Randall Commission, which I sent to Congress with a very strong endorsing message. Nothing could be further from the truth. I thoroughly believe that it is only in a liberalization of trade, an increasing of trade throughout the free world, that we are going to achieve many of the things that I talked about a while ago in answer to questions by Mr. Harsch and others. We have got to do it.

That doesn't mean that the Congress of the United States, which is certainly supposed to be representative of 162 million people, has to take my recommendations, arrived at after months of study with able people, and vote "yes" or "no," and do it now.

It consists of many parts. There are parts involving the increase of tourist's exemptions when they come in, lightening the taxload on investments abroad, simplifying customs procedures, other things of that kind, that can be done now and should be done now.

And there is the heart of the program.

As a matter of fact, there are other things that can be done administratively, and we are pushing ahead on them as hard as we can.

Then there are other things that do take time for the Congress to study because, remember this, every single time that you touch the tariff in one way or another, somebody in the United States is affected. These men and women in Congress represent the people of their districts, and they want to have their voices heard: "Is this industry hurt or is that group of labor going to be hurt?" "Is there going to be some unemployment?" "What is going to happen?"

We must have a strong America. Not only for the benefit of that man who is drawing wages must we have high wages, we must have a high consumptive power in this United States, because we are our own best customers.

Nevertheless, along with that, we must recognize the need for this foreign trade.

Now, the one thing that you must have, that I think should be done immediately over and beyond what I have described as really nonargumentative portions of this program, we should have a simple extension of the Reciprocal Trade Act while Congress makes up its mind about the heart of the program which I proposed, which was the opportunity to reduce by 5 percent a year for 3 years, you will recall, the tariffs on selected items that study reveals is necessary for our general overall good in the world and our economy at home.

Now, to say that I have abandoned, because I don't insist that this thing be all done at once, that is just not true. I believe in it just as strongly as I ever believed in it.

Q. Lucian Warren, Buffalo Courier-Express: Mr. President, last year the House passed the Miller-Capehart bill authorizing private power facilities at Niagara Falls. This week, on Tuesday, the Senate Public Works Committee approved the Case bill which would have the effect of turning the Niagara power facilities over to the New York State Power Authority. I wonder what is your attitude on this legislation?

THE PRESIDENT. Well, you know, strangely enough, here is one argument that has been going on where they haven't come in front of me and argued their cases.

I think all of you know very clearly that I believe that the authority, the political authority, of local governments must be upheld in this country or in the long run we lose our particular form of government. I believe the authority of the municipality, of the State, must be upheld.

In every instance where it is possible, and no other factors enter into the situation, I would like to leave such determinations to the State: what do they want to do? But this particular case has not been argued out in front of me, and I am not going to give a specific answer other than to state what my belief is.

Q. Raymond Brandt, St. Louis Post-Dispatch: Mr. President, there have been rumors that some of the congressional leaders wanted an understanding that you would not negotiate any reciprocal trade agreements if they extended it for 1 more year. Is there any truth in that report?

THE PRESIDENT. I could not possibly make such an agreement.

You know, it seems to me, ladies and gentlemen, I have talked so much this morning and taken so long on some questions, I am almost apologetic; but remember this: we have got people in this country that believe that if we do any trading or anyone does any trading with Iron Curtain countries, it is to our disadvantage; and, therefore, they want to stop it by law, if possible.

We have people who say we must not lend or give or grant any more money. We have others who say we will not take another pound of anything in this country.

Now, ladies and gentlemen, we are trying to build up allies who can make a living.

Isn't it rather odd to say, "We want you as friends, be on our side, but we won't allow you to trade over there, we won't give you any money, we are not going to do anything to defend the trading areas you now have, but you must be our friends and we won't trade with you."

It just doesn't make sense. We have got to decide: are we trying to build up a strong, cooperative family of nations that want to work together and, therefore, show it by our actions as well as our words, or do we not?

Now, as I have said before, it would be a very comfortable feeling in this world, I think, if you could really be an isolationist, if you could believe the United States could retreat into itself, live there safely and alone, with all of the wonderful prosperity that has come to this country; that would just possibly be a wonderful feeling if you could forget your conscience. But if there is anyone here that has got an idea how that can be done, I would certainly like for him to write me a long memorandum on it and explain it in detail, because I don't, and I confess that.

Merriman Smith, United Press: Thank you, Mr. President.

NOTE: President Eisenhower's fortieth news conference was held in the Executive Office Building from 10:33 to 10:59 o'clock on Thursday morning, June 10, 1954. In attendance: 146.

139   ¶ Address at Meeting of District Chairmen, National Citizens for Eisenhower Congressional Committee.   *June* 10, 1954

[Broadcast over radio and television at 9:00 p.m.]

GOOD EVENING TO YOU, my very dear friends, and good evening to each American across this broad land who has allowed me into their living room on their television or their radio receiver.

I prize this opportunity to meet with citizens, dedicated to the policies and objectives of this administration.   These policies and objectives have been placed before the Congress in a legislative program to build a better and a stronger America.   I am delighted that you have come to Washington to pledge your support to those members of the present Congress who are working for this program.   Happily these are both numerous and able—and to be found not only among the leaders and the seniors who helped design the program, but among our younger friends most recently elected to that august body.

Naturally, I am equally pleased that you are pledged to do your individual and collective best to see that there will be many more such men and women in the next Congress.   It would seem redundant for me to say: the more the better.

Now, what we mean by a stronger America is a nation whose every citizen has reason for bold hope, where effort is rewarded and prosperity is shared, where freedom expands and peace is secure.

The legislative program that you and I support is a broad, straight legislative highway to that kind of America.

Tonight, I propose that we talk frankly, even if somewhat sketchily, about that program—now in the Congress.

It was laid before the Congress last January, and was designed to protect our freedoms; to foster a growing, prosperous, peacetime economy; and to fulfill the Government's obligations in helping solve the human problems of our citizenry.

Now, basic to the protection of our freedom is a strong, forthright foreign policy.   This we have been developing.   Our foreign policy is vigorously opposed to imperialistic ambition, but devoted to harmonious cooperation with all nations and peoples who share our will to live in peace with their neighbors. It demands, this policy, unremitting effort to create and hold friends and to encourage them in staunchness of friendship with us. It requires us to be vigilant against those who would destroy us; to be calm and confident in the face of their threats.

Present world conditions require a national defense program, streamlined, effective, and economical, that takes into full account our air and nuclear might. But in the longer range, our foreign and defense policies must be directed toward world disarmament. We must seek for all mankind a release from the deadening burden of armaments. We must continue to seek sensible solutions for the fateful problems posed by the atom and hydrogen bombs. Pursuing these purposes, we have persistently made appropriate proposals to the world—and more particularly to the Soviets—which if honestly accepted would go far toward attainment of these goals.

With our friends, we must strive constantly for a freer system of world trade and investment, for strengthened trade agreement legislation, for simpler rules and regulations under which trade can be carried on. In the meantime, we must continue to render military and economic assistance abroad where our national interest is thereby served.

In this way we not only build up our material and military strength so that we may oppose successfully any rash aggression by the Communists, but we help eliminate those conditions of poverty, disease, and ignorance which provide fertile breeding ground for the exploiters of discontent.

Foreign policy is a complicated and comprehensive subject. It cannot be effectively described in a mere section of a general talk such as this. But because foreign affairs and foreign policy do so vitally affect the lives of each of us and all that we are attempting to do abroad, and here at home, the Secretary of State is at this moment on a trip to the West where he is delivering major addresses that will help clarify for all our citizens the position of America in world affairs.

At home we have sought to preserve the sanctity of our freedoms by denying official posts of trust to the untrustworthy; by intensifying legal action against the members and leaders of the Communist conspiracy; by sharpening our weapons for dealing with sabotage.

Scarcely need I assure such an audience as this that I—and my every associate in Government—will keep everlastingly at the job of uprooting subversion wherever it may be found. My friends, I do not believe that

I am egotistical when I say that I believe that every American believes, at least, that about me.

Now the second part of this program is a strong and a growing economy, shared in, equitably, by all our citizens!

Now, we began this part of the program by uncovering and eliminating needless expenditures within the Federal Government. We proposed a reduction in taxes and reform of the tax system. Other measures involve a new farm program adjusted to current domestic and world conditions; an improved and expanded national highway system; a sound and comprehensive development of water and other natural resources; a broad housing program.

We hope, also, to uproot the ingrained habit of operating the vast Post Office Department in an extravagantly wasteful and unbusinesslike manner. We cannot permit the deliberate operation of our postal department at a gigantic loss because a few are opposed to adequate postal rates. Of course, we must have classification and promotional procedures for postal personnel that will serve the best interests of the Government, the public, and the postal workers themselves.

Now the third great purpose outlined 5 months ago was sympathetic consideration of the human problems of our citizens, and practical assistance in solving them.

Our goal for every American is better schooling; better housing; better health; and a reasonable assurance against the hardships of unemployment, against the impact of accident and illness, against poverty, against insecurity in old age.

This threefold program—national security, economic, human—is the product of intensive effort by a multitude of technical experts and specialists, Government employees and executives, legislative leaders and committee chairmen. They labored diligently for months to evolve measures sound both in concept and in detail. These measures were— and are—badly needed to build the kind of America all of us ardently desire. There is nothing partisan, nothing sectional, nothing partial about them; they are for the security, prosperity, and happiness of all Americans.

Now, my friends, in spite of highly publicized distractions, Congress has been hard at work. Not only have the difficult and time-consuming appropriation bills been acted upon much faster than usual, but the Congress has supported the administration in its efforts to reduce expenditures. Through legislation recently enacted, our people will have better highways. Stifling taxes on consumers have been eased. After more than 40 years of heated debate, the historic St. Lawrence Seaway project is now authorized by law. A mutual security treaty with the Republic of Korea has been approved. Now, these are but a few of a number of major pieces of legislation that have been enacted.

But much still remains that is of vital significance to every American citizen. Tonight I am addressing myself primarily to a few of the important parts of the program that are now under discussion in the Congress and in different stages of the legislative process.

First—the tax revision bill.

I remind you of the $7 billion tax reduction already provided to our citizens. You know, this administration goes on the theory that the private citizen knows better how to spend his money than the Government. This program is designed to accomplish a fairer distribution of the tax burden. It will give more liberal tax treatment for dependent children who work, for widows or widowers with dependent children, and for medical expenses. It will help to expand business activity and so create jobs throughout the country and will also give real encouragement to small businesses.

I cannot overemphasize the importance I attach to the general policies and proposals comprehended in the tax bill, and the need for its early passage.

I am sure you will agree that the Congress should enact this tax legislation, already passed by the House of Representatives. And the point I want to make is this: some of its benefits will begin to accrue to the people of our country as soon as enacted, because then, with tax uncertainties removed, investors, manufacturers, and businessmen will all accelerate their activities thus creating new jobs and increasing the national income. This is an added reason for speed.

Now, another pending measure, vitally necessary to every citizen, is the new farm program. Its purpose is to promote stability and prosperity in agriculture and help assure our farmers a fair share of the national income.

The Nation's present farm law encourages production of great surpluses of a few commodities, and then it prices those commodities out of their traditional markets. As a result, the Government must now spend $30,000 an hour—every hour—just to store these surpluses. That is $700,000 a day. In the last 12 months the Government increased its investment in price supported commodities by $2,800 million. During the next 12 months, the present law would force another increase.

Now, one aspect of this amazing process appears to be little understood. Minority clamor has concealed from the majority the fact that a change from rigid price supports to flexible supports would affect less than one-fourth of the income our farmers receive. Rigid supports do not in any way affect crops that produce 77 percent of our farmers' income.

Five months ago, on the advice of farm organizations, heads of agricultural colleges, a host of individual farmers, and many other experts and businessmen, I recommended that a new farm program be enacted by the Congress. This program proposes price supports with enough flexibility to encourage the production of needed supplies, and to stimulate the consumption of those commodities that are flooding and depressing the American markets. It also proposed gradualism in the adoption and application of certain phases of the new program, so that there could not possibly be an abrupt downward change in the level of price supports on basic commodities.

The plan will increase markets for farm products, protect the consumers' food supply, and move food into consumption instead of into governmental storage. My friends, I remember in 1952, during the political campaign, again and again I pledged one thing: I would always do everything within my power to see that the products of food produced by the sweat and toil of our farmers would never have to be thrown away or allowed to spoil when there were hungry people in the world. Now these surpluses are already getting to the point where only decisive and prompt action on our part is going to keep something of that kind from threatening us seriously, if not happening. Now this program will gradually dispose of the gigantic farm surpluses and promises our farmers a higher and steadier return over the years.

This badly needed, new program has a bipartisan origin. The proposal is, in concept, the same as the law passed 5 years ago by a vast majority of the Members of each of the two parties in the Congress.

And yet—despite the vast accumulation of surpluses in the hands of the Government—despite the declining markets at home and abroad, and increasing regimentation of the individual farmer—despite the fact that only a minority of American farmers are affected by price supports— despite the fact that even among this farmer minority, many are opposed to a program so obviously unsuited to the needs of our country—despite all of these painfully evident weaknesses, a vote, described to me as tentative, which was taken 2 days ago in a committee of the House of Representatives, called for continuance of the present farm program for an additional year. In my opinion, the circumstances are too critical to permit such a delay.

Now, my fellow citizens, many have told me that it would not be good politics to attempt solution of the farm problem during an election year. The sensible thing to do, I have been told, over and over again, was to close my eyes to the damage the present farm program does to our farmers and to the rest of our people—and do this job of correction next year.

Now, I would like to make this one point clear!

In this matter I am completely unmoved by arguments as to what constitutes good or winning politics! And may I remark that, though I have not been in this political business very long, I know that what is right for America is politically right.

In the proposal to correct the deficiencies in our farm program, the administration's concern is for all farmers, regardless of their politics, and for all America.

I earnestly hope that the House of Representatives and the Senate will move promptly on these proposals, so that America may have a sound, stable, and prosperous agriculture.

And I hope you will join me in the determination to see that common-sense, good judgment, and fact will, from now on, guide the formulation of American agricultural policy.

Now, aside from taxes and agricultural programs, other projects occupy legislative attention at this moment!

Some of them are of great personal import to our individual citizens, and some have passed one or the other of the two Houses of the Congress.

Extension of the benefits of unemployment insurance should be authorized, so that these benefits may be made available to more than six million additional workers. When this project becomes law, it will remove inequities and inadequacies which for years have limited the effectiveness of this form of income-insurance. In simple justice to a vast number of American citizens, it demands our enthusiastic support.

Congress is considering increased social security benefits, and the extension of social security protection, to more than ten million additional Americans. Likewise, it has before it strengthened programs to rehabilitate disabled people, and to develop adequate medical facilities for those who suffer the misfortune of chronic illness.

In this same health program are items for the construction of diagnostic centers, for nursing homes, and for rehabilitation facilities. Another measure provides for Government reinsurance to enable private and nonprofit insurance companies to give broader prepaid medical and hospital care, on a voluntary basis, to many more of our people. There is a bill to authorize a new housing program, so that every citizen may aspire to a decent home in a wholesome neighborhood.

We are striving to help assure every willing American a practical opportunity to enjoy good health, a good job, a good education, a good home, a good country. And may I emphasize, we are trying to provide opportunity. We are not trying to be paternalistic with respect to anybody.

Now let us look briefly, once again, at the domestic question of protecting our liberties, because this purpose underlies a number of specific bills now before the Congress. They will, when enacted, powerfully increase the effectiveness of the Government's effort to protect us against subversive activity.

Several of these bills would plug loopholes through which spies and saboteurs can now slip. One would let us bar proven subversives from employment in or admission to any private facility, if the facility is essential to our defense.

Another bill would take citizenship from those hereafter convicted of advocating or attempting violent overthrow of our Government.

Moreover, since Communist conspirators sometimes resort to telephones to plot and pass information, we believe that their own words, as learned by the FBI, should be admitted, under adequate safeguards, as evidence in security cases in Federal courts. Another bill would grant immunity from self-incrimination to selected witnesses, while requiring them to tell the truth about their associates and their fellow conspirators before courts, grand juries, and congressional hearings.

All of this internal security legislation adds up to a potent package of protection against communism, without in any degree damaging or lessening the rights of the individual citizen as guaranteed by our laws and the Constitution. It will greatly assist the FBI and the Justice Department, our best weapons against the secret Communist penetration. That program now awaits congressional approval. And I know that all of us, too, await that approval.

Now, I have talked frankly and simply about these matters this evening, because I want you to know why the legislative program in Congress will, when approved, make our country stronger, and help keep our people prosperous with freedoms secure.

As I said earlier, many members of Congress are as deeply anxious as you and I for the passage of these essential measures. They have worked faithfully for their enactment, and I hope that they know of your support. With our appreciation to them goes also, I am sure, this firm assurance from all of us: that we shall unflaggingly pursue the enactment of the remainder of this program.

We live today in an age of ceaseless trouble and danger. For all of us the challenge is clear. For all of us the future is shadowed by mushroom clouds and menaced by godless men addicted to force and violence and the continuance of anarchy among nations.

Here, in our time, in our hands, and in our own courage, in our own endurance and vision, rests the future of civilization and of all moral and spiritual values of enduring meaning to mankind.

Part—but only part—of our responsibility for preserving these values can be discharged through the legislative structure we propose to enact this year.

Let us, therefore, not rest until these laws are passed.

May I suggest that we have less political fission and more political fusion.

Let us have, in this session of the Congress, approval of this program essential to a stronger, a better, a safer America.

NOTE: The President spoke at the Statler Hotel in Washington.

140 ¶ Statement by the President Upon Signing Bill To Include the Words "Under God" in the Pledge to the Flag. *June* 14, 1954

FROM THIS DAY FORWARD, the millions of our school children will daily proclaim in every city and town, every village and rural school house, the dedication of our nation and our people to the Almighty. To anyone who truly loves America, nothing could be more inspiring than to contemplate this rededication of our youth, on each school morning, to our country's true meaning.

Especially is this meaningful as we regard today's world. Over the globe, mankind has been cruelly torn by violence and brutality and, by the millions, deadened in mind and soul by a materialistic philosophy of life. Man everywhere is appalled by the prospect of atomic war. In this somber setting, this law and its effects today have profound meaning. In this way we are reaffirming the transcendence of religious faith in America's heritage and future; in this way we shall constantly strengthen those spiritual weapons which forever will be our country's most powerful resource, in peace or in war.

NOTE: The joint resolution amending the pledge of allegiance to the flag is Public Law 396, 83d Congress (68 Stat. 249).

141 ¶ Veto of Bill for the Relief of Mrs. Rose Kaczmarczyk. *June* 14, 1954

To the House of Representatives:

I am returning herewith, without my approval, H.R. 898, 83d Congress, "An Act For the relief of Mrs. Rose Kaczmarczyk."

The bill would authorize and direct the Secretary of the Treasury to pay to Mrs. Rose Kaczmarczyk the sum of $4,344, which represents the service-connected death compensation she would have received for the period June 23, 1944, the day following the date of death of her son, William P. Kaczmarczyk, through April 3, 1951, if claim for such compensation had been filed within one year after the death of her son and she had been found to be otherwise eligible.

The evidence discloses that William Paul Kaczmarczyk served in the Army of the United States from June 4, 1942, until his death on June 22, 1944. After receipt of notice from the Department of the Army of the death of the serviceman, the Veterans' Administration, on August 25, 1944, mailed a letter to the mother of the deceased, Mrs. Rose Kaczmarczyk, expressing regret over the death of her son and enclosing an application form for death compensation, which gave instructions for its completion and return to the Veterans' Administration. There was no response to the letter by the mother, or anyone in her behalf, until April 4, 1951, the date of receipt of an application by Mrs. Kaczmarczyk for death compensation. Thereafter, she was awarded death compensation at the rate of $60 per month, effective April 4, 1951, the date of filing such claim with the Veterans' Administration, which is the earliest date from which such benefits are payable under existing law. Payment of such compensation has continued to date.

It appears that favorable action by the Committees which considered H.R. 898 was based on the belief that since the claimant could not read English and did not realize her rights, the delay in filing claim should be excused. It is pertinent to note in this connection that on August 11, 1944, the Veterans' Administration sent Mrs. Kaczmarczyk a form for claiming her son's $10,000 National Service life insurance, and that her completed claim for that insurance was returned to the Veterans' Administration five days later. Mrs. Kaczmarczyk was thereafter awarded payments for life in the amount of $66.50 per month, beginning June 22, 1944.

Further, it is indicated in the Committee reports that had Mrs. Kaczmarczyk filed a timely application for death compensation she would have been entitled to compensation in the sum stated in the bill for the period from June 23, 1944, through April 3, 1951. In order to have been eligible for compensation during the stated period, Mrs. Kaczmarczyk, in addition to filing a timely claim, would have had to establish that she was the dependent mother of the veteran during that period. I am informed that she has not submitted to the Veterans' Administration evidence—and it is not known whether she is in a position to do so— to establish that during the almost seven-year period under consideration she was in dependent circumstances.

The report of the Senate Committee also states their belief that the situation here involved is unique and would not constitute a precedent for future claims. To the contrary, I am informed that there are many other claimants for death compensation benefits, who, like Mrs. Kaczmarczyk, by reason of inaction on their part within the period established by law, are not entitled to retroactive awards of death compensation. To approve this bill therefore would obviously be discriminatory. As I have stated in the past, it is unwise to set aside the principles and rules of administration prescribed in the general laws governing veterans' benefit programs. Uniformity and equality of treatment to all who are similarly situated must be the steadfast rule if the Federal programs for veterans and their dependents are to be operated successfully.

For the foregoing reasons, I am unable to approve H.R. 898, which would authorize payment of compensation from a date almost seven years earlier than the date authorized by the general law and in a case where the evidence of record fails to establish that the claimant is otherwise eligible.

DWIGHT D. EISENHOWER

142 ¶ Veto of Bill for the Relief of Mrs. Josette L. St. Marie. *June* 14, 1954

To the House of Representatives:

I am returning herewith without my approval, H.R. 6452, 83d Congress, "An Act For the relief of Mrs. Josette L. St. Marie".

The bill proposes that Frank P. St. Marie's death in service on March 9, 1943, shall be held and considered to have been in line of duty.

Private St. Marie, then on active service in the United States Army, committed suicide on March 9, 1943, while in confinement because of excessive use of alcoholic beverages. The military department determined that his death was in line of duty, while mentally unsound, and not the result of his own misconduct. The claim of Mrs. Josette L. St. Marie for death compensation as dependent mother was denied by the Veterans' Administration on the ground that death was due to the soldier's own misconduct.

It appears that favorable action by the Committees which considered H.R. 6452 was based upon disagreement with the determination of the

Veterans' Administration and a belief that the military department's determination is entitled to greater weight and should be controlling. The basic issue in this case involves the adjudicative function of evaluation of evidence to determine whether the soldier's death was in line of duty and not due to his own misconduct for purposes of death compensation. The statutory duty of making such determinations is the sole responsibility of the Veterans' Administration. I am informed that the conclusion of the Veterans' Administration in the case is fully substantiated by the evidence of record, and in my judgment it is unwise to adjudicate individual cases by private legislation.

To prefer this case for special treatment to the exclusion of other similar cases would be unwarranted and discriminatory. In this regard, I am advised that during the past six years approximately 1000 claims for service-connected death compensation in World War II cases alone have been denied on the ground that the veteran's death was due to his own willful misconduct. Further, it is understood that there are no dependents of World War II veterans on the death compensation rolls as a consequence of enactment of a private law. Approval of H.R. 6452 could result in the placing of such a dependent on the mentioned rolls, and possibly retroactively for almost a nine-year period. Thus, its approval would constitute a far reaching precedent which I cannot justify.

I am opposed to setting aside the principles and rules of administration prescribed in the public laws governing veterans' benefit programs. Uniformity and equality of treatment to all who are similarly situated must be the steadfast rule if the Federal programs for veterans and their dependents are to be operated successfully. Approval of H.R. 6452 would not be in keeping with these principles.

Dwight D. Eisenhower

143 ¶ The President's News Conference of June 16, 1954.

THE PRESIDENT. A week or so ago I made a pledge to this group that every time I appeared publicly, privately, or anywhere else, I was going to mention my support of the administration's program before the

Congress. For fear there will be no questions asked about it today, I say that now and get it off my chest.

We will go to questions.

Q. Merriman Smith, United Press: Mr. President, I wonder if you could elaborate a little for us on Prime Minister Churchill's forthcoming visit, tell us a little more about the background of it.

THE PRESIDENT. Well, I will be glad to.

Mr. Churchill has, during the 12 or 13 years I have known him, been one of the greatest supporters of close British-American cooperation and, in my opinion, has been one of the most effective supporters of that field.

Now, in dealing with such a question you are often reminded of a sort of figure of speech I saw, talking about such things, to this effect: there is a bridge here across the Potomac, and thousands of people use it every day, and that is not news; but let the bridge fail or fall some place, and it is instantly news.

Now, we are not trying to make news; we are trying to keep the bridge between America and Britain strong.

We communicate all the time. In one of his communications to me was a suggestion that a meeting between us would certainly do much by itself to combat the theory that there are such great rifts occurring among us. He pointed out that such stories could be of value only to our common foes. And I promptly invited him over.

To make it a friendly, informal thing, I invited him to come to the White House and spend a weekend.

He is an old, old friend, as you people know. I haven't the slightest idea of exactly what we will talk about. But I will tell you, very frankly, that I doubt whether there is a subject that anyone could ask a question about this morning of any international concern that we won't talk about. We will talk about everything—I have been in these before.

As you know, again I repeat, I like and admire him, and I look forward to his visit with the greatest of pleasure.

That is the general background today, a feeling that a meeting can do nothing but good.

Q. Mr. Smith: Mr. President, physically, where will the meetings take place? Inside the White House?

THE PRESIDENT. There are going to be no meetings as such. I expect him to stay at the White House with me, and there will be people coming in and out. Mr. Eden, by the way, is staying with me, too, because he is another old wartime friend, as you people well know. The two of them are going to stay with me in the White House, and there will be people of ours in and out. There is going to be nothing formal, no social things or anything of that kind; it is just going to be as informal and comfortable as we can make it.

Q. Alan Emory, Watertown (N.Y.) Times: Governor Dewey of New York visited you here 2 weeks ago, sir. Would you tell us if at that time you urged him to run for re-election this fall?

THE PRESIDENT. At that time? No, I said nothing to him at that time.

Q. Mr. Emory: At any other time, sir? [*Laughter*]

THE PRESIDENT. I have often talked to him about his own situation and convictions, but he has to make his own decisions. I never urge anyone past the point of their own convictions to do anything.

Q. Mr. Emory: Sir, may I ask you one last question on that subject?

THE PRESIDENT. Yes.

Q. Mr. Emory: Would you consider Governor Dewey's presence at the head of the ticket in New York of substantial benefit to the Republicans this fall?

THE PRESIDENT. Well, I can say this: obviously in the past it has been; and I think he is still a pretty strong person. However, let us not forget he has been plugging away in public service for a good many years, and I would think he had earned the right to make his own decisions without any question.[1]

Q. Pat Munroe, Salt Lake City Deseret News: Mr. President, have you any comments on recommendations of the U.S. Tariff Commission to you to invoke higher duties on several imports, including lead and zinc?

THE PRESIDENT. Well, they are all under study now, and they have not yet come to my desk. I believe there are five of these cases now pending. They have not come back to my desk, so I wouldn't want to comment on them now.

Q. Charles von Fremd, CBS Television: The House Agricultural Committee on Monday, sir, came up with a compromise butter and dairy products proposal that would direct the Secretary of Agriculture to give

---

[1] On September 7, after Governor Dewey's withdrawal, the White House announced that the President sincerely regretted the Governor's decision, and that as a voter of New York and personally as a friend the President had hoped that Governor Dewey's great abilities and years of experience would continue to be at the service of his State.

dairy farmers 80 percent of parity instead of the 75 percent, while allowing dairy products to go down in response to supply and demand. Does this proposal have your endorsement?

THE PRESIDENT. Well, as a matter of fact, as a specific measure to be adopted, it hasn't been brought to my attention or brought up to me in that way.

During all of the period of consultation on this thing, we went over the matter with dairy advisers and groups that congregated here.

I don't know exactly what would be a final decision on this particular point because I have not read its exact language; but, as you do know, I am very much in favor of gradualism in everything that the Government does with respect to agriculture.

The thing that hurts agriculture more than anything else, in my opinion, are rapid fluctuations, particularly of course, the rapid downward fluctuations. If you have rapid upward ones, you usually have, sooner or later, rapid downward ones. We are trying to level off those curves, flatten them out; so anything that would operate to do this gradually, without violating the basic principles and leading you into more and more trouble, would always get good consideration from me.

Q. Marvin Arrowsmith, Associated Press: Mr. President, Sherman Adams suggested the other day that loss of control of Congress to the Democrats in the November election might cause you to decide not to run again in 1956. Would such a development have that effect on your plans?

THE PRESIDENT [*laughing*]. Mr. Arrowsmith, to my knowledge, the matter of 1956, and as it possibly develops, has never yet been discussed in the White House since I have been there or by me with anybody else in anything except some most facetious vein.

Now, I am not one to predict. Actually, as I see it, sufficient unto the day are the evils thereof. [*Laughter*] We have got an awfully big problem to solve today: it is strength at home to give us a chance to do our part in solving these critical international problems, and to make certain that our own people are strong in spirit, strong in understanding and in their determination, and, of course, with the economic and military means to support and implement their determinations.

I am not, by any manner of means, casting my mind forward to '56 at this point.

Q. Merriman Smith, United Press: Not casting your mind what?

THE PRESIDENT. Casting my mind forward to '56. I am talking about these problems of today, that's what I am interested in.

Q. Mr. Smith: You mean you have made no decision?

Q. Ray Scherer, National Broadcasting Company: Mr. Adams also suggested there were two other contingencies under which you might not offer yourself for re-election, but he didn't name them. Would you——

THE PRESIDENT. A funny thing—I will tell you this much: as I started over here this morning he said, "You are probably going to get a question about something," and he said, "I have two secret contingencies that I haven't told you about, and someday I am going to tell you." So I am just as ignorant as you are.

Q. George Herman, CBS Radio: Sir, with the Korean phase of the Geneva conference apparently now terminated, would you care to tell us a little about your administration's view of the future of Korea and American troops there, and the unity of that country?

THE PRESIDENT. I think, first, we must get clearly in our minds just exactly what did happen at Korea, and know all of the, you might say, background of this affair.

I am expecting General Smith home next week, and as quickly as convenient thereafter, I am going to invite into the White House members of both Houses, members of both parties, and let them listen to a detailed explanation of everything that went on. I think there are probably gaps even in my understanding of this thing.

Now, the Korean problem itself: I believe the next step is that the 16 nations report to the United Nations their failure to reach a—I am talking now on the terms of the armistice as I remember them—they have to report their failure to reach a satisfactory agreement, and then the United Nations has to take some action. What that will be, of course, I don't know.

Q. Sarah McClendon, El Paso Times: Mr. President, Congressman Martin Dies told the House yesterday that if we really wanted to stop communism dead in their tracks right now, and not just give lip service to it, that we would cut off from Russia the nonstrategic goods, food, and fiber which she needs most, because he says she is spending 80 percent of her productive energy now in making armaments. What would you say about that?

THE PRESIDENT. Well, it is very difficult to know exactly what would occur with any attempt to cease all trade with the Iron Curtain countries, because, you must remember, the satellites—including Red China—are, after all, different from Russia.

Let us assume there is no trade with anybody in the world through that Iron Curtain; the satellite countries, as I see it, then have only one place to go, and that is to Russia, for anything they need. Consequently, you are building up and strengthening ties that gradually become stronger and stronger, because that vast area includes, generally speaking, the raw materials, the skills, and everything else that is needed to produce a highly productive life.

Now, what you really want to set up in that whole complex, if you can, by every means possible, are centrifugal forces; you want the interests and attention, let us say, of Czechoslovakia and of Bulgaria and of Red China even, looking to the outside world and trying to set up forces there, an attraction away from the center instead of toward the center. I would call it centrifugal as opposed to centripetal forces, what you are trying to devise.

If you just cut off all trade and say, "Go your own way," I am not just so sure as to what the result will be. And the only reason I say this, ladies and gentlemen, is this: there are no easy, simple generalizations to solve the problems of the world today. You have got to take each one, you have got to try to hold it against the background of all possible tangents of direction, all possible results of this action, and then do your best with whatever talents you are endowed to find a decision in this case that will advance you a little bit toward the objective we have—which is to establish a stable peace.

So, I shy away from every single generalization. To say, "Just do this and that is peace," that just isn't true.

Q. Harry Dent, Columbia (S.C.) State and Record: Mr. President, now that the farm fight is getting fairly hot, some of your opponents are charging that in 1952 you told the farmers that you favored farm price parities all the way up to 100 percent of parity. I just wondered what you could tell us this morning——

THE PRESIDENT. One hundred percent in the market place is what I said.

I never said rigid governmental supports at 100 percent, make no mistake. I have been thoroughly consistent on this from the beginning of my understanding of this farm problem; I have never implied or insinuated that I would support 100 percent rigid price supports by the Government.

Q. Mr. Dent: Well, the other day, I think Senator Aiken, in debate with Senator Ellender of Louisiana, said that even if Congress did pass a 90 percent extension for 1 year, that you would veto it; and I just wondered if he was speaking with any authority from you or just on his own when he said that, sir.

THE PRESIDENT. I have made a statement to this group time and again, and I hope I am not, at my age, going to be guilty of making wild statements and then repudiating them. I have said I don't predict in advance what I am going to do about vetoing bills. I take the bill when it comes to me, and then study it.

Q. John Herling, Editors Syndicate: Mr. President, last Thursday night in your address to the Nation you referred to the importance of unemployment insurance, what you called one phase of income insurance, and hoped that Congress would extend the coverage of it as you indicated. Now, another phase of your message early in the year had to do with the duration of unemployment insurance and also the amount. That depends on the States. Now, only 14 of the 48 States have had sessions, and only one or two have done anything about that. Since the problem is a continuing one, do you plan to urge special sessions on the part of the States to deal with this specific problem?

THE PRESIDENT. No. I would intend to urge upon them the great advantages of dealing with this problem in this way. I wouldn't presume to tell Governor Arn of Kansas that he should have a special session; he ought to know his own situation better than I do. But I would urge the problem itself and the great advantage to Kansas and to all the Nation of solving it.

Q. Mr. Herling: Do you plan to take that up at the Governors' Conference in July?

THE PRESIDENT. Well, there are always so many things to take up that I am not going to promise now that that is going to be included. I probably will deal informally with the thing, of course.

Q. Norman Carignan, Associated Press: Yesterday Secretary Dulles said that there is a reign of Communist-type terror going on in Guatemala; also there are reports that the Guatemalan army has asked the

President to get rid of the Communists in government.   I was wondering whether you would comment on the general situation in Guatemala?

THE PRESIDENT.   Of course, it is very disturbing to Americans what has happened here within the last few days; the constitutional guarantees and rights to citizens have been suspended, there have been arrests, apparently, of anti-Communists, and others apparently have fled the country.

You have here a situation developing that is in a pattern that we have looked at with great dismay in more than one country.   So this is the kind of situation that the Caracas resolution was intended to deal with; and, consequently, our Government is in touch with other countries in the Americas, calling their attention to the problem, asking for their suggestions and ideas.   It is a matter that is under the most earnest and urgent study.

I couldn't go beyond that in talking about the situation.

Q. Nat S. Finney, Buffalo Evening News: I won't mention names in connection with this, but a member of the Joint Atomic Energy Committee on the Hill, the other day, made the statement that if a majority of the members of the Atomic Energy Commission vote to accept the minority report on Dr. Oppenheimer, that then the members of the Commission will be questioned by the Joint Committee, but that if the majority report is accepted, the Joint Committee will not question the members of the Atomic Energy Commission.   I would like your views, if you are willing to give them, on the question of the propriety of that sort of action or statement in the Congress.

THE PRESIDENT.   I have not heard before this statement you make; consequently, I don't believe it would even be logical for me to start any wild or quick answers to such a question.   I would want to look at it.   After all, the Atomic Energy Commission is part of the executive branch of Government, and I would have to look at my own responsibilities and see what this is all about.   I haven't heard of it before, and I would have to talk with the Commission itself.

Q. Mr. Finney: Will you do that, sir?

THE PRESIDENT.   Well, I don't know; it depends on what I find out from my preliminary inquiries, how serious this is.

Q. Chalmers Roberts, Washington Post and Times Herald: Mr. President, when Mr. Churchill was over here some years ago on one of his trips, one of your predecessors managed to get him into a White

House press conference. I wonder if, when he comes this time, you would ask him if there would be some way that we could see him or if you could bring him——

THE PRESIDENT. I don't know whether this would satisfy the situation, but I was reminded by a British friend the other day that every time he comes over he is always a luncheon guest at the Press Club downtown. Would that meet the situation? I hadn't thought of this, so I am not going to commit myself to putting pressure on my old friend. But if that would meet the situation, why, I would assume that——

Q. Mr. Roberts: We are greedy, sir; we would like to have him both ways.

Q. Sarah McClendon, El Paso Times: Mr. President, I would say that would meet the situation if the men's Press Club lets the women correspondents attend that luncheon.

THE PRESIDENT [*laughing*]. Look, you are taking up questions now that somebody else is responsible for; I am sure I am not responsible for that.

Q. Ethel Payne, Defender Publications: Mr. President, recently two foreign students in Alabama were subjected to discrimination on a bus in interstate travel. There are several bills before both Houses that are in committee on banning segregation in interstate travel, and I understand that the Attorney General was asked to render an opinion on this. I would like to know if you plan to use any action to get these bills voted out of committee?

THE PRESIDENT. The Attorney General hasn't given me any opinion on the bills; I haven't seen them; I know nothing about them.

I think my general views on this whole subject are well known, and you also know that I believe in progress accomplished through the intelligence of people and through the cooperation of people more than law, if we can get it that way.

Now, I will take a look. I don't know what my opinion is, really, at this minute on that particular law.

Merriman Smith, United Press: Thank you, Mr. President.

NOTE: President Eisenhower's forty-first news conference was held in the Executive Office Building from 10:32 to 10:53 o'clock on Wednesday morning, June 16, 1954. In attendance: 138.

144 ¶ Remarks at the Convention of the National Association of Retail Grocers.
June 16, 1954

I THANK YOU SINCERELY, ladies and gentlemen, for the cordiality of your welcome. I feel that I can claim at least one specific item of kinship with this organization. We were both born in 1890.

I suppose there is no individual closer to the affairs, the business, and the feelings of a community than is the local grocer.

There are many other things about your industry that makes this a very wonderful occasion for me. When I was a boy, I was one of six in my family. We had a quarrel daily as to who could go up and do the chore of bringing the groceries down home. They had a practice then, in grocery stores, that I understand growing efficiency has eliminated—always hoping that the grocer would say you can have one of the dried prunes out of the barrel over there. But better than that was the dill pickle jar that you could dive into, sometimes arm deep almost, and try to get one. I understand that they are not that accommodating anymore; we have got too efficient. When you go around picking things off the shelf, you pay for them. These, you understand, were free. That meant a lot to young boys to whom a nickel looked about as big as a wheel on a farm wagon.

So, you people—you representative people—have been not only sort of a social center for small boys and the rest of the community, particularly in the smaller communities, but they are serving a function in the operation of our economy which is almost unique. Traditionally they are small businesses, they are businesses where Americans are displaying their traits of initiative and courage in taking a risk and doing the job themselves, working for themselves with the greatest kind of independence, and always performing a service for those around them.

The groceryman is, of course, the bridge between the farmer and the consumer, and as such must be acquainted with the desires and the needs of both. He is also a local power, a local figure. Because of this position of his, he exercises influence in our local political life. It is as such that I unashamedly bring to your attention this morning—indeed proudly bring to your attention—the fact that there are now programs before the Congress of the United States which if pushed, as they should be, by every single grocer in our Nation, I am sure will result in laws, in developments in this country, that will do much to insure jobs. It will make certain that this country continues on a high level of economic activity and does so without infringing upon the liberties of the grocer, or the farmer, or the working man—or anybody else.

Now, among other things that this program does, is to reduce the amount of the taxes taken from the entire citizenry. Of course, reducing of taxes is always an acceptable sort of move. We believe that at a time when the Government expenditures are high, and if we are going to continue and improve, support, increasing economic activity, we have got to allow people to have more of their own money to spend instead of spending it through governmental agencies.

Fully as important as tax reduction is tax reform—to try to begin the process of differentiating between the fields of taxation that should pertain to the Federal Government, State government, and local, so that every department of government, and particularly the local departments of government, can do their jobs and have the money with which to finance them.

Indeed, let us not forget this: when we read our Constitution we find that it says there that all powers not herein specifically given to the Federal Government are reserved to the States and to the people. We can observe that meticulously. But if we use the taxing powers so that we take away all of the available taxable revenue from the States and localities, where indeed are the localities and the States going to get the wherewithal to exercise their legitimate functions?

In other words, the taxing power, if not wisely used, will result in centralization of authority, in dependence upon Washington. That is the very thing we are trying to prevent and reverse—a trend which has certainly existed in the past.

Now, on the farm program: the farm program is designed, with the help of every kind of farming expert—in the colleges, in different farming areas, with the help of businessmen, retailers and wholesalers, with every kind of individual we could get that knew something about this problem—for one reason: to take the production of America and move it into markets, into consumption, domestic and foreign, and out of storage. Now, it is just as simple as that.

We must quit piling up storage that alarms everybody, and upsets the business and farming community, and get things to be used—to find, establish, and sustain markets everywhere. We must quit encouraging the production of things that we can't handle for the moment, and get things we do need.

To my mind, unless we can get these existing surpluses isolated from the markets, unless we can stop their inordinate growth, there is just no program in the world that can avoid having its back broken after awhile. Then we will have something disastrous for all of us.

We want to sustain a reliable farm income everywhere, doing it without taking the risk of just breaking the back of a program through accumulating surpluses.

Now, as I see it, it is the kind of government that wants to leave in the hands of all citizens the maximum possible amount of their own money to spend, that wants to emphasize the local responsibility and authority in government, that nevertheless wants to do those things that the Federal Government should properly do to help citizens advantage themselves, to encourage them to take risks and to exercise their own initiative. That is the kind of government that I believe is truly liberal.

With respect to this question, Lincoln said: one of the functions— speaking of functions of Government—is to do for people those things which they cannot do at all, or cannot so well do for themselves as can the Government.

Now, if we take that as the limit as to how the Federal Government should participate with States and localities through loans or anything else, there is no question we will get our necessary highways, we will get our schools, we will get everything, because there will be the wherewithal in the localities to do it. The policy of our Government will continue to support and encourage the growth of our economy. There will be more revenues for local, State, and national, each echelon of government to do its job. And we will go ahead with strength at home and security abroad.

Now that, my friends, that is "once over lightly" what this program before our Congress is intended to do. It has in mind every individual of 160 million. It tries to think of the man who has been physically disabled, and how he can be rehabilitated. It tries to think of those who suffer the awful scourge of chronic illness—incurable, chronic illness. It tries to think of our education. But it tries to do these things by encouraging people, so far as possible, to do these things for themselves, but to put behind them the full power and authority of the Federal Government so that everybody knows he is getting the right kind of assistance, the right kind of help, when the burden becomes too great for the localities to handle themselves.

That is the whole theory. That is the whole purpose. That is the kind of thing that I ask you to get busy, to put your shoulders to the wheel and help get across. We need it, and we need it now. The time is late.

Thank you very much.

NOTE: The President spoke at the National Guard Armory in Washington.

145 ¶ Statement by the President Upon Signing Bill Amending the Railroad Retirement Act of 1937. *June* 16, 1954

I HAVE TODAY approved H.R. 356, "To amend the Railroad Retirement Act of 1937, as amended." This bill repeals, effective October 30, 1951, the so-called dual benefits restriction which was incorporated in section 3(b) of the Railroad Retirement Act by Public Law 234, 82nd Congress. That restriction required that a railroad retirement pension or annuity based in whole or in part on untaxed railroad service before 1937 must be reduced if the annuitant was receiving or was entitled to receive old-age benefits under the Social Security Act.

H.R. 356 will increase benefits for about 36,000 annuitants presently on the rolls by an average of $24 a month, or 20 percent of the average annuity, retroactively to October 30, 1951. Over the next 50 years it is estimated that about 120,000 railroad workers will benefit.

The dual benefits restriction was one of several provisions enacted in the Railroad Retirement Act Amendments of 1951. These amendments increased benefits generally and also provided for closer coordination between the financial and benefits features of the railroad retirement and OASI systems. The purpose of the restriction was to minimize duplicate benefits largely made possible by the 1950 OASI "new start" and to help provide funds to pay for the general increase in railroad benefits.

In approving H.R. 356 I recognize the sentiment of the Congress that the dual benefits restriction was not wholly satisfactory because certain weaknesses in it made it less than fair to the annuitants who were affected. These weaknesses were fully brought out in the extensive hearings before the House and Senate committees and are set forth in the reports on the bill. In some cases the restriction operated to reduce the combined railroad retirement and OASI benefits for an annuitant and his family below the amount of railroad benefits the individual would have received if his service had all been counted under the Railroad Retirement Act. The restriction also operated to keep many annuitants from receiving cost of living increases in OASI benefits enacted by Congress subsequent to October 30, 1951.

On the other hand, it is also apparent that repeal of the dual benefits restriction in itself creates several anomalies which should receive the attention of Congress at an early date. For example, the repeal of the restriction makes it possible for former railroad workers who had obtained railroad retirement benefits based on 30 years of partly or wholly untaxed service to qualify also for full Social Security benefits after as little as six quarters of employment covered by the Old Age and Survivor's Insurance provisions of the Social Security Act.

It is vital that retirement programs operated by the Government be so arranged that they conform to a reasonable overall pattern. It should not be overlooked that today, under all of these systems, many opportunities arise for uneven, and sometimes even windfall benefits, because these systems have not been adequately coordinated with the provisions of Old Age and Survivor's insurance.

The importance of this principle of coordination was recognized when the Congress established the Committee on Retirement Policy for Federal Personnel to make recommendations on the relationship of the several retirement systems for Federal employees with OASI. The railroad retirement system, like the Federal employee systems, is essentially a staff pension plan. Its better coordination with OASI, as has been done in the case of many private staff pension plans, would appear to be needed.

One other important matter that should receive the attention of the Congress is an equitable means of financing the benefits which repeal of the dual benefits restriction will provide. Over the next 50 years it will involve aggregate expenditures estimated at $385 million, and will increase the actuarial deficiency in the railroad retirement account from

0.91% of payroll to 1.06%. While this increase is not particularly great, it cannot prudently be disregarded if the railroad retirement system is to be kept actuarially sound.

NOTE: As enacted, H.R. 356 is Public Law 398, 83d Congress (68 Stat. 250).

146 ¶ Remarks to the National 4–H Club Campers.   *June* 17, 1954

Mr. Secretary, and my young friends:

First, of course, it is my privilege on behalf of the administration to welcome you all here to your Nation's Capital. This I do with very real pleasure. Likewise, I hope I can speak for all of you when I welcome to our shores those among you who are from other lands and who will spend some time with us.

Now, sometime ago, I made a vow that I would never meet during the next few months with any group and make public or private statements that did not have some connection with the program that is now before Congress to be enacted into legislation. Having said those words, I will mention only one little phase of it, in which I hope most of you are interested.

One item in that program asked for the vote for people of your age. It seems to be, for the moment, stymied. But I hope that part of it, at least, you will get behind, and work for as hard as you know how. I personally think that your judgments in the destiny of this Nation are about as good as those of some of us who are many years your senior.

Now, I realize that you are interested, first of all, in the basic occupation of our country, the production of foods and fibers and the preservation of our soil and our water, and that kind of thing. And in all of that work, I wish you every kind of success.

By the way, the delegation here from Arkansas, won't you please assure the 4–H Club that gave me the pig, that the pig is doing well—very well.

Now, I was delighted to find that this year this great group had taken as two of the themes to engage its attention, good citizenship and promotion of world understanding.

Indeed, I think these two subjects are identical. I don't believe you can be a good citizen today without helping to promote world understanding. Certainly, we know that no nation in this modern day, however strong, can live alone. Therefore, if we are going to live, we have to do so in some understanding of the hopes and aspirations, and needs and requirements, and the capacities of the other nations, just as we hope they know something about us.

We want to ship to them our surpluses, particularly our farm surpluses, and we, therefore, must buy in return from them certain things. Now this requires earnest study and understanding on our part, because when we begin to buy things from abroad, there are likely to be parts of our economy temporarily damaged, and maybe people thrown out of work. We have got to think these things through. We have got to think of them not merely from our side, but from the other fellow's side. In this exchange program in which you are now engaged, I see tremendous possibilities. I particularly congratulate those among you who are this year having the opportunity to engage in that particular work.

If you are going thoroughly, earnestly, to study this problem of world understanding, you are not going to limit yourself, either, merely to economic matters. You are going to study the histories, the cultures of other nations, how they came to where they are, how much they have contributed to our civilization, how much, in turn, we can contribute to theirs. Because I assure you, if there is one thing of which I know to be true, there is no true peace in the world except through the understanding you people are studying. That is the reason I put so much of my faith in the future of the world in you people, because you are approaching it at the right end: to understand before you make your conclusions, before you reach these pontifical and weighty decisions that affect the lives of all of us. You are trying to understand, and I can't tell you how much I believe in it, support you, and believe in you.

So, as you go about this work, may God prosper you, because in the real success of this kind is our future happiness, prosperity, and peace.

I hope that as time goes on, I will get to see some of you more intimately than is afforded by this one chance to stand up in front of you and expose you to some of the things that I so deeply believe. Maybe, one of these days, I will get a chance to meet with each of you and sit down and let you do the talking—which I greatly prefer.

Thank you for the compliment of asking me out here. It has been wonderful to see you.

NOTE: The President spoke in the Rose Garden. His opening words "Mr. Secre-tary" referred to Secretary of Agriculture Ezra T. Benson.

147 ¶ Statement by the President Upon Signing Bill Concerning Termination of Federal Supervision Over the Menominee Indian Tribe. *June* 17, 1954

I HAVE TODAY signed H.R. 2828 which provides for the method of terminating Federal supervision over the property and affairs of the Menominee Indian Tribe of Wisconsin on December 31, 1958. This bill, developed after extensive consultation with the Menominee people over a period of many months, is the first to be enacted into law as an outgrowth of the Congressional policy on Indian affairs which was embodied in House Concurrent Resolution No. 108 adopted last summer. That policy calls for termination of Federal supervision over the affairs of each Indian tribe as soon as it is ready for independent management of its own affairs.

The Menominees have already demonstrated that they are able to manage their assets without supervision and take their place on an equal footing with other citizens of Wisconsin and the Nation. I extend my warmest commendations to the members of the Tribe for the impressive progress they have achieved and for the cooperation they have given the Congress in the development of this legislation. In a real sense, they have opened up a new era in Indian affairs—an era of growing self-reliance which is the logical culmination and fulfillment of more than a hundred years of activity by the Federal Government among the Indian people.

In the four and one-half years which remain before Federal supervision is terminated, the Menominee Tribe has authority to employ any specialists it may need in developing plans for a sound business organization to carry on the tribal enterprises. The Tribe will also have the active assistance of the Department of the Interior and the State of Wisconsin during this important period of preparation for full and final independence.

All of the problems of withdrawal of the Federal Government from the field of Indian administration have not been solved by the enactment of this one bill. Nevertheless, I am sure that it will provide useful and sound guide lines for authorizing other Tribes to realize their full potentialities as productive citizens of the United States whenever they can advantageously assume complete responsibility for the management of their affairs.

NOTE: As enacted, H.R. 2828 is Public Law 399, 83d Congress (68 Stat. 250).

148 ¶ Exchange of Letters Between the President and President Coty of France After the Fall of the Laniel Cabinet. *June* 18, 1954

[Released June 18, 1954. Dated June 16, 1954]

My dear President Coty:

I write to assure you that in these troubled days my country remains warm in its sympathy and staunch in its friendship for your country.

It is of the utmost concern to my country, and indeed to peoples everywhere, that France should continue to play her historic role as the champion of liberty, equality, and fraternity, and as a master craftsman of new and better human relationships.

The United States hopes to see realized, while the opportunity still exists, the imaginative and epochal French concept for blending national military forces on the continent of Europe so that they will perform a single service of peace and security. I want to assure you that the pledge of support embodied in my message of April 16 to Monsieur Laniel still stands, and will continue available to his successor.

In Indochina our nation has long shown its deep concern by heavy financial and material aid which continues. The proposals for a united defense which we submitted to Monsieur Laniel represented on our part a momentous and grave decision. Nothing has happened here to change the attitude thus expressed, even though the lapse of time and the events which have come to pass have, of course, created a new situation. But I assure you that we shall be ready in the same spirit to open new discussions as the forthcoming French Government may deem it opportune.

I have mentioned two aspects of our relations which imperatively demand high governmental attention. You can be sure that they will be dealt with upon the foundation of the respect and affection for France which is felt by many millions of individual American citizens. Our past associations have brought sorrows and joys which have indelibly pressed their image upon the very heart of our nations and this is, on our side, a guarantee of our future attitude.

I shall be talking informally with Sir Winston Churchill and Mr. Eden next week and I look forward to resuming with the Government of France such intimate conversations as I have had in the past both as President and previously when I served in Europe in our common cause first of liberation from one tyranny and then of defense against another tyranny.

I extend to you, my dear Mr. President, my respectful greetings.

DWIGHT D. EISENHOWER

NOTE: President Coty's letter, dated June 23, follows:

My dear Mr. President:

I am profoundly moved by the sentiments of understanding that you have so kindly expressed to me.

The friendship of our countries is written in history, it is profoundly embedded in the hearts of the French who do not forget the disinterested aid which in the gravest hours the United States has spontaneously provided on two occasions. This friendship confers on our relations frankness and confidence that has always marked our affairs.

The world must face up to tremendous problems. In agreement with their friends and allies, the United States and France are merging their efforts to preserve the freedom of Europe and to put in the background the conflicts of the past, in order to assure, in peace the independence of the peoples of Southeast Asia. As you have been kind enough to suggest, the French Government is always ready to proceed with the United States Government to examine the problems involved in the reestablishment of peace in the Far East.

In searching for a system upon which the future depends, France continues to be motivated by her desire for freedom and peace. United to all the peoples of the Atlantic Community, whose solidarity guarantees independence, France has decided to contribute to a rapid and realistic solution of the problem of the defense of Europe.

You have been kind enough to give me the assurance that the American Government was disposed to examine, in the most friendly spirit, the principal aspects of the relations between our two countries. This undertaking is particularly valuable, coming from the Chief of the great American nation, who was Commander of the Armies of the Liberation, whose victory has maintained this freedom which we defend together. I can on my part assure you of the desire of the head of the French Government to see reopened, between our two Governments, in the near future, conversations of a confidential and intimate character resulting from inalterable sentiments of friendship.

I pray you, my dear Mr. President, to find here the expression of my respectful and faithful friendship.

RENE COTY

For the President's message of April 16, see Item 84.

149 ¶ Remarks at the National Editorial Association Dinner. *June* 22, 1954

President McIntosh, members of this distinguished audience:

Under the impact of the words of the tribute just paid me by this organization, through your President, I know that you will not expect me to be especially eloquent. I think, when the heart is full, the tongue grows clumsy. But I think that possibly you would allow me to talk to you this evening about a few of the things that are very close to my heart, as I try in my own stumbling way to carry out in some faint degree my duties in the style that President McIntosh's great tribute would suppose that I am doing.

Now, first of all, there is no need to sell me the small town of America. I think for any American who had the great and priceless privilege of being raised in a small town, there remain always with him nostalgic memories of those days. And the older he grows the more he senses what he owed to the simple honesty, the neighborliness, the integrity that he saw all around him, in those days, and took for granted, and that he learns to appreciate only as he grows older and dwells more in other places of the earth.

There is no need to sell me the small town paper. I hope there are those among you who are acquainted with and respect the Abilene, Kansas, Daily Reflector and Chronicle, as much as I do. Certainly, there is no other paper in the world that I read for so many years at a stretch as I did that one.

I was particularly interested in what Mr. Keller said, to the effect that a half-truth cannot make you half-free. In various places in his talk to us, he hinted at a very obvious fact—that truth comprises more than knowledge; there must be some understanding. And this understanding—in the hurly-burly of our world, the complexities, the intricate interdependencies that exist in the world—economic, political, and social interdependencies—to get real understanding is difficult, even among the people that we know to be, in relative terms, at least, enlightened.

If you will bear with me, I would like to talk for a few moments about four types of truths, or facts, that are brought to my attention constantly, each of which has its own elements of truth, but each of which, taken by itself, does not represent in any degree the advancement of the welfare of the United States of America.

The first obvious fact is this, repeated to me in many ways, through correspondence and other types of communication: the United States cannot be an Atlas, it cannot by its financial sacrifices carry all other nations of the world on its own shoulders, and we should stop giveaway programs. Now, this is very true. You could not keep any other country in the world free merely by money. You can't buy or import a heart, or a soul, or a determination to remain free. Consequently, the statement that American so-called giveaway programs are not going to keep the world free, is absolutely true.

Next, I am told: why do you allow nations with whom we are allied to trade with the Reds? And they go on, and they make quite a story about its wickedness. It is, of course, true that when others are trying to destroy us, we should by no means provide them with the ammunition, the guns, the planes, or the direct means of making things with which to destroy us. And we should not allow or we should certainly not agree to our allies doing so.

Another thing that we hear: do not let us get involved in southeast Asia. Let not the United States be in the place of defending the whole world in its freedom, when it really doesn't want freedom. Now, my friends, it is, of course, perfectly true that, again, the United States cannot be strong enough to go to every spot in the world, where our enemies may use force or the threat of force, and defend those nations. Again, unless there is a great determination in those places to remain free, they will in one form or another fall prey to some kind of authority other than the rule of their own people.

Again, I am told this, and this is the fourth factor: let us not trade with countries whose labor and living standards are so far below ours that it hurts some of the industries here at home. Let us not try to expand trade, let us rather raise our barriers and protect our people, whether they be in the mines, or in the shops, or working in any kind of industry, or in agriculture—wherever they may be. And again reason; commonsense shows that we must not merely open the gates and let these floods of supplies come in that would reduce our country to a workless, food-line basis of existence.

Well now, my friends, I want to take a situation in the world that focuses all of these considerations and these facts upon one particular problem that we have to solve.   Over in the western Pacific, the key to its defense is Japan.   Japan comprises 85 million people—industrious, hardworking, inventive.   Actually, the power that they developed against us in World War II was such as to be frightening when we saw what they could do alone.   Consequently, it becomes absolutely mandatory to us, and to our safety, that the Japanese nation does not fall under the domination of the Iron Curtain countries, or specifically the Kremlin.   If the Kremlin controls them, all of that great war-making capacity would be turned against the free world.   All of the soldiers, all of the armies, all of the air force, they could use.   Japan would be given the task of producing all the great navies that they need.   And the Pacific would become a Communist lake.

Now, my friends, what is Japan?   Eighty-five million people, living on an area no larger than California.   Now we of course admit that California is a very wonderful and prosperous place, but as yet there are not 85 million people there.   And even if there were, they would have access to all the markets of the United States on a free basis.

Japan cannot live, and Japan cannot remain in the free world unless something is done to allow her to make a living.

Now, if we will not give her any money, if we will not trade with her, if we will not allow her to trade with the Reds, if we will not try to defend in any way the southeast Asian area where she has a partial trade opportunity, what is to happen to Japan?

It is going to the Communists.

Now, no one of these programs pursued alone could possibly help Japan; and any one of them pursued to an extreme would ruin us.

What we must do, what the statesman must do, what the Congressman must do, is find the answer to this: how do we put all four of these tough problems—these tough facts—together, and get the truth that you people must give to 160 million people.

This business of distributing the truth, I beg to say, is far more than printing a newspaper.   It is getting the facts, and with such wisdom as God gave us, with such dedication to our country as we hope we have inherited from our forefathers to try to sum up; to try to work out in our time programs and policies that will further the kind of United States that Mr. Keller so eloquently described as having brought so much happiness to so many people.

587

We learn, then, that freedom, and the defense of freedom, is a collective job. I took only one example, to show you how these conflicting facts, and they are facts, come together. And now wisdom and understanding is demanded, in order that we may get a solution that will serve the United States.

Some weeks ago, I made a vow before a press conference—by the way, I think my dedication to a free press is possibly proven every Wednesday morning—I made a statement at one of these press conferences that hereafter I would never allow myself to appear in public, or in private, and in speaking of a public question, omit or ignore the opportunity to talk about the programs of legislation before our Congress today.

Now, I am not going to take this program, this evening, and outline it again in the pattern of a State of the Union speech to the Congress—not at all. I do want to point out that the job of keeping our freedoms, including our free press, means an America that is free, if not of anxiety, certainly free of hysterical fear from any threat abroad; which has at home a group of dedicated people, alert to dangers from within as well as from without, determined to do everything possible to see that, as we advance through the social developments of our time, people are served by their country—but in such a way as to preserve always the essentials of the individual freedoms guaranteed by our Constitution, and especially its first ten amendments.

The entire program that has been laid before the Congress has, in some form or another, these purposes in view.

Government, in the attempt to serve all the people, is apt to grow sprawling. As a matter of fact, Mr. Keller in certain instances expressed very emphatically, and rather, let us say, sarcastically at times, some examples of how Government is getting into places where it has no business to be—and I agree with him.

Moreover, I think I can say this: where Government must take over the job of regulating or interfering, or being part of our daily lives, we should so far as possible make that governmental function a local one—at city or township or county and State level, and keep it out of Washington.

One thing that always strikes me is this: Washington can print money to pay for its mistakes, and other governments can't.

So we don't want to blot out efficiency. We want to keep the Government out of too much of your affairs. But on the other hand, we cannot have a Government serving 160 million people in this modern, complex difficult time in which we live, if we just revert to, in the words of the old economic textbook, laissez faire—just let things slide. That can't be done. We can keep Government close to people and try to steer that line that does not ignore the rights of people to good health, to education—everything else.

Remember, I am not saying that the Federal Government does this itself. But we cannot ignore it. On the other hand, let us not tell every farmer what he may raise, and indeed let us not try to tell each newspaper what it may print.

And so before the Congress we place agricultural bills designed to protect all farmers against disasters that they could not have foreseen, and against which they could not protect themselves, designed to help move food into consumption instead of into storage bins, into surpluses.

We have devised tax programs to distribute the load equitably and leave to each person as much money as we possibly can so that he may spend it for himself rather than depend on the wisdom of some bureaucrat in Washington. We devise every kind of program affecting health, insurance plans, old age protection, unemployment protection so that people do things for themselves, knowing that a great Government is back of them to protect them only and especially when misfortune, which they could not avoid, overtakes them.

So we steer a line between laissez faire, which would just let these people look out for themselves, all of them, when they are in our economy incapable often of doing so, and on the other hand the rigid control that is a form of statism.

Now, in very simple words, ladies and gentlemen, that is the program that is before Congress. It runs into many forms. It provides additional laws, for example, by which we may honestly and with absolute respect for every American tenet of law, protect ourselves against any Communist infiltration or subversion.

It does not violate the rights of any person. But it does make certain that we have the weapons to combat those who would destroy us. This is the kind of thing of which we are talking.

And so I come back to this: the responsibility of the newspapers, and I mean the small, local newspapers, which provide so much of the reading opportunity for so many millions of our people in the small towns and rural areas of America. I know, because as I said before, I have read them.

I believe that as you understand and tell the truth, the whole truth, including the relationship of one fact to another, I believe we will protect and perpetuate our freedoms and our national security.

I believe as you fail in that, to that extent America and her freedoms are in danger.

I do not believe you will fail.

I have at times, at least in private, talked about some of the frustrating experiences that are encountered in the office that I am now honored to hold. But there are very inspiring experiences, and one of those is the frequency with which a President of the United States, calling upon any other citizen for assistance or help, gets the most inspiring and favorable response you could imagine—men, women, who say, "Well this is a great sacrifice, but if you tell me it is my duty, here we go."

Now, I would like to say to the editor of every single newspaper in the United States, you also have a duty: to find the truth and project it fearlessly, honestly, and to the utmost ability that your heart and head will allow, to every person that you can reach.

For the very great honor you have done me in this plaque, which I will keep so proudly, for the very warm welcome you have accorded me, I thank you all very much indeed.

Good night.

NOTE: The President's remarks followed the presentation of a plaque paying tribute to him for his "stalwart championship of freedom of the press as being the mightiest weapon a citizenry can wield against the dark forces of tyranny, intolerance and injustice". His opening words

"President McIntosh" referred to Alan C. McIntosh, President of the Association, who made the presentation. Later he referred to Ralph W. Keller, manager of the Minnesota Editorial Association. The dinner was held at the Shoreham Hotel in Washington.

150 ¶ Special Message to the Congress on the Mutual Security Program. *June 23, 1954*

To the Congress of the United States:

I herewith transmit recommendations relating to the mutual security program which, I am deeply convinced, are essential to the efforts of the

United States in the fields of international relations and national defense. These recommendations are the outgrowth of painstaking analyses of present mutual security programs, recent world developments and alternative methods of protecting the nation's interests.

Our mutual security program is based upon the sound premise that there can be no safety for any of us except in cooperative efforts to build and sustain the strength of all free peoples. Above all else communist strategy seeks to divide, to isolate, to weaken. The mutual security program is an important means by which to counter this strategy. It helps us to bolster strength in remote areas which are, nevertheless, vital to our own security. It is mutually advantageous to our own economy and to the economies of the countries to which we give assistance. It meets the communist menace at the front line with practical and effective measures. It serves the ultimate purpose of our foreign policy by expanding the area of hope and freedom, and thus it helps to secure the foundations of a free and peaceful world.

For the new program I urge that the Congress authorize new appropriations to the President in the amount of approximately $3,500,000,-000. This amounts to approximately a 40% reduction in two years. Further reductions in the authorized program at this time, in view of the continuing threat to our national safety, would be unjustified and unsafe. Because the new program is in large measure a continuation of existing programs, its success requires reauthorization for expenditure of funds that are still unexpended.

Measured in terms of functions, about $2,748.4 million of the $3.5 billion of new appropriation authority, or 79%, is for programs essentially of a military nature. Of this amount, $1,580 million is for Mutual Defense Assistance (principally military end-items and training); $945 million is for Direct Forces Support (primarily for supplies and equipment for forces in Southeast Asia and the western Pacific); and $223.4 million is for Mutual Defense Support (principally to sustain abnormally large but essential military programs in certain countries). The remainder consists of $241.3 million for programs in Korea, $256.4 million for Development Assistance (largely in the Near East and South Asia), $131.6 million for Technical Cooperation, and $70.5 million for other programs, including contributions to voluntary programs of the United Nations.

Dividing the $3.5 billion into areas, approximately $900 million is for Europe, $570 million for the Near East, Africa and South Asia, $1,770 million for the Far East and the Pacific, and $47 million for Latin America. Some $165 million is requested for non-regional programs.

Today the continued ruthless drive of communist imperialists for world domination places an especially high premium on our maintenance of close relations with friendly nations. We must provide military assistance to some nations, especially to those of strategic military significance which are willing to join in the common defense effort. A major part both of the nearly $5 billions of expenditures in the current fiscal year and the appropriations authorization requested for the coming year is for programs of a military nature. These amounts are, indeed, substantial. But a common defense system evolved in concert with allies is far less expensive to our people and far more effective for the free world than a defense structure erected only on our soil, consisting only of our forces. Such amounts, moreover, are minuscule compared to the cost of global war which these programs help to prevent.

Recent events in Southeast Asia have created grave uncertainty. The security of that region and the interests of the United States and its allies there are clearly endangered. It is, therefore, critically important that the Congress authorize the appropriation of funds needed to provide military and other assistance to this area and that authority be granted to adjust the use of these funds to rapidly changing conditions.

I also recommend continuance of limited authority to transfer, for use in another geographic area or for a different purpose, funds appropriated for one geographic area or purpose. Other forms of flexibility which proved their value during the past year should also be continued. The United States must be in a position to employ these programs with the utmost speed and precision to accomplish our goals under the swiftly-shifting circumstances of the world.

Our country's participation in Technical Cooperation programs must be vigorously advanced. Certain fundamentals are essential to their success. First, they should provide experts and know-how rather than large amounts of funds or goods, although they should not be allowed to fail due to lack of necessary teaching and demonstration equipment. Second, they should be tightly adjusted to the needs of the host countries. Third, they should be so administered as to reach as many people as possible, helping them raise their own standards of living and solve their own problems. Technical Cooperation programs now before the Congress are based on these fundamentals. These programs are our most effective counter-measure to Soviet propaganda and the best method by which to create the political and social stability essential to lasting peace.

Three months ago I advised the Congress that economic assistance on a grant basis should be terminated as swiftly as our national interest would allow. This concept underlies the new programs. In Europe economic assistance is recommended only for a few local programs of especial importance. As rapidly as feasible in our relationships with other countries, these programs are being supplanted by more durable undertakings in the field of mutually profitable private investment and trade. As such trade and investment expands, the need for grant assistance will further diminish. But this expansion takes time and effort. This requires that in strategically located, underdeveloped areas of the world, some grant assistance must be continued for an additional period of time. Such assistance is also needed for certain countries which lack the economic capacity to establish and equip military forces needed for the common defense.

Notwithstanding the continuing need for such grants, we must strive constantly toward relationships with our friends which are more satisfactory, both to them and to us, than grant assistance. This legislation should, therefore, reserve for loans not less than $100 million of the fiscal year 1955 funds. Such loans would be made where there is reasonable chance of repayment in dollars or in local currencies, and should be extended in a manner that would not substantially impair a country's capacity to borrow from private banking sources, the International Bank for Reconstruction and Development, or the Export-Import Bank. This is a vital step toward the general replacement of grant economic assistance. We shall achieve this goal as quickly as world conditions and our national welfare permit.

In the administration of the mutual security program, agricultural surpluses will be used to strengthen the economies of friendly countries and to contribute in other ways to the accomplishment of our foreign policy objectives. We shall also attempt to use other products of our farms and the output of our industries whenever their use is consistent with the essential objectives of the program, after taking into account such factors as availability, price and quality. In the conduct of these and other mutual security programs a Foreign Operations Administration performs a necessary function and should be continued.

The United States has chosen carefully from among many alternatives in order to chart a sound course in the world.

We have chosen to build defenses with our allies rather than go it alone, because we are convinced that this course is more effective and less costly.

We have chosen to help develop and expand world markets, because we believe that this course will strengthen the economies of all free nations, including our own.

We have chosen to exchange technical knowledge and ideas with our friends, because we believe that course will go far toward countering the effects of communist propaganda, while at the same time promoting peace through improved political and economic stability.

Having embarked upon these courses of action, we shall follow them through. We did not choose the gigantic struggle now endangering the world, but surely this is clear: During periods when the contest is hardest, we must not falter, we must not abandon programs of positive action. Instead, at such a time, we must intensify sensible and positive action.

This program of mutual security is such action; it is one of our most effective, most practical, least costly methods of achieving our international objectives in this age of peril.

I therefore strongly urge enactment of mutual security legislation along the lines I have herein generally outlined.

DWIGHT D. EISENHOWER

151 ¶ Remarks at a Breakfast Meeting of the National Cartoonists Society. *June* 24, 1954

President Kelly, and members of this distinguished audience:

I am deeply touched by this symbol of membership in your organization. Not only have I been a follower of probably the oldest of all cartoons that have been in American papers; I still read Mutt and Jeff when I can get hold of it. But I have been carefully instructed by the Treasury Department on exactly how much help you have been through the years in selling our bonds on a very broad basis, and trying to get every American to feel definitely that he is a partner in this great enterprise.

Now, let me refer for a moment to your Toastmaster's observations with respect to the timing of social events in Washington. I want to assure him that for official Washington we are about 30 minutes from lunch time—by stomach-time, anyway, even though the Secretary of the Treasury and I have both the National Security Council and a Cabinet meeting lying between us and when we will actually get there.

I would like to point out that this meeting, in a way, in its purpose, illustrates something of the great interdependencies of the modern world. I suppose the unthinking would say that the cartoonist is concerned primarily with a few moments of recreation and enjoyment for his readers—for his clientele—and that is that.

Actually, here we find the very practical job of preserving the Government's credit through the distribution of its bonds and keeping our business on a sound basis. And we have another that has been adverted to this morning: the influence of the cartoonist on the present and future life of America. I am quite certain that every one of us should view with the greatest concern, as we think of our beloved country, what are we teaching our own people; what by example, what by everything we do, are we placing before the adult of today, so that he may gain a better understanding of the intricacies and complexities of the problems that seem to face us every day in international and national life?

And above all, what kind of ideals, what kind of characters are we forming among those who must so quickly take over from all the rest of us?

I have three grandchildren, the eldest 6 and the next one 5, and already I find that Sunday mornings is the big event of their lives. Because then they seem to get more cartoons than normally, and they are on the floor, and they are with them, living with their heroes that they find there in pen and ink and color.

And, gentlemen, I couldn't think of a greater opportunity, as I sat here and contemplated it this morning, that comes to anyone than is in your hands. The church, the school, the home—all of the indispensable agencies trying to implant truth, some wisdom and the great faith that we need, if we are to battle our way through the complex and intricate problems that face us—are all important. And so are you. Because those minds, picking up true values, proper values, from what you place before them, are reinforced in the faith that they get in their schoolrooms, as they repeat the Pledge to the Flag, that they get in the Sunday School room, what they absorb at their mother's knee.

Now, of course, I am not trying to make a perfect instrument out of anything in this world. We are human. And perfection seems, almost, to repel us at times.

By way of complete digression, I had a teacher once, and I thought I was very smart in getting a solution to a problem directly, and I guess I made a little show of myself. He kept me in, and he said, "I want to tell you one thing, young fellow, if you find that you are never wrong in this world, if you want to get along with people, you had better manufacture a situation in which you can be wrong and get up and say it."

That is what I mean. I am not urging that we not be human. Of course we must be human, because only in that way will we appeal to these young minds. But I am not talking about details. I am talking about standards of truth and honesty, and above all, dedication to a principle, and to a country.

So, for the very great honor you have done me in admitting me, along with our Secretary of the Treasury—if we weren't English-speaking people, if we were Latin, I could pause here and go into some ecstasies about the character of our Secretary of the Treasury; but since we are of the English-speaking race, I'll say: he's pretty good.

But, as you do me the honor of admitting me, along with him, to this honorary membership, I assure you that it is not only with the passing pride that you have so complimented me that I accept it, but it is with a very deep appreciation that I now belong—even if only on this basis— to a group that can and I know will do much to keep our country straight and true and strong in the future.

Thank you very much.

NOTE: The President spoke in the auditorium of the Perpetual Building Association in Washington. His opening words "President Kelly" referred to Walt Kelly, President of the Society and toastmaster for the occasion, who presented President Eisenhower with an engraved T-square as a symbol of his honorary membership.

152   ¶ Statement by the President Upon Signing Bill Relating to the Administrative Jurisdiction Over Certain Public Lands in Oregon.
June 24, 1954

I HAVE TODAY signed S. 2225 "Relating to the administrative juris-diction of certain public lands in the State of Oregon, and for other purposes."

My action in doing so represents the settlement of a controversy over some 462,000 acres of so-called "O and C" lands which has persisted over many, many years. The lands lie within the indemnity limits of the Oregon and California Railroad land grant originally authorized in 1866. Under this Act, the controverted lands will be administered by the Secretary of Agriculture as national forest lands and revenues there-from will be distributed to the Oregon counties in accordance with laws governing distribution of receipts from "O and C" lands. The measure furthermore authorizes land exchanges between the Department of Agri-culture and the Department of the Interior to end the "checker-board" pattern of jurisdiction which has plagued the administration of public lands in Oregon in the past.

I congratulate Senator Guy Cordon and Congressman Harris Ells-worth for the part they have played in bringing this matter to a solution.

NOTE: As enacted, S. 2225 is Public Law 426, 83d Congress (68 Stat. 270).

153   ¶ Letter to Dr. Chester I. Barnard, Chairman, National Science Board, Concerning United States Participation in the International Geophysical Year.   *June* 25, 1954

[Released June 25, 1954. Dated June 24, 1954]

Dear Dr. Barnard:

I appreciate your letter with respect to the United States program for participation in the International Geophysical Year.

51986—60——41   597

I am glad to support this undertaking. It is a striking example of the opportunities which exist for cooperative action among the peoples of the world. As I understand it, some thirty nations will unite their scientific resources for a simultaneous effort, extending over two years, to penetrate the basic geophysical forces which govern the natural environment in which we live. Under especially favorable conditions, scientists of many nations will work together in extending man's knowledge of the universe. The findings of this research will be widely disseminated throughout the world, aiding in the further development of telecommunications, aviation, navigation, and weather forecasting. It is doubtful whether any single nation could undertake such a program. Acting in concert, each participating nation, contributing within its means, secures the benefits of the program.

The United States has become strong through its diligence in expanding the frontiers of scientific knowledge. Our technology is built upon a solid foundation of basic scientific inquiry, which must be continuously enriched if we are to make further progress. The International Geophysical Year is a unique opportunity to advance science, while at the same time it holds the promise of greater technological gains both for ourselves and for other nations. I am sure that our participation in this far-reaching effort will very materially strengthen our bonds with the many cooperating nations and make a constructive contribution toward the solution of mutual problems.

Sincerely,

DWIGHT D. EISENHOWER

NOTE: Dr. Barnard's letter, dated June 22 and released with the President's reply, expressed the Board's appreciation for the President's support of the International Geophysical Year program. The White House release containing the exchange of letters stated that on June 7 the President had transmitted to Congress a request for supplemental appropriations for fiscal year 1955 which included a request for $2,500,000 for the National Science Foundation to permit preparations for U.S. participation in the IGY program scheduled for 1957–58.

154   ¶ Joint Statement by the President and Prime Minister Churchill.   *June* 28, 1954

IN THESE FEW DAYS of friendly and fruitful conversations, we have considered various subjects of mutual and world interest.

I. WESTERN EUROPE

We are agreed that the German Federal Republic should take its place as an equal partner in the community of Western nations, where it can make its proper contribution to the defense of the free world. We are determined to achieve this goal, convinced that the Bonn and Paris Treaties provide the best way. We welcome the recent statement by the French Prime Minister that an end must be put to the present uncertainties.

The European Defense Community Treaty has been ratified by four of the six signatory nations, after exhaustive debates over a period of more than two years. Naturally these nations are unwilling to disregard their previous legislative approvals or to reopen these complex questions.

In connection with these treaties, the United States and the United Kingdom have given important assurances, including the disposition of their armed forces in Europe, in order to demonstrate their confidence in the North Atlantic Community and in the EDC and the Bonn Treaties.

It is our conviction that further delay in the entry into force of the EDC and Bonn Treaties would damage the solidarity of the Atlantic nations.

We wish to reaffirm that the program for European unity inspired by France, of which the EDC is only one element, so promising to peace and prosperity in Europe, continues to have our firm support.

II. SOUTHEAST ASIA

We discussed Southeast Asia and, in particular, examined the situation which would arise from the conclusion of an agreement on Indochina. We also considered the situation which would follow from failure to reach such an agreement.

We will press forward with plans for collective defense to meet either eventuality.

We are both convinced that if at Geneva the French Government is confronted with demands which prevent an acceptable agreement regarding Indochina, the international situation will be seriously aggravated.

III. ATOMIC MATTERS

We also discussed technical cooperation on atomic energy. We agreed that both our countries would benefit from such cooperation to the fullest extent allowed by U.S. Legislation.

IV.

In addition to these specific matters, we discussed the basic principles underlying the policy of our two countries. An agreed declaration setting forth certain of these will be made available tomorrow.

155   ¶ Joint Declaration by the President and the Prime Minister of the United Kingdom. *June 29, 1954*

AS WE TERMINATE our conversations on subjects of mutual and world interest, we again declare that:

(1) In intimate comradeship, we will continue our united efforts to secure world peace based upon the principles of the Atlantic Charter, which we reaffirm.

(2) We, together and individually, continue to hold out the hand of friendship to any and all nations, which by solemn pledge and confirming deeds show themselves desirous of participating in a just and fair peace.

(3) We uphold the principle of self-government and will earnestly strive by every peaceful means to secure the independence of all countries whose peoples desire and are capable of sustaining an independent existence. We welcome the processes of development, where still needed, that lead toward that goal. As regards formerly sovereign states now in bondage, we will not be a party to any arrangement or treaty which would confirm or prolong their unwilling subordination. In the case of nations now divided against their will, we shall continue to seek to achieve unity through free elections supervised by the United Nations to insure they are conducted fairly.

(4) We believe that the cause of world peace would be advanced by general and drastic reduction under effective safeguards of world armaments of all classes and kinds. It will be our persevering resolve to promote conditions in which the prodigious nuclear forces now in human hands can be used to enrich and not to destroy mankind.

(5) We will continue our support of the United Nations and of existing international organizations that have been established in the spirit of the Charter for common protection and security. We urge the establishment and maintenance of such associations of appropriate nations as will best, in their respective regions, preserve the peace and the independence of the peoples living there. When desired by the peoples of the affected countries we are ready to render appropriate and feasible assistance to such associations.

(6) We shall, with our friends, develop and maintain the spiritual, economic and military strength necessary to pursue these purposes effectively. In pursuit of this purpose we will seek every means of promoting the fuller and freer interchange among us of goods and services which will benefit all participants.

DWIGHT D. EISENHOWER
WINSTON S. CHURCHILL

156 ¶ Veto of Bill Conveying Certain Public Lands to Jake Alexander. *June 29, 1954*

To the House of Representatives:

I return herewith without my approval, H.R. 1128, entitled "An Act authorizing the Secretary of the Interior to issue to Jake Alexander a patent in fee to certain lands in the State of Alabama."

This private bill authorizes and directs the Secretary of the Interior to convey without consideration to Jake Alexander 160 acres of unappropriated public lands withdrawn from entry as part of the William B. Bankhead National Forest, Alabama.

I feel that this special legislation is unnecessary because cases of this kind can and should be taken care of under existing law. Public Law 159, 83rd Congress, broadened the Color of Title Act of December 22, 1928 specifically to cover claims similar to the one involved in H.R. 1128.

A basic requirement of the Color of Title Act is payment to the United States of the appraised value of lands patented thereunder. In this respect I feel that H.R. 1128 would discriminate against the interest of the United States, as well as other color-of-title claimants, by exempting this particular claimant from payment of any consideration.

DWIGHT D. EISENHOWER

157 ¶ The President's News Conference of June 30, 1954.

THE PRESIDENT. I understand, ladies and gentlemen, that we are privileged this morning to have quite a group of editors from southeast Asia and Japan with us. For my part, I extend to them a warm welcome, and am delighted they are here.

I have no announcements this morning; I have one request to make on you people. Last year, in the Fourth of July weekend there were 400 Americans killed as a result of holiday activity. Now, I would like to see what this group, through newspapers, television, and radio, can do to cut that in half this year. I would like to get your help now on something and work at it every day from now until the Fourth of July weekend, and through it.

I don't know how much you can do; I don't know how much leeway there is. But I do know that it would be a very worthy cause to devote your energies to.

Thank you very much. We will now have questions.

Q. Merriman Smith, United Press: Mr. President, in connection with the current debate in Congress over your farm program, one of our clients has asked me to ask you this: whether you consider the Republican loss of the House in 1948 to have been due to the farm vote on the issue of flexible supports?

THE PRESIDENT. Well, Merriman, first of all, at that time I certainly was not a political analyst, even if I could so qualify now. I don't know why they lost the House that year and, as you people also know, I am not particularly interested in turning back and trying to unearth every mistake of the past; I never have been.

We have a problem now, and through the past many months I have devoted a real maximum of time to doing my part in developing a program I thought was good for all the United States, including all the farmers in the United States. I believe in that program.

Now, I don't know about '48, but I know in '54 we have to have a program that gets away from the terrible defects of the program that has been on the books.

Q. Kenneth M. Scheibel, Gannett News Service: Mr. President, the House tomorrow is supposed to begin debate or probably vote on the farm bill as it now stands. Do you plan any last-minute appeal to the members to remove the 90 percent provision which is now in the legislation?

THE PRESIDENT. Well, if I can think of any more persuasion to apply, I would certainly put it out in every way I know. I believe that the rigid price supports of these so-called basics is damaging the farmers of the United States, and all the United States. I have put my case as strongly as I know how, so I have no plans at this minute for doing anything additional.

But I must say this: if I thought I could be more persuasive than I have been, I would be right on the job.

Q. Mr. Scheibel: Do you feel that these high price supports are having an effect on the cost of food?

THE PRESIDENT. I think it would be certain they have some, but I do know this: they are encouraging the production of food that is now in such excess, so much in surplus, that we have no place to put it; and we have to ask for more and more money to make these loans. It is getting to be really a back-breaking job.

Now, just exactly how far this is reflected in the cost of food, I can't say because I don't know the statistics.

Q. Chalmers M. Roberts, Washington Post and Times Herald: I would like to ask you, sir, the same question which I put to Prime Minister Churchill at his press luncheon; it is this: what are the possibilities for peaceful coexistence between Soviet Russia and Communist China, on the one hand, and the non-Communist nations on the other?

THE PRESIDENT. Of course, that almost calls for a very long explanation; I will try to limit my comments to a very few.

For a long, long time everybody in the United States has urged that we attempt to reach a proper basis for peaceful coexistence. We have found, though, an aggressive attitude on the part of the other side that has made such an accomplishment or consummation not easy to reach. In other words, there must be good faith on both sides. Moreover, let us make certain that peaceful coexistence does not mean appeasement in the sense that we are willing to see any nation in the world, against its will, subordinated to an outside nation. For an answer on that one, I would refer you to the document we issued yesterday as a statement of purpose.

So, I would say that within the limits I have just so briefly alluded to, why, I say the hope of the world would be that kind of an existence, because, certainly, we don't expect to be eliminated; and certainly, I think, it would be silly to say you can eliminate the other instantly. We have got to find ways of living together.

Q. Mrs. May Craig, New England Papers: Mr. President, does not the British proposal of a nonaggression pact mean that they would ask us to agree not to help unwillingly unsubordinated peoples?

THE PRESIDENT. Not to help——

Q. Mrs. Craig: Yes. If they were unwillingly subordinated and they asked us to help them, would we agree not to help them with force to get them free?

THE PRESIDENT. Well, are you asking this question: are we ready now to go to war to free somebody in the world that we find is not completely free? Is that it?

Q. Mrs. Craig: Not exactly, sir. I am speaking of the Vietnamese, the possible agreement between the Red Chinese and the French to subordinate Vietnamese to the Communists, and our possible agreement that we would support that situation.

THE PRESIDENT. How would we support it? We are not a party to any agreement in the Vietnamese area.

Q. Mrs. Craig: I am asking you if we would support them.

THE PRESIDENT. Did you read that declaration?

Q. Mrs. Craig: Yes, sir.

THE PRESIDENT. I ask you, Mrs. Craig, to read it again, and I mean exactly what I say in it. I will not be a party to any treaty that makes anybody a slave. That is all there is to it.

Q. Norman Carignan, Associated Press: Mr. President, the fighting in Guatemala has apparently ended with the defeat of the Communists.

I wonder if you would give us your views on the significance of what we have witnessed there, the struggle that we have witnessed there?

THE PRESIDENT. You have asked me a different kind of a question; the significance could be very deep, it could be very local. I think it has not yet been analyzed carefully enough so that we know all of its significance. But I understand Secretary Dulles is going on the air this evening to give a rather full explanation of the whole occurrence, as we understand it.

I did hear this morning—my report was—that the Communists and their great supporters were leaving Guatemala. If I would try to conceal the fact that that gives me great satisfaction, I would be just deceitful. Of course it has given me great satisfaction.

Q. Nat Finney, Buffalo Evening News: Mr. President, may we put your statement to the effect that you will not be a party to any treaty that makes anybody a slave, in direct quotations?

THE PRESIDENT. You can.

Q. James B. Reston, New York Times: Does your statement on Indochina, sir, mean that you will not cooperate in any way with an armistice in Indochina that partitions Viet-Nam?

THE PRESIDENT. Oh, no, I don't say that I am going to stand here, and in the absence of studies and analyses of any proposal made, I don't say that I won't go along with some of it.

I say I won't be a party to a treaty that makes anybody a slave; but to make such a statement doesn't mean you are not going to study every single region, every single incident that comes up, and decide what to do at the moment.

Q. Mr. Reston: But if Viet-Nam is partitioned, will not the northern part of the country then be left under Communist control?

THE PRESIDENT. I don't know what kind of a thing it's going to be yet. As a matter of fact, let us assume this: let's assume that there is going to be ample opportunity given for the migration within these areas of any people, not merely the Armed Forces, but any peoples, and ample time to do it if they want to transfer. I don't know what kind of a deal there will be there; I am just as much puzzled as anybody else on that one.

Q. John W. Vandercook, American Broadcasting Company: Mr. President, yesterday afternoon the House Foreign Affairs Committee approved an amendment to the foreign aid bill which, in effect, would deprive any Asian nation which joined in a treaty of the Locarno type from any further American military or economic aid. Do you regard that as harmful or hurtful in the formation of foreign policy?

THE PRESIDENT. I did not read the exact terminology of the amendment itself, but I did have a telephone message sent to find out from our people working on this whether it would limit us in what we are trying to do. The answer was, no, it would be all right.

Q. Mr. Vandercook: It would fit in——

THE PRESIDENT [*continuing*]. I don't know of any difficulty about it.

Q. Sarah McClendon, El Paso Times: Sir, there seems to be some disagreement between you and your Republican congressional campaign committee chairman, Congressman Simpson of Pennsylvania, about the Randall Commission. He told the House that it would be infinitely worse than the present reciprocal trade law, and said, "You would throw up your hands in horror if you would see how those hearings were held; no opportunity for businessmen to come in and tell their tales, no opportunity for cross-examination, and an entirely unfair way to conduct a hearing if you want to find out the effects on the American businessman." He says they will have to throw out the Randall Commission and have extensive hearings to write an entirely new trade bill next year. I wonder if you will be receptive to different views on trade?

THE PRESIDENT. That statement hasn't been made to me, and I think I will wait on that one until it is made to me.

I would remark on this: I think Mr. Randall is a fairly successful businessman.

Q. Douglas B. Cornell, Associated Press: Mr. President, would you care to say anything about the decision of the AEC in the Oppenheimer case?

THE PRESIDENT. No, I don't want to comment on it. The decision was made in the normal procedures. There are men there that I trust. I have not myself studied the findings and the final decision. I just read in the paper, actually, that the vote was 4 to 1.

Q. Robert J. Donovan, New York Herald Tribune: Sir, from what you now hear and know, what do you think the Republican chances are in November?

THE PRESIDENT. There seems to be a very great interest in casting every public figure in the terms of a prophet. Certainly it is something I know very little about.

I will tell you: I have believed from the beginning that the American people want to see a well thought out, comprehensive program, dealing with our principal affairs abroad and our principal affairs at home, put before the Legislature and enacted into law. That program we have labored very earnestly to produce, and we have laid it before the Congress.

Now, no one has ever thought that in every detail it would be enacted. But I do believe that if the results are achieved in Congress that I still believe are going to be achieved, which is that the great bulk of that program is enacted into law, the supporters of that kind of action are going to be favorably considered by the voters.

I am just not going to predict any more accurately than that, but I believe thoroughly that the American people want a constructive program that is concerned with the future of America.

Q. Roscoe Drummond, New York Herald Tribune: Mr. President, after the close of the Mundt hearings, Senator Potter came over to call on you. I wondered if you could tell us anything of your conversations and whether you found yourself in agreement with Senator Potter?

THE PRESIDENT. Well, now, I will tell you perfectly truthfully, Senator Potter has been to see me periodically. I admire and like him, and I don't remember in the slightest degree what was the subject of the last conversation we have had; I simply don't. If it were something that were in the public domain, I would be glad to talk about it; but I just don't recall what it was we talked about at this moment.

Q. Milton Freudenheim, Akron Beacon Journal: Do you feel, sir, that the country is safer and more secure now that Dr. Oppenheimer no longer is working for us?

THE PRESIDENT. I think you had better go and ask the Atomic Energy Commission. They are responsible for this. They have a very delicate and tough job to do; I think they are the ones to ask.

Q. Charles von Fremd, CBS Television: Mr. President, the day before yesterday after the regular morning legislative conference with your legislative leaders, the Speaker of the House and Senator Knowland told us that they had had a briefing from Secretary Dulles in which he said, among other things, that the outlook in the Far East is more encouraging, but they declined to give us the reasons for that outlook on the part of the Secretary of State. I wonder if you can give us any inkling as to why we should now regard the Far East as possibly more encouraging?

THE PRESIDENT. Such an opinion as was expressed is a combination of so many factors, none of which, I think, is decisive in itself, that it would be almost futile, short of an hour's conversation, to try to give you the picture of what's in anyone's mind, including mine.

Let us take one single thing: when Mr. Churchill and Mr. Eden came over here, there was very vast concern in this country about the difficulties seeming to stand in the way of us reaching reasonable agreements about our several problems in the world. I think that visit did much to get this thing back on the rails, recognizing the truth, you might say, to the fore, recognizing that there is no possibility that any two nations will always see eye to eye on every detail. Yet our broad purposes and our actual convictions and beliefs, as to the best application of those purposes in particular areas, were clearly established as common to both of us.

Consequently, I would say that that is one item that gives us greater encouragement and greater belief. You can go into numerous things, certain of the statements of the new Premier of France, and so on, that give some encouragement, but you have to wait to see.

Q. Ray Scherer, National Broadcasting Company: Mr. President, Mr. Churchill had some rather generous things to say about you, and I wonder if you would like a chance, perhaps, to reciprocate? [*Laughter*]

THE PRESIDENT. I would say, with respect to that, I have been saying them ever since I knew him, and I doubt that any further word of mine is necessary to add to the luster of his reputation.

As you people know, I regard him not only as one of my warmest foreign friends, but I have served with him intimately in many kinds of operations now for, well, let's see, 12 years and my admiration for him is as high as ever.

Q. L. Edgar Prina, Washington Star: Mr. President, do you consider the Oppenheimer case closed, or would you, in the event it were made, consider a plea from Dr. Oppenheimer?

THE PRESIDENT. I am one of those persons that believe that any citizen in the world that believes himself abused has a right to appeal. If he wanted to make an appeal, of course he would be listened to. And I would think the next place it would be referred by me would be, let's say, the Attorney General to make a complete analysis and to tell me what my own prerogatives, authorities, and responsibilities in the matter are. I haven't looked up those things in detail.

Q. James Reston, New York Times: Mr. President, could I ask you just one more question about Oppenheimer in order to keep the record straight? You said the case was the responsibility of the Atomic Energy Commission. As I understand it, the Atomic Energy Commission never discussed the case until it received a letter from you on the 3d of December ordering the investigation. Could you tell us about that December 3d meeting, what the background of that was?

THE PRESIDENT. I don't recall any meeting. I recall that I received a report that was very disturbing to me, and I forwarded it to the Atomic Energy Commission with the certainty in my own mind that it would be thoroughly investigated.

Exactly what we said at that time, Mr. Reston, I haven't the slightest idea. I took the action that seemed almost compulsory under the circumstances.

Q. Eliyahu Salpeter, Haaretz (Tel Aviv): Mr. President, it has been reported that in the talks with Sir Winston Churchill, the Middle East has also been discussed. Could you tell us whether an understanding has been reached on a joint policy on the Middle East, particularly on the Suez, on the northern tier, and on Arab-Israel relations?

THE PRESIDENT. No. I think I understand your question, which was: has any specific agreement been reached as to the character of the arrangements we would like to see established in the Middle East?

Q. Mr. Salpeter: Yes.

THE PRESIDENT. I would say that with respect to the Suez Canal, the question is one of the Egyptian Government with the British Government.

Of course, the situation was explained to us when our friends were here; but as far as I know, there is no fixed final position. They gave this merely to us as a matter of information on a confidential basis; I would want to say no more about it.

Q. Richard Wilson, Cowles Publication: Mr. President, to what extent have you and Mr. Churchill discussed the H-bomb, the use of the H-bomb, and the control of it?

THE PRESIDENT. Well, as I think I told you ladies and gentlemen before Mr. Churchill came, I was quite certain there would be no problem of common interest to us extending over the world that we would not discuss; and, of course, we did so.

Now, there were no specifics reached. I told you there was no agenda for this conference, and that was correct; so there were no specific agreements to be signed and sealed or handed to our separate governments. Our conversations were merely searching out our understandings as to how we would approach different problems. There is nothing specific to report on the question that you raised, nothing.

Q. Henri Pierre, Le Monde (Paris): Mr. President, there has been an exchange of letters between you and President Coty of France. Does it imply that a visit of Mr. Mendes-France is considered, and would you welcome that visit?

THE PRESIDENT. You will recall that I expressed in a letter—they were made public, weren't they? [*Chorus of "Yes"*] I expressed in my letter a desire to reopen negotiations; and he replied in the hope that something of that kind could be done.

However, let us remember that Mr. Mendes-France is very preoccupied with a very difficult job. For our part, we will be glad to talk to anybody about these great problems of the world when they are in position to do so.

Q. George Herman, CBS Radio: Mr. President, some weeks ago you told us that the next step for Korean peace would be the return of General Smith and discussions with him. Can you tell us now, sir, what the prospects are for Korean peace and the withdrawing of our troops?

THE PRESIDENT. I would say at the moment there is little change in the situation. As you people know, there was no solid agreement reached there.

Q. Joseph Chiang, Chinese News Service: Mr. President, recently six Far Eastern countries, Hong Kong, the Philippine Islands, Formosa, and others held a collective defense against communism conference at Chinhae, Korea, namely seeking American aid and your great leadership. Would you care to comment, sir?

THE PRESIDENT. I think there has been no specific request placed upon this Government in this respect. Certainly there has been no analysis and study presented to me.

However, it is a question I will be glad to look up and see where we stand. It hasn't been put on my desk yet.

Q. Edward T. Folliard, Washington Post and Times Herald: Mr. President, Vice President Nixon made a speech the other day. His thesis, as I understood it, was that the Acheson foreign policy was to blame for the loss of China, and from that flowed the war in Korea and

the difficulty in Indochina. The Democrats didn't like it very much.
I wondered if you had any observations to make about it?

THE PRESIDENT. First of all, let's recognize this: each individual in
this country is entitled to his own opinions and convictions.

The next thing is, I admire and respect and like the Vice President. I
think he is a very splendid American.

Thirdly, I think my own job is to look at America today and to look
ahead. I carry administrative and executive responsibilities and planning
responsibilities that don't fall on some of the other individuals; so I just
simply haven't time to go back.

My belief is this: we must seek agreements among ourselves, with respect to foreign policy, that are not confined to any party. We must get
every American to studying these things and reaching conclusions regardless of party, because they are too important. Regardless of what party
takes over, there must be a stability or there is no foreign policy.

Now, as to exactly what he said or what this was, taken in context, I
don't know; I have never seen his speech. But as I say, everybody is
entitled, I think, to his own opinion.

Q. Carleton Kent, Chicago Sun-Times: Do your remarks about the
Vice President mean that from now on members of the Cabinet do not
have to clear with you any speeches they may make in the public forum?

THE PRESIDENT. I think you have been here long enough to know that
the Vice President is not a member of the Cabinet; I invite him to all
meetings.

Q. Mr. Kent: Yes, sir.

THE PRESIDENT. No member of the Cabinet, I believe, would make a
foreign policy speech without consulting with the State Department,
and if there is any question in the mind of the Secretary of State, certainly they would clear with me.

In this case, I don't know; but I assume whatever the talk was, it
was made on an individual responsibility. As I say, if he made the
speech, I know this: he believes what he said. But I didn't see the speech.

Q. Edward T. Folliard, Washington Post and Times Herald: Rightly
or wrongly, sir, we are in the habit of saying that a Vice President speaks
for the administration. If he makes a speech of that kind we say that is
the administration viewpoint. Now, perhaps we have been wrong in
saying that. Should we make a distinction?

The President: Well, are you trying to make one swallow a summer? [*Laughter*]

I am saying that normally I think that the Vice President is kept in such close contact with everything that is going on that he would know and would reflect what is administration thinking. Certainly neither I nor anyone else is ready to say that any other individual is always going to state exactly the things the way I would state them, and exactly as I believe.

Now, you are not going to get me in a position of condemning my Vice President, because I repeat, I like and admire and respect him.

The mere fact that I might not have said it doesn't make it something that I am going to be disturbed about too much. But I would say this: you can normally take it, when he talks, he is talking pretty much the language of this administration. I thoroughly have this belief: no President has the right to go through his career here without keeping the next in line thoroughly informed of what are the big problems, so he would know how to take over if misfortune would overtake the Chief Executive. So he stays so close in, and normally we find our minds running so closely the same that I wouldn't try to excommunicate him from this party if I were you. [*Laughter*]

Q. Paul R. Leach, Chicago Daily News: Can you say anything about the conversations with Mr. Churchill on his idea of conferences with Malenkov in Moscow?

THE PRESIDENT. Of course, all of us have announced time and again we are ready to do anything in the world to confer with anyone if we can become convinced, through deeds or any other way, that they are sincere, that the other side is sincere.

We believe—we know we are sincere in the search for peace. If there is any proof of the other side that they will keep their agreements, I think we would be, all of us, quite content to do almost anything to advance that cause.

We talked about it, insofar as I know, only in that regard. He didn't propose to me anything specific or "Let's agree to this deal or that deal or the other," not at all.

Q. Merriman Smith, United Press: Mr. President, could you tell us your reasons for ordering the AEC to make a private power agreement for getting some additional power put in through the TVA?

THE PRESIDENT. It's a rather long and complicated story. I told you people long ago that the TVA was a historical fact, that it was going to be supported, and particularly supported in the purposes written into the law for which it was established.

Now, as time goes on, we find that TVA has gone far beyond the establishment of steam plants to firm up maximum water power developed in the waters of that region. We find projects for installing, building, TVA power plants way out on the periphery of this area, which would mean finally that they could best deliver their power on beyond that; and I know of no way in which this thing would be limited.

The only thing that I want with respect to that is a very good look from every angle—tell us what is the best future for that region, how far we can continue to build up this area at the expense of others. Maybe we should be building the Missouri River or the Susquehanna or the Penobscot or some other.

One of the contentions made was that they were under an immediate shortage, something had to be done because of this great portion of the power taken by the AEC. The AEC says that they have the authority to buy their power for a given number of years under private purchase. The comparisons of cost, as based on original layout and the annual cost of this power, are long and involved, but it looked like a good thing to buy this power privately so that we can get a really good look as to where we are going into the future in terms of expansion. You see, I have States, representatives of Massachusetts, New York, Indiana, coming to me and saying, "You are taking our taxes and building up cheap power some place and taking our industries out."

I don't know exactly where all of the truth lies in this thing, and I am trying to find out. This is just a way to give us a chance to study the thing thoroughly.

Q. Sarah McClendon, Sherman (Texas) Democrat: Mr. President, back to the Nixon speech, Mr. Sam Rayburn, who comes from Sherman Democrat territory, told the House yesterday, he said in so many words, the bipartisan foreign policy you want was threatened by the Nixon speech, and he sort of warned that if any more speeches came out like that, that hurt the Democrats' feelings very deeply, that there might not be any bipartisan foreign policy. Under those circumstances, would you consider asking Mr. Nixon to apologize? [*Laughter*]

THE PRESIDENT. I told you that I liked and respected him, and I think if Dick Nixon ever finds any reason for apologizing for his own actions, he will do it without any advice from me.

Now, I am working for a proper, long-range, commonly supported foreign policy, and I am not going to give up just because someone may hurt my feelings or threaten me or anything else. I am going to continue working.

Merriman Smith, United Press: Thank you, Mr. President.

NOTE: President Eisenhower's forty-second news conference was held in the Executive Office Building from 10:33 to   11:06 o'clock on Wednesday morning, June 30, 1954. In attendance: 184.

158 ¶ Exchange of Messages Between the President and the President of Mexico on the Rio Grande Flood Disaster. *July 1, 1954*

His Excellency
Adolfo Ruiz Cortines
President of the United Mexican States

I join with the people of the United States of America in expressing to Your Excellency and the people of Mexico profound sympathy in the tragic disaster wrought by flood waters along the Rio Grande which has brought untold suffering to many persons in both countries. Our thoughts and prayers go out to those bereaved and left homeless.

DWIGHT D. EISENHOWER

NOTE: The President of Mexico's reply, released July 3, follows:

To the President of the United States:

In thanking your Excellency very cordially for your sympathetic expressions occasioned by the floods along the Rio Grande, may I assure you that the people of Mexico and I share with the Government and the people of the United States of America the same deep feelings with regard to the loss of life and the sufferings which that catastrophe has brought to the people along the border of our two countries.

ADOLFO RUIZ CORTINES

159　❡ Veto of Bill for the Relief of Ralston
Edward Harry.　*July* 3, 1954

To the House of Representatives:

I am returning herewith without my approval H.R. 3350, 83d Congress, "An Act for the relief of Ralston Edward Harry."

This bill proposes to extend to Ralston Edward Harry, a United States citizen, who served in the Canadian Air Force during World War II, the same medical, hospital, and domiciliary care as that to which honorably discharged persons who served in the Armed Forces of the United States from September 1941 to July 1945 are entitled.

Mr. Harry did not serve in the Armed Forces of the United States. On May 14, 1949, four years after his discharge from the Canadian Air Force, Mr. Harry sustained severe injuries in an automobile accident which have and will continue to necessitate extensive medical care and hospitalization.

Under existing law the Veterans' Administration is authorized to enter into reciprocal agreements with our World War II allies to provide medical treatment and hospital care for their veterans upon a reimbursable basis and at the request of the government concerned. Although such an agreement has been entered into with the government of Canada, the Canadian authorities have advised that he has been afforded all the benefits of their laws and is not eligible for further treatment.

The committees of Congress which considered H.R. 3350, agree that Mr. Harry is not eligible for United States veterans' benefits. A majority of both committees recommended favorable consideration of the bill, however, upon the ground that Mr. Harry served honorably with the Royal Canadian Air Force and attempted to transfer to the Armed Forces of the United States upon its entry in the war.

I am advised that many thousands of United States citizens served in the armed forces of governments associated or allied with the United States in World War II. As the minority views of the Congressional committees indicate, approval of this bill would obviously be discriminatory against such veterans who have also returned to the United States and would constitute a far-reaching precedent.

Although I deeply sympathize with Mr. Harry's need, sympathy should not be permitted to abrogate the principles and rules of administration prescribed in the general law. As I have stated in the past, uniformity and equality of treatment to all who are similarly situated must be the steadfast rule if the federal programs for veterans and their beneficiaries are to be operated successfully.

Heeding the special plea or the emotional appeal of hardship cases would eventually destroy the effectiveness of these programs. Approval of HR 3350 would not be in keeping with these principles.

DWIGHT D. EISENHOWER

160   ¶ Message to the Mayor of Philadelphia for the Fourth of July Ceremonies at Independence Hall. *July* 5, 1954

[Released July 5, 1954. Dated June 10, 1954]

Dear Mr. Mayor:

I send warm greetings to all citizens of Philadelphia and the distinguished friends joining them for the Fourth of July ceremonies at Independence Hall.

Because your city was the birthplace of our Declaration of Independence and was closely associated with many of the important incidents and figures of our Revolutionary history, it occupies a high place in American sentiment and memories. For most of us it symbolizes Freedom itself.

During the decades following upon those stirring events in Philadelphia, the march of freedom toward many corners of the globe seemed triumphant and certain to continue. But, beginning a score of years ago, it has suffered notably from forces marshalled by the leaders of Facism and Communism. Though their evil doctrines differ in some respects, they are as one in contempt of our concepts of liberty and human dignity. Both have disdained and attempted to destroy all religious belief and have ruled the millions under their control through cruelty, violence and deceit.

Important parts of these conspiracies have already been stopped by an outraged humanity. Eventually the others are certain to go, because in the long run nothing can stand before man's intense desire for personal liberty and his determination to worship in his own way.

616

On this Fourth of July we confidently strive toward the ultimate triumph of peace and justice in the world. May it be a conquest, we pray, accomplished not by force, but through patient perseverance and the growth of knowledge and understanding among nations and men.

Sincerely,

DWIGHT D. EISENHOWER

NOTE: This message to Mayor Joseph S. Clark, Jr., was used in connection with the ceremonies held on Monday, July 5.

161　¶ The President's News Conference of *July 7*, 1954.

THE PRESIDENT. Ladies and gentlemen, of course no one can say exactly what influence the efforts of your people and of your employers had in effecting a 20 percent reduction in the Fourth of July casualties. So far as I am concerned, something kept 80 families that were last year sorrowing for the loss of a child or a relative, kept them from doing it; and I think you had something to do with it. I thank you, and I am sure that every single American who knows anything about this terrible toll we pay on holidays would thank you also.

I have heard from Mr. Hagerty and others exactly how intensive was the campaign that was carried out, particularly by some of the groups. I am grateful.

With respect to things more intimately connected with my own work, I remind you that some months ago I expressed the great conviction that this fall the issue before the public was going to be the legislative program presented by the administration, and the success in translating it into law.

In the past week there has been such great progress in both Houses that I think the prospects are looking up. As a matter of fact, I would say the prospects are rosy that there will be placed before the public this fall a record of accomplishment of which any Congress, any administration, could be proud; particularly the farm bill that passed in the House and the tax bill in the Senate made my weekend, at least, a very, very much more pleasant affair.

Now, with those two remarks, I think we will go directly to questions.

Q. John Cutter, United Press: Mr. President, since your recent talks with the British Prime Minister, there has been considerable talk in this country about the admission of Communist China to the United Nations; it has been the subject of congressional debate, and so forth like that. I wonder if you could give us today, sir, your own feelings on the admission of the present Communist government of China to the United Nations.

THE PRESIDENT. I would be glad to. As you know, and I have said before this particular group, I am completely and unalterably opposed under the present situation to the admission of Red China into the United Nations. I personally think that 95 percent of the population of the United States would take the same stand.

Now, let's take a look at this thing for a minute, if you will bear with me.

There is a moral question, first of all, that is involved. The United Nations was not established primarily as a supergovernment, clothed with all of the authority of supergovernment and of great power to do things. It was, among other things, an attempt to marshal the moral strength of the world in order to preserve peace, to make certain that quarrels were composed through a decent respect for justice and fairness and right, and to see whether we couldn't avoid resort to force.

Today we have Red China going to Geneva, and instead of taking a conciliatory attitude about anything, it excoriated the United Nations. As a matter of fact, at Geneva it demanded repudiation of the United Nations position. On top of that, Red China is today at war with the United Nations. They were declared an aggressor by the United Nations in the Assembly; that situation has never been changed. They are occupying North Korea; they have supported this great effort at further enslavement of the peoples in Indochina; they have held certain of our prisoners unjustifiably, and they have been guilty of the employment of the worst possible diplomatic deportment in the international affairs of the world.

How can the United States, as a self-respecting nation, doing its best and in conformity with the moral standards as we understand them, how can we possibly say this government should be admitted to the United Nations?

That is the way the case stands now, and that is my position.

Q. Chalmers Roberts, Washington Post and Times Herald: To carry that a little bit further, sir, there have been some suggestions on the Hill that if Red China is admitted over our protest, that the United States should then withdraw from the U.N. Would you comment on that, sir?

THE PRESIDENT. Well, yes, I would. We went into the United Nations under treaty forms. Now, I must say, first, if the United States ever reaches the point that it wants to repudiate solemn treaty obligations, it must do so after the most careful deliberation and study of all of the consequences that could be involved.

Secondly, I repeat, the establishment of the United Nations was an effort to rally the moral forces of the world. I don't see how any state, impartial state, can vote for their acceptance under present conditions; I just don't understand it.

If these people, mistakenly, as we believe, could override us—I don't know that they can, I would fight to the last minute to prove they can't— but if they should, the question of whether we would accomplish more good in the world, whether we could advance the cause of peace and decency better by going out than by staying in, that is something that would have to be decided.

My own feeling is this: I never give up a battle until I am licked completely, utterly, and destroyed. I don't believe in giving up any battle as long as I have got a chance to win.

Q. Mr. Roberts: Sir, is it a fair inference from your remarks then that you oppose any amendment to the foreign aid bill or any current legislation, which would automatically take us out if Red China is admitted?

THE PRESIDENT. Well, as a matter of fact, I don't know that there is any such amendment under consideration of any kind.

Q. Mr. Roberts: It has been suggested in both Houses of Congress.

THE PRESIDENT. Well, I don't believe it is up officially; I don't believe it has been brought up in a way that would cause real study on it. But I would not think that we ought to prejudge cases. I believe we ought to take these problems as they arise, and I doubt that any such amendment will be seriously considered.

Q. Mr. Roberts: Sir, could you tell us if what you have told us here is approximately what you told Senator Knowland yesterday?

THE PRESIDENT. Why, Senator Knowland and I had conversations about many things, programs and everything else; and I think we are, generally speaking, in conformity on most of our ideas and thoughts.

On this one, he did say that he would himself begin to fight for the withdrawing of the United States from the United Nations. I say I have not yet reached any such decision; no, I haven't.

Q. Frank van der Linden, Nashville Banner: Mr. President, Governor Frank Clement of Tennessee has sent you a telegram saying that your remarks here last week regarding TVA were deeply disturbing to him, and asking a chance to meet with you and state his case regarding this new proposal for private utilities to come into TVA territory. Have you decided to give him that conference?

THE PRESIDENT. As a matter of fact, I haven't actually seen the telegram yet, but Governor Clement, like any other Governor in the United States, can come to see me at any time that a convenient time can be arranged.

Q. Andrew Tully, Scripps-Howard: Mr. President, can you think of any circumstances under which you would favor admission of Red China into the U.N.?

THE PRESIDENT. I think there is no use of going forward into all of the things that would, let us say, constitute that record of deeds for which I have so often plead that would change my attitude. But I will tell you this: it would have to be a record of deeds that would prove really good faith and a readiness and a capacity on the part of their country to discharge its obligations in the international field properly and decently.

Q. Mr. Tully: Over a long period of time, sir?

THE PRESIDENT. Well, I don't—you are going to ask me how long is a piece of string pretty quick. [*Laughter*] I don't know exactly. I would say again, it is something to be met as time goes on, and let us see what are the developments.

Q. Wesley G. Peyton, San Jose (Calif.) Mercury: Mr. President, getting back to the legislative program for a minute, a few days ago California Congressman Charles Gubser wrote Chairman Hall of the Republican National Committee, urging the Republican National Committee to withhold the support and sponsorship of the party from all Republican legislators who do not back up your program. Would you care to comment on that, sir?

THE PRESIDENT. I didn't know about that message. No, I think I wouldn't comment on that one.

I do say this: I believe the program that has been put forward, while admittedly still with its imperfections, is a great pattern for the United

States to follow as it pushes ahead—in, as I have explained, my idea—trying to be conscious of the problems of every individual, but trying to run the kind of an economy that gives every individual opportunity and initiative. With that belief, very naturally I want support for it. So when someone suggests different ways of supporting it, why, of course, he has an immediate pathway to my heart; but how these things work out within the political party, that is something for them to decide themselves.

Q. Edward T. Folliard, Washington Post and Times Herald: Mr. President, some time ago, I think it was last fall, you said that if the Republican Party did not enact a good legislative program, that it didn't deserve to remain in power. You said substantially that. In view of what you said this morning, I take it that you think now that it does deserve to remain in power?

THE PRESIDENT. It certainly is establishing a record that looks to me like it.

Now, admittedly, ladies and gentlemen, there are going to be little pieces and parts of this whole program in which I have had my disappointments. I would be just guilty of misrepresentation if I just said all the world is rosy, and all the roses are gilded. But if we had a straightforward, across the board progress, that shows that men have stood up to be counted and had the courage to go ahead in doing what they think is right, then I think we have got a pretty good record, and there is so much of the program being enacted into law, that I think by the end of the month or by the time, whenever it is, that Congress goes out, we are going to look pretty good.

Q. Walter T. Ridder, Ridder Papers: Do you plan in the coming months, sir, personally to tell the American people how good that legislative record is?

THE PRESIDENT. If it is as good as I think it is, I would be proud to.

Q. Sarah McClendon, El Paso Times: Sir, have you promised Senator Price Daniel of Texas that you would name Everett Hutchinson of Austin to the Interstate Commerce Commission as soon as you can get Monroe Johnson off?

THE PRESIDENT [*laughing*]. Well, now, you have asked me sort of whether I have stopped beating my wife.

I don't know that I have promised to get anybody off, and I don't recall that I have promised to appoint any particular individual.

There has been argument advanced that the positions on some of these commissions are allotted geographically in our country, and that this one is the next one that is going to that region. But there is no decision made on any of this, so I don't admit that I am attempting to get anybody off or that I have promised to appoint anybody else to it.

Q. Edward F. Creagh, Associated Press: Can you tell us anything about the labor situation at Oak Ridge or the Paducah A-bomb plants?

THE PRESIDENT. Of course the picket line which was established this morning at one of the plants—the other one, I believe, is an hour or so later in point of time, and we do not know yet whether or not it's been done—it's a serious thing for the United States, beyond all question. It was because of that that I signed the order last night to appoint a fact-finding board of inquiry.

I think there is great hope that the unions will observe the propriety of that action and the law in the matter, and will postpone their strikes and await the outcome of that fact-finding board. I certainly hope so, because it would be most embarrassing and difficult for us if these strikes were maintained.[1]

Q. William M. Blair, New York Times: Mr. President, I would like to ask a question about the farm situation. Do you believe the compromise flexible system passed by the House last week gives you enough flexibility to deal with the present farm situation?

THE PRESIDENT. From my viewpoint, it wasn't even a compromise. If you will read everything I have ever said about this farm program, I have asked for a flexible system gradually applied.

The only thing that the House did by legislative rather than waiting

---

[1] On July 7 the White House released two letters from the Chairman, Atomic Energy Commission, concerning threatened strikes by local unions associated with the A.F. of L. at Oak Ridge, Tenn., and by CIO locals at Oak Ridge and at Paducah, Ky. Also released were Executive Orders 10542 and 10543, dated July 6, 1954, creating emergency boards of inquiry in each dispute, and directing them to report to the President on or before July 20. (For text of orders see 1954 Supplement to title 3, Code of Federal Regulations, page 64).

On July 10 the White House announced that the President had been informed that the work stoppage at Paducah had been ended, and that the CIO workers had voted to return to their jobs. The announcement stated that the President desired to give special public tribute to those A.F. of L. workers at Oak Ridge and the supervisory personnel at both locations who recognized the importance of the national security aspects of their jobs and who did not leave them. It further stated that the President was gratified that the CIO members returned voluntarily to work and that the plants would soon be restored to normal operation.

See also Item 193.

for Executive action, they did provide that in the first year the drop in the price supports of the basics could not be below 82½ percent, a particular provision that I think will have really little, if any, effect upon the situation.

I don't mind telling you that I personally would have prevented any drop in the first year below 80, so I don't even look on it as a compromise. So far as I am concerned, I don't mind telling you I look upon it as a great and sweeping victory; we have got a long-term principle established in a positive way. The first year drop to 82½ was not only acceptable to me, I was delighted with it.

Q. Joseph A. Loftus, New York Times: Mr. President, can you explain, within the area of security, why it is so vital that there be no interruption at Oak Ridge? Is there such pressure to reach a weapons goal, or is it important to maintain uninterrupted production, or what is it?

THE PRESIDENT. Well, there are all sorts of things. Primarily, one of the big troubles is the difficulty that comes about in closing, attempting to close, and then reopening later, some of these very expensive and continuous operations; any interruption in this kind of activity is a very serious matter in every respect. We know that potential enemies are advancing in this field, and we certainly want to keep pushing ahead ourselves.

Now, there are certain fields that have to do with the peaceful use of this; research, many other things of that kind, will be sadly interrupted. But there is no possibility of my here outlining all of the different aspects in which this could look serious, and others which would not be so serious; I could not possibly do it.

Q. Ethel Payne, Defender Publications: Mr. President, we were very happy last week when the Deputy Attorney General sent a communication to the House Interstate and Foreign Commerce Committee saying that there was a legal basis for passing a law to ban segregation in interstate travel. Mr. Rogers also said that in view of the recent decision by the Supreme Court in the schools cases, that such legislation ought to be enacted by Congress at this time, and the Bureau of the Budget approved it. I would like to know if we could assume that we have administration support in getting action on this?

THE PRESIDENT. You say that you have to have administrative support. The administration is trying to do what it thinks and believes to be decent and just in this country, and is not in the effort to support any particular or special group of any kind. These opinions were sent down, these beliefs are held as part of the administration belief, because we think it is just and right, and that is the answer.

Q. Harry W. Frantz, United Press: Mr. President, reverting to your comment on the legislative program, have you abandoned hope of getting legislation for Hawaiian statehood at this session and, if so, will you carry over the campaign into a future Congress?

THE PRESIDENT. No, I haven't entirely abandoned hope. I would be foolish to say that there aren't some very tricky problems involved in it, because the Senate put both of these together; but I haven't abandoned hope at all by any means.

Q. Hazel Markel, Mutual Broadcasting System: Mr. President, I have a biographical question. I think it is pretty generally known that your parents were deeply religious, and I think a number of articles which have been written on your family have stated that they were very strong pacifists, and some other statements have been made that both of them objected to your being a soldier. I interviewed a gentleman yesterday who said that you had corrected him on that; that your father had not objected at all, that it was only your mother who had objected. I wonder if that is true, if you care to comment, and also if she finally was reconciled to it.

THE PRESIDENT. Well, of all the kinds of questions that I never expected to go into here—[*laughter*]—would be to go back that far into my family life.

All such things are normally exaggerated, except the one that they were deeply religious people. They were also rebels in religion. They would join here, and go out to some other place very soon. They had their own religion. It is true that my mother finally became a member of an organization which had definitely pacifistic tenets in its program; but I think that it would be enough to say about my father's belligerency that he was Pennsylvania Dutch and he had all the temper of a Pennsylvania Dutchman; there was nothing pacifist about him. [*Laughter*]

I have also heard that my mother objected strenuously to my going to West Point. I know that she even at that time believed that the world didn't have to go to war, believed it very passionately; but she never said one single word to me.

624

Now, I think, that answers the question as well as I can.

Q. George E. Herman, CBS Radio: Sir, there has been a lot of talk and speculation and rumors about the situation inside CIA, certain charges of infiltration and other things. I think you are the only person in the country who can straighten us out on what is going on in CIA and what is going on in there.

THE PRESIDENT. As you people know, all of the organizational features are to be examined by a task force headed by General Clark, a man that I have known from the time we were both cadets, for whose ability and patriotism and loyalty I have the highest respect, and who I think will do a very grand job.

So far as the head of the CIA is concerned, he has constantly invited Executive examination into his operations, to get some help to see that everything there is being done that can be done to further the purposes for which it was established, for which it is supported, and to make certain it is being done honestly and decently.

Now, all of that goes on all the time on some kind of a routine basis, one or the other.

I assure you that I have the utmost confidence in the integrity and the loyalty and efficiency of the head of the CIA.

Q. Edward T. Folliard, Washington Post and Times Herald: Mr. President, the Ground Observer Corps is having a day soon, July 14. It is made up of 350,000 people trained to watch for enemy planes. I wondered if you cared to give them a word of encouragement. [*Laughter*]

THE PRESIDENT. Not only would I but I think, unless I am mistaken—sometimes a man's memory can be very badly off as to time—I think I have already written a message for use on that day. I personally think that the more we can enlarge that corps, and the more we can impress upon them the responsibility that will rest with them, the better off we will be. I think they are doing a very fine and loyal service.

John Cutter, United Press: Thank you, Mr. President.

NOTE: President Eisenhower's forty-third news conference was held in the Executive Office Building from 10:32 to 10:56 o'clock on Wednesday morning, July 7, 1954. In attendance: 165.

162   ¶ Statement by the President Upon Signing the Agricultural Trade Development and Assistance Act of 1954.   *July* 10, 1954

I AM HAPPY to sign today the Agricultural Trade and Development Act of 1954. It is an essential part of the comprehensive agricultural program which I recommended to the Congress on January 11, 1954. In the face of burdensome and growing stocks of agricultural products, the Administration urged the enactment of legislation providing for flexible price supports and other measures designed to check the accumulation of surpluses. We recommended that the burdensome stocks which had already accumulated be liquidated over a period of time, through disposal programs that would create new markets for United States products, and assist friendly countries.

The Agricultural Trade and Development Act is well designed for its purpose of "providing a means whereby surplus agricultural commodities in excess of the usual marketings of such commodities may be sold." It will lay the basis for a permanent expansion of our exports of agricultural products, with lasting benefits to ourselves and peoples in other lands. The Act also provides authority to give surpluses to meet famine and other emergency requirements, thus enabling us to maintain our American tradition of generous help in time of need.

The Act wisely sets forth the intention of the Congress that it shall expand world trade on a sound basis, and not disrupt it. I am glad that this makes it possible for me to assure normal suppliers to commercial markets at home and abroad that the Act will be administered so that the United States will not be engaging in unfair competition or in other practices which would disturb world markets. Such disturbance to markets would not only cause serious harm to other countries but would harm us most of all, since we are the world's largest exporter. Thus, in following our own broad interests, we shall be reflecting our responsibilities as a member of the family of nations.

NOTE: The Agricultural Trade Development and Assistance Act of 1954 is Public Law 480, 83d Congress (68 Stat. 454).

163 ¶ Letter to Secretary Weeks Establishing a Cabinet Committee on Transport Policy and Organization. *July* 12, 1954

Dear Mr. Secretary:

The vital interests of this Nation require that the transportation industry of the United States maintain itself at maximum effectiveness. The Government must provide effective leadership in assuring that its policies and programs affecting the various forms of transportation, whose services are so necessary to the public and to industry and which have such a vital bearing upon the national security, are best designed to aid them in performing fully the roles for which each is best suited.

Over the past years, studies have been made and recommendations have been presented regarding Government programs affecting particular segments of the transportation industry. Following the recommendations of the original Hoover Commission on Government Organization, considerable progress has been made in the past five years in the centralization within the Department of Commerce of major programs affecting transportation. However, a comprehensive up-to-date review of over-all transportation policies and problems is needed as an aid in assuring the over-all consistency of Government policies and programs concerning particular branches of the transportation industry. Also, the organization of the Federal Government to cope with transportation problems should be reviewed.

The exploration and formulation of policy and organizational recommendations covering the whole field of transportation require a broad perspective which comprehends the over-all needs of the Nation and understands the special problems and capabilities of all forms of transportation. To meet this need, therefore, I am establishing a Cabinet Committee on Transport Policy and Organization whose task will be the presentation of recommendations for my consideration.

Because of your major responsibilities in the field of transportation, I am requesting you to serve as Chairman of this Cabinet Committee. By copies of this letter, I am designating the Secretary of Defense and the Director of the Office of Defense Mobilization to serve as the other members. The Secretary of the Treasury, the Postmaster General, the Secretary of Agriculture, and the Director of the Bureau of the Budget will participate on an ad hoc basis. My Advisory Committee on Government Organization will be glad to cooperate wherever possible.

I am informed that a large fact-finding task will not be required since many studies have been made from which much of the required data can be readily obtained. Accordingly, I request that the Cabinet Committee on Transport Policy and Organization submit its recommendations to me not later than December 1, 1954.

Sincerely,

DWIGHT D. EISENHOWER

164 ¶ Message for the Governors' Conference at Lake George and Request for Recommendations as to a Federal-State Highway Program. *July* 12, 1954

[Text read by the Vice President]

I AM CERTAIN that in meeting with the assembled Governors, you will derive the same inspiration and the same increased confidence in the superiority of our form of government that I never fail to get in like circumstances.

When the Prime Minister of Great Britain recently visited me, he asserted that our federated form of government gave to our country the great advantage of providing 48 training grounds for public service on the national level, while in the case of the most broadly experienced public servant of our time, the distinguished Governor of South Carolina, this process has been successfully reversed.

I am sure that the Prime Minister's observation is valid, but I believe that probably the greatest worth of the American political system is the opportunity it provides for keeping government closer to the people and for performing in our several State and territorial capitals government activities that would otherwise fall to Federal authority.

Because of the size of our country, the climatic differences of its different sections, the economic interdependence of the States, any such centralization would inevitably lead toward greater and greater regimentation of our people. These facts also highlight the great need for cooperation between these two important echelons of government in the United States. Consequently, from the Federal viewpoint, the greatest value of the Governors' Conferences, to which are invariably invited members of the national administration, is in the opportunity presented for discussion among us of problems affecting national and State governments, and every individual.

The recent visit to Korea by three members of the Governors' Conference is merely another example of our great recognition that scarcely any public activity is of exclusive interest to any echelon of government. I would be most appreciative if you would extend to all the Governors present my very best wishes for a successful meeting, and for the happiness and the welfare of each.

DWIGHT D. EISENHOWER

[Before reading the President's message Vice President Nixon spoke from notes prepared by the President and covering matters of common interest to the States and the Federal Government. The Vice President quoted directly the following request relating to the requirements of an adequate Federal-State highway program:]

I hope that you will study the matter, and recommend to me the cooperative action you think the Federal Government and the 48 States should take to meet these requirements, so that I can submit positive proposals to the next session of the Congress.

NOTE: The President was scheduled to address the Governors' Conference, but was unable to be present because of the death of a member of his family. The President's notes, as paraphrased by Vice President Nixon, were released by the White House.

165 ¶ The President's News Conference of *July* 14, 1954.

THE PRESIDENT. Ladies and gentlemen, I have an announcement about President Rhee's visit. I have invited him over here, and he is going to come on July 26th. Rather than take your time to tell about the visit in detail, I merely inform you there is a mimeographed paper outside that will be given to you to tell you about the details.

I want to say one thing about the tax bill which is, I believe, going into conference this morning. I think there has been quite a bit of misunderstanding about this tax bill.

I had this typed out so I would remember it, and give it exactly as I mean it. First of all, of course, I hope we get prompt action, but these are the things that have been forgotten.

This tax bill will help millions of Americans by better tax treatment, and here are a few of them: for child care, retired people and their widows, parents of children who work part time, people with sick and accident insurance, people with medical bills, farmers doing soil and water conservation, taxpayers with nonrelative dependents, and many others.

Then there are provisions for more flexible depreciation and better tax treatment of research expenses. These will help all business to modernize and expand, and be especially helpful to small businesses.

Most important, those provisions, by helping the economy expand, make more and better jobs.

I want to emphasize these points because we lose sight of the great and broad purpose of tax revision in some peculiar revision which we label with our own terms and slogans and headings. I just think we lose sight of these particular points, this kind of purpose that underlies this whole tax program.

Now, we will go to questions.

Q. Robert Clark, International News Service: Mr. President, do you have anything you can tell us generally about the Secretary of State's visit to Paris, particularly as it relates to our future participation in the Geneva conference?

THE PRESIDENT. Well, first of all, let me tell you that I would expect an announcement shortly. I would advise all of you to keep in fairly close touch with Mr. Hagerty during the day; there may be some announcement.

But Mr. Dulles went to Paris because of our great concern to keep a united front in fundamentals, fundamental objectives and aims and principles with our principal allies, Great Britain and France; I mean principal allies in the subject we are now dealing with.

He went over there to see whether there was a common front in basic principle, so that our presence, through ministerial representation of some kind, would be helpful at Geneva and not damaging.

He is coming back soon; he will report to me. After he is here there will unquestionably be more to say on this subject. That is about the answer as it stands.

Q. Merriman Smith, United Press: Mr. President, is Under Secretary Smith going to Geneva?

THE PRESIDENT. I couldn't say, I couldn't answer yes or no at this moment; but I say if you do keep in touch, there may be some announcement on the future activity in which we will engage.

Q. Mr. Smith: In all respect, sir, is that going to be the announcement?

THE PRESIDENT. I don't know whether it will. The announcement may be that under—

I can't tell you, I am not going to predict; but I say it could affect that, of course.

Q. Charles S. von Fremd, CBS Television: Along the same lines, sir, it would seem that there has been growing alarm among our Western allies due to their sudden realization of the fact that they are caught between two tremendous countries, each possessing the A- and H-bomb, and capable, of course, each of delivering it, and possibly devastating their smaller countries.

Do you think that this possibly is the reason for their reluctance to enter into a pact such as EDC or the Far Eastern Alliance, and if so, is there anything that can be done to lessen or erase their fears in this matter?

THE PRESIDENT. I have brought this question up, I think voluntarily, in front of this body before, when I talked about the horrors of bombing, and how differently people feel who have been the victims of such a disaster than do we, who have been relatively free from it.

It is absolutely idle for us to think that we can sit here, in the relative security and assurances with which we have lived over these many years with respect to danger from a foreign foe as affects our homes, and figure out what the people of London and Coventry and Berlin and Essen, and people of that kind feel; so, of course, this has a very, very important influence in their reaching their decisions.

As a matter of fact, you will recall on December 8th I proposed the beginning of a little plan. It was in its way a very modest one, but it was to bring to all the people of the world a definite realization, a definite example, in their own hands and in their own consciences that this new development can help them and not destroy them.

I believe, if we can get the whole world to having right in front of them every day that this great discovery of the great scientists is helping us, it doesn't necessarily have to destroy us, I believe we will marshal a lot of world opinion in getting rid of this horrible cloud of threatened destruction that hangs over the world.

Now, that was really the underlying purpose of that plan and, as a matter of fact, I will just tell you this: I am not going to let it die, if I can possibly help it.

Q. Alan Emory, Watertown (N.Y.) Times: Sir, you have named Governor Jordan of Idaho to be Chairman of the United States section of the International Joint Commission and, I believe, as things stand now, he plans to take the office after his term as Governor expires on December 31st. Do you plan to name any interim chairman, sir, or will the office remain vacant as it has since February 1?

THE PRESIDENT. The particular point hasn't come to me. This is the first time I have thought of it in those terms, and I will have to get the answer. I will try to, and let you have it through Mr. Hagerty.

Q. Sarah McClendon, El Paso Times: Sir, there are two bills put forward by your administration now on Capitol Hill before the Senate Judiciary Committee designed to curb the hundreds of thousands of Mexican wetbacks coming into this country. There is nothing being done now on that in the House. Do you plan to ask your congressional leaders to push this? I believe it is part of your program.

THE PRESIDENT. Well, it is part of the program, although I don't know whether it was one of the items listed in my January 8 presentation or not; but, of course, it is an important problem, and if it is being neglected, why, I will take it up. I didn't realize that it was, as you put it, sort of neglected. I didn't know that.

Q. Edward F. Creagh, Associated Press: Is there any comment, sir, on yesterday's action by the House regarding your health reinsurance program?

THE PRESIDENT. Well, I hope you didn't invite me to use up the rest of our time making a speech.

Ladies and gentlemen, in the campaign I made two promises that have to do with the health of the American people. I said, first, that I was opposed to socialized medicine and would use every single attribute and influence of the Presidential office to defeat any move toward socialized medicine; also, in talking about the great deficiencies in medical care in this country and, particularly, for people who can't afford the expensive type of service that is now available to us in our best hospitals, that something must be done. We were going to study ways and means to bring better medical care to the rural areas, and bring good and fine medical care within reach of the average household budget. This is what we have been trying to do.

I am sure that the people that voted against this bill just don't understand what are the facts of American life.

I don't consider that anyone lost yesterday, except the American people. There is nothing to be gained, as I see it, by shutting our eyes to the fact that all of our people are not getting the kind of medical care to which they are entitled. I do not believe there is any use in shutting our eyes to the fact that the American people are going to get that medical care in some form or other.

As I say, I am the last one to believe that the answer lies in socialized medicine, and I am trying to provide a plan. If they want to amend the plan or to perfect it in some way, go ahead; but when opponents of the plan get up in the House and say that this is only an effort of the Republicans to redeem our campaign promise, I plead guilty. Of course I am trying to redeem my campaign promises, and I will never cease trying.

This is only a temporary defeat; this thing will be carried forward as long as I am in this office.

Q. Nicholas P. Gregory, Philadelphia Inquirer: Mr. President, are you going to send a message to Congress for a rise in the debt limit?

THE PRESIDENT. Well, the whole problem will have to be taken up when all of the appropriation bills are in, when we know exactly where we stand.

Now, as you know, the fiscal situation is a delicate one, it is a tough one to handle all the time. Every time there is a new bill, it seems, new appropriations; and when you are trying to live within your income, it's tough. But I just don't believe, no matter what we have to do in order to meet our current bills, that we can proceed on the theory that we can forever just live on deficit spending; it can't be done.

Q. Chalmers M. Roberts, Washington Post and Times Herald: Mr. President, the implication of the stories which have been coming from Paris on the Secretary's conference there appears to be that the United States is prepared, while not recognizing a Communist state in northern Viet-Nam, to guarantee the independence of the southern half and, possibly, of the other two states through a southeast Asia pact. The further implication is that we would be willing to commit force or use American armed force for that. Is that a fair assumption?

THE PRESIDENT. You ask an odd question, because I must say this: when anything, any plan, any proposition, is the subject of a difficult international conference, I think anyone commenting on it in advance—any responsible official—would be making a great error.

This is what I think: we should make no assumptions whatsoever on the thing until we really have the answer, because to make an assumption on one part can easily prejudice all other parts. So, I wouldn't want to comment.

Q. Lloyd Schwartz, Fairchild Publications: Mr. President, the other day on the Senate floor, Senator Capehart said that you supported his bill which would make the good faith meeting of a competitor's price a complete defense against price discrimination charges under the Robinson-Patman Act; and, as I understand it, since then about all industry groups, mainly in the food industry, have asked you to disavow the support of that legislation. I wonder if you could comment on that?

THE PRESIDENT. No, I can't because you are bringing up something that has not yet been brought specifically to my attention.

Q. Kenneth M. Scheibel, Gannett Newspapers: Mr. President, the Senate Agriculture Committee has put a provision in the farm bill that it is working on now, to raise the price of butter, the support price, to 85 percent of parity. Does this strike you as a reasonable proposal or do you think it will discourage the use of butter?

THE PRESIDENT. I think it is a grave error. I believe that the only way we are going to get dairy products used is to have them used by the American people and at prices at which they will consume them.

Now, the consumption of butter has gone up something in the order of 7 percent since the Secretary, about 3 months ago, reduced the price support.

I would say, now, if you increased suddenly the price support, the people who would profit would be the middlemen who have this butter in their possession, people who have accumulated it at certain prices and have it in their storehouses and warehouses, and now suddenly can take it over to the Government and get a 10 percent increase—it is very nice business. I believe they would be the first ones that would be helped, and it would cost the Government a nice $100 million or something of that kind.

I believe that the dairy industry, in this butter business, is probably in better shape now than it has been for a long time, and we are beginning to get these things consumed almost at the rate produced.

Q. Mr. Scheibel: Sir, to go a bit further on the farm program, Governor Thornton of Colorado the other day said that he thought the farm program, your program, would be the No. 1 domestic issue in the campaign this fall. Do you agree with his assessment?

THE PRESIDENT. I hadn't heard that one. This is what I believe: if we get the essentials of that farm program passed, all of the United States will benefit, and by next fall they will understand that they are benefiting. That is, to my mind, the best kind of politics.

Q. Robert G. Spivack, New York Post: Mr. President, can you tell us how you regard the candidacy of Clifford Case, who has been designated Republican candidate for Senator in New Jersey?

THE PRESIDENT. I am—[*laughter*]—I think I am caught a little bit on the horns of a dilemma, because I believe I said I would not talk about individuals.

I will say this: in all of my dealings with Congressman Case, I found him to be a very splendid American and dedicated to public service.

Q. Glenn Thompson, Cincinnati Enquirer: Mr. President, could you give us some ideas about how the $50 billion in highway building should be financed?

THE PRESIDENT. Well, I don't think there is any one way. As a matter of fact, all I made was a proposition. I believe we are at least $50 billion behind in our road networks. We are suffering from it in losses of life; we are suffering from it every day in terms of inefficient operation of all of our transportation throughout the country.

Every city—even down—I had a report from a city yesterday of 22,000, and it said "Our No. 1 problem is parking." The parking space, the thruways, the great networks that we need, all of these must be done.

Now, in the great part of these I very much favor these self-liquidating projects.

The Government has made the proposition that we are ready to do our part in going forward with this planning and exploring a way. I have no definite plan, although we have been studying it for a year with people from the outside because, of all people, we must have the Governors and legislatures in with us. Until they come to me and show me their proposition and something that we can get together on, it is really idle to say how any single project will be financed.

I think there could be certain cases in which the Federal Government would have to do it all, possibly, because of some particular Federal use; but, by and large, it should be local and, I would say, exploit the self-liquidating idea as far as is possible.

This, I should point out, that I am talking about has nothing to do with the normal road building that is going on now, in which the gasoline taxes and all that were involved. This is entirely over and above that.

Q. Raymond P. Brandt, St. Louis Post-Dispatch: Mr. President, on the gasoline tax, what is your view on letting the States have some of those taxes?

THE PRESIDENT. As I recall, what was at issue this year was one-half a cent, and for the moment, we thought until this whole thing could be worked out and studied, we should continue as we had been rather than trying to make a change from which we couldn't retreat.

I don't believe that there is a final decision made, except this: that everybody to whom I have talked believes that we should put the maximum authority and responsibility in the States that they are capable of taking. If you put responsibilities there, you have got to let them have the money to do it.

Q. Frederick Kuh, Chicago Sun-Times: Mr. President, you said that you did not intend to let the proposal you made for an international pool of fissionable materials die.

THE PRESIDENT. Yes.

Q. Mr. Kuh: I would like to ask whether you discussed with the British when they were here the possibility of going on with that plan, without the Russians; and if so, whether they have agreed to that?

THE PRESIDENT. Well, you put this on a more formal basis than this conference really attained. This was a friendly exchange of views, and

I am sure of this: my old friend would not want us to let this idea die merely because somebody else didn't agree to it.

Q. Martin Agronsky, American Broadcasting Company: There have been a lot of versions, sir, about the last campaign in which you withdrew a reference to General Marshall in the campaign speech in Wisconsin. The latest version comes from Governor Kohler, who said he induced you to withdraw it. I wonder if we could have your version, sir? It is pretty ancient political history now.

THE PRESIDENT. Well, I will tell you, it is ancient, and I never like to say anything or question anybody else's account when I don't have a record, because I have learned to distrust my own memory.

As I recall, and you will recall I hope, in Denver I made quite a little talk on General Marshall, my admiration for him, my belief in him as one of the great patriots that I had ever known, and one of the most selfless men that I had ever known.

Now, the only thing that I recall is that someone said, "Well, you are just going around and you are going to make this your speech. Haven't you said it enough?"

Now, I am not going to question anybody's word. Governor Kohler is a friend of mine, and he probably recalls this exactly. He possibly talked to some of the people around me, and it was just mentioned to me; because I don't recall any conversation, that is all.

Q. Frank van der Linden, Nashville Banner: Mr. President, it seems like it has been some time since somebody asked you if you were going to appoint a new TVA chairman.

THE PRESIDENT. You bet I am.

Q. Mr. van der Linden: Could you say yet who he is going to be, sir?

THE PRESIDENT. No, I can't say this morning. [*Laughter*] I mean, I forget sometimes whether I have made things public already. I know who I am looking at, I will tell you that much. [*Laughter*]

Q. Fletcher Knebel, Cowles Publications: Mr. President, is it your hope, in connection with the tax bill, that the conference committee restores the tax credit on dividend income that the Senate cut out?

THE PRESIDENT. I would like to see the principle preserved. I have never on that particular item been adamant as to a particular scale or how much; I would like to see the principle preserved.

Q. George E. Herman, CBS Radio: Sir, the question of American participation in the Geneva conference brings up the broader question of

American interests in all of southeast Asia. That applies not only to Indochina but, for instance, to Malaya, both of which countries are the provinces of particular Western nations. I would like to ask you, sir, how much you consider the problems, such as Indochina or Malaya, the province of France or England and how much the province of the Western World, the Western alliance, headed by the United States and our Government?

THE PRESIDENT. Why, I consider such problems completely global in character, particularly global as they affect free nations.

Wasn't it to this group that I talked about the importance of this whole area, let us say, to Japan? Didn't I take your time one morning doing that?

Q. Raymond Brandt, St. Louis Post-Dispatch: Yes.

THE PRESIDENT. All right.

How can the free world see Japan go communistic? I mean, if you answer that question, then you say how do we keep Japan out from communism, from falling under the domination, just through the force of economic circumstances? I think that the whole Eastern, or all the Asian problem becomes one that the world just can't ignore.

There is no use in saying because it is just across the Pacific from us, we are more interested than is Western Europe. The world is interested in this region. We want them to have the same rights of self-government, the same opportunity to enjoy freedom, as fast as any one of them are qualified for it, as we do ourselves.

Q. A. Robert Smith, Portland Oregonian: Mr. President, I have been trying to ascertain the administration's position more specifically on statehood for Alaska. At the Interior Department I hear that there are certain defense considerations there, but at the Pentagon there is no apparent apprehension on that count; and in both departments they suggest that at the White House there is a certain feeling in that regard. I wonder if you could clarify this whole matter?

THE PRESIDENT. Well, you are asking my personal opinion; you said "the White House." I suppose you mean me, because I think I know a little bit more about the military than anyone else at the White House. [*Laughter*]

Indeed, I am concerned. Anyone that looks at the map can see what the importance of Alaska, the Alaskan territorial expanse, is to the United States from a security standpoint. So I am very deeply concerned as to the fate of all of those outlying areas that lie, let us say, west of the 150th meridian and, let's say, north of the Yukon or Brooks Range.

Those regions are of tremendous importance, and I don't think I should say any more than that.

Q. John W. Vandercook, American Broadcasting Company: Mr. President, in that same connection, I don't quite understand the theory that a territory is necessarily easier to defend than a State. Could you explain that, sir?

THE PRESIDENT. I would say this: I don't say it is easier to defend; I say it is easier to use, because, in one case, it is under the absolute control of the central government, and in the other case it isn't.

Q. Merriman Smith, United Press: Mr. President, this is a personal question for those of us who have to follow you around. I wonder if you could tell us about your summer plans? We assume you are going to Denver shortly after the close of Congress.

THE PRESIDENT. I don't mind giving you a guess. I hope to go to Denver. Now, from there, I have made some tentative engagements for going to dams and fairs and, possibly, a convention or two. Altogether, I would say about three trips.

I would hope, if all goes well, to be out of here no later than, oh, I don't know, somewhere between August 15th and 17th, along in that region.

Now, if you people think you must go ahead and be a reconnaissance in force, why, I would think that would be all right; but I don't see how I can go much earlier.

Last year, you will recall, I tried to go right after Congress closed, and I had the bills follow me out there. But there are certain bills that you just have to talk over with your principal advisers, and to get that far away makes it a little awkward. I can carry out the personal and simple bills, but some of the others I just have to stay here and work out.

Q. Douglass Cater, The Reporter Magazine: Mr. President, as a Republican, do you have any personal opinion about Senator Flanders' resolution that he promises to call up this week?

THE PRESIDENT. I think I could safely leave that to the Senator.

Merriman Smith, United Press: Thank you, Mr. President.

NOTE: President Eisenhower's forty-fourth news conference was held in the Executive Office Building from 11:01 to 11:27 o'clock on Wednesday morning, July 14, 1954. In attendance: 133.

166   ¶ Statement by the President Upon Signing
Bill Increasing Reenlistment Bonuses for Members
of the Uniformed Services.   *July* 16, 1954

I HAVE TODAY approved a bill which will substantially increase the
size of reenlistment bonuses payable to the men and women in our armed
forces who agree to continue to serve after the termination of their current
enlistment or period of obligated service.   The purpose of these increases
is to offer an added inducement for more people to make the service their
career, thereby increasing the efficiency of our armed service.

Career personnel—trained, seasoned, and experienced—are the backbone of the armed forces.   The weakest aspect of our national defense
today is the low rate of reenlistments in our armed forces.   The rapid
turnover of skilled personnel adversely affects the readiness and effectiveness of combat forces.

In expressing my concern about this situation in the past, I have
outlined some of the steps which, I think, will make life in the service
more attractive insofar as both intangibles and tangibles are concerned.
True pride in service and maintenance of the traditional military benefits
and perquisites go hand in hand, each increasing the other and the basic
strength of our Army, Navy, Air Force, Marine Corps and Coast Guard.

The Secretary of Defense and his principal aides have expressed an
equal concern about this problem.   They have assured me that efforts
to meet it are being made on a broad front.   Constructive action is and
will continue to be taken administratively and, in addition, certain legislative action has been proposed to the Congress.   The bill I signed today
falls into this latter category and there are others, particularly those
authorizing more adequate family housing and medical care for dependents of military personnel, which are still awaiting Congressional
action.   To the extent that such benefits encourage individuals to remain in the service, the increased cost resulting from them will, in my
opinion, be more than offset by savings in the high cost of training replace-
ments.   Even more important, we will have a more effective national
defense.

I shall continue to insist that the Department of Defense do everything possible to improve this serious situation, and I shall seek the cooperation of the Congress in this endeavor.

NOTE: As enacted, the bill is Public Law 506, 83d Congress (68 Stat. 488).

167 ¶ Remarks at Presentation by Field Marshal Alexander of a Portrait of the President. *July* 20, 1954

FIRST OF ALL, you know how much I will prize the portrait that was made by Sir Oswald Birley. To have a replica will be a very great honor, and to have you bring it to me is something that I can scarcely imagine. You know how I have felt toward you all these years. I assure you it will always be the same, and I will always have the same feeling toward all those other people that make up that great band that I am privileged to call my British friends.

Thank you.

NOTE: The ceremony was held in the President's office. The remarks of Field Marshal Alexander were also released.

The original portrait was painted in 1951 at SHAPE headquarters, shortly before the artist's death. Marshal Alexander stated that Birley had painted it as a gift to the American people, and that he had planned to do a replica for presentation to the President. The actual replica, by Sir John Leigh-Pemberton, was arranged for by Birley's British friends.

The original was sent to the Smithsonian Institution for display as part of the National Collection of Fine Arts; the replica, to the Eisenhower Museum in Abilene.

168 ¶ The President's News Conference of *July* 21, 1954.

THE PRESIDENT. Ladies and gentlemen, you know that the meeting at Geneva is still in session; as a matter of fact, I believe there is a plenary session now going on. There are also many details of the agreements that have been reached there, or at least auxiliary parts of the agreement, that we have not been able to study in detail.

In this situation, I have prepared a statement which I shall read. You need not take it down because there are copies that will be provided before this meeting is over.

[*Reading*] I am glad, of course, that agreement has been reached at Geneva to stop the bloodshed in Indochina. The United States has not been a belligerent in the war in which thousands of brave men, while defending freedom, have died during the past 7 years.

The primary responsibility for the settlement in Indochina rested with those nations which participated in the fighting.

Our role at Geneva has been at all times to try to be helpful where desired, and to aid France and Cambodia, Laos and Viet-Nam, to obtain a just and honorable settlement which will take into account the needs of the interested people.

Accordingly, the United States has not itself been a party to or bound by the decisions taken by the conference, but it is our hope that it will lead to the establishment of peace consistent with the rights and needs of the countries concerned. The agreement contains features which we do not like, but a great deal depends on how they work in practice.

The United States is issuing at Geneva a statement to the effect that it is not prepared to join in the conference declaration but, as loyal members of the United Nations, we also say that in compliance with the obligations and principles contained in article II of the United Nations Charter, the United States will not use force to disturb the settlement. We also say that any renewal of Communist aggression would be viewed by us as a matter of grave concern.

As evidence of our resolve to assist Cambodia and Laos to play their parts in full independence and sovereignty, in the peaceful community of free nations, we are requesting the agreement of the governments of Cambodia and Laos to our appointment of an ambassador or minister to be resident at their respective capitals. We already have a Chief of Mission at Saigon, the capital of Viet-Nam, and this embassy will, of course, be maintained.

The United States is actively pursuing discussions with other free nations with a view to the rapid organization of a collective defense in southeast Asia in order to prevent further direct or indirect Communist aggression in that general area. [*Ends reading*]

Now, ladies and gentlemen, because of the delicacy of the negotiations going on, because this matter is at a very critical stage, I think I shall have nothing further to say about the situation this morning.

Q. Merriman Smith, United Press: Mr. President, I wonder if you can bring us up to date on your attitude or your feelings toward the condition in which you find your legislative program?

THE PRESIDENT. Of course, the accomplishments of the Legislature are frequently lost sight of because of the great publicity value of fights and failures.

By and large, there has been such accomplishment of the past 2 to 3 weeks that the prospect that seemed to be generally accepted as sound a few weeks ago has proved to be in error.

I think that it is coming along in good shape; although, of course, there will be, admittedly, features in which I am very deeply interested that are not going to be enacted.

Q. Nicholas P. Gregory, Philadelphia Inquirer: Mr. President, on May 11th, you appointed an interdepartmental economic commission to study the possible rehabilitation of the northeastern Pennsylvania hard coal region. Can you tell us when that report will be released by the White House?

THE PRESIDENT. Well, I can't tell you. They just brought me an interim report that they are working very hard, and there have been a number of specific proposals that have been studied; some they feel have certain validity and virtue, can be supported, and one or two have been impractical. Now, they haven't brought me any further than that.

Q. Robert E. Clark, International News Service: Mr. President, the Democrats have used some pretty strong language on the Hill this week in attacking the administration proposal to grant a private power contract in the Tennessee Valley area. Republican Senator Cooper of Kentucky has also joined critics of the proposal. Is there any chance, any possibility, of the administration changing its position on this issue?

THE PRESIDENT. I constantly state in front of you people that there are always details of anything I propose where, if I am shown there is a better way of doing it, why, I am perfectly ready to do it.

Now, I think I explained this situation here a couple of weeks ago. This area says it needs power because industries want to come into that region.

Long ago, the project of harnessing the streams in the area was completed, and the Federal Government also built the steamplants to firm up the waterpower potential.

In these recent years it has been merely a question of producing steamplants. Well, now, the problem in my mind, and I should think in everybody's, is if the Federal Government goes into the constant production of steamplants, why don't we go now to the Missouri Valley or to the Ohio or to the Connecticut or the Sacramento or the Pecos or anywhere else, and produce steamplants in that region before we go putting more here?

I am trying to find out the facts of this whole situation, what it means.

As I told you before, I am prepared to support the TVA as it now stands with all the strength I have, and anyone who says there is any attempt to destroy the TVA is, to say it in the mildest way I know, in error. There is no such thought at all.

There is the thought of providing the power while we take a new and further look at this whole business because the whole United States is concerned, not simply one little area, and I am working for the United States.

Q. Raymond P. Brandt, St. Louis Post-Dispatch: Mr. President, is Senator Knowland speaking for the administration in his opposition to the Flanders resolution?

THE PRESIDENT. They haven't even asked me about it, they haven't even asked me a thing about it. I have taken no stand whatsoever on it.

Q. Mr. Brandt: You are taking none now?

THE PRESIDENT. None now.

Q. Alan S. Emory, Watertown Times: Sir, a couple of days ago, the Young Democrats of the country, meeting in their convention, endorsed your proposal to lower the voting age to 18 years. Would you consider that this bipartisan backing among the politically conscious youth of the Nation might well be transferred to their seniors in Congress?

THE PRESIDENT. I think you people have often heard me say that I thought all of us older citizens could well learn many things from the younger ones, and now it seems that even political parties should be able to do so. Of course I am for them, and I welcome their support.

Q. Edward Jamieson, Houston Chronicle: Mr. President, last week Senator Daniel, after seeing you, quoted you as saying that you felt and recognized the 10½-mile limit in the offshores of Texas. Since then there have been some statements by other people adding some confusion, or creating some confusion. Has your administration any intention of changing the historic 3-league boundary of Texas in the Gulf of Mexico?

THE PRESIDENT. Let me say, again, back in 1946 or 1947, as I recall, I saw a group of papers that seemed to me to be furnishing conclusive evidence that the proper title to the so-called tidelands to historic boundaries belonged to the States. I took that view then; I have never had any reason to change it. I have supported that view, and by no word or action that I know of have I ever implied modification of that idea. No one has ever brought forward an argument that I thought was valid against it.

I still support it, and if there is any confusion, it certainly is in somebody else's mind, not mine, on that point.

Q. Mrs. May Craig, Maine Papers: Mr. President, President Rhee of Korea will be here soon. Do you regard the partition of Korea as permanent, short of war, and are you including, planning to include, Korea and Free China in any kind of a southeast Asia pact?

THE PRESIDENT. Well, of course, Korea is not in southeast Asia.

Already we have, you know, a treaty of mutual defense with Korea. It has been enacted, it has been approved, by the Senate.

Now, as I understand it, when the Korean war started, the purpose of the United Nations was to prevent any advance by force into South Korea; they did do that.

I know of no one that has ever proposed that we go to war to free North Korea.

As it is, it is an unsatisfactory situation, exactly as exists in Germany, and now apparently is going to exist in part of Indochina.

These are very unsatisfactory situations and, to my mind, will always give reason for aggravating situations that are difficult, at best. But there is no thought on the part of any of us to start an aggressive move for the freeing of that country.

Q. Richard L. Wilson, Cowles Publications: Mr. President, if I understood you correctly, you said earlier that the prospect for a favorable legislative program a few weeks ago is in error. Does that mean that the program is a disappointment to you?

THE PRESIDENT. No. I possibly did not make myself too clear, Mr. Wilson, but I remember a few weeks ago I saw many predictions that the whole program had collapsed, and there would be no major part of it, outside of appropriation bills, enacted.

As the session has gone on, it seems to me that the record is building up constantly in better fashion, and I think now we can easily see that some of the gloomy predictions were in error.

Q. Sarah McClendon, El Paso Times: Sir, several weeks ago Congressmen from the drought-ridden States began asking the Department of Agriculture to set up a new drought program. We have none now. It ended July 15th, and cattle are being dumped on the markets, and many States are affected. I was told today that you might decide if Texas and Wyoming would be declared emergency areas.

THE PRESIDENT. Well, it just happens that those two declarations were signed this morning. I signed declarations for at least, I think, three areas, and this is in addition to the flood relief granted Texas in actual money. I think that Mr. Hagerty will probably have an announcement this afternoon of the exact areas, so you can get it.[1]

Q. Chalmers M. Roberts, Washington Post and Times Herald: Mr. President, when you mentioned Korea and Nationalist China a moment ago, you referred to the fact that we have a Mutual Defense Pact with Korea. There was a story only this morning quoting our Ambassador to Formosa as saying some negotiations were under way for a similar arrangement with Formosa. Is it our intention to go through with that kind of arrangement, thus limiting or voiding the question of whether Formosa should belong to the proposed southeast Asia pact?

THE PRESIDENT. I don't think the two subjects have been considered together or, as you might say, mutually exclusive.

All I know is that with respect to the first one, that is a matter that has been under study for some time and there has been no final decision reached yet.

Q. Nat S. Finney, Buffalo Evening News: Mr. President, do you attach any particular significance or special significance to the apparent fact that for the first time in about 20 years, almost two decades, there isn't a war going on somewhere in the world?

THE PRESIDENT. Well, of course, you could talk about the terrors of

---

[1] On July 28 the White House announced that 83 counties in Texas, Colorado, New Mexico, and Wyoming had already been designated drought disaster areas, and that feed grain from Commodity Credit Corporation stocks would be made available in these areas. The release added that further aid was available through the cooperative Federal-State hay supply program and through Farmers Home Administration loans.

On August 2 the White House announced that 76 counties in Missouri and 26 in Oklahoma had been designated as drought disaster areas, and that the situation in Alabama, Kansas, Kentucky, Georgia, and Tennessee was under continuous study.

war, and you could be a bit emotional on that side, but I don't think it is in that direction we find the true answer.

I have never felt that, except through these satellite excursions, that the Communist world wants any war at this time; in other words, I don't believe they would deliberately challenge us, challenge the free world, to a war of exhaustion.

So the problem, no matter whether you happen to be fighting in one of these areas, remains the same. The loss of great areas through propaganda and deceit and subversion and *coup d'état,* and every means available to a secret, well-financed conspiracy, they are all there. I personally think that if there is one good that can come out of this whole southeast Asian experience, it is this: to get the free world to looking facts in the face, and to seeing what we must do, what we should do, what sacrifices we are ready to make, in order to preserve the essentials of our system.

I think that when the freedom of a man in Viet-Nam or in China is taken away from him, I think our freedom has lost a little. I just don't believe that we can continue to exist in the world, geographically isolated as we are, if we just don't find a concerted, positive plan of keeping these free nations so tightly bound together that none of them will give up; and if they are not weakened internally by these other methods, I just don't believe they will give up. I believe we can hold them.

Q. Robert E. Clark, International News Service: Mr. President, along that line, a number of Congressmen today are branding the Geneva settlement as appeasement. Do you think there are any elements of appeasement in the cease-fire agreement?

THE PRESIDENT. Well, I hesitate, Mr. Clark, to use such words, as I have told you so often. I find that so many words mean so many different things to different people. I would say this, as I said in my statement: this agreement, in certain of its features, is not satisfactory to us. It is not what we would have liked to have had.

But I don't know, when I am put up against it at this moment, to find an alternative, to say what we would or could do. Then if I have no better plan, I am not going to criticize what they have done.

Q. Edward T. Folliard, Washington Post and Times Herald: Mr. President, I hope this is outside of the area of the Geneva conference wherein you didn't want to say any more. But about the time the Geneva conference was starting there was a report from Paris that the French had asked us for war planes manned by Americans to make a strike at that Dien Bien Phu. I asked you about that report at the time, and you said you couldn't comment then. But as I remember it, you suggested that you might be able to talk about it at some later time. I wondered if that time had arrived?

THE PRESIDENT. I'll tell you, Mr. Folliard, we have, at least discussed briefly, and—I am not making this as a promise, I am just saying this as a possibility—we will prepare sort of a paper of the history of this thing, get it all in focus, and try to give you all the information we have. Certain of these things—one reason that you can't talk about them independently is, they mean nothing. If a request comes to you and you say no, that would appear to indicate a harsh and unsympathetic attitude. But if you know the whole long weary route of negotiations that preceded it, and you find that the "no" is merely consistent with what you have been doing and trying to do for months, then it is a different thing.

So, therefore, I think it would be far better if we can possibly give a short history of our relationship to the whole thing.

Q. William M. Blair, New York Times: On your legislative program, sir, there are now some 10 days left before the target adjournment date of July 31st. At the present time the Senate seems more or less bogged down in extended debate over atomic energy and TVA. Does this tend to dismiss chances that you will get all of your program before the Congress leaves?

THE PRESIDENT. Well, as I admitted, I knew there were features that I was not going to get; but I am certain of this: the legislative leaders are working hard and effectively to get the bulk of it through before the adjournment.

Now, it is true, they have had July 31st as a target. I don't know whether they have yet made that a decision that they want to go. I haven't talked to the leaders in the last 2 or 3 days about their ability to stick to the target date.

Q. Milton B. Freudenheim, Akron Beacon Journal: Mr. President, the House voted on a housing bill yesterday, and in the debate some said that it represented a setback for your program as it bore on the low-rent public housing feature. The Senate is supposed to vote on this bill, as it came out of conference, possibly tomorrow. Do you have any comment on this housing bill, sir?

THE PRESIDENT. Well, ladies and gentlemen, very naturally we thought that the program we laid in front of the Legislature was well designed to meet our present and our needs of the immediate future.

Now, practically all of that housing program has been enacted, let's not forget that; but when it came up to this public housing feature, we do know that it has always been a very controversial point.

I believe, as I have so often said, given the right kind of help through localities and municipalities, States, and so on, that private enterprise could finally get into this business and probably do it better than any Government bureaucracy.

But I also believe that, as we are trying to do that and to get this understanding and all these arrangements accepted in the world, there is still a problem of people living in bad houses. So I want the authority to build public housing where that is absolutely necessary.

Most people don't like it; it gives no chance for house ownership. But I wanted 35,000 a year for 4 years; they gave that actual authority only for '56. We now, I believe, have a total authority under that bill of 68,000 through '56.

Now, next year at the very beginning of the session or whenever facts begin to clarify a little bit, I will send messages to the Senate and the House to meet the new situation, whatever it is.

Q. Joseph A. Loftus, New York Times: Mr. President, in connection with your program, can you tell us anything more today about your proposals for handling the debt limit problem?

THE PRESIDENT. No, I can't. It is one that hasn't been up for 2 or 3 days; and anything that is 2 or 3 days old, these days, is forgotten almost.

Q. John Herling, Editors Syndicate: Mr. President, the wetback legislation prepared by Attorney General Brownell is sort of bogged down in the Congress, and at the time it was introduced there was great urgency about it, and it seems to continue to be that. Do you plan to give the idea an additional push?

THE PRESIDENT. Well, wherever I see an opportunity, yes, I will.

This is part of a general program that the Attorney General has to make it possible for him to enforce the laws as written. We want to make sure there is no disposition here in any of these laws to interfere with the transient workers who come in by legal means. They want them, they want to come; it is all on the up and up. The only difficulty is these that come across illegally; it is difficult to control unless he gets these additional measures. I believe there are two of them on that particular subject that should be enacted.

Q. Alan S. Emory, Watertown Times: Sir, during the debate on the atomic energy revisions, Senator Lehman of New York characterized the international exchange section of the bill as a counterpart of the Bricker amendment in that it would restrict the exchange of information to one nation at a time, and would subject your agreements to a check by Congress. Have you any comment on that, sir?

THE PRESIDENT. Well, I don't know exactly what he is talking about, for this reason: there have always been in the atomic energy bill certain provisions where items are taken down and laid in front of the Joint Committee before anything is done about them.

I don't know exactly what Senator Lehman is talking about, but I do know this: the bill, as I last read it, would give us the necessary authority to exchange required information with our allies so that we could work effectively together in the event of emergency.

Q. Kenneth M. Scheibel, Gannett Newspapers: Mr. President, is there anything that you see on the horizon now in either the foreign or domestic front which might require a special session of Congress this fall?

THE PRESIDENT. Of course I can't foresee it, because if I could foresee it exactly, I would tell the leaders about it now and have a big conference.

The very word "special" means that it is really designed to meet an emergency, isn't it? So there are numbers of problems that have to be talked out thoroughly with the leaders before they go so they know what the situation is, and we have got to be in agreement—I am not speaking of leaders now, some of these will be on a bipartisan basis I assume—that will give us an understanding among ourselves how we would handle given situations should they arise.

Q. Doris Fleeson, United Features: Mr. President, one of the major points in the debate on the Atomic Energy Commission-TVA contract today arose out of testimony before the Joint Committee on Atomic Energy that three Commissioners of the Atomic Energy Commission opposed signing the contract. Therefore, the Senators are arguing the question of whether the President has the power to order independent agencies to take action that their administrators or a Commission majority oppose. Would you discuss your attitude toward that problem?

THE PRESIDENT. Well, I am not going to discuss it very greatly, very obviously. I have an Attorney General, and when there is a matter of legality arises, why, I have to be governed by what the legal staff of that office decides is correct. Remember this: it isn't always a matter of taking authority in these cases, it is a matter of somebody exercising responsibility; someone has to do it. Frequently, I suppose lots of people would like to get out of exercising responsibility, but you have to do it when the chips are down.

In this one you are telling me things and you are giving me a premise that I didn't know existed. I will say this: the Atomic Energy Commission I do not believe is an independent commission in the sense that the ICC or FCC is; it is something that I am compelled to take action on and over which to exercise supervision.

Merriman Smith, United Press: Thank you, Mr. President.

NOTE: President Eisenhower's forty-fifth news conference was held in the Executive Office Building from 11:32 to 12 o'clock on Wednesday morning, July 21, 1954. In attendance: 190.

169   ¶ Statement by the President Reviewing the Progress Made Toward a Balanced Budget.
July 22, 1954

THE GOVERNMENT made a better showing than expected in fiscal 1954 by $245 million. This improvement is shown today in the monthly budget statement for June, which reports a $3.029 billion year-end deficit, $245 million less than the $3.274 billion estimated in the January budget.

We reduced the budget proposed by the previous administration by more than $10 billion, and we cut actual spending by more than $6½ billion under the amount spent in fiscal 1953.

We have come over two-thirds of the way toward balancing the budget. And we have done this while putting into effect a tax program which will return nearly $7½ billion to the people.

These fiscal achievements mean a great deal to the American people:

(1) We have made possible a program of tax cuts totaling $7½ billion.

651

(2) We have halted inflation. The purchasing power of the dollar has varied only one half of one cent in the past 18 months.

(3) Our people have new confidence. We are laying a firm base for a healthy and expanding economy for better national security, and for more jobs for more people.

The progressive reduction in estimated budget expenditures and deficits is shown in the following table (in rounded hundreds of millions) :

| | 1953 Actual | 1954 | | |
		In January 1953 Budget	In January 1954 Budget	Figures at Year-end
Budget receipts	$64. 8	$68. 0	$67. 6	$64. 6
Budget expenditures	74. 3	77. 9	70. 9	67. 6
Deficit	9. 4	9. 9	3. 274	3. 029

Attached are (1) a joint statement by the Secretary of the Treasury and the Director of the Budget and (2) the Monthly Statement of Government Receipts and Expenditures for the month ending June 30, and last day of the fiscal year. The figures are subject to final audit, which may result in comparatively minor changes.

NOTE: The joint statement by the Secretary of the Treasury and the Director of the Bureau of the Budget, dated July 22, 1954, contains a detailed breakdown of the figures in the President's statement, showing areas of change in final receipts and expenditures as compared with the original budget estimates. The monthly budget statement for June, entitled "Monthly Statement of Receipts and Expenditures of the United States Government for the period July 1, 1953, through June 30, 1954," contains summary tables for the fiscal year and a detailed comparison of June with the corresponding month of the preceding year. It was prepared by the Treasury Department and printed by the Government Printing Office.

170 ¶ Remarks at the World Christian Endeavor Convention.   *July 25, 1954*

Dr. Poling and friends:

It is indeed a very great honor to be invited to come here to extend to you, on behalf of this Government, a greeting to the Capital of the United States. Those of you who come from our own country, and those who come from abroad, are met here in a fellowship from which we naturally expect much, and because of which we extend to you a greeting that is more than usually sincere.

While I am talking about this matter of just meeting you, I should like to ask each of you a favor. You will return soon to your homes, and I should like for you, whether you live abroad or in America, to take to all your associates personal good wishes, a personal expression of hope from me and from this Government, that all of your labors, all of your meetings, all of your endeavors, will lead ever toward that closer bond of brotherhood and friendship without which this poor old world is indeed in trouble, and which I believe that the young people of this world can do so much to promote.

Now, when we talk about such high moral efforts in this world today, we sometimes encounter in the diplomatic field the statement that if an international relationship does not use moral standards, that it is based upon expedience, or upon practical solutions to practical problems of the moment. And mayhap this is sometimes true, in the temporary sense. But it cannot possibly be true in the permanent sense, if we are to win that security, that peace, for which all mankind so desperately longs.

We must remember the spiritual base that underlies man's existence, and the spiritual base that underlies all free government; else we shall surely fail.

That there is a spiritual base to all free types of government is not difficult to demonstrate, of course. Free government makes as its cornerstone the concept, or the idea, that men are equal—they are equal before the law, they have equal rights and equal opportunities in the governments maintained to protect them.

Now we know that men and women are not equal among themselves, physically; they are not equal among themselves mentally. Consequently, they must be equal, if free government has any validity, in some way that has nothing to do with the physical or intellectual make-up of man. And that can be only his spiritual side.

Therefore, if we do not believe in the spiritual character of man, we would be foolish indeed to be supporting the concept of free government in the world—free government as opposed to dictatorship. But so long as we do recognize the spiritual values in man, his spiritual side, and recognize the dependency of free government upon these spiritual values, then everything that we are trying to do makes sense. Then the words "the dignity of man" assume real meaning. We may work for it with our whole hearts, we may work for true brotherhood among men without any qualification whatsoever, except doing everything honorable to achieve success.

In the great conflict that is going on in the world today, one side upholds the freedom and dignity of man, and therefore recognizes his spiritual character. The other lives by something it calls the materialistic dialectic, meaning only that it denies all the kinds of values that you young people support. It says there are no values in life except the material ones—what you can see or express in the material or intellectual way.

And this, of course, we know to be false. So, not only do you people get the satisfaction that comes to every human in this world, as he labors for the benefit of his brothers and his sisters, you know that in laboring to promote an understanding of these spiritual values, to raise them ever higher in our calculations of everything we do, that you are working for a permanent, lasting, durable peace among all the men of the world who so desperately thirst for it.

And I should like, of course, to give you this one conviction of my own: that all men, all masses, do truly long for peace. They want you to win the struggle you are waging. It is only governments that are stupid, not the masses of people. Governments may seek for power, for the right to dominate, to extend their authority over others. Free people do not seek that.

So your task is to help every man realize that he, himself, because he has been born in this world, is valuable. He is meaningful. He is important to you, because as you defend his rights you are defending your own.

And then we must make men understand that people who believe that way must unite among themselves, if they are to meet successfully the opposition which is united by force, by the threat of the MVD, by the threat of the police, the threat that comes about when child is asked to inform upon its parents, when there is no sanctity left in family life or in community life—anything, indeed, except slavish devotion to the head of the state.

Most of you are still young. You have your whole lives to live. You have, in other words a 60 or 70 year investment in this old earth. People my age, if they are lucky, have 10 or 15 years still invested in it. This earth is very much more important to you, then, possibly, than it is to us elders.

654

I say to you this, as possibly the only worthwhile word I can bring to you: if you remain ever true to the principles lying behind the organization to which you belong, if you believe in them with all your heart, if you live them, and if you get countless others to join with you in supporting those values, then indeed your lives will be fruitful and happy ones, and all those that come after you will be the beneficiaries of your great work.

My friends, though today we must remain strong in all the economic and the scientific affairs of the world, we must remain strong militarily for the protection of our firesides and our rights, to prevent domination by those who would seek to enthrall us. Yet bullets and guns and planes and ships—all the weapons of war—can produce no real or lasting peace. Only a great moral crusade, determined that men shall rise above this conception of materialism, rise above it and live as people who attempt to express in some faint and feeble way their conceptions of what the Almighty would have us do—that is the force that will win through to victory. Then the world will have prosperity and peace—prosperity beyond all the imaginings of the past; science will be developed and devoted to the happiness, the welfare of man, and not to his destruction; and all of us can live together peacefully and happily.

To each of you, wherever you go, I say: good luck and may God bless you.

NOTE: The President spoke at 4:00 p.m. in the main ballroom of the Mayflower Hotel in Washington. Dr. Daniel A. Poling, editor of the Christian Herald, served as chairman of the meeting.

171 ¶ Toasts of the President and President Rhee of Korea at the White House. *July* 26, 1954

Mr. President, Mrs. Rhee, my friends:

I am sure there is no one at this table who does not feel, Mr. President, a feeling of distinction in your visit to this country, and your presence at this table. I think it is not difficult to discover the reasons for this sense of pride and distinction, and I hope I will not be considered guilty of filibustering—(*laughter*)—if I asked you for a moment to go back with me to a lecture I heard in my staff college days.

The lecturer was pointing out that the principal characteristic of life is change. And since he was talking about war, he talked about the changing factors that the fighting man had to consider in his calculations as to war. He pointed out that there are constant changes in the means of transportation, in the weapons to be used, in methods of supply—everything that we do; and that the rules that sometimes obtain among so-called civilized nations, they change.

And then he pointed out that there is one factor that is completely unpredictable, completely unreliable and untrustworthy, and yet never changes—only one—and that is human nature.

In support of his thesis, he pointed out that there is no history so old, no mythology so venerable, that it does not glorify the qualities of courage, of stamina, of reliability, of self-sacrifice, and does not treat with contempt all of the opposites, of intolerance, evil and selfishness.

So I think that in our feeling of pride in the Korean people, and the presence here of their Chief Representative, we are merely responding to an age-old instinct of man, to venerate those qualities that we call ennobling, that we believe are somewhat Godlike in their quality. And we have seen the Korean people through tribulation, through troubles, through enslavement, under brutal attack, respond gallantly and with courage.

It has been a great source of pride to Americans that, with her other allies of the Western World, we could join with Korea in seeing that that country should not be overrun by the invading hordes from the north.

And to the courage of that people, to its prosperity, to its future happiness, I think we may drink a Toast by doing so in the name of their Representative here present—President Rhee.

Ladies and gentlemen, President Rhee.

NOTE: The President proposed this toast at a dinner in the State Dining Room in the White House. President Rhee responded as follows:

Mr. President, Mrs. Eisenhower, ladies and gentlemen:

The honor which has been paid to Korea tonight is beyond any words of mine to express my feelings, and those of my people. I want you, my friends, to know that the Korean hearts, the hearts of the Koreans who are here in our party—the hearts of all the Koreans who are in Korea—are full of gratitude and thanks to you, and to the American Government and the American people.

I would like very much to tell something about what the American aid and assistance have done, what the American fighting men have done in Korea, to save at least half of that war-torn peninsula. And I would like to say how much the American citizens, individually and collectively, have done in the way of relief work for Koreans.

But I can't. I don't know how to start, or how to end.

All that I ask you, my friends, is to know that we are grateful to you for everything you have done, and for everything that you are doing.

We are grateful. And we will remain grateful.

Talk about bravery of the Korean people—the Korean fighting men. Yes. We thank God we were willing to fight, were willing to fight to the finish, as long as there are territories still occupied by a foreign Communist army. And not only soldiers—army, navy, and air, maybe—but the people, the men and women, rank and file, the many—they are all one, in that we cannot live unless we unify our country, unless the aggressive Communist armies are out of our land.

That same spirit is what proved that the Koreans have an army known to be the biggest anti-Communist defensive force in Asia. Yes, I say that they are willing to die, they are willing to give their lives.

Why are these Koreans so brave? Why are they so willing to give up their lives? I will tell you why. Their country was occupied by an alien rule for 40 years. They have experienced how terrible it is to live under a foreign military rule. That gave them the conviction that unless we have our independence and our own government, our lives are not ours, we have no freedom—just as Patrick Henry said he would rather die than live as a slave.

That is the feeling there. But that is not what I mean to say. What I mean to say is that the Koreans must have a wonderful fighting spirit—they are wonderful soldiers, and all that. But not without your aid. Your fighting men came over there and trained them and helped them build up their morale and their spirit. And your weapons! Look what all that has done for them. When I go over to the front lines, they are all standing up, every soldier equipped from head to foot—all from America. This is what makes Korean boys strong fighting men.

Pardon me, I didn't intend to make a speech. I just got up and wished to say a word or two in response to the remarks that President Eisenhower made, which are very complimentary to me. And I want you to know this, you friends who honor me: all this is wonderful to me, and what your President, and Vice President, Mrs. Eisenhower and Mrs. Nixon—all you friends—are doing to welcome me and receiving me in such a magnificent way—it all flashed back to the soldiers of Korea, spread all over the country.

Now your great American President—the American people—are honoring our country, our people. That means so much to us. And I tell you, my friends, I do not know, if I live hundreds of years, we will never be able to do enough to pay our debt of gratitude to you.

I want you to know, my friends, that the Korean people will do anything and everything they can do to accomplish their common objectives: that is, to defeat the Communist aggressors, and to make the world, at least our part of the world, safe for democracy.

I thank President Eisenhower and Mrs. Eisenhower for planning this dinner in such a wonderful way, and all their friends here—every one; if they asked me to make a list of guests to attend this dinner, I would not make it any different, or any better. Thank you, my friends, for your presence here, to make this occasion so wonderful to me.

I wish I could have time to spend 1 hour with each one of my friends here. That would be wonderful. I have so much to talk about. But I mustn't talk any more. I just want you all to know I am so full of gratitude and thanks to you. I sometimes talk too long, but that is what my friends are expecting me to do.

Before I sit down, I should like to ask you to join me in a Toast to the health and success of President Eisenhower, and include Mrs. Eisenhower.

172 ¶ The President's News Conference of July 28, 1954.

THE PRESIDENT. Ladies and gentlemen, we will go right to questions this morning.

Q. Marvin L. Arrowsmith, Associated Press: Mr. President, I wonder if you would give us your appraisal of the recent Chinese Communist attacks on British and American planes particularly in the light of apparent concern on the part of some of our allies that it might touch off another war. Are you disturbed about this situation?

THE PRESIDENT. Of course, things like this always cause deep concern and deep study.

The sequence of events was that we learned of this transport plane being shot down; there were Americans aboard, and so instantly we ordered a task force into the area to pursue rescue operations—not to provoke any incident, but to take any necessary measures to defend themselves while they were doing this task. You know, I think, then the sequence of events; and, of course, when we were attacked, there were two of these Chinese planes shot down. We protested, and then they claimed that these planes were where they shouldn't be. We were perfectly certain they were not only where they should be, but on legitimate business.

The orders of the task force were to stay there as long as there was any hope of finding any of these people. I would assume that period is now at an end, and I would expect them to be leaving the area momentarily, although I don't know the exact hour in which Admiral Phillips has ordered them out. It is his judgment as to when no hope remains.

Now, of course, in the first instance the Communists apologized at once; then when we were involved they took a different attitude. I think it is difficult to calculate with any confidence what that means, but I would say that at the very least it is part of the regular plan of separating the Western allies one from the other, of having a different attitude toward one than it does toward the other—an attempt, therefore, to split us up.

I notice that the dispatches show that in Paris there is anxiety, that we were thought to be impulsive and truculent. We don't mean to be, but we do mean to defend our rights, and our people will defend themselves wherever they are on legitimate business.

That is all, I think, I have to say on that.

Q. Pat Munroe, Salt Lake City Deseret News: Mr. President, my question concerns several proposed water projects in the vicinity of your summer headquarters in the Rocky Mountain area. Frying Pan-Arkansas, of course, is up in the House this afternoon, but there is very violent opposition from southern California water users who are downstream on the Colorado. I wonder if you would have any comment on this.

THE PRESIDENT. I had the matter up for some explanation to me a few days ago. I have not had the complete conclusions of the people within the Cabinet and executive department who have been put, you know, on the Water Resources Board. I am told, however, that there is no water involved except that which, by prior agreement and by law, belongs to Colorado and does not belong to downstream States; this is by some riparian rights. I don't know any further facts on the matter at this time.

I know that some people say it is a very fine project and will work to the welfare of that whole region; others say it is a very, very bad project. But I must say, ladies and gentlemen, those same observations apply to many projects that are brought up.

Q. Alan S. Emory, Watertown (N.Y.) Daily Times: Mr. President, both the farm bills, as approved by the House of Representatives and the Senate Agriculture Committee, contain a provision permitting the Secretary of Agriculture to make direct subsidy payments to dairy farmers under the price support program. Do you see any difference between this proposal and the Brannan Plan, which you attacked so vigorously during the '52 campaign?

THE PRESIDENT. Well, of course, the Brannan Plan, at least, was larger in scope, and wanted to apply the same principle to many products.

I have taken my stand and announced it on the dairy situation. The dairy situation has been improving very markedly in different respects since the rigid price supports were broken down, I believe, the 1st of April—or March. Their market has been growing. We would hope that would continue.

I personally believe that the dairy program should not be disturbed as it now is.

Q. Robert E. Clark, International News Service: Mr. President, the Swiss Government is saying that your action yesterday in boosting watch tariffs is a serious blow to the whole program of free trade. Do you think that boosting tariffs is consistent with the administration's program of increasing trade and lowering tariffs?

THE PRESIDENT. Well, Mr. Clark, you say "boosting tariffs"; this is one specialized instance. I forget how many cases have come from the Tariff Commission to me, all recommending increased tariffs because of their findings that certain segments of our industry are adversely affected.

There was one minor one in which I partially approved their recommendations, and that had to do with a particular kind of clover from Canada, as I recall it. All the rest I disapproved, because I believe we must have a freer and better flow, bigger flow, of international trade.

This one, this watch program and project, has been studied for many years; there have been many actions taken on it. I personally have been studying it intensively for some weeks. I decided finally that the weight of the evidence was on the side of some increase; and, of course, I had to take, on that basis, the recommendations of the Tariff Commission.

Now, I want to point out that this is something that you think is right. I do not claim by any stretch of the imagination that my decisions are sacrosanct and are going to be forever true. I simply say that it looked to me, at this moment, this was the thing to do.

As you know, the Tariff Commission is required to report back to me within 2 years as to the effect of the action just taken, but I am not stopped at any time from asking them to resurvey the whole situation whenever I desire.

Q. Robert W. Richards, The Copley Press: Mr. President, would you discuss the collateral reason why you decided to increase tariffs on Swiss watches, that is, the military significance?

THE PRESIDENT. Well, of course, the legal reason is that which is given by the Tariff Commission; and that is that serious damage is being done to American industry.

But from the standpoint of defense, it seems to me that we must preserve certain kinds of skills in the United States. A particular skill is this ability to deal with very close tolerances, very fine work. When I look at the record of the number of men that were employed in these industries only a matter of 2 or 3 years ago, and what are now employed in this area, it seemed to me that was a collateral reason for trying to save roughly 20 or 25 percent of our market for our own people in this field.

Q. Oscar W. Reschke, German Press: Mr. President, the Senate Foreign Relations Committee called on you yesterday for direct action in case of non-ratification of EDC to restore German sovereignty and permit her to contribute to the Western defense. Would you tell us, please, what steps you would deem necessary or appropriate to restore sovereignty?

THE PRESIDENT. Let me ask, has that report of the Senate gone to the Senate floor?

Q. Mr. Reschke: It will go to the Senate floor, most probably today.

THE PRESIDENT. Well, has it been made public? Has the resolution itself been made public?

Q. Mr. Reschke: Yes.

THE PRESIDENT. Well, of course, I most thoroughly approve then of the resolution itself which was worked out between the Senate committee and the Secretary of State.

Just exactly what measures would have to be taken, of course, cannot be detailed; if they could have been, they would have been, I suppose, included in the resolution. But it does direct the President to take such steps as he finds necessary to effectuate certain parts of the treaty of '52, in spite of the fact that certain of the conditions laid down in that '52 treaty have not been met—namely, the enactment of EDC. So I have to, under this resolution, take such steps as I deem necessary to move along in securing a better relationship with Germany.

Q. Sarah McClendon, El Paso Times: Sir, in the Texas election, Governor Shivers received surprisingly stiff opposition in a race in which his support of you in '52 was somewhat of an issue, and there were five Congressmen who openly or by implication had more or less come out for you, and they either retired voluntarily or were retired at the polls. I wonder if you or your party leaders have analyzed this election yet?

THE PRESIDENT. No. As a matter of fact, it is the other party that is having this election, and—[*laughter*]—no one has said a word to me about it from our own party officials.

I don't mind saying that Governor Shivers is a friend of mine. I have liked him and admired him; I think he has made a good Governor. Not only, of course, was I pleased that personally he found it proper to support me in '52 but, as a person born in Texas myself, why, I have that much interest in him.

Q. Joseph A. Loftus, New York Times: Mr. President, I have a political question, too, sir. In the past few months there has been some modification of your policy with respect to political campaigns; I refer specifically to your support of individual candidacies by name. I wonder if we might expect any further modification of that policy in the coming fall campaign?

THE PRESIDENT. This is what I said, as I recall, and I am subject to correction because I don't claim that my memory is perfect: I said I was not going into different districts stumping for particular candidates; that wherever I spoke and whatever I said or did, I was going to talk about a program; and that if I was in an area where the individual had supported that program, I would expect or hope, at least, that my presence there helped him.

But I don't believe that I pledged myself to abstain from making a speech or going anywhere; I didn't say that.

Now, recently I was asked a question about an individual, and I admitted that I was in a bit of a dilemma, but I did admire and respect that person. I believe that is as much as I have said; that was before this body.

As I say, my statement still stands. I expect to do some traveling, and I certainly hope that it will not damage anyone who supported the program I have laid before the legislature.

Q. Mrs. May Craig, Maine Papers: Mr. President, is there anything you can tell us now about the visit and your conversations with President Rhee?

THE PRESIDENT. Well, very little. He and I have had private conversations.

The Secretary of State is meeting with him this morning. The investigations and conversations are going ahead in two main channels, the military and the economic. They are going ahead now, and I would assume before he leaves we will, following the usual pattern, have a statement to release.

Q. Raymond P. Brandt, St. Louis Post-Dispatch: Mr. President, what standards or qualifications are required for Congressmen to have their pictures taken with you? [*Laughter*]

THE PRESIDENT. You know, after all, there is a bit of a compliment when a Congressman comes up and asks to have his picture taken; at least he seems to imply he is not going to be damaged by that picture. [*Laughter*]

I go on the theory that anyone who comes up is normally someone who believes generally as I do. I do admit that I take a little bit of a check, as much as time gives me, to see whether on the important things in which I believe he has generally been along.

I have told you people time and again, I think, I don't believe that support of an administration or of my views personally has to be 100 percent. We do have different ideas about different things, and that makes democracy. But I do believe that the principles on which I am trying to conduct the business of my office must be observed or I shouldn't try to give help to him.

Q. Mr. Brandt: Have any been refused or will be refused?

THE PRESIDENT. I haven't done it personally. If some of the people around me have, that's different; I don't know.

Q. John W. Vandercook, American Broadcasting Company: Mr. President, on Saturday, I believe, the House Appropriations Committee knocked out an item of some $18 million appropriations for the technical assistance program of the United Nations and, I believe, that was supported by a small vote, but a majority vote, in the House yesterday. Now, that was part of your program, part of your recommendation, and I wondered if you would have any comment to make or propose to take any further action?

THE PRESIDENT. Well, I would take further action in this respect: these things go from one House to another House; when I find something that I deem of importance, and this item has some importance, I take it up then with the second group to deal with it and show them how important I believe it to be so that congressional action can, at least, have the full knowledge of the importance I attach to the point. And so, if they do support me, then they can take it up in conference.

Q. Mr. Vandercook: And you do approve that?

THE PRESIDENT. I think we should have this thing.

Q. Robert E. Clark, International News Service: Mr. President, now that the filibuster is over, do you feel any concern for the rest of your program in Congress?

THE PRESIDENT. I thought I might get that. [*Laughter*] If you don't mind, I will read what I have. [*Laughter*] I just made a list of the items that are still in front of the Senate:

The farm bill—this would begin, as you know I feel, a new and sound agricultural policy for the country;

The tax bill which, as I pointed out to you before, I believe is so necessary for stimulation of business, the creation of jobs, better tax arrangements in this country;

The Attorney General's anti-Communist bills, to punish those who seek to destroy and overthrow our form of Government;

The housing conference report, which will help our cities cope with the growing slums and make it easier for low-income families to obtain housing;

Social security measures to safeguard our citizens against need;

Foreign aid for our allies to strengthen the free world's will to combat Communist aggression.

Now, those things I consider major elements in the program that has been placed before the Congress, their purpose being to strengthen America at home, increase her security abroad. I would be more than bitterly disappointed if there was any failure to enact those measures.

Q. Kenneth M. Scheibel, Gannett Newspapers: Mr. President, in the debate in Congress on the farm program, there have been reports of a consumers' revolt against the high price of food. Now, I was wondering if, in your conversations with people and letters that you get, you have evidence there is a consumers' revolt?

THE PRESIDENT. Well, while here and there I have heard of the high price of food and cost of living—I mean, noticed it advanced in argument—it is usually coming in from someone who is advancing a special case, a governmental employee wanting more money, or something of that kind.

Actually, I think that the history of the cost of living index in the last 18 months has been one that approaches stability about as closely as you could possibly expect it to; so, if prices are high now, they have been awfully high a long time.

Q. Mr. Scheibel: Sir, is it your belief that if the Congress does adopt your farm bill that food prices will come down?

THE PRESIDENT. I think, at the very least, we should have a stabilization, because we hope that the factors of supply and demand will come into closer equality, coordination. We would like to get these great surpluses off the market, and parity then ought to be achieved if your supply and your demand are getting somewhat equal, because parity is simply the comparison of the cost of the things a farmer buys to the things he sells. I hope those factors will become again of more importance.

Q. Edwin Dayton Moore, United Press: Mr. President, you didn't mention raising the debt limit a minute ago. Does that mean that the administration is dropping that?

THE PRESIDENT. I would say that isn't necessarily a part of a program; that is a necessity.

Q. Mr. Moore: It is a necessity?

THE PRESIDENT. That is a necessity. As far as it looks now, I see no escape from it myself; but I didn't put it, as I recall, in my January program.

Q. Joseph A. Loftus, New York Times: Can you tell us now how you propose to go about this debt limit problem?

THE PRESIDENT. There have been many conferences which have been going on between Treasury officials and officials on the Hill that have to do with this problem. I would say that the program itself is not quite ready yet to expose and show exactly what we are going to do.

Q. Robert L. Riggs, Louisville Courier-Journal: Mr. President, you told Mr. Brandt that you wouldn't want to support someone who had opposed you on a major issue. In the last week Senator Cooper of Kentucky has voted twice against the administration—once against the TVA contract, and yesterday or last night, rather, against the entire atomic energy bill. Would you consider that major opposition, sir?

THE PRESIDENT. Well, I think Senator Cooper is mistaken, but I think that Senator Cooper's record in the Senate is one that I couldn't possibly criticize in any serious way.

Now, he has been perfectly honest, he has come to me every time he has had a difference, and I know that it does not make either of us happy. He believes there is a point of legal responsibility and legal authority involved. I think he has been perfectly honest in that, and I respect a man's honest opinions. Don't try to get me to say I am against Senator Cooper; I am not.

Q. Mr. Riggs: I am not trying to. [*Laughter*]

Q. Robert W. Richards, The Copley Press: There has been a good deal of editorial sniping at your majority leader. Would you like to say a good word for him for busting the minority filibuster?

THE PRESIDENT. Well, you know, I rather think he can take care of himself. But I do think this: I think criticism is good, and I think it is awfully easy to make, but I am struck by the number of times that the criticism does not suggest a better course to follow.

So I think that in this case, it is easy enough to make these criticisms, but I think the Senator has given a pretty good account of himself.

Q. Edward T. Folliard, Washington Post and Times Herald: You just said, Mr. President, that you expect to do some traveling in connection with the 1954 campaign.

THE PRESIDENT. Not "campaign"; on my program. Let's make the distinction. [*Laughter*]

Q. Mr. Folliard: Will that be extensive, sir? The reason I ask you, there have been announcements in various parts of the country that you will speak here, you will address this rally; but there has been no confirmation from the White House. Mr. Hagerty told us yesterday you were going to speak in Los Angeles.

THE PRESIDENT. Mr. Folliard, for this there are some very good reasons: it is awfully hard for the President to firm up a program too far in advance, and so you try to avoid making fixed engagements. You say, "Yes, if," and that is the way a good many of them now stand. I say a good many: from the standpoint of a person who would like to get a little bit of rest from the sound of his own tongue, it sounds like a lot; possibly not so many to those who want you to come.

So I think that the announcements will be made as quickly as they know they are firm. There is no attempt here to conceal or to evade, that I assure you. It is just we don't want to put out things that aren't true.

Q. Robert G. Spivack, New York Post: Mr. President, can you tell us something of your conversation with Paul Hoffman 2 weeks ago? I believe you had him at lunch. Was there a special purpose?

THE PRESIDENT. I must assure you that Paul Hoffman and I have been friends, I don't know how many years. Whenever he comes to town, if I possibly can I have him to lunch. I admire the man and his opinions; I listen to him. We cover every subject, I suppose, that any two of you, in just sitting down for a good conversation, would do. I don't recall what it was about specifically.

Q. James B. Reston, New York Times: I wondered, sir, if you had any comment on the apparent improved situation in the Middle East, particularly on the Anglo-Egyptian agreement?

THE PRESIDENT. I couldn't tell you how highly pleased I am that this composition has apparently been reached. I think it is evidence of patience and statesmanship on both sides. I think that the legitimate national aspirations of Egypt have been protected, and the requirements of Western defense are cared for, and I sincerely hope that soon now Egypt can go ahead with her friends in improving both her economic and her security position. I am very highly pleased.

Q. Mr. Reston: Has Egypt undertaken during these negotiations in any way to improve her relations with Israel and the other countries in the Middle East?

THE PRESIDENT. That I can't say; that is the most confused situation, of course. I can say only this: our policies are all directed, in dealing with each of these countries, to promoting friendships in the area.

I think I have expressed my conviction to this body before: I believe there is no future for any country there unless we can bring about something of this kind, and I believe concessions have to be made by both sides. But it is a terribly complicated problem, and just exactly whether Egypt has done anything I am not sure.

Q. Richard L. Wilson, Cowles Publications: Mr. President, would you object to a provision in the atomic energy bill authorizing governmental bodies to manufacture electricity from the power of the atom?

THE PRESIDENT. Governmental bodies? I am afraid I don't know exactly what you mean.

Q. Mr. Wilson: Well, the question goes to this point: the Senate has passed a couple of amendments which authorize the Government to go into the power business; and the House has passed an amendment prohibiting the Government from going into the power business; and those two points of view have to be resolved in conference. I wondered if you had anything you wanted to contribute to the thinking on that subject?

THE PRESIDENT. I think I will have to avoid too specific comment here for the reason I didn't know the issue had met in that head-on fashion.

Naturally, the power that is being developed now is all governmental.

They are not developing it for private sale to anyone because it is still, as you know, on a development basis. It is still very expensive, 5 to 10 times as high as you can do it in a steamplant.

It is a process which we hope is going to be scattered not only through this country some day but through all the world. As I tried to say last December 8, I think all the world ought to recognize and understand that in this new scientific development are possibilities for the betterment of mankind, and it is not to be devoted exclusively to destruction.

Now, that means that lots of people have finally got to use it or we are not going to have that come about. So, as I say, I didn't know that it had come in this head-on fashion; I knew that one had provided it. And I haven't discussed with my chief advisers, on this particular point, just exactly what we would do in a case of a head-on collision like that.

Merriman Smith, United Press: Thank you, Mr. President.

NOTE: President Eisenhower's forty-sixth news conference was held in the Executive Office Building from 10:31 to 10:58 o'clock on Wednesday morning, July 28, 1954. In attendance: 135.

173 ¶ Statement by the President Upon Signing Bill To Provide Water From the Santa Margarita River. *July* 28, 1954

I HAVE SIGNED today H.R. 5731, a bill "To authorize the Secretary of the Interior to construct facilities to provide water for irrigation, municipal, domestic, military, and other uses from the Santa Margarita River, California, and for other purposes."

This legislation grows out of the long-standing controversy between the United States and the Fallbrook Public Utility District and other water users concerning rights to the use of the waters of the Santa Margarita River. The bill will provide authority for the Secretary of the Interior, after certain determinations have been made, to construct storage facilities to satisfy the needs of the Fallbrook District and also of the United States if its water rights would not be jeopardized. I believe this legislation will be helpful to all agencies and persons concerned and I congratulate all those who cooperated in obtaining its enactment.

It is to be noted that, unless otherwise agreed by the Secretary of the

Navy, the facilities authorized by the bill, including the De Luz Dam, are to be operated in a manner which will permit the unobstructed passage of all of the water to which the United States is now entitled. It is likewise to be noted that the bill is not to be construed as a grant or a relinquishment of any of the rights in the Santa Margarita River which the United States now owns. That stream provides the essential supply of water for Camp Pendleton, a naval hospital and a naval ammunition depot. Each of those vital establishments is important for purposes of national defense.

The bill authorizes the Secretary of the Interior to construct the dam and other facilities only after he has determined that the project has economic and engineering feasibility. It is my understanding that such a determination will not be made until he has found that there will be ample water available in the Santa Margarita River for storage at the De Luz Dam, separate and apart from all rights to the use of water of the United States (except any appropriative rights hereafter obtained) and of all claimants on the stream.

In view of litigation now pending between the United States and other claimants to water from the Santa Margarita River, I shall expect the Secretary of the Navy to obtain and be guided by the advice of the Attorney General before taking any steps to acquire additional water rights in the River on behalf of the United States. Furthermore, I expect that the Secretary of the Navy will not agree to the impounding of any water to the use of which the United States is entitled without first consulting with the Attorney General and obtaining from him advice that such impounding will not be a grant or relinquishment of any of the rights to the use of water which the United States of America has acquired in accordance with the laws of the State of California.

NOTE: As enacted, H.R. 5731 is Public Law 547, 83d Congress (68 Stat. 575).

174 ¶ Toasts of the President and President Rhee of Korea at the Dinner for President Eisenhower. *July* 28, 1954

President Rhee, Mrs. Rhee and friends of this distinguished group:

I think I speak for each of us when I assure you, President and Mrs. Rhee, that anyone here would be honored by your invitation to any place. We are delighted that you arranged to have this dinner served in a place where so many of your good friends, friends of ours, of Koreans, could join in order to pay their tribute to your courage, to your friendliness, to your stamina, and to the great gallantry of your people.

We hope that when you go back to your country, you will be able to impart to them something of the warmth that you say you have felt coming from our hearts, from our minds, so that they will understand that in spite of distance, in spite of occasional differences, that those people who love freedom, who are ready to fight for freedom, are truly brothers—are truly comrades-in-arms, and are ready always to sacrifice together.

Methods and means are points on which we meet to discuss and confer. We do not always see the answers clearly in any one day, but we do know, as history has so often shown, that if we remain true to a cause, if we forget not the great spiritual basis that is the foundation for every system of free government, then in the long run tyranny cannot prevail, and freedom will.

So to you and Mrs. Rhee, we thank you for coming over to this country, for taking the trouble to learn again something new about us, possibly. You, who have lived amongst us so long, possibly did not yourselves need such reassurance; but it is possibly very fine for your people that you can come back now and say not only were the American people friends in 1948 and 1950, and 1951 and 1952, but they are still the friends of Korea—and we hope that the Koreans are our friends.

And so I am sure that this company will feel highly honored to join with me now in a Toast to your gallant people, to you and to Mrs. Rhee, drunk in your name as their symbol and their leader.

President Rhee!

NOTE: The dinner was held in the Williamsburg Room of the Mayflower Hotel in Washington. The President's toast was in response to the following one proposed by President Rhee:

Ladies and gentlemen:

I promise not to make a speech.

Of course, we thought it would be very appropriate for us to invite the President of the United States to our own place, however humble that might be. But it had to be large for the great number of friends to be invited, and that house is too small. Therefore, we had to make arrangements to have it here in the Mayflower Hotel—which is our embassy for tonight.

When President Eisenhower came out to visit Korea right after the election, in the cold and freezing weather, in the war time, with Communists supposed to be running loose everywhere, without waiting for the Inauguration, the President flew over ten thousand miles to come and visit Korea, to see how to help Korea.

That was enough to thrill all our people. Of course, we wanted to show a little of our hospitality. But our roofs were all torn down. We could find very little place or shelter for our own heads, and we could not show any hospitality to our great friend and great President at that time.

I am glad we have the Mayflower Hotel to use as an embassy, as under this roof we have the privilege of entertaining in a small way, and visiting with all our good friends, and with the President and Mrs. Eisenhower. And we are very happy to be so honored.

And wherever the President and Mrs. Eisenhower can go to show their interest in Korea, I am sure they will go, anywhere, any time.

I thank you, my friends, for honoring us tonight, and giving us such encouragement as you do tonight. I can express only my feeling that is created inside me when we arrived in Washington. Everywhere people in America cordially received us. Not only that, people in the streets and everywhere we go, they just congregate, waving hands. It is a real touching sight, and we are full of emotions, and go away from here full of encouragement and hope, realizing that not only the Government of the United States but the people of the United States are all our friends. There is no Communist in this United States. [*Applause*]

I promise not to speak—when I was standing at the entrance to this dining hall this evening, and friends were coming in, somebody came to me and told me this: that I must be very tired, and kept so busy. And I said no, when you meet with friends you are not tired. We have to go away very soon, so that our friends may not get tired of us.

Ladies and gentlemen, I just want to propose a Toast to the health and the success of this present administration, the prosperity of the United States, and to peace on earth—and to President and Mrs. Eisenhower.

Of course, all of us want peace on earth, but how to establish lasting peace is our question. I can only hope and pray that God Almighty will find some means to bring us peace on earth.

Now, as I have promised not to speak, I ask you ladies and gentlemen to drink to the health and success of President Eisenhower and Mrs. Eisenhower.

175 ¶ Statement by the President on Extending Aid to Flood Stricken Areas in Eastern and Central Europe. *July* 29, 1954

THE AMERICAN PEOPLE have followed with sympathy and compassion reports of the widespread human suffering which has already resulted from serious flood conditions in large areas of Central and Eastern Europe. Reports indicate that serious damage to homes and crops has occurred all along the Danube, and has been particularly heavy in Germany, Austria, Czechoslovakia, Hungary and Yugoslavia. Moreover, there has been considerable hardship and destruction of property along rivers in East Germany flowing north. The full extent of these losses cannot be known for several weeks.

In West Germany and Austria U.S. authorities have extended emergency assistance in an effort to alleviate the immediate situation. The United States is prepared to extend such aid as is feasible throughout the flood areas. We stand ready to make food available to lighten the burden on flood victims who are struggling to rehabilitate themselves.

The foodstuffs which can be made available without delay could be distributed through a mutually acceptable international agency. Various agencies are under consideration such as the League of Red Cross Societies. We are also making inquiries regarding the need for medical and other supplies.

I have asked our diplomatic missions in each country which has suffered flood damage to make themselves available to the local authorities in such a manner that we can be promptly and effectively of assistance to aid those in distress.

176 ¶ Citation Accompanying the Medal of Freedom Presented to Genevieve de Galard-Terraube. *July* 29, 1954

THE PRESIDENT of the United States of America, authorized by Executive Order, July 6, 1945, has awarded the Medal of Freedom with

Bronze Palm, to Mademoiselle Genevieve de Galard-Terraube, French Airborne Nurse, for meritorious service.

MEDAL OF FREEDOM (WITH BRONZE PALM)

Mademoiselle Genevieve de Galard-Terraube, French Airborne Nurse, by her ministrations to the sick and wounded at Dien Bien Phu, inspired and heartened the entire free world. Her service to her comrades, marked by the courage of a woman in battle and by the devotion of a nurse to her sworn duty, has been unsurpassed in this century. Her supreme fortitude in hours of peril, her unfaltering dedication to her mission reflected the greatness of spirit manifested on many fields, in many centuries, by the soldiers of France.

The Republic she serves so nobly has been an ally of the United States for 178 years. The continuing friendship between the peoples of the two Republics is symbolized today in their joined salute to Mademoiselle de Galard-Terraube. Her service at Dien Bien Phu reflects great credit upon herself and her country and the cause of freedom around the world.

DWIGHT D. EISENHOWER

NOTE: The award was made by the President in his office. Among those present were Ambassador Henri Bonnet and Mme. Bonnet, and Mrs. Eisenhower.

177 ¶ Letter to Joseph T. Meek, Illinois Republican Candidate for the Senate. *July 30, 1954*

[Released July 30, 1954. Dated July 27, 1954]

Dear Mr. Meek:

Thank you very much for your letter of July twenty-third.

Since this Administration took office, it has sought to secure the enactment of a program clearly in the best interests of the people—a program assuring maximum security for the country and prosperity for every citizen. It now is apparent that most of this program will be adopted by the Congress. I am delighted to have your personal assurance that I can count on your loyalty and support in furthering this program and the objectives and purposes of this Administration.

May I say further, that I look forward with anticipation to greeting you on January third as the Junior United States Senator from Illinois.
Sincerely,

DWIGHT D. EISENHOWER

NOTE: Mr. Meek's letter of July 23 was released with the President's reply.

178 ¶ Joint Statement by the President and President Rhee of Korea. *July 30,* 1954

WE HAVE HAD a fruitful and cordial exchange of views on a number of matters of mutual concern. These conversations have strengthened the friendship existing between our two countries and are a further demonstration of our solidarity of purpose.

On August 8, 1953, President Rhee and Secretary Dulles agreed that the United States and the Republic of Korea would again consult if the political conference envisaged in the Armistice of July 27, 1953 failed to produce a satisfactory settlement. This conference was held at Geneva from April 26 to June 15, 1954, but at that meeting the Communists refused to accept any formula for the unification of Korea on the basis of genuinely free elections under UN supervision and instead continued to press for arrangements which would have led directly and inevitably to extinguishing the liberties of the Korean people.

We reaffirm our intention to move forward, in accordance with the Charter of the United Nations and the resolutions of the General Assembly on Korea to achieve a unified, democratic, and independent Korea. In view of the failure of the Conference at Geneva to reach a settlement of the Korean question, we have discussed means for continuing to seek this objective.

Our military and economic advisers will continue with more detailed discussions of the questions of common interest which concern them.

In conclusion, we reiterate our determination to continue to work together in close and reciprocal cooperation to attain our common objectives regarding Korea.

179 ¶ Statement by the President Upon Signing the Housing Act of 1954.   *August 2, 1954*

THE COUNTRY will be benefited by the Housing Act of 1954 which has now become law.

It has been one of our major legislative goals. It will raise the housing standards of our people, help our communities get rid of slums and improve their older neighborhoods, and strengthen our mortgage credit system. In coming years it will also strongly stimulate the nation's construction industry and our country's entire economy.

The new law permits the government to insure larger home mortgage loans, carrying smaller down payments and longer terms. Millions of our families with modest incomes will be able, for the first time, to buy new or used homes. Families will be helped to enlarge or modernize their present homes.

Another feature of the law is especially important. Many families have to move from their homes because of slum clearance and other public improvements. This law provides especially easy terms for these deserving people. The new law makes available, for the first time, a practical way for our citizens, in the towns and cities of America, to get rid of their slums and blight.

The law strengthens private mortgage credit facilities. It does this by reorganizing the Federal National Mortgage Association. This agency will continue to be a support for the mortgage market, but later on it will become independent of Federal capital. Under this new law, private financial institutions have a really good chance to mobilize their own resources to supply adequate mortgage credit without regard to race, creed or color to home owners in every part of our country.

Of course, this is a tremendous job, and it is not all finished. For example, we have 33,000 public housing units available this year and, under this law, 35,000 more next year. We shall need to continue our public housing program until the needs can be met by private industry. Also, the Executive should have broader authority to adjust the terms on home loans to changing economic conditions. Nevertheless, by this new law we have made a major advance toward meeting America's housing needs.

NOTE: The Housing Act of 1954 is Public Law 560, 83d Congress (68 Stat. 590).

180 ¶ Statement by the President Upon Signing the Vocational Rehabilitation Amendments of 1954. *August 3, 1954*

THIS LAW is especially noteworthy in two respects. In the first place, it reemphasizes to all the world the great value which we, in America, place upon the dignity and worth of each individual human being. Second, it is a humanitarian investment of great importance, yet it saves substantial sums of money for both Federal and State governments.

The law lays a foundation for increasing from 60,000 to 200,000 by 1959 the number of disabled people rehabilitated each year. Each State is given more assistance for its rehabilitation program but is enabled to assume more responsibility in the program's administration and operation. The law also provides for special training for rehabilitation specialists, increased research on conditions that result in handicaps, and new benefits for the blind.

A few weeks ago, I approved another law in the four-point health program which we placed before the Congress this year. It will provide hospitals and nursing homes for people with long-term illnesses, and special medical facilities for persons who do not need hospitalization but do need medical attention. It also will provide rehabilitation facilities to serve many thousands of additional disabled people each year.

Our people have no personal concern more important than the maintenance of good health. I am delighted, therefore, that the Congress has passed this important new law to help more of our people meet their essential health needs.

NOTE: The act (Vocational Rehabilitation Amendments of 1954) is Public Law 565, 83d Congress (68 Stat. 652).

181   ¶ Veto of Bill for the Relief of Klyce Motors, Incorporated.   *August 3, 1954*

[Released August 3, 1954. Dated August 2, 1954]

To the House of Representatives:

I return herewith, without my approval, H.R. 5185, "For the relief of Klyce Motors, Incorporated."

The bill proposes to pay Klyce Motors, Incorporated, of Memphis, Tennessee, the sum of $91,000 for alleged losses sustained in connection with the purchase, on May 25, 1946, of 109 surplus trucks from the War Assets Administration.   The evidence discloses that these trucks were represented to be new, disassembled, and boxed for export.   When the trucks were uncrated for assembly, it was discovered that certain parts were rusted and otherwise damaged in a manner necessitating repair or replacement.   Government inspection personnel confirmed that the condition of these trucks did not conform to the warranty made to the purchaser by the disposal agency.   A settlement agreement for breach of warranty was entered into in the amount of $20,710, and the Government was released from further liability.

There must come a time in all negotiations leading to settlement between parties when final commitments can be made and thereafter relied upon by both parties.   In this case, however, equitable considerations indicate that the Government should not insist upon strict adherence to its legal rights.

The records show that when the Company, on April 17, 1947, accepted the settlement of its claim in the amount of $20,710 (5% of the purchase price), they had already incurred a loss of over $30,000 exclusive of assembly costs.   On the other hand, the tabulation of loss elements which was inserted in the committees' hearings appears to include losses for which the Government is not responsible and for which it should not pay.   The figures presented clearly do not justify the $91,000 payment authorized by the bill.

Under the circumstances, I am compelled to withhold my approval from this bill.   I believe, nevertheless, that a compromise adjustment is warranted.   I suggest that the claim be reconsidered by the Congress.   I would approve a measure which appears to be more realistic and which makes a more equitable adjustment and apportionment of the rights of both the Government and the Company.

DWIGHT D. EISENHOWER

182 ¶ The President's News Conference of *August 4, 1954.*

THE PRESIDENT. Ladies and gentlemen, with respect to our offer of food in the flooded areas of Europe, Yugoslavia has not been able to make reply. They don't even know the extent of the damage. Floods are still raging there.

Germany and Austria have replied they are very greatly interested, and we will undoubtedly hear further from them.

There has been no reply from other countries, but I do want to say that as any information comes in, Mr. Hagerty will keep you informed with respect to it.[1]

Wasn't there one other item? Oh, yes.

I just wanted to mention how delighted I was that the law providing for group life insurance for civil service was passed. It is a new idea for the benefit of civilian workers in the Federal Government, one I believe to be highly desirable. I am delighted Congress has passed it.

We will go to the questions.

Q. Robert Clark, International News Service: Mr. President, the Senate controversy over the Flanders resolution appears to be both

---

[1] The White House issued the following announcements with respect to the offer of aid to the flood stricken areas in Europe:

On August 6, that the President was gratified that the offer had been accepted by East Germany;

On August 12, that Hungary had accepted and that Foreign Minister Boldocsky had expressed his government's thanks to the President and to the American people;

On August 24, that Yugoslavia had accepted and that the President hoped that some assistance could be made quickly available through the League of Red Cross Societies;

On December 3, that the first relief cargo for the people of East Germany and Czechoslovakia was due to arrive that day at the East German port of Wismar, and that the shipment had been delayed because of the need for assuring that the relief would be administered under Red Cross principles.

See also Items 175, 195.

678

threatening to do serious harm to party unity and to keep the Senate in session considerably beyond the time when you have planned to leave Washington.

I wonder if you can give us first any appraisal, if not of the effort to censor Senator McCarthy itself, of the effect of this effort on Republican harmony in an election year; and two, any idea of your own plans if the Senate remains in session beyond mid-August—whether you would stay in Washington or go on to Denver.

THE PRESIDENT. Let me answer the second part first. It would seem to me, as I understand it,—now I am not quite clear as to what the plan is—but if the House adjourns and the Senate stays in session for this particular purpose, then there could be no legislation passed, and I would know of no reason why the White House staff and I personally could not follow out the programs we have set up for ourselves. And I might add, I hope that doesn't discommode too much you people who have the task of following along where I go. I don't know your sentiments on it.

Now, with respect to the other, of course, under our system this is clear: the party that has been given responsibility for the Federal Government through the elections to the National Legislature and to the Presidency has its head in the Presidency. The individual occupying the President's post cannot escape, of course, party responsibility, which does not mean by any manner of means that he approves of everything that goes on within the party, and he does his best in the party councils and wherever he thinks it would be effective to keep things going ahead that have an effect on the public mind.

The important thing, however, is a legislative program, things that have some permanent value and effect within the country. He gets the advice that is available to him to devise a program and to push it through. The long-term effects of his incumbency are going to be reflected in that way, in my opinion.

Now, the kind of controversy that is now going on in the Senate, of course is going to affect the party in some way or other. I cannot evaluate exactly what it will be; but until the Senate itself makes up its mind, through any process it wants to choose, exactly what it wants to do, it seems to me it would be not becoming for me to give particular judgments or opinions about it. That is their business. But I do say that anything that tends to divide the party is something that must concern me, and I must take such measures as are available to me to try to avoid it and to ameliorate it.

Q. Edward T. Folliard, Washington Post and Times Herald: Mr. President, Senator McCarthy put a letter in the Congressional Record the other day, and it was from Harry Woodring, former Secretary of War. Mr. Woodring had this to say about General George C. Marshall: "He would sell out his grandmother for personal advantage." He went on to say other things in that same vein. Mr. President, what do you think of that appraisal of General Marshall?

THE PRESIDENT. Ladies and gentlemen, there are some things that cause me to be almost emotional.

Now, I believe that there are many of you here who knew General Marshall well, yourself, all during his war years, the work he did and the way he did it.

I happened to be one of those Army officers that did not meet General Marshall except in the most casual way until the war started. I think I had seen him twice in my life, in neither case not over a minute or two at the time. I was brought in, and my relationships with him have been largely, almost exclusively, official. But I would like to say, and I have been saying this ever since I first knew him well, that he to me has typified all that we look for in what we call an American patriot.

I saw many things he did that were proof to me, at least, of his selflessness. I am quite certain that he did not want to sit in Washington and be a Chief of Staff. I am sure he wanted a field command, but he wouldn't even allow his Chief to know what he wanted, because he said, "I am here to serve and not to satisfy personal ambition."

Now, later, of course, he went—after all, the war was over—to a different post. What the circumstances were of that post, I know nothing. What were his judgments, what were the things that could have been done and were not done or what things were done that should not have been done, I don't know. But I do know that General Marshall served according to his conceptions of his duty to his Chief.

I tried to put this in a book that I wrote once, and maybe somebody heard about it. I tried to say what I thought about him. I have been saying it ever since, and I shall continue to say it until there is evidence that I just don't believe exists in this world that I am wrong.

So I repeat that I think that to reward a man who gave at least 50 years of his life to the service of his country—a great deal of it in junior positions, but if you go back through his record you will find it was a brilliant record, always serving to the best of his ability. I believe as a first lieutenant, if I recall, he was picked out to serve as the Chief of Staff of the greatest maneuvers ever held in the Philippines until that time; it was indicative of his ability and his dedication to his job. And all the way through, his record is studded with that kind of performance.

I think it is a sorry reward at the end of that long term to say that he is not a loyal, fine American, and that he served only in order to advance his own personal ambitions.

I can't imagine anyone that I have known in my career of whom this is less so than it is in his case.

I am sorry if I have made a speech, but that is the way I feel.

Q. Ethel Payne, Defender Publications: Mr. President, some time ago you suggested that the housing agencies be queried on what has been done to implement that section of your message to Congress of January 25, 1954, which said that there must be steps taken to secure decent and well-located homes for all Americans. The housing agencies were asked about this, but no satisfactory answer was received, except an indication from Mr. Cole that there might be called a housing conference on minority problems soon. Six months have passed since your message; and now that the housing bill has passed, could you tell us what will be done to halt the practice of using Federal funds to assist in the promotion of housing from which racial minorities are excluded?

THE PRESIDENT. You have asked me a question that if I would say what was going to be done, I would have to say I haven't any plan here I can expose to you.

I have tried as hard as I know how to have accepted this idea, that where Federal funds and Federal authority are involved, there should be no discrimination based upon any reason that is not recognized by our Constitution. I shall continue to do that.

Now, with respect to the specific nature of your question, the only thing I can do is to ask Mr. Hagerty to go to the agencies involved, find out about it, and to give you the answer as well as he can.

Q. Ray L. Scherer, National Broadcasting Company: Mr. President, I don't think anyone has asked you this for some time. I wonder if you could be specific on what you think the principal issues will be in the fall congressional campaign.

THE PRESIDENT. I think everybody has their own ideas, apparently, of what are going to be the specific issues. I know what mine are going to be: has the man or the individual who may be in question at any moment, has he done his best to help put over a program that is in consonance with the platforms to which we are all pledged in a political party, and the programs that have been devised by the principal leaders, executive and legislative, of that party, for the benefit of America?

Now, the issue is going to be, as far as I am concerned: is the record a good one or is it not. Whether or not everybody else will accept that as the issue, I don't know, but that is mine.

Q. Raymond P. Brandt, St. Louis Post-Dispatch: Mr. President, General Vogel, who is nominated for the TVA, tells us he does not know who sponsored him, and he doesn't know why he was selected other than his his record. Can you tell us how he was selected and for what reason?

THE PRESIDENT. Only because, Mr. Brandt, I was searching this country for a man whose type I described to you some 3 or 4 months ago. There was nobody that sponsored him. It was in a search of all of the available sources that we finally ran across his name, got him in, talked to him, and asked him whether he would do it.

He has not, of course, yet reached the age, I think, of compulsory retirement, but he was the kind of man we wanted, and he agreed to serve if approved.

Q. Mr. Brandt: May I ask one more?

THE PRESIDENT. Yes.

Q. Mr. Brandt: In your specification, you said, "One who agreed with you in a philosophical approach to TVA."

THE PRESIDENT. Yes.

Q. Mr. Brandt: Is there any agreement on that?

THE PRESIDENT. This is all that I asked him to do: I said, "You are competent; I am not going to talk to you at all about the way you run the place as a competent engineer. But I do want to know all the facts about this. And finally, in your recommendations to Congress and to me, base them upon your best judgment as to what should be done in the expansion or anything else about this great organization." And I specifically called his attention to the fact that I am pledged against any action that tends to destroy it.

Q. James B. Reston, New York Times: I would like to ask you, sir, a question about your atomic energy pool, your international pool for atomic energy. I don't think we have ever really had a rundown as to what happened in the negotiations with the Soviet Union, nor are we clear as to where we go from here now that that phase of those negotiations are completed. I wonder, sir, whether you would tell us something of the negotiations and what the future of them seems to be.

THE PRESIDENT. Of course, the second you mention the word "atomic energy," I draw in on myself a little bit, because we have laws that are very strict about what may be revealed, and I am sometimes uncertain of what is in the public domain and what I have read elsewhere in my own confidential reports.

I can tell you this: the proposal as placed before the Soviets was not favorably received. Now, whether or not there have been any details of the correspondence and the talks back and forth, I don't know. But there I would just have to ask that you go to the Secretary of State, because he will know how much of that can be put out.

Now, when that happened, I instantly started studies: "What can we do in any event without the Russians?" Because one of the purposes I think we should attempt to achieve is to make certain that the public opinion of the world knows by demonstration that there is some useful purpose to which this new science can be devoted rather than mere destruction.

We encountered too often—and this is based upon reports that I get from all over the world—"atomic energy is really of interest to only two or three of the great nations and they are going to try to destroy each other with it."

I should like to make every nation in the world know that there is the possibility, the potentiality here, for a great increase in their standards of living of all kinds. Therefore, I don't propose to be defeated in this merely because the Soviets won't go along.

Now, it will take a little bit of doing, because one part of the plan will have to be abandoned. Frankly, I hope that through an arrangement like this, a practical arrangement, there would grow up a field in which we, with our enemies, at least in this cold war, could begin to talk decently and intelligently and constructively, rather than finding it necessary always to stand up and call names and create further division in the world.

I think this: Americans know that we are peaceful; they know that we have no desire to start the great cataclysm of war. They know that what we want for other people are merely the rights that we enjoy ourselves. But the job of getting other people to believe that is terrific—we know that the Soviets are spending literally billions in different kinds of propaganda, ranging all the way from commercial exhibits to every kind of propaganda, subversion, and bribery that they find to be effective.

I think we must be more imaginative in finding ways to combat it; and I think furthermore we must be less niggardly when we do think we have a good way of meeting this thing, we should be less niggardly in doing it.

Permit me one more word. I think we should talk less about American leadership in the world, because we are trying to be a good partner. Leadership, if it is existing, should be acknowledged by others, because as long as we attempt to look upon ourselves as "We know the right answers; now, you get in with them," I think that is poor psychology and poor psychological methods.

We want to do what is right, what is just and what is decent, and try to get them going along because they believe in the same things.

We, though, being the largest and the strongest of this group of nations, we would hope that they finally would come to say, "Well, we must have the United States." To that extent the leadership becomes, let us say, implicit rather than explicitly stated by ourselves, because I just don't think it is good business to be shouting about that all the time.

A platoon leader doesn't get his platoon to go that way, by getting up and saying, "I am smarter, I am bigger, I am stronger, I am the leader." He gets men to go with him because they want to do it for him, because they believe in him.

Q. John Herling, Editors Syndicate: Mr. President, up on Capitol Hill, Senator Cooper and Congressman Frelinghuysen have introduced compatible bills on emergency school construction. Thus far they feel they have a certain amount of backing, but there is a general uncertainty on the Hill as to how much administration support this emergency school building program for $250 million has. Now, sir, are you for such legislation?

THE PRESIDENT. As a matter of fact, I do not know the details of that particular legislation. There are particular kinds of school construction that I have supported all along, and recommended. With respect to this one, I don't know its details, I'd suggest you go to Secretary Hobby to find out where we stand.

Q. Mr. Herling: It has the support of the National Education Association and trade unions, and so on.

THE PRESIDENT. That in itself wouldn't be the influencing factor. I would like to take a look at the whole story. It is their business to get all these facts together and present them to me, and I haven't seen any analysis of these bills.

Q. Joseph R. Slevin, New York Journal of Commerce: Mr. President, could you tell us your reaction to the cut that the Senate voted yesterday in the foreign aid bill?

THE PRESIDENT. I think it is very unfortunate. We in the executive department, in looking at this phase of our security and foreign program, cut as far as we thought was safe and proper. The House took out, I believe, about $100 million, and that is as good a guess as ours. I have no objection.

I think the cuts voted yesterday are too deep and will hurt us badly.

I believe there is some lack of comprehension of what the people on the other side of the Curtain, the people in the Kremlin, are doing. I don't believe there would be so much resentment or so much resistance to this if they could really see that we are desperately trying to build up confidence among the free nations of the world, confidence and some understanding, giving them a chance to have a life of their own.

I should like to point this out: you cannot help a country militarily unless it wants to be free. How can you go into a nation, how can the United States go in anywhere unless the native population asks you in? If you do, you are either a paternalistic sort of dictator in the world or you are an exponent of colonialism, both of which I think America rejects.

Consequently, if they are going to be on our side, they have got to have some chance, some hope of making a living. And that is important, I think.

Q. John D. Morris, New York Times: Mr. President, could we have permission to quote you on your reply to the question about General Marshall?

THE PRESIDENT. Well, I will tell you. If you will allow Mr. Hagerty to look it over so that he sees that I haven't tied up syntax and construction, and ended my sentences with prepositions, why, I don't mind. He might object, because the constant quoting, of course, then finally you ask me a question and I say, "No"—that puts it out of context.

This is what I say: I have said it so often that, this one, I would see no reason for objecting to quoting. But if you will see him, I think he will give it to you.

Q. William V. Shannon, New York Post: Mr. President, are you acquainted with an organization known as the American Assembly?

THE PRESIDENT. Indeed I am.

Q. Mr. Shannon: Well, they went on record last week against allowing Red China into the U.N. at this time, but they also said that they are opposed "to a rigid policy of permanent opposition to admission of this regime," and I was wondering if you would see any merit in their conclusion.

THE PRESIDENT. I think they are being realistic. Might I ask anybody here who, in let us say the winter of '44–45, when we were engaged in the Battle of the Bulge, could have seen the time when we were looking upon Germany and then, applying the same standard, Japan, as people we seek to reach understandings with and to make close associates?

Now, remember, China is a great mass of human beings, hundreds of millions. Those of you who have traveled through China I know have been as astonished as I have that so many people could live in such a space. They have a government of which we violently disapprove, and we are not going to accept them in any organism in which we have any say under present conditions. But for me to say to you here that I know what the conditions 5 years from now are going to be, well, you would know that I was a little bit off my rocker. And so I am not going to try.

So the Assembly, as far as I see it—and I haven't seen that quotation—they are merely saying, "Of course, we are not going to admit them if we can help it at this time." And I think we can help it! But we are always ready to see whether the sinner reforms and comes into the fold; that is the way I feel about it.

Merriman Smith, United Press: Thank you, Mr. President.

NOTE: President Eisenhower's forty-seventh news conference was held in the Executive Office Building from 10:32 to 10:57 o'clock on Wednesday morning, August 4, 1954. In attendance: 140.

183 ❡ Memorandum on the Community Chest and United Fund Campaigns. *August 4, 1954*

To the Heads of Executive Departments and Agencies:

This fall Community Chests and United Funds all over the country will conduct their annual campaigns for financial support of 19,500 separate, local health and welfare organizations as well as for the United Defense Fund. In addition, over 500 of these community campaigns will seek support for such national agencies as the Red Cross and those fighting heart disease, cancer, polio, tuberculosis, cerebral palsy and many other health problems. The goals of these campaigns will aggregate over $290,000,000. Their very size and the wide range of their valued services require that we accord them a primary place in our voluntary giving.

I have assured the leaders of United Community Campaigns of America, representing local Community Chests and United Funds, of the cooperation of the Federal Government. To this end I have approved the appointment of the Honorable George M. Humphrey, the Secretary of the Treasury, as Vice Chairman for the Federal Government of United Community Campaigns.

I am confident that you will extend the full cooperation of your Department in each community throughout the United States and its territories and possessions where it conducts its operations. Such cooperation should include the effective solicitation of all employees, the acceptance of equitable unit goals and the setting up of an adequate collection method for the convenience of those who wish to make contributions on an installment basis.

It is my hope that all employees will give generously—not because they must, but because they may—keeping in mind the wide variety and large number of organizations they will be supporting through their gifts to this single appeal.

DWIGHT D. EISENHOWER

184 ¶ Exchange of Letters Between the President and the Shah of Iran Concerning the Settlement of the Oil Problem. *August 5, 1954*

[Released August 5, 1954. Dated August 4, 1954]

Your Imperial Majesty:

The important news that your Government, in negotiation with the British, French, Dutch and United States oil companies, has reached, in principle, a fair and equitable settlement to the difficult oil problem is indeed gratifying.

Your Majesty must take great satisfaction at the success of this significant phase in the negotiations to which you personally have made a valuable contribution. I am confident that implementation of this agreement, under Your Majesty's leadership, will mark the beginning of a new era of economic progress and stability for your country.

Like myself, all Americans have a deep concern for the well-being of Iran. With them I have watched closely your courageous efforts, your steadfastness over the past difficult years, and with them I too have hoped that you might achieve the goals you so earnestly desire. The attainment of an oil settlement along the lines which have been announced should be a significant step in the direction of the realization of your aspirations for your people.

There is concrete evidence of the friendship that exists between our two countries and of our desire that Iran prosper independently in the family of free nations. We have endeavored to be helpful in the form of economic and technical assistance and we are happy to have helped in finding a solution to the oil problem.

I can assure Your Majesty of the continued friendly interest of the United States in the welfare and progress of Iran, and of the admiration of the American people for your enlightened leadership.

With sincere best wishes for the health and happiness of Your Majesty and the people of Iran,

Sincerely,

DWIGHT D. EISENHOWER

NOTE: His Imperial Majesty's reply, released August 9, follows:

Mr. President:

I am deeply grateful for your letter of August 5th and appreciate the friendly feelings which have inspired it.

It is, indeed, a source of satisfaction to me that my government has been able to arrive, in principle, at a settlement of the oil dispute, which, in the light of present world conditions, appears to be as equitable a solution of a difficult problem as could have been reached.

Ever since nationalization of the oil industry, which corresponded with the aspirations of my people, it has been my constant endeavor to facilitate and hasten a fair agreement within the framework of the relevant laws.

You can rest assured that the valuable contribution which you personally, Mr. President, The American Government and your distinguished Ambassador, Loy

Henderson, have made to this end is highly prized.

It is now my hope that the implementation of the agreement will not be long delayed.

With the attainment of this goal and with increased American assistance, I share your feeling that we may look forward to an era of economic and social development which will improve the lot of my people, as well as further consolidate the security of the Middle East.

I cannot sufficiently lay stress on the fact that American assistance to Iran has been most timely and helpful. My people reciprocate to the full the friendship of your noble nation.

Whilst renewing the expression of my gratitude for your cooperation, I tender warm wishes for the welfare of the American people under your wise leadership.

Yours sincerely,

MOHAMMAD REZA PAHLAVI

185 ¶ Letter to Herbert Hoover, Jr., on His Contribution to the Settlement of the Anglo-Iranian Oil Dispute. *August 7, 1954*

[Released August 7, 1954. Dated August 4, 1954]

Dear Herbert:

I want to express again my deep appreciation of your outstanding contribution to a realistic and equitable settlement of the Anglo-Iranian oil dispute which has so long been a threat to the stability of the Middle East.

My appreciation of the contribution you have made is enhanced by the fact that I have known something of the personal sacrifice you have made in order to assist us. I have in fact felt concerned, as the many months involved went by, by knowing that your absence from your own business affairs was extending far longer than we had originally planned. The fact that you chose, without urging, to stay with the problem until its solution, has been a great source of satisfaction to me and to members of the Cabinet.

The conclusion of this agreement, which promises to further progress in Iran as well as our objective of maintaining peace in the area, is due in significant measure to your expert knowledge of the international oil business, to your persistence and to your skillful diplomacy.

I am personally grateful to you.

Sincerely,

DWIGHT D. EISENHOWER

NOTE: Mr. Hoover served as Consultant to the Secretary of State on international oil matters. The letter was released at Augusta, Ga.

186   ¶ Letter to Ambassador Loy W. Henderson on His Contribution to the Settlement of the Anglo-Iranian Oil Dispute.   *August 7, 1954*

[Released August 7, 1954. Dated August 4, 1954]

Dear Mr. Ambassador:

I want you to know that I personally appreciate the splendid results of your work on the oil problem in Iran. Your knowledge of the situation, your resourcefulness, your judgment and your tireless patience in the face of repeated frustration contributed greatly to the happy arrangements which have now been worked out.

The present solution of the Anglo-Iranian oil dispute, for which you deserve such a large share of the credit, is a major achievement which will not only further our objectives in the Middle East but also contribute to our good relations with our European allies and our friends in other parts of the world as well.

I am most grateful to you for this successful effort on behalf of the Government and people of the United States.

Sincerely,

DWIGHT D. EISENHOWER

NOTE: This letter to the American Ambassador to Iran was released at Augusta, Ga.

187 ¶ Letter to the Governors of the States
Urging Them To Establish Committees To Assist in
Implementing the Refugee Relief Act.
August 7, 1954

Dear Governor ————:

With America's traditional concern for the homeless, the persecuted, and the less fortunate of other lands . . . one of the first acts passed by your 83rd Congress was the Refugee Relief Act of 1953 authorizing the entry into the United States of some 214,000 refugees.

These are men and women of the same character and integrity as their and our ancestors who, generation upon generation, have come to America to find peace and work, to build for themselves new homes in freedom.

Under supervision of the Department of State an almost world-wide organization has been set up to help these refugees from Communist persecution, natural disaster, and military operations. To aid in obtaining the needed sponsorship-assurances for these people, and to assist in the resettlement program, we need your assistance.

It would greatly stimulate the speed and effectiveness of this program if you would consider appointing a Governor's Committee to operate within your state. So that you can give full consideration to our suggestion, I am asking the State Department to forward you a complete Committee Manual explaining the act, functions of the Governor's Committee and other pertinent information.

Your assistance in this great humanitarian program will always be a source of great personal satisfaction and will be a genuine service to many communities within your state.

Sincerely,

DWIGHT D. EISENHOWER

NOTE: This is the text of identical letters sent to the Governors of 47 States on the first anniversary of the Refugee Relief Act. For the text of the letter to the Governor of New York see Item 188.

188   ¶ Letter to the Governor of New York Congratulating Him on Establishing a Committee To Assist in Implementing the Refugee Relief Act. *August 7, 1954*

Dear Governor Dewey:

I have today written to the Governors of each of the other states suggesting that they may wish to appoint committees to cooperate with the Administration in connection with implementing the Refugee Relief Program of 1953. I have not addressed the letter to you because you have already created such a committee and I understand that Commissioner Corsi has already had a meeting with the Administrator of this Program, to the mutual satisfaction of both of them.

I congratulate you on undertaking this work to stimulate the flow of assurances and to aid in the resettlement of these immigrants. I hope you will let Commissioner Corsi know how much we appreciate the cooperation extended by him and his associates.

Sincerely,

DWIGHT D. EISENHOWER

189   ¶ Exchange of Letters Between the President and Chancellor Adenauer Concerning Vested German Assets in the United States. *August 10, 1954*

[Released August 10, 1954. Dated August 7, 1954]

Dear Mr. Chancellor:

I was very much interested in your views on the question of the disposition of vested German assets in the United States, contained in your letter of July 17, 1954; and I appreciate the spirit in which your comments were offered.

You refer particularly in your letter to the hardships imposed on a large number of persons, many now advanced in years and without other

692

means of support, whose small holdings in this country, in the form of pensions, life insurance policies, interests in estates, and bank deposits, have been vested. You state that early action to provide relief in such cases would be a major contribution to the strengthening of the ties of friendship between our two countries.

Because of the great dislocation in the German economy which took place as a result of the war, the Allied Governments decided to look to German assets in their territories as a principal source for the payment of their claims against Germany. The recovery of the German economy, which has progressed so rapidly and so well under your administration, was thus not hampered by a large reparation burden. In considering the problem of the vested assets, it is necessary therefore to take into account legitimate claims on the part of American citizens arising out of the war for which some provision should be made, if the original approach is reversed.

I am aware of the measures taken by the German Federal Government under your high-minded leadership to contribute to the relief of victims of Nazi persecution, and to re-establish normal economic and commercial relations with the countries of the free world. I also share your sympathy with individuals in straitened circumstances in Germany for whom the operation of the vesting program in this country created particular hardships. I am hopeful that it may be possible to take some remedial action in such cases, and at the same time provide some measure of compensation to those American nationals who incurred losses arising out of the war, with resultant hardship in many cases.

As you know, the solution of this complex of problems lies with the Congress. Several bills dealing with the subject are now pending there, and members of my Cabinet and other Government officials have appeared and expressed their views. None of the measures thus far proposed have the approval of my Administration, but you may be assured that this problem is receiving earnest consideration and it is my hope that a fair, equitable and satisfactory solution can be arrived at.

Sincerely,

DWIGHT D. EISENHOWER

NOTE: The German Chancellor's letter of July 17, released with the President's reply, follows:

Mr. President:

The Federal Government follows with special interest efforts of the U.S. Congress to find a solution to the question of seized German assets in the United States. Despite the favorable development of relations between our two countries, this problem has remained unresolved. A solution to it is a special wish of my government. Thousands of Germans who through no fault of their own find themselves in an unfortunate economic situation, old people and pensioners, beneficiaries of insurance policies and inheritances, hope that now, nine years after the end of hostilities, their property will be released. Among them are numerous persons who have lost their means of livelihood and homes as a consequence of the war. For all of them an early release would alleviate their hardships. Many Germans would be able to build their lives anew with these means. Moreover, seizure of these assets has affected precisely those German firms and persons, who through personal and business connections with the United States, have for many years formed the traditional bridge of friendship between our two countries. For them as well, the unresolved problem is an element of uncertainty.

In the opinion of the Federal Government and of the entire German public, the Federal Republic has expressed its will to contribute to reconstruction on the basis of common principles of the Western world through recognition of German foreign obligations in the London debt agreement, through ratification of the Bonn and Paris agreements, and through conclusion of the Israeli agreement. An early solution to this problem lies specially close to the hearts of myself and my government. It would not only have a far-reaching favorable psychological effect in that it would give the German people a feeling of security and increase its moral strength, it would also make a considerable contribution to furthering the friendship between our two peoples, so promisingly begun.

As head of the government of the Federal Republic, may I voice a request to you, Mr. President, that a contribution will also be made from your side that the hopes, so recently given life, will not be disappointed. Accept, Mr. President, the expression of my highest consideration.

ADENAUER

190   ¶ Letter to President Hoover on the Occasion of His 80th Birthday.   *August 10, 1954*

[Released August 10, 1954. Dated August 9, 1954]

Dear Mr. President:

As you celebrate your eightieth birthday this August tenth, I look anew, and with ever increasing admiration, upon your distinguished career. Few men in our country's history have been privileged to serve the nation in so many important capacities as have you, and certainly none has done so with greater brilliance and devotion.

To me it is also remarkable that after so many years given to the public service, you still cheerfully accept new assignments involving governmental responsibilities of the most burdensome character. To justify my own part in asking you to assume some of these additional duties, I merely point out that by virtue of your long experience, wise understanding and eminent position, you are qualified, as almost no other American, to discharge them successfully. Your Party and your country are proud of you; Americans know that you have ever used your great talents in the interests of all.

I wish I could be present to join in the ceremony to honor you, but I know that what I have just stated, and what all of us as Americans feel in our hearts, will be far more eloquently expressed by others present than I could hope to do. May you have many more years of happiness and health, and may we continue to have the benefit of your counsel and judgment.

With warm personal regard,

Sincerely,

DWIGHT D. EISENHOWER

191 ¶ Statement by the President Upon Signing Bills To Modernize the Tanker Fleet.
August 10, 1954

THESE TWO BILLS will help to modernize the tanker fleet under the United States flag, reduce our serious mobilization deficit in such tonnage and create a Government-owned and maintained tanker reserve essential to our mobilization requirements. The bills will also give a much-needed stimulus to our nationwide shipbuilding and associated industries.

One of these measures authorizes the Secretary of the Navy to negotiate with private operators for the 10-year charter to the Government of fifteen fast, commercial-type tankers which will be privately owned and operated. These will be constructed in American shipyards of materials and equipment produced or manufactured in the United States. Private shipyard construction, at Government expense, of five similar tankers is also authorized. The building and use of these twenty modern tankers will enable us to put into reserve thirty-seven World War II-built tankers which are now operated for the Department of Defense by the Military Sea Transportation Service.

The other bill will permit ship owners to trade in, for a government credit allowance, tankers built in World War II. This allowance may be applied on the construction of new, more efficient tankers to be built and operated under the American flag. In addition to stimulating tanker construction for private account, this bill will strengthen the competitive position of our private tanker owners, while increasing the potential of our mobilization tanker reserve.

This legislation will, of course, mean jobs in American shipyards. Teams of specialized workers will stay together and keep at the vital task of building ships; the skill of these men, essential to our security, will not be lost by their dispersion into other forms of employment. I have directed the Secretary of Defense and the Secretary of Commerce to space the new construction in both of these programs in such a manner as to avoid undesirable peaks and valleys in construction and employment.

NOTE: The two bills are Public Laws 574 and 575, 83d Congress (68 Stat. 680, 681).

192 ¶ The President's News Conference of *August* 11, 1954.

THE PRESIDENT. Recently, ladies and gentlemen, there has been presented to me at the White House a very comprehensive series of statistics portraying the conditions of the American economy at midyear. They are quite detailed; most of them are very hopeful.

I have directed Mr. Hagerty to get them ready so that within a day or so they can be published for your information over there, and you may have them.[1]

I think it would be very strange if I didn't mention some satisfaction about the enactment of the farm bill in the Senate. I think Senator Aiken and the leadership did a remarkable job.

I want to make very clear one thing: so far as I am concerned, this is not a political victory. This is merely another step in the program that is designed for the welfare of American farmers, for a stable agricultural economy and, therefore, for the benefit of all of us. I don't regard it in any way as a partisan victory.

---

[1] See Item 194.

As you know, there are several things I still hope to have ironed out in conference, notably the dual price plan for wheat. I want to get the wool program without any time limitation; and, of course, I want the dairy program left alone. There are one or two other items, but those items I am very hopeful will be ironed out.

Now, with that little statement, ladies and gentlemen, we will go to questions.

Q. Merriman Smith, United Press: Mr. President, I wonder if you could tell us how you feel about recurrent suggestions that this country sever diplomatic relations with Russia? The most recent of these comes from General Mark Clark, who also didn't think very highly of the present form of the U.N.

THE PRESIDENT. Well, now, let me make clear, General Mark Clark is an intimate personal friend of mine of some more than 40 years, and he was an extremely capable soldier. The views he expresses, as just outlined here, as you know, are by no means the views of the administration.

I think, of course, instead of really criticizing the United Nations as such, he was criticizing the Communist misuse of the organization.

I am quite certain that the world must retain a forum of this kind, established by the agreement among all the major nations in which to discuss our differences.

I recognize clearly what so many of you do, that it becomes merely a forum for propaganda, a field in which we don't seem to be as skillful as the other fellow. But, by and large, I believe our only hope is to improve this organization, bring it closer in its effect and its operations to the great thoughts that inspired it and were written into its charter. We cannot possibly, as I see it, serve our interests now by just cutting off so-called diplomatic relations.

I really believe that if anyone would sit down and study all of the conflicting considerations, objectively, and not merely shoot from the hip on such questions, they would arrive at a somewhat similar conclusion.

Q. Ray L. Scherer, National Broadcasting Company: Mr. President, there seem to be increasing suggestions that we should embark on a preventive war with the Communist world, some of these suggestions by people in high places. I wonder, sir, if you would care to address yourself to that proposition.

THE PRESIDENT. All of us have heard this term "preventive war" since the earliest days of Hitler. I recall that is about the first time I heard it. In this day and time, if we believe for one second that nuclear fission and fusion, that type of weapon, would be used in such a war—what is a preventive war?

I would say a preventive war, if the words mean anything, is to wage some sort of quick police action in order that you might avoid a terrific cataclysm of destruction later.

A preventive war, to my mind, is an impossibility today. How could you have one if one of its features would be several cities lying in ruins, several cities where many, many thousands of people would be dead and injured and mangled, the transportation systems destroyed, sanitation implements and systems all gone? That isn't preventive war; that *is* war.

I don't believe there is such a thing; and, frankly, I wouldn't even listen to anyone seriously that came in and talked about such a thing.

Q. Harry C. Dent, Columbia (S.C.) State and Record: Mr. President, yesterday you received Ambassador John Peurifoy, and he conferred with you on the situation in Guatemala. I just wondered if you have any comments on his report to you, and do you think he did a good job down there for the United States and the free world?

THE PRESIDENT. I think he did an excellent job, but I have no special comments.

Almost every ambassador who comes back pays a call at the White House. He did fill me in on a number of details. As I say, I think he did an excellent job. As you know, he was ambassador in Greece, and then was moved over to Guatemala because of the confidence in his abilities.

Q. Robert W. Richards, The Copley Press: Mr. President, a couple of world hot spots or potential world hot spots, Suez and Iran, have been cooled by agreements within the last week or two. Could you tell us whether, in your opinion, the international situation elsewhere moves toward war or toward peace?

THE PRESIDENT. Ladies and gentlemen, when you embark upon discussion of such a broad subject, one is very apt to go far afield. I have no objection, if you see me digressing too far from the main theme here, I have no objection if someone suggests that our time is limited—

[*laughter*]—because it is a very comprehensive and it is a very serious question.

I think the best thing we could do would be to go back and review for a second. A year ago last January we were fighting in Korea and in Indochina. We were faced in Iran with a situation that was highly dangerous to the world. Mossadegh was using his power, and the party— I don't know exactly how you pronounce it, but the Communist Party, Tudeh I guess—that party was using their power to lead Iran further and further away from the Western World. It looked almost as if a break was imminent from day to day.

The situation in Egypt was no better, at least in its potential capacity for damage to the United States.

The growing threat in Central America was another place where things looked very bad indeed.

Now, in not all of these instances has the problem been solved with complete satisfaction to us. But remember, the two wars of which we speak were being waged under a political situation and in a political setting that really made a decisive winning of those conflicts impossible; and so any settlement was necessarily going to be less than satisfactory to us.

However, in both places we have a chance now to do something constructive, to build up economic alliances in those areas that will make it possible for those people to make a living, to raise their standards, and to be true partners in a free world economy.

In Iran the situation has been greatly ameliorated; it looks much better, and we are very hopeful that the new agreement will soon bring back income to Iran on the basis that they can continue to advance, raising the standards in that country.

The situation in Egypt is also immeasurably better, since through patience and refusal to get stampeded, refusal to be calling names all over the world, there is finally an agreement that looks like the requirements of the free world are substantially met and the sovereignty of Egypt clearly recognized.

In South America, the situation is of such recent resolution that I think no comment is necessary.

All of this adds up—as I see it, the free world has a better chance than before to use its brains, its intelligence, its understanding and, indeed, its wealth, to build up a structure that will really be impervious to the Communist assault, whether that assault takes its usual form of subversion and bribery and infiltration or whether, in the long run, it might include force.

I believe if we do this intelligently, work effectively toward the end, there will be no war.

Q. Sarah McClendon, El Paso Times: Sir, have you given any thought to asking Congress for legislation that would enable them to enforce integration in public school education, backing up the Supreme Court decrees?

THE PRESIDENT. The subject has not even been mentioned to me.

Q. Charles L. Bartlett, Chattanooga Times: Mr. President, the conference report on the atomic energy revision bill, which is now pending before the Senate, contains a patent licensing provision that is somewhat different than the one which you recommended to the Congress. I wondered if this conference version is agreeable to you?

THE PRESIDENT. Well, the Department of Justice and the Atomic Energy Commission have not been in to see me about it; I am not familiar enough with the details of that bill, I am sorry, as it stands now, to speak about it.

Q. Robert E. Clark, International News Service: Mr. President, this question may sound a little premature in view of the fact you still have the tax bill on your desk, but I wonder if you could look ahead a little for us on the tax and budget fronts. Can you give us something of the budget outlook, as well as the prospect of reducing income taxes, in the next year?

THE PRESIDENT. The general outlook is for reduced income, but it is also for reduced expenditures.

As a matter of fact, I was amazed to pick up a paper not long ago, or have one brought to me, where it made quite a point of an economy directive when, as a matter of fact, we have preached nothing else for 18 months around here. I was a little bit astonished to see that such a document could make the news, because it is no change.

As to what deficits, either administrative or cash budget, would be at the end of '56, I wouldn't want to make any guesses now at all.

Q. Chalmers M. Roberts, Washington Post and Times Herald: Mr. President, in answering that question about preventive war, you confined yourself to military reasons against it. Did you wish to leave the impression that that was the only basis of your opposition to the idea?

THE PRESIDENT. Well, let me make it this way: if you remember, I believe it was Conan Doyle's *White Company,* there was a monk that left the church; he said there were seven reasons, and the first one was he was thrown out; they decided there was no use to recite the other six.

It seems to me that when, by definition, a term is just ridiculous in itself, there is no use in going any further.

There are all sorts of reasons, moral and political and everything else, against this theory, but it is so completely unthinkable in today's conditions that I thought it is no use to go any further.

Q. Jay G. Hayden, Detroit News: Mr. President, you have been criticized at times in the past for your attitude that, as the head of the party, it was your obligation to support whoever a given State nominated. In view of that statement on your part, what is your answer to the New Jersey Republicans who have wired you indicating they would not support Clifford Case and would like your help in getting him out of the race?

THE PRESIDENT. I haven't seen the wire.

Frankly, like everybody else, I think I have made some generalizations that don't stand up. In fact, didn't a Frenchman say all generalizations are false, including this one.

I like to meet my problems as they come up. I told you before that they have nominated a man in New Jersey whose record in Congress I had thought was very fine and satisfactory. I hear that some people criticized it on account of one or two votes; I have found him always an honest, honorable man and, therefore, I think he is the kind of candidate we ought to have.

Q. Joseph A. Loftus, New York Times: Mr. President, 26 Chinese students in this country say they have written you a letter asking that you allow them to go back to their families. They say they have been told that thousands of Chinese students here are not being allowed to go back and won't be, although they say, at the same time, they have read in the paper that 15 have been released. Can you tell us anything about this policy, if not about this particular case?

THE PRESIDENT. I am not too certain, as to the thinking on this project, the point to which it has reached. It has been a troublesome question, we have been thinking about it a long time. I do know that within recent weeks they have started to issue visas for certain of them to go back.

I believe it has been discussed not only among ourselves but, I believe, discussed partially at Geneva. They are starting to go back.

Q. Marvin L. Arrowsmith, Associated Press: Mr. President, the production workers at the Paducah atomic plant voted last night to go out on strike tomorrow, and the situation at Oak Ridge is pretty serious too. Do you plan to ask the Attorney General to seek an injunction under the Taft-Hartley law?

THE PRESIDENT. I hadn't heard about the Oak Ridge situation to this moment.

This is my opinion: here is one field where we cannot tolerate any cessation of work or strike. I am prepared to use any device, any legal device, provided by the Congress and available to the Government to prevent a cessation of work in those places.

Q. William S. White, New York Times: Would you care to discuss the general record of Congress with us a little more than merely this comment on the farm bill, since it is about to end?

THE PRESIDENT. I would; but you know, I think it would be sort of plagiarizing on myself. Right now I am working on a little bit of a talk that I hope to give soon that is going to be on the record of Congress since January 20, 1953. So I don't really want to cheat on myself.

Q. Joseph A. Loftus, New York Times: Mr. President, is this talk you are referring to earlier than the August 19th appointment you have in Illinois?

THE PRESIDENT. I hope so.

Q. Mr. Loftus: Can you tell us when, the occasion?

THE PRESIDENT. No, I don't know when; I don't know when because, after all, I can't talk about the accomplishments of Congress until it quits. I don't know when it is going to quit.

Q. Raymond P. Brandt, St. Louis Post-Dispatch: Mr. President, you are going to the State Fair?

THE PRESIDENT. I am going to the State Fair, but I am not slated there for any major talk. I am going to visit the State Fair as a guest of Governor Stratton. It is a date of long standing. I am going to visit, that same afternoon, World Council of Churches; and I believe I am going to visit Northwestern University at the same time.

Q. Mr. Brandt: How long will you be at the State Fair?

THE PRESIDENT. We will be probably in Springfield 2 hours or 2 hours and a half.

Q. Mr. Brandt: There will be pictures?

THE PRESIDENT. As far as I am concerned. [*Laughter*]

By the way, now that my movements are news, maybe I should have announced something: I have been wanting to have a little bit of an outing with the Cabinet one day, and so on Friday I have transferred the regular Cabinet meeting to Camp David; I am going to have it there.

Q. George Herman, CBS Radio: Mr. President, sometime ago, Sir Winston Churchill told the House of Commons that tremendous changes have taken place in the whole strategic position in the world, which makes the thoughts which were well founded and well knit together a year ago utterly obsolete; and some columnists in the newspapers this morning implied that was entirely because of H-bomb and atomic weapons development. Is that your feeling, sir, or do you think more along the lines you outlined about changes in other countries?

THE PRESIDENT. Well, anyone that ignored the influence of the H-bomb, its influence upon our thinking and very much more on the thinking of those people who feel even more exposed than do we, he would be wrong. Of course, it is influential. But we are living in a time of incessant change. Our law has changed. What we must do is not to be so proud of what we said a year ago or just to insist we were right 6 months ago necessarily, but to find out what is an approach, a program, that is good for today and for the proximate future, let us say, and not be too determined, like some people are, to prove that from the time they were born they were geniuses and right.

I am quite sure I have been wrong my full share of the time, but I am certainly trying to work to the best of my ability to make sure that the solution for tomorrow is a little better.

Q. Nat S. Finney, Buffalo Evening News: Mr. President, you used the expression that you liked to meet your problems as they came up. Would that be a fair maxim for us to use as we go into the campaign as to about what to expect?

THE PRESIDENT. I quoted the old Frenchman, that all generalizations are false, including this one. So I would hesitate to give you a maxim to use; but I do like it.

I do not know whether I can explain it in a few words. After all, I am not supposed to be here, I think, a professor in methodology and so on. I do believe we can fall into grievous errors if you say such and such is the aisle down which I walk, and refuse to admit there are important things going on in the next aisle. I believe you have got to be ready to do the work, to do your homework, try to grasp the essentials of a situation and see what do we do now, what is the nearest to justice and right and the welfare of our people that we can reach.

Q. Merriman Smith, United Press: Mr. President, could you tell us a little bit more about Friday? Is the Cabinet going to spend the weekend with you up there?

THE PRESIDENT. No, I have invited them up there for the day. I hope to have a Cabinet meeting somewhere along about 11, have them for a light lunch, and along about 5:30 or 6:00 have a buffet supper for them.

As you may know, there is a little swimming pool up there. There isn't much to do, but they can at least sit around at an altitude of 1800 feet, which is a little higher than Washington—at least physically, I say.

Q. Alan S. Emory, Watertown Times: In following this "meeting problems as they come up," sir, late last week Governor Adams said on a television program that you were still turning over in your mind your decision as to whether or not you would run again in 1956. Have you come to that decision yet, sir? *[Laughter]*

THE PRESIDENT. There are two things here which I could comment on, I think, with your indulgence: first, the great interest that people take in digging into what are someone else's motives, and the conclusions they reach often on scanty evidence.

Now, I don't know why any member of the staff is saying these things. To the best of my memory, Governor Adams has never spoken to me about it, and no one else in my staff has ever spoken about it. If they want to speculate, I uphold their right to express their opinions, just as I uphold General Clark's right to express an opinion that is directly, almost, opposed to mine.

So I have no objection to their saying what they please; but I wish he would give me whatever facts he has to go on, because I have none.

Q. William M. Blair, New York Times: Mr. President, during consideration of the farm bill, Senator Williams proposed an unsuccessful amendment that would have required States to pay between 25 and 50 percent of the cost of any disaster relief such as drought or flood. Do you favor this approach to a better relationship with the States?

THE PRESIDENT. Well, I don't know how much they should pay, but last year, when I went out to Texas and went into Kansas City and one or two other places, we kept exploring what was the best way here to form a partnership.

One of the factors, one of the problems, you run into always is past history. The grant-in-aid program has often been on a 50–50 basis, and it has frequently been without any financial participation by the States. So you run into what people think is due them, not in this particular situation but in view of past history.

I haven't any specific formula for the situation you describe. But I do believe that in everything we do in this country, certainly with manifest exceptions like in the field of national security and so on, I believe there should be a partnership between the local government and the Federal, if the Federal must participate. If there is not, then what influence, what incentive, is there for the local government to be economical and efficient in the running of this affair? On the contrary, their incentive is to be extravagant because that brings in more money from the general purse to spend there.

The reason that I want a partnership so much is so that there is somebody there who says, "All right, you need help, but I am helping to pay for it and, therefore, we will run it economically." I don't believe that we should be sympathetic merely by distance. I believe, first of all, we should be sympathetic and considerate because it is our neighbor, and then bring in the people who are further away.

Merriman Smith, United Press: Thank you, Mr. President.

NOTE: President Eisenhower's forty-eighth news conference was held in the Executive Office Building from 10:31 to   10:57 o'clock on Wednesday morning, August 11, 1954. In attendance: 138.

193 ¶ Letter Directing the Attorney General To Petition for an Injunction in Labor Dispute at the Atomic Energy Commission Facilities at Oak Ridge and Paducah. *August 11, 1954*

Dear Mr. Attorney General:

On July 6, 1954, by virtue of the authority vested in me by Section 206 of the Labor Management Relations Act, 1947 (Public Law 101, 80th Congress), I issued Executive Order 10542 creating a Board of Inquiry to inquire into the issues involved in a labor dispute between the Union Carbide and Carbon Corporation and certain of its employees represented by Locals 288 and 550, United Gas, Coke and Chemical Workers, CIO, at certain facilities of the Atomic Energy Commission.

On July 10, 1954 I received the Board's written report in the matter. A copy of that report is attached hereto.

Although the strike referred to in said report was discontinued following receipt of the report, the labor dispute which led to the strike and which is referred to in Executive Order 10542 has not been resolved and continues to the present time.

I am informed that there is a threat that the strike or strikes will be resumed at the Atomic Energy Commission's gaseous diffusion plants and their associated shops and facilities at Oak Ridge, Tennessee or at Paducah, Kentucky, or both. Said threatened strike or strikes arise out of the same labor dispute referred to in Executive Order 10542.

In my opinion these unresolved labor disputes have resulted in a strike and threatened strike affecting an entire industry or a substantial part thereof engaged in trade, commerce, transportation, transmission or communication among the several States and with foreign nations which strike, if permitted will imperil the national safety.

I therefore direct you, pursuant to the provisions of Section 208 of the Labor Management Relations Act, 1947, to petition in the name of the United States any District Court of the United States having jurisdiction of the parties to enjoin the resumption and continuance of such strike, at certain facilities of the Atomic Energy Commission at Oak Ridge, Tennessee and at Paducah, Kentucky where such action is necessary to remove a peril to the national safety and to secure a resumption of trade, commerce, transportation, transmission or communication among the several States and foreign nations, and for such other relief as may in your judgment be necessary or appropriate to protect the national interest.

Sincerely,

Dwight D. Eisenhower

NOTE: An injunction was granted on August 11 by the District Court for the Eastern District of Tennessee.

The Board's report of July 10, and its final report of October 11, were made available through the Federal Mediation and Conciliation Service. Final negotiations for settlement of the dispute were concluded on November 7, 1954.

194   ¶ Statement by the President on the State of
the Economy at Midyear.   *August* 12, 1954

1. THE PARAMOUNT FACT about the economy at mid-year is that
the recent decline in economic activity has come to a halt.   For the last
six months, the Federal Reserve index of industrial production has moved
within an extremely narrow range.   At the beginning of the year the index
stood at 125 (average 1947–49=100).   In March and April, the index
registered 123; in May and June, 124.

2. In view of this narrow range of fluctuation in total industrial production during the past six months, we may justly take an average of the
past six months as indicative of the recent level of economic activity.   It
then becomes of interest to compare this level with that attained by the
economy during the first half of 1953, when our Nation was enjoying the
greatest prosperity we have yet known.

3. Making that comparison, we find that industrial production has
been running 8.1% lower in 1954 than in 1953.   But in forming a judgment about the state of the economy, we must bear in mind that the
widely used Federal Reserve index of production covers only manufacturing and mining; that it omits construction, agriculture, transportation,
and the great range of personal services; and that the omitted parts are
much more important sources of employment than the included parts.   It
is desirable, therefore, to look at more comprehensive measures or indicators of economic activity.

4. The most significant of these measures are the following:

(a) Gross national product—which expresses the dollar value of the
Nation's total output of commodities and services.

(b) Nonagricultural employment (as estimated by the Bureau of
Labor Statistics)—which expresses the number of wage and salary workers in business establishments outside of agriculture.

(c) Personal income—which is simply the sum of all individual and
family incomes.

(d) Disposable personal income—which is simply the sum of all individual and family incomes *minus* personal income tax payments.

(e) Bank debits outside New York City—which express debits to
individual and business bank accounts, and thus measure the flow of

money payments in industrial, commercial, and to some degree, financial transactions (New York City debits are omitted because they are dominated by financial transactions).

5. When we now compare the first half of 1954 with the first half of 1953, we obtain the following results:

	Percent change from 1st half of 1953 to 1st half of 1954
Gross national product	−2. 7
Nonagricultural employment	−2. 6
Personal income	+0. 2
Disposable personal income	+1. 4
Bank debits outside New York City	+0. 9

It is fair to conclude from these facts that the recent economic decline, on an over-all basis, has been very small. This conclusion will not be changed if we take account of the increase in population. Thus, while the total disposable personal income increased 1.4%, the disposable personal income per capita declined merely 0.3% between the first half of 1953 and the first half of 1954.

6. In judging the performance of the American economy during 1954, we have taken the first half of 1953 as the standard. It may help us to see the current state of the economy in better perspective if we go one year further back. The first half of 1952 was not characterized by the same intensity of activity, but it was the best year we had experienced prior to 1953. Therefore, while 1952 does not provide us with as high a standard as 1953, it still constitutes a very high standard.

7. If we now compare the first half of 1954 with first half of 1952, the showing of the rather broad indicators to which we have already referred is as follows:

	Percent change from 1st half of 1952 to 1st half of 1954
Industrial production	+3. 3
Gross national product	+4. 4
Nonagricultural employment	+1. 1
Personal income	+7. 2
Disposable personal income	+8. 8
Per capita disposable income	+5. 3
Bank debits outside New York City	+10. 2

Every one of these indicators shows a rise, and some of the increases are not small.

Since 1952 was the best year before this Administration took office, it follows that economic activity of late has been higher than at any time before this Administration assumed responsibility. And since 1953 was a still better year than 1954 is turning out to be, it follows that the over-all performance of the American economy thus far during this Administration has been better than during any earlier time.

8. Some of the economic indicators used above are expressed in a physical unit, others in a monetary unit. It is well, therefore, to say a word about the price level.

When we compare the first half of 1954 with the first half of 1953, we find that the index of wholesale prices is up 0.8% and that the index of consumer prices is up 1.1%. Not only are these increases tiny, but our measures of price movements fail to take account of discounts, concessions, bargain sales, etc., that have been a significant feature of recent markets. If we allow for these developments we can surely say, without the slightest fear of contradiction, that the value of the people's money has remained entirely intact.

This conclusion also holds if we carry comparisons one year further back—that is, if we compare the first half of 1954 with the first half of 1952. On this basis, the index of wholesale prices is down 1.3% and the index of consumer prices is up 1.9%.

9. Let us take note of another fact, namely, that while recent economic activity has been at a high level and the value of the dollar has been stable, the increase in wages—which is one of the principal expressions of the progressiveness of the American economy—has continued.

Average hourly earnings have moved as follows:

	Percent change from the—	
	First half of 1952 to first half of 1954	First half of 1953 to first half of 1954
Manufacturing, total	+9.1	+2.9
Durable	+9.2	+2.2
Nondurable	+7.8	+3.8
Building construction	+13.3	+5.3
Retail trade	+10.8	+4.3

10. The above statistics suggest a high, or even an improving, state of economic welfare. An economic historian of an earlier generation, if confronted with facts such as these, would have felt no hesitation in describing recent times as a period of great prosperity. And if our imag-

inary historian had stopped to take account of the difficulties of shifting from a war to a more nearly peace economy, with government expenditure on national security dropping nearly one-fifth in a year, he might well have described the last year or two as a time when economic miracles were being wrought.

11. Not all of our contemporaries, however, are describing the performance of the American economy in these lyrical terms. The reason is partly that a decline occurred after July 1953 in economic activity, particularly in employment, and that the thinking of many people is geared to the concept of uninterrupted progress. The reason is partly that this rather minor decline has been better advertised than many major declines of our past. The reason is also that, while the decline has been small on an overall basis, it has affected seriously some industries, communities, and groups in our society. Factory employment, particularly in the durable goods industries, has suffered, while agricultural prices and incomes have shown the adverse effects of shrinking export markets and unbalanced production.

12. Unemployment is now greater than during the time of the Korean War, as the following figures indicate:

| | *Unemployment as percent of civilian labor force* | | | | | |
	1949	1950	1951	1952	1953	1954
January–March	5.0	7.2	3.8	3.2	2.8	5.5
April–June	5.4	5.2	2.8	2.7	2.3	5.2
July	6.4	5.0	2.9	3.0	2.4	5.1

It is clear, however, that unemployment in recent months has not been larger than during comparable months in 1949 and 1950.

13. Moreover, the rate of unemployment has shown some tendency to diminish of late. This is one of numerous signs of economic improvement. Retail sales have recently been rising again. Business expenditures on capital expansion and improvement are continuing at a high rate. New construction contracts are running well above the level of a year ago. Inventories have been reduced and are now in better adjustment to current sales. The financial markets have been displaying great strength. The level of business and consumer confidence in the economic future is high and improving.

14. The standards that our generation apply to the performance of an economic system are very different from those that our fathers applied

and even different from those that we ourselves applied only a few years ago. It is a good thing that our standards are higher. Great economic and social achievements will not be made unless we are sensitive to the need for making them.

The economic program being enacted by the present Congress marks a milestone in constructive legislation. It will help to reduce unemployment and to stimulate enterprise and development in all directions. In the months and years ahead, we must continue to bring knowledge, cool judgment, and a concern for people to the consideration of economic problems. In the measure that we do this, we may look forward with great confidence to the future.

195 ¶ Memorandum Directing Use of Agricultural Commodities for Flood Relief in Austria, the Federal Republic of Germany, and Soviet-Occupied Germany.   *August* 12, 1954

Memorandum for:

   The Secretary of State, the Secretary of Agriculture, the Director of the Bureau of the Budget, the Director, Foreign Operations Administration

In accordance with my statement of July 29, 1954, with regard to the extension of aid throughout the flood areas of Eastern and Central Europe, and in accordance with the recommendation contained in the memorandum of August 12, 1954, submitted by the Director of the Foreign Operations Administration, and pursuant to the authority vested in me by Title II of Public Law 480, 83d Congress, 2d Session, I hereby determine that up to $4,000,000 worth of agricultural commodities from the stocks of the Commodity Credit Corporation may be used for the purpose of providing emergency assistance in meeting flood and other urgent requirements in Austria, the Federal Republic of Germany, and Soviet-occupied Germany. The maximum amount of $4,000,000 is computed on the basis of the Corporation's investment in the commodities made available for export, including processing, packaging, inland transportation within the United States, and handling costs.

The Secretary of State shall conclude any necessary bilateral agreements with the governments concerned in connection with the furnishing of this assistance.

Arrangements for the operations of this relief program, including the specifications of the commodities and the provision of Mutual Security funds to cover the costs of ocean transportation of the commodities, shall be the responsibility of the Director of the Foreign Operations Administration and the transfer of the commodities shall be upon such terms and conditions as the Director determines to be appropriate, after consultation with the Secretary of State.

NOTE: On August 14 the White House announced that the President had approved similar emergency assistance under Public Law 480 for the flood victims of Pakistan. Messages of thanks from the Governor General of Pakistan and the President of Austria were released on August 25 and September 4, respectively.

196 ¶ Letter to Chairmen, Senate and House Agriculture Committees, on the Farm Bills in Conference. *August* 12, 1954

Dear ─────────

This letter is prompted by my conviction that decisions to be reached in respect to several items in conference on the farm bill will very seriously affect the well-being of our farming population. I hope my views can receive your colleagues' earnest attention in conference.

I refer, first, to the support level on dairy products. To me, it is inescapable that an increase in this level would be injurious, not helpful, to the dairy industry, for it would diminish the consumption of dairy products, increase the accumulation of surplus stocks, and add needlessly and therefore wastefully to the cost of this program to the public. This would also result in excessive windfall profits to the handlers of dairy products. Any objective analysis of the facts relating to this matter makes it clear, I believe, that the sound course is to continue in the Secretary of Agriculture the authority to keep the support level at seventy-five to ninety per cent.

The two-price plan for wheat is another item occasioning apprehension. I strongly suspect that the House plan would not achieve the desired result. Following preliminary studies on three different occasions, the National Agricultural Advisory Commission recommended against the adoption of the two-price plan. It is obvious that the matter needs further study. I do hope, therefore, that the two-price provision will be eliminated in conference, although retaining direction to the Secretary to study the plan for wheat and possibly rice and to report his findings to the Congress early next year.

Another item of concern is the bill, introduced at my request, relating to management of forest lands used for grazing purposes. The Senate provision is fair to all users of the national forests and a forward step in the management of forest lands. Because its approval would complete the several conservation measures recommended by this Administration to the Congress, I am especially hopeful that it can receive the approbation of your colleagues.

You are aware, of course, of my interest in legislation to promote the production of wool. The House provision would limit the duration of this Act to two years and require the Secretary to maintain about the same level of support for mohair as for shorn wool. Because both of these provisions are clearly at variance with the objectives being sought, I hope they can be withdrawn in your conference deliberations.

By restricting the Secretary's authority to limit the number of terms which a county committeeman may serve, a provision in the Senate bill would undo progress toward broader farmer participation in committee activities. You may recall that the recommendation for improvement of the work of the committees was made following a thorough study in which State ASC committees and the CCC Advisory Board participated. I very much hope, therefore, that this provision in the Senate bill may be eliminated in conference.

I am sending a similar letter to the Chairman of the House (Senate) Committee on Agriculture.

With warm regard,

Sincerely,

DWIGHT D. EISENHOWER

NOTE: This letter was sent to George D. Aiken, Chairman of the Senate Committee on Agriculture, and to Clifford R. Hope, Chairman of the House Agriculture Committee.

The President referred to H.R. 9680 and S. 3052. For the President's statement on signing the Agricultural Act of 1954, see Item 221.

197 ¶ Remarks to Republican Candidates Supported by Citizens for Eisenhower Groups. *August* 12, 1954

IT IS A PLEASURE to greet you, gentlemen. I understand that each of you is a Republican candidate for the Congress, and that each of you is supported by the Citizens for Eisenhower groups in your respective districts.

These groups, of course, are reorganized from the groups of similar names of the 1952 Campaign. I hear they have picked you out for support because you believe in what they believe; that they are going to get behind the legislative program that has been drawn up and submitted in furtherance of the pledges made in 1952, and which still constitute the platform of this Administration, and will continue to do it until it is all enacted into law.

Now, if you people are intending to come here and help on that—and that is what I understand—then I want to say to each one of you a hearty welcome. I believe it is that kind of thing, that kind of program which will make Americans stronger at home in every way—economically, politically, spiritually. And certainly it will make us more secure abroad.

Now that, I think, is our duty to our country, and it will be a great privilege to work with all of you.

I hear I am to have the fun of shaking hands with each one of you.

NOTE: The President spoke in the Rose Garden.

198 ¶ Message for the Ceremonies Marking the 10th Anniversary of Allied Landings in Southern France. *August* 14, 1954

[Released August 14, 1954. Dated August 9, 1954]

TEN YEARS AGO an Allied force landed on the southern coast of France and later joined other Allied forces to liberate France and destroy a tyranny imposed by totalitarian dictators.

The valorous French First Army, led by the late Marshal de Lattre de

Tassigny, was among those forces which on that day demonstrated that there are men in the world strong enough and brave enough to make supreme sacrifices for the ideals in which they believe. The occasion of this landing was only one example of this heroism. Many times thereafter the reconstituted French forces, with their Allies, showed the determination and courage that win and preserve freedom for men.

I have been proud to know the people of the great French nation, and I hold the deepest respect and admiration for their devotion, as individuals and as a nation, to their individual liberties and their country's independence. With them, I pay tribute to this great event now being commemorated; with them, I mourn their lost comrades, many of whom were also comrades of mine. Today, as new perils threaten, may we continue to march unitedly, as we did a decade ago, and together may we continue to strive and to persevere toward the international good will and peace for which we commonly yearn.

NOTE: The message was read by General Jacob L. Devers, USA (Ret.), at the ceremonies held on August 14 at Le Candel in southern France.

199 ¶ Statement by the President Upon Signing Bill Revising the Internal Revenue Code.
August 16, 1954

THIS BILL which today becomes law is the excellent result of cooperative efforts by the Congress and the Department of the Treasury to give our tax code its first complete revision in seventy-five years. It is a good law. It will benefit all Americans.

This law brings tax relief to large numbers of our citizens. It is, in fact, part of a comprehensive tax program which, since January 1 of this year, will have provided for tax cuts totaling $7,400,000,000—the largest dollar tax cut in any year in the nation's history.

It is a law which will help millions of Americans by giving them fairer tax treatment than they now receive. For example:

The parents of dependent children who work can continue to claim their children as dependents, no matter how much the children earn.

Retired people and widows living on retirement income other than social security will receive a tax credit which will in effect be equal to the tax credit now given to people living on social security income.

Taxpayers will now be able to claim as dependents people who are not related to them, so long as they provide more than one-half of such dependents' support.

Farmers active in soil and water conservation will be able to deduct from their income the cost of such conservation work, up to 25 percent of their gross income.

People with large medical expenses will now be able to deduct from their income all such expenses which exceed three percent (rather than five percent) of their incomes, and the maximum amounts deductible will be twice as large as they were in the past.

Working widows and many other mothers with child-care expenses will be able to deduct from their income up to $600 a year for the costs of taking care of their children.

People receiving sick benefits paid by employers will not have to pay any tax on such income up to $100 a week.

In addition to removing inequities in our tax system, this law will help our economy expand and thus add materially to the strength of our nation. It will help our people produce better goods at cheaper prices—and it will help to create more jobs.

This economic growth will be fostered by such provisions as more flexible depreciation and better tax treatment of research and development costs, thus encouraging all business—large and small—to modernize and expand. And, partial reduction of the double taxation of income from dividends will stimulate the investment of savings by our private citizens and so make available the thousands of dollars that provide the plant tools and power needed for each new job in America.

Numerous other provisions will also help to expand the economy. These include the easing of the so-called penalty tax on accumulated earnings when necessary for legitimate business purposes; the extension of the carry-back of net operating losses, and the greater flexibility of the tax treatment of recapitalizations and reorganizations.

Almost balancing the revenue lost through these tax reductions is additional revenue of $1.2 billion gained by an extension of the 52 percent tax on corporation profits. The new law also closes more than fifty loopholes through which, in the past, some taxpayers may have attempted to avoid their fair share of the tax burden.

And, at long last, the American people will have—because of this law—

much needed clarification of many tax provisions which previously have been subject to controversy.

I congratulate the Congress and its leaders for having enacted this monumental tax revision. Its passage is a tribute to a Congress which in this session has made so many major contributions to the prosperity and security of the people of our country.

NOTE: The Internal Revenue Code of 1954 is Public Law 591, 83d Congress (68A Stat. 3).

200 ⁋ The President's News Conference of *August* 17, 1954.

THE PRESIDENT. Please be seated, ladies and gentlemen.

The only announcement I have is that I have just seen word from the Czechoslovakian Government that they accept the American offer to assist the victims of the great Danube floods through their areas, and are ready to discuss methods of implementation.

Now, we will take questions.

Q. Marvin L. Arrowsmith, Associated Press: Mr. President, Stephen Mitchell, the Democratic National Chairman, said yesterday you personally ordered the Dixon-Yates power contract awarded to a firm in which one of your closest friends has an interest, and at $90 million more than a competitor syndicate. His office later identified the friend as Bobby Jones. Do you care to comment on that matter?

THE PRESIDENT. Well, ladies and gentlemen, I knew when I once went into political life that I would be subjected by many types of strange characters to many kinds of innuendo and allegations.

In this case, I must say, I am a little astonished that any kind of such innuendo should include a private citizen of the character and standing of Bob Jones. I think there is no gentleman that I know whose integrity and probity I am more certain of than I am of his.

Now, as to my own actions, I am not going to defend myself, as I have told you time and again I shall not. I merely say this—of course I approved the recommendations for this action—every single official action I take involving the contractual relationships of the United States with anybody, except only when the question of national security is directly involved, is open to the public. Any one of you here present may, singly or in an investigation group, go to the Bureau of the Budget, to the chief of the Atomic Energy Commission, and get the complete record from the inception of the idea to this very minute; it is all yours.

Now, that is all I have to say about it.

Q. Robert E. Clark, International News Service: Mr. President, can you give us your views on the conflicting bills passed by the House and Senate to outlaw the Communist Party?

THE PRESIDENT. Things happened so fast in that procedure, Mr. Clark, as to keep most of us, I think, a bit confused. I thought the bill as it came out of the House yesterday was satisfactory. Now I think all America is just a bit confused.

We recognize the Communist Party as a conspiracy and not as a political party in the accepted meaning of that term here at home. We think, therefore, it has no place on our ballots. But we are puzzled as to exactly how we do this and show the same concern, the same interest, in all of the civil rights of the individual citizen, whoever he may be and wherever he may be, that are required under our form of government.

So I felt that—any act that would tend to vitiate or to obstruct—the great work that has been going on in the FBI and in the Department of Justice under the authority of the Smith Act and the internal security acts should not be interfered with. I think the purpose of the bill that came out yesterday, moving to the outlawing of the party as such, made very sure that none of the work, the accumulated results of that work, under the FBI and the Department of Justice would be vitiated.

I hear, just before I came over here, another amendment has been enacted in the Senate. I don't know its exact language, and I can't comment on it. But I thought the one that came out yesterday was generally satisfactory from my viewpoint.

Q. Merriman Smith, United Press: Mr. President, there have been reports recently of a buildup of Chinese Communist strength across on the mainland from Formosa. There have been reports from the Far East that the Chinese Communists may attack Formosa. What would happen, sir, if the Communists did attack Formosa in force?

THE PRESIDENT. Well, in January or February of 1953 instructions went out to the 7th Fleet. Those instructions regarding the defense of Formosa merely reaffirmed orders that had been in force in that fleet since 1950. Those orders are still in force. Therefore, I should assume what would happen is this: any invasion of Formosa would have to run over the 7th Fleet.

Q. Neal A. Stanford, Christian Science Monitor: Mr. President, it has been suggested that the British Labor Party leaders now in Red China visit the United States on their way back to Britain. Have you considered inviting them or do you see any merit in inviting them?

THE PRESIDENT. Did you say it has been suggested? It had already been suggested?

Q. Mr. Stanford: There have been comments in the paper suggesting it.

THE PRESIDENT. Oh; I hadn't thought about it.

Q. Sarah McClendon, El Paso Times: Sir, my question has to do with the reserve program and the manpower utilization programs which the Defense Department is preparing, I believe under your direction, for presentation to Congress next year. In this connection I asked Mr. Wilson recently if he would agree with this idea that practically all of our citizens just as well prepare themselves to fit in by either skills or combat training in some sort of military organization. He said yes, he would agree to that. Will you please comment on that?

THE PRESIDENT. As a matter of fact, I think you could approach such a question from many different angles. Let me give you one.

War has unfortunately been a phenomenon of the life of every generation in our whole history. One of the reasons for this preparation of which Mr. Wilson spoke is to give the individual maximum chance for survival, not only through fitting his own efforts in with the joint efforts of the Nation so as to insure victory and, therefore, promote his chances of survival, but in the actual combat, learning how to take care of himself and what to do to make himself a better individual.

So I would say, as a matter of general philosophy, with the world in the state it is, that some form of military training or related training for every individual was an advantage to him and to the Nation.

Q. Charles S. von Fremd, Columbia Broadcasting System: There has been deep concern, sir, in some circles over the far-reaching amendments proposed by the French Premier to the European Defense Community Pact; indeed, so much concern that some people wonder whether or not the EDC will ever become a practicing reality. I wonder if you might give us your evaluation of this serious situation.

THE PRESIDENT. Well, ladies and gentlemen, this is one of those questions that I would rather not discuss in any detail.

I suppose most of you know that from the day I was sent back to Europe in January of 1951, I had the task of working for EDC. Because of the prejudices and the tensions that prevailed in Europe, I came to believe it is the only process by which Western Europe can possibly get together on a reasonably effective basis to protect themselves militarily and to support the kind of units they should have.

Certainly, it was the only way I could see that Western Germany can be brought into such a concert of nations without creating, well, such additional tension as to upset the whole equilibrium and, therefore, destroy the object you are seeking.

So, at this moment, when again it has been brought forward by a French Premier, I would not want to express myself too positively on any particular one of his proposals.

I merely say this: there has been a long legislative process that has been gone through by other nations; and if proposals would be so drastic that each of those nations would again have to enter an entirely new process, then I would say it would be quite serious. I do not believe that that would be the purpose of the French Prime Minister.

Q. Charles L. Bartlett, Chattanooga Times: Mr. President, back on the Dixon-Yates thing for a minute, it has been suggested that because you just appointed a new TVA chairman, and because various alternatives to the contract have been proposed, that you might order the contract to be deferred until the new chairman had time to look over the situation and give his evaluation. Is there any truth in those reports?

THE PRESIDENT. As to the exact timing of the execution of that contract, I believe that is a point that has never been brought to my attention.

But I do know this: the new chairman, I believe, is to take over on the 1st of next month. As I think I told you people once before, he has only one instruction—to do his honest best to find the facts there and to make his recommendations according to his own professional training and what is needful in the region.

Q. Kenneth M. Scheibel, Gannett Newspapers: Mr. President, a number of Republican Congressmen are expecting political repercussions in the elections this year over the farm program. Do you look for political reprisals or do you feel the rank and file farmers are going to support your flexible plan?

THE PRESIDENT. As I have so often explained, the plan that went to Congress, the farm plan, was made up through consultation with every single farm group that we could get hold of.

There was one farm group, I recall, that never agreed really with any part of it; it is not as large as the others. But the main farm groups, representatives of the agricultural colleges, of actual farmers themselves, people who are most experienced both legislativewise and executivewise in the governmental phases of this thing, were brought in. So, from my point of view, the majority—I am certain that the majority of farmers in the United States support the bill as a whole; although, I suppose, it would be true that in each district you could possibly find a majority that might object to some specific feature of it.

But the bill is not merely one feature; it is a very broad and comprehensive program designed to produce markets and to get supply and demand back into our farming problem.

Q. Mr. Scheibel: Sir, if you find there is a need at the next session of Congress for changes in the program, would you suggest further amendments?

THE PRESIDENT. Indeed I will. I don't believe I have yet gotten stupid enough to believe I am so smart that I know all of the answers in advance.

Q. Laurence H. Burd, Chicago Tribune: Back to Formosa, sir, in the event of a Communist invasion, are we prepared to use any other forces in addition to the 7th Fleet to defend Formosa?

THE PRESIDENT. It hasn't been brought up. I haven't had a conversation with my military advisers.

Q. Nat S. Finney, Buffalo Evening News: Mr. President, I wonder if you would help me in straightening out a bit of the record. I believe that in your atomic message to Congress, it was stated that the bill on which work is now being completed was not to be considered covering the legislation needed for an international pool. Now, I wondered whether you presently consider that the provisions in this bill—which, I presume, will pass—are adequate to permit you to go ahead on a domestic law basis on an international pool?

THE PRESIDENT. I could speak, I am sorry, only by impression; it is one that I think I should prefer to speak both to the Attorney General and to the AEC chief before I would give you a definitive answer. I will try to do so through Mr. Hagerty before I get away from Washington.

Q. Alice Frein Johnson, Seattle Times: Mr. President, when you issued, or rather, when your Air Coordinating Committee issued the report on Civil Aviation Policy last May, you had a covering letter in which you said you would be guided in the future by that policy in making decisions on civil aviation. Senator Thye and other Republican Senators recently have said that the policy will allow the revival of the "chosen carrier" instrument or monopoly in international trade. Do you believe that that policy will allow competition to be stifled and monopoly to be in force?

THE PRESIDENT. I am afraid you are asking me to be a little bit too accurate in my legal interpretations this afternoon.

I will say this: I don't believe in monopoly; and if that is permissible or encouraged by that act, I would want to take another look at it and decide what to do.

Q. Edwin L. Dale, New York Herald Tribune: Mr. President, the economic statistics you gave us last week dealt, as you know, primarily with the past. I am wondering if your advisers, in light of the fact that business has been rather steady for 3 months, expect it to pick up soon—perhaps in the fall?

THE PRESIDENT. Well, it happens that this morning I was on a plane, and I read a little article by W. I. Myers from Cornell, you know, dean of agriculture from Cornell.

He says business, he believes, will have an upturn this fall; and he says he believes it will be of a character that won't lead us into any inflationary process, but it will be a good healthy upturn.

So far as I can determine, and I do not want to quote anybody else, the mass of opinion from the experts seems to be that we are in a general mild upswing.

Q. Frank van der Linden, Nashville Banner: Mr. President, Vice President Nixon recently told some of us reporters that he didn't plan to campaign in South Carolina this year for congressional candidates because he didn't think the Republicans had much of a chance down there. I wondered if you planned to campaign in some southern States this fall for Republican congressional candidates?

THE PRESIDENT. I thought that my entire itinerary for the fall had already been published. Hasn't it?

Mr. Hagerty: Not quite. [*Laughter*]

THE PRESIDENT. Well, as a matter of fact, I know of no reason why it should be secret. I think that I promised that the second that it is fixed—I suppose there are still one or two tentative dates on it; but I have no plans, so far as I know, to go south.

Q. Harry W. Frantz, United Press, Foreign Service: Mr. President, the Senate Armed Services Committee, I believe, sent a committee resolution recommending in general terms that some United States expedition should resume exploration in the Antarctic. There has been some unofficial discussion of further Antarctic exploration. Has that received your attention as yet, or would you——

THE PRESIDENT. Well, so far it has merely been in the conversational and discussional stage. No specific recommendation has come to me at all.

Q. Norman Carignan, Associated Press: Mr. President, have you made any decision as yet on recommendations by the Tariff Commission for an increased tariff on lead and zinc?

THE PRESIDENT. No, I have not made any.

Q. Edward T. Folliard, Washington Post and Times Herald: Mr. President, is the legislative picture such now that you can say when you will leave for Denver?

THE PRESIDENT. Well, there still are some measures before the Congress which, of course, I would like to have out. There is the reinsurance bill; there are certain parts of the Social Security Act; there is the Renegotiation Act; of course the farm bill has not yet been enrolled and brought up.

But I will tell you what I am doing: I am hoping to leave this city at 9:30 on Saturday morning. Now, if I am too optimistic, why, I will have to give you notice when I find that out; but that is when I am hoping to go.

Q. Richard L. Wilson, Cowles Publications: Mr. President, do you plan to go to the Iowa State Fair?

THE PRESIDENT. I am to—[*confers with Mr. Hagerty*]—I'll tell you what: I am coming here to address the American Legion, and on the way back I am to stop at the Iowa State Fair for a matter of an hour or so, something like that.

Q. Mr. Wilson: What day is that?

THE PRESIDENT. The 30th of August.

Q. Mr. Wilson: Thirty-first?

THE PRESIDENT. Thirtieth, isn't it?

Mr. Hagerty: Thirtieth of August.

Q. Robert J. Donovan, New York Herald Tribune: Sir, just on these plans, are you still contemplating a broadcast on the record of Congress?

THE PRESIDENT. Yes.

Q. Mr. Donovan: That would be before leaving Washington, sir?

THE PRESIDENT. No, I think probably it would have to be done from Denver next Monday or Tuesday night, Wednesday, something like that.

Q. Mr. Donovan: Sir, without pinning yourself down to memory on dates, could you give us just, in general, a little bit of your itinerary this fall?

THE PRESIDENT. Well——

Q. Mr. Donovan: The good dates.

THE PRESIDENT. ——Mr. Donovan, I don't want to cross up my staff. I promised that when they get these plans fairly well in line they will announce them. Now, that does clean up the August dates, doesn't it?

Mr. Hagerty: August, yes.

THE PRESIDENT. All the August dates; that is all of them. The 19th in Illinois with two appearances, the 30th coming back here and then going on to——

Q. Mr. Donovan: Iowa.

THE PRESIDENT. And back to Denver; and then, of course, this talk in Denver early next week.

Q. Richard L. Wilson, Cowles Publications: I just wanted to ask you one more question, sir, with respect to your visit to the Iowa State Fair. Do you expect that the Republican candidates for Congress will be there at the time you are there? [*Laughter*]

THE PRESIDENT. Well, that wasn't in the bargain, Mr. Wilson, but I will tell you this: from all the questions that come to me about such things, I just assume they are going to be. I just don't see any other—[*laughter*]

Q. Mr. Wilson: Did you say, sir, that you would like to have them?

THE PRESIDENT. Surely I do. After all, they are my associates here, I work with them; I like them.

Q. Roscoe Drummond, New York Herald Tribune: Mr. President, in New York your former Army mess sergeant, Marty Snyder, is running for Congress as an Eisenhower Independent. I wondered if you would say whether you think he would be a useful Member of Congress?

THE PRESIDENT. Well, Marty Snyder, as you say, was a sergeant in my headquarters; he ran the headquarters mess.

So far as I know he has been a fine citizen. I don't know anything about him before that moment. He was a good soldier. He certainly got it in his head early to try to make one Eisenhower President of the United States, and stuck with it, and possibly thinks he is a bit responsible. Maybe he is.

Now, I would deduce from that that he would be a loyal supporter if he were down here. [*Laughter*]

Merriman Smith, United Press: Thank you, Mr. President.

NOTE: President Eisenhower's forty-ninth news conference was held in the Executive Office Building from 3:01 to 3:25 o'clock on Tuesday afternoon, August 17, 1954. In attendance: 144.

201   ¶ Statement by the President Upon Signing Bill Amending the Water Facilities Act.
August 17, 1954

I AM HAPPY today to sign into law the amendment to the Water Facilities Act.

This is one of three legislative actions taken by the 83rd Congress which give important new strength to our national efforts to conserve the vital water and soil resources of the United States. This legislation is of high significance in the movement which came to life fifty years ago when Theodore Roosevelt gave new meaning to the word "conservation."

This legislation is significant because it gives new stimulus to local initiative and establishes for the first time a nation-wide program of conservation practices based on the concept that farms, streams, forests, and towns are all inter-related parts of a watershed. It recognizes in practical terms that the upstream part of the watershed, as well as the downstream part, must be taken into our plans if we are to have the water we vitally need and if we are to solve with maximum effectiveness three of our most challenging problems—soil erosion, floods and drought.

The first of these bills is the Watershed Protection and Flood Prevention Act. This Act recognizes by law for the first time the great importance of upstream watershed protection in our over-all water resource policy. For the first time also, this Act provides a broad program of Federal technical and financial assistance to such local watershed groups as are willing to assume responsibility for initiating, carrying out, and sharing the costs of watershed protection which will help conserve water for agricultural uses and supplement any needed downstream flood control measures.

The second bill amends the Water Facilities Act. Formerly limited to the 17 western states, the program established by this Act makes available, throughout the entire nation, loans for developing agricultural water improvements on farms and ranches. In addition, this law establishes a program of direct or insured loans for drainage facilities, reforestation, and other water and soil conservation measures. Farmers and ranchers frequently need credit to take care of the initial investments required in establishing conservation systems, or to tide them over an adjustment period while they shift to a better and, in the long run, more profitable type of land use. These new credit provisions, specially geared to conservation needs, provide a significant means of encouraging and advancing soil and water conservation.

The third legislative action is part of the Congressional revision of the internal revenue laws. It allows farmers and ranchers to treat expenditures for a number of soil conservation measures as current annual expenses which may be deducted from farm income in computing income taxes. This Act therefore gives farmers new tax advantages on these land improvement measures. Not only will these advantages benefit the farmer financially; they will also add incentive to the application of soil and water conservation measures.

These three bills rest on several sound principles.

First, we recognize that it is absolutely urgent to conserve and improve our water resources. For water is essential to every part of our life, and in quantities that are usually unsuspected. It takes 18 barrels of water, for example, to refine a barrel of oil. It takes 85,000 gallons to produce a ton of rubber. It takes something like 800,000 gallons of water to mature an acre of cotton. It takes some 1,300 gallons of water each day to supply the direct and indirect needs of each one of our citizens. As our population increases, so will these demands.

726

Even these statistics do not drive home the urgency of adequate water supplies nearly so well as the personal experiences many Americans have had this very summer—of insufficient water for crops and livestock, of failing wells, of restrictions on use of water in towns. Some of our cities have had to seek means of supplementing their failing or depleted reservoirs. Some have had to haul water from nearby streams. In rural areas, there has been a growing call for water for irrigation. These facts add up to a hard warning: we cannot afford to waste water.

Any attempt to conserve this water should take into account a key fact: that this all-important water—the water we use on our farms, in our homes, in our businesses, or in our factories—has been collected from all the lands of the watershed, beginning at its uppermost limits. Our streams, our deep wells, our storage reservoirs are merely accumulations of water that has fallen on the land in the form of rain or snow. Some of it runs off in creeks and rivers. Some of it evaporates. Some soaks in to nourish crops and trees. Some finds its way into springs or into the sands we tap with our wells. How much water runs off, and how fast, and how much soaks into feed crops and springs—these quantities depend in large measure on what kind of land it falls on, what this land is used for, and what kind of cover—trees, grass—the land has.

For this reason our water management programs must not go to work only in large streams or rivers, though the flood control and other measures there are of enormous importance. Our programs to conserve water must begin where the raindrop falls. And because of the extensive erosion and sedimentation damage which result from floods in headwater streams and small tributaries, and also because these parts of the watershed have up to now been relatively neglected in conservation planning, these programs must put new emphasis on their management.

Under the Watershed Protection and Flood Prevention Act, sound soil conservation plans will be developed to establish the right use for each kind of soil on all the farms of a watershed. Soil conservation will be supplemented where necessary with small detention dams, channel improvements, or other measures to protect the fertile bottom land along these small streams.

These measures will be of pronounced benefit to agriculture. More and more American farmers are coming to realize that good land use and land treatment can help them to conserve water as well as soil. They are seeing the advantages of inducing as much water as possible to soak into the ground where it falls—water which will help grow crops and help recharge underground water supplies that are tapped by farms and by cities and industries. Thus an accelerated soil conservation and watershed program will also benefit urban centers by helping to keep sediment from cutting down the storage capacity of our large city reservoirs. It will reduce the amount of silt that has to be filtered from water before it can be used by city water systems or by industry. And it will help lessen the damage caused by drought and thus help stabilize areas where this hazard has been unusually severe.

Another significant contribution of the watershed legislation is that it gives new force and emphasis to local leadership. Its programs are not Federal work projects; no new agencies will have to be created to carry them out. These programs will be planned only at the instance of local people. They will be planned with the cooperation and participation of local and State governments. They will be initiated only when local people have demonstrated their willingness and ability to share equitably in the cost and to assume responsibility for direction and maintenance of the work.

The watershed and water development programs will also encourage a new and improved means of local-State-Federal teamwork. Locally, rural and urban interests must join forces in sponsoring and contributing to the programs—contributing the funds, labor, materials, lands, easements, and other needs that can best be supplied by local organizations. State and county governments are also involved. Floodwater retarding dams, sediment control structures, channel stabilization measures and the like, on the tributary streams, represent measures which individuals cannot be expected to install by themselves, and which may properly require State or even Federal aid because their benefits extend beyond the local community. The Federal Government also has a major role in providing technical, research, financial, and educational assistance.

To do this work, all levels of government and private endeavor must cooperate. And there will be a call for increased effort in the future. Because our population is growing rapidly, the demands upon the nation's soil and water resources are bound to become heavier in the years ahead. But we do have the resources to match this growth if we manage them wisely. In the long run, it is absolutely vital to the welfare of farm and urban people, and to the strength of the entire nation, that we work soundly and vigorously to protect and develop our nation's vital water supplies and the related resources of farm land, range, and timber. In such a matter of national interest, we must act with effectiveness. These three measures show that we have so acted.

NOTE: As enacted, the bill (S. 3137) is Public Law 597, 83d Congress (68 Stat. 734).

202 ¶ Statement by the President Upon Signing the Federal Employees' Group Life Insurance Act. *August 17, 1954*

I AM HIGHLY GRATIFIED by this new law which makes group life insurance available to Federal employees.

The economic security of an employee's family contributes directly and powerfully to his effectiveness as a worker. Group life insurance has therefore become an important factor in private industry's employer-employee relations. Enactment of this new law is a milestone in the effort to adapt to Federal personnel management the best practices of progressive private employers.

The Civil Service Commission will see that appropriate information is distributed promptly to all Federal employees, so that they will have the benefit of this insurance protection at the earliest possible date.

NOTE: The Federal Employees' Group Life Insurance Act of 1954 is Public Law 598, 83d Congress (68 Stat. 736).

203 ¶ Address at the Illinois State Fair at Springfield. *August 19, 1954*

Governor Stratton, Governor Craig, and distinguished members of this great audience:

For a number of reasons I am highly honored to be with you today. In the first place, I was invited here by your distinguished Governor, one of those young, virile men in our country who is giving his life to public service for the betterment of all of us.

Incidentally, just now, as I left the luncheon table of Governor

Stratton and his charming family, he remarked to me that he had a special reason for being glad I was here; because, he said, otherwise, this being Governor's Day, he would be worrying about a speech. He felt it was quite a job—a good piece of work—if you could pass on your chores to the President.

There is a very deep personal reason for my feeling of gratification in being with you today. Of course, during the last 2 or 3 years, I have been privileged to meet many old friends, to make many new ones, whose friendships I hope will be as durable as the old ones. But more than that, I was born and reared in this great Mississippi Basin. When I get back to the familiar sights of the farmlands, the corn, and the wheat, the vast horizons, the friendly people with whom I was raised, I feel more at home than I do any other place in this world that I have been roaming for long over 40 years.

And then, of course, it is inspiring to visit this spot where Lincoln lived. And by happy coincidence, this is the year—the centennial year—of the party of which Lincoln is still the hero and the everlasting spiritual inspiration.

I want to say that I believe he would be proud of the delegation the party has sent to Washington during this last 2 years. The reason I believe that is this: they have been in the forefront of the battle to get enacted into law a vast program for the betterment of America, for making certain that here at home there is a growing prosperity, a sound economy, a wide sharing of our productivity. And at home—and abroad—an ever-growing security and safety for ourselves.

This delegation of yours has been there to help carry out the promises that they made to you people. They have been helping me carry out my promises, my promises that I made 2 years ago, to go to Washington to work for one thing, and one thing only: the good of the United States of America.

I asserted then that I believed we could have a prosperous economy without war. And that we could begin the process of taking America back from the bureaucrats and giving it back to America.

Now today I could not possibly review for you in detail the long record of constructive accomplishment of that Congress, which is just now engaged in the last of the long series of bills which will be of the most lasting and tremendous importance to every one of us meeting here today.

But I think it would be profitable to take a quick look to see what this Congress, under the leadership of the party of Lincoln, has done if we can hit only the very highest of the high spots.

A year ago, last January, we were still reading casualty lists in our daily newspapers. America's heart was bleeding for all those mothers, brothers, sweethearts, wives, and children who were deprived of a loved one through the operation of that war. Obviously all of us know that the composition that was reached in Korea is not satisfactory to America, but it is far better than to continue the bloody, dreary, sacrifice of lives with no possible strictly military victory in sight.

In Indochina the Communists have added new groups to their already great expanse of people that they are enslaving with the hope of destroying all of us. But even there the composition reached by one of our friends was one that was dictated by almost sheer necessity. In the unhappy circumstances of that land, we at least have a chance now to rally the people of good feeling and goodwill, the people who believe in the dignity of the human man, and make a line to develop a concert of nations that the Communists will not dare attack.

Think what has happened in Iran, a country that we were almost certain was going under the Communist banner—and it is now associating strongly with the Western World.

The long, dreary quarrels in the Suez region have been composed with the greatest possible promise for the security and the prosperity of the west, including the United States of America.

In Guatemala, the people of that region rose up and rejected the Communist doctrine, and said in the terms of the spirit of the agreement at Caracas, "You shall not come here and establish yourselves."

Of course, the international scene is still troubled. It is not the kind of problem that can be solved in a day, but if we make steady progress in the terms of this past year and a half, each day will see the free world stronger, and more and more reach that point where none will dare any aggression against us.

Here at home, my friends, one of the first duties, one of the most pleasurable duties I had was to lift from the economy of the United States the stifling controls that had been called necessary in order to control prices and keep down the cost of living. And the American people proved that if we would let this economy alone, to respond to the natural laws under which it was established and has so far developed, it would be conducted in such a way as to meet the needs of 160 million people.

And so, instead of the great inflation that was predicted, prices have shifted scarcely at all. At this moment there have been effected reductions in the actual expenditures—cash expenditures of government—almost exactly $10 billion below the levels that were scheduled for expenditure 1 year ago last January. There have been laws passed expanding social security and old age pensions. Governmental workers have been insured so that they do not have to look forward to a life of penury. There has been enacted a farm program, my friends, that has a chance to stand solidly behind the agricultural community indefinitely. It is not one that will break down of its own weight because of unmanageable surpluses.

There has been, at long last, after many, many years, a great tax reform. There has been refunded, restored to the American people something of the order of 7 billion dollars, in the belief that they know better how to expend their own money than bureaucrats know how to expend it for them.

These are just a few of the highlights, and during these long months, while this program was being developed and brought before the national Legislature—debated, argued, and enacted—there have been sitting on the sidelines, of course, the prophets of gloom and doom. Some of them saw a great inflation that the policies of the administration in taking off controls was leading to. They have been proved wrong.

Others then started preaching depression. Every time we turned around we were all going to be in the poorhouse. Something has gone wrong with their calculations. They remind me a little bit of the story of Lincoln's crooked fence. You remember he said a farmer built a fence that was so crooked that every time a pig bored a hole through it, he found himself on the same side from which he started.

Now these economic prophets of doom have been building up a lot of fences of what they call economic statistics. But they built them up so crookedly that every time they bored through them, they came out on the side of pessimism and depression. It seems lately that they would like to forget the whole thing. And I think all of us are getting rather tired of crooked-fence economic politics.

Riding out here this morning, ladies and gentlemen, I picked up a paper, published in your neighboring State, and it had a wonderful little editorial about the settling of the Studebaker labor-management argument. A man named Horvath is apparently president of that union. The last sentence of this editorial quoted Mr. Horvath as follows: "When you are allowed to tell the truth, the people will always agree to the right thing."

I wish today I could meet Mr. Horvath and shake him by the hand. I believe he has given us—every man who has the responsibility of public office—a proper philosophy: trying to give people the truth, to do it to the best of his ability, and they will follow the correct line.

Now ladies and gentlemen, I came out here today for the opportunity of greeting you, of seeing you, because I must assure you that in Washington, too often, one gets the feeling that he is drifting just a bit away from the heart of the United States.

True, my mail is vast, and a great portion of it I try to read and answer myself, but there is no substitute for coming out and seeing the people of the United States.

Before I leave here, I want to thank you. I want to thank each person that I have met along your beautiful streets for the warmth of the welcome they have given me, and I hope that they will not consider it a political speech if I should say that in view of the record this Congress has made in advancing your interests, in protecting your country, in making sure that we have a steady, sound prosperity, widely shared, if I should suggest to you the possibility that it might be a good thing to increase the size of the delegation that you send from Lincoln's party to Washington.

Because I must tell you one thing: some months ago I pledged a group with whom I was meeting that never again as long as I was President would I meet privately or publicly with anyone and make a statement for publication, unless I insisted that I wanted every bit of help I could get in enacting that program to make America strong, for you, and for our children and theirs.

Thank you very much.

NOTE: The President spoke at 1:20 p.m. His opening words "Governor Stratton, Governor Craig" referred to William G. Stratton, Governor of Illinois, and George N. Craig, Governor of Indiana. Later in the address he referred to Louis Horvath, President of Studebaker Local 5, United Auto Workers.

204 ¶ Address at the Second Assembly of the World Council of Churches, Evanston, Illinois. *August 19, 1954*

Your Grace, the Archbishop, President Miller, members of the clergy, my fellow citizens and friends:

There are many good reasons why I am so delighted to meet with this assembly of the World Council of Churches on this beautiful campus in this charming city. I think it is very fitting that one of the great universities of our country should be the host of this wonderful body of world representatives.

Now I should like to enumerate a few of the reasons why I believe that I speak for the American people in saying that we are proud that this assembly has chosen to meet here. First of all, the citizens of the United States feel highly honored that you have chosen this country in which to hold your Second Assembly of the World Churches, because you are a world body of spiritual leaders. Here in this land, we sometimes are thought to be too ready to adhere to and to place our trust in material values. Now it is true that in today's world of risks and alarms, we must and we will remain strong, and seek to make our good friends strong in all those scientific, material, and military means that ensure or enhance our safety, and discourage aggression against us or against our friends. But we know that there is no true and lasting cure for world tensions in guns and bombs. We know that only the spirit and mind of man, dedicated to justice and right, can in the long term enable us to live in the confident tranquility that should be every man's heritage.

We are likewise delighted that your conference representing 48 nations and 163 church groups, virtually brings the world to the center of the North American continent. However fervent the citizens of this land may be about our own country—and we are—all of us realize that the problems and hopes before us today are world problems and world hopes. More and more we understand the prophetic wisdom of John Wesley's statement: the world is my parish.

Again, you call yourselves a council. The term suggests that you accept the injunction "Come, let us reason together." Deliberation such as yours, involving long-term as well as immediate objectives, can lend depth and distance to our own thinking. International political conferences deal habitually with crises, and its results often are little more than a series of improvisations. Indeed, responsible officials have no opportunity to deal with the matter until it becomes a crisis.

Woodrow Wilson complained "By the time anything gets to me it is a problem." We in Government today feel the same. In many respects, we envy the chance of the members of your great convocation to meet and plan on a positive basis for the world in the years to come. Still another reason for our gratification in your presence among us is that you are a council of churches. You represent a vast body of believers, of men and women, and you know the power of believing. You are custodians of a great faith, and this in an age of uncertainty and bewilderment. Many of you have what the Quakers call a concern. Your energies are pledged. You are committed to a program that involves personal responsibility for the general good. It therefore heartens us to have an assembly of this sort in the United States of America, and on our part we think it fitting that you meet here.

Almost anywhere you turn in this country you will find a confluence of religious forces producing a person or an institution with service to others as an objective. Moreover, we are a nation of many people, out of many lands; practically every national group is represented in all branches of our Government. With our diversity, if you could look at us from afar, we would be theoretically impossible. But we do exist. And in reasonable harmony. Thus we meet the variety of this great assembly with a variety of our own, and with the feeling that we can understand something of your hopes and aspirations.

So, even as you have announced your aims, we as a people have put our ideals on record. We have chosen to state these ideals for all the world to see.

At our national beginnings, now a century and three quarters gone, we announced what we intended to make out of this country. We proclaimed then the principles on which it was founded, and toward which we continue to strive. We have fallen short, yes. But the ideals we have set forth, that we have blazoned on the record, stand always there to challenge us. Thus we shall view with the greatest of sympathy your own efforts here to set forth a steadily higher ideal toward which man in his growth must always move. We will watch with great interest what you do here, for another reason. We are essentially a religious people. We are not merely religious, we are inclined, more today than ever, to see the value of religion as a practical force in our affairs.

Contrary to what many people think, the percentage of our population belonging to churches steadily increases. In a hundred years, that percentage has multiplied more than three times. Recently, a great bible society announced that it had doubled the distribution of the Scriptures in the United States since 1948. Bible distribution in this country last year rose to almost 10 million volumes, published in 81 languages.

Now, these two facts are not in themselves proof, either of piety or of an approaching millennium. But they are signs—an indication—that our interest in religion is serious and genuine, not merely theoretical. A score of religious faiths, large and small, are represented in the membership of our present Congress, and it will interest you to know that a good many Members of our Congress periodically meet together outside of legislative hours, to consider how religious principles can be applied to the practical affairs of our Government. I think that you ought to feel at home here, and to know that you are among people who feel in harmony with your purposes. Believing as we do in the importance of religion, we shall expect much of this convocation. We hope that you will touch our imagination, and remind us again and again of the vision without which the people perish. Give us criticism in the light of religious ideals. Kindle anew in us a desire to strive for moral greatness, and to show us where we fall short. We shall listen, if you speak to us as the prophets spoke in the days of old.

We look to you for another thing, and that is for a practical demonstration of the Christian ethic. We hope you may show us additional and better ways in which it can be applied to all sorts of problems. This is what you might call the logistics of faith. We as a people have sought, however imperfectly, to carry out in this spirit programs that have been regional and even global in scope.

The war was scarcely over, may I remind you, when American hearts were digging cash out of American pockets to help restore the devastated regions, to relieve suffering. There was finally established the great system of CARE—CARE packages going everywhere in the world to feed the hungry, and to bring a moment of belief and of good feeling to millions who are in despair; the Marshall Plan, and its effort to restore to other nations something of the abilities they had to earn their own livings before the cataclysm of war struck them; the technical assistance that spread around the world from Peru to Pakistan, everywhere that people needed technical help to help themselves. And aside from all these, we have a great record of Red Cross and church and other groups doing their mightiest all the time, to help their brethren who are less fortunate.

Now admittedly, my friends, these programs always reflect our own enlightened self-interest, as well as humanitarian purposes. We know that no nation may live by itself alone. To preserve the individual freedoms we prize so highly, we must not only protect ourselves as a nation, but we must make certain that others with like devotion to liberty may also survive and prosper.

We have wanted a world in which we might live in peace and confidence. And in striving toward that goal, we have understood that to help others was often the best way ourselves to advance. But underlying all these practical considerations has been belief in the dignity of man, and in the rights conferred upon him by his Creator, and so eloquently stated in our Declaration of Independence. Which I hope, by the way, Your Grace, you have read.

Now, my friends of this convocation, there is another thing we can hope to learn from your being with us. I illustrate it by quoting the statement of a former college president, and I can understand the reason for his speaking as he did. I am sure President Miller can.

This President said, "I have two kinds of problems, the urgent and the important. The urgent are not important, and the important are never urgent."

Now this, I think, represents a dilemma of modern man. Your being here can help place the important before us, and perhaps even give the important the touch of urgency. And you can strengthen our faith that men of goodwill, working together, can solve the problems confronting them. Because these men, these people, these devoted people meeting here believe, first of all, always in faith.

Faith is the mightiest force that man has at his command. It impels human beings to greatness in thought and word and deed. I am going to call to your mind just two instances. First, the First Crusade—1096. Five columns of individuals starting in Europe, out of a great burst of faith

737

in their ability to rescue, as they thought, the Holy Land from the infidel. Five columns started out, without taking the slightest thought of military organization, of the terrors and troubles and tribulations on the way. They had no commissaries, lines of supply—they just started toward the Holy Land. Only two reached Constantinople, bedraggled, torn, suffering. But the point is, the other three, lost on the road, their numbers down, had not a thought of turning back. It was their faith! And they moved on into the Holy Land, to carry out the mission for which they started.

Faith unlocked the energies of that whole continent, and carried men forward through sufferings, and hardships that are almost inconceivable.

And then let us come down in years to something nearer our own shores, but of course, in size, much smaller. In 1620 a little group of pilgrims started out from the eastern seaboard of the Atlantic. And they landed at Plymouth Rock, after a passage across a stormy ocean in a ship that today no one in his senses would think of attempting to use. They came across without the slightest diminution in their faith that here in this untrammeled, unfettered land they could build for themselves a place in which they would prosper and they could stand upright before their God.

And they made this compact. It began: "In the name of God, Amen." I cite these two just to show what man can overcome. And I assure you, ladies, when I use the term "men" I mean humanity as a whole. What people can overcome when they believe enough. Those of us who have seen the incredible deeds of devoted and dedicated men on the battlefield, know that you don't have to go back even to the pilgrims to be certain of this same truth.

The achievements of believing men and women, then, in every generation remain a challenge to us, in ours. Faith has indeed moved mountains.

Now, ours is a time when great things must again be dared in faith. Around the world men and women anxiously search the future for the dawning of a just and lasting peace. Its winning cannot be left to the diplomat and the soldier. History is filled with the stories of their failures, no matter how skillful or devoted their efforts. Yet those failures have not destroyed hope. There is no other longing of men so universal and so indestructible as the yearning for a lasting, just, and global peace.

I believe that even if this goal seems for a moment far beyond our reach, there is, nevertheless, much that each of us—you and I—everybody in this audience—can do to help attain it.

Let me speak then, for a moment, not as this Nation's Chief Executive, whose days are largely devoted to the efforts of Government to secure peace, but as a private citizen, a single member of one of the constituent bodies of this Council of Churches.

But I must speak also inescapably as one who has seen at first-hand the almost miraculous battlefield achievements of men bound together by mighty devotion to a worthy cause. A thousand experiences have convinced me beyond room for doubt that common, fervent dedication to a noble purpose multiplies the strength of the individual and the body, and brings within the scope of his capabilities almost any conceivable objective.

Today—now—the campaign for a just and lasting peace desperately needs the lifting and transforming power that comes from men and women the world over, responding to their highest allegiance and to their best motives.

Now, how can we help strike this spark of dedication in receptive hearts around the earth? I believe that you, members of this convocation, spiritual leaders of a great world organization, together with your brethren of other faiths, can lead the way.

The goal should be nothing short of inviting every single person, in every single country in the world, who believes in the power of a Supreme Being, to join in a mighty, simultaneous, intense act of faith. That act of faith might take the form of a personal prayer, delivered simultaneously and fervently, by hundreds upon hundreds of millions who have the devotion, wisdom, and stamina to work unceasingly for a just and lasting peace. If this mass dedication launched an unending campaign for peace, supported constantly by prayer, I am certain wondrous results would ensue.

First, and at the very least, there would be a reminder to each of us that the cause of peace needs God. We would come to know also that responsibility for peace or conflict rests in some degree with each of us. Each would be heartened and strengthened by the certainty of close comradeships in faith and purpose. Thus there would be set in motion a great and growing force that could unify men in peace as a common peril unifies them in war. There would be initiated unceasing and universal study of the principal factors in the global problems that seem to impede progress toward peace.   There would be generated a support for honest and devoted world leaders that would inspire them to plumb new depths of knowledge and understanding, and seek new paths toward conciliation.   There would spring forth and be carried out new projects for defeating the despair and suffering and hopelessness in which millions now live.   And the destruction of the conditions that shrivel the soul and starve the body would add new millions to the soldiers of the faith, the faith that the children of God can live—if they so will—in the climate and the relationships that mean justice and decency and peace for all.

Now, my friends of this great convocation, I hope you do not deem me presumptuous in expressing to you my personal belief in your opportunities and capabilities as spiritual leaders of men.   But if I have, I plead in extenuation the universal realization that the time has come when for mankind there is no substitute for a just and lasting peace. We may have ignorance and selfishness and greed and atheism, and war and destruction.   Or we may have courage and stamina, and understanding, and faith and peace.

None of us is denied the high honor of working in this cause.

May each of us have the vision to recognize his own opportunity to contribute effectively.

May each of us in his own faith find the strength to do his full part.

Thank you, my friends.

NOTE: The President spoke on the campus of Northwestern University at 4:35 p.m. His opening words "Your Grace, the Archbishop" and "President Miller" referred to the Most Reverend Geoffrey Francis Fisher, Archbishop of Canterbury, and Dr. J. Roscoe Miller, President of the University. Following the address Dr. Miller conferred an honorary degree on the President.

205   ¶ Message to Madame de Gasperi on the Death of the Prime Minister of Italy.
August 19, 1954

I HAVE BEEN profoundly moved to learn of the death of your husband. From my long, close and friendly association with him, I know how much the world owes to him for his courageous contribution to the defense of civilization, his devotion to democracy and his dedication to the cause of European integration. He was one of the truly great men of his time and provided an inspiration not only for Italy but for the world that I hope will find reflection in future action. Mrs. Eisenhower and I wish to convey to you our heartfelt sympathy and that of the American people in your loss.

DWIGHT D. EISENHOWER

NOTE: This message was released at the Governor's Mansion, Springfield, Ill.

206 ¶ Veto of Bill Regulating the Election of Delegates From the District of Columbia to National Political Conventions. *August* 20, 1954

To the United States Senate:

I return herewith without my approval S. 1611, an enactment entitled "An Act to regulate the election of delegates representing the District of Columbia to national political conventions, and for other purposes."

This enactment regulates the election of national committeemen and committeewomen and delegates and alternates from the District of Columbia to all conventions of political parties nominating candidates for the Presidency and Vice Presidency of the United States.

The enactment further provides for a Board of Elections, composed of three members appointed by the Commissioners of the District of Columbia. The Board would maintain a permanent registry of electors, conduct the elections, certify nominees and the results of elections, and perform other functions incident to the conduct of such elections.

Section 9 of the enrolled bill exempts the qualified electors of the District of Columbia from the Hatch Act.

I cannot approve the provisions of the enrolled bill which would enable a very limited number of Federal employees to engage in partisan political activities, a privilege denied to all other Federal employees by the Hatch Act. The bill would amend this act by permitting Federal employees living in the District of Columbia to actively participate in the nomination and election of delegates and alternates representing the District at national political conventions and in the selection of members of the national committees of political parties. It is estimated that of the approximately 2,180,000 Federal employees in the United States, only 160,200 or 7 percent work in the District of Columbia. It is impossible to determine how many of the 160,200 live in the District of Columbia and would be privileged to actively participate in elections of party national committeemen, but the number would be extremely small compared to the total number of Federal employees. Thus a tiny percentage of Federal employees would be permitted to be candidates for, and to serve in, the political party offices of national committeemen. They also would be allowed to engage in such partisan political activities as serving on campaign committees, making public addresses in behalf of candidates, soliciting funds, and a variety of other duties incident to political campaigns. If additional political privileges are to be extended to Federal employees it should be on a nation-wide basis. No apparent reason exists for singling out a limited number of Federal employees living in the District of Columbia and permitting them to participate in partisan political activities while all other Federal employees throughout the country are denied this privilege under the Hatch Act.

I take this action with considerable regret. Were it not for this wholly unacceptable exemption from the Hatch Act, this legislation would represent a constructive step toward obtaining suffrage in the District of Columbia. Fortunately, the first election under procedures authorized by this bill would not take place until April 1956. Therefore, there is still ample time for the 84th Congress to consider this matter again. I recommend such action, and I shall be glad to approve a bill from which the defects of the present measure are removed.

DWIGHT D. EISENHOWER

207 ¶ Statement by the President Upon Signing Bill Governing the Keeping and Public Inspection of Arrest Books in the District of Columbia. *August* 20, 1954

I HAVE this day approved S. 3655, a bill which makes mandatory the present practice of the police department in the District of Columbia in maintaining arrest books for all persons taken into custody and keeping them open to public inspection.

The purpose of this bill, to establish by law an additional safeguard against secret arrests, is clearly a sound one.

In connection with the application of the bill to police records for children of juvenile court age—that is, children under 18—questions have been raised as to the consistency of the bill with special standards proposed by interested groups. For example, in its report to the Council on Law Enforcement of the District of Columbia, the Committee on Juvenile Crime recommended that identifying information received by the police department on persons of juvenile court age should be confined to the files of the juvenile squad and kept confidential. Similarly, the Senate Subcommittee to Investigate Juvenile Delinquency has suggested that such information be kept by the police separate and apart from that relating to older persons and be open to inspection only by persons having a legitimate interest in it. And the Standard Juvenile Court Act prepared by the National Probation and Parole Association provides that police records of children shall be kept separate from records of adults and shall not be open to public inspection. The reason for these recommendations is that publication of the identity of individual children who are in trouble is likely to defeat or make more difficult the rehabilitation of the child and tends to undermine the confidentiality of juvenile court records.

However, the press in the District of Columbia and the great body of the press in other places have shown real understanding of this problem and have voluntarily withheld from publication the names of children and other identifying information. I have, therefore, approved this bill in full confidence that the press and all interested members of the community, because of their interest in the protection of children, will continue to cooperate in this fashion.

I am asking the District of Columbia officials to explore the feasibility, from an administrative standpoint, of keeping separate arrest books for adults and children of juvenile court age. The bill, I understand, would not preclude this. In addition, I am asking them to study the actual experience which develops under this law and, if it should appear that the interests of the children of the District of Columbia are not adequately protected by it, to recommend the enactment of appropriate safeguards.

NOTE: As enacted, S. 3655 is Public Law 609, 83d Congress (68 Stat. 755).

208   ¶ Memorandum of Disapproval of Federal Employees' Pay Bill.   *August 23, 1954*

IN ORDER THAT federal workers may not have to undergo a period of uncertainty as to my action on H.R. 7774, "An Act to increase the rates of compensation of classified, postal and other employees of the Government, and for other purposes," I wish to announce that I shall withhold my approval from this bill.

The American people desire to reward properly, even generously, dedicated and faithful service on the part of their Government career employees.   In return for the taxes they pay, they expect to have a civil service system that is free of partisan politics, encourages efficient operation, rewards merit, and provides steady pay increases as the value of each employee increases with service and experience.   I am wholeheartedly in accord with those desires.

Since taking office, this Administration has developed a personnel program applying the best practices of progressive employers to the requirements of public service.   In furtherance of that program, recommendations were made by this Administration to the Congress for reasonable pay increases and adjustments in pay scales.   H.R. 7774 is inconsistent with these principles.   Unfortunately, the general pay increase proposed by this bill ignores and therefore tends to perpetuate the inequities we must correct.

On February 24, 1954 I approved and promptly submitted to the Congress the program to which I have just referred.   It is the broadest and most constructive of its kind ever placed before the Congress.   Most of its important provisions were passed at this session and these measures, in themselves, are so important as to constitute a milestone in the improvement of the Civil Service System.   These provisions include:

1. For the first time an inclusive system of Group Life Insurance and unemployment compensation benefits similar to those enjoyed by workers in private industry, have been provided for Federal employees.

2. Restrictions on permanent promotions and reinstatements of former career employees have been removed.

3. The statutory limit on the number of employees in the Executive Branch has been adjusted to meet present day needs.

4. The incentive awards programs have been liberalized and made applicable to all employees.

5. Arbitrary restrictions upon the accumulation of annual leave have been repealed.

6. Longevity pay increases have been authorized for all except the three highest classified service grades.

7. An equitable system for overtime pay has been established.

These measures not only will benefit our Federal career system and its employees, but also will improve the sound management of the Federal Government, to whose efficiency this Administration is resolutely dedicated. H.R. 7774 is not a part of a progressive and efficient program.

An important part of the Administration's program that was not enacted into law involves general pay increases based upon the purposes of correcting inequities, promoting efficiency and rewarding merit and experience.

In withholding my approval from this bill, I want to make it absolutely clear that the Administration is not departing from the principles and purposes which it has hitherto advocated. I shall continue to urge the enactment of the remaining parts of the personnel program which was submitted to this session of Congress so that obvious distortions in the pay scales of both the postal and classified services can be corrected; so that adjustments and more equitable relationships between grades and steps within those grades can be made, and so that a proper and effective relationship between pay and work performed will be established and maintained.

Legislation is obviously unwise that disregards these principles of sound personnel management and ignores the necessity of revenue to pay for salary increases.

This measure, because it ignores the Administration's recommendations for postal rate increases, would add $112 million to the cost of operating the Post Office Department which is operating at a deficit of $400 million this year. It is well to remember that since 1945 the accumulated postal deficit has reached the staggering total of $4 billion. Likewise, this measure would add more than $200 million to Civil Service pay without providing any revenue to meet it.

My remarks in Washington on June tenth are now particularly pertinent. I then said, "We hope to uproot the ingrained habit of operating the vast Post Office Department in an extravagantly wasteful and un-business-like manner. We cannot permit the deliberate operations of our Postal Department at a gigantic loss because a few are opposed to adequate postal rates. And we must have classification and promotional procedures for postal personnel that will serve the best interest of the Government, the public and the postal workers themselves."

Legislation for pay increases and classification adjustments related to work performed is still vital and urgently needed. The inequities presently existing in pay scales must still be corrected. I shall therefore resubmit to Congress when it convenes in January the recommendations previously made by the Administration, together with such additional recommendations as any change in conditions then existing may warrant.

While this bill is limited to civilian personnel, I must observe, parenthetically, that consideration of a complete Federal personnel program must eventually meet certain imperative needs of the members of the Armed Forces. These patriotic men and women, whose morale, skill and dedication to service are so important to us all, now lack adequate medical care for dependents and reasonable survivorship benefits for their families. It is most important that these needs of Armed Forces personnel, serving their country often in remote corners of the world, engage our serious consideration.

I am confident that the Congress will consider all of these recommendations promptly and that the American people will regard them as fair and just.

Dwight D. Eisenhower

NOTE: This memorandum was released at Lowry Air Force Base, Denver, Colo.

209 ¶ Radio and Television Address to the American People on the Achievements of the 83d Congress. *August 23, 1954*

Good evening, my friends:

Many months ago, I promised you one night that from time to time either I or some member of the administration would appear before you to give you a report on our stewardship of your Federal governmental affairs in Washington.

Now, something like 70 hours ago, the 83d Congress adjourned.   It will not again meet unless there should be some unexpected crisis at home or abroad that would demand it to re-assemble in Washington. In the absence of such a crisis, the 84th Congress will take over next January.

Now, this seems like a good time to report to you about the program that has engaged the attention of Congress, and about how successful we have been in carrying out the pledges we made to you more than 19 months ago.

I must say, in starting, that I salute the membership of that Congress for their hard work, for their effective accomplishments; and I am sure that after you take a quick look at this record, you will join in that salute.

It seems to me that the best way to start this little talk is to do it against the backdrop of 19 months ago.   Remember some of the crises that then existed in the world—crises, at least, as far as we were concerned.   There was in Iran a fanatic in charge, who was supported by the Communist party, and weekly we felt there was a great danger that that huge reserve of oil would fall into the hands of the Communists. Sixty percent of the world's known reserves of oil were at stake.   We had a beachhead of international communism starting in Guatemala.   We had a terrible war in Indochina.   We had a great argument going on in the Suez between two of our great international friends.   And of course, there was the war in Korea, a war around which there had grown up such a political situation that military victory, at least a decisive military victory, was no longer in the cards.   It was a war that brought home to us a daily casualty list, with resulting sorrow in thousands of homes.

At home, aside from those casualty lists, there was the threat of inflation.   It bothered us all.   We were worried about the cheapening dollar and about the mounting prices, in spite of the rigid controls that the Federal Government was attempting to enforce.

Along with this, there was a mounting deficit in the Federal budget. Each year we were falling further and further into debt.   We were spending more than we were collecting, and the situation was such as to cheapen our dollar, to make our debt and our interest payments greater and greater, and to give a resulting load to the taxpayer.

On top of this, for many months there had been an era of falling farm prices, and so the whole farm industry was suffering the effects of paying a lot of money for the things they had to buy, and getting little in return.

Now in this picture—in this situation—the administration took over a year ago last January, and determined on a very broad program for strengthening America, strengthening it at home spiritually, economically, and militarily, and making certain that it would be stronger internationally, insofar as its peace and security were concerned.

Now at home, to make it more secure, there were a number of things to do.   First, there were great and broad economic measures, the relieving of controls, and all that sort of thing.   There was the establishment of security measures, so as to make it difficult, if not impossible, for Communists to penetrate into the Government, or into any of the other great organisms of our country where they could weaken us, particularly in time of a crisis.

It was time for a new era of fair play, in which to treat everybody alike, to have no favored classes; and this administration was pledged to do everything it could for the benefit of 160 million American people, and not for any single group, any single area, or any single geographic section.

And then there was noticeable at that time, you will recall, a growing and continuing trend toward centralization in the Federal Government— centralization of power and authority in Washington—with our affairs more and more being dictated by a bureaucrat in that city.

This administration was committed to decentralization—decentralizing our own individual affairs to ourselves where that was possible, and in Government decentralizing as far as possible to the States.   You will recall that there was even an attempt at that time to take away from some of the States their own property, their own territory.   We passed the tidelands bill to restore to those States their title to their proper lands.

At the same time, we were in all sorts of businesses.   We were making synthetic rubber.   We were operating barge lines.   We were operating coffee roasting plants and clothing stores, and making rope.

Well, we have been getting out of them, so as to return to you, the American people, the maximum of initiative, the maximum responsibility and authority in your own affairs.

Now, in the international field, it was plain, with these mounting deficits, we had to provide for our own security, as economically and effectively, and as efficiently as possible.

That has been the program of the administration.

So defense authorities, instead of just saying, "Let's go out and buy a lot of security," determined priorities in which we should build our defense forces. We have tried to minimize the effort on those that seemed less essential in this day of the atomic bomb, to put our emphasis on those that seemed to offer us the greatest security. This of course applies to our air power, not only in the Air Force, but also in the Navy, which in itself deploys now a tremendous amount of air power and contributes markedly to our defense.

Along with all of this, we tried, through talks—full and frank talks with our allies—to establish better relationships, to get closer to them, to know exactly where we were going, in spirit, in the development of our economic measures, and in the building of our military measures. NATO, of course, existed before this administration came in; I was serving in NATO when I was in Europe during my last tour. It was at the great Caracas conference, where all American countries agreed that any penetration by international communism into this continent would be considered as a threat to all. And that conference had much to do with the final elimination of the threat in Guatemala.

Ever since we came in, we have been trying to establish a concert of nations in Southeast Asia. On April 16, 1953, I made a speech on peace in the world, in which I urged that the free nations undertake that project.

Now, in Indochina, war has ceased, under circumstances that are certainly not satisfactory to all of us. In some respects they are disappointing, but at least we have an opportunity again to tackle that problem of getting a concert of nations that will make the whole region safer and more secure for freedom.

Now this program at home can be defined best, I think, by saying this: that it has been a liberal program in all of those things that bring the Federal Government in contact with the individual, when it deals with the individual and his problems; in this field, the Government tries to be humane, considerate, and sympathetic—and that is true liberalism. But when it comes to the economy of this country, your pocketbook, and your taxes, it tries to be conservative.

So it is conservative in the economy, liberal in human affairs.

We have been developing a program that would bring about a national situation in which every citizen would have reason for bold hope, in which effort would be rewarded, in which prosperity would be shared, freedom would expand, and peace would be as secure as humans can make it.

It is a great program. It is a program to benefit all Americans.

Let's take a look at how it made out.

Now, in discussing what the Congress has done, my friends, I can't possibly take up even the major bills in detail. Literally, there were hundreds of bills passed by this Congress, but many of them are what are called routine or personal.

We calculate that of the bills to promote the program, of which I have been describing the purposes in general terms, there were about 64. Now these bills I couldn't possibly take up, but I will talk about three or four groups of them; and so I shall limit myself to that kind of process this evening.

Now, in the first place, the 83d Congress did two things that previous Congresses have tried time and time again to do and failed.

One, they passed the St. Lawrence Seaway project. Five of my predecessors in office recommended that, and they got nowhere.

The next thing they did was to pass an enormous tax revision bill. I don't mean a reduction of taxes just here and there, but a great tax reform so as to remove inequities and to make more reasonable the basis for your tax dealings with the Government.

Now, I am going to read, in terms that I think will be of interest to a great many of us, a few statistics as to what this tax bill has done, just in the way of looking after people that have had special problems.

First of all, in this matter of dependent children, you parents can now deduct $600 for each child regardless of how much he earns, if he is under 19, and you furnish more than half his support. Now, even if he is over 19, you can deduct the $600 just as before, if he is going to school or taking on-the-farm training. Now, such provisions save you taxpayers $85 million a year.

Take the matter of child care. If you are a single working parent, such as a widow, you can deduct up to $600 more for the expense of child care for each child up to 12 years of age. This will save you $130 million.

Medical expenses—and we know what this means to the ordinary family budget: you can deduct far more for medical expenses than you could under the old law. This will save taxpayers $80 million.

Then, for retired people, all of you who are 65 and older who are retired, including schoolteachers, firemen, policemen, civil servants, and so on, will be exempt, on retirement, up to $1,200 of your income. This will give you a tax cut up to $240 a year. In its total, it will save taxpayers $141 million.

Help for farmers: farmers can now have deductions up to 25 percent of the total farm income for soil and water conservation. They get a faster write-off of the expenses of farm machinery and equipment. Now, these provisions will save farmers $10 million.

Depreciation. All of you will get a more liberal write-off of the cost of new equipment, twice the amount now allowed in the first year. This will save $375 million.

And then, this business of filing your final income tax return. You have an additional month. It is April 15 now, instead of March 15, and you have that much additional time to make your final payment.

Now, here is the significance of all these tax reforms and deductions during the last 19 months. First, they have saved you $7,400,000,000. This is money you spend for yourselves—now—instead of the Government's spending it for you. Moreover, it is money that you are using for all of the things that you need to do—you are following your own decisions, instead of following a bureaucrat's decision.

Now let me ask you this question: How many of you have any faint idea of what $7 billion is?

I had these statistics looked up for me. All the money that the American farmers got last year for all the corn and all the wheat grown in the entire United States—that was $7 billion.

All of the money paid in all of last year for household utilities, and for fuel, amounted to $7 billion.

All the money Americans pay each year for doctor, dentist, medical and hospital bills, is $7 billion.

That gives you some idea of how money has been returned to you, and how much of it has been returned.

Now, along with these two items—the Seaway and the tax reform, which in themselves, with the long study and analysis and work involved, would have made an honorable record—and in addition to the routine bills, there have been many projects undertaken and successfully accomplished that will redound to your great benefit.

You remember I referred to the appalling Federal deficits. We have reduced them two-thirds. And we are well on the way toward a goal, finally, of achieving a balanced budget.

Now, we haven't used any meat-axe in reducing expenditures. It has been a selective type of reduction, and it has taken a very great amount of work, but it is being done under the supervision of Cabinet officials and department heads, and in cooperation with the Congress, so as to bring you one hundred cents for every dollar you spend.

This tax program which I mentioned, incidentally, gives on the average, to each of you, an 11 percent cut in your income taxes.

Now, along with this, the administration has removed 200,000 people from the padded payrolls of the Federal Government; and that in itself is something on the order of a billion-dollar saving.

We are, as I said, on the way to a balanced budget, but in going in that direction we haven't placed the pocketbook above the heart. This is a human administration.

Take housing. The housing measure enacted by Congress, and the programs of this administration that will be fought through to the finish, will make certain that every American family has an opportunity for a decent home, a home in a good neighborhood, among good citizens. In fact, one of the great purposes of this housing program is to produce good citizens, to remove and eliminate those conditions that make crime and disorder rampant in certain sections.

Now, in addition, there are all sorts of social security programs which have gone into effect on a widened basis, reaching more people—with more liberal payments. This brings to the average American home peace of mind, domestic security. That is the kind of thing that is sought in all of these social security programs.

Health—which means so much to all of us. We have gone into a program of hospital construction and the rehabilitation of the permanently disabled, on a very broad basis.

Now we reject socialization of medicine. We don't believe in it. But we know, and everybody must know, that the United States—the people of the United States—are going to have to have access to good medical facilities. And we are attempting to bring about a program, and we will bring about a program, that will make this possible. Scientific research will go on.

Now—the farm problem. When we took over, you will recall, farm income was toppling. And we had unmanageable surpluses which continued to grow at such an alarming rate that they were depressing the market. There was literally nothing you could do, so long as the growth of these surpluses was not checked, to bring prosperity and the promise of real stability to the farmer.

So we started out with the knowledge that every hour we were paying $30,000 of your money—every day $700,000 of your money—just for storage of these crops, which we couldn't dispose of, and which were depressing the market and further cutting our prices.

Now, we have got a program that will encourage efficient production, stimulate consumption, and stabilize farm income. It has been fought through to almost exactly the terms on which it was presented to the Congress.

We went into office last January a year ago, you will remember, in a period of extreme international tension. Now every single part of that problem was patiently studied, often on a bipartisan basis, always with the cooperation of the Legislative leaders, who dealt with the Secretary of State, with me and with others in the executive departments engaged in this problem.

The legislation proposed, and the legislation that has been passed, is concerned with security and peace, and with the building of a strong concert of free nations, because that is the only way in which we can make certain that the Communist menace will be stalled—stopped—in this world, and finally driven back to where it belongs, to its own country.

The foreign aid law is not one merely to help other people for humanitarian purposes; it is serving our own enlightened self-interest, giving us greater security in this country, a feeling of peace and confidence in the world.

Reciprocal trade is another problem that is now under earnest study, and that will be taken up by the next Congress. We have got another year, as a result of the Randall Report, in which to study certain features of this whole business so that our friends could, with us, make a living through profitable trade, which would eliminate the need for these great grants in the future.

Now, at home, we have had to evolve new weapons in order to help defeat internal communism. The great thing we wanted to do was to find effective means of eliminating the Communist or the subversive from any point where he could possibly damage us, but to do it by constitutional process, to make certain that if you or I, or anybody else, were called up to answer questions about communism, he would be protected by the Government.

Now, the Attorney General made up a package program. I think it was a total of 15 bills that he recommended to Congress on this matter, and 13 have been enacted by the Congress. That whole program was made up as a result of the study by the FBI, the Attorney General and all others who have been so experienced in this great matter. It is a record involving not only operation, as we went along getting rid of people, and deporting many people that shouldn't be here, but formulation of the plan that will make us even better and stronger in the future.

Now, how was all this record achieved? One man can't do it. The Congress can't do it alone.

Well, first of all, it was achieved by almost unprecedented coordination—smooth coordination—between House and Senate. Then there was a new era of coordination and cooperation between the legislative branches and the Executive. My Cabinet and I meet frequently with the legislative leaders, and through this process we make certain that we are all going in the same direction.

In addition, in the House and in the Senate there have been energetic legislative captains, the men in responsible positions of leadership in both Houses who carry the responsibility and exercise the authority of committee chairmen.

Of course, in all foreign affairs, there are bipartisan consultations. These take place at frequent intervals, in order that we do not allow this great subject which affects the safety and security of all America, to become a subject of party politics.

That must never happen. And certainly we are doing our very best—and I have always pledged my best efforts—to see that this cannot occur. But all in all, there were 64, as I say, of these legislative projects submitted to the Congress. Now, 54 of them were enacted into law. We did not always make home runs. But we did have 54 hits. Some of them aren't quite what we wanted. But that, after all, is a batting average of .830, and any baseball fan will tell you that is pretty good going in any league.

And the next question is: is the job done?

And the obvious and emphatic answer is no, of course not.

We are at the mid-mark. We will go ahead with this program. We are going to get lots of things done that have not yet been done. We are going to have to re-study this question of making a reasonable reduction in the minimum voting age. Health reinsurance we are going to put before the Congress again, because we must have means in every American family so that it can insure itself cheaply against the possibility of catastrophe in the medical line. The Taft-Hartley Act needs some revisions and, again, they will be proposed to the Congress. I already mentioned the subject of foreign trade. It will be one of our big jobs of the coming year.

Now, I said that I have been disappointed. I don't mean individually, or personally. I am disappointed because this program has been designed, through study and work and cooperation with hundreds and literally thousands of people, for your benefit, for your greater prosperity at home, and your greater security abroad. So, when I am disappointed, I mean I am disappointed for all of us—160 million people. Nevertheless, every American can be proud of this 83d Congress, and can join in my salute to it.

Every fact that we have gives the lie to those prophets of gloom and doom that said that we were going to be in an economic depression, and forming breadlines in this time of our history. Of course, we are going ahead, with bold courage—all of us.

Now—what about the future?

Our domestic house is partially in order. I mentioned a few items we must still get into the hopper and get accomplished, but we are going ahead, and the whole planning and program is founded on respect for human freedom, dignity, rights, and our effort to obtain peace. So our relations with the external world will be the thing which we will have to emphasize during the coming months. We will make certain that our friends understand us better.

I have already mentioned such places as Korea, Iran, Suez, and Guatemala, where great threats to our peace and security have already been removed. I want to say this: the papers right now are filled with gloomy predictions about Europe. Don't be too discouraged. On that continent are great friends of mine. They are great statesmen. They are laboring for peace. They want peace as much as you and I do. And they are not licked yet, and we are certainly not licked. Let us not lose faith in them. There is still something to be done in that region, and we are going to do it. We are going to develop better partners in all parts of the world, between us and our cooperating friends.

And now, my friends, here we are. If we are going ahead with this program, if you want it to go ahead, the decisions are largely up to you. Because it is the character of the 84th Congress that will determine: can we go ahead and push through in all these programs for the benefit of America? Or will we be stopped by some kind of political arguments?

We want to go ahead. We are sure that you want us to go ahead. All my mail shows exactly that: that you, with us, are looking forward to peace abroad, greater security, and greater and greater prosperity at home.

And now, my friends, thank you very much and good night.

NOTE: The broadcast originated in Denver through the facilities of radio and television station KLZ.

210 ¶ Statement by the President Upon Signing the Communist Control Act of 1954.
August 24, 1954

I HAVE TODAY signed S. 3706, An Act to make illegal the Communist Party and to prohibit members of Communist organizations from serving in certain representative capacities.

The American people are determined to protect themselves and their institutions against any organization in their midst which, purporting to be a political party within the normally accepted meaning, is actually a conspiracy dedicated to the violent overthrow of our entire form of government. The American people, likewise, are determined to accomplish this in strict conformity with the requirements of justice, fair play and the Constitution of the United States. They realize that employment of any other means would react unfavorably against the innocent as well as the guilty, and, in the long run, would distort and damage the judicial procedures of our country. The whole series of bills that the Administration has sponsored in this field have been designed in just this spirit and with just these purposes.

The new law which I am signing today includes one of the many recommendations made by this Administration to support existing statutes in defeating the Communist conspiracy in this country. Administratively, we have in the past 19 months stepped up enforcement of laws against subversives. As a result, 41 top Communist leaders have been convicted, 35 more are indicted and scheduled for trial, and 105 subversive aliens have been deported.

The new laws enacted in this session of the Congress provide to the FBI and the Department of Justice much more effective weapons to help destroy the Communist menace. They include the following:

1. Last week I signed a bill granting immunity from prosecution to certain suspected persons in order to aid in obtaining the conviction of subversives. Investigation and prosecution of crimes involving national security have been seriously hampered by witnesses who have invoked the Constitutional privilege against self-incrimination embodied in the Fifth Amendment. This Act provides a new means of breaking through the secrecy which is characteristic of traitors, spies and saboteurs.

2. The Congress has passed a bill providing for the loss of citizenship by those advocating the overthrow of our government by force and violence. In carrying out the Administration's recommendation that any citizen who knowingly and actively participates in the Communist conspiracy to overthrow the government by force and violence should be regarded as renouncing his allegiance to the United States and forfeiting his right to citizenship, the Congress has reinforced our historic concept that citizenship is a right only of those who bear true faith and allegiance to the United States and its free institutions. This bill to which I shall presently give my approval adheres closely to our standards of due process of law and provides that the loss of citizenship shall become effective only upon conviction by a court of competent jurisdiction.

3. My approval has already been given to the bill which carries out the recommendation by this Administration increasing the penalty for harboring or concealing any person who is a fugitive from justice. There are at the present time five Communist leaders who have been indicted or convicted under the Smith Act who are fugitives from justice. This

bill serves notice that any person who assists such fugitives in any way to conceal their whereabouts will be subject to severe penalty.

4. My approval has already been given to a bill designed to serve as an effective additional deterrent to wilful bail jumping by making such act a crime subject to severe penalty.

5. The Congress has passed, and I shall approve, a bill to include within the definition of sabotage, acts involving the use of radioactive, biological and chemical agents not presently covered by the law.

6. The foregoing bill also includes a provision for the death penalty for persons found guilty of peacetime espionage.

7. I have already approved a bill requiring "Communist-Action" or "Communist-Front" organizations, which must register under the Internal Security Act, to submit full information regarding printing equipment in their custody or control.

8. I shall shortly sign a bill preventing the payment of annuities by the United States to former officers and employees who have been convicted of certain criminal offenses. This Act includes those who have made false statements regarding past or present membership in the Communist Party.

In addition to the foregoing measures enacted by the 83rd Congress, the bill which I have signed today further carries out an important part of the recommendations made by this Administration. It creates within the framework of the Internal Security Act of 1950 a new category entitled, "Communist-Infiltrated Organizations." This provision will enable the Administration to assist members of those few labor organizations which are dominated by Communists, to rid themselves of the Communist control under which they have been forced to operate.

In the final days of the session, the Congress added to this measure certain clauses denying to Communists all rights, privileges and immunities which they have under the Federal Government. These provisions also subject members of the Communist Party or its front organizations, having knowledge of their revolutionary aims and objectives, to the provisions and penalties of the Internal Security Act. The full impact of these clauses upon the enforcement of the laws by which we are now fighting the Communist conspiracy in this country will require further careful study. I am satisfied, however, that they were not intended to impair or abrogate any portion of the Internal Security Act or the criminal statutes under which the leaders of the Communist Party are now being prosecuted and that they may prove helpful in several respects.

The Congress has thus enacted a substantial portion of the Administration's recommendations to strengthen our internal security laws.

In order to provide aggressive administration and enforcement of the foregoing measures, I have already strengthened the mechanism for carrying out more effectively our entire anti-Communist program by the creation of the Division of Internal Security in the Department of Justice.

We have made great progress in the past year and a half in prosecuting the leadership of the Communist conspiracy. I am proud that in this battle against the subversive elements in this country we have been able to preserve the rights of the accused in accordance with our traditions and the Bill of Rights. The 83d Congress has added effective new legal weapons to assist us in our fight to destroy communism in this country.

NOTE: As enacted, S. 3706 is Public Law   The statement was released at Lowry
637, 83d Congress (68 Stat. 775).   Air Force Base, Denver, Colo.

2 1 1   ¶ Remarks on the Communist Control Act of 1954. *August 24, 1954*

[Recorded on film]

I HAVE just signed a bill which is designed to place into the hands of our law enforcement agencies, particularly the Attorney General and the FBI, better weapons for combatting the Communist menace in this country. This is one of a series of bills that are designed in this general purpose.

The American people are determined to eliminate from their midst organizations which, purporting to be political parties in the accepted sense of that term, are actually conspirators dedicated to the destruction of our form of government by violence and force.

Now they also are determined to do this by means that are fair, just and in accordance with our Constitution. They well realize that to do it in any other way could affect the innocent adversely as well as the guilty, and could in the long run distort and damage our entire judicial procedures. All of these bills are designed in that spirit and with those purposes.

NOTE: This statement was released at Lowry Air Force Base, Denver, Colo.

212 ¶ Memorandum of Disapproval of a Bill for the Relief of Nina Makeef, Also Known as Nina Berberova. *August 24*, 1954

I AM WITHHOLDING my approval of H.R. 692, "For the relief of Nina Makeef, also known as Nina Berberova."

This alien entered the United States as a visitor and has not departed within the time permitted. She is now unlawfully in the United States. The bill would grant her the status of a lawful permanent resident upon payment of the required visa fee. The alien is a native of Russia, 53 years of age, who apparently is stateless. She entered the United States in November 1950. Prior to that entry she had been a long time resident of France. It appears that she can return to France.

Upon the alien's failure to depart when her period of lawful stay expired deportation proceedings were instituted. She was accorded a hearing and ordered deported. However, the Board of Immigration Appeals granted the alien the privilege of deporting voluntarily from the United States, and alternatively ordered that in the event she failed to depart the order of deportation should be reinstated. She has failed to depart.

This alien has been permitted to remain in the United States beyond the period of time authorized by law and she should be required to depart in accordance with the terms under which she was granted admission to this country. There are many other aliens in foreign countries who are awaiting an opportunity to come to the United States for permanent residence but who are required to follow the regular means of obtaining permanent resident status. There are no facts present in this case justifying the enactment of special legislation granting this alien preferential treatment over others seeking to enter the United States.

The enactment of this bill undoubtedly would encourage other aliens to attempt to enter the United States as visitors for a temporary period and thereafter seek exemption from requirements of the immigration laws through special legislation.

Accordingly, I am constrained to withhold my approval from the bill.

DWIGHT D. EISENHOWER

NOTE: This memorandum was released at Lowry Air Force Base, Denver, Colo.

213 ¶ Statement by the President Upon Signing Bill Amending the Merchant Marine Act of 1936. *August 26, 1954*

I HAVE approved S. 3233, an act "To amend the Merchant Marine Act, 1936, to provide permanent legislation for the transportation of a substantial portion of waterborne cargoes in the United States-flag vessels."

The United States requires a merchant marine which, as I have said before, constitutes our fourth arm of defense. However, I have been concerned over the manner in which this merchant marine is to be maintained.

In transmitting my message on Foreign Economic Policy, to the Congress on March 30, 1954, I stated that we must have a merchant marine adequate to our defense requirements. I also stated that such support of our merchant fleet as is required for that purpose should be provided by direct means to the greatest possible extent. In keeping with this approach, I asked the Department of Commerce to study the extent to which direct means can be utilized in maintaining an adequate merchant marine.

It appears that the major purpose of S. 3233 is to confirm on a permanent basis policies we have been following for a number of years. United States vessels are already carrying better than 50 percent of aid cargoes and cargoes resulting from the Government's stockpiling program. However, certain provisions of this legislation cause me concern and I hope the next Congress will reconsider them. I refer particularly to the provision with regard to currency convertibility which, if it applies to Title I of Public Law 480, 83d Congress, would handicap the disposal of United States agricultural products abroad, and to the provision with regard to offshore procurement which, by forcing United States vessels into trades in which they normally do not operate, could increase the cost of the aid program. I am asking the Attorney General for an opinion on the applicability of the currency convertibility provision.

I am hopeful that the Department of Commerce study will result in some sound suggestions for the maintenance by direct means of a merchant marine adequate to the requirements of the United States. When this study is completed, I may wish to recommend additional changes in this legislation.

NOTE: As enacted, S. 3233 is Public Law   The statement was released at Lowry
664, 83d Congress (68 Stat. 832).   Air Force Base, Denver, Colo.

214 ¶ Letter to Secretary Mitchell Establishing an Interdepartmental Committee on Migratory Labor. *August 26, 1954*

Dear Mr. Secretary:

It is very reassuring that Congressional approval of the Administration's recommendation for new funds for the Department of Labor will enable you to assume leadership in improving the social and economic welfare of our domestic migratory farm workers. A coordinated Federal approach and a full utilization of existing resources will make possible more effective action in the solution of migratory labor problems.

As you have suggested, I am establishing an Interdepartmental Committee on Migratory Labor made up of the Secretaries of the Interior, Agriculture, Labor, and Health, Education, and Welfare and the Administrator of the Housing and Home Finance Agency. I am designating you as Chairman. In addition, there are other departments and agencies which have major interests in specific areas, and I shall expect you, as Chairman, to keep them informed and to invite their participation as needed.

It is my hope that this Committee will aid the various Federal agencies in mobilizing and stimulating more effective programs and services for migrants and in providing service to State and local areas through their constituent members. I believe this Committee can be of great help in developing cooperative relationships between the Federal agencies and the State agencies concerned with these problems.

I shall look forward to having periodic reports from you concerning the progress and recommendations of the Committee.

Sincerely,

DWIGHT D. EISENHOWER

NOTE: This letter to the Secretary of Labor was released at Lowry Air Force Base, Denver, Colo.

215 ¶ Memorandum of Disapproval of Bill for the Relief of George Pantelas. *August* 26, 1954

I AM WITHHOLDING my approval of S. 154, "For the relief of George Pantelas."

The beneficiary of the bill is an alien who is deportable on the ground that at the time of his last entry he was not in possession of a valid immigration visa and because of his record of crimes involving moral turpitude.

The bill would authorize and direct the Attorney General to discontinue the pending deportation proceedings, cancel any outstanding order of deportation, warrant of arrest and bond which may have been issued and would exempt the alien from deportation in the future by reason of the same facts upon which the current proceedings are based.

The alien was born in Greece on February 12, 1903. He originally entered the United States in 1921. On May 3, 1929, he was convicted in California of issuing checks without sufficient funds and sentenced to an indeterminate term of imprisonment for not more than fourteen years. He was subsequently deported from the United States on June 18, 1931, because of his criminal record. Thereafter, the alien re-entered the United States as a temporary visitor on May 28, 1940, under an assumed name. In proceedings before the Immigration and Naturalization Service he testified that in order to obtain a Greek passport in another individual's name he paid $100 for a birth certificate and thereafter committed perjury and forgery in securing the necessary passport visa for his re-entry.

While I am in sympathy with the evident purpose of this legislation to provide support for the family of the alien, the record of bad conduct presented in this case convinces me that the granting of the relief proposed would not be in the best interests of the United States.

Accordingly, I am withholding my approval from this bill.

DWIGHT D. EISENHOWER

NOTE: This memorandum was released at Lowry Air Force Base, Denver, Colo.

216 ¶ Memorandum of Disapproval of Bill for the Relief of the Estate of Mary Beaton Denninger. *August 26, 1954*

I HAVE WITHHELD my approval from S. 3064, 83d Congress, "An Act for the relief of the estate of Mary Beaton Denninger, deceased."

The bill would authorize and direct the Secretary of the Treasury to pay to the estate of Mrs. Denninger the sum of $780.36 in full settlement of all claims of the estate against the United States for payment of certain installments of an indemnity under the Servicemen's Indemnity Act of 1951.

Robert William Denninger died in service on November 20, 1952. The proceeds of a policy of United States Government life insurance, $2,443.27, were paid on behalf of Mary Beaton Denninger, the designated beneficiary. However, in order to determine whether she was also entitled as a widow to an indemnity of $7,000 under the Servicemen's Indemnity Act of 1951, for which no beneficiary had been designated, it was necessary to obtain evidence of the interlocutory judgment of divorce which the serviceman had obtained from her effective March 12, 1952, as well as evidence pertaining to the dissolution of one of her prior marriages. Upon receipt of evidence establishing her eligibility, settlement was authorized on her behalf and, without knowledge that she had died two days previously, a check for $780.36 representing 12 accrued installments of indemnity was mailed to a Veterans' Administration agency on October 27, 1953, for delivery to the payee. Because of the death the check was returned and canceled.

The law prohibited payment to Mrs. Denninger's estate, and thereafter the Veterans' Administration made settlement of the indemnity in favor of the serviceman's parents, the next entitled beneficiaries. This settlement included the installments totaling $780.36 which had accrued during the lifetime of Mrs. Denninger. The bill proposes that, in addition, the Government pay $780.36 to Mrs. Denninger's estate.

Favorable action by the Committees which considered the bill appears to have been based upon the view that the installments which accrued prior to Mrs. Denninger's death became her property and, accordingly, should be paid to her estate. The specific language of the law clearly expresses a contrary intention on the part of the Congress. I cannot agree either that the mandatory provision of the law should be abrogated in this case to the exclusion of other similar cases, or that the Government should be subjected to double payment of those installments of indemnity which accrued during Mrs. Denninger's lifetime. To do so would obviously be discriminatory and precedential.

As I have previously stated, if the law is to be changed it should be changed for all. Uniformity and equality of treatment under general law applicable equally to all must be the steadfast rule if the Federal programs for veterans and their dependents are to be operated successfully. Heeding the special plea of individual cases would obviously destroy the effectiveness of these programs.

For the foregoing reasons, I am unable to justify approval of S. 3064.

DWIGHT D. EISENHOWER

NOTE: This memorandum was released at Lowry Air Force Base, Denver, Colo.

217 ¶ Letter to Harry A. Bullis of Minneapolis on Foreign Economic Policy.   *August* 26, 1954

Dear Harry:

Many thanks for your good letter expressing as it does your sincere interest in a most vital problem confronting our country.

As you know, I fully share your view as to the splendid accomplishments of the Congress in translating so much of my legislative program into reality during the session recently concluded. Several of these enactments required of the Congress the setting of new directions and a fresh pace. That is always a time-consuming and often exacting process.

With respect to the foreign economic policy aspects of the program, it was unavoidable that they reached the Congress well along in the session. Time was not available to consider them adequately. I want to emphasize, however, that my Message of March 30, 1954 to the Congress on this subject remains firmly the Administration position. It is my present intention to give high priority to progress in this whole field in planning for next year's legislative program.

The events of every day bear in heavily upon us the imperative necessity of building stronger economic relations between ourselves and the free world. This is true, first because the growth of our own economy and the attainment of rising standards of living for our people can materialize only in step with economic growth and improvement in the economies of the free world linked to ours. It is more emphatically true because it is in our enlightened self-interest to have economically strong friends throughout the world. The prudent widening and deepening of the channels of trade and investment by us will not only produce good results in themselves but will encourage similar action by our friends abroad. That is the route to better markets and better feeling.

I note what you say on the watch tariff decision. That case, as with the more recent one on lead and zinc, was decided solely on its merits under the law in the light of the United States Tariff Commission's report and with the advice of interested Departments and Agencies of the Executive Branch.

I welcome your support and the support of the many who like you believe that the proposals of my Message of last March are still in the best interest of our people.

Sincerely,

DWIGHT D. EISENHOWER

NOTE: Mr. Bullis' letter and the President's reply were released at Lowry Air Force Base, Denver, Colo. With respect to the watch tariff decision Mr. Bullis wrote that some of the President's friends were fearful of its consequences, and were anxious to be reassured that the Message of March 30 still constituted the administration's foreign economic policy.

218　❡ Memorandum of Disapproval of Bill
Concerning Compensation of Quarantine
Inspection Personnel.　*August 27, 1954*

I AM WITHHOLDING my approval of H.R. 6253, a bill "To amend
Public Law 410, 78th Congress, with regard to compensation for over-
time, Sunday, and holiday work of employees of the United States Public
Health Service, Foreign Quarantine Division."

This bill would amend the Public Health Service Act in two major
respects. First, it would establish special rates of overtime, Sunday,
and holiday pay for certain quarantine inspection personnel of the Public
Health Service comparable to those received by customs inspectors of
the Treasury Department and immigrant inspectors of the Department
of Justice under special premium pay statutes enacted many years ago.
Second, with certain important exceptions, it would require that when
night-overtime, Sunday, or holiday inspections are performed at the
request of the owner, agent, master, or other shipping company representatives, the requesting party shall reimburse the United States for the
extra cost represented by overtime compensation.

It is important to note that no charges would be payable by the carrier
for services performed in connection with the inspection of persons
arriving by (1) international highways, ferries, bridges, or tunnels, (2)
regularly scheduled aircraft or trains, or (3) regularly scheduled Great
Lakes vessels or vessels operated between Canadian ports and Puget
Sound, or for services in connection with the inspection of the conveyances
or vessels in which such persons arrive.

Under existing law, the inspection services are rendered without
charge, regardless of the hour at which they are rendered. However,
the Surgeon General, under his statutory authority to fix the hours during
which quarantine service shall be performed at each quarantine station,
has—at most places other than airports—fixed the regular hours of quarantine service from 6 a.m. to 6 p.m., 7 days a week (Sundays and holidays included). When a vessel arrives within that time, quarantine
service is rendered, and rendered free, even if it extends beyond that
time. If the vessel arrives after 6 p.m., service will be rendered only if
the vessel is in distress, or there is illness aboard, or there are other

emergency conditions; otherwise the vessel is required to anchor at quarantine until the following morning and must await its turn for inspection. The delay incident to this waiting period is expensive to the owner of the vessel—it may run as much as $5,000 per day—and thus the owners are willing, indeed anxious, to pay whatever premium rates for out-of-hours inspection are authorized by law.

Although the bill would require certain reimbursements as indicated above, it would also require all employees performing these inspectional or quarantine services to be paid at the rate of one-half a day's pay for each 2 hours of overtime (or fraction thereof of at least one hour) between 5 p.m. and 8 a.m., with a limit of two-and-one-half days' pay for the full period from 5 p.m. to 8 a.m. For any Sunday or holiday duty, however brief or fleeting, the employee would be entitled to two "additional" days' pay. If the day falls within the employee's regular tour of duty, this would, apparently, entitle him to 3 days' pay. This means that the Government must pay the premium rates in all cases regardless of whether reimbursement is later made. The Federal Employees' Pay Act of 1945, as amended, under which these employees are now paid, provides for twice the regular rate of pay only for holiday work (and correspondingly less for less than a day's work), no extra pay for Sunday work (unless performed in excess of 40 hours a week), and overtime pay at the rate of time and one-half for employees whose annual salaries are less than $2,980. Employees at higher salaries are entitled to overtime pay on the basis of a rate schedule which decreases as the basic salary increases until their overtime rates of pay are less than the rates payable for straight time.

The special rates of pay proposed for these employees have been justified on the ground that these rates, and to a large extent the other provisions of the bill, are patterned after similar legislation which has long been in effect for customs and immigration inspectors, (19 USC 267, 1451; 5 USC 342c) and that, like such inspectors, the irregular, sporadic, and unpredictable nature of their overtime, Sunday, and holiday services is different in character from that to which most other Federal employees are subject and is more burdensome.

These contentions require close examination. The claims of the shipowners for out-of-hours service have merit. The claims of the inspectional employees for equal treatment with other inspectional groups have much merit, but equality of treatment for all inspectional employees is not brought about by this bill. Furthermore, the special pay features of the bill depart from principles of overtime and premium pay set forth in the so-called fringe benefits bill recently enacted by the Congress. This factor and the reimbursement requirement combine to make it impossible for me to give my approval to this bill.

I recognize that the existence of the highly preferential rates of customs and immigration premium pay statutes creates severe administrative problems for the Public Health Service, since quarantine inspectors work in close proximity with these other inspectional services. However, the premium rates for the customs and immigrant inspectors are so far out of line with prevailing industrial and governmental practice that I do not believe extending their use to other groups of Federal employees would be good management. Legislation relating to groups of inspectional employees should seek to improve the overall pattern of premium compensation rather than to attempt to patch the existing uncoordinated pay structure.

In the recently enacted liberalizations of existing law governing overtime and holiday pay there are several special features, for example, provisions for call-back time, standby pay in lieu of overtime, and the like, which will make considerably more equitable the premium pay available to these inspectional employees. Overtime compensation at the full rate of time and one-half will be based on regular pay up to an amount equal to the entrance salary of Grade GS–9 instead of the present $2,980 limit of the Federal Employees' Pay Act. The large majority of these employees are classified in that grade.

In circumstances such as these, I cannot give my approval to H.R. 6253 even though the problems which the bill seeks to solve are real and pressing. I intend to have these problems further explored as they relate to both domestic and international carriers. I shall also direct further study of effective means to rationalize and coordinate overtime and premium pay for all inspectional service in relation to that for other Federal employees. Upon completion of these studies, I hope to be able to make recommendations to the Congress for necessary legislation.

DWIGHT D. EISENHOWER

NOTE: This memorandum was released at Lowry Air Force Base, Denver, Colo.

219 ¶ Statement by the President Upon Signing Bill Establishing a New Limit on the Federal Debt. *August 28, 1954*

I HAVE TODAY signed into law the bill establishing a new limit on the Federal debt.

The record of this Administration fully demonstrates its dedication to thoroughgoing economy and efficiency. Despite the great momentum toward increased government spending which has built up in the past, much progress has already been made in bringing the Federal budget into balance. It is our basic policy to continue this progress.

But in the present state of the world it is equally important to emphasize once again that the Federal Government must always be ready to assure our national security, to carry out its responsibilities under the Employment Act, and to fulfill its other obligations. An essential part of this preparedness is a debt limit high enough to permit the Treasury, if necessary, to borrow the funds required to carry out the Government's obligations under the Constitution and under the laws of the Congress.

The present bill permits a temporary increase of up to $6 billion in the Federal debt outstanding before the close of the current fiscal year. Although this provision may prove inadequate, it does allow some indispensable latitude in conducting the operations of the Federal Government during the current year and is an improvement over the existing situation. The Administration will make every possible effort to carry on the activities of the Government in accordance with this limit.

NOTE: As enacted the bill is Public Law 686, 83d Congress (68 Stat. 895). The statement was released at Lowry Air Force Base, Denver, Colo.

220 ¶ Statement by the President Upon Signing Bills Increasing Payments to Veterans or Their Dependents. *August 28, 1954*

I HAVE TODAY approved H.R. 9020 and H.R. 9962. Both of these Acts provide for an increase in payments to veterans or their dependents—in the one case, for service-connected disability or death compensation, and in the other for nonservice-connected disability pensions.

H.R. 9020 relates to the rate of payments made to veterans or their dependents as a result of wounds, injuries, disabilities, or death incurred as the result of military service. It represents an attempt to compensate them for earning power whose loss is attributable to service in our armed forces. H.R. 9962, on the other hand, relates to the rate of pensions payable to veterans and to the dependents of veterans whose earning power was or is limited by reason of nonservice-connected disabilities; it is designed only to meet minimum economic need.

Since the time of the Revolutionary War, the American people have been determined to demonstrate their recognition of the sacrifices made by those who have served in our armed forces. I share this determination. I deeply believe in the principle of our disability compensation and pension laws. We must remember, too, the difference in the principles upon which these two systems are based. We must also remember their difference in purpose.

I have approved H.R. 9962 solely for humanitarian reasons, for I recognize that many of the individuals who will benefit from this increase are now living under circumstances of extreme hardship. Statistics also show, however, that many will receive this increase who need no additional assistance. In this respect H.R. 9962 is inconsistent with the principles of our pension system and tends to perpetuate inequities and anomalies which have arisen not only within the pension system itself but also in its relation to closely related government programs.

Although additional benefits have been granted from time to time, our basic veteran laws have not changed materially in the last thirty years. We must also recognize the fact that, because of the inauguration and growth of closely related—and uncorrelated—Federal programs designed to provide assurances against want to all of our citizens, there are today many instances of uneven and inequitable benefits. Under the present system, for example, there are no means of taking into account the degree of a veteran's need—no relation between payments received under the veteran pension laws and payments received, for example, under our Old Age and Survivors Insurance system.

It is essential, therefore, that steps be taken to examine the entire structure, scope and philosophy of our veterans benefit laws in relation to each other and to other government programs. I am ordering such a study.   On the basis of this study I shall recommend to the Congress such legislative action as will correlate our many programs and thus strengthen them.   Such action will inevitably be in the interest not only of our 21 million veterans and their families, but of all 162 million Americans.   In this endeavor, I am confident that this Administration will have the full support of all veterans and their organizations.

I should like it also understood that the Administration will continue to watch closely changes in economic conditions and, when warranted by reason of such changes, will seek appropriate adjustments in compensation and pension laws.

NOTE: As enacted, H.R. 9020 and H.R. 9962 are Public Laws 695 and 698, 83d Congress (68 Stat. 915, 916).   The statement was released at Lowry Air Force Base, Denver, Colo.

221   ¶ Statement by the President Upon Signing the Agricultural Act of 1954.   *August 28, 1954*

I AM VERY HAPPY indeed to approve this bill which embodies my major recommendations to the Congress in January.   This new law—the central core of a vigorous, progressive agricultural program—will bring substantial, lasting benefits to our farmers, our consumers, and our entire economy.

Obviously its most publicized feature is the flexible price support system which it places into effect.   At last our farmers are enabled gradually to redirect our agriculture toward better balanced production—and, at last, our farmers are assured of greater freedom instead of the rapidly increasing regimentation and Federal domination they were sure to suffer under a continuation of the present system of rigid price supports.   Those who share my deep feeling about the great importance to our country of preserving the proud independence and initiative of our farming people will share my pleasure in this new law, and will also share my hope that in time nearly all production adjustments can be accomplished through flexible supports instead of direct government controls.

There will be many other important gains from the flexible price support system.

It will help achieve a better balanced agriculture by moving more farm products into consumption.

Over the years, for the farmer, it will mean a healthier, more prosperous farm economy, a more stable income, and a steadier buying power.

Over the years, for the consumer, it will mean adequate, steady supplies of agricultural products at reasonable prices.

Over the years, for all of our people, because of the central economic importance of agriculture, it will mean a stronger national economy.

An especially important provision in this new law authorizes the government to set aside up to $2,500,000,000 worth of its surplus commodities in a reserve insulated from normal trade channels. By this action we can minimize the threat of huge surpluses to current markets and the entire farm support program. Surplus commodities so set aside will be used for many worthwhile purposes—school lunch programs, disaster relief, aid to the people of other countries, and stockpiles at home for use in war or national emergency.

The wide-ranging scope and great public importance of this new law is illustrated by brief reference to some of its other provisions. The new law:

—increases authority for moving dairy products into consumer channels;

—encourages increased domestic wool production;

—continues for two years government assistance to farmers who take steps to conserve their soil;

—authorizes larger normal supplies of wheat and corn to guarantee our nation an adequate amount of these staple grains at all times;

—shifts agricultural attaches in foreign embassies from the Department of State to the Department of Agriculture in order to sharpen the effort to find new world markets for our agricultural products;

—provides that the modernized parity formula will be applied gradually to wheat, cotton, corn and peanuts.

Important though this new farm law is, it is still only a part of a broad program for agriculture. For example—

1. The new tax law signed on August 16 not only accords the farmer benefits accruing to taxpayers generally; it also allows him to depreciate the cost of his heavy equipment on more liberal terms and specifically permits him to deduct soil and water conservation costs up to 25 percent

773

of the gross income he receives from farming. This will benefit some 500,000 farmers. It will save them some $10,000,000.

2. Increased funds have been appropriated for agricultural research. This will advance the development of more efficient and more profitable farming methods.

3. The recently authorized St. Lawrence Seaway will in time result in lower water transportation rates for farm products moving from the Midwest to the Eastern United States and to world markets across the seas.

4. Foreign outlets for American farm products will be expanded by the new Agricultural Trade Development and Assistance Act.

5. A $15,000,000 emergency credit program, administered by the Farmers Home Administration, will make disaster loans available to farmers in amounts up to $15,000.

6. For the first time, an amendment to the Social Security Act will extend the old age and survivors benefits of that law to an estimated 3,600,000 farm operators. For the first time also, these benefits will be extended to a group of about 2,100,000 farm workers who have not previously had these benefits.

7. For the first time, the Watershed Protection and Flood Prevention Act, approved on August 17, recognizes by law the great importance of upstream watershed protection in our overall water resource policy. For the first time also, this Act provides Federal technical and financial assistance to local watershed groups willing to assume responsibility for initiating, carrying out, and sharing the costs of watershed protection which will help conserve water for agricultural uses and supplement downstream flood control measures.

8. Amendment to the Water Facilities Act makes available throughout the nation loans for developing agricultural water improvements on farms and ranches. This law also establishes a program of direct insured loans for drainage facilities, reforestation, and other water and soil conservation measures.

These and many other measures are all parts of an integrated program to foster prosperity and steadily growing opportunity in American agriculture and our national economy. The new farm law is a long step forward in that program.

NOTE: The Agricultural Act of 1954 is Public Law 690, 83d Congress (68 Stat. 897).

The statement was released at Lowry Air Force Base, Denver, Colo.

222 ¶ Memorandum of Disapproval of Bill Providing for Taxation by Wyoming of Property Within Grand Teton National Park.
August 28, 1954

I HAVE WITHHELD my approval from S. 1706, "To provide for taxation by the State of Wyoming of certain property located within the confines of Grand Teton National Park, and for other purposes."

The bill would permit the State of Wyoming and any taxing authority of the State to levy taxes on privately owned hotels or lodging facilities within Grand Teton National Park. It further provides that if the United States acquires such properties in the future, payments in lieu of taxes will be made by the United States in amounts equal to the last annual taxes assessed against the property by the State or locality when it was privately owned.

This legislation is unnecessary for two reasons: First, the State now has authority to tax privately owned hotel or lodging facilities in the park and has collected such taxes for some time. Second, there appears to be no disposition on the part of the United States to acquire any such property in Grand Teton National Park, either through purchase or donation. However, I am withholding my approval not only because the bill is unnecessary but also because of the precedent it might establish for piecemeal action in this field.

The present Congress approved my recommendation that a Commission on Intergovernmental Relations be established to study the means of achieving a sounder relationship between Federal, State, and local governments. I have requested that the Commission's report include recommendations as to how to solve the difficult problems which arise in the field of intergovernmental tax immunities. The Commission has a special study committee on in lieu payments and shared revenues. The Commission's report is expected in the near future, and it is anticipated that the Administration will recommend legislation to accomplish its recommendations shortly thereafter.

I believe that questions of Federal tax immunity should be decided broadly and deliberately, rather than through a succession of piecemeal decisions and that this decision should await the recommendations of the Commission on Intergovernmental Relations on this question.

DWIGHT D. EISENHOWER

NOTE: This memorandum was released at Lowry Air Force Base, Denver, Colo.

223   ¶ Statement by the President Upon Signing the Atomic Energy Act of 1954.   *August 30, 1954*

BECAUSE OF great progress in the field of atomic energy during the past eight years, I recommended early this year that the Congress modernize the Atomic Energy Act of 1946, the basic law governing our vast atomic enterprise. This new legislation was enacted by the Congress in pursuance of that recommendation.

The new Act permits us, under proper security safeguards, to give our allies certain information that they must have for an effective defense against aggression. This information includes data needed for training in the use of and defense against atomic weapons and for evaluating the atomic capabilities of a potential aggressor. Agreements of this type with our allies will greatly strengthen our common defense and security.

This Act also sets up procedures to encourage certain exchanges of non-military atomic technology. Thus it recognizes the excellence of the atomic energy programs in certain other nations, and the groundwork is laid for wider participation in the peacetime applications of atomic energy. For example, under the Act our technicians can assist friendly nations or groups of nations in building reactors for research and power.

Also reflected in the new law is the fervent desire of our people to proceed with a plan for an International Atomic Energy Agency which would advance the peacetime applications of atomic energy, as we proposed last December to the United Nations. Although progress on this plan has been impeded by Soviet obstruction and delay, we intend to proceed—*with* the cooperation and participation of the Soviet Union if possible, *without* it if necessary.

776

That it is time to draw more specifically into the national atomic energy program the initiative and resources of private industry is recognized in the new law. For instance, private industry is enabled to participate more fully in the development of economic nuclear power, while the Government continues to assist this progress with basic research and the building of experimental reactors.

Debate on this legislation revealed some misunderstandings about the effect of certain of its provisions on public and private development of electrical power from the atom. I want our people to know that these provisions are designed eventually to relieve the taxpayer of the enormous cost of the commercial aspects of the enterprise, while fully protecting the public interest in atomic energy. In fact, these provisions carry into effect the 1946 policy declaration of the original Atomic Energy Act, that free competition in private enterprise should be strengthened.

As I sign this bill, I am confident that it will advance both public and private development of atomic energy—that it will thus lead to greater national strength—and that programs undertaken as a result of this new law will help us progress more rapidly to the time when this new source of energy will be wholly devoted to the constructive purposes of man.

NOTE: The Atomic Energy Act of 1954 is Public Law 703, 83d Congress (68 Stat. 919).

224 ¶ Statement by the President Upon Signing Bill Authorizing Construction of Bridges Over the Potomac River. *August* 30, 1954

I HAVE TODAY signed H.R. 1980, a bill authorizing the construction of two bridges over the Potomac River, one from a point at or near Jones Point, Virginia, and the other from the vicinity of Constitution Avenue in the District of Columbia to the Virginia side.

I have signed this enrolled bill because it provides, in Title I, a compromise solution for the long-standing controversy as to the location of a central area bridge across the Potomac. The bill, however, contains serious defects which should be corrected as soon as possible. Certain of the defects can be corrected by Executive action in the form of instructions, whereas others will require amendment of the legislation.

Title I of the enrolled bill, in providing for the construction of the central area bridge by the Commissioners of the District of Columbia, fails to provide statutory recognition and adjustment of the relationship of the bridge, together with its approaches and connecting roads, to existing and potential improvements on park lands. The bridge, with its high traffic volume, will have a serious impact on some of the most important of the National Memorials. It can affect importantly the effectiveness of the memorial concept of Arlington Memorial Bridge, which symbolizes the reunion of the North and South and provides a monumental approach to Arlington National Cemetery. It can infringe upon the Water Gate design as a monumental entrance to the Mall from the Potomac River. Most serious of all could be the effect of the bridge on the beautiful setting of the Lincoln Memorial.

In order to minimize the possible impairment of the monumental design and artistic setting of the Lincoln Memorial and other monumental structures in that area, the Secretary of the Interior should continue to keep control and jurisdiction over all park lands in the vicinity of the bridge except the actual bridge structure and the road and street surface between curbs necessary for maintenance by the District of Columbia. The Secretary of the Interior also should be authorized to approve all plans for the bridge and for approach roads and interchanges at both ends of the bridge since park structures and land are involved. Trucks should be prohibited on the bridge and its approaches, and all passenger-carrying buses now utilizing the Arlington Memorial Bridge should be required to use the new bridge upon its completion.

I feel that Title II of H.R. 1980 improperly vests in the Secretary of the Interior the responsibility for the construction, maintenance, and operation of the Jones Point Bridge. There is, in my opinion, no logical basis for the performance of these functions by that Department since it is not a construction agency and the bridge will not primarily concern or serve areas administered by that Department. The responsibility for the construction, maintenance, and operation of this bridge should be placed in the Bureau of Public Roads, Department of Commerce, or in the Corps of Engineers of the Department of the Army.

I am requesting the Secretary of the Interior to submit to me recommendations for Executive action and amendments of the Act necessary to correct these defects in this legislation.

NOTE: As enacted, H.R. 1980 is Public Law 704, 83d Congress (68 Stat. 961).

225 ¶ Address at the American Legion Convention. *August 30, 1954*

Commander Connell, my fellow veterans, and friends:

For the third time since World War II, I am honored to join a national convention of the American Legion.

With you, I give thanks that at last we can come together at a time when the sounds of battlefields, everywhere in the world, have been stilled.

In such a gathering, made up of those who have served our country in time of war, it seems fitting that we turn our attention to our international affairs and the Nation's security. Now, in saying this, I do not mean that any group or any section of America has a monopoly either of interest or of wisdom in dealing with complex world problems.

The contrary is true. The term "bipartisan participation" is too narrow to describe accurately the attitude that all Americans should maintain in this great area of vital concern. Rather, we should speak of universal or national participation, which would in turn imply serious study, analysis, and debate of every proposal and issue presented.

The world must understand that there is stability in our international purposes. Obviously, this cannot be obtained if there is to be marked change or if the world is to fear a marked change with every varying of partisan political winds. The only answer is that the whole American people must be informed and their decisions be made clear.

Of course, it is obvious that much of the diplomatic work, particularly those efforts classed as preparatory toward the reaching of agreements, be conducted in confidence. The political situations in the several free countries are not identical, and premature disclosures of positions and arguments could very well bar the attainment of any reasonable solution. But on broad objectives and purposes, and on the acceptable methods for obtaining them, the American people must be fully informed. Thus, their decisions will be appropriate to the situation, and the world will know that they are stable in terms of time.

This comprehensive approach is difficult to achieve; perfection cannot, of course, be attained. But the first lesson in today's complicated world affairs is that they are far too important to all of us for any one party or any one group to risk the exclusion of other Americans in

779

reaching answers that will eventually affect the fate of all of us. Success or failure in all we hope to accomplish in attaining a peaceful world may well hinge upon our success in eliminating politics and prejudice from our Nation's efforts toward this goal.

Basic to our analysis of our present world situation is clear recognition of several important truths. I mention only a few of these, but these few we can forget only at our peril.

The first is that the Communist dictatorship—ruthless, strong, insatiable—is determined to establish its sway over all the world. This truth requires no elaboration. All Americans recognize it as a fact.

The second truth is that the Communist dictatorship is adroit in its selection and use of every imaginable weapon to achieve its ends. It uses force and the threat of force. It uses bribery, subversion, and sabotage. It uses propaganda.

This last weapon—propaganda—is one which emphatically requires from us new and aggressive countermeasures. There is a dangerous disproportion between our country's efforts to tell the truth about freedom and our Nation's objectives, on the one hand, and the propaganda of the Red dictatorship on the other. For every spokesman of freedom that we assign to the struggle for men's minds and hearts, the Communists assign scores; for every dollar we spend for informational purposes, they spend fifty in opposition; for every word we utter in the cause of liberty and faith, they utter thousands to extol their system and to degrade and defame the values of the free.

Legionnaires, we must preach, demonstrate, and tirelessly sell the vitality and value of freedom in the world. Nothing is more dangerous to our cause than to expect America's message to be heard if we don't bother to tell it.

We must reaffirm to the oppressed masses of the earth the great truth that the God who gave life to humanity, at the same time gave the right of liberty to man. And in our own interest we must apply both our intelligence and the necessary material means to assist other peoples to realize for themselves the blessings of freedom and of self-government.

Now, another Red weapon which we must vigorously counter is subversion. This phase of the worldwide battle goes on constantly. Fortunately, many nations have become alerted to the dangers of this menace and are taking steps against it.

During the past year the nations of this hemisphere, at Caracas, jointly declared international communism to be a menace to all. Heartened by this resolute stand, the majority of the Guatemalan people rose to defeat the first specific attempt of Communist imperialism to establish a beachhead in this hemisphere.

In the battle against subversion within our own land, I am aware that you of the American Legion have been leaders for a third of a century. For this vigorous stand, the Nation has cause to be grateful. I know that from your determined leadership our people will continue to benefit.

Your Government will continue to wage relentless battle against subversion and infiltration. We shall do so not by half-hearted half measures which complacently accept or ignore the untrustworthy and the disloyal, but by measures realistically adjusted to the nature and magnitude of the Red conspiracy.

We have been intensively using existing laws against subversion. During the past 19 months the rate of convictions and deportations secured by the FBI and the Department of Justice has been stepped up. In addition, with the cooperation of the Congress we have written a number of new laws to help us blot out the Communist conspiracy. While a few of these may need modification based upon experience, the aggregate gain will be very substantial.

And of this you may be sure: as we continue this battle we shall not impair the constitutional safeguards protecting our liberties, yours and mine. Our Nation is too strong to give way to hysterical fear which, under the guise of preserving our institutions, would undermine the principles upon which they rest. I know the American Legion will support this wise, traditionally American approach.

I have dealt with two truths essential to our appraisal of the world situation—the implacability of the Communist drive toward world domination, and the readiness of the Communists to use any weapon to achieve their ends.

A third truth is this: the safety of any single nation in the free world depends directly upon the substantial unity of all nations in the free world. No nation outside the Iron Curtain can afford to be indifferent to the fate of any other nation devoted to freedom.

If each, ignoring all others, pursues only its own course toward its own ends, the Communists would have unlimited opportunity to turn the full force of their power upon any selected victim. Each, beginning with the weakest and the most exposed, might succumb in turn, until the strongest of all—ourselves—would be left alone to face a hostile world. The final result would be fearful to contemplate. We will never permit it to happen.

The free countries of the world have tremendous assets—in people, in productive resources, in the staying power and flexibility of free institutions. How effectively and how unitedly these countries employ these resources may well determine the outcome of the present world struggle.

This is why your national administration tirelessly seeks to solidify partnerships within the free world. I should like to talk to you briefly about certain meanings of those partnerships.

First and foremost, we can have no partnership with any nation that does not itself desire world peace and want to work for it. In this modern age, war as an instrument of deliberate policy is so unthinkable for us that we could not possibly work in permanent harmony with any nation which fails to share our peaceful convictions.

On this basis we participate in alliances with other nations of good will. Today we are allied with thirteen nations under the North Atlantic Treaty, with nineteen American nations in the Rio Pact, and with six nations in the Pacific.

Now, what should we expect of these partners? And what should they expect of us?

The answer should be sharply clear: we must work together on a principle of united freedom. In our common values and purposes, in our common interests and goals, we and our partners must be solidly joined together. To fail in this is to invite peril. At the same time, in our thoughts, in our practical decisions, in our actions as sovereign countries, we and our partners are and must be free. Because we can be at once united and free, we can be strong. And let no one ever mistake the origin of this strength.

This principle makes clear the scope of our mutual obligations. If we ignore it, we create unrealizable expectations on both sides. Then, any divergence in action or reaction is likely to give the impression that one side is "unfaithful" to the other.

In practical terms, this principle means that we are not committed to giving any of our partners a veto over our actions, nor do we have a veto over their actions. We must, therefore, guard against the dangerous assumption that other nations, as our allies, are bound to do what we want. They have never bound themselves in this sense. Nor have we bound ourselves to do what they want.

But all free nations have a continuing obligation to strengthen the recognition of the common values and interests of all peoples menaced by Communist imperialism. We must ceaselessly affirm our belief in the blessings of the hearts of free men, and must inspire their every free action and decision. For in these ideals is a rich and living unity. Free men who have it will never willingly exchange it for the stifling shroud of regimentation under which the Communist despotism hides its silent, captive peoples.

The fourth truth, closely related to the third, is this: from the resources of the free world must be developed the many kinds of strength required to oppose successfully the broad front of Communist pressure.

We and our friends must be strong spiritually and intellectually so that neither fear, nor ignorance, nor lack of determination can lead us into defeat.

There must be a strong, free world economy so that free nations can support the military strength they need and also to help alleviate hunger, privation, and despair, which the Communist leaders so successfully exploit.

The free world must be strong in arms—to discourage aggression, or to defeat it if the Communists are so unwise as to attack.

Now, this task of keeping the free world strong and healthy is complex and continuous. It is indeed difficult to organize world peace. It calls for steady effort by the free nations to work patiently together in solving problems reaching to every corner of the globe. Inevitably this process is marked by setbacks as well as successes. In Europe, for example, the progress of EDC has not fulfilled our hopes. Yet meanwhile, longstanding disputes in Egypt and Iran have been settled, and measures for the collective defense are going forward in Southeast Asia. Neither the ups nor downs justify any slackening of our efforts. The free world must build on its successes and be spurred to new endeavor by its setbacks.

The fifth truth—most important to us as a nation—involves our own place and function in the great cooperative effort to preserve security and peace.

Of all the free nations, our country is in many ways the richest and

783

the strongest. Thus, there is imposed upon us a heavy share of the whole burden of free world security. Obviously, we cannot help others unless we remain strong ourselves—strong in spirit, strong in economy and productivity, and strong in military might.

Now, a few plain statistical facts about our military: our military strength is the product of our scientists, our working men and women, our industrialists, our military leadership—our entire people.

Today the United States has the most powerful and the most efficient fighting force it has ever maintained short of all-out war. In fact, in some respects it is the most powerful ever developed.

We have an Air Force of growing effectiveness. It has 50 percent more jets than it did last year. It possesses awesome power.

We have a mighty Navy, with thousands of active aircraft. It is a world leader in nuclear propulsion.

We have our strongest peacetime Army, equipped with modern weapons, trained under modern doctrine. It is capable of carrying out its assignments in the modern world.

We have a Marine Corps, tough and strong, rightly proud of its traditional esprit and readiness.

And all of this great power is supported by developing intelligence and warning systems of constantly increasing effectiveness and scope.

Perhaps you would permit me to interject here that the civil defense program must be remembered as another arm of our true national defense. What this American Legion can do to inspire people to participate actively as responsible citizens in the civil defense program adds that much to our national and our individual security.

Now, my friends, by no means do I intend this series of facts about the character of our fighting forces to be interpreted as blustering or as a threat to anyone.

Let us always remember that our basic objective is peace. But in our search for peace—indeed, in order to enhance that search—we are determined to remain secure.

Another thing about this fighting force: for a century and a half the Republic has prided itself on its refusal to maintain large standing military forces. We have relied, instead, upon the civilian soldier. But we have done so without being fair either to the private citizen or to the security of the Nation. We have failed miserably to maintain that strong, ready military reserve in which we have believed or professed belief for 150 years.

Now at long last, we must build such a reserve. And we must maintain it. Wishful thinking and political timidity must no longer bar a program so absolutely essential to our defense.

And one point about this needs special emphasis: this reserve will not unfairly burden men who have already served.

Establishment of an adequate reserve—an objective for which the American Legion and other patriotic organizations have vainly fought for a generation—will be a number one item submitted to the Congress next year.

And I repeat: as we contemplate this powerful military system, we must always remind ourselves that we maintain it only because we must. We must remember that armaments alone cannot provide for the world a future that is secure and peaceful and filled with promise for humankind.

Now, my friends, the foreign policy of our country is simply a program for pursuing peace under methods that conform to these and other truths of today's international existence. Essential to its success are the loyal and effective officers of our Foreign Service, serving under the inspired leadership of Secretary of State Dulles. With a few highly publicized exceptions, we have been fortunate in the high competence, professional ability, and devotion of these officers upon whom we must depend in our delicate and difficult negotiations with other nations and in assuring the world of our peaceful purposes.

In respect to that pursuit of peace, America does not change. No responsible individual—no political party—wants war or wants to damage America. The only treasonous party we have is the Communist Party. No matter how deep may be our differences in other fields, in this we are all Americans—nothing else. Of course, we recognize that, in applying such a policy to the many troublesome and difficult problems which beset the free world, there will continue to be differences of opinion and frictions about particular issues.

But difficult as our course is, we would do well to reflect that we can, in wisdom and humanity, choose no other way. To follow the path of isolation would surrender most of the free world to Communist despotism and ultimately forfeit our own security. Deliberately to choose the road to war would needlessly place in jeopardy the civilization which we are determined to preserve.

We shall not be sidetracked into either of these dead ends. We shall continue to give expression to our people's deep-seated desire to live at peace with all nations. In pursuance of this effort, we have loyally supported and worked with the United Nations, which, in its first 9 years, has accomplished much in the cause of peace. Clearly it has often failed to fulfill our hopes. But that is no reason to weaken our support.

In the quest for peace, we have sought to resolve specific international disputes. In June of last year we negotiated a truce which ended the Korean War, preserved the Republic of Korea's freedom, and frustrated the Communist design for conquest. In January, at the Berlin Conference, we sought a Communist agreement to the establishment of a free and united Germany and an Austrian peace treaty. At Geneva in April we sought the peaceful unification of Korea, and tried to help settle the Indochinese war.

We have suggested other means for reducing tensions. In April last year, our Nation outlined general principles for world understanding. Last December we suggested the international pooling of atomic resources for peaceful purposes. Unfortunately, the Communist reaction to both proposals has been indifferent or negative.

This Government will continue, nevertheless, to examine, with our friends, applicable methods for making nuclear science serve the needs of mankind. Moreover, we will continue to give voice to the free world's aspiration for peace. Despite the discouraging results on specific proposals, I believe that continuing United States efforts to persuade the Soviets to consider such solutions advance the cause of peace. And the door will always be open for their participation whenever they demonstrate sincere purpose to do so.

Nor do we despair of eventual success. No human problem is insoluble. In the earnest belief that these basic purposes conform to the will of the Highest of All Rulers, the United States will continue to pursue them. In this paramount cause of this century, this Nation must have the help of all its citizens. It must have their understanding, their determination, their readiness to sacrifice—and, above all, the strength and daring of their faith.

To help keep America strong—to help keep her secure—to help guide her on the true path to peace, there is no group better qualified than you of the American Legion.

Specifically for this reason, I repeat my expressions of pride and distinction in having this opportunity to address you today.

May courage, wisdom and determination guide the deliberations of this convention, and make the American Legion an instrument of ever-increasing value to the whole of America and the free world.

NOTE: The President spoke at the National Guard Armory in Washington. His opening words "Commander Connell" referred to Arthur J. Connell, National Commander of the American Legion.

226 ¶ Address at the Iowa State Fair at Des Moines. *August 30, 1954*

Governor Beardsley, President Hoover, distinguished guests, and my friends:

Before I shall try to communicate to you the thoughts that crowd my mind, I want to straighten out one little announcement of which I thought, on the way out here. I saw in a squib in the paper that there was some anxiety, if not irritation, because it was said I was not going to pay my fifty cents to get into the Fair. Now, on behalf of a former President of the United States and myself, I hereby tender to Governor Beardsley one dollar, and hope that he will pass it on to the proper authorities. *[Laughter]*

Ladies and gentlemen, this is the very first time in my life that I ever paid anything for the privilege of making a speech. *[Laughter]* But today I am so honored to do so that it would be worth many times the price.

I truly feel a deep sense of distinction in being privileged to meet with this gathering. I know of some of the statistics that are quoted by Iowans to prove that their State is the greatest of all. I have two very special reasons. First, it is the native State of one of the truly great Americans, Mr. Hoover. And, very important to me, it is the native State of Mamie Doud Eisenhower. And if I should have failed to say that, I don't think I should have gone home this evening.

Now, ladies and gentlemen, in this day and time, when our hearts are troubled about incidents that daily appear in our press, there are a thousand subjects of which I could speak briefly to you. And in doing so, I might be able to impart to you something of the urgency your Government feels in dealing with the problems that are so important to all of us.

I think I shall talk for just a few moments about the world in which we live: about foreign things. Now, I know that primarily, and from an economic standpoint, Iowa is interested, first of all, in agriculture. So is all the United States. All of us well know without a prosperous agriculture there is no prosperity in America. And you also know that without a prosperous America there is no prosperity for the farmer. And from this kind of reasoning, and this observation, it takes no mental leap at all to understand that without very close and proper relations with a great portion of the world there is no prosperity for any of us. Because, not only do we need imports from other nations, in order that we may have tractors, all of our steel—rubber—tin—and many other things, but we must export. We must export to them the surpluses which keep our economy sound, progressive, and expanding. And from those people we must buy the things with which they can pay for these exports.

Now, I am not going to talk about that particular phase of our foreign relations, the trade and economic phases. I merely want to talk about this: the absolute, utter necessity of every American taking thought about our relations with the world.

Why do we have friends? We are strong, and we are mighty. We are rich. With 6 percent of the world's population, we have so much of the world's resources, our industries, our agriculture is so productive, that we astonish the world.

Why, then, must we have friends? We know that today the central core of the great world problem is the aggressive intent of international communism. If the free world does not hang together, then the unity of communism, achieved by force, by the use of the police outside your door and the spy inside your home, that unity will take one nation at a time, beginning with the most exposed, and subdue it. If this process should be continued, and we made no effort to stop it, eventually the American continent, the American hemisphere—finally, possibly, North America, would be an isolated island of freedom in a sea of communism.

Such a picture does not have to be long held up in front of us, before we understand that we must never let it occur.

We shall not let it occur.

Now, in the conduct of foreign affairs for this great nation of 160 million people, there are successes and there are setbacks. The Iranian oil dispute that has been settled sufficiently so that that country is again oriented toward the West, and marching with us. This great portion of the oil reserves of the world no longer seems in weekly danger of falling to our enemies and excluding us from it.

Incidentally, I should like to pay a tribute to the son of President Hoover, for his great success as a diplomat in handling the American end of that difficult negotiation. I might say I have been lucky enough, also, to recruit him for service.

Another place where we have had a success is in the Suez Canal. There, a situation that looked as if it could cause us a great difficulty— all the free world—seems to be amicably settled, and with the protection of all the interests of the Western World.

The first open, specific attempt of international communism to establish a beachhead on this continent has been repulsed by the majority of the people of Guatemala, and proving again that people who have tasted freedom will not willingly submit to the regimentation of the Red dictatorship.

We have had our setbacks. One of the major setbacks was reported in your papers today: the rejection by the French parliament of the French proposition to establish in Europe the European Defense Community. This was a device, my friends, whereby the free world could establish, without indulging in the traditional fights among themselves in Western Europe, security from any threat from without. This proposal was established to allow Germany—Western Germany—to enter into defensive alliances without any danger whatsoever that it would be in position to start a war or, indeed, to engage in any kind of aggression.

Because of these characteristics of this plan, the United States, Great Britain, and all the Western nations stood for it, and approved this great French plan. Now, there is no disguising the fact that this is a serious setback. But what I want to say to you people is this: the free world is still overwhelmingly strong as compared to the Iron Curtain countries, in the people we have, in their levels of intelligence and understanding, in their skills, in agriculture, and in industry; in their free adherence to a cause, rather than in regimented adherence to a government. Finally, in their tremendous productivity; and indeed, in sum total, in their military might.

All that this world needs—this free world needs to be safe, is a united approach to the problem of security and defense.

Now this does not mean that we expect every nation—every friend— to agree with us, no more than in any one family everybody is always in perfect agreement. We do not expect, always, to agree with them, because this is a characteristic of free life—a free family—a free city—a free State—a free world, as to arguments. But we do adhere to basic principles.

America is strong because we believe in the dignity of man. We believe in the federated plan of forty-eight States. We believe in free enterprise. We are strong because we believe in basic things. Then we argue with all our might about the details, and about the methods.

It is in that sense that the free world must be strong.

Ladies and gentlemen, that is the reason that every American has a duty, a duty to himself and to his country: to study these other nations— their cultures, their histories, their aspirations, their fears, their hopes. In this great field there can be no such thing in America as partisanship. There can be nothing except an American attitude, an attitude that preserves continuity, because it represents the hearts and minds of the American people.

Let us not speak of labels.

Now, ladies and gentlemen, I find, in talking to many Americans on an individual basis, that they say to me: yes, I know that this job of foreign relations is probably the most important thing facing this great country. We want no more war. We are thankful to our God that after all these 20 years, at least the sounds of battlefields are stilled everywhere. We don't want to send our sons to war—our brothers—our husbands.

But what can I do?

I say: grasp enough of this problem that you know the basic principles to which you are adhering, that freedom cannot be divided. If we will be free ourselves, we must be ready to help defend the freedom of those who want to remain free. It is not divisible. We must be united.

Remind yourselves of the strength of America. Think of her spiritual strength that we have inherited, not only from our parents at their knees as we said our prayers, but we inherited from our Founding Fathers the system they gave to us. Remember our schools, our industries, our productivity, the great strength that 160 million people can generate.

When we have our setbacks we are disappointed. But we must not be discouraged.

America has never quit in something that was good for herself, and the world.

We will not quit now. We shall never do so.

In this atomic age, we have tried our best to share with all the world certain of the secrets that we thought, in such sharing, would bring to all the world an understanding that this new science can be devoted to the good of the world, as well as to the destruction of humanity.

We shall continue to try. In this, as in all other things, we cannot, we must not, admit defeat. In this new age, the thing we must hold before us is this: with American faith, with American belief, with American know-how, with our readiness to understand our fellow man and work with him, it can open before the world a true golden age of our civilization.

We need not despair. We must not.

And so, the opportunity to say some of these things to you this evening, at the very moment when this one setback has occurred, makes me feel better.

You inspire me, I assure you—because when I see America represented like this, how can you be fainthearted? It can't be done.

Now, my friends, Mr. Hoover and I have a very important date with a few finny comrades up in the high Rockies, and it is about time we were getting along.

If I have held you here too long, my apologies; but I repeat: for myself and my party this has been a very great honor, one all of us shall long remember.

Good night.

227   ¶ Statement by the President Upon Signing
Bill Increasing Unemployment Compensation
Benefits in the District of Columbia.
August 31, 1954

THIS NEW LAW makes the first major improvement in more than
10 years in the amount and duration of District of Columbia unemployment compensation benefits.   It increases maximum benefits from $20
a week to $30 and increases the outside limit on duration of benefits
from 20 to 26 weeks.

The Act still is not the model law I should like to see for the District
of Columbia, due to such features as an alternative limitation of benefits
to one-third of the workers' past year's earnings, and certain stringent
disqualification provisions; but such defects will be the subject of amendment at the next session of the Congress, so the process of improvement
started by this legislation will continue to be carried forward.

NOTE: As enacted the bill is Public Law   The statement was released at Lowry
721, 83d Congress (68 Stat. 988).   Air Force Base, Denver, Colo.

228   ¶ Memorandum of Disapproval of Bill for
the Relief of Anna K. McQuilkin.
August 31, 1954

I HAVE WITHHELD my approval from H.R. 3516, "For the relief
of Anna K. McQuilkin."

The bill provides for a direct payment award of $6,125 to Mrs. Mc-
Quilkin who claims that her brother, a World War I veteran who died
in the service in 1918, applied for and was issued yearly renewable term
insurance in the sum of $10,000 and that she is entitled to the proceeds
thereof as the sole beneficiary.

The Veterans' Administration and predecessor agencies have disputed
her claim over a number of years, contending that their records and
those of the military department fail to disclose that the brother made
application for insurance.   In 1922 the Veterans' Bureau, after careful

consideration of the evidence presented in support of the claim, rejected it.   Upon this denial, an award of automatic insurance of $25 a month was made to the deceased veteran's father, based on the determination that there had been no application for insurance.   A total sum of $3,875 had been paid to the father at the time of his death in 1930.   The $6,125 proposed for payment by H.R. 3516 represents the difference between the amount paid to the father and the sum of the insurance for which application was allegedly made.

During the period 1920 to 1932 Mrs. McQuilkin engaged the services of a number of attorneys to prosecute her claim.   New counsel in July 1932 instituted suit against the Government in the United States District Court for the Northern District of Illinois and secured a judgment in the amount of $12,592.50.   The lower court decision, however, was reversed on appeal to the Circuit Court of Appeals on the ground that the statutory period of limitations for filing such a suit had expired.

The Judiciary Committees appear to have accepted the lower court decision against the Government as now conclusive of the merits of Mrs. McQuilkin's claim.   This would not seem, however, to be the case in view of the procedural turn of the Circuit Court of Appeals ruling which precluded review of the substantive question of whether there was substantial evidence to support the findings of the District Court.

I also agree with the Veterans' Administration that the case does not present any equitable consideration which warrants the direct gratuity award proposed.   Unfortunately, the procedural reversal by the Circuit Court of Appeals has left the parties in the unsatisfactory position which existed prior to the District Court suit.   The evidence in this case is complex and controversial.   I believe, therefore, that in fairness to Mrs. McQuilkin she is entitled to a day in court for decision of her claim on its merits, and I would be willing to approve a jurisdictional enactment waiving the bar of any statute of limitations.

DWIGHT D. EISENHOWER

NOTE: This memorandum was released at Lowry Air Force Base, Denver, Colo.

229   ¶ Memorandum of Disapproval of Bill for the Relief of S. H. Prather, Mrs. Florence Prather Penman, and S. H. Prather, Jr.   *August* 31, 1954

I HAVE WITHHELD my approval from the bill (H.R. 9357) "For the relief of S. H. Prather, Mrs. Florence Prather Penman, S. H. Prather, Junior."

The bill proposed to pay the sums of $5,000 to S. H. Prather, $2,000 to Mrs. Florence Prather Penman and $1,000 to S. H. Prather, Junior for personal injuries and property damages sustained at Quitman, Georgia, as the result of a collision of their family automobile with a car driven by one Howard Hart, an alleged bootlegger. The Committee report on this bill (H. Rept. No. 2208) indicates that the collision occurred on August 6, 1935, when Hart was being pursued by an investigator of the Alcohol Tax Unit, Bureau of Internal Revenue, Treasury Department, and by a state officer. The report of the Treasury Department embodied in the House Report, states that the officers while traveling at approximately 70 miles per hour, had pursued the car for a distance of about 2 miles but had slowed down, when Hart turned into a dirt side street of the town of Quitman, picked up speed to 75 miles an hour and collided with the Prather car which was proceeding at a lawful rate of 20 to 25 miles per hour. Hart's car contained approximately 43 gallons of illicit whiskey at the time.

The officers in this instance were acting in the performance of their official duties in attempting to apprehend persons who were violating the law in their presence. The report of the Special Investigator of the Alcohol Tax Unit states that Mr. Prather conceded when interviewed that the officers were doing their duty and were without blame "but that he felt someone should compensate him for the damages suffered", since the violators who had caused the wreck had no financial responsibility.

The misfortune suffered by this family as a result of the automobile accident, for which they were in no manner responsible, is most lamentable. While it is true the accident might not have happened if the law enforcement officers had not been pursuing the bootleggers, there is nothing in the file to indicate the law enforcement officers were acting negligently or were doing anything other than their duty.   Unfortunately, the culprits legally and morally responsible for the injuries, cannot be made to respond in damages.   Enactment of the bill would constitute a gratuity and would create a dangerous precedent which might set in motion a chain of endless requests for the payment of damages by the Government arising out of accidents in which law enforcement officers may have been remotely involved.

Accordingly, I am constrained to withhold my approval from the bill.

Dwight D. Eisenhower

NOTE: This memorandum was released at Lowry Air Force Base, Denver, Colo.

230 ❡ Memorandum of Disapproval of Bill for the Relief of the Estate of Carlos M. Cochran. *August* 31, 1954

I HAVE WITHHELD my approval from S. 820, "For the relief of the estate of Carlos M. Cochran".

This enrolled enactment would pay the sum of $5,000 to the estate of Carlos M. Cochran, who was killed in line of duty when he was a member of the Armed Forces in 1942.

The soldier decedent was discovered lying beside a highway just outside the entrance to the military installation where he was stationed. Although he appears to have been temporarily of unsound mind at the time, the sentry at the gate to the installation who discovered him and took him into custody was not aware of this fact.   While the sentry was telephoning for military policemen to come to the gatehouse for the decedent, he attempted to escape.   He failed to obey the sentry's three shouted commands to halt.   The sentry then aimed his shotgun at the decedent's legs and fired.   Just at this moment the decedent jumped into a ditch.   As a result, he was struck in the chest rather than the legs, and was instantly killed.

A board of officers, which subsequently considered the case, determined that the sentry's actions had been reasonable under all of the circumstances.   The board also determined that since the decedent was known to have been in a state of mental confusion at the time of the shooting, his death should be considered to be in line of duty.

The records of Army show that the regular death gratuity was paid in this case and that at the time of the decedent's entry into the military service he was offered but specifically refused national service life insurance.

The decedent's closest survivor seems to be a sister who presumably would be the ultimate beneficiary of the bill. She is not entitled to survivorship benefits under laws administered by the Veterans' Administration since sisters are not included within the categories of survivors eligible to receive benefits under such laws.

Laws administered by the Veterans' Administration and other Federal agencies provide systems of benefits for certain dependent survivors of members of the Armed Forces killed in line of duty. Benefits so authorized are generous and are payable to the specified survivors regardless of whether death results from the negligence or wilful misconduct of fellow servicemen or any other person. Under the circumstances, I think it only fair and reasonable to consider the generous, uniform, and assured protection which these systems afford as the exclusive remedy against the United States on account of the death of a member of the Armed Forces killed in line of duty. Any other view would be productive of anomalies and serious inequities.

The foregoing view accords with that taken by the Supreme Court in denying relief in a negligence case brought under the Federal Tort Claims Act in which, as here, a member of the Armed Forces was killed not only in line of duty but incident to his actual military service. Such a view is in no sense novel. Military and veterans' survivorship benefits are the equivalent of civilian workmen's compensation benefits. The Federal government and most of the States have abolished actions for damages between employers and employees and superseded them with workmen's compensation statutes which provide the sole basis of liability in most cases.

Additionally, as already noted, the decedent had the opportunity to apply for a policy of national service life insurance in the maximum amount of $10,000. He was specifically offered this opportunity but refused to take advantage of it, as is indicated by his service record.

Accordingly, while regretting the tragic death of the decedent, I am constrained to withhold my approval from S. 820.

DWIGHT D. EISENHOWER

NOTE: This memorandum was released at Lowry Air Force Base, Denver, Colo.

231 ¶ Memorandum of Disapproval of Bill for the Relief of Lawrence F. Kramer.
August 31, 1954

I HAVE WITHHELD my approval from the bill (S. 2083) "For the relief of Lawrence F. Kramer."

The bill provides for payment to Lawrence F. Kramer of Paterson, New Jersey, of the sum of $67,500 in full satisfaction of his claim against the United States for (1) compensation for services rendered by him during the period from 1935 to 1952 in assisting and enabling the United States to prosecute successfully criminal proceedings against certain defendants who had defrauded the Government in connection with fixed prices on work projects in the State of New Jersey, and (2) for reimbursement for expenses incurred by him in rendering such services.

It appears that in late 1935, Mr. Kramer complained to the Works Progress Administration concerning the existence of a possible fraud conspiracy, collusive bidding, and bribery in connection with certain sand and stone supply contracts awarded, and to be awarded, by the Works Progress Administration in northern New Jersey. His sole information was that his father, Philip Kramer, operator of a stone quarry at Paterson, New Jersey, had been approached by one George Brooks to participate in the scheme, and had refused, and that as a result of his refusal, stone supplied by him had been rejected by the Works Progress Administration (apparently due to the influence of the conspirators), with the consequence that he suffered heavy business loss.

As a result of this complaint, an investigation was undertaken by the Government which culminated in the conviction of the lawbreakers in 1941 and a civil recovery (by way of settlement) in 1952. Apart from the initial tip concerning the existence of a possible conspiracy, and the furnishing of the names of certain persons having knowledge of the approach made to his father, it does not appear that claimant contributed anything to the successful prosecution and civil recovery.

There is nothing to distinguish this case from any other case in which the Government receives from a private citizen information concerning wrongful action with reference to which criminal proceedings are brought and civil recoveries are obtained. The vast majority of such proceedings are made possible by citizens who either because of their normal interest in law enforcement and good government, or because of self-interest supply law enforcement officers with information of the character here involved.

Even if claimant were to be treated as if he had commenced suit as an informer, he would be entitled to no more than the 10 percent of the civil recovery, whereas the bill proposes to award him 30 percent of that amount.

Dwight D. Eisenhower

NOTE: This memorandum was released at Lowry Air Force Base, Denver, Colo.

232 ¶ Memorandum of Disapproval of Bill for the Relief of Graphic Arts Corporation. *August 31, 1954*

I AM WITHHOLDING my approval from S. 2801, "For the relief of Graphic Arts Corporation of Ohio."

S. 2801 provides that the Secretary of the Treasury be authorized and directed to pay the sum of $84,359.19 to the Graphic Arts Corporation of Ohio, Toledo, Ohio, in full settlement of all claims of the said Graphic Arts Corporation against the United States. The bill would afford financial relief to the Graphic Arts Corporation for losses alleged to have been incurred in the performance of contract W–33–038 ac–2023 with the Army Air Corps during the period 1 January to 1 June 1946.

It is the contention of the Corporation that it was not supplied with the full quantity of work contemplated by the contract during the contract period, and that the contractor was assured by representatives of the Army Air Corps that it would be protected against losses in its operation under the contract. However, it appears that the contractor did accept extensions of time and other amendments to the original contract under various change orders and supplements pertinent thereto by executing said documents. It is reported that payments totaling $2,029,185.29 were made to the contractor.

Insofar as furnishing work under the contract was concerned, it appears that there was substantial compliance by the Government within the contract period as extended.

There is an established rule that a formal written contract entered into on the basis of negotiations between the parties merges all such previous negotiations and is presumed in law to express the final understanding of the parties. Contract W–33–038 ac–2023, as amended, was entered into on a fixed-price basis. It contained no provision for payment of additional compensation merely because the contractor might suffer a loss in performance. Hence, while the contractor's claim is based primarily upon the premise that certain representations were made by Government officers at the time the contract was negotiated, to the effect that the Government would protect the contractor from any loss in performance, the terms of the contract relating to the work to be performed and to the prices to be paid therefor were clear and unambiguous and such extraneous representations, even if established, legally could not be resorted to for the purpose of imposing an additional obligation on the Government. If the contractor felt that the formal contract and change orders and extensions, et cetera, did not afford it sufficient protection against losses in performance, it should not have signed the contract and accepted the extensions. Having done so, it seems clear that there is no liability for any further payment to the contractor, based upon the contract provisions.

Government audit of the contractor's records indicates that this corporation, although claiming a loss of $67,952.31 in the operation of the "Gadi" Division for the five months' period beginning 1 January 1946, actually sustained a loss of only $46,213.94 during that period. Of this amount, the audit report shows only $29,432.29 was applicable to Army Air Corps contract W–33–038 ac–2023. Despite this loss of $29,432.29 on this contract for the first five months of 1946, the contractor actually earned a profit of $34,202.86 on the entire contract. The Audit report also discloses that this contractor earned a profit of $392,329.15 on all other Government business for the years 1944, 1945 and the first five months of 1946. Its commercial business during the same period also operated at a substantial profit.

My approval of this bill would establish the undesirable principle of Government underwriting any wartime losses incurred by contractors providing goods and services to the Government, regardless of the fact that such contractors did not sustain a net loss. I am unable to perceive any circumstances which would warrant preferential treatment for the claimant to the detriment of other wartime contractors. I am satisfied that it is my duty to oppose this bill.

Although my examination of the record in this case does not lead me to believe that there is an equitable basis for this claim, it is possible that a court through judicial processes might be led to determine otherwise. In complex situations like this one, it is my opinion that judicial rather than legislative remedy should be sought. I would, therefore, be willing to give my approval to a jurisdictional bill waiving the bar of any statute of limitations against the claim.

DWIGHT D. EISENHOWER

NOTE: This memorandum was released at Lowry Air Force Base, Denver, Colo.

233   ¶ Statement by the President on the Death of Senator Maybank of South Carolina.
September 1, 1954

I DEEPLY REGRET the untimely passing of Senator Burnet R. Maybank, whom I came to know well through his years of effective service on the old Senate Committee on Military Affairs. He was a dedicated servant of his state and the nation. His passing is a loss much to be regretted by all Americans who want men of integrity and ability in their government.

NOTE: This statement was released at Fraser, Colo.

234   ¶ Statement by the President Upon Signing Bill Providing Benefits for Government Employees.
September 1, 1954

I AM VERY HAPPY to approve H.R. 2263 which provides important benefits for employees of the Federal Government.

In the enactment of legislation benefiting government employees and improving government personnel management, the record of this Congress far surpasses that of any previous Congress. These various laws have largely accomplished the Administration's objectives in the field of personnel management during the 83d Congress. These objectives include:

—more efficient and flexible personnel administration in the Federal service;

—attractive employment conditions in government, more nearly in harmony with practices of progressive private employers;

—a better basis for relationships between the government as an employer and its employees.

Administrative steps to carry out this law include greater encouragement for suggestions, inventions and superior performance of employees, authorizations for longevity pay, and more equitable overtime pay practices. There will be many other administrative improvements under this new law.

Also a result of this legislation is an Executive Order, which I am now issuing, permitting the Civil Service Commission and agency heads to lift temporary limitations on promotions and reassignments of hundreds of thousands of career employees.

NOTE: As enacted, H.R. 2263 is Public Law 763, 83d Congress (68 Stat. 1105). The statement was released at Lowry Air Force Base, Denver, Colo.

235 ¶ Statement by the President Upon Signing the Social Security Amendments of 1954. *September* 1, 1954

I AM VERY HAPPY to sign the Social Security Amendments of 1954. By enabling some 10,000,000 more Americans to participate in the Old-Age and Survivors Insurance Program, it gives them an opportunity to establish a solid foundation of economic security for themselves and their families.

Beyond broadening the coverage of this program, this new law contains four other important provisions:

First, it raises payments to all retired workers by at least five dollars a month. It also raises—by $13.50 a month for retired workers and by $31.25 a month for families—the ceiling on payments to people now receiving monthly checks. People becoming eligible in the future will also receive higher payments, including increases that result from raising from $3,600 to $4,200 the maximum wage base from which the amount of their benefit checks is determined.

Second, the law eliminates the four or five lowest years of earnings from the computation of the OASI checks of workers who retire in the future.   This provision is of great importance to many people whose years of unusually low earnings—for reasons of unemployment, illness, or otherwise—would sharply reduce their benefits.

Third, all retired workers under the program are permitted to earn more without forfeiting OASI checks.   The amount of exempt earnings is increased to $1,200 a year, and this annual exemption is applied equally to wage earners and self-employed workers.

Fourth, the Act preserves the benefits rights, under Old-Age and Survivors Insurance, of those workers regularly covered under the program who become totally disabled for long and indefinite periods.

This new law is an important part of the broad program of the Administration and the 83d Congress to improve the well-being of our people. In the past month I have signed into law a number of other Acts directly affecting the human problems of each family in the land.   These include:

1. More hospitals and nursing homes for persons who are chronically ill, special medical facilities for people not requiring hospitalization, and rehabilitation facilities for disabled people.

2. A start toward increasing from 60,000 to 200,000 by 1959, the number of disabled people rehabilitated each year.

3. Three Acts helping the States and local communities meet the nation's educational problems.

4. Help to provide and improve housing, to prevent and eliminate slums, and to conserve and develop urban communities.

5. Extension of the unemployment insurance program to almost 4,000,000 more workers.

These Acts and the Social Security amendments I have approved today will bolster the health and economic security of the American people. They represent one of the cornerstones of our program to build a better and stronger America.

NOTE: The bill (Social Security Amend-   The statement was released at **Lowry** ments of 1954) is Public Law 761, 83d   Air Force Base, Denver, Colo.
Congress (68 Stat. 1052).

236 ¶ Statement by the President Upon Signing Bill To Extend and Improve the Unemployment Insurance Program. *September* 1, 1954

I AM HAPPY to sign the bill known as H.R. 9709. Not since unemployment insurance was first the subject for Federal legislation has it been so greatly extended and improved as it is by this new law.

This law assures almost four million additional workers that they will have the same type of income protection, when temporarily unemployed, as do those now covered by the system. Almost one-and-a-half million of these workers are employees who were not covered under the previous Act because their employers did not hire eight or more workers; this new Act gives protection to those whose employers hire *four* or more workers. Thanks to this new law, moreover, more than two million Federal civilian workers now will enjoy the same kind of unemployment insurance coverage available to workers in many private industries.

I believe that our citizens now generally accept the principle that insurance against loss of income due to unemployment, to old age or to disability should be provided under law. This is a practical and orderly way to alleviate such personal hardships in a free, private enterprise economy. The enactment of H.R. 9709—together with extension and improvement of Old Age and Survivors Insurance—makes 1954 a year of unusual progress toward greater economic security for all our citizens.

But much remains to be done. I hope that next winter state legislatures will supplement the action of the Congress by passing certain unemployment insurance measures of their own. Through such action our citizens might expect larger benefits and longer duration of benefits, and employees of state and local governments might gain inclusion in unemployment insurance systems established by those governments. This action would affect a total of about 4.2 million additional workers throughout the nation.

NOTE: As enacted, H.R. 9709 is Public Law 767, 83d Congress (68 Stat. 1130). The statement was released at Lowry Air Force Base, Denver, Colo.

237 ¶ Statement by the President Upon Signing Bill Authorizing Construction of Family Housing for Military Personnel and Their Dependents. *September 1, 1954*

I AM VERY HAPPY to sign H.R. 9924, which authorizes construction of some 12,000 sets of family-type quarters for military personnel and their dependents. I most earnestly hope that this legislation is but the beginning of a continuing program to meet the housing needs of our servicemen.

Many of our military installations are remotely located where family housing simply does not exist, or in congested urban areas where such civilian housing as is available is inadequate even for the needs of the non-military population. The result has been that many of our career servicemen have had to be separated for long periods from their families. Many others must pay excessive rentals even to occupy grossly inadequate housing.

The imposition of such irritating hardships and unnecessary sacrifices upon our Service personnel has induced many of them to return to civilian life and greatly complicated the always difficult peacetime task of maintaining an effective professional fighting force. The problem goes beyond housing. It includes medical care and survivorship benefits for dependents, off-duty educational opportunities, and an advantageous retirement system. For generations such so-called "fringe benefits" have characterized our military services. These benefits have helped to compensate our uniformed personnel for expenses and discomforts which are imposed upon them and have served also as a supplement to the historically modest service pay. But during recent years—at a time when our need for experienced service personnel has been the greatest in our peacetime history—we have been energetically curtailing inducements to our citizens to make our armed forces a career.

This new law is, therefore, a good beginning—a start on the larger task of assuring to our trained men and women in uniform the advantages and opportunities and inducements necessary to make them wish to remain permanently in their country's service.

In the next Congress I hope we can carry forward this good beginning in the field of military housing, and I shall recommend that renewed attention be given to the improvement of medical care and survivorship benefits for servicemen's dependents. In this way we shall powerfully strengthen our nation's defense.

NOTE: As enacted, H.R. 9924 is Public   The statement was released at Lowry
Law 765, 83d Congress (68 Stat. 1119).   Air Force Base, Denver, Colo.

238   ¶ Statement by the President Upon Signing Bill Conveying Certain Mineral Rights to Mrs. Pearl O. Marr.   *September 1, 1954*

I HAVE TODAY approved S. 3251, "An Act to provide for the conveyance of certain mineral rights to Mrs. Pearl O. Marr, of Crossroads, New Mexico."

The bill directs the Secretary of the Interior to quitclaim to Pearl O. Marr the oil, gas and other mineral interests reserved by the United States at the time the lands involved were patented to John W. Marr, her husband.

This bill first came to my attention on August 27, 1954. At that time the Department of the Interior advised me on the basis of the information then available to it that there were no special equities in this case to warrant singling it out as an exception to the general law which requires that public lands valuable for certain minerals may be patented only upon condition that the mineral rights are reserved to the United States. Under these circumstances I issued a memorandum of disapproval on August 27, 1954.

It now appears that an error was made.

The Secretary of the Interior advised me today that his attention has been directed to new evidence which indicates that special equities do exist in this case. He informed me that subsequent to the time Mr. Marr was required to file waivers of mineral rights on his homestead, a determination was made by the Department of the Interior that there was no evidence to establish that the lands were prospectively valuable for oil and gas and that as a result of this determination almost all of the homesteaders in that area at that time received patents to their lands without reservation of oil and gas rights. It was then too late to correct the patent which Mr. Marr had received.

The Secretary of the Interior, therefore, now recommends that the bill be approved. Accordingly, I have reconsidered the bill in the light of this additional information and agree that the bill shall be approved. Fortunately, the constitutional time period within which I must act has not yet elapsed.

NOTE: As enacted, S. 3251 is Private Law 988, 83d Congress (68 Stat. A285). The Memorandum of Disapproval dated August 27, 1954, was withdrawn.

The statement was released at Lowry Air Force Base, Denver, Colo.

239 ¶ Memorandum of Disapproval of Bill for the Relief of Mrs. Rosaline Spagnola.
September 1, 1954

I HAVE WITHHELD my approval from H.R. 2881, a bill "For the relief of Mrs. Rosaline Spagnola."

This enrolled enactment would pay to Mrs. Rosaline Spagnola the sum of $675.50 as additional compensation on account of the accidental death of her son in 1947 at Schofield Barracks, Hawaii.

As a member of the Armed Forces, the beneficiary's son had been convicted of housebreaking by a court-martial, sentenced to five years' confinement, and given a suspended dishonorable discharge. While confined in a post stockade he was shot and killed during an abortive jailbreak. It was subsequently determined that the decedent was not involved in the attempted escape in any way, and his death was declared to have occurred in line of duty. On the basis of this determination the beneficiary was paid the usual six months' death gratuity.

Earlier in his military career the beneficiary's son had taken out a $10,000 national service life insurance policy, designating his mother as beneficiary, and paying the premiums on his policy by allotments from his pay. However, since he had forfeited all pay and allowances while in confinement his allotment became ineffective, causing the policy to lapse for lack of premium payment. When the beneficiary made application after her son's death for regular monthly payments under the policy, the Veterans' Administration made such payments to her over a period of several years in an aggregate amount of $4,324.50 before discovering that the policy had not actually been in effect at the time of the son's death. Under discretionary authority which it possesses, the Veterans' Administration waived recovery of the amount thus erroneously paid to the beneficiary on the grounds that she had received it in good faith and to require repayment would work an undue hardship on her. In this connection, it may be noted that the award proposed by the present measure is based on the difference between the aggregate amount of the erroneous insurance payments and $5,000, the sum deemed by the Congress to be a reasonable total payment in the light of the circumstances of the case.

It appears that, even if she were dependent upon her son for support, which she was not, the beneficiary is ineligible for survivorship benefits under laws administered by the Veterans' Administration, because such benefits are denied in cases in which the serviceman died while in confinement, regardless of whether or not his death was incurred in line of duty.

The only question presented by this case is whether its special facts warrant the additional relief which the bill would afford the beneficiary. It might be argued that such relief is warranted not only because the beneficiary, apart from the issue of dependency, is ineligible for benefits under laws administered by the Veterans' Administration even though her son died in line of duty but also because neither she nor her son was ever specifically notified by the Veterans' Administration that this insurance had lapsed. Even if such arguments were valid, and I do not consider that they are, I still believe that there would be no justification for the award proposed here. I believe that any equities which might have existed in favor of the beneficiary were more than satisfied when the Veterans' Administration waived recovery of the insurance payments erroneously made to her.

DWIGHT D. EISENHOWER

NOTE: This memorandum was released at Lowry Air Force Base, Denver, Colo.

240　¶ Memorandum of Disapproval of Bill for the Relief of Raleigh Hill.　*September* 1, 1954

I AM WITHHOLDING my approval from the bill, H.R. 6529, Eighty-third Congress, "An Act for the relief of Raleigh Hill."

The bill would authorize and direct the Administrator of Veterans' Affairs to pay the proceeds of National Service life insurance of Walter H. Nichols, Junior, to Raleigh Hill, uncle of the insured and designated principal beneficiary of such insurance.

National Service life insurance in the amount of $10,000 matured on April 8, 1945, the date of death in service of Walter H. Nichols, Junior. The Veterans' Administration denied the claim of his uncle, Raleigh Hill, the designated principal beneficiary, on the ground that he did not stand in loco parentis to the insured and was therefore not within the permitted classes of beneficiaries, a statutory requirement applicable to National Service life insurance maturing prior to August 1, 1946. The correctness of the Veterans' Administration determination under the applicable law is not disputed.

Favorable action appears to have been predicated on a belief that because the restriction concerning the permitted classes of beneficiaries has been removed as to National Service life insurance maturing on and after August 1, 1946, payment should be made to an ineligible beneficiary in this case involving insurance which matured prior to August 1, 1946, and further, that the Government failed to advise the insured properly concerning classes of eligible beneficiaries. I am advised that the latter view is not supported by the record. As to the former, a similar view was urged in support of H.R. 3733, 83d Congress, which likewise proposed to pay an ineligible beneficiary the proceeds of a National Service life insurance policy. In my message of February 23, 1954, returning the bill without approval, I said that it seemed to me irrelevant and unwise to accept as justification for that bill the fact that the ineligible beneficiary could at the time of the message qualify as a beneficiary under existing law which was not made retroactive. My view has not changed and applies with equal force to the present case.

Furthermore, approval of H.R. 6529 would be discriminatory and precedential. I am advised that of the approximately 3,600 claims for the proceeds of National Service life insurance denied by the Veterans'

Administration because the claimants were not within the classes of beneficiaries permitted by law, it is estimated that a majority were cases similar to Mr. Hill's where the claimants had been designated as beneficiaries.

As stated on previous occasions, I am opposed to setting aside the principles and rules of administration prescribed in the general law relating to veterans' benefit programs. Uniformity and equality of treatment to all who are similarly situated must be the steadfast rule if the Federal programs for veterans and their beneficiaries are to be operated successfully. Approval of H.R. 6529 would not be in keeping with these principles.

Dwight D. Eisenhower

NOTE: This memorandum was released at Lowry Air Force Base, Denver, Colo.

241 ¶ Memorandum of Disapproval of Bill for the Relief of Mrs. Merle Cappeller Weyel. *September* 1, 1954

I AM WITHHOLDING my approval of S. 45, a bill "For the relief of Mrs. Merle Cappeller Weyel."

This enrolled enactment would pay the sum of $5,437.21 to Mrs. Merle Cappeller Weyel in full settlement of her claim arising out of the death of her husband after his release from active duty in the Navy in 1948.

The husband of the beneficiary of this bill was recalled to active duty in 1947, after having been retired following the completion of 30 years of service. Prior to his release from this tour of duty, he was given a particularly thorough physical examination because of indications that he might be suffering from high blood pressure. However, a board of medical survey determined, as a result of this examination, that he was physically qualified for release from active duty, and he was accordingly again returned to his retired status in February 1948.

Subsequently, this officer was treated and X-rayed by a private physician in September 1948. The X-ray disclosed that he was suffering from a malignancy which caused his death in December 1948, after two unsuccessful operations in private hospitals.

This deceased officer's case was twice considered by the Board for the Correction of Naval Records, which was established by statute to correct records where this was necessary to remove an injustice. It was contended by the beneficiary that the malignancy should have been discovered at the time her husband was released from active duty and that, if it had been discovered, he would have been kept on active duty until his death. On the basis of this, it was further contended she was entitled to be paid the usual death gratuity, the difference between her husband's active and retired pay for the period between his release from active duty and his death and the amount of private medical and hospital expenses incurred on his behalf. The present measure is based on these same contentions.

After twice reviewing the case, the Board concluded that it was to be presumed that the malignancy had existed at the time the decedent was released from active duty and that, had its existence been discovered, he would not have been released at the time he was. However, the Board concluded that the decedent would not have been kept on active duty until his death, but in all probability would have been retired for physical disability not later than July 1948.

I can perceive no justification for the payment which the bill would make on account of the cost of private medical and hospital care incurred on behalf of the decedent. He was, at all times, entitled to such care at facilities operated by the Navy Department. There is no showing that any attempt was made to take advantage of these facilities. But, on the contrary, it appears that, for personal reasons, the decedent elected to be treated privately. If the government is to establish medical facilities and make provision for the care of servicemen and veterans, as it has done, it cannot, at the same time, be expected to undertake reimbursement of such personnel when they decide, for personal reasons, to obtain care at their own expense from private physicians and hospitals.

Another reason why I am unable to approve this measure is that, as enacted, it is either unfair to the beneficiary or to the Government. This results from the fact that the bill excludes payment of the death gratuity of six months' pay which was originally claimed by the beneficiary but recognizes and authorizes the payment of the difference between active duty pay and retired pay for the entire period between the date of the decedent's release from active duty and the date of his death. It is obviously inconsistent to exclude the one and recognize the other. If the decedent is to be considered on active duty for the entire period in question for pay purposes, he certainly should be so considered with respect to the payment of the death gratuity. On the other hand, if his active duty is considered to have ended prior to the date of his death, then it is equally obvious an adjustment should be made in the pay differential award. In all fairness, it would appear that this inconsistency should be resolved one way or the other.

It should be stressed that notwithstanding disapproval of the bill, the beneficiary can now have her claim settled administratively. Since the time when the case was last reviewed by the Board for the Correction of Naval Records, legislation has been enacted which permits administrative settlement of claims based on changes in records made by the Board. Reconsideration of the beneficiary's claim under such legislation would result in an award which, I am confident, will be equitable from the standpoint of both the beneficiary and the government. In this connection I should like to express my belief that the Board should take into account, in its reconsideration of the case, the possibility that had it been discovered prior to his release from active duty medical treatment of the decedent's condition might very well have led to his retention on active duty until the date of his death.

DWIGHT D. EISENHOWER

NOTE: This memorandum was released at Lowry Air Force Base, Denver, Colo.

242 ¶ Memorandum of Disapproval of Bill for the Relief of E. S. Berney. *September* 1, 1954

I HAVE WITHHELD my approval from S. 46, entitled "For the relief of E. S. Berney."

This bill would pay to E. S. Berney the sum of $4,750 as compensation for damages allegedly sustained by him as a result of certain representations made by a representative of the Navy during World War II.

It appears that in the summer of 1943 a representative of the Navy discussed with the beneficiary the potential use of his Nevada ranch and certain adjoining ones as a bombing range. Although the evidence on this point is conflicting, it appears that such representative indicated that he expected the Navy to begin operations that fall and that, prior to the beginning of such operations, all livestock would have to be removed from the land. The beneficiary alleges that on the basis of this information he disposed of his cattle and other property and vacated his ranch early in the fall. It developed, however, that the Navy did not need or begin to use his land until the following spring.

In subsequent condemnation proceedings, the Court refused to recognize any damages occurring prior to the time when the Navy began using the land in question in the spring of 1944. On this premise the Court awarded the beneficiary $766.67 for damages occurring after use by the Navy began. The present bill was designed to afford compensation for damages which were excluded by the Court and which the beneficiary alleges were due to the premature vacation of his land.

Conceding the facts in this case to be as stated by the beneficiary, it still does not follow that he is entitled to the award proposed here. It has not been established that the damages allegedly sustained by the beneficiary were due to a reasonable reliance upon the representations of the Navy representative. There appears to have been no such reliance on the part of other ranch owners whose land was taken under similar circumstances and whose statements appear in the Committee reports in support of some aspects of the beneficiary's claim.

In addition, there appears to be confusion as to the basis for measuring the damages which the beneficiary allegedly sustained. He made an unverified claim of damages in the amount of $12,000. Part of the damages so claimed are covered by the $766.67 condemnation award. The Congress reduced the claim to $4,750, with no indication as to how this sum was arrived at.

From the foregoing, it seems to me, that the record in this case is inconclusive both with respect to the merits of the beneficiary's claim and as to the damages which he may have sustained. These uncertainties compel me to withhold my approval from this bill.

I would, however, be willing to approve legislation which would permit adjudication of the case by the appropriate District Court. Such legislation should authorize the payment to the beneficiary of such damages as the Court might determine to be reasonably attributable to his reliance upon the alleged representations made to him by the Navy representative. I believe that only by such means can the rather obscure elements of this case be considered and resolved in a manner fair to both the Government and the beneficiary.

DWIGHT D. EISENHOWER

NOTE: This memorandum was released at Lowry Air Force Base, Denver, Colo.

243 ¶ Memorandum of Disapproval of Bill Concerning Claims Arising as a Result of Construction of Elephant Butte Dam. *September 1, 1954*

I HAVE WITHHELD my approval from S. 417, a bill "Conferring jurisdiction upon the United States District Court for the District of New Mexico, to hear, determine, and render judgment upon certain claims arising as a result of the construction by the United States of Elephant Butte Dam on the Rio Grande."

Under S. 417, jurisdiction would be vested, notwithstanding any statute of limitations or lapse of time, in the United States District Court for the District of New Mexico, "to hear, determine, and render judgment upon any claim against the United States for compensation for the taking of or for damage to real or personal property as a result of the construction by the United States of Elephant Butte Dam on the Rio Grande."

The bill does not identify the persons to whom it would open the doors of the district court. It does not identify the date or dates on which the alleged taking of property or damage occurred. It does not identify the events which might be alleged to have caused the damage or the taking. Its only requirement is that suit be filed within two years from the date of enactment of the bill.

Construction of Elephant Butte dam was commenced by the Interior Department in 1912. Approval of the bill would thus be an open invitation to anyone who believes that he has, at any time over the last 42 years, been injured in his property by the construction of this dam to bring the United States into court, no matter how stale his claim may be.

It appears that the cases around which the hearings on the bill principally turned are those of a number of persons who believe that the existence of the dam, taken in conjunction with the severe floods that descended the Rio Grande Valley in 1929, resulted in the permanent seeping or swamping, from and after that year, of their lands in the neighborhood of the now abandoned town of San Marcial. I am aware of no showing, however, that these landowners did not have an adequate opportunity to pursue their legal remedies within the period prescribed by general law or that there were sound reasons for their failure to do so. Still less am I aware of any reasons for including within the coverage of the bill not only these landowners, but also all others who, regardless of time, attribute a damaging or destruction of their property to the construction of Elephant Butte dam.

The very purpose of a statute of limitations—whether it relates to suits between private citizens or to suits brought against the Government—is to avoid stale claims and to procure a reasonably prompt initiation of judicial action before records are lost or scattered, memories grow dim, and witnesses die or become unavailable. To say this is not to say that compliance with the statute must be insisted upon in cases where its waiver would avoid a clear inequity. The instant bill, however, is not in this exceptional category. On the contrary, the controversies with which it deals necessarily involve the resolution of questions of fact, of which some, at least, would require oral testimony from persons familiar with conditions as they were at the time when the claims originally arose. Thus, the nature of the claims here involved emphasizes the justice and wisdom of the general rule. Against this background, nothing in the terms or history of S. 417 of which I am informed offers any sound ground for the departure from existing law which the bill would sanction.

Beyond these considerations there is, in my judgment, no more merit to waiving the statute of limitations in order to permit the trying of cases which may range over all the 40-odd years of Elephant Butte history than there would be in the case of any other Federal river-control structure. In other words, I am seriously concerned that an exception as broad as that which S. 417 proposes to make in the case of Elephant Butte would be a precedent for attempts to secure similarly over-generous legislation in the case of every other Federal river-control structure that anyone believes has caused him harm, regardless of how long ago the harm occurred.

DWIGHT D. EISENHOWER

NOTE: This memorandum was released at Lowry Air Force Base, Denver, Colo.

244 ¶ Memorandum of Disapproval of Bill Concerning a Claim of the Cuban-American Sugar Company. *September* 1, 1954

I AM WITHHOLDING my approval from S. 3304, which would confer jurisdiction upon the Court of Claims of the United States to consider and render judgment on the claim of Cuban-American Sugar Company against the United States.

The problem at the root of the lawsuit and the private relief bills involves the company's World War I excess profits taxes for the year 1917. The specific facts in this 34 year old controversy are set forth fully in the report of the Senate Judiciary Committee (S. Rept. 1963, 83d Cong., 2d sess.). Basically, the taxpayer, for the year 1917, computed its excess profits tax liability on the invested capital method. Some years thereafter, it felt that its tax liability was excessive and requested the Commissioner to compute the tax under the relief provisions of the law. When this was done, additional taxes were found to be due, and were paid. Several years later, in 1927, a claim for refund was filed on the ground that the tax computation by the relief method was erroneous. This claim was rejected on March 15, 1933, although later that year the taxpayer attempted to amend it, claiming that the invested capital method should be used. This method had been used in a settlement of the years 1918, 1919, and 1920, controversy with respect to which had been going on concurrently. The claim for refund filed in 1933 was rejected on the grounds it was not filed within the statutory period.

The over-all effect of the legislation would be to direct the Court of Claims to determine the 1917 liability of the taxpayer by applying the invested capital method used in settling the years 1918, 1919, and 1920 before the Board of Tax Appeals (even though section 3 of the enrolled enactment states that nothing in the Act is to be construed as an inference of liability on the part of the United States) since, as the Committee Report indicates, there is no question but that the taxpayer's taxes were overpaid.

Since the bill grants relief from the operation of the statute of limitation, special equitable circumstances should appear which require that this taxpayer be singled out for special relief. It is difficult to find such circumstances in this case. Basically, the Senate Report urges that the taxpayer was denied a proper hearing by the Commissioner with respect to this claim. Yet, as the Senate Committee Report itself indicates, both prior to 1921, and after 1927, the taxpayer and the Commissioner's representatives had numerous conferences with respect to the taxpayer's 1917 liability. It would have served no purpose to hold further conferences in 1933 on a refund claim which was filed after the statute had run and based on another method of computation.

It is also suggested that the Bureau of Internal Revenue and the taxpayer "agreed" to postpone any action on the 1927 claim for refund until the 1918, 1919, and 1920 cases were determined.

No valid evidence appears that there was such an "agreement". Indeed, the only information regarding any such discussion is, as the Court of Claims stated in a decision rendered in 1939 on this matter and involving this taxpayer, that a representative of the taxpayer had written a letter to the Bureau "purporting to confirm a conversation" with a representative of the Bureau that further conferences on the year 1917 were to be indefinitely postponed for the reason that nothing further could be done regarding the special assessment question until such question had been settled by the Bureau or the Board of Tax Appeals. This unilateral statement not only does not seem adequate evidence of such an agreement but illustrates the desirability of a statute of limitations which disposes of stale claims and the necessity for retaining or securing evidence with respect thereto.

Finally, the bill requires the Court of Claims to use a specific method of computing invested capital (assuming the taxpayer has overpaid his taxes), to be based upon an amount arrived at in settling the controversy before the Board of Tax Appeals for the years 1918 through 1920. The year 1917 was not involved in that settlement, nor, as the Court of Claims indicated in its 1939 decision, "does the action taken with respect to subsequent years constitute conclusive proof as to 1917". Even assuming the desirability of granting jurisdiction to the Court of Claims for this year, it does not seem desirable to preclude the Court from determining the correct tax liability for the year.

Since the proposed legislation would be discriminatory and would single out a particular taxpayer for relief from the statute of limitations without adequate reason therefor, and since it would preclude the Court of Claims from determining the true tax liability, I feel constrained to withhold my approval of S. 3304.

DWIGHT D. EISENHOWER

NOTE: This memorandum was released at Lowry Air Force Base, Denver, Colo.

245 ¶ Memorandum of Disapproval of Bill for the Relief of Carl Piowaty and W. J. Piowaty. *September 2, 1954*

I HAVE WITHHELD my approval from H.R. 1665, "For the relief of Carl Piowaty and W. J. Piowaty."

This bill authorizes and directs the Secretary of the Treasury to pay to Carl Piowaty and W. J. Piowaty the sum of $4,450 in full settlement of their claim against the United States for war-crop advances made to them by the Regional Agricultural Credit Corporation prior to April 16, 1943.

The claims of the United States against these two persons and their claims against the United States have been adjudicated in the courts where both sides were afforded an opportunity to present all pertinent evidence on the issues involved. The case was tried before a jury in the Circuit Court of Orange County, Florida, on May 22 and 23, 1947, and a judgment was obtained against both Carl Piowaty and W. J. Piowaty for the full amount they owed. They appealed the verdict to the Supreme Court of Florida where the lower court's judgment was sustained on February 13, 1948. Appeal for a rehearing was thereafter denied.

In 1950, W. J. Piowaty and his wife instituted an action in the Circuit Court of Orange County, Florida, seeking a declaratory judgment relieving their real property from the lien of the judgment. That suit was dismissed on motion of the United States. In 1951, suit was filed by the United States against Carl Piowaty, W. J. Piowaty and the Globe Indemnity Company on the bonds which were posted when the appeal was taken to the Supreme Court of Florida. Carl Piowaty and W. J. Piowaty filed an answer in that suit, but on motion for summary judgment, judgment was rendered against all the defendants in favor of the United States on October 29, 1952.

In the light of this history of repeated judicial review, I cannot agree that Carl Piowaty and W. J. Piowaty should be given the special consideration and relief which the bill would provide.

DWIGHT D. EISENHOWER

NOTE: This memorandum was released at Lowry Air Force Base, Denver, Colo.

246 ¶ Memorandum of Disapproval of Bill To Establish the Finality of Contracts Between the Government and Common Carriers. *September 2*, 1954

I HAVE WITHHELD my approval of S. 906, "To establish the finality of contracts between the Government and common carriers of passengers and freight subject to the Interstate Commerce Act."

This legislation provides that rates established under the provisions of Section 22 of the Interstate Commerce Act, when accepted or agreed to by the Secretary of Defense, the Secretary of Agriculture, or the Administrator of General Services, or by any official or employee to whom the authority is delegated by them, shall be conclusively presumed to be just, reasonable, and otherwise lawful, and shall not be subject to attack, or reparation, after one hundred and eighty days, or two years in the case of contracts entered into during a national emergency declared by Congress, after the date of acceptance or agreement upon any grounds except actual fraud or deceit, or clerical mistake.

The determination of what is a just, reasonable, or otherwise lawful rate on interstate shipments is now vested in the Interstate Commerce Commission. All shippers, including the Government, are bound as a matter of contract to pay the agreed rate, whether it be in the form of a tariff rate or a Section 22 Quotation. This contractual obligation is subject, however, to an overriding right of the shipper to appeal to the Interstate Commerce Commission to determine whether the agreed rate is lawful. The statute of limitations for such action in the present law is two years. This Act would require the Government to determine the lawfulness of the rate, with finality, and through agencies other than the Interstate Commerce Commission, within one hundred and eighty days at ordinary times, or within two years during a national emergency declared by Congress. Whereas the commercial shipper could contest the rate while it is in effect, the Government would apparently be required to cancel or refuse the rate and pay higher charges during any test of the lawfulness of the rate.

I am therefore unable to approve this legislation, which relegates the Government in its role as a user of transportation services to a position inferior to that of the general shipping public and restricts its access to the Interstate Commerce Commission, the body of experts authorized by Congress to determine the reasonableness of rates.

I see no reason why the Government should not be subject to the same limitations on retroactive review of its freight charges as the commercial shipper. That result could be accomplished equitably by an amendment to Section 16(3) of the Interstate Commerce Act specifying that the Government shall be subject to the two year limitation presently applicable to commercial shippers. The Government would then be on exactly the same basis under that section as all other shippers, and existing inequities in the present rate-making relationships between the Government and the common carriers would be removed. I recommend that such legislation be enacted at the next Session of the Congress.

DWIGHT D. EISENHOWER

NOTE: This memorandum was released at Lowry Air Force Base, Denver, Colo.

247 ¶ Memorandum of Disapproval of Bill for the Relief of T. C. Elliott. *September* 2, 1954

I AM WITHHOLDING my approval from S. 1687, "For the relief of T. C. Elliott."

The purpose of this enactment is to pay to T. C. Elliott of Daytona

Beach, Florida, the sum of $15,000, as compensation for his services in preparing and furnishing certain information to Members of Congress. The bill provides that payment authorized shall be free of Federal income tax.

This bill is faulty for two reasons. First, the exemption of the award from all Federal income taxes is totally unwarranted. Second, it is stated in the enactment that the payment is "compensation for services rendered." The record demonstrates that the sum to be paid is not true compensation, but a monetary award for special services.

The claimant, T. C. Elliott, was an employee of the Federal Government from November 1, 1900, until his retirement, January 31, 1944. During this period of employment Mr. Elliott was an auditor in the Navy Department, the Treasury Department, and the General Accounting Office. In such a position he became conversant with freight rates and transportation problems and furnished data on these subjects on many occasions to individual Members of Congress and to various Committees of the Congress.

It is conceded that Mr. Elliott, in addition to performing his regular duties, rendered valuable service to Members of Congress. His efforts undoubtedly contributed to a saving to the Government of large sums of money, but the record is also clear that these services were rendered by Mr. Elliott voluntarily, after office hours, on his own time, or on his leave time and were completely aside from his official duties or the requirements of his office. Mr. Elliott, like thousands of other devoted Government employees, is to be commended for the unselfish manner in which he made his knowledge of freight rates available to others.

Each year there accrue to the Government the beneficial results of extraordinary services rendered by interested private citizens and organizations who volunteer much useful information and experience to the Congress, to its individual Members, and to the Executive Branch agencies as well. I do not believe that claims for compensation for such volunteer services should be encouraged. Approval of legislation for that purpose would ratify an irregular and unformalized employment relation, and would also place the Congress and the Executive agencies in an unacceptable and unbusinesslike position. If such services are to be on a regular or recurring or even a sporadic basis, formal arrangements for employment should be made. There are numerous alternatives. A regular full-time or part-time appointment, appointment as a consultant at a per diem or an hourly rate, and performance of work by contract are the most common. If the service is performed outside of a formal employment relationship, whatever recognition may be given to it should not be considered compensation.

I do not want my action in withholding approval of this bill to be construed as derogation of Mr. Elliott's services or as criticism of recognition by the Congress of special services afforded to its members. While I cannot approve the bill in its present form for the reasons given above, I shall be glad to approve a bill which is by its terms an extraordinary monetary award for special service and which removes the tax-free status of the award.

DWIGHT D. EISENHOWER

NOTE: This memorandum was released at Lowry Air Force Base, Denver, Colo.

248 ¶ Memorandum of Disapproval of Bill Relating to the Labeling of Packages Containing Foreign-Produced Trout. *September* 2, 1954

I AM WITHHOLDING my approval from S. 2033, "Relating to the labeling of packages containing foreign-produced trout sold in the United States, and requiring certain information to appear in public eating places serving such trout."

The bill would amend the Federal Food, Drug, and Cosmetic Act by making its criminal sanctions—imprisonment up to 3 years or a fine up to $1,000, or both—and certain civil sanctions applicable to the sale, offering for sale, possessing for sale, or serving of foreign-produced trout in violation of special provisions which the bill would add to the Act with respect to such trout, except a certain species of lake trout largely imported from Canada. (These special requirements would be in addition to any of the other requirements of the Act and to any applicable requirements of State law.)

These special requirements—none of them applicable to domestic trout—are as follows:

1. Foreign-produced trout would have to be packaged and, if the package is broken while held for sale, each unit for sale consisting of one or more trout would have to be in a separate package.

2. Each such package would have to be clearly and conspicuously stamped or labeled, in type or lettering of specified size, with the word "trout" preceded by the name of the country in which such trout was produced.

3. It would be unlawful for any restaurant or other public eating place to possess, in a form ready for serving, any foreign-produced trout unless the restaurant or eating place displayed prominently and conspicuously a notice stating that "———— trout is served in this restaurant," with the name of the country or origin inserted in the blank space.

According to the Committee reports, the bill has the three-fold purpose of (1) protecting the public and consumer against deceptive and unfair acts and practices by requiring truthful disclosure of the origin of the trout being sold, (2) protecting our domestic trout producers against unfair competition from foreign producers of trout, and (3) protecting our source of supply for stocking the streams of our Nation with game trout.

It is claimed that in recent years certain merchants and restaurants have indulged in the practice of serving imported trout to restaurant patrons and other consumers as Rocky Mountain trout, Rocky Mountain rainbow trout, or under other descriptive names which, to the consumer, indicate their domestic origin. If domestic trout producers are deprived of this market, it is feared that they may be unable to continue their other important function of supplying eggs and fingerlings for restocking our streams for the sportsman-angler.

Fraud and deception in the marketing or serving of food or any other product cannot, of course, be condoned. I am convinced, however, that to the extent that the provisions and sanctions of the bill properly involve the Federal functions, they are unnecessary to prevent fraud and deception. The Tariff Act and the Federal Food, Drug, and Cosmetic Act already provide for necessary labeling of imported products. Furthermore, the provisions of S. 2033 are discriminatory and oppressive against foreign trade, and to a very substantial extent they would invade a field of regulation and enforcement which I believe should be left to the States and localities. Finally, the costs of enforcement would be out of all proportion to funds available to the Food and Drug Administration for vital functions affecting the health of the American people.

DWIGHT D. EISENHOWER

NOTE: This memorandum was released at Lowry Air Force Base, Denver, Colo.

249 ¶ Statement by the President Upon Signing the River and Harbor Act and the Flood Control Act of 1954. *September 3, 1954*

BECAUSE its enactment strengthens our control and use of our water resources, I am very happy to approve this bill, H.R. 9859, which authorizes 179 projects for navigation, beach erosion prevention, flood control, and related purposes.

These projects are new or are modifications of projects previously authorized. Their cost to the Federal Government will approximate $1,126,553,814, of which the Act authorizes $1,072,351,814 to be appropriated.

In the development of the nation's water resources, I believe that the Federal role should be cooperative, not preemptive—that the cost of such development should be shared by the Federal Government with the States, local governments and private interests. I believe also that—to the greatest possible extent—those directly benefiting from resource development should be responsible for it and pay for it.

That some of these projects will have inadequate local and State participation is, therefore, very unfortunate, as also is the fact that some flood control reservoirs protecting specific, well-defined localities will have *no* local participation as now authorized.

It is heartening, however, that local participation is prescribed for several flood control reservoirs and that local contributions for such benefits are required in many other projects for navigation and flood protection. My requests for appropriations authorized by this Act will give precedence to projects in whose costs local interests are required appropriately to share.

Section 202 of the Act declares it to be the policy of the Congress that:

"No project or any modification not authorized, of a project for flood control or rivers and harbors, shall be authorized by the Congress unless a report for such project or modification has been previously submitted by the Chief of Engineers, United States Army, in conformity with existing law."

Despite this section, directly conflicting provisions of the same Act authorize eight projects costing $21,331,900. Until reports on these projects have been completed and data essential to their evaluation is available, I will not request appropriations to start their construction.

Aside from these specific deficiencies, most projects authorized by this Act are basically sound, and I am glad to give this important legislation my approval.

NOTE: The River and Harbor Act of 1954 is title I of Public Law 780, 83d Congress (68 Stat. 1248). The Flood Control Act of 1954 is title II of the same public law. The statement was released at Lowry Air Force Base, Denver, Colo.

250 ¶ Statement by the President Upon Signing Bill Making Available Special Nonquota Immigrant Visas to Skilled Alien Sheepherders. *September 3, 1954*

I HAVE TODAY approved S. 2862. This is one of a series of bills enacted by the Congress over the years to provide relief of the sheep raising industry by making available special nonquota immigrant visas to skilled alien sheepherders.

Although this was the sole purpose of the bill when first introduced, it was so amended as to make this measure the first major adjustment of standards for permanent admission to the United States since enactment of the Immigration and Nationality Act of 1952.

I am deeply gratified that the Congress has recognized the need for a more flexible approach to our immigration problems and has taken this first step toward correcting injustices inherent in the system.

NOTE: As enacted, S. 2862 is Public Law 770, 83d Congress (68 Stat. 1145). The statement was released at Lowry Air Force Base, Denver, Colo.

251 ¶ Memorandum of Disapproval of Bill for the Relief of the Trust Association of H. Kempner. *September 3, 1954*

I HAVE WITHHELD my approval from H.R. 951, "For the relief of the Trust Association of H. Kempner."

This bill would provide an indirect means for payment of approximately one million dollars by the United States for certain peacetime commercial losses of the Kempner Trust Association. To accomplish this purpose the bill would require the Court of Claims to determine the amount that the Trust Association lost as a result of cotton sales made to certain private business firms in Germany during 1923 and 1924. The bill would then require that the Court of Claims determine how much of the property seized during World War I by the United States from a German firm wholly unconnected with Kempner or the cotton sales—Germann and Company—had been lost through improper administration by the Alien Property Custodian. The determined amount of the loss of the Germann and Company vested property would be then withdrawn from the War Claims Fund and used to compensate the Kempner Trust Association to the extent of its loss.

Following World War I the Kempner Trust Association through subsidiary corporations entered into contracts for the sale of cotton with a number of German textile manufacturers for future delivery. A fall in cotton prices before delivery led the German firms to breach their contracts with the Association. The amounts payable by the German debtors on account of the breaches of contract, as determined by judgments and negotiated settlements, could not be paid through the subsequent period before World War II because of German foreign exchange controls, and, as a result, the Trust Association lost money on the transactions. These losses would be paid by the United States if this bill were enacted although it is clear that the United States bears no moral or legal liability for the transactions which resulted in the losses in question.

Moreover, the method of payment proposed by the bill raises serious questions of propriety. The matter involving Germann and Company has no relationship to the claim which the Kempner Trust Association seeks to have paid. During World War I the Alien Property Custodian had seized the property of Germann and Company, a firm in the Philippines, as enemy property. When the property was returned to Germann and Company, following enactment of legislation authorizing return of seized property after World War I, it was claimed that the firm's assets had been depleted by approximately one million dollars during the period of its administration by the Alien Property Custodian through allegedly improper payments. The Treaty of Berlin which terminated World War I between the United States and Germany, however, precludes

Germann and Company from asserting any claim against the United States on account of the seizure of its property or any losses during the period it was held by the United States.   There is therefore no valid claim to be asserted by Germann and Company as the basis for the proposed determination by the Court of Claims.   Even if such a claim existed, however, the proposed payment of its proceeds to the Kempner Trust Association instead of to Germann and Company would not appear to be a proper disposition of the rights of the latter company.

Furthermore, the bill confers upon the United States Court of Claims jurisdiction to sit in judgment upon the acts of the former German government with respect to acts committed in Germany.   I am informed that this would be contrary to a well-recognized principle of international law and practice.

For these reasons, the purpose and method of payment would not appear justified.   Moreover, enactment of this bill would establish an undesirable precedent for the assumption by the United States for the commercial losses of American citizens, even where no governmental sponsorship of the commercial venture appeared.   It would also set an undesirable precedent for the use of the German and Japanese assets vested during World War II for commercial losses suffered during peacetime in lieu of their present use through the War Claims fund as the source of payment of the wartime personal injury damages suffered by American nationals.

Accordingly, I am constrained to withhold my approval from the bill.

DWIGHT D. EISENHOWER

NOTE: This memorandum was released at Lowry Air Force Base, Denver, Colo.

252 ¶ Memorandum of Disapproval of Bill Providing for a Commission To Regulate Public Transportation of Passengers in the Washington Area. *September 3, 1954*

I HAVE WITHHELD my approval from H.R. 2236, entitled "An Act to provide for a Commission to regulate the public transportation of passengers by motor vehicle and street railroad within the metropolitan area of Washington, District of Columbia, and for the establishment of a Metropolitan Washington Commission."

Title I of this enactment would establish a Washington Metropolitan Area Transit Commission to regulate public transportation by bus, streetcar and taxicab in the District of Columbia and the counties of Montgomery and Prince Georges in the State of Maryland. The bill would grant to the proposed new Commission, in strengthened form, most of the powers now separately exercised in this regard by the Interstate Commerce Commission and the Public Utilities Commissions of the State of Maryland and the District of Columbia.

Title II of the bill would create a temporary Metropolitan Washington Commission to study, investigate, and make recommendations with regard to certain aspects of the Washington metropolitan area transportation problem.

The regulation of public transportation in the greater Washington area must contend with the growth of an integral economic community spreading far beyond the boundaries of the District of Columbia to include Montgomery and Prince Georges Counties in Maryland and Arlington and Fairfax Counties and the cities of Alexandria and Falls Church in Virginia. Within this community, the daily travel of persons back and forth across State lines has reached dimensions with which present facilities cannot cope. Under these circumstances, it is understandable that the present division of responsibility for regulation among four different agencies no longer meets the needs of the area. This division of responsibility has contributed, as it could not help but do, to the development of an inadequate system of public transportation. The situation plainly requires the unification of regulatory authorities over public transportation throughout the metropolitan area.

The present enactment, however, falls substantially short of this objective. Its failure to include the Virginia segment of the metropolitan area within the jurisdiction of the proposed Commission is a fundamental deficiency. Through this omission of an integral and important part of the greater economic community, a system of fragmented and divided regulatory authority is continued. What is worse, the Federal Government is placed in the position of treating the carriers and persons within one segment of the area on a different and discriminatory basis from those in the remainder of the area. In the absence of any substantial grounds for this differentiation, the measure is unacceptable even as a temporary expedient.

This bill is also unsatisfactory because it extends, without sufficient safeguards, the authority of the Federal Government to matters that have, hitherto, been considered as primarily the concern of the District of Columbia and of the States. The problem is difficult because the urgency of need and the extent of Federal interest in the Nation's Capital both argue for unification of regulatory authorities under Federal auspices, at least for the time being. However, in any such arrangement means must be found to give adequate recognition to the rights and responsibilities of the District and of the States involved. Specifically, provision should be made to enable the States of Maryland and Virginia and the District of Columbia eventually to make arrangements for the exercise of this function under joint responsibility. In this regard, it would appear desirable to explore the feasibility of utilizing an interstate compact or other cooperative arrangement in which the Federal Government would participate and the Federal interest would be fully protected. In addition, every effort should be made to minimize the impact of any new Commission upon the internal affairs of the District of Columbia.

With respect to Title II of the enactment, I agree that further study of metropolitan transportation problems is desirable. The primary mission assigned to the Commission is related directly to highway, bridge and traffic problems. In emphasizing this role rather than consideration of mass transit problems, the bill unnecessarily complicates relationships with the National Capital Planning Commission and the National Capital Regional Planning Council. I believe that further consideration by the Congress will result in a more orderly allocation of responsibilities between the Commission and these existing planning agencies. Title II also establishes undesirable limitations governing the appointment and qualification of members of the Commission.

I hope that the 84th Congress will promptly enact a measure to unify regulatory authorities over public transportation and provide for a further transit study with adequate coverage and recognition of State and District responsibilities. Since Title I of this bill would not have become fully effective until July 1, 1955, there need be no significant loss of time in obtaining its objectives. Similarly, time did not permit the Congress to provide funds for Title II before adjournment. Therefore, since an appropriation cannot be made until after the Congress convenes in January, little time, if any, need be lost in the studies which a revised Title II would encompass.

Dwight D. Eisenhower

NOTE: This memorandum was released at Lowry Air Force Base, Denver, Colo.

253　¶ Memorandum of Disapproval of Bill Permitting Increased Water Diversion From Lake Michigan.　*September* 3, 1954

I HAVE WITHHELD my approval of H.R. 3300, "To authorize the State of Illinois and the Sanitary District of Chicago, under the direction of the Secretary of the Army, to help control the lake level of Lake Michigan by diverting water from Lake Michigan into the Illinois waterway."

The bill would authorize the State of Illinois and the Sanitary District of Chicago, under the supervision and direction of the Secretary of the Army, to withdraw from Lake Michigan, in addition to all domestic pumpage, a total annual average of 2,500 cubic feet of water per second into the Illinois waterway for a period of three years. This diversion would be 1,000 cubic feet per second more than is presently permitted under a decree of the Supreme Court of the United States dated April 21, 1930. The bill also would direct the Secretary of the Army to study the effect in the improvement in conditions in the Illinois waterway by reason of the increased diversion, and to report to the Congress as to the results of the study on or before January 31, 1957, with his recommendations as to continuance of the increased diversion authorized.

The bill specifies that the diversion would be authorized in order to regulate and promote commerce, to protect, improve, and promote navigation in the Illinois waterway and Mississippi Valley, to help control the lake level, to afford protection to property and shores along the Great Lakes, and to provide for a navigable Illinois waterway. No mention is made of possible improvement of sanitary conditions or increase in hydroelectric power generation on the waterway.

I am unable to approve the bill because (1) existing diversions are adequate for navigation on the Illinois waterway and Mississippi River, (2) all methods of control of Lake levels and protection of property on the Great Lakes should be considered before arbitrarily proceeding with the proposed increased diversion, (3) the diversions are authorized without reference to negotiations with Canada, and (4) the legitimate interests of other States affected by the diversion may be adversely affected. I wish to comment briefly on each of these points.

I understand that waterborne traffic on the Illinois waterway has grown in the last twenty years from 200,000 tons to 16,000,000 tons annually. The Corps of Engineers advises, however, that the existing diversions of water are adequate for navigation purposes in the Illinois waterway and the Mississippi River. Surveys are now under way by the International Joint Commission and the Corps of Engineers to determine the best methods of obtaining improved control of the levels of the Great Lakes and of preventing recurrence of damage along their shores. Reasonable opportunity to complete these surveys should be afforded before legislative action is undertaken.

The diversion of waters into and out of the Great Lakes has historically been the subject of negotiations with Canada. To proceed unilaterally in the manner proposed in H.R. 3300 is not wise policy. It would be the kind of action to which we would object if taken by one of our neighbors. The Canadian Government protested the proposed authorization when it was under consideration by the Congress, and has continued its objection to this bill in a Note to the Department of State dated August 24, 1954. It seems to me that the additional diversion is not of such national importance as to justify action without regard to the views of Canada.

Finally, as is clear from the report of the Senate Committee, a major purpose of the proposal to divert additional water from Lake Michigan into the Illinois waterway is to determine whether the increased flow will improve existing adverse sanitation conditions. The waters of Lake Michigan are interstate in character. It would seem to me that a diversion for the purposes of one State alone should be authorized only after general agreement has been reached among all the affected States. Officials of several States adjoining the Great Lakes, other than Illinois, have protested approval of the bill as being contrary to their interests and not in accord with the diversion authorized under the 1930 decree of the Supreme Court. Under all of these circumstances, I have felt that the bill should not be approved.

DWIGHT D. EISENHOWER

NOTE: This memorandum was released at Lowry Air Force Base, Denver, Colo.

254 ¶ Memorandum of Disapproval of Bill To Revise and Codify the Laws Relating to Food, Drugs, and Cosmetics. *September 3, 1954*

I HAVE WITHHELD my approval from H.R. 9728, "To revise, codify, and enact into law, title 21 of the United States Code, entitled 'Food, Drugs, and Cosmetics.'"

The legislative history of this measure indicates that it was enacted in the view that existing law would not be substantially changed by the bill or that no changes in existing law would be made which would not meet with substantially unanimous approval.

Notwithstanding this, the bill makes one very important substantive change and casts serious doubts on the status and interpretation of other statutory provisions. The most important change is the deletion from the multiple seizure powers of the present law the authority which the Food and Drug Administration has had for a number of years to make more than one seizure of food, drugs, and cosmetics, where they bear identical labeling which is believed fraudulent or so materially misleading as to injure or damage the purchaser or consumer. In the cases subject to removal of authority made by the bill, the Food and Drug Administration would be able to seize only one shipment of the articles believed to be so misbranded. Such a limitation would make it possible for fraud and material deception to continue unabated until the validity of the labeling involved in the seizure case is definitely settled by the courts.

The enactment also contains a new substantive provision affecting the administration of the Federal Food, Drug, and Cosmetic Act, the meaning of which is very uncertain, namely, that the Administrative Procedure Act "shall continue to apply to all activities of the Food and Drug Administration." The Administrative Procedure Act already applies to both rule-making and adjudication under this regulatory statute, as it does to other Acts of Congress not expressly excepted. The Federal courts, I am informed, have discussed on several occasions the relationship of these two enactments. The new language, unless it should be regarded as mere surplusage, might be held to effect basic changes in existing procedures, thereby placing the Food and Drug Administration under requirements not applicable to any other Federal agency. Such a change in the scope of the Administrative Procedure Act should not be adopted without full consideration.

The interest of the consumer public is the principal objective of the Federal Food, Drug, and Cosmetic Act. I believe that substantive changes which may seriously affect the administration of this law should not be placed in the statute books without extending to the responsible enforcement agency, the great industries affected, and the consumer public, the full opportunities for hearing and discussion afforded by the usual operation of the legislative process both in the Committees and in both Houses of the Congress.

Finally, the enactment, through oversight, may nullify the provisions of legislation relating to the importation of animals and poultry into the Virgin Islands, approved on July 22 of this year (P.L. 517). The enrolled measure apparently does not take into consideration the amendments to the Organic Act of the Virgin Islands which were made by that Act. Here again the adverse effects would be serious.

DWIGHT D. EISENHOWER

NOTE: This memorandum was released at Lowry Air Force Base, Denver, Colo.

255 ¶ Statement by the President on Highway Safety During the Labor Day Weekend. *September 3, 1954*

A YEAR AGO, at this time, four hundred and five men, women and children, along with millions of other Americans, were looking forward to summer's last big outing—the Labor Day weekend. Three days later, these 405 were dead.

They died in holiday traffic accidents just as similar accidents had taken 480 lives the year before, and 461 the year before that.

I have just been given a grim forecast. The experts say that, over this Labor Day weekend, before our people go back to work on Tuesday, 390 people will lose their lives in this needless way.

Do we have to let this happen? Have we reached the point where we are helpless in the face of a prediction that almost four hundred of us will kill ourselves or someone else over a weekend?

To everyone who gets behind a steering wheel during the Labor Day weekend I make this appeal:

Let's be careful this weekend. Let's stay alert. Let's remember the simple rules of the road. Let's fool the experts. Let's all be alive next Tuesday.

NOTE: This statement was released at Lowry Air Force Base, Denver, Colo.

256 ¶ Remarks at the Airport, Grand Junction, Colorado. *September* 4, 1954

Governor Thornton, members of this distinguished audience:

Your Governor told you the truth when he said this was not a speaking tour. In fact, I never get over being astonished when I look out the porthole of my plane and see a crowd gathering when I was traveling for some purpose other than what is called politicking.

Nevertheless, the first word I want to bring to you is this: a word of profound gratitude for the cordiality you have shown me—first by coming here, and then in the warmth of your smiles.

No American can have any greater honor than to know that other Americans would gather to greet him and to pay him the honor of a smile, a cheery hello, and to know and to be accepted among them as one of them. So, I am extremely grateful; that I assure you.

Now this is, for me, a trip to learn something. I am not out today to do any informing on my own. I am trying to absorb. I have on the plane with me members of the Reclamation Bureau, representatives from your own State, and engineers from the region. I have the Secretary of Agriculture and the Secretary of the Interior.

We are just trying to learn what it is that we can do, down in Washington, to be helpful in this great job that our citizens are doing, in reclamation, in developing the resources of our country.

We do not, as we see it, want to be the great bosses of America. We want to be the servant, the agent that will help our people make for themselves the happiest possible life.

When that calls for Federal direction, or engineering skill, or finances—all right, let's put it in and do it cheerfully, quickly, and promptly. But, let's not make Washington the master of any free American, either through unnecessary direct intervention in his business, or through the indirect method of getting control of all of the power and other resources that he needs in order to make a living.

Now it is in that spirit that we are going around. We are doing our best to learn. And of course, as I stop to think of it, I couldn't possibly witness, I couldn't possibly see the greatest of the resources of this region, unless I did have the opportunity you have given me, to see some of the people—a representative group. Because, after all, it is Americans—it is the American spirit, American faith, American courage, and American stamina that have been the greatest resource of this Nation since the first landing in Virginia.

And so again, I repeat my pride in meeting you, my determination that the Washington Government is doing everything that is feasible and possible and proper to hasten along the development of these great areas so that our country may be more prosperous, stronger at home, and more secure abroad.

It is difficult indeed—when I get a chance to meet with folk that I have known so long, out in this western region of the United States—difficult indeed for me to find the proper terminal facilities and sit down. Today it is almost compelled upon me to get going, because I have, I believe, a total of a 1,500-mile trip today, with two other stops.

So again, my thanks for coming out, and my very great hope that I will learn something of value on this trip today, and those with me will. Good luck to all of you. Thank you.

NOTE: The President spoke at 8:40 a.m.

257 ¶ Remarks at Natrona Airport, Casper, Wyoming. *September* 4, 1954

Mr. Chairman, Governor Rogers, and my fellow Americans:

I am on a very simple trip today, although of some length, with a group from the Department of the Interior and from Agriculture, and with local officers and representatives of those departments. We are making a circuit through Colorado, touched Utah, into Wyoming, Nebraska, and Kansas, to see if we can learn a little bit more about the great interests of these regions, particularly in the agricultural and reclamation areas.

Now I say that because I want to apologize to any group of Americans such as this, for having no particular or specific message to bring to you. I do thank you most earnestly—most profoundly—for doing me the honor of coming out and giving me a chance to meet some of you once again; because I hope some of you will remember a cold morning, right here on this spot, I think, about 2 years ago, when I stood here with a big crowd under different circumstances.

But I think that then I promised you that, should you send me to Washington, I was going to do my best to pick a Cabinet that would do its best, to pick administrators that would do their best, to look at the United States as a whole, to find out those things that are good for 160 million Americans, not to be swayed too much just by the interests of any one group, any one class, any one section. And it is in pursuance of such promises as those that we are here.

What is good for the agriculture and the agricultural interests of the United States, for the natural resources of the United States, is good for all of us, not only now but extending on into the future. Thus we discharge not only part of our debt to the people of today by having our officials and administrators learn about the needs of people in particular areas and relating them to the needs of the whole nation, but we are likewise—as I see it—doing part of our duty to our children and those yet to come.

All of us who are true Americans are certainly interested in those things. Here in this great livestock-producing area, we have just had the opportunity a few moments ago to fly over some of the great reservoirs, on the way up from the Echo Park dam area, to see those great supplies of water that are helping you stabilize the livestock industry and to become a more prosperous, stable industry in that area.

We don't look upon that as something that is important merely to you. Of course, you must be prosperous, else how are we going to get the money to run the Government? But, unless the United States is prosperous, unless each individual feels that glorious right within himself, to do for himself and his family what he can, to get the spiritual uplift of working as hard as he knows how, for himself, and for his neighbors, then the United States is going backward.

What we are thinking about, therefore, is not merely whether you can have a second car. It is whether you can satisfy the great and proper ambitions that reside within yourselves, the ambitions to make of yourselves a true, fine citizen of this great country—so that all of us may work toward a world peace, so that we may pass on to those who come after us a world that has made at least some little step toward the kind of place, the kind of living in which each of us, each under his own religious faith, in his own belief in America, can make of himself what he should like to be.

The nearer we approach that, the nearer we approach perfection for America. And that is why we are here—trying to learn, not merely to make speeches. Anyway, you know that speeches in themselves are nothing. But if they do help us reveal one to the other something of what we believe in this great country, then indeed they are valuable.

And for myself, the chance to mingle once again with the people that I have known in this western country from babyhood, to say good morning, to see your faces, is a very great privilege.

For one—and there's a number here who can testify to the truth this morning—for one who spends far too much of his time in Washington, this is truly something.

Thank you again for coming out—and goodbye.

NOTE: The President spoke at 10:51 a.m. His opening words "Mr. Chairman" referred to Irvin J. Matthews who was in charge of the reclamation project at Casper, Wyo.

258 ¶ Remarks at the Airport, McCook, Nebraska. *September* 4, 1954

Governor Crosby, distinguished guests, my fellow citizens:

First, permit me to thank each of you for the honor you have paid me in coming out today, to give me a chance to bring a word of greeting, and to meet you face to face.

I spent a long time in the Army, and we had textbooks that told why a commander should go around and visit the people who were doing the actual fighting—this was to inspire the troops. I soon found that for my part I seemed to be different. I went around, all right, but it was because they inspired me. Having met—and meeting—young Americans on the battlefields, I could go back to my own job with much greater dedication, much greater belief, and conviction that I could execute it.

I know of nothing—particularly for one who has to spend a great deal of his time in Washington in an official position—that can take the place of going out and trying again to meet Americans that are making a living and paying taxes, rather than just taking it unto themselves to spend the taxes.

While it is true today that my party and I are here on a special kind of fact-gathering trip, always in any kind of trip it is that need we feel, to get out again and to see Americans in their own homes, and in their own cities, making this country what it is.

Now today we are visiting a number of water conservation projects—reclamation projects—to see if we can get a little firsthand practical education in our phase of helping in this great and necessary development of the western country, indeed of all our country.

Now, we have not come with any idea that in Washington reside all the brains that can determine what should be done in these areas. Indeed, we don't believe that Washington should have the right to interfere too specifically with the lives of any of us, or to lay down the rules and regulations as to how everything should be done in the development of this country.

On the contrary, we believe that the people who are farming the land and using the water, who are developing our natural resources, know a little more about it than the people that just are passing laws concerning it.

So we come out here—legislators, administrative officers, and executives—to find out what do the people believe, what do they think?

And one phase of that thinking is not just alone the use of water, the development of the water power and the irrigating water; it is this: what is the proper relationship between the local farmer, between the local area, the State, and the Federal Government—the proper relationship not only in the provision of, let us say, from Washington, the broad national survey, so that everything fits together, but how do we get together to finance these things, and do things so that each does his proper share, and so that every part of the United States may have the proper use of its own resources, and the proper control over them—responsibility for them?

Where the Federal Government has a function, we want to do it adequately and promptly. We want to help. But we don't want to be bosses. That I should like to make clear, and I should like for you to remember it.

Indeed, I think I might remark in passing that those people who believe that a group of men can be gathered together in Washington— and remember, that's all Government is, just a group of men that you select to perform particular jobs—a group of men, sitting in Washington, to run the affairs of this country in its details better than can the people who are actually doing the work, then we have gone a long, long way away from the kind of country that was given to us by our Founding Fathers, and the kind that we hope to pass on.

Washington is there to help coordinate, to help in every kind of thing that, as Lincoln put it: to help in those things which people cannot do for themselves, or cannot so well do for themselves. And nothing else. And when they go beyond that, somebody out there among you ought to be slapping us down.

I believe that in the course of this 1,500-mile trip today we will have gained a lot of things, not only what I have mentioned before, the opportunity to see you face to face, to get some idea of the way you are feeling, through your people, your representatives sitting on the platform here, what they tell me as we travel from station to station, but the actual study of land, of rivers, and the seeing of the reservoirs and the canyons— where they want to put them—the rivers and the lands they want to irrigate. All that is very helpful, and I assure you that is what we will be taking back.

All this will be done, not with any thought that the Government of the United States is taking care of you. It is merely that the Federal Government is doing its part in trying to be your good partner. We want to be no more. And that I assure you.

Now, we still have a day ahead of us. In fact, we are not going to land there but I am going to fly over my own State of Kansas. I was rather amused by Governor Crosby talking about this being a hot day. He ought to have been raised down in Smoky Hill; we have some heat down there. But anyway, I am going to get to go down around there before my party and I land back in Denver.

With me are representatives of the Agriculture Department, Interior Department, with especially the Reclamation Bureau and the local engineers of the services, local officials of the States, and so on. It is a most informative thing.

Thank you again for coming out. Each of you has done me a very great honor, and I am very proud of it.

Thank you very much. Goodbye.

NOTE: The President spoke at 12:57 p.m.

259 ¶ Statement by the President: Labor Day. *September 4, 1954*

ON THIS DAY all Americans once again give thanks that we live in a country which upholds the high belief that every citizen should have the right to seek freely the work he wants to do. To all the world we have shown the incredible results which can be accomplished in a land where every man can choose the job he wants—any job for which his ability fits him; prepare himself for it; and join freely with his fellow-workers in common effort. A slave state may force its masses to brutish, endless toil. But it can never produce that deep and tremendous surge of might which comes to a nation when each man knows that he is driving a wedge or plowing a furrow or operating a lathe purely because he is a free man, and that to this endeavor he freely sets his hand. In this principle lies a true and joyous strength.   May we recognize it today with a new conviction.

DWIGHT D. EISENHOWER

NOTE: This statement was released at Lowry Air Force Base, Denver, Colo.

260 ¶ Radio and Television Remarks on the Occasion of the Ground-Breaking Ceremony for the Shippingport Atomic Power Plant. *September 6, 1954*

Fellow citizens:

On this Labor Day, 1954, we Americans pause to take special note of the dignity and the worth—and the tremendous accomplishment—of the individual worker in our land.   On this day we salute with special pride the unmatched productivity of our working men and women.   All Americans are grateful for this proof of what free people can achieve.

It is our good fortune, therefore, that on this special day we take a historic step forward, opening for all of us new avenues to constructive employment, to prosperity, to respite from burdensome toil.

For today, at Shippingport, Pennsylvania, we begin building our first atomic power plant of commercial size—a plant expected to produce electricity for 100,000 people.   In thus advancing toward the economic production of electricity by atomic power, mankind comes closer to fulfillment of the ancient dream of a new and a better earth.

But we do not stop with this plant, nor, indeed with our own country's hopes and dreams.   Our many proposals for peaceful use of the atom have so far been cynically blocked in the councils of the world, but we shall proceed onward.   We shall proceed now—under safeguards set forth in our law—to share atomic technology with others of good will.

We have just agreed with a number of other nations to go ahead now with the formation of an international agency which will foster the growth and spread of the new atomic technology for peaceful use. Atomic materials for projects sponsored by this agency will be set aside for that purpose.   We hope that no nation will long stand aloof from the work of this agency.

As these arrangements are being made, we will set up a reactor school to help train representatives of friendly nations in skills needed for their own atomic programs. Discussions also will shortly take place on cooperation with countries planning to build their own research reactors.

We are, moreover, about to negotiate with the Government of Belgium on the building of an atomic power reactor in that country. On Thursday of this week, we begin talks on atomic matters with our friends in Canada. Negotiations with other friendly nations will swiftly follow.

My friends, through such measures as these, and through knowledge we are sure to gain from this new plant we begin today, I am confident that the atom will not be devoted exclusively to the destruction of man, but will be his mighty servant and tireless benefactor.

It is, then, with profound hope and confidence—and with prayer for the future ages of mankind—that I now, by this act, begin construction of America's first commercial-size atomic power plant.

NOTE: The President's words were broadcast over radio and television from station KOA–TV in Denver. At the close of his remarks he set in motion, by remote control, a bulldozer at the Shippingport site.

261   ¶ Statement of Policy, Approved and Issued by the President, on Foreign Trade as Related to Agriculture.   *September* 9, 1954

THE GENERAL foreign economic and trade policy set forth in the President's message to Congress of March 30, 1954, is applicable to and in the general interest of American agriculture. United States farm programs, both short-run and long-run, should be consistent with this policy.

United States agriculture, as well as other segments of the economy, stands to gain from such a sustained policy of expanding world trade, based upon the most productive use in each country of the available labor, natural resources and capital. Therefore, it is in the long-run interest of the American farmer, as well as all Americans, for this country to work with other nations in a mutual effort to expand international trade, and to promote the fuller convertibility of currencies, the freer movement of investment capital, and the interchange of technical and scientific information.

Today, the United States agricultural situation is complicated by two factors on the domestic front: (1) prices of many farm products are not competitive with world prices; and (2) production of certain farm products is badly out of balance with demand, thus creating rapidly mounting surplus stocks which overhang and tend to unsettle both domestic and foreign markets. Both of these factors promise to remain operative for some time. It therefore becomes necessary to reckon with them in any formulation of an agricultural foreign trade policy for the United States.

Consistent with the principles set forth in the President's message of March 30, 1954, it is essential that our agricultural foreign trade policy take into account the position of other countries and that our policy be understood by them.

Today, the magnitude of the United States holdings of many commodities is such as to be capable of demoralizing world commodity markets should a policy of reckless selling abroad be pursued. This potential greatly alarms other countries despite the fact that past behavior of the United States has shown no intention of pursuing a harmful policy.

At the same time, the United States cannot accept the role of limiting its sales in world markets until other countries have disposed of their production. The adjustment of world supply to world demand will require adjustments of production in other countries, as well as the United States.

The capacity of certain areas of the world to produce food and fiber in excess of current market takings presents a basis and a hope for improving living standards around the world—provided ways can be found for improving marketing and distribution systems and enlarging the purchasing power of consumers. This represents a challenge to the nations of the world to develop sound means for utilizing their productive capacity in the improvement of living standards.

1. The world supply and demand situation in agricultural products requires in the interest of the general welfare, an orderly and gradual liquidation of our surpluses. Such a policy, arrived at with the full knowledge of friendly nations, would go far to eliminate fear arising from uncertainty.

2. The United States cannot be satisfied with the position of holding

its own supplies off the market and accumulating surpluses while other countries dispose of their entire production. Accordingly, the United States will offer its products at competitive prices. At the same time, the United States will not use its agricultural surpluses to impair the traditional competitive position of friendly countries by disrupting world prices of agricultural commodities.

3. The United States will seek in cooperation with friendly countries to utilize its agricultural surpluses to increase consumption in those areas where there is demonstrable under-consumption and where practical opportunities for increased consumption exist or can be developed in a constructive manner. The United States will attempt to utilize such opportunities in a manner designed to stimulate economic development in friendly countries and to strengthen their security position.

4. The United States recognizes that the movement of goods in foreign trade is dependent upon the enterprise of private business—foreign and domestic. In implementing these policies with respect to agricultural commodities, the United States Government will seek to assure conditions of commerce permitting the private trader to function effectively.

NOTE: This policy statement was issued in connection with Executive Order 10560 of the same date, entitled "Administration of the Agricultural Trade Development and Assistance Act of 1954" (3 CFR, 1954 Supp., p. 70).

Together with the following letters (Items 262, 263), the policy statement was released at Lowry Air Force Base, Denver, Colo.

262 ❡ Letter to Clarence Francis Requesting Him To Serve as Chairman of Interagency Committee on Agricultural Surplus Disposal. *September 9, 1954*

Dear Mr. Francis:

The Executive Order which I have issued today establishing administrative arrangements for the Agricultural Trade Development and Assistance Act of 1954 provides, as you know, for an Interagency Committee on Agricultural Surplus Disposal with a representative of the White House Office as Chairman.

I request you to assume responsibility for organizing this Committee and to serve as its Chairman.   I shall look to you for advice concerning policy issues that may develop.

In connection with the work of your Committee I shall expect you to be guided by the policy statement concerning foreign trade as related to agriculture which I have approved and issued today.   I regard this document as an important announcement of the philosophy of this Administration with respect to agricultural foreign economic policy.   It should generate confidence both at home and abroad as to our purposes in this vital area of international economic relations.

With best wishes,

Sincerely,

DWIGHT D. EISENHOWER

NOTE: Mr. Francis served as Special Consultant to the President.   See notes to Items 261 and 263.

263   ¶ Letter to Members of Interagency Committee on Agricultural Surplus Disposal. *September 9, 1954*

My dear ————:

I have today issued an Executive order providing for the administration of the Agricultural Trade Development and Assistance Act of 1954. It is the purpose of this letter to further define relationships among the several agencies of the executive branch which will have key responsibilities in assuring successful administration of this program.

The act provides for the use of surplus commodities to further many of our existing domestic and foreign programs, and in some instances, it expands or liberalizes them.   These programs are currently carried on by many agencies of the Government.   Accordingly, it is desirable to place the administration of the new act in those agencies and to make it possible for them to make their proper contribution in connection with the disposition of agricultural surpluses.

The very fact that a number of agencies have a responsibility in one or another aspect of surplus disposition makes effective coordination absolutely essential.   It is therefore directed that a committee, to be known as "The Interagency Committee on Agricultural Surplus Disposal," be established to assist the agencies concerned in bringing into harmonious action, consistent with the over-all policy objectives of this Government, the various agricultural surplus disposal activities vested in them by, or assigned to them pursuant to, the Act. The Committee should be composed of a representative of the White House Office, as Chairman, and one representative of each Government department and agency which is, consonant with law, designated by the Chairman to have representation on the committee. I shall look to the Chairman to advise me concerning policy issues which arise. I shall expect the Secretary of Agriculture to assure the effective coordination of day-to-day operations through appropriate interagency relationships.

The following arrangements are prescribed in order to facilitate the best administration of the Act:

1. Existing pertinent interagency coordination arrangements are to be followed.

2. This program must be carried out in accordance with and in furtherance of our foreign policy objectives. I wish to re-emphasize that the Secretary of State is the officer responsible for advising and assisting me in the formulation and control of foreign policy. I look to him as the channel of authority within the executive branch on foreign policy as I do to the Secretaries of Defense and Treasury in their respective fields.

3. The delegation to the State Department of responsibility for negotiations with foreign governments is intended to give recognition to State Department's central responsibility in this area. Other agencies directly concerned with the substance of the negotiation, however, must continue to carry substantial responsibility in such negotiations. Moreover, it is assumed that these other agencies will conduct day-to-day discussions with representatives of the foreign governments in implementing basic agreements reached with such governments. Such discussions, of course, must be in conformance with the foreign policy responsibilities of the State Department and the chiefs of our diplomatic missions.

4. It is imperative that we continue to coordinate United States programs affecting other nations. For this reason, the accompanying Executive order makes this program subject to my previous instructions with respect to coordination of United States activities in foreign countries. Under those instructions, the chief of the diplomatic mission is the principal officer of the United States in each country and has full responsibility and authority for assuring effective action in that country.

5. In order to coordinate most effectively the various agricultural

surplus disposal programs abroad, I shall expect the Secretary of Agriculture to utilize to the maximum extent practicable the facilities, services and experience of the Foreign Operations Administration.

6. I am requesting the Secretary of Commerce to provide the focal point in the Government for assisting private enterprise with respect to barter transactions referred to in the act. This arrangement would be one more step toward assuring the maximum utilization of private channels in the execution of this program.

7. It is contemplated that the Office of Defense Mobilization shall utilize the facilities and services of the General Services Administration for the purchase and handling of materials under section 104(b) of the act.

In January of this year, I stated in my message on Agriculture that surplus agricultural stocks can be used for constructive purposes that will benefit the people of the United States and our friends abroad. Enactment of this legislation is a major step forward in achieving that broad objective. With effective administration, mobilizing the total resources of Government and private channels of trade, we should make substantial strides towards achieving the above goals.

I have forwarded an identical letter to the other officers of the Government principally concerned with carrying out the Executive order.

Sincerely,

DWIGHT D. EISENHOWER

NOTE: Identical letters were sent to the Secretary of State, the Secretary of the Treasury, the Secretary of Defense, the Secretary of Agriculture, the Secretary of Commerce, the Director of the Foreign Operations Administration, the Director of the Bureau of the Budget, the Director of the Office of Defense Mobilization, the Administrator of General Services, the Chairman of the Board of Governors of the Federal Reserve System, and to Clarence Francis, Special Consultant to the President, who was designated Chairman of the Committee by the letter in Item 262 above. See also Item 261 and note.

264 ¶ Exchange of Messages Between the President and the Shah of Iran on the Losses Caused in the United States by Hurricane "Carol." *September* 10, 1954

Your Imperial Majesty:

Your Imperial Majesty's message of sympathy concerning the tragic loss of life and property which a hurricane recently inflicted on the northeastern coast of the United States has touched me deeply. It is further evidence of your humanitarian feelings which are so widely recognized. I appreciate your message and the spirit which inspired it, and I wish to take this occasion to assure you again of my admiration for the way you have led your nation through the difficulties of the past few years to the present point where a future full of opportunity is opening before you and your people.

DWIGHT D. EISENHOWER

NOTE: The Shah's message follows:

Mr. President:

I was deeply distressed by the news of the tragic loss of life and property which the recent hurricane inflicted upon your nation. I would like to express to Your Excellency and to the noble people of the United States the heartfelt sympathy of myself and that of my people.

REZA SHAH PAHLAVI

The messages were released at Lowry Air Force Base, Denver, Colo.

265 ¶ Message to the President of France on the Earthquake in Algeria. *September* 10, 1954

I WISH TO EXPRESS to you in the name of the Government and the people of the United States our profound sympathy for the tragic loss of life and destruction suffered as a result of the earthquake that struck Algeria.

NOTE: This message to President Rene Coty was released at Lowry Air Force Base, Denver, Colo.

847

266 ¶ Statement by the President on the Meeting of the National Security Council in Denver. *September* 13, 1954

YESTERDAY, the National Security Council met with me here in Denver. This was unprecedented, but it was also very natural. I had not met with the Council for more than two weeks, while it happened that yesterday Secretary Dulles reached here on his way back from the Philippines, where he had been conducting difficult negotiations.

We met in order that all of us together could have the benefit of his observations and the details of his report.

No specific decisions were advanced for action. It was merely a consulting together as to the place of the United States in the world today in that particular area—that troubled area of the Western Pacific—and reaffirming our devotion to certain policies.

These are, of course, to defend the vital interests of the United States wherever they may arise, to make better partners of old friends, and to get new friends wherever we can. And of course, where our vital interests demand it, to support them in their security and in their own interests.

The meeting lasted several hours, and broke up last evening.

NOTE: This statement was released at Lowry Air Force Base, Denver, Colo.

267 ¶ Remarks at Dedication of the Boulder, Colorado, Laboratories of the National Bureau of Standards. *September* 14, 1954

Mr. Secretary, Dr. Astin, my friends:

For the past 30 minutes or so, I have had the great privilege of a personally conducted tour through certain of the facilities of these new laboratories.

Now, the things that the layman sees in these laboratories are not to be understood by him. He grasps, though, that something of the most tremendous significance is proceeding here—significant not only to the scientist, to the industry, or the facility that may use the products of that science, and of the discoveries the scientist makes, significant to our Nation and to each of us, to our children, to the progress toward security and prosperity that each of us so desperately longs for.

It seemed to me, as I went through with Dr. Astin, that here we have a new type of frontier. This spot only a few short decades ago was inhabited by the Indians and by buffalo and by, finally, the trappers and the miners. It became the center of a great mining and agricultural region, which has meant so much to the United States in the past—and indeed, does now.

But the frontier days when we could go out and discover new land—new wonders of geography and of nature—has seemed largely in the past. But here, inside this building, we have a frontier possibly of even greater romantic value as well as greater material value to us than were some of the discoveries of those days.

Now another thought came to me as I went through these laboratories. In recent years the scientists have produced so much that terrifies us with its destructive force, that we begin to think of science as only something to destroy man, and not to promote his welfare, his happiness, his contentment—his intellectual and spiritual growth.

But I think, if we think of it this way, we will drop such thoughts from our minds. Almost everything that man has discovered in his long, long journey from darkness toward the light has been capable of two uses: one good, one evil.

Way back, long before history was started, man discovered fire. Without fire we wouldn't be warm, we couldn't cook, we would still be in the depths of savagery. Yet look how destructively fire can operate.

Take dynamite: we think of dynamite as a weapon of war; yet how much of it has been used in your hills here, in developing the great lead, zinc, silver, and gold mines that have made Colorado famous and rich.

I submit that every discovery of science can be used in one or two ways. It is not the fault of science if it is used wickedly. It is within ourselves.

And therefore, in the words of he who gave our invocation, possibly each one of us is a laboratory, to discover what we can contribute toward the growth of that kind of spirit among men that will make all of these discoveries of these dedicated scientists become assets to us, as we try to develop for ourselves and our children a better life, a richer life, one that gives us more opportunity to grow intellectually and spiritually.

And I think it is in those terms that we should think of the growth of science, as we think of these men laboring in this building, of our scientists in our universities, and in the Bureau of Standards in Washington—in the great factories of our Nation.

Having faith that if each of us does his part, then we will steadily go down the ages as a people more prosperous, more happy, more secure, more confident in peace.

Now those are the thoughts that occurred to me as I walked through this building. I believe this region of the United States is fortunate to have this facility here, to remind you of these things day by day, that you may at least in a sense become a part of some of these great discoveries that will be so useful to mankind—now, and through all the years yet to come.

I have now two little duties to perform, one most pleasurable. The first is to thank you—each of you—for your welcome to me, for the cordiality of your reception.

The second is that I am privileged to push a button—and of course, this being a scientific thing, you couldn't do it by just pulling a cord— this is very scientifically done, this dedication. But by pushing this button, they tell me that I am going to release the veil over the cornerstone; and in so doing, it is my high privilege to dedicate this facility of the Bureau of Standards to the welfare of humanity—in America and throughout the world.

NOTE: The President spoke at 10:45 a.m. His opening words "Mr. Secretary, Dr. Astin" referred to Secretary of Commerce Sinclair Weeks and Dr. A. V. Astin, Director of the National Bureau of Standards.

268 ¶ Letter to the Governors Concerning the State and White House Conferences on Education To Be Held in 1955. *September 21, 1954*

[Released September 21, 1954. Dated September 20, 1954]

Dear ――――:

All of us recognize the urgency of solving such serious educational problems as shortages of teachers and school facilities and the loss of needed trained manpower through illiteracy and school drop-outs. Many States and local communities are making progress in dealing with these problems. The facts show, however, that we are falling behind rather than catching up.

I deeply believe that the primary responsibility for meeting these problems must lie with the States and local communities, and that the Federal Government should strengthen and not interfere with State administration of education. It is because our citizens have taken direct responsibility for their schools and colleges that, through the years, American education has flourished.

Public Law 530, just passed by the Congress, conforms to this historic principle of self-reliance. It gives Americans the opportunity to determine what steps they can take at local, State and national levels to insure the best possible education for our youth. This Act authorizes State and White House Conferences at which representative citizens and educators can study their educational problems at all levels and determine what action should be taken. $700,000 has been allocated to the States for defraying a portion of the costs of preparing for and conducting these meetings. I have asked Secretary Hobby to write you more in detail concerning these Conferences.

With this opportunity to know the facts and understand the problems, I am convinced that the people of the United States will develop programs of effective action. It is with this conviction that I ask you to join with me in bringing about the most thorough, widespread and concerted study that the American people have ever made of their educational problems. This study is necessary, I believe, to make citizens realize the importance of immediate and continued action if we are to have agencies that contribute to a well-educated nation.

In my judgment, we have in this program a great opportunity to meet the needs of education in our country.

With best wishes and personal regard,

Sincerely,

DWIGHT D. EISENHOWER

NOTE: This letter, released at Lowry Air Force Base, Denver, Colo., was sent to the Governors of the States and to the principal Executives of the District of Columbia, Alaska, Hawaii, Puerto Rico, and the Virgin Islands.

269 ¶ Statement by the President: National Day of Prayer. *September* 21, 1954

IN COMMON WITH religious people everywhere, we in America know that the true cure for the tensions that threaten and too often produce war lies not in guns and bombs but in the spirits and minds of men. We are firm in the belief that faith is the mightiest force that man has at his command. On September twenty-second, we are therefore observing, with an act of faith, a national day of prayer. Throughout the United States of America, whatever our ancestry, whatever our religious affiliation, we shall offer simultaneously to the Almighty our personal prayers for the devotion, wisdom and stamina to work unceasingly for a just and lasting peace for all mankind.

I most earnestly hope that men and women, boys and girls over all the world will join us on that day in that act of faith. May the many millions of people shut away from contact and communion with peoples of the free world join their prayers with ours. May the world be ringed with an act of faith so strong as to annihilate the cruel, artificial barriers erected by little men between the peoples who seek peace on earth through the Divine Spirit.

NOTE: See also Proclamation 3064, National Day of Prayer, 1954 (3 CFR, 1954 Supp., p. 31). The statement was released at Lowry Air Force Base, Denver, Colo.

270 ¶ Remarks at Dedication of Aerial Fire Depot, Municipal Airport, Missoula, Montana. *September* 22, 1954

Governor Aronson, Congressman D'Ewart, Mr. McArdle, and my friends:

I am more than fortunate to be here today. Long have I wanted to have an occasion where I could join with other Americans in a salute to the Forest Service of the Department of Agriculture, and more particularly to the Smokejumpers of that organization.

I first heard about their work when I was still in the Army. They helped to train the paratroopers who were so valuable to us in the war— their techniques and their practices and all their experiences were passed on to us, to give us some of the finest organizations that America has ever sent to battle.

I am not at all astonished that it is such a good outfit. Within the last week I have had a little proof of the qualities of leadership of Mr. McArdle himself. It has not been my good fortune to know him, but only 2 nights ago, in Fraser, Colorado, I was visited at my cabin by a cook, a cook in the Forest Service. And he said, "I read in the paper you are going to Missoula. There you will see my boss, Mr. McArdle. Give him my greetings and best wishes."

I was long with the Army, and I have seen some of the finest battle units that have ever been produced, and whenever you find one where the cook and the private in the ranks want to be remembered to the General, when someone sees him, then you know it is a good outfit. I pay my salute to Mr. McArdle.

Incidentally, I think it is a happy coincidence that for the only time in my life that I know of, I have been introduced to an audience by an ex-Forest Ranger, my good friend Wes D'Ewart.

Now, I know the establishment of this great training center here is the culmination of long years of work—20 years of work. With units scattered all over, they need a center such as this for training and other experimental and centralized work.

And I want to pledge, here and now, that this kind of effort will have the support of the Federal Government as long as I am connected with it.

To that extent, and in accordance with what Mr. McArdle has told us, possibly I am a vicarious member of the Missoula Chamber of Commerce. If so, I am proud of it.

Now these people, in the course of their service to us, have saved, as Mr. McArdle said, millions of dollars in property. They have saved a crop that means so much to us, not only because of its value as lumber and paper and all that, but the time it takes to grow. Forty years is an average time for a pine tree to grow, and down in the Rockies 150 years for pole pines to grow the way we want them. To think of what one devastating fire can do to such a crop in an instant, and what these people have done to save our crucial values!

Now, as I came up here today, I was told by Secretary McKay of the Interior, that in 1 year they have fought twelve thousand fires. It seems like an incredible number, but I hope he is right, because I am going to quote him whenever I talk about them.   And if he is wrong, I just hope they don't correct me.

Incidentally, you know, as I landed here and saw this great crowd, I was a little alarmed that you expected me to take to a parachute and jump out.   Not only had I no such intention, but I am also delighted that the demonstration was cut short of the place of taking any chances of injuring one of these men, none of whom can we spare.

Now, I am not going to try to recite to such a crowd as this all of the work that the Forest Service does.   I think it is better—more appropriate—that I should call attention to this fact: each of us can do something to assist them, directly or indirectly, in their work.

For us, for our children and our grandchildren, they are saving the priceless assets and the resources of the United States.   And we can help. We can help by avoiding any of those careless acts that sometimes set these fires.   We can help by joining in every kind of conservation practice and conservation organization that helps also to preserve these resources.

In so doing, it seems to me we cannot fail to think more objectively, in a more sincere way, about this country, what the good Lord has given us in the way of priceless resources.

Certain it is that whatever we help to do engages our attention and our interest more deeply than those things that seem to us to be free and to come without effort.   We don't particularly worry about the air that we breathe, but we do worry and think about things we earn by the sweat of our brow and bring home.

Now when we are preserving these resources of the United States, we are helping by the sweat of our own brows or the concerns of our own minds and hearts to save them for the others.

This brings up the basic policy of the administration now in Washington.   It is the intense belief that every citizen of the United States has a part to play in keeping this country great, that we are not wards of a centralized Federal system, that the Federal system is set up by the people to help, when help is indicated for us, but that each citizen in his own right is better qualified to look after himself than is some bureaucrat in far off Washington.

Now, in a very brief and homely way, that states the policy by which this administration tries to live.   Never will we desert any section or any people who, through no fault of their own, suffer disaster and need the help of central Government.   And by the same token, never will we step across that line that permits unwarranted Federal intrusion into your lives.

Lincoln said this better than anybody else.   He said the function of government is to do for people and a community of people those things which they need to have done, and cannot do at all, or cannot so well do for themselves as can the Federal Government.   And he went on to say when people can do these things for themselves, the Federal Government ought not to interfere.

And never has a better philosophy for America been stated than that.

My friends, I am on a hurried trip, and I hope you will allow me to thank each of you for coming out for these few minutes, so that I might greet you—to bring you greetings from your Government, to gain the inspiration that I always gain from association with great groups of Americans; and then, that you will permit me to go to my plane and be on my way, because I believe I am due in Walla Walla in a very short time.

I again assure you that to be here present at the dedication of this training center is a very great honor—one I shall long remember.

Goodbye and good luck.

NOTE: The President spoke at 6:00 p.m. In his opening words he referred to Governor J. Hugo Aronson and U.S. Representative Wesley A. D'Ewart of Montana, and to Richard E. McArdle, Chief of the Forest Service.

271   ¶ Address at the Dedication of McNary Dam, Walla Walla, Washington.
September 23, 1954

Governor Patterson, Governor Langlie, and Members of the United States Congress, distinguished guests, and my fellow Americans:

Before I begin the more serious parts of my address, I wonder if you would mind if I would communicate to you an odd thought that occurred to me, as I sat here.   There was brought to me in emphatic form once, by an old soldier of mine, who reminded me that you could never tell what was around the corner in the world.   When I first came back from Europe 2 years ago, and before my friends found that it was utterly futile and useless to try to make me appear better on the TV by the use of paints and stains, they had me in a little room one night, and the man was working very seriously on my face in an effort to do something about it. Finally, in this very preoccupied sort of job and atmosphere that was prevailing, he suddenly began to laugh. And he said to me, "General, we have got ourselves in a funny fix." He said, "Here you are, an old General, trying to turn politician." And he said, "I am a beautician. Do you know what I was in the war?" I said, "No." He said, "I was one of your paratroopers."

What made me think of that this morning was the fact that when I first met Sam Sturgis, I was detailed as a young officer to coach a football team and I made him an end, and he worked pretty hard under me for some weeks and months.

Today, I think that all of you would like for me to speak for you in commending him as a brilliant head of a great organization which not only here but throughout our land has built up these great works in flood control, in drainage, in water conservation, and power development—an organization of which not only the United States Army but which America is proud.

My friends, to join you in so important a ceremony—here in the heart of the Pacific Northwest—is indeed a privilege. I am delighted to be here with you on this historic spot.

Our Nation was only 16 years old when, from a point near here, two Americans of great courage—Lewis and Clark—pushed off and floated to the mouth of this great river.

A little over a century ago, a man named McKay struggled over primitive paths in this area. A hundred and nine years ago, a frontiersman named McNary, with his family, reached this almost virgin land to establish his home.

Both of these men had famous descendants—men who have contributed much to the extraordinary growth of the Northwest.

From the McKay family came an able Governor and a dedicated Secretary of the Interior—Douglas McKay.

From the McNarys came the great American whose name forevermore will distinguish this monumental work.

Senator McNary believed deeply in the future of this country. He had the grit and determination to help build that future. In this endeavor he worked side by side with those men of vision of this region who, before the turn of the century, sought to open to navigation the upper reaches of the Columbia River. With that drive for an open river for water traffic came the natural development of hydro-electric power.

Ten years ago, death denied Senator McNary the privilege of seeing his dream come true. But the will to build this dam lived after him.

And may I pause to pay my personal tribute to Mrs. McNary, here with us today on the platform. That the will to build this dam survived—and that today this dam is built—are due to the spirit of distinguished citizens of this region. Especially are they due to an Oregonian who carried on Senator McNary's work and for the past 10 years has labored tirelessly to complete this project—my good friend, Senator Guy Cordon.

I am mindful as well of the sustained effort of many Congressmen from this region, including particularly Congressman Hal Holmes, who have worked in behalf of this and other great projects here in the Northwest.

Now, this massive dam, my friends, means much more than the steel and concrete, more than the genius and the effort that went into its building. It means more than the benefits and the progress—however great—that it will bring to this fortunate region.

This structure symbolizes the purpose of using, for the benefit of all our people, the tremendous natural legacy with which the Almighty so abundantly endowed our land. Wisely and providently we must use and develop these resources, so that each succeeding generation of Americans may share in their benefits. It is for us to see that they shall not be wasted or neglected or denied to generations yet to come.

Now, among these treasures of our land is water—fast becoming our most valuable, most prized, most critical resource. A blessing when properly used—it can bring devastation and ruin when left uncontrolled.

It is essential that every drop of water, from the moment that it falls upon our land, be turned to the service of our people. Thus we will save our soil and make it more productive: thus we will develop power, prevent floods, improve navigation, and supply our tremendous and growing domestic and industrial needs for water. So crucial to our future has water become, that I have assigned appropriate surveys and plans concerning it to a special committee of the Cabinet, and to the Hoover Commission as well. These studies, when subjected to Congressional action, will undoubtedly result in the comprehensive water policy that this country has needed since its very beginning.

The wise control of our water resources obviously requires the most skillful and comprehensive planning. This dam, for example, is designed to operate in coordination with similar structures, upstream and down. It is part of a plan to assure the full use of the water resources of this entire river system. McNary Dam is, therefore, representative of the coordination that must mark the development of all of our river systems. It is, moreover, an example of national responsibility properly assumed by the Federal Government.

Just a mile and a half down river is another structure—the bridge at Umatilla. I am sure that you who live here are just as proud of that bridge as you are of this tremendous dam. You have every right to be. That bridge at Umatilla is an example of local responsibility properly assumed.

A major difference between the two undertakings is in size. All of you know that when construction was started on McNary Dam, no local enterprise—public or private—could have financed it, so, realizing that the dam was necessary, the Federal Government gave its support.

The bridge at Umatilla was a much smaller effort. Local enterprise—in this case the county government—was able to shoulder the $5 million loan that made that construction possible. And so, local enterprise did that job.

These two structures illustrate an idea we have been applying in Washington for some 19 months. It is not a new concept. A century ago Abraham Lincoln put it better than anyone else has done. He said, "The legitimate object of government is to do for a community of people whatever they need to have done, but cannot do at all, or cannot so well do for themselves—in their separate and individual capacities."

Now, in keeping with Lincoln's standard, the Federal Government has certain vital responsibilities in such fields relating to the control and use of water as flood control, improvement of navigation, and reclamation and development of land. When in the course of assuming these responsibilities, dams are built, then hydro-electric power is often developed, of great value to the surrounding regions and to the Nation.

I hope that we shall soon have another example of Federal responsibility in the generation of power. I refer to the Libby Dam, which—like this great McNary Dam—is a project requiring the resources of the Federal Government. From its location on the Canadian border, on a tributary of this mighty Columbia River, it will powerfully aid the control of floods, and produce a new means of generating power, all the way to the sea.

I have recently acted to remove obstacles to the construction of that dam. A new site has been selected. A distinguished northwesterner, Governor Jordan of Idaho, has been named Chairman of the International Joint Commission. His intimate knowledge of this area and sound judgment will surely go far to speed fulfillment of our aims, and those of our Canadian neighbors. This project will be brought into existence.

I shall continue to recommend Federal construction of such beneficial projects. New ones will be started.

Such activities as these, my friends, are obviously, as Lincoln said, "the legitimate object of government." But here let us draw our line as he himself did, when he went on to say this: "In all that the people can individually do for themselves, government ought not to interfere."

It is not properly a Federal responsibility to try to supply all the power needs of our people. The Federal Government should no more attempt to do so than it should assume responsibility for supplying all their drinking water, their food, their housing, and their transportation.

To attempt such a centralization of authority and responsibility always starts a deadly cycle.

Parenthetically, may I remark that a region which lets itself become completely dependent upon national funds provided by a Congress— which Congress represents not that region alone but the whole Nation— would frequently find that the funds fail to keep pace with local needs. But the important thing is that as Federal power expands in a region— and I mean Federal authority and responsibility—local enterprise becomes increasingly intimidated and discouraged, even though the needs for energy continue to grow. Thus still more Federal intervention becomes necessary. Such a conversion of local regions into Federal satellites poses a threat deadly to our liberties. The Administration in Washington—and the present leadership in Congress—are unalterably opposed to such malignant growth of bureaucracy.

In our devotion to conservation, let us not forget that there are spiritual as well as physical values to protect. Above all else, we must protect the freedom and the spirit of independence of our people in our States and counties, in our cities and towns. Determination to have this kind of freedom gave us this Nation. It brought your ancestors to this

Western country. That determination is not only the surest protector of our liberties, it is the principal ingredient in our national prosperity.

Yet, there are some who contend that the development and distribution of hydro-electric power is exclusively the responsibility of the Federal Government. They argue that to permit any State or local government or any private company under governmental regulation to develop such power capacity is to give to a special group an asset belonging to all the Nation. Indeed, in some instances, these disciples of centralized responsibility and authority insist that since the Federal Government should provide all hydro-electric power, it should likewise eliminate competition by providing steam-electric power as well.

Only thus, these zealots would have us believe, can we poor citizens be protected against exploitation against what they call the "predatory" exponents of capitalism—that is, free enterprise.

Now, let's have a quick look at this matter.

In the first place it is, of course, not difficult to be generous with someone else's money. So the individual who wants to build power dams only with Federal money is not directly or particularly concerned with the economic necessity of the project or with the suitability of its location. Secondly, these advocates of centralized government shut their eyes to the remarkable development of this Nation during past decades. They must wonder how such prosperity came about when communities and citizens were free to look after themselves—including their own protection against the so-called local "interests."

These believers in centralization fail to warn us that monopoly is always potentially dangerous to freedom—even when monopoly is exercised by the Government. Curiously enough, they proclaim their fear of a private power monopoly in a county, city or State, but they urge upon us all a gigantic, overwhelming, nationwide power monopoly. But, of course, they also see themselves as the all-wise directors of that monopoly—so all would be well.

monopoly, nor do they want a system leading toward it. They know

The American people do not want and do not need to have any such

they can have all the power capacity of our streams developed, as needed, without forfeiting the advantages of local responsibility and participation.

Throughout our country are many public enterprises—organized years ago by States, municipalities, and other public agencies—which have long been in successful operation. In hundreds of other instances, power has been and is being provided by private enterprise under the regulatory processes in the particular governmental agency involved. In each instance the people directly concerned by such operations have themselves decided whether they are best served by public or by private agencies.

The issue is not, therefore, public power versus unregulated private power. The issue posed to us is Federal monopoly of power, as against public or regulated power, freely chosen in each instance by the citizens of each area, with the Federal Government coming in as a cooperating partner where this seems necessary or desirable.

Last year, for example, State and local governments were invited to cooperate in power generation without the threat of Federal power control. During this brief period numerous local public agencies and private investors have applied for licenses to build hydro-electric plants. These applications in this Northwest region amount to nearly six million kilowatts. This represents a prospective investment of not less than one and one-half billion dollars. Well over half of this would be invested by public power—not private power—interests.

But the seekers after Federal control of energy are not silenced even by this array of facts. They say that construction of power projects by local enterprise will impede the comprehensive development of this or other river basins.

Now again—let's take a look at the facts.

What they say just is not true. All power projects must be licensed by the Federal Power Commission. Before the Commission grants a license, it must see evidence that the project makes maximum use of the developed resources. It makes no difference who builds the projects—Federal, State, municipal, or private agencies. These requirements apply—regardless.

We should also get this straight: when a project is licensed before a non-Federal authority, it is not removed from public control. Rates and services remain under regulation. And when the licensing period ends, the site can be assumed by the Federal Government.

I happen to hold this conviction: that, here in the Northwest, your own public agencies and your own private companies—operating under both Federal regulation and your own eagle eyes out here—can work in the public interest at least as well as some far-off Federal agency. They ought to do better.

At this moment there are glowing reports on your regional efforts to work out your own problems. Through the Governors' Power Policy Committee, Governors Langlie, Patterson, Jordan, and Aronson are doing great work in assuring this area of adequate supplies of water. More benefits will flow from efforts to further inter-State cooperation on problems that cross the borders of the Northwestern States.

I am especially happy that the power produced by this great new dam will contribute to the finest type of cooperative effort—your own Northwest Power Pool. This arrangement is an admirable model of voluntary pooling of public and private generating and transmission facilities. Because of it, you citizens of the Northwest have hundreds of thousands of kilowatts of additional prime power that would not exist through independent operation of your various utilities. And in addition—and very important—you have it under your own control—not under the permission of a far-off Washington office holder. This is a splendid partnership—the kind that the Administration will continue to encourage. I might add that this partnership concept has been most ably advanced by your Republican delegation in the Congress, led by Senator Cordon.

My friends, in all of these things that I have mentioned, your goal and the goal of your Government are exactly the same: to assure each citizen of enough kilowatts, when he wants them, where he wants them, at the lowest competitive cost—with the least likelihood of bureaucratic domination from Washington, D.C.

In this effort, we shall avoid extremes. We shall neither withdraw from the power field nor will we federalize all electric power generators in the United States. Instead, we shall continue to advance in a spirit of helpfulness to localities, and in a spirit of cooperation with local citizens.

Where local enterprise can shoulder the burden, it will be encouraged and supported in doing so.

And where local action cannot or should not fully meet the need, we shall have Federal action.

In this way, our people, in their communities and homes throughout America, shall reserve to themselves as many of the basic decisions affecting their lives as possible. In this way, our people will remain free to carve out their destinies as their predecessors did. It was in this spirit that those who preceded you in the great Northwest, in only a century and a half, turned an unsettled wilderness into an inland empire—an empire vastly enriched by this gigantic structure which today we so proudly name the McNary Dam.

Now, my friends, I know that the policy I have outlined for you will satisfy neither group that exists at the extreme ends of this argument. It is not intended to please them. This program, as all other programs in which your Government engages, is designed to benefit the United States of America—160 million people. It is guided and formulated on the advice, the commonsense counsel of the vast majority of Americans. Extremes do not interest me, or the Administration, in the slightest.

Fellow citizens, we have talked today especially of power and water and this great new dam. But it is well that we remind ourselves that these are but part of a commonly-held objective which transcends all partisan and sectional considerations. The objective is that this Republic shall in every way grow ever stronger and more secure—that it may remain at peace in a world freed of the threat of atomic war. We want our America to have an ever growing, vigorous economy. We want every citizen to prosper and advance—with freedoms which daily shine brighter in each community of our land. We shall continue to build the material, moral, and intellectual strength to assure ourselves and our children of an always finer tomorrow.

Toward that stronger and better America, my friends, I know that you will continue to go forward, as self-reliant, courageous descendants of God-fearing pioneers, fortified by your faith in yourselves and in your country.

As you travel that wonderful road, I trust that you will have full confidence, every step of the way, that your Federal Government strides beside you as your true partner. May you always be sure that this Administration is ready to help where necessary, eager as your servant to make the way easier for you and for all. But it will never be willing to assume over you a domination that will rob you of your greatest heritage—your individual liberty and your maximum control over your personal, family and local concerns.

That, my friends, is the kind of government, the kind of America, of which your children and mine will be as proud as we are of our country today.

And now, of course, without a pushbutton, no dedication is possible. General Sturgis has explained to you the workings of this instrument— what will happen about the lights and the sounds—about what will happen in sending an electric current to some machinery—about the lights going on—and then this great and inspiring marvel, the McNary Dam—another portion of it, will be furnishing power to the Northwest Power Pool.

It is with the greatest sense of distinction and pride in the Federal Government's part of what was done in this project that I now, by this act, officially dedicate this McNary Dam.

Thank you very much, my friends—thank you.

NOTE: The President spoke at 10:30 a.m. His opening words "Governor Patterson, Governor Langlie" referred to Governor Paul Patterson of Oregon and Governor Arthur B. Langlie of Washington. He later referred to Maj. Gen. S. D. Sturgis, Jr., Chief of Engineers, U.S. Army.

272 ¶ Remarks at the Airport, Pendleton, Oregon. *September 23, 1954*

Senator Cordon, Governor Patterson, distinguished guests, my fellow Americans:

I can well understand how I am right welcome to the young fry who got out of school to come out here today. But I must tell you all that I am deeply complimented by the presence of every person here today. When this schedule of mine was made up for the day, it was a crowded one. I am to end up this evening in Los Angeles, where again I am to make a speech, so there wasn't time for many little side trips.

I want to tell you one reason I would particularly like to have visited Pendleton. About 15 years ago I acquired a fishing shirt that is my prize possession. I have been wearing it ever since, when I went fishing—and they call it a Pendleton shirt. Now whether that is the right name or not, I don't know; but it's a good reason to visit here, because it's a good shirt.

When I say I am deeply complimented by your presence, I have a very distinct and personal reason for saying so. I have served in many odd corners of the world. I have been far away from America, for years at a time. I have been one of those who because of the services of our American soldiers have been specially honored by foreign governments— because of the services those soldiers performed.

But I have learned this: there is no honor one American can receive that is greater than the readiness of his fellow citizens to meet with him for a brief moment.

The fact you have come out from Pendleton this morning, impels me to try to leave with you an idea of what this administration is trying to do in Washington.

I think I can best say it this way: with everything, and in everything that affects your relationship to your Federal Government, that Government means to be liberal, human, sympathetic—always.

With everything that deals with your money—your pocketbooks—and the economy of your country, that Government tries to be conservative.

That, I think, sums up in about two sentences the philosophy of the Government you now have in Washington.

The colleagues I have—and the fellow workers from your State—have been people that have helped formulate that policy and help to support it.

I trust that it is one that will commend itself to you, because without that kind of philosophy, without that kind of effort, I believe that America's future cannot be as bright as it can be—a future that we all want to be peaceful, to be prosperous—for all of us; where everybody regardless of origin or race or religion has an equal chance; the kind of America that we have dreamed about from babyhood and which we can have, if we want it, and do not let ourselves be led astray by false promises and glittering generalities.

My friends, again thank you so much for coming out. I must be on my way. I am grateful for your presence and for these presents.

NOTE: The President spoke at 1:10 p.m.

273 ¶ Address at the Hollywood Bowl, Los Angeles, California. *September* 23, 1954

MAY I FIRST address the heads of the organizations that are my hosts this evening: Mrs. Kearns, Madam President of the National Federation of Republican Women, Mr. Saunders, Chairman of the Citizens for Eisenhower of Southern California, and Mr. Trippitt, President of the Democrats for Eisenhower—and my fellow Americans:

Incidentally, this is the first time I have had the great privilege of using such words in addressing my hosts.

Now for many reasons I am delighted to be with you. Here I meet again with groups which 2 years ago did so much to reverse the trend toward highly centralized government in our Nation.

Among you are the representatives of the women of the Republican Party, inspired with that wonderful determination for good that has always characterized your activities. Others of you represent other groups bound not by party ties but by a common devotion to good government—government administered by public servants of integrity and purpose.

Naturally, I want, first, to pay my compliments to all of you who have joined together to be my hosts tonight, but far more than this, I feel that I owe to you an accounting of the progress made by the administration that your efforts did so much, 2 years ago, to send to Washington.

I think, too, that it is time that we had a talk about the course of our Government for the next 2 years.

We are meeting in a great State which has furnished the Nation so many distinguished public servants. It is the State which only recently has given our country a man who will be known in history as one of the great Chief Justices of the United States, Earl Warren. It is the home State of another devoted public servant who both here and abroad has been doing such a great job for all of us—our Vice President, Dick Nixon. Here, too, is the home of a man who in the last Congress demonstrated outstanding qualities of ability and leadership—the Majority Leader of the United States Senate, Bill Knowland. And, my friends, I think I speak for everyone present when I say that the prayers of this entire gathering are with Mrs. Knowland, for her early return to health. And, tonight, I am especially happy to be in the company of an able compatriot in the business of government, Tom Kuchel, who as a member of the Senate has ably served his State and our Nation.

My respects go as well to the Congressmen of our party who have worked so diligently to bring success to our cause. And of course, I cannot forget your Governor, who so graciously introduced me to this audience.

Now, all of these men, and all of you here tonight have shown that you are Americans willing to do more than just talk about having a better and stronger Nation—an America willing to work and to fight for the kind of country that you are determined to have. You are among the millions of our citizens who take seriously their obligations of citizenship. You are not content merely to be bystanders in the business of self-government. And because you are leaders—dedicated leaders—you persuade others to exercise their civic responsibilities as well.

Through such selfless devotion, all of America is strengthened, and our freedoms are made more secure.

Our common interest is good government. All good government is produced only by able and dedicated people. Government is people. All of you in this great audience are, therefore, a part of the stuff of which good government is made. Our common purpose is that our Government shall daily advance the good of all of our people, regardless of race or color or creed or political affiliation or regional considerations.

In this effort in the past, you have made speeches. You have button-holed your neighbors. You have pounded the pavements. You have used the telephone. You have addressed envelopes. And you have licked stamps.

And you well know what resulted 2 years ago from all those efforts.

I know that you will again succeed. Because, as good citizens, you know that in the American way, it is not enough to start a job with zeal and enthusiasm. You must also have the stamina and the determination to see it through.

Let us, then, militantly resolve here tonight to carry forward together the great work we undertook 2 years ago.

Now, what did we start out to do? How far have we come? What's left to be done? These are the political questions of our day that are truly important.

Two years ago the people of our country voted to have clean government. What has happened in the 20 months since?

Not one appointee of this administration has been involved in scandal or corruption.

Moreover, in this administration, not politics, nor complacency, nor cronyism, will stay the use of every available legal and investigative process to prevent abuse of the public trust. Integrity and decency and dignity have been restored to the Federal Government. Our Government again stands high in the eyes of our people. This is clean government.

Two years ago the people of our country demanded a cut in the high cost of their Government. They wanted a cut, too, in their high taxes.

And what has been done?

This administration and your Congress, under Republican leadership, have cut the cost of your Government by over eleven billion dollars. This has made it possible for us to pass on to the taxpayer 7 billion 400 million dollars of this saving. This is equal to an annual saving of almost fifty dollars for every man, woman, and child in all America. This is the biggest tax cut in the history of the United States. Now the remainder of this savings in governmental costs is being applied against the previously planned budget deficits, so that our debt—the public debt—will not unnecessarily keep piling up.

This administration believes that the individual knows better how to spend his money than does a bureaucrat in Washington.

And may I emphasize that the tax laws have been executed without political favoritism and without corruption.

Two years ago our people were longing for a prosperous economy—without war. The useless shooting that could lead nowhere except to ever growing casualty lists has been stopped. The tremendous expenditures to support it have been stopped. Nevertheless, the Nation's economy has adjusted to these new conditions with minimum economic detriment to most of our people. This is true even in those areas most directly affected by war production. The year 1954 is, in fact, the best peacetime year in our history.

But we are most certainly not satisfied—far from it. I am keenly aware of the economic dislocation and individual hardships which, in certain locations, are the aftermath of war and inflation. The administration and the Republican Congress have moved and will continue to move with the full force of the Federal Government to ease these problems.

And we have provided many strong protections to strengthen our economy. Among these are tax revisions which encourage new enterprise—and make new jobs. We have new housing programs. And there are no windfall profits in them. The FHA has been overhauled and revitalized and has again become an indispensable and an effective agency in helping to provide homes for those who need them. We have soundly expanded the social security system to include ten million more Americans. We have a broadened unemployment compensation program—for four million more Americans. We have provided advantageous group life insurance for every Government worker.

This evening I met briefly the wife of our Postmaster General, who told me that after this insurance program was effected and accomplished, within 3 days thereafter a man working for the Post Office Department died, and except for this insurance system his wife and family would have been left penniless. Now they have something on which to live.

We have an expanded road program made possible by returning to the States money received from Federal gasoline taxes. We have enacted a farm program that will prevent the accumulation of unmanageable surpluses. This program will lead to full parity in the market place for the farmer, instead of a percentage of parity at some Government warehouse. All of these measures—and there are many more—provide an even stronger economy, an economy that will stay strong, that will continue to grow, an economy under which Americans will continue to prosper.

At last our Nation's economic strength is of an enduring kind.

It is not a prosperity based on the froth of inflation.

We flatly reject the idea that, for America to stay prosperous, we must constantly run an economic fever.

We flatly reject the idea that, for America to stay prosperous, the Government must always spend more than it has.

No longer do we have a prosperity pegged to the battlefield sacrifices of our husbands, our sons, and our brothers.

We do have a prosperous economy—and we have it without war.

We have kept faith with the American people.

And over the world we are building strength where there was weakness. We have brought realism where there was wishful thinking in our foreign dealings. We have brought frankness, candor, and force to a foreign policy which at last insists on distinguishing words from deeds in the conduct of the affairs of the world.

Much of a specific and concrete character has been accomplished in this field.

Two years ago, it looked almost certain that our friends in Iran would bow to communist imperialism. With their downfall the free world would have lost over 60 percent of the known petroleum reserves of the world. The consequences would have been disastrous.

Iran today has new strength, new hope, new determination. Iran has a new tie to the cause of freedom. Disaster has been averted.

At Suez, ancient irritations and quarrels involving two of our friends have been resolved. Peace has been preserved. Progress has been assured in an area vital to Western civilization.

Pakistan has become a valued new ally.

In the Far East, despite the inescapable misfortune of Indochina, the United States Navy has just completed the resettlement of 250,000 evacuees from the Communist-held northern sections, and have transferred them to places where they could live in conditions of freedom. A new concert of nations is building strength in this region, where there was weakness. In that crucial area of the world there has been established for the first time, a solid, enduring relationship between the Western World and the friendly people of Asia.

At Caracas the American Republics joined in a solid working arrangement assuring the defeat of any future attempts to impose communistic imperialism upon the peoples of the Americas.

As a result, in Guatemala, the first beachhead of international communism in the Western Hemisphere has been eliminated.

In spite of recent disappointments in Europe, the growing strength of NATO continues to bring an increased sense of security to the free people of that vital area. We are, with continuing determination and confidence, working with our friends to bring about a new defensive arrangement which will further assure the freedom of the peoples of western Europe.

Throughout the world a series of alliances and improved understandings among our friends has enhanced the strength of the free world, upon which our own security so very greatly depends. These are merely examples of results brought largely about by the tireless efforts of our distinguished Secretary of State, Foster Dulles.

I am gratified to report to this great audience that this administration has maintained a continuing bipartisan discussion of the foreign problems of this Nation—a record of bipartisan consultation unmatched in any previous administration. To you and to all Americans, patriots above all sectional and partisan considerations, I know this accomplishment is of real meaning.

Now at home, what of our national defense?

First and foremost, we have established a business administration in the gigantic defense organization. We are eliminating the waste of duplication and inefficiency.

No longer do we have a feast and famine program of defense. Skyrocketing expansion of our Armed Forces, inspired by hysterical fear, followed by their reckless contraction resulting from complacency, are the most perilous and costly kind of military program.   We have adopted a stable, long-term policy, emphasizing a steady buildup of our military strength with efficiency and with economy.

No longer do we waste vast sums for mothballing and demothballing of ships—on opening and closing of military bases.   No longer do we force in and force out of the Armed Forces young veterans who already have served this Nation in time of war.

No longer do we build combat air wings just on paper.

Instead, today, at a cost of billions less, we have an armed strength far more efficient and better organized than ever before—a defense stronger and readier in peacetime than it has ever been.

Next—today we at last deal effectively with the Communist conspiracy in the United States itself.   This doesn't mean that every citizen should suspect his neighbor or fear the loss of his constitutional rights. But it does mean that we are backing up the FBI and the Department of Justice in dealing forthrightly with any who would plot the violent destruction of our form of Government.   The Congress and the executive branch have taken the statutory and administrative steps necessary to treat this problem with the care and the vigor it requires.   This administration does not look upon the Communist menace as a red herring.

Yes, we promised to strive for a prosperous America, at peace.   We promised an efficient defense against attack from abroad and against subversion at home.   We promised a realistic foreign policy.

As to performance, over and above what I have said, we invite the most rigid scrutiny of the record.

But we said we would do even more than this.

We said we would cut down padded Federal payrolls—that we'd clean out misfits and unfits in the Government service.   And in 20 months padded payrolls have been cut by over 211,000.   Security risks have been removed from sensitive positions.

We said we would reverse the deadly trend toward centralization of Government power in Washington.   This we have done.   In addition, pursuant to an act of Congress, I have appointed a Commission, composed of distinguished Americans, which for months has been examining closely all phases of Federal, State, and local responsibility, and their relationships one to another.

We said we'd remove stifling controls from the Nation's economy.   This was done a year and a half ago, amid dire predictions of carping critics that inflation would follow and prices would soar out of sight. Despite these gloomy predictions, inflation was stopped and the cost of living was stabilized.

As all of this was being done, we were also stopping bureaucrats in Washington from doing a lot of things that you and all enterprising Americans can do better yourselves.

We have tried to live by the maxim of Abraham Lincoln: "The legitimate object of Government," he said, "is to do for a community of people whatever they need to have done, but cannot do at all, or cannot so well do for themselves—in their separate and individual capacities." And he added, "In all that the people can individually do for themselves, Government ought not to interfere."

In keeping with this sound and sage advice, the Government is stopping the manufacture of ice and of cement. It is being stopped from retreading tires, repairing shoes, roasting coffee, making clothes. The Government has been stopped from making rope, operating rubber plants, running a commercial bank.

The Government has been stopped from operating a big fleet of tugs and barges on our inland waterways. All of these things are again in the hands of private citizens—exactly where they belong.

We made another commitment to the American people 2 years ago. We promised a new era of cooperation between the Executive and the Congress—cooperation that would lead to progressive accomplishment for the good of all our people—as visualized by our Founding Fathers when they wrote the Constitution for the United States of America.

For the past 20 months there has been harmony unprecedented in our time between the Executive and the Congress—harmony that has led to progressive accomplishments for the good of all our people. This must be preserved.

Now, on the promises to which I have adverted, we have delivered. Our people know it.

But the program is not completed. There is much to be done. We must keep on working.

We shall keep on, despite those misguided and irresponsible people who, hoping for individual advantage, spread fear—fear of war, fear of atomic disaster, fear of international catastrophe, fear of depression— false fears, my friends, of tomorrow and of ourselves.

Fellow Americans, 2 years ago the people of this country proved that they will not listen to the peddlers of fear.

We shall ride forward over their gloom-filled talk and their cynical doubts.

Our program is for just one thing: the practical good of 160 million Americans. In 2 years we have done much toward that goal. But we have much more to do.

Important legislation must be considered by the next Congress. This would include a great program to expand our foreign trade, a program to promote American investment abroad, a comprehensive water resources program. It will include a tremendous new highway program. It will include legislation to meet the needs of our people in the field of health and medical care—and it will once and for all repudiate the philosophy of socialized medicine. It will include consideration of the very important recommendations that will grow out of the White House Conference on Education. The next Congress will consider legislation of fundamental importance respecting the personnel of our Armed Forces. A new Armed Forces Reserve System will be established. Congress will be called upon to consider the exceedingly important recommendations of the Hoover Commission and also those of the Commission on Intergovernmental Relations and Fiscal Affairs concerning the relations between Federal, State, and local governments.

Many other important problems will command the attention of the next Congress. Among them will be measures for lowering the voting age in Federal elections, statehood for Hawaii, amendments to our labor-management laws, and other as yet unrealized promises in the national platform of the Republican Party. We are determined to fulfill every commitment that we have made to the American people.

Will we be able to go ahead to attain these goals for a better America?

Let us look at a few political facts. Under our system, many millions of our citizens have partisan affiliations. This is as it should be. In no other way can party responsibility be fixed under our system.

But for a political party in our Nation to be held clearly accountable to the people for its political philosophy and programs to guide the course of our Government, it is essential that that party control both the executive and the legislative branches of the Government. This is what all of you worked for in 1952.

When, unfortunately, the Congress is controlled by one political party and the executive branch by the other, politics in Washington has a field day. The conduct of Government tends, under these conditions, to deteriorate into an endless round of contests for political advantage—an endless round of political maneuverings, of stagnation and inaction—of half measures or no measures at all. These are the reasons—the compelling reasons—why the completion of your great program requires the election of a Republican-led Congress.

My friends, 2 years ago I called upon those who believe in the principles and objectives that we commonly share, to fight for their advancement with all their heart and force. Tonight I renew that call. I call upon you for a rekindling of the enthusiasm and determination of 1952. I am convinced that the great majority of Americans believe that we are on the right course. But the very confidence that they now have in our Government has understandably diminished their constant and active participation in its affairs. They think everything is all right. They must make sure that it remains so. It is our task, therefore, to reactivate their participation. It is our task again to organize the hearts and minds and the efforts of this great majority actively in this cause. You are leaders in this task. And as leaders, you must seek the cooperation and fighting support of our people, regardless of party, who, like you, want to support these principles and these objectives.

Let me make this clear: this is the time to go to work. This is the time for rededication, for renewed effort.

We must carry forward our program—a program which in deeds and in facts gives voice to the spirit of America. It is a program whose success will inspire gratitude in the hearts of all of our people, now and in the future.

And now, my friends, before I leave this platform, may I thank you once again for the cordiality of your welcome. I should like also to take this moment to thank all those who, along the streets of this great city today, gave me a smile and a welcome and a "Hi Ike."

Good night, and God bless you.

NOTE: The President spoke at 9:00 p.m.

274 ¶ Remarks at the Breakfast in Los Angeles Given by Republican Groups of Southern California. *September 24, 1954*

Governor Knight, Mr. Chairman, and my friends:

This meeting, insofar as it involves a talk from me, is sort of an added number on my schedule. I have no text, and I think I have no particularly brilliant ideas. But I must say that the great pleasure of meeting with a group of people that you know to be friendly, who wish well to you and to the cause for which you struggle, is a very warm feeling.

And this inspires me to tell you a little bit of what we are trying to do, how truly simple it is, and therefore, to see whether we may not draw even a little closer together because of the simplicity of these ideas and, I think, the fact that we see all right-thinking Americans should be for, in general this kind of thing.

Carter Glass once went to a great university. He was to receive an honorary degree of doctor of laws; and the dean of the law school, in presenting him to the president of the university, read a long citation. This citation had to deal largely, almost exclusively, with the long record of Carter Glass's integrity, his absolute unimpeachable honesty as a public servant throughout his life. It dwelt on this theme in numerous ways and I think even quoted examples.

Finally it was Carter Glass's turn to speak. He said: "My friends, I think I should decline to receive this decoration, because if the time has come when the American people and their great institutions of learning find it proper or necessary or desirable to decorate a man and give him awards because he is honest in the public service, then I despair of the Republic."

"This," he said, "is something you can demand of your public servants; you don't have to reward them for it. You can demand it through the proper use of your authority as an American citizen, through the ballot box, and you can see that you get good men—honest men and women in government."

Now there is a particular reason why this is so important. We are very apt, when we speak about government in Washington, to think of some rather amorphous, distant, bewildering, comprehensive, complex

875

thing. We don't really know what we mean when we say government. We realize there is a President up there, and a few leaders in the Senate and the House, and we sort of have them visualized; and the rest of it is just a bunch of bureaucrats.

And that's largely true.

But what I want to get over is this: government is nothing in the world but men and women that you select and send to fill the several offices.

Now of course, there is an organization roughly outlined by a Constitution, and more crystallized through our laws as the decades have gone on. But the only thing that comprises government is men and women.

Now those men and women, therefore, must be the people that you carefully select.

Frankly, that is all that the administration that you people have sent to Washington is trying to do.

Make certain they are men and women who, first, are unimpeachable in their approach to every public problem; that neither politics nor cronyism, nor hope of reward nor hope of favoring any particular class or group, has any influence on it; that they are motivated and inspired by one thing: what is the good of 160 million people? That must be, of course, the purpose in their hearts, but take a look at their heads.

You have to send people who are, by their reputations in their own localities, fitted to tackle such complex jobs as now plague a government. They have to be men that have established some success. And you have got to work out in your own mind, "What kind of man do I believe is a good Senator, a good Congressman, a good Governor?"

Incidentally, may I pause to say, you have so many good ones in California, you seem to know more about this, maybe, than I do.

But one thing I want to point out is this: we must not have doctrinaires. This world moves. We outlined, through our forefathers, a great set of principles in the Constitution, and that Constitution—through our Supreme Courts, through actions of the Congress and the Chief Executive down through the years—has been molded and modeled to our needs.

Our needs are not what they were 20 years ago. It is just as senseless, today, to talk about the social security of today in the same terms we would have talked about social security when there were free lands everywhere, and this country was a debtor country with great assets and resources yet to be explored, as it is to talk about taking off here and flying to the moon, instead of waiting for the 50 years that it is going to take for the scientists to show how to do it. It is just that silly, to talk about going back to that kind of thing.

Now, how do we get a man that is that flexible, that adjustable? We want men that can take and listen to facts, who are not so doctrinaire that every fact that is brought in front of them, if it doesn't agree with their preconceptions, it is just thrown out in the woodpile. That is a very necessary thing.

And I want to assure you that in the last 20 months I have watched some very great people making up the executive department—I have watched them work. I don't know of a single one who comes in with the theory—into the Cabinet meeting, or anywhere else—and with this theory fixed in the back of his mind forces everything to conform to it.

On the contrary, every one of them is supported by his own selected group of associates, of advisers throughout this country—from trade associations, from every kind of professional group, from businessmen—everywhere. Those people are the ones that come in and help formulate the policies that this group then tries to translate into recommendations for the legislature to consider.

What I am trying to show is this: that throughout the ten governmental departments, through the heads of agencies, of the FOA, and the Office of Defense Mobilization, and everything else, there is a very earnest attempt on the part of these people to get the opinion of the United States. There is a very great conviction there that the commonsense of the United States—if we avoid both extremes, and take the commonsense judgment of the United States, you have got a pretty good guide as to where we should move in legislation and in programs.

I commend, therefore, the kind of man whom you know to be absolutely unimpeachable in his honesty, who has shown by his standing in the community that he deserves the respect of that community, and who has been something of a success, either as a young man or at any stage of life.

And finally, a man who has got the flexibility of brain, in this day and time, to try to adjust the basic principles in which we believe, the liberty of the individual and his rights, and adjust to the problems that face us every day, whether it be in Indochina, Formosa, or whether it be right here in your great city of Los Angeles.

That is the kind of people that we need so desperately in Washington. And I think that you people who helped to send this administration there, if you will look at the character and types of people now occupying the executive positions, all the way from the Secretary of State on down to the newest appointee, that you can take some pride in the people that have been selected.

And largely, after the Cabinet is selected, remember, all these other people are selected by those Cabinet officers. So there is a wide geographical distribution among these people. There is a wide distribution of professional attainment in their particular specialties.

This same applies, of course, in the Congress, by their very nature being so representative. Our leaders—particularly Senator Knowland and his senior associates in the Senate, Joe Martin and the great Charlie Halleck, a very great lieutenant, their associates in the House—are really doing a remarkable job.

So, as we face this coming election, recognizing as we do that if you are going ahead with a positive program—and I am not going to take up your time this morning to outline this program again; it has been recited time and again in the newspapers, it has been on the television. As a matter of fact, some of you may know I made a little speech about it last night.

Now, of course, none of us is in detail going to agree entirely with that program, because no program, if it is made up as I have been trying to describe to you, is reflective of any single person's complete ideas. But if it follows the general purpose, the good of 160 million people, if it is supported by honest men and women who want nothing in the world but the good of those people, and if it has been intelligently, broadly based, then I think we have got something that we ought to be able to sell.

One of the troubles, of course, is that anyone who takes something of that kind to carry to the people is robbed, really, of the drama of the extremes. It is much easier, you know, to get up and say everybody is a so-and-so except my little gang and me, than it is to go out and sell a really constructive truth, because we tend to take it for granted.

Well, I think that the Administration, probably, is not capable of telling anybody how to dramatize these truths, these programs, and carry them out so that people will overwhelmingly accept them.

But I know it can be done. I believe that if you carry the truth to the people, that there will be only one decision from the mass of 160 million Americans.

I am going to end this little talk with a little story.

Not long ago, I went out to Illinois to the State Fair, and on the way I happened to pick up a paper that was on my airplane. And Paul Hoffman had had a little trouble there at Studebaker—you remember he had asked his union to take a lower wage, a wage they agreed was in conformity with the average. Studebaker had been well above it, I understood, so he asked them to go to two dollars-and-something an hour. He got his teeth kicked in, the first time he proposed it, although the president of the union was very much on his side—I believe his name was Horvath. This story was after they had voted the second time and the union had overwhelmingly voted to accept this cut and then go to work.

This union leader was interviewed by the press, and they said to him, "Well, what do you think about all this?" He said, "Well, you know, I have found this: if you can just get time to tell your people the whole truth, they will always go along with the right thing."

It was a rather comforting thought to have this labor leader saying this, when we had so many wise-cracking so called intellectuals going around and showing how wrong was everybody who didn't happen to agree with them.

By the way, I heard a definition of an intellectual that I thought was very interesting: a man who takes more words than are necessary to tell more than he knows.

I hope that no one is going to get up and wisecrack at me and say, "You've already done it."

I think, though, with those thoughts, and I do pray there is a little bit of commonsense and homely philosophy in them, that you will accept, now, my thanks for the cordiality of your welcome, for the great honor you have done me by inviting me to appear before you.

I assure you that within just about a half hour or an hour, I am to appear before another audience who are not going to be nearly as friendly.

Thank you very much.

NOTE: The President spoke at the Statler Hotel at 8:05 a.m. His opening words "Governor Knight, Mr. Chairman" referred to Governor Goodwin J. Knight of California and to George Meany, President of the American Federation of Labor. Later he referred to Paul Hoffman, President of the Studebaker Corporation, and to Louis Horvath, President of Studebaker Local No. 5 of the United Auto Workers.

275 ¶ Remarks to the American Federation of Labor Convention, Los Angeles, California. *September 24, 1954*

President Meany, and my fellow Americans:

I hope you will allow me to say, first, that when I hear any meeting or convention open with a bit of an invocation and such a rendering of The Star Spangled Banner, you do something to the emotions of an old soldier's heart that leaves me a little bit speechless.

Now there are a number of reasons why I am delighted to be with you. The first is this: I would like to ask you a great favor—that as the elected representatives of the tremendous body of organized labor in this country, each of you will convey to those groups that you represent my very best wishes, my warm greeting as great Americans.

Now I recognize, as well as does anybody else, that it is those people whose heads and hearts and hands have created so much of the wealth of this country, who have done so much to give us the country, with its great resources, that all of us enjoy. So that I, an individual dedicated to the welfare of 160 million people, certainly include all of that great group, exactly as I include every other group in my contemplations, in my studies and the plans that I try to make for this country.

Now I can read, and I do read in the papers, that there are certain things that I do of which this group as a body does not approve—that it does not approve of some of the things, apparently, that I believe in. I think that does not affect at all our personal friendships and respect. In this room there are a number of people who have been in my office, and we have had very cordial relationships, in spite of any differences of conviction and opinion. So of course I know that you respect my attitude, my right to think that possibly you are a bit wrong occasionally, just as you think I am wrong. And that hasn't anything to do with what we may say to each other.

I have another reason for being pleased to be here. I understand that by tradition, by history, you are completely and absolutely nonpolitical. I can't tell you what a relief it is to me to address an audience where there is nothing political expected of me one way or another.

There is one place where I know we agree in one specific, concrete objective or purpose, and one where I think it is not out of place for me, in my present office, even, to say that I should like to commend the American Federation of Labor. Your history of absolute opposition to communism in all its forms, in whatever way it may pose a threat, is to me a heartening thing. And at least, in that, we are one—and I am certain there is no difference possible between us.

I think most of you know of the efforts we have made, through new legislation, through enforcing of old legislation, and strengthening of support for the FBI and for the Department of Justice, whereby we are doing our part daily, hourly, in uprooting any possible trace of this terrible conspiracy that we can find in our country.

And I assure you that to this body I look, always, in that respect, for support in doing that, at the same time that we protect absolutely, with all our might, every constitutional right of every individual that lives in this country.

I think there are a couple of other things on which we agree. I don't believe that you would want me to do anything to start up, again, the war in Korea, and start the casualty lists.

I don't believe you want me to oppose the social security expansion and extension of benefits we have tried to put over.

I am certain you would not want me to raise taxes again, and I am certain you wouldn't want me to increase governmental costs.

Now, I just want to point out, as we go along, that it isn't everything that we are differing about. There are a few things, I think, that as Americans we can all get behind. There I have no objection whatsoever, of course, to listening carefully. And I have listened carefully—I think there are a number of people here that will testify to that effect—I have listened carefully to the measures that some of you people, either individually or as an organization, believe should be done about meeting obvious soft spots in our economy. And there are such—and anyone would be idiotic to deny it.

But the only thing I can say is that with the complexities of government, at home and abroad, we are trying to meet all of these situations, as Abraham Lincoln said it: "As God gave us the wisdom to see the right."

Now there is nothing sacrosanct about any views that I hold, and I have never so stated. So I just want to say this: that the views of this convention will be studied, and thoroughly and sympathetically considered, just as will the views of every other great group of Americans that compares to it.

I know that at times we seem to like issues more than reforms and advancement. I saw that I was challenged, in one paper, as to what I was going to say to this Convention about my failure to redeem my pledge to get away from the union-busting provisions in the Taft-Hartley Act.

Well, I can say only this: I regret that failure, and if this were not a completely nonpolitical meeting, I would point out that a solid Democratic vote in the Senate of the United States defeated me.

But that is political, and you shouldn't state it, I believe.

I am going to recommend again to get rid of that provision. I also recommended—and stated that I would recommend—measures for making certain that people in organized labor were not compelled to take an oath they were anti-communistic, when no one else had to. I think it is completely un-American. I will do my best to get rid of it.

I will resort to every effort in order to redeem my promises—and certainly I hope that there is no one that can say I have not made every effort that I know how to make, in order to redeem any pledges I have ever made to any individual in the world, as groups or individuals. If necessary I will take those two and put them in one special package by themselves, in order that I can say to you: I kept that promise.

Now you people, I know, are against vested interests—and so am I. I want to say this one thing: one of my special jobs is to see that the Federal Government does not establish such monopolies over our lives, such directive power in our communities and in our States, that it becomes the greatest vested interest of all and, finally, is an instrument for attacking the individual liberties of each one of us.

One of my tasks is to do just that. I have tried to find a short way of stating the policy of an administration which has to deal with the most complex, the most worldwide problems that it is possible to conceive of in this day and time; just the welfare—the local welfare of 160 million people is certainly enough to tax the ingenuity of the greatest administration that could be put together. And while you are trying to do that, you study all of the interplay of trade and old prejudices and hatreds, and every kind of antagonism between the nations of the world, many of which we must stay close to if we are to continue as a prosperous, great Nation. Then it becomes extremely complex.

So it is not a simple thing to state the policy of the administration. But I do believe this—while an aphorism, a generality which does express our hope is: in everything where the Government deals with the individual human, be he great or be he small, or be he black or white, or whatever his race or religion, to be humane, to be sympathetic, to be understanding, and do your best to be helpful.

And when the Government deals with the economy of all the people—and that means his pocketbook and his money and his taxes—then by all means to be conservative.

I have searched for ways in which I could state this policy briefly, and I think if you will take that and cut it to pieces and criticize it and put it back together again I do believe it represents what is in the hearts of the administration you now have in Washington.

Now there is one other thing—I am sure there is no way of my proving it, and therefore my statement must either be rejected or accepted on faith: I promised in 1952, earnestly, consistently, and persistently, to try to be a friend of every man who works with his hands.

I need not remind you—I think most of you know: I was a very hard worker. Maybe I told you—my last year before I went to West Point was 52 weeks, with each week 84 hours, and not one hour off. So I have very great comprehension of what organized labor has done to this country. I respect this. I admire them for it.

And in spite of these differences to which I refer, I am not only friendly to that group, to my mind they are part, a great part, of the United States of America. And anything that is United States of America engages my attention and my heart—every single second of my life.

NOTE: The President spoke at the Ambassador Hotel in Los Angeles at 9:37 a.m.

276 ¶ Letter to Harvey S. Firestone, Jr., National Chairman, United Community Campaigns of America. *September 26, 1954*

[Released September 26, 1954. Dated September 17, 1954]

Dear Mr. Firestone:

At the opening of this year's Community Chest and United Fund Campaigns, I extend my most sincere wishes for their overwhelming success.

In this drive our people once again make a concerted voluntary effort to help those among us in illness or in need: children who are sick, the physically handicapped, old people unfriended and alone, those whose suffering in body or mind would otherwise go uncared for, those who would otherwise lack assistance to bring them happier, better lives.

Each person contributing to this assistance can know that he has earned the profound gratitude of those whom he helps. But he has an even greater reward in the inner realization that—as a free individual—he has chosen to show sympathy to fellow human beings. I earnestly hope that the American people will earn these rewards anew by contributing to this year's Community Chest and United Defense Funds with an inspired generosity and a true warmth of heart.

Sincerely,

DWIGHT D. EISENHOWER

NOTE: This letter was released at Lowry Air Force Base, Denver, Colo.

277 ¶ Statement by the President on the Occasion of the Jewish New Year. *September 27, 1954*

ON THE OCCASION of the Jewish New Year, my warm greetings go to all Americans of Jewish faith.

For the tens of centuries spanned by the history of the Jewish people, members of your race have given to mankind almost unbelievable examples of courageous devotion to noble principles—to justice, to liberty, to the right of men to worship according to the inner voice of conscience. Such are the principles which can now give the only sure guide to all men as they seek to establish true peace in the world, the peace which common people everywhere long for in their hearts. From this New Year's Day forward, may the inspiration of your devotion to these ideals give an ever more brilliant light to the path which leads to a real harmony and concord among nations.

DWIGHT D. EISENHOWER

NOTE: This statement was released at Lowry Air Force Base, Denver, Colo.

278 ¶ Letter to the REA Administrator Concerning Recent Progress in Rural Electrification. *September 28, 1954*

Dear Ancher:

I understand that some people are busily circulating statements to the effect that this Administration is opposed to rural electrification programs and that these programs are to be drastically curtailed in the coming fiscal year. I am sure you recognize, as I do, that this is part of a general fear psychology now being adroitly generated in many fields by people who evidently have ends to serve that they consider more important than the truth. I am convinced that our rural population will not be misled by such reckless and irresponsible statements.

For the record I should like to emphasize certain facts. During the past year the progress of the REA has been exceptional. Our rural people know it. This progress has been evidenced in this past fiscal year by your speedier handling of loan applications. This will bring electric power to 170,000 additional farm families—almost 10,000 more than in fiscal year 1953 and 33,000 more than in fiscal year 1952. During the past fiscal year almost $75,000,000 in telephone loans were made as compared with $41,000,000 during the previous fiscal year. The fact is that the backlog of both types of loan applications has been reduced to the lowest point since 1947. Moreover, industry cooperation in these programs, which you have initiated, has already reduced the cost of electric power to farmers in large areas and markedly facilitated the extension of telephone service. Because these jobs in this past fiscal year were done at a substantial saving in administrative cost, the accomplishment is even more impressive.

I want to make this clear: The Administration considers these REA programs great advances for rural America.   They have made our farms more productive; they have greatly enriched the lives of our rural families; and they have served as a powerful stimulus to our country's economy. We shall completely meet next year's financing needs for these programs.

It is our determination that these programs shall fully accomplish their purposes.   We shall continue to give them our wholehearted support.

Sincerely,

DWIGHT D. EISENHOWER

NOTE: This letter to Ancher Nelsen, Ad- istration, was released at Lowry Air Force ministrator, Rural Electrification Admin- Base, Denver, Colo.

279   ¶ Statement by the President: National Newspaper Week.   *September* 29, 1954

To the Newspapers of the Nation:

The nation joins the editors, publishers and reporters of this country in observance of National Newspaper Week.   No institution is more necessary to our way of life than a free press.

A sign of free government, a free press is a primary source of that government's strength.   It informs the people so that they may well discharge their responsibilities as citizens.   It provides them and their elected representatives with a wide range of fact and opinion which must be weighed by all who are concerned with the well-being of our country.

Those who struggle to keep America informed can enjoy the satisfaction of knowing that their contribution to the cause of freedom is mighty. They well deserve the respect and gratitude and support of all our people.

DWIGHT D. EISENHOWER

NOTE: This statement was released at Lowry Air Force Base, Denver, Colo.

280 ¶ Message to the King of Cambodia. *October 2, 1954*

[Released October 2, 1954. Dated September 24, 1954]

Your Majesty:

The people of the United States have watched with concern and admiration the struggle of Cambodia against unwarranted Communist aggression. The United States is happy that Cambodia has reaffirmed its independence and that your Kingdom is in a position now to undertake a course which will secure that sovereign freedom for which your people fought.

At this time when Cambodia has so convincingly demonstrated its independence and its stern determination to maintain that independence, I desire Your Majesty to know that my Government will be pleased to consider ways in which our two countries can more effectively cooperate in the joint task of stemming the threats facing your territories and maintaining peace and prosperity in your Kingdom.

With assurances of my personal esteem and high regard,

Sincerely,

DWIGHT D. EISENHOWER

NOTE: This message to His Majesty Norodom Sihanouk, King of Cambodia, was delivered by Robert M. McClintock, Ambassador to Cambodia, when he presented his credentials to the King at Phnom Penh on October 2. The White House release accompanying the message pointed out that Mr. McClintock was the first resident American Ambassador to Cambodia, and that his assignment at Phnom Penh constituted recognition by the United States of the completion of Cambodian independence.

The message was released at Lowry Air Force Base, Denver, Colo.

281　¶ Letter to Dr. Thomas Keith Glennan Reconvening the Board of Inquiry in the Labor Dispute at Atomic Energy Facilities at Oak Ridge and Paducah.　*October 4, 1954*

Dear Dr. Glennan:

This will advise you that on August 11, 1954, the United States District Court for the Eastern District of Tennessee issued an injunction in the case entitled United States of America v. Union Carbide and Carbon Corporation, et al., Civil Action No. 2456, enjoining each of the defendants from encouraging, causing or engaging in a strike or lockout in the atomic energy industry of the United States. The Attorney General will furnish you a copy of the injunction together with copies of all papers filed in the case.

Pursuant to Section 209(b) of the Labor Management Relations Act, 1947, you are hereby reconvened as the Board of Inquiry established under Executive Order No. 10542 dated July 6, 1954, for the purpose of performing such further functions as may be required of you under the said Act.

Sincerely,

DWIGHT D. EISENHOWER

NOTE: See note to Item 193. The letter was released at Lowry Air Force Base, Denver, Colo.

282　¶ Statement by the President on the Nine-Power Conference in London.　*October 4, 1954*

I HAVE, of course, been in constant communication with Mr. Dulles during the progress of the London Conference and talked to him again this morning on his return to Washington.

All of us have reasons to be gratified by the outcome of the session. It appears that the agreements reached at the 9-power conference in London will—when ratified—preserve most of the values inherent in the original European Defense Community proposal. Certainly they carry great promise of a strengthened and unified security arrangement among the

Western European nations, including West Germany, so as to maintain an effective front in defense of freedom.

Secretary Dulles, in cooperation with the other foreign ministers, has accomplished what may be one of the greatest diplomatic achievements of our time because of the potentialities of these agreements for promoting security, prosperity and peace in Europe, with the inevitable benefits of such a development on the United States and the rest of the world.

NOTE: The agreements are published in "London and Paris Agreements, September–October 1954" (Department of State Publication 5659, Government Printing Office, 1954).

The statement was released at Lowry Air Force Base, Denver, Colo.

283 ¶ Exchange of Messages Between the President and President Einaudi of Italy on the Trieste Agreement. *October* 5, 1954

His Excellency
Luigi Einaudi
President of the Italian Republic

I wish to convey to you my profound gratification and that of the American people at the achievement of an agreement on the delicate Trieste problem. This agreement, worked out through long months of difficult but friendly and constructive endeavor, gives testimony to the far-sighted statesmanship and good will of the government of Italy. It is my earnest hope and expectation that this arrangement will usher in a new era of fruitful collaboration that will contribute to the prosperity and security not only of Italy and Yugoslavia but of all the free nations of Europe. We agree, I am sure, that this fine example of the ability of neighbor nations amicably to settle extremely difficult questions will be highly reassuring to our own peoples and those of friendly nations throughout the world.

Please accept, Mr. President, my heartfelt congratulations at the efforts which you and the members of the Italian government have exerted to make possible this agreement which has so materially contributed to the possibility of maintaining peace in the world.

Sincerely,

DWIGHT D. EISENHOWER

NOTE: President Einaudi's reply follows:

Mr. President:

Ambassador Clare Boothe Luce has personally delivered the message you have addressed to me at the moment of the conclusion of the agreement on the problem of Trieste and I wish not to delay in telling you how gratifying is for me this most valuable evidence of the satisfaction with which the American people and their President have welcomed the event.

You have stressed the farsighted and constructive spirit that has animated the Italian Government during this arduous diplomatic issue and have availed yourself of the understanding reached between Italy and Yugoslavia to reaffirm your confidence in a fruitful cooperation of the two bordering nations and in the help that the mutual relations among all peoples will derive from it.

The agreement arrived at by my country will not fail, as you say, to have profound and favorable repercussions on the happier future of a peaceful and strongly united Europe.

In assuring you that Italy is well aware of the friendly contribution brought by the United States of America to the settlement of the question of Trieste, I thank you, Mr. President, in the name also of the Italian Government, for the noble expressions contained in your message, while I beg you to believe me, sincerely yours,

LUIGI EINAUDI

The messages were released at Lowry Air Force Base, Denver, Colo.

284 ¶ Exchange of Messages Between the President and President Tito of Yugoslavia on the Trieste Agreement. *October* 5, 1954

His Excellency
Marshal Josip Broz-Tito
President of the Federal Peoples Republic of Yugoslavia

Permit me on behalf of the American people personally to extend my warm congratulations to you and to the other members of your government at the achievement of an agreement on the Trieste problem. This agreement, worked out with good will, patience and unremitting endeavor, reflects honor upon your government, for the broad, farsighted statesmanship which has made this agreement possible.

I am sure that you share with me the sense of optimism engendered by the agreement. All of the peoples of the free nations of Europe, as well as the American people, will now be encouraged by this arrangement which opens the way to greater security in Southeastern Europe against any possible encroachment and fosters the hope that improved relations between Yugoslavia and Italy will enhance the general welfare and peace in Europe.

I wish to convey to you my deep gratification at this accord which I am convinced will materially contribute to that which is closest to our hearts, the maintenance of peace, of security and of prosperity in the world.

Sincerely,

DWIGHT D. EISENHOWER

NOTE: President Tito's reply follows:

To the President of the United States:

Permit me to thank you most cordially on my behalf as well as on behalf of the members of the Yugoslav Government for the extremely warm congratulation you were kind enough to extend to me on the occasion of the agreement achieved on the Trieste problem.

I avail myself of this opportunity to thank you for your great efforts in this matter which came particularly to expression in your message sent through Mr. Murphy and which greatly contributed to the overcoming of the last obstacles and to the reaching of an agreement. I fully share with you the sense of optimism that this agreement will have great significance both for the normalization of relations between Yugoslavia and Italy and for the strengthening of peace and security, not only here but generally in Europe.

I wish to convince you that, regardless of the sacrifices Yugoslavia has made for this agreement, I as well as the other members of the Yugoslav Government feel a satisfaction that in this part of Europe a problem has been settled which had worried the world.

JOSIP BROZ-TITO

The messages were released at Lowry Air Force Base, Denver, Colo.

285 ¶ Letter to Harvey V. Higley, Administrator of Veterans Affairs, Designating Him Chairman of the Veterans Day National Committee. *October 8, 1954*

Dear Mr. Higley:

I have today signed a proclamation calling upon all of our citizens to observe Thursday, November 11, 1954 as Veterans Day. It is my earnest hope that all veterans, their organizations, and the entire citizenry will join hands to insure proper and widespread observance of this day. With the thought that it will be most helpful to coordinate the planning, I am suggesting the formation of a Veterans Day National Committee. In view of your great personal interest as well as your official responsibilities, I have designated you to serve as Chairman. You may include in the Committee membership such other persons as you desire to select and I am requesting the heads of all departments and agencies of the

Executive branch to assist the Committee in its work in every way possible.

I have every confidence that our Nation will respond wholeheartedly in the appropriate observance of Veterans Day, 1954.

Sincerely,

DWIGHT D. EISENHOWER

NOTE: This letter was released at Lowry Air Force Base, Denver, Colo.

286   ¶ Address at the Republican Precinct Day Rally, Denver, Colorado.   *October* 8, 1954

[Broadcast from the City Auditorium at 7:35 p.m.]

Governor Thornton, Mr. Vice President, distinguished leaders of the Congress, members of this great audience, and my good friends, over all of America:

Tonight, as I speak to my countrymen, I am privileged to address myself especially to my fellow Republican workers, gathered here in Denver and in meetings throughout our land.   To each of you—to your families, to your friends, and to your political associates—I send my warmest greetings.

All of us are happy that tonight Mr. Nixon, Speaker Joe Martin, and the other members of our able legislative team are here with us.   Under the leadership of these men, the 83d Congress made its record of extraordinary success.   They have my respect and admiration for the splendid service they have rendered to the American people.

Tonight, in our meetings over America, we come together as members of the Republican Party.   But in spirit we have also with us the vast army of other Americans who in 1952, and since, have fought alongside us for the great plans and programs for which together we stand.

We assemble here, and all over America, proud of our Party's principles—proud of our Party's record.

Now, what are these principles and that record, and as Republicans, what is our goal?

That goal is not political power for its own sake, but to advance the good of 163 million Americans.

To that end, we are dedicated to the maximum of individual freedom, fostered by a government desiring not to dominate but only to serve—a government kept close to the hearthsides of America—a government liberal in dealing with the human concerns of the people, but conservative in spending their money. From Lincoln's day to this, these have been the fundamental aims of our historic Party.

Republicans believe that such government will best preserve liberty and justice, and prosperity and happiness in our land.

Such a government will best promote an enduring peace throughout the world.

These are the convictions that unite us; this is the cause that inspires us—and our friends—to continued and dedicated effort.

Two years ago the people of our country showed their desire for this kind of government.

Remember election day 1952. In the early hours of morning, in thousands of precincts over America, our citizens eagerly lined up to vote long before the polls were open.

Do you remember why Americans crowded to the polls on November 4th, 1952?

Let's think back.

Two years ago Americans wanted an end to the war in Korea. It was a costly war, allowed to become futile, and seemingly without end.

They wanted something done about our veterans, who suddenly found the country so poorly prepared that they themselves had once again to undergo the dangers of battle, while others remained at home who had never served.

Americans wanted a government thrifty and frugal with the public's money.

They wanted a stop to the endless rise in taxes, taking more and more of the family income to support an overgrown Washington bureaucracy.

They wanted something done about inflation—to end the growing discouragement as day by day pensions and savings and the weekly pay check bought less and less at the corner store.

Americans were determined to eliminate penetration by the communist conspiracy in our government and in our whole society. They did not consider this menace a red herring.

They wanted clean, honest government.

They were anxious to get rid of the antagonism between the Congress and the Executive which hamstrung the processes of government.

All this America wanted two years ago, and you—you, and those like you throughout this great nation—did something about it.

You remember the telephone brigades of two years ago. You remember the "Get Out The Vote" campaigns. You remember the drive, the enthusiasm that in November 1952, surged forth from our people.

And what happened? You got results.

The people of America established in Washington the kind of government they wanted.

In just 20 months, we have come far.

First of all, with the help of thousands of citizens from every walk of life and from every part of America, we devised a comprehensive, progressive program in keeping with the Republican Party's Platform and the pledges made to America during the campaign. Fundamentally, that program has but one purpose—to make America stronger and better, with growing prosperity and happiness for all of our people.

Now that program was made up of many parts affecting every phase of the life of our great nation. Some parts could be accomplished quickly. Others necessarily had to be developed slowly over the months, to assure their fitness and effectiveness. Important sections still remain to be enacted. The program is one, therefore, of continuous and simultaneous study and action. Its completion is essential to the future prosperity, security and peace of the people of America.

So, let's consider this program and what has happened since its inception.

Fourteen months ago, the futile sacrifices in Korea were stopped.

We now have clean, honest, decent government in Washington.

Government spending has been sharply reduced. Stifling controls have been removed from our nation's economy, amid dire predictions of carping critics that inflation would follow and prices would soar out of sight.

In 20 months, this Administration and the Republican-led Congress cut our government's costs by 11 billion dollars.

And at last, we have a tax cut!

Taxes were cut by 7 billion 400 million dollars—the largest tax cut in the history of this nation. It brings benefits to every family in every American home.

At the same time, we smoked out 211 thousand unnecessary positions on the Federal payrolls.

All during this time, our government has been returning to private citizens activities traditionally belonging to private citizens.

It is stopping the roasting of coffee, the baking of bread, the making of paint and clothes. It has stopped running a hotel. It has stopped running a tug and barge business on our inland waterways. In keeping with the philosophy of our whole program, all of these activities have been returned to private citizens—exactly where they belong.

My friends, I could never mention this subject without adverting to a statement of our first and greatest leader, Lincoln. He said, "The legitimate business of government is to do for a people or a community those things which they cannot do at all for themselves, or cannot so well do in their separate capacities; but in all those things that people can do for themselves, the government ought not to interfere."

I think no better philosophy for a free government has ever yet been stated.

Now, Americans wanted a strong national defense at less cost.

We have today the strongest armed forces of our peacetime history. In building them we have saved vast funds. We have cut red tape and eliminated duplication and waste. And let me make this clear: our military strength does not consist of forcibly recalled veterans who have already served our nation in war.

But, of course, our people also wanted a strong peacetime economy. For this, the Congress took many steps. It passed, for example, a new housing program. It passed an expanded highway program. It passed a new farm program to stop the seven-year decline in farmers' income— a program to promote lasting farm prosperity in an America no longer at war. And that program was designed also to remove the great surpluses that were breaking the back of the program then existing.

The Congress extended old age and survivor's insurance to 10 million, 200 thousand more Americans, and raised their benefits. And at last, my friends, these benefits include farmers who have been indirectly helping to pay the cost of the social security system all these years. The Congress extended coverage of unemployment compensation to 4 million more Americans. It passed tax revisions to encourage small business, and to eliminate inequities in the law.

Due to these and other measures, we have at last an economy whose strength is not sapped by the virus of inflation. It is an economy that doesn't compel the piling up of debts for our children—an economy whose strength is not dependent upon the sacrifices of the battlefield.

Without the economic collapse so widely forecast by professional pessimists, our nation has moved from war to peace.

Nevertheless, I am keenly aware that in some American localities, dislocations and hardships do exist. These are the inescapable aftermath of war and inflation. These problems we are striving constantly to ease. In the localities concerned, as well as in the rest of the country, we are taking concrete action to foster strength in the whole economy.

There was something else, two years ago, that all of us especially wanted. We wanted subversives out of the government service.

This Administration and the Congress are dealing decisively with the communist menace. Supported by eleven new laws, we are backing to the hilt the Department of Justice and the FBI. There is no vacillation nor inaction on the part of this Administration in dealing with those who, by force or violence, would overthrow the government of the United States.

And abroad, we have an honest, forthright foreign policy concerned with deeds, not merely words. Over the globe our friends know our devotion to freedom. They know that America joins with those who help themselves in the effort to preserve liberty and peace.

Two years ago, war was raging in Korea and Indochina. All Asia lay exposed to the steady advance of the Reds. Iran, with 60 percent of the world's known petroleum reserves, was in deadly danger. Suez and Trieste posed constant threats to peace in the West. Europe had foundered on century-old differences, unable to build a position of reliable strength. Even in the Western Hemisphere, communist imperialism had ominously appeared.

You know of the events that have since occurred.

In London, a few days ago, an agreement of momentous significance was signed that can powerfully strengthen the defenses of the West. Just this week, after almost a decade of anxious effort, Yugoslavia and Italy, with the encouragement and help of the Western world, settled their differences over Trieste.

For the first time in twenty years, there is no active battlefield anywhere in the world.

And, at last, we are harnessing the atom to the work of peace.

As for nations which, despite our best efforts, are still unfriendly, they harbor no delusions about the determination and the growing strength of the free world.

Recently, communist imperialism discovered that the entire Association of American Republics means business in defending freedom. First at Caracas, then in ten short, determined days, the communist beachhead in Guatemala was eliminated.

In all these ways, then, there has been progress of the most tremendous import to the peace and security of the Western world. Much of this progress is due to the richness of experience, imagination and determination of our distinguished Secretary of State. He and his colleagues in the State Department and the Foreign Service are carrying American prestige to new heights in foreign chancelleries.

Fellow Citizens, I have recited some of the advances made in many fields in a short 20 months. For the most part, they have grown out of a cordial partnership between the Administration and the Congress. This cordiality has been a welcome relief from the bickering and the suspicion that for so long poisoned relations between the Executive and Legislative Branches. In laws passed, and in heightened respect for their government, this harmony has brought immense benefits to the American people.

And now, let's take a quick look at the future.

Many things need to be done.

We must continue to foster the growth of a free economy to provide more jobs and higher living standards.

We must continue our efforts to cut the cost of government, so we can cut taxes still more.

We must continue each year to improve our peacetime farm program.

We must have a vast new highway program.

We must expand our foreign trade and American investment abroad. We must expand markets for America's farms and factories, if we are to keep prosperity within our own land.

We must write into law a national water resources program.

We must help our people meet their critical health and medical needs, while repudiating socialization of medicine.

We must find ways to encourage communities to provide the school-houses they need, and to improve opportunities for their school teachers.

We must build a new and effective reserve program for our armed forces.

We must begin to unravel the confused relations between the Federal, State and local governments, and make still more improvements in the organization of the Federal government.

We must drive through partisan obstructions to achieve statehood for Hawaii, to lower the voting age in Federal elections, and to make our promised changes in the labor-management laws.

We must continue our historic advances in the vital area of civil rights.

We must vigorously push all constructive measures for promoting world peace, always strong and secure, but always fair and conciliatory.

Now, my friends, a cold war of partisan politics between the Congress and the Executive Branch won't give us these goals.

And this brings up a political fact of life.

You know perfectly well that you just can't have one car with two drivers at the steering wheel and expect to end up anyplace but in the ditch—especially when the drivers are set on going in different directions. By the same token, you cannot have efficient Federal government when the Congress wants to follow one philosophy of government and the Executive Branch another.

In our system of government, progress is made when the leaders of the Executive Branch and the majority of the Congress are members of the same political party. The unsurpassed record of the 83d Congress is shining evidence of this truth. Moreover, in no other way can Americans hold one party and one group of people responsible either for success or lack of success.

History shows that when the Executive and Legislative Branches are politically in conflict, politics in Washington runs riot. In these conditions, the public good goes begging while politics is played for politics' sake. Meanwhile, in the eyes of the world, we appear divided in council and uncertain in purpose.

These are the reasons—the compelling reasons—why the completion of your great program requires the election of a Republican-led Congress.

In our effort to keep the kind of government we want, you citizens are on the political front lines—the precincts of America. There you are as much a part of government as the sincere, hard-working men and women in Washington today who are trying to give you the kind of government you want.

As leaders and workers in your precincts, you know that the members of our Party cannot carry this battle alone. We must enlist the spirited support of friends and neighbors, regardless of party, who believe in the same principles and objectives. Happily, we have been blessed with millions of such sturdy allies. For the cause in which we believe is bigger than any political party. To this cause, all Americans, regardless of party, can give their enthusiastic support.

And in this struggle, I know you will have the same determination—the same enthusiasm—the same drive—as you had two years ago.

For only through your effort can our program continue to advance.

Only through your effort will we continue to have the kind of America all of us so earnestly desire.

Together, my friends, we shall forge ahead in this great work we have so well begun, determined to keep America strong and secure—determined that this land of freedom, under Almighty God, will not rest until we see in the world a lasting peace with justice. Together we shall forge ahead to build in our America a steadily growing prosperity and happiness that will bring an ever brighter future for our people and for those who, after we are gone, must carry forward the banner of freedom.

That, my fellow Ameicans, is our kind of America.

Working together with those millions who have made common cause with us in this effort, that is the kind of America we shall have.

Thank you—thank you—and goodnight to all of you.

287 ¶ Remarks to Members of the Olympic Committee, Denver, Colorado. *October* 12, 1954

Mr. Wilson:

Last April the Congress authorized the President to proclaim October 16 as Olympic Day. I signed the Proclamation last week, and I give to you now a copy of the Proclamation that proclaims that day as Olympic Day.

In doing so, I want to give my word of commendation to you people who are doing so much to promote the success of the American Olympic Team, and the Olympic games in general. I thoroughly believe that the participation in athletics is one of the greatest influences in the development of our youth; and I thoroughly believe in the Olympics as one of the means and methods by which some understanding of fair play and justice can be developed among nations.

So, to you, good luck, and especially good luck in getting all the support from our people, not only athletic-wise but financial-wise, to make the games a huge success.

I believe in what you are doing. Good luck to you, and to your team.

NOTE: The President spoke on the steps of the Headquarters Building, Lowry Air Force Base, at 10:20 a.m. His opening words "Mr. Wilson" referred to Kenneth L. Wilson, President of the U.S. Olympic Committee. For the text of the Olympic Day proclamation see title 3 of the Code of Federal Regulations (1954 Supp., p. 33).

288 ¶ Memorandum on Occupational Safety in the Government Service.   *October* 14, 1954

[Released October 14, 1954. Dated October 11, 1954]

To the Heads of all Departments and Independent Agencies:

I am very much concerned with the problem of injuries to Federal workers. The suffering and the wastage of both human and financial resources caused by accidents in the Government service constitute an urgent challenge. This Administration is determined to do everything possible to reduce the rate of such accidents.

While some agencies and departments have shown improvement in their accident record, a greater effort in this respect is essential to efficient operation. I am, therefore, requesting the head of each Government department and agency to review the accident experiences and the safety program of his organization and to take all necessary steps to reduce accidents.

The Federal Safety Council has recommended an annual Presidential safety citation to the agency or department which makes the greatest progress in accident prevention. I have approved this recommendation and have advised the Secretary of Labor to proceed with the necessary arrangements. I have also asked him to provide or arrange for assistance to all departments and agencies in the development, organization, and maintenance of effective accident prevention programs and to report to me from time to time on the progress made.

DWIGHT D. EISENHOWER

NOTE: This memorandum was released at Lowry Air Force Base, Denver, Colo.

289 ¶ Exchange of Messages Between the President and President Magloire on the Hurricane Damage in Haiti. *October* 14, 1954

[Released October 14, 1954. Dated October 13, 1954]

His Excellency Paul E. Magloire
President of the Republic of Haiti
Port-Au-Prince, Haiti

I would like to express the deepest sympathy of the American people to the people of Haiti at this time when reports have been received of a disastrous hurricane which has passed over the western part of your country. I am informed that Ambassador Davis has already arranged for assistance from the United States Armed Forces to survey the damaged area and lend all possible help. I trust you will inform him of any additional ways in which the United States can render aid. I send heartfelt wishes for the safety of the Haitian people and Your Excellency's own welfare.

DWIGHT D. EISENHOWER

NOTE: President Magloire's reply follows:

His Excellency Dwight D. Eisenhower
President of the United States of America

I wish to express to you the thanks of the people of Haiti and the gratitude of their government for the friendly action of the American people and government. I would like to emphasize the valuable cooperation of Ambassador Davis and the members of the American Embassy at Port-au-Prince and also the assistance of Rear Admirals G. B. H. Hall and Taylor and their associates.

The people here were hard hit. All possible help is needed. Please accept my personal appreciation and sincere best wishes for the American people and for your own welfare.

PAUL E. MAGLOIRE

The messages were released at Lowry Air Force Base, Denver, Colo.

290 ¶ Remarks in Indianapolis at the Columbia Republican Club. *October* 15, 1954

Governor Craig, and my friends:

I have often heard that in any political gathering in Indiana it was not very difficult to work up quite a head of steam. I see exactly what they mean.

I have been doing a little traveling over the United States in the past few weeks, particularly the western part. I visited big meetings and big cities and small places—farms, and so forth. And I have been trying to gather impressions. I have been astonished by one thing I have found. Everywhere our Republican groups, either in the organization or our candidates or incumbents in office, would talk about their difficulties, saying that they were greater than they expected to find them, particularly in view of an admitted record of accomplishment in the 83d Congress.

And finally, about a week ago, I ran into a friend of mine who explained it to me in his own way. He said, "Well, General, you oughtn't to be so greatly surprised by this." He said, "You know, in 1952 we got together, and we had a great cause, and we called it a crusade. We believed it was a crusade. We wanted to throw out the New Deal—and we did. And so what have we got to worry about now? Our taxes have been lowered. We have got rid of the abominable excess profits tax. Controls have been taken off our economy. We feel we are more our own men again, making more our own decisions. We are perfectly happy, so why should we get excited?"

Well, this was rather astonishing, still, to me. Because you must remember that I had most of my experience in the Army. And I had 3½ years of rather exciting experiences in the recent war. And I learned one thing: a victory is not won until every objective for which you are struggling has been attained. Time and again, you found units, having gotten off to a good start, everything going pretty well, suddenly being surprised—driven back—sometimes suffering quite a reverse, as at Kasserine Pass in Africa.

Because, in the first flush of victory, they forgot there were no rules applied to this game except winning—in war, I was talking about. I hope I am still not partisan enough that I put any thought of winning above honor and decency. And I don't think the Republican Party does.

So about—let me see, I guess the day before yesterday—maybe 2 days ago—I went to a luncheon where they had the people that were heading the financial affairs of the Republican campaign in Colorado. And in attempting to describe my feelings about this, I recalled to them—and some of you here are old enough to have the same memories—I recalled to them a South American who came up here, a great prizefighter, and he crawled in the ring with a man named Dempsey. And in the first round he knocked Dempsey so far out in the audience that he broke two or three typewriters for the newspapermen. But Dempsey crawled back in the ring and whipped the tar out of him.

Now I don't think the Republican Party has any idea of being a Firpo.

In the 1952 campaign we started something in which we deeply believed. We believed that the Federal Government was penetrating too deeply into our lives, and the lives of our cities, our States, and often of our families, and certainly of our businesses. So we set about reversing this trend. And we have got the new trend started. It started well. The accomplishments of the 83d Congress, I venture to say, when future people look at them with a little bit less impassioned eyes than we possibly do now, will say: there was a Congress that America should have been proud of. And in my opinion they are.

But maybe that pride is just not of the kind to stir us to the action that will let the Congress, under the same leaders, carry forward and finish the job. That is what we are trying to do now. We have got to stir up and obtain the same kind of enthusiasm we had in 1952. And I admit it is not as easy. Because then we had always a symbol. Here was the New Deal standing up there and doing things to us we didn't like, and we really got busy and girded up our loins and went into battle. That is what we have got to do again.

Now in talking to these many people over in Colorado 2 days ago, I told them, "I am not going to talk dollars to you. Dollars are needed, but they are incidental. I want to talk about your hearts. Where is your heart?"

No organization, no battle unit, nobody else, can win a war—can win a battle or a political campaign unless they have got something very deep for which they believe they are fighting. So deeply do they believe it that they hold back nothing. And if it's money that has to be thrown into the pot, why, throw it in. Why not? You throw in your efforts, your time, and your brain. So why not money? And that is the only way that I would ever talk about money to anybody—I don't care how rich he is or how well he was able to support the efforts of the party.

What we have got to do now is to build again that flame, that flame that means good government, decent government, honest government, government of the kind that reserves to every citizen and to every locality the maximum power to determine its own affairs. It is in that kind of government that America has grown great. And it is only in that kind of government that America can continue to grow and be great—the kind of government that respects the human, respects him as an equal before the law and before God. That is the kind of thing in which we must believe—by which we do believe—but which we must build up again into such a cause for which to fight that there will be no question about these things.

Now I should like to make myself clear: I have never made any claim, and I am certain no one in this room does, that all the patriotism in America is the exclusive property of any one party.

We do know that we have a program for establishing the United States on the road of moderate government—decent, moderate government— that does respect the human, that does use the government to support and uphold the individual when he gets in trouble through catastrophes that he can't himself control—that is the kind of thing we want to do. Then I say if we are going to live that kind of thing—believe in it and support it—we have got to get on our horses, get the spurs in the grease and get going.

Now personally, I have never in my life gone into any fight to lose. I believe in faces that go this way, and not this way [broad—not long].

I believe in optimism—enthusiasm—and the confidence that we can do it.

As I tried to say the other night, this is so important because you can't have two drivers at the wheel of an automobile and expect to land anywhere but in the ditch. We don't want one driver—the Legislature; and another driver—the Executive, wanting to go two different places. We want these people working together, doing their task and going to the same place: good government for the United States of America, prosperity and peace and security.

When I came in and I was talking to Governor Craig, he said 2 minutes. I have done far better than—I mean, I have exceeded my welcome by that much; but I have one more message:

Mrs. "Ike," who is still on the plane, charged me specifically with making her apologies. But a long plane trip is a thing that throws her out of kilter a little bit, so I made her stay on the plane and take a nap. So she is not here, not because she did not want to come, but because just the spirit is willing; the flesh is just a little bit weak.

So good night.

NOTE: The President spoke at 6:10 p.m.

291 ¶ Address at Butler University, Indianapolis, Before the National Institute of Animal Agriculture. *October* 15, 1954

Dean Reed, and my fellow Americans:

I hope you will permit me, first, a personal message from my wife who, because of slight indisposition, couldn't come this evening and stayed on her plane. She heard that this magnificent chorus was going to sing "Mamie," and she asked me particularly to thank the chorus on her behalf.

I feel a deep sense of distinction in meeting so many of you tonight, both you in this great hall and those I am privileged to greet by radio and by television in their own homes across this land.

May I, first, on behalf of all of us, pay my respects to the distinguished leaders of American agriculture here with us this evening. Likewise, I salute the leaders in research, science, and industry who are taking part in this meeting through the National Institute of Animal Agriculture.

And, my friends, will you permit me to pay a personal tribute to a former county agricultural agent who is with us tonight. I refer to the most devoted, most dedicated friend of American agriculture I know: our Secretary of Agriculture, Ezra Taft Benson.

Now, my principal purpose this evening is to give you an account of this administration's stewardship in matters specially affecting our agricultural community. In doing so I do not mean to imply that our farmers' interests are limited to farming. Far from it! Nor is a prosperous agriculture of interest to the farmer alone. The welfare of 163 million Americans is bound up with our Nation's agriculture—just as every farmer is affected by all national and world affairs.

First, our farmers, like the rest of us, want and need peace. They want their boys at home, and not at war. So, it is important to all of us that the seemingly endless and frustrating war in Korea was ended 14 months ago. Today we have peace. For the first time in 20 years, there is no active battlefield anywhere in the world. And I pledge to you that every resource of this country is being tirelessly used to make it a lasting peace. Our Nation extends the hand of friendship to all in the world who will grasp it in honesty and good faith. We will confer on this subject with any and all—if only we can have some assurance of sincerity of purpose, which must underlie all progress toward permanent peace. In this I know I speak for every American citizen, regardless of partisan or any other consideration.

Our farmers, just as all of us, want America strongly defended. Now, under methods that assure the least possible cost to the taxpayer, our military strength grows daily. And we have today the strongest Armed Forces in our peacetime history, and by far the most efficient.

Our farmers, like all the rest of us, want relief from oppressive taxation. In 21 months we have cut the cost of Government by 11 billion dollars. This tremendous saving made possible a tax cut of 7 billion, 400 million dollars. It is the largest tax cut in history—an equivalent of about $180 for every family in America.

Our farmers, like all the rest of us, demand efficient Government. In 1½ years 211 thousand excess positions have been dropped from the Federal payroll.

Our farmers, as all of us, want a trustworthy government—a government that deals quickly and effectively with those in its employ who are unfit, or corrupt, or tinged with communism. Misfits are being tirelessly searched out and removed from sensitive government positions. New laws passed by the 83d Congress have powerfully strengthened the efforts of the Department of Justice and the FBI to deal with the Communist menace in our country.

Our farmers, and all of us, want a national economy strong in all its parts, not dependent on the froth of inflation or the blood of the battlefield. We have moved from war to peace without the economic collapse so widely predicted last winter by professionally pessimistic but politically hopeful prophets.   For our Nation as a whole, this year 1954 is the most prosperous peacetime year in our entire history.

Even so, as the inevitable aftermath of war and inflation, economic dislocations and individual hardships exist in some industrial communities and in some farming areas.   My heart truly goes out to every citizen who wants to work and has no job, or who, in other ways, suffers these hardships.   Methods to eliminate distress and to build enduring economic strength in these localities are being thoroughly explored and pursued.

So, peace, lower taxes, honest government, a strong economy, personal security—these we must seek for every American.   We must never forget that the fortunes of all of us are tightly intertwined.   This interdependency applies also among the nations of the world—certainly among the nations which are free.

This was not so widely understood when I was a boy working on the farms of Kansas.   Then, a half-century ago, we were, except for the weekly newspaper, somewhat isolated from the rest of the world.   In those days we plowed with a team of horses and a one-bottom plow.   We stacked our hay by hand.   When a calm stopped the windmill we had to pump countless buckets of water for use in home and stable.   The nearest thing to a tractor we saw were the big engines used for running threshing machines.

And then came automobiles, mechanization, electricity, telephone, radio, and television, and life today on our farms is a far different thing.

And yet, in many ways, it hasn't changed.   Markets and weather are still unpredictable.   Wind and hail, mud and dust, floods and drought still exist.   There are still the insects and plant and animal disease.   Watering and feeding the stock, and milking the cows, still have to be done right on time.   In short, good farming is still sun-up to sun-down work.

But just look at what this hard work has done for America!

A skilled American farm worker today produces food and clothing for eighteen other Americans.   What a contrast with countries where as many as nine must toil to provide food for themselves and one other person.

And yet, in large sections of agriculture, this work has not received its fair reward.   Two years ago, the farmers of America were fearful—they were fearful for reasons that went beyond their suspicions of corruption and subversion in government and the Korean war.   They saw definite signs of impending disaster in farm programs and in our agricultural economy.

They wanted a stop to falling income, a stop to rising farm costs, a stop to the loss of markets, a stop to the piling up of threatening and unmanageable surpluses.

In the 2 years before this administration took office in January 1953, the parity ratio dropped nineteen points.   Our farmers suffered a serious loss in buying power.   Here are the facts.

In 1947, a cotton farmer could buy a pickup truck with 9 bales.   By the end of 1952, it took not 9 but 14 bales.

In 1947, 800 bushels of corn would buy a tractor.   By the end of 1952, it took not 800 but over 1,300 bushels—two-thirds more.

In 1947, 930 bushels of wheat would buy a combine.   By the end of 1952, it took not 930 but over 1,600 bushels—three-fourths more.

My friends, this steady decline in farmers' buying power took place under the old farm law—a law that is still in effect.   Yet, some would have our farmers believe that in the future this law will do what it has failed miserably to do in the past.

Now every farmer knows why his income declined.   Agriculture was losing markets.   Prices were depressed by uneconomic production which was encouraged by the old farm law.

The truth is, this vital problem of markets and surpluses had never been faced head on.   Two wars had postponed the day of inevitable reckoning.

It was war—World War II—which supplied the markets for farm surpluses that had piled up in the late 1930's.

In 1950, another war, this time in Korea, postponed the problem until 1952.

Now, clearly war is not an American solution for any problem.   At Kasson, Minnesota, two years ago, I pledged that a Republican administration would seek a lasting, peaceable agricultural program.

Twenty-one months ago we set out to develop a durable, logical plan. We sought objective, expert advice from practical farmers, farm groups, commodity specialists.   We consulted with educators, law makers, food processors.   The final result was a comprehensive program passed by the 83d Congress, under Republican leadership.

So, at last, we have a program which attacks our farm problem on both crucial fronts—markets and production. We have a farm program geared not to war, but to peace—a program that will encourage consumption, expand markets, and realistically adjust farm production to markets. It will begin the movement toward that full parity in the market place which 2 years ago at Kasson I set as a goal.

By removing from normal trade channels a large part of the stocks now owned by the Government, we have reduced their depressing effect on farm prices and price support levels.

The program provides, of course, for price supports. They are essential. They are, however, only one of many steps essential to a prosperous agriculture—steps that should have been taken long ago.

Now let's review some of the progressive measures passed by the 83d Congress in this general area.

First, it passed a new law to use a billion dollars' worth of our farm commodities to expand our foreign markets.

Second, this same Congress overcame 30 years of frustration and authorized the St. Lawrence Seaway which will bring to millions of farmers low-cost transportation and readier access to foreign markets.

And I warn you, my friends, this list of accomplishments of the 83d Congress is a long one.

Third, this same Congress extended social security to five and a half million farmers and farm workers. For years these farmers had been indirectly helping to pay the costs of the social security system. Now, for the first time, our farmers will receive its benefits.

Fourth, this same Congress permits farmers to deduct for tax purposes up to 25 percent of their income each year for the costs of many soil conservation practices.

Fifth, this same Congress accelerated the depreciation period for newly-constructed grain storage facilities and liberalized depreciation for new farm equipment.

Sixth, this same Congress launched a program that provided storage for more than 500 million bushels of grain.

Seventh, this same Congress provided effective incentives to wool growers.

Eighth, this same Congress gave independence to the Farm Credit Administration and provided for its eventual control by farmers themselves—something that farmers had been demanding for many, many years.

Ninth, this same Congress increased Federal funds for agricultural research.

Tenth, the administration and this same Congress vigorously advanced the farm electrification program. Loans to electric and telephone borrowers during the 1954 fiscal year totaled $242 million. With this help, telephone borrowers provided more modern service, more new lines, and connected more subscribers than during the four previous years combined.

Eleventh, this same Congress passed a law to develop the upstream protection of watersheds by assuring Federal technical and financial help to local groups. And very important, these programs will not be planned by an all-wise bureaucracy in far-off Washington. They will be planned at the instance of local people, with the cooperation and participation of State and local governments.

Twelfth, this same Congress made loans available to develop water improvements on farms and ranches throughout America—loans formerly limited to 17 States.

Thirteenth, this same Congress authorized loans for drainage facilities, reforestation, and other water and soil conservation practices.

Fourteenth, this same Congress authorized the establishment of the Farm Cooperative Service as a separate and vital agency in the Department of Agriculture. This action is in line with our determination to strengthen farmer cooperatives.

Fifteenth, this same Congress, working with the administration, has swiftly met sudden crises in agriculture.

You remember the terrible drought of 1953 and the help provided by the Federal Government. Tragically, it is true that this year, in large regions of our country, a serious drought still exists. Again we are extending help. In 15 States—in more than 850 counties—we are providing credits and low-cost feed.

Recently we worked out with the railroads a 50 percent reduction in all freight rates on hay shipments in the drought areas. This cooperation of the railroads is a valued contribution to the common good. And in your name I thank those railroads.

So, my friends, in 21 months we have gone far toward building for our agriculture a foundation of enduring prosperity, in an America at peace. And yet, much remains to be done.

We must, for example, do more, much more, for the operators of small farms who in programs of previous years have been too often forgotten.

We must advance atomic research to assist and develop low-cost electric power for our farms and increase efficiency in food production and preservation.

We must continue to foster conservation of our valuable soil and water resources and improve the productivity of our land.

We must prepare for that day when our concern will not be surpluses, but the production of enough food for a gigantic population.

We must continue to free our farmers from paralyzing bureaucratic control.

We must constantly improve existing programs, adapting them as new conditions arise.

My friends, all 163 million of our citizens have an enormous stake in making certain that this program is carried through in its entirety. Your leaders in the executive and legislative branches of your Government are determined to bring it to pass.

As we forge ahead with this program, we know that awaiting all of us is opportunity undreamed of but a few years ago. This opportunity is surely ours if we keep vital and strong our unmatched will to advance and grow our individual initiative and our personal freedoms.

Opportunity is ours if we continue to reject policies that lead to ever higher taxes, to regimentation, to dependence on a government far from our homes.

Opportunity will be ours if we keep a government of teamwork—a government of harmony and good will—to continue the advance along the course charted 21 months ago.

We need a Congress and an executive department both guided by leaders of the same general political philosophy. The leaders of both those great branches must be dedicated to the same broad programs and objectives. These are the reasons for my deep conviction that for the next 2 years our national welfare will be best served by a Republican-led Congress.

But, my friends, let us—all of us—strive together for that kind of future for America—a future boundless in opportunity, unlimited in rich promise for our farmers, for all of us, for our children. For it is given to us to do our part in building and preserving America—an America whose shining faith and hope and freedom will continue to

light the way for all in the world who, with us, love liberty and peace.
Thank you very much—thank you.

NOTE: The President spoke at 8:00 p.m. His opening words "Dean Reed" referred to Harry J. Reed, Dean of the School of Agriculture at Purdue University, and chairman of the National Institute of Animal Agriculture.

292 ¶ Remarks of Welcome to President Tubman of Liberia. *October* 18, 1954

Mr. President:

It is a very great privilege to welcome here the Head of the Liberian nation in which, since the founding of your government, our countrymen—our people—have taken a very deep and abiding interest.

And we are delighted that you have found it possible to pay here a courtesy visit, so that we can assure you again of our friendly feelings toward your country.

NOTE: The President greeted President Tubman on the North Portico of the White House at 5:00 p.m. President Tubman responded as follows:

I thank you, Mr. President, and I assure you that the government and people of Liberia are highly honored by this gesture of your regard and consideration of them.

The ties of friendship that have existed between us, that have characterized our two countries for the past—more than a century, shall continue in ever increasing measure in kind.

293 ¶ Toasts of the President and the President of Liberia. *October* 18, 1954

President Tubman, my friends:

I think it would be difficult to conceive of a social occasion in which could be symbolized more of improbable romance and sheer grandeur than we have in this room this evening.

In this House have been entertained proud representatives of proud nations—individuals who, with only an occasional bow to unexplainable twists in the family tree, can go all the way back to the Plantagenets and the Yorks and indeed to Charlemagne.

In 1865 a Negro in Alabama, lately freed from bondage, learned or knew of the rather young nation of Liberia in western Africa. And he left the United States to go there. Some years later, in the early 1870's a young girl from Georgia, apparently going with her parents—although this point I have not checked—also went to Liberia.

Tonight—some 90 years later than that first departure from our country—we meet here to greet, to entertain, and to pay our salute to the grandson of that man—the son of that little girl. If Horatio Alger or G. A. Henty, or indeed Shakespeare could do better than that in writing drama—the drama of real life—into a story, I have yet to find where they did it.

I feel that we meet also with a very deep affection not only for the individual whom we honor, but for the country that he represents and heads. There has been indeed a very close association between America and Liberia. And it is transcendent of mere sentiment. Present with us this evening are the heads of two of America's great industrial corporations. Each has significant—indeed very important—business arrangements and investments in this country of Liberia. Its association with us has, therefore, not been entirely a one-sided arrangement, even in the let us say "sordid" avenues of trade. We as a country have profited because of the great resources of this country, now of two million people— a people whose constitution is written largely in the pattern of our own, for whom—because of their origin, or part of their origin, because of the parenthood of their President and because of our close business connections—we have every kind of intimate association.

Consequently, we are indeed happy and proud that President Tubman has come over here to visit us, to express something of his own nation's readiness to live in friendship with us, to promote that friendship, to learn more of us—although indeed he has been here often enough now that he probably knows us pretty well. But it is the kind of thing that is certainly most welcome to us, one that we respect, one that we welcome from every standpoint.

And for all those reasons, I am sure that everyone here will, with real enthusiasm, rise to join me in a Toast to President Tubman of Liberia.

NOTE: The President proposed this toast at a state dinner at the White House. President Tubman responded as follows:

President Eisenhower, and Mrs. Eisenhower:

I had prepared some written remarks that I had intended to read tonight, be- cause there were some things that I de- sired to say. But President Eisenhower has, by his speech, compelled me to pursue a different course.

I am particularly touched, Mr. Presi- dent and Mrs. Eisenhower, by your most generous gesture in extending to us an invitation to come to Washington in these times of stress, of extreme difficulties, when Washington has become the capital of the world and your hands are so filled with national and international problems—even politics.

The relationship that has existed between our two countries for more than a century has given the people of Liberia an unshakeable confidence and trust in the Government of the United States. And there are several reasons for that. There are several things that justify this position. One of them is that when Liberia was first founded as a colony by the American Colonization Society and other American philanthropic interests, within 25 years thereafter traders refused to recognize the authority of the colony to impose laws and collect excise duties. It was then that the Colonization Society suggested that the only way out of that situation was for them to declare themselves an independent state. And that was the reason why the Republic of Liberia declared herself an independent state so early. On the other hand, we look at that situation and we wonder what would have happened had Liberia been a colony of one of the colonizing powers, within 25 years—what would have happened? One hundred years now, possibly still a colony.

But it was the broad view, outlook of American statesmanship and American policy that enabled us, at the time, to become an independent, a sovereign state, and their contributions from time to time have assisted us to maintain our independence and sovereignty.

And another thing your people—the United States, the people of America, have justified, or one of your greatest poets has written correctly of, and concerning, when he said:

> Be great without seeking to be great
> By fraud and conquest.
> Rich in gold, but richer in the vast
> estate of virtue
> For thy children hold.

Mr. President and Mrs. Eisenhower, I thank you again—to you all.

And it is our ardent desire that the ties of friendship heretofore existing between our two countries, shall be maintained and increased with the years.

I ask you, ladies and gentlemen, in that spirit to rise and join me and drink a Toast to the health of the President of the United States and of Mrs. Eisenhower.

294 ¶ Remarks at the Department of State 1954 Honor Awards Ceremony. *October* 19, 1954

Mr. Secretary and friends:

In his opening remarks the Secretary well described my relationships with this great group, both with the Foreign Service and with the State Department civil personnel. So you can understand why I feel that this is a family gathering. I feel it keenly, and hope you do the same, because you are the people that execute a responsibility that is laid upon me by our Constitution—the responsibility for the foreign affairs of our country.

You are, of course, in carrying this responsibility, concerned with promoting the prosperity and happiness and well being of the United States, through solidifying those relations with other nations that will be helpful in this regard.

Now this can be done only in peace. Since the advent of nuclear weapons, it seems clear that there is no longer any alternative to peace, if there is to be a happy and well world. I often recall an argument I got into once with a foreign diplomat. He was a member of the British Foreign Office. And he was very worried about the arrangement that had been made to place the control of Germany temporarily in the hands of soldiers. He thought—and I don't know why—that those war-weary soldiers would be too anxious to start a war, and finally in rather resentful disgust I said to him, "My friend, I would like for you to know that the soldier has only one excuse for living in this world, and that is to regain the peace that you diplomats lost in the first place."

Now the reason I bring this up is that even if there was a modicum of truth in what I said then, there no longer is. The soldier can no longer regain a peace that is usable to the world. I believe that the best he could do would be to retain some semblance of a tattered nation in a world that was very greatly in ashes and relics of destruction. But possibly he could keep us from immediate and complete domination by some outside force. That would be a poor climate in which to start again the development of a peace. Certainly it would be a far worse opportunity than we now have.

The reason I paint this little picture—even in a sort of digression—is this: we have glorious opportunity ahead of us. Because we have opportunity in a world that has not yet suffered that kind of destruction—pray God must not suffer that kind of destruction.

In these halting words, and with these halting examples, I am trying to impress upon you my opinion of the importance of your work. There is no task facing the world today so important as maintaining a peace and giving to the world confidence that that peace will be just and lasting.

That is the measure of what you people and those like you—those above you and those below you—in these services, must do for America.

Now, some among you today are being rewarded for unusual service. I have been a party to such ceremonies in the military service many times during my lifetime. They reward for courage, unusual ability and devotion and dedication, just as do you people. And I remind you that in my conviction your work is now more important than theirs. But I want to bring out another point. Those experiences I had in the military service convinced me that the gradations in character among the different services, is often difficult to determine. We select one man for a decoration and then another man is not selected. And yet the second man may have faced hardships, dangers, and privation. But you can say, well if this service is not rewarded what shall we do? I think you can only remind yourself of the words on the Iwo Jima Statue, "Uncommon Courage Was a Common Virtue."

So these people, as they come up to be decorated, will be representative of each of you. Each of you will at least vicariously and in some small part be a recipient of that same award. By the same token, one day, undoubtedly, you will be standing there to receive a token that will be representative of the work of a great body. Because only as we think of it in that way, only as we work together from top to bottom, only as we give loyalty and not jealousy and envy, only as we cling together secure in our confidence that we are dedicated to the great ideals of Americanism, justice and decency and fair play—even for those with whom we are dealing, sometimes, at swords-points, across the distances of an ocean—only as we do that can we be truly successful.

If there is any organization that should have the highest morale based firmly in its own convictions, as to the importance of its work, the necessity for successful accomplishment regardless of what critic or opponent may say, a morale based in that high belief in a cause, then that should be the Foreign Service and the State Department—as, indeed, I believe it is.

So you can understand something of the happiness I feel when I gather here with you to witness the decoration of a few among you who, standing as symbols for all, will exemplify and typify the appreciation that your country feels toward them—and each.

Thank you very much.

NOTE: The ceremony was held in Constitution Hall.

295 ❡ Remarks at the Trinity College Convocation, Hartford, Connecticut. *October* 20, 1954

President Jacobs, Trustees, the Faculty, the Student Body, the friends of Trinity's family:

It would be, indeed, difficult for me to find the words in which to express the deep sense of pride I have in accepting the Honorary Doctorate of this College. And my pride does not spring solely from the fact that this is a venerable institution of learning, one with a great standing among the colleges of our country, its academic excellence, not merely because your President happens to be one of my old and valued friends and associates, but more particularly because of my very deep respect for the always great and now rapidly increasing importance of the institution of learning in the life of our Nation and of the world.

Time was when there could be disputes among nations and each could mobilize for itself an army or a fighting force which it could send out; having met the other fighting force upon the field of battle, a decision was reached; the nations and their political agencies and institutions obeyed that decision, and presumably the winner derived some advantage from the contest.

Those days have gradually left us. Professional armies, professional navies, have given way to the Nation in arms; and now we have had science give to us in these modern days weapons that mean not only is the whole Nation in arms, but the whole Nation is constantly exposed to the threat of destruction.

We have arrived at that point, my friends, when war does not present the possibility of victory or defeat. War would present to us only the alternative in degrees of destruction. There could be no truly successful outcome.

Now, many individuals through the ages have attempted, in a sentence, to define exactly what is an institution of learning. One that I think is particularly applicable at this day and time is this: it is a place where young minds are exposed to great minds.

The reason I think that this particular definition has growing applicability is because education, if it ever could, can certainly no longer discharge its responsibility by mere imposing of fact. There must be an understanding, an understanding of the relationships of one fact to another fact, and one community to another, or one trade to another, of one geographical area to another. And above all, one nation to another.

If we are to achieve such understanding, it is not enough that we know the geographical location of a friendly or potentially hostile nation, even that we know its potential strength, even that our intelligence reports on it are accurate to the "nth" degree. If we are to develop the kind of understanding that will avoid the great catastrophe of war, we must know about the cultures of these countries—the history of them. And above all, why do they react to certain actions, certain considerations and circumstances in this world in a different way from which we do? Will we be able to achieve an understanding that shows why they do it, make allowances for it, and then knowing that, go ahead in devising and composing those arrangements in the world that will gradually abolish this terrible scourge?

Indeed, I think we could put it this way: our institutions of learning, and our churches, have become the true mobilization centers of those forces which may now save civilization and preserve those forms of life, those concepts of human dignity and right, on which our civilization has been based. Unless there is this understanding developed in our institutions of learning, and unless that understanding is related to the truth, of the essentially spiritual character of man with his spiritual longings and aspirations, we cannot do our duty by ourselves or to those to whom it is our duty to pass on this civilization and this country of ours.

And so, in these halting words, my friends, my purpose is to try to make you see what is the great privilege and the great opportunity that is yours today in this great institution of learning. All over this land, people—the generation that must very quickly take over—incidentally, let me digress a bit: I most thoroughly believe in young men, and I think it is a very simple proposition, if I am lucky I may own 15 or 20 years of the United States. If each of you is lucky, you own about 60 years. And I think you ought to take a very great comparative interest on that basis.

But, at this very moment, you are passing through that stage of your life when you grasp these relationships and understanding of these relations, between a broad comprehension of tensions and stresses in the world and the spiritual values that must always underlie any solution—moral and spiritual values that must be present in any solution that you can devise and propose for the composition of the world's troubles.

I think there is no use laboring the subject. Let me, for just a moment, in closing, be a bit more personal. To each of you my warmest thanks for the cordiality of your welcome, for the attention you have paid me. I think I would be remiss, also, if I did not thank the Proctor for reciting what I deduce to be complimentary passages with respect to myself— in Latin. Since it was obvious that the tone was friendly, there must have been exaggeration. And the Latin at least had the virtue of concealing these exaggerations from me, and so saving me embarrassment. I assure you I did understand several words, "Dwight David Eisenhower" and "Ike." And that explains to you how far my own Latin is behind, these many years.

To each of you, good luck—God bless you and be with you.

NOTE: The President spoke at 11:20 a.m.

296 ¶ Remarks at the Governor Lodge Birthday Celebration in Hartford. *October* 20, 1954

Governor Lodge, ladies and gentlemen:

After that introduction, my natural question is, Well, whose birthday is this, anyway? I thought I came up here to tell you a little bit of what a great Governor you had. I never, I think, said before, "Happy Birthday" to anyone in front of such a big crowd. And I can't sing Happy Birthday, so I have to say the words.

But I do suggest this one thought. Of course, I am astonished that Governor Lodge is 51. He looked to me 41. But no matter how long he lives, something has been given him today that will be far more valuable to him and his family than will any present of gold or silver or anything else of material kind that he can ever receive.

Here, without regard to any spurious criterion of party, or any other divisive influence in our own country, people gather to say to him "Happy Birthday." The affection that inspired this gathering, I venture to say, is the most valuable commodity—unseen as it is, it is bound to be felt by him today, and in the future.

It means that in the estimation of all of these people, that he, as the first citizen of your State, does a worthy job in your service.

I merely want, therefore, as my part in this celebration, to help him thank you for coming here, because I know that his own heart will be so full of gratitude and humility that he can't say it as eloquently as he should like.

So I help him to say to each of you: thank you so much for coming here to tell him Happy Birthday.

Goodbye and good luck.

NOTE: The President spoke in Bushnell Park at 12:40 p.m.

297 ¶ Address at the American Jewish Tercentenary Dinner, New York City. *October* 20, 1954

My friends:

We have come together in memory of an inspiring moment in history— that moment, 300 years ago, when a small band of Jewish people arrived on the ship "Saint Charles" in what was then the Dutch colony or state of New Amsterdam. It was an event meaningful not only to the Jews of America, but to all Americans—of all faiths, of all national origins.

On that day there came to these shores 23 people whose distant ancestors had, through the Old Testament, given new dimensions of meaning to the concepts of freedom and justice, of mercy and righteousness, kindness and understanding—ideas and ideals which were to flower on this continent. They were of a people who had done much to give to Western civilization the principle of human dignity; they came to a land which would flourish beyond all seventeenth century dreams, because it fostered that dignity among its citizens.

Of all religious concepts, this belief in the infinite worth of the individual is beyond doubt among the most important. On this faith our forefathers constructed the framework of our Republic.

In this faith in human dignity is the major difference between our own concept of life and that of enemies of freedom. The chief among these enemies a decade and more ago were Nazi and Fascist forces which destroyed so many of our fellow men. Today the Communist conspiracy is the principal influence that derides the truth of human worth and, with atheistic ruthlessness, seeks to destroy the free institutions established on the foundation of that truth.

Asher Levy and his party came to this land on that long ago day because even then they had to find a country where they could safely put into practice their belief in the dignity of man.

In this respect—as in so many others—they were no different from scores of other groups that landed on our shores. Only 34 years earlier, another party had landed at Plymouth Rock. That group, too, came here in the hope of escaping persecution, of gaining religious freedom, of settling quietly in the wilderness to build their homes and rear their families.

And there was another noble concept of our common Judeo-Christian civilization shared by these two groups: the ideal of peace.

I recall that wonderful prophecy of Isaiah: "And the work of righteousness shall be peace; and the effect of righteousness, quietness and assurance forever."

The pursuit of peace is at once our religious obligation and our national policy. Peace in freedom, where all men dwell in security, is the ideal toward which our foreign policy is directed.

My friends, I have been thrilled this evening by the historical accounts we have heard of the adventures of those 23 people. That was 300 years ago. That is approximately 10 generations. Now I want to look forward this evening, instead of back. And I want to give you some little conception of what I believe our responsibility to those of 300 years hence is.

If you—each of you—would assume no inter-marriage whatsoever among your progenitors for those ten generations, do you realize that each of you was produced by 1024 people of ten generations ago?

If you invert that pyramid and throw your mind forward ten centuries, you can see the enormous number of people that are going to be directly related to you, perhaps—if you were so fortunate—and your responsibility to them and to all their friends and neighbors.

So I think it is only fitting that while we have heard this saga—the adventures of these 23 people; their origins—if you will allow me to talk a little bit about the hopes and aims of your government in beginning now the movement toward what we hope will be a far better world 300 years from now, that would be the thing I would like to do this evening.

I know that I am speaking to people who deeply love peace. I know that, with all other Americans, you share a profound thanksgiving that for the first time in 20 years there has been for some months no active battlefield anywhere in the world.

Moreover, while fighting has been brought to a halt during the past 21 months, still other developments favorable to the maintenance of peace have been brought about. This has been done through understanding and through persistent and patient work, in which your Government has been a helpful participant. Some of these developments have commanded our headlines—Korea, Egypt, Trieste, Iran, Guatemala.

Our people and their Government are dedicated to making this a just and a lasting peace.

In the years immediately ahead, the advancement of peace will demand much of us—our strength, our patience, our wisdom, our will. It will demand, above all, a realistic comprehension of the world and of its challenging problems. Some of the factors in these problems are new, and some old.

The principal and continuing factor is the persistently aggressive design of Moscow and Peiping, which shows no evidence of genuine change despite their professed desire to relax tensions and to preserve peace. Continuing, also, is the breadth and scope of the Communist attack; no weapon is absent from their arsenal, whether intended for destruction of cities and people or for the destruction of truth, of integrity, or loyalty.

The major new factor in the world today, beside the absence of fighting, is the rapid development in military weapons—weapons that in total war would threaten catastrophe. These products of science alone should be sufficient to stimulate the genuine efforts of all, including the Kremlin, to give to the world a true and permanent peace.

For our part we shall explore every avenue toward that goal. With any and all who demonstrate honesty of purpose, we are happy to confer. But well we realize that, in the circumstances of the moment, America must remain strong—and the community of free nations must likewise remain strong—to discourage the use of force in the world. In this effort we must help to harmonize the divergent views of the many free, self-governing nations, and without encroaching upon rights which all people cherish. For in the diversities of freedom are a tremendous might—a might which the imposed system of communism can never match.

Our Nation, because of its productivity and power, both existing and potential, holds a prime responsibility for maintaining peace. How, then, shall we meet this responsibility? With what policies can we best pursue our goal of peace?

Certain fundamentals are clear. Our Nation does not covet the territory of any people. We have no wish to dominate others. The peace we seek is a secure and a just peace, not bought at the expense of others, not bought at the expense of principle, and not bought by abject surrender of our vital interests. Peace so bought would at best be an illusion, and at worst a permanent loss of all that we hold most dear.

The following avenues must be trod as we make our way toward our peaceful goal.

First, we must tirelessly seek—through the United Nations, through every other available avenue open to us—every means to establish the conditions for an honorable peace.

Second, we must promote the unity and collective strength of other free peoples.

Third, we must maintain enough military strength to deter aggression and so promote peace.

Now, in these thoughts, we Americans overwhelmingly agree.

To examine briefly the first principal avenue, we stand ready to join all others in removing fear among nations. We shall resolutely adhere to the principles of the United Nations Charter. We shall constantly urge the Communist rulers to do the same. We shall keep open the existing channels of negotiations, and shall use them whenever there is any prospect of positive results.

At the Berlin and Geneva conferences our Nation sought serious negotiation on German unity, on a treaty for Austria, and on a political settlement for Korea. Our efforts found no similar response from the Communist side. We will not be misled by proposals intended to divide the free nations and to delay their efforts to build their own defenses. Nevertheless, no matter how discouraging the prospect, no matter how intractable the Communist regimes we shall press on our search for agreement.

We will welcome a workable system for limiting armaments and controlling atomic energy. Moreover, if the armaments burden can be lifted, this Government stands ready to ask the Congress to redeem the pledge I made a year ago last April, to help support, from the funds thus saved, a worldwide development program.

Now, the second road leading toward our peaceful goal concerns our efforts to strengthen and unify other free peoples.

To meet the challenge destiny has laid upon our country, we must strive to help these free peoples achieve their own security and well-being; we must encourage regional groupings of these peoples; we must ourselves foster and practice policies that encourage profitable trade and productivity in the free world.

In these areas there has been heartening progress. We have broadened our alliances. We have helped to remove sources of conflict. We have helped to build firmer foundations for social and economic progress in our quest for peace.

For some years free world nations have sought to associate the Federal Republic of Germany in the Atlantic Community. Rejection of the European Defense Treaty by the French Assembly 7 weeks ago was a setback to that hope. Yet, no nation in Western Europe was willing to accept this setback as final. In the recent meetings at London, the free Western nations reasserted their basic unity and established a new pattern for achieving their common purposes. Then Secretary of State Dulles has just joined our European allies in Paris in further important negotiations to strengthen European cooperation.

In southeast Asia we have sought united action to preserve for the free countries of that area the independence accorded them since the end of World War II. Unfortunately, in recent years no foundation had been laid for effective united action to prevent Communist gains. Because of their consequent isolation, the governments that bore the burden of the Indochina war understandably sought its conclusion in the face of the limitless manpower of China.

But recently at Manila we succeeded in negotiating a treaty with Asian and European countries. This pact symbolizes the desire of these nations to act together against aggression and to consult together on measures against subversion. The Manila Pact, bringing together states of the East and the West, and the related Pacific Charter are a long step toward the peaceful progress to which all Asian peoples aspire, whether or not members of that pact.

Perhaps you would allow me to pause to say here, I have traveled this world in peace and war, and there is one fact to which I can testify with the greatest confidence: all peoples want peace—all peoples. The misunderstandings that keep us apart seem to be of our own making, the making of government, and of selfishness in leaders. Basically the heart of people seems to have a similarity, wherever you find the people.

In this Hemisphere we have strengthened our solid understandings with our American neighbors. At the Caracas conference earlier this year, the American Republics agreed that if international communism were to gain control of the political institutions of any one American state, that this control would endanger them all, and therefore would demand collective action. Recently such a threat arose in Guatemala. The American states were preparing to act together to meet it when the Guatemalans themselves removed the danger. The Caracas agreement will stand as a bulwark of freedom in the Western Hemisphere.

In a number of areas throughout the free world, dangers to peace have been eliminated. The problem of Trieste, a threat to peace for a decade, has now been satisfactorily solved by Italy and Yugoslavia, with friendly assistance from the United States and Great Britain. Egypt and Britain have reached an amicable adjustment of questions centering on Suez. Iran has been helped in settling its difficult internal problems and is moving toward firm and friendly relations with the West.

In the Near East we are all regretfully aware that the major differences between Israel and the Arab States remain unresolved. Our goal there, as elsewhere, is a just peace. By firm friendship toward Israel, and all other nations in that area, we shall continue to contribute to the peace of the world. But I assure you that, in helping to strengthen the security of the entire Near East, we shall make sure that any arms we provide are devoted to that purpose, not to creating local imbalances which could be used for intimidation of or aggression against any neighboring nation. In every arrangement—every arrangement—we make with any nation, there is ample assurance that this distortion of our purposes cannot occur.

The fact that so many stubborn problems have been resolved through patience and forbearance surely justifies our hope that, by similar efforts, the nations of the free world will be able to eliminate other problems. Such efforts themselves tend to bring the free nations closer together. In speaking recently of the London conference, Sir Winston Churchill said of his country and the United States, "True and friendly comprehension between our kindred nations has rarely reached a higher standard."

Since I personally have been in many conferences with my friend Sir Winston during the past 12 years on these subjects affecting the friendship between Britain and America, I can testify with him, and in spite of the differences that seem magnified at times in our public prints, that statement is true—our relations with our British friends are solid and sound.

When we think of these many encouraging developments over the world, and the patient, helpful work that brought them about—when we contemplate the fact that the seemingly endless war in Korea, with its tragic casualty lists, is a thing of the past—and when we see improvement in area after area, from Suez to Iran, from Trieste to Guatemala, from London to Manila—then we indeed take heart.

In addition, we must devise means by which more highly developed countries can assist peoples who face the difficulties of an earlier stage of economic development.

As we continue to assist in these efforts, we shall also contribute much to free world unity by the wise use of our great economic power. We have, in the past, provided indispensable assistance to our partners. We continue to stand ready to help: to repair the ravages of war; to ease economic difficulties caused by their efforts to build needed military strength for the good of all of us; to relieve disasters, and flood or famine.

Economic relations, however, are a two-way street. If the common goal is to be reached, free nations must subordinate the selfish to the general interest. All must bear their fair share of the common burden. All must do more to liberalize the exchange of goods among free peoples. Let us be mindful, of course, of our own responsibility in this field. Bold action could release powerful forces of economic enterprise from which the whole free world would benefit.

And if there were no other reason for national policy concerning itself every day and every minute with the Nation's economy and full employment, it would be justified by the need for this kind of economic strength in meeting our world problems.

We must continue to explore ways in which nuclear discoveries can be turned to the service of man's peaceful needs. Since our Nation's proposal for an international effort toward this end was laid before the United Nations last December, we have taken the initiative in this direction. We would welcome the participation of the Soviet Union. But this great effort for human welfare cannot wait upon their decision.

Our third major road leads us to maintain enough military strength to deter aggression and to help keep peace in the world. This strength is a trust on which rests the current safety of free men.

Neither in size nor in character can our military establishment remain static. With constantly changing dangers, with rapidly changing developments in the science of warfare, our military forces, too, must change. From atomic submarine to atomic cannon, from new weapon systems to new military organizations, this giant, complex structure must respond to the current needs of our time. Above all, its purpose is to prevent aggression and war. Our forces will never be used to initiate war against any nation; they will be used only for the defense of the free world.

Together with the armed strength of other free nations, our military power—the greatest in our peacetime history—is today a deterrent to war. This awesome power we must and shall maintain, for we are determined that at all times, in today's uncertain world, we shall be able to deal effectively and flexibly with whatever situations may arise.

My friends, in these many ways our Nation will continue tirelessly in its quest for peace based on justice. In recent months we have come far—and yet we know that the road ahead is long and difficult. But we shall continue to press on.

As we do so we shall keep faith with those of earliest America who came to these shores three centuries and more ago. They have launched a venture in freedom unparalleled in man's struggle over the ages. They sought peace and freedom and justice, for themselves and for those who were to follow.

Yes, my friends, we know, with the prophet Isaiah, that the work of righteousness shall be peace.

Now let me remind you, when those people came, they didn't come for a negative purpose, just to be free of persecution. They sought the positive right to stand up as free men, as dignified humans; and the struggle that they carried forward to achieve those rights has been described to you eloquently and vividly this evening.

In the same way, in preserving peace in the world, international peace is not a static—is not a negative thing. It is a positive thing, of preparing the world—the conditions in the world, where people may live honorably and upright, and at peace.

And we know this: that as we labor for peace, we labor for all humanity, for all values, for all of enduring meaning to mankind. Never was there a nobler cause. Ringingly, insistently, it calls out to us, all of us, for ardent devotion and advocacy. To work with all our hearts for peace in the world is a task not alone for the soldier, the diplomat, the scholar, the statesman—peace is a job for every one of us, the concern of the working man, businessman, and clerk, the farmer and doctor and engineer—rabbi, clergyman, and priest—the teacher, the parent, and the child.

Let us then, each of us, resolve anew that we shall have peace. Let us then—let each of us—have faith that we shall succeed. Let us strive for peace with all our hearts and minds. From county seat to the conference table among nations—let us talk for peace from the classroom to the congressional hall.

And my fellow citizens, let each of us pray for peace—pray that He who rules over nation and man may guide every human being toward that wisdom and understanding that forever will bar from mankind the scourge of war.

To each of you, my thanks for the warmth and courtesy of your welcome. Thank you for the honor of being with you.

NOTE: The President spoke in the main ballroom of the Sheraton-Astor Hotel in New York City at 10:00 p.m.

298 ¶ Remarks at the New York Republican State Committee Rally, New York City.
October 21, 1954

Governor Dewey, Senator Ives, and my friends:

I am here, I think, possibly more because I am a voter in the State of New York than I am because I am a—a temporary resident in Washington. So in case anyone thinks that my ballot is secret, I will say I am one of those that will vote the straight Republican ticket. And so, with that out of the way—and, I might add, I am going to do it enthusiastically—with that out of the way, we can talk about a couple of things here—since they gave me carte blanche—that are from my heart.

First, I think there was something started 2 years ago that many of us feel was sort of finished, and that is the aspect of our job that I want to talk about. There were a number of things that formed the battlecry of the Republican Party and its affiliated allies—from parties and independents and everything else, 2 years ago.

We wanted clean government. We wanted efficient government. We wanted economical government. We wanted the security of this country looked after. We wanted a program begun in our relationships with other nations that solidified our own security and made the whole free world more certain of its ability to withstand the Communist menace, either in its threat of the use of military force or in its political aspects—the ones that are constantly going on.

Those were the main things. There were added programs, of devising farm plans that would not break down of their own weight, of getting the tax structure revised so that it was more equitable in its incidence upon all our citizens, and so it could be used to create more jobs and to make our economy a better place.

Now not long ago I was talking to one of my Republican friends, and we were talking about how much of this has been accomplished. "Why," he said, "practically everything." He thought things looked well. He said, "We have gotten rid of the excess profits tax, and we have gotten rid of those terrible controls over our economy—amidst the prophets of gloom, that prices would skyrocket and we would have a terrible round of inflation. The Korean War was stopped and we had all sorts of things happening." He was very well satisfied. Indeed, he had no real criticism of what the administration and the Congress had accomplished. So he was very satisfied.

Well, I told him, to start off my argument, I knew about a man named Firpo—and some of you here are old enough to remember the name. He was a South American, who came up here, and he crawled into the ring one night here in New York, with a man named Dempsey, and in the first round Firpo knocked Dempsey out of the ring and he broke three typewriters of the newspapermen. But Dempsey crawled back into the ring and whipped the tar out of him.

Now, as I see it, we have carried the cause through the first round.

We have made a tremendous start on accomplishing the basic objectives of that whole crusade, which is: moderate government in this day and time that is fitted for the economic and the social and the political needs of the United States of America. The things we have done have been important steps in getting over to the United States that this is the kind of government that is now fitted to our needs. We reject the extremes of both sides—the extreme right and the extreme left. We believe they are wrong, and we have the difficult task of dramatizing and selling moderate government, one that is attacked from both sides—and I am proud that it is.

But it does make it a little bit hard to explain and to sell.

Now what I really believe is our job today—the reason that justifies such meetings as this, coming together, to consult among ourselves—is to realize that that job is only partly done, that the great population has not absorbed all of this understanding of what is going on. We have got to go ahead with it. We must not pause along the way.

And so we come down to the fact that we have a battle. Now about battles I think I know a little. And I know this: the one indispensable ingredient of any victory is heart—belief in what you are doing, and the determination that nothing in the world will stop you from succeeding.

In the Army—or the armed services—we called it morale, esprit de corps, all the rest of it—but it is that thing inside the heart of a man, the heart of an organization, that will not accept defeat, and goes out and wins.

I realize that many things are necessary—organization, plans, money. All of these things, as we give them, are merely manifestations of what is in the heart, and how much we believe. How much do we believe that we are really saving the basic principles of the United States of America, the system under which it was developed. And in doing so, we preserve it by adapting all of those principles to the economic and industrial agricultural requirements of the moment—and so we can pass them on sound and unimpaired.

Now, if we believe that is our task, where is the sacrifice too great? How can there be too much time to put into this job? Every step that we have made is merely indicative of what we can do. Much remains to be done, and it seems to me that to entrust our echelons of government, national and State, to the people who have jumped in and carried the job this far, is exactly what we are trying to say and to do now.

In Washington we are trying to keep the same leaders. To do that we have to have the same party predominant so that those leaders can carry on in their responsible positions. In the States in the same way.

Here in this State you have a Senator who has been tremendously helpful in carrying us forward in Washington, now turning and accepting the duty of leading the job here in the State. And it is tremendously important.

I have got just one more word to add. I have probably said this to many of you lots of times. Ladies and gentlemen, again I refer to fighting in its generic sense—contest. I have seen various kinds. I have never yet seen one that was won when the leaders went around pulling their faces up to here. We have got to go that way [demonstrating]. You have got to let people see that you believe in something. You are not ashamed of what you believe in, and that you do not consider your own duty done until not only have you put in every bit of time—the substance—the thought—the heart—the brain that you have got, but that you have induced others to do it also.

And that is what brings victory.

Goodbye.

NOTE: The President spoke in the Roosevelt Hotel's Palm Room at 9:10 a.m.

299 ¶ Remarks at the Manhattan State Hospital, Wards Island, New York City. *October 21, 1954*

Governor Dewey, Senator Ives, ladies and gentlemen, my fellow Americans:

I am afraid that your Governor, although I have rarely found him wrong or mistaken in any statement, has not been to Washington lately. But $10 million does, again, mean an awful lot of money down there.

I came to New York in order that I could go to a dinner tonight, which is called the Al Smith Dinner. But it is staged each year in order to provide voluntary help for the care of the sick, to provide better health facilities in our country.

I think there is nothing that is more important for us than to realize that a healthy nation is a strong nation—strong in its morale, strong in its economy, strong as it faces the world, no matter what threats it may have to face. So this business of health is one that must engage the concern and attention of everybody who occupies a post that designates him a public servant to our body politic. That is the reason that I am to be there this evening, and when I heard of this practical demonstration of some of the funds of the public being put to actual use, I told the Governor not only that I would come but I would be happy to come.

Moreover, I would like to greet each of you, or at least some of you in your particular classes of activity, with respect to this great building.

Of course, to the doctors, nurses, the hospital attendants, all the diagnosticians, and the surgeons—everybody that will work here—this will be a great boon. They will be much better enabled to help our unfortunate people.

But as I look at a work like this, and realize that it is just as much what the plumber does to a pipe as what the doctor does to my appendix, I would like also to thank those people—the men that are putting this thing up, and taking pride in making sure that the doctors are not going to be stopped by the light suddenly going out, the plumbing going wrong, something happening to the elevator—I think each of you should possibly take pride in this work and this kind of constructive job for humanity.

We are, of course, as a nation, dedicated to peace. What does peace mean? It means that we know—each of us—that our best efforts, our substance, goes not to the construction of engines of war and things to kill each other, but those things to make each other happier, to help one another, to be healthier in our bodies, in our requirements, and certainly achieving more of what we want in our hearts with our families and with our children.

So I really feel this morning that every single person that has the slightest thing to do with this hospital, whether he was signing the bill that made the appropriations possible, or whether he is one of the men that smoothed out the roads so the foundation could be laid, or somewhere else, every one of you is to be congratulated.

I bring to each of you my personal greetings, my very deep thanks for your courtesy in receiving me, the warmth of your welcome, and for listening to me.

Goodbye.

NOTE: The President spoke at 10:45 a.m

300 ¶ Remarks at the Dedication of the State University of New York Medical Center, New York City. *October* 21, 1954

Mr. Chairman, Governor Dewey, Senator Ives, my friends:

Governor Dewey spoke very much about this invitation. I must tell you, frankly, I am practically self-invited. So you know I am an added starter up here, and not expecting to take too much of your time, or those back here.

The reason I wanted to come was because of a very long interest in the kind of work that will here be done. In World War II I was shocked to find that the record showed how many of our people were rejected from military service because of physical disability. And many of those disabilities were obviously ones that could have been corrected early in their youth, and they would have been healthy, completely useful citizens. They couldn't even do their tasks in war. Many of you here this morning are people who served with me in that war; we saw an unusually large number of men who fell along the wayside because they didn't have the stamina to go on, on an average march, an average hardship, an average privation, which that soldier has to suffer in war. The most of them went along all right, but there was a very large percentage that did not, and could have been better cured.

Then I came to this city—I went to Columbia. Your Governor was talking about the difficulty of saving $10 million out of the State budget. I would like to see him save $1 million out of the University's budget, and that was what our medical school support cost us each year, over and above revenues. That was tough. All the way along the line, this job of a healthful citizenry, providing the facilities for it, everybody in Government should give some attention to it, even though I subscribe to the view expressed just now: we must have nothing to do with controlling it.

And now, permit me just for a second to advert to what Dr. Carlson said about the job of each of us as a citizen, and particularly the doctor.

I believe that behind the whole purpose of keeping a healthful citizenry must be something that deals with the aspirations of mankind, the aspirations of men and women as we know them to live free and rich and

933

useful lives. That means to live under institutions that give us an opportunity to expand, that we will not be controlled by others—we will not be regimented. The kind of thing that Dr. Carlson brought out so briefly is the kind of thing that I believe each of us, whether he be interne or student or laborer or high governmental official, ought to be thinking about all the time: this America, what it means in terms of our aspirations, our hopes, for ourselves, and our people—and preserving them down through the years. The healthful body in which we do it is only one thing. But the head, the understanding that we have of all of the tensions and the complexities in the world, and what we must do to preserve them; and finally, after all, the heart. What are the fine, decent things we want of life? How much are we prepared to sacrifice for them, and work for them with our whole selves?

Here is one evidence in this great hospital that the people of New York have worked and sacrificed to provide something to make us healthier in body so that we may be healthier and stronger and better in mind, and give, therefore, better opportunity for us to attain the aspirations of our hearts.

Thank you for letting me come to this ceremony. Thank you for these minutes you have given me to address you.

Goodbye.

NOTE: The President spoke at 12:20 p.m. His opening words "Mr. Chairman" referred to Dr. Carlyle Jacobsen, Executive Dean for Medical Education of the State University of New York. Later he referred to Dr. William S. Carlson, President of the University.

301 ¶ Address at the Alfred E. Smith Memorial Dinner, New York City. *October* 21, 1954

Mr. Chairman, Your Eminence, Governor Dewey, Mayor Wagner—and my fellow citizens at this wonderful dinner:

I assure you that never would I have given up anything more cheerfully than a few minutes of the time that has apparently been allotted to me to His Eminence. I thoroughly objected to the sort of "military discipline" they seem to have tried to subject him to.

I would be remiss if I did not, first, try to express to you something of the gratitude I feel for the cordiality of your welcome. And here and on the streets of today, New York seems to remember that for some all too brief years I was privileged to live here. Those years are among the happiest of the lives of my wife and myself. And I want to assure you that we are grateful for every smile we see, and every time I hear "Hi Ike."

First, I would like to crave your indulgence to pay my deep respects to a lady whose early life was devoted to and intertwined with that of the man whose memory we are here to honor. His confidante, his counsellor, an admired citizen in her own right, a worthy daughter of a noble parent—Emily Smith Warner.

On such an evening as this, before such a gathering as this, our attention seems inescapably directed to three subjects, related in our thinking. They are:

First—the man whose memory we honor: Alfred Emanuel Smith.

Second—the practice of charitable giving.

Third—the government and the health of all the people.

None in our generation more warmly sympathized with the needs, the hopes, the aspirations of humanity than did Governor Smith; none more earnestly used government as an instrument for their satisfaction.

Yet none in our generation more acutely recognized the menace of bankrupting waste inherent in a centralized bureaucracy; none more firmly believed in self-dependence and initiative; and none more firmly believed that thrift and solvency are hallmarks of good government.

In all that concerned human beings, he was a true liberal; in all that concerned the economy within which they lived, he was a genuine conservative. In his daily tasks, he was a man of charitable heart; a patriot who loved America and its people. His life made manifest the challenges and opportunities, the responsibilities and rewards which America confers on those who serve their country and their fellow men.

His life did not escape the experience of defeat, but he accepted his defeats calmly, for he knew that if he were right, time would vindicate him and truth would prevail.

He faced his challenges unafraid, for he was armed in honesty of purpose and integrity of soul.

He seized his opportunities eagerly, for he was an alert steward of God-given talents.

He bore his responsibilities serenely, for he sought the counsel of the wise and the help of the Almighty.

935

He accepted his rewards modestly, for he felt those higher inner satisfactions known only to those who dedicate themselves to service to others.

Through a long life he served his city, his State, his country, to the limits of a great capacity. In every task he was impelled by a fiery faith in the decency and dignity of men and in the purposes of America. So impelled, he labored well. His life was a crusade against inequities rooted in such spurious criteria as ancestry and income.

Therefore, the name Alfred E. Smith is enshrined in history. So long as the Republic endures, he will not be forgotten.

But, beyond that, Al Smith, the man, the happy warrior, the American of great mind and great soul, lives in the hearts of people.

Monuments of timber and stone and metal have recorded human accomplishment through the years. In the history of America there are many who have earned such distinction. To only a few, however, in all the years of the Republic has there been paid the highest of all awards: a public resolve that the causes which they espoused shall not be permitted to die with them; that others, inspired by their memory, shall carry on the work to which those few dedicated themselves.

Our assembly this evening is an expression of that public determination, with respect to the causes espoused by Alfred E. Smith.

In our distant and diverse origins, in our present vocations and affiliations and interests, we are the infinite variety of American life. The roll call of this dinner is a roster of the races and religious creeds, the political parties, the economic enterprises, the cultural movements that constitute the Republic. But the common bond of dedication to values that Al Smith upheld converts our multitudinous variety into a purposeful unity. We are a reflection of our basic national unity that is today a towering beacon of hope to torn and divided mankind.

Our gathering to honor this man, to pay our respect to the causes for which he labored throughout his life, symbolizes our unity. We honor him because through his career he gave himself unsparingly to the American dream.

Since the beginning of time men have deluded themselves—or have been deluded by other men—with fantasies of life free from labor or pain or sacrifice, of limitless reward that requires no risk, of pleasure untainted by suffering. From such dreams, the awakening has always been rude and the penalty a nightmare of disillusionment.

936

The American dream is a goal that can be achieved only in work and wise thought, in unity among men and faith in God.

Our forefathers dreamed in terms of hard fact and high ideals. Then, they devised a system for man's self-government. Their system has succeeded beyond all others because it is the political expression of a religious faith that man is free; that man is responsive to the call of conscience and duty; that man is endowed at birth with certain capacities and rights. But they knew that man must earn his freedom, his rights, his way throughout his life.

Al Smith was both a product and an apostle of these concepts and this system. His undivided and passionate loyalty was given to America, and to the spiritual and moral values that mean Americanism. Sympathetic as he was toward differing convictions based in conscience, he was incapable of entertaining or of tolerating a thought directed toward the violent destruction of the governmental system of our free country. He was a deadly foe of such things as communism and fascism. Who can doubt that he would have supported and applauded, if alive in 1954, every one of the laws of the recent Congress to make more certain the discovery of subversives, to speed their removal from influential positions, to mete out to them legal punishment. Though he would have repudiated injustice toward or persecution of any individual, yet he would have been as stern as George Washington in dealing with any properly convicted of betraying this Nation.

Among the fruits enjoyed by those who live under the fundamental concepts and principles that define our system—are an abundance in all that makes a good life, unparalleled in the entire history of tribes and nations and empires.

But, since the earliest days, never has the factual realization of the dream been devoid of imperfections. Happily, their correction has been constant and ceaseless. In every generation there have been mighty voices crying out insistently that this evil be eradicated or that wrong be righted. Al Smith was such a voice. He was a man of many concerns for the betterment of human living.

Not the least of his many concerns is the direct inspiration for our gathering here tonight—the care and the cure of the sick and the ailing.

Created for productive life, endowed with talents of mighty potential, man has the right to enjoy adequate means for the preservation of good

937

health and its restoration whenever injured or lost. The community, whether it be tribe or empire, that ignores this right commits slow suicide.

You, in this room this evening, act in an ancient and firmly rooted tradition of the Jewish and Christian faiths. You are engaged in a noble work of mercy. By your presence here you are witnesses to the everlasting truth of our spiritual brotherhood. This brotherhood requires of us that the fortunate be quick in their aid to the unfortunate.

And here may I salute another lady—the sponsor of this dinner. Hers is truly the spirit that seeks no reward beyond the knowledge of a good task well done. For her name is, at her own request, unknown to us. But, because of her generosity in paying the costs of this dinner, every penny raised goes to the cause of the sick, a cause so close to the life of Al Smith. I know that, with all your hearts, you join me in salute to this bountiful lady.

But the preachers of materialism brand such acts as hers, and the spirit that animates you around these tables, as an obsolescent manifestation of that spiritual force which they term "the opiate of the people."

But should we ourselves ever permit the spirit of charity to weaken among us, we shall by that much weaken America. Thereby, we can lose that will to sacrifice, which in hospital ward and on battlefield, in the daily living of the home and the bustle of an industrial world, only arouses men and women to the heights of greatness. Thereby we can lose the recognition of our spiritual brotherhood, of our duty that the more fortunate help those less fortunate amid the accidents of life. And that recognition is a tie binding tens of millions of Americans into a single family.

There is a responsibility on every one of us that we, by word and deed, further the practice of voluntary giving. This practice is rooted in a spirit that is at once a mark of the American dream and an essential influence toward its eventual realization.

Yet, so important, so grave, is this responsibility for the care of the unfortunate, that it must be borne not only individually but collectively. In these days of complex and mass living, we must recognize that disease and calamity, their prevention and correction, require a broad and concentrated effort, in which the Government has a significant role.

The health of a people, Al Smith realized, is intertwined with and affected by their schooling, their opportunities for leisure and play, their access to hospitals and medicine. Their health concerns their ability to afford more than the bare bones of existence, their hours and their conditions of work; it colors all their present circumstances and all their plans for the future. Within the State of New York, on a many-sided front, Governor Smith fought a long war for man's right to enjoy the best means for the preservation of good health and its restoration whenever injured or lost.

No one dared call his program a wedge for socialism. Rather, we see him as a champion of freedom and opportunity for the individual to plan his own life, in his own way, according to his own conscience. This right is limited only by the equal rights of all others. But we see him, too, as a man of conscience and good will who realized that within an industrialized society no man, no family, no community, no State can stand entirely alone. Illness within a home may be beyond relief by available local measures. Our Government, founded on the free individual, cannot ignore a single home in such plight.

In these late years, another Governor of New York has earned for himself the gratitude of millions by carrying on, in the tradition of Al Smith, the development of state medical facilities. Obviously, I refer to the distinguished leader—Thomas E. Dewey.

It was in full harmony with the convictions of these two great champions of the public good, that 18 months ago there was established in Washington a new cabinet position and the new Executive Department of Health, Education, and Welfare. In many fields of great human concern, this new department of Government helps the individual, the family, the community, the State to do those essential things that they cannot, by themselves, otherwise accomplish. In time, by means of this new department, we can bring into focus the knowledge, techniques, and scientific resources of State, local, and private groups, as a step toward affording every American full opportunity for good hospitalization and adequate medical care.

In recent months, much that is new has already been done.

Newly passed by Congress is a 3-year $180 million program to build diagnostic and treatment centers, hospitals for the chronically ill and impaired, nursing homes and rehabilitation facilities. Through this program, which supplements other funds for general hospital construction, we at last recognize the growing proportion of aged persons in our population and the resulting increases in chronic illnesses.

Newly passed legislation provides more generous tax treatment of some

8,500,000 individuals and families with heavy medical, dental or hospital bills, saving them some $80 million a year in taxes. This new law also liberalizes the tax treatment of sickness or accident benefits.

Newly passed by Congress is a major expansion of Federal-State rehabilitation services to restore disabled people to useful, productive lives—a program of tremendous humanitarian importance. With the cooperation of those concerned in private groups and on all levels of government we expect that in 5 years we will have progressed from the rehabilitation program of about 55,000 persons annually in this program to some 200,000 a year. Our goal is to afford opportunity for rehabilitation to every American who is disabled and can be restored to a useful, self-supporting life.

There is expansion, too, in the crucial field of health research—an intensification of direct governmental research in cancer, blindness, and neurological diseases, and many other ills—all this at the National Institutes of Health. Of special importance to every worker was the opening in Cincinnati this year of the new Taft Sanitary Engineering Center to augment research in environmental and occupational health hazards.

And recent amendments to food and related laws assure better protection of the health of consumers who each year make purchases of $50 billion in this field.

Finally, there was the proposal to encourage the growth and improvement of voluntary health insurance.

This was not passed, but by its passage, millions would have had the opportunity—out of their own provident thrift—to increase their protection against the cost of sickness. In this way we would help ease the catastrophic shock of illness and injury on the individual citizens and families of America.

Some extremists of the bureaucratic type challenge the plan because it does not attempt to remove all local and individual responsibility for the care of the sick and the unfortunate. Our refusal to centralize all responsibility and authority in the Federal Government is deliberate; it is an expression of active conviction that though the central Government may aid and coordinate, local authority and private initiative must be supreme in the normal procedure of daily living, else freedom—unless this is so, we all realize freedom and self-government will be lost.

Others—of the opposite extreme—oppose this legislation on the ground that it might become the entering wedge of socialized medicine. To that kind of service in America, my co-workers and I are emphatically opposed. But I hope that none of us confuses social progress with socialism.

We know that the American people will not long be denied access to adequate medical facilities. And they should not be. The program for voluntary health insurance is one further step in achieving this objective in the American way. It is the logical alternative to socialized medicine. We cannot rest content knowing that modern health services are beyond the financial or physical reach of many millions of our fellow citizens. We must correct these defects. I know that in this purpose the Nation has the full support of our unexcelled medical profession which, like all of us, wants better health for all of America.

A proposal to establish a sound reinsurance program will be submitted to the next session of the Congress. It will be an important part of a health program to fill the great gaps in this field of health preservation.

The start now made is only a first beginning on a vast human enterprise—the health of our Nation. This is a task for the individual citizen, the city, the county, the State, and finally, the Federal Government. We Americans have accomplished near miracles in material things. But we are years behind our potential achievement in the availability and adequacy of health services.

But I repeat, the task does not belong exclusively or even primarily to the Congress and the Government. It belongs to each of us—each of us here—and to the communities in which we live. The inadequacy will be fully remedied only as we—each of us—performs his full duty as an American citizen, certain that in so doing he is not only relieving distress but making a more durable contribution to the Republic.

Our goal is a healthier and therefore a stronger America—

Let us, then, resolve that—

Our forward march will be in the tradition of men like Al Smith:

Using Government as the servant of the people—

And cherishing personal sacrifice and the practice of charitable giving.

And, my friends, we will be confident that a healthier and stronger America will better sustain our freedom; better promote our individual and national prosperity; make more certain our security and constantly enlarge our spiritual stature.

I thank you very much.

NOTE: The President spoke at the Waldorf-Astoria Hotel at 10:30 p.m. His opening words referred to Charles Silver, chairman of the dinner, Francis Cardinal

Spellman, Archbishop of New York,   York, and Robert F. Wagner, Mayor of
Thomas E. Dewey, Governor of New   New York City.

302 ¶ Letter to Senator Capehart on the Investigation of the Federal Housing Administration.   *October 23, 1954*

Dear Senator Capehart:

This will acknowledge your letter of October tenth in which you refer to the shocking testimony before your Committee regarding the Federal Housing Administration.

Since then I have discussed the contents of your letter with the Attorney General and with the Administrator of the Housing and Home Finance Agency. As you know from the cooperation which they have already given your Committee, these two officials have been conducting intensive investigations of the activities of the Federal Housing Administration from 1934 through 1952—the period during which these scandals took place. As you also know, the Attorney General has already obtained 200 indictments returned in Federal Courts in connection with his investigation. He has many additional matters to present to grand juries throughout the country and it is expected that many additional indictments will result.

The Administrator of the Housing and Home Finance Agency reported to me that 21 Federal officials appointed to the Federal Housing Administration prior to 1953 have been dismissed from the Government service as a result of his investigation. There are several similar investigations presently being conducted.

The Administrator also assured me that he is convinced that the loopholes in previous laws which made this costly scandal possible have been closed by the Housing Act passed in the last session of Congress. The applications for federally-insured loans are greater today than at any time before in our history. This is largely due, I believe, to restored public confidence in the operation of the new housing law by public officials dedicated to decent, honest government in the best interests of all the people of our country.

The tragedy of the disclosures made by your Committee, as I see it, is that a great number of innocent Americans have been forced to pay for the wrongful acts of certain public officials and builders. Windfall profits over the years have resulted in higher rentals for unsuspecting tenants. Fraud and misrepresentation in connection with home improvements have cost the small home owner other millions of dollars.

The Attorney General is seeking by civil process to force rebates from the builders who benefited from these huge windfalls. He will continue, at my direction, to take every appropriate legal step against those who have violated their public trust and those who gained easy money at the expense of tenants and the small home owner so that those responsible for what you call "the biggest scandal in the history of the United States" may be brought to justice.

With warm regard,

Sincerely,

DWIGHT D. EISENHOWER

NOTE: Senator Homer E. Capehart of Indiana was Chairman of the Senate Committee on Banking and Currency. His letter, released with the President's reply, stated that the Committee had heard witnesses who admitted total FHA mortgage proceeds of more than $85 million above their total construction costs, and that many FHA employees were shown to have received money or substantial property from builders with whom FHA was doing business.

303 ¶ Remarks at the Pennsylvania Monument, Gettysburg National Military Park.
October 23, 1954

My friends:

I was raised in a profession in which it was a sin ever to be surprised. But someone handed this thing to my hand just this minute, and I am a little bit astonished because I didn't know I was just to drive up here to start to talking.

As I drove on this battlefield just now, it occurred to me, what a spot in which to remind ourselves how much we all want peace. And I want to say this to you folks: today there is going on over in Europe negotiations for which I personally have the greatest of hope. I believe that there we may find that our Secretary of State is able to come back with assurances to us that will add a very great deal to our peace of mind.   Certainly I prayerfully hope so, and I wanted to tell you about those hopes.

I came up today because I learned that I was going to meet a lot of friends—some of them, possibly, also political friends—over at my farm. And so Mrs. Eisenhower and I decided to drive up there.   Then they said, "Will you pass by the Pennsylvania Monument?" And I said, "Why not, because we are going to be citizens of Pennsylvania soon, we hope."

This is the way we have the great privilege of meeting with you folks today.   We are of course in a political campaign now.   I am not going to say one word about it.   This is a nonpolitical meeting so far as I am concerned.   I hope you are neighbors.   I hope you are people we will get to see a lot of in the days to come.   And if all October days in Pennsylvania are this nice, I tell you we have new reason for coming.   And I assure you that one of the things we are looking forward to, more than anything else in our lives, is when that day comes that we can go over here and settle down back of Round Top, and begin to raise a few cows of our own.

In the meantime, thank you all for coming out.   It is a great privilege to meet you.   We are going on, as I say, over to the farm now, where I believe we are expected.

To each of you, good luck and thanks.

NOTE: The President spoke at 12:30 p.m.

304   ¶ Remarks in Gettysburg to a Group of Republican Candidates.   *October 23, 1954*

Mr. Chairman, Governor Fine—and what soon, at least, we can call my fellow Pennsylvanians:

When a little boy does his lesson well in school and then the principal happens to come around, he is frequently called upon to repeat it.   All the other students present are supposed to act a little astonished, even though they have heard it before.

Now the photographers today decided that they liked the message I read to you a little while ago, and they would like to take a picture while it is being read.   So I promised to repeat that particular performance.

This is to the President, from Secretary Dulles.   "I am happy to inform you that everything, including Saar, has now been signed, sealed and delivered. I know you will rejoice with me that the unity and freedom of Europe, to which you contributed so indispensably, seems likely now to be preserved. Faithfully yours, Foster."

I cannot tell you, my friends, how much that message means. I met a group with Mrs. Eisenhower over at the Pennsylvania Monument a few minutes ago, and I told them that as I drove onto the battlefield, a corner of which we are now occupying, I could not help thinking that on this peaceful day how naturally it is that our thoughts should turn to peace. When I stop to think of what the world has to face, unless we do bring about a confidence in a growing world stability and peace, I am inspired to go back to work twice as hard as I did before.

And so you can imagine with what tremendous satisfaction I report to you people today that in my opinion the events of the late months have brought us measurably nearer the day when we not only can say that confidence is growing, but when we can say this dream begins to come definitely within our grasp.

We had seen the terrible threat in Iran disappear. That annoying situation in Suez has been composed. The sensitiveness of the Trieste question has been removed. The first beachhead of communism in the United States, at Guatemala, has been eliminated by the Guatemalans themselves. And the Caracas agreement stands as a sure defense among all Americans that it cannot succeed in establishing itself here.

Now today, after all these years of work and study, and patience—prodding and urging and pleading and arguing: here we have this message. Truly it is one that I think gives us real reason for rejoicing.

Now there is, of course, with respect to this political campaign in which we are all so deeply interested, little of a factual character that I can say to you people today that would be new to you. Most of you are far, far more experienced in politics than I.

There is one field, though, in which I think I am competent to speak a bit, and that is on the general subject of fighting.

And in its way, a political contest is a fight. A fight is half-won when the cause for which any side is fighting is one that fills them with inspiration, one in which they fervently believe, one which represents values which to them are priceless.

That, I submit, the Republican Party has today.

The party of moderation in Government, coupled with progress, with absolute humanity and sympathy toward every person who needs the help of Government, but with absolute conservatism when the economy of this country is involved, that kind of road to progress is one that we see—is that shining road that leads forward to a peaceful, secure, and bright future.   That is what we are working for.

I am often reminded of the story of Cromwell's army.   You know, there has been a sort of understanding, or belief, among many people that an army could not have at one and the same time a very high order of discipline and a very high order of *esprit, élan,* morale.

Well, there probably never was an army so highly disciplined as was Cromwell's, but it was far from being a regimented group.   They went into battle singing hymns.   They went into battle because they wanted to go.   They believed in something.   And no matter how mistaken we may today believe that they were, in their beliefs and in their convictions, it absorbed their whole hearts.   It was almost a glory to die.

We are held together; as I see it, our discipline is devotion to a cause, to furthering the betterment of America.   Our *élan* is because of our belief in that: we know that we shall succeed.   We have both the morale and the discipline—the determination to go ahead.

I realize you people have a number of other engagements for the day. Mine, fortunately, I hope, is going to be a couple of hours of looking at the farm, which I hope soon to spend one night in; and not long thereafter to live in—at least on weekends.

Now, I have, by and large, not indulged in what you might call the personalities of this political campaign.   Today I think I deserve—indeed, I think I possibly owe to myself—a little, let us say, self-given dispensation from this particular inhibition.

I am in the district where my Congressman—or what I soon hope will be my Congressman—is running.   It seems to me I have a right to speak of him.   I am in a State where I hope that my candidate for Governor will be elected.   I know of no reason why I can't exercise the rights of an ordinary citizen, when I am in Gettysburg, and speak out in no uncertain terms in favor of these people.

Now, since my Congressman won't be as powerful down there, unless he is supported by others of his own associations, and beliefs and convictions, I know of no reason why I can't speak out for the Congressmen who are running in Pennsylvania. We want a good solid delegation.

Now, so that all of you can see who I am talking about, I should like, first, for Governor Wood—I will excuse Governor Fine, although we haven't retired him yet—but I want Governor Wood to come up here and look at you. [*The rest of the Pennsylvania delegates came up to the podium and had their pictures taken with the President*]

Now, ladies and gentlemen, for the warmth of your welcome, and for your courtesies to Mrs. Eisenhower and to me, thank you very much.

NOTE: The President spoke in a tent at his Gettysburg farm at 1:58 p.m. His opening words "Mr. Chairman, Governor Fine" referred to Milton G. Baker, Superintendent of the Valley Forge Military School, and to Governor John S. Fine of Pennsylvania. Later in his remarks the President referred to Lieutenant Governor Lloyd H. Wood.

305 ¶ Remarks Recorded for Program Marking the 75th Anniversary of the Incandescent Lamp. *October 24, 1954*

FAITH, faith and the American individual. Yes, it is on these two pillars that our future rests.

It was Thomas Edison who said: "Be courageous; be as brave as your fathers before you. Have faith. Go forward."

Seventy-five years ago this very week, Tom Edison—a humble, typical sort of American—put this credo into action and gave a new light to the world.

It is faith that has made our Nation—has made it, and kept it free. Atheism substitutes men for the supreme creator and this leads inevitably to domination and dictatorship. But we believe—and it is because we believe that God intends all men to be free and equal that we demand free government. Our Government is servant, not master, our chosen representatives are our equals, not our czars or commissars.

We must jealously guard our foundation in faith. For on it rests the ability of the American individual to live and thrive in this blessed land— and to be able to help other less fortunate people to achieve freedom and individual opportunity. These we take for granted, but to others they are often only a wistful dream.

"In God we trust." Often have we heard the words of this wonderful

American motto. Let us make sure that familiarity has not made them meaningless for us.

We carry the torch of freedom as a sacred trust for all mankind. We do not believe that God intended the light that He created to be put out by men.

Soon we will be celebrating one of our holidays, one that typifies for me much of what we mean by the American freedom. That will be Halloween. On that evening I would particularly like to be, of course, with my grandchildren, for Halloween is one of those times when we Americans actually encourage the little individuals to be free to do things rather as they please. I hope you and your children have a gay evening and let's all give a little prayer that their childish pranks will be the only kind of mischief with which we Americans must cope. But it can be a confident kind of a prayer too, for God has made us strong and faith has made and kept us free.

Good night.

NOTE: The President's remarks, recorded on film, were part of a television program carried on all four national networks between 9:00 and 11:00 p.m.

306   ¶ Letter to the President of the Council of Ministers of Viet-Nam Regarding Assistance for That Country.   *October* 25, 1954

[Released October 25, 1954. Dated October 1, 1954]

Dear Mr. President:

I have been following with great interest the course of developments in Viet-Nam, particularly since the conclusion of the conference at Geneva. The implications of the agreement concerning Viet-Nam have caused grave concern regarding the future of a country temporarily divided by an artificial military grouping, weakened by a long and exhausting war and faced with enemies without and by their subversive collaborators within.

Your recent requests for aid to assist in the formidable project of the movement of several hundred thousand loyal Vietnamese citizens away from areas which are passing under a *de facto* rule and political ideology which they abhor, are being fulfilled.   I am glad that the United States is able to assist in this humanitarian effort.

We have been exploring ways and means to permit our aid to Viet-Nam to be more effective and to make a greater contribution to the welfare and stability of the Government of Viet-Nam.   I am, accordingly, instructing the American Ambassador to Viet-Nam to examine with you in your capacity as Chief of Government, how an intelligent program of American aid given directly to your Government can serve to assist Viet-Nam in its present hour of trial, provided that your Government is prepared to give assurances as to the standards of performance it would be able to maintain in the event such aid were supplied.

The purpose of this offer is to assist the Government of Viet-Nam in developing and maintaining a strong, viable state, capable of resisting attempted subversion or aggression through military means.   The Government of the United States expects that this aid will be met by performance on the part of the Government of Viet-Nam in undertaking needed reforms.   It hopes that such aid, combined with your own continuing efforts, will contribute effectively toward an independent Viet-Nam endowed with a strong government.   Such a government would, I hope, be so responsive to the nationalist aspirations of its people, so enlightened in purpose and effective in performance, that it will be respected both at home and abroad and discourage any who might wish to impose a foreign ideology on your free people.

Sincerely,

DWIGHT D. EISENHOWER

His Excellency Ngo Dinh Diem
President of the Council of Ministers
Saigon, Viet-Nam

307 ¶ Remarks in Connection With Secretary Dulles' Public Report at a Cabinet Meeting. *October* 25, 1954

[Broadcast from the Cabinet Room at the White House at 7:00 p.m.]

Mrs. Hobby and gentlemen:

As you know, I asked you to come here this evening so that we could immediately hear a firsthand report from the Secretary of State regarding the negotiations that have just been going on in Europe, and the outcome of those negotiations. I think it is extremely important that all of us have a clear understanding of what was accomplished, and the circumstances under which it was done, and what it will probably mean.

Having determined upon this, when request was made to me that we open this meeting to the television companies, the radio companies, and the newsreels, it suddenly occurred that, for tonight, there is one subject— a very special one—about which to talk, and one which the American people, all of them, without regard to race or party or creed or color or any other thing, will want to hear.

So, for this one time, we are having this meeting of the Cabinet on all of these media of publicity.

Secretary Dulles.

[*At this point Secretary Dulles reported on his trip to Bonn, London, and Paris, and on the negotiations which culminated in the agreements reached in Paris on October 23 terminating the occupation of and restoring sovereignty to Western Germany, providing for its admission to NATO, and establishing a Western European Union to consist of the six EDC nations and the United Kingdom. After a brief further report on the Saar Agreement the President resumed speaking.*]

Yes. Well, Foster, I feel like we almost ought to give you a standing ovation. You know how intensely I believe that the safety and security of the Western World demanded unity and strength in Western Europe.

Now that that gives every promise of coming about, I can't tell you how gratified I am, not just for myself, but for the entire American

950

people; and your colleagues thank you for this brilliant presentation. Really we do.

NOTE: Secretary Dulles' report to the President and the Cabinet was published, together with related documents, in "London and Paris Agreements, September–October, 1954" (Department of State Publication 5659, Government Printing Office, 1954).

On October 24 a White House release stated that the President believed that all Americans would join with him in rejoicing at the success of the Paris conference, and that the agreements reached there represented a historic step toward that unity so necessary for the maintenance of the freedom of Western Europe.

308   ¶ Address at the Forrestal Memorial Award Dinner of the National Security Industrial Association.   *October* 25, 1954

Mr. Chairman, Mr. Folsom, Mr. Chief Justice, my fellow Americans:

It is indeed a high honor that you pay me. I am touched by the terminology in which you have seen fit to commend me, and though I shall be somewhat embarrassed each time I read it, I assure you that my pride will be equal to my embarrassment, and I will read it often.

Moreover, to receive an award bearing the name of James Forrestal is indeed a great distinction. I am deeply grateful to all of you, and to the National Security Industrial Association.

I was privileged to be associated closely with James Forrestal during the final years of his life. He was devoted to the public good. There has been no stauncher patriot nor anyone more far-sighted in perceiving the evil designs of Communist imperialism. At my first meeting with him, during World War II, he expressed his grave fear that Communist Russia would emerge from the war as a threat to individual liberty and freedom. To these he was completely dedicated.

Now, central among the many concerns of his sweeping mind was the great free economy of America. He knew that in peace and war, this economy is the source of our military strength. He knew that unless this economy were kept healthy, strong, and expanding, there would be for the free world neither victory in war nor security in peace.

In the vitality of this system, James Forrestal had complete faith. He did not mistakenly think of our economy merely in terms of broad acres and mighty industries, of railroads and ships, and mines and factories. Though all these we have, he clearly saw that it is America's people— farmers, teachers, shipbuilders, scientists, executives, machinists, truck drivers, all living under a system that encourages individualism—who are directly responsible for the near miracle of our great productivity.

Consequently, he was skeptical of excessive governmental interference with our economy in times of peace. He well recognized the need for the Government to prevent or correct monopolistic concentrations, as well as unemployment and agricultural dislocations. Yet he saw just as clearly the evils of regimentation.

His faith in America was rooted in his conviction that, by and large, and over the long pull, we could and would cooperate, one with another, for the benefit of all. He believed that in an America at peace, a combination of private citizen and local and Federal Government, operating together under wise regulatory laws and accepted practices, would sustain our priceless liberties and rights, while producing for each of us an ever-rising prosperity and standard of living.

Of this economy that so engaged the study and interest of James Forrestal, I shall speak tonight. More specifically, I shall speak of certain functions that, I believe, our Government must perform to keep our economy growing, stable and strong.

It has been truly said that the state of our economy is largely a national state of mind.

For 20 long years, somewhere in the world there has been war—up until a few months ago. Thus, for almost a generation, tragedy and happiness—waste and plenty—foxholes and jobs—have been tightly joined together in people's minds. Many came to believe that these had to live together or not at all—that, without war, without the mountainous demands of the battlefield, modern industrial America would always overproduce, forcing unemployment and a downward economic spiral, and ultimately cascading all of us into the terrible pit of depression.

As war year succeeded war year, this attitude toward our Nation's economy exacted a heavy toll. It stunted growth. It warped economic behavior. It blighted confidence and discouraged needed investments that thrive on confidence. Many of our people were frightened into grasping more for security and protection than for new opportunity and a fuller life.

But, in the past 2 years, there have been heartening events. They should release tremendous economic energies and, for all of us, open the door to a happier future. For, in 2 years, we have again demonstrated that America's prosperity does not necessarily depend on war's sacrifice.

Without war, our economy is working at near record levels. Over 62 million people have jobs. The number is steadily increasing. The hours of work are getting longer. Consumers are spending at a higher rate than ever before. Construction records are being broken month by month. Wage rates are at their all time peak. Weekly earnings in manufacturing are again on the rise. Our people have more personal income after taxes than ever before. Our national production surpasses even the war peak of 1944. It is far above the levels of 1945 through 1952.

We know that, if we act wisely, before us is continuing expansion, with a steady rise in the living standards of all our people.

To foster this expanding economy must be our Government's domestic goal.

In so conducting our affairs, we must never lose sight of the fundamental fact that our economy succeeds only as our people succeed. On the release of the treasure house of energy, brains, and confidence of all 163,000,000 of our people, depends our economic future.

Drawing on the richly varied abilities of our entire citizenry, we can foresee that in less than a decade the national output will increase from today's $356 billion to $500 billion. This would equal an average increase of more than $3,000 for every American family of today. And these can be real dollars—dollars of stable buying power, not simply more dollars of cheapened value.

And while our people in their daily tasks are bringing this about, Government must intelligently and vigorously do its part.

Government must work to stabilize the buying power of the dollar, else the value of the pension, the insurance policy, and the savings bond is eroded away.

Government, through social security and by fostering applicable insurance plans, must help protect the individual against hardship and help free his mind from anxiety.

Government must use its full powers to protect its citizens from depression, unemployment, and economic distress.

Government, my friends, must have a heart as well as a head. It must encourage, guide, backstop, and supplement—but never dominate or attempt to regiment our people.

Events of recent months provide lessons we must not ignore.

A year ago, inflation was halted. Defense expenditures were being reduced. Wartime economic stilts that many thought were essential props for business were being cut down. New floods of automobiles, appliances, and other products had swept away civilian market shortages. We were shifting from the shortage economy of war to the plenty of peace.

And why wasn't the result chaos and economic despair, as many feared?

First, because taxes were cut. Citizens could devote fewer hours to meeting governmental obligations and more to their own living requirements. Seven billion four hundred million tax dollars are being left with our people to spend at a time when their buying power needs to be sustained. This saving is evident every time a citizen opens a pay envelope, goes to the movies, takes a train or a bus trip, buys a refrigerator. For all of our citizens—from working mothers with dependents in their homes, to wage earners with heavy medical bills, to business needing to expand and thereby to create more jobs—the tax burden has been reduced. Thus our national adjustment from wartime to peacetime was eased. And our economy was given added strength.

Now, second, government powers over money and credit were used to stabilize the buying power of the dollar. They were used in January 1953 to stop the spiraling inflation which could have resulted in serious unemployment and depression. Later, as this risk diminished, the process was gradually reversed to ease credit markets and encourage economic expansion. This helped people to buy homes, automobiles, and household appliances. It encouraged them to construct new plants, manufacture equipment, build new shopping centers. It stimulated State and local public works. In these ways, our Nation avoided liquidations which in the past brought on panics, widespread unemployment, and despair.

The objective of these measures, I repeat, was to release individual enterprise and initiative—to maintain confidence among consumers and investors, among businessmen and working people.

Other measures also have helped to sustain our economic strength.

Social security was extended to 10,400,000 more people, including, for the first time more than 5 million farmers. Thus hundreds of millions were added to the buying power of our elderly people.

The protection of unemployment insurance was extended to some 4 million workers not previously covered.

A new housing law helped our people acquire new homes and encouraged building throughout the country.

In carrying out farm laws still in effect, basic crops were supported by loans and purchases amounting to $1,646,000,000 in the current fiscal year. At the same time, a new farm program was carefully evolved to attack the problems of markets, production, and surpluses which, for 7 years, have forced a steady decline in farm income.

Strategic materials, essential to our military strength, are being purchased in an amount of $900,000,000.

A new multi-million dollar program of shipbuilding and repair is keeping in operation needed shipbuilding facilities and creating many jobs.

In these and many other ways, Government has helped to keep our Nation's economy on an even keel. And the result? This year 1954 is our most prosperous peacetime year in all our history.

This picture is marred, of course, by the fact that in certain industries and localities unemployment still exists as the aftermath of war and inflation. It is a matter of deep concern to all of us when people, looking for work, cannot find it. Unemployment figures are far more than statistics. They reflect heartache—anxiety—hardship—and ultimately, loss of confidence in our country's future. It is not only in the interests of the jobless workmen but for the benefit of all of us, that the problem be solved.

It is essential to create more jobs and to ease these war-born hardships. Good progress is being made. Since last spring unemployment has been steadily declining. Still more progress is needed. There is certainly no comfort for us in the mere fact that the unemployment level is much lower today than during the recession of 1949 and 1950, or in the fact that unemployment today is less than one-third its level in the years 1933 to 1940, when as many as 10,000,000 Americans were out of jobs and couldn't find them.

I should like to interrupt myself here, to give you a report that reached me just late this afternoon. It came from the Secretary of Commerce and the Secretary of Labor jointly. It is the latest report on unemployment.

In this month, it has been reduced by 400 thousand jobs.

In that period, unemployment has fallen from 3,100,000 to 2,700,000.

I have asked the Secretary of Labor, incidentally, in a nationwide telecast tomorrow night, to give to the public all of the facts that we have on this employment and unemployment situation.

Incidentally, I might remark, as I look at this head table, this seems to me, or feels to me like the second Cabinet meeting I have had since 7 o'clock this evening.

I sincerely hope that most if not all of you got to hear the report from Secretary Dulles, a report that carries for all of us so much of promise, because of its evidence of growing strength in Western Europe.

I repeat that a central reason for our overall economic growth is confidence that the American economy will meet the tests of peace.

I believe that it is high time, in this great, growing, productive land of ours, to put behind us the rash of fears that for so long have haunted some among us—fear of war, fear of unemployment, fear of ourselves—fear of the future.   Certainly, we know now that one such fear—the fear of paralyzing depression—can be safely laid away.

But we must not rest.   In our economy, to stand still is to fall behind. Our labor force is growing.   Productivity is rising.   We must do more than simply to plan against trouble or accept unemployment at its present level.   Rather, we must advance toward and beyond the goal I mentioned earlier—within 10 years, a national production of 500 billion dollars.

This means that we must do a number of things.

First, we must develop a foreign economic program that will expand trade, encourage investment, help bring about currency convertibility, and reduce the need for direct aid to other countries.   This program will expand markets for our goods abroad.   It will help improve our standard of living, as well as the security and solidarity of the entire free world. Our economy can grow only as part, though a vastly important part, of a growing free world economy.   Just as there is no security for America in isolation, neither is there durable prosperity.

Second, we must continue to reduce the cost of Government, so we can have more tax cuts.   Already in 2 years we have cut Federal costs by 11 billion dollars.   To the limit that national security will permit, we must make more savings and return them, in the form of lower taxes, to the American people.   Tax cuts will add still more to private income and expenditure.   They will stimulate the continued growth of the economy.   For every dollar cut down on Federal expenditures, I believe we can, with reasonable assurance, expect a two-dollar expansion in our private economy.

Third, we must give America a modern highway system.   In addition to easing the Nation's traffic problems, we will, by this great program, powerfully stimulate healthy economic growth and strengthen the Nation's security.

Fourth, we must continue to improve our farm program.   As the American farmer keeps on increasing his productivity—already the highest in the world—he must be helped to gain his fair share of the steady increase in our national income.

Fifth, we must speed the conversion of the atom to the peaceful service of mankind—incidentally, a program on which we never give up for one minute.   We proceed with all of our friends in working out ways and means for doing this.

Sixth, we must work for more and better schools and homes.   We must improve opportunities for teachers.   We must further improve our social security system.   We must provide better protection against the hardships of old age, ill health, poverty, and unemployment.

Seventh, in partnership with States, local communities, and private citizens, we must develop the water, power, and soil resources of our great river valleys.

In these and other ways, we shall continue economic progress for all America in a world at peace.   Thus we shall assure every citizen of maximum opportunity to enjoy good health and a good job, a good home and a good education, and a rising standard of living.

Three basic facts are important in this forecast.

First, of course, is our free way of life.

Second is our rapidly growing population.

Third is the amazing variety of new products of our technology.

Our population grows at a rate of five new Americans every minute. We have grown by 20 million in the past 10 years.   By 1970 we will number 200 million souls.   Simply to keep up with our needs for homes, and factories, and schools, and roads, and goods for all these additional Americans will powerfully stimulate expansion of our economy.   And, to provide us a higher standard of living, it must expand even more.

This expansion is entirely within our power.   Doubters need only to look at some of the new frontiers science opens to us almost daily—in plastics, new metals, peacetime atomic developments, antibiotics, television, aeronautics. Today more than twice as many of our people work in research and development as were so working a dozen years ago. America now invests four billion dollars a year in scientific research and development. No money is better invested in our Nation's future.

In my own lifetime, from my boyhood in Kansas to this day, I have seen automobiles, radio, television, telephones, electricity, tractors, power machinery, new insecticides, fertilizers, good roads, and modern schools all come to rural America. If in this time—because I'm not so awful old—so much could be done, I know that America's tomorrow will be still more exciting, still more productive, filled with more and better things for all our people.

We must, therefore, encourage our economy along the ways of healthy expansion and be vigilant to keep it vigorous and free.

My friends, there remains one thought, the most important of all, that I must leave with you. It is that only when we win the struggle for permanent peace can we devote the full power of this mighty country of ours to the advancement of human happiness.

America's greatest hope and opportunity is to make strong and lasting the present uneasy peace that has so lately come to the world. With our great economic strength, we have no reason for fear. If we exercise wisdom, if we maintain our faith in the genius and energy of our people, if we avoid the centralization that is the refuge of fear, our economy will remain healthy and growing and strong.

With this strength, with this confidence, our Nation will be fortified in its quest for world peace—a quest that must never cease, never slacken, until the final goal has been attained.

This, our deepest aspiration, a precious dream that was shared by James Forrestal, will, with God's help, one day be realized. Then the true road to enduring happiness and prosperity will open to us and to all the world.

My friends, again permit me to express my very great pride in this award and in the compliment that I have been paid by this entire gathering.

Thank you.

NOTE: The President spoke at the Mayflower Hotel in Washington at 10:30 p.m. His opening words "Mr. Chairman, Mr. Folsom" referred to R. C. Simmons, Secretary of the Association, and Frank M. Folsom, Chairman of the James Forrestal

Memorial Award Committee. The first Forrestal Memorial Award, a medal bearing the likeness of Secretary Forrestal in low relief, was presented to President Eisenhower "for distinguished service to national security."

309 ¶ Letter to Harvey V. Higley, Administrator of Veterans Affairs, on the Elimination of Segregation in Veterans Facilities.
October 26, 1954

[Released October 26, 1954. Dated October 25, 1954]

Dear Harvey:

I greatly appreciate your report on the success of the Veterans Administration program to eliminate segregation in all VA hospitals and domiciliaries. You and all who cooperated with you in this program are to be highly commended.

In making the success of your program possible, our people have once again demonstrated their social maturity and their determination to have in America fair play and equal opportunity. In your accomplishment, Americans everywhere can take a great and justifiable pride.

With warm regard,

Sincerely,

DWIGHT D. EISENHOWER

NOTE: Mr. Higley's final report, in the form of a brief letter to the President, was released with the President's reply. The report stated that the Veterans Administration, in keeping with the President's policy of eliminating segregation in all Federal activities, had launched its program in October 1953. It further stated that segregation had been eliminated in all VA hospitals and domiciliaries, and that the agency's experience with the integration of patients had been most satisfactory.

310   ¶ Remarks at the Conference of the National Women's Advisory Committee on Civil Defense. *October 26, 1954*

Mrs. Howard and ladies:

I suppose there are a dozen places in which I could logically start the little talk I should like to make to you. As one who has some acquaintanceship with war, I could go into some description of its horrors, its privations, its suffering—which would seem to be useless even if it could be a bit logical. I could roam over the whole field of our past experience in this country, and in different countries, what we might expect—talk about the probabilities of future destruction in the event of war, and all that sort of thing.

I would rather start at a very much different place, and that is spirit.

I would like first of all to make the point that we are not met—you in giving of your time and effort—are not met merely to save homes and lives. Underneath it all is a way of life—a way of life—a conception of how people ought to live, people created in the image of their Maker, and their rights, and so on. So that we want to live under a system that first of all we want to preserve.

To do that, we of course have to preserve humans, because that system is based on the theory that the human is all-important. So we start in, then, with a very wonderful conception of our duty. It is not one in which we necessarily have to fire ourselves—to work up enthusiasm. We are talking about the very basis of our living: freedom—liberty—a system that preserves those freedoms and liberties; and then of course, the lives of our loved ones and ourselves.

We know that if we would suffer great destruction, this system would be gone, to say nothing of the millions that would pay the price. Then we begin to calculate in our minds, what can we do? And your presence here is proof that you have gone through all this line of thinking, and you know there is much that you can do.

One of the phenomena of war is how easily panic can overtake humans, when they have not been prepared for some particular surprise. One of the things that I noticed in war was how difficult it was for our soldiers, at first, to realize that there are no rules to war. Our men were raised in sports, where a referee runs a football game, or an umpire a baseball game, and so forth. They had sort of the idea that there were sort of hours for fighting a war; and to catch an attack at 10 o'clock at night, with a half-dozen men killed and the rest running for their lives, you could see the resentment boiling up inside them, because they had not been quite prepared for that kind of rough stuff.

Now one of the things, then, we have to do is to prepare ourselves, in our minds and in our hearts and in our spirits, for any catastrophe that might come to us. We have got to recognize that war is no longer something that is neatly packaged, divided into parts, and there are soldiers off some place, and we are doing our best through the Red Cross, the USO, and knitting the things to send to them. It is not that remote any longer from us—it is right on our doorstep, right squarely there.

And so every woman, every child, has practically the same duties in war as does any man, no matter where he is. It is a frightening and revolutionary thought. It of course highlights the tremendous necessity that the statesmen of the world—and the so-called statesmen of the world—have for pursuing peace with all of the energies of which they are possessed, tirelessly, constantly, insistently, leaving no stone unturned in order to find it.

But in the meantime, the strength of the United States is represented first of all, then, in the spirit that you women show, not only in your comprehension of what this thing is about, and what you must do, but your readiness to do it—another attribute of free nations—volunteering to do these things. That in itself makes us stronger.

A well-disciplined company loses through a blast right in its center, they lose a third of a company, and the rest close in and form up; and they are still a fine outfit. An undisciplined, unready company loses a couple of wounded on the end from a stray shot, and it takes a very good man to find the whole company very soon. It is a difference between thinking and preparation—the readiness of the spirit and of the mind, as well as the readiness of the body.

Now you have a peculiar difficulty to overcome, which again I saw in war. Americans have a very great fear of being thought a little "boy scoutie," or maybe I should say "girl scoutie"; that is, being a little bit too naive, too child-like in their approach.

I saw individuals in the world war, when they were on bombing drill or fire drill, trying to carry a bucket of sand, and practically speaking, trying to cover it with a raincoat to hide the bucket of sand so people would not know what they were doing.

Well, you have got to overcome—you have got the job as leaders—to overcome the reluctance of people, of our people, to do something constructive, to prepare themselves just to be ready with the little bit of routine action that would be necessary in war, whether it be in the first aid, helping the wounded, or whether it be helping to put out a fire, or merely directing somewhere at a crossroads people where they could go in a hurry.   There is so much that can be done, to remove the fear, the danger of panic from our lives, that I couldn't possibly find words in which to thank you people for getting into this job and helping.

And I am sure that you understand this: any man that has been married as long as I have, doesn't underrate the persuasive powers of a lady.   And so I am particularly pleased that this is the Women's Advisory Committee, and there are the groups of State directors, regional directors, that are doing this work, meeting together and getting all the techniques and plans that you are going to use.

Because I will tell you: I think, first, as this is understood in the world, what we are doing, you have lessened the chances of war, exactly as we believe that a bombing squadron or a good regiment, we believe with that much, it lessens the chances of war.

And I assure you, if war ever comes, the value of your work will be so overwhelming, so incalculable, that it couldn't possibly be gauged in any mere words or by any comparison.   It could well mean the difference between victory—or put it this way: between defeat and averting defeat. Because I really doubt whether, in modern times, in global war, there is any victory.

So I came over this morning, as you can see, not to attempt to make you any speech, but to attempt, rather, to express to you some of the thoughts in my mind, the instinct and the feelings that are in my heart.   And above all, to thank you.   Thank you, because by your presence you show your continuing indestructible interest in the United States of America—all of the system that makes up the United States, and the people that inhabit it.

I trust that you will find your meeting here, ladies, just as enjoyable as it is interesting, and that you will go back not only feeling that you have profited, I say professionally, and in the work that you have undertaken so

voluntarily and so well, but that also it will be a very enjoyable memory.
Thank you very much.

NOTE: The President spoke in the Executive Office Building at 11:00 a.m. His opening words "Mrs. Howard" referred to Katherine G. Howard, Deputy Administrator, Federal Civil Defense Administration.

311 ¶ The President's News Conference of *October 27, 1954.*

THE PRESIDENT. Ladies and gentlemen, it, of course, has been some time since I have seen a great many of you. I have nothing to announce, no speeches to make, at least unless provoked. [*Laughter*] And so I came over because it occurred to me there might be a question or two that some of you might have on your mind.

Q. Merriman Smith, United Press: Mr. President, to put it mildly, there has been some confusion about your plans for this weekend. I wonder if you could tell us whether or not you plan any last minute tour in behalf of the Republicans on Friday and Saturday?

THE PRESIDENT. Well, an examination of my schedule, which of course has to precede any decision of this kind, shows that the only possible day that I could leave Washington is Friday. Whether or not I can go has not been quite definitely determined. I should like to dramatize my desire to see everybody vote in this election. I should like to do a little bit of stirring up, but whether or not I can do it, whether all of the details can be worked out, I am not certain at this moment.

However, certainly within the course of the next few hours it must be determined. The second that it is, I will let Mr. Hagerty know; and he will notify you, and exactly what points would be involved.

Q. Harry C. Dent, Columbia (S.C.) State and Record: Mr. President, do you have any comments on the race in South Carolina between the two Democrats, Strom Thurmond, who is a write-in candidate, and Edgar Brown, who is a committee nominee running for the United States Senate?

THE PRESIDENT. Well, I think my comment is contained in your question, they are two Democrats running for Congress. [*Laughter*]

Q. Charles S. von Fremd, CBS News: Mr. President, the Chairman of the Republican National Committee, Len Hall, turned a new word or phrase just recently regarding the Federal housing scandals. He called it a "stealaway."

THE PRESIDENT. A what?

Q. Mr. von Fremd: He called it a "stealaway" and attributed it to the Democrats, which probably has something to do with the close proximity of November 2d.

I wonder, sir, if you feel that there is any laxness on the part of your administration regarding the Federal housing disclosures, and also what the people of the country may expect now that these disclosures have been made. Is there any chance of getting back some of the windfall profits, any chance for lower rents?

THE PRESIDENT. Well, I thought that the Attorney General had made some announcements in this field.

Let me make clear, I am not a court of law, I am not trying to adjudge guilt, and neither by implication or direct statement do I mean to say so-and-so was guilty.

My report from him is that he has secured a number of indictments, that he is instituting civil suit to recover the money that innocent tenants suffered as a result of the so-called windfalls.

As you know, the law under which it was done expired back as far as 1950, and I think that all building operations under that law must have ceased, say, by the end of '52 or somewhere along there—maybe it was before that.

But in any event, the Attorney General is progressing with all of the facilities available to him to do what he can to correct what has happened, one, to recover the money, and the other to punish people that are guilty. That is all there is.

Q. Ray L. Scherer, National Broadcasting Company: Mr. President, the forecasters have all made their predictions, and most of them say the Democrats. I wondered if you would care to risk a prediction on the event of next Tuesday?

THE PRESIDENT. I don't think I have ever predicted. You people know what I believe, and I am not going to take up this entire period to repeat it to you. I am working for something, I believe in it, and I want to continue during these next 2 years to get that done as nearly as possible. So I am not going to predict, but I can certainly hope.

Q. Alan S. Emory, Watertown Times: Continuing that thought, sir, several months ago you told us that you thought the major issue of this campaign should be your legislative program, and indicated at the time that you did not think the Communist issue should be a major one in the campaign.

Now, of late, the Republican leaders who have been campaigning around the country, with the exception of yourself, sir, have seemed to shift emphasis from the accomplishments of the Congress and your legislative program to the Communist issue. I would like to know, sir, first, whether they have consulted you on that decision and, second, whether it has your approval?

THE PRESIDENT. Well, you base your whole question on a statement that you say appears to be a Republican attitude at the moment. I have not read the speeches. I have listened lately to two or three talks here in town, and I didn't hear the word "Communist" mentioned—I mean they have originated here in town.

As far as I am concerned, none of these people have come to me about the details of their talks. They know what I believe, and they are going out doing their best in their own way and, I suppose, answering questions or attempting to answer or to present the case as they see it. But I couldn't possibly comment in detail on the whole generality.

Q. Marvin L. Arrowsmith, Associated Press: Mr. President, on another subject, Prime Minister Churchill said yesterday that he would be willing to meet with Premier Malenkov of Russia at an appropriate time and place, but he spoke out against any meeting of the Western powers with Russia before ratification of the Paris agreements. Could you tell us what your position is on a possible meeting with Malenkov, either before or after ratification?

THE PRESIDENT. Well, in both cases I would have to answer what has been said before. I believe that this is not a time to project or to hold a four-power meeting while these discussions and this plan have gone to this stage of development.

Now, as far as appropriate time for talking with the Communist authorities, whenever that time is appropriate and we have a reason to believe they are sincere, why, we will talk any time with anyone who wants sincerely to promote peace.

Q. Joseph A. Loftus, New York Times: Mr. President, the Budget

Bureau last June distributed a memorandum to all Federal agencies having to do with surveillance of the behavior of Government employees. It has nothing to do with security. The Bureau up to this moment has declined to answer any questions about it, and only a few days ago made public the text, after it had already been published.

My question, sir, is does this secrecy have your approval and, in a larger sense, would you comment on the question of secrecy in Government where security is not involved?

THE PRESIDENT. Of course, in certain activities it is obvious that secrecy must be maintained, let us say, in the departments that are working out the forecasts of crops for next year, and so on. Until the thing is ready for publication, to release it to any individual ahead of time would be a gross violation of the public trust. So I want to be understood that my general attitude toward this thing is not to run contrary to commonsense in specific cases. I am against secrecy where the security is not involved in the ordinary sense or in the ordinary case.

Now, what this order is—if I have seen it and gone over it, it slipped my mind; I don't recall it and, consequently, I could not comment on what this thing is.

As we know, the Director of the Budget Bureau is the business manager of the Government. What he has published in the way of procedural affairs for handling personnel I don't know at this moment, so I would have to have more details before I could comment.

Q. Chalmers M. Roberts, Washington Post and Times Herald: Sir, one of the officials in Governor Adams' office has recently sent out a letter and some charts on personnel management program having to do with employment of new Government employees, through the Republican National Committee. One of the documents issued over the name of the Office of the Assistant to The Assistant to the President says in the corner: "Checked and/or approved by the President."

Could you tell us, sir, whether you have, in fact, approved this method of recruitment through the party machinery?

THE PRESIDENT. Indeed I have. It is nothing in the world but an effort to get the best kind of people applying for governmental service that you can get, to get the White House out of the channel, so far as possible, to get these people recommending to the Civil Service Commission or to the departments in question, and to make a record of the people who do so recommend these individuals so that if we have any difficulty we know exactly who is responsible. Now, it is a generality, it is a long detailed thing, but it is to get it away from the White House as far as we can.

Q. Robert E. Clark, International News Service: Mr. President, you spoke in a speech the other night of the continued reduction of Government spending and tax cuts to the limit that the national security will permit. Can you say anything more definite at this time about the prospects of future tax cuts?

THE PRESIDENT. No, I can't.

Now, I do have constant reports from officials within the Defense Department that there are still areas in which, in the administrative and logistic fields, we can save a bit more money without being hurt and without reducing our combat strength. So to the extent that savings can be made, well, of course, they will be passed on. But I would say as of this moment we could not expect any major diminution in security strength, which bars any talk of great reductions in major sums; although, of course, there will be additional money found every month as there has been for the last two.

Q. Raymond P. Brandt, St. Louis Post-Dispatch: On this secrecy of documents, and so forth, why can't we get the Dixon-Yates contract? We got a copy but other people didn't. [*Laughter*]

THE PRESIDENT. As a matter of fact, I probably, if I had anything to do with it, would discipline the person that gave you the copy, if I knew them. I don't know.

Here are the facts. I promised all the documents in the negotiations leading to the making of this contract and, as far as I know, everybody has been able to see them. Next, there is a contract made. The law provides that that contract, when made, is placed before the Congress, and is to remain there until, I believe it is the Joint Committee, the Joint Atomic Energy Committee, has the full opportunity to investigate it and go through its details. When that is done, then it will undoubtedly be made public. But until it has finished its tour in front of the Atomic Energy Committee, I doubt that it would be proper to release it.

Q. Mr. Brandt: On that point, sir, do you wish the Joint Committee to waive that 30-day period for inspection and have the contract——

THE PRESIDENT. No one has asked me to ask them to waive any period.

967

Now, this is what I do know: the Federal Power Commission says this is a proper contract and fair to the Government and all concerned; the TVA authorities have gone over it and say, after incorporation of certain changes they wanted, that it is perfectly satisfactory; the Congress has the last word in the situation, and can go after it if they want to. So I feel that the Government is perfectly and splendidly protected.

Q. Clark R. Mollenhoff, Des Moines Register and Tribune: The Senate Committee has raised some question about the ethics of the actions of some subsidiaries of the Dixon-Yates group. I wonder if that has any effect on your thinking on the Dixon-Yates people, and the fact that the contract was let without bid?

THE PRESIDENT. I can't think of any man in Government whom I trust more as to his integrity, his commonsense, and his business acumen than Lewis Strauss.

Now, he was the one that was at the focal point of making this contract. I quoted the Federal Power Commission, I quoted the TVA; the congressional committee has its right to go over it in detail. If they find anything wrong, I am sure there will be someone that will make it public. Up until that moment, I have nothing further to do with it. I haven't seen the contract in its detail, and I haven't any more comments to make about it.

Q. John Herling, Editors Syndicate: Mr. President, the Census Bureau last night reported that nonfarm employment rose by 285,000 in October, but there was a decline of 288,000 farm jobs which more than offsets the gain. Do you care to comment on that in relation to the other figure in which unemployment is reported as going down 358,000?

THE PRESIDENT. That is right; it went down to 2,741,000.

Q. Mr. Herling: Yes.

THE PRESIDENT. The figures you just gave me have not been brought to my specific attention. I suggest you take it to Secretary Mitchell and ask him to explain them.

Q. Mr. Herling: This is Secretary Weeks, sir. But I would suggest that usually both figures on unemployment and employment are released at the same time, but this was a little early for that type of report. And interpretations by some of the experts indicate that the decline in unemployment, taken in connection with these other figures, would indicate there was actually a withdrawal of people from the labor force rather than actual return to work.

THE PRESIDENT. The report made to me—and, after all, I would hardly defend myself against the charge that I am [not] an expert in this field—the report made to me was that this is not merely a seasonal upturn; this is obviously the result of an upturn in the entire economy, in construction, in purchasing, in renewed and increased activity.

Now, as I say, if there is any detail of this thing, I suggest you take it to the Secretary of Commerce and the Secretary of Labor, and see what the answer is; I haven't heard of this seeming paradox that you quote.

Q. Sarah McClendon, El Paso Times: Sir, following Mr. Roberts' question about this personnel management chart that came from Mr. Willis' office, you said that was an attempt to get the best kind of people that you could get; but this is all geared to working through the Republican National Committee and the Republican Congressmen and Senators. Do you feel that only through the Republican National Committee and Republicans can we get the very best people?

THE PRESIDENT. I have no doubt that others will make their recommendations—not at all.

Q. John Scali, Associated Press: Mr. President, one of our subscribers in Rome, Italy, has requested that we ask you about your views about appointing an American ambassador to the Vatican. Could you say something about that, please?

THE PRESIDENT. Who did you say asked for it?

Q. Mr. Scali: One of our subscribers in Rome, Italy.

THE PRESIDENT. I have expressed myself on it so emphatically and so often that I think I would merely ask you to go back and see what I have said about this in the past.

Q. Hazel Markel, Mutual Broadcasting System: Mr. President, you have a very distinguished visitor coming today. I wonder if you care to make a comment on his visit.

THE PRESIDENT. You mean Mr. Adenauer. I have Mr. Adenauer coming, Mr. Yoshida of Japan, Mendes-France from France, and, of course, the Queen Mother. At least two of them are old and good friends of mine, which, of course, adds a personal pleasure along with our official satisfaction.

I consider Mr. Adenauer one of the great statesmen of our time, and one of the best informed men on Western European affairs that I have met. I find him a man animated by good sense, dedication to his people and to the peace of the world. I can only say that it is with tremendous satisfaction that we will have him here.

Q. Lawrence Fernsworth, Concord (N.H.) Monitor: Mr. President, I refer to the vacancy in the United States Supreme Court. There have been criticisms of the political nature of some of these appointments. The question is raised whether judges with distinguished records on the State or the Federal bench may not aspire to promotions to the highest court of the land, whether the selection of judges from among the judiciary might not be a desirable practice or policy. Would the President care to comment on that?

THE PRESIDENT. You say "some of these appointments"; you must be referring to someone else, I have made only one.

Q. Mr. Fernsworth: Yes, sir.

THE PRESIDENT. From my viewpoint, in the average case, the normal case, for the Associate Justices, I should think it would be a good practice to bring in people who have had real experience on the courts. I think at the same time the Chief Justice presents a very special problem, and everybody has to follow his own conscience when he is in a position of responsibility to solve that problem.

However, I do believe that the Supreme Court, as a whole, ought to offer great opportunity to judges who have served on a court.

Q. James B. Reston, New York Times: Mr. President, I wondered if we could get your personal philosophy about the meaning of this election. There has been some controversy on that point. Do you, for example, regard the election as a vote of confidence in you personally and in your administration?

THE PRESIDENT. No. As a matter of fact, I am now quoting the messages that come to me from all over this land, which are to the general effect that people won't put me into the election; that seems to be the complaint that I, at least, get from the Republican side.

I don't know—the biggest complaint I get is one of apathy. This I don't understand, but this is probably because I am working every single day of my life in these vital problems, domestically and in the foreign field, that affect us so seriously. Possibly I lose a little bit of a sense of perspective, which is one reason I like to get down with people and talk to them about the things that are occupying their mind.

So I can't understand the apathy at this time, but it does seem to be there.   And I will go back and say that one of my reasons that I would really like to get out and sort of dramatize for a day, for 1 day if I can, the need for getting out the vote is sort of to emphasize the importance of this election as well as those when the Presidency is at stake.   I can't comment on it much more than that.

It does occur to me, though, as this political question recurs and recurs, I should have said in answer to one question about this business of appointing individuals to Government service, there is no responsible official in this department that hasn't had orders that, in recruiting for the civil service, a man's party affiliation will make no slightest difference and give him none.   Those orders have been issued emphatically.

Q. Mrs. May Craig, Maine Papers: Mr. President, will you send any nominations, treaties, or other matters to the special session of the Senate beginning November 8th?

THE PRESIDENT. I think there will be some little things they can take care of; I mean little in volume, important in the individual cases.

Q. Clark R. Mollenhoff, Des Moines Register and Tribune: Mr. President, there have been some security-firing figures released recently, and there has been some effort to obtain information as to whether that is Democratic appointees or Republican appointees; and there was one story which said figures would indicate that 75 percent of those were Republican appointees.   I wonder if you could comment on that and tell us whether there is any reason why there should be any secrecy around whether these were Republican or Democratic appointees.

THE PRESIDENT. Well, I think the answer there is, when were these people appointed.   I don't know.   There have been Democrats in positions, I guess, that carry appointive power in the organizations today, and there have been Republicans, undoubtedly, in the past.   I believe that there is a number, it is in the small hundreds, that were appointed, but only tentatively appointed, since January 1953 that are included in this group.   It may be 275, something of that kind.   They got provisional appointments pending the completion of their total field inspections, and when those were done and there was reason to believe that they were not good material, they were let go.   But that is the only one, so far as I know, involved since January 1953.

Q. Elie Abel, New York Times: Can you tell us, sir, whether the recent Soviet nuclear explosions indicate any change in the relationship between the United States and the Soviet Union in atomic technology?

THE PRESIDENT. No. I would not think so. As a matter of fact, I don't have anything to say about that at all, other than the mere announcement that Admiral Strauss made either yesterday or the day before on the subject.

Q. George E. Herman, CBS Radio: Mr. President, Dr. Vannevar Bush has commented recently that the morale among our scientists, especially those working for Government in military installations, is dangerously low, and he gave it as his opinion that we may be a year or so behind where we should be in continental defense for that reason. I wonder if you would comment on that, sir?

THE PRESIDENT. Dr. Bush is entitled to his opinion. But I must say this, the scientists who have come to see me exhibit no such attitude.

Q. William M. Blair, New York Times: Mr. President, you mentioned a moment ago your receiving reports of apathy among voters. To what do you ascribe this apathy? Is it a disenchantment with the program of the last 2 years, sir?

THE PRESIDENT. What would you expect me to answer to that? [*Laughter*]

I answered Mr. Reston's question as fully as I knew how. I don't know why there is apathy. I will tell you what one reason given to me is: that the United States feels that they have gotten what they want, and why worry; that is the reason that is given to me. Far from disenchantment, it is just too much satisfaction from it. [*Laughter*]

Q. Alice F. Johnson, Seattle Times and Alaskan Papers: Mr. President, the Republicans recently experienced an almost 100 percent disaster in the Alaskan election; and both the Republicans and the Democrats, those who won and those who were defeated, attributed the Democratic victory to the feeling of Alaskans' disappointment that they were not included in the statehood move. Will this lead you to explain further to the people of Alaska your position?

THE PRESIDENT. Well, I can't say what I will comment on this. As a matter of fact, I haven't seen all of these records, I haven't seen these statements; but if I have anything to say, I will say it, I assure you.

Q. Kenneth M. Scheibel, Gannett Newspapers: Mr. President, speaking of these nominations to the Senate, might the new Comptroller General be named then?

THE PRESIDENT. I am not certain. You see, there was a Joint Resolution passed that I could fill that when I found the right man, without regard to that law which requires if a vacancy has existed 30 days before the termination of the Congress you can't fill it as an interim appointment. I do have authority to make that *ad interim,* and I am not sure therefore whether I will send it up.

Q. Joseph C. Harsch, Christian Science Monitor: I would like to ask the President a nonpolitical question, if I may. Last week you made two speeches in which you mentioned matters of foreign policy. In one of those you referred to the persistently aggressive design of Moscow and Peiping which you said shows no evidence of genuine change; and in another one of your speeches you made a remark to the effect that there is no longer any alternative to peace. I was wondering if you could open to us any thinking you may have in that area that lies between those two matters.

THE PRESIDENT. First of all, the latter of those two statements certainly ought to stand without argument. There is just no real alternative to peace, as I tried to express it. The results of any war, as I see it, would be only the choice between destruction and defeat and the averting of complete defeat.

I also believe that these fanatic pursuers of the communistic theory have not changed their mind.

But there has been evidence of a growing realization in the free world as to the very great importance of the basic issues on which we are united—the need to preserve freedom, the need to conduct ourselves so as to support our systems of government. That means to hang together, it means to be united in that conviction and, therefore, united in our strength to support that conviction. I believe that that strength, as it grows—and I think there is all sorts of evidence that it is growing. If we start right in and go around the world, to include such trouble spots as Iran and Suez and Trieste and Guatemala, even Korea and Indochina, SEATO, and this new and great advance in Western Europe, there is evidence that we are drawing closer together in fundamentals.

That, to my mind, is the channel or the direction that we must pursue and explore in all its angles to see whether finally there is some diminution of the intractibility of the other side's position, and finally better chances for negotiation.

I think one of the sort of auxiliary activities that ought to go along with this is the peaceful use of the atom, something we are pursuing with our friends. If the Soviets won't come in, it is too bad; we are not going to stop.

We are going to keep it going—every kind of thing to show the world that we are not just sitting off here alone and trying to protect our own money and ourselves, but we are recognizing that the freedom of the world demands we all hang together, and we are going to do it.

By the way, in this foreign field, let me repeat again so I am not misinterpreted: basic foreign policy must be a bipartisan, nonpartisan, affair. The thin line or the thread of direction that dictates objectives and aims, it must be an American thing. The handling, the operational, and the day-by-day work—that, of course, requires a certain set of leaders, and they have to take their responsibility when they are in power. But the whole thing, the basis of it, I am not trying to quote any partisan side; I am trying to quote what I believe is strictly American policy.

I believe America's success, therefore, over these last 2 years in that foreign field, and at home in going from a war to a peace economy without real depression—which has been customary and historical and is almost expected—those two things are the great significant events of our time.

I believe we have got better reason to hope today for peace than we did. One of the reasons is we are maintaining our strength at home in order to help this whole amalgamation of the free world around basic principles.

Q. Merriman Smith, United Press: Mr. President, to get back to the trip for a moment, if you do make this trip Friday, will it be a flying trip that covers several cities?

THE PRESIDENT. If I make the trip it will be in a chartered plane. It would be, I would say, covering a maximum of four stops, and merely at airfields; no attempt to leave the airfield, I simply haven't the time.

Now, as I say, whether I can dramatize what I would like to dramatize, whether I have the time and whether it would fit in, are all questions that are not quite settled yet.

Q. Chalmers M. Roberts, Washington Post and Times Herald: Mr. President, to get back to foreign affairs for a minute, does it follow from your answer to Mr. Harsch's question that you consider that foreign policy has not been an issue in this campaign, and that the result——

THE PRESIDENT. Oh, no. As a matter of fact, so far as I am concerned, there seems to be no issue you can keep out of a campaign, because they challenge the method, the way it is done; they challenge the attitude and the personality of the individual conducting these things. So you can't really keep it out.

The only thing I am trying to say is that our broad basic purposes of solidifying the free world around concepts of freedom and human dignity, leading them forward into better standards of living so that we have got greater intellectual, economic, and military strength to oppose this great menace, that must be nonpartisan; and it has been, so far as I know. I have never heard any quarrel on the basic principles in the long months I have been here.

Q. Mr. Roberts: May I ask the other part of the question, sir: does it follow that that basic principle, as apart from the actual conduct of it, would be unaffected whichever way the election turned, in your view?

THE PRESIDENT. If ever I attempt to make foreign policy, basic foreign policy, a partisan issue, I wish one of you people would remind me very forcefully. I simply reject it with everything I have; and as far as I know, every leader on both sides, when you come down to these fundamentals, has expressed that same view and feeling.

Merriman Smith, United Press: Thank you, Mr. President.

NOTE: President Eisenhower's fiftieth news conference was held in the Executive Office Building from 10:30 to 11:05 o'clock on Wednesday morning, October 27, 1954. In attendance: 203.

312 ¶ Letter to the Vice President in Appreciation of His Contribution to the Campaign. *October* 28, 1954

[Released October 28, 1954. Dated October 27, 1954]

Dear Dick:

Whenever my burdens tend to feel unduly heavy, I admire all the more the tremendous job you have done since the opening of the present campaign. You have personally carried a back-breaking load of hard, tedious, day by day and state by state campaigning. And in doing so you have been undismayed by problems of time, distance, and physical effort.

I know we share the urgent hope that there may be returned to the Congress a Republican majority that will work with the Executive Branch in completing the program that we believe is in the best interests of all America. No man could have done more effective work than you to further that hope. Whatever the outcome next Tuesday, I can find no words to express my deep appreciation of the contribution you have made toward that goal.

Please tell Pat, too, that she has aroused my admiration as an able campaigner; there is no question but that she is the most charming of the lot.

With warm regard,

As ever,

D. E.

313   ¶ Letter to Representatives Broyhill, Hyde, and Small on Legislation Benefiting Federal Employees.   *October* 28, 1954

[Released October 28, 1954. Dated October 27, 1954]

Dear ————:

I appreciated your writing me and telling me about misunderstandings you believe exist in the minds of some Federal workers about the Administration's attitude toward pay legislation.

The Administration is strongly committed to the principle that the Government must be a good friend and a good employer to its workers. Because of this, the Administration proposed, during the last session of Congress, legislation to eliminate existing inequities in the present unfair and outmoded job classifications. The legislation so proposed, had it been enacted, would have given a pay increase to every postal and every classified employee.

I appreciate the concern that the Congress had for the pay of Federal workers, and I regret that I could not conscientiously approve its approach to the problem. I do, however, feel confident that an equitable pay program can and will be enacted in the next Congress if members of our Party are retained in positions of leadership.

While both of us are, of course, disappointed that the Administration pay program was not enacted this past session, the record of the Republican-led 83d Congress in the passage of legislation of benefit to Government workers was outstanding:

(1) Group life insurance at low cost was authorized and is now available to all Federal employees and their families.

(2) Unemployment insurance was for the first time extended to Federal employees, and beginning January 1, 1955, these employees will have the protection of unemployment insurance coverage.

(3) Permanent promotions and reinstatements for Federal employees with Civil Service status were authorized for the first time in five years.

(4) Permanent status for "indefinite" employees was made possible.

(5) Premium pay practices were broadened and made more equitable.

(6) An allowance of $100.00 for uniforms was made possible for those employees who are required to wear uniforms on their jobs.

(7) Sick leave payments up to $100.00 a week were exempted from income tax when the employee is ill for seven days or more.

(8) The first $1200.00 of an employee's retirement annuity was exempted from income tax, resulting in a tax benefit of as much as $240.00 a year to every retired Federal employee.

These are some of the accomplishments that came about through the cooperation of Congress and the Administration in our joint effort to provide improved personnel management and sound benefits for Federal employees. We hope to be able to continue this progress. With understanding and support among Federal employees, I know we will succeed.

Sincerely,

DWIGHT D. EISENHOWER

NOTE: Identical letters were sent to Representatives Joel T. Broyhill of the 10th Congressional District of Virginia, DeWitt S. Hyde of the 6th Congressional District of Maryland, and Frank Small, Jr., of the 5th Congressional District of Maryland.

314 ¶ Joint Statement by the President and Chancellor Adenauer. *October* 28, 1954

I.

During this morning's conversations we took an opportunity to renew the spirit of friendship and confidence which has marked our relationship in the past, especially in our efforts to overcome the very serious situation which faced us during the past few months. We reviewed the decisions taken at London and Paris and we are convinced that with the coming into effect of the Agreements signed this past weekend, the road towards a strong and united Europe will have been paved. We view the understanding reached between the Governments of France and the Federal Republic of Germany as an especially encouraging step towards lasting peace in Continental Europe. This understanding was greatly furthered by the commitment on the part of the United Kingdom to maintain forces on the Continent. The basis for a European community has thus been established.

The continued interest in and support of this community by the United States was reiterated. Together with the strengthened North Atlantic Treaty Organization, now to include the Federal Republic of Germany, these new agreements will, we are convinced, serve to reinforce the defense system of the free world.

II.

We particularly addressed ourselves to the question of German reunification. The demand for a reunited Germany in freedom is viewed by us as the legitimate demand of the German people. We are agreed that this aim shall be achieved only by peaceful means. We are convinced of the necessity of continued efforts towards this goal and are agreed that such efforts will be made by the United States and the Federal Republic of Germany together with the Governments of the United Kingdom and France.

In this connection, we exchanged views on the latest Soviet note. It is our initial view that this does not seem to offer any new proposal on the part of the Soviet Union; it appears essentially as a reiteration of the positions taken by Mr. Molotov at the Conference in Berlin regarding Germany and European security.

We have no doubt that the strengthening of free Europe which will result from the recent London and Paris Agreements, will aid our efforts to bring freedom and unity to all of the German people.

III.

We discussed the unfortunate fact that large numbers of German prisoners of war and civilian deportees are still held in custody in areas behind the Iron Curtain, mainly the Soviet Union. The Chancellor requested the continued assistance of the United States in obtaining the release of these prisoners. This question has for some time been the subject of investigation by a United Nations Commission. The Chancellor was assured that the United States stands ready, now as in the past, to offer every support and assistance considered useful in accomplishing this end.

IV.

We also discussed the question of German assets in the United States. The President expressed sympathy for the problem raised by the Chancellor in his letter of July 17, 1954, to him on this subject and again expressed his willingness to explore such problems along with the question of American war claims. We were agreed that conversations between representatives of our two Governments will soon begin.

315 ¶ Statement by the President on the Floods and Landslides in Italy. *October 28, 1954*

FLOODS and landslides have caused great devastation in the region around Salerno, Italy.

The American people are keenly aware, as a result of their own recent experiences with hurricanes and floods, of the serious human sufferings that can be created by such a disaster. I wish to extend the sincere sympathy of the American people to our stricken friends in the Salerno area.

I have asked the Secretary of State to pursue every possible means to provide emergency relief, calling on the Secretary of Defense for any assistance his Department may give. The Director of the Foreign Operations Administration has also been notified to give every consideration to further measures of assistance.

NOTE: On November 1 the White House announced that the Italian Cabinet had expressed thanks for the offer of assistance, and that American voluntary relief agencies were actively cooperating with Italian authorities and the Italian Red Cross in the distribution of food, clothing, and medicine to the people of the Salerno area.

316 ¶ Address at Eisenhower Day Dinner Given by the Citizens for Eisenhower Congressional Committee for the District of Columbia. *October 28, 1954*

My good friends:

For both Mamie and myself, let me first say that it is wonderful to be with you again. It is wonderful to see the bandwagon and the Ike balloon, even if only in the moon. Everything about this meeting is one to give me a lift. In fact, I came here this evening with the mission of seeing whether I could help you go out through the land to stir up the sense of duty and the enthusiasm among the voters of this country that they need.

I must tell you, I can add nothing to what you people can do. If I could only shift to this country, to each corner, some of your fervor, some of your enthusiasm, some of your great faith and readiness to work, some of your youth, not merely youth in years but youth in outlook, how happy I would be.

In 1952, I met so often and so happily with the "Citizens" groups, that to renew the experience here this evening gives me a heart-warming feeling just of coming home.

You and I, and thousands of others were the partners in a political campaign. Together we built our platform of convictions and pledges.

Two busy years have passed since we crowded to the polls in the cities and towns and villages of our country to establish the kind of government in which you and I believe. By the tens of millions, Americans of all parties, all callings, all races emphatically made their wishes known.

You remember what we worked so hard for 2 years ago.

We worked to get honest and efficient government—the kind of government pledged by the Republican Party and its great allies, the citizens groups of Independents and of Democrats.

You and I worked for the kind of government that stays close to the homes of America.

Especially we fought for government that would concern itself with all the people—and that would make America strong abroad and strengthen prosperity and freedom at home.

And above all, we wanted progress toward peace.

To this kind of government we have dedicated ourselves. For it, for 21 months, my associates and I in the Congress and the Executive Branch have been working incessantly. With your support, we have made real progress.

The question now is: "Are we to continue that advance?" To forge ahead requires us to keep in positions of legislative responsibility the team of leaders who have been guiding this program through our Congress. This requires another Republican-led Congress.

Now, how far have we come in these 21 months?

First—where do we stand today in the world as compared to January 1953?

Two years ago there was a costly and apparently endless war in Korea which daily and weekly was taking the lives of America's youth. All the world was restless and irritable. Hot spots glowed threateningly in Iran, Trieste, Suez. In Europe, disunity and dissension hindered progress toward world security. Even here in the Western Hemisphere, in Guatemala, international communism was raising a menacing head. Each of these trouble spots threatened to flame, without warning, into disaster.

But gradually crisis was forced to give way to promise.

In Korea, 14 months ago, the futile waste of American life and treasure was stopped.

In Europe, only a few days ago, we saw an historic step toward unity and strength. It may well prove to be the greatest stabilizing accomplishment of this century in world affairs.

Meanwhile, two of our friends, Yugoslavia and Italy, cleared up years of trouble over Trieste.

Two other friends, England and Egypt, solved long-standing differences over Suez.

Strategic Iran, with its vast oil riches, threw off a threat of Communist domination and came strongly to our side.

The Communist foothold in our hemisphere was eliminated.

In southeast Asia, threatened by the Communist advance, a security coalition has at last been developed.

In all these heartening events, America was privileged to participate as an understanding and helpful friend.

The brightened prospects for free world security and eventual peace must be classed as one of the most important facts of recent years.   I deeply believe that the foreign policy of America is a bipartisan matter. More than any previous Administration, this one has observed the requirements of this truth.   Consultations with leaders of the other party in this delicate, vital area of government have been candid and open, and more frequent than ever before.

Nevertheless, my friends, in this field, as in all others, America needs a close-working Executive-Legislative team.   It needs undivided leadership which all of us can hold responsible for results; we cannot pursue peace so effectively when divided leadership can provide evasion of responsibility, and can afford to both parties alibis for failure.

At home, we have redeemed our pledge of 1952 to give America clean and efficient government.

We have moved decisively to root out subversion in this land.

We have removed from the government employ, people who failed to meet the high standards of public trust.

Along the way, we dropped 211 thousand excess positions from the Federal payroll.

Then, with the cooperation of the Congress, we redeemed another pledge by making possible the biggest tax cut in America's history, and I remind you, the only tax reform in many years.

Government spending was slashed by billions.

Social security benefits were accorded to 10 million more citizens.

Unemployment insurance was extended to 4 million more citizens.

A new housing program was started so that every American can have a decent home.

A new farm program was passed designed to stop the many years of decline in farm income.

Two years ago we also demanded peace and prosperity.   Thanks to a good Congress, thanks to hard work by many people in Washington and throughout the land, we have made the most significant domestic accomplishment of recent decades.

We have proved at last that America can go from war to peace without a terrifying depression.

By every measure of a nation's increase in wealth and productivity, 1954 is by far our most prosperous year of peace in all our history. Sensible handling of money supply and money rates, expansion of social security, tax reductions and reform, hard work, public and private building of confidence all across the broad economic front—these have at last eliminated from American life the dreaded specter of economic collapse.

But we know that still today, as an aftermath of the war and the inflation it brought, some unemployment persists amidst our general prosperity. So long as any citizen wants work and cannot find it, we have a pressing problem to solve. This Administration is working vigorously to bring about a lasting solution. Indeed, only this month unemployment dropped by hundreds of thousands. Unemployment today stands much below the levels of 1950. It is not even one-third of the 1940 level. In both those years, millions of people had been without jobs for long periods. And they did not get jobs until the nation went to war. Then workers got jobs in uniform or in war plants.

No wonder—no wonder many had come to believe that America could prosper only when American blood was flowing on the field of battle. Happily, faith in our system, confidence in the future, cooperation between industry and government, and wise decisions have dispelled that defeatist attitude. In twenty months, we have eliminated fears rooted in 20 years of economic discouragement and war.

And so, my good friends, this is how far we have come since January 1953.

We have an America at peace.

We have a prosperous America.

We have an America whose government is honest and efficient.

We have an America confident of the future.

And now I repeat: the question before our people tonight is, shall we continue this program? Shall we carry it on to full completion?

I believe that the overwhelming majority of the American people want this kind of progress to continue.

Of course, the Presidency is not at stake, but this election will have a heavy impact upon the future of all our people.

To explain why this is so requires some frank talk about how our Congress works.

The Congress in Washington is made up of over half a thousand men and women, Republicans and Democrats. Under our system, when there are more Republicans than Democrats, the Republicans run the Congress. When there are more Democrats, they run the Congress. And the party that runs the Congress also runs the Committees of the Congress. And it is mainly in these 30-odd Committees that the laws for our country are written.

When pressures of party loyalty and obligations influence legislative leaders and Committee Chairmen to oppose the Executive, there are many things they can do. History shows that both Parties have indulged in these obstructionist practices, sometimes at grave risk to our country's good.

Legislative leaders can stop essential bills in the Legislative Committees, in the Rules Committee, or kill them in the Senate or House of Representatives.

They can refuse to approve appointments to public offices.

They can put political amendments on good laws to force the President to veto the whole, or to accept the amendment in order to get the good law.

For political reasons, they can bottle up program after program to keep the President from doing something no matter how much the people may want it.

Now, my friends, this is no exaggeration. Neither is it accusation. It is simply the way politics has often been played in Washington. One Republican and two Democratic Presidents have, in this generation, testified to the stagnation, frustrations, and political feuds that result when one Party controls the Congress, the other the Executive Branch.

Now, in our system, of course, normally the two Parties, day by day, normally work well together. But they can't both serve efficiently—and at the same time—as the Captains of the Ship of State. When divided control between the Executive and Legislative Branches inspires each party to try to be Captain, which one can then be held responsible by the American people, either for putting the Ship on the rocks or for a successful voyage? For the next 2 years, the Executive Branch will be Republican. Confusion can be avoided and steady progress assured only by electing a Republican majority to the Congress.

I am not talking theory. I am talking hard facts. Here are just a few examples of what we could expect.

If the Democrats should take over the Congress, the Committee which handles your tax laws would be in charge of a man who supported the Administration on only 8 percent of the issues on which the leaders of the two Parties disagreed.

In the Senate and House Committees which handle laws respecting all judicial matters and our courts, the Chairmen would be men who supported the Administration on only 5 percent of those same issues.

The Senate and House Committees handling laws affecting American business would be headed up by men who supported the Administration on only 4 percent of these same issues.

These are just examples. But they illustrate the innumerable obstacles to steady progress if your government team is made up of a Congress controlled by one party and the Executive Branch by the other.

For the good of America, our governmental traffic must be efficiently handled. We won't get anywhere with red lights at all the governmental crossroads. Add to this, two drivers at every governmental steering wheel, each trying to go in a different direction, and we shall certainly end up in a hopeless traffic jam.

You and your friends and I—all of us—made solemn pledges to our country. We have come a long way toward fulfilling them. To go ahead, we must prevent a split government. The job is clear. The progressive program which the vast majority supported in 1952 needs now the reinforcement of their 1954 votes. So the job is to get the voters to the polls. Thus we will keep our government from political fiddling while the world burns. Thus we can go ahead, in this age of peril, building a stronger, better America, and a lasting peace in the world.

Now, my friends, all Americans sincerely long for peace. Neither party needs yield to the other in this regard. But do we want to interrupt the work of proved leaders and impede the progress they have helped so much to bring about in the past 2 years? Do we want uncertainty and confusion to replace certainty and confidence? Do we want divided responsibility or single responsibility? To ask these questions is to answer them. America needs another Republican-led Congress.

This calls upon us for the same enthusiasm and fervor with which we burned 2 years ago. And if this meeting—if this meeting is anything at all like the rest of the Citizens for Eisenhower groups throughout this United States, there is no question—you would wonder why I am talking. I am talking because I believe this so much. I believe, with you, we must go ahead.

Now, if we are to do this, it means, of course, talking to your neighbors, using the telephone, ringing doorbells, getting out the vote as you did then.

And I ask you these questions:

Is steady and sure progress toward world peace worth this kind of hard work?

Is prosperity worth it?

Is efficient, honest government worth it?

Are tax cuts, good homes, loyal employees, alertness against subversion and preventing inflation worth this hard work?

Of course they are. You have proved it by your acts.

Well, then, let's all of us—you and I—no matter how much we put forth before, let's roll up our sleeves and go harder to work—for a stronger America, good government, and a world at peace.

Let's have another Republican-led Congress.

NOTE: The President spoke at the Statler Hotel in Washington at 9:30 p.m.

317 ¶ Remarks at the Municipal Airport, Cleveland, Ohio. *October* 29, 1954

Mr. Bender, ladies and gentlemen:

These are busy days for all of us. I certainly found them to be very busy ones for me. But I decided to make this trip today, in order to urge upon all of us—all Americans everywhere—the importance of voting.

The reasons for this are simple. There are going to be great issues decided on November 2d. America cannot afford to have those issues decided by a minority vote. There is even a further reason. I am convinced—I am sure every single Republican is convinced—that the program for which we fought so earnestly in 1952, and was approved by such a vast majority of American citizens, is still approved by that vast majority of American citizens.

Consequently, if they only come out to vote, there is no question as to the outcome.

I can go to only a few places. I was disappointed to find that limitations of time and space would not let me visit every single State of the Midwest, as I originally intended. But I certainly hope that those States where I cannot go will understand that whatever I am trying to do, applies exactly to them as to any place where I am fortunate enough to meet with my fellow Americans.

Now, this State, this is my first visit since the tragic death of the late great Senator Taft. I want to say that during the final weeks of his life—the 12 or more weeks preceding the end—he became my greatest political friend and adviser in Washington. We were very close. No one could have lost more than I lost with his passing. And I could not come here without attempting to pay my tribute to a very great Ohioan—to a very great American.

Two years ago, we voted for a very great change. And I think it would be well to take just a few moments to recall to ourselves what was the change we wanted.

First, we wanted clean Government. We were tired of hearing the word "Communist" every time it was mentioned being called a red herring. We were tired of scandals in the Internal Revenue department, and other places of Government. We wanted clean Government.

Ladies and gentlemen, there has been no single appointee of this administration who has been confirmed by the Senate who has later been charged with any kind of wrongdoing, dismissed from the service, or indicted. They have a record of spotless integrity in your service.

Throughout the Government, from top to bottom, there has been applied a security program, a security program that is tough and thorough, but is absolutely fair. No man can say that his civil rights have been unjustly damaged through the operation of that security program.

And then we wanted prosperity. And we wanted prosperity in a world at peace. We wanted an end to the Korean war. The Korean war, with its futile casualty lists and loss of Americans, has been ended. And following that war, measures were instantly instituted to see that this country should pass from war production to peace production without the terrifying depressions that have always characterized such transitions in the past. This has been done.

First we started out and we removed controls from the economy. Do you remember when we said we were going to take off price controls?

And the prophets of gloom stated—they said that prices would go out of sight, that food prices, clothing prices, rents, would be impossible for the average citizen? We proved they were wrong.

The money policies of the Government have been adjusted to our needs. There has been a vast extension of the social security system, for old age pensions, for unemployment insurance. A housing program has been established that makes certain that every American can have a good home.

And finally, we tackled the problem of the farm. For 7 long years farm prices have been dropping. Since January 1951 the parity index has dropped by 25 points, and 19 points of that loss occurred before January first, 1953, when the new administration came in.

And even more than this, my friends, just a few days ago I had a letter from my home State of Kansas, and a farmer said to me, "My income is off this year, look what your program has done to me." My friends, I am sorry, but we are still operating under the rigid price support system that has been invoked for these many years. No new price support system in the farm area is yet operating, and it cannot operate until the crops of 1955 are in.

Then we tackled the problem of unemployment. Now I shall not weary you with going through the long list of things that have been done, but let me give you just a few facts:

Unemployment within this past month has dropped almost 400,000. It now stands at 2,741,000, and is going down. But let me tell you something else about this: we have been accused of many things by our political opponents, that we have caused unemployment. Unemployment today is far less than it was in 1949 and 1950; and my friends, it is less than one-third of what it was in 1940. And those people in 1940 and 1950 who were without work got jobs only when we went to war, and they either went into uniform or into war plants.

Now, do we want war in order to solve our economic difficulties? Of course we don't.

Nevertheless, in spite of all this great progress, I do assure you this: as long as there is a single American without work, who is able to work, and honestly seeks it, this Government will seek to find a better solution than has yet been brought out. We will never give up on this matter.

The only thing we bar is: we won't go to war in order to get work.

And now my friends, let me talk for just a moment about the great problem that besets the world: the problem of the pursuit of world peace.

When your administration took over in January 1953, do you recall the things going on in the world? War in Korea, war in Indochina, Iran threatening to fall under Communist domination, Suez, Trieste—points of irritation, ready to break out into sudden disaster at any moment? In Guatemala, communism already raising its ugly head.

Where are those spots? All gone—all gone.

But more important than these, perhaps, is this fact: the peace of the free world demands—literally demands—unification and working together in Western Europe. For many years we have been trying to aid in bringing that about. Within the last few days, the greatest Secretary of State of our time came home and reported to us that this is now well on the road to accomplishment.

I should say, my friends, that this incident—this development—can well be listed finally in our schoolbooks as the greatest development toward world peace of this century.

Now, with all this kind of record, with all this progress toward the things for which we launched that crusade in 1952, let us take a look at the purpose of my visit: the vote.

It is easy to say that one vote doesn't count. My friends, there have been three Presidents elected by one electoral vote in the electoral college; and one of those Presidents, my friends, the vote that elected him, because it was finally put in the House of Representatives, was by a representative from Indiana, whose margin of victory was one vote. And that one vote was from a sick constituent who insisted on being carried from his bed to the voting booth so he could register his opinion on the decisions of that day.

And there have been five States admitted to the Union by the margin of one vote.

Now let me bring this closer to home. How many of you remember the majority by which the Democrats won Ohio in 1948?

Well, it was 7,100. And you had more than eight thousand election precincts. One more vote in each election precinct on the right side and you would have been in the right column.

Now ladies and gentlemen, I am trying to show you that your vote is important.   Not only because you owe it to yourself, to the Government under which you are living, to register your convictions as to the political developments and programs of this country, but because of the potential meaning of that vote in what is going to happen to this country during the years to come.

Now you have made the first great step.   You have nominated—put into nomination—a great group of Republicans to fill the important positions in your States and in your Federal complement of Senators and Congressmen.   With that kind of group to serve you—to represent you—why is there any doubt as to what we must, what we can, and what we will do.   And I do not mean, in this case, merely taking your vote up to the poll.

I believe that every one of you, this afternoon, ought to call up every friend that you can think of, and remind them of these issues and their importance, and make them agree to remind others, and to keep it going until there will be such a sweep of votes that Ohio will not only be in the right column, but from Senator and Governor and Congressmen, and all your State offices in the right column by such a majority that you will be an example.

Thank you very much.

NOTE: The President spoke at 9:05 a.m.   to U.S. Representative George H. Bender
His opening words "Mr. Bender" referred   of Ohio.

318   ¶ Remarks in Cadillac Square, Detroit, Michigan.   *October* 29, 1954

Mr. Mayor, Senator Ferguson, Mr. Leonard, my fellow Americans:

First of all, permit me to thank each of you for the cordiality of your welcome.   I am truly grateful from the bottom of my heart.

Now I have come to talk to you a little while today about one of the most important things any American can do.   That is to vote—to register his opinion as to his Government and the kind of Government he wants.   And I have come for another reason.   As most of you are aware, we are in a bit of a fight these days.   And I have been in them before—but a different kind.

I think there is among this great audience many thousands of people who served with me in the armed services. Those men well know that it was my habit, when battles reached their climax, to try to get down and see what the people who were really doing the work were thinking and wanted to do—what was their state of mind, and how were things going with them.

I am out today to try to get as close to the people of this great city, and two or three others, in the few hours available to me.

How are we doing? I think, of course, we are doing fine.

Now, at such a time as this, there are a thousand things to talk about. There is peace, there is the progress toward a firm and secure peace, there are all phases of our economy, there is every kind of political doctrine and tenet to discuss, if we wanted to cover the whole field.

I am going to talk about something today that I think is of particular and important interest to all of you—that is, some of the dislocations that come about as a nation passes from war to peace, and what your Government can and is doing about them.

This kind of subject is of tremendous importance to a city like Detroit, because here is centered these great industrial facilities that make so much of our war munitions. Consequently, as we pass to peace—to a peace economy, a greater dislocation occurs here than it does in most places.

The goal of your Government, the goal of all Americans, is a strong, stable, growing, expanding economy, an economy that will bring higher standards of living to all of us, greater prosperity and strength at home, so that we can support the kind of military strength that makes us safe abroad.

Now for 20 years we have lived under a false belief that the only time America is really prosperous is when she is at war. The only time in 20 years we have had full employment has been at the height of the war years. And we had gotten to the impression that the two words war and prosperity were connected.

My friends, if there is one accomplishment that I believe your Government has some justifiable right to brag about, it is that in the last 2 years it has succeeded in working with industry in developing a cooperative attitude that has brought us from a war economy to a peace economy with a minimum of dislocation, and at this moment a growing prosperity throughout the land.

Now this outcome does not agree with the predictions of many of the prophets of gloom and doom. Sometimes, it seemed almost like they were anticipating this great and terrifying depression that they predicted with some satisfaction, in order to show that their opponents were not so smart.

Now maybe their opponents are not so smart, but when you take America's heart and America's industry and America's working man and work in cooperation with him, he can win the battle of peace as well as he proves so well in war he can win the battles of war.

So of course we know that good times in Detroit, in a great manufacturing city like this, demand good times throughout the country. You are a part—a very important part—of the whole economy. And that whole economy must prosper, if you are to prosper.

What have we done about this whole economy? The first thing we did, and the first thing that brought down these dire predictions of disaster, was to remove the controls from wages and prices a year ago last spring. And did all the disasters occur that were predicted? Not a bit of it.

American industry, released from these controls, functioned exactly as you would expect it to: more efficiently than ever before.

And then, my friends, we cut taxes—the biggest tax cut in history—$7,400,000,000. And how was that brought about? By saving governmental expenditures. Governmental expenditures have been cut by more than $11 billion, and that has made possible this tax cut, returning money to the people who we think know better how to spend it for themselves than Government does for them.

Within the last 2 years, my friends, social security has been made available to 10 million more Americans that did not have it before. Unemployment insurance is available to 4 million Americans that did not have it before. Great housing programs have been pushed ahead. Today—this month—there's 25 percent more construction going on in the United States than there was this same month last year. This is the greatest construction program in the entire history of the Nation.

There has been an expanded program—a regular program of road construction—which has been expanded and made bigger than ever before.

A farm program has been designed that will bring to an end the 7-year decline in farm income. Now, since January 1951 there has been a 25-

point drop in the parity index of the farmer. Nineteen of those points occurred before January 1, 1953. And we are still, my friends, operating under the laws that have been on the books for a long time. The new program is not yet in effect. But it will be started next year. We will get rid of these surpluses that overhang the market, and the farmers' future will be a brighter one.

My friends, after decades of frustration and effort of all kinds, this Congress and this administration passed the St. Lawrence Seaway Act.

The health of the people has engaged the attention of the Congress and the administration. Great new hospitals are being built to fill the requirements of our big cities and our rural populations alike. In every possible way, research in medicine is being pushed in order that we can bring health not only to the wealthy and the well-to-do, but to every man, woman, and child of this United States.

Now, by every measure—by every index by which we measure the wealth of a nation, this is by far the best peacetime year of our whole history. And I am quite sure that Americans don't want to pay for any pseudo or false prosperity in the blood of their sons and brothers on the battlefields.

Today, my friends, 62 million Americans are working, with good jobs. The workweek is lengthening, the steel output climbing, consumer spending is at an all-time peak. Personal incomes, after taxes, are greater than ever before. Construction is setting record peaks, wage rates the same. Weekly earnings are on the rise again. And the national output exceeds even that great war year of 1944.

Now, let's look for a moment at this always troublesome question: unemployment.

In this month, unemployment is down 400,000. It stands at 2,741,000, as of my last report, and is still going down. The great employers of this city have reported to me that they are calling back men to work every day, and on October 15, in this city alone, 60 thousand more people were working than on September 15.

Now, the number of men and women who want work and are unemployed today is one-third the number that were unemployed in 1940, despite our much greater population. There are not nearly so many as were unemployed in 1950.

And how did those people who were unemployed in 1940 and in 1950 get jobs? Because they either went to war or they went into war plants.

And we are getting employment without that.

Now this does not mean by any means, that I come to you, my fellow Americans, and talk about unemployment in mere terms of statistics. Unemployment is not that.   Unemployment is heartache, it is privation, it is discouragement—and we know it.   I assure you of one thing.   You have got a Government with a heart as well as a head.

As long as there is a single American citizen who honestly wants work, is able to work, and can't find it, there's a problem that your Government will try to help solve.

Now, as I say, this is the finest economic year in our history, and we are on the upgrade by every index that we have.

And I hope you will allow me to mention just a word or two, now, about the subject that I believe is of the greatest importance to all Americans: the growth, the development, the progress toward peace.

My friends, 2 years ago, if you will cast back your minds for a moment, there was war in Korea, in Indochina; daily we feared that we would pick up our papers and read that Iran, with 60 percent of the oil reserves of the world, was under Communist domination.   Trieste was a terrible problem, causing trouble in a sensitive spot.   Suez was another.   In Guatemala, communism was already raising its ugly head.   And in Europe there was discouragement and disillusionment.

All those hot spots have been cooled off.   They are gone.   They are not troubling us.   We don't read about them.

And in Europe, my friends, only a few days ago, there came back to report to you, and to all of us, the greatest Secretary of State of our time, on the developing plans in that area that bring to us promise of increased strength in the free world, that we can reside in our homes with greater confidence that this menace of international communism heading up in the Kremlin is not going to be successful in its efforts against us and our friends all over the world.   Growing confidence everywhere that we can live in peace, a peace that will grow to be a permanent and lasting and just peace—that is what we are talking about.

And now, I have only one or two points I want to mention briefly before I go.   I said things are on the upswing.   The best analyst in this whole motor field, in which you are interested, says that in December we will be up to a peak production of 615,000 motor vehicles.   What a wonderful prediction and outlook on the economic side. We are pushing ahead with a great road program, a road program that will take this Nation out of its antiquated shackles of secondary roads all over this country and give us the types of highways that we need for this great mass of motor vehicles. It will be a nation of great prosperity, but will be more than that: it will be a nation that is going ahead every day. With Americans being born to us—with our population increasing at five every minute, the expanding horizon is one that staggers the imagination.

And as, along with that, our economy advances and keeps up with that kind of rate, we are of course, certainly within 10 years, we are going to see a year when we will have a $500 billion income, meaning $3,000 more to every family now existing in the United States.

That is the kind of future we are looking for—and we are going to have!

And so, as I say goodbye, I want to remind you of this: I have tried to give you a few of the reasons why you should vote. I want to point out the importance of one vote. Three Presidents of the United States have been elected by one electoral vote. One of those had the election thrown into the House of Representatives, and he was elected in the House by one vote. And the Congressman who cast the deciding vote was elected in his District in Indiana by one vote. And that one vote was of a sick man who ordinarily could not have gone to the polls, but he insisted they put him on a litter and take him to the polls where he voted. That, my friends, is some measure of the value of one vote. Five States have been admitted to the Union by one vote in the Congress.

That is why we need every voter to come out and make certain that we have a Congress that continues under the leadership that we have had in the last 2 years, to bring about these great things I have been telling you about so roughly and so briefly.

That means that from this great State of Michigan we want that part of the leadership. After all, you have the Senator who is the head of the Republican Policy Committee in the Senate body. By all means you must send him back and support him with the big delegation that you are capable of sending.

You have nominated great State and national tickets, your Governor, your Senators, your Congressmen, your State officers.

Do the rest of the work, and elect them.

995

Please vote!
Goodbye.

NOTE: The President spoke at 11:45 a.m. His opening words referred to Mayor Albert E. Cobo of Detroit, U.S. Senator Homer Ferguson of Michigan, and to Donald S. Leonard, President of the Detroit City Council and candidate for Governor.

319   ¶ Remarks at Standiford Airport, Louisville, Kentucky.   *October* 29, 1954

Senator Cooper and my friends:

I am on a trip today to remind all my friends in this Nation of a very important duty they have.   It is to vote.   It is to exercise the greatest right that free government can confer upon a citizen.

Now, of course, I would like for you to vote for Senator Cooper and all the rest that are running on the Republican ticket from this State. But above all, it is your duty to vote.   So I feel, also, that if there are enough people who vote, we will be all right, because I am quite certain that the great vast majority that voted in 1952 still feels the same way. Now if that vast majority votes again, then we will have Senator Cooper and those like him back in the Senate, and will have a Republican-led Congress in both Houses.

Now in 1952 this vast majority was made up of Republicans, and of independent-minded citizens of all kinds.   Some were called Citizens for Eisenhower, Independents for Ike and Dick, Democrats for Eisenhower, and so forth.   In any event, they believed and were conducting a crusade.   And I have thought often of the simplicity of the crusade, the simplicity of the cause that was at the bottom of that crusade. Actually, as I see it, we were trying to substitute one three-letter word for one two-letter word in United States thinking.

For 20 years we had come to think of peace *or* prosperity.   And these crusaders said we could have and would have peace *and* prosperity.

Now of course, this was only a change of a small word, but in meaning and significance a change of the most profound importance.   All those years from 1933 to 1940 we continued to have very large unemployment; even when we began the preparation for war in 1940, unemployment was still, in that year, at an average of 8,100,000.

And then again in 1950, even though in that year we began again the great preparations for the Korean war, unemployment never fell to the 3 million mark. At the peak in that year, in February, it was 4,900,000.

Now these people in 1940 who had been without work for a long time, how did they get jobs? They went into the armed services or they went into war plants. And this happened again in 1950.

Is it any wonder, then, that the United States came to believe that we could have peace or we could have full employment or prosperity?

Now the crusaders said you can have both. For 2 years those crusaders—your representatives in the Congress, in the executive branch, and with your support—have been busy proving that formula ever since. And the record is a great one. It has been brought about through cooperation instead of division within our great economy—within our Nation. Government has tried to work with people, rather than to try to dominate them—rather than to boss them. There has been a new spirit of working together, of teamwork throughout—from the remotest hamlet in the middle of the country right on down to Washington, between the farm and the city, between Government and citizen.

In this matter of unemployment, we have seen a steady decline from the peak of last winter. Only this month there was another 400 thousand reduction. We are down to approximately 2,700,000 at this moment. Unemployment is still going down, and employment is still going up. There are 62 million Americans working—working at profitable wages. The weekly wage is still going up. The amount of money left the American people for expenditures after taxes is at its all-time high. Construction is breaking records every single month. Construction this month is 25 percent higher than last year, which was supposed to be the peak of all time.

Ladies and gentlemen, by every measure that we can determine the increase in the wealth and productivity of a nation, we are prosperous, we are going up; and this in spite of the fact that in certain areas there still is unemployment. And that unemployment engages the attention of your Government, and its cooperating municipalities and States and industry, every second of the day. As long as there is a single American citizen that wants a job, is capable of working, and can't find it, the Government will never let up on this.

We have prosperity—by far the most prosperous peacetime year in our whole history.

But now we said also, remember, peace and prosperity. Now by peace, if we are honest with ourselves, we don't mean merely an absence of shooting. We thank the Almighty every day of our lives that no longer do we read the casualty lists from those barren mountains of Korea, and we are glad, of course, that the shooting and the killing has stopped in southeast Asia. But we are talking about progress toward a peace of confidence and security, one in which we can believe, when we can begin to turn the full productivity of this great and prosperous economy to the advancement of human happiness.

We don't mean that we have really reached peace when we have to devote—and all the world is still devoting—so much of its sweat and toil and productivity to making the engines of war, in order that we can remain secure.

Now what have we done in the last 21 months? You remember where we were in January 1953? We were still losing American boys in Korea, and the fighting was going on in Indochina. Beyond that, day by day we expected to pick up our papers and read that Iran with its great resources, 60 percent of the world's known reserves of petroleum, had fallen into Communist hands. And Suez: we expected to pick up the paper and read that it was going to flame into open disaster; Trieste, bothering our friends and the Italians and all Western Europe—those age-old irritations between Italy and Yugoslavia. And even in Guatemala, in our own hemisphere, the ugly head of communism—international communism—was menacing us.

Now, through patient work, through persistent work, through friendly partnership, all of these sore spots have either disappeared or have been so greatly accommodated that they are no longer the dangers that they once were. So that there has been developing a constantly better atmosphere in which the statesmen and diplomats of the world could work for peace.

Now, far more important, even, than these specific incidents of which I have spoken, is the better situation in Western Europe. Frequently we ask ourselves, well what about Western Europe, why do we worry?

My friends, we know what the menace in the world today is: it is international communism under the direction of the men in the Kremlin, who have announced their intent by aggression, by violence, by any way that is appropriate to them, or feasible or expedient, to destroy free government, to destroy your freedoms and mine, and those of every other citizen of the free world.

Now they have a vast empire. Right now they control at least 800 million souls, parts of it very productive. But think of Western Europe: 250 million more people, with a skilled labor element almost twice as strong as our own. Suppose all those people with their vast productivity fell under the domination of the Communists? The threat to the rest of the free world, specifically to the United States of America, would be so grave and so great that what we are spending now for national defense would be a drop in the bucket.

So, ladies and gentlemen, Western Europe is not something that we can say is across the Atlantic. It is right here in Louisville, Kentucky, in its significance to our safety.

Now 2 years ago, we had been working for a long, long time to bring about some unity and strength in that region. It looked rather dismal. Prospects didn't look too good. They weren't good. But again, patient work, refusal to be defeated on the part of all the Western allies, with Great Britain and our own country acting as friendly partners throughout, finally the greatest Secretary of State of our time could come home and report to you people that a new spirit had been developing, a new pact was on the way for signature, which would guarantee the security of that nation, and therefore work to the great benefit of the United States and all the free world.

Now ladies and gentlemen, most sketchily but certainly I think most accurately, that is a rough outline of how far we have come on these twin-roads of prosperity and peace in 21 months. That has been brought about by the cooperation of many people. And particularly in this area of foreign relations, let me make myself crystal clear: no one believes in bipartisan direction of foreign affairs more than I do. In the basic elements of our foreign policy, we must be America—we must not be parties. The world must know that when America speaks, it means to speak for this year and until some great change in circumstances forces America—not some political party—to change its mind.

But even in this field, my friends, leadership is necessary. The day by day operation of foreign affairs, the headaches and other incidents that come up that must be taken care of, demand a team of leaders.

Now in this whole economic development, this leading toward prosperity, this leading toward peace, you have had a team, a team of legislative leaders in the Senate and in the House, operating with their confreres and with their associates in the executive department.

What this election is all about, the one in which I am asking every one of you to vote, is to determine whether we are to have a continuation of the kind of progress I have so roughly sketched out for you.

I tell you, my friends, the traffic of Government must not encounter red lights at every crossroads in Washington. We must all want it to flow ahead on proper lines in the same direction. And certainly, above all means, though two parties can work together, we must not conclude that both can at the same time be captains of the Ship of State. It just simply can't be. Somebody must, and one Party must, be responsible, so that you—you—the United States of America—you voters—can hold somebody responsible.

We must not by split Government, give to each Party a chance to alibi against the other, to give to us excuses for failure.

Now, make no mistake, my friends. This decision is yours. Whatever your decision is is going to be loyally accepted by the people that are serving you in Washington. And I assure you, whatever your decision, no less devoted and dedicated will be my own efforts, or the executive branch's effort, to bring about this great prosperity and more and better peace.

But I say also: that as long as you have—as you must have—an executive branch in control of one Party for the next 2 years, progress toward peace will be more rapid, more assured and toward prosperity will be more certain, if we do not break up the team at this point.

And so I repeat, if we want the crusade that started 2 years ago to be guided through to fruition, let us all vote.

Thank you very much for the cordiality of your welcome.

Goodbye—God bless you.

NOTE: The President spoke at 1:50 p.m.

320 ¶ Remarks at New Castle County Airport, Wilmington, Delaware. *October* 29, 1954

Senator Williams, Congressman Warburton, Mrs. Martin—my fellow Americans:

This has been a busy day for me, one that was fitted into a schedule we already thought was fairly tight. But there had been rumors that came into Washington that people who joined in the crusade of 1952 felt so sure that their program was going ahead, that they forgot that it was time to bring up some reinforcements, that apathy was creeping over the strength of our old crusaders, and it was time to do something about it.

Moreover, there was another reason for going out. There are in this crowd, I know, a lot of people who served with me in the armed services. Some of them were undoubtedly with me in the European theater. Every time a climax of the fighting or campaign approached, I found it a very useful thing to go out and see how the men were feeling, the people that had to do the slugging, the people that had to be on the firing line.

Now the textbooks used to say that the reason the commander did this was to go out to inspire the troops to fight better. It has always worked differently with me. Every time I came back from those visits, I was inspired to do my own job better.

I have found that out today, my friends. By going out, far from finding the apathy they talked about, far from finding any need on my part to tell people, let's roll up our sleeves and get to work, I feel like I haven't been working hard enough. I have encountered enthusiasm, a belief, a confidence, that I wish you could feel. As a matter of fact, I think you do feel it, because you show it here.

The only regret I have about today's trip into Cleveland, up to Detroit, down to Louisville, is that there is only so much time in a day, and I could go no further. I would have loved to have visited every single State that I could have reached in 3 or 4 days, to go and tell everybody what I have been seeing—that they are on the march, the crusade is still going.

Now I want to tell you one thing about votes. It is this: I think we are frequently apt to underestimate the importance of one vote. It means a lot of things. First, what does it mean to you—you. With your own conscience you have done your duty as an American citizen. You have registered your decision. Whatever it may be, you have done it.

But in a more practical sense, do you realize that three Presidents have been elected by one electoral vote, or in one case where it was referred to a commission, by one vote in that commission? And my friends, even more dramatic than that, in the case where it was done by commission, the one decisive vote was cast by a man who in his District had been elected by a majority of one. One vote made a President of the United States. Five states have been admitted to the United States by one vote in the Congress.

Now this is very important to me because one of the States was that of my birth, and if it hadn't been elected, I wouldn't have been a citizen.

But I want to get over what your one vote can mean, both in terms of your own satisfaction, and in terms of what it can mean in a practical sense, and one other. What does it mean to those around you who watch you and believe in you, have some confidence in you? Joe voted—I'll vote. It is what your example does. Moreover, if I could give you one suggestion, after this meeting—you know, if everybody here in this audience would go home this evening and start calling up, and each would call up 10 voters and ask them to call up 10 voters, and so on, you would cover the State of Delaware with every man, woman, and child in about 2 hours. Think how fast that would multiply. You would reach millions in that time. That is what we want, all the votes out.

Now why do Republicans want all the votes out? Because this crusade was put on the road by a vast majority of the American people. That vast majority of the American people still believes the same way.

If everybody votes, we are in!

Now let's go back to 1952 for just a few minutes. You remember we wanted to clean out the scandals. We wanted clean government. We wanted dignity in high places, and there were a number of other things we wanted. But our real slogan was a very simple and short one. It was *peace and prosperity*.

Now let me speak about that just a second. The important word in that phrase is the simple little conjunction *and*. Peace *and* prosperity.

For 20 years we were gradually absorbing the idea in this country that you could have peace *or* prosperity. Our crusade was really nothing but substituting and for or in that phrase.

Now to look at it—in 1940 there were still, after years of talk, and a lot of other things, there were more than 8 million unemployed. In 1950, in February, at the peak of unemployment of that year, there were 4,900,000 still unemployed. The average for the year, even though we went to war, you will recall, of July 1950, was 3 million, one.

Now, my friends, is it any wonder that we had come to believe we couldn't have full employment in this country unless we got it by going into the armed services or into war plants? If you wanted prosperity, the belief was growing you had to have a battlefield.

We rejected that in 1952, and said you can have peace *and* prosperity.

Now, in both these things, I am just going to run over the record, just very briefly, to show you that there has been real progress in peace *and* in prosperity in 21 months.

First, let's take the prosperity angle. Unemployment following upon the end of the war, rose to a peak, last February and March. Ever since, it has been steadily declining. Only this last month—the month we are now in—it has gone down 400,000 more. It reached on my last reports about 5 days ago, 2,741,000. And it is still going down.

I do not mean to say that as long as there is any unemployment in any spot brought about by the aftermath of war and inflation, that we are going to be satisfied. Far from it. Unemployment is not just statistics. Unemployment is heartaches, it is privation, it is discouragement, it is suffering.

And this Government that you have has a heart, as well as a head, and as long as there is any unemployment, this is going to be a major problem of attack for them.

There are worlds of useful work that this Nation has to do. We have great highway programs to build. We still have hospitals to build, and all of the other things in which Federal and State and county and private enterprise can cooperate. And we need have no unemployment even at this level, and we are not going to have.

Now let's take other things. Money available to all of us, after taxes, is at an alltime peak for spending. By every measure of production—the construction industry this year, this month, is 25 percent higher than it was this month last year, which was the peak year of all time; the workweek is lengthening in hours, wages are at their alltime high.   By every index that we have, it is the most prosperous peacetime year of our history. And I was assured by the President of the Retailers Association that he believed this year would exceed in sales even last year.   We are prosperous, and getting more prosperous.

This economy is expanding at such a rate, my friends, under wise policies of money management, instilling cooperation in our people instead of domination, that within—certainly within 10 years, we are going to have a $500 billion national product every single year.   That will mean an increase of $3,000 per family—of the families in the United States today.

We are going up and up.   We are not stopping here.   And we are going to need all these people that haven't got jobs this minute.

Now along with this, while this has been going on, how about peace? Well now, in January 1953 the casualty lists were still coming in from Korea, in that war that was seemingly endless and had certainly become futile and useless.   There was a war in Indochina.   There was a terrible situation existing in Iran, every day we expected the news that that country, with 60 percent of the oil reserves of the world, had fallen to the Communists.   In Trieste, there was a trouble spot that threatened to explode.   In Suez was another.   In Guatemala, international communism was already trying to establish a beachhead.

What has happened to all these spots?   Patient work, hard work, intelligent cooperation on a friendly basis with all our partners, has eliminated them.   They are no longer threatening our peace.   The atmosphere is improved.   And along with this, 2 years ago, the situation in Europe was still uneasy and tense.   Age-old hatreds and prejudices were threatening to break up every attempt at establishing a coalition that could keep that country secure.   It was a very bad situation.   Because, my friends, Europe—Western Europe—is not just a country that happens to lie straight across the Atlantic from here, and is of no importance to us except as a place to visit.   Did you ever stop to think what would be our situation if the Communists of today, with their great ruthless power, already controlling more than 800 million people, could get Western Europe with its great productive power, more than 22 million skilled workers in great vast industrial plants, all put up in the pattern of the American industrial plan?   What would happen, with their great productivity, their nearness to us, their immediate threat to our friends in Britain, and in the African area? We would be under deadly peril, and our expenditures for security would be so great as to dwarf those we are making today.

And that, my friends, is all changed.

Only a few nights ago, the greatest Secretary of State of our time came back and made his report to you, that this danger has been averted. Western Europe is growing together, is getting into a position where they can support their own troops and can make certain that their security is such that we will not have this threat to face.

And in terms of the prospects for peace, this means just this: with these developments around the world, with the new coalition developing in southeast Asia, with Japan leaning our way, with Iran oriented toward us, with this agreement in Western Europe, there is a growing strength that is born of unity—unity in basic spirit and conviction and determination that the Communists dare not attack.

Which means we can pursue peace in confidence, standing up straight and not being afraid, not cringing, standing up and saying, here is what is right and here is what must prevail in this world, and doing it from a position of security.

Ladies and gentlemen, in this postwar world, the prestige and position of the United States in the world today is at its record peak.

I have just one thought to add. In this business of foreign affairs, foreign relations, foreign operations, there must be bipartisanship. Let us not mistake ourselves. No one party has a monopoly on patriotism and dedication to this country. And if we do not have bipartisanship in the main basic threads of our national policy, then with one from year to year, from administration to administration, we would be weakened because of lack of stability of policy in the world.

But I must point this out, that although this administration has pursued this truth, and acted in this truth more firmly than any of its predecessors, has had more meetings in determining what these basic foundations of our policy should be, yet when it comes to the day by day operation, leadership is still necessary.

There is a team, a team made up of congressional leaders and executive leaders that has been responsible for the operation, the carrying out, the execution, of these policies. And so the question is: since this same team has to deal with our policies at home and abroad, do we now, with this great progress achieved, and so much more still to be done, do we want to break it up, do we want to split this team and make part of it one thing and part of it another?

That is what this election is about. Do you want to keep this team together that has brought and is bringing peace *and* prosperity?

So my friends, let me emphasize: when I ask you to vote, I am not asking you to vote merely so that one party can have the great honor and distinction—responsibility—of representing you in Washington. I am placing these issues before you to show you that your vote means the progress in the peace and prosperity—the continuation of the progress they have so far achieved.

And that is the reason that you must have a Senator Warburton to help Senator Williams—and in the other House, Mrs. Martin to represent you. The executive department must remain Republican during this coming 2 years—by constitution.

When I say Republican, we do not mean that we hope to represent only Republicans, or occupy and fulfill those jobs in any narrow way. We know that it is Republicans, and open-minded independents—and understanding Democrats—that have sent this team of legislative and executive leaders to Washington.

Now you send them back, and this work will go forward. That I promise you.

Good night. God bless you.

NOTE: The President spoke at 6:05 p.m. Mrs. Lillian I. Martin to whom he referred in his opening remarks, was Republican candidate for U.S. Representative at Large from Delaware.

321 ¶ Radio and Television Remarks on Election Eve. *November 1, 1954*

GOOD EVENING. And now we come again to the end of a political campaign. The candidates have presented their arguments. The shouting dies away. And now it is up to you, the American citizens. Tomorrow you sit as judges on all this, and make your decisions. The farmers, the lawyers, the teachers, the preachers, the taxicab drivers, the miners—

all of us—all of us march to the polls tomorrow, where every single American is the equal of every other American, and there register those decisions that will affect our national life and our personal lives for the next 2 years—and even on far beyond that.

Now the decision is not an easy one. Issues are often intricate, not easily understood, and of course they are normally presented from a partisan standpoint. And so each citizen has to decide for himself just where the truth does lie.

The fact that these decisions are difficult was brought emphatically to my attention the other day. You know that most of the prayerbooks in our churches have special prayers for the welfare, the prosperity, the safety, the peace, of the United States of America. I ran onto one that addressed itself particularly to election day. It sought divine guidance for each citizen in making the decisions that you have to make. And we, knowing how difficult those decisions are, can understand the reasonableness of such a prayer.

Now the first point I should like to make with you is this: you inescapably must participate in this decision. You may do this in two ways. You may do it in a positive way. By that I mean you may vote for the program in which you believe, and for the personalities that you believe will carry out that program. In this way you do your best to see that those things in which you believe for America come into effect as a policy and a governmental program, in the State, in the municipality, or in the Federal Government.

Now, you may not vote. Suppose you don't. Then the effect of that is that you double the value of the vote of anyone who does not believe in the things that you believe in. By staying away from the polls, you have, then, participated in the decision; and this means there is no such thing as sitting out an election. There is no such thing as escaping responsibility for your own decisions in this matter, and you cannot escape the consequences of that decision. Either negatively or positively, you are voting for what you believe in.

Well, some may say, "But of course, there is no one that I believe in implicitly." Maybe so. There is nothing perfect in humanity. And all humans make mistakes and certainly all political parties do. But you can make your decision as to what you believe to be more in line, what program, to be more in line with your own thinking; and certainly you can make up your mind as to whether you will get the greatest prudence, the greatest honesty, the greatest integrity, the greatest businesslike methods and economy in Government.

So for now, and for the future, you are tomorrow participating either positively or negatively in this great decision.   Now this is very important to you—to all of us—for this reason.   From the time we are born and the date of our birth is registered in the governmental registry office, until we are interested in old-age pensions, somewhere along the line we are forever touching Government, or Government is touching our lives.   Now just think of such things as schools and hospitals and roads—all provided by the Government in some form or other.   The regulation of our utilities— the levying of our taxes—and the value of our money—keeping our money solid, so that people of modest income—like most of us—can be sure that our pensions are going to be worth what we put into them, that our savings accounts are not going to be ruined, our insurance policies will be worth just as much when we finally draw them as when we pay the premiums.

So, such other things as social security, and the economic programs that affect the farmer—labor-management—all are intended to prevent depression and the loss of employment.   Our unemployment insurance. Measures against subversion.   Civil rights programs.   And the national security—and all the money we must pour into these military establishments, and economy and efficiency in doing so.   Think what all these things mean to you.   And then, of course, always, matters of foreign policy and our quest for peace.

Now, my friends, if you don't vote for what you believe in, then it is easily possible that minorities—either minorities or pressure groups—can take over and establish the policies for our Government for the next 2 years, and indeed possibly on long beyond that, for you and for your children.   But if all America votes, then America will get the kind of Government in Washington, and in your State, that America wants.

Now 2 years ago there were 61½ million people went to the polls. That was a Presidential year, and so it is possible we won't have that many tomorrow.   But here is a very important point we must all remember: no matter how few people might go to the polls, the rest of us are compelled to observe and honor their decision for the next 2 years.   If we did not honor that decision, no matter how few turned out to make it, we would be disloyal to our country, to the ideals for which she stands.   We are not going to do that.

So, my friends, you owe it to yourself, you owe it to your country, you owe it to your children, to turn out and vote tomorrow.   Now, in that way you not only do your duty, you also do this: you exercise the greatest right and privilege of the American citizen.

And let me give you one more little suggestion: the other day, in answer to letters from some friends of mine, I called them up and said, "Why don't you call up 10 of your friends and ask them to call their friends to vote.   Not how to vote.   Just vote."   Now, why don't you check up tomorrow and call up 10 of your friends and say "Just vote."   If you do that, that will be a voluntary act on your part, just over and beyond your own duty of voting.

And now, for both Mamie and me, good night.

NOTE: The President spoke at 9:20 p.m. at a studio of the Columbia Broadcasting System in Washington.

322   ¶ The President's News Conference of *November* 3, 1954.

THE PRESIDENT. Good morning.   I hope you have had some sleep. [*Laughter*]

There are, of course, a lot of things we could talk about, about this election, if we wanted to devote a half hour to that subject.   I will frankly admit in a lot of cases I am absolutely astonished and surprised; I have even heard a few of you people say that you were a bit that way. So I suggest with that one we just wait and see what happens.

There is a very important development in one field, and I wrote out a statement to read to you.   It is about the progress on this use of atomic energy for peaceful purposes in establishing an international agency. I will read it so I don't make any error even in wording.

[*Reading*] Today the Secretary of State, Mr. Dulles, is delivering to Mr. Zaroubin, the Soviet Ambassador, our reply to the Soviet aide memoire of September 22d.

You will recall that this Soviet message indicated that they apparently wanted to renew the negotiations to implement the proposal that I made to the United Nations last December for an international pool of fissionable material and information.   Now, I hope that this will start a new phase in the U.S.-U.S.S.R. negotiations which will be more fruitful than the first phase, during which the Soviet showed a lack of interest in cooperating with the United States to further international cooperation in developing peaceful uses.

Later on this week, Ambassador Lodge is going to give a report on American preliminary plans in connection with the international agency and the political committee of the United Nations.

This project, of course, is very close to my heart. I am glad to see that we are making good progress toward establishing the agency. We are determined to get on with this international project whether or not the Soviets participate; although, of course, we are very anxious for their participation.

I am glad to be able to tell you that Morehead Patterson of New York has agreed to serve under Mr. Dulles—to head up the United States group, act as our representative—to conduct the diplomatic negotiations looking toward United States participation in the International Atomic Energy Agency.

I am going to see Mr. Patterson tomorrow to tell him about the importance I attach to this project. [*Ends reading*]

I thought you would be interested in that statement. Now, we will go to questions.

Q. Marvin L. Arrowsmith, Associated Press: Mr. President, do you see any disapproval of administration policies in the Republican loss of the House?

THE PRESIDENT. No, I don't. As a matter of fact, Mr. Arrowsmith, I haven't attempted to make any analysis of my own about this development as yet. I shall, of course, when I get the complete returns and statistics on the districts to see what was made the principal issue in each district, but I haven't done so yet.

Q. Joseph A. Loftus, New York Times: Mr. President, the one branch of the Congress will be Democratic. Can you tell us what your plans are with respect to meeting the legislative leaders regularly? Would you meet with the Democratic leaders alone or with the Republicans?

THE PRESIDENT. Well, I have no specific plans. As you know, other Presidents have had this same job. I suppose that one of the things that one would do would be to look up historical precedents on how these things have been handled in the past. I just assure you of this: I have certain beliefs, you people know what they are. I believe in certain programs which, I think, represent progress for America. I am going to continue to work for them; and if there are any roadblocks thrown in the way of cooperation, I am not going to be responsible. I am going to do my very best right down the line to keep the business of the Government moving as well as we possibly can.

Q. Robert J. Donovan, New York Herald Tribune: Sir, in whatever thinking you may have about 1956, does the result today affect it at all?

THE PRESIDENT. Well, certainly it hasn't so far. [*Laughter*] No, I wouldn't say that any results of today would. I suppose you are referring to my own personal plans and ideas?

Q. Mr. Donovan: Yes, sir.

THE PRESIDENT. As I have told you before, I don't try to predict too far in advance, even with respect to myself. I am trying to do a job, and I think we will have plenty of time to see what I will do.

Q. Frank van der Linden, Nashville Banner: Mr. President, during your campaign recently you said that you found it difficult to work with some of the Democratic committee chairmen in the House. You mentioned Ways and Means as one. Do you think you will have any trouble working with Mr. Jere Cooper on the Ways and Means Committee?

THE PRESIDENT. A lot of these people are my personal friends. I have been around Washington, as some of you may know, in and out, for a good many years—far too many.

Now, I quoted this: the number of times that on specific divisions, where the leaders of the two parties in the Congress divided, how often these particular chairmen voted with the administration program; I said that represented a difference in philosophy.

I have always cheerfully admitted their right to have this different philosophy. I was talking about smoothness in cooperation.

Q. Sarah McClendon, El Paso Times: Mr. President, you had such good personal relations with the individual members of the House last year, and especially they all seemed to enjoy your luncheons, I wonder if you feel—I mean they enjoyed the personal visits. [*Laughter*] I don't mean they just enjoyed the food; it was good, too. [*Laughter*] But, sir, do you feel that your campaigning for the party, as you did, will have any effect on your personal relations with these people?

THE PRESIDENT. Well, ladies and gentlemen, I don't see why it should.

I have never in my life spoken badly of another individual in public, that I know of.   I have never attacked any man's motives; I have talked about policy, about beliefs, about convictions or about the practices of an administration.   I have never assaulted any man's good name, and I don't see any reason why these people shouldn't be my friends, that have been my personal friends in the past.

Q. Merriman Smith, United Press: While you haven't attacked people by name, sir, during the course of the campaign, I believe you forecast a degree of political chaos in case the Democrats won control of the Congress.   Do you still feel that way, sir?

THE PRESIDENT. Well, no.   As a matter of fact, "chaos" is possibly a bit strong, I should think, Mr. Smith.

What I have said, I don't see how we can expect people of differing political faiths, with different party loyalties, to produce the same degree of cooperation as if those leaders belonged to the same party.

I am talking about the business of the Government and getting it done; and I repeat, there is going to be no initiative on my side that can possibly lead toward lack of cooperation.

Q. Robert J. Donovan, New York Herald Tribune: Sir, when you said at the outset that you were astonished and surprised, did you mean at the total picture or in individual cases?

THE PRESIDENT. As a matter of fact, I was thinking really of a number of individual cases.   Of course, I was pleased with all the reports I have seen as to the size of the vote.   I asked the last minute for an estimate of the number of people who voted, I didn't get it.   We haven't it, maybe you people have.   I was quite astonished with that, and very pleased about that one.

Q. John Herling, Editors Syndicate: Mr. President, I don't want to belabor a phase of this subject you have already discussed, but, sir, you did use the word, the expression, during the campaign of a "cold war" between the legislative branch and the executive branch in case of the Democratic leadership.   Do you anticipate any overt or covert action of that sort, or do you feel that——

THE PRESIDENT. As I recall, I used the expression that a cold war of partisan politics could develop; and I have no doubt my expression was too strong for what I had in mind.   I merely meant that there were new forces and influences thrown into the relationship, that tended toward pulling apart rather than pulling together.   If I used too strong a term, why, I would regret it, because I don't mean that we apply the "cold war" as between forces in the world—which is a great deal more antagonism than there is between me and some of my friends in the other party.

Q. Alan S. Emory, Watertown Times: Sir, have you any comment on the close New York gubernatorial election where Mr. Harriman narrowly defeated Senator Ives?

THE PRESIDENT. No, I don't want to comment on particular races. I don't know anything about the local influences that affected these races.

I find that some people get up in front of the television and say, "This has national influence," and another one says, "This was wholly local."

I know nothing about it, and I would rather not comment on particular races.

Q. Joseph A. Loftus, New York Times: Mr. President, I am not sure that I followed the reading of that paper closely, but I am wondering if there is any information or intimation you could give use of what is in your reply to the Soviet or when we might expect to get something, or does it modify the United States position?

THE PRESIDENT. As a matter of fact, I didn't check the point with the Secretary of State. But obviously, I wouldn't give anything out until the Soviets have had it and studied it. So I think it will have to be confidential for a moment.

Q. Mrs. May Craig, Maine Papers: Mr. President, are you considering calling back the present House for action on legislation before the new Congress comes in, in January?

THE PRESIDENT. I hadn't thought of it; I hadn't even considered it, no.

Q. Edward T. Folliard, Washington Post and Times Herald: Mr. President, to go back to Mr. Arrowsmith's question, Chairman Hall was talking last night about the closeness of this election. It is very close, probably one of the closest in our history. He pointed out that the party in power usually loses seats in an off-year election, and pointed out further that the average loss is about 40 seats; and in this election the Republican loss is nowheres near that. Hall said that this proves to him that there has been no breakaway from the Eisenhower administration. Could you go along with that without looking into these causes in the various districts?

THE PRESIDENT. As a matter of fact, without trying to interpret the election, after all, I have been in a very great number of States. In some of those States I have talked to people who are rather astute. I firmly believe, without any apology whatsoever, that the great mass of the people believe in the, you might say, the moderate attack on this great problem of governmental relationships to our economy and to our people. I believe that they feel that they want to avoid extremes. That is what I stand for, and try to implement that thought by putting it into definite legislative programs. I honestly believe the people approve of that.

I have talked to people. Some of you that were in Denver know I had groups of workmen together; I talked to them, I talked to businessmen, I talked to political leaders and publishers, and I find a very great sentiment that way. I think that the United States really—I believe that is its general political conviction these days; that is what I think.

Q. Mr. Folliard: Yes, sir. You are saying that——

THE PRESIDENT. I am just saying that I hesitate to interpret elections. You people know how little experience I have had with elections. This was really my second one that I know anything about, and so I don't want to interpret figures where I would be talking a little bit beyond my field. But I do believe that I can sense the feeling of people pretty well; that I have been trying to do for a good many weeks now.

Q. Mr. Folliard: Is this a correct interpretation of that, Mr. President—that there has been no repudiation of the administration program?

THE PRESIDENT. So far as I can see, no.

Q. Mr. Folliard: Pretty general agreement with it?

THE PRESIDENT. That is what I think.

However, in an election as close as this one, as you point out, traditionally one where the party in control usually loses seats, every kind of local crosscurrent comes into it.

Last night, when I went to bed, one of our Senators was so far behind, I believe they were talking of conceding; the other side was claiming. This morning I find our man is a few hundred ahead. When we left Colorado, you remember the odds that were quoted against Republicans. Well, one of them looks like he has done pretty well.

All of these things are sort of local things which I think don't have much to do with the national sentiment.

Q. Robert W. Richards, Copley Press: Mr. President, about the forepart of October the experts were predicting a Democratic landslide. Do you think that if you had moved into the picture earlier in the campaign—

they said the Republican campaign moved up when you entered into it about 2 weeks ago—do you think you might have turned it?

THE PRESIDENT. Actually, I don't know just what the influence of a particular individual dropping into a particular place, I don't know what that influence is; and I must say that there are always plusses to be weighed against minuses, and you finally decide such-and-such is a good thing. But we were particularly anxious to have a big vote, and it was thought I could help that way.

Now, I didn't enter this campaign just 2 weeks ago. I think it was the day after I got to Denver this year, I went on the television to tell what the record of the Republican-led 83d Congress was. As far as I am concerned, that was trying to show the people the things that I believed ought to be the issues of this campaign, do they approve of that program or do they not.

If you mean if I had stayed with that kind of thing would it have made any difference—I mean all summer long—I don't know and I am not going to guess, either.

Q. Harry C. Dent, Columbia (S.C.) State and Record: Mr. President, I notice the Republican Party seemed to do pretty well in the South. In fact, in the House election they seemed to do better in the South than they did anywhere else. [*Laughter*] And I just wondered if you don't think there is a good possibility now, in an off-year election gaining a seat in Florida and holding one in North Carolina and some in Virginia, that maybe a two-party system can be——

THE PRESIDENT. Don't forget Texas.

Q. Mr. Dent: Yes, sir—a two-party system might be entrenched a little deeper than it is down there, sir? Do you think there is much possibility of it?

THE PRESIDENT. Well, of course, we are always hopeful that the South will develop a two-party system; because I feel that until they do, the South is not exercising the influence in the affairs of this Nation that it should. It can be too often ignored. So I would be hopeful at least that these are signs of some break in that solid wall, and that the South is really going to adopt a two-party system so they can really exercise the kind of influence they should.

Q. Raymond P. Brandt, St. Louis Post-Dispatch: Mr. President, I think one of the figures of speech you used in one of your addresses was that you couldn't have an automobile trying to drive in opposite directions. Would it not be possible to plan with the Democratic leaders on the course you are going to have?

THE PRESIDENT. Well, I am certainly going to try, no question about that.

Q. Merriman Smith, United Press: Are you going to try to plan with the Democrats, sir?

THE PRESIDENT. Of course I am.

Q. Robert W. Richards, Copley Press: Were you speaking of it from the past record of divided Government?

THE PRESIDENT. Of what?

Q. Mr. Richards: Of the past record of divided Government. President Truman had one, President Taft and President Hoover.

THE PRESIDENT. Mr. Wilson had one. The history of them is, I think, summed up about as well in Mr. Hoover's book as almost any place I have seen them. The history is that such experiences are filled with frustrations and difficulties.

But I say this: the harder the problem, the harder you have to try to solve it, because the business of the Government just won't wait.

Now, the quest for peace in this world is too important to let any particular political situation here stand in our way. There is the one field, hopefully, and I really believe, the one field where we ought to have the greatest possible chance to get ahead, because all through these last 2 years there have been frequent, incessant consultations with the leaders of the other party in order to establish the basic directions and channels of our foreign policy.

But the business all the way through is too important just to say, "Oh, this is difficult," and, therefore, hide behind an alibi. I say to you I am not going to do that, and I am sure the others won't.

Q. Clark R. Mollenhoff, Des Moines Register and Tribune: Mr. President, I wondered if you thought the vote in the Midwest gave any indication of a support or a repudiation of your farm program?

THE PRESIDENT. Well, I would say again that you would have to wait for the actual returns by districts. I had two or three reports from Indiana where the districts were, let's say, one-third industrial, two-thirds farm, and they have looked very, very fine; and then I saw one which seemed to be the other way. I think you would have to wait and make a real analysis; I couldn't guess.

Q. Merriman Smith, United Press: Mr. President, could you give us any indication of the mechanics whereby you will consult with the Democrats in the development of a program?

THE PRESIDENT. No. I think that after I have made up my mind on that point completely, I will invite them to do so-and-so. After all, they are of another party, and they may have ideas differing from mine, but I will invite them to do certain things, and to meet me on certain basis.

Now, I don't know just how often that will be or how that will be. Naturally, I am going to continue to meet with the legislative leaders of my own party, I am sure you understand that. Just how it will work out I can't say.

Q. Laurence H. Burd, Chicago Tribune: Mr. President, you spoke of planning with Democratic leaders—I didn't get all of that; is that what you said?

THE PRESIDENT. I don't remember what word I used; I meant conferring.

Q. Mr. Burd: What I meant to inquire on that basis was, would you consult with them in advance on domestic policy decisions?

THE PRESIDENT. Well, if they control the House, they certainly control the order in which bills can come up.

It would seem to me to be the part of wisdom when you are dealing with humans to meet with them and see what you can get done; just to butt your head up against a stone wall is no good. So I think there has to be conferring probably on every important measure—"Are you ready to take this up," "Will you take it up if I send it down"; there are all sorts of things that strike me will be the subjects of conferences, necessary conferences.

Now, I can't at this moment establish the limits as to how far you go and how far you don't go.

Q. Mrs. May Craig, Maine Papers: Mr. President, might I ask a second question, please? I am interested in your approval of the two-party system in the South. Would you also approve the two-party system in the reverse, for instance, in Maine? [*Laughter*]

THE PRESIDENT. Well, you know, strangely enough, I do. [*Laughter*] I do. I believe in the two-party system.

There is an old saying in the military services, "That which is not inspected deteriorates." I believe that in the political life, you have got to have two groups, one watching the other all the time. I just think that is a matter of philosophy, and I believe that almost everybody that I know of in this political life would agree to some such aphorism or statement.

Q. John Herling, Editors Syndicate: Mr. President, another question. Do you expect the first 2 years of your administration to be inspected by the new leadership of the Congress?

THE PRESIDENT. By the what?

Q. Mr. Herling: By the new leadership of the Congress, such as the——

THE PRESIDENT. As a matter of fact, I have tried to conduct the business of the executive department—and I think all of its principal officials will so tell you—so that to the greatest possible extent they not only can be laid out for the inspection of anybody in the Government, but the entire public. I find at times my policy runs into a roadblock here and there, and has to be straightened out; but that, nevertheless, is the policy we try to effect.

Q. George E. Herman, CBS Radio: Mr. Herman, George [*laughter*]—I got in reverse there—sir, you were widely quoted on the famous remark of having said that "sometimes a man gets tired of all this political clackety-clack." Now that it is out of the way, I wonder if you will tell us about your personal plans, of what next you will tackle in the major fields before you——

THE PRESIDENT. In the program?

Q. Mr. Herman: ——either in the program or your personal plans or problems or what you will bring up next.

THE PRESIDENT. Well, I'll tell you. I find this: the whole problem of foreign relations is engaging the attention of every thoughtful person in Government almost every day; that always takes precedence. Because here is, as I say, not only the quest for peace, but it is the day-by-day security of the United States, the firming-up of friendships, dealing with old friends. I am having, as you know, new heads of state coming here, or governments, soon—of course, the Queen Mother is not the head of a state, but Premier Yoshida comes right after.

Everything we are doing, all the time, that seems to color everything; it sort of dictates the size of our budget, it affects us in many ways, this whole multitudinous array of problems.

Now, behind that, I think that the general outlines of the program, except for certain specifics in the economic field, foreign economic field, have been rather well laid out already. I will pursue that same program, trying to get it enacted.

Merriman Smith, United Press: Thank you, Mr. President.

NOTE: President Eisenhower's fifty-first news conference was held in the Executive Office Building from 10:30 to 10:54 o'clock on Wednesday morning, November 3, 1954. In attendance: 148.

323 ¶ Memorandum on the Administration of Foreign Aid Programs.   *November 6, 1954*

To: The Secretary of State, The Secretary of the Treasury, The Secretary of Defense, The Secretary of Agriculture, The Secretary of Commerce, The Director of the Foreign Operations Administration, The Director of the Office of Defense Mobilization, The Chairman of the Board of Directors of the Export-Import Bank of Washington, The Director of the United States Information Agency

I have today signed an Executive order which is designed to carry out the provisions of the Mutual Security Act of 1954.

My letter of June 1, 1953, regarding the organization of the executive branch for the conduct of foreign affairs, continues to represent my instructions on the subjects discussed in that letter. This letter supplements my previous letter and the Executive order signed today.

The Director of the Foreign Operations Administration is responsible for coordinating all operations of the foreign assistance programs. He should establish appropriate machinery to achieve this coordination and to assure that all aspects of the mutual security program are consistent with and further the attainment of foreign policy, military policy, and financial and monetary policy objectives. This should include provisions for the Secretaries of State, Defense, and Treasury to receive adequate reports on the operations and projected plans with respect to each program under the Mutual Security Act.

The delegation to the Secretary of State of responsibility for negotiations with foreign governments is intended to give recognition to the central responsibility of the Department of State in this area. Other agencies directly concerned with the substance of the negotiation must continue to carry substantial responsibility in such negotiations, however. Moreover, it is assumed that these other agencies will conduct day-to-day discussions with representatives of the foreign governments in implementing basic agreements reached with such governments. Such discussions, of course, must be in conformance with the foreign policy responsibilities of the State Department and of the chiefs of our diplomatic missions.

The Director of the Foreign Operations Administration will coordinate the implementation of the statutory requirement that a certain minimum amount of the Mutual Security funds be used to finance the export and sale for foreign currencies of surplus agricultural commodities. He shall coordinate this surplus disposal program with that under the Agricultural Trade Development and Assistance Act of 1954. He shall consult with the interagency committee established by the President to assist in the administration of that Act, but I am looking to the Director for the successful implementation of this important part of our mutual security program.

The Secretary of Commerce is designated as the officer to carry out the program to encourage travel. This assignment in no way diminishes the responsibilities of the Department of State or the Foreign Operations Administration to operate exchange and technical assistance programs, nor does it affect the responsibility of the Department of State to carry on diplomatic negotiations with other countries regarding the removal of legal barriers to international travel and similar matters.

The responsibility of finding opportunities for investment and development abroad under the Mutual Security Act is delegated to the Director of the Foreign Operations Administration. The Secretaries of State and Commerce are to continue their regular work through the Foreign Service relating to finding opportunities abroad. The Secretary of Commerce shall be responsible for the regularized publishing and circularization to American business of opportunities abroad, but the Director may continue his normal, direct contacts with individual business firms that arise as a result of his other functions under the Act, such as making investment guarantees and promoting economic development. The Departments of State and Commerce and the Foreign Operations Administration should make arrangements for appropriate consultation and cooperation in respect of their programs relating to encouraging American private investment abroad.

The arrangements described above and in the Executive order issued today are to continue in effect during fiscal year 1955 or until other arrangements for the administration of foreign aid functions are prescribed by the President after further study has been given to this problem in the executive branch of the Government.

DWIGHT D. EISENHOWER

NOTE: The Executive order of November 6, 1954, is published in the 1954 supplement to title 3 of the Code of Federal Regulations (EO 10575, p. 79). The letter of June 1, 1953, is published in the Department of State Bulletin (vol. 28, p. 855).

324 ¶ Letter to the Chairman of the United States Delegation to the Ninth Session on the General Agreement on Tariffs and Trade.
November 8, 1954

[Released November 8, 1954. Dated November 4, 1954]

Dear Mr. Waugh:

Since you are soon leaving to participate in the Ninth Session on the General Agreement on Tariffs and Trade in Geneva, I should like to ask that you convey to your fellow delegates the importance that we attach to a successful outcome of the forthcoming renegotiation and review of the Agreement.   The task before the contracting parties at this Ninth Session is one of crucial significance to the further economic growth of the free world.

At the time of the Eighth Session, the United States and other countries were reappraising their international economic policies.   Based upon such a review in the United States, I recommended in March of this year a program for expanding international trade and overseas investment, for promoting currency convertibility, and for reducing the need for economic aid.   Some portions of this program have already been put into effect.   The remaining parts, especially the heart of the program—extension and amendment of our Trade Agreements Act—will, as you know, be pressed at the session of the Congress which begins in January, and I look forward to early action.

That program envisages United States participation in a multilateral approach to tariffs and trade. The General Agreement has made a useful contribution to the postwar recovery and restoration of the economic vitality of the free world. It was established at a time when the economies of most countries had been seriously weakened. The trade rules of the Agreement recognized that the objective of the widest possible movement of goods among the countries of the world could not be immediately realized, but the goal was set with confidence that it would be progressively achieved. I am convinced that economic reconstruction and growth has now reached a point in many countries to warrant further development of the Agreement, so that we may progress with even more assurance toward our ultimate objective. It would also seem essential that an effective organization be established for the administration of the Agreement and otherwise to promote an expansion of world trade.

The interests of the participating countries may at times seem to conflict. Our mutual goal is of such importance to the economic strength and well-being of all our peoples, however, that this session must be a practical demonstration of the ability of free countries to reach agreement on difficult issues. I am hopeful that ways and means of moving forward now toward our common goal will be found and that the Ninth Session of the Contracting Parties will be one of high achievement.

Sincerely,

DWIGHT D. EISENHOWER

NOTE: The Chairman of the U.S. delegation, Samuel C. Waugh, was Assistant Secretary of State for Economic Affairs.

For the President's March recommendations, see Item 67.

325   ¶ Address to the National Council of
Catholic Women, Boston, Massachusetts.
November 8, 1954

Your Excellency, Madam Chairman, my friends:

First, I should like to thank His Excellency most profoundly—most sincerely—for the prayer he just offered before this congregation.   Next, I should like to thank each of you for the cordiality of your welcome, and through you I should like to thank all those people that I saw along the streets as I came down from the airport.

There was an official representation participating in this welcome. There was your Mayor—Mayor Hynes, your Governor—Governor Herter, and Senator Saltonstall.   And all of them expressed sentiments in which I am sure you would be glad to join, and that is that Senator Kennedy may soon be restored to full health, and he can be assured of our prayers to that happy event.

My visit today happily coincides with the tenth anniversary of Archbishop Cushing's formal installation as Archbishop of Boston.   To him I offer my cordial felicitations.   With you I most earnestly hope that a benign Providence will permit continuance of his splendid service for many years to come.   This convention held in Boston under his auspices for the past 4 years typifies his great contributions to American spiritual strength.

Now, to appear before this national council, representative of millions of American women, at once brings to mind the problems and concerns of our Nation's families.

And this, in turn, brings to my mind two of the oldest stories in the world.   One is a nation's search for a home—the story of the Israelites seeking the Promised Land.   The other is the story of a wanderer who, after many hardships, returned home to find rest and peace.   This is the story of the Prodigal Son.

The human feeling on which these stories rest is one of the deepest man can know.   Reflected in them is love of family, love of hearth and home, and that tie between parent and child which is older than Abraham and Isaac, and as young as the newest-born infant.

To Americans, for more than three centuries, the love of home and family has been a source of the deepest, most intense spiritual strength. Of course the external characteristics of home are not the same for each of us. On the coasts of Maine, families may labor to bring in their livelihood from the gray sea. In the vast reaches of the West, many families live isolated from their neighbors. For each American, the meaning of home is unique and personal.

But something of its general meaning for most of us is bound up symbolically in two great religious holidays: Thanksgiving and Christmas. Whatever our callings, wherever we pursue them, on those days we reunite with our loved ones. The spiritual ties which bind us are restored. The wanderer returns to home and family.

To our Nation this family emotion is profoundly important. Always it has been so. In 1837 a young immigrant observed that America's "domestic virtue" is "the principal source" of all her other qualities. "It acts," he said, "as a promoter of industry, as a stimulus to enterprise. . . . It ensures the proper education of children, and acts, by force of example, on the morals of the rising generation; in short, it . . . is a better guarantee for the permanency of the American government than any written instrument, the Constitution itself not excepted."

In our own time, we have seen a vast nation—which today threatens the free world—threaten the family structure within its own borders, and it has failed miserably in the attempt.

But in our own land, it is largely through the family that our national character is formed. Americans love fair play, bravery, hard work, and believe in human brotherhood because American fathers and mothers, by precept and example, teach these virtues to their children. So long as these ennobling qualities are passed from generation to generation in America, our Nation will remain strong and secure and great.

Faced with this fact, it is imperative that our Government never rest in its task of serving the American home. All of us must work to help remove from the shoulders of American families burdens which reduce their ability to live and to work happily within the home for one another as well as for their fellow-citizens. In every way possible, we must keep our families spiritually rich, strong, and free.

To this end many groups—health, educational, welfare, religious and, finally, governmental—must work together to supplement the efforts of the family itself. This work to strengthen the American home is not sheer humanitarianism on the part of any of these citizen groups or of the Government. It is done in clear appreciation of the great national need for keeping our families strong and healthy. The work of these groups and of the Government is a priceless investment in the national well-being.

Thus it is that our Government helps our disabled citizens to live more productive and happier lives for themselves and for those who are close to them—that our system of Social Security is being steadily expanded to help remove the fear of poverty of our elderly people—that through special tax relief and survivors' benefits we ease the heavy burdens borne by widows and working mothers with dependent children. Thus it is, too, that we actively combat the growing problem of juvenile delinquency—that we work continually to remove from among our people the fear of economic disaster through illness. These measures all evidence the fact that to keep America strong, our Government must have a heart and a head.

Even so, let us be clear that in this field the Government's action must remain secondary and of a buttressing nature. The primary initiative and effort rest with our people themselves, grouped into family units, private institutions and local, State, or national charitable organizations. These efforts the Government must supplement and advance, ever realizing that the Nation's first reliance is the continuing responsibility and self-reliance of our individual citizens.

Now, ladies, there is nothing accidental at all about my making— before such a group—the home as my principal topic of conversation, the sanctity of that home and the strength of the institution that is the family.

Not only have we always recognized that the woman—the mother— is the center of that institution, and the home, but possibly we have not recognized clearly enough how definitely the future of this Nation, in its character as a spiritual and intellectual and material, economic leader of the world, depends upon what we teach in our homes.

As we seek peace, unless peace is taught in the home by the mother, during that age where everything that is learned and absorbed stays with us so strongly, unless we do this, my friends, there is going to be no peace.

Peace is the problem of the American people.

Of course, we would like, through some engagement—some conference—to accomplish all these things in a single day, or a single month. We have not eliminated tuberculosis and cancer, and other dread diseases of mankind in a month. We still labor. We don't give up.

I say with all the earnestness that I can command, that if American mothers will teach our children that there is no end to the fight for better relationships among the people of the world, we shall have peace. Because, as they do this, other mothers will do it; and gradually the age-old longing of humankind for peace will be reflected in better governmental structures, governmental structures that will be forced to comply with the demands of the great and enlightened citizenry throughout the world.

And so, far greater in importance to every American family than any of these activities I have been describing, is the patient, tireless effort of our Government to establish a just peace among nations.

Now today presents another coincidence to me, though not so happy as the first I mentioned.

Twelve years ago today, the first American troops landed in North Africa. I was in command of those troops in the European theatre, and on that day started the great ground conflict by American troops in Europe that did not end until Hitler was dead and Germany had surrendered. Now as we look back on that day, and on the most terrible war in human history, we again resolve that there must never be another war.

Today the fathers and mothers of our land rejoice that the possibility of permanent peace is more promising than at any time in recent years. They are grateful for the ending of bloodshed in Korea and Southeast Asia, the repulse of communism in Guatemala, the easing of tensions in Iran, Suez and Trieste, and the promising agreement recently reached in Western Europe. They are heartened, too, by the building of strength where there was weakness throughout the Pacific. Despite such instances of provocation as that which occurred yesterday off the coast of Japan, all of us are profoundly thankful that the terrible specter of war looms less threateningly over all mankind.

Now to convert this uneasy global armistice to a lasting peace, with justice for all people everywhere, is the longing of the parents of America's children. To attain this enduring peace, while living in freedom, must ever be the overriding goal of our American foreign policy.

Without exciting fears or false hopes, without magnifying difficulties or dwelling upon mistakes, we must squarely face every obstacle to peace and attempt to overcome it. This means patience, courage, profound confidence in the common yearnings of the people of the world. This determination, this confidence, must become a spiritual and an instinctive part of each American beginning at every mother's knee.

Through the United Nations—through every possible means—we must strive to build an honorable peace. I know all Americans are hopeful that our proposal for an international pool of atomic energy will inaugurate a new phase in negotiations between the United States and the Soviet Union. I deeply believe that, regardless of the Soviet decision, the cause of peace will be furthered as we go ahead with friendly nations to turn this new science to the arts of peace.

At the same time, we must strive to maintain the collective, united strength of free peoples. By broadening alliances, by strengthening our cultural ties with peoples of other lands, we build a firmer foundation for permanent peace throughout the world.

And it is not paradoxical in our peaceful efforts that we maintain powerful military forces. For in a world partly dominated by men who respect only guns, planes, and tanks, these weapons are essential to our survival.

And let us remember this: war and peace, struggle and resolution, hatred and concord are not merely the concerns of Government and diplomacy. They well up from the emotions and impulses in the hearts of individual men and women, in every nation of the world.

These emotions, from generation to generation, are passed on from parent to child. The problems these emotions create are incredibly complex. Why must a country fight to the death to hold seemingly worthless territory? Why must a nation passionately strive to maintain an apparently meaningless boundary? Why must the people of one nation continue to hate or fear the people of another, for reasons lost in the dimness of the past?

Solution of these problems requires more than skillful diplomacy. Essential to lasting peace is a genuine desire of the individual citizens of each nation to understand the traditions and hopes and desires of the citizens of all other nations. We in America must strive to understand the emotions and attitudes, instilled in other peoples from childhood, which lie at the heart of vexing international difficulties. Above all we need the religious quality of compassion—the ability to feel the emotions of others as though they were our own. If the mothers in every land could teach their children to understand the homes and hopes of children in every other land—in America, in Europe, in the Near East, in Asia—the cause of peace in the world would indeed be nobly served.

But still more is essential to our cause than the capacity to understand the motivations which, ingrained in nations, divide them. We must probe through these to the more fundamental urgings, the bonds which make brothers of all men.

The desire to be free, the desire to realize one's own capacities, the desire for justice, the respect for reason, willingness to sacrifice for one's children, love of home and love of peace—all these lie deep in the hearts of all peoples.

It must be so.

It is this Divinely inspired faith which gives promise to our quest for peace.

May this faith be ever nourished and strengthened in the families of America.

For these are the foundations, my friends, on which the men and women of our Nation and of all nations which cherish freedom and peace can build an abiding happiness, for themselves, and for their children.

And now, my friends, again my very earnest and humble thanks for the cordiality of your welcome, for the courtesy you have paid to me in listening to me so patiently. Thank you.

NOTE: The President spoke in Symphony Hall at 11:05 a.m. His opening words "Your Excellency, Madam Chairman" referred to The Most Reverend Richard J. Cushing, Archbishop of Boston, and to Mrs. William H. Dalton, President of the National Council of Catholic Women.

326 ¶ Remarks to a Representative Group Receiving Citizenship Papers on Veterans Day. *November* 9, 1954

WELL, I can almost say "my new fellow citizens": It is really a privilege to welcome you, not only to all of the rights and the freedoms that go with

American citizenship, but to remind you—as you already know—that it has very serious obligations.

We expect you to carry on the obligations just as you enjoy the rights and the privileges. That is what every good citizen does. You are following in the footsteps of millions that have come before you, to build this country—of intermingling races and bloods and cultures. You will add your part to this great Nation that we call America.

Through you, I would like to extend my very warm greetings, my very sincere welcome, to all the fifty thousand who—with you—on Armistice Day will take the formal oath of allegiance to the United States.

I wish that I could be with you on that date, because I know it will be very significant to you.

Thank you very much for coming and giving me a chance to say hello to you.

NOTE: The President spoke in the Rose Garden at 11:25 a.m.

327 ¶ Remarks to the First National Conference on the Spiritual Foundations of American Democracy. *November* 9, 1954

Dr. Lowry, ladies and gentlemen:

It is one of the happier duties that devolve upon the President that he is privileged occasionally to greet and welcome to this city—to the Capital City of our country—groups that have joined together in some great civic enterprise.

Usually there is some thought that occurs to me, when I perform this pleasant duty, that I think is appropriate to the occasion. But I must confess, I am having a little trouble today.

We are talking about the spiritual foundations of our form of government, and I meet with the spiritual leaders of the Nation, and I am one of these poor laymen, and it looks to me it's a little bit like Daniel in the lion's den in reverse.

Now Dr. Lowry said something about my having certain convictions as to a God in Heaven and an Almighty power. Well, I don't think anyone needs a great deal of credit for believing what seems to me to be obvious.

I remember once that Carter Glass was given a decoration, an honorary doctorate at a university, and the citation read in his behalf stressed very greatly that he was an honest man. And finally, when he got up, he said he thought he ought to decline this decoration because if the United States had gotten to the point that they had to decorate a man because he was honest, well, he despaired of the Republic.

Now it seems to me that this relationship between a spiritual faith, a religious faith, and our form of government is so clearly defined and so obvious that we should really not need to identify a man as unusual because he recognizes it.

Now I am not going to go into any long dissertation today. That is not my purpose in coming and telling you how much I support the work that you are now initiating. I do believe we need this kind of thing. But as we go back and trace, let us not go back to the Judeo-Christian tradition and try to introduce it into the forms of man's attempts at self-government, but let us just come down to modern times since the Reformation.

Milton asserted that all men are born equal, because each is born in the image of his God. Our whole theory of government finally expressed in our Declaration, you will recall, said—and remember the first part of the Preamble of the Declaration was to give the reasons to mankind why we had established such a government: "Man is endowed by his Creator." It did not assert that Americans had certain rights. "Man" is endowed by his Creator—or "All Men" I believe was the expression used.

So this connection is very, very clear. And no matter what Democracy tries to do in the terms of maximum individual liberty for an individual, in the economic and in the intellectual and every other field, no matter what it tries to do in providing a system of justice, and a system of responsibility—of public servants to all the people—and identifying the people as the source of political power in that government, when you come back to it, there is just one thing: it is a concept, it is a subjective sort of thing, that a man is worthwhile because he was born in the image of his God.

And so it seems to me that the spiritual foundation is not so much the effort we have now, to prove it, as it is to make people recognize it and live accordingly. Because if we are going to have maximum freedom in carrying on the business of government, then there must be self-discipline, a fervor that establishes self-discipline; because if we don't, freedom runs so far that we cannot meet the challenges of today.

The challenges of today, I think, probably are of two kinds, one from within ourselves, because our fervor, our strength, in our spiritual convictions as to the worth-whileness of this form of government, weakens; and on the other side we are attacked by the Communists who in their own documents state that capitalism—Democracy—carries within itself the seeds of its own destruction, and give, as you know, several reasons why they claim that.

So we are under tremendous attacks. But it is not that we have just to establish the fact. We have to establish the fervor, the strength of our convictions, because fundamentally Democracy is nothing in the world but a spiritual conviction, a conviction that each of us is enormously valuable because of a certain standing before our own God.

Now, any group that binds itself together to awaken all of us to these simple things, and to discover new ways and means by which they are brought home to us through our surroundings, through our relationships with other nations, our relationships with one another, and through our peering into the future, any organization such as that is, to my mind, a dedicated, patriotic group that can well take the Bible in one hand and the flag in the other, and march ahead.

Now that is what I am for. And I am delighted, therefore, that you have met here, that you are having this kind of convention which I hope will, as one of its results, grow and grow and grow until this kind of thing is habitual in every city, town, and hamlet of the United States, back to the remotest village.

Again my thanks for your welcome. I will watch with keen interest the outcome of your work, and I am sure that the United States cannot fail to prosper through what you are doing.

Goodbye.

NOTE: The President spoke at 12:02 p.m. at a luncheon meeting at the Sheraton-Carlton Hotel in Washington. His opening words "Dr. Lowry" referred to the Rev. Charles W. Lowry, chairman of the Foundation for Religious Action in the Social and Civil Order, which sponsored the conference.

328 ¶ The President's News Conference of *November* 10, 1954.

THE PRESIDENT. Please be seated. I understand, ladies and gentlemen, that there are present this morning two groups of additional reporters, one from NATO countries, and one who came with the Premier from Japan. For my part, I heartily welcome them here in this company.

I have no announcements to make, so we will go right to questions.

Q. Robert E. Clark, International News Service: Mr. President, the shooting down of one of our B–29's recently by Russian fighters is the latest in a series of incidents in which the Soviet has both rejected our claim for reparations and brushed aside our protest notes. Is there anything we can do to guard against such incidents and force reparations, aside from filing formal protests?

THE PRESIDENT. You raise a very complicated, in some ways tricky, problem.

The world, enjoying what we call a peace, is nevertheless very watchful of its own borders.

Now, with respect to this last incident, let me show you some of the cloudy features of it.

I believe it is the Habomai Islands, right off the coast of Hokkaido—range from two miles, the closest one, on out to several miles. Now, back in the World War, the Kuriles were turned over by agreement to the Russians. No matter what you think of the wisdom or unwisdom of that agreement, there was the further complication itself that the southern boundary of the Kuriles was apparently not definitely defined; and since then the Soviets have claimed that the little islands right off of Hokkaido were part of the Kuriles.

This incident took place right in that area. Naturally, since it is a disputed area, they are very jealous in keeping hold of it—I guess they are going on the theory that possession is nine points; I don't know. But in any event, this isn't one of those clear-cut things where you can just say this, this, this, this must be so, and that is that.

Now, on the other hand, when we do have this type of incident, we believe we are the aggrieved party, I think that we are entitled to courteous answers and examination into the matter. In this latest incident there was, I would say, a very considerably different attitude shown on the part of the others than there has been in the past.

Just exactly what will come out of this one, I cannot say.

I do want to point out, though, that these things are not always so completely clean-cut as they might look on the surface. But we think we are aggrieved, we believe that the plane had a right to be where it was; and so, therefore, our protest—which was, of course, done at my direction and my approval. That is where the case stands.

Q. Edward T. Folliard, Washington Post and Times Herald: This question, Mr. President, is related to Mr. Clark's question. Chip Bohlen, our Ambassador to Russia, attended an anniversary party in Moscow the other night. Now, he has been criticized for that because of this plane incident. Do you see anything unbecoming in his conduct?

THE PRESIDENT. Of course, decisions about such things are usually made as much by the emotions and the sentiments as they are by calm, logical thought.

As I understand it, Mr. Bohlen got this news some 30 minutes before he was going to a party that was a very formal affair in the capital. He obviously could not have known anything of the details; he couldn't even make up his mind, possibly, as to whether this was an accident where one of our planes had gotten lost or what had happened. He had to make up his mind on the spur of the moment. And I believe this: I believe we have a good group of foreign officers, as I have repeated time and again. I believe they can be trusted to act with good judgment so far as the facts present with them at any time will permit them to act; and I am not going to sit here this far off and say this man was wrong for going to that meeting. He had to make up his own mind, and that's that.

Q. Robert W. Richards, Copley Press: Whatever possessed us to give away the Kuriles?

THE PRESIDENT. I really haven't the slightest notion. It happens that I did not attend any of the conferences during the war when our people were conferring with what has turned out to be the opposite side, with the Soviets. So I don't know what the influences were, and it is one thing concerning which I have never talked to any of the principals. So except for the papers that have been published on these things, I know nothing about it.

Q. Sarah McClendon, El Paso Times: Sir, I believe it was in 1950 that President Truman, in an effort to achieve more bipartisan foreign policy, appointed John Foster Dulles and John Sherman Cooper as consultants for the State Department, their main mission being, I believe, to contact Senators and Congressmen on Capitol Hill. I wonder if you plan to do the same thing?

THE PRESIDENT. I don't know exactly what method will be pursued in this thing. But I think, as I explained before, as far as personal contacts and friendships are concerned, I have many personal friends among the leaders of the other party. I personally anticipate no difficulty in meeting with these leaders and talking to them about our mutual problems. Now, just exactly how we will do it, I don't know.

Q. Charles S. von Fremd, CBS News: Mr. President, there have been several stories during the past week—I don't know whether or not they are strictly speculative or not—reporting that Chiang Kai-shek and the Chinese Nationalists have been ordered by this country not to attack the Chinese Communist mainland, and that their forces are to be used— land, sea, and air forces—are to be used only as a defensive device. Can you tell us whether or not that is true?

THE PRESIDENT. Well, now, first of all, we try to deal with out partners as such; we do not give orders. We do make agreements about the possible and proper use of certain of the materials we furnish; those are made in advance.

Now, with Nationalist China, there are constant talks going on as to what is wisdom at the moment, what is wisdom for the future, what should be our relationships. Those go on all the time. But I would say that there is no atom of truth in the statement that we have issued orders to Chiang Kai-shek. We just don't do that.

Q. William M. Blair, New York Times: Mr. President, Mr. Thomas Murray, a member of the Atomic Energy Commission, testified before the Joint Committee this week that the top level management of the Atomic Energy Commission was being diverted from its primary mission by what he described as a political controversy over the Dixon-Yates contract. Would you agree with this conclusion and discuss with us, sir, your views on whether the Atomic Energy Commission should be a nonpolitical or a political body?

THE PRESIDENT. I think, of course, that any business organization working for the Government should be nonpolitical, and I deplore any thought that there had been an effort to make this matter political. On the contrary, this contract—to which has been raised some objection—there was no effort to keep that under cover until after the elections. It was laid out and spread out on the record as fast as it could be—first, the negotiations, and after the contract was once in the hands of the Congress, then the country.

Possibly I had better straighten out once again my attitude toward this whole business.

It was represented to me that there was going to be an acute power shortage in the TVA area by 1957. Now we have an area in which the Federal Government has not only fully developed the waterpower, has then built the steamplants to firm up that waterpower, then has built additional steamplants, and is still enlarging some of them.

The question becomes how long does this go along at Federal expense unless we do it in the Smoky Hill Valley and in the Penobscot Valley, and in the Hudson Valley, and all the rest of the world. It would look like it was time to take a look at this. So, consequently, I said, "How can we supply that need without putting the Government in position that in perpetuity it is going to continue to build steamplants anywhere anyone wants them?"

Now, one way to do it was to take the needs of the AEC and to see whether they could be supplied and, therefore, provide this extra 600,000 watts it was then predicted they were going to need in 1957; then you wouldn't damage the people of the area, and you would go ahead and give everybody time to take a good look at this and study it out.

There is nothing in this contract that can raise by a single cent the prices that TVA charges its customers for power. And the contract was gone over, as I told you before, by the Federal Power Commission, by TVA and, I believe, the General Accounting Office, all of whom found it a satisfactory contract.

So if there is anything political in it, someone is making it that way; it is nothing political from my viewpoint.

I appointed a man to head the TVA who, as far as I know, has never had a political affiliation in his life, who has got a long professional career, competent in this field of hydroelectric engineering. He has got one order: to find out the facts and advise the President and the Congress as to what he believes to be right. So if there is any politics in this thing, it is not by my choosing.

Q. John M. Hightower, Associated Press: Mr. President, could you tell us anything about the possible use of fighter escorts under the present policy or whether the policy might be changed with respect to these aircraft?

THE PRESIDENT. You are bringing up again this B–29?

Q. Mr. Hightower: Yes, sir.

THE PRESIDENT. My own feeling is that when we use planes for any necessary or desirable purpose in areas that are risky, they ought to be planes that fit that particular specification; we shouldn't use them as just sitting ducks.

So if a fighter escort is necessary where we know we have got a right to go, then we ought to use them.

For example, you will remember some time back there was a plane downed at sea, a British plane. We knew there were Americans aboard, and we wanted to pursue rescue operations. The forces going in there were directed to protect themselves because they were in an area we knew they had a right to be. I think we should—we must do that.

Q. Robert L. Riggs, Louisville Courier-Journal: Mr. President, this week, one of your strong supporters journalistically, the Scripps-Howard Papers, called on you to let go of the Dixon-Yates contract. They said it was a dangerous thing politically and would hurt you. Have you changed your mind any on supporting the Dixon-Yates contract, or are we to understand that it is going to go?

THE PRESIDENT. Well, I haven't changed my mind for this simple reason: no better contract has been offered. If we are going to get power in that region, and if we are going to get it in this amount, I know of no better way to get it. No better way has been offered, so until there is some better way offered, I have got to stick with this one.

Q. Raymond P. Brandt, St. Louis Post-Dispatch: Mr. President, on that point, why were not the specifications laid down for this, and competitive bids asked?

THE PRESIDENT. I don't want to be quoted here too exactly that I can't change my mind; but, as I remember it, I was informed that they put this matter up before a number of utilities and there were only two offers received. One was, they thought, completely unacceptable, because there was no risk whatsoever.

You remember, in contracts of the past where the AEC has made contracts, they have been strictly cost-plus. I rejected those; I thought they weren't good for the Government. I thought we ought to have a contract where there is some risk shared by the building companies, so I insisted on that.

The other plan, as I understand it, that was submitted, was again one which the building companies took no risk on.

Q. Mr. Brandt: As I understand, the specifications were very general, and there was only one other company made a bid. And I also understand that TVA was not consulted in the initial steps.

THE PRESIDENT. Well, you would have to check that up with AEC and with the Bureau of the Budget. I can't be expected to recall every detail, but I do know they came and sat in front of me often enough, and I assume TVA knew about it.

Q. Mr. Brandt: The previous Chairman of TVA testified that he was not called in on the initial proceedings to give the expert advice.

THE PRESIDENT. Well, I do believe this: I believe that the prior Chairman's whole attitude toward this particular matter was well-known; but I don't recall, and I think that you have got good places to find out that detail.

Q. Mr. Brandt: May I ask one more question, please?

THE PRESIDENT. Yes.

Q. Mr. Brandt: Are you adamant against TVA expanding further?

THE PRESIDENT. You say "adamant." I hope that I am old enough that I don't think there is anything particularly sacrosanct about my decisions and conclusions.

I do believe this: that if we continue to expand there, what are we going to do about the other sections of this country. I think there has got to be a policy deliberately adopted by the United States before we make things so lopsided; because, let me tell you, for every argument I have had for TVA, there are many, many people, political leaders, business leaders, come to my office and say: "Why do you continue to give them cheap power and take away our industries, and then we pay taxes to support them?"

Now, I don't know that there is any justice to that argument. And, as I told you again and again, I have put a man down there from whom I believe we can all expect absolutely objective and complete reporting on the thing. I hope we get it, because I would like to know what the answer is.

Q. Robert L. Riggs, Louisville Courier-Journal: Mr. President, could I ask one more?

THE PRESIDENT. Yes.

Q. Mr. Riggs: There are two kinds of expansions, sir: one is geographical and the other one is expanding power production——

THE PRESIDENT. That is right.

Q. Mr. Riggs:——inside TVA's area. Now, do you oppose expansion both ways?

THE PRESIDENT. Well, again, I say, I don't know too much about it. Look—if the Federal Government is committed just to building power in the TVA and giving them 100 percent of all they will ever want in their estimates for the next 5 years, why don't I do it in the Mississippi Valley? That is what I want to know, and no one answers for me. I ask them—— the TVA people come in my office and stand around and argue, and I say, "Well, now, are you ready to support, before you get any more, are you ready to support this kind of development for the upper Mississippi?" And they just look at me and say, "That is outside the question." But it isn't to me; I believe that the United States should be treated fairly all the way through.

Q. Mr. Riggs: Their argument down there is that the Federal Government is their power monopoly in that area. Any expansion they get in that region must come from the Federal Government.

THE PRESIDENT. Well, to my mind, I would hate to be admitting that I am completely and absolutely dependent upon the vagaries of the Federal Government that might do anything at any moment. I don't believe any section of this country has to be completely dependent upon the Federal Government unless it is the District here.

Q. Paul Scott Rankine, Reuters: Mr. President, could I ask another question?

THE PRESIDENT. Yes.

Q. Mr. Rankine: About the plane incident, you said that this was not one of those clear-cut things. Now, could you tell us what it is that isn't clear-cut? Is it the issues, the territory, or the facts?

THE PRESIDENT. Well, I said—I thought I explained it very carefully—that the Soviets are claiming title to this little group of islands well to the south of the Kuriles, and one of which is only a matter of 2 or 3 miles off Hokkaido.

Now, that has never been accepted by the United States, and never been accepted by Japan. I believe that line came about because it was an occupational line agreed upon by the Supreme Commander right after the war, and so it is now called a part of the Soviet territory by them, but we don't admit that. So that is where you have—it isn't one of these cases where a plane has come out in the middle toward Hawaii and shot you down.

Q. Robert E. Clark, International News Service: Mr. President, one more question on this: you also said that there has been a very considerable difference of attitude shown in this case than in previous instances. Do you mean the Russians have been more receptive to our protests this time?

THE PRESIDENT. Well, I am saying this: the general attitude here seemed to be more conciliatory than it has been in some former instances. Actually, I can say no more than that at the moment, because I don't know whether the note itself was released or not; I have forgotten.

Q. John Herling, Editors Syndicate: Mr. President, this being American Education Week, and so designated by you, I wonder whether, as President of the United States and as former president of a great university, you would care to comment on the anti-intellectual trend in our country which expresses itself in hostility to new ideas or different ideas or even traditional ideas?

THE PRESIDENT. I think I have made speeches on this subject, and I would have thought that my attitude would be clearly understood.

I believe that when people get so frightened of new ideas that they can't tolerate them, they are getting frightened of themselves.

I want to make it very clear, I do not and would not tolerate anyone anywhere that was openly preaching the destruction of the United States form of government by violence. That, to my mind, is not mere idea, that is one type of war.

But anyone who wants to talk a philosophy, a philosophy of life, of an economy, of a government, or of a social order, I think if we don't examine them and look at them, we are confessing a fear which I, for one, do not feel.

I believe the United States system can stand on its own feet. I believe it will be upheld by our people in the face of really open and exhaustive discussion. And I deplore any idea that you can shut off thoughts, ideas, and grow strong; I just don't.

Q. George E. Herman, CBS News: Mr. President, George Herman, CBS—I have been rehearsing it all week. [*Laughter*]

Sir, along those same lines of education, there has been a survey or series of surveys lately that said that the Soviet Union's output of science students has been vastly increasing in quality and in quantity, and that our own output of students who are interested in science seems to be on a dangerous downtrend, continually decreasing. Have you any thoughts on the part of the Government in that sense?

THE PRESIDENT. I believe that here is one place where people in Government should be very alert, and if we find anything like that, there are numbers of ways open to us that can correct the situation without waiting for the economic influences to do it.

We know this: if you get few enough scientists, they can command prices that you will have a rush to the scientific colleges. But we can't wait for that, so I believe the Federal Government could establish scholarships. I would not want the Federal Government to go in and support a particular college or university, and then say, "Now, go there." But you could support scholarships which could be used at any outstanding university, and in a number of ways could encourage this kind of education.

I haven't talked lately to any of my scientific friends on this subject; I am just saying what could be done and, possibly, will have to be done. I don't know.

John L. Cutter, United Press: Thank you, Mr. President.

NOTE: President Eisenhower's fifty-second news conference was held in the Executive Office Building from 10:30 to 10:53 o'clock on Wednesday morning, November 10, 1954. In attendance: 169.

329 ¶ Special Message to the Senate Transmitting the Southeast Asia Collective Defense Treaty and Protocol Thereto.
November 10, 1954

To the United States Senate:

With a view to receiving the advice and consent of the Senate to ratification, I transmit herewith a copy of the Southeast Asia Collective Defense Treaty and the Protocol thereto, both signed at Manila on September 8, 1954.

I transmit also for the information of the Senate a copy of a declaration known as the Pacific Charter which was drawn up at Manila and signed on that same date. The Charter proclaims the dedication of the signatory governments to the ideals of self-determination, self-government, and independence. It is a declaration of principles and does not require the advice and consent of the Senate.

There is further transmitted for the information of the Senate the report made to me by the Secretary of State regarding the Southeast Asia Collective Defense Treaty and the Protocol thereto. I concur in the recommendation of the Secretary that the "unanimous agreement" required by Article IV, paragraph 1, for the designation of States or territories, by Article VII for the invitation to States to accede to the Treaty, and by Article VIII for a change in the treaty area is to be understood in each instance as requiring the advice and consent of the Senate.

The Treaty is designed to promote security and peace in Southeast Asia and the Southwestern Pacific by deterring communist and other aggression in that area. It is a treaty for defense against both open armed attack and internal subversion. Included in the Treaty is an Understanding on behalf of the United States that the only armed attack in the Treaty area which the United States would regard as necessarily dangerous to our peace and security would be a communist armed attack. The Treaty calls for economic cooperation to enable the free countries of this area to gain strength and vigor, not only militarily, but also socially and economically.

The Southeast Asia Collective Defense Treaty complements our other security treaties in the Pacific and constitutes an important link in the collective security of the free nations of Southeast Asia and the Pacific.

I recommend that the Senate give early and favorable consideration to the Treaty and Protocol submitted herewith, and advise and consent to the ratification thereof subject to the understanding of the United States contained in the Treaty.

DWIGHT D. EISENHOWER

NOTE: The treaty and related papers are printed in Senate Executive K (83d Cong., 2d sess.). The treaty and protocol were approved by the Senate on February 1, 1955, and after ratification entered into force February 19, 1955 (6 UST 81).

330   ¶ Joint Statement Following Discussions With Prime Minister Yoshida of Japan. *November* 10, 1954

PRESIDENT Eisenhower and Prime Minister Yoshida met on November 9 and reaffirmed the spirit of friendly cooperation characterizing the relations between the United States and Japan. The Prime Minister also met with Secretary of State Dulles, Secretary of Treasury Humphrey, Secretary of Defense Wilson, and Director Stassen of the Foreign Operations Administration. The Prime Minister and Secretary Dulles at their meetings this week, after a full and frank exchange of views on matters of mutual interest, reviewed the conversations held during the past three weeks by representatives of the two governments.

I.

The President and the Prime Minister agreed that the solidarity and determination of the free nations had greatly advanced the cause of world peace. They declared that their governments would, in cooperation with the free nations of Asia, continue their united efforts to maintain and promote the peace and prosperity of Asia. The Prime Minister reaffirmed his government's determination to make a full contribution to those efforts and in particular stressed Japan's desire to cooperate, wherever possible, in the development of economic strength by the free nations of Asia.

The President and the Prime Minister declared that the goals of their governments are peaceful and that their peoples desire peace and liberty for themselves and their neighbors.

II.

Representatives of both governments discussed Japan's economic situation in detail. It was agreed that the economic well-being of the Japanese people is a matter of importance to the entire free world. The achievement of improved economic conditions in Japan depends partly upon the ability of the Japanese people themselves to pursue sound and constructive internal monetary and other economic policies and partly upon Japan's ability to expand its trade with other countries. By various means since the end of the war the United States has been able to contribute substantially to the economic progress which Japan has achieved. The United States is aware of the efforts which Japan is making to solve its difficult economic problems and will continue to examine sympathetically means whereby it can assist the Japanese people to advance their well-being.

A number of specific measures were discussed in the recent talks. General agreement was reached that the United States would cooperate with Japan in its efforts to expand its foreign trade and achieve a better balance in its foreign economic relations. It was further agreed that the United States would sell to Japan agricultural commodities and that a substantial portion of the proceeds of these sales will be used for Japan's domestic economic improvement and defense support and for regional economic development. Other steps were discussed, such as the establishment of a productivity program in Japan and the mutual benefits which might arise from Japan's participation with the other free nations of South and Southeast Asia in the economic development of that area. Both sides agreed that these measures would be of marked benefit to Japan by improving its economic position and facilitating its efforts to attain a higher standard of living.

III.

United States representatives expressed regret over the incident on March 1 in which 23 Japanese fishermen were injured—one fatally—by the fall-out of radioactive materials following a nuclear test in the Pacific. They emphasized their belief that peaceful uses of atomic energy would be steadily developed and would eventually become of great value to Japan and other friendly nations throughout the world.

IV.

There was also discussion of the disposition of Japanese assets vested by the United States and representatives of the United States stated that this matter is under consideration. Among other subjects reviewed were Communist efforts to weaken and discredit the operations of free governments in Asia, the request of Japan for expedited consideration of the cases of war criminals, and the status of the Ryukyu and Bonin Islands in the light of the present international situation as well as the desire of Japan for the return to the Bonin Islands of former inhabitants.

331 ¶ Remarks at the Dedication of the Eisenhower Museum, Abilene, Kansas. *November 11, 1954*

Governor Arn, my good friends:

Knowing that I was going to be privileged to attend this ceremony today, I seriously considered the idea of preparing for it a talk. I decided that upon reaching here I would be so swept with waves of emotion that anything that I did in advance would be utterly useless and would be thrown away as I stood before you. And so I decided that whatever I should feel upon my arrival here I should try to communicate to you in a few simple words as I performed my small part in the dedication of this memorial.

First, may I express on behalf of every member of the Eisenhower family our very warm thanks to each individual here attending today. You typify for us that great spirit of America, indeed maybe we could say Kansas, cordiality and hospitality that we have come to expect every time we come back to Dickinson County and Abilene. We are more than grateful for every smile we have seen, for every shout that we have heard. I am certain also that you would expect me, on this day, to have a special feeling for the Armed Forces of America.

I am delighted that some portions of the Armed Forces, both in the professional, the civilian and the cadet formations, could find it possible to be here today. I spent 40 years of my life among them. I came on the battlefields of the world, and in times of peace, to have for them a respect, an admiration, which will never die.

And finally I should like to compliment the particular members of this parade on their performance. I have witnessed ceremonies throughout our country many times, and I have seen none that I thought exceeded in its exhibition of skill, in marching, and music, the one I saw today.

But another feeling is also deeply imbedded in my heart today. My brother in his talk expressed something of this feeling that we all have for the priceless gift of American citizenship, what it means, what features of it do not change, even though the world about us changes with bewildering speed.

And so it is, of course, of tremendous gratification for one who necessarily at the moment holds and carries great responsibilities in the development of America of the future, to know that here is an organization and an activity devoted to the promotion of good citizenship in America. I feel that there is nothing—nothing else—that could ever have induced the Eisenhower brothers to attach their name to something which inescapably would have certain elements, let us say, of self-glorification, except that that project was presented as something for the future good of America, the future validity and value of all of those teachings that will produce the citizens of the future America; the kind of thinking that will continue to pass on from generation to generation; the priceless gifts of freedom, of freedom of speech, and of worship, and of the right of earning; to work for yourself and your family and, as my brother said, for opportunity; the preservation of opportunity for each individual to fulfill himself both in the material and economic way, and in the intellectual and spiritual.

And finally, of course, that tremendous satisfaction that comes from knowing that your neighbors and your old friends that have been so helpful to you during your life—indeed, let me remark, there is present today a gentleman who way back in 1910, 44 years ago, was one of those who worked so hard to allow me to embark on a military career; I should like to take advantage of this little digression to thank personally Mr. Harger for all he did for me in those days.

It is very wonderful to think that such old friends, those that knew you in boyhood, and those that you have met since, should gather together and want to do something to commemorate the Armed Forces of the

United States—a body to which, as I say, I belonged for 40 years—and to put their efforts, their substance, their time and their thought in making certain that the privileges of citizenship that were so well exemplified by my father and mother, and which their sons have so haltingly and at times so feebly tried to carry forward, are to be here enshrined forever.

And so I am bold enough to speak for every Eisenhower I know, or have known, for those representatives of six generations of Eisenhowers who lie buried in this county and the neighboring county of Geary, for all of them, for the generations to which they belong, and for those who shall bear our name or be related to us in the future, in expressing our humble pride that today we may be here to participate in this ceremony, as I am privileged, to dedicate this shrine to the future citizens of a great and glorious America.

Thank you very much, my friends.

NOTE: The President spoke at 11:15 a.m.   Harger, editor of the Abilene Reflector-
In his remarks he referred to Charles M.   Chronicle.

332 ¶ Special Message to the Senate Transmitting Protocols to Treaties Relating to the Federal Republic of Germany. *November* 15, 1954

To the United States Senate:

I transmit herewith for the consideration of the Senate a certified copy of the Protocol on the Termination of the Occupation Regime in the Federal Republic of Germany, signed at Paris on October 23, 1954, to which are annexed five schedules, and a certified copy of the Protocol to the North Atlantic Treaty on the Accession of the Federal Republic of Germany, also signed at Paris on October 23, 1954. I request the advice and consent of the Senate to the ratification of these two documents.

In addition, I transmit for the information of the Senate a number of related documents. These include a report made to me by the Secretary of State on the present agreements; the Final Act of the Nine Power Conference held at London, September 28–October 3, 1954, with annexes; three resolutions adopted by the North Atlantic Council on October 22, 1954; four protocols to the Brussels Treaty signed at Paris on October 23, 1954, together with the text of the Brussels Treaty signed on March 17, 1948; a declaration dated October 23, 1954, of the states signatory to the Brussels Treaty inviting Italy and the Federal Republic of Germany to accede to the Treaty; a resolution on the production and standardization of armaments adopted by the Nine Power Conference at Paris on October 21, 1954; the Convention on the Presence of Foreign Forces in the Federal Republic of Germany signed at Paris on October 23, 1954; the Tripartite Agreement on the Exercise of Retained Rights in Germany signed at Paris on October 23, 1954; certain letters relating to the Termination of the Occupation Regime in the Federal Republic of Germany, dated October 23, 1954, together with the texts of letters exchanged in 1952 referred to therein; and a statement on Berlin made by the Foreign Ministers of France, the United States, and the United Kingdom in Paris on October 23, 1954.

I know the Senate is aware of the very great importance of these agreements to the security of the United States and to the cause of peace and freedom in the world as a whole. The agreements represent the culmination of a joint effort, extending over several years, to promote closer cooperation in security matters among the nations of Western Europe and to find a way of associating the great potential strength of the Federal Republic of Germany with that of the free world in a manner which will ensure freedom and equality for the people of Germany and at the same time will avoid the danger of a revival of German militarism. The Congress of the United States has recognized on several occasions that the effectiveness of the entire Atlantic relationship depends to a very great extent upon the attainment of these objectives, and last summer the Senate adopted a resolution (S. Res. 295, July 30, 1954) expressing the sense of the Senate that steps should be taken to restore sovereignty to Germany and to enable her to contribute to the maintenance of international peace and security.

It was hoped that these objectives would be accomplished through the Treaty constituting the European Defense Community, together with the Bonn conventions of May 26, 1952, which were designed to terminate the occupation regime in the Federal Republic. But the Treaty constituting the European Defense Community failed of ratification, and the conventions, being dependent on the Treaty, could not be brought into effect. Accordingly, it became necessary to devise a set of alternative arrangements by which the nations of the North Atlantic community might pursue their common security objectives, and these new arrangements are embodied in the present agreements.

In accordance with these arrangements, the Federal Republic will be invited to accede to the North Atlantic Treaty and, along with Italy, to the Brussels Treaty. Furthermore, important changes will be made in the military arrangements under the North Atlantic Treaty Organization and in the basic nature of the Brussels Treaty to which Belgium, France, Luxembourg, the Netherlands, and the United Kingdom are already parties. These changes will have the effect, not only of placing certain agreed controls on European armaments, but also of strengthening and reinforcing both the North Atlantic Treaty Organization and the new Brussels Treaty Organization, the Western European Union.

In NATO, the powers of the Supreme Allied Commander, Europe, will be strengthened in the fields of assignment and deployment of forces, inspection, and logistical organization. In addition, the principle of integration of units may be carried to lower echelons than is now the case. These measures are desirable in their own right because they increase the general effectiveness of NATO forces. At the same time, they create a degree of mutual inter-dependence among national forces assigned to NATO that will effectively limit the ability of any one nation to take independent military action within SACEUR's area of command.

The Brussels Treaty is modified so as to establish a new Council for Western European Union, and promotion of European integration becomes a new purpose of the Treaty. The Council is given important powers in the fields of controlling forces and armaments. The continental forces of the Brussels Treaty countries are set at specified limits, conforming, for those countries which would have been members of the European Defense Community, to the limits set by the EDC Treaty. These limits cannot be changed except by the unanimous consent of the Council. In addition, the United Kingdom has agreed that it will continue to maintain on the mainland of Europe forces of the level presently committed there. Further safeguards are provided in the armaments field. The Federal Republic has renounced the right to manufacture atomic and certain other weapons. Major types of conventional weapons will be subject to control. An Agency for Control of Armaments is to be set up for the purpose of enforcing these arms limitations.

It has also been agreed that the occupation regime must be brought to an end and the Federal Republic will assume the full authority of a sovereign state in its external and internal affairs. This will be accomplished by the Protocol on the Termination of the Occupation Regime in the Federal Republic of Germany, which amends the conventions which were placed before the Senate in 1952 and brings them into effect as amended. The amendments are designed principally to bring the Bonn Conventions into harmony with the new arrangements for a German defense contribution and with German membership in the North Atlantic Treaty Organization. The greater part of the Conventions has been left unchanged. They will provide, as before, for the revocation of the Occupation Statute, the abolition of the Allied High Commission, and the settlement of numerous problems arising out of the war and the occupation. The convention regulating the status of Allied forces in Germany will continue until it is replaced by new arrangements based on the NATO Status of Forces Agreement, supplemented by such provisions as are necessary in view of the special conditions with regard to forces stationed in the Federal Republic. New arrangements will also eventually have to be concluded on the support of foreign forces in the Federal Republic. Of the special rights retained by the United States, the United Kingdom, and France in the original conventions, those relating to Berlin and to Germany as a whole will be kept on the same terms as before, and the right to station forces in Germany will, after German admission to NATO, be exercised with the consent of the Federal Government insofar as the Federal territory is concerned.

Of the four conventions which are to be amended by the protocol and placed in effect as amended, only one (the Convention on Relations between the Three Powers and the Federal Republic of Germany) was submitted to the Senate for its advice and consent to ratification. The other conventions were in the nature of implementing administrative agreements, for which the Senate recognized that formal approval was unnecessary and, furthermore, was undesirable, inasmuch as they might require technical revision from time to time to meet changing conditions. Approval of the Protocol on the Termination of the Occupation Regime in the Federal Republic of Germany will not change the nature of those related conventions.

While the arrangements embodied in these agreements are complex, their purposes are simple. The Federal Republic is placed on a basis of full equality with other states. The military strength of the Federal Republic will be combined with that of the other countries in the Atlantic community in such a way that the development and use of the German military contribution will be in accordance with the common need. The Federal Republic will be fully associated with the Atlantic community through membership in the North Atlantic Treaty Organization, and with the European community through membership in the Western European Union established under the Brussels Treaty. Both of these organizations will be strengthened internally. The procedures and institutions which are the subject of these agreements make it inevitable that the states involved will act closely together in the matters most important to their security. This concert of action will, I am convinced, foster the spirit of cooperation and desire for continuing association which have been evident in the free nations and which are essential for their future safety and welfare.

One of the principal specific consequences of the new arrangements will be the addition of a substantial increment of German resources to the Atlantic defense system. At the same time, I want to emphasize the fact that these agreements are founded upon the profound yearning for peace which is shared by all the Atlantic peoples. The agreements endanger no nation. On the contrary, they represent one of history's first great practical experiments in the international control of armaments. Moreover, their fundamental significance goes far beyond the combining of strength to deter aggression. Ultimately, we hope that they will produce a new understanding among the free peoples of Europe and a new spirit of friendship which will inspire greater cooperation in many fields of human activity.

I urge the Senate to signify its approval of this great endeavor by giving its advice and consent to ratification of the protocols on the admission of the Federal Republic to the North Atlantic Treaty Organization and on the termination of the occupation regime. I hope these instruments may be studied with a view to enabling the Senate to act promptly on these matters when it meets for its new session in January.

DWIGHT D. EISENHOWER

NOTE: The protocols and related papers are published in "London and Paris Agreements, September–October 1954" (Department of State Publication 5659, Government Printing Office, 1954). The protocols were approved by the Senate on April 1, 1955, and after ratification entered into force May 5, 1955 (6 UST 4117, 5707).

333 ¶ Remarks to the American Council To Improve Our Neighborhoods.
November 15, 1954

General Irving, ladies and gentlemen:

It is indeed a rare privilege to have this opportunity to come over here to welcome this particular group to the Capital City.

First, I must remark on seeing General Irving here in the position of presiding officer and understanding he is president of this organization. Old soldiers are, after all, supposed to fade away. We just seem to reappear.

It does give me the opportunity to congratulate you on securing such a president for this organization. After long experience and association with him in the Army, I wouldn't hesitate to write a rather large blank check as to the character of performance you will get from him.

Now, I can think of a dozen reasons why I am particularly delighted to see this organization meeting and starting to work on the purposes for which you have been organized. I like your title. As a matter of fact, I think you worked up the initials and then worked out a title to go with the initials. And it's the kind of thing, of course, that appeals to a soldier's heart: decide what to do, and then do it, and stop the talking about it.

I am particularly pleased, though, of course, by the fact that this group seems to represent, to me, much more definitively, and much more emphatically than do most, almost the philosophy of government by which I try to live: that Federal Government has certain functions, but that Federal Government, or any other government of the kind that we have and under which we live, can succeed only as the locality and as the individual citizen does his full part and seeks ways of organizing and combining together to do his part collectively and locally—else something is going to happen to us that we don't like.

So, with the million houses, I am told, becoming slums each year, to find the local people undertaking to do something about this to stop this kind of economic deterioration, is very wonderful.

But it seems to me to be even more wonderful when we understand what this means in stopping the erosion that takes place in the sense of dignity and decency, in the pride of the individual American, when we are trying to preserve for him a good home, and where we can't preserve it, then to get busy and build them so that he can have that great sense of high pride that goes with living as a good American in this great country.

I couldn't possibly find words in which I could describe to you the sense of admiration I feel for each of you in joining up with this group. But the gratitude I feel is because it means we are all jumping in to-gether—we in the Federal Government, and you as the local citizenry and groups—to do a job that must be done.

You know about the hearings and finally the bills that were passed at the last session of the Congress to help along in this way. But again and again we come back to the theory that the mainspring of all authority in this country is the people. So is the mainspring of all energy and real constructive thinking. It comes from this great mass we call America.

So, for your meeting, my very best wishes for an interesting and en-joyable time. And for the work you are going to do, my profound grati-tude and the assurance that I will follow it every step of the way, certain that you are doing a great job for the United States of America.

Thank you very much.

NOTE: The President spoke at a luncheon at the Mayflower Hotel in Washington at 12:30 p.m. His opening words "Gen- eral Irving" referred to Maj. Gen. F. A. Irving, USA (Retired), Chairman of the Council.

334   ¶ Remarks on Receiving the Frank H. Lahey Award From the National Fund for Medical Education.   *November* 16, 1954

THANK YOU very much. Quite naturally, I am very proud to receive an award from such an Association, from such a group. There is an added distinction because it bears the name of one of our greatest pro-fessionals and our greatest citizens.

On the other hand, Mr. Colt, I rarely felt quite so unworthy of re-ceiving an award because my part in the organization of this National Fund was really getting someone else to do the work. It would be far more fitting this morning if I were presenting this to you, because you have been President of that Association from the beginning.

But I can say this: I don't know of any group that is doing more necessary and worthwhile work than making certain that our medical schools have ample funds from private sources to keep running, because this is one profession we don't want to get under the dead hand of bureaucracy, I assure you.

Thank you again, Mr. Colt—and Mrs. Lahey, may I thank you for being with us.

NOTE: The President spoke in the Conference Room at the White House at 9:05 a.m. He referred to S. Sloan Colt, President of the National Fund for Medical Education. The award, a medal inscribed "For Outstanding Leadership in Medical Education" was established in 1954 under the joint sponsorship of the National Fund, the American Medical Association, and the Association of American Medical Colleges.

335   ¶ Remarks at Annual Meeting of the Association of Land-Grant Colleges and Universities.   *November* 16, 1954

President Hovde, former Presidents of this Association, and ladies and gentlemen:

Although I am exceedingly proud of the associations I was privileged to have with the educators of this country, I must confess that before such a body as this I still feel a bit of an interloper, particularly if I am to talk about matters affecting the education of our youth.

However, both as a military man, and since, I have been interested in the act that gave birth to the land-grant colleges of the United States. Of course, I am not going to trace the legislative history of that act. All of you know it better than I do. But there are two or three things I think that I can mention about that act which would lead me to the principal thought I should like to leave with you this morning.

First of all, that act had as one of its purposes the training of young men for service in the Armed Forces. I am one of those who can bear sincere witness to the efficacy of that training, and to the very great services you people and your predecessors have rendered to the United States of America on the field of battle.

And I think I would be remiss in my capacity as Commander in Chief, should I fail to pay my tribute to all of that great body of individuals who have graduated from the military sections of your colleges, and to those who dedicated their talents to helping in that education.

Now secondly, in 1862, we know that higher education was largely confined to the classical—the lawyer, the teacher, and the preacher who was educated. And it was expected that he should have a very large view of our country and our society, our history—world history—in order that he could help those more ignorant.

But the practical side of our education had been very largely neglected. In fact, West Point was the first engineering school established in this country, and for a long time provided the only engineers we had. And it is for that reason, I think, that to this day military engineers are in charge of all our rivers and harbors work, and so on.

But this act did bring a certain practical streak, both in the agricultural, mechanical, and industrial arts, into our education that was sadly needed and, up to then, lacking.

But you will remember that Mr. Morrill also said, as he was advocating the enactment of his bill, that one of the purposes was to bring education into the outlying portions of our country, to bring education closer to the people—higher education—and at a price they could afford. And moreover, he said, not only a practical education but a liberal education.

Now I have no particular admiration for my own definition of "liberal," but it doesn't agree with many of the definitions you sometimes read in the papers. But I conceive liberal to mean that type of education that lays the groundwork of understanding of our society, the kind of education that allows an individual to relate one fact to another, to get the whole in the proper perspective with relationship to the society in which we live, including the world society.

As distinguished from mere fact and knowledge, and technique and practice, it means, in my mind, understanding of knowledge rather than mere knowledge.

Now this leads me to the thought I should like to leave with you: there is no aspiration, there is no dream on the horizons of man's hopes and beliefs and faiths that is so strong, so vivid, as the dream of peace—lasting peace.

There are many things that must be understood, and many things that must be done, if we are to make progress toward the realization of that dream.

But there is one thing, I think, that educators cannot afford to forget, and that is this element of understanding as opposed to mere knowledge.

We know, let us say, that the people of a certain country are suspicious of our motives, when we know those motives to be good; or are so ignorant of what we are trying to do in the world that our efforts to help are translated into efforts to dominate.

Now, unless we make the effort—and I mean the effort right down at the grass-roots level of our country—to understand something of the culture of that people, of its history, its aspirations, the tribulations and trials through which that people may have passed—unless we understand that, we will never comprehend why our motives are misunderstood.

In like fashion, unless those people can gain some understanding of us—of our great amalgamation of races and colors and religions and nationalities—unless they can understand how we feel, what are our loftiest aspirations, then how can we expect them to believe that someone is truly altruistic in his purposes—or let us put it more specifically, can any nation be altruistic?

You will recall the famous article of only a few years ago, which said the greatest mistake that America makes is to assume there is morality in international relationships. But how are we going to have long-term peace without morality? So by all means let us make the pragmatic approach, meeting the temporary and short-term problem: let us be strong, but don't let us be strong only in tanks, guns, and planes and ships. There is no lasting peace there. The most they can do is to protect you in what you have for the moment.

But we want to progress. We want to lighten the burden of carrying things, to use our substance and our man-hours, and our sweat and our toil and our brains, to raising the standards of a people, its spiritual standards, its intellectual standards, and its capacity for happiness, that is what we really mean; and in doing so, raise the standards of the world in these same regards. Only as we can do that, can we look toward permanent peace.

You can achieve great progress, of course, by successful conferences addressed to particular things, as long as you are strong, know what you want, and don't deviate from what you know to be the right.   But over the long-term, when we think of our children and our grandchildren, I think it is enough to say that peace is not primarily in the hands of elected political leaders, it is in the hands of the family, the home, the church, and the school.

And if the purpose of the Morrill Act was to bring higher education and understanding closer to the people, then I should say that this group has not only a wonderful challenge in front of it, but it possibly has the broadest opportunity now open to any comparable group in the United States of America.

I hope I have not sounded either visionary or pontifical.   I have told you only what I believe.

Thank you very much.

NOTE: The President spoke at the Statler Hotel in Washington at 10:15 a.m.   His opening words "President Hovde" re-ferred to Frederick L. Hovde, President of the Association and President of Purdue University.

336   ¶ Statement by the President: Safe Driving Day.   *November* 16, 1954

My fellow citizens:

December fifteenth this year will be Safe Driving Day—a day proclaimed throughout America by your governors, mayors and county officials in cooperation with the President's Action Committee for Traffic Safety.   This Committee is a volunteer group of citizens working, at my request, to reduce fatalities and accidents on our nation's streets and highways.

All of us agree with the purpose of Safe Driving Day.   It is to save lives and to prevent injuries.   No endeavor could be more worthy of our universal cooperation.   None is more urgent.

On this December fifteenth I hope that every American will help make it a day without a single traffic accident throughout our entire country.

How can we best do this?   Three things are essential.

First, let's each of us make sure that we obey traffic regulations.

Second, let's follow common sense rules of good sportsmanship and courtesy.

Third, let's each one of us resolve that, either as drivers or as pedestrians, we will stay alert and careful, mindful of the constant possibility of accidents caused by negligence.

If every one of us will do these three things, Safe Driving Day can be a day without a traffic accident in all of America.

Last year, when I called a national conference on highway safety, Americans were being killed in traffic accidents at the rate of 38,000 a year. A million more were being injured.

This year, although we are driving more cars more miles than ever before, the number of deaths and injuries from accidents is smaller. Clearly we have found that it is not necessary to have more and more deaths and injuries.

I believe we can do even better—and that we must do better. Each of us must help.

Won't you do your part on December fifteenth to help stop death and injury on the highways and roads of America? Let's make Safe Driving Day an overwhelming success, and our nation's standard for the future.

337 ¶ White House Statement Following Bipartisan Conference on Foreign Affairs and National Security. *November* 17, 1954

AT THE INVITATION of the President, legislative leaders of both parties and the Chairmen and ranking members of three Committees of both Houses of the Congress met this morning in the Cabinet Room at the White House.

The President opened the meeting by saying it was essential to have a continuing bi-partisan approach to foreign affairs and national security matters that would represent the best interests of our nation, regardless of which political party controlled the Congress.

The Secretary of State, as he has done many times in the past, presented a complete review of the international situation—this time bringing the legislative members up to date on foreign developments since the adjournment of the Congress last August. He discussed the participation by the United States in the Manila, London and Paris Conferences, the Trieste and Saar settlements, and the President's proposal to the United

Nations for an "atoms for peace" pool. Against this background, the Secretary outlined the policies which would guide the future conduct of our international relations.

In this connection, the President and the Secretary urged the legislative leaders to give early consideration at the next regular session of the Congress to ratification of the Manila Pact and those sections of the Paris Agreements which would grant sovereignty to the Federal Republic of Germany and admit that nation to membership in the North Atlantic Treaty Organization. Such action by the Congress would greatly strengthen the defenses of the free world against Communist aggression.

Together with the Secretaries of State and Defense, the President discussed with the leaders the security and defense plans of our Country and the steps we have taken and propose to take to strengthen the armed forces of our friends and allies throughout the world.

A general discussion and exchange of views were held thereafter on these subjects.

338 ¶ Remarks to Executive Committee of the United States Junior Chamber of Commerce and Directors of the Canadian Chamber of Commerce. *November* 19, 1954

I HOPE the acceptance of this makes me a public supporter of your Creed.

It is good to see all of you here, and I am particularly happy to know that this is a combined meeting of Canadian and American businessmen, senior and junior.

It is a great advance, I think, when civilians not only of any one country but of more than one country meet to make certain that their respective countries are going—industrially, economically, politically—in the direction that they believe to be correct.

If your meetings are conducted in the spirit of this code that we just heard read, I certainly have no fear for the future of the North American Continent.

Thank you very much.

NOTE: The President spoke in the Cabinet Room at 9:15 a.m., following the presentation to him of a plaque inscribed with the Creed of the U.S. Junior Chamber of Commerce.

339 ¶ Statement by the President on the Death of Governor William S. Beardsley of Iowa.
November 22, 1954

I WAS SHOCKED to hear of the tragic accident which took the life of Governor William S. Beardsley of the State of Iowa. The people of Iowa have lost a devoted public servant whom they elected three times as Chief Executive of their State. Mrs. Eisenhower and I extend to Mrs. Beardsley our deep sympathy in the great personal loss she has sustained.

340 ¶ Message to the Conference of Ministers of Finance and Economy Meeting in Rio de Janeiro.
November 22, 1954

I AM VERY PLEASED to send greetings and best wishes to the Meeting of Ministers of Finance and Economy of the American family of nations, convened in Rio de Janeiro, the capital of our great sister nation, Brazil. I am happy to send this message through our Secretary of the Treasury, Mr. George M. Humphrey who, as Chairman of the United States Delegation, speaks for our nation and will authoritatively present our policies.

I am confident that this Conference will advance still further the unique relationships which have developed among the peoples and nations of this Hemisphere. As those relationships evolved and grew, the people of the United States learned to call their own attitude toward their sister nations the policy of the Good Neighbor. Today, the bonds which unite us as sovereign equals who are working side by side for the betterment of all of us—nations and citizens—have elevated this neighborly relationship to one of genuine partnership.

No longer is it sufficient to maintain the mutual respect and cordiality of neighbors, useful and pleasant as that is. In the world of today, the well-being and the economic development—as well as the security—of all peace-loving nations are so closely interrelated that we must be partners. If this is true in the larger context, it is especially true among the American Republics where we share the same traditions and many of the same favorable circumstances for progress.

As the Conference discusses a wide variety of measures for economic and financial cooperation in this Hemisphere, and endorses those that are sound and durable, I earnestly hope that the meeting as a whole may join with the Delegation of the United States in common dedication to the Policy of the Good Partner.

To this may I add my best wishes for the success of the Conference and warm personal greetings to each of its members.

NOTE: The message was read by Secretary Humphrey at the plenary session on No-   vember 23, 1954, as part of his address.

341 ¶ The President's News Conference of *November 23, 1954.*

THE PRESIDENT. I have no announcements, ladies and gentlemen, so we will go right to questions.

Q. John L. Cutter, United Press: Mr. President, Senator Knowland has expressed fears that Russia promotes a policy of peaceful coexistence as a sort of a Trojan horse to lull the free world into a false sense of security which would lead to disaster. Do you feel there are any grounds for such fears?

THE PRESIDENT. I have always urged that we must be alert and vigilant and strong.

This word, the adjective, you put in front of "coexistence," of course, gives it a special meaning. Coexistence, after all, of which we hear so much, has relatively a simple meaning. You either live with someone in this world or you are fighting him and trying to kill him; and as long as you are not trying to destroy, you are coexisting.

Now, when you say "peaceful," "peaceful" is an adjective that has many connotations. If we two individuals are standing here calling each other names, it may be called peaceful, but in the general sense, we think of peaceful as rather friendly. So, if we are talking these terms of "peaceful" and "friendly" in the sense of attempting to lull us into complacency, well, then, of course it is something to watch very closely.

Under our Constitution, I and, as my chief assistant, the Secretary of State are charged with this whole field of which you are talking—foreign relations. I assure you there is no tendency on our part to take anything for granted in this whole field.

Q. David P. Sentner, Hearst Newspapers: As a postscript, Mr. President, would you care to comment on the proposed four-power meeting in Paris?

THE PRESIDENT. Well, there have been proposed, you know, from time to time these four-power meetings. We have stated—well, first of all, there will be quite an explanation made of this whole thing on Monday night. The Secretary of State is making a foreign policy speech in Chicago, and there will be quite an explanation, but I will just advert to it briefly.

First of all, until these accords are signed [ratified] to the Paris agreements, why, we are not going to agree to such a conference; secondly, there should be some evidence or, let us say, a promise of real fruitfulness in going through such a conference; and, thirdly, of course, there must be time for its preparation.

To go to these conferences merely for, you might say, a new or almost *ad hoc* opportunity to promote additional propaganda is without any virtue. So there would have to be some time for the preparation of the conference before we could go into it.

But I repeat, as I have repeated every time I have had a chance since I came on this job, whenever we have any reason to believe that anyone wants to talk earnestly or sincerely about peace, we will talk to them.

Q. Chalmers M. Roberts, Washington Post and Times Herald: Mr. President, you used the phrase "a promise of fruitfulness," I believe. Does that represent a change from what I understood was the previous position of deeds, not words?

THE PRESIDENT. Not at all, not at all. We want some kind of evidence. While I can't in advance say exactly what it will be, you will remember in the April 16 speech in 1953 I suggested that a very definite agreement as to the Austrian treaty would be taken as a deed that would indicate real sincerity on the part of the Communist world to go into further negotiations. Now, that doesn't mean that all the provisions of the treaty have to be executed instantly, but the mere fact they say, "All right, on such-and-such a date we will agree to it."

Q. Mr. Roberts: Could I ask a second question, sir?

THE PRESIDENT. Yes.

Q. Mr. Roberts: In relation to this Big Four meeting suggestion the French Premier made at the U.N., do you have any personal feeling that such a meeting should be on the foreign ministers level or on the heads of state level?

THE PRESIDENT. I don't know exactly what the proposal would be at that particular time, but I can't conceive of an initial meeting of the heads of state being a fruitful thing. I would think that the foreign ministers would have to meet and work out a lot of details and programs, and then if there was any worthwhile agreement it would be possible that the heads of state should meet for signing. I don't know, I can't guess really as to what would be the circumstances. I merely say there is going to be no standing on protocol or anything else if we can make a real step toward advancing the peace of the world.

Q. Chester M. Potter, Pittsburgh Press: Mr. President, last week Senator Duff and Representative Bonin reported to you their reasons for the defeat of the Republicans in Pennsylvania, and gave you their ideas for rejuvenating the party. Would you comment upon that, sir?

THE PRESIDENT. No, but I will tell you what I would do: I would have no objection to their telling you exactly what they told me. As long as there is firsthand evidence available, I would be really out of line to try to remember the details of what they said to me, because they mentioned personalities as well as ideas. So I would rather they tell you their story.

Q. Robert E. Clark, International News Service: Mr. President, the decision by the Democratic leadership to put over until the new Congress any nominations on which there is any controversy is holding up several of your appointments, including that of Judge Harlan to the Supreme Court; this, in turn, is holding up the Supreme Court's action on school segregation. Do you have any objections to this?

THE PRESIDENT. This is the way I feel, Mr. Clark: the business of Government must go on. Now, where there is legitimate reason for controversy, I can understand they can't use up the short time in committee work, of this session, to handle these controversial ones; but where the controversy is not deep or real, I believe it would serve the best interests of the Government to get that type of appointment confirmed just as fast as possible. It is a serious matter to keep these offices from being filled by able and capable men, and I do assure you that we spend a lot of time looking for them.

Q. Nat S. Finney, Buffalo Evening News: Mr. President, in another connection, apparently two of your appointments to the Atomic Energy Commission have been held up. Can you give us any comment on those nominations?

THE PRESIDENT. No, I think they will have to just work that out in the Senate. I don't know exactly what the reasons are lying behind it, but they will just have to work it out down there.

Q. Francis M. Stephenson, New York Daily News: I was wondering, Mr. President, if you plan to confer with Republican leaders in Congress again this year before the session?

THE PRESIDENT. When are they coming back, on the 29th? Well, I have no doubt that I would see them again, although the House leaders will probably not be here. But it has been such a periodic thing in the past, I think it would be almost routine to see them sometime along the line.

Q. William H. Lawrence, New York Times: Mr. President, I think that Mr. Stephenson may have meant—and I know what I had in mind was—that last December when you were preparing your State of the Union Message you had in the committee chairmen, you had in a whole raft of people, quite apart from the technical leaders.

THE PRESIDENT. Yes, I remember.

Q. Mr. Lawrence: And I think—I know I was wondering whether you had any such meeting in mind for this year.

THE PRESIDENT. Well, there will be some of it all right, although possibly not on quite as formidable a basis as last year, Mr. Lawrence. You must remember, then the program was a new thing, and the program now is really a means of rounding out what we didn't get done before. We will have to have certain people in, unquestionably, but I don't think it will be done on quite as formal and exhaustive a basis.

Remember we met from December 17th to 19th, inclusive, wasn't it——

Mr. Hagerty: Yes, sir.

THE PRESIDENT. ——3 days of meetings just on ironing out details. I think there will be nothing that formidable this time.

Q. Mr. Lawrence: If I may follow up that question, sir, even if you do have a less formidable session, would you, perhaps, bring in the prospective Democratic chairman?

THE PRESIDENT. Well, I think in the conferences with them, as I explained to you before, on all foreign affairs and security things, we will seek opportunities to make certain we are in agreement in advance, we are advancing on the same line. When it comes to other things, I think that each case will probably have to be decided on its merits, what you do at a particular moment.

Q. Sarah McClendon, El Paso Times: Mr. President, following a visit to you recently of about 20 Senators who asked for more spending on public works and irrigation, some of them were a little—well, they differed as to what was said about your policy on permitting new projects to get started in the next fiscal year. Will you tell us what you told them?

THE PRESIDENT. Really what I did, I went back to a statement that I had already given to the Congress, I mean in its intent and meaning, as to the need for a great water survey of this country.

I repeat, water is rapidly becoming the most valuable natural resource of the United States, and it must be dealt with in a very comprehensive and broad way. I believe thoroughly we must have these projects integrated into a big broad program.

Now, as to new starts, as long as we have got projects that fit into a survey like that partially completed, we are sure they are not just off, individual, by themselves in a river basin, why then, of course, we want to start them.

Remember this: in the early years of starting those things, there is not very much money involved. You go through exploration, surveys, planning, borings, and all that sort of thing. That really takes 5 or 6 years before you really start to spend money, so we must get started if we are going to do anything about it at all. Surely I am for some starts.

Q. Marvin L. Arrowsmith, Associated Press: Mr. President, to go back to Mr. Cutter's opening question on Senator Knowland's views, what do you think of the propriety of the Senate majority leader questioning publicly the administration's foreign policy?

THE PRESIDENT [*laughing*]. You seem to have thought most of the morning to work that one out. [*Laughter*]

I would only say this: I think I would repeat what I said before, that I am charged by the Constitution with the conduct of foreign affairs. I have the Secretary of State as my chief assistant, and when anything is in the nature of a binding agreement of the United States, partakes of a treaty, it must have the concurrence of two-thirds of the Senate.

Now, in doing all this, I strive my best to get legislative consultation and approval in advance. So I would explain to you my side, and let anybody else explain their own particular position.

Q. Robert G. Spivack, New York Post: Mr. President, in the aftermath of the John Paton Davies case, there were some suggestions in some quarters that, perhaps, the Government security program needed an overhauling. I wonder if, after watching it now for 2 years, you feel the security program has worked satisfactorily or does need some revisions?

THE PRESIDENT. I, of course, can't answer that in complete detail.

I would say this: I think scarcely a week goes by that some phase of that security program isn't brought up to me and made the subject of a very earnest and prayerful conference of some kind.

I have only recently been engaged in the business of studying its whole aspect and the details of the thing. I am not certain in my own mind exactly what kind of a move I will make to help me get a new examination of the program, but I will say this: it never stops; the revision, at least so far as my own mind is concerned, goes on constantly. The second that I find something that I believe to be really wrong with it, I won't hesitate to change it.

I assure you there is no authorial pride that stands in the way of revision the second I believe it necessary.

Now, as far as the Davies case is concerned, I only know one thing: that is that John Foster Dulles spent many prayerful days reviewing a record that was formidable in its size, going through it and reaching a decision as a very earnest public servant, and not merely as someone who has had a preconception of it.

Q. Harry C. Dent, Columbia (S.C.) State and Record: Mr. President, all interested States and groups have now filed their briefs with the Supreme Court as to when and how they would like segregation ended in the public schools, and some have said they want no delay, and others have said they want much delay. And I just wondered if you have your own personal views on that you could give us.

THE PRESIDENT. Not particularly. I will tell you: as you know, the Attorney General is required to file his brief; and I guess because he went to South America, I think he has 2 or 3 days' delay. But the Supreme Court has ruled what is the law in this case, what the Constitution means.

I am sure America wants to obey the Constitution, but there is a very great practical problem involved, and there are certainly deep-seated emotions. What I understand the Supreme Court has and has undertaken as its task, is to write its orders of procedure in such fashion as to take into consideration these great emotional strains and the practical problems, and try to devise a way where under some form of decentralized process we can bring this about. I don't believe they intend to be arbitrary, at least that is my understanding.

Q. Martin S. Hayden, Detroit News: Mr. President, in connection with the Senate debate on peaceful coexistence, the very start of it raises the suspicion in a lot of people's minds that something has happened that may change our attitude toward Russia. Do you know of anything that indicates the Russians want any different kind of coexistence than we have had?

THE PRESIDENT. I didn't get your name.

Q. Mr. Hayden: Hayden, Detroit News.

THE PRESIDENT. No, I know of nothing. Of course, as you know, the Russians have lately been talking a different tone than they have for some time past, but every study that I have ever seen about communism, going back to the very earliest analyses, says there is one underlying, unchanging motive—world revolution and the dominance of a Communist centrally controlled state. That remains the same.

Methods and tactics—if you read some of their books, their processes and tactics of retreat and advance and every kind of thing that is useful in bringing this about, they assert to be good for the world. So I think that any thought of losing sight of the basic objective would be the greatest error we could make.

Q. Lawrence Fernsworth, Christian Century: Mr. President, by request for the Christian Century:

The World Council of Churches at Evanston, recently set forth certain objectives in the international order. The Christian Century asked me to call your attention to several of them briefly:

1. "That Christians can never accept as the only kind of existence open to them a state of perpetual tension leading to inevitable war.

"It is resolved: We appeal to the statesmen and the leaders of public opinion to refrain from words and actions that are designed to inflame enmity and hatred."

2. —And I will go very briefly—"Reconciliation in a Christian spirit with potential enemy countries and a conviction that it is possible for nations and people to live together in a divided world." The Council avoided the use of the moot term "coexistence."

3. "An end to a suicidal competition in arms and to a situation which is unfit to be described as peace."

It asks—I am quoting all along, Mr. President—"Universal enforceable disarmament through the United Nations."

4. "Elimination and prohibition of atom and hydrogen bombs and other weapons of mass destruction, and the insistence that nations carry on tests only within their respective territories or, if elsewhere, only by international clearance and agreement."

The Christian Century feels that the Christian world is anxious to know the President's views on these questions.

THE PRESIDENT. Well, I wouldn't undertake to answer in detail all of the matters that are brought up either directly or by implication in those questions.

I think most of you have listened to college commencement addresses, and nearly always there is a sentence that, either directly or by implication, states: "Keep your head in the clouds and your feet on the ground."

I know of no better advice in this day and time.

Of course, we understand that in one of its deepest aspects this is a struggle between a civilization that is firmly based in a religious faith, and atheism or materialism; that is inescapable. You will recall—I think I have said to you so often before—I am always struck with the fact that our own ancestors, attempting to explain the new form of government they were setting up, wrote in the Declaration of Independence in its opening paragraph, ". . . men are endowed by their Creator"— meaning the only way they could explain free government is that men are endowed by some supernatural force with certain rights; they didn't try to claim those rights as the result of any other circumstance of life.

So, it is a civilization based upon some kind of religious belief and conviction and faith. If that is so, then, of course, all of these ideals for which this Christian paper, Christian Century, is struggling, are something that must animate us. We must think about them, we must live with them; but we must not forget also that man isn't made up entirely of noble qualities and the ennobling virtues that send him doing his duty for his fellow man. He is also made up of a lot of selfish and greedy and ignoble qualifications and qualities; and that we have got to prepare for, because we are of a dual nature. And if anybody thinks that the United States can be in better position in the pursuit of peace by being weak, I must say I disagree with him 100 percent.

We must be strong, and we are going to be strong. When we are secure and safe, they will find nobody more anxious than everybody I know in the United States—not only its Government, I am not trying to speak for any particular clique—to meet anybody half way in good will and with the hope and purpose of devoting the sweat and toil of peaceful folk to their own advancement and not to their own destruction.

I just can't say this thing too emphatically. But let us not try again to find peace in the world by ourselves disarming and being weak and unready; I just can't go with that.

Q. James T. Rogers, Gannett Newspapers: Mr. President, the debating teams at West Point and Annapolis are being kept out of debate on the question of recognizing Red China. I wonder whether you feel that that coincides with your views of intellectual freedom that you expressed at your last meeting with us?

THE PRESIDENT. I must say that there are Superintendents at these two academies that I admire and respect, and I have no doubt that their reasons for whatever instructions they gave were very sincere, and that they thought it was the right thing to do.

Of course, no member of the armed services questions and attacks in public a policy that has been adopted officially by his Commander-in-Chief. But I look upon these cadets, although they are technically of the armed services, they are students. They have very splendid instructional courses, both in the scientific side and in the liberal arts; and I really believe that I would trust the judgment of the cadets. If they wanted to argue this point, I would allow them to do it just as strongly as they wanted to.

I personally think you might find a difficult time to get some of them to argue certain points—since I was a cadet myself once, I think I know something of their feelings—but I would never stand in the way of taking any question that troubles the world, no matter what our Government's position on it, and let cadets debate it to their hearts' content. I think it would be all right.

But, as I say, I don't know the details, how this thing came up in the first place. Actually, it hasn't been reported to me officially. I know only about what I have heard, and that is my attitude.

Q. Donald Irwin, New York Herald Tribune: Mr. President, have you received any reports from General Collins on Indochina as yet, and have you any comment on the situation there?

THE PRESIDENT. I have seen only preliminary reports, and I am sure they were on a very secret basis as they were submitted up to this point; so I couldn't comment on it.

Q. Kenneth M. Scheibel, Gannett Newspapers: Mr. Rayburn said the other day that one of the first things he wanted the House to do was to set aside your farm law and put it back on the old standard. Do you expect next year to have to fight this thing all over again?

THE PRESIDENT. I simply would say that if my sampling of farmer opinion during the summer was accurate at all, it was that the farmers don't agree with him. That is all I would say.

Q. John L. Cutter, United Press: Mr. President, there has been some recent interest in the subject of dependents of our military men joining them overseas, sometimes in potential trouble spots around the world; and I wondered if you, as an old soldier, shall we say, believe—[*laughter*]

THE PRESIDENT. Make no mistake, I am proud of the title. [*Laughter*]

Q. Mr. Cutter: It is the "old" I was questioning—[*laughter*]—believe that there is a military asset in having the wives and children of the servicemen with them overseas; and in the event of a sudden enemy attack, what would their presence mean?

THE PRESIDENT. Of course, to take your last part first, if there is a sudden enemy attack, their presence would cause very acute problems.

But let us not forget this: we are in a cold war; we want to present our best foot, let us say; we want people of high morale; we want to look confident.

If every place we sent our soldiers today in the world we broke our old custom of letting dependents go along, it would look like we were frightened to death and expecting an attack momentarily.

Some of you here probably may have been in Europe in January 1951, when I went over there; and you will recall, possibly, also that my wife went with me. The tension was so great at that moment—and you may have forgotten—the tension was so great that a few, 2 or 3, months later the head of one of the principal travel agencies of the United States came to me and said that the mere fact that my wife went over there with me, took a season where there was going to be practically no travel at all and made it one of the finest travel seasons of their whole career.

In other words, the showing of confidence on the part of leaders and people of a nation—as long as it is not truculent, if you are not being, you might say, bombastic and truculent and ill-mannered—I think that such things as that really encourage confidence.

Now, by the same token, there are areas where there are no fit quarters, and you can't send dependents. I think it is unfortunate; committed now to an indefinite period where we have to have some 3 million Americans in the services, I think it is too bad if we have to keep them separated from their families too long.

Q. Mrs. May Craig, Maine Papers: Mr. President, if I might go back to the questions about the Senate majority leader, is it not true that he was elected to that position by his Republican colleagues, that he is their agent and not the agent of the Executive or of the Republican Party, and that only they can rebuke and replace him?

THE PRESIDENT. I think that is true.

John L. Cutter, United Press: Thank you, Mr. President.

NOTE: President Eisenhower's fifty-third news conference was held in the Executive Office Building from 10:31 to 10:59 o'clock on Tuesday morning, November 23, 1954. In attendance: 154.

342 ¶ Message to the Relatives of Americans Held Prisoner by the Chinese Communists. *November 25, 1954*

Mrs. Mary I. Arnold
8 National Street
Montgomery, Alabama

I am truly distressed to learn that your husband is one of those Americans who are now prisoners of the Chinese Communists.

I assure you that I am keenly aware of the deep distress you are suffering. It is my hope that you and John's family secure some consolation in the thought that he was serving his country when taken prisoner and that this Nation is grateful for that service.

It is tragic that the feeling of thankfulness you must have in hearing at last that he is alive must now be joined with the heartache of concern for his wellbeing.

You may be very sure that your government is using every feasible means to bring your husband and all other Americans now in Communist hands, to freedom and to secure their proper treatment so long as their confinement continues. These efforts will be carried forward resolutely and tirelessly.

With assurance of my profound sympathy.

DWIGHT D. EISENHOWER

NOTE: Identical messages were sent on Thanksgiving Day to the relatives of other Americans held prisoner by the Chinese Communists. The message was released at Augusta, Ga.

343 ¶ Letter to Heads of Departments Constituting the Interdepartmental Committee on Narcotics.   *November 27, 1954*

Dear ——————:

It is gratifying to know that your representatives have been meeting with representatives of the other Departments concerned with the problem and with my Special Counsel as an informal committee to review and coordinate the Federal Government's programs to combat narcotic addiction in this country.

In order to define more clearly the scope of the problems which we face and to promote effective cooperation among Federal, State and local agencies, a comprehensive up-to-date survey on the extent of narcotic addiction is urgently needed and should be made by the Committee. A determination of what the States and local agencies have accomplished and what they are equipped to do in the field of law enforcement and in the rehabilitation of the victims of the scourge should also be included in the survey. In this, I know, the Committee will have the enthusiastic cooperation of State and local authorities.

Receipt of the Committee's report on both subjects as promptly as possible will expedite systematic review and improvement of our narcotics programs—local, national and international. I know that devoted and strenuous attention is being given to the problem on a number of fronts; but we should omit no practical step to minimize and stamp out narcotic addiction.

Sincerely,

DWIGHT D. EISENHOWER

NOTE: Identical letters were sent to the Secretary of State, the Secretary of the Treasury, the Secretary of Defense, the Attorney General, and the Secretary of Health, Education, and Welfare. The Committee's report was transmitted to the President on February 1, 1956. (See Public Papers of the Presidents, 1956, p. 226.)

344 ¶ Message to Sir Winston Churchill on the Occasion of His 80th Birthday.
November 29, 1954

The Right Honorable Sir Winston Churchill
K.G., O.M., C.H., M.P.
The Prime Minister
London, England

Dear Winston:

I know I speak for my fellow countrymen as I enthusiastically do for myself, in sending you warmest congratulations on reaching a new landmark in a life that is in itself a series of great landmarks.

We Americans have known you and of you over the years—as roving war reporter, as adventurous soldier, as administrator and parliamentarian and, increasingly with each passing year, as statesman and defender of freedom.

We have seen the great Anglo-American partnership grow and flourish with you as one of the staunch advocates. In the dark times of war, and the anxious ones of uncertain peace, this partnership has sustained us all and given us strength.

Now, as you reach four score, we Americans salute you as world statesman, as unconquerable warrior in the cause of freedom, as our proven friend of many valiant years.

With warm personal regard,

As ever,

DWIGHT D. EISENHOWER

345 ¶ The President's News Conference of
December 2, 1954.

THE PRESIDENT. Ladies and gentlemen, two or three points that I should like to mention before we start the question period:

Just a few minutes ago I was informed that the Vatican announced that the Pope is seriously ill. I have met him personally and not only liked him as a person, but have always admired his strong stand for peace, for liberty and freedom in the world, and his stand against communism. So I think that all of us would like to join and really and fervently hope that he will soon recover.

The Rio conference ends today, and while its beginnings were attended by some apparent misunderstandings, the results, in my opinion, will be very much to the good. It will further the good partnership policy which we have maintained with the American nations, and will make it easier for us to cooperate with them to our mutual advantage in the future.

We owe a very great deal to our Secretary of the Treasury, who is head of our delegation, and after he left, the same to the Under Secretary, Herbert Hoover, Jr.

This afternoon, the Secretary of State and Foreign Minister George Yeh will sign the treaty on behalf of America and the Republic of China concerning our mutual defense treaty.

I want to talk for just a moment, with your indulgence, about 13 American prisoners. And you cannot possibly talk about them in any isolated sense.

At the risk of boring you with some repetition, I repeat: the world is in an ideological struggle, and we are on one side and the Iron Curtain countries are on the other.

This struggle we now are in, we call the cold war. The great hope of mankind is that we can find methods and means of progressing a little bit, even if by little steps, toward a true or real peace, and that we do not go progressively toward war.

Now, on our side we must make certain that our efforts to promote peace are not interpreted as appeasement or any purchase of immediate favor at the cost of principle; but we must, on the other hand, be steady and refuse to be goaded into actions that would be unwise.

To fit this incident into the global picture, let me remind you these prisoners have been held by the Chinese for 2 years, so their selection of a time of announcement was, of course, a deliberate act. In fact, we find little evidence in all of the actions of the Communist States that indicates any haphazard actions on their part. Everything they do is deliberate and well thought out. I do not mean to say that everything in Russia is completely coordinated with everything that is happening in China.

I do say that when one of these governments permits anything to happen or makes any announcement, it does it deliberately and with a deliberate purpose.

Now, if this is a deliberate attempt out there, as it appears to be, to goad us into some impulsive action in the hope of dividing us from our allies, breaking down and destroying all the work that has been going on over the past years to build up a true coalition of free governments, then it certainly makes a mockery of the softer tone that has been used in Russia towards Western Europe at times lately, even approaching the tone of blandishment.

We must not forget what the aims of communism have always been, announced by themselves: to divide the free world, to divide us among ourselves as the strongest nation of the free world, and by dividing to confuse and eventually to conquer, to attain through those means their announced aim of world domination.

For us there are two courses, and here I should like, in a way, to talk a little bit personally: in many ways the easy course for a President, for the administration, is to adopt a truculent, publicly bold, almost insulting attitude. A President experiences exactly the same resentments, the same anger, the same kind of sense of frustration almost, when things like this occur to other Americans, and his impulse is to lash out.

Now, I want to make quite clear that when one accepts the responsibilities of public office, he can no longer give expression freely to such things; he has got to think of the results.

That would be the easy way for this reason: those actions lead toward war. Now, let us think of war for a second. When this Nation goes to war, there occurs automatically a unification of our people. Traditionally, if we get into trouble that involves war, the Nation closes ranks behind the leader. The job to do becomes simply understood—it is to win the war. There is a real fervor developed throughout the Nation that you can feel everywhere you go. There is practically an exhilaration about the affair.

The great Lee said, "It is well that war is so horrible; if it were not so, we would grow too fond of it," because in the intellectual and spiritual contest of matching wits and getting along to see if you can win, there comes about something, an atmosphere is created, and an attitude is created to which I am not totally unfamiliar.

But, ladies and gentlemen, I have also had the job of writing letters of condolence by the hundreds, by the thousands, to bereaved mothers and to bereaved wives and others who have lost dear ones on the battlefield. That is a very sobering experience. It means that if we are going ever to take such a fateful decision as leads us one step toward war, let us, by no means, do it in response to our human emotions of anger and resentment; but let us do it after we have prayerfully considered it and found, as Wilson expressed it, "no other means of protecting our rights."

Let us recognize that we owe it to ourselves and to the world to explore every possible peaceable means of settling differences before we even think of such a thing as war.

The hard way is to have the courage to be patient, tirelessly to seek out every single avenue open to us in the hope even finally of leading the other side to a little better understanding of the honesty of our intentions. There is no question; they honestly, in certain instances, do question our intentions. They do not believe always, or at least universally, that we are peaceably inclined. We have got a job yet of our own to do—as well as to demand action from others—the courage and the patience to keep after this kind of thing.

Now, I just want to say one word about the idea of blockade. It is possible that a blockade is conceivable without war; I have never read of it historically.

A blockade is an act in war intended to bring your adversary to your way of thinking or to his knees. In fact, in the rules of war that were studied in my former life, were clearly established the conditions that must prevail before you could legally proclaim a blockade. You couldn't, even if you were a belligerent, merely say, "We blockade Antarctica," or any other country. You had to make the blockade effective, and you were not justified in stopping anyone's ship unless you had the means present at the spot to make that blockade effective, indicating that the word "blockade," is, so far as I know, an act of war, a part of war. I have not checked this idea with the constitutional lawyers, but I believe it to be true.

So far as I am concerned, if ever we come to a place that I feel that a step of war is necessary, it is going to be brought about not by any impulsive individualistic act of my own, but I am going before the Congress in the constitutional method set up in this country, and lay the problem before them with my recommendation as to whatever it may be.

In the meantime, I have got one thought that I must express: at least 11 of these soldiers, by the Communists own propaganda and testimony made public, were in uniform. They were soldiers captured in the Korean war. Consequently, they were to be treated as prisoners of war under the terms of the armistice.

Moreover, those men were there in conformity with obligations incurred under the United Nations, and were there, in fact, in accordance with the specific request and resolution of the United Nations.

How the United Nations can possibly disabuse itself of a feeling of responsibility in this matter and retain its self-respect, I wouldn't know; and so, I think that the United States does not stand alone. Merely indicating that we are yet far from exhausting all of our resources, I mention only one of those that is available to us.

So far as the honor of the United States is concerned, I merely hope that I shall not live long enough to find myself accused of being insensible to the honor of the United States and the safety of her men and soldiers, no matter where we send them.

Now, I am sorry I have taken up so much of your time with my talk. We will go to questions.

Q. Marvin Arrowsmith, Associated Press: Mr. President, do you care to comment on the way the Senate vote is going thus far on the censure of Senator McCarthy issue?

THE PRESIDENT. No, I have no comment on that. This is a matter of the Senate, as I understand it, determining what is required in the preservation of the dignity of the Senate; and no one else is in it.

Q. Charles S. von Fremd, CBS News: There has been some speculation, sir, recently because of some of the actions on Capitol Hill that, before the Republican Convention in 1956, there might be a split within the Republican Party, with the so-called conservative members being unhappy about being hard on Communist infiltration, and the carrying out of the foreign policy. If such reports ever were given to you, sir, by people that you listen to, would it affect in any way your own strong drive towards a sound middle-of-the-road policy?

THE PRESIDENT. I see no connection between trying to be tough on communism and still being progressive.

Now, if anyone thinks I have got any love in my heart for the concept of communism—normally, I have been accused here of being too tough in my search and efforts to get out anybody that might be guilty of subversion or otherwise in our Government—I must say that on that point I hope again I don't have to defend myself.

I believe that a political party, to be a useful agency in this country for the promotion of the happiness of our people, must be a progressive, dynamic force; it must have a doctrine, a program, legislative and otherwise, that is moderate in its approach, avoiding extremes of right and left.

As I have told you before, I think it must be liberal when it is talking about the relationship between the Government and the individual; conservative when talking about the national economy and the individual's pocketbook.

That is my rough conception of progressivism, and I believe the Republican Party must be that or it won't be any force long in American life. I just don't believe that Americans, 163 [million] intelligent Americans, are going to be satisfied either with the action or with such a distinct trend toward centralization and paternalism in our Government that it becomes difficult to detect it from a socialistic form. So I don't care when this occurs; I am not talking about conventions, I am not thinking of such things. I am thinking merely of where does a great party like the Republican Party, what direction does it have to take, if it is going to be a useful agency for America.

Q. Robert E. Clark, International News Service: Mr. President, Senator Knowland's opposition to the administration on several recent issues has been viewed in some quarters as a threat to Republican harmony in the new Congress, particularly in the Senate. Do you see any peril in the fact that the man chiefly charged with guiding the administration's program through the Senate is often in opposition to your own view?

THE PRESIDENT. I noticed that he said the other day, after reading Secretary Dulles' speech, that he thought the difference had been exaggerated.

I, as you know, have always acknowledged the right of any individual to differ from me, violently and persistently; but I would hope that the men with whom I have to work would not be differing greatly from me in the main issues in which we have to work, or it would be extremely difficult.

But, again, in the times that Senator Knowland and I have frequently discussed these matters, at that moment I have found little between us in the way of differences in philosophy in foreign policy, in domestic policy.

I note that he makes statements at times that do not conform to my approach, but they do normally affect method rather than principle.

Q. Carroll H. Kenworthy, United Press: Will you give us your views, sir, on Prime Minister Churchill's disclosure that as long ago as in 1945 he favored saving German arms to use them against Russia if it undertook to spread further across Europe?

THE PRESIDENT. I understand he explained the thing himself, and I guess I had better let that stand.

He made a statement, and then he got up and made another statement including, as I understand it, something of an apology for misinforming the House of Commons; so I think that answers the question itself.

Q. Frederick Kuh, Chicago Sun-Times: Mr. President, would you care to say what character, what type, of action you think the U.N. should take on behalf of the 13 prisoners?

THE PRESIDENT. No, I can't say because just as in a court or anything else, I don't prejudge the action; I don't know anything about it.

I just feel that the United Nations, as a body, to retain its self-respect, indeed in the future to handle a similar case as that which arose in the Korean war, that they now have a certain sense of responsibility they cannot escape.

Q. Joseph A. Loftus, New York Times: Mr. President, can you tell us the purpose of the meeting this morning of the Defense Mobilization Board?

THE PRESIDENT. It was a regular meeting in which I wanted to participate. I participated only in a few of them, and lately there have been questions that I had, and it was just easier to meet with the Board and discuss these questions directly than it was to have a report on them. There were a number of questions brought up, but all of a general nature.

Q. Ruth S. Montgomery, New York Daily News: Mr. President, can you tell us whether Chip Bohlen brought you any ray of hope from Russia concerning world peace?

THE PRESIDENT. Well, Chip Bohlen is a very realistic person, and I don't think he would be one to go around spreading, let's say, false hopes.

I will tell you what I will do: I just came from this conversation a little while ago, and I will check up with my people to see whether they consider this a confidential report or not. There wasn't anything of profound importance, but it might be that I was violating a confidence. If not, I will tell you next week about it.

Q. Joseph C. Harsch, Christian Science Monitor: Sir, is there anything in this case of the prisoners which is at all comparable to the case of the plane shot down over the Habomai Islands, where you said it was cloudy and there might have been a different feeling on their part about the merits than on ours? Or is this totally different?

THE PRESIDENT. Might be different——

Q. Mr. Harsch: In regard to the Habomai Island incident of the plane, you said the merits of the thing were clouded and that the opponent probably, perhaps, thought he had a right to do what he was doing; is this at all comparable or is it different?

THE PRESIDENT. No, not in my opinion, Mr. Harsch. In the Habomai Islands, you remember that the Supreme Commander out there established a dividing line for occupation, which allowed the Russians to come into those islands for occupational purposes.

Now, we have never recognized those islands as belonging to the Kuriles, and it was the Kuriles that the conference at Yalta yielded to Russia, not these Habomais which are just off the coast of Hokkaido. But nevertheless they moved in.

You will remember there have been numerous instances all around this great periphery; whenever any plane approaches within a certain distance, there is trouble. You remember last year, or maybe it was 2 years ago, two Swedish planes were shot down; we had a Navy plane once in the Baltic Sea; and we had that trouble with the British ship that would seem to be a perfectly flagrant case—you know, the British fleet that was flying up from Hanoy, or somewhere down there, into Hong Kong. So they are very sensitive, and respond to any such thing very quickly, particularly in areas that they claim; and they do claim those islands, although we don't admit it.

But this last case to my mind, with respect to the 11 uniformed soldiers, was completely indefensible, and they should be home right now.

Q. Frank van der Linden, Charlotte (N.C.) Observer: Mr. President, I have a request from Charlotte to ask you if this bill you signed yesterday regarding the reduction in the number of Government vehicles is based on the measure which was sponsored by your friend, Congressman Charles Jonas?   [*Laughter*]

THE PRESIDENT. Well, I forget the exact language of his bill, but you do remember the old saw, "He is a great man, he thinks like I do." [*Laughter*]   So if he was for it, why then I, of course, must consider him a very great man and give him full credit for his idea.   [*Laughter*]

[*Confers with Mr. Hagerty*]

Mr. Hagerty tells me something I didn't know, that the legislation actually asked the Executive to take action; so, in that sense, it is the inspiration for the order of yesterday.

Q. Harry Flannery, Mutual Broadcasting System: Mr. President, do we intend to take up the matter of the 13 prisoners in the United Nations or is it our position that some other nation would preferably bring that up?

THE PRESIDENT. That will be up to the State Department entirely, how they do it; the actual manner of doing that, you would have to ask the Secretary of State.

Q. Roscoe Drummond, New York Herald Tribune: Mr. President, some have recently advocated that the United States should break diplomatic relations with the Soviet Union.   I would like to ask if you think such an action would be useful at this time?

THE PRESIDENT. Well I will tell you, frankly, no, I don't.   To give you the full reasons again would be a bit of repetition of the story I have given you before.   And I say, taking any specific action, I don't believe it can be considered alone; it can't be considered only in its effect in one area, but its effect throughout the world.

Let us remember—you will have to forgive me for adding this one thought—ever since about '46, certainly ever since the beginning of the Marshall Plan, one of the great objectives of Communist propaganda has been to break up, destroy, prevent, any type of growing union and strength in Western Europe.

We know, of course, that Western Europe is a great prize toward which they have turned their eyes a long time.   It is a region that has 22 millions of skilled workers; it is a region of great productive capacity, and added to the present Communist capacity would constitute a threat in the world that would be almost insupportable.

Now, what happens?   Every time anything happens over there, there's all sorts of trouble created in the world. They try blandishment, mixed with threats on the Western nations. First of all, they offer a conference. Then they have a conference of their own, they organize a general staff and a joint staff, and they say that the most dire consequences will first of all follow along the formation of NATO, then EDC. Unfortunately, we fell down on EDC. The Western nations were expedient enough, resourceful enough, that they came up with a new solution, and this is all started over again.

Now, all of these things are directed towards this one thing; and I believe that, rather than just breaking off relations and saying, "We are going to ignore that you exist," the thing we must do is to give our attention to the positive business of building up strength among ourselves. Above all, I am one of those that believe that as long as we are strong, as long as we look to our own arms, to our own readiness, to our own mobilization capacity, and build up our nations in that, then we can afford to be more patient than could weaker nations.

I believe that we must constantly increase our strength, to reason and talk to these people from a position of strength, and try to achieve that thing that is so often called *modus vivendi;* I don't know of any brighter hope that there is on the horizon today. But I don't believe that this is going to be advanced merely by pretending they don't exist.

Q. Edward T. Folliard, Washington Post and Times Herald: Mr. President, I hope we may be authorized to quote that statement you made at the outset, the general philosophy about the world situation.

THE PRESIDENT. Well, if you will give me my usual privilege of having Mr. Hagerty look it over and see how many grammatical errors I made in an off-the-cuff talk, if it looks all right to him, why, he could release it.

Q. Mr. Folliard: Now, Mr. President, I would like to ask a purely local question, if you don't mind, that my paper is interested in. William Zeckendorf has said that you are much interested in the plan to redevelop the southwest section of Washington—that is what they call a blighted area. Would you care to comment on the prospect for a face-lifting of that southwest area?

THE PRESIDENT. As a matter of fact, I don't know what the prospects are, Mr. Folliard, right now, but I do know this: Mr. Zeckendorf came in one day, and I listened, I think, for a half hour to his layout with drawings, architect drawings, and plans. It made of that section, which is now called a blighted area, just a perfectly beautiful addition to this city.

No one despises and hates slums more than I do, and believes they should be gotten rid of; and this plan looked to me a good one.

He came to see me because there would be a certain Federal connection; the Federal Government would have to lease buildings that they would build for a certain number of years.

Q. John M. Hightower, Associated Press: Is there anything you can say, sir, about the status of the other 2 men, in addition to the 11 men who were in uniform?

THE PRESIDENT. Well, it is cloudy, and I couldn't discuss it in detail.

Q. Sarah McClendon, San Antonio Light: Sir, there are so many men leaving the Air Force now, men who are trained in mechanics and radar, going into private industry, and they say we are going to have to spend billions in the next 3 years to retrain new men to take their places. I wonder if you plan any legislation to seek in Congress that would correct these conditions and help the men to stay in the Air Force?

THE PRESIDENT. You are getting to a subject very close to my heart, I will tell you. I have lived with the services and with their esprit, their rights, for a great many years.

I don't believe that soldiers, sailors, or airmen and marines go into the service for a career just for money. Naturally, they like to be respected; but, above all things, they like to know that while they are doing the jobs to which they are ordered, and with no request or any initiative on their own part, that their families are properly taken care of. They like to know that they are living in respectable houses, that they are respected citizens of the community.

I believe that if we provide the proper medical care for the dependents of all these trained career people you are talking about, if we give them decent housing, if we stop moving them every other day so that they never have a chance to establish a home life, if we make some allowances for the leave privileges they should have and which they so often have to use up just in going from station to station, to take their goods with them—if we do a number of things like that, the increase in pay, while I think there should be probably a slight raise, I think that is nominal compared to these other things. Above all, residual rights for their widows and their dependents and their retirement—today I believe this to be a fact: if a captain of the Regulars is killed in action, I think his widow gets, let's say, $30 to $40 a month; is that about right?

Mr. Hagerty: That is right.

THE PRESIDENT. If he is Reserve, she gets $500. Now, I may be wrong; don't quote me exactly. But that is the kind of thing that must be corrected, and you won't have any trouble with the morale and the career people, I am sure of it.

Merriman Smith, United Press: Thank you, Mr. President.

NOTE: President Eisenhower's fifty-fourth news conference was held in the Executive Office Building from 2:32 to 3:06 o'clock on Thursday afternoon, December 2, 1594. In attendance: 141.

346 ¶ Remarks to the Washington Conference of Mayors. *December 2, 1954*

THANK you very much. It is getting to be a habit of mine, but for that reason a privilege no less valued, to appear before the assembled Mayors of our country with a word of welcome. I assure you that it is, on my part, an honor to be able to occupy such a position, to extend to you the greetings of this Government—the administration—as you meet in conclave to discuss problems among yourselves, and those problems that are either common to the municipality and the Federal Government, or have at least a common impact upon the two echelons of government.

I think one reason that I am always so delighted to meet with Mayors, you typify especially one of those concepts of government in which I so fervently believe: decentralization.

I believe there are many things wrong with centralization of authority and responsibility, and I have always been struck also by that observation of a rather wise old fellow once who said, "Centralization is the refuge of fear."

And the more I ponder over those words, the more I see what he meant and the more I am convinced that that is exactly what it is.

We centralize things in ourselves, or in an individual, or a centralized authority, because we fear that our associates—often of our own choosing—are not capable of carrying out those responsibilities. And so we create great blocks in progress due to the inability of one human or one organism of government to do all those things which a people need to have done.

So I always have a special feeling of satisfaction in meeting with Mayors who, as the executive heads of our municipalities, do represent that great element in our governmental structure which means local authority and local responsibility.

I think there is another reason, in these days, that gives special meanings to meetings such as yours. When our Constitution was founded, of course, the great division that was expected to persist—when the Constitution was written, I should have said—the great governmental division that was to exist was visualized as that between the Federal Government and the State. And, of course, that is still important. It is not only important, but I think it has been abused in some ways; we have a very splendid Commission studying those proper relationships, and I believe you are to hear tomorrow from Mr. Kestnbaum, its head.

But in these latter days, a special relationship arising in the national security function of the Government has arisen directly between the city and the Federal Government. That is because the city, presumably the special or favored target of some of the modern weapons of war which are capable of such destruction as to appall the imagination, are after all moving to the front line much faster than is a rural area which would not be a favored target for such weapons. And since the Federal Government is charged with the national defense, there is instantly created between the city and the Federal Government—indeed, between the Mayor of the city and the Chief Executive of the United States—a relationship which up until that moment, apparently, was either unimportant or did not exist at all.

Of such things we in the Federal Government are acutely aware and for that reason are delighted that you come here to meet with our people who are studying these things all the time in order that we may devise ways and means, in this critical problem, for the safety of our country, and particularly for the protection of the cities in case of emergency.

I do not mean, by any manner of means, to belittle or minimize those other great problems that we have in common, functions in which each branch of government is absorbed—in education, in combatting juvenile delinquency, in the health of our people, in child welfare, prevention of crime. All of these things are common responsibilities, and they in themselves would constitute and give to us ample reasons for meeting and consulting together, for out of these consultations should come some clear understanding of the capacities of each echelon of government to do its own job, to fit best with the other echelon, and indeed to further the basic concept of democracy, which is the solution of group problems by cooperation, not by coercion.

So, for all these reasons I am delighted that you are here and again meeting with our people on these serious and ever present questions.

On the more personal side, I hope that through the people you meet— General Clay discussing the highway problem, our Secretary of State explaining to you something of the world situation—I hope through these personal contacts you will feel closer to your Federal Government, more privileged, more ready to submit your ideas in particular lines when you believe they would be helpful in the solution of problems. I hope that there will be friendships growing up that will be helpful to us all, as each of us in all echelons of government struggles to do his part in furthering the best interests of the people of the United States.

For yourselves, I do most sincerely hope that while you are here you will find your work informative and interesting, and very, very enjoyable so that you will come back again.

For the privilege of appearing before you, my thanks and gratitude.

NOTE: The President spoke at the Departmental Auditorium. He referred to the Commission on Intergovernmental Relations, under the chairmanship of Meyer Kestnbaum. Later he referred to General Lucius D. Clay, Chairman of the President's Advisory Committee on a National Highway Program.

347   ¶ The President's News Conference of *December 8, 1954.*

THE PRESIDENT. Please be seated. Ladies and gentlemen, we have got three short announcements this morning. The first one, I hope, you won't interpret as a mixing into your business, but I would like to submit a petition, and I believe you do uphold the right of petition.

I have designated December 15 as Safe Driving Day, and I have got a tremendous conviction the United States can do anything it wants to. I would like to get you to transmit requests to all your bosses—editors and the publishers and everybody else, the people that run the radio and television and telenews, and everything. Let's get safe driving in the headlines and prominent places on December 14th and 15th, and see what a record we can make for December 15.

This is, I say, a request, and it is not trying to tell anybody his business.

Today is the anniversary of the talk I made to the United Nations in submitting an atoms-for-peace proposal.

At my request, the Secretary of State this afternoon, I believe at 4 o'clock, will have a record of the exact things that have been done under that proposal in this year. Obviously, they are below the level of, not expectation, of hope, but still they constitute a considerable accomplishment. If you are interested, he will have it.

The only other announcement is that next week I have scheduled two meetings to which I have had the necessary acceptances. On Monday I shall meet with Republican leaders of both Houses in a review of the administration program, and with the necessary changes brought about in the experience of a year. We will go over it. And on Tuesday I have a bipartisan meeting at which will be invited chairmen and principal members of Foreign Relations, Foreign Affairs, of National Security, and I believe of the Appropriations Committees.

Mr. Hagerty: Armed Services.

THE PRESIDENT. Yes, Armed Services—well, Security—and Appropriations.

At that meeting will be gone over all of our present proposals, our suggestions or thoughts we have in these fields of foreign affairs, foreign aid, national security; and they will be, of course, discussed.

Now we will go to questions.

Q. Robert E. Clark, International News Service: Senator McCarthy has accused you of a shrinking show of weakness against Red China, and a failing to wage a vigorous fight against homefront communism. I wonder, in view of the strong personal nature of his attack, you might have a reply for the Senator; and, two, what danger you see in what appears to be a declaration of war by McCarthy, what danger do you see to the Republican Party?

THE PRESIDENT. Well, now, in the first part the answer is, no. I do not indulge in personal vituperation or quarrels of any kind. I stand for positive things.

I have always upheld the right of the Congress to make legitimate investigations into the affairs and conduct of the executive departments, subject only to requirements of national security and very clear public interest.

As far as the civil rights of our people are concerned, I have tried to champion those in dozens of ways. I have even selected particular individuals and named them by name where I thought their services to our country had been unjustly deprecated.

I believe in positive things. I shall continue to believe in those things, and I am not going to engage in any kind of a personal quarrel with anybody on any subject that I can think of.

As for the effect on the Republican Party, I would suggest you go over and ask the Chairman, Mr. Hall, what his conclusions are on this thing, and what effects he sees.

Q. Ray L. Scherer, National Broadcasting Company: Mr. President, there seems to be a conflict of opinion amongst some of the Cabinet members both as to the efficacy and the method of financing of a proposed economic aid program for Asia. Would you comment on that, sir?

THE PRESIDENT. The proposal has not been brought far enough along that it has been argued in front of me.

I know of no subject important to the United States that does not develop conflicting opinions. I would be frightened if it didn't; and, so, when the matter finally comes up to the point of settlement, why, there will be timely announcements made. It hasn't been argued yet in front of me.

Q. Chalmers M. Roberts, Washington Post and Times Herald: On that same subject, sir, the Secretary of State told us yesterday that he felt it was very likely there would be a program submitted to the next Congress. Is that a fair estimate of how far the matter has gone?

THE PRESIDENT. Oh, there will be some program, of course, because our interest in Asia, as you know, is intimate and continuous. There are backward areas that need help; you can start with Japan and go all along the Pacific coast. Of course there is going to be some kind of a program sent up.

Q. Mr. Roberts: But, sir, you mean a program different in type and scope from what we currently are doing in that part of the world?

THE PRESIDENT. Oh, I can't say what the changes will be, I don't know. The specialists and the people that are particularly concerned, the Secretaries, have not yet laid out what they believe to be the specific needs of each of these areas.

Q. Martin S. Hayden, Detroit News: Mr. President, I hope this question won't require that you have a personal conflict, but there seems to be a prospect that the extreme right wing of your Republican Party might follow Senator McCarthy into a new party in 1956. I would like to ask you, sir, as the leader of the party, if you feel that would kill Republican chances of remaining in power?

THE PRESIDENT. Well, after all, I have no crystal ball, but I believe this: from the beginning I have tried to stand for something that is positive and progressive. I believe that the Federal Government has a continuous, definite obligation to study the needs of 163 million people, our standing abroad, our security from attack, and the arrangement of the connections between Government and our economy, our industries, and our individuals. These things must be studied intelligently, and they must be so provided for that the great productivity of our economy is shared in to the greatest possible extent by all of us.

That is the kind of a program that I stand for, and if there are enough people wanting to go along with it, then we have no fear. If people want to split off because of some other secondary or lesser consideration, that will have to be their business.

But I do know that so far as I can determine, the great mass of the people of the United States want intelligent and what I would call a group of progressive moderates handling their business. And that is exactly what I am working for.

Q. David P. Sentner, Hearst Newspapers: Mr. President, the Communist Chinese Government is reported to be taking the position regarding the U.N. charges that they never did sign any Korean peace and, therefore, cannot be charged with any violation. Would you comment?

THE PRESIDENT. I haven't heard this; consequently, my comments would have to be very general for the simple reason that they may be arguing certain technical facts that have no application whatsoever in the moral field.

Now, we know that Chinese forces were fighting in Northern Korea, and we know that we lost prisoners of war who, by the open admission, published admissions, of the Chinese Government, were in uniform and were properly carrying out legitimate missions at the time of their capture.

We know that the armistice provided for the exchange of prisoners.

Now, someone has violated and, at the very least, these people have the right or have the power to control whoever violated it.

The only reason I don't try to answer more specifically is because I can't be expected to recall every detail and every technical point even of that armistice, but that is my feeling. Morally, the situation is just as clear as it can be.

Q. Roscoe Drummond, New York Herald Tribune: Mr. President, if you should decide not to be a candidate in 1956, would you be disposed to use your influence to bring about the nomination of a Republican nominee who would be in support of the policies and the program which you have been carrying out?

THE PRESIDENT. Well, I would put it this way: if I see the Republican nominee whom I believe to support the general philosophy of government in which I believe and which I have so often tried in my rough way to expound, of course I would be for him. I would be for him very, very strongly.

Now, you proposed a question: would I try to help bring about his nomination? Don't ask me to foresee exactly what the conditions of that moment are going to be, but I will support anybody that is the nominee that believes in that general philosophy.

Q. Edward Jamieson Milne, Providence Journal-Bulletin: Mr. President, would you yourself be more or less likely to run again if the party were faced with a split in '56?

THE PRESIDENT. I haven't the slightest idea. And that is not being facetious; I just haven't.

There are so many things—I'll tell you: some day we'll take a half hour, and I'll try to give you my thinking maybe on these things, but I have no decision.

Q. Sarah McClendon, El Paso Times: Sir, there have been some expressions by individual members of the Republican National Committee and officials of Citizens for Eisenhower individually in Washington, of late, that there is a great trend throughout the country for people to vote for the man and for the program, and not for the party label. Would that be in line with your thinking?

THE PRESIDENT. Of course, you always run into this great problem of smooth operations between the legislative and the executive department.

What I would hope is that we produce a group of fine, energetic, idealistic candidates, men and women of experience, and who believe in this program; then I don't have that problem to settle, and I can just go out and support Republicans.

But I do believe that we must adopt and think in terms of what I would call moderate progressives—I don't know of any better word—moderate in your attitude toward the functions of government, but progressive in carrying out those things that our people need.

Q. Clark R. Mollenhoff, Des Moines Register and Tribune: Mr. President, your statement of congratulation to Senator Watkins last week is what apparently set off this McCarthy controversy; and I wonder if you would want to explain precisely what you meant in your congratulation; if Watkins was taking the kind of positive action you spoke of here before.

THE PRESIDENT. No, I don't mind answering at all.

When Senator Watkins was given this task he, by chance, was in my office, and I told him that I thought he had been given one of the toughest jobs that ever faced a United States Senator, and that I knew that he would handle it with the dignity, with the sense of justice I had come to expect of him. He was a judge at one time, you know, and I was perfectly certain of the manner in which he would perform his duties.

When he came in, all I did, I said, "Well, I congratulate you. You certainly lived up to everything that I expected of you." I made no comment about the justice or injustice of voting. I talked about his conduct of a tough job, and I still think that it was one so tough that no one wanted it.

Q. Jerry W. Poole, Pulliam Papers: Mr. President, did Secretary of Labor Mitchell's speech to the CIO convention yesterday in Los Angeles, in which he came out strongly against the so-called State right-to-work laws, did his speech represent your thinking and the views of your administration on that subject?

THE PRESIDENT. He did not attempt to express any administration view, and I believe made that clear. He has long believed that that was sort of a paradox in the law, but he did not represent necessarily the administration views in any part of his speech.

We do have, of course, the rights of Cabinet officers to express their own views on particular points very emphatically, particularly during the stages that policies are being made up. That is his view.

Q. Douglass Cater, Reporter Magazine: Mr. President, Senator McCarthy said that he was sorry that he had asked the people to vote for you in '52. I wonder if you exchanged the sentiment? [*Laughter*]

THE PRESIDENT. Obviously, you don't expect an answer. [*Laughter*]

Q. Alan S. Emory, Watertown Times: Sir, in New Orleans at the Democratic National Committee meeting, a group of Democratic Governors and Governors-elect, including Harriman of New York, Freeman of Minnesota, and Williams of Michigan, signed a statement that the dairy farmer and the dairy industry, as a whole, were being made the whipping boys of the farm problems now facing the country. Sir, do you believe that the dairy farmer is being unjustly picked on in an attempt to solve the farm problem?

THE PRESIDENT. I had a report just within the last day or so that the average level of the prices received by the dairy farmers of the United States this minute are above those that were applicable at the moment that the 90-percent rigid price support was abandoned.

I don't believe he is a whipping boy at all. There is no group in which I have taken more interest. I hope that all of you have heard about my milk luncheon the other day; if you haven't, I will take time off to speak about it. [*Laughter*]

But I am told this: the dairy problem disappears the second that we get every person in the United States to drink 1½ ounces more milk per day. The further statement is made that this is something that wouldn't be substituting for something else because we need this 1½ ounces. So here is a case that all we have to do is do what is good for us and we have helped the dairy industry so much there will be a shortage.

Q. Charles E. Shutt, Telenews: Aside from the present situation in China of the imprisoned airmen, sir, would you say the chances for a continuing peace are brighter now than any other time since you have been in office?

THE PRESIDENT. Well, I dislike to have to take so much time to answer each question, but it is quite difficult to answer some of these things yes or no.

Don't forget what you mean by "peace," and an armistice is not peace.

What we really mean by peace is that situation in the world where we have confidence, justifiable confidence, that a situation is going to prevail where we can devote the vast majority of our resources, of our work, of our sweat, of our brains to doing those things which are for the good of the people and not merely to protect ourselves or to destroy others.

Now, that isn't, frankly, the kind of a situation in which we are now.

I believe this: I believe that the fears the free world had of a global war, say, at the time that I was sent to SHAPE—when I left Columbia to go over there to work on that problem—I believe the fears that the free world had of global war are below, are less, at a lower level than they were at that time.

Q. Kenneth M. Scheibel, Gannett Newspapers: Mr. President, speaking of a legislative program, do you think your relations with the Congress are going to suffer as a result of the split in the party over this censure proceeding?

THE PRESIDENT. Well, I don't know. I would just say this: I am going to do my best. I recognize that many people approaching specific problems reach different answers.

What I am trying to ask is that people see the wisdom of the broad kind of program I have so often tried to picture to you people, and to get behind that and put their shoulders to the wheel to put it over for the United States.

Now, whether the job will be tougher or easier, that remains to be seen.

Q. Clark R. Mollenhoff, Des Moines Register and Tribune: Mr. President, there was only one other censure problem on which you expressed an opinion earlier; that was relative to the treatment of General Zwicker, and you stated that you disapproved of the way General Zwicker was treated.

THE PRESIDENT. I said, I expressed before this group my confidence in General Zwicker and my belief that he was a patriotic American who deserved credit rather than condemnation.

Q. Mr. Mollenhoff: I wondered if, in the light of the action taken by the Senate, you felt they had turned their back on you with regard to the Zwicker count?

THE PRESIDENT. No, I have no feeling about that.

But I do want to point out this: I think I said before, this morning, let's don't confuse these issues with the fundamental right of the Congress to make legitimate investigations of the executive departments. I believe in that, and I not only believe in it, I believe it is contemplated and directed in the Constitution. I believe we would certainly begin to go downhill unless we had it.

Q. Mrs. May Craig, Maine Papers: Sir, how do you reconcile an expanded foreign aid program with our continued deficit financing in this country?

THE PRESIDENT. As a matter of fact, I don't know and never thought of it in those terms; I don't know that I do completely reconcile it.

But let us remember this, to be repeated every time you say the words "foreign aid," I don't think those are good words. I think the word that we ought to use is "mutual security." Anything that we go into in the world ought to be for the enlightened self-interest of 163 million people.

And we ought to judge—permit me to go on—we ought to judge every single one of these programs in which we are trying to assist Iran or Indochina or Indonesia or Japan or France or anybody else, we ought to weigh them, always starting from this viewpoint: what does the enlightened self-interest of the United States lead us to.

Then we also know that a balanced budget is good for a nation; because if you don't, you tend toward inflation and toward the cheapening of money. That can lead to disastrous consequences.

You have to put these two requirements constantly against each other; and when you meet your minimum costs of Government and of this kind of thing, you have to say, "Now, how much taxes is good for our country?" because now you have another indeterminate factor entering this equation. If you relieve taxes on industry, how fast will it expand and give you more income at a lower tax rate? So you have constantly a changing equation of variables that never at any 2 successive days gives you exactly the same answer.

But I do say I don't think I quite can reconcile completely the two except in the terms I have just given you.

Q. John M. Hightower, Associated Press: Will you tell us, sir, whether you have any plans to appoint Nelson Rockefeller as an Administrative Assistant in foreign affairs?

THE PRESIDENT. The only thing I can say about that is that Nelson Rockefeller, among others, has been constantly—we have been constantly examining our situation. I need somebody in that place, but Mr. Rockefeller already occupies a very important position in Government. It is a question of getting the very best answer we can. No definite decision has been made, and there will be a proper announcement at the proper time.

Q. Harry C. Dent, Columbia (S.C.) State and Record: Mr. President, yesterday the District Commissioners announced that they are going to try to test old antidiscrimination laws in the District by hailing barbers, and so forth, anybody that operates a public place, into court in case of discriminating against anyone because of race; and Eugene Davidson, the president of the local NAACP chapter, said the Commissioners are only following a mandate from President Eisenhower to abolish every vestige of segregation and discrimination. And I just wondered if that is true that they are just following——

THE PRESIDENT. I never heard of this particular point. Whatever it is, I think the courts should decide whether there is any injustice done here or not. I never heard of this point.

Q. Richard L. Wilson, Cowles Publications: Mr. President, do you think it is possible or practical to have a political grouping of these progressive moderates of whom you speak from both political parties, who would be more representative of the wishes of the people than either the Republican or the Democratic Party?

THE PRESIDENT. You raise a question in which there would be many imponderables. For example, just take a simple and material one. I understand that many State laws contemplate only two parties, and allow only two—I say many States—several States. So you would have to start in changing the State laws before you could do any such thing to start with.

But I think that we have got to probably use the mechanisms already devised and so well known to our people, and get one of them, at least, to stand in behind this doctrine; and I believe the Republicans should— behind this doctrine and this kind of a program—very earnestly and so seriously that the words "progressive," "moderation," in Government becomes synonymous with the party label.

That is really what I believe. And I think that can be probably better and more effectively done than you could make the kind of a regrouping which would be, as I understand what you mean, a third party, start a new party; it would be, I think, very difficult.

Q. Marvin L. Arrowsmith, Associated Press: Mr. President, the new Chairman of the Democratic National Committee, Paul Butler, said over the weekend that you personally have shown a lack of capacity to govern and unite the American people. Do you care to make any comment on that remark?

THE PRESIDENT. Well, again, I am not going to reply to an individual. I have heard these remarks before.

I will say this: I think too often politicians look into a looking glass instead of through a window. [*Laughter*]

The United States presents a broad vista of thinking, and I have a tremendous and profound faith in the general commonsense approach of the American people to our great problems. I believe, in general, they go along very earnestly with what we would call a progressive program, with moderation, in the terms that I have explained it before to you people.

Now, as to my abilities and inabilities, I hope I am not one of the egoists that can think only in terms of the vertical pronoun.

I suggest this to you, gentlemen, and ladies: for 2 years I have been meeting in front of this body, the personnel of which doesn't seem to reflect any great change from week to week. I really believe you are better judges of interests, breadth of interests, and capacities and the kind of things we are trying to do, than is some politician who, looking in the glass, sees only reflections of doubt and fear and the kind of confusion that he often tries to create.

So, ladies and gentlemen, that particular question will have to be answered by you.

Q. A. Robert Smith, Portland Oregonian: Mr. President, we have had numerous reports stemming, apparently, from the outcome of the Oregon election, that Secretary McKay was to be replaced. Could you make any comment on those rumors?

THE PRESIDENT. Well, I have heard a number of new ideas this morning, but that is the newest. No, I hadn't heard it.

Q. James B. Reston, New York Times: Last week, sir, you told us that you were personally studying the security, the internal security system of the Government.

THE PRESIDENT. Yes.

Q. Mr. Reston: Have you reached any conclusions about that?

THE PRESIDENT. No, it is still undergoing study.

Merriman Smith, United Press: Thank you, Mr. President.

NOTE: President Eisenhower's fifty-fifth news conference was held in the Executive Office Building from 10:33 to 11:02 o'clock on Wednesday morning, December 8, 1954. In attendance: 209.

348 ¶ Letter to Joseph M. Dodge Designating Him as Special Assistant to the President and as Chairman, Council on Foreign Economic Policy. *December* 11, 1954

[Released December 11, 1954. Dated December 1, 1954]

My dear Mr. Dodge:

It is my desire that we proceed as rapidly as possible to bring about improvements in the organization of the Executive Branch for the development and coordination of foreign economic policy, including its relation to domestic economic policy where it is involved. I have discussed the objectives of this program with the Cabinet, my Advisory Committee on Government Organization, the Director of the Bureau of the Budget, and with you.

I am most pleased that you have agreed to continue to serve the Government and to organize on my behalf this very important undertaking. Effective immediately I am designating you as Special Assistant to the President to assist and advise me in accomplishing an orderly development of foreign economic policies and programs and to assure the effective coordination of foreign economic matters of concern to the several departments and agencies of the Executive Branch.

More particularly, in respect to foreign economic matters, I shall look to you to provide for the anticipation of problems and issues, ensure advance preparation, analyze information for the purpose of clarifying and defining issues, and determine the primary responsibilities of the executive agencies for the preparation of original documents and for any other steps necessary to produce a coordinated and agreed upon governmental position.

There now are numerous standing and ad hoc interdepartmental coordinating mechanisms, as well as a complex of overseas departmental operations, each dealing with a limited aspect of our foreign economic policy. I expect that the arrangements established by this letter, with the cooperation and assistance of the Director of the Bureau of the Budget and his staff and with the benefit of other studies in this field of activity now underway, will lead to a substantial simplification of the present structure.

You are authorized to establish and to serve as the chairman, of a Council on Foreign Economic Policy through which executive agencies can participate effectively in this undertaking. The Secretaries of State, Treasury, Commerce, Agriculture, and the Director of the Foreign Operations Administration, or their principal deputies, should comprise the initial basic membership of the Council. All of them are regular members of the Cabinet and three of them are regular members of the National Security Council.

In addition, ex officio members will be my Administrative Assistant for Economic Affairs, my Special Assistant for National Security Affairs, and a member of my Council of Economic Advisers. The heads of other departments and agencies should be invited by the chairman to participate in meetings of the Council when matters of direct concern to them are under consideration.

You may provide yourself with such staff as is necessary to assist you in connection with these duties. In addition, I anticipate that from time to time provision will need to be made for a limited number of special task forces for the review of specific foreign economic matters that are so extensive or complicated as to make it advisable to organize them as special projects.

Because the formulation of foreign economic policy in many instances is an integral part of the formulation of national security policy or of international financial policy, I want you, as quickly as possible, to establish appropriate working relations with the National Security Council and the National Advisory Council on International Monetary and Financial Problems, respectively, to the end that in those instances referred to the desired integration will be effected. The achievement of such integration will be furthered by your attendance at such meetings of those organizations as you consider necessary, as well as attendance by a representative of those organizations at meetings of the Council on Foreign Economic Policy when appropriate.

Sincerely yours,

DWIGHT D. EISENHOWER

349 ¶ White House Statement Following Meetings With Republican Leaders of Congress on the Legislative Program. *December* 13, 1954

THE PRESIDENT invited the Republican leaders of the Senate and the House of Representatives to meet with him today for a general preliminary discussion of some of the legislative program which the President will submit to the Congress at the next session.

Today's conference dealt primarily with the domestic program of the Administration.   Other domestic recommendations to be made by the President will be discussed at later meetings.

A bi-partisan conference will be held tomorrow on the subjects of foreign policy, mutual security and national defense.

At the conference this morning the Director of the Bureau of the Budget and the Secretary of the Treasury presented an analysis of our present fiscal situation and the prospects for our estimated position at the end of the present fiscal year.

The Secretary of State then outlined the present state of affairs throughout the world, and will continue tomorrow with detailed suggestions for legislative action.

The Secretary of Defense discussed the need for salary increases for the military, increased medical care, survivors' benefits and better housing for families of military personnel.   Together with the President, the Secretary will join in a presentation of the security plans for the nation at the meeting tomorrow morning.

The Director of Foreign Operations briefly outlined the work of his agency and will return tomorrow for a further discussion of mutual security requirements for the coming fiscal year.

During the morning session, other subjects discussed were:

1. Extension of the Reorganization and Defense Production Acts.
2. Continuation and expansion of the Small Business Administration.
3. Statehood for Hawaii.
4. Revision of the Constitution to lower the voting age.
5. Legislation dealing with suffrage and self-government in the District of Columbia.
6. The foreign economic policy recommendations growing out of the report of the Randall Commission.

At the afternoon session six additional subjects were discussed. They were:

Highway Program—The Assistant to the President outlined proposals made to date, including those of the Governors' Conference, for the establishment of a ten-year national highway construction program. Final recommendations on this program await the report of the President's Committee on a National Highway Program, to be submitted before the Congress convenes in January.

Health Program—A national health program, including an improved health reinsurance program was outlined by the Secretary of Health, Education and Welfare.

Labor Program—Suggested revisions of the Fair Labor Standards Act and amendments to the Labor-Management Relations Act were discussed by the Secretary of Labor.

Civil Service and Postal Pay Increases—The Postmaster General and the Chairman of the Civil Service Commission outlined proposals for wage adjustments and the elimination of inequities in pay scales in the postal and classified Civil Service systems. It was pointed out that any increase in postal pay should be coordinated with corresponding increases in revenue.

Public Housing—The Housing and Home Finance Administrator discussed the program for public housing to be undertaken by the agency for the next two years. He also reviewed briefly the results of the "windfall" investigation within the Housing Administration.

Agriculture—The Secretary of Agriculture presented a review of the farm situation and discussed various proposals that are presently being considered by the Department to permit operators of small farms greater opportunities of sharing the benefits of the agricultural programs.

350 ¶ Remarks Recorded for the Dedication of the Memorial Press Center, New York City. *December* 13, 1954

WE ARE HERE tonight to salute the eyes and ears of our Free Nation—the men and women of our Free Press. We are here to dedicate a living memorial to those members of the Fourth Estate who have given their lives, in war and in peace, in pursuit of truth—the key to freedom.

Through many years, I have had good reason to count the Press Corps as a vital arm of the forces of freedom. In war, I saw its members strive tirelessly, endure hardship, dare battlefield peril that our people might be fully and quickly informed; on every front, they were worthy comrades of our fighting men. Now, as President, I find that each emphasizes anew for me the fairness, the discernment, the dedication of the American reporter; in peace, he is still a valiant warrior for the truth that makes men free.

In establishing a Memorial Press Center in New York City, one of the great crossroads of communications, members of the Overseas Press Club, their fellow journalists and the American public remember the men and women who died in the service of a Free Press, as they would want to be remembered.

In the unending struggle to maintain our freedom, the American reporter is ever in the front line. For as long as faith and knowledge endure, freedom is certain to survive.

NOTE: The President's remarks were recorded on December 10 in the Broadcast Room in the White House for use at the dedication of the Overseas Press Club Memorial in New York.

351 ¶ White House Statement Following Bipartisan Conference on Foreign Affairs, National Defense, and Mutual Security.
December 14, 1954

TODAY'S bi-partisan meeting of the leaders of both political parties in the Senate and the House of Representatives dealt with the problems of foreign affairs, national defense and mutual security.

At the start of the conference, the President thanked the leaders for accepting his invitation to discuss these subjects in advance of his submission of the State of the Union Message. He will present the State of the Union Message to the Congress on January 6th.

The Director of the Budget and the Secretary of the Treasury presented a review of the budget and the general fiscal situation, particularly as it will be affected by national defense expenditures and those for mutual assistance.

The Secretary of State recommended that the Senate give early consideration to the ratification of the Manila Pact and the Mutual Defense Treaty with the Republic of China, as well as those sections of the London-Paris Agreements dealing with the restoration of German sovereignty and the admission of that country to the North Atlantic Treaty Organization. He also stressed the importance he and his Department attached to the economic aspects of our foreign policy, particularly in view of a stepped up campaign by the Soviet world in this regard.

Mr. Randall followed the Secretary of State and presented the recommendations which will be made to the Congress as a result of the study of the Randall Commission in this field. In general, these recommendations closely follow the proposals made by the President last year, with the addition of the establishment of an International Finance Corporation under the auspices of the World Bank which was endorsed at the recent Rio Conference of American Finance Ministers.

In a discussion of national defense, the President said that the security of the nation in this age of atomic bombs and long-range aircraft depended not only on a hard-hitting retaliatory combat force and an expanded reserve force but also on a strong and prosperous economy here at home. He emphasized that the decisions respecting the force levels of the military establishment will be designed to meet fully national needs in the light of continually developing new weapons and subsequent changes in military strategy.

Assistant Secretaries Burgess and McNeil discussed proposals to increase the reserve strength of the military forces, career incentive pay increases for military personnel and the defense budget. Under further discussion were other proposals to provide additional benefits for the military—increased medical care for dependents, survivors' benefits and better housing for their families.

The final topic of the meeting was the mutual security program for the coming fiscal year. The Director of Foreign Operations detailed the steps he believed were necessary to assist our friends and allies throughout the world to strengthen their own economy and to maintain their own adequate defense forces to help in the protection of the free world. Assistant Secretary Hensel gave a report of the military-aid program and prospective needs to carry on this part of the Administration's recommendations.

A general discussion was held on each subject as it was presented.

352 ¶ Message Recorded on Film in Connection with the Observance of Safe Driving Day. *December* 14, 1954

AT THE REQUEST of the Governors and other officials, I have designated tomorrow, December 15, as Safe Driving Day.

I have a deep conviction that the United States can do anything to which 160 million citizens set their hearts and minds. If we are determined to have a day without a traffic accident in all of America, we can have it.

So let us see how many highway deaths and injuries we can prevent by obeying traffic regulations, following simple rules of good sportsmanship and courtesy, and staying alert and careful—whether we are driving or walking.

Let us establish an unblemished record of safety on Safe Driving Day, and then make that record our standard for the future.

353 ¶ The President's News Conference of *December* 15, 1954.

THE PRESIDENT. Good morning. I suppose you would expect me to mention that this is Safe Driving Day, and I am really hoping for the very best.

I was notified there was a petition on the way to my desk, somewhere in the mailroom, from 20,000 people from one city offering their cooperation. I hope it is certainly effective, not only in that city but everywhere.

I should like just to mention briefly the great satisfaction that the administration and I take, and I am sure the whole American people, in the visit of the Shah to our country, with his lovely wife.

You know, a matter of a year and a half ago, how badly things were going in Iran, from the standpoint of the Western World. It looked like Iran was on the way to becoming another of the so-called satellites. So this meeting seems to have not only significance in itself, but as symbolizing a great contrast in the conditions, at least in that country, between a year and a half ago or 16 months ago, and today. It is a matter of great satisfaction to us.

That is all I have. We will go to questions.

Q. Merriman Smith, United Press: Mr. President, we have heard something of this from other sources, but we wonder if you could tell us about the reasons and your plans to ask Congress to postpone the corporation and excise tax reduction next year?

THE PRESIDENT. Well, it is a very simple process.

As I have told you before, the financial affairs of the Government are really very complicated, and they have numbers of unknown factors. One of them is the expenditures, what they are going to be, which always have to be estimated in advance. Another is income. And the other, of course, is the deficit and its effect on the value of the dollar, which introduces, definitely a variable factor.

This administration has been very much in favor, as you know, of extending such things as social security coverage, unemployment coverage, and all that sort of thing. There are two reasons for that—there are three reasons: one, of course, is the humanitarian, giving to these people a feeling of security and confidence. Two, the added stability you get in times of recession; you keep up the income of the mass of people, and keep up their purchasing power. But, three, all of this falls by the board unless your money stays stable. A pension plan is worth nothing if you pay for it in dollars that are now worth a hundred cents, and finally you draw it down in terms of 2-cent dollars.

So, this whole business of the financial affairs of the country, you have to take all of these things into account simultaneously.

Now, to lower taxes, you first must lower expenditures; and we have cut expenditures as, I think you will see when the figures finally come out, to what we consider the safe minimum.

But if you still have a deficit that begins to loom up as having a real effect on the value of your dollar, then you must keep up your taxable income. That taxable income, as we see it now forecast, will require the continuation of the 5 percent extra on the corporations, and these excise taxes as they now stand. Of course, they were already reduced last year. That takes positive action on the part of the Congress, because they are due to expire—those two taxes—as you know, on April 1st I believe it is.

So it is merely a question of keeping all of these matters in balance, as we see it, to the good of the whole country.

Q. Raymond P. Brandt, St. Louis Post-Dispatch: Mr. President, will you ask a 1-year extension or 2 or 3 years' extension of these taxes?

THE PRESIDENT. I don't believe that the point has been discussed in detail. I had thought of it in terms of 1 year, but it may be that the Treasury Department has some other term in mind. I can't give you an exact answer because that particular point hasn't been discussed.

Q. John Herling, Editors Syndicate: Mr. President, in the past year the Secretary of Labor has come up with at least two major ideas: one, the raising of the minimum wage from the present 75-cent level, and, two, the opposition to the anti-union shop laws in States now permitted under the Taft-Hartley law. Does the Secretary of Labor——

THE PRESIDENT. You are talking about the right-to-work laws of the States?

Q. Mr. Herling: Well, the proponents call them right-to-work laws, and the opponents don't; yes, sir.

Does the Secretary of Labor then have your support on the increase in the minimum wage and, second, do you yourself favor the position of the Secretary of Labor in regard to the so-called right-to-work laws?

THE PRESIDENT. With regard to the first, the whole question of increase in minimum wages was discussed, as I recall, in the last Economic Report that I submitted to the Congress. This administration does stand in favor of the adjustments, I believe I said then, at the proper time; and the proper time is certainly an expanding period in the economy. This matter has been under discussion; not ready to make a final announcement, but it is a matter that is under intensive study at the moment.

Now, on this point of the right-to-work laws: I have heard it discussed ever since I have been in my present office, pro and con. Of course, labor unions are very much against it. But States, and many States even that don't have them, are very much for them because they say this represents the inalienable and constitutional rights of a State to act in certain fields.

So you have here, to my mind, a matter that sort of hoists you on the horns of a dilemma if you believe, as I do, very firmly in constitutional government.

I am not particularly certain in my own mind just where the right does lay here. Of course, the Supreme Court has held under the Interstate Commerce provisions that the Federal Government has a right to operate in all these areas and should assume responsibility. But also there is the provision in the Constitution of the reservation of certain rights to the States. I myself couldn't say that I have reached an irrevocable decision. It is one that has been argued in front of me. Until finally the revision of the Taft-Hartley Act is taken up seriously by Congress, and this thing exhaustively and completely argued out, I just don't know exactly what my decision will be.

But, in the meantime, I have upheld the right of Secretary Mitchell to express his own convictions, because he has always held them, and so notified me, even before I appointed him.

Q. Mr. Herling: Sir, may I ask whether—the Secretary of Labor is your chief labor adviser, is he not?

THE PRESIDENT. That is right; indeed, he is.

Q. Mr. Herling: May I ask would it be——

THE PRESIDENT. But listen, I will make this clear: I have no adviser who can take over from me the responsibility for making a decision for my own action as final. I am the responsible one, no matter if I have advisers who are chief or even sole. I have finally to take the responsibility for my own actions.

Q. James B. Reston, New York Times: As I understand it, sir, the North Atlantic Council in Paris this week is going to discuss the question of the atomic defense of Western Europe. Would you give us the benefit of your thinking as to who has the power of decision in the event of an attack, the power of decision of using atomic weapons in Western Europe?

THE PRESIDENT. As a matter of fact, you raised the very question that is under discussion this week; and I think it would be most unwise for me to give my own convictions publicly when my own representatives are engaged in the negotiations on this point.

In certain areas and in certain fields, of course, our own right to act as we see fit is unquestioned.

When you have allies, if you are going to treat them as partners, you have to take into consideration their beliefs, their convictions. If they differ from yours, there is often very good reasons for it; and, therefore, you have to negotiate it out and see where you come out.

I will probably be ready to say a little bit more about this after this meeting is over; but, as it is now, I think that is about all I should say.

Q. Daniel Schorr, CBS News: Mr. President, it has been reported that the administration is planning a further cut of a hundred thousand——

THE PRESIDENT. To do what?

Q. Mr. Schorr: ——a further cut of 100,000 in Army strength in the next fiscal year, and the withdrawal of the 1st Marine Division from the Far East. If that is so, could you explain the thinking behind it?

THE PRESIDENT. Where was this reported?

Q. Mr. Schorr: On CBS, sir. [*Laughter*]

THE PRESIDENT. Well, I guess I must accept that as authoritative. [*Laughter*]

The only reason I am a little hesitant about giving you my thinking on this matter is that a full exposition would require probably more time than we should like to give to it.

I can say this, and it is in an attempt to, you might say, almost epitomize my thinking: the United States, as a nation, never had any reason to be particularly fearful of direct attack upon itself until the advent of two things—one, the long-range bomber or a means of delivering weapons upon us; and, secondly, of very destructive weapons. This, then, points— as I say, I am really cutting corners—this fact points to this one great need on our part: ways of blunting any attack against us, and ways of trying to deter it, preventing it from ever occurring. Here is where comes in the philosophy, you know, of retaliation, to make certain that no one can ever attack us and hope to gain by that kind of attack. If you can prevent that, then, as has been traditionally the case, the economy, the great industrial power, of the United States can unquestionably be decisive again.

In the meantime, of course, with these modern conditions we have accepted, we have recognized new problems—the terrific importance to us of a centrally controlled dictatorship getting sway over such industrial complexes, such productive nations and regions as, let us say, Western Europe and Japan.

So we have, with our own particular interest centered on continental defense, and, let us say, this power of ours to deliver more severe blows than we would get, we have also that problem of preventing the fall of those areas into the hands of someone who could exploit them.

All of this means, as I see it, that our immediately active forces are donated largely to the first task.

Secondly, to prevent all of the disastrous occupations and attacks against these vital areas concerned, we must have a proper reserve system that will enable us, both from a material and manpower standpoint, to bring our power to bear as rapidly as possible.

We can never do this across the oceans in a hurried fashion. The transport of troops and all of these things must follow curves that are determined by the amount of shipping, the amount of escort vessels, the safety of the oceans, and many other factors; so it can't be done hurriedly. So we can depend there, and must depend largely, on a fine Reserve system; which means that when we are calculating where our greatest value that we get, greatest defense value, out of every dollar is concerned, we can cut back on personnel in the active forces as long as we keep our continental defense, our striking power, and our Reserve system operating at its maximum character.

So this means, as I see it, that we should be very concerned in keeping the minimum of people in other places in our defense forces during the time of peace, so we can get the greatest dollar value out of every dollar we spend.

Q. Joseph C. Harsch, Christian Science Monitor: Two weeks ago you told us that you would look into the matter of whether there was anything in Ambassador Bohlen's report to you which you can pass on to us. Have you done so? Can you tell us anything?

THE PRESIDENT. Yes, and I am sorry to tell you that the reports and advice that I get are not very encouraging on the side of talking in this way. Mr. Bohlen gave me his impressions very honestly and openly; the State Department pointed out that if I wanted to receive that kind of information always from the Ambassadors coming back, as they always do visit me, that I would just have to regard them as confidential because the man does not gauge his report to me in the terms of how it might be received in other quarters—I mean abroad. So it just seems to me that that must be governing in this case.

Q. Roscoe Drummond, New York Herald Tribune: Mr. President, may I ask two related questions? Growing out of the Monday conference with the Republican leaders, could you tell us the kind of support for your program you expect to get from your own party; and growing out of Tuesday's meeting, do you think that you observed a show of bipartisanship or do you feel there was substance and spirit behind the bipartisanship that appeared to be manifested?

THE PRESIDENT. Well, I will answer them in reverse order.

I think that yesterday the attitude toward all of these questions—we brought up not only foreign policy in its political or diplomatic sense, but foreign economic aid, mutual security programs, and the national security programs—I believe, in these, cooperation will be very real.

One reason I am encouraged in that regard is that numbers of times I have appeared before both Foreign Affairs and Foreign Relations Committees of the Congress, and before the security committees—now called the Armed Services Committee in the House and in the Senate—and in those cases I never yet found the matters that I was presenting treated or decided upon partisan grounds. In some of those committees they have almost a tradition, it seems to me, of dividing according to conviction and not necessarily according to party.

I am very hopeful, and had every reason to believe in the conference yesterday, that that is very real.

Now, as far as concerns the kind of support that I am going to get for the carrying out of the administration program in all other fields from the Republican side, the matter didn't come up in those terms, and so I cannot be expected to comment exactly in detail on it. But I was given no reason to believe that the support wasn't genuine.

There are, as we all know, some differences, very earnest differences of conviction as, for example, concerning the Randall report. I don't suppose that any kind of a meeting will completely eliminate those differences. But I'd say, by and large, I would expect a very maximum of cooperation from my own party.

Q. Chalmers M. Roberts, Washington Post and Times Herald: Mr. President, in answering the question a moment ago about the change in the size of our troop commitments, you referred to the philosophy of retaliation. Does that change in our troop commitment mean any change in our ability to fight the so-called little wars, especially nonatomic wars?

THE PRESIDENT. I wouldn't think so.   As a matter of fact, little wars as distinguished from big wars, I think you have a bit of an artificial distinction.

What you are trying to do is to conduct or develop a program that meets the overall national needs in the best way.   I would rather improvise and resort to expediency in little wars than I would in big wars. I would rather cast and mold my security arrangements to meet the great threats to the United States, and take the others, as far as I could, in my stride.

Q. Mr. Roberts: You don't, sir, do you, rule out the possibility that we might have a situation in which you had what has been referred to as a little or nonatomic war?

THE PRESIDENT. Well, if you had a little war, I would say this: if you can win a big one, you can certainly win a little one.   That would be my general attitude.

In other words, I believe this: after you get so far in the expenditure of money for planes and tanks and guns and men in the services, you reach a point of very sharply diminishing returns.   I believe it is far better from there on to devote whatever resources you must put into this thing, into getting a proper mobilization base in terms of productivity, where necessary stockpiling, and the training and organization of men for moving into this thing when they have to.

I just don't believe you can buy 100 percent security in every little corner of the world where someone else wants to start trouble.   I think you have to go ahead, taking certain calculated risks.

Here is the one crucial thing you must remember with respect to our Defense Establishment: it isn't one to meet a problem this year; we must be prepared from now on, as long as we have this kind of a threat in the world, which means that we have got to have one that is carried forward under a free enterprise system, with the full support of a population that knows it must bear the taxes to carry it on.   It must be one that can be carried for 50 years, if necessary.   I hope and pray that we are not going to carry it 50 years, but that is the way we must design it.

Consequently, you cannot be 100 percent ready to meet every little trouble that can arise, otherwise you would have to have troops stationed in every place in the world where trouble might arise, in advance.   That would be your best protection.

You have to do it as it comes up, and I believe that the kind of system we are trying to develop is best developed, best molded, best devised for that kind of a theory.

Q. Clark R. Mollenhoff, Des Moines Register: Mr. President, it has been reported in the last week that Senator John Williams of Delaware had to enlist your personal support to get the Treasury to take action on some personnel cases involving persons linked with the Truman administration tax scandals. I wonder if you could tell us precisely what you did in that; whether it was a routine referral or there is some follow through, and what your policy is when these things come to your attention?

THE PRESIDENT. Frankly, I don't recall any specific report to me. I have talked to Senator Williams from time to time, starting before I was inaugurated. I always listened to whatever he has to report to me, and I passed it along, because I believe we have there a very honest, concerned individual. But I can tell you what the policy is without any question whatsoever.

Everybody in this Government who has a position of responsibility is instructed if there is anything that comes to his attention that looks like it is off-color or there is someone that has been criminally negligent or is otherwise to blame for anything that goes wrong in Government, it is to be immediately reported to the proper authorities, and the prosecution to the limit.

Now, there are no exceptions to it.

Q. Mr. Mollenhoff: Have you had any indication, either from Senator Williams or from any other Cabinet members, of his dissatisfaction since his meeting with you last April? At a press conference on April 29, you did confirm that you had talked with Senator Williams with regard to a bad situation in the Internal Revenue Service.

THE PRESIDENT. Well, I haven't had another word about it that I know of; so far as I can remember, not a one.

Q. Garnett D. Horner, Washington Star: Mr. President, if I can change the subject rather drastically, recent news reports indicate that some European governments are investigating quite seriously the flying saucer problem. And not too long ago there was a book published in this country that purported to show that our Air Force thought that some of these flying objects, at least might come to be of extraterrestrial origin. I wonder if you could tell us if our authorities really do suspect something of that kind or, if not, what is the form of the things?

THE PRESIDENT. Well, with regard to these recent reports, nothing has come to me at all, either verbally or in written form. And I must say, when I go back far enough, the last time that I heard this talked to me, a man whom I trust from the Air Forces said that it was, as far as he knew, completely inaccurate to believe that they came from any outside planet or otherwise.

Q. Raymond P. Brandt, St. Louis Post-Dispatch: Mr. President, have you worked out the mechanics of consultation with the Democratic leaders step by step?

THE PRESIDENT. As a matter of fact, I don't know, Mr. Brandt, whether it will just conform to any pattern.

I made this one statement yesterday, and it probably was published: I invited them at any time that they saw fit—responsible officials on the Hill—that they saw anything in this whole field we covered yesterday, that they believed would need my attention, to bring it up.

But beyond that, I am preparing a draft now, asking each of the Cabinet officers that deal with these subjects, any time that they are proposing a new plan, before it is crystallized, before it is presented to Congress, themselves to confer with the security committees, the foreign committees, and so on.

Q. Edward T. Folliard, Washington Post and Times Herald: Mr. President, your able Press Secretary, Mr. Hagerty, made some news the other night. He was on a radio program, and he was asked this question: "Mr. Hagerty, would it be foolhardy for the Republican Party to approach the 1956 election with any other idea than to draft President Eisenhower as a candidate?" Mr. Hagerty gave it as his personal opinion that it would be foolhardy.

Mr. President, is there any point in asking you to comment? [*Laughter*]

THE PRESIDENT. Well, I would like to say this: Mr. Hagerty is included as one of those staff officers, I have told you before, to whom I accord the great privilege of having his own opinion; and, as a matter of fact, as long as he expresses it, and there has been no established administration policy, why, I support his right as Voltaire did to say what he thinks. [*Laughter*]

Q. Mrs. May Craig, Maine Papers: Mr. President, some time ago Secretary Humphrey said on a television program that he approved of the elimination of all restriction on earned income by social security pensioners. Do you approve of that elimination and will it be in the next budget?

THE PRESIDENT. That particular point hasn't been suggested to me as one of the eliminations.

I think it is probably a little bit too serious just to start shooting wildly on. My impression, my instincts are, yes. When you have gotten to that point, it seems to me that income tax has once been paid on that. Now, I am not going to commit myself irrevocably.

Q. Mrs. Craig: Well, sir, you are aware that people who get unearned income, the pensioners, who get unearned income, do not lose because they have unearned outside income, but those who do earn now over more than a certain amount outside of their pension, do lose their pensions.

THE PRESIDENT. After they get a certain amount.

Q. Mrs. Craig: Yes.

THE PRESIDENT. Yes; that is right. Well, now, I will tell you, I will have a talk with the Secretary of State [Secretary of the Treasury]. But you are getting into a very technical question, and I would not want to answer it carelessly here.

Q. Marvin L. Arrowsmith, Associated Press: Mr. President, some of the congressional leaders, after their meeting with you yesterday, talked about a new military manpower reserve program which Senator Lyndon Johnson said would be a modification of UMT. Could you tell us anything about the nature of the plan?

THE PRESIDENT. Well, I think it is really a far cry from UMT; in other words, it is rather drastic. But I think, if I am not mistaken, that Secretary Wilson and his manpower secretary, Mr. Burgess, are going to have a press conference on the details of this plan very soon. [*Confers with Mr. Hagerty*]

It is on Friday, and I think it would be better to take these specific questions to that press conference.

Q. Nat S. Finney, Buffalo Evening News: Mr. President, in your discussions with the Republican leaders was anything said or done about a renewed debate on the so-called Bricker amendment?

THE PRESIDENT. No, it wasn't mentioned.

Merriman Smith, United Press: Thank you, Mr. President.

NOTE: President Eisenhower's fifty-sixth news conference was held in the Executive Office Building from 10:35 to 11:03 o'clock on Wednesday morning, December 15, 1954. In attendance: 152.

354   ¶ Letter to Nelson A. Rockefeller Appointing Him Special Assistant to the President. *December* 16, 1954

[Released December 16, 1954. Dated December 15, 1954]

Dear Mr. Rockefeller:

An outstanding characteristic of our nation, I believe, is a constant endeavor to insure each citizen the fullest possible opportunity to develop himself spiritually, socially and economically. Faith in the individual, in his dignity and in his capacity for achievement is a basic principle of our system. The history of America is the story of men and women who came to these shores from all parts of the world and who have made full use of their opportunities, not only for themselves but in order that others might benefit. Of such is our strength.

It is my conviction that all the peoples of the world share the same human cravings for freedom and for opportunities to win economic and social advancement. In keeping with our heritage we seek to join with all peoples in a common effort to achieve and sustain the basic essentials of human dignity.

It is time for all of us to renew our faith in ourselves and in our fellow men. The whole world has been far too preoccupied with fears. It is time for people throughout the world to think again of hopes, of the progress that is within reach.

So that these matters may have the increased degree of attention they deserve, not only in the Departments and agencies but especially within my immediate staff, I hereby appoint you as Special Assistant to the President. I shall look to you for advice and assistance in the development of increased understanding and cooperation among all peoples. I shall also look to you for assistance in reviewing and developing methods and programs by which the various Departments and agencies of the government may effectively contribute to such cooperation and understanding.

You are requested to attend the meetings of the Cabinet, the National Security Council, the Council on Foreign Economic Policy, and the Operations Coordinating Board.

Sincerely,

DWIGHT D. EISENHOWER

355 ¶ Remarks at the Pageant of Peace Ceremonies. *December 17, 1954*

[Broadcast over radio and television at 5:30 p.m.]

Mr. Secretary, and members of this audience, my fellow citizens, at home and across the seas; my fellow men and women of all the Americas, and of all nations:

Christmastide is a season of hope—of heartening hope—for peace on earth, good will among men. This year, even as two thousand years ago, when the Prince of Peace was born into the world, the drums of war are stilled. In their silence, after a whole generation of almost ceaseless beating, many people—already become fathers and mothers— enjoy the first peaceful Christmas they have known. So—mankind's unquenchable hope for peace burns brighter than for many years.

Our hope, true enough, is blemished by some brutal facts. Oppression, privation, cruel suffering of body and mind imposed on helpless victims— these scourges still wound in too many places the daily living of mankind.

Even at this happy season, we dare not forget crimes against justice, denial of mercy, violation of human dignity. To forget is to condone and to provoke new outrage.

Neither dare we forget our blessings. To count them is to gain new courage and new strength, a firmer patience under test and a stouter faith in the decency of man and in the providence of God.

Among the greatest of man's blessings this Christmas is his strengthened hope of lasting peace. But hope without works is the prelude to disillusionment. They, whose cause is just, must be prepared to meet the harsh challenge of inertia; privation; despair; statism; materialism. This bright Christmas must not be followed—ever—by a Christmas of universal tragedy.

We Americans know that a mighty part of promoting and serving peace is ours to do. With our friends we must enlarge the design of our partnership so that we, who marched together in evil days when war and fear of war darkened the earth, shall enjoy together in days of light the rich rewards of a secure and stable era.

There are some who have believed it possible to hold themselves aloof from today's worldwide struggle between those who uphold government based upon human freedom and dignity, and those who consider man merely a pawn of the state. The times are so critical and the difference between these world systems so vital and vast that grave doubt is cast upon the validity of neutralistic argument. Yet we shall continue faithfully to demonstrate our complete respect for the right of self-decision by these neutrals. Moreover, because they hate aggression and condemn war for conquest, even as we, there is provided a strong foundation upon which we can proceed with them to build mutual understanding and sympathy.

Now, with those who stand against us, in fear or in ignorance of our intentions, we have chosen the hard way of patient, tireless search in every avenue that may lead to their better understanding of our peaceful purposes. They know, as well as we, that the world is large enough, the skills of man great enough, to feed and to clothe and to house mankind in plenty and in peace. This universal knowledge could be the fruitful beginning of a prosperous life together.

America speaks from strength—strength in good allies, in arms, in readiness, in ever-increasing productivity, in the broader sharing of the abundant fruits of our economy, in our unchanging devotion to liberty and to human justice. Her voice is for peace based upon decency and right. But let no man think that we want peace at any price; that we shall forsake principle in resigned tolerance of evident evil; or that we may pawn our honor for transitory concession.

At this Christmas season, America speaks too in humble gratitude for the friendship of peaceful peoples across the world. Without their warm confidence and faithful partnership, this earth would be a bleak ground of aimless and endless clash and conflict.

And America joins with all believers of every faith in a prayer of thanks and a plea that, whatever lies ahead, we may be strong and courageous and wise in the doing of our own task in accord with the Divine will.

To all the dwellers of the earth, I speak for this Republic—and directly from the heart of every one of its citizens—when I say that this Nation prays for you—all of you—the fullness of the Christmas spirit, peace and good will.

And now, please permit me a personal note. My wife and I wish to all of you here, and to all peoples everywhere, a very merry Christmas. As I light the Nation's Christmas tree, "God rest you . . . Let nothing you dismay."

And now, good night and again, Merry Christmas!

NOTE: The President spoke just before lighting the National Community Christmas Tree at the Pageant of Peace Ceremonies on the Ellipse. His opening words "Mr. Secretary" referred to Douglas McKay, Secretary of the Interior.

356 ¶ Memorandum on the Red Cross Campaign. *December* 21, 1954

To the Heads of Executive Departments, Commissions and Agencies:

In peace and war, at home and abroad, the work of the American Red Cross symbolizes American courage and compassion. Through its blood program for civilians and the armed forces, services for American troops in foreign countries, relief work after flood, fire and hurricane, safety and nursing services—in these and many other ways this organization tirelessly serves human need.

That this work may continue, I know all Federal employees will want to join with their fellow-citizens in supporting the 1955 Red Cross Fund Campaign. I have asked the Honorable Sinclair Weeks, Secretary of Commerce, to act as the Chairman of the Government Unit. I urge you personally to consult with him and to request all officials and employees of your department, in Washington and the field, to cooperate with their respective local chapters and to form an organization adequate to raise the amount desired from your department.

If each of us does his full share, this great humanitarian program will be a brilliant success.

DWIGHT D. EISENHOWER

357   ¶ Statement by the President on the Vote by the French Assembly To Ratify the Paris Treaties. *December 30, 1954*

THE RECENT series of actions taken by the French Assembly is a matter of great gratification, not only to the United States but to the entire free world.

There are, of course, further steps to be taken, both in France and elsewhere, before a satisfactory foundation for Western Defense has been achieved. But of particular importance is the fact that the French Deputies, after initial hesitations against bringing Germany into Western Defense arrangements, have now voted to ratify the new treaties signed at Paris last October.

The French action is all the more significant since it follows the vote on ratification taken last week by the Italian Assembly, which approved Western Defense plans by a decisive majority.

Once sovereignty is restored to the Federal Republic, with German participation in the North Atlantic Treaty Organization, there will be added defensive strength and general solidarity in Western Europe. As decisive cooperation supplants age-old antagonisms the prospects for a general and lasting peace will be definitely improved, and a measure of encouragement may therefore even now be felt by all who are earnestly striving to maintain and improve the unity and harmony of the free world.

Appendix A—White House Press Releases, 1954

NOTE: Includes releases covering matters with which the President was closely concerned, except announcements of Presidential personnel appointments and approvals of legislation with which there was no accompanying statement.

Releases relating to Proclamations and Executive Orders have not been included. These documents are separately listed in Appendix B.

For list of Press and Radio Conferences, see subject index under "News Conferences."

Appendix A

1120

Appendix A

1121

April	Subject
16	White House statement on directive to agencies to cooperate in the investigation of the Federal Housing Administration
16	Exchange of messages between the President and the President of France and the Chief of State of Viet-Nam concerning the defenders of Dien Bien Phu
16	Statement by the President regarding the United States position on the proposed European Defense Community
16	Telegram inviting Governors of the States afflicted by dust storms to attend conference at the White House
19	Statement by the Secretary of State after his report to the President of his trip to London and Paris
22	Remarks to the National Society of the Daughters of the American Revolution
22	Address at the dinner of the American Newspaper Publishers Association, New York City
23	White House statement on the forthcoming Governors Conference
23	Remarks at the birthplace of Abraham Lincoln, Hodgenville, Ky.
23	Address at Transylvania College, Lexington, Ky.
26	Remarks at the 42d Annual Meeting of the U.S. Chamber of Commerce
26	Recorded interview by Mrs. John G. Lee, National President, League of Women Voters
29	Remarks to the leaders of the United Defense Fund
29	Special message to the Congress transmitting Reorganization Plan 1 of 1954
29	Special message to the Congress transmitting Reorganization Plan 2 of 1954
29	Remarks to the President's Committee on Employment of the Physically Handicapped
29	Message to the Congress transmitting 35th Report on Lend-Lease Operations
30	Remarks to the Defense Advisory Committee on Women in the Services
30	Memorandum directing the departments and agencies to take part in a civil defense test exercise

April	Subject
30	White House announcement of delegates and alternates to the Seventh World Health Assembly

May	
3	Message to the Congress transmitting Report on Lend-Lease Operations
4	Statement by the President on the dust bowl emergency
4	Letter to the Administrator of the Civil Defense Administration authorizing allocation of funds to aid drought areas
4	Remarks to the President's Conference on Occupational Safety
5	Statement by the President on the conference in Geneva
6	Statement by the President upon signing the Federal-Aid Highway Act
6	Remarks at the 22d Annual Convention of the Military Chaplains Association
7	Message to the President of France on the fall of Dien Bien Phu
7	Message to the Chief of State of Viet-Nam on the fall of Dien Bien Phu
11	Remarks at the Capitol at the dedication of the Rotunda Frieze
11	Letter to Chairmen, Senate Finance and House Ways and Means Committees, on tariff on scissors and shears
12	Remarks at the Annual Conference of the Society for Personnel Administration
12	Statement by the President on the death of Senator Hoey of North Carolina
13	White House statement announcing the prospective visit of the President of Liberia
13	Remarks upon signing the St. Lawrence Seaway Bill
13	Messages from the President of France and the Chief of State of Viet-Nam in response to the President's messages on the fall of Dien Bien Phu
14	Remarks at the Armed Forces Day Dinner
17	Letter to General Wladyslaw Anders of the Polish Armed Forces in Exile on commemoration of the Battle of Monte Cassino

Appendix A

June	*Subject*	*July*	*Subject*

15 Letter accepting resignation of William M. Rand, Deputy Director, Foreign Operations Administration

15 Letter accepting resignation of H. Lee White, Assistant Secretary of the Air Force

16 Remarks at the Convention of the National Association of Retail Grocers

16 Statement by the President upon signing bill amending the Railroad Retirement Act of 1937

17 Remarks to the National 4–H Club Campers

17 Statement by the President upon signing bill concerning termination of Federal supervision over the Menominee Indian Tribe

18 Letter to President Coty of France after the fall of the Laniel Cabinet

22 Remarks at the National Editorial Association dinner

23 Special message to the Congress on the mutual security program

23 Statement by the Press Secretary concerning payment of retirement benefits to persons convicted of a felony

24 Remarks at a breakfast meeting of the National Cartoonists Society

24 Statement by the President upon signing bill relating to the administrative jurisdiction over certain public lands in Oregon

25 Letter to the Chairman of the National Science Board concerning U.S. participation in the International Geophysical Year

26 Letter from the President of France in response to the President's letter of June 18

28 Joint statement by the President and Prime Minister Churchill

29 Joint declaration by the President and the Prime Minister of the United Kingdom

29 Veto of bill conveying certain public lands to Jake Alexander

30 White House statement on proclamation concerning tariff on alsike clover seed

1 White House statement on reports of Boards of Visitors to the Naval and Military Academies

1 Letter accepting resignation of Mrs. Katherine G. Howard, Deputy Administrator, Federal Civil Defense Administration

1 Letter from Chancellor Adenauer of Germany concerning the discussions with Prime Minister Churchill

1 Message to the President of Mexico on the Rio Grande flood disaster

2 Letter to Chairmen, Senate Finance and House Ways and Means Committees, on tariff on groundfish fillets

3 Veto of bill for the relief of Ralston Edward Harry

3 Message from the President of Mexico in response to the President's message on July 1

5 Message to the Mayor of Philadelphia for the Fourth of July ceremonies at Independence Hall

9 Report of the Governors' trip to Korea with a supplemental report on Japan

10 Statement by the President upon signing the Agricultural Trade Development and Assistance Act of 1954

10 White House statement concerning the work stoppage at the Paducah atomic energy plant

12 White House statement upon signing bill providing for a Federal-State program to build medical facilities

12 Letter to the Secretary of Commerce establishing a Cabinet Committee on Transport Policy and Organization

12 Message for the Governors' Conference at Lake George and request for recommendations as to a Federal-State highway program

14 White House announcement of forthcoming visit of President Rhee of Korea

16 Statement by the President upon signing bill increasing reenlistment bonuses for members of the uniformed services

16 Letter accepting resignation of Ralph A. Tudor, Under Secretary of the Interior

Appendix A

Appendix A

Appendix A

1127

September   *Subject*

4 Remarks at the Airport, Grand Junction, Colo.

4 Remarks at Natrona Airport, Casper, Wyo.

4 Remarks at the Airport, McCook, Nebr.

4 Statement by the President: Labor Day

4 Message from the President of Austria concerning assistance to flood victims

6 Radio and television remarks on the occasion of the ground-breaking ceremony for the Shippingport Atomic Power Plant

7 White House statement on the decision of Thomas E. Dewey not to be a candidate for Governor of New York

7 White House announcement of appointment of members to the President's Advisory Committee on a National Highway Program

8 White House statement concerning the delegation of certain civil defense responsibilities to departments and agencies

9 Statement of policy, approved and issued by the President, on foreign trade as related to agriculture

9 Letter to Clarence Francis requesting him to serve as chairman of Interagency Committee on Agricultural Surplus Disposal, and letter to members of the Committee

9 Letter to Chairmen, Senate Finance and House Ways and Means Committees, on imports of hand-blown glassware

10 Exchange of messages between the President and the Shah of Iran on the losses caused in the United States by hurricane "Carol"

10 Message to the President of France on the earthquake in Algeria

11 White House announcement of report by the Tariff Commission on imports of dried figs

12 News conference of the Attorney General and the Director of the Federal Bureau of Investigation

12 News conference of the Secretary of State on the Manila Pact and the Pacific Charter

September   *Subject*

13 Statement by the President on the meeting of the National Security Council in Denver

13 White House announcement of resignation of Raymond A. Hare, Ambassador to Lebanon

14 Remarks at dedication of the Boulder, Colo., Laboratories of the National Bureau of Standards

15 Letter accepting resignation of Dr. Henry DeWolf Smyth, member, Atomic Energy Commission

15 Final tabulation of bills approved or vetoed during the 2d Session of the 83d Congress

21 White House announcement of prospective visit of President Magloire of Haiti

21 Letter to the Governors concerning the State and White House Conferences on Education to be held in 1955

21 Statement by the President: National Day of Prayer

22 White House announcement of a meeting of the President's Advisory Committee on a National Highway Program with interested associations

22 Remarks at dedication of Aerial Fire Depot, Municipal Airport, Missoula, Mont.

23 Address at the dedication of McNary Dam, Walla Walla, Wash.

23 Remarks at the Airport, Pendleton, Oreg.

23 Address at Hollywood Bowl, Los Angeles, Calif.

24 Remarks at breakfast in Los Angeles given by Republican groups of southern California

24 Remarks to the American Federation of Labor Convention in Los Angeles

26 Letter to Harvey S. Firestone, Jr., National Chairman, United Community Campaigns of America

27 Statement by the President on the occasion of the Jewish New Year

28 Letter to the REA Administrator concerning recent progress in rural electrification

29 Statement by the President: National Newspaper Week

Appendix A

Appendix A

Appendix A

Appendix B—Presidential Documents Published in the Federal Register, 1954

PROCLAMATIONS

Appendix B

Appendix B

Appendix B

Appendix B

Appendix B

PRESIDENTIAL DOCUMENTS OTHER THAN PROCLAMATIONS AND EXECUTIVE ORDERS

Appendix C—Presidential Reports to the Congress, 1954

Subject	Published	Sent to the Congress	Date of White House release
Report on Inclusion of Escape Clauses in Existing Trade Agreements	H. Doc. 296	Jan. 12 (S) Jan. 14 (H)	Jan. 12
	H. Doc. 470	July 8	. . . .
Foreign Service Retirement and Disability Fund for fiscal years ended June 30, 1952 and 1953 .	H. Doc. 297	Jan. 12 (S) Jan. 14 (H)	. . . .
National Science Foundation, Third Annual Report for the year ending June 30, 1953 . . .	H. Doc. 301	Jan. 15 (S) Jan. 18 (H)	. . . .
Railroad Retirement Board Report			
For the fiscal year ended June 30, 1952. . . .	H. Doc. 181	Jan. 18	. . . .
For the fiscal year ended June 30, 1953 . . .	H. Doc. 276	May 10	. . . .
Commodity Credit Corporation for the fiscal year ended June 30, 1953	H. Doc. 299	Jan. 18	
Panama Canal Company and the Canal Zone Government, First Annual Reports for the fiscal year ended June 30, 1952.		Jan. 20	
National Advisory Committee for Aeronautics, Thirty-ninth Annual Report for the fiscal year 1953	S. Doc. 79	Jan. 25	. . . .
Economic Report of the President	H. Doc. 289	Jan. 28	Jan. 28
National Capital Housing Authority for the fiscal year ended June 30, 1953		Feb. 2	. . . .
National Advisory Council on International Monetary and Financial Problems	H. Doc. 338	Mar. 1	. . . .
	H. Doc. 490	Aug. 9	. . . .
Report on the Mutual Security Program . . .	H. Doc. 337	Mar. 8	Mar. 8
	H. Doc. 495	Aug. 20	. . . .
United States Civil Service Commission			
For the year ended June 30, 1953.	H. Doc. 261	Mar. 22	. . . .
For the period of January 1, 1951, to June 30, 1953	H. Doc. 489	Aug. 9	. . . .
Report on Operations of the State Department .	H. Doc. 365	Apr. 7	. . . .
Thirty-fifth Report on Lend-Lease Operations .	H. Doc. 366	May 3	May 3
Report of the Office of Alien Property, Department of Justice, for the fiscal year ended June 30, 1953		June 7	. . . .
Report on Disaster Relief	H. Doc. 479	July 24 (S) July 26 (H)	July 24
Report on Participation in the United Nations, for the year 1953.	H. Doc. 492	Aug. 10	. . . .

Appendix D—Rules Governing This Publication

[Reprinted from the Federal Register, vol. 24, p. 2354, dated March 26, 1959]

TITLE 1—GENERAL PROVISIONS

Chapter I—Administrative Committee of the Federal Register

PART 32—PUBLIC PAPERS OF THE PRESIDENTS OF THE UNITED STATES

PUBLICATIONS AND FORMAT

Sec.

32.1 Publication required.
32.2 Coverage of prior years.
32.3 Format, indexes, ancillaries.

SCOPE

32.10 Basic criteria.
32.11 Sources.

FREE DISTRIBUTION

32.15 Members of Congress.
32.16 The Supreme Court.
32.17 Executive agencies.

PAID DISTRIBUTION

32.20 Agency requisitions.
32.21 Extra copies.
32.22 Sale to public.

AUTHORITY: §§ 32.1 to 32.22 issued under sec. 6, 49 Stat. 501, as amended; 44 U.S.C. 306.

PUBLICATION AND FORMAT

§ 32.1 *Publication required.* There shall be published forthwith at the end of each calendar year, beginning with the year 1957, a special edition of the FEDERAL REGISTER designated "Public Papers of the Presidents of the United States." Each volume shall cover one calendar year and shall be identified further by the name of the President and the year covered.

§ 32.2 *Coverage of prior years.* After conferring with the National Historical Publications Commission with respect to the need therefor, the Administrative Committee may from time to time au-

thorize the publication of similar volumes covering specified calendar years prior to 1957.

§ 32.3 *Format, indexes, ancillaries.* Each annual volume, divided into books whenever appropriate, shall be separately published in the binding and style deemed by the Administrative Committee to be suitable to the dignity of the office of President of the United States. Each volume shall be appropriately indexed and shall contain appropriate ancillary information respecting significant Presidential documents not published in full text.

SCOPE

§ 32.10 *Basic criteria.* The basic text of the volumes shall consist of oral utterances by the President or of writings subscribed by him. All materials selected for inclusion under these criteria must also be in the public domain by virtue of White House press release or otherwise.

§ 32.11 *Sources.* (a) The basic text of the volumes shall be selected from the official text of: (1) Communications to the Congress, (2) public addresses, (3) transcripts of press conferences, (4) public letters, (5) messages to heads of state, (6) statements released on miscellaneous subjects, and (7) formal executive documents promulgated in accordance with law.

(b) Ancillary text, notes, and tables shall be derived from official sources only.

FREE DISTRIBUTION

§ 32.15 *Members of Congress.* Each Member of Congress shall be entitled to one copy of each annual volume upon application therefor in writing to the Director.

§ 32.16 *The Supreme Court.* The Supreme Court of the United States shall be entitled to twelve copies of the annual volumes.

§ 32.17 *Executive agencies.* The head of each department and the head of each independent agency in the executive branch of the Government shall be entitled to one copy of each annual volume upon application therefor in writing to the Director.

PAID DISTRIBUTION

§ 32.20 *Agency requisitions.* Each Federal agency shall be entitled to obtain at cost copies of the annual volumes for official use upon the timely submission to the Government Printing Office of a printing and binding requisition (Standard Form No. 1).

§ 32.21 *Extra copies.* All requests for extra copies of the annual volumes shall be addressed to the Superintendent of Documents, Government Printing Office, Washington 25, D.C. Extra copies

shall be paid for by the agency or official requesting them.

§ 32.22 *Sale to public.* The annual volumes shall be placed on sale to the public by the Superintendent of Documents at prices determined by him under the general direction of the Administrative Committee.

* * * * *

ADMINISTRATIVE COMMITTEE OF THE FEDERAL REGISTER,
WAYNE C. GROVER,
Archivist of the United States,
Chairman.
RAYMOND BLATTENBERGER,
The Public Printer,
Member.
WILLIAM O. BURTNER,
Representative of the Attorney
General, Member.
Approved March 20, 1959.
WILLIAM P. ROGERS,
Attorney General.
FRANKLIN FLOETE,
Administrator of General Services.

[F.R. Doc. 59–2517; Filed, Mar. 25, 1959; 8:45 a.m.]

INDEX

[References are to items except as otherwise noted]

Index

Index

Index

Index

[References are to items except as otherwise noted]

Index

[References are to items except as otherwise noted]

Index

[References are to items except as otherwise noted]

Index

[References are to items except as otherwise noted]

Budget, Bureau of the, Director (Joseph M. Dodge)
　News conference remarks on, 50, 68
　Resignation, letter, 65
　See also Dodge, Joseph M.
Budget, Bureau of the, Director (Rowland R. Hughes), 169, 348, 349, 351
　Flood relief in Europe, memorandum, 195
Bulgaria, compensation claims of U.S. nationals, 94
Bullis, Harry, letter, 217
Burd, Lawrence H., 25, 50, 101, 115, 129, 200, 322
Bureau of Advertising, 87
Bureau of Engraving and Printing, fair employment practices, 92
Bureau of Foreign Commerce, 14 (p. 181)
Bureau of Land Management, 14 (p. 170)
Bureau of Mines, 14 (p. 171)
Bureau of Public Debt, 14 (p. 187)
Bureau of Public Roads, 14 (p. 176)
Bureau of Reclamation, 256, 258
　Budget message, 14 (pp. 167, 168)
Burgess, Carter L., 351, 353
Burns, Arthur F., 107, 129
Bush, Vannevar, 311
Business and Defense Services Administration, 14 (p. 181)
Business Economics, Office of, 14 (p. 181)
Business loans
　RFC program, liquidation, 14 (p. 181)
　Small business loans, 14 (p. 181)
Butler, Paul, 347
Butler University, 291
Butter
　Consumption, 165
　Price supports, 25, 39, 143, 165
　Surpluses, 25, 39, 50
Buy American Act, 67, 115
Byrd, Sen. Harry F., 115
Byrnes, Gov. James F., 115, 164

Cabinet meeting, report of Secretary Dulles on negotiations in Europe, 307
California, 39
　Condon, Repr. Robert L., 18

California—Continued
　Gubser, Repr. Charles S., 161
　Hanford, 14 (p. 128)
　Holifield, Repr. Chet, 12 n.
　Knight, Gov. Goodwin J., 274
　Knowland, Sen. William F., 9, 33, 48, 129, 157, 161, 168, 172, 273, 274, 341, 345
　Kuchel, Sen. Thomas H., 273
　Los Angeles, 273, 274, 275
　San Francisco, 14 (p. 134)
California and Oregon Railroad grant lands, 152
Cambodia
　Communist aggression in, 280
　Membership in defense alliance, question of, 107
　News conference remarks, 101, 107, 168
　Norodom Sihanouk, message, 280
　U.S. Ambassador Robert M. McClintock, 280 n.
Camp Blanding Military Reservation, Fla., conveyance of lands within, veto, 121
Camp David, 50, 192
Canada
　Agreement with U.S. on civil uses of atomic energy, 260
　Chamber of Commerce, remarks, 338
　Heeney, A. D. P., 110 n.
　International Joint Commission, 165, 271
　Massey, Vincent, 101
　Position on Great Lakes water diversion, 253
　Royal Canadian Air Force, 159
　St. Lawrence Seaway projects, 3, 14 (pp. 175, 176)
　U.S. tariffs on Canadian clover, 172
Canal Zone, 14 (p. 190)
Candidacy for second term, comment on 9, 143, 192, 322, 347, 353
Candidates for public office, 177
　Campaign remarks, 304, 317, 318, 319, 320
　Equal time for radio and television appearance, 50

Index

Index

[References are to items except as otherwise noted]

Index

[References are to items except as otherwise noted]

Coal, commission on rehabilitation of Pennsylvania hard coal region, 168

Coast and Geodetic Survey, 137

Coast Guard, 137
Budget message, 14 (p. 175)

Cobo, Albert E., 318 n.

Cochran, Carlos M., estate, relief of, disapproval, 230

Coffee prices, Federal Trade Commission investigation, 18, 25, 39, 50, 57

Coffee and Sugar Exchange, 18

Cohn, Roy M., 115

Coinage of 50-cent pieces for commemorative events, vetoes
Louisiana Purchase, sesquicentennial, 29
New York City, tercentennial, 28
Northampton, Mass., tercentennial, 27

Cole, Albert M. See Housing and Home Finance Agency, Administrator (Albert M. Cole)

Cole, Repr. W. Sterling, 57, 129

Collective bargaining, 5

Collective security, 6, 38, 45, 72, 73 ftn. (p. 384), 84, 91, 297, 329
News conference remarks, 101, 115, 157, 168, 311
See also North Atlantic Treaty Organization; Southeast Asia Treaty Organization

Colleges and universities
Association of American Medical Colleges, 334 n.
Association of Land-Grant Colleges and Universities, 335
Butler University, 291
Columbia University, 39, 118, 128, 300, 347
Cornell University, 12 n., 200
Duke University, 33
Emory University, 33
Federal aid for medical research, 14 (p. 143)
Harvard University, 129
Housing, 14 (pp. 87, 151)
Howard University, 14 (pp. 153, 154), 33
Northwestern University, 192, 204

Colleges and universities—Continued
Purdue University, 291 n., 335 n.
Southern Methodist University, 12 n.
State University of New York, 300
Transylvania College, 89
Trinity College, 295

Collins, Gen. J. Lawton, 341

Colonialism in Indochina, 39

Colorado
Boulder, 267
Denver, 101, 165, 182, 200, 209 n., 260, 286, 287
Releases from, 210–222, 227–232, 234–255, 259, 261–266, 268, 269, 276–285, 288, 289
Fraser, 233 n., 270
Grand Junction, 256
Millikin, Sen. Eugene D., 33
Thornton, Gov. Dan, 35, 39, 85 n., 99, 165, 256, 286

Colorado River development, 101, 172
Recommendations on, statement, 62

Colt, S. Sloan, 334

Columbia Institution for the Deaf, 14 (p. 155)

Columbia Republican Club, Indianapolis, remarks, 290

Columbia River, 271

Columbia University, 118, 300, 347
Bicentennial, 39, 128

Commemorative occasions. See Addresses, remarks, etc., on commemorative or dedicatory occasions

Commerce, Department of
Budget message, 14 (pp. 178, 181, 182)
Business programs, reorganization, 14 (p. 181)
Employment and unemployment information, 39, 107, 308
Merchant marine, study of, 67
Transportation programs, 163

Commerce, Secretary of (Sinclair Weeks), 37, 267, 311
Chairman, Red Cross campaign, 356
Foreign aid, memorandum, 323
Highway, study, 102
Letter, 163

1151

Index

[References are to items except as otherwise noted]

Index

Communist Party in United States, outlawing of, 48, 200
 Approval of act, 210
Communists in French armed forces, handling of, 48
Community Chest campaign, 132, 183, 276
Community development, budget message, 14 (pp. 146–151)
 Table, 14 (p. 147)
Comptroller General of the United States, filling of vacancy, comment on, 311
Comptroller General of the United States (Lindsay C. Warren), 73
 Retirement, letter, 69
Condon, Repr. Robert L., 18
Conduct of Government employees, 92, 302, 311, 353
Congress
 Committee investigations, comments on, 48, 57, 63, 72, 92, 101, 107, 113, 115, 129, 302, 347
 Immunity of witnesses, 139
 Power to declare war, 57, 92
 Record of, 192, 200, 322
 Broadcast, 209
 Relations with, 33, 273, 286, 322, 347
Congress, letters to Members of
 Aiken, Sen. George D., farm bill, 196
 Broyhill, Repr. Joel T., Federal employees benefits, 313
 Capehart, Sen. Homer E., Federal Housing Administration investigation, 302
 Hope, Repr. Clifford R., farm bill, 196
 Hyde, Repr. DeWitt S., Federal employees benefits, 313
 President of the Senate, Congressional election campaign, efforts toward, 312
 Small, Repr. Frank, Jr., Federal employees benefits, 313
Congress, messages to
 Agriculture, 4
 Atomic Energy Act, amendment, 38
 Economic report, 21
 Foreign economic policy, 67
 Germany, protocols to treaties re, 332

Congress, messages to—Continued
 Group life insurance for Federal employees, 116
 Health program, 11
 Housing, 17
 International Labor Organization
  Convention on social security standards, 126
  Recommendations on collective agreements and voluntary conciliation and arbitration, 125
 Labor-management relations, 5
 Mutual Defense Treaty, U.S.-Korea, 6
 Mutual security program, 150
 Public assistance programs, 10
 Reorganization Plan 1 of 1954, 94
 Reorganization Plan 2 of 1954, 95
 Social security, 10
 Southeast Asia Collective Defense Treaty, 329
 State of the Union, 3
 Vetoes
  Alexander, Jake, conveyance of lands to, 156
  Camp Blanding Military Reservation, Fla., conveyance of lands within, 121
  Carlson, Theodore W., relief of, 134
  Court of Claims jurisdiction in overtime compensation case, 41
  District of Columbia, election of delegates to national political conventions, 206
  Engelbert, Wilhelm, relief of, 58
  Harry, Ralston E., relief of, 159
  Holder, Anna, relief of, 42
  Kaczmarczyk, Rose, relief of, 141
  Klyce Motors, Inc., relief of, 181
  Louisiana Purchase, sesquicentennial, coinage of 50-cent pieces in commemoration, 29
  New York City, tercentennial, coinage of 50-cent pieces in commemoration, 28
  Northampton, Mass., tercentennial, coinage of 50-cent pieces in commemoration, 27

Index

Index

Index

Index

[References are to items except as otherwise noted]

1157

Index

[References are to items except as otherwise noted]

Index

Index

Index

Index

Index

[References are to items except as otherwise noted]

Index

Index

Index

Index

[References are to items except as otherwise noted]

Index

Index

Index

Index

Index

[References are to items except as otherwise noted]

Index

[References are to items except as otherwise noted]

Index

Index

[References are to items except as otherwise noted]

Index

[References are to items except as otherwise noted]

Index

Index

Index

Index

Index

Index

[References are to items except as otherwise noted]

Index

Index

Index

[References are to items except as otherwise noted]

Index

Index

Randall (Clarence B.) Commission. *See* Commission on Foreign Economic Policy
Rankin, Karl L., 168
Rankine, Paul Scott, 63, 328
Rastovorov, Yuri A., 25
Rayburn, Repr. Sam, 57, 157, 341
Reactors, nuclear, 38, 260
　Construction, 14 (p. 129)
Reading, the President's
　Abilene *Reflector-Chronicle*, 149
　Mutt and Jeff cartoon, 151
Recession, question of, 25, 26, 33, 129
Reclamation, Bureau of, 256, 258
　Budget message, 14 (pp. 167, 168)
Reconstruction Finance Corporation, 18
　Budget message, 14 (pp. 150, 178–181)
　Business loan program, liquidation, 14 (p. 181)
　Liquidation under Reorganization Plan 2 (1954), 95
　Production programs, 14 (pp. 179–181)
Records
　Federal Housing Administration, 81
　See also Information
Records management, 14 (pp. 187, 188)
Red Cross, 183, 204, 310
　Campaign
　　Memorandums, 1, 356
　　Statement, 46
　In Korea, 48
　Italian, 315 n.
Red Cross Societies, League of, 175, 182 ftn. (p. 678)
Red Feather campaign. *See* Community Chest campaign
Reed, Repr. Daniel A., 48
Reed, Harry J., 291
Reenlistment bonuses for military personnel, approval of bill, 166
Refugee Relief Act, 63
　Letter to Gov. Dewey, 188
　Letter to Governors, 187
Refugees
　Admission to United States, 92
　Governors' Committee proposed, 187, 188

Refugees—Continued
　Indochinese, 273
　New York State committee on, 188
Religious Action in the Social and Civil Order, Foundation for, 327 n.
Renegotiation Act of 1951, extension, 3
Reorganization and Defense Production Acts, extension proposed, 349
Reorganization Plans
　No. 1 of 1954, message, 94
　No. 2 of 1954, message, 95
Reports to the President
　Air Coordinating Committee, 123, 200
　Board of Inquiry on labor dispute at atomic facilities, 193
　Chairman Strauss, nuclear tests in Pacific, 68 n.
　Commission on Foreign Economic Policy, 16, 18, 67, 68, 90, 101, 209, 349, 351, 353
　Department of Justice record of action on subversives, 129, 130
　Secretary Dulles, Mutual Defense Treaty with Korea, 6
　Tariff Commission, wool imports and price supports, 49
　Veterans facilities, elimination of segregation, 309 n.
Reports to the President, letters, statements, etc., in response to
　Air Coordinating Committee, U.S. aviation policy, 123
　Commission on Foreign Economic Policy, 16
　Department of Justice record of action on subversives, 130
　National Security Training Commission, reserve forces, 7
　Veterans Affairs Administrator, segregation in VA facilities, 309
Republican Committee of New York State, remarks, 298
Republican National Committee, 22 n., 77 n.
　News conference remarks on, 33, 50, 311, 347

1187

Index

Index

Index

Index

Index

Index

Index

Index

Index

Index

Index

Index

[References are to items except as otherwise noted]

Index

[References are to items except as otherwise noted]

Index

HETERICK MEMORIAL LIBRARY

3 5111 00357 3965